BA 243

ENVIRONMENTS OF BUSINESS

THE SMEAL COLLEGE
OF BUSINESS ADMINISTRATION

The Pennsylvania State University

The McGraw-Hill Companies, Inc.
Primis Custom Publishing

New York St. Louis San Francisco Auckland Bogotá
Caracas Lisbon London Madrid Mexico Milan Montreal
New Delhi Paris San Juan Singapore Sydney Tokyo Toronto

McGraw·Hill

A Division of The McGraw·Hill Companies

BA 243
ENVIRONMENTS OF BUSINESS

Acknowledgements:
Business, Government, and Society, Eighth Edition by George A. Steiner and John F. Steiner. Copyright © 1985, 1988, 1991, 1994, 1997 by Irwin/McGraw-Hill, The McGraw-Hill Companies, Inc.
Business and Society, Fifth Edition by Heidi Vernon-Wortzel. Copyright © 1977, 1981, 1985, 1990, 1994 by Irwin/McGraw-Hill, The McGraw-Hill Companies, Inc.
Business Law and the Regulatory Environment, Ninth Edition by Michael B. Metzger, Jane P. Mallor, A. James Barnes, Thomas Bowers, Michael J. Phillips, Arlen Langvardt. Copyright © 1946, 1951, 1955, 1959, 1963, 1966, 1970, 1974, 1978, 1982, 1986, 1989, 1992, 1995 by Irwin/McGraw-Hill, The McGraw-Hill Companies, Inc.
Business and Society, Second Edition by Alfred A. Marcus. Copyright © 1993, 1996 by Irwin/McGraw-Hill, The McGraw-Hill Companies, Inc.

McGraw-Hill's Primis Custom Series consists of products that are produced from camera-ready copy. Peer review, class testing, and accuracy are primarily the responsibility of the author(s).

1 2 3 4 5 6 7 8 9 0 BBC BBC 9 0 9 8 7

ISBN 0-07-014349-8

Editor: Linda Kozar DuPlessis
Cover Design: Rob Winter, Winter Digital Art
Printer/Binder: Braceland Brothers, Inc.

Contents

Chapter One

INTRODUCTION TO

THE FIELD

Exxon

Every large corporation in the United States and many smaller ones are concerned with the wide range of forces in the business-government-society (BGS) interrelationship. Exxon provides a good example of its complexity.

Exxon is one of the largest and oldest of the world's industrial enterprises. It was the largest industrial company in the United States in 1995 as measured worldwide by sales of nearly $122 billion. It engages in virtually every major type of basic energy production, from exploration of oil and gas to mining coal, and other minerals. It operates fleets of ships, airplanes, and helicopters, and employs 82,000 people.

The company is deeply intertwined with governments all over the world. It deals with governments in over eighty countries of the world. It explores for petroleum in six continents and in offshore waters. It has an interest in more than thirty oil refineries in eighteen countries and owns or has a share in nearly 27,000 miles of pipelines transporting crude oil, natural gas, and petroleum products. It has a fleet of tankers and other vessels.

The U.S. federal government has roughly 300 primary agencies, virtually all of which affect Exxon's operations. There are agencies in each of the fifty states with whom Exxon has relations. Relations became tense and bitter with the State of Alaska and several federal government agencies (including the Department of Justice and the Environmental Protection Agency) when a company tanker, the *Exxon Valdez*, spilled 11 million gallons of oil into Prince William Sound on March 24, 1989. This disaster created enormous legal, political, and social problems for Exxon with these government entities and environmentalists.

Exxon's long and outstanding reputation for attentiveness to its social responsibilities has been tarnished by the criticisms it received as a result of the oil spill. The company was accused of laxity in its ship operations, ill-conceived management response to public concerns about the spill, and sluggishness in cleaning up the mess.

A prominent feature of Exxon's social posture for years has been its very large philanthropic contributions, amounting to $55.4 million in 1995. In 1995 the company's Exxon Education Foundation observed its fortieth anniversary. During this period its grants totaled $406 million to a broad range of programs designed to improve education from kindergarten through college. In addition to cash grants its employees are deeply involved in helping educational institutions.[1]

This brief sketch of the BGS relationships of a large company is illustrative of the position of thousands of companies. Such interrelationships are of cardinal importance to, and a clear reflection of, the ways in which our entire political-economic-social system functions. They also reflect and affect the changing role of the United States in the world.

Business, Government, and Society, Eighth Edition, by George A. Steiner and John F. Steiner. © Irwin/ McGraw-Hill, The McGraw-Hill Companies, 1985, 1988, 1991, 1994, 1997.

We begin the chapter with two questions: What is the BGS field? Why is the field important to managers? Then we present major conceptual models which people use in thinking about the BGS interrelationship. This is followed with a brief note on the BGS relationship in other highly industrialized nations. Finally, we discuss the main characteristics of the analysis of this book.

What is the Business-Government-Society (BGS) Field?

First, we define what is meant by business, government, and society. *Business* is a broad term encompassing a range of actions and institutions. Included are activities of small enterprises such as hamburger stands to giant corporations such as Exxon. The term covers manufacturing, finance, trade, service, and other economic activities of business firms.

Government covers a wide range of organizations. Included are local, state, and federal governments. Government may be defined as the structures and processes through which public policies, programs, and rules are authoritatively made for society. In this book we are most interested in the economic and regulatory powers of government, especially those of the federal government, and their impact on business.

As used in this book, the term *society* means generally this nation, or the American civilization. Inherent in this concept of society are three fundamental, interrelated parts: (1) ideas or beliefs, (2) institutions, and (3) material things.

Ideas include attitudes, ideologies, and beliefs. They establish the broad goals of life expressed in terms of what is considered to be good, true, right, beautiful and acceptable. Ideas and beliefs underlie and dominate the systems of institutional arrangements in society, of which business is one.

Institutions are those more or less formalized ways by which society tries to do something. Examples of institutional systems are the business system, the political system, labor unions, the educational system, the language system, and the legal system.

The third element in society encompasses tangible, material things such as stocks of resources, land, and all manufactured goods. These help shape, and are partly products of, our institutions, ideas, and beliefs. Our economic institutions, together with our stock of resources, determine in large part the type and quantity of our material goods. As our types and quantities of material things change, so do our ideas and beliefs.

Both business and government are institutions operating within society. We distinguish among these entities to help focus on each one and their relationships to one another. The above definitions apply to foreign nations as well as the United States, and we shall have occasion throughout this book to examine them as they relate to U.S. companies doing business abroad.

The BGS field covers the broad areas defined above. However, in this book the focus is considerably narrower. Our focus is on business management. More specifically, we are concerned with the most significant forces in the BGS relationship that impact importantly on the broad acceptance of the business institution in society, and the social and ethical dimensions of the behavior of business and business managers.

The titles of the chapters in this book define our view of the principal elements of the BGS field. There are many other subjects that affect business management and which could be chapter headings. For example agriculture, national security, demography, weather, the money and banking system, and the insurance system could be discussed. Sometime in the future one or more of these subjects might properly be included as chapters in a text such as this. To illustrate, fifty years ago pollution and consumerism would not have been found in an academic study of BGS. Certainly, from 1950 to 1953 the Korean War was prominent in the BGS relationship. And before that, World War II dominated the field. The topics discussed in this book are those we consider at this time to be currently the more important ones in the BGS relationship from a managerial point of view.

Why is the BGS Field Important to Managers?

To be successful in meeting its objectives, it is necessary for a business to be responsive to both its economic and its noneconomic environment. General Motors Corp., for example, must be efficient in producing cars that meet the demand of consumers at competitive prices. GM must not only react to current economic forces, but anticipate them as well. It did not perform this function very well in the 1970s and opened the door for Japanese companies to penetrate the American market. From virtually no share of the American automobile market in 1974 the Japanese now have almost one-third.

What is most important is that management realize that it must consider the impact of every business policy and business action upon society. It has to consider whether the action is likely to promote the public good, to advance the basic beliefs of our society, to contribute to its stability, strength, and harmony.

Source: Peter Drucker, *The Practice of Management*, New York: Harper & Row, 1955, p. 342.

Properly responding to economic market forces fifty years ago was about all GM and other businesses had to do to survive profitably. Not today. Now there are powerful nonmarket forces to which every business, especially the larger ones, must respond appropriately. For example, GM was required, by regulations of the National Highway Traffic Safety Administration (NHTSA), to equip the 1990-model automobiles with a driver-side passive-restraint system such as an air bag or an automatic shoulder harness. General Motors and other automobile companies must comply with scores of other governmental rules affecting cars. There are many other powerful noneconomic forces, such as community demands for less-polluting automobiles and improved safety features, to which GM and other automobile companies must respond. Identifying and dealing with nonmarket forces such as these today commands a higher and higher proportion of the attention of business managers.

It is important to recognize that the business institution was created and accepted by society. If society does not accept its functioning, the business institution as we know it will either be regulated or redefined. At any one point in time there is a basic agreement between business institutions and society known as the social contract. This contract defines broad relationships between the business institution and society. The contract is partly expressed in legislation and law. It is also reflected in generally accepted customs and values that govern business activity. Unfortunately for business managers, this contract is not as clearly delineated as are the economic forces a business faces, as complex and ambiguous as they often are. For example, it is widely recognized today that business has social responsibilities other than just following regulatory mandates. If a business does not meet them it may suffer. But precisely what are they? To what extent must a business comply when they are not written into law? To what extent does the social responsibility of a large company differ from that of a small one? These are questions that will be addressed at length in the book.

It should be underscored that if a business manager ignores or violates in any important way the social contract, as vague as parts of it may be, he or she is courting disaster. Not only must a manager react to today's noneconomic environment but to that which is perceived in the future. So, the response to the question of why the BGS field is important to managers is: to be successful business managers must understand, respond properly to, and anticipate demands of the noneconomic environment as well as the economic environment.

Another answer to the question concerns business participation in the debate about social and ethical demands made on the business institution. If business responds appropriately to societal demands it will have more credibility when it engages in debate about its responsibilities. As David Rockefeller said in 1971:

> It is vital that social accountability become an integral part of corporate conduct, rather than a philanthropic add-on. Only in that way will the economic development of the private sector move forward within an acceptable framework of public purpose. Only in that way will corporations assure the healthy social climate vital to their own future economic prosperity.[2]

This is a position that many prominent managers have taken. At stake is the definition of the role of business in this society. Business managers, of course, must be engaged in formulating that role.

Basic Conceptual Models of the BGS Relationship

People view the BGS field from different perspectives. They have frames of reference, or models, through which they evaluate the interplay of economic, political, and cultural forces. Depending upon their chosen model, they may reach entirely different conclusions about central issues in the BGS field. They may differ fundamentally, for example, about the scope of business's power in society, the key criteria for making business decisions, the extent of corporate social responsibilities, the ethical dimensions of management decisions, and the need for regulation of business. Therefore, it is important to know the model or conceptual framework, that people have in mind.

What follows are four basic models that represent fundamental alternatives for conceptualizing the BGS relationship. These models are simple abstractions. Each is a simple representation of a more complex reality and each encompasses a variety of opinions among those who adhere to it.

The Market Capitalism Model

The market capitalism model, as shown in Figure 1-1, has been popular with business managers and many economists for more than two centuries. This conceptual model visualizes the business system as substantially sheltered from the direct impact of the social forces in its environment and focuses on the primacy of market economic forces. It depicts business and industry as existing in a market environment that is influenced and shaped both by business decisions and by impinging social, political, legal, and cultural forces. The market environment in the model acts as a buffer between business units and nonmarket environmental forces.

The system depicted in this model is called capitalism. It is a system in which the bulk of economic activity is carried on by private enterprise operating in a competitive market. The efficient operation of this system is based on a number of fundamental assumptions.[3]

One assumption is that government interference in economic life will be held to a minimum. Government intervention in the market is not only inappropriate but also unnecessary. It is inappropriate because it will lessen the efficiency with which the free enterprise system will operate to benefit consumers. It is unnecessary because market forces are sufficient to channel business efforts to meet social needs. Noneconomic goals or performance measures are not legitimate guideposts for judging the contributions of business. Market performance should be the only accepted measure of social performance. It is the function of government, not the free enterprise system, to minister to social problems. Managers, therefore, should define the interests of their companies, narrowly, as profitability and greater efficiency in using scarce resources. Business makes its primary contribution to society by providing wealth for society as a result of its profitable operations.

FIGURE 1-1
The market capitalism
model

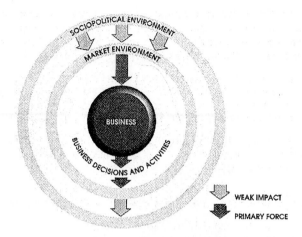

Another fundamental assumption is that individuals have maximum freedom to pursue their own self-interests and that they will do so. Each individual, it is reasoned, is interested in bettering himself or herself. If each has economic freedom each will, by pursuing his or her individual self-interest, ensure economic progress.

The model assumes also that individuals can own private property and are free to risk investments in business firms. Under these circumstances businesses are powerfully motivated to make a profit for their owners. If there is free competition in the market, profits will be held to a minimum and the quality of products and services will rise as firms try to attract more buyers. If one enterprise tries to increase profits by charging higher prices, consumers will buy from another producer. If one producer produces higher-quality products, others will be forced to follow. The free market system, therefore, is a strategic regulator of business that converts competition into social benefits.

Space does not permit further elaboration of assumptions but we should indicate here a few. For example, individuals must have full knowledge of products and prices to make the best decisions; there will be many producers in the competitive market; the interests of enterprises and consumers are closely related; and there will be necessary institutions, such as a reliable banking system, to facilitate free competition.[4]

This model has been a powerful basis for resistance to government regulations throughout our history. There is validity in parts of the model, but today the emphasis is distorted in light of current realities. Today, for example, the social responsiveness of business is not as limited as this model would indicate, and many of the assumptions upon which it is based are contrary to reality. Contemporary managers, if their enterprises are to succeed, must respond to forces in the sociopolitical environment. Today, demands of society have resulted in massive intrusions of government in the marketplace. Nevertheless, this model is still widely used as a lens through which many people, particularly managers, view the BGS relationship. The theory of capitalism still dominates economic values in the United States today, but great social regulation and a changing social environment necessitate modification of the model if it is to reflect reality. But, in its pure form it still is the ideal many managers, economists, and others believe should define reality.

The Dominance Model

The dominance model conceptualizes a second basic way of looking at the BGS relationship. It represents a perspective attractive primarily to business critics. In it, business and government dominate the great mass of people and groups in society. This idea is represented in the pyramidal, hierarchical image of society shown in Figure 1-2. Those who subscribe to this model believe that a small elite sits astride a system that works to increase and perpetuate wealth and power for a privileged few at the expense of the welfare of common people. Such a system is, of course, undemocratic. In democratic theory government and leaders represent interests expressed by the people.

FIGURE 1-2
The dominance model

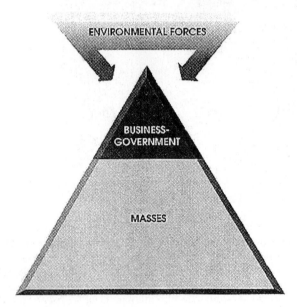

In the United States the dominance model appeared as a way of conceptualizing the BGS relationship during the latter half of the nineteenth century when large trusts emerged and corruptly manipulated politicians and legislatures. Beginning in the 1870s, farmers and other critics of big business based a reform movement called populism on a view of the BGS relationship like that in the dominance model.

This was an era when the actions of powerful business magnates and financiers shaped the destinies of common people and they openly displayed their power. For example, when a reporter told William Harriman, a railroad baron, that he had a responsibility to the public he snapped, "The public be damned. I am working for my stockholders."[5] Later, when some business leaders became worried about antitrust initiatives by the federal government Edward Harriman, another railroad giant, said that he was not worried and "declared that if he wanted state legislation, he could buy it and that if necessary he could buy Congress and the judiciary as well."[6]

The populist movement failed in its effort to reform the BGS relationship. But its critical perspective about big business lived on. Today it continues to have a lively existence among radical critics of business. Following are the words of one recent critic.

> We are ruled by Big Business and Big Government. . . . Corporate money is wrecking popular government in the United States. The big corporations and the centimillionaires and billionaires have taken daily control of our work, our pay, our housing, our health, our pension funds, our bank and savings deposits, our public lands, our airwaves, our elections and our very government.[7]

This 1900 political cartoon illustrates a central theme of the dominance model, that powerful business interests act in concert with government to further selfish money interests. Although the cartoon is old the idea remains compelling for many.

In the hands of his philanthropic friends.

Marxism, a philosophy opposed to industrial capitalism which emerged in Europe in the nineteenth century, contains ideas in accord with the society depicted in the dominance model. In capitalist societies, according to Karl Marx, an elite ruling class dominates the economy and other institutions, including government. This has led many radical critics worldwide to advocate socialist governments which, based on Marx's theory, can achieve more equitable distributions of power and wealth.[8]

In the United States today the dominance model, in its most unadulterated form, is a theory opposed by considerable scholarship which holds that pluralistic forces in society check and control corporate and government power in the public interest. However, there is considerable attraction to elements of the dominance model in the American population, which is traditionally suspicious of centralized power in business or government. It remains one of the fundamental alternative perspectives of the BGS relationship. At times in our past history, as in the post-Civil War era, it was in close accord with reality. It also is close to the reality of the BGS relationship in some other nations, including Japan, China, and Korea.

The Dynamic Forces Model

The dynamic forces model, shown in Figure 1-3, pictures the BGS relationship as a system of interactions. As complicated as the model appears it does not fully reveal the extraordinary intricacies of influence-response interrelationships among the major elements of society. But it does clearly show dominant flows of influence in the BGS relationship as far as business is concerned. It shows that the main influences on business come from changes in environmental forces, both economic and noneconomic; their impact on public values, expectations, demands, and so on; and the influence of these forces on the political processes, which in turn affect corporations and other businesses. In addition, the model shows that business influences all the other elements in society.

FIGURE 1-3
The dynamic forces
model

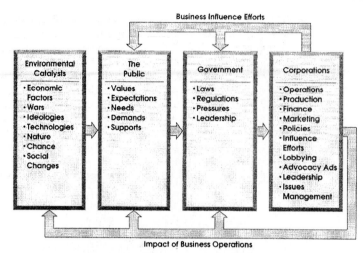

This is a dynamic model of multiple, or pluralistic forces. The forces operate differently and with varying impacts, depending on a wide range of factors such as the subject or policy at issue, the power of competing groups, the intensity of public feelings, and the effectiveness of government and business leadership. The dynamic forces model differs fundamentally from the dominance model, which depicts a system strongly dominated by economic interests over a wide spectrum of issues. Many of the forces shown as important in the dynamic forces model would be regarded as of negligible importance in the dominance model.

What overarching conclusions can be drawn from this model?

1. Business is deeply integrated into the environment and must respond to many forces, both economic and noneconomic, impinging upon the business system. It is not isolated from its environment, nor is it dominant.
2. Business is a major initiator of change in its environment, especially through its interaction with government and the introduction of new products or services.
3. Ours is an open society of complex interactions in which many forces exert pressures on both government and business. Society is not hierarchial or dominated by a small group but is an interacting network of influences.
4. Broad and underlying public support of the business enterprise depends on its adjustment to many different environmental forces. To survive, business must react to a mixture of social, political, and economic forces.
5. Support for business will be greatest when the impacts of the business system on its environment are more positive than negative, that is, when benefits provided are greater than costs imposed. This, of course, is difficult to measure in practice, but the underlying idea is important.
6. BGS relationships continuously evolve as changes take place in the main ideas, institutions, and processes of society.

The Stakeholder Model

In the stakeholder model the business firm is at the center of a set of mutual relationships with individuals and groups called *stakeholders*. Stakeholders are those who are benefited or burdened by the firm's operation, that is, they have a stake in it. For a large corporation this definition of stakeholder includes a wide range of entities, which can be divided into two categories based on their relative importance. *Primary* stakeholders are those that are essential to the survival of the firm. These include owners, customers, employees, communities, and government and may include others such as suppliers or creditors. *Secondary* stakeholders include other groups or individuals not essential to the survival of the firm, but which are affected by its operations. Secondary stakeholders might include interest groups such as environmentalists, the media, intellectual critics, trade associations, and even competitors.[9] Figure 1-4 shows an expansive view of possible stakeholders for a large corporation. Among those who subscribe to the stakeholder model there is debate over the exact identification of stakeholders. Some use a very broad definition and include, for example, future generations and natural entities such as the earth's atmosphere, oceans, terrain, and living creatures because corporate activity has an impact on them.[10]

FIGURE 1-4
The stakeholder model

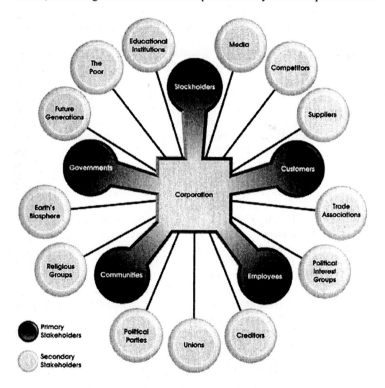

The stakeholder model fundamentally redefines the priorities of management away from what they are under the market capitalism model. In the market capitalism model the corporation is the private property of the owners who invest capital. It combines capital from investors with materials from suppliers and labor from employees into products which are sold to satisfy consumer demand. The dominant purpose of the firm's operation is to benefit one group of stakeholders—investors. In the stakeholder model, however, the welfare of each stakeholder must be considered as an end in itself, not simply as a means to enrich investors. Put differently, "stakeholders are defined by *their* legitimate interest in the corporation, rather than simply by the corporation's interest in *them*."[11] Managers should be strongly responsive to multiple stakeholders and because of this the interests of owner/investors receive less emphasis.

The way of looking at the corporation prescribed by the stakeholder model then, emphasizes duties toward many groups in society, duties that are not emphasized in traditional economic theory. The traditional theory of the corporation encourages the corporation to dominate its environment and minimize benefits for other stakeholders, all for the benefit of owners. The stakeholder theory asserts a moral duty for management to recognize and work toward the satisfaction of a much broader range of stakeholder interests.

Advocates of the new stakeholder perspective have focused on developing new rules which should guide corporations in their relations with stakeholders. One scholar, for example, argues that stakeholders are "moral agents" entitled to common rights and considerations. To ensure regard for these rights, corporate directors should have a "duty of care" to see that the corporation is managed "in the interests of its stakeholders."[12] This concept requires more ethical consideration about the impact of corporate actions on various stakeholders than is presently practiced by managers. Another scholar argues that "maximum consideration of stakeholders is paramount" and advocates a system of "moral strategic management" to develop and implement policies that are sensitive to the rights of various stakeholders.[13] If multiple stakeholder interests must be considered in corporate strategies a further logical step is to call for stakeholder groups to participate in corporate governance and corporate decisions.

Overall, the stakeholder model is more than a descriptive model of how corporations relate to their environment. It is intended by its advocates to fundamentally redefine the corporation. The stakeholder model rejects the traditional view of the corporation which emphasizes profit making for stockholders. "The plain truth is," write two of its advocates, "that the most prominent alternative to stakeholder theory (i.e., the 'management serving the shareowners' theory) is morally untenable."[14] It seeks to substitute a doctrine of ethical duties toward multiple stakeholders that would shift power in the corporation, reducing that of owners and increasing that of other primary stakeholders.

The stakeholder model of the BGS relationship not only rejects central elements of the market capitalism model, but is fundamentally different from the other two models set forth in this chapter. It is the opposite of the dominance model, which describes a world in which corporations exercise control over a range of stakeholders rather than interact with genuine concern for their interests. And it is at odds with the dynamic forces model. The dynamic forces model diagrams important forces, or power flows, between the corporation and its environment. These power flows are estimates of reality, not prescriptions for an ideal that might be achieved if the corporation changed. The focus of the dynamic forces model is broader; it displays a wide range of environmental factors including, but not limited too, stakeholders.

The Meaning of the Four Models

All the models are both descriptive and normative, meaning that they describe how the BGS relationship works and also prescribe judgments about how it should work. Persons or groups that subscribe to one of these models see reality in a way which leads them to certain moral conclusions.

The market capitalism model is dominant in the thinking of a majority of managers in business, especially in small enterprises. Because of its influence, many conclude that their decisions should be most heavily influenced by economic considerations and that solving social problems is a secondary, even an inappropriate, goal. However, managers fully understand the perspective of the dynamic forces model, which shows how corporations are exposed to multiple groups and forces that can dramatically affect their operation. From this perspective they may conclude that corporations should put energy into monitoring and interacting with noneconomic forces in their environment. The stakeholder model depicts a world in which the corporation is at the center of multiple interests. From this perspective it is a short step to the conclusion that managers have a moral obligation to more deeply consider in their decisions the well-being of all these groups.

The dominance model is held principally by some, but by no means all, critics of business. This model depicts a world which diverges from democratic theory and violates fundamental principles of equality and justice. Those who use this model conclude that business is too powerful and reform or radical change of the system is necessary. Most managers shun this model.

The models are too simple to fully show the relative power of forces within BGS relationships. For instance, the market capitalism model does not explain the degree to which the market environment protects business from specific noneconomic environmental forces. The stakeholder model fails to explain how much influence each constituent has on a corporation. It should be recognized also that these models are not static. The relationships they depict change over time.

The BGS Relationship in Other Highly Industrialized Nations

The relationships among business, government, and society also vary widely among nations. For instance, corporations in the United States pay much more attention to shareholders than corporations in Japan, Germany, or France.[15] Workers in the United States have much less influence on the management of the companies where they work than workers in many European countries. The basic relationship between business and government in the United States is adversarial, following the market capitalism model. In Japan and Korea it is highly cooperative and is closer to the dominance model. In China the central government exerts authoritarian controls over all activity, except in a few free trade areas which the government has established.

What are the Main Characteristics of the Analysis of This Book?

As you have seen, the interrelationships among business, government, and society are many and can be approached in different ways. The principal characteristics of our analysis in this book follow.

Focus on Strategic Management

Strategic management is a term now in vogue. It describes the formulation and implementation of strategies that adapt a company to its changing environment. By "strategic management" we refer to the formulation of a company's missions, purposes, and objectives; the policies and programs to achieve them; and the methods needed to assure that they are implemented.

The concept of strategic management does not imply that managements formulate strategies only in response to current events. Quite the contrary, it means that managers try to anticipate future environmental forces so that they can take proactive measures to deal with them.

More specifically, we are concerned with the way environmental forces enter into the formulation and implementation of such strategies as the following:

- Those that spell out the social responsibilities of the company.
- Those that react to changing social values with respect to such matters as the nature of the company's products or the changing aspirations of employees.
- Those that respond to government regulations concerning such matters as pollution, product safety, and equal opportunity.
- Those that determine when and how the company will try to influence political processes.
- Those that change the structure and processes by which the firm responds to environmental forces.
- Those that affect the ethical standards according to which decisions are made in a company.

Interdisciplinary Approach with a Managerial Focus

A large number of disciplines must be considered in dealing with theory, practice, and policy issues in the BGS interface. The more prominent ones are economics, political science, law, philosophy, sociology, science, history, and management. Our approach is an eclectic one in which we attempt to use the most relevant disciplines associated with a particular theory, practice, or policy issue. It is possible to analyze the BGS relationship in an interdisciplinary way but with a dominant disciplinary orientation, such as economics, political science, or law. Our orientation, as we have said, is managerial.

Comprehensive Scope

We have sought to make this book comprehensive in scope. We have tried to cover a large canvas, sketching out the most important interrelationships among business, government, and other societal forces. This approach is in contrast to that of selecting and concentrating intensively and exclusively on a few areas such as business social responsibility, pollution, consumerism, equal opportunity, and antitrust. We believe that it is far better for students in a basic course covering the BGS relationships to study many interrelationships, even if the exposure is often light, than to explore only a few areas.

Focus on Theory

We have tried to emphasize theoretical concepts appearing to have some permanence and providing valuable normative guides for understanding environmental forces, the managerial responses to them, and the way in which the business role is changing. We recognize, however, that there is no underlying theory integrating the entire field, nor is there likely to be one in the foreseeable future. The field is extremely diverse, complex, and fluid, and there is no consensus about its precise boundaries.

One can say tentatively, however, that the beginnings of an underlying theory of business and its relationship to society are emerging, but the profile is not clear. There is growing agreement, for example, about the theoretical obligations of corporations to respond to social pressures. In a number of major areas, useful theories are rooted in relevant disciplines. For example, there are tested political theories concerned with business power, scientific theories concerned with pollution issues, legal theories concerned with manufacturer liability, and economic theories concerned with government regulations to mention a few. We have sought to emphasize such theories where they are relevant to the subject matter of this book.

The Historical Perspective

To the extent practicable we set forth a historical perspective for discussion of major topics. We believe that one cannot fully understand the present—or the future—without some comprehension and appreciation of the past. With history as a base, it is easier to avoid being deceived by clichés, "red herrings," and irrelevant observations. As Justice Holmes once suggested, history is the first step toward an enlightened skepticism. Furthermore, it is important to know that there are historical causes for current events and that the pattern of future events is being shaped today.

History is not useful in the sense that a knowledge of chemistry is. But it can be at least as valuable in providing insights into how we got where we are today, the creditability of solutions proposed for burning current issues, and where we may be heading. "A moment's insight," wrote Justice Holmes, "is worth a lifetime of experience."

Global Perspective

In a limited way we seek a global perspective on selected subjects. Our interest, of course, is in comparisons with the principal foreign competitors to U.S. companies, countries in which our corporations operate, and countries with which we have significant trade relationships.

Endnotes

1. See, for example, *"We Were Only Limited by Our Imagination and Creativity:" Exxon and Education*, New York: Exxon Corporation, 1995.
2. David Rockefeller, *The Corporation in Transition: Redefining Its Social Charter*, Washington, D.C.: Chamber of Commerce of the United States, 1973, p. 23.
3. The model was built in consideration of the way in which the ideal operation of the free enterprise system was first enunciated by Adam Smith in his *Wealth of Nations* (published in 1776), a book which has been influential throughout the history of free enterprise and democratic countries.
4. For a brief discussion of the assumptions, see George A. Steiner, *Business and Society*, New York: Random House, 1971, Chapter 3, "The Theory of Capitalism."
5. Cited in Clifton Fadiman, ed., *The Little, Brown Book of Anecdotes*, Boston: Little, Brown, 1985.
6. James A. Barnes, *Wealth of the American People*, New York: Prentice-Hall, 1949, p. 630.
7. Ronnie Dugger, "Real Populists Please Stand Up," *The Nation*, August 14/21, 1995, p. 159.
8. See, for example, Michael Parenti, *Democracy for the Few*, 5th ed., New York: St. Martin's Press, 1995.
9. See, for example, Max Clarkson, "A Stakeholder Framework for Analyzing and Evaluating Corporate Social Performance," *Academy of Management Review*, January 1995, pp. 106-7.
10. See, for example, Mark Starik, "Essay by Mark Starik," *Business and Society*, April 1994, pp. 92-93.
11. Thomas Donaldson and Lee E. Preston, "The Stakeholder Theory of the Corporation: Concepts, Evidence, and Implications," *Academy of Management Review*, January 1995, p. 76. Emphasis in original.
12. R. Edward Freeman, "The Politics of Stakeholder Theory: Some Future Directions," *Business Ethics Quarterly*, October 1994, p. 417. See also Freeman's landmark book *Strategic Management: A Stakeholder Approach*, Boston, Mass.: Pitman, 1984.
13. Archie B. Carroll, "Stakeholder Thinking in Three Models of Management Morality: A Perspective with Strategic Implications," in Jahu Nasi, ed., *Understanding Stakeholder Thinking*, Helsinki, Finland: LSR Publications, 1995, p. 68.
14. Donaldson and Preston, "The Stakeholder Theory of the Corporation," p. 88.
15. See Charles Hampden-Turner and Alfons Trompenaars, *The Several Cultures of Capitalism*, New York: Doubleday, 1993. In this study the authors surveyed 15,000 managers in seven countries considered to have capitalistic systems. The countries were: the United States, the United Kingdom, Sweden, France, Japan, the Netherlands, and Germany. The authors found major differences in the value systems among these countries and thus in the way capitalism operated.

Chapter Two

THE BUSINESS

ENVIRONMENT

Enron Corp

In January 1995, a consortium headed by Enron Corp. (with Bechtel, Inc., and General Electric's GE Capital Corporation) completed the paperwork to begin construction of a $2.8 billion power plant at Dabhol in the state of Maharashtra, India. In February an election was held in that state and the Hindu nationalist party (BJP) teamed up with a splinter group and gained control of the government of Maharashtra. In August 1995, after Enron and its partners began construction and spent some $300 million, the new government based in Bombay "repudiated" the contracts Enron had negotiated with the previous government and with the national government in New Delhi and vowed to "throw Enron into the sea" and not pay Enron and its partners 1 penny.

This action should be considered in light of a crippling power shortage in the state of Maharashtra, one of the major industrial areas of India, and the promise that the investment of Enron and its partners would stimulate substantial further investment in the poverty-stricken country. Furthermore, it was the previous Maharashtra state government that invited Enron to build the plant. This was in accord with a policy of the national government in New Delhi to welcome foreign investment. What happened?

The political environment for Enron changed radically. The BJP is a left-wing group that fanned the flames of anti-foreign influence that existed in Maharashtra and in other areas of India. So, it was natural that when it gained control of the government it would reflect that sentiment.

Many charges were levied against Enron. It was accused of getting the contract without competitive bidding, of being too costly, of harming the environment, of fraud and misrepresentation, and of making bribes to get the contracts. Enron vehemently rejected these charges and none were proven.

An expert committee was formed to renegotiate the contract and agreement with the Dabhol partners, which was reached and announced in early 1996. All approvals have been received at the state level and, upon central government and lender approval, construction is expected to resume in the second quarter of 1996.

Enron is a major integrated natural gas company with worldwide operations, based in Houston, Texas. Its 1995 sales are estimated at $9.8 billion.

The situation of Enron is illustrative of uncertainties of foreign environments in which U.S. companies operate. In this chapter we first discuss the volatility of the business environment throughout our history. This is meant to provide a perspective for the remaining discussion of the chapter, which is divided into two parts. The first part pertains to the historical forces that have evolved over a long period of time and that underlie short- and medium-range trends in the business environment. The second focuses on the current business environment, external and internal. We conclude with comments about the impact of business on the environment and the implications for business and the business institution.

The Volatility of the Business Environment

In 1844 Philip Hone, mayor of New York City, was baffled by the volatility of his environment. "This world is going on too fast," he wrote. "Improvements, Politics, Reform, Religion—all fly. Railroads, steamers, packets, race against time and beat it hollow. Flying is dangerous. By and by we shall have balloons and pass over to Europe between sun and sun. Oh, for the good old days of heavy post-coaches and speed at the rate of six miles an hour!"[1]

Hone's views reflect what people have experienced throughout history, including today. From ancient to modern times environments have been volatile and generally unpredictable. For example, the Black Death in the middle of the fourteenth century killed one-third of the population of Europe and completely changed that world. The industrial revolution in the eighteenth century in England was unforeseen and changed the world significantly for all time. Businesses in the American colonies in the seventeenth and eighteenth centuries were more and more restrained by so-called navigation acts imposed by the British Parliament to control exports from and imports to the colonies in the interests of England. Throughout the eighteenth and early nineteenth centuries in the United States most businesses were able to exploit a vast continent with unbounded resources and friendly governments. That freedom was considerably reduced in the late nineteenth and twentieth centuries as business became subject to ever widening and more restrictive government regulations.

Throughout history, people in business who have been unaware of or ignored their changing environments have, at best, lost opportunities for profit and, at worst, led their companies to disaster. Look at the Baldwin Locomotive Works, for example. That firm was started by Matthias W. Baldwin, a watch-maker, to make steam locomotives. The first engine he produced—"Old Ironsides"—was built in 1832. It was one of the first steam engines made in this country. By the time of Baldwin's death in 1866 the plant had built 1,500 locomotives for American and foreign railroads. As we all know the railroads, facilitated by the steam locomotive, shaped the development of this country. As the years went by Baldwin's company prospered and had a virtual monopoly on the production of steam locomotives in the United States. However, its management failed to see the significance of the diesel locomotive and the company went bankrupt. On the other hand, General Motors seized the opportunity offered by diesel technology and profitably exploited it.

Currently, changing conditions here in the United States and around the globe bewilder people in and out of business with their volatility and power. For business, for example, global competition poses serious threats to some companies and great opportunities for others. Our textile manufacturers, for example, have felt the sting of global competition. Our pharmaceutical firms, on the other hand, have met foreign competition and thrived in the new global marketplace.

Underlying Historical Forces Changing the Business Environment

We believe that in a broad sense, order can be found in the swirling patterns of current events; that there is a deep logic in the passing of history; and that change in the business environment is the result of elemental historical forces trending in roughly predictable directions. Henry Adams defined a historical force as "anything that does, or helps to do, work."[2] The work that Adams refers to is the manifest power to cause events. Change in the business environment is the work of events caused by the seven deep historical forces or streams of related events discussed below. Corporate strategy is the effort of business to adapt to the continuous changes caused by these forces.

The Industrial Revolution

The first historical force is the industrial revolution. The breakup of small, local economies and the invention of new machinery and manufacturing techniques in seventeenth-century Europe led to expanded markets and mass-production technology that combined capital, labor, and natural resources in dynamic new ways. The growth of mass-consumer societies and a world economy in the twentieth century are but two recent echoes of this industrial "big bang." The ramifications of the industrial revolution ripple out through time to define the strategic business environment in many ways. For example, new and larger factories, massive capital accumulation, management techniques for organizing huge corporations, and the interdependence of financial markets all articulate its centuries-old premise.

Dominant Ideologies

A second historical force is the impact of dominant ideologies. An ideology is a worldview which is built upon and reinforces a set of beliefs and values.[3] For example, the idea of progress, which has been a defining ideology in Western civilization, was built on a set of beliefs that arose with industrialism. Adam Smith taught that market economies were a great advance that harnessed human greed for the public good. Charles Darwin wrote that the biological world was characterized by constant improvement and Herbert Spencer argued in what later came to be called social Darwinism that competition in the business world weeded out the unfit and drove humanity in upward motion toward betterment. The idea of progress reinforced values of particular importance to business such as optimism, thrift, competitiveness, individualism, and freedom from government interference.

A small number of powerful, well-developed doctrines define a worldview for millions of people. Americans and Western Europeans largely adhere to ideologies of capitalism, constitutional democracy, and the major western religions of Catholicism and its offshoot, Protestantism. Other nations, facing different historical challenges, have been attracted to different ideologies. In Russia the populace accepted autocratic ideologies such as Czarism and Communism as the price of having a ruling power capable of maintaining national boundaries.

Tensions frequently arise between ideologies. For example, the accumulation of great wealth is justified by capitalism, but when this wealth is translated into social power it conflicts with tenets of democracy that give mass populations the right to check ruling classes in the exercise of power. Tensions between these two ideologies have ignited political movements and led to redistribution of power.

Inequality of Human Circumstances

From time immemorial, societies have been marked by status distinctions, class structures, and gaps between rich and poor. Inequality is ubiquitous, as are its consequences—jealousy, demands for equality, and doctrines that justify why some people have more than others. The basic political conflict in every nation is the result of economic antagonism between rich and poor.[4] This is the conflict, manifest in the competition between Athens' democracy and Sparta's oligarchy, that debilitated and eventually tore apart ancient Hellenic civilization. In the modern world industrialism has accelerated the accumulation of wealth without solving the persistent problem of its uneven distribution. The current emphasis on corporate social responsibility in the business environment is, in a general sense, based on the need to mitigate the appearance of remote and unresponsive concentrated wealth.

Science and Technology

The great scientific developments of civilization since Leonardo da Vinci in fifteenth-century Italy have been fuel for the powerful engine of commerce. From the water wheel to recombinant DNA, business has utilized new discoveries to more efficiently convert basic resources into equity. The development of the microchip brought changes in virtually every facet of the business environment. Like the automobile in its time, it has changed society.

Nation-States

The modern nation-state system arose in an unplanned way out of the wreckage of the Roman Empire as princes and monarchs expanded and consolidated empires in Europe after the Peace of Westphalia in 1648. The institution of the nation-state was well-suited for Western Europe, where boundaries were contiguous with the extent of languages. But the nation-state idea was subsequently transplanted to territories in Eastern Europe, Southwest Asia, and the Middle East, partly by force of colonial empires and partly by mimicry among non-Western political elites for whom the idea had attained high prestige. And where it was transplanted, nations were often irrationally defined and boundary lines divided natural groupings of culture, ethnicity, and language.

Today the world is a mosaic of independent countries, each with a separate government to impose social order and economic stability over its territory. And in each there develop feelings of nationalism or loyalty to a national identity. The dynamics of this system are a powerful force in the international business environment. Conflict among nations seeking to aggrandize their power and wealth is frequent, as occurred in the 1930s when Japan colonized South Asian countries to gain access to oil and bauxite. Conflict between culture groupings across nation-state boundaries is today increasingly prominent.[5] The nationalistic feelings of Palestinians deposed from Israeli territory and living in other countries have affected American companies in many ways, from oil companies that have been caught in Middle East conflicts to airlines that lose passengers afraid of terrorism. For many reasons, the nation-state system is one of the major sources of turbulence in the business environment.

Great Leadership

Great leaders have brought beneficial as well as disastrous changes to societies and businesses. In the third century B.C., Alexander the Great imposed his rule on the Mediterranean world and created new routes of trade on which Greek merchants flourished. On the other hand, leaders such as Adolph Hitler in Germany and Joseph Stalin in the Soviet Union brought to their societies disaster that retarded industrial growth.

There have been many business leaders whose actions had great impact. Probably no industrial leader in American history had a more profound influence on the nation than John D. Rockefeller. His Standard Oil Company of Ohio, from its inception in 1870 to its breakup by a Supreme Court antitrust decision in 1911, grew to completely dominate the oil industry and, in the process, changed the American economic, political, and social landscape. Its offspring are still among great oil companies which dominate the global petroleum market. Today William Gates of Microsoft inspires comparisons to Rockefeller as the strategies of his company increasingly define how telecommunications technologies will be used in society.

There are two views about the power of leaders as a historical force. One is that leaders simply ride the wave of history. "Great men," writes Arnold Toynbee, "are precisely the points of intersection of great social forces."[6] The other is that leaders themselves change history rather than being pushed by its tide. "The history of the world," wrote Thomas Carlyle, "is at bottom the History of the Great Men who have worked here."[7] The cases and stories of business leaders in this text provide instances for debate of this provocative clash of views.

Chance

When change occurs we seek causes. If two or more lines of action intersect in an event its cause is known, as when the technological innovation of the diesel locomotive and the steam-locomotive-based strategy of the Baldwin Locomotive Company intersected to produce failure. But where lines of action cannot be observed or seem to be random, then the concept of chance can be used to explain an event. The first Tylenol murders occurred in September 1982, when seven people died from capsules filled with cyanide. This event, perhaps the work of one person, was followed over the years by recurrent and mysteriously random product tampering to poison consumers. This tampering created a major change in the production and marketing environments of food and over-the-counter drug companies. Was the initial tampering a random act unrelated to the actions of the corporations and victims it affected, without which this change in the business environment would not have occurred? Or can its causes be explained?

Many scholars are reluctant to use the concept of chance, accident, or random occurrence as a category of analysis. Yet some changes in the business environment may best be explained as the product of unknown and unpredictable causes. No less perceptive a student of history than Niccolo Machiavelli observed that fortune determines about half the course of human events and human beings the other half. We cannot prove or disprove this estimate, but we note it. The student of the world surrounding business must recognize the role of caprice.

Six Key Environments of Business

Figure 2-1 shows the six major environments affecting business today. From time to time, other environments such as national security may significantly affect business, but these six have the greatest impact today.

Today's business environment challenges managers in far more different ways and is more uncertain than any since World War II. We seem to be at a critical stage in world and U.S. history, with turning points in many important areas. Note, for example, the ending of the Cold War and the forces that are operating throughout Eastern Europe and Russia to support free markets and democratic governments. It is no wonder that business executives are spending more of their time, indeed most of their time, dealing with environmental forces. The requirement today is that managers throughout an organization, not just the chief executive officer and staff, be continuously committed to understanding and adapting to environmental developments that can affect operations.

We turn now to thumbnail sketches of each of the dominant environments of business and selected forces operating in them. We will dig deeper into these environments throughout the book.

FIGURE 2-1
The six key
environments of
business

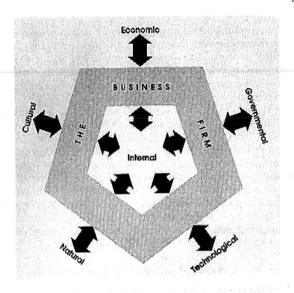

The Economic Environment

The economic environment covers a vast territory and is, of course, of primary significance to business. The economic forces of concern to a company range from overall economic activity, as measured by the gross domestic product (GDP), to a competitor's actions in a local market. We illustrate next a few dimensions of the scope, turbulence, complexity, and power of the economic environment of business.

Overall economic activity as measured by GDP has fluctuated widely from the end of World War II to the present. When GDP is rising robustly, it stimulates business growth and profitability. When it is growing slowly or declining, business activity is depressed and profits drop or disappear.

The many different components within GDP tend to fluctuate much more than the GDP total. Thus, changes will vary more in such economic forces as consumer and wholesale prices, employment, wage rates, worker productivity, steel production, automobile sales, house construction, and inventories.

Every important economic force has an impact on a wide range of other economic forces, which in turn affect others. The patterns of change vary with time and in intensity. To illustrate, commodity prices have fluctuated significantly in recent years and will doubtless do so again in the future, a matter of concern to business as well as consumers. But when and by how much will prices change? What will be the economic implications? No one really knows. Major changes in the general level of commodity prices will affect interest rates, consumer purchasing, stock and bond prices, basic raw material prices, and wage-rate demands, to mention but a few activities. Each of these forces affects other phenomena. For example, rising commodity prices tend to generate forces that lift interest rates. This, in turn, increases the cost of capital to business and dampens business borrowing for expansion. Rising interest rates also will bring a decline in bond prices. But rising, or lowering, interest rates result not only from commodity price increases. Higher interest rates can result from a too rapid expansion of general economic activity and rising demand for capital, a decline in savings, or rising interest rates in a major foreign country that attract our limited capital.

These broad changes in the economic environment narrow down to specific impacts on an individual business and necessitate some difficult and often fateful decisions in dealing with them. A chief executive must answer such questions as the following: How will my costs of operations change? Wage rates? Raw materials? Health and benefit costs for my employees? Interest rates on my borrowing? What new competition will I face in the global market? How will the economic unification of Europe affect my business? Will my competitors here at home steal my market? How can I expand the demand for my products? How much research and development expenditures for new products shall I authorize?

Such underlying economic forces operate in every free enterprise and democratic country in the world, but differently in each one. For example, all countries have protective tariffs, but greater efforts are made in Japan to protect selected manufacturers and farmers from foreign competition than in the United States. In Europe, business in every country that is a member of the new European Union is being affected by the new Union rules. Central banks in these European countries used to exert unchallenged control over the monetary system, but no more. Today, global capital markets challenge their power with daily trades of $1 trillion worth of currency. Recently, both the Federal Reserve Bank in the United States and the Central Bank of Japan tried to raise the world price of the dollar versus the yen, but with little result.

The Technological Environment

New technology can and often does change the entire way of life, thinking, values, habits, and even the political processes of a nation. The automobile is a classic example of a new technology that enormously affected every aspect of life here and in many other countries of the world. The United States has gone through one technological revolution after another and continues to do so. For example, technology is new in computer science, biotechnology, medicine, robotic factories, telecommunications, and microelectronics, to mention just a few areas. The list of new technologies today is awesome. In the next two decades technology changes will reshape virtually every product, every service, every job in the United States. The forces generated will shake the foundations of the most secure businesses. The choices will powerfully affect options available to consumers, the rate and growth of different business sectors, the role of business in the world, and the standard of living in the United States.

There also occurred a certain important development in technology. I would bet not more than three people here have heard about it. England ran out of firewood, they had burned too much of it. And, because of that, they had to turn to a poor and dirty substitute: coal. It was soon found that coal burned at a higher temperature and that you could now handle iron very much better than you could handle it before. The price of iron came down below that of bronze. The iron age really started at that time because prior to that iron could be used only for some particularly important purposes, like art or war.

Source: From Edward Teller, "The Next Hundred Years," in *Technological Planning on the Corporate Level*, James R. Bright, ed., Cambridge, Mass: Harvard University Graduate School of Business Administration, 1962, p. 151

A few illustrations make the point that in the immediate future there will be mind-boggling new technological inventions. New biogenetics will cure some of the most intractable human diseases. Micromotors no larger than the period at the end of this sentence, which now exist, will be inconspicuously inserted into the human body to snip tumors, repair artery walls, unclog blood vessels, and provide television transmission of interior conditions. Advancing computer technology will be unparalleled in its impact on every facet of society. Since the 1970s, about every 2½ to 3 years we have had a new generation of computers. The trend has been to make them smaller and smaller and cheaper and cheaper. This movement continues and will carry us into what is currently called the *information highway.* It is envisioned as a seamless global web of communications networks, computers, databases, and consumer electronics, that will instantly provide users with enormous amounts of information. This infrastructure will integrate information services (voice, video, and data) into an advanced high-speed, interactive, broadband, digital communications system.[8] Among other things, this technology will carry us into a new era where the production and distribution of knowledge will be more important than the production and distribution of products. We cannot today imagine all the consequences of such developments on business.

The Governmental Environment

This environment covers a range of subjects, from federal government regulations to local party politics. We shall be dealing in depth with various aspects of government relations with business throughout this book. Here we briefly comment on a few highlights of concern to business.

There is today practically no aspect of business that governments cannot and will not regulate if the occasion arises and popular or legislative support exists. In recent years, governments have responded affirmatively a wide range of public concerns about such matters as product safety, product labeling, advertising, minority employment, pollution, and worker safety, to mention a few. Accordingly, laws have been passed to deal with these concerns. These, when added to the accumulated volume of past laws, have resulted in more government control of business than at any peacetime period in our history. Furthermore, the direction of many of these laws has been to involve government in detailed managerial decision making.

Not many years ago the principal legal worries of a large company centered on antitrust matters, and everything else was lumped together as a poor second. Today major areas of legal concern to business, in addition to antitrust, are securities and stockholder matters; consumer complaints; fair employment practices; product safety; worker safety and health; government contracts; and air, water, and noise pollution. Not only have legal actions against business in all areas increased rapidly, but potential liability for business has also risen. Corporations are exposed considerably more than in the past to legal liabilities for injuries from their products. Also, directors, officers, and other managers of businesses are subject to vastly expanded legal liabilities for their actions and, often, for those of their subordinates.

U.S. companies, of course, are subject to the politics and laws of foreign governments. Illustrative of uncertainties they face was the decision by the government in the state of Maharashtra, India, concerning Enron as explained at the beginning of this chapter.

The Cultural Environment

In 1979, when Coca-Cola returned to China, it discovered that Mao's simplification of Chinese characters translated Coca-Cola to mean "Bite the Wax Tadpole." The company solved the problem by using four Mandarin characters that translated as "Can Happy, Mouth Happy."

This simple anecdote illustrates the necessity for a company doing business in foreign countries to understand the culture of the host country. There are subtle and striking differences between the culture of the United States and the foreign cultures in which our companies do business. In addition, the cultures of individual companies differ from those of the foreign companies with whom they do business, further complicating matters. The most trivial and the most important aspects of business can be affected by those cultures.

Culture, among other things, includes the system of values, beliefs, attitudes, ideas, customs, manners, and rituals of people.[9] Culture provides a code which determines human thinking and behavior. George P. Murdock, a well-known anthropologist developed a list of seventy "cultural universals" or elements that exist in every culture.[10] In the following discussion we can touch on only a few to illustrate the major implications of others for U.S. business managers.

Laissez-Faire

Throughout our history, a fundamental dogma of people in business has been minimum government interference in the economic system. The term laissez-faire, first used by the French, meant literally that government should "leave us alone." This, of course, is inherent in the market capitalism model. Despite the fact that government today intrudes substantially in business, the fundamental value of laissez-faire is still strongly held by people in business. One result is that in the United States business exists in an adversary relationship with government.

This value is in sharp contrast to that held by people in business in Japan. The relationships there are generally cooperative and often involve close collaboration on shared goals. In Germany the relationship is also collaborative, but operates differently than in Japan. German ministries are required to consult with business and union members when drafting new legislation, but do not promote industry as much as in Japan.

Individualism

This value also is in conformance with the market capitalism model discussed in Chapter 1. Individuals in the United States seek a maximum of freedom to pursue interests relatively unimpeded by government. Today, the older view of unrestrained individualism has been modified by concepts of equality, government protection of the individual against adverse market forces, and more participation of the individual in organizations.

In Japan, people tend to see themselves as part of a group. They consider harmony in and success of the group to have a higher priority than individual welfare. Individualism is less a dominant cultural value in France, Germany, and the United Kingdom, than in the United States.

Profit

The old view, inherent in the market capitalism model, is no longer accepted. Profit is still considered necessary by a majority, but attitudes about it are changing. Society is coming more and more to expect that societal interest be considered as well as business self-interest in the pursuit of profit objectives. This is inherent in the dynamic forces model and the stakeholder model, both discussed in Chapter 1. Business managers today take the view that concern for the interests of the dominant sociopolitical stakeholders in their companies is the best route to expanding profits for shareholders.

In a study by Hampden-Turner and Trompenaars, 15,000 managers worldwide were asked to make the following decision: Choose one of the following as an accurate statement of the proper goals of a company: "(a) The only real goal of a company is making profit. (b) A company, besides making profit, has a goal of attaining the well-being of various stakeholders, such as employees, customers, etc." Only 40 percent of managers in the United States chose (a). At the other extreme, only 8 percent of the Japanese chose (a). At the lower end were Singapore, France, and Germany. Close to the United States were Australia, Canada, and the United Kingdom.[11]

There are dozens more cultural values of importance to business, so the previously-mentioned study is no more than the tip of the iceberg. Some other cultural issues of concern to business are the loyalty of people in organizations, the role of women in organizations, the type of clothing people wear in business situations, ethical codes, norms of gift giving and gratuities, organization hierarchy, the meaning of time, and the optimism of people. Our main point is that such differences constitute a major force in the cultural environment for business at home and abroad.

The Natural Environment

Included in this environment are issues associated with air and water pollution, hazardous waste disposal, unsafe pesticides, automobile emissions, ozone depletion, global warming, protection of endangered species, weather, land usage, and so on. There is an intricate and significant interrelationship of industrial activity and the natural world. Industrial activity consumes, contaminates, and shapes the natural world. Interest groups pressure corporations to change impacts. This often raises difficult questions for managers who must balance their decisions about producing things people want against pressures to preserve nature. Sometimes, they face disaster from unexpected events such as floods, tornadoes, or earthquakes.

An example of how one group of environmental activists gave managers of a large corporation a large headache concerns Royal Dutch/Shell Group, a giant oil company with headquarters in the Netherlands, and Greenpeace, a worldwide environmental group. Shell had an oil rig called the *Brent Spar*, built in 1970 and now obsolete, that it wanted to dump in the Atlantic Ocean 150 miles west of Scotland. There the ocean was 1½ miles deep and Shell said that any pollution resulting from the dumping would have insignificant impact on marine life. The rig had served as a floating oil tank, built to hold 300,000 barrels of oil produced in nearby fields. The oil was removed, of course, but there remained 100 tons of oil-related sludge in the tanks. Greenpeace said the dumping would release pollutants that would adversely affect sea life. Shell began towing the rig in mid-June 1995 and Greenpeace attempted to board the rig by aircraft in order to stop the towing, but was repulsed by water cannons. Pictures of the fracas were distributed worldwide and agitated environmentalists, especially in Germany. One result was a boycott of Shell products. German sales were off 20 to 30 percent. At that point Shell rescinded its decision to dump the rig in the ocean in favor of land disposal.

"You could argue in retrospect that we should have been more up front and explained what we were doing," said Christopher Pay, chairman of the Shell U.K. unit directly responsible for the *Brent Spar*.[12] Shell and observers concede that a big mistake was made in not coordinating the issue with environmental stakeholders of the company.

The Internal Environment

The internal environment like the external environments, can change over time and, like the external environments, have a catalytic effect on business operations. It can be described in several ways. One is to view it as being coterminous with the company culture, which has been briefly mentioned. Another approach is to identify the main classes of people in an organization. This approach is shown in Figure 2-2. Each group in the chart has different goals, beliefs, needs, and so on, which managers must coordinate to achieve overall company goals. The fundamental characteristics of the groups are readily known and need no further elaboration here. Later in the book, we will intensively examine the changing internal life of organizations.

FIGURE 2-2
Major stakeholders in
the internal business
environment

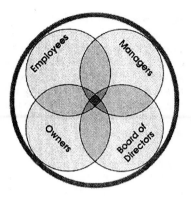

Business's Impact on Its Environment

Business is not simply a passive entity that moves with historical and environmental forces like a billiard ball reacting to impacts. On the contrary, while business is strongly constrained by forces in its environment, it also has a powerful capacity to shape societies and change history.

The evolution of the automobile is a good example of how business and its products can affect our lives. The auto industry has been a prime mover of the American economy in the twentieth century, at one time accounting directly or indirectly for one of every eight jobs and a large proportion of our GDP. It encouraged an expansive highway system. It depleted world oil reserves and caused a decline in our railroads. It worsened noise, water, and air pollution. Socially, it changed patterns of courtship, accelerated movement from farms to urban centers, encouraged a connection between status and ownership of material objects, and expanded tourism. It introduced assembly-line technology in manufacturing, encouraged a strong highway lobby, and expanded the field of insurance. These are but a few impacts. No business in this century up to the present time has created more intentional and unintentional changes in our society. Figure 2-3 illustrates the dynamic interconnection of the historical forces, business, and business environments discussed in this chapter. The deep historical forces act to shape the current major environments, both external to the corporation and internal, while the actions of corporations constantly influence not only current environments but may be powerful enough to influence the course of history. The next chapter is devoted to a discussion of the power that business has over its environment.

FIGURE 2-3
The dynamic interaction
of historical forces,
business environment,
and corporate actions

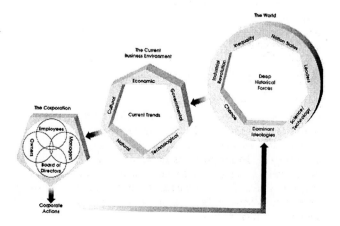

Concluding Observation

The environments of business have vast and profound implications for the management of business enterprises, as well as the role of the future business institution in society. Top managers today, especially of larger corporations, spend a large part of their time dealing with environmental problems. These include responding to economic environments, and also addressing social concerns, complying with new social legislation, communicating with legislators and government executives about proposed laws and regulations, meeting with various interest groups concerning their demands and/or grievances, and administering their organizations in a way that is responsive to the changing attitudes of people working there. This agenda is in sharp contrast to that of a top executive of a major corporation sixty years ago, whose decision making was based almost wholly on economic and technological considerations.

Endnotes

1. Quoted by John Steel Gordon in "When Our Ancestors Became Us," *American Heritage*, December 1989, p. 108.
2. In the essay "A Dynamic Theory of History (1904)," in Henry Adams, *The Education of Henry Adams*, New York: The Modern Library, 1931, p. 474; originally published in 1908.
3. See a similar definition by Gerald F. Cavanagh in *American Business Values*, 3d ed., Englewood Cliffs, N.J.: Prentice-Hall, 1990, p. 2.
4. Mortimer J. Adler, *The Great Ideas*, New York: Macmillan, 1992, pp. 578-79.
5. This thesis is found in Samuel P. Huntington, in "The Clash of Civilizations?" *Foreign Affairs*, Summer 1993.
6. *A Study of History*, vol. XII, *Reconsiderations*, London: Oxford University Press, 1961, p. 125.
7. In "The Hero as Divinity," reprinted in Carl Niemeyer, ed., *Thomas Carlyle on Heroes, Hero-Worship and the Heroic in History*, Lincoln, Neb.: University of Nebraska Press, 1966, p. 1. This essay was originally written in 1840.
8. See U. S. General Accounting Office, *Information Superhighway: An Overview of Technology Challenges*, Washington, D.C.: Government Printing Office, January 1995.
9. Scholars have not agreed upon a single definition of culture, but we use this one as a working definition. Furthermore, there is a distinction between basic cultural values, attitudes, beliefs, and other words noted in our definition. For discussion of these concepts see Milton Rokeach, *The Nature of Human Values*, New York: Free Press, 1973.
10. George P. Murdock, "The Common Denominators of Culture," in Ralph Linton, ed., *Science of Man in the World Crises*, New York: Columbia University Press, 1945.
11. Charles Hampden-Turner and Alfons Trompenaars, *The Seven Cultures of Capitalism*, New York: Doubleday, 1993, p. 32.
12. Quoted in Bhushan Bahree, Kyle Pope, and Allanna Sullivan, "How Greenpeace Sank Shell's Plan to Dump Big Oil Rig in Atlantic," *Wall Street Journal*, July 7,1995.

Chapter Three

STRATEGY IMPLEMENTATION

AND EVALUATION

Strategy implementation and formulation are highly interrelated activities. The issues addressed in this chapter are both fundamental to accomplishing corporate goals. This chapter examines the key elements of the process that move the company from analysis toward getting the job done and evaluating the results.

Environmental scanning and analysis, introduced in the previous chapter, links strategy formulation and implementation with evaluation. Once the company has collected the best and most useful information about the economic, social, legal/political, and technological environments, managers must be able to identify the stakeholders and the issues that directly and indirectly influence the firm.

Stakeholder Analysis

In their book *Strategy in Action*, Boris Yavitz and William H. Newman note that "success and, indeed, survival of every business depends on either obtaining the support or neutralizing the attacks of key actors in its environment."[1] They go on to explain that "we live in a highly interdependent world. To steer a course through this ever changing structure, we need a keen insight into the behavior of those actors who affect our fate."[2] We call these key actors *stakeholders*. A stakeholder is any individual or group who believes it has a stake in the consequences of management's decisions and has the power to influence current or future decisions. Even before managers begin the environmental scanning and analysis process, they should ask, "Who are the actors or players who have the greatest stake in a given issue or management decision?"

Stakeholders may be religious groups, employees, unions, environmentalists, or consumerists. They include government agencies (e.g., the Occupational Safety and Health Administration, the Equal Employment Opportunity Commission, the Securities and Exchange Commission), local chambers of commerce, Mothers Against Drunk Driving (MAAD), the National Association for the Advancement of Colored People (NAACP), and the Gray Panthers. They may also include the traditional industry participants who affect the fate of companies such as suppliers, buyers, and competitors. Stakeholders are also you, me, our families, and our neighbors.

The stakeholder influence map (SIM) in Figure 3-1 provides a conceptual framework for understanding the roles and influence of various stakeholders and issues. This map does not include every player in every circumstance, but it creates a foundation for categorizing

Business and Society, Fifth Edition, by Heidi Vernon-Wortzel. © Irwin/McGraw-Hill, The McGraw-Hill Companies, 1977, 1981, 1985, 1990, 1994.

people and organizations involved in implementing and evaluating the firm's social responsiveness strategy.

FIGURE 3-1
Stakeholder Influence
Map (SIM)

	Direct	Indirect
External	Suppliers Customers Competitors Potential entrants Government	Social activist groups Religious institutions Regulators Local community members Media Trade associations Lobbies and PACs
Internal	Board of directors Employees	Unions Shareholders

Stakeholders hold widely varying expectations and opinions about particular issues. Some stakeholders represent the views of large numbers of people; others speak for just a few; still others speak only for themselves. The amount of power and influence stakeholders wield also runs a wide range, as does the intensity of their feelings about any given issue. Stakeholders may be actively involved in one set of issues and relatively passive in their reactions to another.

Stakeholders play a central role in determining whether or not a company achieves its strategic objectives. All firms face major challenges in balancing the legitimate claims of groups ranging from suppliers to employees to environmentalists. This chapter analyzes stakeholder activities according to their position inside or outside the firm, their vested interests in a particular issue, the depth of their involvement, and their power to affect company strategy.

The Stakeholder Influence Map

Figure 3-1 classifies stakeholders into four groups along two dimensions. The dimensions are:

- *Location:* whether stakeholders are internal (work inside the firm's structure) or external (work outside the firm).
- *Influence:* the way they exert this influence on the firm, either directly or indirectly.

For example, the upper left quadrant of the SIM includes suppliers, customers, and competitors, which are external to the firm and exert their power directly. Much of their ability to influence the firm comes from their economic power—the power to offset competition within an industry or industries. Employees and the board of directors occupy the lower left quadrant. They are internal to the company and directly affect its policies. In the upper right quadrant are a variety of stakeholders external to the firm whose influence varies from issue to issue. In the lower right quadrant are unions and shareholders. These groups are part of the company "family" and exert power over the firm intermittently and less directly than the company's employees do.

In Figure 3-2 R. Edward Freeman combines stakeholder analysis with Michael E. Porter's five variables (discussed shortly) and refers to the combination as the "six forces that shape strategy."[3] To control the strategy formulation and implementation process, management must build a coalition of diverse stakeholders. The process requires considerable analysis, negotiation, persuasion, and exercise of power. If a company hopes to continue achieving its objectives, its stakeholder management effort must be continuous. According to Yavitz and Newman, "shaping external alignments is a never-ending task. Even with the most thorough analysis of each key actor and the wisest choice of relationship, tomorrow will present new problems."[4]

FIGURE 3-2
Six forces that shape
competitive strategy

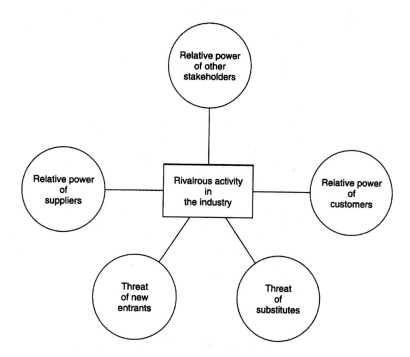

Source: R. E. Freeman, *Strategic Management: A Stakeholder Approach* (Boston: Pitman Publishing, 1984), p.78.

Elective Stakeholder Management

Freeman suggests that organizations with high stakeholder management capability are likely to possess the following attributes:

- They design and implement communication processes with multiple stakeholders.
- They actively negotiate with stakeholders on critical issues and seek voluntary agreements.

- They take a marketing approach to serving multiple stakeholders. They spend heavily on understanding stakeholder needs and use marketing research techniques to segment stakeholders and understand their needs and aspirations.
- In formulating strategy, they draw on members of their management teams who are knowledgeable about stakeholders.
- They take a proactive stance, attempt to anticipate stakeholder concerns, and try to influence their stakeholder environment.
- They allocate resources in a manner consistent with stakeholder analysis.
- Their managers think in "stakeholder-serving" terms.[5]

External Direct Forces

Michael E. Porter's analytical framework helps managers analyze the impact of these external direct stakeholders.[6] Figure 3-3 shows the forces that drive industry competition and play a central role in determining the company's profitability. In the following discussion, we will see how these stakeholders influence telecommunications companies in the United States and abroad.

FIGURE 3-3
External direct forces

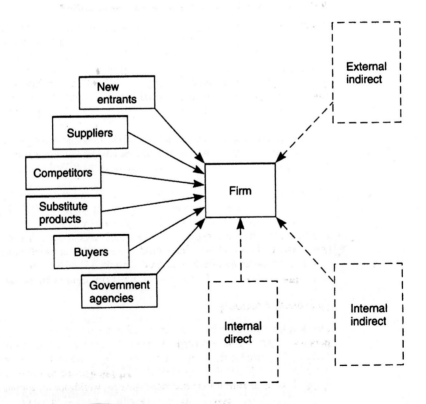

New or Potential Entrants

New or potential entrants to an industry present current players with all kinds of problems and opportunities. Sometimes new entrants bring substantial resources and have the power to change the "rules of the game." For example, those who add capacity cut prices to utilize their capacity efficiently and increase their market share.

In the 1990s, deregulation of the telecommunications industry across Europe weakened traditional national monopolies. The British government decided to grant licenses to a number of new entrants. In the spring of 1993, potential international competitors challenged British Telecommunications (BT) and its smaller rival, Mercury Communications, with a wide range of problems, opportunities, and choices in international calling.

In April 1993, AT&T applied to the British government for permission to start telephone services. AT&T was the latest of 18 companies to apply for various kinds of basic telephone service licenses. Other participants included Sprint International, a unit of U.S.-based Sprint Corporation, the Australian and Swedish phone companies, and Nationwide Linkline Europe, an eight-employee company that planned to offer specialized discounted services such as voice mail and fax.

As deregulation gained momentum, experts expected BT's share of Britain's telecommunications service market to drop from 95 to 83 percent by 1998. They also expected a decline in phone rates as companies competed for customers. What strategy would BT and Mercury Communications adopt to meet these external direct forces?[7]

Intensity of Rivalry among Existing Competitors

If a number of powerful, aggressive, and well-entrenched competitors exist in an industry, the rivalry is likely to be very intense. Such fierce rivalry characterized the Canadian telecommunications industry as Stentor, Unitel, MCI, and AT&T battled for the long-distance telephone market. For years, Stentor, a consortium of Canadian utilities, held a monopoly on domestic trunk services. In 1992 Unitel, the former telegraph service of the Canadian Pacific and Canadian national railways, received government permission to break Stentor's grip. Immediately the Canadian companies developed new alliances for a major battle.

Unitel sold a 20 percent stake (the highest stake permitted by Canadian law) to AT&T. It received access to AT&T's switches, transmission facilities, and other network technologies. Unitel also obtained the right to adapt AT&T's U.S. products to the Canadian market.

Stentor formed a consortium with MCI, a Washington-based firm that held 17 percent of the U.S. long-distance market. Stentor was attracted by MCI's low costs, sophisticated telecommunications software, and aggressive corporate culture.

Canada's communications minister predicted these alliances would foster fierce competition that would bring new products and services to telephone users and stimulate Canada's "premier high-tech industry." In addition, the cross-border partnerships would foster closer integration of telephone services between the United States and Canada.[8]

Substitute Products

Products that may be substituted for the offerings of a given industry place a ceiling on the potential returns of an industry. Perhaps the greatest environmental threat any industry faces is the prospect that someone will develop a product or service that will render the industry's traditional offerings obsolete. This happened to rotary dial phones when their Touch-Tone replacements were integrated into new, worldwide telecommunications systems.

In July 1993, AT&T began marketing a hand-held computer called the Personal Communicator 440. The $3,000 machine was part computer and part cellular telephone. Users could send faxes and electronic mail by writing on a small display screen with a special pen. The computer could make cellular telephone calls in addition to transmitting and storing voice messages.

In August, Apple Computer unveiled the Newton, its own version of a similar machine. When the Newton was presented at the MAC exposition in Boston, it was an immediate and fabulous success. Industry observers predicted it would turn around Apple's recent decline.[9] The miniaturization and flexibility of products like the Newton threaten to make larger, single purpose devices obsolete.

Bargaining Power of Buyers

According to Porter, "Buyers compete with the industry by forcing down prices, bargaining for higher quality or more services, and playing competitors against one another—all at the expense of industry profitability."[10] Buyers are in a powerful position if they are large in size, are limited in number, and account for a large percentage of industry participants' total revenues. A buyer's position may be even more powerful if the firm is partially integrated or is capable of integrating backward. Buyers' bargaining power extends to consumers, wholesalers, and retailers. For example, a large retailer of consumer electronics can negotiate better terms with suppliers than a small, independent retailer can.

Bargaining Power of Suppliers

Powerful suppliers are in a position to charge higher prices or offer lower levels of service or quality of goods. Weak suppliers, in contrast, must deliver more for less and thus allow industry participants to enjoy higher profits.

AT&T's top management vowed to become the world's telecommunications "global outsourcer." In May 1993, AT&T launched World Source, a set of customized international business telecom services. The goal was to become a "one-stop shop" for 2,500 multinational corporations. World Source was designed to manage and integrate international networks and offer the latest in data and voice facilities through a single point of contact. To facilitate this integration, AT&T planned to develop partnerships with several other international carriers.

British Telecom promoted its own global outsourcing venture, Syncordia, in 1991.[11] At first, BT decided to go it alone. But in June 1993, BT formed an alliance with MCI Communications to bolster its strength.

Although Robert Allen, AT&T's CEO, declared, "A partnership like World Source has better opportunities than a single alliance," it remains to be seen which supplier will be most successful.[12] Which of these giants will determine the base line for prices, quality, and service?

Government Agencies

The government can directly influence a company's competitive position in two ways. First, as a large-scale purchaser or supplier, it affects the competitive position of firms from which it buys or to which it sells. Its purchases thus indirectly affect the positions of all the other firms in the industry. Second, government can alter the position of a firm or industry by providing subsidies or imposing regulations.

The role of national governments in the telecom industry is just beginning to wane. In recent years, deregulation has opened up telecom markets worldwide. Even Japan's Nippon Telegraph and Telephone Company, two-thirds of which is owned by the Japanese government, lowered its barriers to competition. After years of trade friction over telephone equipment between the United States and Japan, NTT agreed to buy a dozen advanced central office telephone switches from AT&T. This transaction probably would not have taken place had the U.S. government not pressured Japan to increase its purchases from non-Japanese suppliers.

The announcement of the NTT purchase coincided with the Clinton administration's review of the issue of classifying imported minivans and sport-utility vehicles as trucks instead of cars. If they were classified as minivans or sport-utility vehicles, the tariff would go up by 25 percent, a move that would protect Detroit automakers while hurting Japanese producers.

The Japanese government has a long record of making concessions on contracts at politically opportune times. However, both the Japanese and U.S. governments preferred not to link the situations publicly. AT&T's vice chairperson said simply that officials at the State Department and other agencies "have certainly been helpful to us in engineering, as nearly as they could, a level playing field."[13] Japan's economic minister contended the deal had nothing to do with political pressure because NTT had been increasing its purchases since the early 1980s.[14] Despite the disclaimers, even the casual observer can readily understand the power the U.S. and Japanese governments exercised on their industries' behalf.

Internal Direct Forces

Employees

As Figure 3-4 shows, employees at every level exert internal direct force on corporate decision making. Their stakeholder force is both economic and noneconomic. Economic issues that overlap with social issues are comparable worth, equal pay for equal work, and compensation through benefits such as retirement, maternity policies, and medical benefits. Additional issues that directly involve employees include safety and stress in the workplace, privacy, sexual harassment, equal access to training programs, and hiring and firing practices. Employees who abuse drugs and alcohol cost companies in terms of absenteeism, sick leave, poor-quality work, and potential danger to co-workers or the public. Co-workers who are not abusers pay in both monetary and psychological terms for those who are. Abusers can make nonabusers subject to drug testing and invasion of privacy.

Boards of Directors

The other group of internal direct stakeholders, boards of directors, set policy for their firms and are responsible for the companies' financial well-being. They are often involved in the establishment of social issues programs and may even take leadership in this area. In fact, it would be virtually impossible for a company to formulate a social issues agenda without the approval and participation of its board.

Walter J. Salmon wrote in the *Harvard Business Review* that boards have a role in crisis prevention.[15] Board composition and oversight have improved significantly since the 1970s. Salmon points to surveys showing the typical board today consists of nine outside directors and three inside directors, as opposed to five inside and eight outside directors 20 years ago. In Salmon's view, the only insiders who belong on boards are the CEO, the chief operating officer (COO), and the chief financial officer (CFO). The CEO should routinely initiate discussions between board members and senior managers.

A properly informed board should be able to spot problems early. Although directors should not micromanage (become overly involved with) issues, they have a responsibility to get involved in long-range planning and identify areas of concern. Effective directors speak their minds, engage in constructive discussion, make tough decisions, and exhibit impeccable personal integrity.

Board members of large corporations often receive retainers of $25,000 and a variety of additional perks such as meetings in posh resorts, gifts of company products, and pension plans. They should *earn* this generous compensation. Each board member's activities should be regularly assessed and evaluated. If a particular member is not fulfilling the oversight obligation, he/she should be replaced.[16]

FIGURE 3-4
Internal direct forces

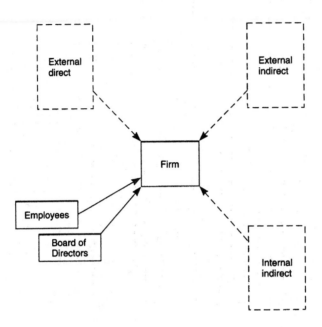

External Indirect Forces

Figure 3-5 shows the groups of stakeholders in the upper right quadrant. They are external to the firm and wield varying degrees of indirect influence. External indirect stakeholders include social activist groups; some government agencies (especially those not specifically tied to the firm's economic position in the industry); members of the local community; industry trade associations; and religious organizations, lobbies, and PACs.

Companies and communities need to coordinate their programs to satisfy all of these stakeholders. If, for example, 25 percent of the workforce in a given company needs child care, this need can have profound implications for stakeholders in the local community. If a child care center is located on company property, local providers may lose their livelihood. If it is located in the community, local government agencies may be asked to participate or religious institutions may be chosen as sites. Teachers may need both local and state certification. School-age children may need transportation to the child care center.

Communities often benefit from corporate perquisites that extend to family members. For instance, AT&T sponsors the U.S. Chamber of Commerce ConSern Loans for Education program. All employees and family members are eligible for student loans to secondary schools, accredited colleges, and universities. Family includes children, grandchildren, siblings, spouses, and even nephews and nieces. Qualified applicants can receive low-interest loans for up to $25,000 per year for tuition, room and board, and books. They may even receive $3,000 for a personal computer.

AT&T has huge installations in central New Jersey. The flow of money into area educational institutions will have an extremely beneficial effect on local communities. Indirect benefits include continued employment of school faculty, support staff, and administrators. Local businesses prosper by offering goods and services to students and school employees.

FIGURE 3-5
External indirect forces

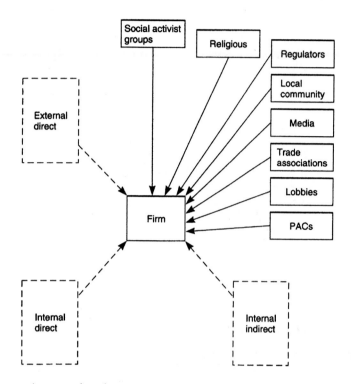

Access to these loans may make the difference between an employee staying at AT&T, and contributing to the local tax base, or leaving for a more lucrative position elsewhere. Extended families that take advantage of the program but are not employed by AT&T also contribute to their local communities.[17] A ripple effect occurs as these external indirect stakeholders affect and are affected by company policies.

Internal Indirect Forces

As Figure 3-6 shows, unions and shareholders belong in the lower right quadrant of the stakeholder influence map. They are part of the company but do not always influence it directly. Unions may work with management to develop programs or take an adversarial approach by making demands management is unwilling to consider. Indirectly, union demands affect external competition if workers strike or gain concessions. Unions can also affect the quality of work life within the firm.

The U.S. telecommunications industry is only partly unionized. Neither MCI nor Sprint has a union, nor do the U.S.-based subsidiaries of Canada's Northern Telecom or Germany's Siemens. AT&T is, in fact, the only major unionized U.S. telecom company. Between the 1984 breakup of AT&T and 1993, AT&T halved its hourly workforce. As a result of the cutbacks and other issues, the company was hit by strikes in 1986 and 1989.

FIGURE 3-6
Internal indirect forces

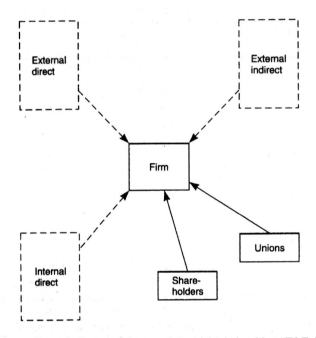

Instead of perpetuating an adversarial relationship, AT&T decided to give the unions a larger role in worker participation and consult with top union officials on a range of issues. The 1992-1995 labor contract contained a promise by AT&T and its two biggest unions, the Communications Workers of America (CWA) and the International Brotherhood of Electrical Workers (IBEW), to create a "workplace of the future." Business-unit planning councils bring together top managers of strategic business units and local presidents and top officials of unions several times a year. The purpose of the meetings is to set future business strategy. The new relationship between AT&T and its unions is in its early stages. It remains to be seen how much power these internal indirect stakeholders will exercise.[18]

Traditionally most shareholders have been content to sign over their voting proxies to corporate appointees. But in recent years, a new kind of shareholder has emerged. Today some shareholders, primarily large institutional investors, such as pension funds, are taking a real interest in the companies in which they have invested. They are asking tough questions of boards of directors and are not automatically assigning voting proxies for the stock they own. This interaction, called *relationship investing*, usually concentrates on profits and governance. The U.S. Council on Competitiveness, the congressionally sponsored Competitiveness Policy Council, and the Twentieth Century Fund have all endorsed the idea of relationship investing.

There is no structural reason to exclude social issues from relationship-investing concerns. In fact, the close ties between corporations and these large investors should provide an ideal climate for defining and implementing a social issues strategy.

Corporate Partners, a major mutual fund, is an affiliate of Lazard Frères & Company. Since 1989, it has made big stock purchases in seven companies and sits on their boards of directors. Corporate Partners invests in companies in which its capital and management expertise will help the firms solve problems. It always investigates management expertise before making the investment. It also insists on having a board seat to monitor management's progress against a mutually agreed-on strategy.

Supporters of relationship investing point to two major advantages: long-term investing and increased management accountability. Relationship investors provide "patient" capital that focuses on long-term goals. In theory, top managers should be freer to concentrate on productivity and prospects without the pressure of quarterly returns.

Supporters declare this new breed of large shareholder holds the CEO to account. The board of directors can no longer automatically rubber-stamp decisions made by an "imperial" leader. In fact, studies show few CEOs are deposed by activist shareholders. A *Wall Street Journal* study determined that large companies are fairly unresponsive to shareholder threats of bad publicity or proxy fights. According to a University of Rochester study, small and mid-size companies are much more likely to react to shareholder criticism and their CEOs are slightly more likely to lose their jobs than are those at larger firms.[19] Relationship investing is still a new idea, and its effectiveness and influence have yet to be fully felt and assessed.

Stakeholders' Power to Affect Firm Affairs

R. Edward Freeman and Daniel R. Gilbert, Jr., point out that "power is an interesting concept . . . because it signifies that those who have it control those who do not.[20] Seemingly powerless stakeholders can, if aroused, exert considerable power. Most stakeholders tend to be fairly passive toward a company's affairs unless they see themselves as personally threatened or potentially benefited by the company's actions.

For example, women who used the Dalkon Shield first were threatened by the product's damaging effects but later saw great potential benefit in bringing suit against the company. As individuals they wielded little power, but when organized into a class action group they gained considerable power. As another example, stakeholders who lived near nuclear power plants marshaled their forces after the Three Mile Island incident. In both cases, groups of stakeholders successfully wielded influence through the media and the courts. They took action at the point at which they perceived they *could* affect company strategy. Unless top managers can anticipate the activity and potential power of stakeholders, they may find themselves simply reacting rather than formulating and implementing a well-thought-out strategy.

Stakeholders's Resources

Porter perceives power differently than Freeman and Gilbert do. Porter points out that in economic terms, stakeholders possess power only if their resources influence the elements of return on investment (ROI).[21] When social issues are a concern, stakeholders can affect a firm's financial results through the pressure they apply to its buyers, suppliers, and customers.

After the *Exxon Valdez* disaster, activists tried to organize a boycott of Exxon. The boycott failed for several reasons. The boycotters had few resources compared to the giant oil company. There was no loss of human life, the oil spill was in a remote area, and most observers realized they could not meaningfully affect Exxon's ROI.

In contrast, INFACT's boycott against Nestlé was very successful and sufficiently powerful to interfere with Nestlé's buyer and customer relations. Helpless babies' lives were at stake, the moral outrage was sustainable, and a dedicated group of stakeholder activists pursued the issue over a long period of time.

Selection of Alternatives

Managers must understand whether they or stakeholders control the selection of alternative courses of action. The power struggle between stakeholders and managers often revolves around this selection. Active stakeholders try to control management actions and preempt management's choice of alternatives by publicly displaying their particular viewpoints. These stakeholders use common tools such as picket lines, demonstrations, and effective use of the media.

The debate over whether nuclear energy is a societally acceptable source of energy provides a graphic example of how stakeholders have used their power to dictate management and industry policy. Figure 3-7 shows a partial list of nuclear energy stakeholders.

FIGURE 3-7
Stakeholder influence map: nuclear energy issue—partial list of stakeholders

	Direct	Indirect
External	Alternative energy suppliers Nuclear Regulatory Commission Banks Creditors Commercial and residential customers	Local governments State governments Media Public interest groups Industry lobbyists Citizens' groups Other environmental groups
Internal	Employees at operating plants Boards of directors of utilities	Unions Construction companies

The fiasco at Three Mile Island turned passive stakeholders into active opponents of the development of nuclear energy resources. In 1986, the disaster at the Chernobyl plant in the USSR further strengthened the position of antinuclear energy forces, particularly those in the United States. The nuclear energy industry was forced to seriously consider the concerns of a variety of stakeholders. It could not escape nightly television broadcasts of demonstrators locked to chain-link fences that surrounded nuclear plants. Utility companies, in full view of television cameras, authorized police to drag demonstrators to jail.

Public-interest groups went to the courts to prevent plants from coming "on-line." State politicians refused to file evacuation plans, further stalling the start-up process. Public-interest groups made sure antinuclear energy questions were put on state and local ballots. Stakeholders generated both financial and humanpower resources to constrain the industry's selection of alternative actions. As a result, nuclear power companies became increasingly unwilling to commit to ordering new nuclear facilities.

In addition to the public's concerns about radioactive leaks and potential cancer epidemics, reports of unsafe operations inside a number of nuclear plants proliferated. The Critical Mass Energy Project of Public Citizen, a stakeholder group that published an annual compilation of NRC reports, cited 2,810 accidents in commercial nuclear power plants in 1987. Employee error caused many of those accidents.

Unsafe operating practices continued despite adverse publicity. The Nuclear Regulatory Commission reported the New York Power Authority failed to ensure that certain backup systems were operating properly at its Indian Point 3 plant. Between May 1992 and July 1993, the power authority paid $762,500 in fines for safety violations at Indian Point 3 and an additional $300,000 in fines for problems at the Fitzpatrick nuclear power plant in Scriba, New York.[22]

Industry inertia led to widespread personnel problems and poor managerial practices in other states as well. One stakeholder group, the Institute of Nuclear Power Operations, referred to Philadelphia's Peach Bottom plant as "an embarrassment to the industry and to the nation." The Nuclear Regulatory Commission eventually closed the Peach Bottom plant because workers were sleeping on the job.[23]

In addition to the stakeholders already mentioned, active players included state and other government officials, local town and city officials, and an assortment of citizens' groups. All had huge stakes in the consequences of managements' decisions about whether to bring new plants online, rehabilitate old ones, or abandon nuclear energy altogether.

By 1993, the U.S. nuclear industry was on its way to extinction. Even plants that were still operating were struggling with radioactive waste disposal problems. The Department of Energy, which was supposed to build a permanent storage facility in Nevada in 1988, had not yet done so. Most nuclear facilities stored tons of waste on site but were running out of room. Portland General Electric, for example, decided to close down its Trojan plant 20 years early rather than deal with the estimated cost of tearing the plant down and disposing of 20 additional years of nuclear waste.[24]

Company management of substance abuse in the workplace is another issue in which firms can take many alternative actions. This issue involves stakeholders in all quadrants of the stakeholder influence map. Approximately 25 percent of an average workforce suffers from abuse of either drugs or alcohol.[25]

Companies must address several issues. Should they carry out involuntary testing, voluntary testing, or no testing at all? Should they begin a formal program to help alcohol or drug abusers? How should they address employee concerns about confidentiality or job security? Should supervisors be given the responsibility of identifying and reporting abusers? Should managers have to use their operating budgets for rehabilitation programs? How should managers integrate the firm's activities with the community? Finally, how, if at all, will the strategy the firm adopts affect its competitive position in its industry?

Each of these questions has several defensible answers. But before a company can formulate and implement a strategy to deal with substance abuse, it must correctly assess the power different stakeholders hold and the degree to which each is actively or passively involved in the issue. The company can be sure that as this issue continues to evolve, it will receive input from stakeholders who are both external and internal to the firm and are involved both directly and indirectly.

Managing for Social Responsiveness

Obviously companies cannot attend to all issues, and not all stakeholders care equally about particular issues. To deal systematically and effectively with its complex environment, a firm must answer four questions:

- How can managers identify relevant issues?
- How can they classify issues?
- How can these issues be managed?
- How can managers evaluate performance on the issues?

Peter F. Drucker stresses that "social impacts and social responsibilities are areas in which business—and not only big business—has to think through its role, has to set objectives, has to perform. Social impacts and social responsibilities have to be managed."[26]

Classification of Major Social Issues

After completing its environmental scanning and analysis, the company needs to classify the major social issues it confronts into meaningful subjects. Five major categories cover most of the significant issues even large, diverse enterprises face:

1. *Community and political responsiveness:* the effectiveness with which the company manages its affairs in the political and legal environment and responds to the economic and other expectations of the domestic and international communities in which it operates (e.g., job creation, philanthropy).
2. *Human investment:* the provision for the physical, psychological, and economic welfare of present, potential, and retired employees. Also includes the creation of an environment in which people are treated fairly and are given an opportunity to grow, meet challenges, and enjoy satisfaction.
3. *Openness of the system:* the company's willingness to communicate honestly and openly with its employees and external stakeholders, including the news media, to establish an effective governance system and to assure employees of due process and protection of their rights.
4. *Consumer welfare:* the provision of quality products and services to prospective buyers in an honest and comprehensive manner to reasonably assure their safety, well-being, and satisfaction.
5. *Ecology and energy:* the company's efforts to minimize the negative impact of its operations on the natural environment (water, air, plants, wildlife, microorganisms) and the structural environment (buildings, farms, homes) and to conserve natural resources such as energy.

Determine Priorities and Collect Data

Table 3-1 combines these five categories, a few selected issues, and several concerned stakeholder groups. Just as a company sets priorities for expenditures in functional areas, it must rank social issues in their importance to the firm. Some firms may decide to consider only issues for which reliable data exist or for which they can generate good data.

However, not all social issues are data oriented. For example, it is almost impossible to measure the benefit of a contribution to a symphony orchestra or the benefit of hosting a fund-raising gala. Likewise, it is difficult to measure employee satisfaction and greater productivity due to a company sponsored child care program. Data on such an issue are elusive at best.

| TABLE 3-1 | | Matrix of Issues with Social Consequences and the Affected Stakeholders | | | | | | | | | | | |

	Stakeholders											
Social Issues	Stock-holders	Nonmanagement Employees	Managers	Retired Management and Nonmanagement Employees	Customers	Suppliers	Lenders	Competitors	Government	Neighbors or Local Communities	Activist Groups
Community and political responsiveness											
1. Relations with regulatory agencies											
2. Corporate giving											
3. Support of minority-owned business											
Human investment											
1. Minority participation											
2. Health and safety											
3. Treatment of retired workers											
Openness of the system											
1. Relations with the news media											
2. Composition of the board of directors											
3. Financial disclosure											
Consumer welfare											
1. Handling of customer complaints											
2. Customer satisfaction											
3. Product recalls											
Ecology and energy											
1. Pollution abatement											
2. Energy conservation											

In reality, most companies do not even care about measuring benefit. Key managers are simply committed to the cause. Top management determines the relative urgency of corporate priorities. As is often the case in other management decision-making areas, management must make tradeoffs in targeting certain social issues. If management decides it is critical to improve the company's record for equal employment opportunity, it may postpone its attention to one or more other issues, just as it may delay introducing a second new product until it is sure its first entrant will succeed. The social assessment system (SAS) we will introduce later seems to have its greatest impact on improving a company's social performance when it selects four to six *key indicators* for attention and corrective action.

Select a Plan or Policy

If possible, companies should measure their current performance before they act. Creativity and cooperation are important to the SAS process in developing sound measures. Three types of measures exist for the quantification of social performance: (1) actual performance, (2) level of effort, and (3) surrogates (substitutes that appear to approximate the underlying phenomenon). Measures of actual performance are possible in certain areas, such as the frequency of disabling injuries or the number of product recalls.

Managers must be careful when developing measures of actual performance. The data must be consistent in definition and truly represent performance on the underlying issue. For example, minority employment is an area for which actual performance measures are available.

Where actual performance may not be readily quantifiable in commonly understood terms, companies may measure the effort expended in dealing with a given problem. For example, annual expenditures for pollution control equipment would be a measure of level of effort.

The third type of measure utilizes surrogates of performance. Employee satisfaction is an example of an important issue that is not readily measurable. Management may use absenteeism, turnover, and measures of worker output as appropriate surrogate indicators of employee satisfaction.

Endnotes

1. B. Yavitz and W. H. Newman, *Strategy in Action* (New York: The Free Press, 1982), p. 74.
2. Ibid.
3. R. E. Freeman, *Strategic Management: A Stakeholder Approach* (Boston: Pitman Publishing, 1984), p. 78.
4. Yavits and Newman, *Strategy in Action*, p. 85.
5. Ibid., pp. 78-80.
6. M. E. Porter, *Competitive Strategy: Techniques for Analyzing Industries and Competitors* (New York: The Free Press, 1980), p. x.
7. R. L. Hudson, "BT Faces a Line of Potential International Competitors," *The Wall Street Journal*, April 29, 1993, p. B4.
8. B. Simon, "Unlikely Allies Fight Canada's Telephone War," *Financial Times*, February 25, 1993, p. 15.
9. T. McCarroll, "How AT&T Plans to Reach Out and Touch Everyone," *Time*, July 5, 1993, pp. 44-46.
10. Porter, *Competitive Strategy*, p. 24.
11. "AT&T Targets Telecom Needs of Multinationals," *Financial Times*, May 27, 1993, p.23.
12. "AT&T Seeks Partners to Help It Enter European Market," *The Wall Street Journal*, July 8, 1993, p. B3.
13. K. Bradsher, "AT&T in a Deal in Japan," *The New York Times*, April 27, 1993, p. Dl.
14. Ibid.
15. W. J. Salmon, "Crisis Prevention: How to Gear Up Your Board," *Harvard Business Review* (January/February 1993), pp. 68-75.
16. Ibid.
17. "Student Loans Available for Family Members," *Focus: For and about the People of AT&T*, July/August 1993, p. 41.
18. "Rocking the Boat," *The Economist*, May 8, 1993, p. 71.
19. "Relationship Investing," *Business Week*, March 15, 1993, pp. 68-75; J. Kim, "Companies to Activists: Let's Make a Deal," *USA Today*, March 23, 1993; S. Mieher, "Shareholder Activism, Despite Hoopla, Leaves Most CEOs Unscathed," *The Wall Street Journal*, May 24, 1993, p. Al.
20. R. E. Freeman and D. R. Gilbert, Jr., *Corporate Strategy and the Search for Ethics* (Englewood Cliffs, NJ: Prentice-Hall, 1988), p. 172.
21. M. E. Porter, *Competitive Advantage*, (New York: The Free Press, 1985), p. 5.
22. "Nuclear Regulators Propose $300,000 Fine for New York Plant," *The Wall Street Journal*, July 23, 1993, p. B5B.
23. M. L. Wald, "The Peach Bonom Syndrome," *The New York Times*, March 27, 1988, p. Fl.
24. M. L. Wald, "Nuclear Power Plants Take Early Retirement," *The New York Times*, August 16, 1992, p. E7.
25. J. T. Wrich, "Beyond Testing: Coping with Drugs at Work," *Harvard Business Review* (January/February 1988), p. 120.
26. P. F. Drucker, *Management: Tasks, Responsibilities, Practices* (New York: Harper & Row, 1974), p. 325.

Chapter Four

CRITICS OF

BUSINESS

Sisters of Loretto

The Sisters of Loretto are an order of Roman Catholic nuns. There are about 600 Sisters in the order, 300 of whom are retired. Like other Roman Catholic orders, the Sisters of Loretto have an investment portfolio. To manage it, they have an eight-member investment committee composed of representatives from houses around the country.

Their investment philosophy is different from that of the typical Wall Street investor. The Sisters want their investments to help the poor, and they put their money into low-income housing projects and small minority-owned businesses where risk is higher and returns are often lower than with traditional investments. However, the Sisters also buy small amounts of stock in some blue-chip corporations and use their shareholders' rights to promote their views on social justice.

The Securities and Exchange Commission (SEC) permits shareholders to bring a resolution before all corporation shareholders for a vote. Sponsors of these resolutions must meet certain technical requirements. They must, for example, have at least $1,000 worth of stock and show that the issue they raise is material to the corporation's business. The resolution is printed in the corporation's annual proxy statement and presented verbally at its annual meeting. All shareholders can vote on it. If it passes, the corporation must do what it requires.

In the early 1980s, the Sisters decided to fight militarism in American society and picked General Dynamics Corporation, which was headquartered in St. Louis where many of the Sisters live, as their main target. At the time, General Dynamics was the nation's second largest defense contractor, making F-16 Falcon jet fighters, Tomahawk cruise missiles, *Seawolf* and *Trident* nuclear submarines, and M1A1 Abrams tanks. In 1983 the Sisters, joined by three other Roman Catholic orders, qualified a resolution asking that the company withdraw its bid for a contract to manufacture cruise missile components and retrain cruise missile workers for civilian occupations. Together, these groups had 740 shares, or one ten-thousandth of 1 percent of General Dynamics' outstanding shares.

The Sisters interpret Catholic theology to hold that production of nuclear weapons and their delivery systems is immoral. They believe that papal teachings and biblical text condemn the manufacture of forces so potentially destructive of God's creation. In 1983 the secretary of General Dynamics who dealt with shareholder resolutions was John McGuire. McGuire, who was also Catholic and had three priest brothers, believed that Church theology permitted production of nuclear weapons and delivery systems for use in deterring a catastrophic third world war. He also believed that it was improper for critics to buy an infinitesimal share of General Dynamics stock and use the shareholder resolution machinery to pursue values so divergent from those of the company and other shareholders.

Business, Government, and Society, Eighth Edition, by George A. Steiner and John F. Steiner. © Irwin/ McGraw-Hill, The McGraw-Hill Companies, 1985, 1988, 1991, 1994, 1997.

continued

Only 1 percent of General Dynamics shareholders voted with the Sisters back in 1983. But they have kept trying. Each year they have fought to get a vote on a resolution and have gotten votes as high as 9 percent. General Dynamics fights back and has twice succeeded in getting the SEC to disqualify resolutions on technicalities. But the Sisters are unrelenting. In 1992, when the SEC disqualified their resolution to require a study of ethical criteria for military contracts, the Sisters showed up at the shareholders' meeting anyway to confront its executives about their high compensation. Sister Mary Ann McGivern rose and scolded General Dynamics' then-chairperson, former astronaut William A. Anders: "Shame on you, Mr. Anders," she said, "You're robbing us blind."[1]

The Sisters have tried to negotiate with the company issues related to weapons production, conversion of defense facilities to civilian production, and ethical criteria for accepting military contracts. Sister McGivern indicates, however, that relations with the company are strained. The shareholder resolutions, which never pass, are a double-edged sword. They alienate company executives, yet without them the Sisters have no leverage and cannot keep their agenda in play. As it stands, they find themselves unable to get access to executives at higher decision-making levels.

In 1996 the Sisters succeeded, along with the Glenmary Fathers of St. Louis, in qualifying a resolution for the shareholders which would require a report on what General Dynamics is doing to transfer military technology to civilian uses that will solve social needs.

The Sisters disdain profit from defense industry investment. They own shares in a number of defense companies so that they can join other religious groups in shareholder battles. But when they sell shares, for instance after stock splits, they give any profits to charity. This reflects the Sisters' negative feelings about investing in a business system that promotes values that they oppose. The order's treasurer, Sister Swain, once said: "There's no way to participate in the American economic system and be pure."[2] Today the Sisters own 100 of General Dynamics' 63 million shares.

Corporations today are attacked by a wide spectrum of stakeholders. The story of the conflict between the Sisters and General Dynamics is but one of thousands that could be told. It illustrates the difficulty of conflict resolution when corporations confront visionary critics. But there are many types of critics and innumerable criticisms. In this chapter we will elaborate on both.

Historical Attitudes Toward Business

Throughout recorded history, merchants and businesses have been regarded with suspicion. We preface our discussion of types and sources of current business criticism with a look at the past. Although criticism of business has always existed, it deepened and changed its nature after the industrial revolution.

The Ancient and Medieval Worlds

The earliest societies such as ancient Egypt and Mesopotamia, the Inca and Aztec societies, old China, and the ancient Hindu kingdoms of Southeast Asia were agrarian societies. An *agrarian society* is a pre-industrial society in which economic activity, government, and culture are based on traditions arising from agriculture. In these societies the great mass of people tilled land for subsistence. Upper social classes were comprised of wealthy landowners. No industry or mass-consumer markets existed, so business activity was only a tiny part of these ancient economies. In this setting the activities of merchants were often viewed as indecent because their sharp trading practices and temporizing ethics clashed with the traditional, more altruistic values of family and clan relations among farmers. Merchants were typically given lower class status than government officials, farmers, soldiers, artisans, and teachers.

Both Greece and Rome were based on subsistence agriculture and economic activity by merchants, bankers, and manufacturers was limited. The largest factory in Athens, for example, employed 120 workers making shields.[3] Commercial activity was greater in Rome, but it was still fundamentally an agrarian society. Merchants in both societies achieved middle-class status below an upper class of landed aristocrats.

However, because industrial activity was so limited in Hellenic civilization no accurate, coherent economic doctrines were developed to explain or justify commercial activity.[4] Into this vacuum of economic understanding stepped some great philosophers who encoded the idea that wealth, particularly wealth from commercial activity, was associated with greed and corruption—an idea that has left a lasting legacy of cynicism about business activity in Western society.

Greed was regarded as particularly suspect in the limited economy of ancient Greece because of the popular belief that the amount of wealth was fixed. If so, an individual seeking to increase wealth did it only at the expense of the share of others. This belief was responsible for the idea that material acquisitiveness is not a noble motive in the same way as, say, desire for knowledge. The latter does not create social injustice; the former may, and is dangerous to society. The Greeks also believed that the acquisition of wealth freed individuals from certain restraints and let them pursue selfish desires that might be immoral.

These views were reflected in Greek—and later Roman—culture. In the utopian society described in The Republic, for example, Plato prohibited the possession of private property by its rulers for fear of corruption and the rise of tyrants; they were forbidden even to touch gold or silver.[5] In his Politics, Aristotle argued that retail activity for the purpose of monetary gain—as opposed to simply acquiring necessary commodities—is a "perverted or unsound" activity.[6] He also described the lending of money for interest as a "hateful" activity.[7]

Later, Roman law would forbid the senatorial class to make business investments (and the law would be widely circumvented). Likewise, the Stoic philosophers of Rome, such as Epictetus and Marcus Aurelius, taught that the truly rich person possessed inner peace rather than capital or property.[8] These thinkers looked down on merchants of their day as materialists who, in pursuit of wealth, sacrificed the opportunity to develop character. Needless to say, this did not deter the merchants from accumulating fortunes and neglecting the study of ideals.

During the Middle Ages, the prevailing theological doctrines of the Roman Catholic Church were intolerant of profit making. Christianity, of course, created a doctrine opposed to the values of the wealthy ruling class, which had debilitated Rome in its waning years. It rejected a focus on wealth accumulation and sought special status for the poor. The Church was deeply suspicious of commerce because it diverted merchants from devoutness. Merchants were exhorted to charge a *just price* for their wares, a price that was just adequate to maintain them in the social station to which they were born. The just price stands in contrast to the modern idea of a *market price* determined by supply and demand. But today we hear echoes of medieval theology when consumers complain that high prices for a product are unjust, unfair, or unethical. The Roman Church also condemned *usury*, or the lending of money for interest. By the twelfth and thirteenth centuries, however, the money supply and economic activity had expanded greatly and interest-bearing loans were commonplace. "Commercial activity," notes historian Will Durant, "proved stronger than fear of prison or hell."[9] Church scholars such as St. Thomas Aquinas began to back away from the dogma of the just price and the sin of usury, though they never fully embraced market pricing or lending for interest. In fact, Church doctrine making lending money for interest a sin was not officially repealed until 1917.

As industrial activity accelerated during the Renaissance new economic theories arose to justify business activities that had previously been condemned. Aristotle's belief that profits and wealth were corrupting was contradicted by Adam Smith's theory that free markets harnessed greed for the public good. The Church's insistence on the concept of a just price was contradicted by Smith's theory that competitive markets protected consumers from unfair prices. And the idea that only a fixed amount of wealth existed in a society was countered by clear experience with growing economies.

However, at the same time that old beliefs lost their hold, the industrial revolution created new tensions that became sources of critical attitudes about business. These new tensions arose as industrialism began to change agrarian societies and challenged their traditional values with modern alternatives.

Agrarian societies are fundamentally different from industrial societies; in the fire of industrialization they undergo rapid change. Agrarian societies are rural and slow-paced; they are stable and cling to traditional ethics and values passed down over generations. They revere nature, value independence and equality, and emphasize humanitarian ethics of interpersonal relations such as the Golden Rule. With industrialization such societies undergo dramatic, rapid change. They become urban and fast-paced; organizational complexity of institutions grows. Awe of nature is replaced by conquest of nature. New values and habits insert themselves; consumption, for instance, replaces thrift and saving. More emphasis is placed on growth, development, and commerce. The historian Henry Adams put this colorfully and through the lens of a critic when, in 1905, he looked back on the growth of big business in America:

> The Trusts and Corporations . . . were obnoxious because of their vigorous and unscrupulous energy. They were revolutionary, troubling all the old conventions and values, as the screws of ocean steamers must trouble a school of herring. They tore society to pieces and trampled it underfoot.[10]

In conclusion, although the antiquarian values of Greek and Roman thinkers may still shine through in the charges of critics, fundamental societal change from industrialization soon became the great source of raw material for critics of business. We will examine the impact of this change in the United States.

Attitudes Toward Business in American History

Much higher levels of public confidence in business existed during the early years of our nation than exist now. Historians record generally positive feelings toward entrepreneurs, companies, and the business system until the growth of giant trusts in the latter half of the nineteenth century.

The earliest colonies were formed by English trading companies operated by private individuals for profit. In some cases the motive for colonization was to avoid religious persecution, but the backers of the Pilgrims, for instance, hoped to make a profit. The commercial spirit manifested itself in different ways in colonial America, but it was dominant in most walks of life. The farmer was not a peasant bound to the soil with a pattern of life dictated by custom. Although his way of life was different from that of the retail merchant in the town, they both engaged in buying and selling. As the farmers accumulated wealth, they built and ran grain mills and in other ways employed their capital exactly like the merchants. Merchants of great wealth rose to top status in colonial society in part because there was no tradition of a landed or hereditary aristocracy, as there was in Europe.

By 1850, America was a predominantly rural, agrarian society of small, local businesses. But explosive industrial growth rapidly reshaped it, creating some severe social problems in the process. Cities grew as farmers left the land and immigrants swelled slum populations. Most cities were run by corrupt political machines which failed to ameliorate parlous conditions. Simultaneously, in many industries companies merged into huge national monopolies. These changes were the raw material of two movements critical of big business.

The first was the *populist movement*, a farmers' protest movement that began in the 1870s and led to formation of a new political party, the People's party, which met its ultimate defeat in 1896. Here is how the movement started. Soon after the Civil War, farmers began to suffer from a persistent drop in crop prices. Falling prices were caused mainly by overproduction because of the efficiencies of new farming machinery, and by competition from foreign farmers because of new transportation methods. At the time, farmers did not understand these factors and blamed their distress on railroad companies, the largest and most visibly corrupt businesses of the day, which frequently overcharged farmers when hauling crops, and on "plutocrats" such as J. P. Morgan and others in the eastern banking community, who controlled finance and industry and sometimes foreclosed on their farms. In a typical tirade, Mary Lease, speaking on behalf of the Farmers' Alliance ticket in 1890, complained:

> Wall Street owns the country. It is no longer a government of the people, by the people and for the people, but a government of Wall Street and for Wall Street. The great common people of this country are slaves, and monopoly is the master. The West and South are bound and prostrate before the manufacturing East.[11]

To solve agrarian ills, the populists advocated government ownership of railroads, abandonment of the gold standard, and measures to control the influence of big business in politics, including direct election of U.S. senators.

Historian Louis Galambos believes that despite the populist critique, there existed a great reservoir of respect for and confidence in business until the late 1880s.[12] Thereafter, analysis of newspaper and magazine editorials shows mounting hostility toward large trusts. Soon the populists succeeded in electing many state and local officials, who enacted laws to regulate the railroads and provided the political groundswell behind creation of the federal Interstate Commerce Commission in 1887 to regulate railroads. Despite efforts, populists were never able to forge a national coalition with labor organizations. The movement died in 1896 with the decisive defeat of William Jennings Bryan, the People's party candidate for president. But it had refined a logic and lexicon for spotlighting the business system as the source of social ills. Populists blamed adverse consequences of industrialization on monopoly, trusts, Wall Street, "silk-hatted Easterners," the soulless "loan sharks" and shameless "bloodhounds of money" who foreclosed on farms, and corrupt politicians who worked as errand boys for the "moneybags" in a system of "plutocracy" (or rule by the wealthy). Their criticisms were harsh and colorful. In an essay on the superior virtues of farming as an occupation, Bryan wrote that for farmers "even the dumb animals are more wholesome companions than the bulls and bears of Wall Street."[13]

It was, of course, too late in the day for America to return to farming. This did not diminish the appeal of the populist message. On the contrary, continued industrial growth has caused it to resurface time and again up to the present day, each time its critical message refurbished to fit current circumstances.

The second movement was the *progressive movement*, a broader reform movement lasting from about 1900 until the end of World War I in 1918. Fueled by great moral indignation about problems of industrialization, it incorporated the urban middle class as well as farmers. Although a short-lived Progressive party was formed and unsuccessfully nominated Theodore Roosevelt for president in 1912, both the Democratic and Republican parties had powerful, dominant progressive wings. Unlike populism, progressivism was a mainstream political doctrine. Like populism, it was at root an effort to cure social ills by controlling perceived abuses of big business.

The Wonderful Wizard of Oz

The Wizard of Oz is known as a book for children.[14] But it has another dimension. Written by an author of children's books, Lyman Frank Baum (1850-1919), in 1900 as an allegory of the populist dream, it satirizes the evils of an industrial society run by a moneyed elite of bankers and industrialists. "Oz" is the abbreviation for ounce, a measure of gold. It and the Yellow Brick Road allude to the hated gold standard. The characters all represent major groups in society. Dorothy represents the common person. The Scarecrow is the farmer. The Tin Woodsman is industrial labor. His rusted condition recalls the closing of factories in the depression years of the 1890s and his lack of a heart reminds readers that factories dehumanized workers. The Cowardly Lion is William Jennings Bryan, the defeated People's party candidate, whom Baum regarded as lacking sufficient courage. The Wicked Witch of the East was intended by Baum to parody the capitalist elite. She kept the munchkins, or "little people," in servitude. At the end of the Yellow Brick Road lay the Emerald City, which was Washington, D.C. When the group arrived, they were met by the Wizard, who stood for the president of the United States. At the end Dorothy melted the Wicked Witch of the East, the Wizard flew off in a balloon, the Scarecrow became ruler of Oz and the Tin Woodsman took charge of the East. This ending was the unrealized populist dream.

Capitalism. Art Young, a radical cartoonist of the Progressive era, had an Impish ability to highlight the excesses of the industrial age. This cartoon, typical of many at that time drawn by Young and others, first appeared in 1912.

Because of broad popular support, progressives were far more effective than populists in their reform efforts, and during their era a reform tide washed over business. Progressives broke up trusts and monopolies, made federal campaign contributions by corporations illegal, imposed federal regulation on consumer products, restricted child labor, started a corporate income tax and inheritance taxes, and regulated safety conditions in factories. "Turn the waters of pure public spirit into the corrupt pools of private interests," wrote Ernest Crosby, editor of *Cosmopolitan* magazine, "and wash the offensive accumulations away."[15] Progressivism further refined the antibusiness lexicon of the populists and carried their legacy into the twentieth century.

After the triumph of progressive reforms, there was a period of high public confidence in big business during the prosperous, expansive 1920s. This rosy era ended abruptly with the stock market crash of 1929, and business once again came under sustained attack. During the 1920s, the idea that business knew how to achieve continuing prosperity had been advanced and widely accepted. The depression of the 1930s disproved this view and, in addition, brought to light much ineptness, criminal negligence, and outright fraud on the part of prominent business executives. There was a popular feeling that the economic collapse would not have occurred if business managers had been more capable. Criticism of business was intensified by the callous-appearing reaction of the conservative business community, which believed that government should not intervene to relieve human misery caused by the depression.

As criticism of business grew, the old lexicon of populism reemerged. In the Senate, for example, Huey Long, a colorful populist Democrat from Louisiana who claimed to be the advocate of the poor against the rich, rose to condemn a "ruling plutocratic class" controlled by the "fortune-holding elements of Morgan, Mellon, and Rockefeller."[16] In 1934, Long introduced a plan to redistribute wealth which would annually tax large fortunes and corporate assets and redistribute the money by guaranteeing every family a gift of $5,000 and an annual income of $2,500. To promote his plan, Long established a Share Our Wealth Society which attracted over 5 million members in 1935, but he was assassinated before its enactment, and the milder reforms of President Franklin D. Roosevelt's New Deal proved sufficient to placate his supporters.

During World War II support for business rebounded. Industry wrapped itself in patriotism, and its high output of war material proved essential to Allied victory. As a result, business was seen as the "arsenal of democracy," not as a bloated plutocracy. In a postwar poll only 10 percent of the population believed that where "big business activity" was concerned "the bad effects outweighed the good."[17] This renascence of respect lasted into the 1960s before the populist seed sprouted once again.

Recent Antibusiness Sentiment

Strong public support for business collapsed in the mid-1960s. It was a time of unrest. Social movements attacked basic institutions for their failure to solve major problems. Government, labor, the military, churches, higher education, medicine, the press, and, of course, business all suffered diminished public confidence. Here are examples of polls that reflect the extraordinary negative trend in public attitudes toward business.

- In 1968, 70 percent agreed that business tried to strike a fair balance between profits and the public interest. By 1970 the figure had declined to 33 percent, and in 1976 it had plummeted to 15 percent. This was a drop of 55 points in eight years.[18]
- Two polls, the first in 1966 and the second in 1979, showed that the percentage of Americans expressing a "great deal of confidence" in the leaders of major companies declined from 55 percent to 19 percent."[19]

- Between 1965 and 1977 the average favorability ratings for eight industries fell from 68 percent to 36 percent. Approval of twenty-two large companies declined from an average rating of 74 percent in 1965 to 48 percent in 1975.[20]

Scholars who studied the polls theorized that the period of turmoil in American society in the 1960s created a "confidence gap," or a gap between public expectations about how institutions should perform and public perceptions of how they actually did perform. This gap has now persisted for three decades. In 1994 only 26 percent of Americans expressed "a great deal" or "quite a lot" of confidence in big business, the same percentage as in 1973.[21]

Factors Underlying Negative Attitudes Toward Business

What causes this confidence gap to persist? At a high level of abstraction the fundamental source of critical attitudes toward business is industrial development. But additional explanation of complex historical, cultural, and psychological factors is required to understand more precisely the origins and persistence of business critics. Here we discuss some significant forces underlying business-directed opprobrium.

Traditional American Antipathy to Centralized Power

Deeply fixed in the bedrock belief system of American political culture is the fear of concentrated power. Sources of this fear are the experiences of colonial America with an imperious England and the popularity in the revolutionary era of the political theories of the English philosopher John Locke, who wrote that human beings are naturally free and equal. Political power should be accountable to the consent of the governed and be used to protect individual rights to life, liberty, and property. Locke believed that popular majorities have the right to influence and check powerful executives and legislators.[22]

After the Civil War, when giant trusts grew to dominate markets and suborn politicians, Locke's ideology of popular checks on centers of power was advocated by critics. To this day many critics fear the motives of managers and regard large corporations as remote, impersonal entities that cannot be trusted any more than the colonists trusted King George. In 1941 a poll found that 59 percent of Americans agreed that "there is too much power in the hands of a few rich men and large corporations."[23] Over fifty years later the perception of oppressive corporate power seemed even more widespread: 76 percent of those surveyed in 1992 agreed that "there is too much power concentrated in the hands of a few big companies."[24]

Conspiracy Theories

Throughout American history it has been alleged that some group (and the list includes Jesuits, city women, European monarchs, immigrants, Jews, blacks, Communists, Masons, Darwinians, munitions manufacturers, international bankers, oil companies, and Wall Streeters), acting in secret for its own self-interest, is out to do the public in. This mindset, which has been called the "paranoid style" by historian Richard Hofstadter, is distinguished by the belief that a vast conspiracy is the motive force of history.[25]

The number of people who believe that conspiracies exist can be large. In 1974, for instance, 43 percent of Americans believed that the energy shortage was "contrived" by the oil companies to exploit the public.[26] In 1985, according to 67 percent, "the oil companies are just waiting for a chance to create another oil shortage so they can increase their prices again like they did in the 1970s."[27] In 1990 the public affirmed its suspicious prophecy. When oil companies raised gasoline prices after Iraq invaded Kuwait, 84 percent believed that "they deliberately tried to rip off the American motorist."[28]

Conspiracy theories such as these are difficult to combat because their circular logic is airtight. Because undiscovered conspiracies are by definition secret, they cannot be directly observed or verified. The most straightforward appeal of conspiracy theories is that they provide simple explanations for complex events and relieve the mind of the necessity for strenuous thought. Hence, intricate reality is reduced to the existence of a hidden conspiracy that explains everything. The persistence of conspiracy theories about business reflects bedrock cynicism in the population.

Rumors About Business

Rumors are factually unverified stories created in conversation. Many are credible-sounding and may achieve broad circulation. They can be costly to business. In the 1940s, for example, the first king-sized menthol cigarette, called Spud, failed in the market because of a groundless rumor that a leper worked where it was made. Rumors are present at all times, but proliferate in times of social and economic change when people are confronted with unfamiliar, anxiety-causing circumstances. Their telling satisfies a variety of motives: to demystify puzzling circumstances; to vent anger, aggression, and fear; or simply to attract favorable attention to the teller.

Because there is widespread anxiety about business power, it is not surprising that large corporations are the subjects of rumors that reflect mistrust. For example, the persistent rumor that an oil company has purchased a carburetor that gets 100 miles per gallon and is hiding it in a warehouse and paying hush money to the inventor reflects great cynicism about the motives of corporate leaders. Such rumors may express attitudes about capitalism which cannot be articulately expressed as abstract theory.

One measure of public anxiety about big business is that rumors tend to focus on large corporations. In the late 1970s a rumor started in Tennessee that Wendy's hamburgers, which were advertised as "hot and juicy," contained worm meat. Within a year, however, McDonald's became the company named in the rumor and sales of McDonald's hamburgers declined. Why did the worms crawl from Wendy's to McDonald's? The answer lies in the *Goliath effect,* which is that as rumors are reconstructed in conversations over time the dynamics of perception lead people to substitute the names of bigger corporations for smaller ones because large firms are the conspicuous source of mass fears and suspicions.[29] Rumors which are told to release fears and anxieties about the powerlessness of common people are most effective when they focus on dominant corporations.

Tension Between Capitalism and Democracy

There is a natural, built-in tension between capitalistic economies and democratic governments because they embody equally legitimate but competing value systems. Capitalist values include economic efficiency, self-interest as a major motivator, and allocation of resources through an impersonal market mechanism. Unfettered, these values would create enormous inequalities of wealth and circumstance. Democracy is a combination of popular sovereignty, political equality, and majority rule. These characteristics are leveling forces. American society continuously seeks to reconcile these competing value sets.

In the capitalist-democracy synthesis business can expect persistent attack. This attack occurs because democracies tend to have leftward centers of gravity, since over time more and more have-nots are included in the electoral process. Stable democracies often have an inherent leftward drive, and leftwing parties win support by promising to increase the well-being of the lower strata. In this process, leftist politicians and political parties appeal to the masses by attacking wealth and privilege.

Operation of the Business Cycle

The recurrence of recession and depression in American history has ensured periodic concern about the role of economic institutions and their performance and relationship to government. Panics in the nineteenth century led to public rage directed at the financial community. The stock market scandals of the 1930s associated with the 1929 market crash tainted business for years. Opinion polls show that people rate economic problems among the most important problems. Polls also show that people may blame business for their economic ills. Lipset and Schneider correlated surveys of confidence in institutional leadership between 1966 and 1980 with rates of unemployment and inflation and found that as unemployment and inflation rose, confidence in the leadership of major companies and other institutions declined.[30] Historically, economic fluctuation also has been shown to detonate and give expression to underlying trends such as fear of power and belief in business conspiracy.[31]

The Image of Business in Media and the Arts

Values are both shaped and reflected by images of business in journalism, literature, and the visual arts.

A longstanding adversarial relationship exists between business and journalists representing the print and broadcast media. Corporations want to see positive images conveyed through newspapers, magazines, radio, and television. The job of editors, reporters, and producers, on the other hand, is to seek out and publish accurate information in a way that attracts audiences. The result of this difference of mission is that self-interested companies sometimes accuse the news media of distortion, bias, simplification, and omission in business reporting. Journalists, in turn, complain of executives "unavailable" for comment, unreturned phone calls, terse news releases, and overprotective public relations offices that shield top managers from the press. Three other basic factors underlie the friction between journalism and business.

First, many business and economic stories are complex, yet strong forces in the media work against in-depth, sophisticated reporting. Television journalists are usually generalists, not specialists in business affairs. They face short deadlines for stories, and unless the story is a blockbuster, news program editors rarely give it more than ninety seconds. Television news, owing to the visual nature of its presentation, tends to emphasize colorful, emotional, visually exciting, and dramatic stories involving conflict, but not all or even the most important business news fits these criteria. The dynamics of print journalism are less restricting. The most sophisticated daily newspapers, such as the *New York Times* and the *Washington Post*, have specialist business reporters and may devote many pages to a story to achieve in-depth reporting, although their deadlines are also short. Weekly newsmagazines have longer deadlines and are able to do more research on stories.

Second, surveys have shown that journalists have different values than business executives. For example, journalists tend to be liberals and Democrats, whereas executives are the reverse. They have lower income and different educational backgrounds than the managers they cover, and they tend to have different public policy preferences.[32] Thus journalists may put an indirect liberal spin in their stories. Of course, large media corporations frequently own the news organizations that employ journalists. Such ownership ties raise delicate issues. In corporate-owned media, owners and editors do not ham-handedly forbid certain topics or kill big stories. But they have the more subtle power to choose subjects which will be treated in greater depth and with more frequency.

A third factor underlying friction between business and journalism is the tradition of muckraking in the profession. This tradition began during the progressive era after 1902 when a group of moralistic writers published exposes of business corruption in emergent mass-circulation magazines. Ida M. Tarbell, for instance, began her famous two-volume *History of the Standard Oil Company* as a series of articles in *McClure's* beginning in 1903.[33] Other writers skewered trusts in meat packing, railroading, tobacco, banking, and life insurance. Basic to the writings of the muckrakers was faith in the righteousness of an informed, aroused public. Today's journalists carry on this tradition.

The image of business in literature reflects a mixture of attitudes among novelists. It is often negative and business values have been derided by some of the most famous American novelists. At the turn of the century Frank Norris, in his aptly titled novel *The Octopus* portrayed railroads as corrupt and greedy.[34] Upton Sinclair attacked the greed and disregard for workers in the meatpacking industry in *The Jungle*, his tragic narrative of an immigrant's life in Chicago's slaughterhouses.[35] And a few years later Sinclair Lewis used the vacant character George Babbitt to depict a business world that lacked excitement and meaning.[36] This tradition has continued. Tom Wolfe's recent *Bonfire of the Vanities* rose to the top of the *New York Times* best-seller list with the story of a rich, pretentious Wall Street bond trader whose life in business is frivolous and amoral.[37] As the plot unfolds his pretensions of superiority are destroyed by the "little people," the street punks, police, and courts of New York. It is a novel the populists would have loved.

Although some of America's greatest novelists have treated business with scorn and contempt, others have affirmed business values. Horatio Alger's popular formula novels about business success are an example. Alger wrote more than 100 novels between 1867 and 1899, all with the same inspirational story line. In books with titles such as *Mark the Matchboy* and *Ragged Dick*, impoverished street urchins display strong character values of integrity and hard work. Fortuitously, these values attract the attention of titans of industry who then open the doors to opportunity and boundless wealth. One literary historian, who studied 450 novels with business themes, concludes that novelists have admired virtues such as hard work, achievement, and integrity. Some writers, however, portrayed these traits as being at odds with business life.[38] Another historian argues that novelists stand for the individual in the struggle against self, society, and corporation, and not against business per se.[39]

By contrast, on entertainment television the image of business is often strikingly negative. A landmark study of 620 prime-time shows in the thirty seasons between 1955 and 1986 found that business characters were depicted more negatively than any others. Though making up only 12 percent of the characters, they committed 32 percent of the crimes, including 40 percent of the murders. Only 37 percent of business people on TV played positive roles.[40] The researchers found a trend over the seasons toward increasingly negative depictions, whereas other types of characters remained unchanged. This was attributed to a shift in program content from 1950s storylines that conformed with general public attitudes to images in the 1970s and 1980s that increasingly reflected the antibusiness, liberal, left-wing attitudes of writers and producers, which have been documented in surveys.

Current Criticism of American Business

The list of specific criticisms of corporations is virtually endless. But all are based on the same idea, which is that people in business place profit before enduring values such as honesty, truth, justice, love, devoutness, aesthetic merit, respect for nature, and so forth. For example, commercialism has eroded the meaning of Christmas, according to two critics who say it has turned "the day commemorating the birth of Jesus Christ into an unparalleled orgy of consumption."[41] In this instance divinity is sacrificed for profit. To critics the profit motive is less noble than contrasting humanitarian motives because it is seen as selfish. This idea, an echo from ancient Greece, is at the root of the following generic categories of criticism. Each broad category, in turn, includes many specific criticisms.

"Modern Man Followed by the Ghosts of His Meat," by Sue Coe. Coe is an artist who attempts to provoke anger and unease. Her paintings are often bleak because she believes that the presence at injustice in her subjects leaves no beauty to be depicted. This painting is one of a series Coe did after visiting slaughterhouses and meatpacking plants. The image challenges values that support meat eating and includes a McDonald's logo that implicates corporations in the unnecessary, mass slaughter of animals.

Source: Sue Coe. "Modern Man Followed by the Ghosts of his Meat." © 1988 Sue Coe. Courtesy Galerie St. Etienne, New York.

1. Business activity has a corrosive effect on a range of cherished cultural values.
2. Business cheats and harms consumers.
3. Business exploits and dehumanizes workers.
4. Business degrades nature and the environment.
5. Business manipulates government and undermines the public interest.

Basic criticism of the profit motive raises two important questions. First, is profit making an inferior motive? Without the profit motive, levels of business efficiency, innovation, and production would crash; profit cannot be seen solely as avarice with no compensating societal benefit. Second, is profit necessarily ever or frequently opposed to other important values? The Artist's Rights Society once refused to allow a French manufacturer to use a Matisse painting in an ad for a toilet, scolding the company by saying that Matisse would have been insulted and that artistic integrity would be sacrificed for profit. The company responded that it was a French toilet and a fine toilet and, moreover, the ad educated the public about art. Which side was correct? Was there a conflict between profit and the integrity of artistic genius?

A wide range of critics differ in the nature of their attacks and their prescriptions to eliminate perceived ills. To oversimplify, there are five basic groups of critics.

Activist Reformers

The first group, activist reformers, is composed of individuals and groups who accept the basic legitimacy of the business system, but see flaws and work with companies and/or through political processes for reform. The philosophy of the activist reformer is exemplified by consumer advocate Ralph Nader, who accepts American capitalism in its democratic setting but sees an "imbalance of power between the people and the plutocracy."[42] For thirty years Nader has worked to redress this imbalance by building an organization of public interest groups through which he and his disciples pressure business and government to accomplish reform.

Some activism is the product of lone individuals who are galvanized by personal situations. Phil Sokolof, for example, was the president of an Omaha metal parts company. When he had a heart attack he wrote letters to cookie and cereal manufacturers asking them to take high-fat coconut oil out of their products. They failed to respond, so he ran full-page newspaper ads which pictured Hydrox cookies, Cracklin' Oat Bran cereal, and other products under the headline "The POISONING of AMERICA." Within months large firms such as Kellogg Co. dropped coconut oil. A second set of ads picturing a Big Mac and French fries pressured McDonald's Corp. to introduce the McLean Deluxe burger and switch to lower-fat cooking oils for fries. Sokolof has spent over $8 million of his own money and is currently attacking the dairy industry in ads which warn the public that "lowfat" milk contains more fat than the average consumer suspects.[43] The most forceful activism, however, usually comes not from individuals, but from groups, including consumer, labor, environmental, civil rights, and religious groups.

Activists use a wide range of tactics. Common, low-key pressure tactics include negotiation, letter writing, speeches, lobbying legislatures and regulatory agencies, research, and editorial writing. Labor unions frequently picket companies. A number of activist organizations use lawsuits to challenge business. Sometimes, activists resort to harassment, as when they sue corporations based on trumped-up charges such as racketeering or disrupt the lives of executives and their families by picketing their homes, demonstrating at their children's schools, and interrupting services at their churches.

There are several additional tactics used by activists which take advantage of the corporation's market orientation.

- *Shareholder Resolutions.* American rules of corporate governance permit individuals and groups holding the stock of a publicly traded company to sponsor resolutions on which all shareholders may vote at corporate annual meetings. If the resolutions pass, they are binding on management. Religious groups such as the Sisters of Loretto have led in sponsoring such resolutions. The Interfaith Center for Corporate Responsibility in New York coordinates a coalition of over 100 Protestant, Roman Catholic, and Jewish denominations which, in 1995, generated 180 shareholder resolutions aimed at 133 companies.[44]

- *Boycotts.* A boycott is a call to put pressure on a company by not buying its products and services. For example, INFACT, a worldwide network of consumer groups formed in 1977 "to stop life threatening abuses by transnational corporations," has conducted three powerful boycotts. A seven-year boycott of Nestlé ended in 1984 when the company agreed to alter infant formula marketing practices. A six-year boycott of General Electric ended in 1986 when GE sold its nuclear weapons production facilities. Currently, INFACT is boycotting Philip Morris and R. J. Reynolds to stop tobacco ads that target children.[45] There are dozens of boycotts at any given time.

- *Selective Purchasing and Investment Laws.* Some groups have pressured government agencies to stop them from purchasing supplies and services from allegedly irresponsible corporations. For instance, in the 1980s the Africa Fund, Transafrica, labor unions, and civil rights groups were successful in getting more than 100 such laws passed in states, counties, cities, and agencies prohibiting purchase of supplies and services from companies doing business in South Africa. In 1995 the City of Berkeley, California, at the urging of the Pepsi-Burma Boycott Committee, adopted a law prohibiting buying from or investing in any company doing business in Burma, where critics argue that corporations are supporting a military regime that abuses human rights.

Liberal Intellectuals

This group is composed of thinkers who share a broad approach to social problems which they express with the pen rather than the sword of activism. This group believes that (1) human rights should be protected and enhanced, (2) there is a need to restrain corporate power, (3) social arrangements can be improved through reform, and (4) government should be used to correct problems in society. Liberal intellectuals have a basic faith in democratic capitalism, but they find blemishes and suggest remedies consonant with their ideology. The writings of intellectuals with these broad beliefs have over the years been a source of great insight and timely ideas for reform.

The liberal reform tradition surfaced as America industrialized. As economic activity accelerated in the nineteenth century intellectuals began to be bothered. "Commerce," complained Ralph Waldo Emerson in 1839, ". . . threatens to upset the balance of man, and establish a new, universal Monarchy more tyrannical than Babylon or Rome."[46] Over time, intellectual inquiry made visible many problems that reformers grappled with during the populist, progressive, and New Deal eras.

Today, the intellectual tradition continues. In his 1956 book, *The Organization Man*, sociologist William H. Whyte, Jr., argued that big organizations produced undesirable conformity in employees, and economist John Kenneth Galbraith has written numerous books over forty years advocating greater government control of business to reverse the loss of consumer sovereignty that he attributes to the growth of large corporations.[47] Some writers do not challenge business directly, but their work changes social values. The 1962 book *Silent Spring* by naturalist Rachael Carson[48] warned of the danger of pesticides, and came at just the right time to galvanize the environmental movement and quicken the pace of attack on industrial pollution. Peter Singer's 1975 book *Animal Liberation*[49] is a philosophical tract, which created a comprehensive justification for animal rights that changed the environment for the animal agriculture, cosmetics, fur, and restaurant industries.

Marxists

Marxist critics reject current institutional structures and demand replacement with a collectivist state. Unlike reform-oriented critics, this group believes that the faults of capitalism cannot be ameliorated through gradual reform. Basic institutions such as the free market and private capital must be swept away.

Marxists base their critique on the philosophical and economic theories of their intellectual progenitor, Karl Marx (1818-1883). They attack traditional scholarship for failing to see the abusive aspects of current economic arrangements. Orthodox views of the market, they say, fail to reveal how capitalism creates worker exploitation, imperialist expansion overseas, resource waste, racial and sexual discrimination, income inequality, militarism, and other evils.

Historically, Marxist critics have been persistent antagonists of business. Although the tide of history has gone against them in the United States, Marxists have reached high water marks in three eras when grave social problems called into question the legitimacy of the business system. The first was during the progressive era, when in 1912 the Socialist party presidential candidate, Eugene V. Debs, attracted 6 percent of the popular vote. The second was in the depression era of the 1930s, when attacks on free enterprise abounded. And the third was during the 1960s and 1970s, when social movements challenged the establishment, including business. In each case, however, moderate reform defeated the socialist agenda.

Marxist thinkers have been influential, but today their influence is waning. The overthrow of Marxist governments in Eastern Europe in 1989 and 1990 and the deteriorated economies of the former Soviet republics have blunted the appeal of their critique. Though the movement is moribund, to dismiss it now might be premature.

Radical Non-Marxists

Like Marxists, radical non-Marxist critics see industrial society as beyond redemption and advocate replacement of its basic principles and restructuring of its institutions. Unlike Marxists, they do not coalesce around any general theory of what is wrong, what should be done, or how to do it. Radical criticism of industry has a long history in American society; in the last century the first radical critics tried to cling to the values and life of an agrarian society being swept away as they watched.

In the 1840s Brook Farm in Massachusetts and similar agrarian communes were founded by radical critics of industry. In these communes, values prized in industrial society— materialism, competition, individualism, and tireless labor—were rejected. Instead, an effort was made to substitute moderation, cooperation, group harmony, and leisure. These utopias soon failed, of course, their example fated by industrialization.

In 1863 the cantankerous Henry David Thoreau wrote to reject a world where the poetry and grace of everyday life was being smothered by business values.

> This world is a place of business. What an infinite bustle! I am awaked almost every night by the panting of the locomotive. It interrupts my dreams. There is no sabbath. It would be glorious to see mankind at leisure for once. It is nothing but work, work, work. I cannot easily buy a blank-book to write thoughts in; they are commonly ruled for dollars and cents. . . . I think that there is nothing, not even crime, more opposed to poetry, to philosophy, ay, to life itself, than this incessant business.[50]

The ideas of Brook Farm and Thoreau failed to spread. But the tradition of radical rejection of industrial society is continuously renewed. In the last twenty-five years, for example, a school of thought has emerged which would radically restructure the economy by limiting or ending growth. Economist E. F. Schumacher, for example, wrote *Small Is Beautiful*, in which he urged a new society in which people would live in harmony with nature instead of dominating and destroying it. David Foreman, a founder of the radical activist group Earth First! believes in dismantling much of industrial civilization, tearing up roads, and returning to an earlier kind of life.[51] Another recent radical critic, Kirkpatrick Sales writes that industrialism is "seriously endangering stable social and environmental existence on this planet" and must be opposed.[52] He argues that corporations and governments which were originally designed to focus on human needs must be reoriented to have "spiritual identification" with all species, large organizations with global perspectives must be replaced by small communities, and industrial capitalism must be converted to a system of cooperation rather than competition. These ideas, of course, come straight from the book of agrarianism.

Reactionaries

Reactionary critics assail corporations for responding to liberal critics, going too far in the direction of nonmarketsocial responsibilities, or taking political and moral stands that conflict with conservative positions. To illustrate, the Ku Klux Klan has boycotted Philip Morris for supporting black civil rights groups. And economist Milton Friedman scolds business for undertaking social responsibility activities that depart from its traditional economic role.

One of the most tenacious conservative business critics is a fundamentalist minister from Mississippi, Rev. Donald Wildman. In 1986 he masterminded an antipornography campaign that pressured Southland Corp. to stop newsstand sales of *Playboy* and *Penthouse* in 7-11 stores. Two years later, he threatened a Christian boycott of Pepsi unless PepsiCo, Inc., dropped a $10 million contract with Madonna. Wildman objected to "a pop star who goes around in her concerts with sex oozing out, wearing a cross" becoming a role model in Pepsi ads. The Pepsi campaign was canceled. Wildman's group monitors every prime-time network program and records offensive material. It has boycotted companies that sponsor programs with "gratuitous sex, violence, and anti-Christian stereotyping," including Clorox Corp. and Burger King, calling off the boycotts when the companies changed their criteria for sponsorship.[53] Currently, Wildman is boycotting Holiday Inns for providing adult movies in rooms.

Conclusion: What Should We Think of Critics?

In this chapter we have set forth a long history of negative attitudes toward business and discussed specific criticisms. In doing so, we have not analyzed the merits of particular criticisms, but have simply noted them. The fundamental response to critics of industrial society is as follows.

There is no question that industrial capitalism as it exists in the United States and elsewhere is a historical force that creates fundamental, continuous social change; it is, as the economist Joseph Shumpeter wrote in 1942, "a perennial gale of creative destruction," which destroys institutions and challenges existing authority.[54] The great issue is how to regard this change.

The defense of industrial capitalism is that the changes in companies, governments, values, technologies, and living patterns that it creates represent progress, a condition of improvement for humanity. As against promoting greed and avarice, it has rather promoted positive cultural values such as imagination, innovation, organized cooperation, hard work, and the interpersonal trust necessary to conduct millions of daily business transactions on faith. It operates in a democratic political system which has ably reformed abuses over the years. And it has improved living standards for millions. As one defender of the "spirit of capitalism" notes, during the last century even as critics attacked its deplorable impact, it was actually:

> . . . prompting inventions and improvements that systematically came to the assistance of the neediest: eyeglasses for those of weak eyesight, lamps for those in darkness, new medicines for the ill, mechanical aids to replace brute human strength, and ever-greater ease of transport. Life became softer, even as intellectuals described it in terms of the jungle. The spirit of capitalism may in fact be portrayed more accurately as leading to excessive comfort than as reincarnating the law of survival.[55]

Whether or not we agree with their ideas, business critics play an important role. There are legitimate criticisms of business that demand attention both by corporations and governments. If criticism is properly channeled it can preserve the best of the business institution and bring wide benefit.

Endnotes

1. In Adam Goodman, *"General Dynamics' Bonus Plan Approved,"* St. *Louis Post-Dispatch*, January 16,1992.
2. John Curley, "Religious Order Faces a Dilemma in Profiting from Firms It Opposes," *Wall Street Journal*, October 7, 1983.
3. Will Durant, *The Life of Greece*, New York: Simon & Schuster, 1939, p. 272.
4. John Kenneth Galbraith, *Economics in Perspective*, Boston: Houghton Mifflin, 1987, pp. 9-10.
5. Trans. E M. Cornford, New York: Oxford University Press, 1945. See pp. 155-168.
6. Trans. Ernest Barker, New York: Oxford University Press, 1962 p. 27. Originally written c. 335 B.C.
7. Ibid., p. 29.
8. "Asked, 'Who is the rich man?' Epictetus replied, 'He who is content.'" *The Golden Sayings of Epictetus*, trans. Hastings Crossley, in Charles W. Eliot, ed., *Plato, Epictetus, Marcus Aurelius*, Danbury, Conn.: Grolier, 1980, p. 179.
9. In *The Age of Faith*, New York: Simon & Schuster, 1950, p. 631.
10. Henry Adams, *The Education of Henry Adams*, New York: Modern Library, 1931, p. 500. This passage was written in 1905.
11. In John D. Hicks, *The Populist Revolt*, Minneapolis: University of Minnesota Press, 1931, p. 160.
12. Louis Galambos, *The Public Image of Big Business in America, 1880-1940*, Baltimore: Johns Hopkins University Press, 1975, chap. 3. Galambos examined 8,976 items related to big business that were printed in eleven newspapers and journals between 1879 and 1940 using content analysis to reconstruct a rough measure of public opinion among influential groups in the population.
13. William Jennings Bryan, "Farming as an Occupation," *Cosmopolitan*, January 1904, p. 371.
14. First published in 1900 under the title *The Wonderful Wizard of Oz*, Chicago: Reilly & Britten, 1915. Eventually there were fourteen Oz books. The classic interpretation of symbolism in *The Wizard of Oz* is Henry W. Littlefield, "The Wizard of Oz: Parable on Populism," *American Quarterly*, Spring 1964.
15. "The Man with the Hose," August 1906, p. 341.
16. *Congressional Record*, 73d Cong., 2d sees., 1934, p. 6081, speech of April 5.
17. Burton R. Fisher and Stephen B. Withey, *Big Business as the People See It*, Ann Arbor, Michigan: University of Michigan Microfilms, December 1951, p. xiii.
18. Seymour M. Lipset and William Schneider, "How's Business? What the Public Thinks," *Public Opinion*, July-August 1978.
19. Philip Shaver, "The Public Distrust," *Psychology Today*, October 1980.
20. Seymour M. Lipset and William Schneider, *The Confidence Gap*, New York: Free Press, 1983, p. 31.
21. Frank Newport and Lydia Saad, "Confidence in Institutions," *The Gallop Poll Monthly*, April 1994, pp. 5-6.
22. See *The Second Treatise of Government*, Thomas P. Reardon, ed., Indianapolis: Bobbs-Merrill, 1952. Originally published in 1690.
23. George H. Gallup, ed., *The Gallup Poll: Public Opinion 1935-1971*, vol. 1, New York: Random House, 1972, p. 277.
24. A Gallup/Times Mirror poll cited in "Opinion Outlook," *National Journal*, July 25, 1992, p. 1750.
25. *The Paranoid Style in American Politics and Other Essays*, New York: Knopf, 1966.
26. In Clarence H. Danhoff and James C. Worthy, eds., *Crisis in Confidence II: Corporate America*, Proceedings of the Second Annual Intersession Public Affairs Colloquium, Springfield, Ill.: Sangamon State University, 1975, p. 39.
27. Edward Byers and Thomas B. Fitzpatrick, "Americans and the Oil Companies: Tentative Tolerance in a Time of Plenty," *Public Opinion*, December/January 1986, p. 44.
28. "Opinion Outlook," *National Journal*, February 2, 1990, p. 295.
29. Gary Alan Fine, "The Goliath Effect: Corporate Dominance and Mercantile Legends," *Journal of American Folklore*, January-March 1985.
30. Lipset and Schneider, *The Confidence Gap*, p. 62.
31. W. W. Rostow, "Business Cycles, Harvests, and Politics," *Journal of Economic History*, November 1941.
32. See Stanley Rothman and S. Robert Lichter, "Media and Business Elites: Two Classes in Conflict," *The Public Interest*, Fall 1982; William Schneider and I. A. Lewis, "Views on the News," *Public Opinion*, August/September 1985; and S. Robert Lichter, Stanley Rothman, and Linda S. Lichter, *The Media Elite*, Bethesda, Maryland: Adler & Adler, 1986.
33. Ida M. Tarbell, *The History of the Standard Oil Company*, Gloucester, Mass.: Peter Smith 1963, 2 vols. Originally published in 1904.
34. New York: Doubleday, Page, 1901.
35. New York: Doubleday, Page, 1906.
36. Sinclair Lewis, *Babbitt*, New York: Harcourt, Brace, Jovanovich 1922.

37. New York: Farrar, Straus, & Giroux, 1987.
38. Howard P. Smith "Novelists and Businessmen: Schizophrenia in the Complex Society," *Journal of Contemporary Business*, Autumn 1976.
39. Robert P. Falk, "From Poor Richard to the Man in the Gray Flannel Suit: A Literary Portrait of the Businessman," *California Management Review*, Fall 1958.
40. S. Robert Lichter, Linda S. Lichter, and Stanley Rothman, *Watching America: What Television Tells Us about Our Lives*, New York: Prentice-Hall Press, 1991, pp. 131-33.
41. Michael F. Jacobson and Laurie Ann Mazur, *Marketing Madness: A Survival Guide for a Consumer Society*, San Francisco: Westview Press, 1995, p. 203.
42. Ralph Nader, "Breaking Out of the Two-Party Rut," *The Nation*, July 20/27,1992, p. 98.
43. Connie Koenenn, "Attack of the Anti-Fat Man," *Los Angeles Times*, May 4,1995, p. E1.
44. "Corporate Responsibility Challenges 1995," *The Corporate Examiner*, 1994, vol. 23, no. 7-8, p. 1.
45. Kathy Mulvey, "INFACT: Campaigning for Corporate Accountability," *The Boycott Quarterly*, Spring 1994, pp. 10-11.
46. Quoted from Emerson's *Journals*, vol. V, pp. 285-86, in Vernon Louis Parrington, *Main Currents in American Thought*, New York: Harcourt, Brace, 1927, p. 386.
47. William H. Whyte, Jr., *The Organization Man*, New York: Simon & Schuster, 1956. For Galbraith see, for example, *The Affluent Society*, Boston: Houghton Mifflin, 1958; or *The New Industrial State*, Boston: Houghton Mifflin, 1967.
48. Boston: Houghton Mifflin, 1962.
49. New York: New York Review of Books, 1975. Revised edition by Avon Books, 1990.
50. Henry David Thoreau, "Life without Principle," *The Atlantic Monthly*, October 1863, p. 484-85.
51. Dave Foreman, *Confessions of an Eco-Warrior*, New York: Harmony Books, 1991.
52. Kirkpatrick Sales, *Rebels against the Future*, Reading, Mass.: Addison-Wesley, 1995, pp. 276-77.
53. Patrick M. Fahey, "Advocacy Group Boycotting of Network Television Advertisers and Its Effects on Programming Content," *University of Pennsylvania Law Review*, December 1991, pp. 660-62.
54. *Capitalism, Socialism and Democracy*, New York: Harper & Row, 1976, p. 143. Originally published in 1942.
55. Michael Novak, *The Catholic Ethic and the Spirit of Capitalism*, New York: Free Press, 1993, p. 26.

Chapter Five

ETHICS IN THE

BUSINESS SYSTEM

Correct Craft

In 1925 Walter C. Meloon started a little business in Florida to make recreational boats. W. C., as he was known, was a high school dropout who had become a Christian to obtain the hand of his devout new bride, Marian. He wanted to glorify God and follow the Golden Rule in his business dealings.

Meloon's company, Correct Craft, barely survived the depression years of the 1930s, but during World War II it prospered making boats for the armed services. In January 1945 General Dwight D. Eisenhower was driving toward Berlin ahead of schedule and set March 10, 1945, as the date for crossing the Rhine. However, there was a critical shortage of the 17-foot, spoon-shaped assault boats that carried soldiers on such river crossings.

Correct Craft was given an urgent order for 300 of these boats by the Army. The company had only eighteen days to build them; its normal output was forty-eight boats per *month*! Immediately, a government expediter demanded that Meloon go to a seven-day workweek, but he refused, saying that it was not God's plan to work on the Sabbath. The expediter gave in. Correct Craft went on to produce 306 boats four days ahead of schedule, without working on Sundays, and another 100 boats when other companies were unable to meet their schedules.

At a second Correct Craft plant, where Meloon built boats for the U.S. Navy, a government inspector tried to speed production by stopping weekly chapel services for the employees. Meloon told him: "If we can't serve the Lord and the U.S. Navy at the same time, we just won't serve the navy."[1] The inspector relented.

After World War II Correct Craft prospered as the second largest builder of sport boats and yachts in the nation. Then, in 1957, the company got a big U.S. Army contract for 3,000 fiberglass boats. One day a government inspector demanded that the Meloons set up a special account for "inspector's expenses." This was a request for a bribe.

By this time W. C.'s equally principled sons, Walter O. and Ralph, managed daily operations. The family prayed for guidance. The payments were small compared to the income at stake. But bribery was wrong. The payments were not made. "If you have made a decision based only on money," said W. C., "you have made a bad decision."[2] Soon the inspectors began to use trivial blemishes as pretexts for rejecting finished boats. In the end they rejected 640 boats. Correct Craft lost $1 million on the contract and in 1958 went into Chapter 11 bankruptcy proceedings. It owed $500,000 to 228 creditors.

Knowing the situation, every Correct Craft employee resigned. Walter O. and Ralph rehired only those with essential jobs. Their wives worked at the switchboard. Walter O. returned his new Lincoln to the dealer. Other family members mortgaged their homes and sold their cars. All adopted a frugal lifestyle.

The company barely avoided liquidation. First came a loan from a friend. Then the government of Pakistan bought 239 of the fiberglass boats that the inspectors had rejected. In early 1965, after years of hardship, a bankruptcy judge released the company from Chapter 11 when 127 remaining creditors agreed to repayment at 10 cents on the dollar.

continued

But despite the agreement, the Meloons struggled for the next nineteen years to repay 100 percent of their debt. As the years passed it became hard to locate some creditors. The family worked to find them. In some cases they were deceased and payments were made to surprised widows or relatives. In one case Ralph flew to Michigan to search for a creditor when telephone calls proved fruitless. In May 1984 the last payment was made. The family had paid 100 percent of its debt!

Today Correct Craft is a profitable company known for its line of inboard-engined recreational boats, including the Ski Nautique, a towboat preferred by water skiers because of

its flat wake. Correct Craft boats are sold worldwide. The third generation of Meloons is in charge; Walter N., son of Walter O., is president. Walter O. and Ralph remain on the board of directors and a third brother, Harold, has been company chaplain since 1974.

Correct Craft is a company driven by ethical values. These values, derived from the philosophy and example of its founder, permeate the company culture to direct employees and influence strategic decisions. Its story illustrates how ethical values can have a continuous impact on the fortunes of a business.

This picture from the December 1945 *National Geographic* magazine shows the road in front of Correct Craft littered with finished plywood assault boats. It was taken on Wednesday, February 21, 1945.

In this chapter we explain sources of ethical guidance in the societal environment of the corporation, discuss ethical practice within corporations, and describe current methods of managing corporate ethics. In the next chapter we focus on guidelines for making ethical decisions.

What are Business Ethics?

Ethics is the study of what is good and evil, right and wrong, and just and unjust. *Business ethics*, therefore, is the study of good and evil, right and wrong, and just and unjust actions in business. Ethical managers try to do good and avoid doing evil. A mass of principles, values, norms, and thoughts concerned with what conduct *ought* to be exists to guide them. But in this vaporous mass the outlines of good and evil are indistinct. Usually they are clear enough, but often not. Hence, the application of ethics in business is an art, an art which requires judgment about both the motivations behind an act and the act's consequences.

Discussions of business ethics frequently emphasize refractory and unclear situations, perhaps to show drama and novelty. Although all managers face difficult ethical conflicts, the vast majority of ethical problems yield to resolution through the application of clear guidelines. The Eighth Commandment, for example, prohibits stealing and clearly makes practices ranging from theft of a competitor's trade secrets to taking a screwdriver home from work unethical. A misleading or lying advertisement violates a general rule of the Western business world that the seller of a product should not purposely deceive the buyer about its price or quality. This general understanding stems from the Mosaic law, the Code of Hammurabi, Roman law, and other sources and is part of a general ethic favoring truth that has remained unchanged for at least 3,000 years.[3]

In general, ethical traditions that apply to business favor truth telling, honesty, protection of human and animal life and rights, respect for law, and operation in accord with policies adopted by society to achieve justice for citizens. Some of these touchstones go back thousands of years. Other ethical standards, such as the principle that a corporation is responsible for worker safety and health, have emerged only recently. In keeping with this long and growing ethical heritage, most business actions can be clearly judged ethical or unethical; it may be difficult to eliminate some unethical behavior, such as bribery or embezzlement, but knowing the rightness or wrongness of actions usually is not difficult.

This does not mean that ethical decisions are always clear. Some ethical issues are difficult because although basic ethical standards apply there are conflicts among them that defy resolution.

Lockheed Aircraft Corp. made large campaign contributions to Japanese officials intended to influence the Japanese to buy airplanes. This saved jobs for American workers. But even though such contributions were not an unusual practice in Japan and for the international aerospace industry in general, they violated domestic business norms. Lockheed's actions are still debated over twenty years later.

Some ethical issues are hidden, at least initially, and hard to recognize.

The A. H. Robins Co. began to market its Dalkon Shield intrauterine device through general practitioners while competitors continued to sell them primarily through obstetricians and gynecologists. This strategy was wildly successful in gaining market share and did not, initially, appear to raise an ethical issue but, when dangerous health problems with the Shield began to surface, general practitioners were slower to recognize them than specialists. Robins's failure to make extra efforts to track the safety of the device then emerged as an ethical shortcoming.

And some ethical issues are very subtle, submerged in everyday workplace behavior. Managers must often work in a world of uncertainty and act or pass judgment without complete knowledge of facts. The following case involves a commitment, a promise.

A regional manager says that replacement equipment for a factory with production problems that are due to breakdowns will be ordered from this year's budget. At the end of the year, however, the equipment has not been ordered because, as the regional manager explains, "there just wasn't enough money left to do it." Is the plant manager entitled to expect the budget to be managed so that the commitment could be kept? Why was the commitment not kept? Poor planning? Disguised withdrawal of cooperation? Another reason?

Two Theories of Business Ethics

There is a debate about whether ethics in business may be more permissive than general societal or personal ethics. There are two basic views.

The first, the *theory of amorality*, is that business should be amoral, that is, conducted without reference to the full range of society's ethical ideals. Managers may act selfishly because the market mechanism distills their actions into benefits for stakeholders and society at large. Adam Smith noted that the "invisible hand" of the market assures that "by pursuing his own interest [a merchant] frequently promotes that of the society more effectively than when he really intends to promote it."[4] In this way capitalism provides moral justification for the pursuit of profit through behavior which is not purposefully ethical.

The apex of this view came during the latter half of the nineteenth century when doctrines of laissez-faire economics and social Darwinism were popular. It was widely believed that business and personal ethics existed in separate compartments, that business was an ethical sanctuary in which less idealistic ethics were permissible.[5] Dan Drew, a builder of churches and the founder of Drew Theological Seminary, typified the nineteenth-century compartmentalization of business decision making in these words:

> Sentiment is all right up in the part of the city where your home is. But downtown, no. Down there the dog that snaps the quickest gets the bone. Friendship is very nice for a Sunday afternoon when you're sitting around the dinner table with your relations, talking about the sermon that morning. But nine o'clock Monday morning, notions should be brushed aside like cobwebs from a machine. I never took any stock in a man who mixed up business with anything else. He can go into other things outside of business hours, but when he's in the office, he ought not to have a relation in the world—and least of all a poor relation.[6]

The theory of amorality has far less public acceptance and luster than it did in Drew's day, but it quietly lives on for many managers. For them the competitive pressures of the market continue to justify behavior that would be condemned in private life; the theory of amorality continues to release these managers from a burden of guilt that they otherwise might feel.

The second basic ethical orientation is the *theory of moral unity*, in which business actions should be judged by the general ethical standards of society, not by a special set of more permissive standards. Only one basic ethical standard exists, making it possible to harmonize principled behavior with the demands of business life.

Many managers are attracted to this position now and were even in the nineteenth century. An example is James Cash Penney. Although we now remember Penney for the successful construction of a chain of retail outlets, his first enterprise was a butcher shop. As a young man, Penney went to Denver and, finding notice of a shop for sale, wired his mother for $300 (his life savings) and purchased it. The departing butcher advised that Penney's success would depend heavily on trade from a nearby hotel. "To keep the hotel for a customer," the butcher explained, "all you have to do is buy the chef a bottle of whiskey a week." Penney regularly made the gift, and business was good, but gradually the opinion of his father, who reviled alcohol, preyed more and more on his mind. He resolved not to make profits in such a manner, stopped giving the bribe, and at the age of 23 was flat broke when the shop failed. Penney later started the Golden Rule Department Store in Denver and argued that his principles of honesty contributed to his ultimate success. A number of companies, such as J. C. Penney's, have successfully operated on religious principles and high moral standards, and their example counterbalances the gamesmanship ethos.

To those like J. C. Penney who adhere to the theory of moral unity, existence of the market is not a reason or excuse to neglect principled behavior. Although the general welfare of society is advanced through selfish economic transactions, profit making is not the only or the highest standard. Without reference to ethical standards the means of profit making may assume greater importance than the end of societal welfare. The market is not an excusing condition for misconduct and managers cannot exist in ethical sanctuaries. As J. Irwin Miller of Cummins Engine Company argues: "The idea that there is some place where principles of right action or good behavior are to be locked out fascinates me. This is a great thing if we can pull it off. But this is about like saying that there is some area in which the law of gravity does not apply or where two and two may equal five."[7]

Although many managers continue to practice the theory of amorality, the theory of moral unity better spells out the expectations of society today.[8] Ethical conflicts cannot be avoided simply because they occur in business.

We are left with an intriguing question: Are there any factors that excuse or diminish ethical responsibility in business? Surprisingly the answer is yes. Perhaps no explication of these factors in the last 2,000 years has improved much on the way they were first set forth by Aristotle.

According to Aristotle, ethical behavior is a state involving voluntary choice and only unethical actions that are involuntary can be excused. The two factors that may lead to involuntary behavior are *ignorance* or *incapacity*. A person may be ignorant of facts or the consequences of an act. For example, a manager may approve production of a new product not knowing that its chemical formula was stolen from a competitor by subordinates who have kept their espionage secret. Although it is wrong to put the stolen formula into production the manager cannot be condemned; ignorance of the facts absolves him or her of bad intentions. (Naturally, negligence in getting facts or intentional ignorance increases culpability.) Incapacity arises from circumstances that render actions involuntary. Circumstances leading to incapacity arise when: (1) a course of action may impose unrealistically high costs—for example, an automobile manufacturer cannot be expected to prevent all traffic deaths since the costs of a perfectly safe vehicle in materials, design, and production would be staggering; (2) there may be no power to influence an outcome—for example, a manager of an oil company doing business in the Middle East cannot end national frictions or religious differences; (3) no alternative exists—in Fascist Germany, for example, corporate managers had to go to Nazi officials in charge of government boards to get allocations of raw materials such as rubber or steel, import-export licenses, and a variety of permissions necessary to conduct business since the Nazis demanded bribes and businesses could not function without paying them; and (4) external force may compel action—for example, a manager may pay excessive and unjust taxes in a foreign country because a corrupt ruler demands them.

Aristotle cautions, however, that "[t]here are some things such that a man cannot be compelled to do them—that he must sooner die than do, though he suffer the most dreadful fate."[9] Unlike cases of ignorance, unethical behavior involving circumstantial coercion may not be completely involuntary if a manager can simply refuse to comply with the external force. Executives and scholars who argue that the market is an irresistible force overriding individual values give too little credit to the strength of human will.

Major Sources of Ethical Values in Business

Managers in every society are influenced by four great repositories of ethical values: religion, philosophy, cultural experience, and law. These repositories contain unique systems of values that exert varying degrees of control over managers. A common theme, the idea of *reciprocity*, or mutual help, is found in all these value systems. This idea reflects the central purpose of all ethics, which is to bind the vast majority of individuals in society into a cooperative whole. Ethical values are a mechanism that controls behavior in business and in other areas of life. Ethical restraint is more efficient with society's resources than are cruder controls such as police, lawsuits, or economic incentives. Ethical values channel individual energy into pursuits that are benign to others and beneficial for society.

Religion

One of the oldest sources of ethical inspiration is religion. More than 100,000 different religions exist. But despite doctrinal differences, the major religions, including the Judeo-Christian tradition prominent in American life, converge in the belief that ethics are an expression of divine will that reveals to the faithful the nature of right and wrong in business and other areas of life. The world's great religions are also in agreement on fundamental principles which are similar to the building blocks of secular ethical doctrine. The principle of reciprocity toward one's fellow humans is found, encapsuled in variations of the Golden Rule, in major religions such as Buddhism, Christianity, Judaism, Confucianism, and Hinduism. The great religions preach the necessity for a well-ordered social system and emphasize in their tenets the social responsibility to act in such a way as to contribute to the general welfare, or at least not to harm it. Built upon such verities are many other rules of conduct.

In the Judeo-Christian heritage, the Ten Commandments, the Golden Rule, and the Sermon on the Mount have often been mentioned as guides for managers. Donald V. Seibert, former chairman of J. C. Penney Company, Inc., advocates daily Bible reading for executives and says that two books are particularly relevant. "Proverbs," he writes, "is replete with references to the proper approach to business transactions, such as 'A wicked man earns deceptive wages, but one who sows righteousness gets a sure reward' [11:18]. And Jesus's teachings and parables in Matthew have enough practical wisdom in them to provide a blueprint for almost an entire working experience."[10]

Although the Bible does not discuss modern corporate life, many managers find it to be an inspirational wellspring of stories and analogies that teach important lessons. The story of the rich man and Lazarus (Luke 16:19-31), for instance, teaches concern for the poor and challenges Christian managers to improve living conditions of the less privileged. The parable of the prodigal son (Luke 15:11-32) sets out an image of an unconditionally merciful father—a model applicable to ethical conflicts in superior-subordinate relationships in corporations.[11]

Across the United States about 7,000 Christian-based firms, mostly smaller companies, try to operate on biblical principles. The founders of the motel chain Days Inns of America, Inc., for example, consciously adopted a Christian-based strategy of not serving alcohol, of giving away Bibles, and of catering to families. Until the chain was sold by the founders, four full-time roving chaplains were available to help employees. A Christian fast-food chain based in Atlanta, Chick-fil-A Inc., refuses to open on Sunday, a long-standing policy which has excluded it from some desirable mall locations.

Biblical standards for business can be high. Consider the following case used by a financial counselor to Christian businesses.

> John ran a large wholesale shoe company in which he purchased large quantities of athletic shoes from manufacturers and sold them to discount chains. When competition increased John found that he had to sell his shoes at growing discounts, sometimes below his cost. John rationalized that selling below cost was essential to maintain customers until higher prices could be charged again. But as he continued to order shoes he fell further and further behind. John began to stretch out accounts payable, paying many invoices when they were past due and sometimes only when suppliers refused to ship more merchandise. In this way, John continued to stay in business.

In this case, according to counselor Larry Burkett, John was operating according to a prevailing business practice, that is, when funds are tight stretch out accounts payable. It costs less to finance cash flow by stringing along suppliers than by paying interest on a bank loan. But for the Christian in business this practice violates Proverbs 12:22: "Lying lips are an abomination to the Lord/But those who deal faithfully are His delight." When John ordered shoes he made a clear promise to pay for them. When he failed to pay he had, in effect, lied.[12] Burkett also argues that owners of companies should not use company cars, phones, or copiers on minor personal business. These are not perks, but "snares set by Satan, who knows that if someone cheats a little bit the next step will be easier."[13]

Philosophical Systems

A Western manager can look back on over 2,000 years of philosophical inquiry into ethics. This rich, complex, classical tradition is the source of a variety of notions about what is ethical in business. Every age has added new ideas to this tradition, but it would be a mistake to regard the history of ethical philosophy as a single debate which, over the centuries, has matured to bear the fruit of growing wisdom and clear, precise standards of conduct. Even after two millennia, there remains considerable dispute among ethical thinkers about the nature of right action. If anything, standards of ethical behavior were arguably clearer in ancient Greek civilization than they are in twentieth-century America.

In a brief circuit of milestones in ethical thinking, we turn first to the Greek philosophers. Greek ethics, from Homeric times onward, were embodied in the discharge of duties related to social roles such as shepherd, warrior, merchant, citizen, or king. Expectations of the occupants of these roles were clearer than in contemporary America, where social roles such as those of business manager or employee are more vague, overlapping, and marked by conflict.[14] Socrates (469-399 B.C.) asserted that virtue and ethical behavior were associated with wisdom and taught that insight into life would naturally lead to right conduct. He also initiated the idea of a moral law higher than human law, an idea that protesters have used to demand supralegal behavior from modern corporations. Plato (428-348 B.C.), the gifted student of Socrates, carried his doctrine of virtue as knowledge further by elaborating the theory that absolute justice exists independently of individuals and that its nature can be discovered by intellectual effort. In *The Republic*, Plato set up a fifty-year program to train rulers to rule in harmony with the ideal of Justice.[15] Plato's most apt pupil, Aristotle, spelled out virtues of character in *The Nicomachean Ethics* and advocated study to develop knowledge of ethical behavior.[16] A lasting contribution of Aristotle is the doctrine of the mean (or golden mean), which is that people can achieve the good life and happiness by developing virtues of moderation. To illustrate, courage was the mean between cowardice and rashness, modesty the mean between shyness and shamelessness.

The Stoic school of ethics, which spans four centuries from the death of Alexander to the rise of Christianity in Rome, furthered the trend toward character development in Greek ethics. Epictetus (A.D. 50-100), for instance, taught that virtue was found solely within and should be valued for its own sake, arguing that virtue was a greater reward than external riches or outward success.

In business, the ethical legacy of the Greeks and Romans remains a conviction that virtues such as truth telling, charity, obeying the law, good citizenship, justice, courage, friendship, and the correct use of power are important ethical qualities. Today an unethical manager may still try to trade integrity for profit; we condemn this, in part, because of the teachings of the Greeks.

Ethical thinking after the rise of Christianity was dominated by the influence of the great Catholic theologians St. Augustine (354-430) and St. Thomas Aquinas (1225-1274). Both believed that humanity should follow God's will; correct behavior in business dealings and all worldly activity was necessary to achieve salvation and life after death. Christianity was the source of ethical expectations as revealed in specific rules such as the Ten Commandments. Christian theology created a lasting reservoir of ethical doctrine, but its domination of ethical thinking declined during the historical period of intellectual and industrial expansion in Europe called the Enlightenment. Secular philosophers such as Baruch Spinoza (1632-1677) tried to demonstrate ethical principles with logical analysis rather than ordain them by reference to God's will. So also Immanuel Kant (1724-1804) tried to find universal and objective ethical rules in logic. Kant and Spinoza, and others who followed, created a great estrangement with moral theology by believing that humanity could discover the nature of good behavior without reference to God. To this day, there is a deep divide between Christian managers who look to the Bible for guidance and other managers who look to human writings for ethical wisdom.

Other milestones of secular thinking followed. Jeremy Bentham (1748-1832) developed a utilitarian system as a guide to ethics. Bentham observed that an ethical action was the one among all alternatives which brought pleasure to the largest number of persons and pain to the fewest. The impact of this ethical philosophy is almost impossible to overestimate. The legitimacy of majority rule in democratic governments rests in large part on Bentham's theory of utility as refined later by John Stuart Mill (1806-1873). Utilitarianism also sanctified industrial development by legitimizing the notion that economic growth benefits the majority; thus the pain and dislocation it brings to a few may be ethically permitted.

John Locke (1632-1704) developed and refined doctrines of human rights and left an ethical legacy supporting belief in the inalienable rights of human beings, including the right to pursue life, liberty, and happiness, and the right to freedom from tyranny. Our leaders, including business leaders, continue to be restrained by these beliefs.

A "realist" school of ethics also developed alongside the "idealistic" thinking of philosophers such as Spinoza, Kant, the utilitarians, and Locke. The "realists" believed that both good and evil were naturally present in human nature; human behavior inevitably would reflect this mixture. Since good and evil occurred naturally it was futile to try to teach ideals. Ideals could never be realized because evil was permanent in human nature. The realist school, then, developed ethical theories that shrugged off the idea of perfect goodness. Niccolò Machiavelli (1469-1526) argued that important ends justified expedient means. Herbert Spencer (1820-1903) wrote prolifically of a harsh ethic that justified vicious competition among companies because it furthered evolution—a process in which humanity improved as the unfit fell down. Friedrich Nietzsche (1844-1900) rejected the ideals of earlier "nice" ethics, saying they were prescriptions of the timid, designed to fetter the actions of great men whose irresistible power and will were regarded as dangerous by the common herd of ordinary mortals.

Nietzsche believed in the existence of a "master morality" in which great men made their own ethical rules according to their convenience and without respect for the general good of average people. In reaction to this "master morality" the mass of ordinary people developed a "slave morality" that shackled the great men. For example, according to Nietzsche, the great mass of ordinary men celebrated the Christian virtue of turning the other cheek because they did not have the power to revenge themselves on great men. He felt that prominent ethical ideals of his day were recipes for timidity and once said of utilitarianism that it made him want to vomit.[17] The influence of realists on managers has been strong. Spencer was wildly popular among the business class in the nineteenth century. Machiavelli is still read for inspiration today. The lasting appeal of the realist school is that many managers, deep down, do not believe that ideals can be achieved in business life.

In conclusion, the legacy of over 2,000 years of recorded ethical debate is such that no single approach or principle has proven superior to others as a guide to right conduct in business. Indeed, right conduct may be less clear today than it was in the age of Pericles.

Cultural Experience

Culture may be defined as a set of traditional values, rules, or standards transmitted between generations and acted upon to produce behavior that falls within acceptable limits. These rules and standards always play an important part in determining values, because individuals anchor their conduct in the culture of the group. Civilization itself is a cumulative cultural experience in which people have passed through three distinct stages of moral codification.[18] These stages correspond to changing economic and social arrangements in human history.

For millions of generations in the *hunting and gathering stage* of human development, ethics were adapted to conditions in which our ancestors had to be ready to fight, face brutal foes, and suffer hostile forces of nature. Under such circumstances a premium was placed on pugnacity, appetite, greed, and sexual readiness, since it was often the strongest who survived. Trade ethics in early civilizations were probably deceitful and dishonest by our standards, and economic transactions were frequently conducted by brute force and violence.

Civilization passed into an *agricultural stage* approximately 10,000 years ago, beginning a time when industriousness was more important than ferocity, thrift paid greater dividends than violence, monogamy became the prevailing sexual custom because of the relatively equal numbers of the sexes, and peace came to be valued over wars, which destroyed crops and animals. These new values were codified into ethical systems by the philosophers discussed in the previous section. Hence, great ethical philosophies that guide educated managers today are products of the agricultural revolution. Included would be the ethical teachings of the church, which provide the reward for good conduct—salvation and everlasting peace.

Two centuries ago, society entered an *industrial stage* of cultural experience, and ethical systems once more began evolving to reflect the changing physical, cultural, institutional, and intellectual environment. Large factories and corporations, population growth, capitalist and socialist economic doctrines, and new technologies have all assaulted the ethical standards of the agricultural stage. Industrialism has not yet created a distinct ethic, but it has created tensions with old ethical systems based on the values of agricultural societies. It does this by changing values related to what is good and bad. For example, the copious outpouring of material goods from factories has encouraged materialism and consumption at the expense of older virtues such as moderation and thrift. Managers run an industrial apparatus on the cutting edge of cultural experience. The tensions their actions create make business more ethically complex. For example, the widespread use of computers for data storage and communication raises new issues of privacy and individual expression unlike those present in agrarian societies when biblical injunctions were written.

The Legal System

Laws are rules of conduct, approved by legislatures and courts, that guide behavior in society. They codify ethical expectations and change over time as new evils emerge. But laws cannot cover all ethical expectations of society; they simply cannot blanket every area of conduct. Law is reactive; new statutes and enforcement always lag behind the opportunity for corporate expediency.

Over the past twenty-five years an explosion of new government regulations, changes in common law in such areas as product liability, lawsuits by stakeholders and new criminal statutes have enforced rising standards in business. Both civil and criminal liability of executives and corporations have expanded. In addition, today the administrative and legal weapons for enforcing standards of conduct on corporations are more powerful. Three main types of sanctions for illegal acts are fines, punitive damages, and prosecution of individual managers. Though each can be an effective deterrent for corporate illegality, none is unflawed.

Fines often do not hurt large firms. In 1991 the Department of Labor fined Jack In The Box $94,000 for child labor violations, but because the firm's annual revenues were $700 million, this was the equivalent of a $94 traffic citation for a person with a yearly income of $700,000. Similarly, when GE recently paid the government $1.84 million in fines and reimbursement to settle a billing fraud case, it was the equivalent of a $25 parking ticket for a person with a $50,000 annual income. In the past, regulatory agencies and courts have hesitated to impose devastating fines because their burden would fall partly on innocent bystanders—shareholders, workers, suppliers, and others who had no knowledge of or control over the corporation's deviant behavior but whose livelihood depends on its benefactions.

In 1991 the United States Sentencing Commission, a small, nine-member judicial agency in the federal government, released a new set of detailed guidelines for sanctioning corporations that break federal laws.[19] The guidelines require corporations to remedy any harm they cause by reimbursing damaged parties if possible. Beyond this, they establish a fine range based on the type of crime, the level of monetary gain to the company or loss to victims, company size, past criminal convictions, cooperation with law enforcement, and the presence of programs designed to prevent and detect illegal acts. Based on these factors, corporations can be fined as little as $5,000 or as much as $290 million.

In civil cases, juries may assess *punitive damages*, or monetary compensation in excess of a wronged party's actual losses. These may be awarded only if malicious and willful misconduct exists. In one case, a regional manager for Browning-Ferris Industries ordered a district manager to drive a small competitor in Vermont out of business using predatory pricing. His instructions were: "Do whatever it takes. Squish him like a bug."[20] Subsequently a jury awarded the competitor $51,146 in actual damages, then added $6 million in punitive damages. In another case, an insurance agent pocketed a woman's premium payments, absconded, and left her with $3,500 in uncovered medical bills. A jury awarded her $840,000 in punitive damages.[21]

The purpose of punitive damages is to punish and deter crime, so they must be large enough to be painful. The West Virginia Supreme Court divides corporate defendants in punitive damage cases into two categories, "really stupid" and "really mean." Really stupid defendants may get punitive damages up to five times the actual cost of compensatory damages to victims; really mean ones can be hit with up to 500 times such damages.[22] In 1991 this court upheld a $10 million punitive damages award against a "really mean" oil and gas production company which was 526 times higher than actual damages of only $19,000.

Corporations have for years argued that such punitive damage awards are unfair and arbitrary, especially since, given similar offenses, juries assess larger damages against a big corporation than against a small one simply to make certain the penalty hurts. But the Supreme Court upheld the awards in all three cases mentioned here and has refused to define a level of punitive damages that would be unconstitutional.[23]

The third type of sanction for corporate crime is prosecution of individual managers. In the past, judges have often been reluctant to sentence managers to jail terms for fraud, embezzlement, illegal toxic waste disposal, and other so-called white-collar crimes. Managers ordinarily do not violently endanger society, may not have the motive to repeat a crime, and would further crowd prisons. The new federal sentencing guidelines mentioned above, however, now contain a quantitative formula that judges must use for sentencing. This formula requires uniform prison terms with length based on the type of crime and factors such as prior convictions and the amount of money involved.

Investigating corporate crimes is difficult for prosecuting attorneys, who are faced with a mass of highly technical corporate documents to review, a network of subtle organizational relationships to sort out, and the conflicting priority of violent street crime to compete for their time. Corporations hire stellar defense lawyers; the state's case is often championed by less experienced attorneys with thin staff support. For these reasons, U.S. and state attorneys may find it easier to pursue simple indictments for street criminals and shy away from the complex corporate cases.

Other methods for punishing corporate crime exist. One guideline for applying them is that they should not cripple or render inefficient legitimate corporate activity. The new federal sentencing guidelines provide for corporate probation periods during which steps can be taken to eradicate loose controls and unethical cultures. Courts have also required advertisements and speeches to publicize wrongdoing. Some corporations have paid their fines to charities, and executives have been ordered to do community service.

Ethical Climates in Other Countries

Ethical practice in business differs among countries and regions of the world because of the way environmental factors shape ethical values. Some simplified illustrations of these factors and how they operate follow.

Historical experience is a broad factor that can shape ethical environments for business that are radically different. The case of Russia is instructive. Russia has had a long history of autocratic, oppressive rule lasting for centuries under the Orthodox Church and czarism and culminating in this century with Communist rule. This history of oppression led to the development of dual ethical standards for personal and business dealings akin to practice of the theory of amorality.[24] High ethical standards were always important in dealing with friends and family, but deception and intrigue in dealing with tyrannical officials grew to be permitted through the centuries. This ethical split carried over into business life where it remains today. Authoritarian rule also created a system of *blat*, or the custom of informal, sometimes corrupt, use of favors to get official action.

Under Communism, party officials planned business activity in intricate detail, promulgating hundreds of thousands of laws, rules, and orders affecting every industry. Because it was impossible to comply with all these dictates and be efficient in business Soviet managers routinely broke rules, manipulated production data, and fabricated accounts to accomplish business goals. The use of *blat* to get ministers to act was widespread and fostered a climate of corruption.

With the downfall of the Soviet regime an entrepreneurial, free enterprise system is growing in Russia alongside state-owned enterprises. But the ethics of this new business system are low by American standards. Under Communist ideology entrepreneurship itself was unethical because individuals were supposed to work for the collective good of the state. The Communist regime taught the Russian people a stereotyped image of "wild capitalism" that conformed to Karl Marx's worst nightmare. Now, not only are the great majority of Russians hostile toward people who start private companies, but the image of capitalism gone wild has become the template that shapes the behavior of the new capitalists. As a result, free enterprise in Russia is chaotic, characterized by corruption, lack of trust, and unpredictability.[25] If history can be viewed as an experiment, Russia is an example of how not to create a favorable climate for business ethics.

The *stage of economic development* in a country is another factor. In countries where the market economy is not supported by institutions and traditions the way it is in developed economies, basic trust may be missing. This is the case in Russia, where many activities that are critical for free enterprise are illegal or unprotected by law.[26] For instance, "speculation," or profit making, was a criminal offense under Communism and is now a gray area. No laws exist to regulate bankruptcy, mergers, contract disputes, and other important activities and, even worse, no independent judiciary exists to settle disputes. This climate of lax regulation incubates unethical behavior.

In many underdeveloped and impoverished countries, including many African nations, the structure of civil institutions also fails to support high ethical standards. In these countries businesses must fight to survive and they see high ethics as an unaffordable luxury. The people of these countries also struggle to survive; many earn their livelihood from criminal activity. Few of these countries have democratic institutions and, in any case, their citizens have low levels of literacy and civic participation. In this situation consumers, workers, and others injured by unethical business conduct have neither the opportunity nor the experience to work through groups and governments for improved behaviors.[27]

In more industrialized countries legal and regulatory institutions and established public values demand consistently honest market behavior and punish transgression. This is a basic difference in the ethical climate and one that cannot be underestimated in its impact on managerial virtue.

The *nature of the political system* is another important factor. In European social democracies such as England, France, and the Netherlands, where governments have traditionally taken responsibility for alleviating social problems, corporations have had comparatively less voluntary discretion than American firms. European companies are less likely to think in terms of ethical standards that are independent of government legal requirements. One reflection of this is that they are much less likely to have formal, written ethics codes than U.S. companies.[28]

In developing countries various pathologies of government may lead to a climate of corruption. If the government is highly bureaucratic, as in Venezuela or Italy, there are so many rules and restrictions that bribery, corruption, and personal favoritism are rampant. Red tape is circumvented by bribes and friends are given favors in preference to strangers. In both countries government officials have been known to paralyze business activity by strict application of myriad laws until they receive payoffs.

Finally, *philosophy and religion* may have a deep impact on ethical values. Asian countries are deeply influenced by lines of thought that originated in ancient China. Asian managers, who are inclined to philosophy, study Bing Fa, a form of strategic thinking developed in Chinese military doctrine beginning around 700 B.C.[29] Bing Fa is based on the study of historic warfare. Asians believe that all parts of human existence are interconnected and that universal principles discovered in one area are at work in all areas of life. So, ancient battles and strategies are tirelessly studied to reveal universal truths that can be applied in business. For Asian managers, then, the conduct of business shades into warfare. A greater range of tactics is seen as legitimate than is the case in the West.

In Bing Fa texts, the most popular of which is Sun Tzu's *Art of War*, deception is often a highly valued tactic.[30] Western managers are sometimes outraged in business negotiations with Chinese, Japanese, or Korean managers when the Asians hide their purpose through indirection or distraction that to the Westerner is deceitful. Chinese, Japanese, and Koreans directly pry into trade secrets and delight in purposeful competitor intelligence gathering. They may infringe on patents in part because they see the marketplace as a battlefield where manipulations considered unethical in America are considered justified by the lessons of Bing Fa.

One remarkable variation in business ethics arises from the emphasis on individualism in U.S. culture as opposed to the emphasis on groups in many other cultures. Individualism in American social philosophy makes individual conscience the source of ethical control; the individual sin concept in Christianity makes personal guilt the penalty for bad conduct. But in other countries, a combination of the underlying factors discussed above has created far different ethical values.

The Japanese, for instance, have a strong ethic of fidelity to work groups and corporations. Beginning in about the sixth century Japan, like other Asian societies, began to borrow and adapt Chinese culture. Traditional values in China stressed that an individual's primary obligation was not to self but to others, including family, clan, and government. The Japanese also built a strong ethic of loyalty to superiors from the emphasis on fidelity in Chinese Confucianism. In medieval times the extreme of loyalty was seen in samurai, who gave their lives for feudal lords. Today it is seen in corporate employees who do ordinary jobs with life-or-death urgency. The concept of sin is foreign to Eastern religion and philosophy, so the Japanese are not controlled by guilty consciences. Rather, they are shamed by group disapproval.

The collectivist ethic in Japan has many consequences. Japanese employees do not blow the whistle on their companies in the face of wrongdoing; they are restrained by loyalty to employers. A Japanese corporation will fire an employee for the breach of simply interviewing with another firm. Loyalty is so strong that if a company does wrong, all employees feel shame. In one case a number of Japanese working for a camera firm in Tokyo grew ashen-faced, left their desks, and started milling in the halls when they heard that the firm was being sued by a German camera company for design imitation. They were close to bolting from the building and had difficulty understanding that lawsuits are a competitive tactic for European firms. In Japan, where group norms control behavior, resort to legal sanctions is reserved for the most heinous crimes, crimes for which the Japanese would feel strong collective guilt. In another instance, reporters from Japan visited Lockheed headquarters in Burbank, California, during the time when the Lockheed payoff scandals were disgracing a Japanese prime minister and his government. They were amazed to see Lockheed employees walking around, looking happy, and behaving normally. They wrote that the Lockheed workers "had no sense of shame."[31]

The Confucian ethic of obedient loyalty is prominent in other Asian economies and creates some surprising ethical idiosyncrasies. For example, a study of Hong Kong managers showed that older managers more readily agreed to unethical practices than younger ones, just the reverse of the typical U.S. situation. Younger managers are more tightly constricted in their behavior by work-group norms than are older managers, who have more independence to depart from rigid integrity.

As this discussion shows, *ethical relativism,* or the variance of ethical climates among different cultures, exists. Are some cultures correct about what constitutes proper business ethics and others wrong? Many business ethicists and foreigners believe that American companies have the highest ethics of all. Should America impose its standards on other countries? The answer to this question hinges on whether ethical knowledge, like scientific knowledge, can be objectively determined. There are two schools of thought.

The first holds that in terms of biological and psychological needs human nature is everywhere about the same. Hence, there is a transcultural ethic because behavior that fulfills basic needs should be the same in all cultures—for example, following basic rules of justice. Basic justice might be achieved, however, through emphasis on group or individual ethics, leaving room for varying cultural tastes.

The second holds that although human biology is everywhere similar, cultural learning creates widely diverging values, including ethical values. Because ethics are value judgments, there is no method for proving them right or wrong like scientific facts. Therefore no single culture can know that its ethical values are superior and impose them as a standard on other cultures.

We cannot settle this old debate, but it has sharp meaning for protagonists in an arena of multiple, dissimilar ethical climates. Appraise, for example, the following story of contact between two ethical climates as told by the CEO of a large multinational corporation.

[The CEO] remarked on a plant in southern Europe where air emissions significantly exceed the company's standard. He noted with some mixed feelings that the town was otherwise heavily polluted, and bringing this plant to company standards would make no noticeable difference to the town. The company will be prepared to control its emissions when the community as a whole is prepared to act on its broader problem.[32]

Ethical Practice in American Business

Opinion polls show that Americans are very cynical about ethical standards in business. In one recent survey, 64 percent of American CEOs felt that their corporations were "highly ethical" places to work—but only 27 percent of employees felt the same way.[33] In some other countries even top management perceives a disappointing level of ethics. In a recent poll of senior managers in Hong Kong, 74 percent believed that levels of ethics in the "business community in general" were moderate to low.[34]

Unfortunately, ethical behavior in business is not subject to an accurate aggregate measure. It may, however, be analyzed at four levels. First is the level of the *business system*, at which the total impact of all economic activity on society is assessed. Historically, industrial activity has been supported as having beneficial effects that far outweigh costs. But ethical questions exist. For example, the U.S. Catholic Bishop's Conference stated that the economy operates unjustly, failing to meet the needs of the poor.[35]

Second, ethics may be examined at the *industry* level. There is evidence that ethical standards differ among industries. In a survey of corporate directors and officers, 87 percent believed that this was so. They ranked commercial banking; utilities; and drugs, pharmaceuticals, and cosmetics as the most ethical.[36] A recent study of Fortune 500 companies found that firms in the food, lumber, petroleum refining, and auto industries were more likely to have broken laws than firms in other industries.[37] Because industries vary greatly in their structures and competitive dynamics, firms in them face varied ethical environments and pressures.

Third, *companies* differ in ethical practice. A number of firms, such as Levi Strauss, Merck, and Johnson & Johnson are consistently noted for high ethics and have institutionalized a concern for ethics in their operating policies. A few companies have exhibited frequent unethical behavior. It is, of course, awkward to label an entire company unethical, because misbehavior mentioned in the press is often counterbalanced by socially responsible actions that receive little publicity.

Last is the *individual* level of ethical behavior. The ethical behavior of individuals varies greatly. At one extreme are people of exceptional integrity. At the other are sociopaths with no conscience. But for most people, honesty is not an all or nothing construct and ethics varies in response to opportunities and restraints in the workplace. The following section is devoted to a discussion of these workplace factors.

Factors that Influence Managerial Ethics

Many managers have high ethical standards and in surveys will indicate that honesty is a highly valued trait in business.[38] Yet indications are that dishonest behavior not only occurs, but is widespread. For instance, a 1981 survey found that about one-third of American managers from the supervisory to the top executive level believed that their bosses sometimes acted unethically. When the survey was repeated ten years later there was little change.[39] More recently, 10,000 employees in six industries were asked: "Have you seen violations of your company's ethical standards during the past year?" Forty-two percent had.[40] These surveys are not unusual; they are typical of others over many years.

Every manager faces ethical issues. Why do large numbers of managers who, if asked, say that they place a high value on honesty, ultimately act unethically? The answer is that there are strong forces at work in the business environment which can, depending on how they are managed, pull people toward more or less elevated behavior. We will discuss here four prominent and interrelated forces that shape ethical standards.

Leadership

The behavior and example of leaders is the single most important influence on ethical standards in a company. Not only do leaders set formal policies of conduct, but by their example they communicate the importance of ethical behavior or tolerance for unethical behavior. Subordinates are keen observers and quickly notice if standards are, in practice, being upheld or corroded. At companies such as Correct Craft and J. C. Penney the high ethical standards of founders supported people who wanted to act virtuously. But at many companies, managers communicate by their actions that there is a difference between formal policies and how things are actually done. If a sales manager instructs subordinates to use deceptive sales practices with customers and later to lie about sales figures in a meeting with superiors, a powerful message is sent about accepted behavior. Diverting blame for mistakes, placing self-interest above company goals, or intentionally failing to support others in the organization send strong messages. Consider the teaching by example implied in the following story.

> Ed was a fast-track manager assigned to run a bottling plant in a highly competitive beverage container market. By observing past promotion practices in the company he concluded that he would probably be in the position no longer than two years before reassignment. Knowing that he would be judged on short-term results and wishing to ensure his next promotion Ed took steps to produce a high return on assets (ROA). He did this by reducing costs relative to plant assets. He cut maintenance and repair budgets, deferred major capital expenditures, and cut inventories. Work force costs were reduced by not replacing retirements, stretching work loads for those remaining, and cutting annual raises from the usual 10 percent to 8 percent. After 18 months Ed had increased ROA by 21 percent and was reassigned to a larger plant.[41]

Strategy and Performance

A critical function of managers is to create strong competitive strategies that enable the company to meet financial goals without encouraging ethical compromise. In companies with deteriorating positions, managers have great difficulty meeting performance targets and may feel pressure to compromise ethical standards to do so. Even excellent overall strategies need to be implemented with policies that support honest achievement. Managers can be pressured by unrealistic performance goals or compromised by unwise reward or compensation systems. Such factors are considerations in the following story.

> George L. Ball, the chairman and CEO of Prudential-Bache Securities set out to build an empire. Over a two-year period he increased the number of branch offices by a third and he hired 3,600 new brokers. This growth strategy created huge overhead costs and for its success demanded the generation of enormous revenues. To get them the company sold $8 billion in rickety limited partnerships between 1980 and 1990 to investors who were misled by exaggerated marketing claims about their safety, returns, and tax consequences. To encourage sales, brokers who sold the partnerships were given commissions of 7 or 8 percent, compared to about 1 percent on a stock sale. Additionally, Pru-Bache took a 3.5 percent management fee and a 4 percent charge for organizing the partnership in the first place. Investors, therefore, went into the investment with an immediate 15 percent loss—and most never recovered. Brokers who questioned orders to push sales, or "jam the product," were fired. Ultimately Pru-Bache customers suffered huge losses. A lawsuit by 137,000 investors created major financial and image problems for Pru-Bache and its parent, Prudential Insurance Co. of America.[42]

Corporate Culture

Corporate culture refers to the set of values, norms, rituals, and behavior patterns that characterize a company. Every corporate culture has an ethical dimension which is enforced not primarily by formal policies, but by daily habit and widespread beliefs about which behaviors are rewarded and which are penalized.

Recent graduates of the Harvard MBA program who were interviewed about ethical climates in their organizations revealed the strong presence of four informal but powerful "commandments" which were communicated to them early in their careers.

> First, performance is what really counts, so make your numbers. Second, be loyal and show us that you're a team player. Third, don't break the law. Fourth, don't overinvest in ethical behavior.[43]

The young managers believed, in the face of these informal norms, that if questionable behavior was accompanied by achievement it advanced careers. They were in fear of taking ethical stands or blowing the whistle and not without reason. When one manager persisted in challenging false figures that her superior used she discovered that she was in trouble.

> He started treating other people better. He wasn't on my side anymore, and you needed him on your side to do things. He wasn't my buddy anymore . . . there were other cases of this. He did it by acting like you weren't that smart anymore. It made it really difficult to get the kind of support you needed to be a really top performer.[44]

One factor that contributes to lowered ethical climates in corporations is the inability to raise and discuss ethical issues among managers. This phenomenon, which was studied by Bird and Waters and labeled "moral muteness," is widespread.[45] In their study, Bird and Waters found that "managers seldom discuss with their colleagues the ethical problems they routinely encounter."[46] Indeed, of 300 cases of ethical issues they discovered through interviews with managers, only 12 percent were ever openly discussed. There are a number of reasons for this inability to talk about ethical issues. Some managers believe that making ethical judgments of others is confrontational; it involves placing blame and creates anger or grudges. In organizations where formal standards are not followed and deceit is rewarded ethical arguments have little legitimacy and lack force. In addition, people in business have a sophisticated vocabulary and logic for discussing business issues but lack these assets in the moral realm and so have a tendency to redefine ethical issues into business matters. For example, if someone lays out a fraudulent ad in a committee meeting, those in attendance will not react by accusing the person of dishonesty, but will discuss possible loss of sales and revenue if the misrepresentation is discovered—even if their primary motive for opposing the ad is a desire to be honest. The tendency toward "moral muteness" may be present to some degree in every company.

Individual Characteristics

It is important to have honest people in an organization. Unethical managers may create costly operating or image problems. They may also demoralize good people who see standards undermined.

Ethical behavior is motivated by a mixture of internal disposition and situational incentives. In a corporation with a poor ethical climate, corrupt leaders, and high pressure to achieve numbers, otherwise honest individuals may behave unethically. But all things being equal, it is better to have employees who are internally disposed to act ethically. People differ greatly in their drives, ambitions, neuroses, and penchants for ethical behavior.

Approximately 100 statistical studies have been done in the field of business ethics to discover what individual and organizational factors are associated with ethical behavior. Two recent reviews of these studies indicate that their findings are too limited to say much with great confidence.[47] In many cases the studies are not comparable, disagree in result, or are too few in number to confirm early indications. Still, a few findings are established. High ethical behavior is clearly associated with strong religious conviction. In addition, there are indications that higher ethics are associated with advancing age, length of work experience, and amount of education. Of fourteen studies of gender, seven found that women acted more ethically than men and seven found no difference in ethical beliefs.[48] Managers have been found to give more ethical responses to survey questions than business students.[49] Individuals seem to act less ethically as corporations increase in size, but tend to be more ethical where companies have codes of conduct.

At lower levels dishonest job applicants can be weeded out by paper-and-pencil honesty tests which ask questions about past theft, criminal habits, drug use, and fighting. But at managerial levels there is no test or standard interview procedure to detect an unethical person. Much depends on how managers are evaluated and rewarded once hired. Jack Welch, CEO of General Electric, describes how critical choices about a corporation's values are part of evaluating managers.

> In our view, leaders, whether on the shop floor or at the tops of our businesses, can be characterized in at least four ways.
>
> The first is one who delivers on commitments—financial or otherwise—and shares the values of our company. His or her future is an easy call. Onward and upward.
>
> The second type of leader is one who does not meet commitments and does not share our values. Not as pleasant a call, but equally easy.
>
> The third is one who misses commitments but shares the values. He or she usually gets a second chance, preferably in a different environment.
>
> Then there's the fourth type—the most difficult for many of us to deal with. That leader delivers on commitments, makes all the numbers, but doesn't share the values we must have. This is the individual who typically forces performance out of people rather than inspires it: the autocrat, the big shot, the tyrant. Too often all of us have looked the other way—tolerated these "Type 4" managers because "they always deliver"—at least in the short term.[50]

Interrelatedness

The factors that influence ethical behavior in organizations are interrelated. Leadership, particularly, is important in all four. In the next section we examine how some companies have set up comprehensive management systems to mold these factors and encourage higher ethics.

We live in a world of transgressions and selfishness, and no pictures that represent us otherwise can be true; though happily for human nature, gleaming of that pure spirit in whose likeness man has been fashioned, are to be seen, relieving its deformities, and mitigating, if not excusing its crimes.

Source: James Fenimore Cooper, *The Deerslayer* (1841).

Managing Ethics at the Corporate Level

In the past it was assumed in most companies that ethics were a matter of individual conscience. A few pioneers made formal efforts to manage companywide ethics. In 1913 James Cash Penney introduced a conduct code for employees in his department stores. In

1945, Robert Wood Johnson, of Johnson & Johnson, wrote the formal credo of fair relations with stakeholders. But these firms were unrepresentative; until recently, most companies made no specific effort to manage ethics.

Today, however, many corporations are using managerial techniques that are designed to encourage higher ethics. And in some cases companies have set up comprehensive ethics programs which use a wide range of interventions in the formal and informal organization to raise standards. Two recent events have encouraged such actions. First, the 1986 Defense Industry Initiative contained guidelines that required defense contractors to adopt codes of ethics, train employees about ethics and legal compliance, create an atmosphere in which employees could discuss and report code violations, and monitor compliance. Over fifty defense firms initiated ethics programs in response. And second, since 1991, federal sentencing guidelines for corporations allow dramatic reductions in fines and sentences for companies that have formal internal programs for preventing and reporting criminal behavior.[51]

The sentencing guidelines focus on compliance with the law; indeed, the word ethics is nowhere used in them. In some companies *compliance programs* undertaken because of the guidelines are handled by general counsel and focus on the limited, specific goal of reducing illegal behavior. These programs emphasize rule enforcement, audits, controls, and sanctions for misbehavior. In other companies *comprehensive ethics programs* are undertaken with the broader goal of improving employee ethics in addition to achieving legal compliance. These programs place less emphasis on control and emphasize instead interventions designed to foster norms of integrity in the corporate culture, supervision, decision making, and communication.[52] Within these two types of programs corporations adopt widely varying methods for improving employee behavior.

In the following section we discuss the structure of one of the earliest, broadest, and most widely followed programs—that of General Dynamics Corporation. This program has confronted some of the difficulties inherent in trying to elevate corporate ethics and the results are instructive.

The General Dynamics Program

In May 1985, Navy Secretary John Lehman suspended Navy contracts with General Dynamics worth over $1 billion, citing as one reason a "pervasive corporate attitude" inappropriate to the public trust. The company had been caught in a series of illegal acts. Managers were shifting expenses from fixed price contracts to contracts that permitted cost overruns. The company had given expensive gifts to an admiral and his wife. Executives charged country club dues to military contracts, and Chairman David Lewis billed the government for flights from company headquarters to his farm in Georgia. Top executives eventually negotiated an agreement with the Navy under which payments for contracts resumed. This agreement required changes in corporate policies and behavior, including a corporate-wide ethics program.

General Dynamics set up an expansive program in 1985. The strategic objectives of the program were to make government contracts secure by ending illegal actions and to improve the image of the company. The implied goals of the program were broader, and included achieving an ethical organization, promoting open communication about ethical problems, and improving trust in relationships with customers, suppliers, employees, shareholders, and communities.[53]

As the program began, a twenty-page booklet, *General Dynamics Standards of Business Ethics and Conduct*, was distributed to all employees. Distribution began when Chairman Stanley C. Pace handed it to all persons reporting to him. In turn, these managers distributed the booklet in person to their subordinates, and so forth, until the *Standards* had cascaded to the lowest organizational level. The *Standards* instructed employees to "observe a basic code of conduct in the workplace," and defined appropriate conduct in selling and marketing; billing; time card reporting; supplier relations; bribery, kickbacks, and illegal payments; political contributions; and environmental protection. Specific policies were very strict. A draconian policy on giving and accepting gifts prevented employees from accepting even trivia like calendars or pens from subcontractors. Military officials visiting General Dynamics facilities had to pay 25 cents for a cup of coffee. Over 60,000 suppliers and subcontractors also received the *Standards* and were asked to abide by it.

To oversee the program, General Dynamics set up a board committee on corporate responsibility and hired a staff vice president of business ethics who supervised ethics program directors at each company facility and reported directly to the chief executive. All employees were required to attend an ethics training workshop led by a General Dynamics manager and by 1986 all 103,000 had gone to one.

New communications channels were opened to air ethical concerns. All managers were instructed to maintain a workplace climate where ethical issues could be frankly and openly discussed without fear of reprisal. Annual bonuses were based in part on the ethical dimension of leadership. The company also set up ethics hotlines, special numbers answered by the ethics directors, which employees or suppliers could call to ask questions, seek advice, or allege wrongdoing. Callers could remain anonymous. After business hours, hotlines were connected to answering machines in locked rooms or compartments so that confidential messages were received twenty-four hours a day. In the first six years of the program, employees made almost 30,000 contacts with ethics directors at a rate of between 5½ and 6 contacts per 100 employees per year.

When violations of the *Standards* were discovered, company policy made punishment mandatory. After six years, 1,419 sanctions had been made. Most were warnings (508) or reprimands (432), but 165 employees were discharged.[54]

The results of the General Dynamics ethics program have been mixed. The program achieved its strategic objective, which was to ensure continued Navy and government defense contracts by ending illegal behavior. Navy contracts continued and by 1991 General Dynamics was not under investigation by the Department of Defense for any illegal activity, despite a record number of criminal investigations in the industry as a whole. On the other hand, the program fell short of achieving its broader goals of creating new ethical norms and of building trust between superiors and subordinates. After four years of operation, surveys in one division revealed that only 27 percent of employees thought that the company was genuinely interested in their welfare, about one-third believed that they were not treated with dignity, and two-thirds were afraid of reprisals for using the ethics hotline.[55] Eighty percent of a panel of professional and hourly workers interviewed thought that the program was a "sham" and "simply a whitewash scheme to present a false front to [the government]."[56]

General Dynamics built its ethics program on the need to get out of trouble with the Navy and some employees were cynical about whether management genuinely intended it to do more than achieve economic goals. Many employees reacted defensively and negatively to discussions of ethics. Some resented training sessions for implying that their personal integrity was deficient. Another problem was that during the program General Dynamics nearly halved its work force because of defense contract cutbacks. It was difficult to build trust with employees while so many were being laid off.

Guidelines for Managing Ethics Programs

The General Dynamics program exemplifies a state-of-the-art effort to create an ethical corporate culture. Its mixed results show the formidable resistance in large companies to elevating standards. The following elements, all of which were important at General Dynamics, are critical to the success of ethics programs if they are to overcome factors that tend to depress ethical behavior.

Top Management Leadership

The chief executive officer should initiate the ethics program and clearly state the importance of legal and ethical behavior. A vivid illustration of how this can be accomplished is offered by the actions of Robert Cushman, CEO of the Norton Company, an abrasives manufacturer with plants in twenty-seven countries. After introducing a strong ethics code, Cushman presented it at a conference for his international managers. A vice president in attendance that day remembers how he was challenged.

> During a panel discussion, some of the key Europeans were particularly animated in objecting to the code's stringent rules on certain kinds of payments which were standard in their countries. Cushman acknowledged their differences of opinion openly and then reiterated what "the Company" expected them to do. He was decidedly unapologetic about taking an authoritarian stance: "I've had to live by certain rules, and so do you." [Some were] taken aback by Cushman's words, but found the session to be a real eye opener about just how strongly top management meant the code to be enforced.[57]

In addition, management must avoid adopting business strategies, time lines, and reward systems that place unreasonable pressure on employees.

Codes of Ethics

Codes of ethics have become popular—about 95 percent of Fortune 500 companies have them.[58] Codes vary from book-length formulations to succinct statements which in one or two pages express a general philosophy for managing conflicts. One of the simplest codes on record was that of the Samsonite Company, which used to issue to its sales force small marbles printed with the Golden Rule.

Developing a code is an occasion for a corporation to think through characteristic ethical problems and conflicts. When Security Pacific Bank developed its code, it enlisted seventy volunteer senior managers to meet in groups to discuss ethical dilemmas. Their dialogues identified central needs that the bank's credo eventually addressed. In addition to being specific to the company and giving concrete directions about pertinent problems, codes need to be well-communicated and well-enforced.

Changes in Organization Structure

General Dynamics anchored responsibility for its ethics program in committees at the board of directors and senior management levels. It put ethics program directors in major locations and involved all functional areas and the internal auditing staff in code enforcement. Hotlines were set up to establish new communications channels between work locations and higher management. In theory, opening multiple upward channels facilitates the ventilation of allegations, since many employees fear speaking to their immediate supervisors. In practice, however, employees were suspicious of the hotlines and feared retaliation. Workers typically are intimidated and with good reason. Interviews of

1,700 whistle-blowers in the nuclear power industry found that 90 percent had experienced bad consequences.[59] Some experts recommend using independent outside contractors to receive hotline calls but, of course, once internal investigations begin, whistle-blowing employees are at risk of being identified.

Training Sessions

Approximately half of Fortune 500 companies conduct some kind of ethics training.[60] At General Dynamics, most workers went to half-day workshops where they learned about the ethics program, watched two videotapes, and discussed case studies. At Citicorp, among other activities attenders in ethics workshops play a game called Work Ethic. Players draw cards printed with brief ethical dilemmas and multiple-choice answers. They may then earn points or even be "discharged" depending on the answers they pick.

Generally speaking, ethics training is most effective when it is conducted by company managers, and is steered away from abstract philosophical discussions to focus on specifics from the work environment of those attending.

Enforcement

A number of mechanisms may be used to get compliance with ethics policies. At General Mills, employees must sign annual compliance affidavits. At Chemical Bank internal auditors establish and check on controls designed to ensure ethical practices. These extend down to levels that in some companies would not be regarded as having ethical significance. For example, in the human resources area there is a requirement that statistics be kept about whether letters expressing regret are sent to rejected job applicants within thirty days.[61] At Boeing, managers are told that a scandal in their plant or program will lead to a severe reduction in pay—even if they are not guilty of personal wrongdoing.

Of course, violators of standards must be dealt with. Their treatment enters organizational folklore and conveys by example whether top management is really serious or winks at violations. While some punishment is necessary, there is a need to reinforce positive behavior rather than focus on bad behavior. At General Dynamics statistical summaries of types of violations and kinds of punishments were published annually. This may have frightened some workers and reinforced their feelings that ethics were about wrongdoing, not uplift.

Other Measures

There are many other steps that can be taken individually or as part of broader ethics programs. Some companies use ombudsmen to resolve disputes. At Texas Instruments a weekly electronic newspaper carries information on ethics and cases about which employees around the world can send in comments. Some companies use paper-and-pencil honesty tests to select ethical employees.

Overall, ethics programs require a set of reinforcing actions tailored to individual companies. If such actions are taken, lawbreaking can be reduced and a more elevated ethical culture may be nurtured. But problems, including employee cynicism, resistance, and fear are numerous and difficult to overcome.

Conclusion

Although the environment of business is rich in sources of ethical values there are strong forces in competitive markets and within companies that depress aggregate levels of behavior. A number of managerial techniques can be used to discourage lawbreaking and encourage higher ethics. Some companies have combined a wide range of managerial interventions into comprehensive programs to elevate ethics. These programs have had some success, but there is no proof that aggregate ethical behavior is higher today than at any time in the past. In the next chapter we will discuss the nature of ethical decisions to explain why they are often difficult.

Endnotes

1. Quoted in Robert G. Flood, *On the Waters of the World: The Story of the Meloon Family*, Chicago: Moody Press, 1989, p. 18.
2. Quoted in John S. Tompkins, "These Good Guys Finish First," *Reader's Digest*, June 1992, p. 140.
3. See George C. S. Benson, *Business Ethics in America*, Lexington, Mass.: Heath 1982, p. xvi.
4. Adam Smith, T*he Wealth of Nations*, Edwin Cannan, ed., New York: Modern Library 1937, p 423. Originally published in 1776. Smith also believed that merchants must abide by prevailing societal ethics.
5. This view was encouraged in the writings of the social Darwinist Herbert Spencer, who believed that there were two sets of ethics. *Family ethics* were based on the principle of charity and benefits were apportioned without relation to merit. *State ethics* were based on a competitive justice and benefits were apportioned on the basis of strict merit. Family ethics interjected into business or government by well-meaning people were an inappropriate interference with the laws of nature and would slowly corrupt the workings of Darwinian natural selection. See "The Sins of Legislators" in *The Man versus the State*, London: Watts, 1940. Originally published in 1884. Dual ethical perspectives have developed in other cultures such as Slavic cultures which assert one set of ethical standards for personal relationships and a second set which justifies less perfection for business matters. See Sheila M. Puffer, "Understanding the Bear: A Portrait of Russian Business Leaders," *Academy of Management Executive*, February 1994, p. 47.
6. Quoted in Robert Bartels, ed., *Ethics in Business*, Columbus: Bureau of Business Research, College of Commerce and Administration, Ohio State University, 1963, p. 35.
7. In David Bollier, *Servant Leadership: The Story of J. Irwin Miller*, Stanford, Calif.: Business Enterprise Trust, 1992, p. 29.
8. This conclusion is reinforced in a discussion of the intellectual history of these two ideas. See Jon M. Shepard, Jon Shepard, James C. Wimbush and Carroll U. Stephens, "The Place of Ethics in Business: Shifting Paradigms?" *Business Ethics Quarterly*, July 1995.
9. *The Nicomachean Ethics*, trans. J. A. K. Thomson, New York: Penguin, 1953, p. 112. Originally written c. 334-323 B.C.
10. Donald V. Seibert and William Proctor, *The Ethical Executive*, New York: Simon & Schuster, 1984, pp. 119-20.
11. See Oliver F. Williams and John W. Houck, *Full Value: Cases in Christian Business Ethics*, New York: Harper & Row, 1978, for discussion of these and other biblical sources of managerial inspiration.
12. Larry Burkett, *Business by the Book: The Complete Guide of Biblical Principles for Business Men and Women*, Nashville, Tenn.: Nelson, 1991, pp. 55-56.
13. Ibid., p. 64.
14. Alasdair MacIntyre, *After Virtue: A Study in Moral Theory*, South Bend, Ind.: University of Notre Dame Press, 1981, p. 115.
15. Trans. F. M. Cornford, New York: Oxford University Press, 1945.
16. *The Nicomachean Ethics*, trans. Thomson, p. 51.
17. His exact words were: ". . . 'the general welfare' is no ideal, no goal, no remotely intelligible concept, but only an emetic . . ." In *Beyond Good and Evil*, New York: Vintage Books, 1966, p. 157. Originally published in 1886.
18. Will Durant and Ariel Durant, *The Lessons of History*, New York: Simon & Schuster, 1968, pp. 37-42.
19. United States Sentencing Commission, *Guidelines Manual*, Washington, D.C.: Government Printing Office, November 1, 1991, pp. 347-79.
20. *Browning-Ferris Industries v. Kelco Disposal*, 57 LW 4986 (1989).
21. *Pacific Mutual Life Insurance Company v. Cleopatra Haslip*, 59 LW 4157 (1991).
22. See *TXO Prod. Corp. v. Alliance Resources Corp.*, 419 S.E. 2d 870 (W. Va. 1992).
23. See *Kelco, Haslip, and TXO Prod. Corp. v. Alliance Resources Corp.*, 113 S. Ct. 2711 (1993).
24. Puffer, "Understanding the Bear," p. 47.
25. Sheila M. Puffer and Daniel J. McCarthy, "Finding the Common Ground in Russian and American Business Ethics," *California Management Review*, Winter 1995.
26. Stephen Handleman, "The Russian 'Mafiya,'" *Foreign Affairs*, March/April 1994, p. 89.
27. G. J. Rossouw, "Business Ethics in Developing Countries," *Business Ethics Quarterly*, January 1994.
28. Catherine C. Langlois and Bodo B. Schlegelmilch, "Do Corporate Codes of Ethics Reflect National Character? Evidence from Europe and the United States," *Journal of International Business Studies*, Fourth Quarter, 1991, p. 522.

29. *Bing* literally means "soldier" and *Fa* means "doctrine." Both may be translated into "the art of war." Min Chen, *Asian Management Systems*, New York: Routledge, 1995, p. 39. See also Chin-Ning Chu, *The Asian Mind Game*, New York: Rawson Associates, 1991, pp. 10-82.

30. Sun Tzu, *The Art of War*, trans. Samuel B. Griffith, London: Oxford University Press, 1963. Originally written c. 500 B.C. Another popular text studied by Asian managers is Miyamoto Musashi *A Book of Five Rings* (*Go Rin No Sho*), trans. Victor Harris, Woodstock, N.Y.: Overlook Press, 1994. Originally written in 1645.

31. Jack Seward and Howard Van Zandt, *Japan: The Hungry Guest*, rev. ed., Tokyo: Yohan Publications, 1987, pp. 277-78.

32. John F. Magee and P. Ranganath Nayak, "Leaders' Perspectives on Business Ethics: An Interim Report," *Prism*, First Quarter 1994, pp. 72-73.

33. Gene R. Laczniak, Marvin W. Berkowitz, Russell G. Brooker, and James P. Hale, "The Ethics of Business: Improving or Deteriorating?" *Business Horizons*, January-February 1995, p. 40.

34. "Major Findings of a Survey on Business Ethics, Corruption and Fraud," *Ethics in Practice*, Hong Kong Ethics Development Centre, April 1995, p. 3.

35. National Conference of Catholic Bishops, *Economic Justice for All: Pastoral Letter on Catholic Social Teaching and the U.S. Economy*, Washington, D.C.: National Conference of Catholic Bishops, November 14,1986, chap. 3 (B).

36. Touche Ross, *Ethics in American Business: A Special Report*, Chicago: Touche Ross, 1988, p. 69.

37. Melissa S. Baucus and Janet P. Near, "Can Illegal Corporate Behavior Be Predicted? An Event History Analysis," *Academy of Management Journal*, March 1991, pp. 27-28.

38. David J. Fritzsche, *Business Ethics: A Global Managerial Perspective*, New York: McGraw-Hill, 1997, chap 4.

39. Barry Z. Posner and Warren H. Schmidt, "Values and the American Manager: An Update Updated," *California Management Review*, Spring 1992, p. 86.

40. Gary Edwards, "And the Survey Said . . .," in Stephen J. Garone, ed., *Business Ethics: Generating Trust in the 1990s and Beyond*, New York: The Conference Board, 1994, p. 26.

41. This case is based on events described by Robert Jackell in *Moral Mazes*, New York: Oxford University Press, 1988, chap. 4.

42. For the fun story, see Kathleen Sharp, *In Good Faith*, New York: St. Martin's, 1995.

43. Joseph L. Badaracco, Jr., and Allen P. Webb, "Business Ethics: A View from the Trenches," *California Management Review*, Winter 1995, p. 11.

44. Ibid.

45. See Frederick B. Bird and James A. Waters, "The Moral Muteness of Managers," *California Management Review*, Fall 1989.

46. Ibid., p. 74.

47. See Robert C. Ford and Woodrow D. Richardson, "Ethical Decision Making: A Review of the Empirical Literature," *Journal of Business Ethics*, March 1994; and David J. Fritzsche, *Business Ethics: A Global Managerial Perspective*, chap. 4.

48. Fritzsche, *Business Ethics: A Global Managerial Perspective*, chap. 4.

49. James R. Glenn, Jr., and M. Frances Van Loo, "Business Students' and Practitioners' Ethical Decisions Over Time," *Journal of Business Ethics*, November 1993, p. 844.

50. Quoted in Francis J. Aguilar, *Managing Corporate Ethics*, New York: Oxford University Press, 1994, p. 115.

51. You start with a five-point culpability score, and can subtract three points if the company had an ethics program. United States Sentencing Commission *Guidelines Manual*, Washington D.C.: Government Printing Office, November 1, 1991, footnote 40, p. 360.

52. The distinction between these two kinds of approaches is discussed in Lynn Sharp Paine, "Managing for Organizational Integrity," *Harvard Business Review*, March-April 1994, p. 106.

53. Richard A. Barker, "An Evaluation of the Ethics Program at General Dynamics," *Journal of Business Ethics*, March 1993, pp. 166, 171.

54. *Standards of Business Ethics and Conduct: The First Six Years*, St. Louis: General Dynamics Corporation, November 1991.

55. Barker, "An Evaluation of the Ethics Program at General Dynamics," p. 172.

56. Ibid.

57. Laura Nash "The Norton Company's Ethics Program," in *Corporate Ethics: A Prime Business Asset*, New York: The Business Roundtable, February 1988, p. 120.

58. Edwards, "And the Survey Said . . .," p. 25.

59. Marcy Mason, "The Curse of Whistle-Blowing," *Wall Street Journal*, March 14, 1994, p. A14.

60. Edwards, "And the Survey Said . . .," p. 25.

61. "How Chemical Bank Audits Compliance with a Code of Conduct," *Ethikos*, January/February 1993, p 12.

Chapter Six

MAKING ETHICAL

DECISIONS IN BUSINESS

JCPenney

Ethical decisions are sometimes difficult. Here is how one company tries to help its employees.

In 1913, James Cash Penney met with a group of his partners in a Salt Lake City hotel room to create a set of principles upon which to run their fledgling business, the Golden Rule Store Company. The short set of statements they called "The Penney Idea" concluded with the principle "To test our every policy, method and act in this wise: 'Does it square with what is right and just?'" As the Golden Rule Store Company metamorphosed into the giant modern-day retailer we know as J. C. Penney Company, Inc., the seed of an ethics policy contained in that final principle also grew.

As the years passed, many internal policy statements were written about such matters as accepting gifts, entertaining suppliers, and using proprietary information. Since 1986, however, the major elements of these disconnected policy statements have been condensed into a seventeen page "Statement of Ethics," which is distributed to all employees. The ethics code contained in the "Statement of Ethics" is divided into three parts. Part I deals with "Compliance with Law," Part II is on "Conflicts of Interest," and Part III is on "Preservation of Company Assets."

A unique didactic feature of the code is the illustrative short cases. An analysis accompanying each case exemplifies correct interpretation of the code. The following two cases, for example, help explain conflict-of-interest situations involving competing companies. The word "associate" is used to refer to Penney's employees.

Each Penney employee, upon receipt of the code, is required to sign an attached certificate of compliance, which states in part: "I am in compliance and will continue to comply, with the policies set forth in the booklet. . . ." If there is doubt about compliance, the individual is instructed to approach his or her unit manager or department head to ask advice. Under three conditions an employee is, however, instructed to go directly to the general counsel at headquarters in New York City. These urgent exceptions are cases that (1) threaten the overall integrity of the company, (2) raise the possibility of major financial loss or criminal penalty, and (3) endanger human life.

At the end of the "Statement of Business Ethics," employees are given notice that "failure to comply with the principles described in this booklet, including the disclosure requirements, may result in termination of employment."

The "Statement of Ethics" seems to help Penney managers make uniform decisions. One Christmas season a supplier for Penney, Schmidt-Canon International, sent out desk clocks worth $2 to buyers at Penney and a number of other companies. These clocks had Schmidt-Canon's corporate name and phone number on them. An executive at Schmidt-Canon recalls that the "clocks were kept by all of our buyers except those at Penney, where we received virtually every clock back with a nice note saying 'thanks,' but they could not accept it."[1]

THE OFFICIAL J. C. PENNEY POLICY STATEMENT

Each Associate of the Company shall avoid any activity, interest or relationship with non-Company persons or entities which would create, or might appear to others to create, a conflict with the interests of the Company.

EXAMPLE A
A newly employed Associate has worked for a major competitor of the Company, and during the course of that previous employment has acquired shares of stock which amount to a very small percentage of the outstanding stock of the competitor. A question has arisen as to whether ownership of that stock will constitute a conflict of interest.

Analysis of Example A Ownership of stock in a competitor will not be deemed a conflict of interest if both of the following conditions exist: (a) the stock is publicly traded, and (b) the amount owned by the Associate and his or her "relatives" (as defined in this booklet) does not exceed one-tenth of 1 percent of the amount outstanding.

EXAMPLE B
A Company store manager proposes to buy a substantial number of shares of stock of a corporation formed to operate a women's apparel shop. The shop will be located in a shopping center which also contains a Penney store and will carry similar merchandise.

Analysis of Example B A conflict of interest would exist. The apparel shop is a competitor because of its location and because of the merchandise it carries. In addition, the proposed purchase of stock by the Associate does not meet the guidelines described in the Analysis of Example A above.

This chapter focuses on philosophical and practical guides for making decisions about ethical problems in both business life and in case studies such as those in this book. Ethical decisions cannot be programmed like production and inventory decisions, but methods discussed in this chapter may be used by individuals to structure them in helpful ways.

Principles of Ethical Conduct

Over the centuries, attempts have been made to discover rules that lead to just actions. Plato thought he had found the right method of moral decision making when he described an intuitive leap of revelation that would take place after years of study and character development in a utopian society. St. Augustine suggested that virtue came from an interior illumination that was a gift of God. St. Thomas relied on painstaking research of Scripture to reveal the true path, and a sense of complete certainty pervades his massive twenty-three-volume *Summa Theological*, in which moral questions are examined. Recent efforts to find a methodology for business decisions regarding ethics have been less mystical and elaborate. They are described later in the chapter.

We begin, however, with a compendium of ethical principles—some ancient, some modern—that are alternative decision rules for managers. We list them alphabetically. These principles are a distillation of 2,000 years of ethical thought. To the extent that they offer ideas for resolving ethical dilemmas, they are not vague abstractions but useful, living guides to conduct.[2] Some principles are more reflective of ideals, others of a lower reality, but all have adherents.

The Categorical Imperative

The categorical imperative (meaning, literally, a command that admits no exception) is a guide for ethical behavior set forth by the German philosopher Immanuel Kant in his *Foundations of the Metaphysics of Morals*, a tract published in 1785. In Kant's words: "Act only according to that maxim by which you can at the same time will that it should become a universal law."[3]

In other words, one should not adopt principles of action unless they can, without inconsistency, be adopted by everyone. Lying, stealing, and breaking promises, for example, are ruled out because society would disintegrate if they replaced truth telling, property rights, and vow keeping. Using this guideline, a manager faced with a moral choice must act in a way that he or she believes is right and just for any person in a similar situation. Each action should be judged by asking: "Could this act be turned into a universal code of behavior?" This quick *test of universalizability* has achieved great popularity.

Kant was an extreme perfectionist in his personal life. He walked the same route each day at the same time, appearing at places along the route so punctually that neighbors set their clocks by him. Before leaving his house he attached strings to the top of his socks and connected them to a spring apparatus held by his belt. As he walked the contraption would pull the slack out of his socks. To no one's surprise, his ethical philosophies are perfectionist also, and that is their weakness. Kant's categorical imperative is dogmatic and inflexible. It is a general rule that must be applied in every specific situation; there are no exceptions. But real life challenges the simple, single ethical law. If a competitor asks whether your company is planning to sell shirts in Texas next year, must you answer the question with the truth?

The Conventionalist Ethic

This is the view that business is analogous to a game and special, lower ethics are permissible. In business, people may act to further their self-interest so long as they do not violate the law. This ethic, which has a long history, was popularized some years ago by Albert Z. Carr in *Business as a Game*.[4] "If an executive allows himself to be torn between a decision based on business considerations and one based on his private ethical code," explained Carr, "he exposes himself to a grave psychological strain."[5]

Business may be regarded as a game, such as poker, in which the rules are different from those we adopt in personal life. Assuming game ethics, managers are allowed to bluff (a euphemism for lie) and to take advantage of all legal opportunities and widespread practices or customs. Carr used two examples to illustrate situations where game ethics were permissible. In the first, an out-of-work salesman with a good employment record feared discrimination because of his age—58. He dyed his hair and stated on his resume that he was 45. In the second, a job applicant was asked to check off magazines that he read and felt justified in not placing check marks by *Playboy*, *The Nation*, or *The New Republic*. Even though he read them, he feared being labeled controversial or politically extreme. He checked conservative magazines such as *Reader's Digest*.[6]

The conventionalist ethic has been criticized by those who make no distinction between private ethics and business ethics. They argue that industrial activity defines the life chances of millions and is not a game to be taken lightly. As a principle, the conventionalist ethic provides no way to elevate business practice. It is a thin justification for deceptive behavior in business situations.

The Disclosure Rule

This rule has been popular in recent years and is found in many company ethics codes. The way it is stated in IBM's Business Conduct Guidelines is, "Ask yourself: If the full glare of examination by associates, friends, even family were to focus on your decision, would you remain comfortable with it? If you think you would, it probably is the right decision."[7]

When faced with an ethical dilemma, a manager asks how it would feel to explain the decision to a wide audience. Sometimes newspaper readers or television viewers are substituted for acquaintances as the disclosure audience. One advocate of this ethic, Richard J. Stegemeier, chairman and chief executive officer of UNOCAL, says:

> [W]e advise our employees to use a simple test to distinguish between right and wrong.
> The test goes as follows.
> When evaluating the rightness or wrongness of a business action, ask yourself these two questions.
> Would you be ashamed to describe the full details of this action to your family?
> Would you be embarrassed to read about it on the front page of your local newspaper?[8]

This rule screens out base motivations such as greed and jealousy, which are unacceptable if disclosed, but does not always provide clear guidance for ethical dilemmas in which strong arguments can be made for several alternatives. Also, an action that sounds acceptable if disclosed may not, upon reflection, always be the most ethical.

The Doctrine of the Mean

This ethic, set forth by Aristotle in *The Nicomachean Ethics* and sometimes called the "golden mean," because of subsequent but un-Aristotelian embellishment, calls for virtue through moderation.[9] Right actions are located between extreme behaviors, which represent excess on the one hand and deficiency on the other. When faced with a decision, a decision maker first identities the ethical virtue involved (such as truthfulness) and then seeks the mean or moderate course of action between an excess of that virtue (boastfulness) and a deficiency of it (understatement). Likewise, according to Aristotle, modesty is the mean between shyness and shamelessness. The doctrine of the mean is today little recognized and mostly of historical interest, although the notion of moderation as a virtue lives on.

The doctrine of the mean is inexact. To observe it is simply to act conservatively, not extremely. The moderate course and specific virtues such as honesty, however, are defined only in terms of what they are not. What they are is open to differing interpretation.

The Golden Rule

An ideal found in the great religions, the Golden Rule has been a popular guide for ethical decisions for centuries. Simply put, it is: "Do unto others as you would have them do unto you." It includes not knowingly doing harm to others. A manager trying to solve an ethical problem places himself or herself in the position of another party affected by the decision and tries to determine what action is most fair to that person.

A problem with the Golden Rule is that people's ethical values differ, and they may mistakenly assume that their preferences coincide with others'. It is primarily a perfectionist rule for interpersonal relations. It is sometimes hard to apply in corporations where the interests of individuals are subordinated to the needs of the firm and where competitive activities demand selfish behavior. Marketing strategies, for example, do not treat competitors with kindness, but are based on self-interest.

The Intuition Ethic

This ethic, as defined by philosophers such as G. E. Moore in his *Principal Ethica* (1903), holds that what is good is undefinable. Rather, it is simply understood. That is, people are endowed with a kind of moral sense by which they can apprehend right and wrong. The solution to moral problems lies simply in what you feel or understand to be right in a given situation. You have a "gut feeling" or "fly by the seat of your pants."[10]

This approach is subjective. No standard of validation outside the individual exists. Self-interest may be confused with ethical insight. Worse, intuition may fail to give clear answers. It is nevertheless correct that most managers rely on *intuitive* reasoning to resolve ethical dilemmas rather than on *principled* reasoning, which requires a disciplined thought process and the application of abstract principles.

The Market Ethic

This principle was sanctioned in the world of commerce by Adam Smith in his Wealth of Nations. Implicit in Smith's description of a market economy is the idea that selfish actions in the marketplace are virtuous because they contribute to efficient operation of the economy. This efficient operation is in turn responsible for the higher goods of prosperity and optimum use of resources. Decision makers may take selfish actions and be motivated by personal gain in their business dealings. They should ask whether their actions in the market further financial self-interest. If so, the actions are ethical.

This form of ethical guidance is applicable only in market situations. It is not useful in interpersonal relations and therefore is not a universal principle. Also, there are areas of market behavior where society has determined that the broad public interest is not furthered by unrestrained profit-seeking. Antitrust statutes are a prime example of legislated ethics here.

The Ends-Means Ethic

This principle is age-old, appearing as an ancient Roman proverb, *existus acta probat*, or "the result validates the deeds."[11] It is often associated with the Italian political philosopher Niccolò Machiavelli, who wrote interpretive essays about Roman history. In *The Prince* (1513), Machiavelli argued that worthwhile ends justify efficient means, that when ends are of overriding importance or virtue, unscrupulous means may be employed to reach them.[12] When confronted with a decision involving an ethically questionable course of action, a decision maker should ask whether some overall good—such as the survival of a country or business—justifies corner cutting. This was the thinking of John D. Rockefeller during the period when his Standard Oil trust carried out a triumphant strategy of horizontal integration at the refinery level, choking competitors and requiring employees to undertake ruthless predations that surely chilled some hearts. Late in his life, Rockefeller argued that only by smashing his competitors and controlling refining capacity could he tidy up the oil industry and rescue it from the chaotic price fluctuations that marked its infancy in the 1860s.[13] He may have been correct.

By using unscrupulous means a manager concedes the highest virtue and accepts the necessity of ethical compromise. But in solving ethical problems means may be as important or more important than ends. For instance, employees subjected to hidden video surveillance in restrooms will not celebrate the manager who has thereby caught a drug user or petty thief. In addition, the process of ethical character development can never be served by the use of expedient means.

The Might-Equals-Right Ethic

This ethic defines justice as the interest of the stronger. It is represented by Friedrich Nietzsche's "master-morality," Marx's theories of the dominance of the ruling class, and in the practiced ethics of drug cartels. The rationale for some competitive strategies and marketing tactics reflects this thinking. What is ethical is what an individual or company has the strength and power to accomplish. When faced with an ethical decision, individuals using this ethic seize what advantage they are strong enough to take, without regard for lofty sentiments.

In the 1860s Ben Holladay, owner of the Overland Stage Line, perfected a competitive strategy based on this thinking. He entered new routes with lowball coach fares and subsidized his stages with profits from monopoly service elsewhere until local competitors went bankrupt. In 1863 a small stage line between Denver and Central City in Colorado, for example, was charging $6 per run. Holladay put a lavish new-model stage, a Concord Coach with a leather interior, on the line and charged only $2. The competing line soon folded, whereupon Holladay replaced the new Concord Coach with primitive stages resembling freight wagons and raised the fare to $12.

The weakness of the might-equals-right ethic lies in its confusion of ethics with force or physical power. Exerting such force or power is not the same as acting from ethical duty. An ethical principle that can be invalidated by its foundation (e.g., physical force) is not a consistent, logical, or valid principle. The might-equals-right ethic is not seen as legitimate in civilized settings. Its observance invites retaliation and condemnation, and it is not to be used for long-term advantage. Seizure by power violates established rules of cooperation and reciprocity on which societies are based, and the social fabric would be torn apart by widespread use of this principle. Holladay, incidentally, sold the Overland Stage Line to Wells, Fargo & Company in 1866 when he sensed that railroads were about to end the dominance of stages in transportation west of the Mississippi. He started a railroad, which failed, and died an alcoholic in 1887.

The Organization Ethic

Simply put, this principle is: "Be loyal to the organization." It helps organizations endure. Many employees have a deep sense of loyalty to their organization that far transcends their self-interest. We have seen people jeopardize their health and work excessively long hours without pay, contrary to their selfish interests, because of their loyalty to their task and/or company. Similar personal loyalties are found within organizations from one individual to another—such as the loyalty of a subordinate to a supervisor—when they are acting in official capacities.

In practice, the organization ethic implies that the wills and needs of individuals should be subordinated to the greater good of the organization (be it church, state, corporation, university, or military). An individual should ask whether actions are consistent with organizational goals and do what is good for the organization.

The weakness of this principle is that service to the organization is a tempting way to rationalize behavior that would be unethical for an individual. The Nuremberg trials, which tried Nazis for war crimes, taught that Western society expects members of organizations to follow their conscience. Just as no Nazi war criminal argued successfully that he was forced to follow an order in an impersonal military chain of command, so no business manager may claim to be the helpless prisoner of corporate loyalties that crush free will and justify unethical actions. Of course, the greatest virtue may result when individuals are served by organizations rather than subservient to them.

The Practical Imperative

In addition to the categorical imperative, a second and related imperative or universal ethical command suggested by Immanuel Kant in the *Foundations of the Metaphysics of Morals* is: "Act so that you treat humanity, whether in your own person or in that of another, always as an end and never as a means only."[14] Simply translated, this principle admonishes a manager to treat other persons as ends in themselves and not means to ends or objects of manipulation. Each person, by his or her very existence as a rational, thinking being, is entitled to be treated in this fashion. No person should manipulate others for selfish ends. A manager may comply with this dictum by using the *test of reversibility*, that is, by asking if he or she would change places with the person affected by the contemplated policy or action. The practical imperative, like the categorical imperative, is an ideal often breached in practice. Generals send soldiers to die, and corporations move managers away from their families. In modern organizations people often deal with each other in terms of occupational roles rather than as individual human beings and in such cases they pursue their role-based self-interest rather than the ideal of treating the other person as an end. Thus a plant manager may pressure other managers at corporate headquarters for a bigger capital expenditure budget or a sales representative may maneuver a purchasing agent into an order. Unless lying occurs, these actions are ethically acceptable. But, since they involve the use of another person as a means they do not meet the high ideal of the practical imperative.

The Principle of Equal Freedom

This principle was set forth by the philosopher Herbert Spencer in his 1850 book *Social Statics*. "Every man may claim the fullest liberty to exercise his faculties," said Spencer, "compatible with the possession of like liberty by every other man."[15] Thus, a person has the right to freedom of action unless such action deprives another person of a proper freedom. Spencer believed that this was the first principle of ethical action in society. He thought it essential to protect individual liberty from infringement by others; his deep faith that human progress was based on such free action was unshakable.

In applying this principle, a decision maker asks if a contemplated action will restrict others from actions that they have a legitimate right to undertake. This principle is still well known. One version is "Your right to swing your fist ends where my nose begins."

A problem with this principle is that it does not provide a tie breaker for situations in which two rights or interests conflict. Such situations require invocation of an additional principle to decide which right or freedom is more important. Another difficulty is that some ethically permissible management decisions may circumscribe the rights of some for the benefit of others. For example, all employees have broad privacy rights, but management may abridge them when it hires undercover detectives to investigate thefts.

The Proportionality Ethic

Proportionality, a concept incubated in medieval Catholic theology, is an ethical doctrine designed to evaluate actions which have both good and evil consequences. For example, the manufacture of small-caliber, short-barreled, low-priced handguns which are irreverently called Saturday Night Specials has a dual impact on society. It makes cheap, easily concealable weapons available to criminals. But it also creates a supply of inexpensive self-defense weapons for poor people in high-crime areas who cannot afford large-caliber, expensive handguns costing as much as $500. In this and similar cases, where a manager's action results in an important good effect but also entails an inevitable harmful effect, the concept of proportionality may be useful.

A classic formulation is that of Thomas M. Garrett, a Jesuit priest who wrote about business ethics. Garrett developed a "principle of proportionality" which stated that managers are ethically responsible for their actions in situations where both good and evil effects might occur. They are ethically permitted to risk predictable, but unwilled, negative impacts on people or society (for example, innocent people being shot by handguns) if they carefully consider and balance five factors. First, according to Garrett, managers must assess the type of good and evil involved, distinguishing between major and minor forms. Second, they should calculate the urgency of the situation. For example, would the firm go out of business unless stockholder dividends were cut? Third, they must assess the probability that both good and evil effects will occur. If good effects are certain and risks of serious harm are small or remote, the situation is favorable. Fourth, the intensity of influence over effects must be considered. In assessing handgun injuries, for instance, manufacturers might assume that criminal action was an intervening force over which they had little control. And finally, the availability of alternative methods must be considered. If, for instance, an advertisement subtly encourages product misuse, a more ethical action might be to change the ad. Garrett believed that an overall assessment which took all these factors into consideration would bring out fully the ethical dimension in any decision.[16]

A simpler ethical principle derived from the concept of proportionality is the *principle of double effect*. It states that in a situation from which both good and evil consequences are bound to result, a manager will act ethically if: (1) the good effects outweigh the evil, (2) the manager's intention is to achieve the good effects, and (3) examination reveals that no better alternative is available.

These are complex principles, involving a wide range of considerations. Their complexity is a strength if it forces fuller consideration of relevant factors. But proportionality may be used disingenuously to justify harmful acts. What kind of otherwise questionable acts, for instance, may a failing firm take that are justified by the potential harmful effects of the impending evil of bankruptcy?

The Professional Ethic

In an age of specialization and education in complex skills, this ethic has gained importance. In simple form, it holds that you should do only that which can be explained before a committee of your peers.

This ethic is applied by doctors, engineers, architects, college professors, lawyers, and business executives in resolving the special problems of their professions and fields of interest. It is similar to and an application of the disclosure ethic discussed previously.

Professional people have strongly internalized ethical codes that guide their actions. Many of these ethical standards are deep-seated. For instance, we are convinced that the high standards of most engineers in the aerospace industry would prevent them from making a cheap lawn mower. They are so used to working with exceedingly close tolerances and high quality that they could not bring themselves to the task; the acceptance of lower standards would be morally repugnant to them.

The professional ethic is not a universal principle; it does not apply outside professional settings. In addition, most ethical problems in a profession can be resolved by reference to more basic principles.

The Rights Ethic

Rights protect people against abuses and entitle them to important liberties. A strong philosophical movement defining *natural rights*, or rights that can be inferred by reason from the study of human nature, grew in Enlightenment Western Europe as a reaction against medieval religious persecutions. Over time many "natural" rights were given legal status and became legal rights. Basic rights that are today widely accepted and protected include the right to life; personal liberties such as expression, conscience, religious worship, and privacy; freedom from arbitrary, unjust police actions or unequal application of laws; and political liberties such as voting or lobbying.

Rights imply duties. Because individuals have rights, many protected by law, other people have clear duties to respect them. For example, management should not permit operation of an unsafe machine because this would deprive workers of the right to a safe workplace. This right is based on the natural right to protection from harm by negligent actions of others and is legally established in common law and the Occupational Safety and Health Act. If some risk in operating a machine is unavoidable, workers have the right to be given an accurate risk assessment.

Theories of rights have great importance in American ethical debates. A problem caused by our reverence for rights is that they are sometimes wrongly expanded into selfish demands or entitlements. Rights are not absolute and their limits may be hard to define. For example, every person has a right to life, but industry daily exposes people to risk of death by releasing carcinogens into the environment. An absolute right to life would require cessation of much manufacturing activity (for example, petroleum refining). Rights, such as the right to life, are commonly abridged for compelling reasons of benefit to the overall public welfare.

The Theory of Justice

A theory of justice defines what individuals must do for the common good of society. Maintaining the community is important because natural rights, such as the right to life, are reasonably protected only in an orderly, civil society. A basic principle of justice, then, is to act in such a way that the orderly bonds of community are maintained. In broad terms this means acting fairly toward others and establishing institutions in which people are subject to rules of fair treatment. In business life, justice requires fair relationships within the corporate community and establishment of policies that treat its members fairly.

In society, a person's chances for justice are determined by basic economic and political arrangements. The design of institutions such as business corporations and political constitutions has a profound effect on the welfare and life chances of individuals. A contemporary philosopher, John Rawls, has developed an influential set of principles for the design of a just society. Rawls speculates that rational persons situated behind a hypothetical "veil of ignorance" and not knowing their place in a society (i.e., their social status, class position, economic fortune, intelligence, appearance, or the like) but knowing general facts about human society (such as political, economic, sociological, and psychological theory) would deliberate and choose two rules to ensure fairness in any society they created. First, "each person is to have an equal right to the most extensive basic liberty compatible with a similar liberty for others," and second, "social and economic inequalities are to be arranged so that they are both (a) reasonably expected to be to everyone's advantage, and (b) attached to positions and offices open to all."[17] In general, inequality would only be allowed if it would make better the lot of the most disadvantaged members of society.

The impartiality and equal treatment called for in Rawls's principles are resplendent in theory and may even inspire some business decisions, but they are best applied to the analysis of broad societal issues. Acting justly in business, on the other hand, is a matter of daily application of more concrete maxims of fair treatment. Managers may find guidelines in three basic spheres of justice.

Distributive justice requires that the benefits and burdens of company life be distributed according to impartial criteria. Awarding pay raises based on personal friendship rather than performance criteria is unfair. All laws, rules, and administrative procedures should apply equally to each employee. *Retributive justice* requires that punishments should be evenhanded and proportionate to transgressions. A cashier should not be fired for stealing $5 if an executive who embezzled $10,000 is allowed to remain on the job while paying it back. And *compensatory justice* requires fair compensation to victims. A corporation that damages nearby property must restore it to its original state; one that hurts a customer must pay damages. The general thrust of fairness in just action is useful to maintain an orderly community or organization in which individuals secure rights and meet needs.

The Utilitarian Ethic

The utilitarian ethic was developed between the late eighteenth century and the mid nineteenth century by a line of English philosophers including Jeremy Bentham and John Stuart Mill. The principle of utility, on which this ethic is based, is that actions which promote happiness are right and actions which cause unhappiness are wrong. The utilitarians advocated choosing alternatives which led to the greatest sum of happiness or, as we express the thought today, "the greatest good for the greatest number."

In making a decision using this principle, one must determine whether the harm in an action is outweighed by the good. If the action maximizes benefit, then it is the optimum choice among other alternatives that provide less benefit. Decision makers should try to maximize pleasure and reduce pain, not simply for themselves but for everyone affected by their decision. Utilitarianism facilitates the comparison of the ethical consequences of various alternatives in a decision. It is a popular principle. Cost-benefit studies embody its logic and its spirit.

The major problem with utilitarianism is that in practice it has led to self-interested reasoning. Its importance in rationalizing the social ills of capitalism can hardly be overestimated. Since the 1850s, it has been used to argue that the overall benefits of manufacturing and commerce are greater than the social costs. Since the exact definition of the "greatest good" is subjective, its calculation has often been a matter of expediency. A related problem is that because decisions are to be made for the greatest good of all, utilitarian thinking has led to decisions that permit the abridgment of individual or minority group rights. Utilitarianism does not properly relate individual and community ends in a way that protects both.[18]

Reflections on the Uses and Limits of Principles

The foregoing ethical principles are derived primarily from the Western philosophical tradition. Other principles, important to managers in other cultural settings, exist. For example, the *principle of nonaction* (*wu wei*) in Taoism, which seems mystical to a Westerner, is that all worldly events are the manifestation of Tao, the creative force. Managers following this principle should act in harmony with nature, which encompasses everything.[19]

Because this textbook is a secular work, we have not catalogued additional guidelines derived from theology; for example, in Catholicism the *doctrine of community* holds that individual worth is derived from membership in the community of humans created in God's image. Because of this an ethical economic system should serve the ends of the community primarily and individuals less so.[20]

In addition, some evidence exists that the ethical perspective of women may be different from that of men and that women tend to examine ethical conflicts using a viewpoint akin to a principle. Carol Gilligan studied male and female thought processes and found that men see themselves as autonomous, separate individuals in a competitive, hierarchical world of superior-subordinate relationships.[21] As a result, male ethical thinking stressed protection of individual rights and enforcement of principled rules to channel and control aggression. Women, on the other hand, tended to see a world of relationships rather than individuals, a world in which people were interconnected in webs rather than arrayed in dominance hierarchies. Women did not think in terms of abstract rules and principles that set sharp boundaries on individual behavior; they focused on the importance of compassion, care, and responsibilities arising in relations with others.

A *feminine care ethic*, then, is that a person should have compassion for others, avoid hurt in relationships, alleviate suffering, and respect the dignity of others. The care ethic would be violated in business by, for example, cruelty toward subordinates, exploitation of consumers, lack of trust or deceit in relationships, or focus on individual performance coupled with indifference toward colleagues or the welfare of one's company. This ethic creates a stereotype of how women think. Male and female managers cannot be divided neatly into two categories of ethical thinking and studies do not yet support a firm conclusion that men and women make different decisions when faced with the same ethical problems.[22]

Why Principles are Important

The importance of ethical principles is that their use can harmonize ethical decisions with a long tradition of cultural experience. Much ethical common sense, such as be honest, help others, avoid harm, tell the truth, be fair, and respect the life and property of others, can be derived from them. For example, the categorical imperative dictates that individuals tell the truth because truth telling can be made universal, unlike lying, the universalization of which would cause chaos. Standards created by individual managers, companies, or nations might lack consistency or might bear the impress of self-interest. The great principles transcend parochialism and contain enduring wisdom. Years ago, J. Irwin Miller of Cummins Engine Company noted that "the tenor of all the major religions of the world, and of all the great philosophers, is that the rules of behavior are about as inexorable as the laws of mathematics or physics. You violate them at your own peril."[23]

The use of ethical principles, as opposed to the intuitive use of ethical common sense, may improve reasoning, especially in complex situations. Say a cashier pockets $20 from the register at the end of the day. The person's supervisor strongly feels that stealing is wrong and fires the cashier. Ethical common sense is all that is needed in this situation. But consider the following situation.

Richard White, the night manager at an electroplating plant in a southern city, recently surprised everyone when he revealed to coworkers that he was proud to be a member of the Ku Klux Klan. Some of the employees on the culturally diverse night shift have found it more difficult to cooperate with him and accept his authority since this disclosure. White has tried to perform his job without confrontation, but a series of minor social abrasions have occurred between him and other workers on the shift. Absenteeism has risen, the rejection rate on completed jobs has increased by 5 percent, and there have been two minor injuries in the past month traceable to inattentiveness of machine operators. Earl Mizushima, the assistant night manager, is popular with the workers and well trained. He has hinted he is anxious for advancement. Should Richard White be moved from his position?

You are sailing to Rome (you tell me) to obtain the post of Governor of Cnossus. You are not content to stay at home with the honours you had before; you want something on a larger scale, and more conspicuous. But

when did you ever undertake a voyage for the purpose of reviewing your own principles and getting rid of any of them that proved unsound?

Source: Epictetus, *The Discourses* (c. A.D. 120).

An ethically insensitive manager might perceive this case solely as a problem of productivity, see White as a drag on efficiency, and remove him from the position. But let us apply three important ethical principles to the case: utilitarianism, rights, and justice.

From a utilitarian standpoint, management must calculate which course of action would result in the greatest net benefit for the plant and all its workers. In this situation it might be reasonable to decide that removing White would increase productivity and build morale among many workers while hurting only one person, White.

From the standpoint of the rights ethic, however, employers must consider the idea that employees have the right to freedom of conscience and political belief. In American society, workers are entitled to hold unpopular political and philosophical views in their private lives. Although White has brought his affiliation into the workplace by telling others about it, there is no evidence that his personal opinions are part of his management style or that he has been argumentative.

From the standpoint of justice, corporations are required to promote fair, evenhanded treatment of employees. If management allows other workers to be Republicans, environmentalists, or Muslims off the job, the same permission must be granted to White the Klan member.

Readers may make up their own minds about the case. If the productivity problem is substantial, management must intervene. But when ethical concerns about employee rights and equitable treatment are carefully weighed, management may consider alternatives to replacing White, including mediation by an ombudsman, counseling, or removing one or more workers for insubordination to White. At some point, however, management may need to invoke the utilitarian argument and remove White if his supervision becomes ineffective. The rights of one individual cannot, in this instance, jeopardize the benefits many others derive from the company.

This case is one that might be discussed in a corporate ethics training session. The reasoning process illustrates the application of three important and mutually reinforcing principles in a way similar to that used in a decision technique that is popular in the literature of management ethics.[24]

Why Principles are Not the Complete Answer

There are drawbacks to principled reasoning. As noted, specific principles have weaknesses. Some are based on flawed thinking. There is no agreement as to which is best. And, as John Dewey once wrote, they are "not a catalogue of acts nor a set of rules to be applied like drugstore prescriptions or cookbook recipes."[25] Their use demands interpretive thought. And such thinking is learned only in the process of character development. Character development is a source of ethical behavior separate from the use of principles. The theory that character development rather than principled reasoning is the most effective source of ethical behavior might be called the *virtue ethic*. It originates in Aristotle.

Aristotle wrote that moral virtue is the result of habit.[26] Ethical decisions by their nature require choice, and we build virtue, or character, by habitually making ethical choices. Ethical choices are those which accord with appropriate, natural human needs and do not give in to wrong desires for false pleasures.

Application of the virtue ethic requires conscious effort to develop a good disposition by making right decisions over time. Actions are not judged by supreme rules such as the categorical imperative or the principle of utility. Such overarching rules may apply poorly to the multitude of specific, concrete situations they purport to judge. Rather, acts are judged by whether they reflect the disposition of virtuous character, acquired by habitual use of common sense. An act stemming from this character is ethical; an act which is out of character and unguided by correct motives is unethical.

The attractive logic of the virtuous character does not require rejection of the ethical principles presented earlier in the chapter. Virtuous individuals might be more sophisticated in their principled reasoning than less virtuous individuals who have less insight about principles or situations.

Practical Suggestions for Making Ethical Decisions

Individuals in business can take a number of steps to see and resolve ethical problems.

First, learn to think in principled terms, and use concepts like universalizability, reversibility, utility, equity, and other ethical guidelines suggested by the list of principles earlier in this chapter. These principles are powerful decision criteria that enhance the capacity to discover or create ethical alternatives. Use a principle that is meaningful to you. As the famous anthropologist Sir James Frazer remarked: "Once the harbor lights have been passed and the ship is out of stormy waters, it matters little whether the pilot steered by a jack-o-lantern or the stars."

Second, consider some decision tactics that illuminate moral choices. The philosopher Bertrand Russell advocated imaginary conversations with a hypothetical opponent as an antidote for certitude. Have a conversation or debate with an intelligent person who takes a different view. Seek out a more experienced, ethically sensitive person in the organization to be your adviser. This variant of a mentor relationship is of great value in revealing the ethical climate of your company and industry. Alternatively, write an essay in favor of a position and then a second opposed to it. Write a case study in the third person about your situation. Try to apply ethical principles in answer to questions raised by the case.

More than 200 years ago, a balance sheet of pros and cons was proposed as an approach to decision making by Benjamin Franklin. Since that time numerous decision makers have used a balance sheet approach. Richard Nixon, as President, was fond of writing down pros and cons in columns on a yellow legal pad and then crossing out roughly equal considerations until a preponderance was left on one side or the other.

The balance sheet has advantages. First, it organizes information. Studies have shown that the human brain can grapple with only between five and nine bits of information simultaneously. Because many decisions, including moral ones, involve more considerations than this, a balance sheet may prevent chaotic thinking. Second, the use of such a procedure forces decision makers to make entries in a number of relevant categories, and new or unconscious considerations may be brought to light.

Another useful method of applying principles is to draw them out in the form of questions a manager might ask when contemplating a decision. This is known as the "critical questions approach." John Leys surveyed the systems of the great philosophers and derived thirty-six critical questions for the decision maker.[27] The following are a few examples: What are the authoritative rules and precedents, the agreements, and accepted practices? If there is a conflict of principles, can you find a more abstract statement, a "third principle," that will reconcile the conflicting principles? What is not within our power? What are the undesirable extremes in human dispositions? A shorter set of leading questions by ethics consultant Laura Nash is designed to avoid the abstract level of reasoning characteristic of broad principles. This list is shown in Table 6-1.

TABLE 6-1	Twelve Questions for Examining the Ethics of a Business Decision

1. Have you defined the problem accurately?
2. How would you define the problem if you stood on the other side of the fence?
3. How did this situation occur in the first place?
4. To whom and to what do you give your loyalty as a person and as a member of the corporation?
5. What is your intention in making this decision?
6. How does this intention compare with the probable results?
7. Whom could your decision or action injure?
8. Can you discuss the problem with the affected parties before you make your decision?
9. Are you confident that your position will be as valid over a long period of time as it seems now?
10. Could you disclose without qualm your decision or action to your boss, your CEO, the board of directors, your family, society as a whole?
11. What is the symbolic potential of your action if understood? If misunderstood?
12. Under what conditions would you allow exceptions to your stand?

Source: "Ethics without the Sermon," Laura L. Nash, *Harvard Business Review*, vol. 59, no. 6 vol. 59, no. 6 (November/December 1981).

Third, sort out ethical priorities before problems arise. If you do, you will get the benefit of considering alternatives when you are not under stress. Clear ethics reduce stress by reducing temptation, deflating conscience as a source of anxiety, and eliminating conflicts of interest in your decisions. When doing the ethical thing is not the most profitable financially, for instance, it helps to decide in advance that you will put ethics before tainted profits.

Fourth, commit yourself publicly on ethical issues. Examine your work environment, and locate potential ethical conflicts. Then tell coworkers of your opposition to padding expense accounts, stealing supplies from the company, discriminating against minorities, price fixing, or harming nature. They will be less tempted to approach you with corrupt intentions, and your public commitment will force you to maintain your integrity or risk shame.

Fifth, set a good personal example for employees. This is one of the basic managerial functions. An ethical manager can create a morally uplifting work environment. An unethical manager may make money, but he or she and the organization pay the price—and the price is one's integrity. Employees who see unethical competitive behavior, for instance, may wonder when their superiors will turn on them.

Sixth, note and resist the ethical temptations to which you are most prone. Aristotle advised:

> We must notice the errors into which we ourselves are liable to fall (because we all have different natural tendencies—we shall find out what ours are from the pleasure and pain that they give us), and we must drag ourselves in the contrary direction; for we shall arrive at the mean by pressing well away from our failing—just like somebody straightening a warped piece of wood.[8]

Hence, examine your personal traits. Are you marked by greed, prejudice, sadism, cowardice? Work to overcome these, just as the ancient Greeks worked to develop character. Ethical behavior is conditioned by practice.

Seventh, cultivate sympathy and charity toward others. The question "What is ethical?" is one on which well-intentioned people may differ. Marcus Aurelius wrote: "When thou art offended at any man's fault, forthwith turn to thyself and reflect in what like manner thou cost err thyself; for example, in thinking that money is a good thing, or pleasure, or a bit of reputation, and the like."[29] Reasonable managers differ with respect to the rightness of factory closings, genetic testing of workers, leveraged buyouts, and other nettlesome ethical questions. Do not be unforgiving because of pride in high standards.

Eighth, translate your thoughts into action—display courage. Knowing and doing are different. It is often easier to reach an ethical judgment than to act on it. Taking an ethical stand can create anger in others or cost a company profits and there can be personal risks such as termination of employment.

Finally, ethical perfection is illusory. We live in a morally complex civilization with profuse rules, norms, obligations, and duties existing like road signs that generally point in the same direction, but sometimes do not. No method of decision making ends conflicts, no principle penetrates unerringly to the Good, no manager achieves an ethical ideal. There is an old story about the inauguration of James Canfield as president of Ohio State University. With him on the inaugural platform was Charles W. Eliot, president of Harvard University for twenty years. After receiving the mace of office Canfield sat next to Eliot, who leaned over and whispered, "Now son, you are president, and your faculty will call you a liar." "Surely," said Canfield, "your faculty have not accused you of lying, Dr. Eliot." Replied Eliot, "Not only that, son, they've proved it!"

Why Ethical Decisions are Difficult

Why are ethical problems refractory even in the presence of principles and methods to guide resolution? In this section we list nine reasons.

First, managers confront a distinction between facts and values when making ethical decisions. Facts are statements about what *is*, and we can observe and confirm them. Ethical values, on the other hand, are statements about what *ought* to be and are held by individuals independently of facts. For example, some years ago Burroughs Wellcome Co., a British firm, was accused of overcharging for azidothymidine (AZT), the drug that slows replication of the AIDS virus. A capsule that cost $.30 to manufacture had a retail price of $1.60 to $1.80. For AIDS victims the annual cost was $10,000. AZT was expensive to research and develop and the company felt a high price was justified. Was Burroughs Wellcome exploiting desperate AIDS patients, or was it entitled to retrieve AZT's high cost of research and development and earn a profit above that? Facts, such as prices, do not logically dictate values about what is ethical in such a situation. What *is* never defines what *ought* to be. Pressure from gay activists led to two price cuts. But yielding to political force does not answer the question "What ought to be?" either.

Second, it is often the case that good and evil exist simultaneously, in tandem and interlocked. Nestlé's sales of infant formula in countries such as Kenya and Zambia have led to infant deaths as mothers mixed the powdered food with contaminated local water and their babies died of dysentery. But evidence also shows that sales of formula have led to the saving of other infants' lives when the mother is not available, the infant will not breast-feed, or dietary supplementation is indicated. Evil should be minimized, but in some cases it cannot be eliminated.

Third, knowledge of consequences is limited. Many ethical theories, for instance the utilitarian theory of the greatest good for the greatest number, assume that the consequences of a decision are knowable. But the impact of business policy is uncertain in a complex world. In 1977, for example, General Motors substituted Chevrolet engines in Pontiacs, Oldsmobiles, and Buicks, with a policy that extended an old industry practice of parts switching to entire engines. The intention of the policy was to achieve the salutary effect of making more large-block engines available over a wider range of automobiles to satisfy consumer demand. Unpredictably (for General Motors), consumers looked on the engine switching as an attempt to manipulate buyers and rob owners of status—an ethical implication perhaps entirely at odds with corporate motivations.

Fourth, the existence of multiple stakeholder groups exposes managers to competing and conflicting ethical claims. To illustrate, tobacco firms are in a crossfire of competing ethical claims. Customers assert their right to smoke and demand cigarettes. Tobacco farmers, representing over 275,000 farming families, give ethical priority to maintenance of the tobacco economy in southern states. Stockholders urge the priority of profits. Many third world governments encourage sales of tobacco products; they provide sorely needed economic benefits. On the other hand, the surgeon general's office and doctors condemn smoking for harming health. Feminist and minority groups condemn advertising that targets women and minorities. Public interest groups condemn advertising which appeals to children. Of course, companies in other industries also see conflicting stakeholder values.

Fifth, antagonistic interests frequently use incompatible ethical arguments to justify their intentions. Thus, the ethical stand of a corporation is often based on entirely different premises from the ethical stand of critics or constituent groups. Many members of the Animal Liberation Front believe that animals are entitled to rights similar to those enjoyed by humans, including the right to life. The group raided a northern California turkey farm, causing $12,000 in damage and freeing about 100 turkeys, which were taken to "safe homes." Later, members broke into a Delaware poultry farm, taking twenty-five hens and drawing an analogy between Nazi death camps and factory farms in the scrawled message they left behind: "ANIMAL AUSCHWITZ." Poultry growers, on the other hand, accept the utilitarian argument that raising food animals brings benefits to society. A publicist for the industry stated that the group's viewpoint was "an insult to victims of the Holocaust."[30]

Sixth, some ethical standards are variable; they may change with time and place. In the 1950s, American corporations overseas routinely made payoffs to foreign officials, but managers had to curtail this practice after public expectations changed and a new law, the Foreign Corrupt Practices Act of 1977, prohibited most such expenditures. Certain bribes and payments are accepted practice in Asian, African, and Latin American countries but are not regarded as ethical in the United States. Doing business with close friends and family is standard practice in the Arab world, but in the United States or Western Europe the same actions are often regarded as nepotism.

Seventh, ethical behavior is molded from the clay of human imperfection. Even well-intentioned managers may be mistaken in their judgment or motivation. Dennis Levine was an ambitious Wall Street executive who worked hard. He rose from humble origins to make over $1 million a year honestly at Drexel Burnham Lambert. Yet for seven years he also traded on insider information through a bank account in Switzerland. He was prosecuted and jailed. He had never intended to be a criminal, but temptation gradually eroded his honesty. "My ambition was so strong," he later wrote, "that it went beyond rationality, and I gradually lost sight of what constitutes ethical behavior."[31]

Eighth, the late-twentieth century presents managers with newly emerged ethical problems that are not solved easily with traditional ethical guidelines. For example, modern ethical theory has not yet developed an adequate principle for weighing human life against economic factors in a decision. Cancer studies may predict that workers exposed to chemicals will become ill in small numbers far in the future. How should this information be balanced against costs of regulation, capital investment, or job loss? Other examples of tough new ethical problems exist. By using a gas chromatograph to chemically analyze a perfume's ingredients, entrepreneurs are now able to make nearly exact copies of expensive designer perfumes such as Ralph Lauren's Polo and Calvin Klein's Obsession. Because a scent cannot be trademarked like a brand name, the imitations are legal and can be sold cheaply enough to undercut the established brand and piggyback on the expensive advertising that built the foundation of its popularity. Of course, product imitation is an ancient problem. But here the technology has outraced legal remedy and ethical consensus.

Finally, growth of large-scale organizations in the twentieth century gives new significance to ethical problems such as committee decision making that masks individual responsibility, organizational loyalty versus loyalty to the public interest, and preferential hiring of affirmative action candidates. These are ethical complexities peculiar to large organizations.

Concluding Comment

There are many paths to ethical behavior. Not all managers may appreciate the repertoire of principles and ideas available to help resolve problems of business ethics. By studying the principles and guidelines presented here, a person can become more sensitive to the presence of ethical issues and more resolute in correcting deficiencies. In addition, these principles and guidelines are applicable to ethical issues that arise in the case studies in this book. We encourage students to refer to this chapter for conceptual tools.

Endnotes

1. Joseph J. Schmidt III, "At Penney We Found Fairness and Honesty," *Wall Street Journal*, February 27, 1995, p. A13.
2. Empirical studies show that people in business find most of the principles listed here helpful. See Phillip V. Lewis, "Ethical Principles for Decision Makers: A Longitudinal Survey," *Journal of Business Ethics*, April 1989; T. K. Das, "Ethical Principles in Business: An Empirical Study of Preferential Rankings," *International Journal of Management*, December 1992; and Scott K. Jones and Kenneth M. Hiltebeitel, "Organizational Influence in a Model of the Moral Decision Process of Accountants," *Journal of Business Ethics*, July 1995.
3. Emmanuel Kant, *Foundations of the Metaphysics of Morals*, trans. Lewis White Beck, Indianapolis: Bobbs-Merrill, 1969, p. 44. Originally written in 1785.
4. Albert Z. Carr, *Business as a Game*, New York: New American Library, 1968.
5. "Is Business Bluffing Ethical?" *Harvard Business Review*, January-February 1968, p. 149.
6. Carr, *Business as a Game*, p. 142.
7. International Business Machines Corp., *Business Conduct Guidelines*, Armonk, N.Y: IBM, updated p. 6.
8. Richard J. Stegemeier, "Corporate Ethics and the CEO," in *Developing and Maintaining an Ethical Corporate Culture*, Los Angeles: College of Business Administration, Loyola Marymount University, February 1992, pp. 44-45.
9. *The Nicomachean Ethics*, trans. J. A. K. Thomson, New York: Penguin Books, 1982, Book II, chap. 6.
10. *Principia Ethica*, New York: Cambridge University Press, 1948 (reprint).
11. Eugene Ehrlich, *Amo, Amas, Amat and More*, New York: Harper & Row, 1985, p. 123.
12. Niccolò Machiavelli, *The Prince*, trans. T. G. Bergin, ed., New York: Appleton-Century-Crofts, 1947. Written in 1513 and first published in 1532.
13. Allan Nevins, *Study in Power: John D. Rockefeller*, vol. 2, New York: Scribner, 1953, p. 433.
14. *Foundations of the Metaphysics of Morals*, trans. Beck, p. 54.
15. Herbert Spencer, *Social Statics*, New York: Robert Schalkenbach Foundation, 1970, p. 69. First published in 1850.
16. Thomas M. Garrett, *Business Ethics*, New York: Appleton-Century-Crofts, 1966, p. 8.
17. John Rawls, *A Theory of Justice*, Cambridge, Mass.: Harvard University Press, 1971, pp. 60-71.
18. See, for example, Mortimer Adler, *Desires: Right and Wrong*, New York: Macmillan, 1991, p. 61. John Stuart Mill's famous essay "Utilitarianism" deals directly and brilliantly with these and other criticisms. It is reprinted in Mary Warnock, ed., *Utilitarianism and Other Writings*, New York: New American Library, 1962, pp. 251-321.
19. Lao Tzu, *Tao Te Ching*, trans. D. C. Lau, London: Penguin, 1963, pp. 33-34.
20. Louke Van Wensveen Siker, James A. Donahue, and Ronald M. Green, "Does Your Religion Make a Difference in Your Business Ethics? The Case of Consolidated Foods," *Journal of Business Ethics*, November 1991, p. 819.
21. Carol Gilligan, *In a Different Voice*, Cambridge, Mass.: Harvard University Press, 1982.
22. For more on the role of this ethic in the firm and in business education, see John Dobson and Judith White, "Toward the Feminine Firm," *Business Ethics Quarterly*, July 1995.

23. From a 1964 speech quoted in David Bollier, *Servant Leadership: The Story of J. Irwin Miller*, Stanford, Calif.: Business Enterprise Trust, 1992, p. 29.

24. See, for example, Gerald F. Cavanagh, *American Business Values*, 3rd ed., Englewood Cliffs, N.J.: Prentice-Hall, 1990, pp. 194-199. More recently, the originators of this method have added a "feminist ethic of caring" to their ethical decision model. See Gerald F. Cavanagh, Dennis J. Moberg, and Manuel Velasquez, "Making Business Ethics Practical," *Business Ethics Quarterly*, July 1995. For differing decision models, see Joseph L. Badaracco, Jr., "Business Ethics: Four Spheres of Executive Responsibility," *California Management Review*, Spring 1992; and David J. Fritzsche, *Business Ethics: A Global Managerial Perspective*, New York: McGraw-Hill, 1997, chap. 6.

25. John Dewey, *Reconstruction in Philosophy*, New York: Holt, 1920, pp. 169-70.

26. *The Nichomachean Ethics*, trans. Thomson, p. 91.

27. In *Ethics for Policy Decisions*, Englewood Cliffs, N.J.: Prentice-Hall, 1952.

28. *The Nichomachean Ethics*, trans. Thomson, p. 109.

29. *The Meditations of Marcus Aurelius Antoninus*, trans. George Long, Danbury, Conn.: Grolier Enterprises, 1980, p. 281. Originally written c. A.D. 180.

30. Quoted in Kevin Thompson, "Meat Is Murder?" *Meat and Poultry*, September 1987, p. 39.

31. Dennis Levine, "The Inside Story of an Inside Trader," *Fortune*, May 21, 1990, p. 82.

Chapter Seven

CORPORATE SOCIAL

RESPONSIBILITY

Merck

There are many stories of social responsibility in business. The one that follows is singular and remarkable.

For centuries river blindness, or onchocerciasis (on-ko-sir-KIE-a-sis), has tortured humanity in equatorial regions. The disease is caused by a parasitic worm that lives only in humans. When bitten by female blackflies, which swarm near fast-moving rivers and streams, people are infected by the worm's tiny, immature larvae. The larvae settle in human tissue and form colonies, where adults grow up to 2 feet long. These colonies are often visible outside the body as lumps the size of tennis balls. Mature adults live for 7 to 18 years intertwined in these internal nodes, where they mate and continuously release tens of thousands of microscopic new worms, called microfilariae. These offspring migrate from the internal nodes back to the skin, where they cause disfiguring welts, lumps, and discoloration. The itching they cause is so terrible that suicide is not uncommon. Eventually they migrate to the eyes, causing blindness. The cycle of infection is renewed when blackflies bite victims, ingesting tiny microfilariae from their blood, and later bite an uninfected person, passing parasitic larvae to them.

Over 20 million people have the parasite, almost all of them in the river regions of twenty-eight African nations. There the disease has sapped economic activity by blinding and enervating a large portion of the work force and by driving people away from fertile regions to dry areas less suited for farming. Extensive regions in these countries have been abandoned, regions which if farmed could feed millions.

Until recently, there was no effective treatment for river blindness. Two drugs existed, one which killed adult worms and one which killed their larvae, but both had frequent, dangerous side effects, including death when taken by some heavily infected individuals. The World Health Organization had undertaken ambitious pesticide spraying programs to kill blackflies, but it was tough going. Winds carried flies up to 100 miles from their breeding grounds.

Then in 1975 researchers at Merck & Co., a pharmaceutical firm headquartered in New Jersey, discovered a compound that killed animal parasites. By 1981 this compound had been synthesized and introduced as a successful animal drug. But Merck scientists had a strong hunch that it also would be effective in humans against *Onchocerca volvulus*, the river blindness parasite.

Merck faced a hard decision. It costs an average of $230 million to bring a new drug to market and more to manufacture it later.[1] Yet the people who had the disease were among the world's poorest. Their villages had no doctors. Should Merck develop a drug which might never be profitable? The company chose to go ahead, in large measure because its research scientists were motivated by humanitarian and scientific goals and it was difficult to restrain them in a corporate culture that strongly rewarded innovation. Donations from governments and international foundations could pay for much of the cost later, management reasoned.

Clinical trials of the drug, called ivermectin, were held in Senegal and other countries beginning in 1981 and confirmed its effectiveness. A single low dose

continued

dramatically reduced the population of the tiny worms migrating through the body and impaired reproduction by adult worms.[2]   Ivermectin did not cure river blindness, for it did not kill the adult worms, but it miraculously stopped itching, prevented blindness, and did so with no major side effects. A series of largescale human studies confirmed its suitability for mass use with minimal medical supervision.[3]

After analyzing the markets with river blindness, Merck concluded that those in need or their governments could not afford to buy the product. So in 1987 Merck announced that it would manufacture and ship ivermectin at no cost to areas of the world where it was needed for as long as it was needed to control river blindness. Governments and private organizations were asked to set up distribution programs. Currently, Merck

is donating 1 million doses per month, saving or improving the lives of millions. Some experts predict that as Ivermectin distribution widens river blindness can be wiped out—perhaps by around the year 2000.

For a drug company to go through the new drug development process and then give the drug away was unprecedented. However, Merck believes that, although developing and donating Ivermectin is costly, humanitarianism and enlightened self-interest vindicate the decision. Merck's Ivermectin program has dramatic potential for reducing human suffering. Not many corporations have similar opportunities, but most today initiate activities that go beyond normal business operations and are intended to improve society in some way. In this chapter we will discuss and illustrate the idea of social responsibility in business.

The Evolving Idea of Social Responsibility

The fundamental responsibility of business is to use power in keeping with a social contract. Since this contract is continually evolving, the theory and practice of business social responsibility have likewise evolved over time. Here, we briefly review this evolution.[4]

Business Social Responsibilities in Classical Economic Theory

Throughout American history classical economic theory, which is the basis for the market capitalism model has been the fundamental inspiration of people in business. In the classical economic view, a business is acting in a socially responsible fashion if it utilizes resources as efficiently as possible to produce goods and services that society wants at prices consumers are willing to pay. The sole object of business is to maximize profits while operating, of course, within the law. If this is done, say classical theorists, firms carry out their major responsibility.

This easily understood goal, derived from Adam Smith's *Wealth of Nations*, was never sought in business practice without reservations.[5] Even Adam Smith voiced a surprising number of exceptions to his principles for social reasons.[6] Throughout our history, business and business people have modified the strict profit maximization principle to address social concerns—not much at first, but more and more over time. Nevertheless, today this fundamental classical ideology remains entrenched.

The Eighteenth and Nineteenth Centuries

In the colonial era businesses were very small. Merchants practiced thrift and frugality, which were dominant virtues then, to an extreme. But charity was a coexisting virtue and the owners of these tiny enterprises made contributions to schools, churches, and the poor. They did this as individuals, but still exemplified the historical lesson that although American business has often been depicted as a jungle of profit maximization, people in business have always been concerned citizens.[7]

In the early nineteenth century companies were not effusive in their social concerns. Charitable contributions continued and grew over time as great fortunes in business were made. In most cases, wealthy entrepreneurs who gave their fortunes to benefit society did so without any reference to the interests of the companies that were the fountainheads of their wealth. One of the earliest of these philanthropists was Steven Girard, a shipping and banking tycoon. When he died in 1831, the wealthiest person in the country, he made generous charitable bequests in his will, the largest of which was $6 million to establish a school for orphaned boys.[8] Following Girard, others donated money to social endeavors and they began to do so during their lifetimes. The first great living philanthropist was George Peabody, a merchant and financier, who gave away $9 million in the 1850s to promote education and provide housing for the poor.[9]

Other, better-remembered business donors followed Peabody's example. For instance, John D. Rockefeller, who accumulated a fortune in the second half of the nineteenth century, gave in his lifetime more than $550 million and endowed the Rockefeller Foundation, "to promote the well-being of mankind throughout the world." Andrew Carnegie gave away $350 million during his lifetime to social causes, built 2,811 public libraries, and gave 7,689 organs to American churches. Carnegie authored a famous article entitled "The Disgrace of Dying Rich" and said that it was the duty of a man of wealth ". . . to consider all surplus revenues . . . as trust funds which he is called upon to administer."[10] These philanthropic donations, however, were individual actions, not corporate ones. When, for example, Rockefeller gave $8.2 million to construct a medical school in Peking, China, to meet the need for physicians there it was a gift from him, not the Standard Oil Company.

Not all business leaders, however, gave as effusively. Some moderated their giving because of the doctrine of social Darwinism, which held that charity interfered with the natural evolutionary process in which society shed its less fit to make way for progress by the better adapted. Well-meaning people who gave to charity interfered with this natural law by propping up failed examples of the human race. The leading advocate of this astringent doctrine, Herbert Spencer, wrote in a tremendously popular book in 1850:

> It seems hard that a laborer incapacitated by sickness from competing with his stronger fellows should have to bear the resulting privations. It seems hard that widows and orphans should be left to struggle for life or death. Nevertheless, when regarded not separately, but in connection with the interests of universal humanity, these harsh fatalities are seen to be full of the highest beneficence—the same beneficence which brings to early graves the children of diseased parents and singles out the low-spirited, the intemperate, and the debilitated as the victims of an epidemic.[11]

Spencer did approve of some charity, though only because it raised the character and superiority of the giver.

More than simple belief in classical economic doctrine and the doctrine of social Darwinism constrained business from undertaking voluntary social action during this period. There were significant legal restrictions on how managers could use company funds. Courts consistently held that a corporation did not have the power to act beyond its specific charter provisions. To do otherwise was to act *ultra vires*, a legal phrase for acting beyond corporate powers. A corporation acting in an ultra vires manner was subject to stockholder lawsuits. Standard Oil Company, for example, would have invited stockholder lawsuits by funding a medical school in China. A few exceptions to this doctrine were granted by the courts to permit the building of schools and churches in company towns. But social programs that large corporations undertake today, for example Merck's program to cure river blindness, would have run afoul of the ultra vires doctrine had they been attempted in the last century.

In addition, the classical ideology was still a mountain of resistance to expanding the idea of business social responsibility. Overall, the spirit of the time is captured by the nineteenth-century poet James Russell Lowell in the following rhyme:

> Not a deed would he do
> Not a word would he utter
> Till he weighed its relation
> To plain bread and butter.

Changing Views of Social Responsibility in the Late Nineteenth and Early Twentieth Centuries

During the latter part of the nineteenth century and into the twentieth, a number of forces converged to lead business leaders, especially of the larger corporations, to address social problems out of self-interest. Vigorous industrial growth had many negative social impacts. Critics called into question the cruel aloofness of social Darwinism. Business feared new government regulations and sought to blunt their urgency. Business leaders, many of whom by this time were not the original entrepreneurs, but owned only a small part of the stock of the companies they managed, felt freer to use corporate assets for social action. Business sought and found arguments to circumvent the ultra vires doctrine.

By the 1920s three interrelated themes had emerged to justify broader business social responsibility. First, managers were *trustees,* that is, agents whose corporate roles put them in positions of power where they could enhance the welfare of not only stockholders, but others such as customers, employees, and communities. Second, managers believed they had an obligation to *balance* the interests of these groups. They were, in effect, coordinators who reconciled the competing claims of multiple stakeholders on their enterprises. And third, many managers subscribed to the *service principle*, a principle with two distinct definitions. One definition was a near-spiritual belief that business, simply by operating for profit, had the power to redeem society by creating a broad general welfare. Individual managers served society by making a business economically successful; the aggregate business system would then work to eradicate social injustice, poverty, and other ills. A second understanding of the service principle, however, was that although the capitalist system elevated humanity, individual companies and managers were still obligated to undertake social programs to benefit, or serve, the public.[12]

These three interrelated ideas—trusteeship, balancing of interests, and service—were accepted by more and more business and opinion leaders. Although uplifting, they did not foster lavish contributions for social programs, nor did they divert most individual managers from their laissez-faire attitudes and dominant emphasis on profits. For instance, Elbert H. Gary, chairman of U.S. Steel, saw no inconsistency in serving society and at the same time opposing labor unions and the eight-hour day. Others believed that the benefits of efficiency justified the use of child labor.

A few business leaders implemented practices consistent with the new mixture of ideas about business responsibility. One was General Robert E. Wood, who led Sears, Roebuck and Company from 1924 to 1954. He believed that a large corporation was more than an economic institution; it was a social and political one as well. In the Sears *Annual Report* for 1936 he wrote:

> In these days of changing social, economic, and political values, it seems worthwhile . . . to render an account of your management's stewardship, not merely from the viewpoint of financial reports but also along the lines of those general broad social responsibilities which cannot be presented mathematically and yet are of prime importance.

He outlined the ways in which Sears was discharging its responsibilities to what he said were the chief constituencies of the company—customers, the public, employees, sources of merchandise supply, and stockholders.[13]   In speaking about constituents, General Wood repeatedly put the stockholder last "not because he is least important," he said, "but because, in the larger sense, he cannot obtain his full measure of reward unless he has satisfied customers and satisfied employees."[14]

General Wood was an exemplar of the theory of business responsibility in his day, but in his actions he was far ahead of most managers. Nevertheless, in the 1920s and thereafter, corporations found various ways to support community services of all types. Organized charities were formed, such as the Community Chest, the Red Cross, and the Boy Scouts, to which they contributed. They became deeply involved in giving advice and counsel to some city governments to help in a variety of causes, from improving educational systems to public health. Trade associations became involved in a wide variety of community functions. In the 1940s and thereafter, corporations established foundations to which they contributed cash and stock to administer their philanthropic activities. Virtually every large corporation today, and many small ones, have foundations. They are tax-exempt and legally independent of the company. Finally, in 1953 the ultra vires doctrine breathed its last gasp after the Supreme Court of New Jersey found it unreasonably restrictive and refused to uphold it.[15]

This brief history shows that the concept of business social responsibility has slowly expanded against the resistance of classical economic doctrine. The tension between these two doctrines has been ceaseless and will continue.

The Contemporary View of Corporate Social Responsibility

In the last forty years the concept of business social responsibility has continued to evolve and expand. Today, the efficient use of resources to make a profit is still seen as the primary social responsibility of business. But added to economic performance are the ideas of previous eras about the meaning of social responsibility. The view that total social responsibilities are broader than simple economic responsibilities has become more compelling, more accepted by managers, and more widely put into practice than ever before.

The range of social programs assumed by business has continuously expanded since the early years of the century. Today corporations carry out a wide array of social actions. The span includes programs for education, public health, employee welfare, housing, urban renewal, environmental protection, resource conservation, day-care centers for working parents, and many others. In each of these areas the programs that different corporations have implemented number in the thousands.

The fundamental reason why the concept and range of social responsibilities have expanded is that accelerating industrial activity continuously changes society. In this situation social responsibilities arise from the impacts of corporate actions on society. And we know more today about adverse consequences of some business activities. For example, early in this century carcinogens in industrial effluents were unknown. Statistics which would have shown racial discrimination in hiring were not yet kept. Today, then, some corporate impacts are more visible.

Corporate social programs also arise from a second source—intractable social problems in the corporation's environment. "A healthy business and a sick society are hardly compatible," notes Peter Drucker.[16] Racism, wars, violent crime, epidemics such as AIDS, and failing schools are societal pathologies a corporation has not caused but may benefit from mitigating.

The Expansive Concept of Corporate Social Responsibility

The modern, expansive notion of social responsibility, which has come to be called *corporate social responsibility*, has been articulated by both scholars and managers. Many efforts have been made to encapsulate this new, broadened definition of social responsibility in a few words. Here is a sampling from academicians:

- Obligations to pursue those policies, to make those decisions, or to follow those lines of action which are desirable in terms of the objectives and values of our society.[17]
- . . . [D]ecisions and actions taken for reasons at least partially beyond the firm's direct economic or technical interest.[18]
- The social responsibility of business encompasses the economic, legal, ethical, and philanthropic expectations placed on organizations by society at a given point in time.[19]

Some scholars have defined a concept called *corporate social performance* which is intended to encompass a broad standard for corporate social responsibility. It has been defined as "a business organization's configuration of principles of social responsibility, processes of social responsiveness, and policies, programs, and observable outcomes as they relate to a firm's societal relationships."[20] The corporate social performance concept is a broad view implying that business should be judged not only by its acceptance of the idea of social responsibility, but for its overall performance in seeking out societal needs, implementing projects to help with these needs, and assessing the impacts of these projects. The corporate social performance concept is a further expansion of the social responsibility idea of the kind that has been going on since the colonial era.

Business leaders have also articulated a vision of expanded corporate social responsibility. In 1971 the Committee for Economic Development (CED), an old organization of prominent business leaders throughout the nation, issued a milestone statement which boldly stated that "business functions by public consent, and its basic purpose is to serve constructively the needs of society—to the satisfaction of society." Society today, said the report, has broadened its expectations of business into what may be described as "three concentric circles of responsibilities:"[21]

- The *inner* circle includes the clear-cut basic responsibilities for the efficient execution of the economic function—products, jobs, and economic growth.
- The *intermediate circle* encompasses responsibility to exercise this economic function with a sensitive awareness of changing social values and priorities: for example, with respect to environmental conservation; hiring and relations with employees; and more rigorous expectations of customers for information, fair treatment, and protection from injury.
- The *outer circle* outlines newly emerging and still amorphous responsibilities that business should assume to become more broadly involved in actively improving the social environment.[22]

Classical ideology focused solely on the first circle. The new view is that managerial responsibilities go much beyond this point. But this does not mean diminished profits. On the contrary, say top executives in larger corporations, it is in the self-interest of corporations to assume social responsibilities.

In its 1981 *Statement on Corporate Responsibility* the Business Roundtable, a group of 200 leaders of the largest corporations, said that the pursuit of profit and assumption of social responsibilities were compatible:

Economic responsibility is by no means incompatible with other corporate responsibilities in society. In contemporary society all corporate responsibilities are so interrelated that they should not and cannot be separated. . . .

A corporation's responsibilities include how the whole business is conducted every day. It must be a thoughtful institution which rises above the bottom line to consider the impact of its actions on all, from shareholders to the society at large. Its business activities must make social sense just as its social activities must make business sense.[23]

Evolution of Areas of Social Responsibility

Figure 7-1 shows the relative magnitudes of three basic elements of social responsibility in the totality of decisions in an enterprise. The illustrated proportions are our estimates for three historical eras which show in rough measure how the elements of social responsibility have evolved in response to societal changes.

FIGURE 7-1
Principal elements of business social responsibility and their evolving magnitudes in company operations

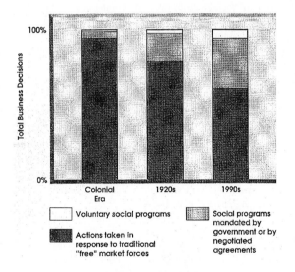

The first element is actions taken in response to market forces. The dominant magnitude of these actions in all three eras shows that market forces have always constituted the bulk of activity and continue to do so. When a corporation responds to the marketplace it is being socially responsible. Some critics believe that certain business operations, for instance gambling, defense, tobacco, or alcohol, are irresponsible no matter how well conducted. Such value judgments do not invalidate the general rule that the greatest impact on society, hence, the greatest test of responsibility, comes from normal market operations.

This is illustrated by General Motors. In 1993, GM employed 711,000 people in fifty-three countries who made 7.8 million vehicles sold through 17,865 dealers. The dealers, in turn, employed another 650,000 people. GM paid $4.3 billion in taxes of all kinds worldwide, and withheld from the wages of U.S. employees an additional $4.2 billion which it remitted to the federal government for income and social security taxes. General Motors customers paid another $4.7 billion in taxes worldwide when purchasing GM products. These statistics partially illuminate the huge aggregate societal impact of GM's routine, everyday, ongoing business operations.[24] These operations broadly support the general welfare; they are, in a sense, GM's biggest social program.

The second category of decisions are for social programs that business undertakes as mandated by government, for example, equal opportunity hiring programs—or as mandated in agreements negotiated with stakeholders, for example, contractual arrangements made in negotiations with labor unions. The proportion of decisions in this category has grown over the years primarily during several eras of regulatory expansion.

GM is exposed to multiple regulations in many nations, dictating a range of decisions. For example, in the United States, GM vehicles must comply with tailpipe emission standards; its fleet must achieve a federally mandated average fuel economy. Its plants must comply with rules limiting air and water discharges. Its work force must meet federal equal opportunity standards. Hence, regulatory guidelines codify for GM many societal expectations for responsible operations. General Motors has also responded to stakeholder pressures. In 1989, for example, GM signed a "fair share" agreement with the NAACP committing it to go beyond federal and state laws in hiring minority employees and using minority-owned suppliers.

The bulk of social actions taken by companies fall into the first two categories, but the third category represents decisions to undertake voluntary social programs. Within the voluntary area are three zones of action. First are programs that might be called "legal plus." These programs go beyond present statutes to enhance societal benefits in areas such as minority subcontracting, workplace safety, or pollution abatement. Second are programs that respond to a national consensus, such as contributing to charities or to improved adult literacy. Third is an area about which there is no consensus. For instance, some religious and radical groups condemn defense contractors for making weapons. Others, however, disagree and regard military contracts as responsible. This voluntary area is small relative to the total, but it has grown rapidly since the 1960s and is of great significance for large corporations. With few exceptions, individual proprietorships and small businesses, including small corporations, struggle to survive and devote few resources to these voluntary programs. A few critics of business define corporate social responsibility almost entirely in terms of this voluntary area; but this view neglects much other corporate activity of importance and, hence, is deficient.

General Motors, of course, undertakes many voluntary social programs. Some of these fall into the legal plus category, such as its WE CARE (or Waste Elimination and Cost Awareness Reward Everyone) program designed to reduce pollution and waste beyond legal requirements. Other voluntary programs commit GM to help society in nonregulated areas related to its primary business. The GM Mobility Program gives $1,000 to disabled persons installing adaptive driving equipment on GM vehicles. In 1993 the GM Foundation donated $54 million to educational, cultural, and arts programs, many of which were unrelated to making cars and trucks.[25] GM has not undertaken some activities for which there is no consensus in society. For example, it has for years opposed demands by religious groups that it adopt controversial guidelines for hiring Protestants in its Northern Ireland plant.

The Dominant Stakeholders

Managers generally agree that their primary responsibilities are to five groups, which may be called dominant stakeholders: customers, stockholders, employees, governments, and communities.[26] Managers often express their responsibilities to these groups in corporate statements of philosophy or, as they are also called, mission statements or credos. A well-known example is the credo of Johnson & Johnson shown in the accompanying box. This credo is chiseled in stone at corporate headquarters.

However, there are many other stakeholders, some of whom may from time to time become dominant. For example, when a firm is heavily in debt the financial community and creditors may take the forefront. For a very large corporation there are many other stakeholders whose multiple demands conflict and can never be completely met. So each company must set priorities to determine where, within its limited resources, it should meet legitimate demands.

Our Credo

We believe our first responsibility is to the doctors. nurses and patients,
to mothers and fathers and all others who use our products and services.
In meeting their needs everything we do must be of high quality.
We must constantly strive to reduce our costs
in order to maintain reasonable prices.
Customers' orders must be serviced promptly and accurately.
Our suppliers and distributors must have an opportunity
to make a fair profit.

We are responsible to our employees,
the men and women who work with us throughout the world.
Everyone must be considered as an individual.
We must respect their dignity and recognize their merit.
They must have a sense of security in their jobs.
Compensation must be fair and adequate,
and working conditions clean, orderly and safe.
We must be mindful of ways to help our employees fulfill
their family responsibilities.
Employees must feel free to make suggestions and complaints.
There must be equal opportunity for employment, development
and advancement for those qualified.
We must provide competent management,
and their actions must be just and ethical.

We are responsible to the communities in which we live and work
and to the world community as well.
We must be good citizens—support good works and charities
and bear our fair share of taxes.
We must encourage civic improvements and better health and education.
We must maintain in good order
the property we are privileged to use,
protecting the environment and natural resources.

Our final responsibility is to our stockholders.
Business must make a sound profit.
We must experiment with new ideas.
Research must be carried on, innovative programs developed
and mistakes paid for.
New equipment must be purchased, new facilities provided
and new products launched.
Reserves must be created to provide for adverse times.
When we operate according to these principles,
the stockholders should realize a fair return.

Johnson & Johnson

Debate about the Extent and Meaning of Corporate Social Responsibility

Throughout American history, and in recent years also, managers and scholars have advanced arguments for and against expanding corporate social responsibility. Here we summarize main arguments in this long-standing debate.

The Case for Business Assumption of Expansive Social Responsibilities

There is no single all-encompassing idea in the argument that business has expanding social responsibilities. Rather, there are three core ideas, not mutually exclusive: (1) corporations are creatures of society and must respond to societal demands; (2) the long-run self-interests of business are served by energetic social responsibility; and (3) exercising responsibility is a way to reduce or avoid public criticism that leads to government regulation.

Society Expects Business to Assume Social Responsibilities

The argument is that corporations are creatures sanctioned by society, and when society's expectations about their functioning change, so should corporate actions. A manager operates within a set of economic, political, cultural, and technical constraints. They are powerful, and as societal expectations change corporate actions must conform. This is the equation of legitimacy. Professor S. Prakash Sethi argues that there exists a "legitimacy gap" between the response of business to nonmarket social forces and societal expectations of what business should be doing.[27] If this gap grows too large, the corporation will be brought to heel. History confirms that an institution with power that is not used in conformity to society's desires will lose that power.

Long Run Self-Interest of Business

The belief of business leaders in this notion is affirmed in the Business Roundtable's *Statement on Corporate Responsibility*, mentioned previously: "Business and society have a symbiotic relationship. The long-term viability of the corporation depends upon its responsibility to the society of which it is a part. And the well-being of society depends upon profitable and responsible business enterprises."[28] It would profit business little to ignore social problems. In the long run, violent cities, deteriorating schools, pollution, poverty, and other problems are the ingredients of economic stagnation, not corporate welfare.

Ben Cohen and Jerry Greenfield, the founders of Ben and Jerry's, the Vermont ice cream company, run company operations on a principle they call "linked prosperity." To them this means that as the company prospers it is obligated to conduct programs that avoid harm and encourage societal prosperity.[29] Each year Ben & Jerry's plants enough trees to replace those cut down to make sticks for its chocolate-covered Peace Pops. The company waives its $25,000 franchise fee when franchises are set up by organizations that benefit inner-city youth, the homeless, and the handicapped. As these examples show, business leaders believe that the fates of corporation and society are intertwined.

Avoidance of Government Regulation

When corporate actions affect major social problems but corporations are inattentive the result is often new government regulation. A classic case of corporate avoidance occurred in the early 1960s when racial tensions in Birmingham, Alabama, gathered explosive force until finally, in 1963, race violence erupted. During this period there had been pressure on U.S. Steel, the largest Birmingham corporation, to use its influence to do something about race issues. But Roger Bloush, the company's chief executive declined, saying that ". . . any attempt by private organizations like U.S. Steel—to impose its views, its beliefs and its will upon the community by resorting to economic compulsion or coercion would be repugnant to our American constitutional concepts."[30]

Within a year Congress passed the Civil Rights Act of 1964, including language which has for over thirty years been used by regulators to shrink the discretion of corporations in hiring and promotion decisions. Since the 1960s many other areas of government regulation have greatly expanded. Such laws create compliance costs and reduce managerial discretion; hence, managers prefer undertaking voluntary social programs.

The Case Against Expansive Social Responsibilities

No worthy argument can be made that corporations have no social responsibilities. But the classical economic view resists expanding these responsibilities beyond market decisions, holding that a business is *most* responsible when it operates efficiently to make profits, not when it goes out on a limb to solve social problems. There are several variations on this theme.

Contrary to the Basic Functions of Business

The core of the strongest arguments against business's assuming any responsibilities other than to produce goods and services efficiently and to make as much money as possible for stockholders is that business is an economic institution and economic values should be the sole determinant of performance. This is called the classical view because it hews closely to the dictates of classical economic theory. A pertinacious exponent of this view is Nobel laureate Milton Friedman, a respected economist who makes this clear statement on the side of the classicists:

> There is one and only one social responsibility of business—to use its resources and engage in activities designed to increase its profits so long as it stays within the rules of the game, which is to say, engages in open and free competition, without deception or fraud. . . . Few trends could so thoroughly undermine the very foundations of our free society as the acceptance by corporate officials of a social responsibility other than to make as much money for their stockholders as possible. This is a fundamentally subversive doctrine.[31]

Friedman argues that in a free-enterprise, private-property system, a manager is an employee of the owners of the business and is directly responsible to them. Because stockholders want to make as much profit as possible, the manager's sole objective should be to try to do this. If a manager spends stockholder money in the public interest, he or she is spending it without stockholders' approval and perhaps in ways they would oppose. Similarly, if the cost of social action is passed on to consumers in higher prices, the manager is spending their money. This "taxation without representation," says Friedman, should be rejected.[32] Furthermore, if the price on the market for a product does not truly reflect the relative costs of producing it, but includes costs for social action, the allocative mechanism of the marketplace is distorted. The rigors of the market will endanger the competitive position of any firm that adds to its costs by assuming social responsibilities.

Social Responsibility Invites Oppression by Corporations

Friedman also believes that if business assumes expansive social responsibilities it may threaten political freedoms. He argues that the doctrine of social responsibility means acceptance of the socialist view that political mechanisms rather than market mechanisms are the appropriate way to allocate scarce resources to alternative uses. A corporation undertaking extensive social programs is performing a political function as well as an economic one. The fusion of both political and economic power controlled by corporate managers is dangerous. The two kinds of power ought to be kept separate. The market mechanism, which itself fragments economic power, is a counterbalance to political power. If they become fused under the control of managers a powerful barrier to tyranny is removed.

Others agree with Friedman. According to Peter Drucker:

> Milton Friedman's position . . . that business should stick to its business . . . is indeed the only consistent position in a free society. Any other position can only mean that business will take over power, authority, and decision making in areas outside of the economic sphere, in areas which are or should be reserved to government or to the individual or to other institutions.[33]

Liberal and radical business critics also sometimes oppose business' assumption of social responsibilities. They believe that government, not business, should take the lead in solving social problems. More regulation is preferable to permitting corporations to decide what is in the public interest. Leftist radicals also argue that the corporate social responsibility doctrine lulls a gullible public to sleep while an exploitive managerial elite advances its agenda.[34] In sum, those fearing oppression from expansive corporate social actions cover a spectrum from the most conservative to the most radical.

Are Social Responsibility and Financial Performance Related?

Is there a reward for virtue? Are socially responsible companies more profitable than those less responsible? Is their stock a better investment? Or is there a cost penalty for social responsibility? Over the past twenty years a large body of scholarly research has been generated to study these questions.

Scholarly Studies

To explore the relationship between social responsibility and profit scholars compare the financial performance of corporations with a high reputation for social responsibility to the financial performance of corporations with no such reputation. At least 50, and perhaps as many as 100 such studies have been undertaken and they show, overall, that there is neither a great reward nor a great penalty for having a socially responsible reputation.

A recent review of twenty-one published studies, for example, found that in twelve studies highly socially responsible firms were more profitable than less socially responsible firms, in only one study were socially responsible firms found to be less profitable, and in eight studies no relationship between responsibility and profits could be measured. From this the reviewers concluded that "socially responsible firms certainly perform no worse and, perhaps, perform better than non-socially responsible firms."[35] This seems as accurate a conclusion as any.

A Story of Two Executives

Theories of corporate social responsibility are only snippets of logic on dry paper until animated by flesh and blood in the real business world. This is the story of two executives, each committed to an opposing theory.

The first, Harold Geneen, took over International Telephone and Telegraph Corporation (ITT) in 1959. He was tough, demanding, and results-oriented. His goal was to increase earnings per share 10 percent annually "under any conditions." He believed that managers had to achieve goals. Excuses were never acceptable. In his autobiography, *Managing*, he is categorical: "Management *must* manage."[36]

He worked hard. Late one night as an afterhours meeting at a restaurant dragged on, the lights began to flicker. "Hal, it's late," a colleague said. "Even the lights are getting tired."

"Only the lesser lights!" replied Geneen. The meeting continued.

Under his leadership between 1959 and 1977, ITT merged with 275 companies; sales rose from $766 million to $2 billion. One hundred and thirty of his subordinates moved on from ITT to lead other companies. He was called one of America's greatest managers. Yet he rejected any focus on corporate social goals.

Geneen believes that economic performance is all that counts. He argues that many companies have underperformed because their executives shifted attention from operations to social projects, diverting themselves from their primary economic responsibility. Worse, getting involved in speeches, fund drives, and civic activities is often a sign of rampant "executive egoism," which Geneen compares to severe alcoholism in its cost to the company in lost time and efficiency. "The egotist may walk and talk and smile like everyone else; still, he is impaired as much by his narcissism as the alcoholic is by his martinis."[37]

The second executive, William Norris, founded Control Data Corporation in 1957 and built it to annual earnings of nearly $300 million in the early 1980s. The company made mainframe computers and peripherals and offered data services.

Norris believed that social problems such as racism, poverty, unemployment, and crime were not being adequately addressed and that corporations should start programs to mitigate them. He believed that there were business opportunities in meeting social needs and he set out to find them. He developed a sophisticated computerized learning system to improve education. It could, for instance, teach grade school and high school subjects to prisoners with unparalleled speed. It worked beautifully, but it was too expensive for most prisons. Norris insisted on locating manufacturing plants in inner-city areas to provide jobs for minorities. He moved company work to prisons. He started a for-profit company to do urban renewal in Minneapolis.

To sell his ideas, Norris gave 238 speeches between 1980 and 1985.[38] Unfortunately, Control Data fell on hard times. Earnings plummeted from a record $289 million in 1981 to a disastrous $567 million loss in 1985. Thousands of workers lost jobs. Communities suffered. Stockholders lost money. Financial analysts, who had criticized Norris's social diversions all along, now blamed him for the problems. Norris was forced to retire in 1986.

In fact, Control Data faltered because its mainstream computer products failed to keep up with the market. Social projects tied up only about 5 percent of the firm's assets and were holding their own. But were critics in the financial community wrong? Did Norris stumble while his attention was diverted from the core business? Geneen wrote that successful companies faltered when an executive lost tight focus on the basic business which he knew well, sometimes to shift his attention to "the broader burdens of the sociological problems of his community, state, or nation, which he knew hardly at all."[39] Was he thinking of Norris?

Both Geneen and Norris were managers of exceptional vision. By conventional benchmarks Geneen succeeded and Norris failed. In the end, Geneen would have criticized Norris with his biting aphorism "Managers must manage!" Does this prove the superiority of Geneen's philosophy? Or is the Control Data experiment worth trying again?

The inconsistency of results from study to study is not surprising because researchers face extraordinary problems. To begin, it is difficult to define social responsibility in an uncontroversial, objective way so that corporations can be ranked as more or less responsible.

People disagree, for example, about the propriety of manufacturing cigarettes, land mines, or war toys. Many academic studies utilize rankings of social responsibility created by organizations, such as the Council on Economic Priorities, which have liberal perspectives. Others rely on social responsibility rankings made by executives of Fortune 500 firms who have a more conservative perspective and tend to ascribe a "halo effect" to highly profitable companies and rank them as highly responsible also. In addition the actions that make a firm highly responsible are often unique. Which social responsibilities are the same for two or more firms? And last, it may seem very objective to quantify financial performance, but among measures of profitability such as return on assets, earnings per share, or net income which should be used?

One other point deserves mention. The profitability of a company can be a precondition related to the kinds of voluntary social responsibilities that a corporation assumes. A company that is financially prosperous can do more. For instance, when the pharmaceutical firm Eli Lilly and Company restructured in 1993 and 1994 it had to cut back about 3,000 jobs. It could have simply laid off workers but chose instead to offer early retirement incentives in which workers opting to leave got extra years of service credit to boost their pensions and a full year's pay. The cost of doing this was $535 million.[40] Had Lilly not been able to afford this voluntary expenditure such a socially responsible downsizing could not have occurred. In some cases, then, profits lead to social responsibility and it is not surprising to find a positive relationship between the two. On the other hand, a company that is doing poorly may cut back on its social programs. This makes it unclear whether social responsibility in some way leads to profits.

Individual Programs

Specific corporate social programs may or may not be profitable for individual companies. Some programs are direct costs. McDonald's, for example, has a McPride program designed to promote achievement at school in which employees earn an hour's wages for studying schoolwork for an hour before their shifts. Other programs reduce costs or bring in revenue. At Ben & Jerry's a recycling program has both reduced the company's use of paper and plastic and saved tens of thousands of dollars.

Hanna Andersson, a children's clothing mail-order sales firm, has a Hannadowns Program in which customers can return used clothes that their children have outgrown in exchange for a credit of 20 percent of the original price to be applied toward future purchases. Returned clothing is given to needy children. The Hannadowns Program helps the poor, but it also generates much repeat business.

The impact of still other social programs on profits is unclear. To teach managers teamwork, many companies have outdoor retreats in which teams compete in races and aggressive games. For the same purpose, the Plastics Division at General Electric has its managers work together restoring houses and community buildings in decaying neighborhoods. Do the visible, socially positive achievements of the GE managers lead to better morale, wiser decisions, and a stronger competitive team? The answer is unclear. As all of these examples indicate, the connection between responsibility and profits for individual corporate programs is complex and varied.

Corporate Social Responsibility in Other Nations

The corporate social responsibility idea has spread around the world. But it has developed differently in other nations because of unique histories, cultures, and institutions. Where the idea of corporate social responsibility is less expansive than in the United States, it is usually because greater emphasis on economic performance fits national expectations.

In Japan, because of historical circumstance and the influence of Confucianism, the idea of corporate social responsibility has developed slowly. Prior to 1800, Japan was a divided society ruled by feudal lords, deeply influenced by Chinese culture, but virtually isolated from contact with Western nations. After 1800 America and European nations aggressively pursued trade with the Japanese. When the xenophobic Japanese tried to stop the influx, they were militarily crushed. Feudal samurai were no match for Western industrial-era weapons. The defeats of the 1850s and 1860s are to this day in Japan seen as a source of shame.

In 1868 Emperor Meiji issued an "imperial oath" which called upon the people to overcome feudal divisions and to rise above their humiliation by making Japan a world power. He called for modernization, to be achieved by borrowing knowledge and technology from the West. The emperor's plan became a national obsession and has been a guiding principle for Japan for over 125 years. Its significance for business, and for corporate social responsibility in Japan, is profound.

Following the emperor's declaration, the government began to play a major role in promoting economic development. The central role of business became to make the country dominant and ensure preservation of the Japanese race in a hostile world. After the deflation of the military in 1945, the role of business became even more important. The people, previously loyal to feudal lords, in time transferred their loyalty to companies. In Japan, individuals believe that they make a national contribution by their work in a corporation. Large corporations in turn adopt a paternalistic attitude toward employees.

Since the time of Emperor Meiji big companies have built housing, roads, and public facilities for workers. The Japanese company accepts all-encompassing responsibility for its community of employees. But while it cossets employees it does not have a broad conception of societal involvement. This limited conception of social responsibility is based partly on Confucian doctrine. Confucianism spells out strict ethical duties and responsibilities, but traditionally they apply only to persons in direct relationships. Thus, companies embrace responsibility for employee welfare, but do not feel as obligated to stakeholders in the outside community. Government must legislate solutions for other groups and corporate responsibility is to follow the law.

The Japanese cultural environment has supported an emphasis on corporate economic performance. Compared to the United States, stakeholder groups apply much less pressure for social performance.[41] Labor unions are weak; to challenge the economic juggernaut would be unpatriotic. Consumer interests have lower priority than industry interests. Environmental interests, though stronger, have had far less public support than in the United States. There are few minorities in Japan, where racial purity is openly discussed as a virtue; no strident civil rights movement confronts business. Wide acceptance of the Confucian teaching that women are lesser beings has slowed a nascent feminist movement.[42]

Professor Richard E. Wokutch observes that the relatively placid societal environment of Japanese firms did not fully prepare them for the more turbulent U.S. environment.

> Japanese firms that have made major blunders include but are not limited to Sumitomo Bank and Honda, which had to pay sex and/or race discrimination settlements to employees; Hitachi, which got caught in an FBI sting operation trying to buy IBM trade secrets and then was criticized for trying to buy public favor when it set up the largest Japanese foundation in the United States; Suzuki Motors, which has had to endure ridicule from virtually every U.S. comic because of the rollover problems with its Samurai utility vehicle; [and] Japanese manufacturers of all-terrain vehicles, which have been involved in numerous product liability suits.[43]

Because of such experiences, and because stakeholder pressures are increasing with the maturation of Japan's industrial society, Japan's corporations are adopting more expansive social programs.[44] Some of these social programs are ingeniously related to the firm's business activity. The Yakult Honsha Corporation, which employs "Yakult ladies" to deliver its milk-based drinks door-to-door throughout Japan, has them check on elderly persons who live alone as they do their routes. The Asahi Beer Co. has established a lavish clinic in Tokyo for backache sufferers. Liquor store delivery people must climb countless flights of stairs in the city's many high-rise apartment buildings and frequently develop backaches. The Asahi Tower Clinic is there to help. Overall, however, the Japanese conception of social responsibility is narrower than the American and probably will be for some time.

In European countries corporate social responsibility has also evolved to accommodate national cultures. In France, and to a lesser extent in Britain, Germany, and Italy, social responsibilities refer primarily to labor issues such as wages, working conditions, and employment security. In these countries conflict between labor unions and employers is old and deep, and reflects in part an aging socialist tradition in which corporate capitalism has been seen as exploiting workers who therefore need government protection.[45]

Unique industrial regulations reflect this emphasis on responsibility toward workers. In France, for example, companies must spend 1 percent of total wages on worker education programs. The French parliament also required in 1977 that large companies draw up an annual social report for the government, focused mainly on employee relations. Powerful unions are today pressing a platform of "social policy" which would extend advanced legal precedents on worker rights throughout the European Union, but this is being resisted by industry, which must face world labor markets with relatively high labor costs and wants to see deregulation.[46]

In European social democracies, governments have taken broad responsibility for alleviating societal problems. Traditionally, these governments have used high taxes to fund far-reaching social programs. Some parliaments have nationalized industries and tried to achieve social objectives through state-owned firms. As a result, there has not been great pressure on private European companies to address a broad range of social problems other than labor problems. The development of an ideology of social responsibility similar to that in the United States has, therefore, been slower. European companies are more likely to believe that they have met their obligations by paying taxes and following regulations.

Less-industrialized nations may emphasize strong corporate social responsibility if this is supported by their history, culture, and stage of development. India is an example. Although Indians have followed the development of social responsibility doctrine in the United States, their thinking is deeply influenced by the doctrine of trusteeship set forth by Mahatma Gandhi in the 1940s. Gandhi believed that all money and property belongs to society and is held in trust by rich people and business organizations. Persons or businesses that accumulate great wealth are obligated to use it for social welfare activities. Ownership of private property has a narrow meaning and Gandhi intended the doctrine of trusteeship to moderate the tendency toward disparities of wealth and poverty in capitalism. Said Gandhi:

> Suppose I have earned a fair amount of wealth either by way of legacy or by means of trade and industry. I must know that all that belongs to me is the right to an honourable livelihood no better than that enjoyed by millions of others. The rest of my wealth belongs to the community and must be used for the welfare of the community.[47]

After World War II the Indian government stressed economic performance by business in a series of five-year plans. But because of Ghandhi's tremendous prestige the doctrine of trusteeship continued to inspire business practice even during these years. Since the mid-1960s Indian business groups have held conferences and produced a series of statements that connect Gandhi's doctrine to the ideology of business responsibility. Indian companies undertake widespread and significant social actions to an extent unusual for a developing nation.

India is a largely rural and agricultural nation which suffers from poverty and bad infrastructure, so many corporate programs are in these areas. For example, Ahmedadad Industries built twelve textile mills to employ rural workers. Associated Cement Companies Ltd. builds and donates cattle sheds, wells, and manure pits for rural farms. Brooke Bond, Ltd., a tea company, sends a mobile artificial insemination unit to rural areas to help impoverished farmers breed more cattle. Cadbury India, Ltd., buys otherwise useless apples that peasants pick up from the ground and makes a carbonated apple drink from them. Other companies build roads and schools and operate buses between towns.

In less developed countries (LDCs) there often is no indigenous sense of corporate social responsibility. For example, many small African and Latin American nations have massive social problems but their economies limp along because of low incomes, high inflation, weak financial institutions, and capital flight. In such situations the primary social responsibility of business is economic. Professor James E. Austin, an expert on less developed nations, argues that "the extremity and pervasiveness of poverty in LDCs places a special social responsibility on business as a vehicle for creating economic progress that will help alleviate this deprivation."[48] Because industry may be weak in such countries the burden of social responsibility falls on foreign multinationals. There are many examples of foreign companies attending to social needs in poorer countries. Levi Strauss & Company organizes its employees into small teams which identify local problems and use company resources to solve them. A team in the Philippines got $9,500 from the company to fence a schoolyard at the Mambog Elementary School in Manila, where wandering farm animals disrupted classes and children fell into open sewers near the yard.

In sum, the ideology of corporate social responsibility has developed differently in other nations. In countries such as Japan and India, its meaning has been defined by the context of history, culture, and institutional arrangements, particularly the business-government relationship. Especially in less developed nations its meaning is still largely confined to economic performance. However, there is a worldwide movement, now confined mainly to industrialized nations but spreading, to encourage voluntary responsibility.

Criteria for Determining the Social Responsibilities of Business

There is no magic touchstone or standard for determining social responsibilities. Because there is debate about the definition of the concept, managers must be thoughtful about responsible corporate behavior. What guides to social responsibility exist? We suggest the following five.

First, there is no one formula for all business or any single business. At least in the area beyond legal and regulatory requirements, each firm must decide for itself what it will or will not do, what it can and cannot do effectively. The first social responsibility of each business, before taking action, is to think carefully about what its social responsibilities are.

Second, business must be considered predominantly an economic institution with a strong profit motive. Business should not be expected or required to meet noneconomic objectives in a major way without financial incentives. As the Business Roundtable says in its Statement on Corporate Responsibility: "If the bottom line is a minus, there is no plus for society."[49] Companies may responsibly incur substantial short-run costs to correct social problems that threaten long-term profitability. And they may be encouraged to find profitmaking opportunities in solving social problems. But business performance should be judged primarily on economic criteria. Social responsibility may complement, but cannot replace, the profit motive.

Third, corporations have social responsibilities to correct the adverse social impacts they cause. Without responsibility the exercise of corporate power is illegitimate. For example, a corporation should seek to internalize *external costs*, or costs of production borne by society. A factory dumping toxic effluents into a stream creates costs—perhaps human and animal disease, perhaps the destruction of natural beauty—that are borne by innocents in society, not by the company or its customers. Corporations should not "maximize" profits by disclaiming external costs, but should seek to minimize these costs.

Fourth, social responsibility varies with company characteristics. Companies vary in size, products, strategies, manufacturing processes, marketing techniques, locations, internal cultures, external group pressures, and managerial values. Thus, a multinational chemical manufacturer has a much different impact on society than a small, local insurance company and its social responsibilities are both different and greater. Responsibilities also vary with national problems. A survey of 12,000 managers in twenty-five countries revealed great international variation concerning the priority of social issues a firm should respond to.[50] Lack of consensus is not surprising because of the great variation in cultural environments.

Fifth, managers can be guided by the general direction of public policy in a country. Lee Preston and James Post believe that managers should follow a "principle of public responsibility"; that is, they should determine responsibility by studying the overall "framework" of public policy, which includes "not only the literal text of the law and regulation, but also the broad pattern of social direction reflected in public opinion, emerging issues, formal legal requirements, and enforcement or implementation practices."[51] Public policy guidelines require interpretation and may be controversial, but they provide general direction for corporate social actions.

Emerging Views of Corporate Social Responsibility

Since the colonial era the idea of social responsibility has evolved to become more expansive. Expansion will continue. Today the boundaries of the current idea of corporate social responsibility are being pushed in both scholarly research and managerial practice.

Scholarly Thinking

Many scholars are attracted to the stakeholder model in which the corporation is at the center of a web of stakeholders; that is, all the groups and interests affected by the firm.[52] In stakeholder theory, the corporation must manage in a responsible way direct relationships with multiple stakeholders. Acceptance and development of this stakeholder perspective may lead to an expansive inclusion of stakeholders, each one having a claim on the corporation to act responsibly toward its interest. Corporations would be required to move further beyond regulatory compliance than they do now if they accepted explicit duties toward stakeholder groups to distribute fairly the benefits and burdens of business operations. Scholars who support the stakeholder model intend that it describe a world of broadened social responsibilities.

Emphasis on stakeholder relationships is either the basis for, supportive of, or not inconsistent with a number of other university-incubated proposals to expand corporate social responsibility.

Another approach is the idea that the concept of corporate social responsibility is moving through a series of developmental stages. William Frederick believes that modern debate beginning in the 1960s has moved through two stages and is now in a third stage. In the first stage managers, after much debate, came to accept the idea that they had social responsibilities. In the second stage they learned how to establish and implement social programs within corporate bureaucracies. According to Frederick, we are now in a third stage, in which scholars and managers are seeking to find ethical criteria to guide corporate social behavior.[53] Frederick believes that these criteria can be discovered in core cultural values from which ethical principles are derived.[54] Managers must learn to understand and apply these principles.   This perspective suggests further expansion of the social responsibility idea because managers are expected to apply ethical principles to decisions that would add elements, encode new lines of judgment, and require consideration of more duties than are commonly recognized today.

Another approach, that of *contractarianism,* is that the obligations of corporations are spelled out in a broad social contract between business and society. The contract, which may differ in its terms in culturally distinct societies, is defined as a set of arrangements that business and other groups would voluntarily agree are mutually beneficial. Groups such as employees and stockholders also enter into more specific social contracts with corporations. Using this theory, it is the responsibility of the corporation to uphold its contract obligations to various stakeholders.[55] This contract theory, in fact, provides a way to study the corporation's obligations to stakeholders. The idea of a social contract is a very abstract notion, but it implies that corporations must meet public expectations. Contractarianism is an expansive notion of corporate responsibility because it cements obligations to many elements of society without precisely defining their limits.   Corporations may, philosophically, be given more kinds of obligations than they would voluntarily assume today.

Managerial Practice

While academics stretch theoretical boundaries, a small number of companies stretch the boundaries of practice with unusual social programs. Most of these companies are small, but there are some giants as well. They share in common a commitment to stakeholders so great as to stretch traditional business values. In some cases these companies claim to exist to serve society primarily and to make a reasonable profit only as a secondary goal.

Stonyfield Farm Yogurt exemplifies a small company with a strong social mission. The company was founded by two entrepreneurs in 1983 as a means of raising funds to promote better farming methods. It has been a financial success and dedicates 30 percent of profits to programs that fulfill its social mission.[56] The Body Shop started out as a single store in Brighton, England, run by Anita Roddick, who believed that the cosmetics industry scared women into buying frivolous products through exaggerated images of glamour. She committed her company to improving society and ecology. All actions are weighed against their energy, environmental, or social costs. At one time she asked employees to ride bicycles to work to avoid pollution caused by cars. Each Body Shop retail outlet sponsors a social project to better its local community. Although Roddick has become wealthy, she speaks disparagingly of her shareholders.

> They play the market without much concern for the company or its values. Most are only interested in the short term and quick profit; they don't come to our Annual General Meeting and they don't respond to our communications. As far as I am concerned, I have no obligations to these people at all.[57]

Although growth in size puts pressure on the kind of social values exemplified by Stonyfield Farms Yogurt and Body Shop, a handful of the world's larger companies are driven by similar values. For example, a Swiss conglomerate with $10 billion in annual revenues, Migros, is also driven by values that emphasize service to society. It was founded in 1925 by an entrepreneur who believed that "the public wealth must at all times take precedence over the interests of the Migros Community."[58] To this day parts of the company are assessed ½ to 1 percent of annual gross sales to fund wide-ranging social programs. The company even helps consumers by refusing to maximize profits. It sets prices based on a standard, low markup over cost rather than demand.

These companies, small and large, are rare and unique but their actions may raise public expectations. As small value-driven companies grow or face difficult competitive conditions they sometimes must choose between social values and market imperatives. At Ben & Jerry's a long-standing policy was that the highest-paid executive could not earn more than seven times the annual income of the lowest. But as the company grew it faced difficult marketing, production, and distribution problems that the two co-founders failed to resolve. When a CEO with appropriate experience was brought in from the outside, market forces in executive compensation required that the 7 to 1 ratio be exceeded and it was (to an undisclosed amount). On this occasion, Ben & Jerry's was criticized for failing to live up to its ideals by some, just as Body Shop was criticized when it was found that some of its cosmetics contained synthetic rather than natural ingredients. Growth and competition may make ideals elusive, but the success of some highly responsible companies indicates that capitalism and compassion can be mixed.

Conclusion

Throughout American history, corporations have been driven primarily by the classical economic ideology. As they have grown in size and power the concept of social responsibility has expanded to justify responding to public expectations. This has also been the experience in foreign countries. This dynamic interaction between corporate power and values of corporate social responsibility will continue. Corporations will be expected to assume more voluntary social programs, become more sensitive to a larger array of impacts on stakeholders, and conform to more regulatory mandates. At the same time they will be expected to manage efficiently the resources at their disposal and be highly competitive in both local and global markets. Exceptional managers will be required to do all these things.

Endnotes

1. David Bollier, *Merck & Company*, Stanford, Calif.: Business Enterprise Trust, 1991, p. 5.
2. Mohammed A. Aziz et al., "Efficacy and Tolerance of Ivermectin in Human Onchocerciasis," *The Lancet*, July 24, 1982.
3. See, for example, Michel Pacque et al., "Community-Based Treatment of Onchocerciasis with Ivermectin: Safety, Efficacy, and Acceptability of Yearly Treatment," *Journal of Infectious Diseases*, February 1991.
4. We use the phrase *business social responsibility* here although it is of modern usage. The word business was seldom used in our history until the end of the nineteenth century. The words most commonly used in our early history were commerce and merchant. The phrase social responsibility was not generally used until well into the twentieth century. Corporate managers spoke of social programs in terms of good citizenship, service, or trusteeship. The phrase *corporate social responsibility*, which we use later in this chapter, came into common usage in academic literature in the 1960s.
5. Adam Smith, *An Inquiry into the Nature and Causes of the Wealth of Nations* (1776), reprint, New York: Modern Library, 1967.
6. Jacob Viner, "Adam Smith and Laissez-Faire," *Journal of Political Economy*, April 1927.
7. For an excellent overview of the charitable impulse in business see Mark Sharfman, "The Evolution of Corporate Philanthropy, 1883-1952, *Business & Society*, December 1994.
8. The school became known as Girard College, which the senior author of this book attended; it still exists in Philadelphia.
9. Geoffrey T. Hellman, "The First Great Cheerful Giver," *American Heritage*, June 1966.
10. Andrew Carnegie, *The Gospel of Wealth* (1901), reprint, Edward C. Kirkland, ed., Cambridge, Mass: Harvard University Press, 1962, p. 25.
11. Herbert Spencer, *Social Statics*, New York: Robert Schalkenbach Foundation, 1970, p. 289. First published in 1850.
12. Rolf Lunden, *Business and Religion in the American 1920s*, New York: Greenwood Press, 1988, pp. 147-150.
13. James C. Worthy, *Shaping an American Institution: Robert E. Wood and Sears, Roebuck*, Urbana: University of Illinois Press, 1984, p. 173.

14. Ibid., p. 63.
15. *A. P. Smith Manufacturing Co. v. Barlow*, 98 A.2d 581 (N.J. 1953).
16. Peter F. Drucker, *Management: Tasks, Responsibilities, Practices*, New York: Harper & Row, 1973, p. 341.
17. Howard R. Bowen, *Social Responsibilities of the Businessman*, New York: Harper, 1953, p. 6.
18. Keith Davis, "Can Business Afford to Ignore Social Responsibilities?" *California Management Review*, Spring 1960, p.70.
19. Archie B. Carroll, *Business & Society: Ethics and Stakeholder Management*, 3rd ed., Cincinnati, Ohio: South-Western Publishing Company, 1996, p. 37.
20. Donna J. Wood, "Corporate Social Performance Revisited," *Academy of Management Review*, October 1991, p. 693.
21. Committee for Economic Development, *Social Responsibilities of Business Corporations*, New York: CED, 1971, p. 11.
22. Ibid., p. 15.
23. New York: The Business Roundtable, October 1981, pp. 12, 14.
24. Figures in this paragraph are from General Motors Corporation, *1994 GM Public Interest Report*, Detroit: General Motors Corporation, 1994, p. 3.
25. Ibid., p. 29.
26. This is the order of priority revealed to surveys of 220 CEOs of large U.S. companies. See Linda D. Lerner and Gerald E. Fryxell, "CEO Stakeholder Attitudes and Corporate Social Activity in the Fortune 500," *Business & Society*, April 1994, table 2. See also Tammie S. Pinkston and Archie B. Carroll, "Corporate Citizenship Perspectives and Foreign Direct Investment in the U.S.," *Journal of Business Ethics*, March 1994, showing that managers of chemical firms headquartered in seven countries rank stakeholders similarly.
27. "A Conceptual Framework for Environmental Analysis of Social Issues and Evaluation of Business Response Patterns," *Academy of Management Review*, January 1979, p. 65.
28. In What Corporate Social Responsibility Means to Me," *Business and Society Review*, Spring 1992, p. 87.
29. Stephanie Weiss, *Gail Mayville*, Stanford, Calif.: The Business Enterprise Trust, 1991, pp. 7-8.
30. Quoted in James W. Kuhn and Donald W. Shriver, Jr., *Beyond Success: Corporations and Their Critics in the 1990s*, New York: Oxford University Press, 1991, p. 49.
31. *Capitalism and Freedom*, Chicago: University of Chicago Press, 1962, p. 133. For a more recent affirmation of this position see "Freedom and Philanthropy: An Interview with Milton Friedman," *Business and Society Review*, Fall 1989.
32. "The Social Responsibility of Business Is to Increase Its Profits," *New York Times Magazine*, September 13, 1970.
33. Drucker, *Management: Tasks, Responsibilities, Practices*, p. 348.
34. See, for example, Russ Bellant, *The Coors Connection: How Coors Family Philanthropy Undermines Democrat Pluralism*, Boston: South End Press, 1991.
35. Moses L. Pava and Joshua Krausz, *Corporate Responsibility & Financial Performance: The Paradox of Social Cost*, Westport, Conn.: Quorum Books, 1995, pp. 8, 56.
36. Harold Geneen, *Managing*, New York: Doubleday, 1984, p. 111.
37. Ibid., p. 77.
38. James C. Worthy, *William C. Norris: Portrait of a Maverick*, Cambridge, Mass.: Ballinger Publishing, 1987, p. 184.
39. Geneen, *Managing*, p. 18.
40. Dale Kurschner, "Interview: Randall Tobias," *Business Ethics*, July/August 1995, p. 32.
41. See Richard E. Wokutch *Worker Protection, Japanese Style*, Ithaca, N.Y.: ILR Press, 1992, pp. 47-54.
42. Chin-Ning Chu, *The Asian Mind Game*, New York: Rawson Associates, 1991, p. 183.
43. Wokutch, *Worker Protection, Japanese Style*, p. 50.
44. Arie Y. Lewin, Tomoaki Sakano, Carroll U. Stephens, and Bart Victor, "Corporate Citizenship in Japan: Survey Results from Japanese Firms," *Journal of Business Ethics*, February 1995.
45. Vivien A. Schmidt, "An End to French Economic Exceptionalism? The Transformation of Business under Mitterrand," *California Management Review*, Fall 1993, p. 85.
46. See Ruth Nielsen and Erika Szyszczak, "The Social Dimension of the European Community," Copenhagen: Handelshøjskolens Forlag, 1993.
47. In *Young India*, November 6, 1932, quoted in K. M. Mital, *Social Responsibilities of Business*, Delhi: Chanakya Publications, 1988, p. 134.
48. *Managing in Developing Countries*, New York: Free Press, 1990, p. 47.
49. Business Roundtable, *Statement on Corporate Responsibility*, p. 5.
50. Rosabeth Moss Kanter, "Transcending Business Boundaries: 12,000 World Managers View Change," *Harvard Business Review*, May-June 1991, p. 156.
51. Lee E. Preston and James E. Post, *Private Management and Public Policy: The Principle of Public Responsibility*, Englewood Cliffs, N.J.: Prentice-Hall, 1975, p. 57.
52. See Max Clarkson, ed., "The Toronto Conference: Reflections on Stakeholder Theory," *Business & Society*, April 1994, p. 93.

53. William C. Frederick, "From CSR1 to CSR2:   The Maturing of Business-and-Society Thought," *Business & Society*, August 1994; and William C. Frederick, "Toward CSR3: Why Ethical Analysis Is Indispensable and Unavoidable in Corporate Affairs," *California Management Review*, Winter 1986. Frederick names the three stages "corporate social responsibility" or CSR1, "corporate social responsiveness" or CSR2, and "corporate social rectitude" or CSR3.

54. William C. Frederick, *Values, Nature, and Culture in the American Corporation*, New York: Oxford University Press, 1995. Frederick also argues that central values in corporations derive from the evolutionary operation of forces in the natural world.

55. See, for example, Thomas W. Dunfee and Thomas Donaldson, "Contractarian Business Ethics," *Business Ethics Quarterly*, April 1995.

56. Allan Reder, *In Pursuit of Principle and Profit*, New York: Putnam, 1994, p. 11.

57. Anita Roddick, *Body and Soul*, New York: Crown, 1991, p. 22.

58. Gottlieb Duttweiler, quoted in Edmund R. Gray, "Gottlieb Duttweiler and the Perpetuation of Social Values at Migros," *Journal of Business Leadership*, Fall 1993, p. 58.

Chapter Eight

MANAGING SOCIAL

ISSUES

Hewlett-Packard

The Hewlett-Packard Company (HP) designs and manufactures computers, calculators, test equipment, medical equipment, and scientific instruments. In 1994 it was the nineteenth largest industrial corporation in the United States, with total sales of $25 billion and net earnings of $1.6 billion. Almost half its business is generated outside the United States. The company employs 98,400 people.

From the beginnings of HP its founders David Packard and Bill Hewlett thought about their social responsibilities. Packard, in his history of how HP was built, expressed it this way:

> Today Hewlett-Packard operates in many different communities throughout the world. We stress to our people that each of these communities must be better for our presence. This means being sensitive to the needs and interests of the community; it means applying the highest standards of honesty and integrity to all our relationships with individuals and groups; it means enhancing and protecting the physical environment and building attractive plants and offices of which the community can be proud; it means contributing talent, energy, time, and financial support to community projects.[1]

A tangible expression of this commitment is embodied in its philanthropic and employee volunteer programs. HP is among the top half-dozen largest philanthropic donors among industrial corporations, a position it has held for many years. In 1994 its giving amounted to $64.4 million. The largest part of the company's grants programs is in equipment. Noncash philanthropy (e.g., company-supported employee volunteers in community activity) is large, but there is no dollar measure of its value.

Universities and hospitals received the largest contributions in 1994. These totaled $30.4 million in equipment and cash grants. Sixty percent of the grants were for graduate and undergraduate instruction and the rest were made to support specific research.

A primary purpose of national grants is to improve the quality of higher education through donations of equipment that will enhance student and faculty exposure to leading edge machines, increase access to technology, improve the efficiency of teaching techniques, and strengthen curricula. An expressed purpose also is to "Stimulate technical and business careers, especially among historically underrepresented segments of the population, to address society's employment needs and to promote a more technically and scientifically literate populace."[2] HP employees are involved with schools and colleges helping teachers use equipment, serving on curriculum committees, and teaching.[3]

It should be added that David Packard and William Hewlett have for many years been active philanthropists. Individually they have given tens of millions of dollars to educational institutions and other organizations.

More will be discussed about philanthropy later in this chapter. Before that we shall discuss the nature of social issues management, why it is important, the life cycle of an issue, and how policy decisions made about social issues are implemented in corporations. We then discuss environmental assessments of social issues. This is followed with a discussion of crisis management, philanthropy, and business aid to education.

What Is Social Issues Management?

Issues management may be defined narrowly as the identification of and response to a few selected controversial social or political issues which may be of concern to managers. Issues management is sometimes defined broadly as the entire process of identifying a wide range of environmental issues, formulating company policy to deal with them, and, once a decision has been made about them either by the company or government, implementing that policy. Both definitions are used in the literature on this subject. We use the latter in this book as it relates to social issues.

There is growing interest in both the academic and business worlds about social issues management. Enough business practitioners of issues management were found in 1982 to begin a new society, the Issues Management Association. The Issue Exchange, with about 125 corporate representatives, is currently a more active organization concerned with issues management than the Issues Management Association.[4]

Why Is Issues Management Important?

In 1993 Home Depot, a worldwide home-supply chain, mailed a questionnaire to its 300 foreign suppliers asking whether they employed children and/or prison convicts. A reply was demanded within seventy-two hours. Home Depot took this action because the media were accusing some U.S. companies with purchasing products from foreign enterprises that employed children as young as 9 years old. Home Depot wanted to make sure that its own suppliers were free of child labor or other rights abuses. The company obviously wished to avoid charges that it was selling products made under such circumstances. This is by no means an isolated case of preemptive action by a company to avoid damaging publicity. Under considerable pressure from animal rights activists to save dolphins, the H. J. Heinz Company, for example, announced in 1990 that its Star-Kist brand would buy its tuna only from fishing boats that used fishing methods which would not entrap dolphins. Sears, and a number of other companies, have said they will not buy products made by forced labor in China.[5]

Today people individually and in groups are increasingly exerting strong pressures on both corporations and governments to take social actions they consider desirable. Furthermore, many of these individuals and groups are unwilling to compromise but insist action be taken as they demand. If companies do not respond to their liking, threats are made to commence adverse publicity, organize product boycotts, file lawsuits, or take direct action that interrupts the normal functioning of the business. At the same time, or in addition, they may pressure governments to strengthen old or pass new laws governing business actions.

Corporations, of course, wish to avoid such potentially costly disruptions and thus take them seriously in decision-making processes. Where there is a definable social need, a potential source of serious stakeholder concern, or the likelihood of government action, corporations today seek to resolve an issue before it gets to a critical stage. This is why issues management in more and more companies is no longer considered an unnecessary cost, but an important function of successful operations. There is literally no end to the list of actions that individuals and organized groups want corporations to take. It therefore becomes very important for a company to identify issues that are of concern to it and decide what action, if any, should be taken.

Patterns of Social Response

Corporate response to these pressures can be classified into five broad basic categories, as follows. First is *rejection*, a strategy in which a company denies any responsibility for taking action on a social issue. Although Philip Morris conducts extensive voluntary social programs to help communities and funds a wide range of charities it rejects demands to end lifestyle tobacco advertising and to stop its aggressive efforts to increase smoking in less developed nations. Sometimes a strategy of rejection is justified, as when fringe groups make unreasonable demands on corporations. In other cases, rejection and other defensive strategies invite more pressure and a fight in which the corporate image can be damaged.

Second is the *adversary* strategy in which a firm fights to avoid having to take social actions but will, under severe pressure, grudgingly give in. A good example is the battle waged by Firestone Tire & Rubber to avoid recall of its ill-starred Firestone 500 steel-belted radial tires. Over a six-year period in the 1970s the excessive failure rate of these tires led to hundreds of accidents causing thirty-four deaths and sixty injuries. Firestone challenged and resisted efforts by the National Highway Traffic Safety Administration to get the tire off the market. Ultimately Firestone was forced to conduct huge and costly recalls.

Third is a *resistance* strategy in which a corporation may make token moves or act slowly to satisfy demands that it assume more social responsibilities than it deems appropriate. For example, at hundreds of oil and gas company facilities birds fly into unprotected exhaust stacks of fire-driven equipment where they are burned to death. A very weak regulatory effort by the Bureau of Land Management required facilities on its plants to install stack caps to protect birds. Companies did comply with this regulation but slowly. In 1993, however, the group People for the Ethical Treatment of Animals (PETA) sent letters to every oil and gas producer requesting that they put inexpensive caps on all open stacks to prevent bird deaths. The companies wrote back stating concern for the birds, but none would cover its stacks. PETA then targeted Mobil Corporation. It started a boycott, organized demonstrations at facilities in three counties in which replicas of *Sesame Street*'s Big Bird were set on fire, and incited so many phone calls to Mobil that receptionists were exhausted. The company agreed to cap its stacks by 1995.[6] In this case resistance and token compliance were overcome by stakeholder pressures.

Fourth is the *accommodation* strategy in which a firm voluntarily undertakes social programs to meet public expectations. Firms in this category do not oppose, strongly resist, or act reluctantly. They develop social programs to meet the observed or expressed needs of communities. Coca-Cola is especially responsive to black causes. The soft drink industry is one in which companies aggressively fight for small fractions of a percent of market share. It cannot afford to alienate any group of consumers by failing to meet their expectations. Although a black boycott in 1981 placed the company under pressure to leave South Africa, both before and after the episode, Coca-Cola has taken many voluntary efforts to promote minority business relationships and improve minority, especially black, communities.

Fifth, the *proaction* strategy is used by companies that take actions designed to promote societal welfare before stakeholder demands or pressures exist. The mail-order clothing company Patagonia reflects its founder's deep environmental commitment. In 1992, Yvon Chouinard, the founder, undertook an environmental audit which found that the process used in making clothing polluted the environment. Polyester was made from petroleum. Cotton was grown using pesticides. Much wool came from large herds of sheep which trampled fragile grazing land in arid countries. As a result of this audit, and without public pressure, the company began using organic cotton and now buys wool only from temperate areas. It dropped 30 percent of its clothing line and offered fewer styles.[7]

Conceptual View of the Entire Issues Management Process

Figure 8-1 is a simplified model of the entire process of issues management, as we defined the term. It shows a process which begins with the development of the issue life cycle to the point where a decision is made to take action to deal with the issue. The figure then shows in detail how the decision is implemented in the company.

FIGURE 8-1
A conceptual model of
the process of issues
management

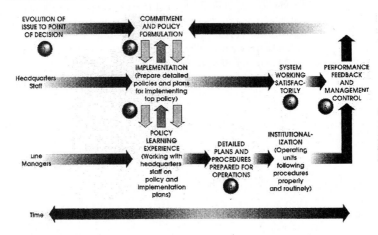

Life Cycle of an Issue

Figure 8-2 is a conceptual model of step 1 in the entire process shown in Figure 8-1. There is general agreement about the basic stages of an issue's life cycle but no consensus of the precise details.[8] We picture the life cycle of an issue in four phases: issue formation, shaping public opinion, legislation, and compliance.

FIGURE 8-2
Issue life cycle

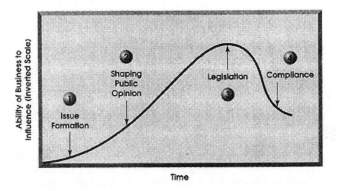

Issue Formation

Generally, issues do not suddenly appear. There are underlying forces and changes in society which may lead to problems that demand concerted attention either by business acting alone or by new government regulations. These conditions may continue for years before there is sufficient public agreement that something should be done. There are many illustrations in our history. For example, in the latter part of the nineteenth century, the merger of companies into giant monopolies at first generated no public concern. Eventually, however, public outrage at their perceived excesses led to government antitrust controls.

The earliest phase of this stage is the evaluation by a company of the changing social issues environment. All companies assess and react to the evolving environment in one way or another. Some meet each day as it comes while others attempt to look ahead and prepare to exploit opportunities or avoid threats. Some of these emerging threats come, of course, from new competition. But, increasingly today significant social threats arise. These may well result eventually in government mandates to take specific actions unless they are satisfactorily addressed through voluntary company programs. (This evaluation process will be discussed later in the chapter.)

Shaping Public Opinion

In this phase a variety of influences are focused on identifying the specifics of an issue and clarifying a solution. The process can begin with some triggering event that provokes the public to demand action. For instance, for many years people were concerned about contaminated food. It was not until Sinclair Lewis published his book *The Jungle*, which described the revolting conditions in meat-packing plants in Chicago, that the public became aroused.[9] The result was the Food and Drug Act of 1906. Similarly, people increasingly became concerned about environmental pollution. It was not until Rachel Carson wrote her book *Silent Spring*, however, that the public became incited about the issue.[10] The result was the nation's first major environmental policy, the National Environmental Policy Act of 1969. Ralph Nader's book *Unsafe at Any Speed*, published in 1966, helped crystallize public opinion that resulted in the creation of the National Highway Traffic Safety Administration (NHTSA) in 1966.[11]

Various activist groups seek to influence the public to demand some action from either businesses or government, or both, to resolve a particular issue. Human rights, animal rights, environmentalists, clergy, think tanks, academics, and many other groups are constantly seeking to arouse the public to get on their side of an issue. The mass media further popularizes the issue. Politicians promise action and begin congressional hearings that further expand public knowledge and attract additional individuals and groups to focus on the issue.

Legislation

In this phase bills are drafted in the legislature, discussed, and passed. This process can proceed very rapidly or take many years. Usually it takes a number of years. As noted above, Rachel Carson's book was published in 1962 but it was not until 1969 that Congress took action to deal with our polluted environment. On the other hand, Nader's book was printed in 1966 and NHTSA was established by Congress the same year.

This does not mean, of course, that there was a cause-effect connection between these books and legislation. Much went on before. Issues usually are very complex, and it often takes time before public opinion crystallizes enough to support legislation.

Compliance

Once a bill is passed and approved by the president, its administration begins both in Washington, D.C., or in states where legislatures are involved, and business complies.

Frequently the legislation and/or the administration of it may be contested in the courts. Both corporate compliance and legal challenges may be undertaken at the same time.

Deviations from the Conceptual Life Cycle Model

Once action is taken either by a company or the legislature an issue may fade in public interest. Some issues, however, are revived in new form. Water pollution and health, for example, are examples of issues that continuously appear in one form or another on the radar screen of public opinion, and a new life cycle begins.

Some issues never go through the full life cycle. For instance, in 1994 the executive branch, Congress, and the country were engrossed in national comprehensive health reform, but the matter for many reasons did not result in legislation. Issues may jump from discovery to resolution very quickly. This happened when thalidomide, a drug prescribed for women in pregnancy, was found to cause deformities in babies. The sale and use of the drug were immediately banned.

Corporations often decide to act before an issue gets to the point of hearings and legislation. When a gas leak at the Union Carbide plant in India killed thousands of people and injured thousands more, chemical concerns throughout the world immediately took action to prevent a similar accident in their plants. At the same time, states and cities passed a number of "right-to-know" laws about toxic discharges of plants, and Congress was inspired to pass a law requiring disclosure of toxic chemical emissions from plants. Proaction was the case with dolphins and foreign human rights issues noted above.[12] There are literally hundreds of issues of public concern that corporations address before they become public policy issues crying for legislation. Many corporations are voluntarily recycling paper, disposing of hazardous waste, supporting employees who teach science and mathematics in elementary schools, repackaging their products to prevent tampering, giving managerial advice to nonprofit organizations, to name a few.

Business Options During Life Cycle

The options open to a company change over the life cycle and become fewer and fewer. During the first stage the company has a free hand in devising policies to deal with a potential controversial social issue. In the initial stages of formation of public opinion, the company can conduct a wide range of publicity campaigns, including advocacy advertising, press releases, public policy speeches by managers and staffs, public reports and studies, and participation in TV and radio talk shows. When the issue moves into legislative hearings and the writing of bills a company has fewer options, but still some powerful ones. To influence the legislative process, activities may include coalition building with other like-minded companies and groups, such as lobbying, making political contributions, and issuing public statements. Finally, when laws are passed, options are limited to methods of compliance and engaging in litigation.[13] Later, when a bill becomes law, corporations can and do seek to influence the drafting of detailed regulations to implement the law and the way regulators go about implementing the rules.

Steps in Implementing the Issues Management Process

Once a decision is made to take action to deal with a social issue the next step is to implement it. Note again that a stimulus to corporate action can come from government regulations as well as from voluntary social programs undertaken by a company.

Stimulus to action can come from settled company policy. Many large companies have written statements or creeds that contain social philosophies and policies. (Note the Hewlett-Packard discussion at the beginning of this chapter.) Such policy statements are expressed at a high level of abstraction and need detailed specification for proper implementation. Forging this detail and assuring the proper response throughout a company can be difficult and time-consuming. Things are not necessarily done automatically in a company because a broad mission statement or credo exists.

The processes to implement a specific policy can differ. For example, a government mandate to permit only so much air emission from a factory chimney must be complied with meticulously and it may require the creation of an elaborate system of compliance throughout the company. At the other extreme, the Home Depot action noted above was simple and quick.

The implementation process begins in step 2 of the model. Here policies and strategies are formulated for action. In this step, of course, the issue to be addressed becomes better defined and detailed plans and programs are prepared for its implementation.

In step 3, policies and plans are revised and perfected through continuous dialogue among top managers, division managers, and staffs.

In a fourth step, tactical plans are translated into more specific procedures and rules and become part of the daily decision-making routine of operating personnel. This step should serve to eliminate operational problems and assure smooth implementation of company policy and plans.

In a fifth step, the system is working satisfactorily and the strategies and policies are fully implemented.

A final step is management control and performance feedback. To assure proper implementation it may be necessary to employ a full range of managerial surveillance and control systems. Included would be reports to management of performance so that corrective action can be taken if needed. Monsanto, for example, has a comprehensive audit system for environmental management. It began with "The Monsanto Pledge," formulated at the highest levels of the company in 1990. See Figure 8-3. Each of Monsanto's sites worldwide has a copy of guidelines written by a corporate environmental group to guide implementation of the pledge. Part of the system is thorough auditing that reports on compliance.[14]

The European Union (EU) has issued a regulation calling for a "voluntary" environmental management system that includes auditing. The International Standards Organization of the EU has set up strategy groups to study methods to install the system in all member countries by the year 2000.

Institutionalizing Social Policies

From a societal standpoint, as well as from that of top managers who accept the idea of social responsibilities for their firms, it is desirable to have corporate social policy institutionalized. This means that once a top social policy has been formulated, its implementation becomes a part of the day-to-day processes of decision making throughout the company. Managers consider the policy in their decision making without continuous surveillance by higher-level managers. When an activity is not institutionalized, it is likely to be periodic, separate from the critical activities of the business, easily forgotten by busy managers, and perhaps controversial.

We distinguish here three types of social action programs. First are the programs pursued because of legislation, such as equal opportunity or worker safety. In this category also are programs undertaken because of contractual arrangements with labor unions, such as those concerning equitable hiring, promoting, and firing of employees. The second category is company social programs that top management decides voluntarily to undertake. Included here would be programs initiated by managers in the organization without pressure from inside or outside. Also included would be programs undertaken as a result of pressures from groups inside or outside. In the third category are social programs undertaken by managers throughout an organization on a voluntary basis and not dictated by higher-level managers.

FIGURE 8-3
The Monsanto pledge

The Monsanto Pledge

It is our pledge to:

- *reduce all toxic and hazardous releases and emissions, working toward an ultimate goal of zero effect;*

- *ensure no Monsanto operation poses any risk to our employees and our communities;*

- *work to achieve sustainable agriculture through new technology and practices;*

- *ensure groundwater safety;*

- *keep our plants open to our communities and involve the community in plant operations;*

- *manage all corporate real estate, including plant sites, to benefit nature; and*

- *search worldwide for technology to reduce and eliminate waste from our operations, with the top priority being not making it in the first place.*

Monsanto
January 1990   Richard J. Mahoney
                        Chairman and CEO
                        Monsanto Company

If a company is to avoid legal penalties for noncompliance, it must, in the case of the first class of actions, establish policies, plans, procedures, control mechanisms, and incentives to ensure that goals are achieved in conformance with law and contract. In this way, the social program is entwined in the decision-making processes of the company, from top to bottom. If this is not done and if top management does not continuously survey activities, lower-level managers may sabotage the program if they find themselves in opposition to it on value, economic, or other grounds.

Similarly, actions of the second type may not be undertaken in organizations even when policy has been announced, in the absence of implementation procedures, rewards, and penalties. The problem here is somewhat different, however, because the motivating force results from greater top-management interest and not from any legal compulsion. Lower-level managers not in complete sympathy with the program may be more difficult to persuade than when legal sanctions are involved.

Finally, it is even more difficult for top managers to get lower-level managers to act in the third category if they are not disposed to do so.

There are many barriers to the implementation of social policies. For example, a traditional response of many managers, when faced with pressures to do something new, is to deal with the matter in an ad hoc, firefighting mode on the assumption that the issue is temporary and will go away. Or managers may file directives to take social action until it is clear that top management really means business. Some managers may have strong reservations about a corporation's responsibility to undertake social programs not required by law. These managers may only sluggishly comply with top-management directives to undertake social programs. There are many things a company can do to overcome such barriers as these. By far the most important is for top management to take leadership in implementation.

Top Management Leadership

If top management does not express and show by example its commitment to making social policies fully operational, there will be indifferent or no implementation of them in the organization. This is not an easy responsibility to discharge, for reasons noted previously. It requires constant attention and leadership by top managers, beginning with the chief executive officer. In addition, it requires attuning the corporate culture to social concerns, making the necessary organizational changes, training and selecting managers for their social awareness, relating performance measurement and reward systems to social concerns, and developing information flows that illuminate community concerns.

Environmental Assessments of Social Issues

Part of the process of issues management, as noted above, is the environmental assessment for social issues of importance to a company. There are multiple purposes of such analyses.

- They may provide mind-stretching exercises for managers and staff to make them more aware of evolving societal trends. It may help managers to focus on environmental matters continuously rather than sporadically, systematically rather than randomly. This is important as it is easy for managers to stay focused solely on day-to-day operations.
- They identify threats and opportunities so that risks can be contained, crises avoided, and opportunities exploited. In this way, they are basic assumptions to aid in the formulation of company policy and strategy.
- They help managers set priorities for the formulation of company creeds, mission statements, policies, and strategies.
- They provide a foundation for managers who take a proactive stance in public debates.

Who Makes the Evaluations?

Corporate planning staffs in larger corporations frequently make social, political, and ecological environmental evaluations. In many companies, however, these evaluations are made in public affairs offices. These offices are deeply involved in identifying public issues for corporate attention; setting priorities for dealing with these issues; providing forecasts of social and political trends to corporate planning staff, divisions, and departments; and reviewing corporate and division plans for sensitivity to emerging social and political trends. There are also many independent companies that make these evaluations. For some types of social issues, newspapers, magazines, and university research reports may provide sufficient information for informed judgment by managers about a particular social issue that the company should address.

Methodology in Making Evaluations of Social Issues

The palette of analytical techniques that can be employed in making evaluations is large, ranging from the intuitive search to comprehensive, systematic, and interdisciplinary computer models. In a comprehensive analysis a great many separate techniques can be employed. Space and time allow us to mention but a few of the methodologies.

Intuitive Search

For analyses in which the dominant focus is sociopolitical, both short- and long-range, the most widely employed method by far is the intuitive search. This technique is used by all managers who concern themselves with the changing environment. It involves a random, unsystematic, qualitative search for information, by means of which the manager comes to conclusions about forces in the environment of concern to him or her and the company. The selection of information and its evaluation are based upon experience, judgment, insight, and "feel." When done by experienced managers who continuously survey the evolving environment, it is more powerful than any other technique.

Scenarios

These are credible descriptions of the future based upon careful analysis of complex, interacting forces. They are not predictions of the future but disciplined and structured judgments of future possibilities. They set forth fundamental projections about anticipated trends and their outcomes. Generally, they describe different possible pictures, or alternatives. They are stories of what might happen in the future.[15] Scenarios can be used to look at possible social, political, and ecological events, but more frequently they embrace all relevant environmental forces. They can be made for rather narrow subjects, such as the future of the automobile, or for more comprehensive events such as the outlook for family life in the United States in the year 2025.

Scenarios have been an important part of strategic management at Royal Dutch/Shell for more than twenty-five years. Indeed, this company was one of the originators and perfecters of this methodology. This company has a staff with responsibility for scenario planning and is continuously engaged in this activity.[16] Many of our large corporations either prepare scenarios with their own staffs or employ outside consultants to work with staff to create scenarios for their management. Government agencies also use scenarios to look ahead. For example, Battelle consultants worked with the Los Angeles Department of Water and Power to prepare scenarios concerning energy requirements for Los Angeles by the year 2007.

Probability/Impact Matrix

In this technique, events foreseen for the future are analyzed in terms of their probability and potential impact on the company. The matrix used is shown in Figure 8-4. This is a straightforward but really powerful tool. If an evaluation places an issue, likely occurrence, or trend in the upper left corner of the matrix, it should be a matter of concern to a company. If, on the other hand, an event is judged to fall in the lower righthand corner, it will be given a low priority for action. Forces falling in the medium-priority areas raise questions about what action, if any, should be taken. The General Electric Company used a matrix like this for a number of years with significant results.

Crisis Management

Crisis management is a form of issue management, but considerably different from that which was described previously. The need for crisis management arises when some event becomes dramatically critical to the viability if not the survival of a company. For example, in 1982 Johnson & Johnson was shocked to learn that someone in the Chicago area had injected deadly poison into capsules of its painkiller Extra Strength Tylenol. Tragically eight people died after taking only one capsule apiece. J&J immediately went into action. A top executive was named to head a committee to deal with the crisis, all Tylenol capsules were removed from the market, and the company executives made themselves available to the media to respond to massive consumer concerns and interest. Heretofore, the company had remained aloof from the media. But not with this crisis. The team brought in others from around the company to design a new "tamper-resistant" package. This was marketed, but unfortunately in 1986 another capsule was filled with poison and one person died. Lessons learned in the earlier crisis helped in this crisis. The capsule form of pill was abandoned and J&J decided to make a solid, smooth, capsule-shaped pill that would be difficult to contaminate. The monetary costs of these crises to J&J were about $500 million. No estimate can be made, of course, for the costs of the deaths, the emotional strains of the families, and consumer anxieties.

FIGURE 8-4
Probability/impact
matrix

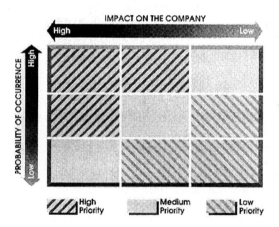

There are many different types of crises and they range widely in their potential impact on a company. For instance, one can include product or service defects, sabotage, natural disasters, industrial accidents, and unexpected substantial pollution of air or water.[17] Crisis management is as necessary to nonprofit organizations as to profit enterprises.[18]

At no time in our past history have the probabilities of such crises been greater for corporations. There is no way to forecast the type and timing of crises that could have serious or even terminal implications for a company. But they do occur and wise managements lay plans to meet them on a when-as-and-if basis.

Here are three basic conceptual steps companies take in preparing for crises:

First, assess realistic possibilities of crises. It is especially important to identify, if possible, warning signs of trouble ahead. J&J, of course, had no warning signs. But in other crises there were. For example, there were warnings that dangerous leaks might occur in the Union Carbide plant in Bhopal, India. When a major leak did occur thousands of people were killed or injured. Evaluations in this step can be similar to those made in the first step in issues management noted above.

Second, prepare plans for meeting the crisis when it occurs. Usually, in the event of a severe crisis such as that described for J&J a top-management team is identified to go into action. For a major fire in the computer room, a different more detailed type of plan might be made, such as making arrangements with another company to use its computers, or duplicating critical records and locating them outside the company.

We do not mean that a set of plans must be prepared to be followed without deviation. The idea here is to prepare an organization to think about crises and to be ready to act appropriately in an emergency. As Christine M. Pearson and Ian I. Mitroff note, on the basis of interviews in 200 companies, "A fixed preparation for all crises is not a sensible target. However, a systematic, integrative process of crisis management is a proper and attainable goal. Anything less invites disaster."[19] This suggests the following step.

Third, game the crisis. This follows the military practice of simulating situations. A scenario of a crisis is prepared and the team goes into action just as if a crisis actually occurred. This means, for example, not only the event itself, but make-believe frightened and irate consumers (if the crisis deals with a product), TV cameras, newspaper reporters, and coordinating action required by the crisis among major functions (production, marketing, finance, etc.).

Hopefully, when a crisis does actually take place the plans and experience with gaming will provide the specifications for getting the coordinating team in place, satisfactorily dealing with the crisis, and creating the means to repair or alleviate the damage to the company.[20]

The Management of Corporate Philanthropy

Philanthropy is a different form of issues management. It means the giving of money, time, products, or services to help the needy or to support institutions working to better human welfare. It is a synonym for charity. As we noted in the preceding chapter, people in business throughout our history thought about their social responsibilities.[21] Also, as we noted, businesses did make charitable contributions for social purposes throughout our history but the amounts were not large. One reason was that courts of law held that such actions by a business were ultra vires acts (beyond the powers of the corporation) and illegal.

The first major break from the narrow interpretation of the legality of corporate giving came in 1935 with the passage of the Revenue Act of that year. Congress made it possible for corporations to deduct from taxable earnings their charitable contributions, up to 5 percent of net profits before taxes. (This was raised to 10 percent by the Economic Recovery Act of 1981.) The legal requirement that directors of corporations must exercise sound business judgment and act in a fiduciary capacity to corporate interests was not relaxed.

The legality of using corporate funds for purposes other than clearly charitable giving under the Revenue Act, however, continued to be very doubtful and corporations were not particularly generous for fear of stockholder suits. The legal restraint on corporate giving was removed in 1953 by the case of *A. P. Smith v. Barlow* in which the Supreme Court refused to review a decision of the highest court in New Jersey allowing the A. P. Smith Company to give Princeton University money for general maintenance. The New Jersey Supreme Court, affirming a lower-court decision, said in part, "Such giving may well be regarded as a major, though unwritten, corporate power. It is even more than that. In the Court's view of the case, it amounts to a solemn duty."[22]

Corporate Philanthropic Allocations

Corporate giving, which includes cash as well as in-kind gifts such as a company's products, was $6.11 billion in 1994, a 1 percent rise from 1993. After adjusting for inflation, this was a decline from 1993 of 2 percent. This was the seventh year that corporate giving did not keep pace with inflation. As large as corporate giving is, it was only 4.7 percent of total philanthropic giving in the United States of $130 billion in 1994.[23]

In 1993 the corporate contributions pie was distributed as follows: education, 38.3 percent; health and human services, 26.3 percent; culture and arts, 11.2 percent; civic and community, 10.5 percent; and all other, 13.6 percent.[24] This pattern of distribution has been rather steady for a number of years.

Few individual corporations have ever come close to giving 10 percent of their pretax revenue to philanthropic purposes. Actually, business contributions have averaged between 1 and 2 percent of pretax revenue over the past twenty years. In only one year was it over 2 percent; that was in 1986 when it was 2.38 percent.

Relating Philanthropy to Self-interest

Corporate philanthropic giving did expand following the *A. P. Smith* decision. Much of it went to organized charities such as the Community Chest (precursor of United Way), the Red Cross, the YMCA, and so on. These were gifts of cash, generally made by foundations funded by the corporations, given without particular reference to company interests. Gradually, corporate philanthropy became more and more related to self-interest until today, in many of the largest corporations, corporate philanthropy is connected directly to the strategic goals of the company.

Craig Smith, president of Corporate Citizen, calls this policy *strategic philanthropy*.[25] Strategic philanthropy tries to tie giving to the basic mission statement, the major strategies, and the primary objectives of the company.

In employing the strategic philanthropy approach corporations coordinate giving by their functional divisions and with corporate-level giving. For instance, Sara Lee chose to support antihunger organizations. The company arranged for its marketers to donate a portion of their product sales to antihunger organizations. Volunteers in the program were chosen from the human resources staff. The operating divisions donated free food. And top managers joined the board of Chicago-based Second Harvest, the food industry's antihunger voice.[26] Nike Inc., a sports shoe and clothing maker, ties its giving to sports events at boys and girls clubs. J&J supports training of hospital administrators and nurses. HP emphasizes computers. However, virtually all companies and their foundations that have strategic philanthropy policy also make some room for altruistic programs that benefit society but may have no direct relevance to corporate interests.

Corporations are creating coalitions to underscore their concern about issues related to their broad corporate interests. For example, a coalition of outdoor and out-of-home advertising companies organized a campaign to distribute in thirty countries around the world a poster supporting an antiviolence campaign. The poster appears on donated ad space, such as billboards, airport walls, subway placards, and so forth, worth about $20 million.[27]

Cause-related marketing is another type of philanthropy practiced by a number of companies. It seeks to have customers reach for products because of the maker's support of some worthwhile cause. For example, General Foods has donated 25 cents to scholarships for African American college students with the use of a specially marked coupon for Stove Top Stuffing and other products. Late in 1994 American Express donated 2 cents per transaction to Share Our Strength, an antihunger organization. These programs have been criticized as being insincere since such a small fraction of the sales price goes to the worthy cause. However, consumers have responded favorably to many of these cause-related marketing campaigns. For some products the programs have not affected sales.[28]

One of the reasons for the relative drop in corporate philanthropy totals noted above is that these aggregates do not include the noncash contributions. Corporate cash distributions have dropped in favor of other kinds of aids. For example, corporations are supportive of employee volunteers for all types of community activities, from teaching in secondary schools to contributing to blood drives. Many corporations make substantial contributions of both old and new equipment to a variety of organizations. For example, the Lucille Packard Foundation and the National Semiconductor Corporation made grants to establish The Computer Recycling Center in Mountain View, California, to take old computers donated by corporations, repair them, and distribute them to needy schools. Corporate managers give expertise and time to community groups.

In sum, the policy of strategic philanthropy benefits the community as well as the corporate self-interest. For the corporation with such a policy it is hoped that employee loyalty and productivity will be improved, the image of the company will be enhanced, cooperation among the functional groups in a corporation may be stimulated, and profits may be enhanced in both the short run and long run.[29]

Business in Education

Business leaders have always been interested in education, but in recent years their concern has expressed a new urgency. They are well aware of the sad performance of many of our schools and the fact that some high school graduates can barely read their diplomas. They know that a poorly educated population is detrimental to the type of community in which their companies can thrive. They see that their companies are not getting the skills required for competition in global markets. For example, modern factories using advanced equipment require that workers use high school-level mathematics. Lincoln Electric, of Euclid, Ohio, requires skilled workers to operate microprocessor control equipment, for example. It has difficulty in finding workers with such skills but is willing to train applicants. However, it finds too few who have the needed elementary mathematics to profit from the training. Experiences such as Lincoln's lead many corporations to become involved in education.[30]

Overview of Business Educational Activity

In surveying what companies are doing in this area, several conclusions seem warranted. First, company managers are increasingly interested in doing something to help improve the quality of education. Second, companies are contributing not only cash but also managerial and employee volunteers in support of their many different programs. Third, whereas in the past companies focused the major part of their educational philanthropy on higher education they are now increasing their support to K through 12 grades. Fourth, many companies have established a staff position at their central headquarters to implement educational policy. For example, in 1989 HP created the position of educational relations manager.

Examples of Business Aid to Education

Aside from cash grants, the programs being undertaken by business cover virtually every important facet of the educational system. Programs range from preventing school dropouts to broad educational reform. Employees of companies volunteer as tutors and mentors, classroom teachers, teachers of teachers, and advisers in preparing new curricula. Companies arrange partnerships with schools and form coalitions to aid education.

A good example is the CIGNA Corporation which, through its CIGNA Foundation, has dedicated significant efforts and resources to improving educational opportunities for children. It has a multiyear cooperative partnership with five schools in Philadelphia that supply employees to the company. The partnership provides planning, financial support, and encouragement to students throughout their academic careers. It contributes computers and trains students in their use. Company volunteers tutor students, help them with homework, and serve as role models. More than 6,000 students have benefited from the partnership programs.[31]

Here are a few other brief examples chosen randomly from detailed illustrations published by the Council for Aid to Education, the Business Roundtable, and the Center for Corporate Public Involvement.[32] Rockwell International's educational program is aimed at increasing student interest and achievement in science and math, strengthening teachers' knowledge and skills, and improving teaching methods and educational processes. Eastman Kodak trains its employee volunteers in teaching techniques and knowledge about the culture and diversity of students with whom they deal, from preschool onward. Procter & Gamble has many projects involving hundreds of mentors, tutors, and other volunteers. Seventeen Chicago companies (among them AT&T, Chubb Corporation, Shell Oil Company, General Motors Corporation, General Electric Company) sponsor INROADS. This is a program for college-bound African American, Hispanic, and Native American students interested in careers in business and engineering. Each company in the program selects one or more students as interns and helps them complete their college education, providing they meet prescribed academic standards. INROADS also has a program to aid high school students.

Some companies have established schools to aid education. For example, Merck has set up the Merck Institute for Science Education where employees train to become mentors in local schools and where teachers can advance their knowledge of science. Honeywell opened New Vistas High School at company headquarters where teen mothers and their children attend. Ford Motor Company established the Ford Academy of Manufacturing Sciences at Michigan's Novi High School to prepare students for careers in manufacturing, engineering, and skilled trades.[33]

Critics of Business Educational Activities

Not everyone approves all that business is doing for education. On the one hand are those educators who resent business people "getting into our sandbox." They believe they know more about how to educate young people than people in business. On the other hand are those who not only welcome business support but hope that it will increase and intensify. We believe the latter are in a substantial majority. Richard Riley, when Secretary of Education, said "I know from my own experience (as a former governor of South Carolina) that the push and muscle of the business community is an absolute necessity to make education reform happen."[34]

Concluding Comment

The demands that corporations, especially larger ones, continue to expand their efforts to help society achieve its economic and social objectives are strong, growing, and not likely to diminish. In addition, government-mandated regulations are more likely to grow than decline. To meet these demands corporations will continue to improve social issue management in their companies.

Endnotes

1. David Packard, *The HP Way: How Bill Hewlett and I Built Our Company*, New York: Harper Business, 1995.
2. *Philanthropy Guidelines: U.S. University Equipment Grants*, Palo Alto, Calif.: Hewlett-Packard, April 1995.

3.   For specific grants see *1994 Philanthropy Annual Report*, Palo Alto, Calif.: Hewlett-Packard, February 1995.

4.   See, for example, *Issue Management Bibliography*, Leesburg, Va.: Issue Action Publications, 1995.

5.   For other illustrations, see John McCormick and Marc Levinson, "The Supply Police," *Newsweek*, February 15, 1993.

6.   David Cantor, "Mobil Goes to Bat for Birds and Bats," *Business and Society Review*, Summer 1995.

7.   Alan Reder, *In Pursuit of Principle and Profit*, New York: Putnam, 1994, pp. 125-26.

8.   For an early listing see James E. Post, *Corporate Behavior and Social Change*, Reston, Va.: Reston Publishing Company, 1978. For a later exposition of steps, see Barbara Bigelow, Liam Fahey, and John Mahon, *A Typology of Issue Evolution*, Monograph No. 5 in a Series on Issue Management, Leesburg, Va.: The Issue Exchange, circa 1995.

9.   Sinclair Lewis, *The Jungle*, Doubleday, Page, 1906.

10.   Rachel Carson, *Silent Spring*, Greenwich, Conn.: Fawcett, 1967 (paperback); first published by Houghton Mifflin, Boston, Mass., 1962.

11.   Ralph Nader, *Unsafe at Any Speed*, New York: Pocket Books, 1966.

12.   For other forces causing deviations, see John F. Mahon and Sandra Waddock, "Strategic Issues: An Integration of Issue Life Cycle Perspectives," *Business and Society*, Spring 1992.

13.   See Rogene A. Buchholz, "Adjusting Corporations to the Realities of Public Interests and Policy," in Robert L. Heath and Associates, *Strategic Issues Management*, San Francisco: Jossey-Bass, 1988.

14.   Colin Wiltshire, "Environmental Management," *Responding to Europe's Environmental Laws*, New York: The Conference Board, Report 1076, 1994.

15.   It should be noted that the nomenclature of assessments or projections of sociopolitical phenomena varies widely among academicians and practitioners. For example, scenarios have been referred to as futures research, future explorations, alternative futures, survey research scanning, exploratory planning, vision, and environmental forces.

16.   See Peter Schwartz, *The Art of the Long View*, New York: Doubleday Currency, 1991. Schwartz helped Shell establish its scenarios and this book contains a detailed series of steps in producing scenarios.

17.   For examples of many actual crises, see Ian I. Mitroff and Ralph H. Kilmann, *Corporate Tragedies: Product Tampering, Sabotage, and Other Catastrophes*, New York: Praeger, 1984; Steven Fink, *Crisis Management: Planning for the Inevitable*, New York: Amacom, 1986; and Gerald C. Meyers, *When it Hits the Fan*, Boston: Houghton Mifflin, 1986.

18.   See, for example, Judith Blumenthal, "Crisis Management in University Environments," *Journal of Management Inquiry*, vol. 4, Issue 3, September 1995.

19.   Christine M. Pearson and Ian I. Mitroff, "From Crisis Prone to Crisis Prepared: A Framework for Crisis Management," *Academy of Management Executive*, February 1993, p. 29.

20.   For other steps see Ibid, p. 58; and Ian I. Mitroff, Paul Shrivastava, and Firdaus E. Udwadia, "Effective Crisis Management," *The Academy of Management Executive*, November 1987.

21.   Morrell Heald, *The Social Responsibilities of Business: Company and Community, 1900-1960*, Cleveland, Ohio: Press of Case Western Reserve University, 1970.

22.   *A. P. Smith Manufacturing Company v. Barlow et al.*, 26 N.J. Super. 106 (1953), 98 Atl. (1962). For an excellent short article on the history of corporate philanthropy during the 1883-1953 period, see Mark Sharfman, "Changing Institutional Rules: The Evolution of Corporate Philanthropy, 1883-1953," *Business & Society*, December 1994.

23.   *Giving USA 1995: The Annual Report on Philanthropy for the Year 1994*, New York: American Association of Fund-Raising Counsel, 1995.

24.   *Corporate Contributions*, 1993, New York: The Conference Board, 1994.

25.   Craig Smith, "The New Corporate Philanthropy," *Harvard Business Review*, May-June 1994, p. 105.

26.   Ibid., p. 106.

27.   Stuart Elliott, "A Simple Yet Captivating Image in the Campaign to Curb Violence," *New York Times*, January 30, 1995. We checked with the office of Don W. Davidson, president and CEO of Gannett Outdoor Group, a leader in organizing the campaign, and confirmed that the campaign did in fact take place.

28.   Geoffrey Smith and Ron Stodgill II, "Are Good Causes Good Marketing?" *Business Week*, March 21, 1994, p. 64.

29.   Curtis G. Weeden, "How Much Should a Company Give?" *Los Angeles Times*, May 30, 1995.

30.   Telephone conversation with Richard Sabo, Assistant to the Chairman, Lincoln Electric, January 31, 1996.

31.   *CIGNA Foundation Annual Report*, 1994, Philadelphia: CIGNA Foundation, 1995, plus printed descriptions of programs.

32.   See, for example, *Business and the Schools: A Guide to Effective Programs*, 2nd ed., New York: Council for Aid to Education, 1992; Eric Wentworth, *Agents of Change: Exemplary Corporate Policies and Practices to Improve Education*, Washington, D.C.: c. 1995; and *To Make a Difference; Reinforcing the Commitment of the Insurance Industry to America's Schools*, Washington, D.C.: Center for Corporate Public Involvement, Washington, D.C., c. 1995.

33.   For a long list of programs supported or created by corporations, see Nancy J. Perry, "School Reform: Big Pain, Little Gain," *Fortune*, November 29, 1933.

34.   Quoted in Ibid, p. 131.

Chapter Nine

CONSUMERISM

Wal-Mart

Samuel Moore Walton opened a new variety merchandise store in Rogers, Arkansas, on July 2, 1962. A sign across the front said WAL-MART. On one side of the sign was "We Sell For Less." On the other was "Satisfaction Guaranteed." These two cornerstone philosophies still guide the company. Overall, there was and still is complete dedication to the consumer.

This new store began a revolution in retailing as great as that started by J. C. Penney, F. W. Woolworth, and Sears & Roebuck at the beginning of the century. Wal-Mart's sales were about $1 million the first year, compared with $2 million for another variety store in the town. But the underlying philosophies and managerial strategies developed by Sam Walton led to fabulous growth.

In 1995 total sales were over 93.6 billion and Wal-Mart became the fourth largest corporation in the United States in terms of revenues. Profits were $2.7 billion and the company had over 630,000 employees domestically. The company had outlets in every state in the United States.

In his autobiography Sam Walton succinctly stated the core philosophy of his company: ". . . the secret of successful retailing is to give your customers what they want . . . if you think about it from your point of view as a customer, you want everything: a wide assortment of good quality merchandise; the lowest possible prices; guaranteed satisfaction with what you buy; friendly, knowledgeable service; convenient hours; free parking; a pleasant shopping experience. You love it when you visit a store that somehow exceeds your expectations, and you hate it when a store inconveniences you, or

gives you a hard time, or just pretends you're invisible."[1]

Throughout the development of Wal-Mart Walton constantly traveled to visit his stores. From the beginning he flew his own airplane so he could more easily visit stores and spot new locations.

When Sam visited a store he led the following cheer:

> Give me a W!
> Give me an A!
> Give me an L!
> Give me a Squiggly!
> (Here, everybody sort of does the twist.)
> Give me an M!
> Give me an A!
> Give me an R!
> Give me a T!
> What's that spell?
> Wal-Mart!
> What's that spell?
> Wal-Mart!
> Who's No. 1?
> THE CUSTOMER.[2]

He said that because everyone worked hard there was no reason for them not to have fun, do silly things, and be cheerful. It is a sort of "whistle while you work" philosophy, he said. He and his employees (he called them "associates") did crazy things to attract the attention of customers. In 1984, for example, he promised to do the hula down Wall Street if the profits of the company rose above 8 percent. They rose 8.04 percent and he fulfilled his promise.

continued

Walton believed that everyone should share in profits, and in 1971 set up a profit-sharing plan for all associates. While he believed that profit sharing was important, he realized that much more was needed to motivate people. One of his rules was to think constantly, each day, of ways and means to motivate and challenge his associates. He believed that it was important to communicate with them everything that was important, including most of the numbers about the business. He listened to them because he said they were on the firing line and had much to contribute to making the company a success. He constantly sought to have everyone think small, to avoid creating a huge bureaucracy, to ignore conventional wisdom, to remember always that the associates were small-town merchants and that the company was built store by store. Above all, he wanted everyone to strive to exceed the expectations of the customers.

For years before his death on April 5, 1992, Sam Walton was hailed as a genius, a hero, the epitome of entrepreneurship, who brought good merchandise at low prices to locations neglected by large discounters. President Bush awarded him the nation's highest civil tribute, the Medal of Freedom, for his accomplishments. But he was not universally loved.

James McConkey was forced to close his hardware store in Albany, Missouri, population 2,100. On Christmas Eve 1985 he looked at his stock of brand-new bicycles and the appliances filling his shelves. His store and downtown Albany were festooned in Christmas decorations. All was festive except for one thing: there were no customers. They all were at a Wal-Mart store in Maryville, population 9,500, and 34 miles west of Albany.[3]

This is a typical experience for merchants in small towns located near Wal-Mart stores. The only way they can compete is to find a niche not served by Wal-Mart and exploit it. That, however, is very difficult for the typical small-town merchant. Wal-Mart not only has changed the facade of commercial areas in many small towns, but in the process has ended a way of life in the towns.

Observers maintain that Wal-Mart cannot be blamed as the sole cause of change in small-town business. Many other factors have been at work and Wal-Mart has merely speeded the process that began in the 1950s.

On the other hand, Wal-Mart has had beneficial impacts on small towns. Professor Kenneth Stone of Iowa State University, who has studied the Wal-Mart influence on small towns, concludes that most of the merchants who have survived the competition of Wal-Mart are doing more business than before because of the attraction of Wal-Mart.[4]

Sam Walton commented on this point in his autobiography. "Of all the notions I've heard about Wal-Mart, none has ever baffled me more than this idea that we are somehow the enemy of small-town America. Nothing could be further from the truth: Wal-Mart has actually kept quite a number of small towns from becoming practically extinct by offering low prices and saving literally billions of dollars for the people who live there, as well as creating hundreds of thousands of jobs in our stores."[5]

The story of Wal-Mart serves as a fitting backdrop for this chapter. The consumer movement has certainly undergone significant changes in the past twenty-five to thirty years.

The Consumer Movement

Consumerism is a movement to improve the rights and powers of consumers in relation to the sellers of products and services. It is also a protest movement of consumers against what they or their advocates see as unfair, discriminatory, and arbitrary treatment. There is nothing new about the idea of consumerism. It is as old as business. Indeed, many current consumer issues are similar to those which existed in the Civil War and beyond. The current consumer movement began in the mid-1960s but its momentum has diminished over the past fifteen years. The current movement differs from the past in the intensity with which it has been pursued and the unprecedented volume and detail of state and federal legislation it has produced.

Its beginning was a special message from President Kennedy to Congress on March 15, 1962. In that message President Kennedy said that consumers had certain rights and that these rights had been violated. These included the rights to make intelligent choices among products and services; to have access to accurate information; to register complaints and be heard; to be offered fair prices and acceptable quality; to have safe and healthful products; and to receive adequate service.

President Kennedy's message, called by some the *magna carta* of consumers, reflected widespread consumer discontent at the time, a discontent that still exists despite the expansive protections in recent legislation. It seems paradoxical that the American consumer is the envy of the world for the quality and abundance of the products and services he or she consumes, and yet is dissatisfied with those products and services. Why the paradox? There are many explanations.

This is an age of discontent, of skepticism, and of challenge to authority. Today's consumers are better educated than those of the past, and they challenge practices that previous generations bore in silence. They question the authority of the uncontrolled marketplace. This is an age, too, of vocal expression of discontent; and consumers, fed up with actual or perceived bad treatment at the hands of manufacturers, advertisers, merchants, and repair services, are voicing their complaints.

Are complaints justified? Every consumer would say yes, because every consumer has been frustrated with a variety of consumption problems. Business people, however, claim that dissatisfied consumers represent only a small fraction of the total. Nevertheless, people in business have become much more conscious of consumers and the importance of focusing attention on them. In *The Practice of Management*, Peter Drucker wrote thirty years ago, "There is only one valid definition of business purpose: *to create a customer*. . . . It is the customer who determines what a business is. . . . The customer is the foundation of a business and keeps it in existence."[6] This idea was not generally translated into practice and it remained for Peters and Waterman in a best-selling business book *In Search of Excellence*, written in 1982, to highlight for business the importance of focusing attention on consumers. They pointed out that the most profitable companies give primary attention to customers.[7] This book galvanized widespread managerial thinking and action about the importance of consumers as major stakeholders.

Momentum of the Consumer Movement

In the 1960s and 1970s one piece of major consumer legislation after another passed in Congress. The Bush administration was somewhat more sympathetic to consumer legislation and some new legislation was passed. The Clinton administration has been in favor of fully implementing legislation already passed and has supported some new legislation, but Republicans in Congress are currently seeking to remove some consumer protections, such as limiting punitive damage awards, and to curtail the aggressive implementation of legislative enactments. In the meantime, of course, state and local governments have differed much in the passage and implementation of consumer protections. But the broad thrust is strengthening the consumer's shield against abusive business practices.

Consumer Advocates

One phenomenon of today's consumerism, in contrast with that of the past, is the rise and influence of consumer advocates. These self-appointed promoters of the consumer are numerous.

Probably the most publicized and highly influential is Ralph Nader. His role has been partly like that of the muckrakers of the past. But it goes much further, to active representation of the consumer in the courts, government agencies, legislatures, and corporations. Nader has been fiercely attacked by businesspeople, many of whom consider him a dangerous radical. Some businesspeople view Nader as being obsessed with what he considers business abuses of the public and as pursuing a vendetta against business. Most people, however, including many businesspeople, believe he has sought to achieve his objectives through, not against, our legal and political systems. They see his motivation as reform of the system to benefit consumers. Many observers believe he has distorted or exaggerated facts in numerous cases, but others believe his work has resulted in needed legislation.

Nader graduated cum laude from Princeton and then got a law degree at Harvard Law School in 1958. His first major move into consumerism was in 1965 with the publication of his book *Unsafe at Any Speed*.[8] This book dealt with what he called dangerous designs in American cars, especially General Motors' Corvair. General Motors hired private investigators to seek evidence to discredit Nader but instead faced a lawsuit for invasion of privacy which the company settled in 1970 for $425,000. This money provided the financial support for Nader's Center for the Study of Responsive Law, which he started in 1968.

Over the years Nader has built a network of more than sixty groups and employed thousands of people to push for legislation to protect consumers. In 1971 Nader founded Public Citizen, his umbrella organization. Under it are twenty non-profit organizations, in which he has varying degrees of control, such as the Health Research Group, Citizen Action Group, Congress Watch, Tax Reform Research Group, and Litigation Group.

In 1978 Nader and a coalition of consumer activists lobbied to create a cabinet-level department in the federal government to protect consumer rights. They failed, but Nader has been influential in the passage of many other significant statutes. For example, he was instrumental in the creation of the National Highway Traffic Safety Administration, the Consumer Product Safety Commission, and passage of the Freedom of Information Act. His groups have provided legal services to those who could not afford legal council, fought for endangered species, alerted consumers to potential hazards in medical devices and drugs, fought for lower prices of drugs, and pushed for warning labels on dangerous products, to mention just a few activities.

Nader's influence has been waning in recent years. This may be due to the fact that he is a victim of his own success. As he says, "Our success has made corporations smarter and tougher."[9] Clearly, Congress in the past twenty-five years has established formidable protections for consumers in major areas and that does not leave as much to be done. The success of the Republicans in gaining control of both houses of Congress and their commitment to reforming the federal regulatory process has also slowed the consumer movement.

There are many other important consumer advocacy groups. To mention a few, the Consumer Federation of America, founded in 1967, brings together about 200 organizations (mostly state and local) with consumer interests. This organization represents over 30 million people. Consumers Union, founded in 1936, is basically an organization that disseminates information to consumers, especially through its magazine Consumer Reports. A few others whose names indicate their activities are Accuracy in Media, Action on Smoking and Health, Advocates for Highway & Auto Safety, American Heart Association, Citizens for Reliable & Safe Highways, Citizens for a Tobacco-Free Society, Friends of the Earth, National Citizens' Coalition for Nursing Home Reform, and Public Voice for Food and Health Policy.

Fundamentally, consumer advocates are reformists. On balance, they probably have served the best interests of consumers, business, and the community. However, many of them are polemicists, and their "factual" assertions, arguments, and policy recommendations must be examined critically in that light.

Business Oriented Interest Groups and Organizations

To round out the picture of the interest groups that address consumer issues, we should mention many groups inside and outside of business organizations that have responded to consumer advocates, sometimes positively and sometimes negatively, and also have initiated programs in the interests of consumers. For example, business organizations such as the U.S. Chamber of Commerce, the National Association of Manufacturers, and the Business Roundtable vigorously advance the business point of view, especially in legislative debates.

The Consumer's Protective Shield

Today there is a massive statutory shield to protect consumers from abuses, real and imagined, from the operation of the free competitive market. In this book we have dealt mostly with federal regulations but there are other significant protections. A primary one is the legal system which we will discuss later in the chapter. Every state and local government has extensive laws to protect consumers ranging from uniform electrical connections to fraudulent billing. An important protection exists in the dissemination of information in the mass media and the growth of investigative reporting.

Well over fifty federal agencies and bureaus are directly active in consumer affairs. The six most important ones are the Federal Trade Commission (FTC), the Consumer Product Safety Commission (CPSC), the National Highway Traffic Safety Administration (NHTSA), the Food and Drug Administration (FDA), the Food Safety and Quality Service (FSQS) of the Department of Agriculture, and the Environmental Protection Agency (EPA). We shall discuss briefly activities of the first five in this chapter. This list of agencies might well include the Securities and Exchange Commission (SEC), which protects investors; the Department of Energy, which is concerned with nuclear waste hazards; and the Federal Deposit Insurance Corporation (FDIC), which protects depositors of financial institutions.

Consumer Product Issues and Decision Making

Before discussing specific consumer issues it is instructive to comment on the cost-price-quality questions that arise in both business and governmental decision making about products and services. Generally speaking, the decision making processes in business involve many complex trade-offs among various forces. For example, product quality is one variable in decisions concerning a product. The higher the quality sought, the higher the price that must be charged. The higher the price, the lower will be the demand for the product. The lower the demand, the fewer products will be produced. If more products are produced, the cost per unit can be reduced. At what point do price, potential sales, quality, product design, and other factors balance? Balancing such factors is an extremely intricate process for which there usually is no formula to produce the decision. Human judgment is an essential and generally final, determinant of a decision. This concept of trade-offs is very important in appraising the managerial response to consumerism.

Highly relevant in this discussion is a point made previously that government regulatory standards set without any reference to costs can be extremely and unnecessarily expensive to the general public. It seems that a sensible approach to regulation is to weigh the costs and benefits of a proposed regulation to determine whether the equation is balanced properly. Although a final standard may not be determined by the cost-benefit equation, the method raises appropriate questions about a proposed standard. In government, as in business, decision makers must consider and balance a multiplicity of factors.

Federal Consumer Protections of Three Agencies

Before discussing significant consumer issues, it is useful to summarize the scope of activity of three dominant consumer protective agencies. They are the CPSC, NHTSA, and FDA.

Consumer Product Safety Commission (CPSC)

This agency is directed by six major pieces of legislation. These laws mandate it to:

1. Protect the public against unreasonable risks of injury and death associated with consumer products.
2. Assist consumers to evaluate the comparative safety of products.
3. Develop uniform safety standards for consumer products and minimize conflicting state and local regulations.
4. Promote research and investigations into the causes and prevention of product-related deaths, illnesses, and injuries.

This is a formidable charge. The CPSC regulates every consumer product except guns, boats, planes, cars, trucks, foods, drugs, cosmetics, tobacco, and pesticides, which are in the province of other government agencies. Even with these exclusions, the agency's mandate is enormous, since it must oversee 15,000 classes of products, work with thousands of manufacturers, and address the complaints of millions of consumers.

Unfortunately, from the creation of the CPSC in 1972 the agency has faced serious barriers in achieving its mandated goals. While it was the Nixon administration that gave birth to the agency, the political environment was difficult. The agency became embroiled in political battles in both the Ford and Carter administrations. President Reagan wanted to abolish it but could not. Instead he drastically cut its budget. Currently the agency is threatened with substantial budgetary cuts by the Republican-controlled Congress. So, lack of resources will likely continue to hamper the operations of the agency.

By far, most of the activity of the agency concerns the development with industry of voluntary safety standards. For example, the commission has worked with manufacturers to set specific standards for bicycles, bunk beds, toys, lawn mowers, cigarette lighters, swimming pool covers, spas, and thousands of other products. The commission has also set limits on the amount of chemicals in products, such as methylene chloride in paint strippers, paint thinners, spray paints, and adhesive removers.

The Commission has banned products that do not meet specified standards. Examples include hazardous toys, charcoal lighter fluid, bicycles, and lawn darts. The Commission has initiated recalls of products including playground equipment, toys using lead paint, and children's furniture. Toys and children's products are a prime concern of the Commission. Other product categories in which recalls were made include home electrical appliances, gas furnaces, fireworks, and smoke detectors. In addition, imported products are inspected and some have been detained. They include mostly toys, fireworks, bicycles, and children's sleepwear.[10]

An agency with such a broad mandate, limited resources, and political embroilment has attracted many critics. Critics claim that the agency relies too much on voluntary agreements and industry self-policing. They argue that the recall program should be severely cut back or stopped because the agency expends too many resources on the program, costs to manufacturers are substantial, and the program saves few lives. They say that it would be much better if the agency spent its money on informing consumers about product safety rather than on regulating the products themselves.[11] Of course, these are debatable propositions.

National Highway Traffic Safety Administration (NHTSA)

This agency has authority to:

1. Mandate minimum safety standards for automobiles, trucks, and their accessories.
2. Establish fuel economy standards.
3. Administer state and community highway safety grant programs.
4. Conduct research, development, and demonstration of new vehicle safety techniques.

The agency has initiated many automobile safety features. A short list of programs to protect occupants would include air bags, safety belts, energy absorbing or collapsible steering columns, penetration-resistant windshields, recessed door handles, breakaway rearview mirrors, padded dashboards, crushable front ends, passenger compartment designs to resist crushing, and tire standards. The agency can order recall of defective products.

Automobile companies have complained about the costs of many of the agency's mandates, but there is no doubt that the regulations have saved thousands of lives. Some critics claim that some of the programs cost too much and that less expensive alternatives exist for saving lives, such as better lighting on highways, limiting highway speeds, installing breakaway traffic lights and signs, padding abutments, and so on.

The Food and Drug Administration (FDA)

This agency operates on the basis of no less than twenty-six major legislative enactments which include its original legislation, the Food and Drug Act of 1906, and amendments. For example, the original legislation, gives it power to regulate in interstate commerce misbranded and adulterated foods, drinks, and drugs; the Public Health Service Act of 1944 gives it authority to ensure safety, purity, and potency of vaccines, blood, serum, and other biological products; the Nutrition Labeling and Education Act of 1990 mandates the agency to develop uniform nutrition labeling on packaged food items; and the Generic Drug Enforcement Act of 1992 permits it to oversee the generic drug industry.[12]

The FDA is a tenacious watchdog of the public health whose jurisdiction ranges over an estimated $1 trillion of products from breast implants to orange juice. In one ten-day period in December 1995 the FDA ". . . approved a new AIDS drug, issued new rules on seafood safety, approved the first treatment for Lou Gehrig's disease and banned nighttime laser shows in Las Vegas."[13] Despite an outpouring of actions to protect consumers the agency has been severely criticized by consumers, economists, politicians, and others[14] for being too slow in granting approval for new drugs and medical devices. FDA Commissioner David Kessler responds that the agency now takes about nineteen months to approve a new drug compared with thirty-three months in 1987. Kessler comments that people want new drugs in a hurry but if anything goes wrong they blame the FDA for moving too fast.

The agency periodically becomes a highly publicized target for specific issues. Such is the case with nicotine in tobacco. The agency currently is determining whether nicotine is a drug. If it is so determined the agency has a mandated responsibility to control it. Legally, the FDA apparently has the power to declare nicotine a drug, but to do so will subject the agency to a thicket of powerful opposition in Congress and among a large segment of the population.[15]

Risk and Product Safety

The FDA, like other consumer protection agencies, faces enormously difficult questions. Where is the balance between accepting a new technology and protecting the consumer? At what point does the benefit of a regulation equal the cost burden on the public? How safe is safe enough? How much risk should consumers be expected to assume? What is the role of government in balancing risk, safety, and other considerations in consumer protection? One might oversimplify by saying that the moment one jumps out of bed in the morning, one assumes risk and faces product safety questions. Chlorine can react with organic matter in drinking water to produce carcinogens. Stored peanuts can develop a mold that produces a potent carcinogen named aflatoxin. Aspirin is safe and therapeutic when properly used, but when used improperly it can kill.

"Too safe" may involve costs so high that consumers cannot buy the product; "too unsafe" causes needless injuries and loss of lives. Acceptable risks must be tolerated. But what are such risks? What is a minimum risk? Can a $20 power tool be expected to be as safe as a $500 one? Are products supposed to be safe even when used by boobs and idiots?

There are no general measures of minimally safe levels of many environmental substances. Much the same thing can be said for risks in product use.

Yet regulatory agencies of necessity have had to address the question: What is a "reasonable" risk? Alfred Edwards defined a reasonable risk

> as one where a consumer (a) understands by way of adequate warning or by way of public knowledge that a risk is associated with the product; (b) understands the probability of occurrence of an injury; (c) understands the potential seventy of such an injury; (d) has been told how to cope with the risk; (e) cannot obtain the same benefits in less risky ways at the same or less cost; (f) would not, if given a choice, pay additional cost to eliminate or reduce the danger; and (g) voluntarily accepts the risk to get the benefits of the product.[16]

These are lofty but useful generalizations. Still, how is a reasonable risk established for a particular product? How does one calculate risks of safety for a large commercial aircraft with its thousands of parts, or for the space shuttle? How far should an agency go in protecting consumers from specific product hazards? How far should the CPSC go, for example, in protecting consumers from hazards associated with electric lawn mowers? How far should NHTSA go in trying to protect drivers of automobiles?

The following discussion illustrates a few of the complex difficulties in resolving product risk and safety issues.

Food Safety

We probably have the world's safest food supply. Food is relatively cheap, plentiful, and wholesome. But is it safe enough? Various studies have estimated that thousands of lives are lost and millions of illnesses created by food borne diseases. The cost of this is estimated to be in the tens of billions of dollars.[17]

We have a complex array of laws to protect our food supply. Twelve major agencies have responsibility in this area but the most important lies with the FDA, the Department of Agriculture, and the EPA. The FDA has responsibility for the safety of food additives, food processing, food labeling, and fish and seafood inspection. The Food Safety Inspection Service of the USDA has responsibility over meat, poultry, and egg inspection. The EPA has authority over pesticides.

Despite this comprehensive attention, there are important questions about the safety of our food supply. We here address two: issues surrounding food additives and the question of "how safe is safe."

The Delaney Clause and Food Additives

The Delaney clause is one of the most stringent and controversial laws in the area of consumer protections. This clause, a 1958 amendment to the Food, Drug, and Cosmetic Act of 1938, allows no flexibility in its prohibition against the addition to food of any substance known to produce cancer in any species, in any dosage, and under any circumstances. Applying this clause has raised enormous administrative problems but efforts to alter it have been stopped in Congress and in the courts.

The first major ruling under this clause was the decision by the Secretary of Health, Education, and Welfare to remove from the market after January 1, 1970, all cyclamate-sweetened soft drinks and soft-drink mixes. This ruling was made on the basis of research showing that six of twelve rats that were given the equivalent of fifty times maximum recommended lifetime daily consumption developed an "unusual" form of bladder cancer. (For a person to ingest as much cyclamate as the rats, it would be necessary to drink several cases of cyclamate-sweetened soft drinks every day for most of a normal human life span!) Since this decision was made, a number of other products have been removed from the market because of similar tests on laboratory animals.

One can expect continuing controversy over the Delaney clause. The FDA has primary responsibility for food safety with respect to 2,700 "direct" food additives, thirty-three color additives, and thousands more indirect additives that may get into foods through ingredients in packaging materials. The issue therefore is not a negligible one.

This point is confirmed by the fact that the Delaney clause has proved to be an open invitation for ingenious toxicologists to find cause for outlawing even the most innocuous substances. For example, experimentalists have created tumors with hundreds of common food substances, from eggs to salt. New instruments are capable of detecting traces of substances at the level of one part in a trillion. "The result," says one observer,

> is that almost everything anyone eats can be shown to contain carcinogens. If, for instance, a tin can is soldered, and if the solder contains lead, and if lead is a carcinogen in test animals, and if detectable traces of it migrate into the contents of the can—all of which is indisputably the case—why, then, the FDA can be accused of being less than diligent if it doesn't outlaw tin cans.[18]

The FDA has sought to avoid banning substances that were in minuscule quantities in foods and that cause no harm. A door was opened for the agency in 1979 by the U.S. Court of Appeals for the District of Columbia Circuit in *Monsanto Company v. Kennedy.*[19] The court said: "There is latitude inherent in the statutory scheme to avoid literal application of the statutory definition of 'food additive' in those *de minimus* situations that, in the informed judgment of the Commissioner, clearly present no public health or safety concerns." Thus, under the de minimus legal doctrine, the FDA might know that a substance was present in a food but disregard it. (The de minimus doctrine means that the law does not concern itself with trifles.)

In 1986 the U.S. Supreme Court (in an 8 to 1 decision) upheld FDA authority to establish minimum standards for poisonous and deleterious substances in food when the public health was protected. In this case, the FDA authorized the shipment of a harvest of corn to be used for livestock and poultry feed so long as aflatoxin in the grain did not exceed 100 parts per billion. Aflatoxin is a potent carcinogen, but the FDA said that in the small quantities allowed it was not injurious to public health.[20]

Then in 1993 the U.S. Supreme Court affirmed a decision by the U.S. 9th Circuit Court of Appeals that reaffirmed the strict language of the Delaney clause. In this case, the EPA under authority granted to it in the Federal Insecticide, Fungicide, and Rodenticide Act of 1947 permitted the use of four pesticides as food additives although they had been found by the agency in 1988 to induce cancer. (The pesticides were benomyl, mancozeb, phosmet, and trifluralin.) The EPA said the four were permitted on the grounds that the cancer risk they posed was de minimus.

The court applied the Delaney clause to the EPA decision and prohibited the EPA to allow the use of the pesticides. The court stated: "The language [of the Delaney clause] is clear and mandatory. . . . The statute provides that once the finding of carcinogenicity is made, the EPA has no discretion." The court explained, "Congress intended the very rigidity that the language it chose commands." Later in the decision the court said: "The EPA in effect asks us to approve what it deems to be a more enlightened system than that which Congress established. . . . Revising the existing statutory scheme, however, is neither our function nor the function of the EPA. . . . If there is to be a change it is for Congress to direct."[21]

Here is a case, of course, where two legislative enactments overlap. The decision can be applied to many other pesticides that cause cancer, but when used in very small quantities pose no threat to humans. There have been repeated efforts by opponents of the Delaney clause and the pesticide prohibitions of the Federal Insecticide, Fungicide, and Rodenticide Act to get Congress to repeal and modify them, but to no avail. The Clinton administration advanced a proposal in a pesticide reform package which would abolish the Delaney clause and in its place permit the use of pesticide residues when it is estimated that the cancer risk is no more than 1 in 1 million. This proposition got nowhere.[22]

How Safe Is Safe?

How safe is food? Most scientists believe that the cancer threat from pesticides is minuscule compared with risks of smoking, drinking chloroform in ordinary tap water, or eating natural substances in foods. However, there are enough uncertainties about what is known about pesticides and other food hazards, as well as what happens in the processing and distribution of foods, to raise questions about the adequacy of current regulations and practices. This subject is far too big and complex to be treated here, but a few comments are appropriate.

The case of Alar, a chemical used to regulate the growth of some red apples, illustrates a worrisome type of consumer problem. In late February 1989, a public interest group published a report that said schoolchildren faced serious risks from eating chemically treated apples and apple products. The story was aired on talk shows and in the newspapers. Immediately, school boards removed apples from school lunches, grocery stores stopped selling apples, sales of apples and apple juice plummeted, and the FDA and EPA were accused of failure to stop the use of Alar.

The scientific community almost unanimously said the risks of cancer from eating apples treated with Alar were virtually nil. An ad hoc group of fourteen prominent scientists called the risks from approved agricultural chemicals negligible or nonexistent and said flatly that the "public's perception of pesticide residues and their effects on the safety of the food supply differs considerably from the facts."[23] The fact is that Alar does produce a possible carcinogen (daminozide), but in minute quantities. Anyway, only 5 to 10 percent of apple orchards were treated with Alar at the time.

A troubling aspect of the Alar incident is that a complicated scientific issue was decided by individuals throughout the country rather than by officials charged with the responsibility for determining what should and should not be tolerated in foods. The case was decided not upon any hard evidence but by a frightened public acting on incorrect media reports. Professor Bruce Ames, chairman of the biochemistry department at the

University of California, Berkeley, tells us that many foods contain natural toxins at much higher levels than residues of dangerous pesticides. Fruits and vegetables produce such substance, he says, to repel insects, fungi, and other predators. Ames points out that up to 10 percent of a plant's weight is made up of natural pesticides. The ordinary potato contains 150 chemicals before it is sprayed with pesticides. Most scientists affirm that by the time a food gets to the market, very little pesticide residue remains.[24]

Nevertheless, there are troubling aspects to potential hazards of contaminants in the food supply. For example, there are thousands of chemicals, animal drugs, and microbiological organisms in food, some of which may be dangerous to human beings. But which ones, and how dangerous? Identifying and testing them is a gigantic task which has only partly been accomplished. Critics point to the fact that restrictions in foreign countries on the use of pesticides and additives are not as strong as in this country, and we import as much as 25 percent of our fruit and vegetables. Little of this produce is tested when it arrives on our shores. Critics also claim that the EPA has no way to measure the combined effects on humans of ingesting many different pesticides. A significant concern of the FDA is the growing microbiological contamination of food.

This area swirls with controversy among scientists. This is partly because not nearly enough is known about linkages between cancer and human health with specific food contaminants, the degree of dosages which human beings can tolerate, and the value of feeding animals huge amounts of chemicals to determine risks to humans.

Products Liability Law

Consumers have legal recourse to compensation for injury of person, property, or reputation by individuals or corporations. This includes, of course, automobile accidents, medical malpractice, professional malpractice, products liability, and so on. One area of special concern is products liability, especially punitive damages, so we briefly discuss this area here.

For most of our history consumers had little recourse in being compensated for defective products. Today, however, manufacturers or other sellers of products can be held liable for defective products under three fundamental theories of law, namely, negligence, strict liability, and breach of warranty.

Negligence

Under this theory, manufacturers have an obligation to do what a reasonable person could be expected to do. Not only the manufacturer but all those in the stream of events leading to the final sale to a customer must exercise reasonable care. They can be held liable today even for injury resulting from unintended but reasonably foreseeable misuse.

Years ago an injured plaintiff was seldom able to collect damages. He or she faced legal barriers that protected the manufacturer and everyone in the chain of distribution up to the consumer.

This legal protective wall for manufacturers was broken by the milestone case of *McPherson v. Buick Motor Company*, in 1916.[25] McPherson was injured when a wooden spoke in a wheel of his Buick collapsed and he was injured. General Motors claimed that the car was bought from a dealer and the company had no liability. The court disagreed and said the company was negligent in not properly inspecting the wheel. Furthermore, said the court, General Motors was responsible irrespective of who was in the chain of events prior to the sale.

This legal philosophy has been vastly stretched in subsequent decisions. For example, General Motors was held responsible by the court for designing products that minimized risks in collisions. If it did not do so it was liable for damages.[26] The New Jersey Supreme Court said in effect that the manufacturer had the responsibility for warning of dangers that were not only undiscovered but scientifically undiscoverable at the time the products were first introduced for use in the workplace.[27] This is a puzzling rule for a company to follow. However, it may provide major protection for injured consumers, as it did for workers injured by inhaling asbestos.

Warranties

A manufacturer or seller can be held liable for a breach of warranty, either explicit or implied. An express warranty is an explicit claim made by the manufacturer to the seller. It can be stated on a card or on labels, packages, or advertising. The Magnuson-Moss Warranty Improvement Act of 1974 sets forth federal standards for written consumer product warranties.

When a product is sold there is an automatic implied warranty that the product is for the ordinary use to which it is likely to be used. The landmark case about implied warranties is *Henning v. Bloomfield Motors, Inc.*[28] In this case Claus Henning bought a Plymouth automobile. A few days after purchase, the steering mechanism failed and his wife, who was driving, crashed the car and was injured. The dealer and the company claimed that when the purchase contract was approved by Henning he had signed a disclaimer appearing on the back of the contract. (Included in eight inches of fine print was a sentence saying there was agreement that there were no warranties express or implied by either the dealer or the manufacturer on the vehicle or its parts.) The court said the automobile company was legally responsible for making cars good enough to serve the purpose for which they were intended.

Strict Liability

This legal weapon makes it possible for injured consumers to hold all those in the chain of distribution responsible for defective products. This theory puts the focus on the product, not the reasonableness of the producer or seller. A manufacturer can be held liable for any defects arising from deviation from the producer's standards. If there are no defects in the design of the product but the product is inherently dangerous, a producer will be held liable for injury if customers are not properly warned about its use.

A landmark case in the development of strict liability was *Greenman v. Yuba Power Products, Inc.*[29] The court said that "a manufacturer is strictly liable when an article he places on the market, knowing that it will be used without inspection, proves to have a defect that causes injury to a human being."

The scope of liability was further broadened by a concept of "joint-and-several liability." It works this way. The driver of a bumper car at Disney World was injured when her car was struck by the bumper car driven by her fiancé. The jury found the fiancé 85 percent responsible for the injury, the plaintiff 14 percent responsible, and Disney World 1 percent responsible. Later, but before the trial, the plaintiff married her fiancé. Under Florida law the husband was immune from suit by the wife. As a result, Disney World had to pay for all of the damages not attributable to the plaintiff.[30]

Pressures to Reform Products Liability Law

A number of forces joined with an expansion of the legal doctrine of strict liability to generate a rapid growth of product liability suits. Among them have been the aggressiveness of some trial lawyers in pressuring consumers to bring suit, the development of more complicated products, and the feeling that if anyone is injured by a product she or he deserves to be paid for damages incurred. In addition juries have become more willing to punish manufacturers with punitive damage awards when they perceive outrageous wrongdoing.[31]

Trends in Product Liability Cases

Studies show no major increases or decreases in either civil products liability suits or punitive damage awards in recent years. The trend for both the number of products liability suits and the dollar totals of punitive damages have been slightly down in the 1990s compared with the 1980s.[32] A large number of products liability suits and awards have been associated with asbestos, the Dalkon Shield, and more recently silicon-gel breast implants. A large number of products liability cases are settled out of court but no one knows how many.

Punitive awards capture public attention because some of them are spectacular. For example, in November 1995, a state court jury in Indianapolis awarded $62.4 million in damages against the Ford Motor Co. because two teenagers were injured in the rollover accident of a Ford Bronco. In September 1994, an Alaskan jury hit Exxon with the largest jury punitive damage award in history of $5 billion for the damages caused by the 11-million-gallon oil spill of the *Exxon Valdez* in Prince William Sound in 1989.

Such huge punitive damage awards are very few, and rare, relative to the total number of products liability suits with average punitive damage awards that are not large. For example, in San Francisco the average was $97,000 during 1990 to 1994; but the maximum was $12 million.[33] Because of appellate court action or settlement both compensation and punitive awards are usually substantially reduced by judges.

Business Wants Products Liability Reform

The business community, stung by increased liability suits, rising liability insurance costs, differing state liability laws, and high-profile business bankruptcies because of products liability awards (e.g., Dow Corning, A. H. Robins, and Manville), has for years pressed Congress to reform and make uniform the nation's products liability standards. Opponents of congressional action have been powerful consumer groups, plaintiffs' lawyers, and some conservative thinkers.

The business community seeks a number of reforms. First, business wants Congress to pass legislation that will establish uniform liability standards across the states. Second, business wants to eliminate a manufacturers' liability when products made today may cause injuries in the future that cannot be determined today. Third, business wants reform of strict liability to shift the burden of proof to consumers rather than the current system where manufacturers must prove that they were not negligent. Fourth, business wants a cap on total punitive awards. Fifth, business wants to eliminate joint-and-several liability. Finally, business wants judges to determine punitive damages, not juries. This is because judges award lower punitive damages than juries.

Congressional Action

Congress has not yet responded to business demands for reform. But, one of the major goals of conservative Republicans in Congress is reform of products liability law. Comprehensive bills have been passed in both the House and the Senate, but problems in reconciliation have delayed final passage. Among other things, these bills would provide uniform standards that would supersede state laws with respect to limits on punitive damages, strict liability, joint-and-several liability, a cap on punitive damages, and degree of fault of manufacturers. For example, the House bill caps punitive damages at three times the sum of compensatory and pain-and-suffering damages. The Senate cap is two times.

In the meantime, President Clinton signed into law the General Aviation Recovery Act, which limits the products liability claims against small aircraft producers. As a result, insurance liability costs have been reduced for manufacturers and production of small aircraft, which had been in decline, now has revived.

Impact of Products Liability on Business

The impact of the current status of products liability law varies much among companies. Most companies are concerned about the possibility of large liability awards. Some companies have dropped products because of the fear of liability. In this class are football helmets and off-road vehicles. Many companies try to settle suits by out-of-court settlements, a practice which has grown in recent years. Arbitration, in which both parties to a dispute accept an arbitrator to decide competing claims, is also a much-used alternative. Probably the most significant alternative has been improvement in the quality of products in order to compete better in domestic and global markets, avoid liability suits, and limit the chances that a federal regulatory agency will order a product's recall. A significant impact, of course, is increasing pressure by business interests to get Congress and state legislatures to pass laws limiting products liability suits and awards. They have been successful among the states where joint-and-several liability has been narrowed, punitive damages reduced, and attorneys penalized for bringing frivolous suits to court, but, as noted, not yet in the Congress.

False and Deceptive Advertising

Advertising is ubiquitous. We cannot escape it on TV, in the media, on billboards, and on packaging. Tens of billions of dollars are spent each year to advertise consumer products. A number of federal and state agencies protect consumers against abuses in advertising. The dominant ones are the FTC and the USDA.

Fundamentally, the purposes of advertising are to make the consumer aware of a product or service, inform the customer of its characteristics, and then persuade the customer to buy it. A wide range of policy issues flow from this simple purpose. For example, what should consumers be told about product contents, use, maintenance requirements, and warranties? What is the impact of advertising on social values? How should products be advertised? How far should government go in regulating advertising?

These are significant issues but space limitations permit us to discuss only false and deceptive advertising to illustrate but one dimension of social issues. Advertising is false when its claims are explicitly, literally untrue. Some years ago the Kenmore dishwasher was advertised to completely clean dishes, pots, and pans "without prior rinsing or scraping." This was found to be utterly false by the FTC.[34] But, advertising can be explicitly true and produce false meanings. The result is deceptive advertising. One is reminded of words attributed to Mark Twain: "When in doubt, tell the truth, it will amaze most people, delight your friends, and confuse your enemies." American advertisers apparently have not heard or been convinced of Twain's recommendations.

Federal Trade Commission Guidelines

Advertisers today employ a wide range of deceptive practices. Here are a few illustrations of rulings of the FTC concerning false and deceptive advertising.

An advertisement for a medicine that offers relief for a symptom is unlawful if it implies an ultimate cure for an illness. Warner-Lambert asserted that its Listerine mouthwash helped prevent colds and sore throats. The advertising also used such phrases as "for colds," "kills germs by the millions," and "those (colds) we catch don't seem to last as long" when Listerine mouthwash was used. The FTC said that this falsely implied that the mouthwash "will cure colds," which simply is not so.[35]

Significant implications in advertising are unlawful when they cannot be substantiated. General Foods Corporation had to stop advertising Gainesburgers as having all the milk protein a dog needs. Dogs, said the FTC, have no special need for milk.[36]

If a product is contrasted with another and the implication made is untrue, the FTC says this is contrary to its guidelines. Thus, when Aspercreme was compared to oral aspirin in advertisements, the implication was that Aspercreme is aspirin in cream form, according to the FTC. The advertisement was stopped. The FTC held that the advertisement had no express representation that Aspercreme contained aspirin, but the words left the false impression that the cream did in fact contain aspirin.[37]

On the other hand, the FTC accepts certain types of puffery. The agency will not stop puffery when exaggeration appears obvious. Thus, "Coke is the real thing" or "Mac's hamburgers are the best in town" is accepted. But if the advertisement says "the lowest prices in town," the FTC wants solid evidence that this statement is true. Otherwise it is unlawful.

This is a small sample of a long list of guidelines that the agency has established over the years. Other guidelines have been set for the use of endorsements and testimonials, deceptive pricing, the use of the word "free" and similar representations, allowances and other merchandising payments and services, private vocational and home-study school product guarantees, and bait-and-switch advertising (that which is offered to get the consumer to buy something else).

Most deceptive advertising is for product brands. The reason for this, says Ivan L. Preston is that ". . . brands in many product categories have no natural physical differences. The resulting desire to make up differences is what prompts deceptiveness and is the primary engine that runs it."[38]

States Move Aggressively

States have been more active in recent years than the federal government in this area. The attorneys general in the states have been unhappy with what they call Washington's laissez-faire approach to advertising regulation, a condition of the last fifteen years. As a result they have become more aggressive in bringing multistate lawsuits against large national advertisers and have prepared their own guidelines to fill what they say is a federal void in prosecuting false and deceptive advertising.

For example, in 1987 Procter & Gamble agreed to pay the state of California $350,000 because the state said that during the test marketing of Citrus Hill Plus Calcium orange- and grapefruit-juice beverages, these products were promoted as "juices" when they each contained only 60 percent real juice. The state of New York and Kellogg Company recently reached an agreement over the company's Rice Krispies cereal advertisements that claimed the food had "more energy-releasing B vitamins than ever" and as part of a good breakfast could "help give you some get up and go." The company admitted no liability or violation of law but agreed to pay the state $10,000 for the costs of its investigation.

In recent years the states have taken forceful action against what they see as false or deceptive advertising with respect to health and environmental claims. For example, Texas has challenged Sara Lee for suggesting that its "light" cheesecake is low calorie. Several states have challenged Kellogg Co. for its advertising of the nutritional benefits of its cereals. Quaker Oats settled a challenge by the state of Texas over its claims that oatmeal can help reduce cholesterol. Seven states have sued Mobil for claiming that its Hefty garbage bag is biodegradable. Ten states have established environmental guidelines which would ban such phrases as "earth friendly" but allow such terms as "recyclable" only in markets where recycling facilities are available.[39]

There are other important issues in advertising, but space limitations prevent our discussing them. In mind are issues such as using scantily clad women in advertising, the morality in some advertising, ethnic issues, medical issues, the overcommercialization of life in the United States exhibited in advertising, and special problem areas such as alcohol and tobacco advertising.

Ethical Standards for Advertisers

The American Association of Advertising Agencies (AAAA) has a laudable ethics code for all its members. The code appears to be one of the most ignored in the corporate world, but some of its major provisions are worth noting as follows:

Specifically, we will not knowingly create advertising that contains:
a.   False or misleading statements or exaggerations, visual or verbal
b.   Testimonials that do not reflect the real opinion of the individual(s) involved
c.   Price claims that are misleading
d.   Claims insufficiently supported or that distort the true meaning or practicable application of statements made by professional or scientific authority
e.   Statements, suggestions, or pictures offensive to public decency or minority segments of the population.[40]

Food Labeling

The American people have become much more health conscious. Prior to the FDA food labeling requirements mandated in 1994, food processors seized on this interest to sell products proclaiming their health benefits. As a result, if one walked down the aisles of a supermarket, said Commissioner David Fesler of the FDA, one might think that they were in a drugstore. The messages on food packages told the consumer that the product would lower cholesterol, ward off heart disease, reduce weight, and so on, without specification of calories, food content, sodium, or other nutritional facts. The result was increasing pressure on Congress to do something. Congress did so with the passage of the Nutrition Labeling and Education Act of 1990, which gave the FDA and the USDA authority to assure truthful and uniform nutritional labeling on all foods regulated by the two agencies.

In conformance with this legislation, the FDA, in November 1992, issued 5,000 detailed pages of new labeling rules, covering some 15,000 product classes, which went into effect in 1994. By now every consumer is familiar with the standard label on packaged food items which informs the consumer about calories, fat, sodium, and so forth, contained in a specified portion of the foods.

In late 1995 the FDA vastly expanded the way in which seafood is inspected. Seafood processors are now required to identify points in the process where contamination or other health problems may arise. They then must monitor the problems and make reports to the

FDA. The idea is to prevent problems rather than try to solve them after they have created difficulties for consumers.

In late 1995 the FDA issued new labeling rules for bottled water. Consumers pay about $4 billion a year for bottled water but up to now did not know that about 25 percent of it came from the same municipal sources that supplied water to homes. Beginning in May 1996 suppliers were required to state the precise source of the bottled water as well as the amount of some minerals in it.

Concluding Comment

There is no question that today business is increasingly concerned about the interests and demands of consumers, government regulations (federal, state, and local) concerning them, and pressures of consumer advocacy groups. This medley of forces will become more complex in the future as the population grows, product choices of consumers expand, technology changes the nature and content of products, and competition intensifies both at home and globally. We can expect, therefore, even more attention to consumers in business, government, and society.

Endnotes

1. Sam Walton with John Huey, *Sam Walton: Made in America*, New York: Doubleday, 1992, p.173.
2. Ibid., p. 157.
3. Hugh Sidey, "Stack It Deep, Sell It Cheap, Stack It High and Watch It Fly!" *Time*, April 20,1992.
4. Cited in Jenny C. McCune, "In the Shadow of Wal-Mart," *Management Review*, December 1994; and Kenneth R. Sheets, "How Wal-Mart Hits Main St.," *U.S. News & World Report*, March 13,1989.
5. Walton and Huey, Sam Walton, p. 177. For an excellent account of the history of Sam Walton and Wal-Mart, see Sandra S. Vance and Roy V. Scott, *Wal-Mart: A History of Sam Walton's Retail Phenomenon, 1962-1992*; and Vance H. Trimble, *Sam Walton: The Inside Story of America's Richest Man*, New York: Dutton, 1990.
6. Peter F. Drucker, *The Practice of Management*, New York: Harper, 1954, p. 37.
7. Thomas J. Peters and Robert H. Waterman, Jr., *In Search of Excellence: Lessons from America's Best-Run Companies*, New York: Harper &: Row, 1982.
8. Ralph Nader, *Unsafe at Any Speed*, New York: Pocket Books, 1966.
9. Quoted in Rich Thomas, "Safe at This Speed?" *Newsweek*, August 22,1994.
10. *U.S. Consumer Product Safety Commission, 1993 Annual Report*, Washington, D.C.: U.S. Consumer Product Safety Commission, 1994.
11. Paul H. Rubin, "Why Regulate Consumer Product Safety?" *Regulation*, Fall 1991.
12. *Congressional Quarterly's Federal Regulatory Directory*, Washington, D.C.: Congressional Quarterly Inc., 1994.
13. Leon Jaroff, reported by Hannah Bloch "The Commish Under Fire," *Time*, January 8, 1996, p. 60.
14. See, for example, Robert M. Goldberg, "Breaking Up the FDA's Medical Information Monopoly," *Regulation*, No. 2, 1995.
15. Laurie McGinley, "What David Kessler Wants and How He'll Try to Get It," *Wall Street Journal*, June 23, 1994.
16. Alfred L. Edwards, "Consumer Product Safety Challenge for Business," *University of Michigan Business Review*, 1975, p. 19.
17. John M. Antle, *Choice and Efficiency in Food Safety Policy*, Washington, D.C.: AEI Press, 1995, pp. 5, 35.
18. Tom Alexander, "Time for a Cease Fire in the Food Safety Wars," *Fortune*, February 26, 1979, p. 94.
19. 613 F.2d 947, 954 (D.C.Cir. 1979).
20. *Frank Young, Commissioner of Food and Drug Administration, Petitioner v. Community Nutrition Institute et al.*, No. 85-664, argued April 30, 1986, decided June 17, 1986.
21. *Kathleen E. Les et al. v. William K. Reilly, U.S. Court of Appeals for the Ninth Circuit*, No. 91-70234. 56 Fed. Reg. 7750, July 8, 1992, affirmed U.S. Supreme Court, February 22, 1993.
22. For pros and cons of the issue see Victor J. Kimm, "The Delaney Clause Dilemma," *EPA Journal*, January 1993; Al Meyerhoff, The Delaney Clause: Point/Counterpoint," *EPA Journal*, February 1993; and Clausen Ely, "The Delaney Clause: Point/Counterpoint (continued)," *EPA Journal*, March 1993.
23. Marcolm Gladwell, "A Consuming Matter of Apples," *Washington Post National Weekly Edition*, May 17,1989.

24. Gisela Bolte and Dick Thompson, "Do You Dare to Eat a Peach?" *Time*, March 27, 1989; and John F. Ross, "Risks, Where Do Real Dangers Lie?" *Smithsonian*, November 1995.

25. 217 N.Y. 382,111 N.E. 1050 (1916).

26. *Larson v. General Motors Corporation*, 391 F. 2d 495 (8th Cir., 1968).

27. *Beshada et al. v. Johns-Manville Products Corporation et al.*, 51 U.S. 2038 (N.J. Supreme Court, July 7,1982).

28. N.J. Supreme Court, 161 A. 2d 69 (1960).

29. Supreme Court of California, 27 Cal. Reptr. 697, 377 R2d 897 (1962).

30. *Walt Disney World Co. v. Wood* 515 So. 2d 198 (Flat 1987).

31. Jury awards are given to plaintiffs for injury, and punitive awards to punish defendants. Compensation may be awarded for economic (out-of-pocket) loss, medical expenses, lost income, and noneconomic loss such as pain and suffering. Punitive damages penalize outrageous wrongdoing that is malicious, willful, and wanton, or evil. All these injuries are called torts and the legal system to protect individuals is the tort system.

32. Erik Moller, *Trends in Punitive Damages: Preliminary Data from California*, DRU-1059-ICJ, Santa Monica, Calif.: RAND Institute for Civil Justice, April 1995, and Joseph F. Delfico et al., *Product Liability: Verdicts and Case Ran Resolution in Five States*, Washington, D.C.: General Accounting Office, September 1989; and Terrence Dungworth, *Product Liability and the Business Sector: Litigation Trends in Federal Courts*, Santa Monica, Calif.: RAND Institute for Civil Justice, 1988.

33. Moller, *Trends in Punitive Damages*.

34. Sears, Roebuck, 95 F.T.C. 406 (1980).

35. *Warner Lambert*, 86 F.T.C. 1398, 1489-90 (1975), *aff'd* 562 F.2d 749 (D.C.Cir. 1977) *cert denied*, 435 U.S. 950 (1978).

36. *General Foods Corp.*, 84. F.T.C. 1572-1573 (1974).

37. *Thompson Medical Co.*, 104 F.T.C. 648, 690, 792-93 (1984).

38. Ivan L. Preston, *The Tangled Web They Weave: Truth, Falsity, and Advertisers*, Madison: University of Wisconsin Press, 1994, p. 207.

39. Mark Landler, Zachary Schiller, and Tim Smart, "Suddenly, Green Marketers Are Seeing Red Flags," *Business Week*, February 25, 1992.

40. *American Association of Advertising Agencies Roster Organization, '95, '96*, New York: American Association of Advertising Agencies, 1996.

Chapter Ten

THE CHANGING FACE

OF ORGANIZATIONAL LIFE

Ford

Henry Ford (1863-1947) was a brilliant inventor. After incorporating the Ford Motor Company in 1903, he designed one car after another, naming each chassis after a letter of the alphabet. In 1908 he began selling the Model T, a utilitarian, crank-started auto which came only in black. The Model T cost $850, but Ford introduced the first moving assembly line and by 1924 mass production had lowered the price to $290. He sold 15.5 million of the cars before production ended in 1927 and the Model A was introduced.

Contained within the success story of the Model T, and less known, is the darker story of the Ford Motor Company organization. Henry Ford was an obstinate man. He was obsessed with power and refused to acknowledge the authority or ideas of others. He was brutal with hourly workers. "The assembly line," he said, "is a haven for those who haven't got the brains to do anything else."[1] There were no job titles for managers; they were not allowed to establish organizational power bases. Sometimes he assigned two men the same job and watched to see which one survived the competition. He demanded the complete, unquestioned obedience of subordinates.

As the firm grew, Henry Ford's authoritarian style was institutionalized in its informal culture. Over time, independent managers left and he was surrounded by sycophants who would have jumped into the Detroit River if Ford had asked. They, in turn, were ruthless and autocratic with their subordinates.[2]

This internal culture consolidated power in Henry Ford's hands, but it did not facilitate adaptation to external forces. Despite warnings in the form of fast-dropping market share in the mid-1920s, Ford Motor

Company failed utterly to anticipate a major transformation in the auto market. It clung to the spartan Model T even as consumer demand moved toward the styling changes, closed body design, and model hierarchy offered by General Motors. Finally, in 1927, Ford had to suspend production at its great River Rouge assembly plant while the Model A was being designed. It never recovered the market share leadership it had held.

Although the company regained its footing and marketed successful new models over the years, the authoritarian leadership style remained firmly entrenched. In 1945 Henry Ford himself felt its sting when he was ousted in a coup engineered by family members. He was replaced by his grandson, Henry Ford II, who also proved to be an autocratic manager.

In the early 1980s Ford suffered three years of disastrous losses, mainly because of heightened international competition. Japanese auto companies had captured 20 percent of the domestic market. The company studied Japanese management and decided to emulate its focus on quality and teamwork. It set out to make an innovative world-class sedan using teams similar to those used by Japanese car makers. It emphasized continuous improvement in productivity and quality.

In Japanese management philosophy, competing personalities and individualism are thought to hamper productivity. So Ford made an effort to change its corporate culture. Over the years it had tended to select autocrats for management positions. A study of 2,000 Ford managers classified 76 percent as "noncreative types who are comfortable with strong authority."[3] (Only about 38 percent of the population at large would fall into this category.)

continued

To facilitate change, thousands of Ford managers were sent to workshops on participative management.

Ford was rewarded for its efforts when the innovative Taurus sedan was introduced in 1985. It was a quick success and became the bestselling car in America between 1993 and 1995. In 1994, Ford made an extraordinary $5.3 billion in profits, a sum exceeded by only one other company in the world (Royal Dutch/Shell with $6.2 billion). But in that year a new Ford chairman, Alexander Trotman, started a sweeping change program called Ford 2000 to prepare the company for an even more competitive international environment. Trotman, who decorates his office with hood ornaments from cars made by failed companies, believes that in the next century a few giant firms, including Ford, General Motors, and Toyota, will compete for dominance in world auto markets. Currently, Ford is behind GM in market share in the United States and Europe, trails Toyota in production efficiency, and trails both in quality measures.

Ford 2000 is a plan to catch and surpass the others. To cut costs, it requires that major worldwide facilities be closed and 25,000 employees contracted into five centers—four in Dearborn, Michigan, and one in Europe. The centers will create basic car designs that can be modified for sale in the markets of many countries. Ford 2000 also places extreme emphasis on teamwork. Hierarchies are being abolished. Layers of middle management have disappeared. Tasks are now defined in meetings instead of by orders from a superior and conflicts are worked out by mediators in positions called "nodes."[4]

All of these recent changes have caused turbulence in Ford's work force. Like many other companies, Ford was forced into massive layoffs and restructuring in the 1980s. Between 1978 and 1996 it cut its work force by 64 percent, from 289,000 workers to 105,300.[5] Many with low seniority were laid off, so the average age of Ford employees has risen. Because its work force is rapidly aging, the company faces a high attrition rate and will need to hire an estimated 10,000 workers each year for the next three years.[6] To increase labor force flexibility many of these workers will not be offered traditional jobs. In 1995, for example, 3,000 jobs in product development centers were filled with contract workers.[7] Irrespective of their status, new workers must come from a labor market with an increasingly varied gender, ethnic, and racial mix. The incorporation of these new hires will further strain and challenge Ford.

This short history of Ford Motor Company illustrates how a set of forces—leadership of a founder, changes in management philosophy, international competition, technological change, and demographic change—shape the workplace. In this chapter we discuss these forces and further illustrate their significance.

The Nature and Meaning of Work

Those who work are performing a timeless, basic task. We define work as sustained effort designed to produce something of value for other people. At an elemental level, work is essential. Humans must manipulate their environment to live. The underlying moral basis of work is that each person is a burden on society and should contribute a fair share of the expenditure of human energy necessary for survival.

Work has an important psychological dimension. The clinician Karl Menninger saw work as one of two constructive outlets for aggressive impulses, the other being play.[8] Psychoanalyst Harry Levinson speaks of work as a central means for accomplishing the "twin unconscious drives of love and hate." "The carpenter who hammers nails," says Levinson, "is not only discharging his aggressions but also building a shelter."[9]

Work may give one a sense of mastery, provide legitimate expression for inner drives, placate a stern conscience, or divert attention from emotionally harmful anxieties. Studies show that fired and laid-off workers are at greater risk of accident, illness, suicide, and marital problems than those who remain employed. A landmark study of the years 1922 to 1971 showed an inverse relationship between economic conditions and admission to mental hospitals.[10] Another study found that suicides by white males rose and fell with the unemployment rate between 1940 and 1984.[11] Despite the generally salutary benefits of work, however, the workplace often is highly stressful and competitive. Even emotionally healthy people may have difficulty adapting to its pressures, frustrations, and conflicts.

The meaning of work has been different in other societies, past and present, from what it is in the United States today. In the ancient civilizations of Greece and Rome, work—in the sense of hard physical labor—was associated with degradation and slavery. Aristotle, for example, believed that hard labor deprived a person of the leisure necessary to develop character. Early Christians believed that God commanded men and women to work for subsistence, and work gradually came to be associated with spiritual betterment. Later, the Protestant Reformation in Europe created a new work ethic which made hard work, thrift, and honest dedication necessary for salvation. God called every person into a work role in their community and their labor in this role glorified God. Hard labor might result in material reward, even great wealth, and this was a sign of God's approval. This set of ideas became known as the *Protestant ethic*. It began as a religious teaching in the fourteenth century and carried across the centuries from medieval Europe to the American colonies.

Today the work ethic in the United States has lost most of its religious overtones, but in the colonial period farmers and artisans, who worked very hard to survive, were inspired by the religious obligation in the Protestant ethic. Workers also took great pride in their skills and crafts. Mundane tools such as saws, shovels, and knives had ornate engraving and were fondly passed from father to son.

After 1850 the industrial revolution attracted farmers and immigrants to cities, where they hoped to work their way to riches. Instead, they often found alienating work with low wages, long hours, tedium, danger, and pitiless supervision. In the early twentieth century, business applied "scientific management" to factories. Scientific management was a school of thought inspired by the influence of Frederick Taylor, an engineer who tried to increase work productivity using time and motion studies to make tasks specialized, routine, and quick. Gone were the days of ornamental shovels. Taylor ushered in an era of utility.

In reaction to this treatment of workers as machines, a school of thought developed that applied psychology to workers and encouraged employers to increase their productivity by nurturing their social needs. During World War II, the driving motive behind work became patriotism. From the end of the war through the 1950s, work was seen by Americans mainly as a source of status and income.

In the morning when thou risest unwillingly, let this thought be present—I am rising to the work of a human being. Why then am I dissatisfied if I am going to do the things for which I exist and for which I was brought into the world? Or have I been made for this, to lie in the bedclothes and keep myself warm? But this is more pleasant. Dost thou exist then to take thy pleasure and not at all for action or exertion? Dost thou not see the little plants, the little birds, the ants, the spiders, the bees working together to put in order their several parts of the universe? And art thou unwilling to do the work of a human being, and dost thou not make haste to do that which is according to thy nature?

Source: Marcus Aurelius (circa A.D. 174-180), *Meditations*.

But by the 1980s, work came increasingly to be seen as a means of self-fulfillment. In a 1983 survey, for example, salary and regular promotions ranked seventh and eighth on a list of ten indicators of career success, behind self-fulfillment measures such as "achievement of personal life goals" and having the "opportunity and means for achieving a fulfilling, happy home and social life."[12] In a similar survey of employed adults in 1991, high income and promotions ranked eleventh and fourteenth on a list of job attributes; "interesting works ranked second (behind having health insurance).[13] As these surveys indicate, most workers want to fulfill a variety of inner needs beyond simple survival.

External Forces Changing the Workplace

Those who work today, especially those who work in large corporations, are swept up in turbulence caused by five environmental forces (1) demographic change, (2) technological change, (3) structural change, (4) competition, and (5) government intervention. These powerful forces interact and together create more rapid change than the country has seen since the 1930s. A discussion of each one follows.

Demographic Change

First, population dynamics are slowly but continuously altering the labor force. Out of a 1994 population of 261 million Americans, about half, or 131 million, composed the civilian labor force as either working or unemployed (the rest were retired, disabled, students, homemakers, children under age 16, or not counted because they got unreported wages).

Historically, the American labor force has grown rapidly and continuously. It continues to grow, but more slowly now. In the last decade the number of workers grew by 1.4 percent each year. But between now and 2005 it is expected to grow by only about 1 percent a year, mainly because of slower growth in the general population.[14] Amidst this slower overall work force growth, however, the number of workers in some demographic categories is growing faster than in others, producing incremental but significant changes. Table 10-1 shows data for the current labor force and projects the results of existing trends to the year 2005.

TABLE 10-1	The Changing Civilian Labor Force: 1994-2005 (In Thousands)				
	1994	Percent of labor force	2005	Percent of labor force	Percent growth
Total	131,056	100	147,106	100	12
Men	70,817	54	76,842	52	9
Women	60,239	46	70,263	48	17
White	111,082	85	122,867	84	11
White male	54,246	41	56,429	38	4
Black	14,502	11	16,619	11	15
Asians*	5,474	4	7,632	5	39
Hispanic†	9,576	7	16,330	11	71

*"Asian" includes Asians, Pacific Islanders, Native Americans, and Alaskan natives.
†"Hispanic" persons may be of any race.
Data are based on employment projections made by the Bureau of Labor Statistics from the January 1994 Current Population Survey.

As Table 10-1 shows, on a proportionate basis both Hispanics and Asians are increasing their participation faster than whites and blacks. Since the 1970s, women have increased participation more rapidly than men and although this trend is slowing, it will continue for at least the next decade. The long-term participation rate for men, on the other hand, is declining. This is thought to be caused by continuing structural shifts in the economy which have hit less-skilled job categories in industry and mining where men predominate.

These changes mean that the work force will become more diverse in gender and ethnicity. In terms of percentages, the change is not great. The percentage of white males, for example, will decline only 2 percent and because of rising participation rates by white females, whites will decline by only 2 percent overall. Hispanics will increase by 4 percent and Asians by 1 percent. Blacks will increase in number but will remain about 11 percent of the work force. However, businesses in very cosmopolitan areas will experience more rapid diversity changes than these national rates suggest.

The work force is also aging. High fertility rates following World War II created a "baby-boom" generation born between 1946 and 1961. As this generation entered the labor market in the 1970s the median age of the work force began to decline, reaching a low of 34.6 years in 1980. The baby boomers are now a bulge of workers in their late thirties to early fifties which constitutes 45 percent of all workers. As this group ages the median age of the work force rises. It stood at 37.6 years in 1994 and will rise to 40.6 years in 2005.[15] Because the nation's fertility rate has been declining, cohorts of workers following the baby boomers are smaller. This means that there are fewer entry- and lower-level workers, while the statistical crowd of baby boomers, now seasoned in middle-management positions, will confront a bottleneck at the top, competing for fewer and fewer vacancies where the organizational pyramid constricts.

The aging of the work force is a worldwide phenomenon and aging trends are more rapid in Western European nations and Japan.[16] The twelve European Union nations have an average birth rate slightly below replacement rate. Because fewer younger workers will arrive in the next ten to twenty years industrialized nations face a challenge in filling entry- and lower-level jobs. While some developed nations face population declines and all have aging work forces, some third world nations have explosively growing, relatively youthful populations.

The United States, which will average net immigration of almost 900,000 persons yearly in the next several years, may have a long-run competitive advantage in international labor markets.[17] Japan and European countries have much more restrictive immigration laws. The Japanese want to preserve racial purity and have had difficulty incorporating non-Japanese into their work force. Many European nations are strongly ethnocentric and prohibit most immigration. But immigration brings an influx of younger workers who are less costly and more adaptable.

Technological Change

Technological change has many impacts on work. It affects the number and type of jobs available. Invention of the airplane, for example, created new job titles such as pilot and flight attendant. New machines are used by management to raise productivity and reduce costs. Automated teller machines at banks, for instance, increase the number of daily transactions possible and simultaneously reduce the number of employees necessary to handle them. Robots in auto manufacturing made American companies more competitive in cost and quality with Japanese car makers.

Automation has a turbulent impact on employment because it creates jobs for the architects of the machine age while displacing traditional manufacturing and service jobs. Overall, the number of jobs available in the United States has continuously increased and this is projected to continue. But automation has caused significant job loss in less-skilled manufacturing and mining jobs. In the coal-mining industry, for example, mechanization has eliminated 300,000 pick-and-shovel jobs since the 1950s. In underground mining a single huge machine called a continuous miner has replaced five separate pieces of equipment used in older mines. Other machines mine by remote control and the industry has become heavily computerized. Because of the introduction of such technology, output per employee has increased about 4.4 percent per year while the number of mining jobs has declined by 1.8 percent per year.[18]

The movement to robotics in the 1980s put almost 40,000 robots on U.S. assembly lines and eliminated roughly two-thirds of all assembly-line jobs by 1990. This trend continues. For example, Pulaski Furniture Corp. recently built a new Plant 12 in Virginia where computer-run lasers cut wood pieces eight at a time, doing in moments what previously took skilled craft workers four hours. Plant 12 has only 125 workers, but it makes more furniture than the company's other plant which employs 600. The workers at the new plant are different from the old. "They have good educations and they know about computers," comments an older worker with forty years of experience making furniture by hand, "but they don't know a lot about building furniture."[19]

Structural Change

Our economy is being reconfigured by three structural trends common to industrialized nations. The long-term effect of these trends has dramatically reshaped the job landscape.

First, the agricultural sector has declined from predominance to near insignificance as an occupation. In colonial America farming occupied 95 percent of Americans, but today it employs only 2.9 percent as fewer and fewer large farms deliver the nation's food supply using intensive and highly automatic crop and animal agriculture.[20] In the 1920s, for example, the largest poultry farm in the country had a flock of 500 chickens; today up to 100,000 birds are raised in a single long, narrow poultry building and multibuilding operations raise several million birds at once. The Bureau of Labor Statistics predicts that agricultural workers will dwindle further, to 2.3 percent of the labor force in the year 2005.

Second, employment in manufacturing has declined for many decades. In 1950 manufacturing jobs dominated the work force, occupying 78 percent of workers, but by 1994 manufacturing jobs had lost their prominence and occupied only 19 percent. By 2005 they are predicted to slump further to 16 percent. There are many reasons for the fall of manufacturing work, but perhaps the two most significant are automation and relocation of manufacturing to lower-wage countries. In steel production, for example, competition from Japan, Korea, and Brazil has caused a reduction in U.S. jobs from a peak of 620,400 in 1953 to only 250,000 in 1992, and the number continues to fall. Since 1970, however, the amount of steel produced per hour by each U.S. worker has more than doubled because of automated production techniques. Structural change away from manufacturing is also occurring in other industrialized nations. Germany, for example, lost 15 percent of its manufacturing jobs between 1991 and 1996.[21]

Third, there is explosive growth in the service sector, which includes jobs in retailing, transportation, health care, and other occupations that add value to manufactured goods. Service jobs increased from 10 percent of the work force in 1950 to 70 percent in 1994 and are predicted to grow to 74 percent in 2005. An example of this explosive growth is in business computer services which employed 271,000 people in 1979 and then grew by 207 percent to employ 831,000 in 1992.

Because of these structural trends the fastest-growing occupations are those which require more education. Less-skilled occupations predominate in the declining manufacturing sector, but even there traditional blue-collar jobs such as tool and die maker now require math and computer skills. Women, Hispanics, and blacks are underrepresented in the fastest-growing occupations in part because their educational attainments are, overall, less than those of white males. This raises new issues of education and training for employers who are pressured to show equity in job categories.

Structural change has been a major force in the decline of labor unions. Before the wave of protective legislation passed in the 1930s unions represented only 5 percent of industrial workers, but this tripled to 15 percent by 1940 and reached a zenith of 25 percent in the 1950s.[22] Unions raised wages and increased benefits for blue-collar workers and these improvements rippled out through the manufacturing sector because nonunionized companies needed to approximate the welfare levels of union workers if they wished to prevent unionization.

In the 1970s, however, union membership began a long slide as structural change eroded its base of factory workers. Employment shifted to service industries and high-tech companies which were hard for industrial unions to organize and to low-wage countries where unions were illegal or weak. By 1996 unions represented only 10 percent of private-sector employees in the United States and as the ranks of factory workers continue to thin so do union membership rosters. The upward push on wages and benefits that unions provide for both members and non-members has weakened commensurately. In Europe, on the other hand, union membership rose over the past two decades and roughly half of all workers are unionized in European Union countries, with the exception of France with under 20 percent. This is the main reason why labor costs are higher in many European nations than in the U.S.[23]

Competitive Pressures in the World Economy

Competitive forces have always been strong in the U.S. economy, but recent trends have intensified them. Customers are demanding higher quality, more speed of service, and faster new product development. In the United States deregulation of large industries such as airlines, telecommunications, trucking, and electrical utilities has stirred formerly complacent rivals. Foreign trade has grown from just 9 percent of the U.S. economy in 1960 to 23 percent in 1995.[24] Over this period U.S. firms have increasingly been challenged by foreign competitors in both domestic and foreign markets. These foreign competitors have seized upon a number of advantages, including lower labor costs outside the United States, a strong dollar, and in some cases higher worker productivity.

American workers, and also workers in other industrialized countries such as Japan and Germany, are increasingly exposed to a global labor market that contains pools of low-cost workers. In less-affluent, less-industrialized countries wages are lower for many reasons, including oversupply of labor relative to demand, low living standards, industrialization policies in authoritarian regimes where workers have no political power, and wage competition among countries seeking to attract MNCs (multinational corporations).

In the United States the average hourly compensation for a manufacturing worker in 1993 was $16.79, but in Korea it was $5.37, in Portugal $4.60, in Mexico $2.65, and in Sri Lanka less than $0.50.[25] Given this wage discrepancy, companies in some industries can no longer afford to do low-skilled manufacturing or service work in the United States and contract to have it done in a foreign country. Nike, for example, manufactures all its athletic shoes in low-wage countries. Citibank puts credit card receipts on airplanes and flies them to the Dominican Republic where low-wage keypunch workers prepare customer's bills. If the bills were prepared in Manhattan, Citibank would be uncompetitive with its rivals.

Low-cost foreign labor is also available for highly skilled knowledge work. Circuit board designers in California's Silicone Valley make $60,000 to $100,000 per year, but similarly qualified electrical engineers now do the same job for $25,000 a year in Taiwan. The majority of motherboards used in computers manufactured by American companies are now made in Taiwan; in the early 1990s most were made in the United States.[26] Engineers in India and China, equally qualified, are increasingly available to do the same design work for $10,000 a year, so the days of the Taiwanese designers are numbered.

In order to match competitors who take advantage of foreign low-cost labor American firms must either contract to have work done overseas themselves, and many have, or they must increase the productivity of domestic labor by reducing employees to a minimum and applying technology to enlarge their output. Either way, there are generally fewer jobs for American workers in the occupation affected.

Government Intervention

Historically, there was a strong laissez-faire current in American economic philosophy and governments at all levels were reluctant to interfere with the *employment contract*, or the agreement by which an employee exchanges his or her labor in return for specific pay and working conditions. Today government intervention is extensive and growing, but this is a twentieth-century trend.

Before 1860 the number of persons employed as wage earners in factories, mines, railroads, and other workplaces was relatively small. But with industrialization their numbers skyrocketed. Between 1860 and 1890 the number of wage earners rose from 1.33 million to 4.25 million, an increase of 320 percent.[27] This rapid growth in numbers, which would continue into the 1930s, created a new class interest, and it was an aggrieved one. In the hard-hearted wisdom of the day employers treated workers as simply production costs to be minimized, there was relentless downward pressure on wages and reluctance to improve working conditions.

Liberty of Contract

Prior to the 1930s there was little government intervention on behalf of workers, and what there was consisted mostly of feeble state safety regulations and laws to limit working hours. In the late nineteenth and early twentieth centuries strong majorities on the Supreme Court adhered to the *liberty of contract doctrine*. This doctrine held that employers and workers should be free from government intervention to negotiate all aspects of the employment contract, including wages, hours, duties, and conditions.[28] For many years the Court struck down state and federal laws that interfered with this theoretical freedom. Such laws were regarded as "meddlesome interferences with the rights of the individual."[29]

The great flaw in the liberty of contract doctrine was that it assumed equal bargaining power for all parties, whereas employers unquestionably predominated. For employers, liberty of contract was the liberty to exploit. Employees could be fired at will and had to accept virtually any working conditions. The unchallenged dominion of employers led to negligent treatment of workers and eventually created and fueled the labor union movement, a social movement to empower workers. But employers resisted the establishment of unions and their demands for more humanitarian treatment of workers.

Waves of Regulation

It was not until the 1930s that government regulation of the workplace began to redress the huge power imbalance favoring employers. One major step was the Norris-La Guardia Anti-Injunction Act of 1932, which struck down a type of employer-employee agreement that angry unionists colorfully labeled "yellow dog contracts." These were agreements that workers would not join unions. Employers virtually extorted signatures on them when workers were hired. Workers had little choice but to sign if they wanted to keep their jobs—and jobs were scarce in the 1930s. If union organizing began, employers went to court, where judges enforced the yellow dog contracts by prohibiting workers from holding union membership. The Norris-La Guardia Act outlawed this tactic, overruling a 1908 Supreme Court decision which had upheld yellow dog contracts under the liberty of contract doctrine.[30]

Turn-of-the century cartoonist Art Young drew this cynical view of the lopsided employment contract in the days before labor unions and laws protecting worker rights

The Norris-La Guardia Act encouraged unionism. It was soon followed by the National Labor Relations Act of 1935, which guaranteed union organizing and bargaining rights, and by other laws which fleshed out standards and rules for labor relations. After the 1930s employers still dominated the employment contract, but company power over wages and working conditions was increasingly checked by unions.

Figure 10-1 shows how this first wave of federal workplace regulation, which established union rights, was followed by two subsequent waves. A second wave, between 1963 and 1974, moved federal law into new areas to protect civil rights, worker health and safety, and pension rights. And a third wave, between 1986 and 1993 broadened the scope of federal law to address additional, and somewhat narrower, employment issues. During this period Congress enacted the following laws.

- A provision in the Comprehensive Omnibus Budget Reconciliation Act of 1986 allows separated workers to continue in group health plans for up to eighteen months at their own expense.
- The Immigration Reform and Control Act of 1986 protects work rights of legal aliens and prohibits hiring illegal aliens.
- The Worker Adjustment and Retraining Act of 1988 which requires companies with more than 100 workers to give sixty days' notice prior to plant closings or large layoffs.
- The Employee Polygraph Protection Act of 1988 prohibits the use of lie detectors to screen job applicants and narrows grounds for using the tests to detect theft or sabotage by employees.
- The Drug Free Workplace Act of 1988 requires companies with federal contracts to take measures to stop abuse.

- The Americans with Disabilities Act of 1990 prohibits discrimination against disabled persons and requires employers to make reasonable accommodations so that people with substantial physical or mental impairments can perform essential job duties.
- The Family and Medical Leave Act of 1993 protects job rights of employees who take up to twelve weeks of unpaid leave for family reasons such as childbirth or illness.

FIGURE 10-1

This figure shows the historical march of major statutes (and one executive order) regulating labor-management and employer-employee relations. Note the existence of three rough clusters or waves of intervention. Space prohibits a description of each law.

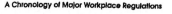

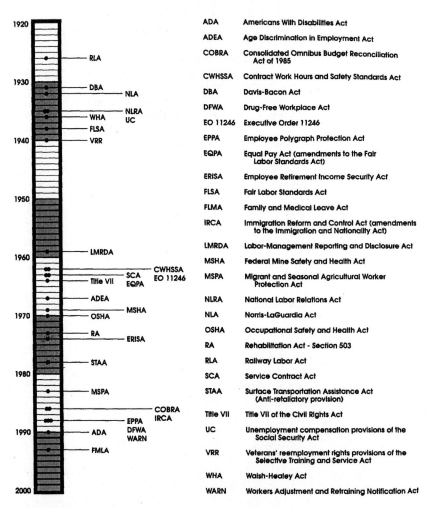

A Chronology of Major Workplace Regulations

ADA	Americans With Disabilities Act
ADEA	Age Discrimination in Employment Act
COBRA	Consolidated Omnibus Budget Reconciliation Act of 1985
CWHSSA	Contract Work Hours and Safety Standards Act
DBA	Davis-Bacon Act
DFWA	Drug-Free Workplace Act
EO 11246	Executive Order 11246
EPPA	Employee Polygraph Protection Act
EQPA	Equal Pay Act (amendments to the Fair Labor Standards Act)
ERISA	Employee Retirement Income Security Act
FLSA	Fair Labor Standards Act
FLMA	Family and Medical Leave Act
IRCA	Immigration Reform and Control Act (amendments to the Immigration and Nationality Act)
LMRDA	Labor-Management Reporting and Disclosure Act
MSHA	Federal Mine Safety and Health Act
MSPA	Migrant and Seasonal Agricultural Worker Protection Act
NLRA	National Labor Relations Act
NLA	Norris-LaGuardia Act
OSHA	Occupational Safety and Health Act
RA	Rehabilitation Act - Section 503
RLA	Railway Labor Act
SCA	Service Contract Act
STAA	Surface Transportation Assistance Act (Anti-retaliatory provision)
Title VII	Title VII of the Civil Rights Act
UC	Unemployment compensation provisions of the Social Security Act
VRR	Veterans' reemployment rights provisions of the Selective Training and Service Act
WHA	Walsh-Healey Act
WARN	Workers Adjustment and Retraining Notification Act

Source: Adapted from General Accounting Office, Testimony: *Rethinking the Federal Role in Worker Protection and Workforce Development*, 1995, p. 5.

Altogether, approximately 200 federal laws have been enacted since the 1930s, including amendments to original statutes, so only the major ones are shown in Figure 10-1. These laws have been based on the dominant perspective of 1930s reformers that the relationship between labor and management is antagonistic. Based on this model, a broad and complex regulatory structure has been created over nearly seventy years to counterbalance the perceived weakness of workers in the employment contract with corporations.

Federal regulations are only part of the growing web of regulation that fetters employers. State courts and legislatures have created additional rules that employers must follow. Legislatures in many states have enacted laws that go beyond federal requirements. For example, California requires that employers must retain and "reasonably accommodate" workers in drug or alcohol rehabilitation programs unless it can be documented that the worker is unable to perform his or her duties or cannot work safely. In Kansas, large layoffs or dismissals in designated industries must be approved in advance by the state's Secretary of Human Resources. In Maine, workers must be paid one week's wages when companies close.

Federal laws typically apply only to firms with more than a specified number of employees—usually 50 or 100. States have often enacted laws that extend the same employee protections to smaller firms. The federal Family and Medical Leave Act, for example, entitles employees of firms with fifty or more workers to take as long as twelve weeks of unpaid leave for family matters such as adoption, illness, or birth. But Oregon lowers the size of the company to twenty-five workers and Vermont to fifteen. The federal law requiring sixty-day advance notification of plant closings applies only to companies with 100 or more workers, but in Hawaii employers with fifty or more workers must give forty-five-day notice. These state actions enhance worker protections and make them more expensive.

State courts have also expanded workplace regulation. While federal courts often decide issues of constitutionality and statutory interpretation, they have not expanded workplace rights beyond the statutes. State courts, on the other hand, have applied doctrines of common law, to establish and expand employees' rights even in the absence of legislation. A leading example of the power of state courts is how in recent years they have revised the common law doctrine of employment-at-will, shriveling perhaps the most fundamental right of an employer—the right to hire and fire.

Erosion of the Employment-at-Will Doctrine

In the United States there is a body of common law, or law derived from judicial decisions, known as "agency," which governs employer-employee relationships. The general provisions of agency hold that employers and employees may enter into voluntary agreements of employment and that either party may freely terminate these agreements at any time.

While employed, an employee must act "solely and entirely" for the employer's benefit in all work-related matters or be liable for termination and damages. Furthermore, the law stipulates that when a conflict arises between an employee and employer, the employee must conform to the employer's rules. The common law of agency is derived from paternalistic English common law which, in turn, was influenced by Roman law that framed employment in terms of a master-servant relationship. Under agency, employers have had extensive rights to restrict employee freedom and arbitrarily fire workers.

Until the recent past, an extreme interpretation of agency prevailed. It resounds in this oft-quoted statement by a Tennessee judge over 100 years ago: "All may dismiss their employees at will be they many or few, for good cause, for no cause, or even for cause morally wrong without being thereby guilty of legal wrong."[31] *Employment-at-will,* therefore, was traditionally defined as an employment contract that could be terminated by either party without notice and for any reason.

Recently, however, absolute discharge rights have eroded. Federal and state laws have restricted the right to fire employees for reasons related to age, sex, race, union activity, physical handicap, religion, or national origin. In addition, courts in many states have introduced three common-law exceptions to termination at will.

First, an employee may not be fired for complying with the dictates of public policy. In *Petermann v. International Brotherhood of Teamsters*, a California worker was asked by his supervisor to lie in answering certain questions before a legislative committee investigating unions.[32] When the worker answered honestly, he was fired. Even though the employee was subject to firing at will in his position, the court did not uphold the termination, stating that there was an overriding public interest in ensuring truthful testimony at legislative hearings. In another case, *Sabine Pilot Service, Inc., v. Hauck*, a deckhand in Texas was fired after being ordered to pump bilges from a boat into waterways and refusing to do so because this is illegal. The Texas court held that an employer could not fire a worker for refusing to violate environmental laws.[33]

Second, courts are limiting the employer's ability to fire if an implied covenant of good faith is breached. In *Cleary v. American Airlines*, an employee of eighteen years in a position subject to arbitrary dismissal was fired.[34] Company personnel policy contained a specific statement that the firm reserved the right to terminate an employee for any reason, but the court became convinced that the firing was done to avoid payment of a sales commission to the employee. It awarded the fired worker punitive damages.

A third check on freedom to fire is recognized where an implied contract exists. In *Foley v. Interactive Data Corp.* managers made oral statements that an employees' job was secure and over seven years gave the person regular promotions and raises. When the employee was fired a California court held that the company had violated an implied contract.[35] The court found evidence that at the time of the man's hiring he had been promised permanent employment so long as his performance was satisfactory. As a result of such decisions, companies are removing implied promises of job tenure from personnel manuals.

The states vary in the extent to which these exceptions to employment-at-will have been adopted. Only five states have failed to take up any of the new exceptions and eight states have adopted all of them. The great majority of states have adopted one or more of the exceptions and the overall trend is toward greater restrictions on the employer's ability to terminate. One state, Montana, has passed a law that permits employers to discharge workers only for "good cause."

Is Workplace Regulation in Need of Reform?

The three waves of federal statutes passed since the 1930s and recent state court decisions protect workers from abuses and expand important rights. But while government action creates highly visible entitlements, it also raises costs and reduces flexibility of employers. Several concerns are paramount.

First, the laws impose large direct costs and administrative burdens on employers. The Family and Medical Leave Act creates an entitlement for employees to go on leaves for up to twelve weeks each year. During this period employers must continue to provide medical, dental, and optical insurance for the absent worker at an average cost of $1,995 each and must pay the cost of recruiting and training a replacement worker.[36] When the on-leave worker returns he or she must be given the same or an equivalent position. Across the nation, this law imposes hundreds of millions of dollars in costs and productivity declines annually on companies with fifty or more employees, with little or no compensating benefit.

Employee protection laws also create large administrative expenses. The managers of an electronics manufacturing company recently complained about the burden of dealing with numerous regulatory agencies and burdensome paperwork requirements.

There are too many different agencies and laws regulating the workplace. . . . Congress should look to consolidate some of these agencies and streamline some of the many federal statutes in a more rational manner. An example of the variation in regulation is the large number of postings and notices employers must comply with. These notifications come from many state and federal government agencies and can fill up an entire plant wall.[37]

Second, there are indirect, hidden costs associated with protective laws and these costs may fall on workers. The direct costs of labor regulation, including administrative costs and rising legal fees because of litigious employees, make hiring more expensive. Over the past twenty years the cost of hiring a manufacturing worker has risen by 5.5 percent a year.[38] The hidden costs of the regulations include lower employment, lower wages, lost productivity, and businesses that are not started or do not survive because of higher labor costs. It has been estimated, for example, that the sum total of the costs of workplace regulation has caused a decline in employment roughly equivalent to that which would occur if the government required a national 10 percent wage increase.[39] And data reveal that employment growth has been as much as 2 percent lower in states where courts have embraced exceptions to employment-at-will.[40]

Finally, labor laws enacted over a half century ago and based on a vision of antagonistic worker-employer relations have hampered the implementation of modern management techniques that emphasize worker-management teamwork. The National Labor Relations Act (NLRA), for example, was passed in 1935 to force managers to deal in good faith with labor unions. Among other things, the NLRA prohibited company unions, or puppet committees of workers set up and dominated by management in order to preclude genuine worker's unions. In 1947 the Labor-Management Relations Act gave an expansive definition of these sham unions that encompassed even groups that lacked formal structures, bylaws, or officers.

These laws protected early unions from unfair resistance by management, and necessarily so, but decades later they have reemerged as roadblocks to popular team management concepts. To meet stiff international competition many corporations, including most of the largest U.S. companies, use employee teams. Management methods fostering teams have many names, for example, job enrichment, quality circles, total quality management, and customer satisfaction groups. But in recent landmark rulings such teams have been ordered disbanded because they violate half-century-old labor laws.

Du Pont had set up a total quality management (TQM) program at a unionized chemical plant using seven committees to address health and safety. The committees included managers and rules required unanimous decisions before action was taken. Over time the committees acted on safety issues and when one committee recommended construction of an employee fitness center the company built it. The union objected to the committees, arguing that since decisions had to be unanimous they were dominated by management and were, in effect, sham unions. No action could be taken by a committee without a positive vote by the manager on it. In addition, the union believed that the committees were bargaining about working conditions that were properly the union's province. In a 1993 ruling the National Labor Relations Board held that the TQM committees constituted an unfair labor practice and ordered them disbanded.[41]

So far there have been at least twenty similar rulings striking down management teams and, while this is not yet a widespread trend, a bill has been introduced in Congress to amend the NLRA to legalize employee-involvement teams dealing with workplace issues.

U.S. firms have struggled in global product markets with foreign competitors in countries that lack such comprehensive and costly workplace regulations. Many in business believe that the pendulum has now swung too far in the direction of protecting workers. They complain about costly and unproductive requirements that add to administrative and legal costs without increasing productivity, efficiency, or competitiveness.[42]   What is needed, according to one scholar of labor law, is "a new vision of the employment relationship that emphasizes common interests to promote the success of the firm in an uncertain world."[43]

Worker Protection in Other Industrialized Notions

The level of benefits and protections for U.S. workers is extensive but not exceptional compared to other industrialized nations. Elsewhere, workers benefit from similar and even greater welfare guarantees. Cultural differences are evident in how worker rights are provided. But in every nation where strong measures of welfare for workers are in place the cost of labor is high.

Japanese workers are now among the world's most expensive. In 1994 the average hourly compensation for a manufacturing worker in Japan was $19.20, compared to $16.36 for an American counterpart.[44]   The fringe benefits of Japanese workers in the largest companies that employ about 40 percent of the work force typically include company housing, family allowances, meals, child education expenses, and paid vacations. Many Japanese men in these large firms enjoy virtual lifetime employment. When they die, Japanese workers are often buried in corporate cemeteries. These benefits are provided voluntarily by paternalistic Japanese companies.

Japanese history and culture in part explain why their companies are so generous. Japan's long feudal period embedded cultural patterns based on values derived from the spread of ancient Chinese culture to the islands. The values that developed at this time included belief in rigid status hierarchies, strong duties of loyalty owed to rulers, emphasis on group rather than individual welfare, and a belief in paternalistic government that would provide for the welfare of citizens. Today these values have been molded to fit the relationship between the worker and the corporation. Just as the feudal Japanese vassal owed great loyalty to a lord, workers now give such loyalty to their company and place work group interests above individual interests. In return, the company has a duty of parent-like beneficence and generously helps its workers.

In the United States antagonistic unions had to demand federal laws protecting their right to organize and then fight companies and industries for higher wages and benefits. But in Japan the centuries-old Confucian tradition of harmonious human relationships has prevented similar fissures from developing. Labor unions have never grown strong and unified. Most are company unions and they rarely strike or make strident demands. In the Japanese political system corporations cooperate closely with government ministries to promote economic growth; they do not struggle with dozens of regulatory agencies enforcing workplace rules as U.S. companies do. Similar approaches to worker welfare are found in other Asian nations, including Singapore, Taiwan, and South Korea.[45]

Industrialized nations in northern Europe also provide high wages and comprehensive benefits for workers. This is reflected in average hourly compensation for workers of $19.12 in Denmark, $20.20 in Austria and Norway, $21.38 in Belgium, $22.66 in Switzerland, and highest of all, $25.56 in Germany.[46] These countries have strong unions organized to negotiate wages and benefits over entire industries. Many European countries have had strong socialist parties and this has given unions longstanding political strength.

In Germany, which has the highest labor costs in the world, the government participates in union-employer negotiations and workers sit on corporate boards where they help run companies. The benefits and protections achieved by German workers are unmatched anywhere. German workers are entitled to generous government pensions, health care insurance, and unemployment benefits. Taxes for these and other benefits increase labor costs for German companies 80 percent over the average manufacturing worker's total pay. A complex network of laws, union agreements, and customs makes the German labor market very inflexible. For example, laws prescribe the hours when factory machines can run, prohibit factories from operating on weekends, prohibit almost all labor during an official Sunday "pause" (exceptions are gas station attendants and bakery clerks), and require that workers be given six months' notice that they will be terminated. The average German works only 36.6 hours per week compared to 40 hours for a U.S. counterpart.[47] This blanket of privilege for German workers has led to high unemployment which moved over 11 percent in 1996. The response of German unions has been to suggest that the workweek be reduced to four days.

In sum, nations have different philosophies and approaches to worker welfare. Of course, regulations and benefits help only workers who have a job. In the United States and elsewhere competitive forces and structural change have created great job insecurity. In the next section we discuss the tenuous position of many workers whose jobs are insecure.

The Turbulent Workplace of the 1990s

The combined impact of the five major forces changing the workplace has created uncertainty and reduced opportunity. Two illustrations of this are corporate downsizing and wage stagnation. Because of the changes going on today some scholars believe that a new employment contract between employees and companies is emerging to replace the old one.

Corporate Downsizing

In recent years many corporations have reduced the size of their work forces, often by announcing huge job cuts. This phenomenon has been given many names in the press and management literature, including downsizing, restructuring, and reengineering. Downsizing occurs for many reasons. When IBM announced layoffs of 60,000 workers in 1993 it was responding to technological advances in computing which had caused revenues from its traditional mainframe business to plummet. When Chemical/Chase Manhattan made 12,000 layoffs in 1995 it was eliminating duplicate positions and reducing costs following a merger. When AT&T made 34,000 layoffs in 1996 it was responding to the imperative of a law passed by Congress which opened AT&T's long-distance business to competition by the regional Bell companies and allowed AT&T to enter local telephone markets. Other companies have shed workers when domestic labor became too expensive and when technology became available to substitute for human labor.

Downsizing has been going on for many years. According to one estimate, 43 million jobs in the United States were permanently lost between 1979 and 1995.[48] Most of these were blue-collar and less-skilled administrative jobs, although middle managers and professionals have been caught by downsizing as well. During this period, however, more new jobs were created than were lost. There was a net gain of 28 million jobs and the number of employed persons in the work force rose. And since the recession of 1981-1982 the unemployment rate has declined from a high of 11 percent to 5.6 percent in early 1996.

Nevertheless, corporate downsizings reflect a new philosophy for managing human resources. In the past, job reductions were often temporary and laid-off workers were called back within a year or less. Today, however, job reductions reflect the permanent elimination of positions. Job creation and unemployment statistics miss the fact that when downsized workers find new jobs they often earn less and lack the generous benefits of previous jobs with large companies. In 1995 a *New York Times* survey found that only 35 percent of workers who lost a full-time job found a new job that paid as well or better and after four or five years 24 percent had not returned to employment.[49]

Downsizing has been attacked on many grounds. It is seen as unfair to make workers bear most of the burden for adjusting to powerful environmental forces. Until recently, mass layoffs were used only as a last resort and were an embarrassing sign of management failure. Today layoffs are no longer a source of shame; in fact, top managers often make record salaries in downsizing years and investors are enriched by short-term jumps in share prices after big layoffs. In the year that AT&T announced that it would shed 40,000 workers its CEO Robert Allen made $3.4 million.

Generous executive compensation seems obscene in contrast to the real pain and suffering of economic adjustment passed on to workers. This anguish is reflected in the following story about a secretary named Linda, told by a human relations manager participating in a mass layoff in which workers were called without notice to a conference room and read a prepared statement which terminated them.

> We avoided looking at each other as I spoke. When I finished, she didn't move for several long seconds; then she stood up and paced the length of the room and started wringing her hands. "What am I supposed to do?" she pleaded, not waiting for the answer that we couldn't give. "I am a single mother, my parents are gone, and I just closed on a house two weeks ago. I *need* my job," she said as the tears started to flow. My reaction was to offer some comfort, at least offer some words of encouragement, but we had been strictly warned by the company attorney not to do anything of the sort. It was for the good of the company that we restrain ourselves, lest we make some passing promise that would end up in court later. We all just sat there until she gathered her papers and walked out.[50]

Another argument against downsizings is that they do not always bring about the desired results. Studies have shown that companies which shed workers do not necessarily prosper. One analysis found, for example, that downsizing hindered product innovation because removing people broke down networks of informal relationships that were crucial in championing ideas and cutting across functional lines.[51] Two surveys have found that only about one-third of downsizing companies achieve their original profit and productivity targets.[52]

Downsizings are defended as necessary responses to pressures on firms in a turbulent environment. If downsizing strengthens a specific firm it enhances the job security of workers who remain and the financial security of current and retired workers who, through pension funds, own approximately 30 percent of corporate equity. If downsizing leads to profits the firm can attract more investors and will have more money to invest in new facilities and new technologies. Corporations cannot control structural and global forces that define how they must compete and cannot be locked into outmoded, less efficient, and more labor-intensive practices to avoid dislocating worker's lives. In fact, one of the strengths of the American economy compared to, for example, the German economy, is the relative ease with which labor is shifted from declining sectors to rising ones. It would be hardest on workers in the long run if American firms, bloated with workers, grew uncompetitive with foreign rivals. According to Albert Dunlap, the CEO of Scott Paper who once laid off 11,000 employees:

> The job of industry is to become competitive—not to be a social experiment. God help us if we pass legislation to make American companies less productive and compromise our global competitiveness. Then it won't be a case of a relatively small number of people losing their jobs. It will be huge numbers losing jobs—and the death of the American free-enterprise system as we know it.[53]

There is validity in the arguments of critics of downsizing. But a better way of navigating currents of change is elusive. Downsizing is occurring in all advanced industrial nations exposed to winds of global competition. In Europe, strong unions have forced companies to retain workers, but this has made many European firms less competitive and led to high unemployment anyway, in this case unemployment resulting from economic stagnation. The chairman of Volkswagen, for example, has publicly stated that the company's German work force of 101,000 is about 30,000 larger than necessary.[54] But downsizing is prevented by the German state of Lower Saxony, which owns 20 percent of Volkswagen, and by powerful unions. The result has been that rivals such as Ford and Audi underprice it, styling is changed more slowly, it has the lowest net return on sales among major competitors, and it makes fewer cars per worker than other large European auto firms. If American corporations are prevented from shedding workers, automating, and creating high profits to attract investors they will soon fall behind global rivals.

Wages and Productivity

Following World War II wage earners in the American economy experienced income growth that allowed them to rapidly raise their standard of living. Between 1948 and 1973 the average worker's compensation (including wages plus benefits) rose 3 percent yearly. This was enough to double the standard of living every twenty-five years. This rising compensation did not make the American worker uncompetitive. The real measure of work force competitiveness is worker output compared to worker cost. This worker output is called productivity, which is measured as output per hour of work. Even when a nation's workers receive comparatively high wages they can be low cost if their productivity is high enough. Between 1948 and 1973 the productivity of American workers rose an average 2.5 percent yearly, one of the highest rates in the world.[55]

Around 1973, however, a slowdown in both compensation and productivity growth set in and between 1973 and 1993 compensation grew just 0.7 percent yearly and productivity just 0.9 percent yearly. At such a glacial rate, average wage earners must wait sixty-five years to double their standard of living. This slowing trend, however, masks a striking bipolarity in which one part of the work force experiences financial decline while another finds unparalleled prosperity. Unskilled and uneducated workers have suffered large declines; for example, hourly wages (adjusted for inflation) for male high school graduates declined by 20 percent. Even workers with college degrees, but no further education, saw their wages drop 9 percent. Workers in less-skilled manufacturing, construction, and mining occupations were the hardest hit. At the same time, highly educated professionals, sales workers, and executives saw their earnings rise.

This bipolar compensation pattern is troubling. Between 1973 and 1993 median family income has remained virtually level, but again, this statistic masks diverging fortunes. Incomes fell by 15 percent among the poorest fifth of families and the national poverty rate rose by 4 percent to 15 percent, while at the same time incomes rose by 25 percent for the wealthiest fifth of households. The precise causes of these inequities in wages and household income are elusive, but experts agree that competition in global labor markets, the shift away from manufacturing, computerization of work, and the declining fortunes of unions as wage-setting institutions are all important. Demographic change is less of a factor. Although immigration brings many unskilled workers into the country the Council of Economic Advisers reports that this influx is responsible for less than 1 percent of the decline in wages among less-educated workers.[56]

A Revised Employment Contract

In the current turbulent setting of work, the outlines of the traditional job are fading. Yesterday, work was done in eight-hour days on rising trajectories of pay and power within hierarchical, pyramid-shaped, corporate organizations. The largest of these organizations, firms such as IBM, AT&T, and General Motors, were insulated in a domestic market and protected by their market power from fierce competition. They could offer unwritten promises of lifetime employment and did so, silting-up with unnecessary workers over time.

In this setting the unwritten employment contract was an exchange of the worker's time, skill, and loyalty for a career of growing compensation, status, and security provided by the company. Now, though, this contract equation no longer works. Competitive and global forces have altered every aspect of it. Downsizing has flattened organization structures, extending work hours for remaining employees and removing many higher positions in the pyramid to which they could have aspired. Real compensation has not risen for the average family in over two decades. And there is less job security.

In this turbulent, transitional period, the outlines of a new employment contract are emerging. In the new contract employees will trade their time, energy, and skills for compensation and the opportunity to work in a company that provides learning, training, and perhaps feelings of self-worth in team settings.[57] Unlike the old contract, the employee will not give a high level of loyalty and the organization will not promise long-term employment. In a competitive global economy companies will need a lean and highly flexible work force. To promote adaptive and rapid decisions in this environment they will move further away from hierarchical forms of organization and toward more participatory management, team-oriented work assignments, and flexible work hours. To attract the most skilled people they will need to provide training and educational opportunities for workers who expect to move sequentially from one employer to another over their working lifetimes. The security of these employees will lie in their marketability, not in promises of long-term work by their immediate employer.

Conclusion

This chapter began with the story of how Ford Motor Company evolved from an authoritarian, entrepreneurial enterprise to a globe-spanning company with a team orientation. The changes at Ford can be traced to the workings of the five major environmental forces discussed in this chapter—demographic change, technological change, structural change, competition, and government intervention. These forces will continue to reshape Ford, other companies, and the U.S. and foreign economies and workplaces. Along with this change the employment contract will shift to accommodate new realities.

Endnotes

1. Quoted in *New United Motor Manufacturing, Inc.*, Freemont, Calif.: New United Motor Manufacturing, February 1992, p. 18.
2. Anne Jardim, *The First Henry Ford: A Study in Personality and Business Leadership*, Cambridge, Mass.: MIT Press, 1970, pp. 114-15.
3. Melinda G. Builes and Paul Ingrassia, "Ford's Leaders Push Radical Shift in Culture as Competition Grows," *Wall Street Journal*, December 3, 1985.
4. Alex Taylor III, "Ford's Really Big Leap at the Future," *Fortune*, September 18, 1996, p. 142.
5. Figures are from Gary W. Loveman and John J. Gabarro, "The Managerial Implications of Changing Work Force Demographics: A Scoping Study," *Human Resource Management*, Spring 1991, p. 25; and Donald W. Nauss, "Auto Maker Job Boom Seen as Workers Retire," *Los Angeles Times*, February 27, 1996, p. A1.
6. Donald W. Nauss, "Auto Maker Job Boom Seen as Workers Retire," *Los Angeles Times*, February 27, 1996, p. A9.
7. Oscar Suris, "Ford's Rebates Spell Trouble as New Models Fail to Excite Buyers," *Wall Street Journal*, January 10, 1996 p. A10.
8. Karl Menninger, *The Vital Balance*, New York: Viking, 1963, p. 141.
9. Harry Levinson, *Executive*, Cambridge, Mass.: Harvard University Press, 1981, p. 29.

10. Harvey M. Brenner, *Mental Illness and the Economy*, Cambridge, Mass.: Harvard University Press, 1976.

11. Bijou Yang, "The Economy and Suicide: A Time-Series Study of the U.S.A.," *American Journal of Economics and Sociology*, January 1992.

12. George F. Breen, *Middle Management Morale in the '80s*, New York: American Management Association, 1983, p. 16.

13. Larry Hugick and Jennifer Leonard, "Job Dissatisfaction Grows; 'Moonlighting' on the Rise," *Gallup Poll Monthly*, September 1991, p. 9.

14. Ronald E. Kutscher, "Summary of BLS Projections to 2005," *Monthly Labor Review*, November 1995, p. 3.

15. Howard R. Fullerton, Jr., "The 2005 Labor Force: Growing, But Slowly," *Monthly Labor Review*, November 1995, p. 42.

16. "The Economics of Aging," *The Economist*, January 27, 1996, Survey, p. 5.

17. U.S. Department of Labor, *Report on the American Workforce*, Washington D.C.: U.S. Government Printing Office, 1994 p. 25.

18. Bureau of Labor Statistics, *Technological Change and Its Impact on Labor in Four Industries*, Washington, D.C., 1992, pp. 10-12.

19. Quoted in Keith H. Hammonds, Kevin Kelly, and Karen Thurston, "Rethinking Work," *Business Week*, October 17, 1994, p.80.

20. Sector employment figures in this section are derived from Kutscher, "Summary of BLS Projections to 2005," Table 4, and from various editions of the *Statistical Abstract of the United States*. Sector employment for 1994 does not add up to 100 percent; the missing increment of 7.9 percent includes private household wage and salary earners and nonagricultural self-employed.

21. Nathaniel C. Nash "In Germany, Downsizing Means 10.3% Jobless," *New York Times*, March 7, 1996, p. C3.

22. U.S. Bureau of the Census, *Statistical Abstract of the United States: 1956*, Washington, D.C.: U.S. Government Printing Office, 1956, Table 271.

23. Sanford M. Jacoby, "Social Dimensions of Global Economic Integration," in Sanford M. Jacoby, ed., *The Workers of Nations: Industrial Relations in a Global Economy*, New York: Oxford University Press, 1995, p. 10.

24. Council of Economic Advisers, *The Annual Report of the Council of Economic Advisers*, Washington, D.C.: U.S. Government Printing Office, February 1996, p. 225.

25. U.S. Department of Labor, *Report on the American Workforce*, Washington, D.C.: U.S. Government Printing Office, 1994, Table 44, p. 201.

26. Pete Engardio et al., "High-Tech Jobs All Over the Map," *Business Week*, November 18, 1994, p. 113-14.

27. Arthur M. Schlesinger, *Political and Social Growth of the United States: 1852-1933*, New York: Macmillan, 1935, p. 203.

28. The liberty of contract majority first emerged in *Allgeyer v. Louisiana*, 106 U.S. 578 (1897), where Justice Rufus W. Peckham grounded it in the due process clause of the Fourteenth Amendment, which states that no state can deprive a person of life, liberty, or property without due process of law.

29. Justice Rufus W. Peckham, writing for a 5-4 majority in *Lockner v. New York*, 198 U.S. 61 (1905). The decision struck down an 1897 New York State law limiting bakery employees to sixty-hour weeks.

30. *Adair v. United States*, 291 U.S. 293.

31. *Payne v. Western & Atlantic R.R. Co.*, 81 Tenn. 507 (1884).

32. 344 Cal. App.2d 25 (1959).

33. Cited in Cameron D. Reynolds and Morgan O. Reynolds, "State Court Restrictions on the Employment-at-Will Doctrine," Regulation, Vol. 18, no. 1 1995, p. 60.

34. 168 Cal. Reptr. 722 (1980).

35. 765 R 2d 373 (1988).

36. Gary Klotz, "The High Cost of 'Employees' Rights," *Wall Street Journal*, August 3, 1993, p. A14, citing an estimate by the Small Business Administration.

37. General Accounting Office, *Workplace Regulation: Information on Selected Employer and Union Experiences*, GAO/HEHS-94-138, June 1994, vol. 1, pp. 79-80.

38. Janet Kmitch et al., "International Comparisons of Manufacturing Compensation," *Monthly Labor Review*, October 1995, p. 4.

39. Richard Edwards, "Using the Market to Find Common Ground," *Regulation*, vol. 16, no. 4, 1994, p. 71.

40. Reynolds and Reynolds, "State Court Restrictions on the Employment-at-Will Doctrine," p. 65, citing a RAND Corporation study.

41. Randall Hanson, Rebecca I. Porterfield, and Kathleen Ames, "Employee Empowerment at Risk Effects of Recent NLRB Rulings," *Academy of Management Executive*, vol. 9, no. 2, 1995, pp. 48-49. See 311 NLRB no. 88, May 28,1993.

42. See Gary Klotz, "The High Cost of 'Employees' Rights, *Wall Street Journal*, August 3, 1993, p. A14.

43. Samuel Estreicher "The Dunlop Report and the Future of Labor Law Reform," *Regulation*, vol. 18 no. 1, 1995, p. 29.

44. U.S. Department of Labor, *Report on the American Workforce*, Table 44, p. 201.

45. Sanford M. Jacoby, "Social Dimensions of Global Economic Integration," in Jacoby, ed., *The Workers of Nations*, pp. 21-22.

46. U.S. Department of Labor, *Report on the American Workforce*, Table 44, p. 201.

47. Mary Williams Walsh, "Germany's Reckoning," *Los Angeles Times*, February 25, 1996, p. D13.

48. Louis Uchitelle and N. R. Kleinfield, "On the Battlefields of Business, Millions of Casualties," *New York Times*, March 3, 1996, p. 16.

49. Uchitelle and Kleinfield, "On the Battlefields of Business, Millions of Casualties," p. 16, based on a survey of workers losing their jobs in 1991 and 1992.

50. Alan Downs, *Corporate Executions*, New York: Amacom, 1995, p. 76.

51. Deborah Dougherty and Edward H. Bowman, "The Effects of Organizational Downsizing on Product Innovation," *California Management Review*, Summer 1995, p. 29.

52. See, for example, studies by Wyatt Company and the American Management Association cited in William McKinley, Carol M. Sanchez, and Allen G. Schick, "Organizational Downsizing: Constraining, Cloning, Learning," *Academy of Management Executive*, August 1995, p. 33.

53. Allan Sloan, "The Hit Men," *Time*, February 26, 1996, p. 48.

54. David Woodruff et al., "VW Is Back—But for How Long?" *Business Week*, March 4, 1996, p. 66.

55. Wage, productivity, and income figures in this section are from *The Annual Report of the Council of Economic Advisers*, Washington, D.C.: U.S. Government Printing Office, February 1995, chap 5.

56. *Annual Report of the Council of Economic Advisers*, February 1995, p. 181.

57. For more ideas on an emerging employment contract see Barbara W. Altman and James E. Post, *Beyond the "Social Contract"—An Analysis of Executives' Views at 25 Large Companies*, paper presented at Academy of Management Meeting, Vancouver, 1995; William J. Byron, S.J., "Coming to Terms with the New Corporate Contract," *Business Horizons*, January–February 1996; and Rosabeth Moss Kanter, *World Class: Thriving Locally in the Global Economy*, New York: Simon & Schuster, 1995, chap. 6.

Chapter Eleven

THE PROMISE OF TECHNOLOGY: ECONOMIC

GROWTH AND PROSPERITY

Our decisions to do something positive, the full consequences of which will be drawn out over many days to come, can only be taken as a result of animal spirits—of a spontaneous urge to action rather than inaction, and not as the outcome of a weighted average of quantitative benefits multiplied by quantitative probabilities . . . Thus, if the animal spirits are dimmed and the spontaneous optimism falters, leaving us to depend on nothing but a mathematical expectation, enterprise will fade and die . . . [and] individual initiative will only be adequate when reasonable calculation is supplemented and supported by animal spirits, so that the thought of ultimate loss which often overtakes pioneers, ... is put aside as a healthy man puts aside the expectation of death.

John Maynard Keynes, *General Theory Of Interest, Employment, and Money*[1]

Introduction

This chapter is about the contributions that technology can make to economic growth and prosperity. The roles played by entrepreneurs, innovative companies and products, investors, and government are discussed. Technological forecasting is important particularly for managers. Why do some technologies succeed, while others fail? Key technologies of the future and technological developments in Japan are considered. This chapter concludes with a description of the innovation process, emphasizing the important social role of technology.

The Importance of Technology

Economic growth—the capacity of a nation to produce the goods and services its people desire—depends on an array of factors including the quantity and quality of labor and natural resources; capital, machines and equipment; management; and values that encourage hard work, diligence, and thrift. Other elements critical for economic growth are a high level of technology and the knowledge to convert the factors of production into goods and services. Technology leads to increasing mechanization and gives rise to an efficient of labor, which improves productivity and permits the accumulation of capital.

Technology is both the cause of many of the world's environmental problems and the best hope for their cure. All the classical economists of the late 18th and early 19th centuries, including Adam Smith, David Ricardo, and John Stuart Mill, stressed technology as a critical component of economic development.[2] Thomas Malthus's pessimism that runaway population would lead to increasing misery as the world's population

Business and Society, Second Edition, by Alfred A. Marcus. © Irwin/McGraw-Hill, The McGraw-Hill Companies, 1993, 1996.

expanded more rapidly than the food supply was based on the premise that technological developments would fall behind population growth.

Technological pioneers often are stubborn dreamers who stick tenaciously to their vision despite the odds against their succeeding. Since few new ideas bear fruit, it sometimes takes foolhardy optimism to overcome a natural inclination toward caution. For innovation to work, at least five elements are needed: entrepreneurs, innovative companies and products, investors, government, and the determination to overcome the many obstacles that inevitably arise.

Entrepreneurs

Small companies employing less than 500 employees have accounted for a large proportion of U.S. job growth since 1988. A new breed of entrepreneur has played an important role. Many entrepreneurs are refugees from large corporations where they gained the solid business experience that results in their success. The rule that a majority of businesses fail in the first five years did not apply to the early 1980s; close to 80 percent of the companies started during that time were still functioning in the early 1990s.[3] The difficulties of being an entrepreneur today—health costs, taxes, government regulation, access to capital, competition, and acquiring a workforce—deterred many from the task. Those who did inaugurate new businesses tried to avoid the risks. Thus, they would commence with a niche in a business they already knew, take on experienced partners, perhaps start with a franchise, and make adjustments quickly when their efforts were not working.

Besides corporate refugees, the new breed of entrepreneurs consisted of many women. A high percentage of the new firms also were started by traditional inventors who were not interested in managing a large enterprise; they lacked people skills and, when they had achieved success, quickly sold out to larger companies. Other entrepreneurs were well-connected individuals who had access to investment bankers and venture capitalists.

Innovative Companies and Products

Two companies known for their innovative products are 3M and Sony (see the next Real-World Example). 3M's innovations extend from low-tech Post-It notes to futuristic synthetic ligaments.[4] More than 30 percent of its revenues came from the 200 or more new products introduced each year during 1985-1990, when 3M's net income doubled. During the recession of the early 1990s, it was careful to limit layoffs of employees and to continue spending 6.6 percent of its total sales on research, about double the U.S. industry average. 3M modernized its factories to cut manufacturing costs and expanded its product line.

Because 3M was a major supplier to the auto industry, many of its products were vulnerable to the recession, and the company faced stiff price competition on its computer diskettes from Japanese companies such as Sony. 3M's products in less recession-prone businesses, like health care, also faced challenges as the United States moved toward cutting these costs. 3M tried to address the needs of other companies during the recession by offering products that would be perceived as cost-saving devices. It tried to speed up product development cycles by getting its design, production, and marketing teams to work more closely together.

Throughout the recession, 3M continued overseas expansion. Its businesses in the Far East enjoyed average yearly growth rates of 20 percent and more. In Europe, however, 3M faced serious difficulties; to save money, it consolidated operations there, linked customers to subsidiaries by computers so that orders could be processed more quickly, and established four large warehouses to replace 17 minidistribution centers. To reduce customer complaints it focused on the smallest details of its businesses. For instance, it reduced the time to process complaints in its medical products division by having sales representatives carry preaddressed, postage-paid labels.

Investors

In the early 1990s, venture capital investments declined by about a half from $4.2 billion in 1987 to slightly over $2 billion in 1991.[5] Investments became concentrated in fewer deals. Initial public offerings of stock replaced venture capitalists as the financial supporters of the ablest entrepreneurs. Venture capitalists too often tended to have arm's length relationships with those they funded, watching only the financial aspects of the business and not offering strategic guidance or practical help. Those venture capitalists who had money during the recession became more specialized and demanding, and they gave more careful scrutiny to the deals they made.

Real-World Example

Sony

Like 3M, Sony has been a consistently innovative company,[6] producing many high-technology successes from the transistor radio to the camcorder, compact disk player, Trinitron television, and Walkman. The company also has had its share of failures, including the Beta Max videocassette recorder. Sony's repeated success at innovation differentiates it from companies like Atari, which invented the videogame, but had no successful follow-ups. Unlike companies like Casio, Samsung, and Sanyo, which try to copy products made by others and sell them cheaply, Sony's goal is to release 1,000 new products per year, 800 improved ones, and 200 that open entirely different markets.

Among its workforce of 112,000, Sony employs more than 9,000 scientists and engineers. It spends 5.7 percent of its revenues on product research and development, and like 3M, its corporate research department organizes an annual exposition, which is open only to employees, where scientists exhibit what they are doing. Sony also wants its products to have a distinct character, so it employs many artists as well as engineers in a strong design center.

The company founder, Masaru Ibuka, articulated the company's vision as "never to follow others." However, while Sony follows typical Japanese practices of lifetime employment, company slogans and attire, long hours, and a rigid pay ladder, it also makes a point of not relying on specialists. Sony employees are supposed to be openminded and optimistic and have wide-ranging interests. The company moves them from one product group to another and tries to instill in them the ambition to create new products. Talented young people are given key positions in new product development teams. These newcomers have the freshness of vision to create entirely new products, while experienced engineers find better ways to manufacture existing products.

Sony always has concentrated on the consumer market, which was largely ignored by U.S. electronics firms that worked on military and space applications. Its distinctive capacity was to package the latest technology into small, inexpensive items that consumers found easy to use. Sony continues to bring out numerous new products, including the Palmtop pocket-sized notepad computer that reads writing and keeps track of appointments, addresses, telephone numbers, and personal memos; and the Data Discman, a portable, paperback-size electronic book that displays text and graphics and has audio output.

Sony has not had unbroken successes, however. Its move into the U.S. entertainment industry through the acquisition of Columbia Pictures was an uncharacteristically big risk that brought Sony unaccustomed difficulties.

Public offerings were the main alternative to venture capital. Wall Street investors supported the biotechnology industry although the biotech firms were slow to develop new products and few earned profits. Given that it takes a decade or more to move a product from the laboratory to the marketplace, the patience of the backers of biotechnology was remarkable. Without collateral, banks found it impossible to extend loans to finance this type of development.

Government

Government's role in technological innovation was important because the payoff to society was greater than it was to the individual company or investor. Without government, innovation would be underfunded. Rational companies and individuals would forgo the advantage of being first as the innovator and produce imitations instead, because copying was almost always cheaper than innovation. Though innovation benefited all of society, it was not in the interest of a specific group other than government to provide for it.[7]

All major industrial nations had technology policies. The post-World War II technology policy of the United States was based on government support for basic research, which it was hoped, would benefit society at some point in time. The U.S. government was a leader in financing many discoveries, but it lagged behind other nations in applying the research to commercialize products.[8] For that reason, Congress has shown less willingness to pay for it. Instead, it has promised increased financing for civilian technologies. Seven hundred national labs were eager to get involved, and they formed more than 1,000 cooperative R&D arrangements (CRADAS) with private companies. The National Institute of Standards and Technology (NIST) started an Advanced Technology Program (ATP), which gave grants to companies developing promising but risky technologies. ATP did not single out industrial sectors for help (e.g., silicon technologies versus steel) nor did it emphasize generic technologies (e.g., advanced material processing or high performance computing). The amounts APT gave were relatively small and the companies it considered for grants had to convince NIST that their ideas had technical merit, practicality, and commercial prospects. Among the 1992 winners were optical computers and advanced plastics for automobiles. In addition, the Commerce Department developed a strategic partnership initiative, in which companies that produced new technologies had the opportunity to meet people from the companies that might use it.

The Pentagon remained the largest financial backer of research in the United States. At first, it gave its support almost exclusively to its suppliers, who were largely sheltered from the civilian market. Increasingly, however, it came to rely on innovations from the civilian economy. Defense Advanced Research Products Administration (DARPA) funding for **dual-use technologies** (military and commercial) was very successful. Germany, Switzerland, and Japan mostly had market-driven technology policies, while the technology policies of the United States, the United Kingdom, and France were more government-directed and military-driven.

dual-use technologies
Technologies with military and civilian applications..

Overcoming Obstacles to Innovation

It was not easy to build competitive advantage on the basis of scientific advances alone. U.S. scientists were as good as any in the world, but the United States was not a leader in making their inventions into commercial successes.[9] At least eight reasons explain why innovation is hard to accomplish:

1. Companies that come up with the discoveries do not always profit from them. The EMI scanner was an enormous scientific discovery—as large as anything since X rays—but EMI suffered great losses in developing it and sold the rights to the technology at a cut-rate price.

2.   Companies that make discoveries do not always use them. Drug companies exploit their own inventions, but relatively small engineering companies routinely make discoveries, such as the bar code readers at supermarket checkout counters, that others use. Suppliers originate many new ideas for their customers.

3.   Innovation rarely is instantaneous. Technologies improve in reliability, quality, and flexibility as they diffuse. In a series of small steps and refinements, they develop an evolving range of applications.

4.   Innovation usually starts as a solution to a narrow problem. The innovators rarely know all the ramifications. Thomas Watson at IBM, for instance, thought the computer would be of limited use. He believed that the single computer his company made in 1947 would solve scientific problems, but it would have limited commercial application.

5.   Diffusion is very uneven. It follows the classic S-shaped curve. The first to adopt new technology are daring; the great mass of people are much slower to change.

6.   Large firms in rapidly growing industries sometimes make innovations first because of their financial strength and access to information, but this is not always true. Some innovators are small unknown firms, like Microsoft, that rapidly rise to the pinnacles of success. The early market for innovation cannot be easily established, and it is not easy to tell in advance who will dominate this market.

7.   The expectation that prices for a new product will fall retards adoption. People wait to buy because they believe further technological progress will drive prices down—think of the market for personal computers! Meanwhile, the inventors and developers who have endured most of the risk may not have staying power. Their inventions are then exploited by the **second and third movers**, those companies that later enter an industry.

8.   Developers frequently do not profit from the commercial application of their ideas. Since imitators face lower costs, the incentive to create is not large. Patent protection does not always help.

second and third movers
Imitators who do not bear the cost but enjoy the benefits of commercially exploiting new technologies.

In short, the path to successful innovation is strewn with many obstacles.

Waves of Innovation

The Russian economist Nikolai Kondratiev (1892-1938) expounded a theory that economic progress was not linear but took place in long waves, each of them lasting about half a century.[10] Each wave had periods of prosperity, recession, depression, and recovery. Joseph Schumpeter, the Austrian economist, connected these waves of growth to technological innovations. The first period (1782-1845) saw major innovations in steam power and textiles; the second (1845-1892) in railroads, iron, coal, and construction; and the third (1892-1948) in electrical power, automobiles, chemicals, and steel.[11]

Technological change, according to Schumpeter, is like a "series of explosions" with innovations concentrating in specific sectors, or leading-edge industries that provide the momentum for growth. These leading sectors propel the economy forward; without them, economic growth is not possible.

creative destruction
Process that replaces old technologies with new ones.

Entrepreneurs, seeing the opportunities for profit, vigorously exploit the new technologies. The pioneers are followed by a swarm of imitators. The combined activity of the pioneers and followers generate boom conditions. Soon, however, there are so many imitators that prices fall and an economic bust follows. This process is one of "**creative destruction**" in which lagging sectors fall behind. Their time passes; they wither and die or are kept afloat by government subsidy and bailout. To spur a revival, new innovation is needed.

Alternative Futures

The prosperity of the post-World War II period was built on innovations in semiconductors, consumer electronics, aerospace, pharmaceuticals, petrochemicals, and synthetic and composite materials (see Figure 11-1). A dynamic growth phase existed shortly after World War II. The middle to late 1960s was a period of consolidation. This was followed by a period of maturity beginning at the end of the 1960s, when many markets were saturated.

FIGURE 11-1
Waves of innovation

1782-1845 Steam power, textiles
1845-1892 Railroads, iron, coal, construction
1892-1948 Electrical power, automobiles, chemicals, steel
1948-1973 Semiconductors, consumer electronics, aerospace, pharmaceuticals, petrochemicals,
           synthetic and composite materials

Source: R. Rothwell and W. Zegveld, *Reindustrialization and Technology* (Armonk, N.Y: M. E. Sharpe, 1985); J. A. Scumpeter, *Business Cycles* (New York: McGraw-Hill, 1939).

As markets stagnated, unemployment in manufacturing grew. Many companies lowered production costs by making incremental manufacturing improvements and exporting jobs to foreign countries where labor costs were lower. After 1973, growth rates declined worldwide, and the post-World War II boom lost its momentum.

Postindustrial Society

Sociologist Daniel Bell constructed the model of a postindustrial society to explain the diverse changes that were occurring in society.[12] A postindustrial society differed from an industrial society in five ways:

1. The economic sector changed from producing *goods* to producing *services*.
2. A *professional and technical class* became dominant in society.
3. *Theoretical knowledge* became the central source of innovation.
4. The *control of technology* and *technological assessment* became primary activities.
5. *New intellectual technologies* (modeling, simulation, cybernetics, decision theory, and systems analysis) influenced decision making.

"The Powers of the Mind"

The popular writer George Gilder extended Bell's vision of postindustrial society. He claimed that "wealth in the form of physical resources" was losing value and importance to "the powers of the mind," which were gaining the upper hand "over the brute force of things." Economic activity in earlier periods centered on physical labor, natural resources, and capital. Today, ideas and technology, not material resources, are the hallmark of ascendant nations and corporations.[13]

Electronics, computer software, and telecommunications relied upon human creativity. They emancipated human beings from their dependence upon the physical world. The microchip, according to Gilder, symbolized this "worldwide shift of the worth of goods from materials to ideas" as the material costs of the product constituted only about 2 percent of the total costs of production.[14] The most valuable part of the microchip was the idea for its design. The rise of the mind as a source of wealth that spanned industries was among the most important forces in the 21st century.

Technological Forecasting

These trends suggest that managers need to forecast technological change and anticipate breakthroughs early when response times are long and they are in a better position to take advantage of them. Technology is dynamic and has many important implications for business expansion and contraction. An estimated 25 percent of existing technology is replaced every year. Managers can understand these changes through simple trend analysis, monitoring expert opinion and other sources of information for indications of changes, and constructing alternative scenarios.[15]

Trends

Trends in one area often lead to the forecasting of trends in another (e.g., military jet speeds foretell commercial jet speeds). The number of components needed to manufacture one product can help managers to estimate the number needed to manufacture a similar product. But trends must be analyzed with caution. Simple extrapolation can be deceiving if it does not take into account the impact of one trend on another, ignores how the human response can change the direction of a trend, and leaves no room for surprises. Economic forecasts are good at predicting the future based on the past so long as the future resembles the past in important ways, but radical breaks that no economist can predict may take place (e.g., the 1973 Arab oil embargo).

Experts

Expert opinion can be used, but experts make mistakes. The British Parliament established a committee of experts at the end of the 19th century to investigate the potential of Thomas Edison's incandescent lamp. It found the idea "unworthy" of attention. During World War II, a panel of experts selected by the federal government did not believe that an intercontinental ballistic missile could accurately deliver its payload 3,000 miles away. The Rand Corporation, a think tank in Southern California, devised the "Delphi method" to aggregate the beliefs of experts about particular issues. Each expert is asked to predict important events and to clarify the reasons why he or she believes the event is likely to occur. Successive requestioning in light of the answers helps to sharpen the results.[16]

Alternative Scenarios

When the future is uncertain, managers can construct alternative scenarios. They can create a series of possible sequences of future events that take into account the uncertainty. In 1972, Shell Oil forecast and assessed the implications of three different energy scenarios: immediate (2 years), middle range (10 years), and long range (25 years). This exercise forced Shell's managers to think through what they would do if unfavorable circumstances should arise and provided them with the opportunity to better manage future contingencies should they occur.[17]

Managers need to monitor the environment for signals that may be the forerunners of significant changes. To do so, they have to clarify their ideas about which indicators to follow. Then they have to understand how to put the information together and interpret it for the purposes of decision making. In a free society, the amount of information produced is immense. Professional conferences, technical papers, and the media yield data that vie for a manager's attention. What to focus on and what to ignore is a perpetual problem.

The Next Wave of Innovation

For economic growth to take off, a new wave of innovation is needed. Where will it come from? The following technologies may play an important role.[18]

- *Artificial intelligence.* Computer use will continue to expand into areas where human intelligence formerly was applied. The computers will be able to carry out such activities as learning, adapting, recognizing, and self-correction.
- *Genetic engineering.* The genetic code of living organisms will be mapped, restructured, and remodeled to enhance or eliminate certain traits. This potential will allow scientists to predict and correct genetic diseases. It should allow them to create crops that are resistant to pests and drought.
- *Advanced computers.* Evolving chip technologies open up the promise of the development of faster and more powerful computers. Sarnoff chips, which contain 100 or more tiny lasers, have been used to create the first functional optoelectric integrated circuit. They could be used in powerful new desktop computers in the future.
- *Bioelectricity.* Damaged or dysfunctioning nerves, muscles, and glands can be stimulated to promote their repair and restore their health so they function properly. Currently, this technique can be used in humans with severed bones and defective hearts and lungs. It speeds the healing rates of wounds and is an alternative to addictive painkillers.
- *Multisensory robotics.* Robots can be made that can perform more than simple, repetitive tasks. Useful service robots, such as smart shopping carts and mobile helpers for factory and personal use, are in the works.
- *Parallel processing.* This technique permits many computers to be used simultaneously in solving a problem. It greatly enhances computer power and performance and thereby increases the complexity of the scientific and technical tasks that can be handled.
- *Digital electronics.* Information from audio, video, and film sources can be digitized for more rapid retrieval. The use of optical memory systems such as optical disks, film, and bar code readers is likely to be expanded.
- *Lasers.* Lasers are light amplified by the stimulated emission of radiation. They permit holography (3-D imagery), which may become more common in advertising. Microwave scalpels equipped with lasers have already begun to replace the old metal scalpels used in surgery.
- *Fiber optics.* Fiber optics carry up to four signals at once (television, telephone, radio, and computer). They promise to greatly improve and expand communications.
- *Microwaves.* New applications are being developed beyond the wireless digital information sent on satellite dishes and used on heating devices such as the microwave oven. Possibilities also include microwave clothes dryers and cancer treatment systems.
- *Advanced satellites.* As more countries send satellites into orbit, satellites will be used for new purposes including oil and mineral exploration and pinpoint surveillance and mapping.
- *Solar energy.* Photovoltaic cells convert sunlight to energy. New uses will be developed beyond pocket calculators and remote power applications. Solar technologies also can be used for rural electrification projects in the developing countries and as alternatives to automobile and jet fuel.

- *Microtransistors.* A quantum transistor 100 times smaller and 1,000 times faster than current transistors has been developed. If mass-produced, it would revolutionize the electronics industry.
- *Molecular design.* Supercomputers can design new materials molecule by molecule and atom by atom. Tailor-made enzymes for industrial use have been developed. Additional products made in this way promise to move out of the laboratory.
- *New polymers.* Lighter, stronger, heat resistant, and able to conduct electricity, new polymers can be used in many products ranging from garbage bags to army tanks, ball bearings, moldable batteries, and running shoes.
- *High-tech ceramics.* These materials promise to be resistant to corrosion, wear, and high temperatures and will be used to create lighter-weight cars and cleaner-running engines. They open up the possibility of a new, more efficient engine design that creates less pollution.
- *Fiber-reinforced composites.* These lightweight and noncorrosive composite materials often are stronger than steel, and they can be used in the construction of buildings, bridges, and aircraft.
- *Superconductors.* These materials carry electricity without loss of energy. They make possible less expensive but more advanced magnetic resonance imaging (MRI) machines for hospitals. They can be used in TV antennas and faster computer circuits. New developments in superconductors could permit the construction of trains with magnetic levitation.

All of these technologies have a wide variety of uses, from telecommunications and computers to health and transportation. They rely on new materials and manufacturing processes for their realization. They promise to extend human sensory capabilities and intellectual processes. By making machines capable of imitating the functioning of the human brain, a computer could process many types of information simultaneously. Mathematical data could be processed at the same time the computer received spoken commands in English or a foreign language.[19]

Obstacles to Adopting Promising Technologies

In theory, these technologies are very promising, but formidable obstacles stand in the way of their widescale adoption and use. A promising idea, commonly referred to as an invention, is not the same as an innovation.[20] An invention is merely the creation of the idea in the laboratory. It is the test of a certain principle, an act of technical creativity that describes a concept that may be suitable for patenting. By contrast, **innovation** puts this idea into widespread use; commercial exploitation assures broad application. The following sections describe some of the obstacles that have been encountered in commercializing two of the technologies previously listed.

innovation
Putting an idea created in a laboratory into practical and widespread use.

Artificial Intelligence

The marketplace applications of artificial intelligence have been very disappointing. Many companies established in the mid-1980s have ceased to exist, and others have shrunk in size and cut back their workforces. Sales that were supposed to reach into the billions of dollars did not exceed $600 million in 1990. Much of the venture capital funding and many of the talented technical people who were attracted to the field abandoned it.[21]

Artificial intelligence (AI) allows computers to mimic ordinary human intelligence. It includes systems that help machines in factories "see," that enable computers to analyze aerial photographs, and that permit language recognition for translation or dictation. Security applications for guarding warehouses have been developed, but AI's greatest promise is in expert systems—software packages that can imitate the reasoning and decision processes of specialists in various fields based on the rules of thumb they use and the data they have available.

The American Express Company successfully applied artificial intelligence in its credit authorization department. It developed a program to review cardholder requests for money to make big purchases. The customer's credit history was reviewed in an instant; if problems existed, they were identified immediately for employees to investigate.

Despite the promise of this type of application, the developers of artificial intelligence have not understood potential markets. For instance, Applied Expert Systems tried to sell a $50,000 software package to professional financial planners. The company claimed that the computer could produce a better financial plan than the planners. Understandably, the professional planners felt threatened by this claim and refused to buy the package. Applied Expert Systems next tried to sell it to banks and insurance companies, which were less threatened.[22]

Another artificial intelligence program, called LISP, was simply too expensive. LISP Machine Inc., Xerox, and Texas Instruments all had workstations that used LISP, but the cost of at least $100,000 was more than most customers were willing to pay.[23]

The problems in the artificial intelligence industry may have been the lack of a good sense for market forces on the part of its founders, many of whom were researchers. Initially, they were very well funded and spent money freely without a sense of the limits of either time or budgets which are needed to make a commercial success.

Genetic Engineering

Genetic engineering companies fared somewhat better than the artificial intelligence companies. The technology was very seductive; entrepreneurs and scientists alike hyped the chances of its success. However, scientists not only had trouble focusing on the products they would make, but they frequently misjudged the time required to prove that the products worked and to obtain regulatory approval. For example, Liposome Company believed that fatty, water-filled membranes could be used to deliver drugs more effectively through the membranes. But to figure out five diseases where this would work, it had to screen more than a million possibilities and then develop a method of delivering the drugs. Finally, it required large-scale manufacturing methods.

Federal regulators, too, have been an obstacle to the commercialization of biotechnology products because five federal agencies each have some jurisdiction and guidelines are not clear. Many companies have had to maintain manufacturing facilities that they could not run at full capacity and sales forces that could not market a product while they waited for regulatory acceptance. To get around the regulatory process, biotechnology companies have looked for applications of their products that need little or no regulatory approval. They also have allied themselves with large drug and chemical companies that are experienced at obtaining approval. Large manufacturers also help them shoulder the risks and furnish marketing capabilities.

Large manufacturers that have entered the biotechnology business on their own have not always been successful. Monsanto, for instance, made a huge investment in biotechnology research.[24] It developed a bovine growth hormone (BGH) to boost the milk production of cows. BGH is a protein similar to the one cows make naturally. It is injected into the cows twice a month and increases milk yields by 10 to 20 percent. However, Monsanto's product was banned by the governor of Wisconsin after opposition from dairy farmers who supposedly would be the product's main customers. Farmers feared that a milk glut would lower prices. Consumer anxieties about artificial foods and the fears of giant grocery chains that people would not buy milk from cows injected with BGH initially prevented the product from being widely used.

Monsanto has also been criticized by environmentalists about another genetically engineered product—a new strain of cotton and soybean plants that can withstand spraying from Monsanto's herbicide Roundup. Environmentalists wonder why Monsanto cannot work on pest-resistant crops rather than crops that resist pesticides.

Biotechnology has great promise. It might be possible to use plant cells to make valuable substances in large quantities that plants make in small quantities.[25] Genetically manufactured products such as melanin could offer protection from skin cancer. Other genetically manufactured products would modify or enhance the flavor of fruits and vegetables, help in the petroleum refining process, and protect people inadvertently exposed to radiation. However, these products can only be developed if they can overcome the regulatory hurdles and gain public acceptance.

Why Technologies Fail

However promising, many ideas fail to find widescale application (see Figure 11-2). Only a small percentage of projects succeed depending on the industry and the circumstances. After a commercial launch has occurred and less-attractive R&D projects and proposals have been weeded out, the success rate is higher. Still, failure is common, and managers have little control over it: it is hard to pick winners.[26]

FIGURE 11-2
Obstacles to the commercializaiton of technologies

Artificial intelligence	Failure to understand potential markets
Genetic engineering	Unclear regulatory responsibilities
	Consumer anxieties
	Environmental criticism

risk
Conditions where the odds of economic success are known with certainty, as opposed to uncertainty, where the odds of success are unknown.

Economists distinguish between conditions where the odds of success are known with certainty (e.g., flipping a coin), which they call **risk**, and conditions where the odds of success are unknown, which they call *uncertainty*. Classification is a question of degree. The art of assigning statistical probabilities is just that—an art. Better management does not easily reduce the failure rate, nor can managers always manipulate the situation to their liking or produce the results they desire. After the fact, it may be easy to say why success or failure occurs, but it is not easy to know what to do beforehand.[27]

Technical and Commercial Feasibility

Most managers have powerful to keep risk to a minimum. In deliberating whether to undertake a particular project, they have to consider technical and commercial feasibility. They have to estimate:

1. Probable development, production, and marketing costs.
2. The approximate timing of these costs.
3. Probable future income streams.
4. When the income streams are likely to develop.

All of these calculations are fraught with uncertainty. The only way to reduce uncertainty is to undertake safe projects. Thus, managers tend to be biased toward innovations where success is easy—simple, well-tread areas where fundamental research and invention is not necessary.[28]

Managers establish new generations of existing products, introduce new models, and differentiate a product further rather than create different products and new product lines. They reduce uncertainty by licensing other people's inventions, imitating other people's product introductions, modifying existing processes, and making minor technical improvements. An automobile with a new type of engine, for instance, is less likely to be introduced than an auto with simple modifications of an existing engine.

Optimistic Bias

Managers must have an optimistic bias to launch a new product. Without it, the contemplation of failure overwhelms the inclination to proceed. An optimistic bias affects all types of investment decisions; innovations are no different. If the actual chances of success were based on entirely sober and realistic assessments, fewer innovations would occur. Engineers, for instance, make optimistic estimates of development costs, but actual costs and the probabilities of technical success are hard to determine.[29]

Predicting Market Success

It is also difficult to predict market success. Market launch and growth in sales are distant in time, and future conditions vary. No one knows what the reaction of competitors will be to the threat of new products. Not only is it difficult to achieve an advance understanding of the costs, given changing economic circumstances, but also it is hard to know in advance how long a product will be on the market and how dominant, given the threat of technical obsolescence, it will be.

The empirical evidence confirms that "early estimates of future markets have been wildly inaccurate."[30] The successful developers of computers thought that fewer than 4,000 would be sold in the United States by 1965. They did not dream that over 20,000 units would be sold in the United States by 1965 and that the potential market was unlimited.

Even with sophisticated techniques for estimating project success, companies make flagrant errors. For instance, no firm was more experienced than Du Pont with new product introductions, yet the company has lost large sums with some products before it withdrew them from the market. Three types of uncertainty that affect new product development—technical, business conditions and the market, and government—have to be considered.

Technical Uncertainty

After prototype testing, pilot plant work, trial production, and test marketing, technical uncertainty is likely to exist in the early stages of introducing products (see Figure 11-3). The question typically is not whether a product will work but one of degree—of standards of performance under different operating conditions and of the costs of improving performance under these conditions. Unexpected problems can arise before a product reaches the market, in the early stages of a promising commercial launch, and after product introduction, as the examples below illustrate.

FIGURE 11-3
Technical uncertainty

- Whether product will work
- Performance under different operating conditions:
  Before product reaches market
  In early stages of promising commercial launch
  After product introduction

Before a Product Reaches the Market

Unexpected problems affected the pharmaceutical company Syntex even before it got a new product on the market. Syntex's patent on its major money-maker, Naprosyn, an anti-inflammatory drug, was about to expire. The company created a new ulcer drug, Enprostil, which not only eased the pain of ulcers but also lowered cholesterol. With about 23 million people worldwide suffering from ulcers, drugs that treat the problem, like SmithKline Beecham's Tagamet and Glaxo Holdings' Zantac, yielded substantial profits. However, the principal researcher who pioneered Enprostil's development spotted evidence of dangerous blood clots that might produce new ulcers or pose a risk of heart attack or stroke. Enprostil failed to win FDA approval and was not a commercial success.[31]

The Early Stages of Production

Serious setbacks can also occur in the early stages of a promising commercial launch. For instance, Weyerhaeuser Company sought to become an important player in the disposable diaper market with its Ultrasofts product. Ultrasofts had superior features—a clothlike cover and superabsorbent pulp material woven into the pad designed to keep babies dry. Consumer tests showed that parents favored it two to one over competing brands. The advertising and promotion campaign offered coupons saving parents $1 per package to try the product. Procter & Gamble and Kimberly-Clark, which together controlled 85 percent of the $3.8 billion baby diaper market, came back with aggressive cost cutting and promotion campaigns to keep customers loyal. Meanwhile, manufacturing problems occurred in Weyerhaeuser's Bowling Green, Kentucky, plant. The system that sprayed the superabsorbent material into the diapers started to break down and a fire broke out. Weyerhaeuser had to raise prices to retailers by 22 percent to cover the unexpected expenses. The retailers refused to give the product shelf space, and Weyerhaeuser was forced to withdraw the product from the marketplace.[32]

After a Product Is on the Market

Serious setbacks also take place when a product is on the market. At General Electric (GE), the appliance division's market share and profits had been falling. Its cumbersome 1950s technology took three times as long to make compressors as it took Japanese and Italian manufacturers. The compressor, a pump that creates cold air in a refrigerator, is as crucial to it as an engine is to a car. GE committed $120 million to building a factory to manufacture a newly designed compressor that had parts made of powdered metal instead of hardened steel. Powdered metal was more easily fabricated to the extreme tolerances that were needed and it was cheaper than steel. Evaluation engineers, however, told the designers that powdered metal had not worked in air conditioners. Designers discounted their views, test data showed no failures, and a technician's observation of excessive heat was ignored. Field testing was limited to about nine months instead of the usual two years, because managers wanted the product on the market immediately. GE scrapped its old compressors and proudly declared that an American company could still take the lead in world manufacturing. Consumers bought the refrigerators with the new compressor in record numbers, with GE increasing its market share by 2 percent, its best showing in years. However, some compressors began to fail after about a year on the market, and GE, which had sold the refrigerators with five-year warranties, decided to recall and replace them.[33]

General Business Uncertainty

General business uncertainty also affects the introduction of new products. It had a negative effect on General Motors efforts in bringing Saturn to the market. Saturn's introduction at a time of poor economic conditions and overcapacity in the industry meant initially disappointing sales. GM was hurt by the changing business conditions of the early 1990s when Saturn was introduced.[34]

The Role of Customers

Pioneering new technologies carries great uncertainties in knowing what consumers want and providing it to them in a timely fashion. Having a good idea is not enough. Models of innovation that start with scientific and technological advances miss the important role that customers play both in the adoption decision and in subsequent refinements.

For example, Motorola's excellence as an engineering company is widely recognized. Still, it has been unable to keep its customers from defecting to such rivals as Intel, Sun Microsystems, and MipsComputer Systems. Motorola's obsession with technological excellence—its engineers had to create the best-designed, fastest, and highest quality product possible—prevented it from meeting market needs in a timely fashion. While competitors were already shipping products to customers, Motorola was still making revisions. IBM chose Intel's chip to be the standard in personal computers, not because Motorola's was technically inferior, but because Intel was more responsive to its needs. Motorola did capture nearly 80 percent of the market for microprocessors used in workstations, but this market was much smaller than the personal computer market. Transferring technology from the laboratory to the market is not easily accomplished when technology-oriented managers dominate.[35]

Uncertain Government Support

New products also can be hurt by uncertain government support. For instance, high-definition television (HDTV) was once a favorite among politicians and business lobbyists in Washington, D.C. Sharp images, perfect sound, and the convenience of large, thin screens had great appeal. The consumer market was estimated at more than $100 billion. Government and business officials met to map out a strategy for developing a new technology to compete with Japan and other foreign nations. However, the Bush administration did not cooperate because it believed that support for research that had commercial potential should come only from the private sector. It cut government support for HDTV. The only American firm willing to take on the risks by itself was Zenith. All other companies backed out because the government would not subsidize the high costs of development.[36]

Striving for Constant Innovation

These examples illustrate the lesson that an innovator cannot afford to rest on its laurels. Past success does not guarantee success in the future. Firms must strive for constant innovation.

For instance, SmithKline Beckman scored a great success with Tagamet, the ulcer medicine it introduced in 1976. For years the biggest problem the company faced was meeting demand. However, Glaxo Holdings, developed a competing drug, Zantac, with fewer side effects. SmithKline, meanwhile, was unable to come up with new blockbuster drugs despite spending vast sums on research.[37] In retrospect, it is easy to say that SmithKline did not act quickly enough to build up a world-class research capability. However, in the pharmaceutical industry, luck may play as much of a role as talent and organization and SmithKline's management could do only so much. Still, the lesson is this: to maintain technical and market leadership, a firm has to strive for constant innovation.

Technology Push and Market Pull

The "technology-push" model of innovation starts with discoveries in basic science and engineering. From these discoveries new goods and services come to the marketplace. However, numerous empirical studies and descriptions of innovation demonstrate the importance of a clear perception of market needs. Successful innovations need both scientific/technical advances and market appeal (see Figure 11-4).

FIGURE 11-4
Evaluating new products: the commercial and technical screen

		Technical Potential	
		High	*Low*
Commercial promise	*High*	Sure success	Need technical breakthrough
	Low	Need market acceptance	Sure failure

Von Hippel shows that the amounts of innovation from scientific/technical people and from manufacturers and users are about equal. Frequent interactions between these groups are important. Users must be sophisticated enough to make technically relevant recommendations and be able to purchase and use the products that incorporate their suggestions.[35]

The challenge innovators face is to match technological opportunity with market need. For managers, this means bringing together the different in-house functions (such as marketing, R&D, and manufacturing) that have a knowledge of consumer needs and scientific and technical developments. Exclusively, technology-push or **market-pull** models are now viewed as atypical examples of a more general process in which constant inter-action takes place between market requirements and scientific achievement.[39]

Although more R&D does not necessarily result in more innovation, market need alone may yield such simple, incremental innovations that they do not add up to much in the long run.[40] In the end, different types of innovation, science and technology-based and market-driven, exist at different stages in the product life cycle.

market pull
Theory that consumer demand, not new discoveries in science and engineering, drive innovation.

Japanese Innovation

Japanese innovation—more of the market-pull variety—had relied on imitation, purchase, and copy of foreign technology. Its improvements have been incremental and involved modest, but commercially extremely important, refinements of inventions made elsewhere, most often in the United States.[41]

Buying Western Technology

From 1950 to 1980, Japan bought Western technology through more than 30,000 licensing and technology importing agreements for which it paid more than $10 billion.[42] The videotape recorder, for instance, was an American invention, created by Ampex Corporation for television productions. Sony made the changes necessary in video recording to appeal to a mass consumer market.

Japan has excelled in this type of applied research. However, it has been trying in recent years to go beyond applied research and the adaptation of Western technologies. The nation's leaders realize that it needs to be able to achieve the kinds of scientific and technical breakthroughs that can create new industries and transform an entire economy. Spurred by a desire for self-reliance and national pride, the leaders have been trying to shift Japanese research priorities toward basic science and research.[43]

Obstacles to Ascendancy in Basic Research

Creativity is necessary for success in basic research. The emphasis in Japanese education, however, has been on rote learning and brute memorization, which are designed to give students the skills to pass rigorous standardized tests. The Japanese have succeeded in lifting their average student above the educational levels generally found in the United States. Thus, the average Japanese blue-collar and salaried worker is better educated and more disciplined than the average blue-collar or salaried worker in the United States. However, American elites are probably more skilled than those in Japan. Japan has had few Nobel Prize winners in the sciences while Germany has had 4 times as many, Great Britain 10 times as many, and the United States 30 times as many.[44]

Since Japanese culture stresses consensus and conformance to group norms, intellectual dialogue and confrontation are not as common. The individual genius who shows disdain for what others do and succeeds despite breaking all the rules is not accepted in Japanese society. In areas where creativity is called for, such as computer software, Japan is lagging behind the United States and other Western nations.

The number of graduate students in Japan is about 3 percent of the total student population compared with about 12 percent in the United States.[45] Most Japanese research is carried out in corporations, not universities, and the corporations emphasize finding practical, commercial applications and solving real-world problems, not basic research.

The Japanese, however, understand that to maintain economic leadership they will have to extend their technical competence beyond incremental innovations. They will have to emphasize basic discoveries. The Japanese also realize that they can no longer live off Western technology; to succeed in the long run they will have to export original ideas.

The Japanese have begun to make great strides. About half the patents filed worldwide now come from Japanese corporations.[46] Japanese technological advances are mostly in hardware areas and they show the continued Japanese genius for manufacturing. Nevertheless, the Japanese have not caught up with the United States and other Western nations in the creative industries of movies, records, and pharmaceuticals.

Product-Focused Research

Japan has more technical and scientific workers per capita than any nation in the world (5,000 per million of population compared with 3,500 in the United States and 2,500 in Germany), and it spends as much on research and development as a percentage of GNP as the United States and more than any single European nation.[47] While U.S. research directed toward military needs is likely to decline somewhat under budgetary restraints and the end of the Cold War, Japan's research has long been more product oriented. Japan also has the capital derived from a high rate of savings to spend on new factories to manufacture the new products. It is beginning to export much of the manufacturing technology to other countries in the Pacific Rim where labor costs are cheaper than in Japan.

Japan's successes in technology are based on many factors (see Figure 11-5):

fusion factor
The ability to blend incremental improvements from sometimes alien fields to create a product with entirely new features.

1. *Fusion factor.* The ability to blend incremental improvements from sometimes alien fields to create a product with entirely new features is known as the fusion factor. The heavy investment by Japanese industrial groups (*keiretsu*) in each other's companies facilitates this process.

2. *Linking innovations.* The Japanese recognize that making a fundamental breakthrough is by itself insufficient. To be really successful at innovation, it is necessary to devise a better way to manufacture and help customers use the product. For instance, Corning Glass, a U.S. company, first developed fiber optics, but Japanese companies solved the practical problems that prevented customers from using this product—they fell apart too easily and the messages sent were often lost during transmission. Robots with various forms of "soft automation" have given the Japanese great advantages in easily redesigning their production facilities in response to changing consumer preferences. Japanese engineers also consider cost and manufacturability from the beginning while American engineers are more concerned about the technical feasibility of a project.

3. *Less reliance on rate-of-return criteria.* Japanese managers do not rigidly adhere to rate-of-return criteria in assessing new projects because they believe that one successful innovation is likely to breed another and that waves of innovation cannot be predicted by conventional rate-of-return techniques. For example, a new optical chip fashioned from gallium arsenide could promote new tools for chip manufacture and solve remaining problems in developing high-definition television (HDTV), thereby speeding innovations in both areas.

4. *Speed in marketing a product.* The Japanese believe that speed in getting a product to the market is critical. Even if the product is not perfect, it is better for customers to buy the product and get used to it. This process enables companies developing the product not only to earn needed income but also to receive invaluable feedback about what the next generation of the product should be like. This feedback cannot be obtained from conventional marketing studies. U.S. scientists at MIT developed a machine capable of recognizing over 400 words, but they had no plans to bring this machine immediately to the market. In contrast, the Japanese telecommunications giant Nippon Telegraph and Telephone developed a machine that recognized only 32 words, but the company already was working on a commercial application.

5. *Refusal to accept failure.* Japanese engineers do not know the meaning of failure. They push on to success regardless of the obstacles. Studies of the working habits of Japanese and American engineers show that after a hard day of work, American engineers go home to their families. Japanese engineers are more willing to stay on the job and continue what they are doing; to retreat or give up would be accompanied by great shame.

FIGURE 11-5
Characteristics of
Japanese innovation

- Fusion—a blend of incremental improvements from different fields.
- A recognition that marketing and manufacturing innovation have to go hand in hand with product innovation.
- Less reliance on conventional rate-of-return criteria and belief in waves of innovation.
- Insistence on speed in getting a product to market in effort to obtain feedback from customers.
- Persistence and refusal to accept failure.

As U.S. scientists become more reluctant to share their technology with the Japanese, the Japanese will have to build their success on an indigenous capability for invention.[48] Nonetheless, they have developed many important and unique qualities that have led to technological successes, and these qualities are likely to persist.

The Innovation Process

New ideas rarely are carried out as expected, product gestation periods are often longer than anticipated, and R&D costs are often underestimated while markets are overestimated. After analyzing numerous innovations, Van de Ven and his colleagues concluded that the innovation process typically consists of the following stages:[49]

1. The gestation period of an invention, which lasts for many years, after which seemingly coincidental events occur that set the stage for the innovation to be initiated.
2. Internal or external shocks to an organization often get things going; without them the level of apathy is great.
3. Dissatisfaction is needed to move people from the status quo.
4. The plans submitted by the developers of an invention to the "resource controllers" are in the form of "sales pitches," not realistic assessments of the costs and the obstacles.
5. Once development begins, those involved usually disagree and have a lack of clarity about what the innovation is supposed to entail.
6. Ideas about what should be done proliferate, making the challenge of managing the innovation extremely difficult.
7. Continuity among innovation personnel is broken as people come and go for many reasons including frustration with the process or alternative career opportunities.
8. Emotions run high and frustration levels build as normal setbacks are encountered, mistakes made, and blame apportioned.
9. At first, schedules are adjusted and additional resources are provided to compensate for the unanticipated problems, but as the problems snowball, the patience of the resource providers weakens.
10. The goals of the resource providers and innovation managers begin to diverge and a struggle for power emerges about project goals and evaluation.
11. Resources tend to get tight and run out before the dreams of the developers are fulfilled.

Innovations often are terminated because new resources are not forthcoming. The ideas continue to show promise, but the resource providers lose patience. The ability to see a project to the end is critical to the successful completion of an innovation.

No project evaluation technique has been developed to make this process smoother or to resolve the difficulties inherent in it. Advanced portfolio methods created by statisticians and management consultants typically are not used.[50] Elements of critical success include the enthusiasm and commitment of a project leader, the skills and abilities of the people involved, unanticipated spin-offs from and to other projects, relationships forged by the innovators with customers and resource providers, and intangibles that cannot be assessed with certainty beforehand.

Hunches and Persistence

Hunches and persistence, the elements most feared by cautious investors, are also needed for innovations to succeed. The acceptance of a high degree of uncertainty associated with an innovation usually is confined to special cases: small entrepreneurs willing to take a big gamble, large firms with a portfolio of innovations where one major success or many small ones can compensate for inevitable failures, large firms with substantial resources and few constraints on their use, large and small firms persuaded by the enthusiasm of inventors and product champions to overlook the sober assessments of financial analysts, and government-subsidized research that is allowed to proceed despite financial risks because of some pressing need such as national security.[51]

The social importance of technology, even with all the problems in its development, remains high. Technology promises to aid the visually impaired with products such as a closed-circuit television device that enlarges print up to 60 times its normal size, to produce a safe and effective birth control pill that can terminate an unhealthy pregnancy up to seven weeks after the last onset of menstruation, to make plastics more recyclable, to help doctors predict who will get cancer, to repair the stagnant economies of Eastern Europe, and to do much more.[52]

Conclusions

Economic progress occurs in stages that are driven by new technologies. At present, it is unclear which technologies will drive economic growth and which will prevail in the future.

The technical, economic, and political obstacles that stand in the way of the development of new technologies are substantial. These obstacles affect the entire development process. Evaluating the promise of a technology requires careful assessment of both the technology's maturity and the market potential, which work together in its successful launching.

Japanese innovation is distinguished by the ability to fuse incremental improvements from many fields, the attention paid to manufacturing and marketing as well as new product development, the disregard for strict rate-of-return assessments, the rush to put products on the market, and the drive to succeed at all costs. This chapter has stressed the many difficulties in developing new technologies, the social importance of technology, and the need for creative entrepreneurs to play their hunches and be persistent despite the odds against success.

Discussion Questions

1. Why is technology important?
2. What five factors drive technological innovation? Discuss the role of each.
3. Describe Schumpeter's theory. What current relevance does it have?
4. What are the arguments of the technological pessimists? What are the arguments of the optimists? What does Daniel Bell say? What do you believe?
5. What are the differences between simple extrapolation, expert advice, and scenario building in forecasting the future?

6. Select a technology that has promise (e.g., cellular communications, biotechnology). Chart what has been accomplished in bringing this technology to market and what must still be accomplished. Give your estimate of the technology's potential.
7. What kind of estimates do developers of technology have to make? Why are these estimates inherently uncertain? What kind of system would you set up in a company so that better estimates could be made?
8. What problems did Enprostil encounter? What problems did Ultrasofts encounter? What problems did GE encounter with its refrigerator compressor? What could have been done to avoid these problems?
9. Analyze Motorola's problems in the chip market.
10. Will the United States be competitive in the market for HDTV? Why or why not?
11. Why do firms have to strive for constant innovation?
12. Which is dominant in innovation—the technology-push or market—pull models? Why?
13. What are Japan's strengths and weaknesses as an innovator?
14. What role do hunches and persistence play in innovation?

Endnotes

1. John Maynard Keynes, *General Theory of Employment, Interest and Money* (New York: Macmillan, 1936), cited in C. Freeman, *The Economics of Industrial Innovation*, 2nd ed. (Cambridge, Mass.: MIT Press, 1982), p. 156.
2. James D. Gwartney and Richard L. Stroup, *Economics: Private and Public Choice* (New York: Harcourt Brace Jovanovich, 1987).
3. Ronald Henkoff, "Where Will the Jobs Come From?" *Fortune*, Oct. 19, 1992, pp. 58-64; Kenneth Labich, "The New Low-Risk Entrepreneurs," *Fortune*, July 27, 1992, pp. 84-92; "On Birth and Business," *Economist*, Oct. 5, 1991, p. 71.
4. "3M Run Scared?" *Business Week*, Sept. 16, 1991, pp. 60-62.
5. "Venture Capital," *Business Week*, Dec. 2, 1991.
6. Brenton Schlender, "How Sony Keeps the Magic Going," *Fortune*, June 18, 1991, pp. 76-84; "Sony," *Economist*, May 30, 1992, p. 67.
7. Stephen Sacks, "Science and Technology Industrial Policy," paper delivered at the Annual Meeting of the American Political Science Association, 1991.
8. "American Technology Policy," *Economist*, July 25, 1992, pp. 21-23.
9. "Innovation," *Economist*, Jan. 11, 1992, pp. 17-19.
10. Nikolai Kondratiev, "The Major Economic Cycles," *Voprosy Konjunitury* 1 (1925), pp. 28-79; English translation reprinted in *Lloyd's Bank Review*, no. 129, 1978.
11. I. M. Kirzner, *Perception, Opportunity, and Profit: Studies in the Theory of Entrepreneurship* (Chicago: University of Chicago Press, 1979); J. A. Schumpeter, *Business Cycles: A Theoretical, Historical and Statistical Analysis of the Capitalist Process* (New York: McGraw-Hill, 1939).
12. Daniel Bell, *The Coming of Postindustrial Society: A Venture in Social Forecasting* (New York: Basic Books, 1973).
13. George Gilder, "The World's Next Source of Wealth," *Fortune*, August 28, 1989, pp. 116-20.
14. Ibid.
15. G. Starling, *The Changing Environment of Business*, 3rd ed. (Boston: PWS-Kent Publishing, 1988).
16. Ibid.
17. R. E. Willis, *A Guide to Forecasting for Planners and Managers* (Englewood Cliffs, N.J.: Prentice Hall, 1987); P. Wack, "Scenarios: Uncharted Waters Ahead," *Harvard Business Review*, Sept.-Oct. 1985, pp. 89-99; M. Magnet, "Who Needs a Trend-Spotter?" *Fortune*, Dec. 9, 1985, pp. 51-56.
18. D. A. Burrus, "A Glimpse of the Future: Twenty New Technologies That Will Alter the Career Paths of the Class of '91," *National Business Employment Weekly*, Spring 1991, p. 6; "A Survey of Artificial Intelligence," *Economist*, March 14, 1992, special report.
19. "White Collar Computers," *Economist*, Aug. 1, 1992, pp. 57-58.
20. W. M. Bulkeley, "Bright Outlook for Artificial Intelligence Yields to Slow Growth and Big Cutbacks," *The Wall Street Journal*, July 5, 1990, p. 81.
21. Ibid.
22. Ibid.
23. Ibid.
24. R. Koenig and R. Smith, "Drop in Tagamet Sales Is Putting SmithKline in Danger of Takeover," *The Wall Street Journal*, Jan. 13, 1989, p. A1; A. Newman, "Biotech Shares May Soon Fulfill Profit Promise," *The Wall Street Journal*, Oct. 8, 1990, p. C1.
25. Bylinsky, 1988; Freeman, *The Economics of Industrial Innovation*.
26. Frank Knight, *Risk, Uncertainty, and Profit* (New York: Houghton Mifflin, 1921).

27. Knight, *Risk, Uncertainty, and Profit*; Freeman, *The Economics of Industrial Innovation.*

28. Ibid.

29. Ibid.

30. Ibid., p. 155.

31. M. Chase, "Did Syntex Withhold Data on Side Effects of a Promising Drug?" *The Wall Street Journal*, Jan. 8, 1991, p. A1.

32. A. Swasy, "Diaper's Failure Shows How Poor Plans, Unexpected Woes Can Kill New Products," *The Wall Street Journal*, Oct. 9, 1990, p. B1.

33. T. F. O'Boyle, "GE Refrigerator Woes Illustrate the Hazards in Changing a Product," *The Wall Street Journal*, May 7, 1990, p. A1.

34. J. B. White and M. G. Guiles, "GM's Plan for Saturn, to Beat Small Imports, Trails Original Goals," *The Wall Street Journal*, July 9, 1990, p. A1.

35. R. Rothwell and W. Zegveld, *Reindustrialization and Technology* (Armonk, N.Y.: M. E. Sharpe, 1985); S. K. Yoder, "Motorola Loses Edge in Microprocessors by Delaying New Chips," *The Wall Street Journal*, March 4, 1990, p. A1.

36. B. Davis, "High-Definition TV, Once a Capital Idea, Wanes in Washington," *The Wall Street Journal*, June 1, 1990, p. A1.

37. Koenig and Smith, "Drop in Tagamet Sales"; R. Koenig, "Rich in New Products, Monsanto Must Only Get Them on Market," *The Wall Street Journal*, May 18, 1990, p. A1.

38. Schumpeter, *Business Cycles*; J. Schmookler, *Invention and Economic Growth* (Cambridge, Mass.: Harvard University Press, 1966); M. Betz, *Managing Technology: Competing through New Ventures, Innovation, and Corporate Research*; E. Von Hippel, *Appropriability of Innovation Benefit as a Predictor of the Functional Locus of Innovation*, working Paper 1084-79, Sloan School of Management, MIT, Cambridge, Mass., 1979; E. Von Hippel, "The Dominant Role of Users in the Scientific Instrument Innovation Process," *Research Policy* 5 (1976); E. Von Hippel, "Users as Innovators," *Technology Review* 80 (1978).

39. D. C. Mowery and N. Rosenberg, "The Influence of Market Demand upon Innovation: A Critical Review of Some Recent Empirical Studies," *Research Policy* 8 (1978).

40. R. H. Hayes and W. J. Abernathy, "Managing Our Way to Economic Decline," *Harvard Business Review*, July-Aug. 1980.

41. E. Mansfield, "Industrial R&D in Japan and the United States: A Comparative Study," *Innovation and Change in Japan and the United States* 2 (1988), pp. 223-28; S. Lehr, "The Japanese Challenge: Can They Achieve Technological Supremacy?" *New York Times Magazine*, July 8, 1984, pp. 18-23; "Thinking Ahead," *Economist*, Dec. 2-8, 1989.

42. "Thinking Ahead."

43. Lehr, "The Japanese Challenge."

44. Ibid.

45. "Thinking Ahead."

46. Ibid.

47. Ibid.

48. A. Murray and U. C. Lehner, "What U.S. Scientists Discover, the Japanese Convert—Into Profit," *The Wall Street Journal*, June 25, 1990, p. A1.

49. A. H. Van de yen, H. L. Angle, and M. S. Poole, eds., *Research of the Management of Innovation* (N.Y.: Harper & Row, 1989).

50. Freeman, *The Economics of Industrial Innovation.*

51. U. Gupta, "Watching and Waiting: Biotechnology Holds Great Promise, but Investors Are Still Waiting for the Payoff," *The Wall Street Journal*, Nov. 13, 1989, p. R32; Freeman, *The Economics of Industrial Innovation.*

52. S. C. Bakos, "Abortion Pill Ready for Use in Five Countries," *Minneapolis Star Tribune*, Oct. 2, 1988, p. 1E; Chase, "Did Syntex Withhold Data on Side Effects of a Promising Drug?"; A. K. Naj, "GE Pushes to Develop Recyclable Plastic," *The Wall Street Journal*, Aug. 13, 1990, p. B5; R. Brenner, *Betting on Ideas: Wars, Inventions, Inflation* (Chicago: University of Chicago Press, 1985); M. Waldholz, "A Genetic Discovery Helps Doctors Predict Who Will Get Cancer," *The Wall Street Journal*, Oct. 31, 1989, p. A1; R. Ricklefs, "Firms Introduce Products Aimed at Visually Impaired," *The Wall Street Journal*, Sept. 28, 1988, p. B25.

Chapter Twelve

THE NATURE

OF LAW

Introduction

Today, businesspeople confront the law at every turn. For example, business firms continually utilize the law of property, contract, and agency. Indeed, business could hardly function without these and other basic bodies of law. In addition to facilitating business activity, the legal system restricts it as well. Today, government regulates most aspects of a firm's operations—for example, advertising, product safety, employee relations, the issuance of securities, and behavior toward competitors.

Thus, business people constantly use, rely on, react to, plan around—and sometimes violate—innumerable legal rules or "laws." For this reason, managers should have a general knowledge of the legal system and the most important legal rules affecting their firms. This text discusses many such rules, often in detail. But your ability to use and apply the legal rules affecting business is incomplete unless you also understand law's general nature, its functions, and how judges interpret it. This understanding could go some way toward reducing business complaints about the law and lawyers.

Four Perspectives on Law

This chapter examines law's nature from four different angles. First, it describes, classifies, and ranks the various kinds of rules that are regarded as law in the United States—the *types* of law. This discussion, however, only partly conveys law's general nature. Thus, the chapter's second section discusses a subject known as *jurisprudence* or legal philosophy. Jurisprudence tries to establish a general definition of law, and each of the competing definitions we examine highlights an important facet of law's many-sided nature. Shifting from the theoretical to the pragmatic, this chapter's third section examines some of the *functions* law serves—what it *does*. The chapter concludes by discussing legal reasoning, the set of techniques judges use when interpreting legal rules. This discussion should help dispel the common misconception that the law consists of clear and precise commands that judges merely look up and then mechanically apply.

Business Law and the Regulatory Environment, Ninth Edition, by Michael B. Metzger, Jane P. Mallor, A. James Barnes, Thomas Bowers, Michael J. Phillips, Arlen Langvardt. © Irwin/McGraw-Hill, The McGraw-Hill Companies, 1946, 1951, 1955, 1956, 1963, 1966, 1970, 1974, 1978, 1982, 1986, 1989, 1992, 1995.

Types and Classifications of Law

The Types of Law

Constitutions

Constitutions, which exist at the state and federal levels, have two general functions.[1] First, they establish the structure of government for the political unit they control (a state or the federal government). This involves stating the branches and subdivisions of the government and the powers given and denied to each. Through its **separation of powers**, for example, the U.S. Constitution establishes a Congress and gives it power to legislate or *make* law in certain areas, provides for a chief executive (the president) whose function is to execute or *enforce* the laws, and helps create a federal judiciary to *interpret* the laws. The U.S. Constitution also structures the relationship between the federal government and the states. In the process, it respects the principle of **federalism** by recognizing the states' power to make law in certain areas.

The second function of constitutions is to prevent other units of government from taking certain actions or passing certain laws. Constitutions do so mainly by prohibiting government action that restricts certain individual rights. The Bill of Rights to the U.S. Constitution is an example.

Statutes

Statutes are laws created by Congress or a state legislature. They are stated in an authoritative form in statute books or codes. As you will see, however, their interpretation and application are often difficult.

Throughout this text, you encounter state statutes that were originally drafted as **uniform acts**. Uniform acts basically are model statutes drafted by private bodies of lawyers and/or scholars. They do not become law until they are enacted by a legislature. Their aim is to produce state-by-state uniformity on the subjects they address. Examples include the Uniform Commercial Code (which deals with a wide range of commercial law subjects), the Uniform Partnership Act, the Revised Uniform Limited Partnership Act, and the Revised Model Business Corporation Act.

Common Law

The **common law** (also called judge-made law or case law) is that law made and applied by judges as they decide cases not governed by statutes or other types of law. In theory, it exists at the state level only. The common law originated in medieval England. It developed from the decisions of judges in settling disputes. Over time, judges began to follow the decisions of other judges in similar cases. This practice became formalized in the doctrine of *stare decisis* (let the decision stand). As discussed later in this chapter, *stare decisis* has enabled the common law to evolve to meet changing social conditions. Thus, the common law rules in force today often differ considerably from the common law rules of earlier times.

The common law came to America with the first English settlers and was applied by courts during the colonial period.[2] It continued to be used after the Revolution and the adoption of the Constitution, and still governs many cases today. For example, the rules of tort, contract, and agency discussed in this text are mainly common law rules. However, the states have codified (enacted into statute) some parts of the common law. They have also passed statutes superseding judge-made law in certain situations. For example, the states have established special rules for contract cases involving the sale of goods by enacting Article 2 of the Uniform Commercial Code.

This text's torts, contracts, and agency chapters often refer to the *Restatement* (or *Restatement (Second)*) rule on a particular subject. The *Restatements* are collections of common law (and occasionally statutory) rules covering various areas of the law. Because they are promulgated by the American Law Institute rather than by courts, the *Restatements* are not law and do not bind courts. However, state courts often find *Restatement* rules persuasive and adopt them as common law rules within their states. Usually, the *Restatement* rules are the rules actually followed by a majority of the states. Occasionally, however, the *Restatements* stimulate changes in the common law by stating new rules that the courts later decide to follow.

Equity

The body of law called **equity** has traditionally tried to do discretionary rough justice in situations where common law rules would produce unfair results. In medieval England, common law rules were technical and rigid and the remedies available in common law courts were too few. This meant that some deserving parties could not obtain adequate relief in the common law courts. As a result, the chancellor, the king's most powerful executive officer, began to hear cases that the common law courts could not resolve fairly.

Eventually, separate equity courts emerged to handle the cases heard by the chancellor. These courts took control of a case only when there was no adequate remedy in a regular common law court. In equity courts, procedures were flexible, and rigid rules of law were de-emphasized in favor of general moral maxims. Equity courts also provided several remedies not available in the common law courts (which generally awarded only money damages or the recovery of property). Perhaps the most important of these *equitable remedies* is the **injunction**, a court order forbidding a party to do some act or commanding him to perform some act. Others include the contract remedies of **specific performance** (whereby a party is ordered to perform according to the terms of her contract), **reformation** (in which the court rewrites the contract's terms to reflect the parties' real intentions), and **rescission** (a cancellation of a contract in which the parties are often returned to their precontractual position).

Like the common law, equity principles and practices were brought to the American colonies by the English settlers. They continued to be used after the Revolution and the adoption of the Constitution. Over time, however, the once-sharp line between law and equity has become blurred. Most states have abolished separate equity courts, now allowing one court to handle both legal and equitable claims. Also, equitable principles have been blended together with common law rules, and some traditional equity doctrines have been restated as common law or statutory rules. Finally, courts sometimes combine an award of money damages with an equitable remedy.

Administrative Regulations and Decisions

Throughout this century, the *administrative agencies* established by Congress and the state legislatures have acquired considerable power, importance, and influence over business. A major reason for the rise of administrative agencies was the myriad of social and economic problems created by the industrialization of the United States that began late in the 19th century. Because legislatures generally lacked the time and expertise to deal with these problems on a continuing basis, the creation of specialized, expert agencies was almost inevitable.

Administrative agencies get the ability to make law through a *delegation* (or handing over) of power from the legislature. Agencies normally are created by a statute that specifies the areas in which the agency can make law and the scope of its power in each area. Often, these statutory delegations are worded so broadly that the legislature has, in effect, merely pointed to a problem and given the agency wide-ranging powers to deal with it.

The two kinds of law made by administrative agencies are **administrative regulations** and **agency decisions**. Like statutes, administrative regulations appear in a precise form in one authoritative source. However, they differ from statutes in that the body enacting them is an agency, not the legislature. In addition, some agencies have an internal court structure that enables them to hear cases arising under the statutes and regulations they enforce. The resulting agency decisions are another kind of law.

Treaties

According to the U.S. Constitution, treaties made by the president with foreign governments and approved by two thirds of the U.S. Senate are "the supreme Law of the Land." As we note shortly, treaties invalidate inconsistent state (and occasionally federal) laws.

Ordinances

State governments have subordinate units that exercise certain functions. Some of these units, such as school districts, have limited powers. Others, such as counties, municipalities, and townships, exercise a number of governmental functions. The enactments of municipalities are called **ordinances**; zoning ordinances are an example. The enactments of other political subdivisions may also be referred to as ordinances.

Executive Orders

In theory, the president or a state's governor is a chief executive who enforce the laws but has no lawmaking powers. However, these officials sometimes have the power to issue laws called **executive orders**. This power normally results from a legislative delegation.

Priority Rules

Because the different types of law conflict, rules for determining which type takes priority are necessary. Here, we briefly describe the most important priority rules.

1. According to the principle of federal supremacy, the U.S. Constitution, federal laws enacted pursuant to it, and treaties are the supreme law of the land. This means that federal law defeats conflicting state law.
2. Constitutions defeat other types of law within their domain. Thus, a state constitution defeats all other state laws inconsistent with it, and the U.S. Constitution defeats inconsistent federal laws.
3. When a treaty conflicts with a federal statute over a purely domestic matter, the measure that is latest in time usually prevails.
4. Within either the state or the federal domain, statutes defeat conflicting laws that depend on a legislative delegation for their validity. For example, a state statute defeats an inconsistent state administrative regulation.
5. State statutes and any laws derived from them by delegation defeat inconsistent common law rules. For example, either a statute or a state administrative regulation defeats a conflicting common law rule.

Concept Review
The Types of Law Compared

	Who Enacts?	State and/or Federal?	Stated in One Authoritative Form?	Remarks
Constitutions	U.S. Constitution originally ratified by states; complex amendment process. States may vary.	Both	Yes, see constitutional decision making	Defeat other forms of positive law within sphere (federal or state)
Statutes	Legislatures	Both	Yes, but see this chapter's discussion of statutory interpretation	Normally defeat other forms of positive law within sphere (federal or state) except constitutions
Common Law	Courts	In theory, state only	No. See this chapter's discussion of legal reasoning	Law of tort, contract, and agency mainly common law
Equity	Formerly, equity courts; now usually courts in general	In theory, state only. But equitable principles pervade federal law as well.	No	Traditional separation of law and equity now virtually gone
Administrative Regulations	Administrative agencies	Both	Yes	
Administrative Decision	Administrative agencies	Both	No	
Treaties	President plus two thirds of Senate	Federal	Yes	Defeat inconsistent state law
Ordinances	Usually, local government bodies	State (mainly local)	Yes	
Executive Orders	Chief executives	Both	Yes	Usually based on delegation from legislature

Classifications of Law

Cutting across the different types of law are three common *classifications* of law. These classifications involve distinctions between: (1) criminal law and civil law, (2) substantive law and procedural law, and (3) public law and private law. One type of law might be classified in each of these ways. For example, a state statute might be criminal, substantive, and public.

Criminal and Civil Law

Criminal law is the law applied when the government prosecutes someone for the commission of a crime. **Civil law** is the law applied when one party sues another party because the other did not meet a legal duty owed to the first party. Civil lawsuits usually involve private parties, but the government may be a party to a civil suit (as, for instance, where a city sues, or is sued by, a construction contractor). Criminal penalties (e.g., imprisonment or fines) differ from civil remedies (e.g., money damages or equitable relief).

Even though the civil law and the criminal law are distinct bodies of law, the same behavior can violate both. For instance, if due to A's careless driving his car hits and injures B. A may face both a criminal prosecution by the state and B's civil suit for damages.

Substantive Law and Procedural Law

Substantive law sets the rights and duties of people as they act in society. **Procedural law** controls the behavior of government bodies (mainly courts) as they establish and enforce rules of substantive law. A statute making murder a crime, for example, is a rule of substantive law. But the rules describing the proper conduct of a criminal trial are procedural. This text mainly discusses substantive law.

Public and Private Law

Public law concerns the powers of government and the relations between government and private parties. Examples include constitutional law, administrative law, and criminal law. **Private law** establishes a framework of legal rules that enable private parties to set the rights and duties they owe each other. Examples include the rules of contract, property, and agency.

Jurisprudence

The types of law are sometimes collectively referred to as *positive law*. Positive law comprises the rules that have been laid down (or posited) by a recognized political authority. Knowing the types of positive law is essential for understanding the American legal system and the business law topics discussed in this text. But defining *law* by listing these different kinds of positive law is much like defining the word *automobile* by describing all the vehicles going by that name. To define law properly, we need a general description that captures its essence.

The field known as **jurisprudence** or legal philosophy tries to provide such a description. Over time, different schools of jurisprudence have emerged, each with its own distinctive view of law. The differences among these schools are not merely academic matters. As Figure 12-1 suggests, their conceptions of law often affect their approach toward real-life issues.

FIGURE 12-1
A brief sketch of the jurisprudential schools

	Definition of Law	Relation between Law and Morality	Practical Tendency
Legal Positivism	Command of a recognized political authority	Separate questions: "law is law, just or not"	Valid positive law should be enforced and obeyed, just or not
Natural Law	All commands of recognized political authorities that are not unjust	"Unjust law is not law"	Unjust positive laws should not be enforced and obeyed
American Legal Realism	What public decisionmakers actually do	Unclear	"Law in action" often more important than "law in the books"
Sociological Jurisprudence	Process of social ordering in accordance with dominant social values and interests	Although moral values influence positive law, no way to say whether this is right or wrong	Law inevitably does (and should?) follow dominant social values and interests

Legal Positivism

One feature common to all types of positive law is their enactment by a recognized political authority such as a legislature or an administrative agency. This common feature underlies the definition of law adopted by the school of jurisprudence called **legal positivism**. Legal positivists define law as the *command of a recognized political authority*. To the British political philosopher Thomas Hobbes, for instance, "Law properly, is the word of him, that by right hath command over others."

The commands made by recognized political authorities can be good, bad, or indifferent in moral terms. But as Figure 12-2 demonstrates, to legal positivists such commands are valid law regardless of their goodness or badness. For positivists, in other words, legal validity and moral validity are different questions. Sometimes this view is expressed by the slogan: "Law is law, just or not." For this reason, some (but not all) positivists say that every properly enacted positive law should be enforced and obeyed, whether just or not. Similarly, positivist judges usually try to enforce the law as written, excluding their own moral views from the process.

FIGURE 12-2
The positivist and natural law definitions of law

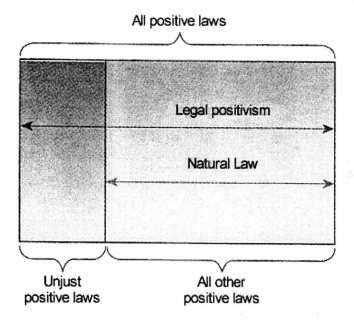

Natural Law

At first glance, legal positivism's "law is law, just or not" approach may seem like perfect common sense. But it presents a problem, for it could mean that any positive law (no matter how unjust) is valid law and should be enforced and obeyed so long as some recognized political authority (no matter how wicked) enacted it. Here, the school of jurisprudence known as **natural law** takes issue with legal positivism by rejecting the positivist separation of law and morality.

The basic idea behind most systems of natural law is that some higher law or set of universal moral rules binds all human beings in all times and places. The Roman statesman

Marcus Cicero described natural law as "the highest reason, implanted in nature, which commands what ought to be done and forbids the opposite." Because this higher law determines what is ultimately good and ultimately bad, it is a criterion for evaluating positive law. To Saint Thomas Aquinas, for example, "every human law has just so much of the nature of law as it is derived from the law of nature." To be genuine law, in other words, positive law must resemble the law of nature by being good—or at least by not being bad. This suggests the practical natural law definition of law depicted in Figures 12-1 and 12-2—that natural law equals *those commands of recognized political authorities that do not offend the higher law by being unjust.*

Unjust positive laws, on the other hand, simply are not law. As Cicero put it: "What of the many deadly, the many pestilential statutes which are imposed on peoples? These no more deserve to be called laws than the rules a band of robbers might pass in their assembly." This view is sometimes expressed by the slogan: "An unjust law is not law." Because unjust positive laws are not truly law, many natural law thinkers conclude that they should not be enforced or obeyed.

As compared with positivist judges, therefore, judges influenced by natural law ideas are more likely to read constitutional provisions broadly to invalidate positive laws they regard as unjust. They also are more likely to let morality influence their interpretation of the law. Of course, neither judges nor natural law thinkers always agree on morality's *content*, and this is a major difficulty for the natural law position. This difficulty allows legal positivists to claim that only by keeping legal and moral questions separate can we get any stability and predictability in the law.

American Legal Realism

To some people, the debate between natural law and legal positivism seems unreal. Not only is natural law pie-in-the-sky, such people might say, but sometimes positive law does not mean much either. For example, juries often pay little attention to the legal rules that are supposed to guide their decisions, and prosecutors frequently have discretion whether or not to enforce criminal statutes. In some legal proceedings, moreover, the background, biases, and values of the judge—and not the positive law—determine the result. As the joke goes, justice sometimes is what the judge ate for breakfast.

Remarks like these typify the school of jurisprudence known as **American legal realism.** Legal realists regard the positivist law-in-the-books as less important than the *law in action*—the conduct of those who enforce and interpret the positive law. Thus, American legal realism defines law as the *behavior of public officials (mainly judges) as they deal with matters before the legal system.* Because the actions of such decisionmakers—and not the rules in the books—really affect people's lives, the realists say, this behavior is what counts and what deserves to be called law.

It is doubtful whether the legal realists have ever developed a common position on the relation between law and morality or the duty to obey positive law. But they have been quick to tell judges how to behave. Many realists feel that the modern judge should be a kind of social engineer who weighs all relevant values and considers social science findings when deciding a case. Such a judge would make the positive law only one factor in her decision. Because judges inevitably base their decisions on personal considerations, the realists seem to say, they should at least do this honestly and intelligently. To promote this kind of decisionmaking, the realists have sometimes favored fuzzy, discretionary rules that allow judges to decide each case according to its unique facts.

Sociological Jurisprudence

The term **sociological jurisprudence** is a general label uniting several diverse jurisprudential approaches whose common aim is to examine law within its social context. Their outlook is captured by the following quotation from Justice Oliver Wendell Holmes:

> The life of the law has not been logic: it has been experience. The felt necessities of the time, the prevalent moral and political theories, intuitions of public policy, avowed or unconscious, even the prejudices which judges share with their fellow-men, have had a good deal more to do than the syllogism in determining the rules by which men should be governed. The law embodies the story of a nation's development through many centuries, and it cannot be dealt with as if it contained only the axioms and corollaries of a book of mathematics.[3]

Despite this common outlook, there is no distinctive sociological definition of law. If one were attempted, it might go as follows: *Law is a process of social ordering reflecting society's dominant interests and values.*

Different Sociological Approaches

By examining a few examples of sociological legal thinking, we can put some flesh on the definition just offered. The "dominant interests" portion of the definition is exemplified by the writings of Roscoe Pound, an influential 20th-century American legal philosopher. Pound developed a detailed catalog of the social interests that press on government and the legal system and thus shape positive law. During his life, Pound's catalog changed along with changes in American society. An example of the definition's "dominant values" component is the *historical school* of jurisprudence identified with the 19th-century German legal philosopher Friedrich Karl van Savigny. Savigny saw law as an unplanned, almost unconscious, reflection of the collective spirit (*Volksgeist*) of a particular society. In his view, legal change could only be explained historically, as a slow response to social change.

By emphasizing the influence of dominant social interests and values, Pound and Savigny undermine the legal positivist view that law is nothing more than the command of some political authority. The early 20th-century Austrian legal philosopher Eugen Ehrlich went even further in rejecting positivism. He did so by distinguishing two different "processes of social ordering" contained within our definition of sociological jurisprudence. The first of these is "state law," or positive law. The second is the "living law," informal social controls such as customs, family ties, and business practices. By regarding both as law, Ehrlich blurred the line between positive law and other kinds of social ordering. In the process, he stimulated people to recognize that positive law is only one element within a spectrum of social controls.

The Implications of Sociological Jurisprudence

Because its definition of law includes social values, sociological jurisprudence seems to resemble natural law. But most sociological thinkers are only concerned with the *fact* that moral values influence the law and not with the goodness or badness of those values. In Chapter 14, for instance, we note that laissez-faire economic values were widely shared in 19th-century America and strongly influenced the contract law of that period. But we do not say whether this was good or bad. Thus, it might seem that sociological jurisprudence gives no practical advice to those who must enforce and obey positive law.

However, sociological jurisprudence has at least one practical implication—a tendency to urge that the law must change to meet changing social conditions and values. This is basically the familiar notion that the law should keep up with the times. Some might stick to this view even when society's values are changing for the worse. To Holmes, for example, "[t]he first requirement of a sound body of law is, that it should correspond with the actual feelings and demands of the community, *whether right or wrong.*"[4]

Comparing the Schools

The following *Rochin* case helps illustrate the differences among the schools of jurisprudence. To highlight those differences, consider the following questions about *Rochin*. Despite Justice Frankfurter's denial, doesn't the Supreme Court's reasoning in *Rochin* resemble natural law's unjust-law-is-not-law approach? What *observation* would almost any American legal realist make about this case? Would most legal positivists approve of the *Rochin* decision? With the benefit of hindsight, it looks as if *Rochin* was a precursor of the many liberal criminal procedure decisions of the 1960s—decisions that probably had their roots in changed social values. If so, what might an exponent of sociological jurisprudence say about *Rochin*?

Rochin v. California[5]

In 1949, three Los Angeles County deputy sheriffs heard that Antonio Rochin was selling narcotics. In search of evidence, they entered Rochin's home one morning and forced open the door to his bedroom. They spotted two capsules on a nightstand beside the bed on which the half-clad Rochin was sitting. After the deputies asked, "Whose stuff is this?" Rochin quickly put the capsules in his mouth. The deputies then jumped Rochin and tried to force the capsules from his mouth. When this proved unsuccessful, they handcuffed Rochin and took him to a hospital. Over Rochin's opposition, they had a doctor insert a tube into his stomach and force an emetic (vomit-inducing) solution through the tube. This stomach pumping caused Rochin to vomit. Within the material he disgorged were two capsules containing morphine.

Rochin then was tried and convicted for possessing a morphine preparation in violation of California law. The two morphine capsules were the main evidence against him, and the trial court admitted this evidence over Rochin's objection. An intermediate appellate court and the California Supreme Court affirmed the conviction. Rochin then appealed to the U.S. Supreme Court. The main issue before the Court was whether the methods by which the deputies obtained the capsules violated the Due Process Clause of the U.S. Constitution's Fourteenth Amendment, which states that "No state shall . . . deprive any person of life, liberty, or property, without due process of law."

Note: At the time this case was decided, evidence obtained through a forced stomach pumping probably was admissible in a majority of the states that had considered the question. Also, the Supreme Court did not then require that state courts exclude evidence obtained through an illegal search or seizure.

Source: 342 U.S. 165 (U.S. Sup. Ct. 1952)

Frankfurter, Justice

The requirements of due process impose upon this Court an exercise of judgment upon the proceedings resulting in a conviction to ascertain whether they offend those canons of decency and fairness which express the notions of justice of English-speaking peoples even toward those charged with the most heinous offenses. These standards of justice are not authoritatively formulated anywhere as though they were specifics. Due process of law is a summarized guarantee of respect for those personal immunities so rooted in the traditions and conscience of our people as to be fundamental, or implicit in the concept of ordered liberty.

The vague contours of the due process clause do not leave judges at large. We may not draw upon our merely personal and private notions and disregard the limits that bind judges. These limits are derived from considerations that are fused in the whole nature of our judicial process. These are considerations deeply rooted in reason and in the compelling traditions of the legal profession. The due process clause places upon this Court the duty of exercising a judgment upon interests of society pushing in opposite directions. Due process thus conceived is not to be derided as a resort to the revival of "natural law."

Applying these general considerations to the present case, we conclude that the proceedings by which this conviction was obtained do more than offend some fastidious squeamishness or private sentimentalism about combating crime too energetically. This is conduct that shocks the conscience. Illegally breaking into the privacy of Rochin, the struggle to open his mouth and remove what was there, the forcible extraction of his stomach's contents—this course of proceeding is bound to offend even hardened sensibilities. They are methods too close to the rack and the screw to permit of constitutional differentiation. **Judgment reversed in favor of Rochin.**

The Functions of Law

In traditional societies, people often viewed law as a set of unchanging rules that deserved obedience because they were part of the natural order of things. By now, however, most lawmakers treat law as a flexible *tool* or *instrument* for the accomplishment of chosen purposes. For example, the law of negotiable instruments, discussed later in this text, is designed to stimulate commercial activity by promoting the free movement of money substitutes such as promissory notes, checks, and drafts. Throughout the text, moreover, you will see courts manipulating existing legal rules to get the results they desire. One strength of this *instrumentalist* attitude is its willingness to adapt the law to further the social good. One weakness is the legal instability and uncertainty those adaptations often produce.

Just as individual legal rules advance specific purposes, *law as a whole* serves many general social functions. Among the most important of those functions are:

1. *Peacekeeping.* The criminal law rules best further this basic function of any legal system. Also, one major function of the civil law is the resolution of private disputes.
2. *Checking government power and thereby promoting personal freedom.* Obvious examples are the constitutional restrictions on government regulation.
3. *Facilitating planning and the realization of reasonable expectations.* The rules of contract law help fulfill this function of law.
4. *Promoting economic growth through free competition.* The antitrust laws are among the many legal rules that help perform this function.
5. *Promoting social justice.* Throughout this century, government has intervened in private social and economic affairs to correct perceived injustices and give all citizens equal access to life's basic goods. One example is the collection of employer-employee regulations.
6. *Protecting the environment.*

Obviously, the law's various functions can conflict. The familiar clash between economic growth and environmental protection is an example. The Rochin case illustrates the equally familiar conflict between effective law enforcement and the preservation of personal rights. Only rarely does the law achieve one end without sacrificing others to some degree. In law, as in life, there is generally no such thing as a free lunch. Where the law's ends conflict, lawmakers can only try to strike the best possible balance among those ends. This suggests limits on the law's usefulness as a device for promoting particular social goals.

Legal Reasoning

This text's main aim is to describe the most important legal rules affecting business. Like virtually every other business law text, it states those rules in what lawyers call "black letter form," using precise sentences saying that certain legal consequences will occur if certain events happen. Although it enables a clear statement of the law's commands, this black letter approach can be misleading. It suggests definiteness, certainty, permanence, and predictability—attributes the law frequently lacks. To illustrate this and to give you some idea how lawyers think, we now discuss the two most important kinds of legal reasoning: case **law reasoning** and **statutory interpretation**.[6] However, we first must examine legal reasoning in general.

Legal reasoning is basically deductive, or syllogistic. The legal rule is the major premise, the facts are the minor premise, and the result is the product of combining the two. Suppose that a state statute says that a driver operating an automobile between 55 and 70 miles per hour must pay a $50 fine (the rule or major premise) and that Jim Smith drives his car at 65 miles per hour (the facts or minor premise). If Jim is arrested, and if the necessary facts can be proved, he will be required to pay the $50 fine. As you will now see, however, legal reasoning is often more difficult than this example would suggest.

Case Law Reasoning

In cases governed by the common law, courts find the appropriate legal rules in prior cases or *precedents*. The standard for choosing and applying prior cases to decide present cases is the doctrine of *stare decisis*, which states that like cases should be decided alike.[7] That is, the present case should be decided in the same way as past cases presenting the same facts and legal issues. If a court decides that an alleged precedent is not like the present case and should not control the decision in that case, it *distinguishes* the prior case.[8]

Because every present case differs from the precedents in *some* respect, it is always theoretically possible to distinguish those precedents. For example, one *could* distinguish a prior case because both parties in that case had black hair, while one party in the present case has brown hair. Of course, such distinctions are usually ridiculous because the differences they identify are insignificant in moral or social policy terms. In other words, a good distinction of a prior case involves a widely accepted policy reason for treating the present case differently from its predecessor. Because people disagree about moral ideas, public policies, and the degree to which they are accepted, and because all these factors change over time, judges may differ on the wisdom of distinguishing a prior case. This is a significant source of uncertainty in the common law. But it also gives the common law the flexibility to adapt to changing social conditions.

The following *MacPherson* case illustrates the common law's ability to change over time. In the series of New York cases *MacPherson* discusses, the **plaintiff** (the party suing) claimed that the **defendant** (the party being sued) had been negligent in manufacturing or inspecting some product, thus injuring the plaintiff, who later purchased or used the product.[9] In the mid-19th century, such suits often failed due to the general rule that a seller or manufacturer was not liable for negligence unless there was *privity of contract* between the defendant and the plaintiff. Privity of contract is the existence of a direct contractual relationship between two parties. Thus, the noliability-outside-privity rule prevented injured plaintiffs from recovering against a seller or manufacturer who had sold the product to a dealer who in turn sold it to the plaintiff. Over time, however, courts began to allow injured plaintiffs to recover from sellers or manufacturers with whom they had not directly dealt. These courts were creating *exceptions* to the general rule; that is, they were distinguishing prior cases announcing the rule and creating new rules to govern the situations they distinguished. *MacPherson* describes the gradual enlargement of such an exception in New York. Eventually, the exception "consumed the rule" by covering so many situations that the original rule became relatively insignificant.[10]

MacPherson v. Buick Motor Co.

One wheel of an automobile manufactured by the Buick Motor Company was made of defective wood. Buick could have discovered the defect had it made a reasonable inspection after it purchased the wheel from another manufacturer. Buick sold the car to a retail dealer, who then sold it to MacPherson. While MacPherson was driving his new Buick, the defective wheel collapsed and he was thrown from the vehicle. He sued Buick for his injuries in a New York trial court, alleging that it had negligently failed to inspect the wheel. Buick's main defense was that it had not dealt directly with MacPherson and thus owed no duty to him. Following trial and appellate court judgments in MacPherson's favor, Buick appealed to the New York Court of Appeals, the state's highest court.

Source: 111 NE. 1050 (N.Y. Ct. App. 1916)

Cardozo, Justice

The foundations of this branch of the law were laid in *Thomas v. Winchester* (1852). A poison was falsely labeled. The sale was made to a druggist, who sold to a customer. The customer recovered damages from the seller who affixed the label. The defendant's negligence, it was said, put human life in imminent danger. A poison, falsely labeled, is likely to injure anyone who gets it. Because the danger is to be foreseen, there is a duty to avoid the injury. *Thomas v. Winchester* became quickly a landmark of the law. In the application of its principle there may, at times, have been uncertainty or even error. There has never been doubt or disavowal of the principle itself.

The chief cases are well known. *Loop v. Litchfield* (1870) was the case of a defect in a small balance wheel used on a circular saw. The manufacturer pointed out the defect to the buyer. The risk can hardly have been an imminent one, for the wheel lasted five years before it broke. In the meanwhile the buyer had made a lease of the machinery. It was held that the manufacturer was not answerable to the lessee. *Loop v. Litchfield* was followed by *Losee v. Clute* (1873), the case of the explosion of a steam boiler. That decision must be confined to its special facts. It was put upon the ground that the risk of injury was too remote. The buyer had not only accepted the boiler, but had tested it. The manufacturer knew that his own test was not the final one. The finality of the test has a bearing on the measure of diligence owing to persons other than the purchaser.

These early cases suggest a narrow construction of the rule. Later cases evince a more liberal spirit. In *Devlin v. Smith* (1882), the defendant contractor built a scaffold for a painter. The painter's workmen were injured. The contractor was held liable. He knew that the scaffold, if improperly constructed, was a most dangerous trap. He knew that it was to be used by the workmen. Building it for their use, he owed them a duty to build it with care. From *Devlin v. Smith* we turn to *Statler v. Ray Manufacturing Co.* (1909). The defendant manufactured a large coffee urn. It was installed in a restaurant. The urn exploded and injured the plaintiff. We held that the manufacturer was liable. We said that the urn was of such a character that it was liable to become a source of great danger if not carefully and properly constructed.

It may be that *Devlin v. Smith* and *Statler v. Ray Manufacturing Co.* have extended the rule of *Thomas v. Winchester*. If so, this court is committed to the extension. The defendant argues that things imminently dangerous to human life are poisons, explosives, deadly weapons—things whose normal function is to injure or destroy. But whatever the rule in *Thomas v. Winchester* may once have been, it no longer has that restricted meaning. A scaffold is not inherently a destructive instrument. No one thinks of [a coffee urn] as an implement whose normal function is destruction.

We hold, then, that the principle of *Thomas v. Winchester* is not limited to things which are implements of destruction. If the nature of a thing is such that it is reasonably certain to place life and limb in peril when negligently made, it is a thing of danger. If to the element of danger there is added knowledge that the thing will be used by persons other than the purchaser, then, irrespective of contract, the manufacturer is under a duty to make it carefully.

The nature of an automobile gives warning of probable danger if its construction is defective. This automobile was designed to go 50 miles an hour. Unless its wheels were sound and strong, injury was almost certain. The defendant knew the danger. It knew that the car would be used by persons other than the buyer, a dealer in cars. The dealer was indeed the one person of whom it might be said with some certainty that by him the car would not be used. Yet the defendant would have us say that he was the one person it was under a legal duty to protect. The law does not lead us to so inconsequent a conclusion. Precedents drawn from the age of travel by stagecoach do not fit the conditions of travel today. The principle that the danger must be imminent does not change, but the things subject to the principle do change. They are whatever the needs of life in a developing civilization require them to be.

Judgment for MacPherson affirmed.

Statutory Interpretation

Because statutes are written in one authoritative form, their interpretation might seem easier than case law reasoning. However, this is not so. One reason courts face difficulties when interpreting statutes is the natural ambiguity of language. This is especially true when statutory words are applied to situations the legislature did not foresee. Also, legislators may deliberately use ambiguous language when they are unwilling or unable to deal specifically with each situation the statute was enacted to regulate. When this happens, the legislature expects courts and/or administrative agencies to fill in the details on a case-by-case basis. Other reasons for deliberate ambiguity include the need for legislative compromise and legislators' desire to avoid taking controversial positions.

Due to problems like these, courts need and use various techniques of statutory interpretation. Figure 12-3 states the most common of these techniques, relating them to the steps in the passage of a statute. As you will see shortly, different techniques can dictate different results in a particular case. Moreover, judges sometimes employ the techniques in an instrumentalist or result-oriented fashion, emphasizing the technique that will produce the result they want and downplaying the others. Thus, it is unclear which technique should control when different techniques yield different results. Although there are some "rules" on this subject, courts often ignore them.

Plain Meaning

Courts begin their interpretation of a statute with its actual language. Where the statute's words have a clear, common, accepted meaning, some courts employ the *plain meaning rule*. This rule states that in such cases, the court should simply apply the statute according to the plain, accepted meaning of its words, and should not concern itself with anything else.

FIGURE 12-3

The steps in a statute's passage and the techniques of statutory interpretation

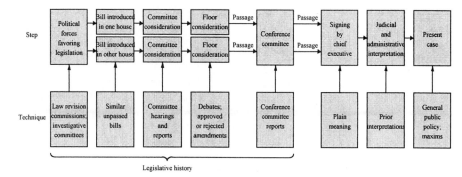

Legislative history

Legislative History

Some courts, like the Supreme Court in the following *Weber* case, refuse to follow a statute's plain meaning when its legislative history suggests a different result. And almost all courts resort to legislative history when the statute's language is ambiguous. A statute's legislative history includes the following sources: the reports of investigative committees or law revision commissions that led to the legislation, the hearings of the legislative committee(s) originally considering the legislation, any reports issued by such a committee, legislative debates, the report of a conference committee reconciling two houses' conflicting versions of the law, amendments or defeated amendments to the legislation, other bills not passed by the legislature but proposing similar legislation, and discrepancies between a bill passed by one house and the final version of the statute.

Sometimes a statute's legislative history provides no information or conflicting information about its meaning, its scope, or its purposes. Also, some sources are more authoritative than others. The worth of debates, for instance, may depend on which legislator (e.g., the sponsor of the bill or an uninformed blowhard) is quoted. Some sources are useful only in particular situations; prior unpassed bills and amendments or defeated amendments are examples. To illustrate those sources, consider whether mopeds are covered by an air pollution statute applying to "automobiles, trucks, buses, and other motorized passenger or cargo vehicles." If the statute's original version included mopeds but this reference was removed by amendment, it is unlikely that the legislature wanted mopeds to be covered. The same might be true if six similar unpassed bills had included mopeds but the bill that was eventually passed did not, or if one house had passed a bill including mopeds but mopeds did not appear in the final version of the legislation.

Courts use legislative history in two overlapping but distinguishable ways. They may use it to determine what the legislature thought about the specific meaning of statutory language. They may also use it to determine the overall aim, end, or goal of the legislation. In this second case, they then ask whether a particular interpretation of the statute is consistent with this purpose. To illustrate the difference between these two uses of legislative history, suppose that a court is considering whether the pollution statute's "other motorized passenger or cargo vehicles" language includes battery-powered vehicles. The court might scan the legislative history for specific references to battery-powered vehicles or other indications of what the legislature thought about their inclusion. However, the court might also use the same history to determine the overall aims of the statute and then ask whether including battery-powered vehicles is consistent with those aims. Because the history probably would reveal that the statute's purpose was to reduce air pollution from internal combustion engines, the court might well conclude that battery-powered vehicles should not be covered.

General Public Purpose

Occasionally, courts construe statutory language in the light of various *general public purposes*. These purposes are not the purposes underlying the statute in question; rather, they are widely accepted general notions of public policy. In one case, for example, the U.S. Supreme Court used the general public policy against racial discrimination in education as one argument for denying tax-exempt status to a private university that discriminated on the basis of race.[11]

Prior Interpretations

Courts sometimes follow prior cases (and administrative decisions) interpreting a statute regardless of the statute's plain meaning or its legislative history. The main argument for following these *prior interpretations* is to promote stability and certainty by preventing each successive court that considers a statute from adopting its own interpretation. The courts' willingness to follow a prior interpretation depends on such factors as the number of past courts adopting the interpretation, the authoritativeness of those courts, and the number of years that the interpretation has been followed. Note that in *Weber* the Supreme Court arguably did not follow one of its own prior interpretations.

Maxims

Maxims are general rules of thumb employed in statutory interpretation. There are many maxims, and courts tend to use them or ignore them at their discretion. One example of a maxim is the *ejusdem generis* rule, which says that when general words follow words of a specific, limited meaning, the general language should be limited to things of the same class as those specifically stated. Suppose that the pollution statute quoted earlier listed 32 types of gas-powered vehicles and ended with the words "and other motorized passenger or cargo vehicles." Here, *ejusdem generis* would probably dictate that battery-powered vehicles not be included.

United Steelworkers v. Weber

As part of its collective bargaining agreement with the United Steelworkers of America, the Kaiser Aluminum and Chemical Company established a new on-the-job craft training program at its Gramercy, Louisiana, plant. The selection of trainees for the program was based on seniority, but at least 50 percent of the new trainees had to be black until the percentage of black skilled craft workers in the plant approximated the percentage of blacks in the local labor force.

Brian Weber was a rejected white applicant who would have qualified for the program had the racial preference not existed. He sued Kaiser and the union in federal district court, arguing that the racial preference violated Title VII of the 1964 Civil Rights Act. Section 703(a) of the act states: "It shall be an unlawful employment practice for an employer . . . to discriminate against any individual with respect to his compensation, terms, conditions, or privileges of employment, because of such individual's race, color, religion, sex, or national origin." Section 703(d) has a similar provision specifically forbidding racial discrimination in admission to apprenticeship or other training programs. Weber's suit was successful, and the federal court of appeals affirmed. Kaiser and the union appealed to the U.S. Supreme Court.

Source: 443 U.S. 193 (U.S. Sup. Ct. 1979)

Brennan, Justice

The only question before us is whether Title VII forbids private employers and unions from voluntarily agreeing upon bona fide affirmative action plans that accord racial preferences in the manner and for the purpose provided in the Kaiser-USWA plan. That question was expressly left open in *McDonald v. Santa Fe Trail Transp. Co.* (1976), which held, in a case not involving affirmative action, that Title VII protects whites as well as blacks from racial discrimination.

Weber argues that Congress intended in Title VII to prohibit all race-conscious affirmative action plans. His argument rests upon a literal interpretation of sections 703(a) and (d) of the act. Those sections make it unlawful to discriminate because of race in the selection of apprentices for training programs. Since, the argument runs, *McDonald* settled that Title VII forbids discrimination against whites as well as blacks, and since the Kaiser-USWA plan discriminated against white employees solely because they are white, it follows that the plan violates Title VII.

Weber's argument is not without force. But it overlooks the fact that the Kaiser-USWA plan is an affirmative action plan voluntarily adopted by private parties to eliminate traditional patterns of racial segregation. It is a familiar rule, that a thing may be within the letter of the statute and yet not within the statute, because not within its spirit. Sections 703(a) and (d) must therefore be read against the background of the legislative history of Title VII and the historical context from which the act arose. Examination of these sources makes clear that an interpretation that forbade all race-conscious affirmative action would bring about an end completely at variance with the purpose of the statute and must be rejected.

Congress's primary concern in enacting the prohibition against racial discrimination in Title VII was the plight of the Negro in our economy. Before 1964, blacks were largely relegated to unskilled and semi-skilled jobs. Because of automation the number of such jobs was rapidly decreasing. As a consequence the relative position of the Negro worker was steadily worsening. Congress feared that the goal of the Civil Rights Act—the integration of blacks into the mainstream of American society—could not be achieved unless this trend were reversed. Accordingly, it was clear to Congress that the crux of the problem was to open employment opportunities for Negroes in occupations which have traditionally been closed to them, and it was to this problem that Title VII's prohibition against racial discrimination in employment was primarily addressed.

Given this legislative history, we cannot agree with Weber that Congress intended to prohibit the private sector from taking effective steps to accomplish the goal that Congress designed Title VII to achieve. It would be ironic indeed if a law triggered by a nation's concern over centuries of racial injustice and intended to improve the lot of those who had been excluded from the American dream for so long, constituted the first legislative prohibition of all voluntary, private, race-conscious efforts to abolish traditional patterns of racial segregation and hierarchy.

Judgment reversed in favor of Kaiser and the union.

Limits on the Power of Courts

By now, you may think that anything goes when courts decide common law cases or interpret statutes. However, many factors discourage courts from adopting a completely freewheeling approach. Due to their legal training and mental makeup, judges tend to respect established precedents and the will of the legislature. Many courts issue written opinions, which expose judges to academic and professional criticism. Lower court judges may be discouraged from innovation by the fear of being overruled by a higher court.

Finally, certain political factors inhibit judges. For example, some judges are elected, and even judges with lifetime tenure can sometimes be removed.

An even more fundamental limit on the power of courts is that they cannot make law until some parties present them with a case to decide. In addition, any such case must be a *real dispute*; that is, courts generally limit themselves to genuine, existing "cases or controversies" between real parties with tangible opposing interests in the lawsuit. Thus, courts generally do not issue *advisory opinions* on abstract legal questions unrelated to a genuine dispute. Nor do they decide *feigned controversies* that parties concoct to get answers to such questions. Also, courts may refuse to decide suits that are insufficiently *ripe* to have matured into a genuine controversy, or that are *moot* because there no longer is a real dispute between the parties. Expressing similar ideas is the doctrine of **standing to sue**, which generally requires that the plaintiff have some direct, tangible, and substantial stake in the outcome of the suit.

Nonetheless, state and federal **declaratory judgment** statutes allow parties to determine their rights and duties even though their controversy has not advanced to the point where harm has occurred and legal relief may be necessary. This enables them to determine their legal position without taking action that could expose them to liability. For example, if Joan thinks that she is not obligated to perform her contract to Jim, she may seek a declaratory judgment on the question rather than risk Jim's lawsuit by breaking the contract. Usually, though, a declaratory judgment is awarded only when the parties' dispute is sufficiently advanced to constitute a real case or controversy.

Ethical and Public Policy Concerns

1. What might be troubling about the result in this chapter's *Rochin* case? *Hint:* Today, what aspect of the case is commonly regarded as one of the country's most serious problems? As discussed moral philosophers sometimes distinguish *deontological* ethical theories from *consequentialist* (or teleological) ethical theories. Strict or extreme deontological theories say that certain actions are right or wrong and should be pursued or avoided, *no matter what the consequences of doing so.* Consequentialist theories, on the other hand, assess the moral worth of actions by looking to their consequences. Which of these approaches best describes the Supreme Court's decision in *Rochin*?

2. Earlier in this chapter, we quoted Justice Holmes's statement that "[t]he first requirement of a sound body of law is, that it should correspond with the actual feelings and demands of the community, whether right or wrong." This statement may mean that the law should reflect prevailing moral views, whatever they happen to be. What is good about such an approach to the law and to lawmaking? What is bad about it?

3. Legal positivists often say that even morally bad laws are still law and that such laws (or some of them, at least) should still be enforced and obeyed. What moral arguments can you make for this position?

Appendix

Reading and Briefing Cases

Throughout this text, you encounter cases—the judicial opinions accompanying court decisions. These cases are highly edited versions of their much longer originals. What follows are explanations of the format of the cases presented in this book, plus some pointers to assist you in studying these cases.

1. Each case has a *case name* that includes at least some of the parties to the case. Because the order of the parties may change when a case is appealed, do not assume that the first party listed is the plaintiff (the party suing) and the second the defendant (the party being sued). Also, because some cases have many plaintiffs and/or many defendants, the parties discussed in the court's opinion sometimes differ from those found in the case name.

2. Each case also has a *citation*, which includes the volume and page number of the legal reporter in which the full case appears, plus the year the case was decided. *United Steelworkers v. Weber*, for instance, begins on page 193 of volume 443 of the United States Reports (the official reporter for U.S. Supreme Court decisions) and was decided in 1979. (Each of the many different legal reporters has its own abbreviation, and they are too numerous to include here.) In the parenthesis accompanying the date, we also give you some information about the court that decided the case. For example: "U.S. Sup. Ct." is the United States Supreme Court, "3d Cir." is the U.S. Court of Appeals for the Third Circuit, "S.D.N.Y." is the U.S. District Court for the Southern District of New York, "Minn. Sup. Ct." is the Minnesota Supreme Court, and "Mich. Ct. App." is the Michigan Court of Appeals (a Michigan intermediate appellate court).

3. At the beginning of each case, there is a *statement of facts* containing the most important facts that gave rise to the case.

4. Immediately after the statement of facts, we give you the case's *procedural history*. Basically, this history tells you what courts previously handled the case you are reading, and how they dealt with it.

5. Next comes your major concern: the *body of the court's opinion*. Here, the court typically determines the applicable law and applies it to the facts to reach a conclusion. The court's discussion of the relevant law may be elaborate; it can include prior cases, legislative history, applicable public policies, and more. The court's application of the law to the facts usually occurs after it has arrived at the applicable legal rule or rules, but it may also be intertwined with its legal discussion.

6. At the very end of the case, we complete the procedural history by stating the court's *decision*. For example, "Judgment reversed in favor of Smith" says that a lower court judgment *against* Smith was reversed on appeal, which means that Smith's appeal was successful and Smith wins.

7. The cases' main function is to provide concrete examples of rules stated in the text. (Frequently, the text tells you what point the case illustrates.) In studying law, it is easy to conclude that your task is finished once you have memorized a black letter rule. In real life, however, legal problems rarely present themselves as abstract questions of law; instead, they are implicit in particular situations you encounter or particular actions you take. Without some sense of a legal rule's concrete application, therefore, your knowledge of that rule is incomplete. The cases help provide this sense.

8. You may find it helpful to *brief* the cases. There is no one correct way to brief a case, but most good briefs contain the following elements: (1) a short statement of the relevant facts, (2) the case's prior history, (3) the question(s) or issue(s) the court had to decide, (4) the answer(s) to those question(s), (5) the reasoning the court used to justify its decision, and (6) the final result. Using "P" and "D" for the plaintiff and the defendant, a brief of the *Weber* case might look like this:

United Steelworkers v. Weber

Facts   The Ds were a private employer and a union that had voluntarily established a craft training program through a collective bargaining agreement. The procedures for selecting the program's trainees favored black workers over white workers by establishing an effective 50 percent quota for the former. P, a white worker who was denied access to the program, would have qualified had the racial preference not existed.

History   P sued the Ds under Title VII of the 1964 Civil Rights Act, which forbids employment discrimination on the basis of race. He won in federal district court and the court of appeals affirmed. The Ds appealed to the U.S. Supreme Court.

Issue   Does this voluntary racial preference favoring blacks violate Title VII's ban on racial discrimination in employment?

Answer   No.

Reasoning Even though Title VII's plain meaning favors P and a prior interpretation holds that Title VII forbids racial discrimination against both whites and blacks, neither point is decisive. The reason is that holding for P would frustrate Title VII's purpose. Title VII's legislative history and its historical context make clear that its aim was to integrate blacks into the American mainstream. This was especially true in the area of employment, an area in which blacks were falling behind. The Ds' preference helped further this purpose because it helped blacks get better jobs, and declaring the preference illegal would have frustrated the purpose.

Result   Court of appeals decision reversed; Ds win.

Problems and Problem Cases

1. In which way do administrative regulations resemble statutes? In which way do they differ from statutes?
2. Suppose that Congress passes a federal statute that conflicts with a state constitutional provision. The state argues that the constitutional provision should prevail over the statute because constitutions are a higher, more authoritative kind of law than statutes. Is this argument correct? Why or why not?
3. Suppose that someone objects to the president's promulgation of an executive order by claiming that the U.S. Constitution only gives the president the power to *execute* the laws, not the power to make them. What concept explains the president's power to make law through executive orders? Explain its meaning.
4. State A passes a statute declaring that those who sell heroin are to receive a mandatory 30-year prison sentence. Describe this statute in terms of the three classifications of law stated in the text—criminal/civil, substantive/procedural, and public/ private.
5. Nation X is a dictatorship in which one ruler has the ultimate lawmaking power. The ruler issues a statute declaring that certain religious minorities are to be exterminated. An international convocation of jurisprudential scholars meets to discuss the question, "Is Nation X's extermination statute truly law?" What would be the typical natural law answer to this question? What would be the typical legal positivist response? Assume that all of those present at the convocation think that Nation X's statute is morally wrong.

6. Nation Y has enacted positive laws forbidding all abnormal sexual relations between consenting adults. However, the police of Nation Y rarely enforce these laws, and even when they do, prosecutors never bring charges against violators. What observation would American legal realists make about this situation? In order to determine what a believer in natural law would think about these laws, what else would you have to know?

7. Many states and localities used to have so-called Sunday Closing laws—statutes or ordinances forbidding the conduct of certain business on Sunday. A few may still do so. Often, these laws have not been obeyed or enforced. What would an extreme legal positivist tend to think about the duty to enforce and obey such laws? What would a natural law exponent who strongly believes in economic freedom tend to think about this question? What about a natural law adherent who is a Christian religious traditionalist? What *observation* would almost any American legal realist make about Sunday Closing laws? Looking at these laws from a sociological perspective, finally, what social factors help explain their original passage, their relative lack of enforcement today, and their continuance on the books despite their lack of enforcement?

8. The Supreme Court of State X is about to decide on the constitutionality of a statute restricting some controversial activity. Three of the court's justices—Justices A, B. and C—are taking the coming decision very seriously. In an effort to determine the true rule of law that governs the case, Justice A is reading and rereading all the relevant precedents and legislative history. In order to determine what result is morally right, Justice B is reading books on moral philosophy. To determine what the public thinks, finally, Justice C is reading every available public opinion poll on the behavior at issue in the case. Which jurisprudential schools do Justices A, B, and C most nearly exemplify?

9. Although you would not know this from reading the *MacPherson* case in this chapter, two of the cases mentioned there distinguished *Thomas v. Winchester* (the case involving the falsely labeled poison) in a certain way. The courts in *Loop v. Litchfield* (the circular saw case) and *Losee v. Clute* (the steam boiler case) both distinguished *Thomas v. Winchester* because in *Thomas*, the thing that caused the injury—a poison—was *by its nature intended to cause harm*. In other words, these courts held that a poison should be treated differently from a circular saw that flies apart or an exploding steam boiler. If the relevant public policy here is to allow recovery for injuries caused by highly dangerous products, does this distinction make any sense?

10. In 1910, the White Slave Traffic Act (usually known as the Mann Act) went into effect. Congress passed the act in response to an alleged white slave traffic in which gangs of certain nationalities were said to be forcing or luring American women into prostitution. One portion of the act stated that "any person who shall knowingly transport or cause to be transported . . . any woman or girl for the purpose of prostitution or debauchery, or for any other immoral purpose, . . . shall be deemed guilty of a felony." In 1913, F. Drew Caminetti was indicted for transporting a woman from Sacramento, California, to Reno, Nevada, to be his mistress. Which technique of statutory interpretation would you use in arguing that Caminetti is guilty under the Mann Act? Which technique would you use to argue that Caminetti should not be guilty under the act?

Endnotes

1. Chapter 26 contains more detail on how the U.S. Constitution performs these functions.
2. However, Louisiana adopted the Code Napoléon, which was based on Roman law.
3. Holmes, *The Common Law* (1881).
4. The italics have been added for emphasis.
5. At this point, you may want to examine this chapter's appendix on the reading and briefing of cases.
6. The reasoning courts employ in constitutional cases resembles that used in common law cases, but it is often somewhat looser.
7. *Stare decisis* should be distinguished from the doctrine of *res judicata*, which says that a final judicial decision on the merits conclusively settles the rights of the *parties to the case.*
8. Also, while they exercise the power infrequency, courts sometimes completely *overrule* their prior decisions.
9. Negligence law is discussed in Chapter 23.
10. The present status of the old no-liability-outside-privity rule in sale-of-goods cases is discussed in Chapter 21.
11. *Bob Jones University v. United States*, 461 U.S. 574 (1983).

Chapter Thirteen

THE RESOLUTION OF

PRIVATE DISPUTES

Introduction

Most business law consists of substantive legal rules. The courts apply such rules when they decide civil cases.[1] Because courts play such an important role in formulating and enforcing substantive rules, your understanding of business law is incomplete unless you know something about the various kinds of courts, the cases they decide, and the procedures under which they operate in civil suits.

The United States has 52 court systems—a federal system, plus a system for each state and the District of Columbia. This chapter first describes the various state and federal courts. Included in this discussion is the jurisdiction of these courts—their power to decide certain kinds of cases. Then the chapter examines the procedures courts follow in civil cases. Because private disputes are increasingly being resolved outside the formal court system, the chapter concludes by discussing alternative dispute resolution.

State Courts and Their Jurisdiction

Courts of Limited Jurisdiction

Minor criminal matters and civil disputes involving small amounts of money are frequently decided in *courts of limited jurisdiction* (also called courts of inferior or special jurisdiction). Examples include municipal courts, justice of the peace courts, and stroll claims courts. Such courts often handle a large number of cases. Their procedures may be informal, the presiding judicial officer may not be a lawyer, and the parties may argue their own cases. Also, courts of limited jurisdiction are usually not courts of record; that is, they ordinarily do not keep a transcript of the testimony and proceedings. Thus, appeals from their decisions require a new trial (a trial *de novo*) in a trial court.

Trial Courts

Courts of limited jurisdiction find the relevant facts, identify the appropriate rule(s) of law, and combine the facts and the law to reach a decision. State trial courts do the same, but they differ from inferior courts in at least three ways. First, they are not governed by the limits on civil damages or criminal penalties that govern courts of limited jurisdiction. Thus, cases involving significant dollar amounts or major criminal penalties usually begin at the trial court level. Second, trial courts are courts of record that keep detailed records of their proceedings. Third, the trial court judge almost always is a lawyer. The trial court's fact-finding function may be handled by the judge or by a jury. Determination of the applicable law is the judge's responsibility.

FIGURE 13-1
An illustrative state
court system

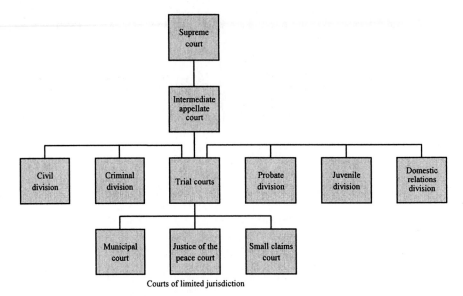

Courts of limited jurisdiction

States usually have one trial court for each county. It may be called a circuit, superior, district, county, or common pleas court. Trial courts often have civil and criminal divisions. They may also contain divisions set up to hear particular matters—for example, domestic relations courts, probate courts, and juvenile courts.

State Appeals Courts

In general, state appeals (or appellate) courts only decide *legal* questions. Their judges do not make factual findings and they have no jury. Thus, although appellate courts can correct legal errors made by the trial judge, they generally accept the trial court's findings of fact. Appellate courts may also hear appeals from state administrative agency decisions. Some states have only one appeals court (usually called the supreme court), while others also have an intermediate appellate court. The U.S. Supreme Court sometimes hears appeals from decisions of the state's highest court.

State Court Jurisdiction and Venue

The party who sues in a civil case (the plaintiff) cannot sue the defendant (the party being sued) in any court he chooses. Instead, the chosen court must have **jurisdiction** over the case. Jurisdiction is a court's power to hear a case and to issue a decision binding on the parties. As Figure 13-2 indicates, in order to render a binding decision in a civil case, a state court must have *both*: (1) subject-matter jurisdiction, and (2) *either* in personam jurisdiction or in rem jurisdiction. Even if a court has jurisdiction, it also must meet the state's **venue** requirements in order for the suit to proceed there.

FIGURE 13-2
State court jurisdiction

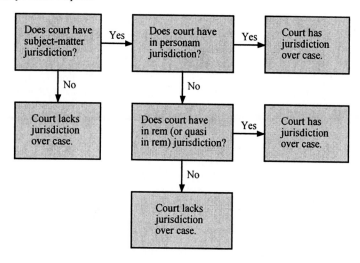

Subject-Matter Jurisdiction

Subject-matter jurisdiction is a court's power to decide the *type* of dispute involved in the case. Criminal courts, for example, cannot hear civil matters, and a $500,000 suit for breach of contract cannot proceed in a small claims court.

In Personam Jurisdiction

Even a court with subject-matter jurisdiction cannot decide a civil case unless it also has either **in personam jurisdiction** or **in rem jurisdiction**. In personam jurisdiction is based on the residence, location, or activities of the defendant. A state court has in personam jurisdiction over defendants who are citizens or residents of the state (even if situated out of state), who are within the state's borders when process is served against them (even if nonresidents),[2] or who consent to the suit (for instance, by entering the state to defend against it).[3]

In addition, many states have enacted "long-arm" statutes that give their courts in personam jurisdiction over certain out-of-state defendants. Under these statutes, nonresident individuals and businesses may become subject to the state's jurisdiction by doing business within the state, contracting to supply goods or services within the state, or committing a tort (a civil wrong) within the state. As the following *Knowles* case indicates, a state's assertion of in personam jurisdiction over an out-of-state defendant is subject to federal due process standards.

Knowles v. Modglin

Albert Knowles, an Alabama truck driver, died of natural causes in California while hauling produce from Alabama to California. After Knowles's body was discovered inside his truck, it was taken to Hems Brothers Mortuaries, where an autopsy was performed by Damon Reference Laboratories at the request of the local coroner. Both Hems and Damon did business in California. After a request from an Alabama funeral home, Hems prepared Knowles's body for shipment and arranged for it to be flown to his hometown. Hems billed the Alabama funeral home for these services and for the price of a casket; it also mailed a statement to Knowles's wife.

continued

Mrs. Knowles did not view her husband's body after its return to Alabama and before its burial, and no one positively identified the body as that of Mr. Knowles during this period. After the burial, Mrs. Knowles received an autopsy report from Damon describing a body that was different from her husband's body. As a result, she had the buried body exhumed and personally viewed it to verify that it was her husband's body—which it was. However, Mrs. Knowles also found that the body had been buried nude, had been packed in cotton in a "disaster pouch," was terribly discolored, and was lying in an awkward position. She described it as looking like "a monster."

Mrs. Knowles then sued Hems and Damon in an Alabama trial court for the wrongful mishandling of her husband's body. Both Damon and Hems had no contacts with Alabama other than those just described, and each moved to dismiss the claim because the court lacked in personam jurisdiction. After the court granted Damon's motion but denied Hems's motion, both Mrs. Knowles and Hems appealed to the Alabama Supreme Court.

Source: 553 So. 2d 563 (Ala. Sup. Ct. 1989)

Houston, Justice

The issue is whether, consistent with the Due Process Clause of the Fourteenth Amendment to the United States Constitution, the defendants have sufficient contacts with this state to make it fair and reasonable to require them to come here to defend against the present action. Due process requires that to subject a defendant to a judgment in personam, he have certain minimum contacts with it such that the maintenance of the suit does not offend traditional notions of fair play and substantive justice. Alabama's long-arm statute has been interpreted to extend the jurisdiction of Alabama courts to the permissible limits of due process.

A relevant factor in a due process analysis is whether the defendant should have reasonably anticipated that he would be sued in the forum state. In determining [this question], it is essential that there be some act by which the defendant purposefully avails itself of the privilege of conducting activities within the forum state, thus invoking the benefits and protections of its laws. Other relevant factors include the burden placed on the defendant, the interest of the forum state in adjudicating the dispute, the plaintiff's interest in obtaining convenient and effective relief, and the interstate judicial system's interest in obtaining the most efficient resolution of the controversy.

The trial court did not err in dismissing Damon for lack of in personam jurisdiction. It does not appear that Damon ever had any contacts with Alabama, with the exception of mailing the autopsy report to Mrs. Knowles. Damon could not have reasonably anticipated that Mr. Knowles's body would make its way to Alabama, that it would not be positively identified by anyone before burial, and that, thereafter, Damon would be haled into an Alabama court to defend against a suit based on a misdescription contained in the autopsy report.

However, Hems established significant contacts with this state by agreeing to prepare and ship Mr. Knowles's body here. In addition, Hems sold Mrs. Knowles a casket, and later solicited payment by mail in Alabama. Hems purposefully availed itself of the privilege of conducting business in Alabama [and] should have reasonably anticipated being summoned to an Alabama court to answer any charges of misconduct in the handling and shipment of Mr. Knowles's body. Furthermore, given the progress in communications and transportation in recent years, we cannot say that it would be unduly burdensome for Hems to defend against the suit in an Alabama court. Considering the nature of Hems's activity, the resultant foreseeability of its being required to defend an action in Alabama, the obvious interest of the plaintiff in obtaining convenient and effective relief, and the relative lack of inconvenience that would be incurred by Hems in appearing and defending, it is fair and reasonable to require Hems to defend against this action in Alabama.

Trial court decision dismissing Mrs. Knowles's suit against Damon for lack of jurisdiction and finding jurisdiction over Hems affirmed.

In Rem Jurisdiction

In rem jurisdiction is based on the presence of *property* within the state. It empowers state courts to determine rights in that property even if the persons whose rights are affected are outside the state's in personam jurisdiction. For example, a state court's decision regarding title to land within the state is said to bind the world.[4]

Venue

Even where a court has jurisdiction, it may be unable to decide the case because venue requirements have not been met. In general, a court has venue if it is a territorially fair and convenient forum in which to hear the case. Venue requirements are typically set by state statutes, which normally determine the county in which suit must be brought. For instance, the statute might say that a suit concerning land must be brought in the county where the land is located, and that other suits must be brought in the county where the defendant resides or is doing business. In certain cases where justice so requires, the defendant may obtain a *change of venue*. This can occur when, for example, a fair trial is impossible within a particular county.

Federal Courts and Their Jurisdiction

Federal District Courts

In the federal system, lawsuits usually begin in the federal district courts, which basically are federal trial courts. Like state trial courts, the federal district courts determine both the relevant facts and the applicable law. The fact-finding function may be entrusted to either the judge or a jury, but determining the law is the judge's responsibility. Each state has at least one district court, and each district court has at least one judge.

District Court Jurisdiction and Venue

There are many bases of federal district court civil jurisdiction. The two most important are **diversity jurisdiction** and **federal question jurisdiction**. Diversity jurisdiction exists when: (1) the suit is between citizens of different states, and (2) the amount in controversy exceeds $50,000. Diversity jurisdiction also exists in certain suits between citizens of a state and citizens or governments of foreign nations where the amount in controversy exceeds $50,000. Under diversity jurisdiction, a corporation is normally a citizen of both the state where it has been incorporated and the state where it has its principal place of business.

Federal question jurisdiction exists when the case arises under the Constitution, laws, or treaties of the United States. The "arises under" requirement normally is met when a right created by federal law is a basic part of the plaintiff's case. There is no amount-in-controversy requirement for federal question jurisdiction.

A district court's diversity or federal question jurisdiction usually includes only those defendants who would be subject to the in personam jurisdiction of the state where the district court sits. Further limiting the plaintiff's choice of federal district courts are the federal system's complex venue requirements. These requirements, which have recently been amended by Congress, are beyond the scope of this text.

Concurrent Jurisdiction and Removal

The federal district courts have *exclusive jurisdiction* over some matters—for example, patent and copyright cases. This means that such cases *must* be heard in federal district court. Often, however, the district courts have *concurrent jurisdiction* with state courts; here, both state and federal courts have jurisdiction over the case. For example, a plaintiff might assert state court in personam jurisdiction over an out-of-state defendant or might sue in a federal district court under that court's diversity jurisdiction. Also, a state court may decide a case involving a federal question if it has jurisdiction over that case. Where concurrent jurisdiction exists and the plaintiff opts for a state court, the defendant sometimes can *remove* the case to a federal district court.

Specialized Courts

The federal court system also includes certain specialized federal courts, including the Claims Court (which hears claims against the United States), the Court of International Trade (which is concerned with tariff, customs, import, and other trade matters), the Bankruptcy Courts (which operate as adjuncts of the district courts), and the Tax Court (which reviews certain IRS determinations). Usually, the decisions of these courts can be appealed to one or more of the federal courts of appeals.

Courts of Appeals

Like state intermediate appellate courts, the U.S. courts of appeals do not have a fact-finding function, and review only the legal conclusions reached by lower federal courts. As Figure 13-3 illustrates, there are 13 federal courts of appeals: 11 organized territorially into circuits covering several states each, one for the District of Columbia, and the Court of Appeals for the Federal Circuit.

FIGURE 13-3
The thirteen federal
judicial circuits

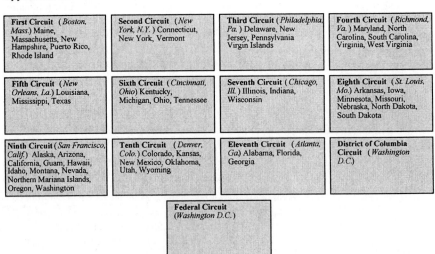

Except for the Court of Appeals for the Federal Circuit, the most important function of the U.S. courts of appeals is to hear appeals from decisions of the federal district courts. Appeals from a district court ordinarily proceed to the Court of Appeals for that district court's region. Appeals from the District Court for the Southern District of New York, for example, go to the Second Circuit Court of Appeals. The courts of appeals also hear appeals from the Tax Court, from many administrative agency decisions, and (via appellate panels they appoint) from some Bankruptcy Court decisions. The Court of Appeals for the

Federal Circuit hears a wide variety of specialized appeals, including some patent and trademark matters, Claims Court decisions, and decisions by the Court of International Trade.

The U.S. Supreme Court

The United States Supreme Court is mainly an appellate court. Thus, it only considers questions of law when it decides appeals. Most of the appeals handled by the Supreme Court come from the federal courts of appeals and the highest state courts.[5] Today, most appealable decisions from these courts fall within the Supreme Court's *certiorari* jurisdiction, under which the Court has discretion whether or not to hear the appeal. The Court hears only a small percentage of the many appeals it receives through its certiorari jurisdiction.

Virtually all appeals from the federal courts of appeals are within the Court's discretionary certiorari jurisdiction. Appeals from the highest state courts are within the certiorari jurisdiction when: (1) the validity of any treaty or federal statute has been questioned; (2) the validity of any state statute is questioned because it is repugnant to federal law; or (3) any title, right, privilege, or immunity is claimed under federal law. The Supreme Court generally defers to the highest state courts on questions of state law, and normally does not hear appeals from those courts if the case only involves such questions.

In certain rare situations, finally, the U.S. Supreme Court has **original jurisdiction**, which means that it acts as a trial court. The Supreme Court has *original and exclusive* jurisdiction over all controversies between two or more states. It has original, but not exclusive, jurisdiction over cases involving foreign ambassadors, ministers, and like parties; controversies between the United States and a state; and cases where a state proceeds against citizens of another state or against aliens.

Figure 13-4 combines the state and federal court systems.

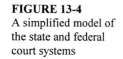

FIGURE 13-4
A simplified model of the state and federal court systems

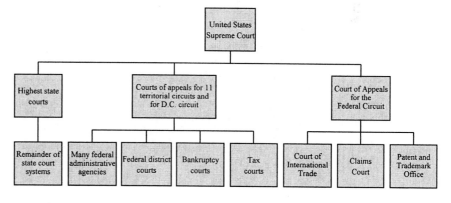

Civil Procedure

Civil procedure is the set of legal rules governing the conduct of a trial court case between private parties. Because this law sometimes varies with the jurisdiction in question,[6] the following presentation is only a summary of the most widely accepted rules governing civil cases in state trial courts and the federal district courts. Knowing about these basic procedural matters is useful if you become involved in a civil lawsuit. Such knowledge also helps you understand the cases in this text. Figure 13-5 presents the major steps through which a civil case normally proceeds and the most significant motions the parties (or *litigants*) can make at each step.

FIGURE 13-5

The most important stages and motions in civil litigation (appeals assumed)

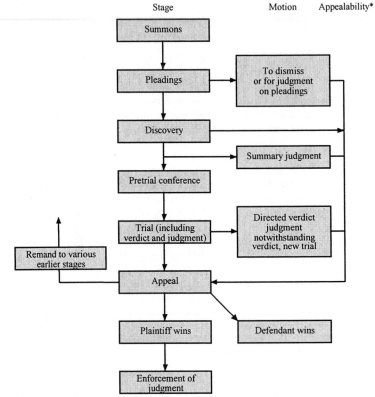

Stage   Motion   Appealability*

Summons

Pleadings → To dismiss or for judgment on pleadings

Discovery

Summary judgment

Pretrial conference

Trial (including verdict and judgment) → Directed verdict judgment notwithstanding verdict, new trial

Remand to various earlier stages

Appeal

Plaintiff wins   Defendant wins

Enforcement of judgment

*As discussed later in the chapter, many other trial court rulings also are appealable.

The Adversary System

In any civil case, the *adversary system* is at work. Through their attorneys, the litigants present contrary positions of fact or law before a theoretically impartial judge and possibly a jury. To win a civil case, the plaintiff must prove each element of his claim by a *preponderance of the evidence.*[7] That is, the plaintiff must show that the greater weight of the evidence—by credibility, not quantity—supports the existence of each element. In other words, the plaintiff must convince the fact finder that the existence of each factual element is more probable than its nonexistence. Thus, the lawyers for each party present their clients' version of the facts, try to convince the judge or jury that this version is true, and attempt to rebut conflicting factual allegations by the other party. Each attorney also seeks to persuade the judge that her reading of the law is correct.

     Supporters of the adversary system believe that allowing the litigants to make competing arguments of fact and law gives the judge and jury the best chance of making accurate determinations because it enables the presentation and criticism of all relevant arguments. The system's critics contend that rather than promoting the disinterested search for truth, it encourages the parties to employ incomplete, distorted, and even false arguments whenever such arguments seem useful. Defenders of the adversary system reply that attacks from the other party and the rulings of an impartial judge should weed out such arguments. This weeding-out process, however, may proceed unequally if one party has superior resources and thus can obtain better representation.

Service of the Summons

The function of the **summons** is to notify the defendant that he is being sued. The summons typically names the plaintiff and states the time within which the defendant must enter an *appearance* in court (usually through an attorney). In most jurisdictions, the summons is accompanied by a copy of the plaintiff's complaint (which is described below).

The summons is usually delivered, or served, to the defendant by an appropriate public official after the plaintiff has filed his complaint with the court. To ensure that the defendant is properly notified of the suit, statutes, court rules, and constitutional due process guarantees set standards for proper service of the summons in particular cases. For example, personal delivery of the summons to the defendant almost always meets these standards, and many jurisdictions also permit the summons to be left at the defendant's home or place of business. Service to corporations often may be accomplished by delivery of the summons to the firm's general or managing agent. Many state long-arm statutes permit out-of-state defendants to be served by registered mail. Although inadequate service of process may sometimes defeat the plaintiff's claim, in most jurisdictions the defendant must make his objection early or it will be waived.

The Pleadings

The **pleadings** are the documents the parties file with the court when they first state their respective cases. They include the **complaint**, the **answer**, and (in some jurisdictions) the **reply**.

The Complaint

The complaint states the plaintiff's claim in separate, numbered paragraphs. It must contain sufficient facts to show that the plaintiff is entitled to legal relief and to give the defendant reasonable notice of the nature of the plaintiff's claim. The complaint also must state the remedy requested by the plaintiff.

The Answer

Within a designated time after the complaint has been served, the defendant normally files an answer to the plaintiff's complaint. The answer responds to the complaint paragraph by paragraph. Usually, it admits the allegations of each paragraph, denies them, or states that the defendant lacks the information to assess the truth or falsity of the allegations (which has much the same effect as a denial).

The answer may also include an **affirmative defense** to the claim asserted in the complaint. A successful affirmative defense would enable the defendant to win the case even if all the allegations in the complaint are true and, by themselves, entitle the plaintiff to recover. For example, suppose that the plaintiff bases her suit on a contract that she alleges the defendant has breached (broken). The defendant's answer may admit or deny the existence of the contract or the assertion that the defendant breached it. In addition, the answer may make assertions that, if proven, would show that the defendant has an affirmative defense because the plaintiff's fraud induced the defendant to enter the contract.

The answer may also contain a **counterclaim**. A counterclaim is a *new* claim by the defendant arising from the matters stated in the complaint. Unlike an affirmative defense, it is not merely an attack on the plaintiff's claim but is the *defendant's* attempt to obtain legal relief. In addition to using fraud as an affirmative defense to a plaintiff's contract claim, for example, a defendant might counterclaim for damages caused by that fraud.

The Reply

In some jurisdictions, the plaintiff is allowed or required to respond to an affirmative defense or a counterclaim by making a reply. The reply is the plaintiff's point-by-point response (a kind of answer) to the allegations in the affirmative defense or counterclaim. However, many jurisdictions do not allow a reply to an affirmative defense; instead, the defendant's new allegations are automatically denied. Usually, though, a plaintiff who wishes to contest a counterclaim must reply to it.

The Functions of the Pleadings

Traditionally, the main function of the pleadings has been to define and limit the questions to be decided at later stages of the case. Only those issues raised in the pleadings have been considered part of the case; points omitted from the pleadings have been excluded from further consideration; and few, if any, amendments to the pleadings have been permitted. Also, litigants usually have been bound to allegations admitted in the pleadings; only those allegations that have not been admitted have been regarded as in dispute. Many jurisdictions retain some of these rules. Over time, however, the main purpose behind pleading rules has shifted from defining and limiting the questions to be resolved in the case to affording the parties notice of each other's claims. Accompanying this shift have been a greater tendency to decide cases on their merits, a more relaxed attitude toward technical defects in the pleadings, and a greater tendency to permit amendments to the pleadings.

Motion to Dismiss

Sometimes it is evident from the complaint or the pleadings that the plaintiff has no case. Here, it is wasteful for the suit to proceed further, and it is useful to have a procedural device for ending it. This device has various names, but it is commonly called the **motion to dismiss**. This motion is often made after the plaintiff has filed his complaint. A similar motion allowed by some jurisdictions, the **motion for judgment on the pleadings**, normally occurs after the pleadings have been completed. A successful motion to dismiss means that the defendant wins the case; if the motion fails, the case proceeds further.

The motion to dismiss may be made on various grounds—for example, inadequate service of process or lack of jurisdiction. The most important type of motion to dismiss, however, is the motion to dismiss for failure to state a claim upon which relief can be granted, sometimes called the **demurrer**. This motion basically says "So what?" to the factual allegations in the complaint. It asserts that the plaintiff cannot recover even if all these allegations are true because no rule of law entitles him to win on those facts. Suppose that Potter sues Davis on the theory that Davis's bad breath is a form of "olfactory pollution" entitling Potter to recover damages. Potter's complaint describes Davis's breath and the distress it causes Potter in great detail. Even if all of Potter's factual allegations are true, Davis's motion to dismiss almost certainly will succeed. Thus, Davis will win the case, for there is no rule of law allowing a civil recovery for bad breath.

Discovery

Litigants sometimes lack the factual information to prove their cases when the suit begins. To help them prepare their arguments and to narrow and clarify the issues for trial, all jurisdictions permit the parties to undertake extensive **discovery** of relevant information. The most common kinds of discovery are **depositions** (oral examinations of a party or a party's witness by the other party's attorney), **interrogatories** (written questions directed to a party, answered in writing, and signed under oath), **requests for admissions** (one party's written demand that the other party agree to certain statements of fact or law), **requests for documents and other evidence**, and **physical and mental examinations**. The permissible limits of discovery are set by the trial judge, whose rulings are controlled by the procedural law of the jurisdiction. In an effort to make civil litigation less of a battle of wits or a sporting event and more of a disinterested search for the truth, many jurisdictions have liberalized their discovery rules to give parties freer access to all relevant facts.

The jurisdiction's law of evidence determines whether or when discovery findings are admissible trial evidence. However, almost all jurisdictions allow some discovery findings to be employed at trial for certain purposes. Depositions, for instance, may sometimes be used as "paper testimony" from dead or distant witnesses, or to attack the credibility of a witness whose trial testimony differs from statements made at the deposition.

Summary Judgment

The proceeding accompanying a motion for **summary judgment** has been described as a trial by affidavit. The summary judgment is a device for disposing of relatively clear cases without a trial. It differs from a demurrer because it involves factual determinations. To prevail, the party moving for a summary judgment must show that: (1) there is no genuine issue of material (legally significant) fact, and (2) he/she is entitled to judgment as a matter of law. A moving party satisfies the first element of the test by using the pleadings, discovery information, and affidavits (signed and sworn statements regarding matters of fact) to show that there is no real question about any significant fact. He/she satisfies the second element by showing that, given the established facts, the applicable law directs that he/she win.

Either or both parties may move for a summary judgment. If the court rules in favor of either party, that party wins the case. If no party's motion for summary judgment is granted, the case proceeds to trial. The judge may also grant a partial summary judgment, which settles some issues in the case but leaves the others to be decided at trial.

The Pretrial Conference

Depending on the jurisdiction, a **pretrial conference** is either mandatory or at the discretion of the trial judge. At this conference, the judge meets informally with the attorneys for both litigants. The judge may try to get the attorneys to *stipulate*, or agree to, the resolution of certain issues to simplify the trial. He may also encourage them to get their clients to *settle* the case by coming to an agreement that eliminates the need for a trial.[8] If the case is not settled, the judge enters a pretrial order including the attorneys' stipulations and any other agreements. Ordinarily, this order binds the parties throughout the remainder of the case.

The Trial

Once the case has been through discovery and has survived any pretrial motions, it is set for trial. The trial may be before a judge alone, in which case the judge makes separate findings of fact and law before issuing the court's judgment. But if the right to a jury trial exists and either party demands one, the jury handles the fact-finding function, with the resolution of legal questions still entrusted to the judge.[9] At a pretrial jury screening process known as *voir dire*, most jurisdictions: (1) allow biased potential jurors to be removed *for cause*, and (2) give the attorney for each party a certain number of *peremptory challenges*, which allow each attorney to remove potential jurors without any cause.

The Basic Scenario

At either a judge or a jury trial, the attorneys for each side typically begin by making opening statements explaining what they intend to prove. After this, the plaintiff's witnesses and other evidence are introduced, and these witnesses are cross-examined by the defendant's attorney. This may be followed by the plaintiff's redirect examination of his witnesses, and perhaps by the defendant's recross-examination of those same witnesses. Then, using the same procedures, the defendant's evidence is presented. Throughout each side's presentation, the opposing attorney may object to the admission of certain evidence. Using the law of evidence, the judge then decides whether the challenged proof is admissible. After the plaintiff and defendant have completed their initial presentations of evidence, each is allowed to offer evidence rebutting the other's evidence. Once all the evidence has been presented, each attorney makes a closing argument summarizing her position. In nonjury trials, the judge then makes findings of fact and law, renders judgment, and states the relief to which the plaintiff is entitled if the plaintiff is victorious.

Jury Trials

At the end of a jury trial, the judge issues a **charge** or **instruction** to the jury. The charge sets out the law applicable to the case. The judge may also summarize the evidence for the jury. Then the jury is supposed to make the necessary factual determinations, apply the law to these, and arrive at a **verdict** on which the court's **judgment** is based.

The most common verdict is the **general verdict**, which only requires that the jury declare which party wins and the relief (if any) awarded. Because the jury need not state its factual findings or its application of the law to those findings, the general verdict gives the jury freedom to ignore the judge's charge and follow its own inclinations. Arguably, this freedom allows the jury to soften the law's rigors by bringing common sense and community values to bear on the case, but it also weakens the rule of law and allows juries to commit injustices. The **special verdict** is one response to this problem. Here, the jury only makes specific findings of fact, and the judge then applies the law to these findings. The decision whether to utilize a special verdict is usually within the trial judge's discretion.

Directed Verdict

Although the general verdict gives the jury considerable power, the American legal system also establishes devices for limiting that power. The special verdict is one of these devices. Another, the **directed verdict**, essentially takes the case away from the jury and gives a judgment to one party before the jury gets a chance to decide. The motion for a directed verdict can be made by either party; it usually occurs after the other (nonmoving) party has presented his/her evidence. The moving party basically asserts that, even when read most favorably to the other party, the evidence leads to only one result and need not be considered by the jury. Courts differ on the test governing a motion for a directed verdict: Some deny the motion if there is *any* evidence favoring the nonmoving party, while others deny the motion only if there is *substantial* evidence favoring the nonmoving party.

Judgment Notwithstanding the Verdict

On occasion, the case is taken away from the jury and one party wins a judgment even *after* the jury has reached a verdict *against* that party. The device for doing so is the **judgment notwithstanding the verdict** (also known as the *judgment non obstante veredicto* or judgment n.o.v.). Some jurisdictions require that, in order to make a motion for judgment n.o.v, the moving party must previously have moved for a directed verdict. In any event, the standard used to decide the motion for judgment n.o.v. is usually the same standard the jurisdiction uses to decide the motion for a directed verdict.

Motion for New Trial

In a wide range of situations that vary among jurisdictions, the losing party can successfully move for a new trial. Acceptable reasons for granting a new trial include errors by the judge during the trial, jury or attorney misconduct, new evidence, or an award of excessive damages to the plaintiff.

Concept Review
The Major Civil Motions Compared

Motion	When Typically Made	By Whom Typically Made	Typical Test	Typical Effect if Successful
To Dismiss or for Judgment on the Pleadings	After complaint or pleadings	Defendant	Assuming the facts in the complaint are true, can plaintiff win as a matter of law?	Defendant wins case
For Summary Judgment	Varies; often after discovery	Either party	No genuine issue of material fact, and moving party entitled to judgment as a matter of law	Moving party wins case; partial summary judgment also possible
For Directed Verdict	After other party has presented evidence at trial	Either party	Two versions. Moving party loses if: (1) *any* evidence favoring non-moving party; or (2) *substantial* evidence favoring nonmoving party	Moving party wins case
For Judgment Notwithstanding Verdict	After adverse jury verdict	Losing party	Same test jurisdiction uses for directed verdict	Moving party wins case
For New Trial	After adverse judgment or jury verdict	Losing party	Wide range of possible grounds	New trial ordered

Appeal

Appellate courts normally consider only alleged errors of law made by the trial court. As Figure 13-5 indicated earlier in the chapter, among the matters ordinarily considered "legal" and thus appealable are the trial judge's decisions on a motion to dismiss or a motion for judgment on the pleadings, the scope of discovery, a motion for summary judgment, a motion for a directed verdict or for judgment notwithstanding the verdict, and a motion for a new trial. Other matters typically considered appealable include any trial court rulings on service of process, its rulings on the admission of evidence at trial, its legal findings in a nonjury trial, its instruction to the jury in a jury trial, and the damages or other relief awarded.

Appellate courts may, among other things, *affirm* the trial court's decision, *reverse* it, or affirm one part of the decision and reverse another part. As Figure 13-5 also suggests, one of three things ordinarily results from the appellate courts' disposition of the appeal: (1) the plaintiff wins the case; (2) the defendant wins the case; or (3) if the case is reversed in whole or in part, it is *remanded* (returned) to the trial court for further proceedings. For example, if the plaintiff appeals a trial court decision granting the defendant's motion to dismiss and the appellate court(s) affirm that decision, the plaintiff loses. On the other hand, where an appellate court reverses a trial court verdict and judgment in the defendant's favor, the plaintiff might win outright, or the case might be returned to the trial court for further proceedings not inconsistent with the appellate decision.

Enforcing a Judgment

In this text, you occasionally see cases where someone was not sued even though he appeared to be liable to the plaintiff, and where another party was sued instead. One explanation is that the first party was "judgment-proof"—so lacking in assets as to make a civil suit for damages impractical. The other party's financial condition also affects a winning plaintiff's ability to actually recover whatever damages she has been awarded.

When the defendant fails to pay as required after losing a civil suit, the winning plaintiff must enforce the judgment. Ordinarily, the plaintiff will obtain a *writ of execution* enabling the sheriff to seize designated property of the defendant and sell it at a judicial sale to satisfy the judgment. A judgment winner may also use a procedure known as *garnishment* to seize property, money, or wages of the defendant that are in the hands of a third party. If the property needed to satisfy the judgment is located in another state, the plaintiff must use that state's execution or garnishment procedures. Under the U.S. Constitution, the second state must give "full faith and credit" to the judgment of the state where the plaintiff originally sued. Finally, when the court has awarded an equitable remedy such as an injunction, the defendant may be found in contempt of court and subjected to a fine or imprisonment if he fails to obey the court's order.

Class Actions

So far, our civil procedure discussion has proceeded as if the plaintiff and the defendant each were a single party. Actually, several plaintiffs and/or defendants can be parties to one lawsuit. Also, each jurisdiction has procedural rules stating when other parties can be *joined* to a suit that begins without them.

One special type of multiparty suit, the **class action**, allows one or more persons to sue on behalf of themselves and all others who have suffered similar harm from substantially the same wrong. Class action suits by consumers, environmentalists, women, minorities, and other groups are now common events. The usual justifications for the class action are that: (1) it allows legal wrongs causing losses to a large number of widely dispersed parties to be fully compensated, and (2) it promotes economy of judicial effort by combining many similar claims into one suit.

The requirements for a class action vary among jurisdictions. The issues addressed by class action statutes include the following: whether there are questions of law and fact common to all members of the alleged class, whether the class is small enough to allow all of its members to join the case as parties rather than use a class action, and whether the plaintiff(s) and their attorney(s) can competently represent the class without conflicts of interest or other forms of unfairness. To protect the individual class member's right to be heard, some jurisdictions have required that unnamed or absent class members be given notice of the suit if this is reasonably possible. The damages awarded in a successful class action usually are apportioned among the entire class. Establishing the total recovery and distributing it to the class, however, pose problems when the class is large, the class members' injuries are indefinite, or some members cannot be identified.

Alternative Dispute Resolution

Courts are not the only devices for resolving civil disputes. Nor are they always the best means of doing so. Settling private disputes through the courts can be a cumbersome, lengthy, and expensive process for litigants. With the advent of a litigious society and the increasing caseloads it has produced, handling disputes in this fashion also imposes ever-greater *social* costs. For these and other reasons, the various forms of **alternative dispute resolution (ADR)** have assumed increasing importance in recent years.

Common Forms of ADR

Settlement

The settlement of a civil suit is not everyone's idea of an alternative dispute resolution mechanism. But it is an important means of avoiding protracted litigation, one that is often a sensible compromise for the parties. Many cases settle at some stage in the civil proceedings described previously. The typical settlement agreement is a contract whereby the defendant agrees to pay the plaintiff a sum of money, in exchange for the plaintiff's promise to release the defendant from liability on the claims in his suit. Although courts are predisposed to enforce settlement agreements, such agreements still must satisfy the requirements of contract law discussed later in this text. In some cases, moreover, the court must approve the settlement in order for it to be enforceable. Examples include class actions and litigation involving minors.

Arbitration

Arbitration is the submission of a dispute to a neutral, nonjudicial third party (the *arbitrator*) who issues a binding decision resolving that dispute. Arbitration usually results from the parties' agreement. That agreement is normally made before the dispute arises (most often through an *arbitration clause* in a contract), but it can occur after the dispute begins. Arbitration may also be compelled by statute. One example is the *compulsory arbitration* many states require as part of the collective bargaining process for certain public employees.

Arbitration is normally less formal than regular court proceedings. The arbitrator need not be an attorney; often, she is a professional who may be expert in the subject matter of the dispute. Although arbitration hearings often resemble civil trials in their broad outlines, the applicable procedures, the rules for admission of evidence, and the recordkeeping requirements typically are not as rigorous as those governing courts. Also, arbitrators have some freedom to ignore rules of substantive law that would bind a court.

The arbitrator's decision, called an *award*, is filed with a court, which will enforce it if necessary. The losing party may object to the arbitrator's award, but the courts' review of arbitration proceedings is limited. Possible grounds for overturning an arbitration award include: (1) its procurement by fraud, (2) the arbitrator's partiality or corruption, and (3) other misconduct by the arbitrator (e.g., refusing to hear relevant evidence).

Court-Annexed Arbitration

In court-annexed arbitration, certain types of civil lawsuits basically are diverted into arbitration. One example might be cases where less than a specified dollar amount is at issue. Most often, court-annexed arbitration is mandatory and is ordered by the judge, but some jurisdictions merely offer litigants the option of arbitration. The losing party in a court-annexed arbitration still has the right to a regular trial.

Mediation

In mediation, a neutral third party called a *mediator* helps the parties reach an agreeable, cooperative resolution of their dispute by facilitating communication between them, clarifying their areas of agreement and disagreement, helping them to see each other's viewpoints, suggesting settlement options, and so forth. Unlike arbitrators, mediators cannot make decisions that bind the parties. Instead, a successful mediation process typically results in a *mediation agreement*. Such agreements normally are enforced under regular contract law principles.

Mediation is used in a wide range of situations, including labor, commercial, family, and environmental disputes. It may occur by agreement of the parties after a dispute has arisen. It may also result from a previous contractual agreement by the parties. Increasingly, moreover, court-annexed mediation is either compelled or made available by courts in certain cases.

Summary Jury Trial

Sometimes settlement of civil litigation is impeded because the litigants have different perceptions of the merits of their cases. In such cases, the summary jury trial may give either or both parties a needed dose of reality. As its name suggests, the summary jury trial is an abbreviated, nonpublic mock jury trial that does not bind the parties. Often, this "trial" occurs before a real judge, with jurors chosen from the regular pool of jurors. If the parties do not settle after completion of the summary jury trial, they are still entitled to a regular court trial. Also, there is some disagreement over whether courts can compel the parties to undergo a summary jury trial in the first place.

Minitrial

A minitrial is an informal, abbreviated private "trial" whose aim is to promote settlement of disputes. Normally, it arises out of a private agreement, which also describes the procedures to be followed. In the typical minitrial, counsel for each party present their cases to a panel composed of senior management from each side. Sometimes a neutral adviser such as an attorney or a retired judge presides. This party may also offer an opinion about the case's likely outcome in court. After the presentations, the managers try to negotiate a settlement.

Other ADR Devices

Other ADR devices include: (1) *med/arb* (a hybrid of mediation and arbitration in which the third party first acts as a mediator, and then as an arbitrator); (2) the appointment of *magistrates* and *special masters* to perform various tasks during complex litigation in the federal courts; (3) *early neutral evaluation* (ENE) (a court-annexed procedure involving early, objective evaluation of the case by a neutral private attorney with experience in its subject matter); (4) *private judging* (in which litigants hire a private referee to issue a decision that may be binding but that usually does not preclude some recourse to the courts); and (5) *private panels* instituted by an industry or an organization to handle claims of certain kinds (e.g., the Better Business Bureau). Also, some formally legal processes are sometimes called ADR devices; examples include small claims courts and the administrative procedures used to handle claims for veterans' benefits or social security benefits.

The Pros and Cons of ADR

Taken collectively, the various forms of ADR have many advantages over litigation before a court. These advantages include:

1. *Quicker resolution of disputes.* This is due mainly to the relative informality of most ADR proceedings and their ability to promote settlement of the case.
2. *Lower costs in time, money, and aggravation for the parties.* Again, these benefits flow mainly from the relative informality and speed of many ADR procedures, and from their ability to spur a settlement.
3. *Reduced strains on an overloaded count system.*
4. *The possible availability of expert decision makers.* For example, arbitrators may possess special expertise in the subject matter of the disputes they handle.
5. *Flexibility and consensus-building.* Mediation, for instance, often avoids the adversarial climate and tendency toward either/or decisions that characterize formal litigation. Thus, it can promote consensus and compromise solutions by the parties themselves.

However, ADR also has a number of possible disadvantages. These include:

1. *A tendency to undermine the rule of law.* At its best, the civil law states general norms that apply uniformly to all the private disputes they cover. ADR decisions, on the other hand, sometimes are ad hoc affairs in which rules of substantive law play little role and precedent even less. Thus, the widespread use of ADR tends to undermine the uniformity and predictability associated with the rule of law.
2. *Inaccurate or biased decision making processes.* One reason for the complexity of the rules of civil procedure and evidence is that they try to give each party the utmost in procedural protection and to ensure that factual determinations are as accurate as possible. The relatively relaxed procedures and evidentiary rules—not to mention the occasional absence of lawyers—in some ADR proceedings may mean that these ends are less likely to be served under ADR.
3. *Second-class justice for the relatively powerless in their disputes with the powerful?* Sometimes, agreements to submit disputes to alternative dispute resolution are buried in complex standard-form contracts drafted by a party with superior knowledge and business sophistication and are unknowingly agreed to by less knowledgeable parties. Sometimes, too, such clauses compel ADR proceedings before decision makers who may be biased in favor of the stronger party. Occasionally, courts strike down arbitration clauses for these reasons.

Ethical and Public Policy

1. As you might expect, the preceding arguments against ADR often come from the legal profession. Are these self-serving arguments? Who stands to lose money and influence if ADR becomes more popular? Assuming that these arguments are self-serving, is this fact alone enough to rebut them?

2. The *Knowles* case presented earlier in this chapter used a style of legal reasoning. This style, which might be called *factor-based balancing*, appears from time to time in this text. Courts using this style of reasoning typically consider several factors (values or policy goals) when deciding. They assess a particular result in light of each factor, trying to determine whether that result advances or frustrates the values embodied in each factor. Then, they try to assess the overall desirability of that result by weighing its positive and negative effects against each other and determining whether the result has a positive or negative effect on balance. Such determinations naturally vary depending on the facts of the case. In *Knowles*, the decision was easy, because almost all the factors the court considered pulled in the same direction.

    What is good about this kind of legal decision making? What is bad about it?

3. Debates in the ethics and business ethics literature have sometimes involved clashes between *utilitarian* ethical theories and *deontological rights-based* ethical theories. Utilitarians normally say that we should maximize aggregate satisfaction, and they tend to approve measures that disadvantage particular individuals so long as those measures actually produce maximum total satisfaction. Such theories occasionally use social wealth maximization as a rough measure of total satisfaction. Deontological rightsbased theories generally urge that some rights are so important that they can only be overridden by certain other rights, and *not* by maximum aggregate utility.

    Speaking generally, into which category would many foes of ADR fit? Assume that these people oppose ADR because they feel that due to the sloppiness of its procedures, it causes injustices to individuals—injustices that could be avoided were normal court procedures used. Although the use of such procedures costs more money than ADR, they assert, this is of no consequence because basic issues of *justice* are involved.

    Speaking generally, into which category would many proponents of ADR fit? Assume that these people stress the social and economic costs created by the court system and argue that the widespread use of ADR would free money and resources for other purposes, thus making people wealthier and happier. This increased wealth and happiness, they would add, easily outweigh the personal suffering caused by whatever injustices ADR permits.

Problems and Problem Cases

1. Peters sues Davis. At trial, Peters's lawyer attempts to introduce certain evidence to help make his case. Davis's attorney objects, and the trial judge refuses to allow the evidence to be admitted. Peters eventually loses the case at the trial court level. He appeals, his attorney arguing that the trial judge's decision not to admit the evidence was erroneous. Davis's attorney argues that the appellate court cannot consider this question, because appellate courts only review errors of *law* (not fact) at the trial court level. Is Davis's attorney correct? Why or why not?

2. Phillips sues Dilks for $500,000 in a state small claims court set up to handle cases where the amount in controversy does not exceed $5,000. The court clearly does not have jurisdiction over the case. What *kind* of jurisdiction is absent here?

3. Dial, a resident of Indiana, vandalizes a parked car in Columbus, Ohio. This action results in harm to the car and also prevents the owner from using it for a period of time. In the meantime, Dial has fled to Indiana and remains there. The owner, an Ohio resident, plans to sue Dial for trespass to personal property. He claims $5,000 in damages and wants to sue either in an Ohio trial court or in a federal district court. Do each of these courts have jurisdiction over the case? Why or why not? Assume for purposes of this problem that: (a) subject-matter jurisdiction is present, (b) Dial has had no other contacts with the state of Ohio, and (c) Ohio has a long-arm statute with all the features described in the chapter.

4. State *two* differences between the motion to dismiss for failure to state a claim upon which relief can be granted (or demurrer) and the motion for summary judgment.

5. In a suit by Pierce against Dodge, the jury has rendered a verdict in favor of Dodge. Pierce and her attorney think that the evidence was overwhelmingly in Pierce's favor. They also have reason to believe that the jury was bribed by someone connected with Dodge. What *two* motions can Pierce's attorney make in an attempt to overturn the jury's verdict?

6. While driving to work one day, Dember runs over Pearson, causing him severe injuries. Pearson sues Dember in a state trial court. His complaint alleges that Dember's negligent driving caused his injuries. The law of the state declares that if the plaintiff's own negligence contributed to his injury, the defendant has a complete defense and the plaintiff cannot recover. Dember wants to argue that whether he was negligent or not, Pearson's own negligence helped cause his injuries and that Pearson therefore has no case. In order to be *sure* of his ability to raise this argument at trial, what should Dember's attorney do in response to Pearson's complaint?

7. What is the main difference between a motion for a directed verdict and a motion for judgment notwithstanding the verdict?

8. The state of Mississippi is planning to sue the state of Massachusetts. Mississippi's attorney general wants to sue in an appropriate federal district court. Do the federal district courts have jurisdiction over this case? If not, which federal court does have jurisdiction? You can assume that Mississippi's suit involves issues of federal law, and that the amount in controversy exceeds $50,000.

9. Jackson was born in Texas but has had absolutely no contact with that state for 20 years. Jackson's father dies, and a Texas court interprets his will so that Jackson receives none of his father's property, which is located in Texas. Assume that the court had jurisdiction to make this decision. What *kinds* of jurisdiction did it have?

10. Pike sues Dillon, alleging that his parked car was destroyed due to Dillon's negligent driving. After the pleadings and discovery have been completed, Pike's attorney concludes that the case is an obvious winner on both the facts and the law. What motion should the attorney make in an attempt to win the case without having to go to trial?

11. Does ADR really resolve disputes without any help from the courts? Give two examples of ADR processes that depend on courts for their operation or their effectiveness, and state how they depend on the courts.

Endnotes

1. See Chapter 12 for the distinctions between civil law and criminal law and between procedural law and substantive law.
2. Service of process is discussed later in this chapter.
3. In some states, however, out-of-state defendants may make a *special appearance* to challenge the court's jurisdiction without consenting to that jurisdiction.

4.   Another form of jurisdiction, *quasi in rem jurisdiction* or *attachment jurisdiction*, is also based on the presence of property within the state. Unlike cases based on in rem jurisdiction, cases based on quasi in rem jurisdiction do not necessarily determine rights in the property itself. Instead, the property is regarded as an extension of the out-of-state defendant, which enables the count to decide claims unrelated to the property. For example, a plaintiff might attach the defendant's bank account in the state where the bank is located, sue the defendant on a tort or contract claim unrelated to the bank account, and recover the amount of the judgment from the account if the suit is successful.

5.   There are, however, situations in which the Supreme Court will hear appeals directly from the federal district courts.

6.   In the following discussion, the term *jurisdiction* refers to 1 of the 50 states, the District of Columbia, or the federal government.

7.   However, in a criminal case the government must prove the elements of the alleged crime *beyond a reasonable doubt*.

8.   Settlement of a civil case is discussed in more detail later in this chapter.

9.   The rules governing availability of a jury trial are largely beyond the scope of this text. The U.S. Constitution guarantees a jury trial in federal court suits "at common law" whose amount exceeds $20, and most of the states have similar constitutional provisions. Also, Congress and the state legislatures may allow jury trials in various other cases.

Chapter Fourteen

INTRODUCTION TO

CONTRACTS

Introduction

Scholars and courts have formulated numerous definitions of the term *contract*. The *Restatement (Second) of Contracts* defines a contract as "a promise or set of promises for the breach of which the law gives a remedy, or the performance of which the law in some way recognizes as a duty."[1] The essence of this definition for our purposes is that a contract is a *legally enforceable promise or set of promises*. In other words, parties to contracts are entitled to call on the state to force those with whom they have contracted to honor their promises. However, not all of the promises that people make attain the status of contracts. We have all made and broken numerous promises without fear of being sued by those to whom our promises were made. If you promise to take a friend out to dinner but fail to do so, you do not expect to be sued for breaching your promise. What separates such social promises from legally enforceable contracts?

The Nature of Contracts

Over the years, the common law courts have developed several basic tests that a promise must meet before it is treated as a contract. These tests comprise the basic elements of contract. Contracts are *agreements* (an *offer*, made and *accepted*) that are *voluntarily* created by persons with the *capacity* to contract. The objectives of the agreement must be *legal* and, in most cases, the agreement must be supported by some *consideration* (a bargained-for exchange of legal value). Finally, the law requires *written* evidence of the existence of some agreements before enforcing them (see Figure 14-1). The following chapters discuss each of these elements and other points that are necessary to enable you to distinguish contracts from unenforceable, social promises.

The Social Utility of Contract

Contracts enable persons acting in their own interests to enlist the support of the law in furthering their personal objectives. Contracts enable us to enter into agreements with others with the confidence that we may call on the law, and not merely the good faith of the other party, to ensure that those agreements will be honored. Within broad limits defined by contract doctrine and public policy, the contract device enables us to create the private law that governs our relations with others—the terms of the agreements we make.

FIGURE 14-1
Getting to contract

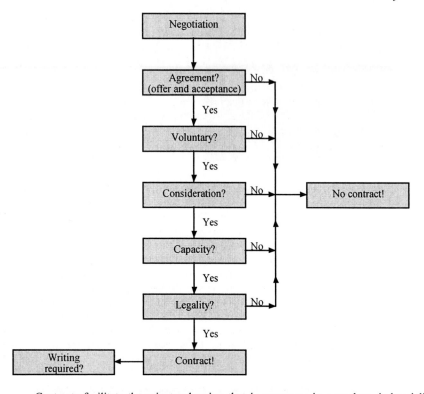

Contracts facilitate the private planning that is necessary in a modern, industrialized society. Few people would invest in a business enterprise if they could not rely on the builders and suppliers of their facilities and equipment, the suppliers of the raw materials necessary to manufacture products, and the customers who agree to purchase those products to honor their commitments. How could we make loans, sell goods on credit, or rent property unless loan agreements, conditional sales agreements, and leases were backed by the force of the law? Contract, then, is an inescapable and valuable part of the world as we know it. Like that world, its particulars tend to change over time, while its general characteristics remain largely stable.

The Evolution of Contract Law

Classical Contract Law

The contract idea is ancient. Thousands of years ago, Egyptians and Mesopotamians recognized devices like contracts; by the 15th century, the common law courts of England had developed a variety of theories to justify enforcing certain promises. Contract law did not, however, assume major importance in our legal system until the 19th century, when numerous social factors combined to shape the common law of contract. Laissez-faire (free market) economic ideas had a profound influence on public policy thinking during this period, and the Industrial Revolution created a perceived need for private planning and certainty in commercial transactions. The typical contract situation in the early decades of the 19th century involved face-to-face transactions between parties with relatively equal bargaining power who dealt with relatively simple goods.

The contract law that emerged from this period was strongly influenced by these factors. Its central tenet was *freedom of contract*: Contracts should be enforced because they are the products of the free wills of their creators, who should, within broad limits, be free to determine the extent of their obligations. The proper role of the courts in such a system of contract was to enforce these freely made bargains but otherwise to adopt a hands-off stance. Contractual liability should not be imposed unless the parties clearly agreed to assume it, but once an agreement had been made, liability was near absolute. The fact that the items exchanged were of unequal value was usually legally irrelevant. The freedom to make good deals carried with it the risk of making bad deals. As long as a person voluntarily entered a contract, it would generally be enforced against him, even if the result was grossly unfair. And since equal bargaining power tended to be assumed, the courts were usually unwilling to hear defenses based on unequal bargaining power. This judicial posture allowed the courts to formulate a pure contract law consisting of precise, clear, and technical rules that were capable of general, almost mechanical, application. Such a law of contract met the needs of the marketplace by affording the predictable and consistent results necessary to facilitate private planning.

Modern Contract Law Development

As long as most contracts resembled the typical transaction envisioned by 19th-century contract law, such rules made perfect sense. If the parties dealt face-to-face, they were likely to know each other personally or at least to know each other's reputation for fair dealing. Face-to-face deals enabled the parties to inspect the goods in advance of the sale, and since the subject matter of most contracts was relatively simple, the odds were great that the parties had relatively equal knowledge about the items they bought and sold. If the parties also had equal bargaining power, it was probably fair to assume that they were capable of protecting themselves and negotiating an agreement that seemed fair at the time. Given the truth of these assumptions, there was arguably no good reason for judicial interference with private contracts.

America's Industrial Revolution, however, undermined many of these assumptions. Regional, and later national, markets produced longer chains of distribution. This fact, combined with more efficient means of communication, meant that people often contracted with persons whom they did not know for goods that they had never seen. And rapidly developing technology meant that those goods were becoming increasingly complex. Thus, sellers often knew far more about their products than did the buyers with whom they dealt. Finally, the emergence of large business organizations after the Civil War produced obvious disparities of bargaining power in many contract situations. These large organizations found it more efficient to standardize their numerous transactions by employing standard form contracts, which could also be used to exploit disproportionate bargaining power by dictating the terms of their agreements. Figure 14-2 summarizes the factors that shaped modern contract law.

The upshot of all this is that many contracts today no longer resemble the stereotypical agreements envisioned by the common law of contract. It has been estimated that over 90 percent of all contracts today are form contracts.[2] How should courts respond to contracts where the terms have been dictated by one party to another party who may not have read or understood them, and who, in any event, may have lacked the power to bargain for better terms? Contract law is changing to reflect these changes in social reality. The 20th century has witnessed a dramatic increase in public intervention into private contractual relationships. Think of all the statutes governing the terms of what were once purely private contractual relationships. Legislatures commonly dictate many of the basic terms of insurance contracts. Employment contracts are governed by a host of laws concerning maximum hours worked, minimum wages paid, employer liability for on-the-job injuries, unemployment compensation, and retirement benefits. In some circumstances, product liability statutes impose liability on the manufacturers and sellers of products regardless of the terms of their sales contracts. The avowed purpose of much of this public intervention has been to protect persons who lack sufficient bargaining power to protect themselves.

FIGURE 14-2
Factors that shaped
modern contract law

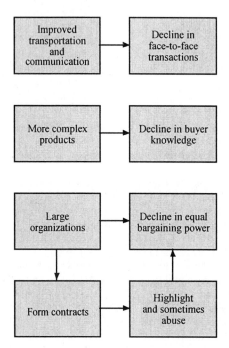

Nor have the legislatures been the only source of public supervision of private agreements. Twentieth-century courts have been increasingly concerned with creating contract rules that produce just results. The result of this concern has been an increasingly hands-on posture by courts that often feel compelled to intervene in private contractual relationships to protect weaker parties. In the name of avoiding injustice, some modern contract doctrines impose contractual liability, or something quite like it, in situations where traditional contract rules would have denied liability. Similarly, other modern contract doctrines allow parties to avoid contract liability in cases where traditional common law rules would have recognized a binding agreement and imposed liability.

In the process of evolving to accommodate changing social circumstances, the basic nature of contract rules is changing. The precise, technical rules that characterized traditional common law contract are giving way to broader, imprecise standards such as good faith, injustice, reasonableness, and unconscionability. The reason for such standards is clear. If courts are increasingly called on to intervene in private contracts in the name of fairness, it is necessary to fashion rules that afford the degree of judicial discretion required to reach just decisions in the increasingly complex and varied situations where intervention is needed.

This heightened emphasis on fairness, like every other choice made by law, carries with it some cost. Imprecise, discretionary modern contract rules do not produce the same measure of certainty and predictability that their precise and abstract predecessors afforded. And because modern contract rules often impose liability in the absence of the clear consent required by traditional common law contract rules, one price of increased fairness in contract cases has been a diminished ability of private parties to control the nature and extent of their contractual obligations.

This change in the nature of contract law is far from complete, however. The idea that a contract is an agreement freely entered into by the parties still lies at the heart of contract law today, and contract cases may be found that differ very little in their spirit or ultimate resolution from their 19th-century predecessors. It is probably fair to say, however, that these are most likely to be cases where 19th-century assumptions about the nature of contracts are still largely valid. Thus, these cases involve contracts between parties with relatively equal bargaining power and relatively equal knowledge about the subject of the contract. Despite the existence of such cases, it is evident that contract law is in the process of significant change. Subsequent chapters highlighting the differences between modern contract rules and their traditional common law forebears render this conclusion inescapable. Before discussing particular examples of this new thrust in contract law, however, we should familiarize ourselves with the basic contract terminology that is used throughout the text.

Basic Contract Concepts and Types

Bilateral and Unilateral Contracts

Contracts have traditionally been classified as bilateral or unilateral, depending on whether one or both of the parties has made a promise. In unilateral contracts, only one party makes a promise. For example, if a homeowner says to a painter, "I will pay you $1,000 if you paint my house," the homeowner has made an offer for a unilateral contract, a contract that will be created only if and when the painter paints the house. If the homeowner instead says to the painter, "If you promise to paint my house, I will promise to pay you $1,000," he has asked the painter to commit to painting the house rather than just to perform the act of painting. This offer contemplates the formation of a bilateral contract. If the painter makes the requested promise to paint the house, a bilateral contract is created at that point.

In succeeding chapters, you will learn that unilateral contracts cause some particular problems related to offer and acceptance and to mutuality of obligation. These problems have caused many commentators to argue that the unilateral-bilateral contract distinction should be abandoned. The *Restatement (Second) of Contracts* and the Uniform Commercial Code, both of which are discussed later in this chapter, do not expressly use unilateral-bilateral terminology. However, both of these important sources of modern contract principles contain provisions for dealing with typical unilateral contract problems. Despite this evidence of disfavor, the courts continue to use unilateral contract terminology, in part because it enables them to do justice in some cases by imposing contractual liability on one party without the necessity of finding a return promise of the other party. For example, many recent employment cases have used unilateral contract analyses to hold employers liable for promises relating to pension rights, bonuses or incentive pay, and profit-sharing benefits, though the employees in question did not make any clear return promise to continue their employment for any specified time or to do anything else in exchange for the employer's promise.[3]

Valid, Unenforceable, Voidable, and Void Contracts

A **valid contract** is one that meets all of the legal requirements for a binding contract. Valid contracts are, therefore, enforceable in court.

An **unenforceable contract** is one that meets the basic legal requirements for a contract but may not be enforceable due to some other legal rule. Chapter 20, Writing, discusses the statute of frauds, which requires written evidence of certain contracts. An otherwise valid oral contract that the statute of frauds requires to be in writing, for example, may be unenforceable due to the parties' failure to reduce the contract to written form. Another example of an unenforceable contract is an otherwise valid contract whose enforcement is barred by the applicable contract statute of limitations.

Voidable contracts are those in which one or more of the parties have the legal right to cancel their obligations under the contract. They are enforceable against both parties unless a party with the power to void the contract has exercised that power. Chapter 19, Reality of Consent, for example, states that contracts induced by misrepresentation, fraud, duress, or undue influence are voidable at the election of the injured party.

Void contracts are agreements that create no legal obligations because they fail to contain one or more of the basic elements required for enforceability. A void contract is, in a sense, a contradiction in terms. It would be more accurate to say that no contract was created in such cases. A contract to commit a crime, such as an agreement for the sale of cocaine, does not create a binding legal obligation. Nonetheless, practical constraints may some times encourage a party to such a contract to perform his agreement rather than raise an illegality defense.

Express and Implied Contracts

In an **express contract**, the parties have directly stated the terms of their contract orally or in writing at the time the contract was formed. As the following *Cook v. Cook* case illustrates, however, the mutual agreement necessary to create a contract may also be demonstrated by the conduct of the parties. When the surrounding facts and circumstances indicate that an agreement has in fact been reached, an **implied contract** (also called a contract implied in fact) has been created. When you go to a doctor for treatment, for example, you do not ordinarily state the terms of your agreement in advance, although it is clear that you do, in fact, have an agreement. A court would infer a promise by your doctor to use reasonable care and skill in treating you and a return promise on your part to pay a reasonable fee for her services.

Executed and Executory Contracts

A contract is **executed** when all of the parties have fully performed their contractual duties, and it is **executory** until such duties have been fully performed.

Any contract may be described using one or more of the above terms. For example, Eurocars, Inc., orders five new Mercedes-Benz 500 SLs from Mercedes. Mercedes sends Eurocars its standard acknowledgment form accepting the order. The parties have a *valid, express, bilateral* contract that will be executory until Mercedes delivers the cars and Eurocars pays for them.

Cook v. Cook

Intending to marry as soon as Donald's divorce became final, Rose Elsten and Donald Cook moved to Tucson in 1969 and lived there together until 1981. Although they did not marry, Rose used Donald's last name and they represented themselves to the community as husband and wife. Both parties worked throughout most of the relationship, pooling their income in two joint accounts and acquiring a house, two cars, and a number of shares of stock, all owned as joint tenants with right of survivorship. Rose left Donald in 1981. Of their joint assets, she received only one car and a few hundred dollars; Donald retained the balance.

Rose filed suit against Donald, arguing that he had breached their agreement to share their assets equally. In her deposition she said: "[E]verything we did and purchased, whether it be a vacuum cleaner or a car, was together as husband and wife. It was just something *that we agreed on*, that is how we were going to do it." When the trial court ruled against her, she appealed.

Source: 691 P.2d (Ariz. Sup. Ct.. 1984)

Feldman, Justice

The *sine qua non* of any contract is the exchange of promises. From this exchange flows the obligation of one party to another. Although it is most apparent that two parties have exchanged promises when their words express a spoken or written statement of promissory intention, mutual promises need not be express in order to create an enforceable contract. Indeed, a promise "may be inferred wholly or partly from conduct," and "there is no distinction in the effect of the promise whether it is expressed in writing, or orally, or in acts, or partly in one of these ways and partly in others." *Restatement (Second) of Contracts.*

Thus, two parties may by their course of conduct express their agreement, though no words are ever spoken. From their conduct alone the finder of fact can determine the existence of an agreement. Although isolated acts of joint participation such as cohabitation or the opening of a joint account may not suffice to create a contract, the fact finder may infer an exchange of promises, and the existence of the contract, from the entire course of conduct between the parties.

The conduct of the parties certainly demonstrates such an agreement and intent. Rose and Donald maintained two joint accounts, a checking account and a credit union savings account, in the names of "Rose and Don Cook" and held them as joint tenants with right of survivorship. Neither Rose nor Donald maintained a separate account. Both deposited portions of their paychecks into the accounts and used the funds to pay for household expenses and various assets they purchased. In addition, Rose and Donald held jointly a number of shares of Southwest Gas stock purchased with funds from the credit union account. In 1972 they purchased a house, taking the deed as husband and wife in joint tenancy with right of survivorship. Both signed the mortgage, incurring liability for the full purchase price of the house, and payments on the mortgage were made out of the joint checking account. There is ample evidence to support a finding that Rose and Donald agreed to pool their resources and share equally in certain accumulations; their course of conduct may be seen as consistently demonstrating the existence of such an agreement. **Judgment reversed in favor of Rose; case remanded for further proceedings.**

Quasi-Contract

The traditional common law insistence on the presence of all the elements required for a binding contract before contractual obligation is imposed can cause injustice in some cases.

One person may have provided goods or services to another person who benefited from them but has no contractual obligation to pay for them because no facts exist that would justify a court in implying a promise to pay for them. Such a situation can also arise in cases where the parties contemplated entering into a binding contract but some legal defense exists that prevents the enforcement of the agreement. Consider the following examples:

1.   Jones paints Smith's house by mistake, thinking it belongs to Reed. Smith knows that Jones is painting his house but does not inform him of his error. There are no facts from which a court can infer that Jones and Smith have a contract, because the parties have had no prior discussions or dealings.
2.   Thomas Products fraudulently induces Perkins to buy a household products franchise by grossly misstating the average revenues of its franchisees. Perkins discovers the misrepresentation after he has resold some products that he has received but before he has paid Thomas for them. Perkins elects to rescind (cancel) the franchise contract on the basis of the fraud.

In the preceding examples, both Smith and Perkins have good defenses to contract liability; however, enabling Smith to get a free paint job and Perkins to avoid paying for the goods he resold would *unjustly enrich* them at the expense of Jones and Thomas. To deal with such cases and to prevent such unjust enrichment, the courts imply *as a matter of law* a promise by the benefited party to pay the *reasonable value* of the benefits he received. This idea is called **quasi-contract** (or contract implied in law) because it represents an obligation imposed by law to avoid injustice, not a contractual obligation created by voluntary consent. Quasi-contract liability has been imposed in situations too numerous and varied to detail. In general, however, quasi-contract liability is imposed when one party *confers a benefit* on another who *knowingly accepts it* and *retains it* under circumstances that make it *unjust* to do so without paying for it. So, if Jones painted Smith's house while Smith was away on vacation, Smith would probably not be liable for the reasonable value of the paint job because he did *not* knowingly accept it and because he has no way to return it to Jones. The following *Corrado* case highlights the centrality of the unjust enrichment idea to quasi-contract liability.

Anthony Corrado, Inc. v. Menard & Co.

Hart Engineering Company (Hart) was the general contractor for the construction of the Fields Point Waste Water Treatment Facility. Hart posted the necessary bond for the project, and Seaboard Surety Company (Seaboard) wrote the bond. Hart subcontracted with Menard & Co. Building Contractors (Menard) to do the masonry work. Menard purchased certain building materials for the project from Corrado, who supplied the materials but was never paid by either Menard or Hart. Corrado later sued Hart, Seaboard, and Menard. He won a summary judgment against Menard, but the trial court granted summary judgments in favor of Seaboard and Hart because Menard, not Hart or Seaboard, had ordered the materials. Corrado appealed.

Source: 589 A.2d 1201 (R.I. Sup. Ct. 1991)

Per Curiam

Corrado argues that under quasi-contract, he had a cause of action against Hart and Seaboard for unjust enrichment. In order to recover under quasi-contract, a plaintiff is required to prove three elements: (1) a benefit must be conferred upon the defendant by the plaintiff, (2) there must be appreciation by the defendant of such a benefit, and (3) there must be an acceptance of such benefit in such circumstances that it would be inequitable for a defendant to retain the benefit without paying the value thereof.

In reviewing a motion for summary judgment, a trial justice must determine, after an examination of the pleadings, affidavits, admissions, and answers to interrogatories, viewed in the light most favorable to the opposing party, whether there is a genuine issue regarding any material fact that must be resolved.

In his affidavit Frank Rampone, president of Hart, avers that from time to time Menard would submit an application for payment and that periodic payments were made to Menard. He further averred that Hart had no contractual relationship with Corrado and that it was Menard's obligation to pay Corrado directly from the periodic payments made to it. Hart never agreed to pay Corrado directly.

It is obvious from the record that there is no genuine issue regarding any material fact that must be resolved. No conflicting evidence was introduced to establish that Menard was not paid in full by Hart. Moreover, there was no evidence that would establish that Hart received any unjust enrichment from Corrado's building materials since Hart made periodic payments to Menard.

Judgment for Hart and Seaboard affirmed.

Promissory Estoppel

Another very important idea that 20th-century courts have developed to deal with the unfairness that would sometimes result from the strict application of traditional contract principles is the doctrine of **promissory estoppel**. In numerous situations, one person may *rely* on a promise made by another even though the promise and surrounding circumstances are not sufficient to justify the conclusion that a contract has been created because one or more of the required elements is missing. To allow the person who made such a promise (the promiser) to argue that no contract was created would sometimes work an injustice on the person who relied on the promise (the promisee). For example, in *Ricketts v. Scothorn*, a grandfather's promise to pay his granddaughter interest on a demand note he gave her so that she would not have to work was enforced against him after she had quit her job in reliance on his promise.[4] The Nebraska Supreme Court acknowledged that such promises were traditionally unenforceable because they were gratuitous and not supported by any consideration, but held that the granddaughter's reliance prevented her grandfather from raising his lack of consideration defense. In the early decades of this century, many courts began to extend similar protection to relying promisees. They said that persons who made promises that produced such reliance were *estopped,* or equitably prevented, from raising any defense they had to the enforcement of their promise. Out of such cases grew the doctrine of promissory estoppel. Section 90 of the *Restatement (Second) of Contracts* states:

> A promise which the promiser should reasonably expect to induce action or forbearance on the part of the promisee or a third person and which does induce such action or forbearance is binding if injustice can be avoided only by enforcement of the promise. The remedy granted for breach may be limited as justice requires.

Thus, the elements of promissory estoppel are a *promise* that the *promiser should foresee is likely to induce reliance, reliance* on the promise by the promisee, and *injustice* as a result of that reliance.

When you consider these elements, it is obvious that promissory estoppel is fundamentally different from traditional contract principles. Contract is traditionally thought of as protecting *agreements* or bargains. Promissory estoppel, on the other hand, protects *reliance*. Early promissory estoppel cases applied the doctrine only to donative or gift promises. As subsequent chapters demonstrate, however, promissory estoppel is now being used by the courts to prevent offerors from revoking their offers, to enforce indefinite promises, and to enforce oral promises that would ordinarily have to be in writing. Given the basic conceptual differences between estoppel and contract, and the judicial tendency to use promissory estoppel to compensate for the absence of the traditional elements of contract, its growth as a new device for enforcing promises is one of the most important developments in modern contract law. Figure 14-3 summarizes the ways in which contract differs from quasi-contract and promissory estoppel.

FIGURE 14-3
Contract and
contractlike theories of
recovery

Theory	Key Concept	Remedy
Contract	Voluntary agreement	Enforce promise
Quasi-Contract	Unjust enrichment	Reasonable value of services
Promissory Estoppel	Foreseeable reliance	Enforce promise or recover reliance losses

The Uniform Commercial Code

Origins and Purposes of the Code

The Uniform Commercial Code (WCC) was created by the American Law Institute and the National Conference of Commissioners on Uniform State Laws. All of the states have adopted it except Louisiana, which has adopted only part of the Code. The drafters of the Code had several purposes in mind, the most obvious of which was to establish a uniform set of rules to govern commercial transactions, which are often conducted across state lines in today's national markets. Despite the Code's almost national adoption, however, complete uniformity has not been achieved. Many states have varied or amended the Code's language in specific instances, and some Code provisions were drafted in alternative ways, giving the states more than one version of particular Code provisions to choose from. Also, the various state courts have reached different conclusions about the meaning of particular Code sections. Work is currently under way to revise many basic sections of the Code, so uniformity will continue to be a problem as states adopt the revised sections at different rates and to different degrees.

In addition to promoting uniformity, the drafters of the Code sought to create a body of rules that would realistically and fairly solve the common problems occurring in everyday commercial transactions. Finally, the drafters tried to formulate rules that would promote fair dealing and higher standards in the marketplace.

Scope of the Code

The Code contains nine substantive articles. The most important Code article for our present purposes is Article 2, the Sales article of the Code.

Nature of Article 2

Many of the provisions of Article 2 exhibit the basic tendencies of modern contract law discussed earlier in this chapter. Accordingly, they differ from traditional contract law rules in a variety of important ways. The Code is more concerned with rewarding people's legitimate expectations than with technical rules, so it is generally more flexible than contract law. A court that applies the Code is more likely to find that the parties had a contract than is a court that applies contract law [2-204] (the numbers in brackets refer to specific Code sections). In some cases, the Code gives less weight than does contract law to technical requirements such as consideration [2-205 and 2-209].

The drafters of the Code sought to create practical rules to deal with what people actually do in today's marketplace. We live in the day of the form contract, so some of the Code's rules try to deal fairly with that fact [2-205, 2-207, 2-209(2), and 2-302]. The words *reasonable, commercially reasonable,* and *seasonably* (within a reasonable time) are found throughout the Code. This reasonableness standard is different from the hypothetical reasonable person standard in tort law. A court that tries to decide what is reasonable under the Code is more likely to be concerned with what people really do in the marketplace than with what a nonexistent reasonable person would do.

The drafters of the Code wanted to promote fair dealing and higher standards in the marketplace, so they imposed a **duty of good faith** [1-203] in the performance and enforcement of every contract under the Code. Good faith means "honesty in fact," which is required of all parties to sales contracts [1-201(19)]. In addition, merchants are required to observe "reasonable commercial standards of fair dealing" [2-103(1)(b)]. The parties cannot alter this duty of good faith by agreement [1-102(3)]. Finally, the Code expressly recognizes the concept of an unconscionable contract, one that is grossly unfair or one-sided, and it gives the courts broad discretionary powers to deal fairly with such contracts [2-302].

The Code also recognizes that buyers tend to place more reliance on professional sellers and that professionals are generally more knowledgeable and better able to protect themselves than nonprofessionals. So, the Code distinguishes between **merchants** and nonmerchants by holding merchants to a higher standard in some cases [2-201(2), 2-205, and 2-207(2)]. The Code defines the term *merchant* [2-104(1)] on a case-by-case basis. If a person regularly deals in the kind of goods being sold, or pretends to have some special knowledge about the goods, or employed an agent in the sale who fits either of these two descriptions, that person is a merchant for the purposes of the contract in question. So, if you buy a used car from a used-car dealer, the dealer is a merchant for the purposes of your contract. But, if you buy a refrigerator from a used-car dealer, the dealer is probably not a merchant.

Application of the Code

Article 2 expressly applies only to *contracts for the sale of goods* [2-102]. The Code contains a somewhat complicated definition of *goods* [2-105], but the essence of the definition is that *goods* are *tangible, movable, personal property*. So, contracts for the sale of such items as motor vehicles, books, appliances, and clothing are covered by Article 2. But Article 2 does not apply to contracts for the sale of real estate, stocks and bonds, or other intangibles. Article 2 also does not apply to *service* contracts. This can cause confusion because, although contracts of employment or other personal services are clearly not covered by Article 2, many contracts involve elements of both goods and services. As the following *Advent* case illustrates, the test that the courts most frequently use to determine whether Article 2 applies to such a contract is to ask which element, goods or services, *predominates* in the contract. Is the major purpose or thrust of the agreement the rendering of a service, or is it the sale of goods, with any services involved being merely incidental to that sale? This means that contracts calling for services that involve significant elements of personal skill or judgment in addition to goods probably are not governed by Article 2. Construction contracts, remodeling contracts, and auto repair contracts are all examples of mixed goods and services contracts that may be considered outside the scope of the Code.

Two other important qualifications must be made concerning the application of Code contract principles. First, the Code does not change *all* of the traditional contract rules. Where no specific Code rule exists, traditional contract law rules apply to contracts for the sale of goods. Second, and ultimately far more important, the courts have demonstrated a significant tendency to apply Code contract concepts by analogy to contracts not specifically covered by Article 2. For example, the Code concepts of good faith dealing and unconscionability have enjoyed wide application in cases that are technically outside the scope of Article 2. Thus, the Code is an important influence in shaping the evolution of contract law in general, and if this trend toward broader application of Code principles continues, the time may come when the dichotomy between Code principles and traditional contract rules is a thing of the past.

Advent Systems Ltd. v. Unisys Corporation

Advent Systems Limited (Advent), a British company engaged primarily in the production of computer software, developed an electronic document management system (EDMS), a process for transforming engineering drawings and similar documents into a computer database. Unisys Corporation (Unisys), an American computer manufacturer, decided to market Advent's EDMS in the United States. In 1987, Advent and Unisys signed two documents, one labeled "Heads of Agreement" and the other "Distribution Agreement," in which Advent agreed to provide the software and hardware making up the EDMS, as well as sales and marketing material and the technical personnel to work with Unisys employees in building and installing the document systems. The agreement was to continue for two years, subject to automatic renewal or termination on notice.

During the summer of 1987, Unisys attempted to sell the document system to a large oil company but was unsuccessful. Nevertheless, progress on the sales and training programs in the United States was satisfactory. But Unisys, then in the throes of restructuring, decided it would be better off developing its own document system, and in December 1987, it told Advent that the agreement was ended. Advent filed suit, alleging breach of contract, among other things. Unisys argued that the agreement with Advent was covered by the UCC and that it failed to contain an express quantity provision that the UCC statute of frauds requires. The trial court ruled, however, that the agreements were not covered by the Code because their services aspect predominated. When the jury awarded Advent $4,550,000 for breach of contract, Unisys appealed.

Source: 925 F.2d 670 (3d Cir. 1991)

Weis, Circuit Judge

As the district court appraised the transaction, provisions for services outweighed those for products and, consequently, the arrangement was not predominantly one for the sale of goods. The agreements provided that Advent was to modify its software and hardware interfaces to run initially on equipment not manufactured by Unisys but eventually on Unisys hardware. "In so far as Advent has successfully completed [some of the processing] of software and hardware interfaces," Unisys promised to reimburse Advent to the extent of $150,000 derived from a "surcharge" on products purchased.

Advent agreed to provide twelve man-weeks of marketing manpower, but with Unisys bearing certain expenses. Advent also undertook to furnish an experienced systems builder to work with Unisys personnel at Advent's prevailing rates, and to provide sales and support training for Unisys staff as well as its customers.

The Distribution Agreement begins with the statement "Unisys desires to purchase, and Advent desires to sell, on a nonexclusive basis, certain of Advent hardware products and software licenses for resale worldwide." Following a heading "Subject Matter of Sales," appears this sentence, "Advent agrees to sell hardware and license software to Unisys, and Unisys agrees to buy from Advent the products listed in Schedule A." Schedule A lists twenty products, such as computer cards, plotters, imagers, scanners and designer systems.

Because software was a major portion of the "products" described in the agreement, this matter requires some discussion. Computer systems consist of "hardware" and "software." Hardware is the computer machinery, its electronic circuitry and peripheral items such as keyboards, readers, scanners and printers. Software is a more elusive concept. Generally speaking, "software" refers to the medium that stores input and output data as well as computer programs. The medium includes hard disks, floppy disks, and magnetic tapes.

In simplistic terms, programs are codes prepared by a programmer that instruct the computer to perform certain functions. When the program is transposed onto a medium compatible with the computer's needs, it becomes software. The increasing frequency of computer products as subjects of commercial litigation has led to controversy over whether software is a "good" or intellectual property. The Code does not specifically mention software.

In the absence of express legislative guidance, courts interpret the Code in the light of commercial and technological developments. The Code is designed "to permit the continued expansion of commercial practices" [1-102(2)(b)]. The Code applies to "transactions in goods" [2-102], which are defined as "all things (including specially manufactured goods) which are moveable at the time of the identification for sale" [2-105(1)].

Our Court has addressed computer package sales in other cases, but has not been required to consider whether the UCC applied to software per se. Computer programs are the product of an intellectual process, but once implanted in a medium are widely distributed to computer owners. An analogy can be drawn to a compact disc recording of an orchestral rendition. The music is produced by the artistry of musicians and in itself is not a "good," but when transferred to a laser-readable disc becomes a readily merchantable commodity. Similarly, when a professor delivers a lecture, it is not a good, but, when transcribed as a book, it becomes a good.

That a computer program may be copyrightable as intellectual property does not alter the fact that once in the form of a floppy disc or other medium, the program is tangible, moveable and available in the marketplace. The fact that some programs may be tailored for specific purposes need not alter their status as "goods" because the Code definition includes "specially manufactured goods." The topic has stimulated academic commentary with the majority espousing the view that software fits with the definition of a "good" in the UCC.

The relationship at issue here is a typical mixed goods and services arrangement. The services are not substantially different from those generally accompanying package sales of computer systems consisting of hardware and software. Although determining the applicability of the UCC to a contract by examining the predominance of goods or services has been criticized, we see no reason to depart from that practice here. We consider the purpose or essence of the contract. Comparing the relative costs of the materials supplied with the costs of the labor may be helpful in this analysis, but not dispositive. In this case the contract's main objective was to transfer "products." The specific provisions for training of Unisys personnel by Advent were but a small part of the parties' contemplated relationship.

The compensation structure of the agreement also focuses on "goods." The projected sales figures introduced during the trial demonstrate that in the contemplation of the parties the sale of goods clearly predominated. The payment provision of $150,000 for developmental work which Advent had previously completed was to be made through individual purchases of software and hardware rather than through the fees for services and is further evidence that the intellectual work was to be subsumed into tangible items for sale.

Applying the UCC to computer software transactions offers substantial benefits to litigants and the courts. The Code offers a uniform body of law on a wide range of questions likely to arise in computer software disputes: implied warranties, consequential damages, disclaimers of liability, the statute of limitations, to name a few. The importance of software to the commercial world and the advantages to be gained by the uniformity inherent in the UCC are strong policy arguments favoring inclusion. The contrary arguments are not persuasive, and we hold that software is a "good" within the definition of the Code.

Judgment reversed and remanded for further proceedings consistent with the Court's opinion.

Figure 14-4 illustrates when the Uniform Commercial Code applies.

FIGURE 14-4
When the uniform
commercial code applies

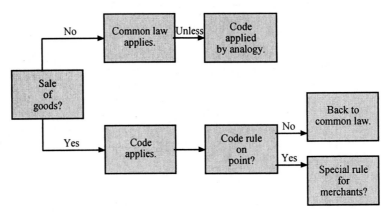

Restatement (Second) of Contracts

Nature and Origins

In 1932, the American Law Institute published the first *Restatement of Contracts*,[5] an attempt to codify and systematize the soundest principles of contract law gleaned from thousands of often conflicting judicial decisions. As the product of a private organization, the *Restatement* did not have the force of law, but as the considered judgment of some of the leading scholars of the legal profession, it was highly influential in shaping the evolution of contract law. The *Restatement (Second) of Contracts*, issued in 1979, is an attempt to reflect the significant changes that have occurred in contract law in the years following the birth of the first *Restatement of Contracts*. The tone of the *Restatement (Second) of Contracts* differs dramatically from that of the first *Restatement*, which is often characterized as a positivist attempt to formulate a system of black letter rules of contract law. The *Restatement (Second)*, in contrast, reflects the "shift from rules to standards" in modern contract law—the shift from precise, technical rules to broader, discretionary principles that produce just results.[6] The *Restatement (Second)* plainly bears the mark of the legal realists, discussed in Chapter 12, and has been heavily influenced by the UCC. In fact, many *Restatement (Second) of Contracts* provisions are virtually identical to their

Code analogues. For example, the *Restatement (Second)* has explicitly embraced the Code concepts of *good faith*[7] and *unconscionability.*[8]

Impact

The *Restatement (Second) of Contracts*, like its predecessor, does not have the force of law, and its relative newness prevents any accurate assessment of its impact on contemporary contract cases. Nonetheless, given the influential role played by the first *Restatement* and the previously mentioned tendency of the courts to employ Code principles by analogy in contract cases, it seems fair to assume that the *Restatement (Second)* will serve as a major inspiration for contract developments in the decades to come. For this reason, we give significant attention to the *Restatement (Second) of Contracts* in the following chapters.

Ethical and Public Policy Concerns

1. Compare and contrast the ethical values at the heart of classical contract law with those at the heart of modern contract law. If all contracts today fit the typical model assumed by classical contract law, would we necessarily feel ethically compelled to treat them differently than they were treated under classical contract law?
2. Do a brief social cost-benefit analysis of the "shift from rules to standards" that has occurred in modern contract law. Do a contrasting cost-benefit analysis of the rule-oriented approach of classical contract law.
3. The idea that contracts should be enforced because they are voluntary agreements can obviously be justified on ethical grounds. What ethical justifications, if any, can you give for departing from the notion of voluntary agreement in quasi-contract and promissory estoppel cases?

Problems and Problem Cases

1. In 1973, Baker and Ratzlaff entered a contract requiring Ratzlaff to grow 380 acres of popcorn and Baker to buy it at $4.75 per hundredweight. The contract gave Ratzlaff the right to terminate if Baker failed to pay for any of the popcorn on delivery. Early in 1974, Ratzlaff made the first two deliveries under the contract to Baker's plant. Baker's plant manager gave Ratzlaff weight tickets acknowledging receipt of the popcorn. Ratzlaff was not given payment and did not ask for it. Nor did he stop by Baker's business office, which was on a direct route between his farm and Baker's plant, to ask for payment. When Baker called to ask for further deliveries, Ratzlaff offered excuses, but did not mention payment. Ratzlaff later told Baker he was terminating due to Baker's failure to pay upon delivery, selling the remaining 1.6 million pounds of popcorn elsewhere for $8.00 per hundredweight. After hearing evidence that Baker's normal practice was to make payments at its office on the basis of copies of weight tickets sent from the plant, and that Baker would have paid promptly had Ratzlaff requested payment, the trial court ruled that Ratzlaff's termination was a breach of his duty to act in good faith. Was this ruling proper?
2. In April 1988, Reifschneider, a farmer since 1957, orally agreed to sell Grain Company 12,500 bushels of corn for $2.25 per bushel. The corn was to be delivered as harvested in October 1988. Shortly thereafter, Grain Company mailed Reifschneider a written confirmation of the oral agreement, with instructions to sign it and return the original. Reifschneider neither signed nor returned the confirmation, and in late June he told

Grain Company that he felt no contract existed and would not deliver the corn. Reifschneider continued to refuse to acknowledge the contract, and ultimately sold his crop elsewhere. To cover his default, Grain Company bought 12,500 bushels of corn from another farmer, paying $8,425 more for it than it had agreed to pay Reifschneider. When Grain Company sued Reifschneider for breach of contract, he raised the Code statute of frauds [2-201] as a defense, arguing that his failure to sign the confirmation meant that it could not satisfy the writing requirement against him. Grain Company countered by arguing that he was a merchant, and pointing to Code section 2-201(2), which says that merchants who fail to object in writing to written confirmations they receive from other merchants within 10 days of receipt lose their statute of frauds defense. Was the trial court justified in ruling in favor of Grain Company?

3.   When Thomas and Sandra Cole were divorced in 1983, Sandra received a judgment against Thomas of $36,556. In May and June 1985, Thomas incurred a hospital bill of $5,985. After discussing the matter with him, Sandra paid the bill with her own funds even though he still owed her $11,884 on the marriage dissolution judgment. When Thomas died in April 1986, Sandra filed claims against his estate for the balance due her under the marriage dissolution judgment and for the hospital bill. The estate challenged Sandra's claim for the hospital payment, arguing that she had paid it voluntarily and had no contractual right to recover the amount she paid. Was the trial court right in ruling in Sandra's favor?

4.   First National Bank filed suit against Jessie Ordoyne and Patricia Ordoyne Bordelon for failure to pay sums due on a Visa card account. Ordoyne argued that he did not know that the account existed until the bank called him to inquire about his failure to make payments. He then told the bank that he and Patricia were divorced and that she must have forged his signature to the account application form. The bank argued that he was nonetheless liable on a quasi-contractual basis, although it failed to prove that he had received any of the merchandise charged to the card. Was the trial court's decision in Jessie's favor correct?

5.   Chow arranged through a travel agent to fly from Indianapolis to Singapore on June 27, 1986. Singapore Airlines gave him a round-trip ticket that included a TWA flight to Los Angeles. Shortly before the trip, Chow's flight was rerouted so that he had to fly to St. Louis first and then to San Francisco. During the St. Louis stopover, the flight developed engine trouble, causing a substantial delay. TWA personnel assured Chow that if he missed his connecting flight, TWA would arrange for him to take the next Singapore flight out of San Francisco. After the engine problem was fixed, TWA delayed the flight's departure an additional two hours to board additional passengers. Chow was again assured that if he missed his scheduled flight, TWA would make arrangements for him. Chow missed his Singapore flight by minutes, and was housed overnight at TWA's expense in San Francisco after once more being assured that TWA would make arrangements to get him on the next Singapore flight. When he called Singapore Airlines the next morning to see whether TWA had made him a reservation, Chow was told that no arrangements had been made. When he contacted TWA, he was told TWA would make the arrangements immediately. After waiting several hours, Chow learned TWA had still not made the arrangements and was told that TWA could no longer help him. Because Singapore Airlines no longer had economy class seats available, Chow had to buy a business class seat at an additional cost of $928. When he filed suit against TWA for that amount, TWA argued that the Conditions of Contract printed on Chow's ticket disclaimed any liability for failure to make connections. Did Chow have a valid claim against TWA?

6.   Commercial Cornice, a subcontractor, entered a contract with Camel Construction, a general contractor, to furnish labor and materials for a construction project owned by

Malarkey's, Inc. Commercial completed its obligations under the contract but only received $78,000 of the $177,773. When Commercial filed suit against Camel and Malarkey's for the remaining $99,773, Malarkey's moved to dismiss Commercial's claims against it on the ground that Commercial's only contract was with Camel. The trial court granted Malarkey's motion, despite the fact that the evidence indicated that Malarkey's had never paid Camel for the work. Was the dismissal of Commercial's claim against Malarkey's proper?

7. Early in 1986, Gray Communications contacted various television tower builders concerning the manufacture and erection of a television tower. After several discussions with Kline Iron & Steel, Gray received a signed written proposal from Kline to build and install the tower for $1,485,368. The proposal said that it could be revoked or modified by Kline prior to acceptance by Gray, and it required Kline's approval after acceptance by Gray. Gray refused to sign the proposal after Kline would not lower its bid to meet a competitor's lower bid, and Kline filed suit for breach of contract. At trial, Gray argued that no contract existed, and that even if a contract existed it was unenforceable because Gray had never signed the writing the UCC requires for all contracts for $500 or more. Kline argued that the contract was not covered by the UCC because it was a services contract. The evidence at trial indicated that the service component of the agreement amounted at most to 26 percent of the total cost. Should the court apply the UCC?

8. Dr. Monteleone, a neurologist, entered into a lease-purchase agreement for a turnkey computer system from Neilson Business Equipment Center, Inc. The system included both hardware and software recommended by Neilson after two Neilson representatives studied Dr. Monteleone's manual billing system. When the computer was delivered in July 1982, serious problems immediately developed. Neilson's attempts to modify the software, which it had acquired elsewhere and renamed the "Neilson Medical Office Management System," were unsuccessful. Dr. Monteleone notified Neilson that he was terminating the lease for cause and later filed suit against Neilson. The trial court awarded him $34,983.42 in damages for breaches of the implied warranties of merchantability and fitness for a particular purpose. Did the trial court err in holding that the case was governed by the UCC?

9. Stephen Gall and his family became ill after drinking contaminated water supplied to their home by the McKeesport Municipal Water Authority. They filed suit against the utility, arguing, among other things, that the utility had breached the UCC implied warranty of merchantability when it sold them contaminated water. The utility moved to dismiss their complaint, arguing that since water was not "goods," the UCC did not apply. Should the Galls' complaint be dismissed?

10. In February of 1981, Salamon, a builder, entered into written agreements to buy two lots owned by Terra for $9,000 each. The agreement provided that Salamon would take possession of the lots by April 15, 1981, but would not have to pay the bulk of the purchase price ($8,500 per lot) until delivery of the deeds in August 1981. Salamon intended to build a house on each lot and then sell the houses to third parties, paying off Terra with the proceeds of the house sales. Salamon partially completed the two houses but was unable either to obtain financing to complete them or to find purchasers for them. Terra extended the date of performance under the purchase agreements by several months, but because Salamon was never able to pay for the lots, he retained ownership of them. Salamon filed a quasi-contract suit against Terra to recover the value of the partially completed houses. The trial judge ruled that Terra had been unjustly enriched in the amount of $15,000. Had Terra been unjustly enriched?

11. Jeff went to look at a car owned by Acme Motors. He wanted to buy the car and tentatively agreed on a price with Marx, but he asked if he could wait until his wife could see the car that evening. Acme agreed, promising in writing not to sell the car to anyone else in the interim. When Jeff and his wife returned to Acme that evening, however, they found that Acme had sold the car to another buyer. Jeff filed a breach of contract suit against Acme, pointing to a section of the UCC that provides that merchants can't revoke signed written offers. Should Jeff win?

Endnotes

1. *Restatement (Second) of Contracts* § 1 (1981).
2. Slawson, "Standard Form Contracts and Democratic Control of Lawmaking Power," 84 *Harv. L. Rev.* 529 (1971).
3. See Petit, "Modern Unilateral Contracts," 63 *B.U.L. Rev.* 551 (1983).
4. 57 Neb. 51, 77 N.W. 365 (1898).
5. See Chapter 12 for a general discussion of the *Restatement* phenomenon.
6. Speidel, "Restatement Second: Omitted Terms and Contract Method," 67 *Cornell L. Rev.* 785, 786 (1982).
7. *Restatement (Second) of Contracts* § 205 (1981).
8. *Restatement (Second) of Contracts* § 208 (1981).

Chapter Fifteen

THE AGREEMENT:

OFFER

Introduction

The concept of mutual agreement lies at the heart of traditional contract law. Courts faced with deciding whether two or more persons entered into a contract look first for an *agreement* between the parties. Because the formation of an agreement is normally a two-step process by which one party makes a proposal and the other responds to the proposal, it is customary to analyze the agreement in two parts: offer and acceptance. This chapter, which concerns itself with the offer, and the next chapter, which covers acceptance, focus on the tools used by courts to determine whether the parties have reached the kind of agreement that becomes the foundation of a contract.

The Objective Theory of Contract

At the outset, it is important to clarify one aspect of what is meant by the word *agreement*. In determining whether the parties reached an agreement, should courts look at what each party actually, in his own mind (*subjectively*) intended? Or should an agreement be dependent on the impression that each party has given to the rest of the world through words, acts, and circumstances that *objectively* indicate that intent? Early American courts took a subjective approach to contract formation, asking whether there was truly a "meeting of the minds" between the parties. This subjective standard, however, created uncertainty in the enforcement of contracts because it left every contract vulnerable to disputes about actual intent. The desire to meet the needs of the marketplace by affording predictable and consistent results in contracts cases dictated a shift toward an *objective theory of contracts*. By the middle of the 19th century, the objective approach to contract formation, which judges agreement by looking at the parties' outward manifestations of intent, was firmly established in American law. Judge Learned Hand once described the effect of the objective contract theory as follows:

> A contract has, strictly speaking, nothing to do with the personal, or individual, intent of the parties. A contract is an obligation attached by the mere force of law to certain acts of the parties, usually words, which ordinarily accompany and represent a known intent. If however, it were proved by twenty bishops that either party when he used the words intended something else than the usual meaning which the law imposes on them, he would still be held, unless there were mutual mistake or something else of that sort.[1]

What is an Offer?

The *Restatement (Second) of Contracts* defines an **offer** as "the manifestation of willingness to enter into a bargain, so made as to justify another person in understanding that his assent to that bargain is invited and will conclude it."[2] An offer says, in effect, "This is it—if you agree to these terms, we have a contract." An offer is a critically important first step in the contract formation process. The person who makes an offer (the **offeror**) gives the person to whom she makes the offer (the **offeree**) the power to bind her to a contract simply by accepting the offer. If no offer was ever made, however, there was nothing to accept and no contract results.

Traditional contract law rules on contract formation are designed to ensure that persons are never bound to contracts unless they clearly intend to be bound. Therefore, the basic thing that the courts require for the creation of an offer is some objective indication of a *present intent to contract* on the part of the offeror. Two of the most important things from which courts infer an intent to contract are the *definiteness* of the alleged offer and the fact that it has been *communicated to the offeree*.

Definiteness of Terms

If Smith says to Ford, "I'd like to buy your house, and Ford responds, "You've got a deal," has a contract been formed? An obvious problem here is the parties' lack of specificity. A proposal that fails to state specifically what the offeror is willing to do and what he asks in return for his performance is unlikely to be considered an offer. One reason for the requirement of definiteness is that definiteness and specificity in an offer tend to indicate an intent to contract, whereas indefiniteness and lack of specificity tend to indicate that the parties are still negotiating and have not yet reached agreement. In the conversation between Smith and Ford, Smith's statement that he'd like to buy Ford's house is merely an invitation to offer or an invitation to negotiate. It indicates a willingness to contract in the future if the parties can reach agreement on mutually acceptable terms, but not a present intent to contract. If, however, Smith sends Ford a detailed and specific written document stating all of the material terms and conditions on which he is willing to buy the house and Ford writes back agreeing to Smith's terms, the parties' intent to contract would be objectively indicated and a contract would probably be created.

A second reason definiteness is important is that courts need to know the terms on which the parties agreed in order to determine if a breach of contract has occurred and calculate a remedy if it has. Keep in mind that the offer often contains all the terms of the parties' contract. This is so because all that an offered is allowed to do in most cases is to accept or reject the terms of the offer. If an agreement is too indefinite, a court would not have a basis for giving a remedy if one of the parties alleged that the "contract" was breached. The following case, *Vian v. Carey*, presents an example of a situation in which the terms of the alleged contract were too indefinite.

Vian v. Carey

Mariah Carey is a famous, successful, and apparently wealthy entertainer. Joseph Vian, Carey's stepfather before she achieved stardom, was in the business of designing, producing, and marketing gift and novelty items.

He claimed that Carey agreed orally to give him a license to produce "Mariah dolls," which would be statuettes of the singer that would play her most popular songs. Vian asserted that this right was given in exchange for his

continued

financial and emotional support of Carey, including picking her up from late-night recording sessions, providing her with the use of a car, paying for dental care, allowing her to use his boat for business meetings and rehearsals, and giving her various items to help furnish her apartment. Vian based his claim of an oral contract on three conversations, twice in the family car and once on Vian's boat. Vian said to Carey, "Don't forget about the Mariah dolls," and "I get the Mariah dolls." According to Vian, on one occasion, Carey responded "Okay"; on other occasions, she merely smiled and nodded. Although Carey admits that Vian mentioned the dolls two or three times, she testified that she thought it was a joke. Claiming that Carey breached the contract to license dolls in her likeness, Vian brought this action for breach of contract. Carey moved for summary judgment.

Source: 1993 U.S. Dist. LEXIS 5460 (U.S. Dist. Ct. S.D.N.Y. 1993)

Mukasey, District Judge

An oral contract can form a binding contract. However, the prerequisites to contract formation must be satisfied. In determining whether a contract exists, what matters are the parties' expressed intentions, the words and deeds which constitute objective signs in a given set of circumstances. The issue is whether the objective circumstances indicate that the parties intended to form a contract. Without such an intent, neither a contract nor a preliminary agreement to negotiate in good faith can exist. In making such a determination, a court may look at whether the terms of the contract have been finally resolved. In addition, a court may consider the context of the negotiations. Vian has adduced no evidence that Carey ever intended by a nod of her head or the expression "okay" to enter into a complex commercial licensing agreement involving dolls in her likeness playing her copyrighted songs. The context in which this contract between an 18-year-old girl and her stepfather allegedly was made was an informal family setting, either in the car or on Vian's boat, while others were present. Vian's own version of events leads to the conclusion that there was no reason for Carey to think Vian was entirely serious, let alone that he intended to bind her to an agreement at that time.

There can be no meetings of the minds, required for the formation of a contract, where essential material terms are missing. Thus, even if the parties both believe themselves to be bound, there is no contract when the terms of the agreement are so vague and indefinite that there is no basis or standard for deciding whether the agreement had been kept or broken, or to fashion a remedy, and no means by which such terms may be made certain. As the New York Court of Appeals has held, "definiteness as to material matters is of the very essence of contract law. Impenetrable vagueness and uncertainty will not do."

Licensing contracts such as the one Vian claims a right to exploit normally are intricate business. They involve details. Even if the agreement was merely to agree on terms at some future time, under New York law, a mere agreement to agree, in which a material term is left for future negotiations, is unenforceable. The word "license" was not even used. As Carey points out, no price nor royalty term was mentioned, nor was the duration or geographic scope of the license, nor was Carey's right to approve the dolls. Vian has not raised a triable issue of fact as to the existence of a contract.
Summary judgment granted in favor of Carey.

Definiteness: Traditional Approach

Classical contract law took the position that courts are contract enforcers, not contract makers. The prospect of enforcing an agreement in which the parties had omitted terms or left terms open for later agreement was unthinkable to courts that took a traditional, hands-off approach to contracts. Traditionally, contract law required a relatively high standard of definiteness for offers, requiring that all the essential terms of a proposed contract be stated in the offer. The traditional insistence on definiteness can serve useful ends. It can prevent a person from being held to an agreement when none was reached or from being bound by a contract term to which he never assented. Sometimes, however, it can operate to frustrate the expectations of parties who intend to contract but, for whatever reason, fail to procure an agreement that specifies all the terms of the contract. Although vague agreements such as the one alleged in the *Vian* case are too indefinite to constitute a contract, the trend of modern contract law is to tolerate a lower degree of specificity in agreements than did classical contract law.

Definiteness and Modern Contract Law

Modern contract principles, with their increased emphasis on furthering peoples' justifiable expectations and their encouragement of a hands-on approach by the courts, often create contractual liability in situations where no contract would have resulted at common law. Perhaps no part of the Code better illustrates this basic difference between modern contract principles and their classical counterparts than does the basic Code section on contract formation [2-204]. Sales contracts under Article 2 can be created "in any manner sufficient to show agreement, including conduct which recognizes the existence of a contract" [2-204(1)]. So, if the parties are acting as though they have a contract by delivering or accepting goods or payment, for example, this may be enough to create a binding contract, even if it is impossible to point to a particular moment in time when the contract was created [2-204(2)]. The fact that the parties left open one or more terms of their agreement does not necessarily mean that their agreement is too indefinite to enforce. A sales contract is created if the court finds that the parties intended to make a contract and that their agreement is complete enough to allow the court to reach a fair settlement of their dispute ("a reasonably certain basis for giving an appropriate remedy" [2-204(3)]). The Code contains a series of gap-filling rules to enable courts to fill in the blanks on matters of price [2-305], quantity [2-306], delivery [2-307, 2-308, and 2-309(1)], and time for payment [2-310] when such terms have been left open by the parties.[3] Of course, if a term was left out because the parties were *unable* to reach agreement about it, this would indicate that the intent to contract was absent and no contract would result, even under the Code's more liberal rules. Intention is still at the heart of these modern contract rules; the difference is that courts applying Code principles seek to further the parties' underlying intent to contract even though the parties have failed to express their intention about specific aspects of their agreement.

The *Restatement (Second) of Contracts* takes an approach to the definiteness question that is quite similar to the Code approach. It seeks to further the intent of the parties and, where intent to contract is indicated but some essential terms are left open, "a term which is reasonable in the circumstances is supplied by the court."[4] Unlike the Code, however, the *Restatement (Second)* indicates that a party's reliance on an indefinite agreement may justify its full or partial enforcement.[5] This provision highlights one of the most intriguing recent developments in contract law—the use of **promissory estoppel** to enforce indefinite agreements.[6]

Promissory Estoppel and Indefinite Agreements

It has long been the rule that promissory estoppel could not be used to enforce indefinite agreements because their indefiniteness meant that the court was left with no promise capable of being enforced. Sometimes people do, however, act in reliance on indefinite agreements, and to protect that reliance a few courts have deviated from the general rule. In such cases, it is common for courts to overcome the indefiniteness problem by awarding damages based on the promisee's losses due to reliance rather than by attempting to enforce the indefinite agreement.

   Hoffman v. Red Owl Stores, Inc., is probably the most famous case of this type.[7] Hoffman wanted to acquire a Red Owl franchised convenience store and, in reliance on Red Owl's promises during their negotiations, sold his bakery at a loss, bought a small grocery to gain experience, moved his family, and bought an option on a proposed site for the franchised store. The negotiations fell through, and when Hoffman sued, Red Owl argued that no contract resulted because the parties had never reached agreement on the essential terms governing their relationship. The Supreme Court of Wisconsin agreed, but nonetheless allowed Hoffman to recover his reliance losses on the basis of promissory estoppel. In doing so, the court noted that nothing in the language of section 90 of the *Restatement* required that a promise serving as the basis of promissory estoppel be "so comprehensive in scope as to meet the requirements of an offer." Another example of both modern standards regarding definiteness and the use of promissory estoppel is seen in the following *Arok Construction Co. v. Indian Construction Services* case.

Arok Construction Co. v. Indian Construction Services

Indian Construction Services (ICS) is a general contractor. AROK Construction Co. is a drywall and stucco contractor. AROK and the principal owners of ICS had entered into contracts on three occasions prior to this case, using in all three situations identical standard form contracts.

   In 1985, Window Rock Unified School District solicited bids for the services of a general contractor on its construction project. ICS submitted a bid to act as the general contractor, listing AROK in its bid as subcontractor for the drywall and stucco portions of the project. AROK had first submitted its bid over the telephone to ICS for $1.549 million. Before bid closing, however, ICS asked AROK to reduce its bid to $1.42 million. AROK's president told ICS's project manager that AROK would reduce its bid even further to $1.4 million if, as a result, ICS would agree to contract with AROK if the school district awarded the job to ICS. ICS's project manager stated that in exchange for AROK's further reduction to $1.4 million, "If [ICS] gets

the job, [AROK] gets a job." AROK sent a letter to ICS confirming the $1.4 million quote and enclosed a detailed bid confirmation. The school district awarded the contract to ICS. After receiving notice to proceed with the project from the school district, ICS requested that AROK perform "value engineering" services with regard to its bid. (Value engineering involves changing the bid structure to lower the overall bid price without changing the profit structure for either the general contractor or the subcontractor). AROK complied and worked approximately 8 to 10 hours further reducing the subcontract price. Several months later, a dispute arose between ICS and AROK over the amount of the contract price, and ICS entered into subcontracts with two other companies to perform the drywall and stucco work. AROK brought suit for breach of contract. The trial court granted summary judgment in favor of ICS, and AROK appealed.

Source: 848 P.2d 870 (Ariz. Ct. App. 1993)

Lankford, Judge

The old "formalist" view limited the agreement to written terms and emphasized rules of contract, such as the requirement that the agreement include all material terms. This has long since given way to the "realist" approach exemplified by the Uniform Commercial Code and the Second Restatement of Contracts. The latter emphasizes standards rather than rules, and assigns to courts the task of upholding the agreements parties intended to make.

ICS concedes for purposes of this appeal that its conditional promise, "If we get the job, you get the job," is an acceptance of AROK's promise to perform the work for a reduced price. ICS contends, however, that the parties failed to specify other terms essential to indicate their intent to be bound: the manner and time of payments, penalty provisions, time for completion, and bonding. ICS argues that as a result of the missing terms, no enforceable contract exists as a matter of law.

Is the agreement too uncertain to enforce? *Restatement (Second) of Contracts* section 33 establishes "reasonable certainty" as the standard for enforcement. The Restatement rule exemplifies the policy of the law to uphold agreements. Courts are never eager to undo agreements. Only when courts ensure that promises create obligations do promises have real meaning. Only then can those in the marketplace rely on their bargains to allocate their resources and plan for the future. For example, AROK presented evidence that it did not bid for other jobs because it had a contract with ICS. If that contract is not enforced, and AROK's resources were idled as a result of ICS's promise and breach, then one of the goals of contract law—economic efficiency—would be thwarted.

The enforcement of incomplete agreements is a necessary fact of economic life. Business people are not soothsayers, and can neither provide in advance for every unforeseen contingency nor answer every unasked question regarding a commercial agreement. This is especially so with a complex contract for a major construction project. Nor are entrepreneurs perfect at drafting legal documents. Finally, parties may want to bind themselves and at the same time desire to leave some matters open for future resolution in order to maintain flexibility. Thus, courts are often presented with incomplete bargains when the parties intend and desire to be bound. Refusing the enforcement of obligations the parties intended to create and that marketplace transactions require hardly seems the solution.

The standard for contract enforceability is not whether the agreement included a resolution of every matter and anticipated every contingency. "The terms of a contract are reasonably certain if they provide a basis for determining the existence of a breach and for giving an appropriate basis for determining the existence of a breach and for giving an appropriate remedy." *Restatement (Second) of Contracts* section 33(2). If a court can determine the existence of a breach by ICS and fashion an appropriate remedy for AROK, then the terms of their agreement are reasonably certain and enforceable. Thus, "gaps" or omitted terms, or vague and indefinite terms, are not invariably fatal to the rights of the parties to obtain enforcement of their bargain.

The terms of this contract are sufficiently certain for two independent reasons. First, ICS breached the contract at a point when the only terms necessary to determine the existence of the breach (scope of the work) and for giving an appropriate remedy (agreed-upon price) were present. Second, there was evidence of a course of dealing involving a standard form contract which could be used to supply any missing terms. We hold that the agreement is sufficiently definite to be enforceable.

AROK also claims that it is entitled to relief based upon promissory estoppel. We hold that this is a proper claim for relief as an alternative to the contract claim. If AROK can show that it acted or detrimentally relied upon ICS's promise to award the contract, then promissory estoppel is available. For example, AROK performed "value engineering" allegedly in reliance upon ICS's promise. AROK may also have forgone other work because it anticipated employing its resources in performing this contract. *Restatement (Second) of Contracts* section 90(1) states:

A promise which the promisor should reasonably expect to induce action or forbearance on the part of the promisee or a third person and which does induce such action or forbearance is binding if injustice can be avoided only by enforcement of the promise.

However, the remedy under this theory may be more limited than damages for breach of contract. In particular, relief may sometimes be limited to restitution or to damages or specific relief measured by the extent of the promisee's reliance rather than by the terms of the promise. Thus, AROK may be entitled to recover only the value of its work in "value engineering" unless it can show greater loss due to its reliance.
Reversed and remanded in favor of AROK.

Communication to Offeree

When an offeror communicates the terms of an offer to an offered, he objectively indicates an intent to be bound by those terms. The fact that an offer has *not* been communicated, on the other hand, may be evidence that the offeror has not yet decided to enter into a binding agreement. For example, assume that Stevens and Meyer have been negotiating over the sale of Meyer's restaurant. Stevens confides in his friend, Reilly, that he plans to offer Meyer $150,000 for the restaurant. Reilly goes to Meyer and tells Meyer that Stevens has decided to offer him $150,000 for the restaurant and has drawn up a written offer to that effect. After learning the details of the offer from Reilly, Meyer telephones Stevens and says, "I accept your offer." Is Stevens now contractually obligated to buy the restaurant? No. Since *Stevens* did not communicate the proposal to Meyer, there was no offer for Meyer to accept.

Special Offer Problem Areas

Advertisements

Generally speaking, advertisements for the sale of goods at specified prices are *not* considered to be offers. Rather, they are treated as being invitations to offer or negotiate. The same rule is generally applied to signs, handbills, catalogs, price lists, and price quotations. This rule is based on the presumed intent of the sellers involved. It is not reasonable to conclude that a seller who has a limited number of items to sell intends to give every person who sees her ad, sign, or catalog the power to bind her to contract. Thus, if Customer sees Retailer's advertisement of WhizbangXL laptop computers for $2,000 and goes to Retailer's store indicating his intent to buy the computer, Customer is making an offer, which Retailer is free to accept or reject. This is so because Customer is manifesting a present intent to contract on the definite terms of the ad.

In some cases, however, particular ads have been held to amount to offers. Such ads are usually highly specific about the nature and number of items offered for sale and what is requested in return. This specificity precludes the possibility that the offeror could become contractually bound to an infinite number of offerees. In addition, many of the ads treated as offers have required some special performance by would-be buyers or have in some other way clearly indicated that immediate action by the buyer creates a binding agreement. The potential for unfairness to those who attempt to accept such ads and their fundamental difference from ordinary ads justify treating them as offers. *Jackson v. Investment Corporation of Palm Beach* presents an example of an advertisement that was held to constitute an offer.

Jackson v. Investment Corp. of Palm Beach

John Jackson read an ad in the *Miami Herald* stating that the Pic-6 Jackpot for the last evening of the dog track racing season would be $825,000. Jackson went to the track on that date, picked the winner in the six designated races, and won the jackpot. However, Investment Corporation of Palm Beach, the owner of the dog track, contended that it should not have to pay more than $25,000 because it had intended the amount of the jackpot to be $25,000, not $825,000. The mix-up occurred when Investment submitted to the newspaper a prior ad with the following words written on the face of it: "Guaranteed Jackpot $25,000 must go tonight," and the newspaper employee who prepared the final draft of

the ad mistook the dollar sign with only one slash-mark to be the number 8. Investment paid Jackson $25,000 on the night of the races, but Jackson later brought suit to claim the balance. At trial, the judge instructed the jury that it should find for Investment unless the evidence supported the claim that Investment intended by its newspaper advertisement to make an offer to pay a guaranteed jackpot of $825,000. The jury returned a verdict in favor of Investment and the trial judge entered judgment on the verdict. Jackson appealed, claiming that this instruction to the jury was erroneous.

Source: 585 So.2d 949 (Flat. Ct. App. 1991)

Downey, Judge

There was no evidence adduced that Investment intended the jackpot to be $825,000. Jackson concedes that Investment never intended the jackpot to be the larger amount. The point is that Investment's subjective intent was not material in determining what the contract was between the parties. As the Florida Supreme Court said in *Gendzier v. Bielecki*, quoting from Justice Oliver Wendell Holmes:

> The making of a contract depends not on the agreement of two minds in one intention, but on the agreement of two sets of external signs—not on the parties having meant the same thing but on their having said the same thing.

Professor Williston, in his work on Contracts, describes the test as:

> [T]he test of the true interpretation of an offer or acceptance is not what the party making it thought it meant or intended it to mean, but what a reasonable person in the position of the parties would have thought it meant. 1 *Williston on Contracts* sec. 94, 339-40.

It appears to us that the law, applicable to offers of a reward, is also applicable to the type of advertisement involved in this case. The offer is a mere proposal or conditional promise which, if accepted before it is revoked, creates a binding contract. We have given due consideration to Investment's argument regarding the advertisement as an "invitation to bargain," but find it inappropriate here. The "invitation to bargain" rule appears to be applied in advertising wherein:

> Neither the advertiser nor the reader of his notice understands that the latter is empowered to close the deal without further expression by the former. Such advertisements are understood to be mere requests to consider and examine and negotiate; and no one can reasonably regard them otherwise unless the circumstances are exceptional and the words used are very plain and clear. 1 *Corbin on Contracts* sec. 25 (1963).

Here there are no further negotiations indicated. If a member of the public buys a winning ticket on six races, he has accepted the offer and the parties have a contract. We

thus hold that the trial court erred in instructing the jury as it did and we reverse the judgment appealed from and remand the cause for a new trial.
Judgment reversed in favor of Jackson.

Rewards

Advertisements offering rewards for lost property, for information, or for the capture of criminals are generally treated as offers for unilateral contracts. To accept the offer and be entitled to the stated reward, offerers must perform the requested act—return the lost property, supply the requested information, or capture the wanted criminal. Some courts have held that only offerers who started performance with knowledge of the offer are entitled to the reward. Other courts, however, have indicated the only requirement is that the offeree know of the reward before completing performance. In reality, the result in most such cases probably reflects the court's perception of the equities of the particular case at hand.

Auctions

Sellers at auctions are generally treated as making an invitation to offer. Those who bid on offered goods are, therefore, treated as making offers that the owner of the goods may accept or reject. Acceptance occurs only when the auctioneer strikes the goods off to the highest bidder; the auctioneer may withdraw the goods at any time before acceptance. However, when an auction is advertised as being "without reserve," the seller is treated as having made an offer to sell the goods to the highest bidder and the goods cannot be withdrawn after a call for bids has been made unless no bids are made within a reasonable time.[8]

Bids

The bidding process is a fertile source of contract disputes. Advertisements for bids are generally treated as invitations to offer. Those who submit bids are treated as offerors. According to general contract principles, bidders can withdraw their bids at any time prior to acceptance by the offeree inviting the bids, and the offeree is free to accept or reject any bid. The previously announced terms of the bidding may alter these rules, however. For example, if the advertisement for bids unconditionally states that the contract will be awarded to the lowest responsible bidder, this will be treated as an offer that is accepted by the lowest bidder. Only proof by the offeror that the lowest bidder is not responsible can prevent the formation of a contract. Also, under some circumstances discussed later in this chapter, promissory estoppel may operate to prevent bidders from withdrawing their bids.

Bids for governmental contracts are generally covered by specific statutes rather than by general contract principles. Such statutes ordinarily establish the rules governing the bidding process, often require that the contract be awarded to the lowest bidder, and frequently establish special rules or penalties governing the withdrawal of bids.

Which Terms are Included in the Offer?

After making a determination that an offer existed, a court must decide which terms were included in the offer so that it can determine the terms of the parties' contract. Put another way, which terms of the offer are binding on the offeree who accepts it? Should offerers, for example, be bound by fine print clauses or by clauses on the back of the contract? Originally, the courts tended to hold that offerers were bound by all the terms of the offer on the theory that every person had a duty to protect himself by reading agreements carefully before signing them.

In today's world of lengthy, complex form contracts, however, people often sign agreements that they have not fully read or do not fully understand. Modern courts tend to recognize this fact by saying that offerers are bound only by terms of which they had actual or reasonable notice. If the offeree actually read the term in question, or if a reasonable person should have been aware of it, it will probably become part of the parties' contract. A fine-print provision on the back of a theater ticket would probably not be binding on a theater patron, however, because a reasonable person would not expect such a ticket to contain contractual terms. By contrast, the terms printed on a multipage airline or steamship ticket might well be considered binding on the purchaser if such documents would be expected to contain terms of the contract.

This modern approach to deciding the terms of a contract gives courts an indirect, but effective, way of promoting fair dealing by refusing to enforce unfair contract terms on the ground that the offeree lacked reasonable notice of them. Disclaimers and exculpatory clauses (contract provisions that seek to relieve offerors of some legal duty that they would otherwise owe to offerers) are particularly likely to be subjected to close judicial scrutiny.

Termination of Offers

After a court has determined the existence and content of an offer, it must determine the duration of the offer. Was the offer still in existence when the offeree attempted to accept it? If not, no contract was created and the offeree is treated as having made an offer that the original offeror is free to accept or reject. This is so because, by attempting to accept an offer that has terminated, the offeree has indicated a present intent to contract on the terms of the original offer though he lacks the power to bind the offeror to a contract due to the original offer's termination.

Terms of the Offer

The offeror is often said to be "the master of the offer." This means that offerors have the power to determine the terms and conditions under which they are bound to a contract. As the following *Newman* case indicates, an offeror may include terms in the offer that limit its effective life. These may be specific terms, such as "you must accept by December 5. 1994" or "this offer is good for five days," or more general terms, such as "for immediate acceptance," "prompt wire acceptance," or "by return mail." General time limitation language in an offer can raise difficult problems of interpretation for courts trying to decide whether an offeree accepted before the offer terminated. Even more specific language, such as "this offer is good for five days," can cause problems if the offer does not specify whether the five-day period begins when the offer is sent or when the offeree receives it. Not all courts agree on such questions, so wise offerors should be as specific as possible in stating when their offers terminate.

Newman v. Schiff

Irwin Schiff, a self-styled tax rebel who had made a career out of his tax protest activities, appeared live on the February 7, 1983, CBS News "Nightwatch" program. During the course of the program, which had a viewer participation format, Schiff repeated his longstanding position that "there is nothing in the Internal Revenue Code which says anyone is legally required to pay the tax." Later in the program, Schiff stated: "If anybody calls this show and cites any section of this Code that says an individual is required to file a tax return, I will pay them $100,000."

Attorney John Newman failed to see Schiff live on "Nightwatch," but saw a two-minute taped segment of the original "Nightwatch" interview several hours later on the "CBS Morning News." Certain that Schiff's statements were incorrect, Newman telephoned and wrote "CBS Morning News," attempting to accept Schiff's offer by citing Internal Revenue Code provisions requiring individuals to pay federal income tax. CBS forwarded Newman's letter to Schiff, who refused to pay on the ground that Newman had not properly accepted his offer. Newman sued Schiff for breach of contract. The trial court ruled in Schiff's favor, and Newman appealed.

Source: 778 F.2d 460 (8th Cir. 1985)

Bright, Senior Circuit Judge

It is a basic legal principle that mutual assent is necessary for the formation of a contract. Courts determine whether the parties expressed their assent to a contract by analyzing their agreement process in terms of offer and acceptance. An offer is the "manifestation of willingness to enter into a bargain, so made as to justify another person in understanding that his assent to that bargain is invited and will conclude it." *Restatement (Second) of Contracts* § 24 (1981). Schiff's statement on "Nightwatch" that he would pay $100,000 to anyone who called the show and cited any section of the Internal Revenue Code "that says an individual is required to file a tax return" constituted a valid offer for a reward. If anyone had called the show and cited the code sections that Newman produced, a contract would have been formed and Schiff would have been obligated to pay the $100,000 reward.

Newman, however, never saw the live CBS "Nightwatch" program on which Schiff appeared and this lawsuit is not predicated on Schiff's "Nightwatch" offer. Newman saw the "CBS Morning News" rebroadcast of Schiff's "Nightwatch" appearance. This rebroadcast served not to renew or extend Schiff's offer, but rather only to inform viewers that Schiff had made an offer on "Nightwatch." An offeror is the master of his offer and it is clear that Schiff by his words, "If anybody calls this show," limited his offer in time to remain open only until the conclusion of the live "Nightwatch" broadcast. A reasonable person listening to the news rebroadcast could not conclude that the above language constituted a new offer rather than what it actually was, a news report of the offer previously made, which had already expired.

Although Newman has not "won" his lawsuit in the traditional sense of recovering a reward that he sought, he has accomplished an important goal in the public interest of unmasking the "blatant nonsense" dispensed by Schiff. For that he deserves great commendation from the public. Perhaps now CBS and other communication media who have given Schiff's mistaken views widespread publicity will give John Newman equal time in the public interest. **Judgment for Schiff affirmed.**

Lapse of Time

Offers that fail to provide a specific time for acceptance are valid for a reasonable time. What constitutes a reasonable time depends on the circumstances surrounding the offer.

How long would a reasonable person in the offeree's position believe she had to accept the offer? Offers involving things subject to rapid fluctuations in value, such as stocks, bonds, or commodities futures, have a very brief duration. The same is true for offers involving goods that may spoil, such as produce.

The context of the parties' negotiations is another factor relevant to determining the duration of an offer. For example, most courts hold that when parties bargain face-to-face or over the telephone, the normal time for acceptance does not extend past the conclusion of their conversation unless the offeror indicates a contrary intention. Where negotiations are carried out by mail or telegram, the time for acceptance would ordinarily include at least the normal time for communicating the offer and a prompt response by the offeree. Finally, in cases where the parties have dealt with each other on a regular basis in the past, the timing of their prior transactions would be highly relevant in measuring the reasonable time for acceptance.

Revocation

General Rule: Offers are Revocable

As the masters of their offers, offerors can give offerers the power to bind them to contracts by making offers. They can also terminate that power by revoking their offers. The general common law rule on revocations is that offerors may revoke their offers at any time prior to acceptance, *even if they have promised to hold the offer open for a stated period of time.* In the following situations (summarized in Figure 15-1), however, offerors are *not* free to revoke their offers.

FIGURE 15-1 When offerors cannot revoke	**Options**	Offeror has promised to hold offer open and has received consideration for that promise
	Firm Offers	Merchant offeror makes written offer to buy or sell goods, giving assurances offer will be held open
	Unilateral Contract Offers	Offeree has started to perform requested act before offeror revokes
	Promissory Estoppel	Offeree foreseeably and reasonably relies on offer being held open, and will suffer injustice if it is revoked

1. *Options.* An **option** is a separate contract in which an offeror agrees not to revoke her offer for a stated time in exchange for some valuable consideration.[9] You can think of it as a contract in which an offeror sells her right to revoke her offer. For example, Jones, in exchange for $5,000, agrees to give Dewey Development Co. a six-month option to purchase her farm for $550,000. In this situation, Jones would not be free to revoke the offer during the six-month period of the option. The offeree, Dewey Development, has no obligation to accept Jones's offer. In effect, it has merely purchased the right to consider the offer for the stated time without fear that Jones will revoke it. The traditional common law rule on options requires the actual payment of the agreed-on consideration before an option contract becomes enforceable. Therefore, in the above example, if Dewey Development never, in fact, paid the $5,000, no option was created and Jones could revoke her offer at any time prior to its acceptance by Dewey Development.

2. *Firm offers for the sale of goods.* The Code makes a major change in the common law rules governing the revocability of offers by recognizing the concept of a **firm offer** [2-205]. Like an option, a firm offer is irrevocable for a period of time. In contrast to an option, however, a firm offer does not require consideration to be given in exchange for the offeror's promise to keep the offer open. Not all offers to buy or sell goods qualify as firm offers, however. To be a firm offer, an offer must:

- Be made by an offeror who is a *merchant*.
- Be contained in a signed[10] writing.
- Give assurances that the offer will be kept open.

An offer to buy or sell goods that fails to satisfy these three requirements is governed by the general common law rule and is revocable at any time prior to acceptance. If an offer *does* meet the requirements of a firm offer, however, it will be irrevocable for the time stated in the offer. If no specific time is stated in the offer, it will be irrevocable for a *reasonable* time. Regardless of the terms of the firm offer, the outer limit on a firm offer's irrevocability is *three* months. For example, if Worldwide Widgets makes an offer in a signed writing in which it proposes to sell a quantity of its XL7 Turbo Widgets to Howell Hardware and gives assurances that the offer will be kept open for a year, the offer is a firm offer, but it can be revoked after three months if Howell Hardware has not yet accepted it.

In some cases, however, offerers are the true originators of an assurance term in an offer. When offerers have effective control of the terms of the offer by providing their customers with preprinted purchase order forms or order blanks, they may be tempted to take advantage of their merchant customers by placing an assurance term in their order forms. This would allow offerers to await market developments before deciding whether to fill the order, while their merchant customers, who may have signed the order without reading all of its terms, would be powerless to revoke. To prevent such unfairness, the Code requires that assurance terms on forms provided by offerers be separately signed by the offeror to effect a firm offer. For example, if Fashionable Mfg. Co. supplies its customer, Retailer, with preprinted order forms that contain a fine-print provision giving assurances that the customer's offer to purchase goods will be held open for one month, the purported promise to keep the offer open would not be enforceable unless Retailer separately signed that provision.

3. *Offers for unilateral contracts.* Suppose Franklin makes the following offer for a unilateral contract to Waters: "If you mow my lawn, I'll pay you $25." Given that an offeree in a unilateral contract must fully perform the requested act to accept the offer, can Franklin wait until Waters is almost finished mowing the lawn and then say "I revoke!"? Obviously, the application of the general rule that offerors can revoke at any time before acceptance creates the potential for injustice when applied to offers for unilateral contracts because it would allow an offeror to revoke after the offeree has begun performance but before he has had a chance to complete it. To prevent injustice to offerees who rely on such offers by beginning performance, two basic approaches are available to modern courts.

Some courts have held that once the offeree has begun to perform, the offeror's power to revoke is suspended for the amount of time reasonably necessary for the offeree to complete performance. Section 45 of the *Restatement (Second)* takes a similar approach for offers that unequivocally require acceptance by performance by stating that once the offeree begins performance, an option contract is created. The offeror's duty to perform his side of the bargain is conditional on full performance by the offeree.

Another approach to the unilateral contract dilemma is to hold that a bilateral contract is created once the offeree begins performance. This is essentially the position taken by section 62 of the *Restatement (Second)*, which states that when the offer invites acceptance either by a return promise or performance, the beginning of performance operates as an acceptance and a promise by the offeree to render complete performance.

4. *Promissory estoppel.* In some cases in which the offeree relies on the offer being kept open, the doctrine of promissory estoppel can operate to prevent offerors from revoking their offers prior to acceptance. Section 87(2) of the Restatement (Second) says:

An offer which the offeror should reasonably expect to induce action or forbearance of a substantial character on the part of the offeree before acceptance and which does induce such action or forbearance is binding as an option contract to the extent necessary to avoid injustice.

Many of the cases in which promissory estoppel has been used successfully to prevent revocation of offers involve the bidding process. For example, Gigantic General Contractor seeks to get the general contract to build a new high school gymnasium for Shadyside School District. It receives bids from subcontractors. Pliny Electric submits the lowest bid to perform the electrical work on the job, and Gigantic uses Pliny's bid in preparing its bid for the general contract. Here, Pliny has made an offer to Gigantic, but Gigantic cannot accept that offer until it knows whether it has gotten the general contract. The school district awards the general contract to Gigantic. Before Gigantic can accept Pliny's offer, however, Pliny attempts to revoke it. In this situation, a court could use the doctrine of promissory estoppel to hold that the offer could not be revoked.

Effectiveness of Revocations

The question of *when* a revocation is effective to terminate an offer is often a critical issue in the contract formation process. For example, Davis offers to landscape Winter's property for $1,500. Two days after making the offer, Davis changes his mind and mails Winter a letter revoking the offer. The next day, Winter, who has not received Davis's letter, telephones Davis and attempts to accept. Contract? Yes. As the following *Lyon* case indicates, the general rule on this point is that revocations are effective only when they are actually *received* by the offeree. The basic idea behind this rule is that the offered is justified in relying on the intent to contract manifested by the offeror's offer until she actually knows that the offeror has changed his mind. This explains why many courts have also held that if the offered receives reliable information indicating that the offeror has taken action inconsistent with an intent to enter the contract proposed by the offer, such as selling the property that was the subject of the offer to someone else, this terminates the offer. In such circumstances, the offered would be unjustified in believing that the offer could still be accepted.

The only major exception to the general rule on effectiveness of revocations concerns offers to the general public. Because it would be impossible in most cases to reach every offered with a revocation, it is generally held that a revocation made in the same manner as the offer is effective when published, without proof of communication to the offeree.

Lyon v. Adgraphics

Edward Sherman engaged V. R. Brokers as listing agent for the sale of Adgraphics, his business. On December 5, 1985, William Lyon made a written offer to purchase the business for $75,000 and attached certain conditions to the offer. Later the same day, Sherman signed a written counteroffer offering to sell for $80,000 and rejecting two of the conditions contained in Lyon's offer. On December 7, at 11:35 A.M., Lyon signed the counteroffer before a notary public and then brought it to the office of V. R. Brokers around noon on that day. Before Lyon could hand the signed counteroffer to Robert Renault, the principal of V. R. Brokers, Renault told him that Sherman wanted to cancel his counteroffer. Lyon filed a breach of contract suit, and, when the trial court ruled in his favor, Sherman appealed.

Source: 540 A.2d 398 (Cone. Ct. App. 1988)

Borden, Judge

It is a basic principle of contract law that in order to form a binding contract there must be an offer and acceptance based on a mutual understanding of the parties. The counteroffer by Sherman created a power of acceptance in Lyon. That counteroffer, however, was revocable by Sherman at any time prior to acceptance by Lyon.

The trial court's conclusion that Lyon's acceptance of the counteroffer was effective when he signed it was contrary to our law. Revocation of an offer in order to be effectual must be received by the offered before he has exercised his power of creating a contract by acceptance of the offer. Acceptance is operative, if transmitted by means which the offeror has authorized, as soon as its transmission begins and it is put out of the offeree's possession. Lyon's act of signing the written counteroffer failed to communicate the acceptance to Sherman or his agent and failed to put the acceptance out of Lyon's possession. It was, therefore, ineffective to create a contract.

When Sherman, through his agent, informed Lyon that the counteroffer was withdrawn, Lyon's power to accept the counteroffer no longer existed. This was done before Lyon had properly accepted the counteroffer by transmitting the signed counteroffer to Renault. Accordingly, no enforceable contract between the parties was ever created. **Judgment reversed in favor of Sherman.**

Rejection

An offered reject an offer by indicating that he is unwilling to accept it. He may also impliedly reject it by making a counteroffer, an offer to contract on terms materially different from the terms of the offer.[11] As a general rule, either form of rejection by the offered terminates his power to accept the offer. This is so because an offeror who receives a rejection may rely on the offeree's expressed desire not to accept the offer by making another offer to a different offeree.

One exception to the general rule that rejections terminate offers concerns offers that are the subject of an option contract. Some courts hold that a rejection does not terminate an option contract and that the offerer who rejects still has the power to accept the offer later, so long as the acceptance is effective within the option period.[12]

Effectiveness of Rejections

As a general rule, rejections, like revocations, are effective only when actually received by the offeror. This is because there is no possibility that the offeror can rely on a rejection by making another offer to a different offered until she actually has notice of the rejection. Therefore, an offered who has mailed a rejection could still change her mind and accept if she communicates the acceptance before the offeror receives the rejection.[13]

Death or Insanity of Either Party

The death or insanity of either party to an offer automatically terminates the offer without notice. A meeting of the minds is obviously impossible when one of the parties has died or become insane.[14]

Destruction of Subject Matter

If, prior to an acceptance of an offer, the subject matter of a proposed contract is destroyed without the knowledge or fault of either party, the offer is terminated.[15] So, if Marks offers to sell Wiggins his lakeside cottage and the cottage is destroyed by fire before Wiggins accepts, the offer was terminated on the destruction of the cottage. Subsequent acceptance by Wiggins would not create a contract.

Intervening Illegality

An offer is terminated if the performance of the contract it proposes becomes illegal before the offer is accepted. So, if a computer manufacturer offered to sell sophisticated computer equipment to another country, but two days later, before the offer was accepted, Congress placed an embargo on all sales to that country, the offer was terminated by the embargo.[16]

Concept Review
What Terminates Offers?

- Their own terms
- Lapse of time
- Revocation
- Rejection
- Death or insanity of offeror or offerer
- Destruction of subject matter
- Intervening illegality

Ethical and Public Policy Concerns

1. Classical contract theory has traditionally found strong ethical justification in the notion of voluntary consent. To parties who want out of their contracts and ask why they should be held to them, the law has often responded: "Because you agreed to them." How does this ethical justification square with the objective theory of contract, which can in some cases result in holding people to agreements that are inconsistent with their subjective intent? Is there some other ethical justification for holding people to the objective manifestations of consent, regardless of their actual or subjective intent?

2. Compare and contrast the underlying ethical justifications of the classical and modern contract positions on what terms are included in offers. Is it ethical for businesses that deal with consumers or other unsophisticated parties to "hide" contract terms under misleading headings, in small print, or on the reverse side of contracts? What about putting form contracts in complex, technical language that consumers are unlikely to understand?

3. As you learned earlier in this chapter, there are now a number of exceptions to the traditional rule that offerors can revoke at any time prior to acceptance, even if they have promised not to. Is there an ethical basis for each of these exceptions? If so, what is it?

Problems and Problem Cases

1. In 1989, the New Jersey Highway Authority increased its tolls from 25 cents to 35 cents. In connection with this increase, it authorized the sale of tokens for a discounted price—$10 for a roll of 40 tokens, a savings of $4 per roll for customers—for a limited time. The authority advertised this sale through several media, including signs on the parkway itself. Shortly after the discount sale began, complaints were made that the tokens were not available. The authority explained that

the shortage probably resulted from an unanticipated demand for the tokens resulting from purchasers hoarding them. The authority then began limiting the sales to certain days of the week, but even with that limitation, the demand could not be satisfied. Schlictman, a motorist who used the toll roads, sued the authority for breach of contract after trying unsuccessfully, on five different occasions within the authorized sale dates and times, to buy the discounted tokens. What should the result be?

2. In 1985, First Colonial Savings Bank ran a newspaper advertisement that stated in part:

You Win 2 Ways
WITH FIRST COLONIAL'S
Savings Certificates

1 Great Gifts   2 & High Interest

Saving at First Colonial is a very rewarding experience. In appreciation for your business we have Great Gifts for you to enjoy **NOW**—and when your investment matures you get your entire principal back **PLUS GREAT INTEREST**.

Plan B: 3½ Year Investment

Deposit $14,000 and receive two gifts: a Remington Shotgun and GE CB Radio, OR an RCA 20" Color-Trac TV, and $20,136.12 upon maturity in 3½ years.

Relying on this ad, the Changs deposited $14,000 with First Colonial on January 3, 1986. They received a color television that day from First Colonial and expected to receive the sum of $20,136.12 upon maturity of the deposit in three and one-half years. First Colonial also gave the Changs a certificate of deposit when they made their deposit. When the Changs returned to liquidate the certificate of deposit upon its maturity, they were informed that the advertisement contained a typographical error and that they should have deposited $15,000 in order to receive the sum of $20,136.12 upon maturity of the certificate of deposit. First Colonial did not inform the Changs, nor were the Changs aware, that the advertisement contained an error until after the certificate of deposit had matured. First Colonial did display in its lobby pamphlets that contained the correct figures when the Changs made their deposit. The Changs sued First Colonial to recover the $1,312.19 difference between the $20,136.12 amount in the advertisement and the $18,823.93 that First Colonial actually paid to the Changs. Should they prevail?

3. On August 4, 1980, Normile made a written offer to buy property owned by Miller. Miller signed and returned the offer after making several substantial changes in its terms and initialing those changes. The executed form was delivered to Normile by Byer, the real estate agent who had shown him the property. In the early afternoon of August, 1980, Miller accepted an offer by Segal to buy her property on terms similar to those in the modified offer she had returned to Normile. At 2:00 P.M. that day, Byer told Normile: "You snooze, you lose; the property has been sold." Shortly thereafter, Normile attempted to accept Miller's proposal. Was the trial court correct in ruling that Normile and Miller had no contract?

4. In April 1981, Action Ads, Inc., hired Judes as a salesperson. The employment contract provided that: "Sixty days from your date of hire, Action Ads will provide a medical insurance program for you and your dependents." Judes was not very successful as a salesperson for Action, earning only $580.09 in commissions during the entire tenure of his employment with the company. Action never provided the promised medical insurance, a fact Judes learned when he inquired about whether he was covered in August of 1981. Judes did little or no solicitation for Action after

August, and the last order he placed with Action was in October 1981. During the period in which he was purportedly working for Action, Judes held himself out as unemployed, collecting $2,448 in unemployment benefits. In November 1981, Judes was seriously burned in a gas explosion at a mobile home. He filed suit against Action to recover his medical expenses, arguing that Action had breached the employment contract by failing to provide insurance coverage for him. Action Ads asserted that the agreement to provide "a medical insurance program" was too indefinite to be enforceable because the parties' agreement did not cover anything specific about the nature of the insurance coverage. What should the result be?

5. Less than an hour before his estranged wife underwent emergency surgery for an ectopic pregnancy caused by another man, McAdoo was asked to sign a standard form contract prepared by St. John's Episcopal Hospital. McAdoo testified that at the time he signed the form his wife's physical appearance and declared mental state convinced him that she was near death. Further, he stated that, under such circumstances, it did not occur to him to read carefully or question the implications of the papers he was being asked to sign. The form contained a provision that read as follows:

> ASSIGNMENT OF INSURANCE BENEFITS: I hereby authorize payment directly to the above named hospital of the hospital expense benefits otherwise payable to me but not to exceed the hospital's regular charges for this period of hospitalization. I understand that I am financially responsible to the hospital for the charges not covered by my group insurance plan.

McAdoo's wife survived and was discharged from St. John's eight days later. McAdoo did not visit her after the day of the operation and had not had any further contact with her when the hospital filed suit against him to collect her hospital bill. Should St. John's be able to enforce the agreement against McAdoo?

6. Phyllis Chaplin filed a class action suit against Consolidated Edison (Con Ed) for allegedly discriminating against epileptics in violation of the Rehabilitation Act of 1973. In August 1981, Con Ed's lawyer sent Chaplin's lawyer a settlement offer. Chaplin's lawyer replied by saying that Chaplin had "objections" to the proposed settlement. On September 16, 1981, Con Ed's lawyer replied, saying: "Any further negotiation is an impossibility; if this agreement is not satisfactory to your client in its present form, I must withdraw all offers of settlement." In a letter dated September 17, 1981, Chaplin's lawyer answered that "after careful consideration" Chaplin still had "objections" to Con Ed's offer. Later on September 17, a federal appellate court ruled that private suits such as Chaplin's were not allowed under the Rehabilitation Act. On September 30, 1981, Chaplin's lawyer told Con Ed's lawyer that Chaplin had "a change of heart" and was accepting the settlement offer. Con Ed's lawyer replied that the settlement was no longer acceptable. Was Con Ed bound by the settlement offer?

7. In October 1981, Christy and Andrus were involved in an automobile accident. On November 8, 1982, Aetna Casualty and Surety Company, Andrus's insurer, sent a letter to Christy and his insurer, The Travelers Insurance Company, offering to settle Christy's claim against Andrus for $8,507. Neither Christy nor The Travelers responded to this letter until February 4, 1984, when an attorney for The Travelers sent Aetna a letter attempting to accept the settlement offer. Aetna then responded that any claim Christy had against Andrus was barred by the state's two-year statute of limitations and that The Travelers' attempt to accept was not timely. Christy filed suit against Andrus end Aetna, arguing that they were bound by the settlement. At trial, Aetna introduced uncontradicted testimony that customary practice in the insurance

industry was to respond to settlement offers within a few weeks. Was the trial court decision in Aetna's favor correct?

8. In March 1985, Cagle, a potato farmer, entered into a written agreement to buy seed potatoes from H. C. Schmieding Produce Company. The terms of the contract obligated Cagle to pay a portion of the purchase price immediately, with the balance to be paid when the crop to be raised from the seed potatoes was harvested. Cagle paid the preharvest portion of the price and proceeded to cultivate the potatoes. He failed to harvest most of the resulting crop, however, or to pay Schmieding the postharvest portion of the purchase price. When Schmieding sued him for breach of contract, Cagle filed a counterclaim arguing that Schmieding had breached a second contract, which obligated him to purchase Cagle's crop. According to Cagle, this second contract resulted from two telephone conversations with Schmieding's employees, occurring in late February 1985 and in May 1985. Cagle introduced evidence to show that Schmieding had agreed in those conversations to pay him $5.50 per bag for approximately 10,000 bags of white potatoes and to pay him market price at harvest time for all of his red potatoes grown on 30 acres of land. Cagle also introduced a letter from Schmieding, dated May 26, 1985, which said: "We are looking forward to working with you on the shipment of your crop," and asked him to "give us a week notice before you are ready to ship, in order for us to prepare our sales orders." Was this contract sufficiently definite to be enforceable?

9. In June 1973, Berryman signed an agreement giving Kmoch, a real estate broker, a 120-day option to purchase 960 acres of Berryman's land in exchange for "$10.00 and other valuable consideration," which was never paid. Kmoch hired two agricultural consultants to produce a report that he intended to use in order to interest other investors in joining him to exercise the option. In late July 1973, Berryman telephoned Kmoch and asked to be released from the option agreement. Nothing definite was agreed to, and Berryman later sold the land to another person. In August, Kmoch decided to exercise the option and contacted the local Federal Land Bank representative to make arrangements to buy the land. After being told by the representative that Berryman had sold the property, Kmoch sent Berryman a letter attempting to exercise the option. Kmoch argued that the option was still in effect and that, in any event, Berryman was estopped from revoking it. Was Kmoch right?

10. Warner Electric, an electrical subcontractor, submitted a bid to the Utah Subcontractors Bid Depository Service for the electrical subcontract on the construction of the General Services Administration (GSA) Metallurgy Research Center in Salt Lake City, Utah. Warner based its bid on specifications and bid forms supplied by the GSA. John Price Associates, a general contractor, used Warner's subcontract bid, which was the lowest submitted, in preparing its bid for the general contract. Price was the lowest bidder and was awarded the contract for the project. A few days after Price had signed a contract with the GSA, Warner told Price that it had a problem with its subcontract bid because the bid did not include certain laboratory work described in section 11600 of the GSA plans, work which Warner had thought would be performed by the general contractor. Warner refused to sign the subcontract without a promise of additional payment for the section 11600 work. Price notified Warner by mailgram that it was accepting Warner's bid. Later that day, Warner's attorney delivered a letter to Price withdrawing Warner's bid. Price then contacted the other subcontractors and ultimately hired another subcontractor for $94,845 more than Warner's bid price. Was Warner free to revoke its offer?

11. A couple read three advertisements: The first was a newspaper ad for a new Mark 12 Luxury Automobile for $9,999. Although they thought the ad might be a

typographical mistake, there was no fine print in the ad and the two decided to go to the dealership and see if it would "make good on the offer." Once there, they learned that the price of the car was $29,999, not $9,999. The salesperson stated that the advertised price was an obvious typo. Is the dealership obligated to sell the car for $9,999?

The second was a flyer from a supermarket inviting customers to "Come celebrate good old-fashioned values for our 25th anniversary." The flyer advertised New York strip steak for $.99 per pound. Upon arrival at the store, however, the couple learned that the ad was an error and the price was intended to be $7.99 per pound, not $.99. The employee pointed to a memo posted in the store that announced that the ad was an error. Was the ad an offer? If it had been an offer, would the memo posted in the store be a valid revocation?

The third ad was a flyer from an electronics superstore that stated, "Dear Preferred Customer: special close-out of Ubachi VCRs. Only three available at this unbelievable price, first come, first served, no rain checks." The couple camped outside the store all night to be first in line, but the store refused to sell the advertised item and tried to sell them a different, higher-priced model instead. Was this ad an offer?

12. "Roof Repair." Roofer had submitted a bid to resurface a roof on the Bobco factory in Industrial Park. He had gotten encouraging signals about getting the job and was just about to get a signed contract to do the work when the Bobco factory burned to the ground. What is the status of Roofer's offer to resurface the roof?

See also "Car Deals" and "Martin Manufacturing."

Endnotes

1. *Hotchkiss v. National City Bank*, 200 F. 287 #293 (S.D N Y. 1911).
2. *Restatement (Second) of Contracts* § 24 (1981).
3. Chapter 14 discusses these Code provisions in detail.
4. *Restatement (Second) of Contracts* § 204 (1981).
5. *Restatement (Second) of Contracts* § 34(3) (1981).
6. See the general discussion of promissory estoppel in Chapter 14.
7. 26 Wis.2d 683, 133 N.W.2d 267 (Wis. SUD. Ct. 1965).
8. These rules and others concerned with the sale of goods by auction are contained in § 2-328 of the UCC.
9. Chapter 17 discusses consideration in detail.
10. under UCC § 1-201(39), the word *signed* includes any symbol that a person makes or adopts with the intent to authenticate a writing.
11. Chapter 16 discusses counteroffers in detail.
12. Section 37 of the *Restatement (Second) of Contracts* adopts this rule.
13. Chapter 16 discusses this subject in detail.
14. Death or insanity of a party that occurs after a contract has been formed can excuse performance in contracts that call for personal services to be performed by the person who has died or become insane.
15. In some circumstances destruction of the subject matter can also serve as a legal excuse for a party's failure to perform his obligations under an existing contract.
16. In some circumstances intervening illegality can also serve as a legal excuse for a party's failure to perform his obligations under an existing contract.

Chapter Sixteen

THE AGREEMENT:

ACCEPTANCE

Introduction

The preceding chapter discussed the circumstances under which a proposal would constitute the first stage of formation of an agreement: the offer. This chapter focuses on the final stage of forming an agreement: the acceptance. The acceptance is vitally important because it is with the acceptance that the contract is formed. This chapter discusses the requirements for making a valid acceptance as well as the rules concerning the time at which a contract comes into being.

What is an Acceptance?

An **acceptance** is "a manifestation of assent to the terms [of the offer] made by the offeree in the manner invited or required by the offer."[1] In determining if an offeree accepted an offer, thus creating a contract, a court will look for evidence that the offeree intended to enter the contract on the terms proposed by the offeror and that he communicated his acceptance to the offeror.

Intention to Accept

In determining whether an offeree accepted an offer, the court is looking for the same *present intent to contract* on the part of the offeree that it found on the part of the offeror. The difference is that the offeree must objectively indicate a present intent to contract on the terms of the offer before a contract results. As the master of the offer, the offeror may specify in detail what behavior is required of the offeree to bind him to a contract. If the offeror does so, the offeree must ordinarily comply with all the terms of the offer before a contract results.

Intent and Acceptance on the Offeror's Terms

Traditional Mirror Image Rule

The traditional contract law rule is that an acceptance must be the *mirror image* of the offer. As the following *Benya* case indicates, attempts by offerers to change the terms of the offer or to add new terms to it are treated as counteroffers because they impliedly indicate an intent by the offeree the offer instead of being bound by its terms. However, if an offeree merely asks about the terms of the offer without indicating its rejection (an *inquiry regarding terms*), or accepts the offer's terms while complaining about them (a *grumbling acceptance*), no rejection is implied. Also, recent years have witnessed a judicial tendency to apply the mirror image rule in a more liberal fashion by holding that only *material* (important) variances between an offer and a purported acceptance result in an implied rejection of the offer. Distinguishing among a counteroffer, an inquiry regarding terms, and a grumbling acceptance is often a difficult task. The fundamental issue, however, remains the same: Did the offered objectively indicate a present intent to be bound by the terms of the offer?

Benya v. Stevens and Thompson Paper Co.

On September 24, 1979, Vincent Benya's agent presented Stevens and Thompson Paper Company (S&T) with a sales agreement to purchase 5,243 acres of timber land owned by S&T for $605,366.50. S&T's lawyer made several modifications to the agreement, raising the cash to be paid at closing from $5,000 to $10,000, raising the interest rate on the mortgage S&T would hold on the property until it was fully paid for from 9 percent to 10 percent, providing for quarterly rather than annual payments on the mortgage, and changing the deed S&T was to provide from a warranty to a special warranty deed. S&T's vice president then initialed each change and signed the document, which was mailed back to Benya's agent. In early November, S&T received a new sales agreement from Benya, which differed from the two previous versions in a number of ways. S&T neither signed this agreement nor responded to it in any way. On November 7, S&T sold the property to someone else. Benya filed suit for breach of contract, and, when the trial court ruled in his favor, S&T appealed.

Source: 468 A.2d 929 (Vt. Sup. Ct. 1983)

Billings, Chief Justice

The trial court found that the September 24th sales agreement constituted a binding contract as both parties had signed it. The court concluded that the changes made by S&T to Benya's sales agreement were minor since the purchase price, closing date and deposit were substantially the same, and therefore did not constitute a counteroffer.

The law relative to contract formation has long been well settled in Vermont and elsewhere. For an acceptance of an offer to be valid, it must substantially comply with the terms of the offer. An acceptance that modifies or includes new terms is not an acceptance of the original offer; it is a counteroffer by the offeree that must be accepted or rejected by the original offeror. The offeror's acceptance of the offeree's counteroffer may be accomplished either expressly or by conduct.

On the record before us it is clear that the September 24th purchase and sales agreement was an offer from Benya to S&T that S&T never accepted. Instead, S&T significantly altered the terms of Benya's offer. These changes were not, as characterized by the trial court, minor and therefore of no effect on Benya's offer. Taken together, they constitute S&T's proposal for a new deal, or, more precisely, a counteroffer. Also clear from the record is that Benya never accepted, either expressly or otherwise, S&T's counteroffer. After Benya and his agent discussed S&T's counteroffer, the decision was made to draft a third proposal, which in turn altered the deposit and time of payment terms of S&T's counteroffer. S&T never signed or in any other way expressed its assent to this proposal. Additionally, the conduct of the parties demonstrates their understanding that agreement had not yet been reached.
Judgment reversed in favor of S&T.

The UCC and the "Battle of the Forms"

Strictly applying the mirror image rule to modern commercial transactions, most of which are carried out by using preprinted form contracts, would often result in frustrating the parties' true intent. Offerors use standard order forms prepared by their lawyers, and offerees use standard acceptance or acknowledgment forms drafted by their counsel. The odds that these forms will agree in every detail are slight, as are the odds that the parties will read each other's forms in their entirety. Instead, the parties to such transactions are likely to read only crucial provisions concerning the goods ordered, the price, and the delivery date called for, and if these terms are agreeable, believe that they have a contract.

If a dispute arose before the parties started to perform, a court strictly applying the mirror image rule would hold that no contract resulted because the offer and acceptance forms did not match exactly. If a dispute arose after performance had commenced, the court would probably hold that the offeror had impliedly accepted the offeree's counteroffer and was bound by its terms.

Because neither of these results is very satisfactory, the Code, in a very controversial provision often called the "Battle of the Forms" section [2-207] (see Figure 16-1), has changed the mirror image rule for contracts involving the sale of goods. As you will see in the following *Union Carbide* case, section 2-207 allows the formation of a contract even when there is some variance between the terms of the offer and the terms of the acceptance. It also makes it possible, under some circumstances, for a term contained in the acceptance form to become part of the contract. The Code provides that a *definite and timely expression of acceptance* creates a contract, even if it includes terms that are *different from those stated in the offer* or even if it states *additional terms* that the offer did not address [2-207(1)]. An attempted acceptance that *was expressly conditioned* on the offeror's agreement to the offeree's terms would *not* be a valid acceptance, however [2-207(1)].

FIGURE 16-1
The "battle of the forms"—a section 2-207 flowchart

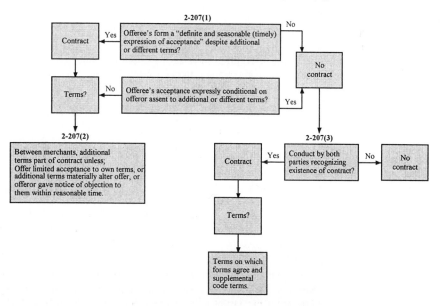

What are the terms of a contract created by the exchange of standardized forms? The *additional* terms contained in the offeree's form are treated as "proposals for addition to the contract." If the parties are both *merchants*, the additional terms become part of the contract unless:

1. The offer *expressly limits acceptance* to its own terms,
2. The new terms would *materially alter* the offer,
    or
3. The offeror gives notice of objection to the new terms within a reasonable time after receiving the acceptance [2-207(2)].

The *Union Carbide* case shows how courts analyze whether a term contained in the acceptance has become part of the contract.

When the offeree made his acceptance expressly conditional on the offeror's agreement to the new terms or when the offeree's response to the offer is clearly not "an expression of acceptance" (e.g., an express rejection), no contract is created under section 2-207(1). A contract will only result in such cases if the parties engage in conduct that "recognizes the existence of a contract," such as an exchange of performance. Unlike his counterpart under traditional contract principles, however, the offeror who accepts performance in the face of an express rejection or expressly conditional acceptance is not thereby bound to all of the terms contained in the offeree's response. Instead, the Code provides that the terms of a contract created by such performance are those on which the parties' writings *agree*, supplemented by appropriate gapfilling provisions from the Code [2-207(3)].

Union Carbide Corp. v. Oscar Mayer Foods Corp.

Union Carbide sold Oscar Mayer plastic casings that Oscar Mayer uses in manufacturing sausages. The prices in Union Carbide's invoices to Oscar Mayer included two 1 percent sales taxes that are applicable to sales that originate in Chicago. In 1980, another one of Oscar Mayer's suppliers of plastic sausage casings began charging a price that was 1 percent lower than Union Carbide's. This supplier had begun accepting orders at an office outside of Chicago and had decided that therefore it did not have to pay one of the sales taxes. When Oscar Mayer informed Union Carbide of this, Union Carbide instructed its customers to send their orders to an address outside Chicago, too, and it stopped paying both sales taxes and therefore deleted them from the invoices it sent Oscar Mayer. Thus Union Carbide had met and indeed beat the other supplier's discount by lowering its price 2 percent compared to the other supplier's reduction of 1 percent.

In 1988, the Illinois tax authorities decided that the two sales taxes were due notwithstanding the change of address and assessed Union Carbide $88,000 in back taxes on sales to Oscar Mayer and $55,000 in interest on those sales. Union Carbide paid this and then brought this suit to recover what it had paid from Oscar Mayer, claiming that Oscar Mayer had agreed to indemnify it for all sales tax liability. It relied on the following provision printed on the back of its invoices to Oscar Mayer and also in a "price book" that it sent its customers:

> In addition to the purchase price, Buyer shall pay Seller the amount of all governmental taxes . . . that Seller may be required to pay with respect to the production, sale or transportation of any materials delivered hereunder.

The trial court granted a summary judgment in favor of Oscar Mayer, and Union Carbide appealed.

Source: 947 F.2d 1333 (7th Cir. 1991)

Posner, Circuit Judge

The common law rule was that if the purported acceptance of an offer was not identical to the offer, the acceptance was a fresh offer and had to be expressly accepted by the original offeror for the parties to have a contract. This "mirror image" rule was widely believed to take insufficient account of the incorrigible fallibility of human beings engaged in commercial as in other dealings, and is changed by the Uniform Commercial Code, which allows an acceptance to make a contract even if it adds terms to the offer. Moreover, if it is a contract between "merchants" (in the sense of "pros," UCC section 2-104(1)—as Union Carbide and Oscar Mayer are), the additional terms become part of the contract. But not any additional terms; only those to which the offeror would be unlikely to object, because they fill out the contract in an expectable fashion, and hence do not alter it materially. If a term added by the offeree in his acceptance works a material alteration of the offer, the acceptance is still effective, but the term is not; that is, the contract is enforceable minus the term the offeree tried to add. An alteration is material if consent to it cannot be presumed. What is expectable, hence unsurprising, is okay; what is unexpected, hence surprising, is not.

This is not the end of the analysis, however. Even if the alteration is material, the other party can, of course, decide to accept it. Put differently, consent can be inferred from other things beside the unsurprising character of the new term: even from silence, in the face of a course of dealings that makes it reasonable for the other party to infer consent from a failure to object. An offeror can protect himself against additional terms, material or not, by expressly limiting acceptance to the terms of the offer.

The record does not reveal the origins of Union Carbide's dealings with Oscar Mayer. All we know is that in 1980 the parties' method of dealing was as follows. Oscar Mayer would from time to time send large purchase orders to Union Carbide which would not be filled immediately but instead would be filed for future reference. When Oscar Mayer actually needed casings it would phone Union Carbide and tell it how many it needed and Union Carbide would ship the casings the next day. After the casings arrived Oscar Mayer would send Union Carbide a purchase order for the shipment on the same form used for the standing orders. These "release orders," as the specific purchase orders were called, were like checks written against a bank account—only this was a sausage—casings account. At about the same time that Oscar Mayer sent Union Carbide a release order, Union Carbide would send Oscar Mayer an invoice for the shipment—and the so-called indemnity clause was on the back of the invoice and also in a price book that Union Carbide sent its customers from time to time. So every actual purchase of sausage casings involved an exchange of four documents: the standing order, the price book, the release order, the invoice. Such a pattern of sequential exchange of documents governing a single sale is a prototypical situation for the application of UCC section 2-207. Union Carbide does not question that for purposes of our decision the purchase orders by Oscar Mayer are the offers and Union Carbide's invoices are the acceptances, and that the price book, if it be assumed to be an offer, was never accepted. So the indemnity clause was binding on Oscar Mayer only if the clause did not work a material alteration of the terms in the purchase orders.

Those orders don't exactly *discuss* taxes, but they contain a space for sales tax to be added into the purchase price, and Union Carbide points out that, consistent with this indication of willingness to pay sales tax, Oscar Mayer paid uncomplainingly all sales taxes that appeared on Union Carbide's invoices. If the sales tax rates had risen, Oscar Mayer would have had to pay the higher rates. What difference does it make, asks Union Carbide, if the increase took the form of an assessment of back taxes? It makes a big difference, amounting to a material alteration to which Oscar Mayer did not consent either explicitly or implicitly. If a tax increase showed up on an invoice, Oscar Mayer would have to pay but might then decide to cease buying casings from Union Carbide, as it had every right to do; it did not have a requirements contract with Union Carbide but could switch at will to other suppliers some of whom might not be subject to the tax. To assume responsibility for taxes shown on an individual invoice is quite different from assuming an open-ended, indeed incalculable, liability for back taxes. The tax clause altered the contract materially; and since the clause was at best ambiguous, this is not a case where consent can realistically be inferred from Oscar Mayer's silence in the face of a succession of acceptances (Union Carbide's invoices) containing the new term. There was no breach of contract.

Judgment affirmed in favor of Oscar Mayer.

Acceptance in Unilateral Contracts

A unilateral contract involves the exchange of a promise for an act. To accept an offer to enter such a contract, the offeree the requested act. As you learned in the last chapter, however, courts applying modern contract rules may prevent an offeror from revoking such an offer once the offeree has begun performance. This is achieved by holding either that a bilateral contract is created by the beginning of performance or that the offeror's power to revoke is suspended for the period of time reasonably necessary for the offeree to complete performance.

Acceptance in Bilateral Contracts

A bilateral contract involves the exchange of a promise for a promise. As a general rule, to accept an offer to enter such a contract, an offeree *must make the promise requested by the offer*. This may be done in a variety of ways. For example, Wallace sends Stevens a detailed offer for the purchase of Stevens's business. Within the time period prescribed by the offer, Stevens sends Wallace a letter that says, "I accept your offer." Stevens has *expressly* accepted Wallace's offer, creating a contract on the terms of the offer. Acceptance, however, can be *implied* as well as express. Offerers who take action that objectively indicates agreement risk the formation of a contract. For example, offerees who act in a manner that is inconsistent with an offeror's ownership of offered property are commonly held to have accepted the offeror's terms. So, if Arnold, a farmer, leaves 10 bushels of corn with Porter, the owner of a grocery store, saying, "Look this corn over. If you want it, it's $5 a bushel," and Porter sells the corn, he has impliedly accepted Arnold's offer. But what if Porter just let the corn sit and, when Arnold returned a week later, Porter told Arnold that he did not want it? Could Porter's failure to act ever amount to an acceptance?

Silence as Acceptance

Since contract law generally requires some objective indication that an offeree intends to contract, the general rule is that an offeree's silence, without more, is *not* an acceptance. In addition, it is generally held that an offeror cannot impose on the offeree a duty to respond to the offer. So, even if Arnold made an offer to sell corn to Porter and said, "If I don't hear from you in three days, I'll assume you're buying the corn," Porter's silence would still not amount to acceptance.

On the other hand, the circumstances of a case sometimes impose a duty on the offeree to reject the offer affirmatively or be bound by its terms. These are cases in which the offeree's silence objectively indicates an intent to accept. Customary trade practice or prior dealings between the parties may indicate that silence signals acceptance. So, if Arnold and Porter had dealt with each other on numerous occasions and Porter had always promptly returned items that he did not want, Porter's silent retention of the goods for a week would probably constitute an acceptance. Likewise, an offeree's silence can also operate as an acceptance if the offeree has indicated that it will. For example, Porter (the *offeree*) tells Arnold, "If you don't hear from me in three days, I accept."

Finally, it is generally held that offerees who accept an offeror's performance knowing what the offeror expects in return for his performance have impliedly accepted the offeror's terms. So, if Apex Paving Corporation offers to do the paving work on a new subdivision being developed by Majestic Homes Corporation, and Majestic fails to respond to Apex's offer but allows Apex to do the work, most courts would hold that Majestic is bound by the terms of Apex's offer.

Acceptance When a Writing Is Anticipated

Frequently, the parties to a contract intend to prepare a written draft of their agreement for both parties to sign. This is a good idea not only because the law requires written evidence of some contracts,[2] but also because it provides written evidence of the terms of the agreement if a dispute arises at a later date. If a dispute arises before such a writing has been prepared or signed, however, a question may arise concerning whether the signing of the agreement was a necessary condition to the creation of a contract. A party to the agreement who now wants out of the deal may argue that the parties did not intend to be bound until both parties signed the writing. As the following *Texaco* case indicates, a clear expression of such an intent by the parties during the negotiation process prevents the formation of a contract until both parties have signed. However, in the absence of such a clear expression of intent, the courts ask whether a reasonable person familiar with all the circumstances of the parties' negotiations would conclude that the parties intended to be bound only when a formal agreement was signed. If it appears that the parties had concluded their negotiations and reached agreement on all the essential aspects of the transaction, most courts would probably find a contract at the time agreement was reached, even though no formal agreement had been signed.

Texaco, Inc. v. Pennzoil Co.

On December 28, 1983, in the wake of well-publicized dissension between the board of directors of Getty Oil Company and Gordon Getty, Pennzoil announced an unsolicited, public tender offer for 16 million shares of Getty Oil at $100 each. Gordon Getty was a director of Getty Oil and the owner, as trustee of the Sarah C. Getty Trust, of 40.2 percent of the 79.1 million outstanding shares of Getty Oil. Shortly thereafter, Pennzoil contacted both Gordon Getty and a representative of the J. Paul Getty Museum, which held 11.8 percent of the shares of Getty Oil, to discuss the tender offer and the possible purchase of Getty Oil.

The parties drafted and signed a Memorandum of Agreement providing that Pennzoil and the Trust (with Gordon Getty as trustee) were to become partners on a 3/7ths to 4/7ths basis, respectively, in owning and operating Getty Oil. The museum was to receive $110 per share for its 11.8 percent ownership, and all other outstanding public shares were to be cashed in by the company at $110 per share. The memorandum provided that it was subject to the approval of Getty Oil's board. On January 2, 1984, the board voted to reject the memorandum price as too low and made a counterproposal to Pennzoil of $110 per share plus a $10 debenture. On January 3, the board received a revised Pennzoil proposal of $110 per share plus a $3 "stub" that was to be paid after the sale of a Getty Oil subsidiary.

After discussion, the board voted 15 to 1 to accept Pennzoil's proposal if the stub price was raised to $5. This counteroffer was accepted by Pennzoil later the same day. On January 4, Getty Oil and Pennzoil issued identical press releases announcing an agreement in principle on the terms of the Memorandum of Agreement. Pennzoil's lawyers began working on a formal transaction agreement describing the deal in more detail than the outline of terms contained in the Memorandum of Agreement and press release.

On January 5, the board of Texaco, which had been in contact with Getty Oil's investment banker, authorized its officers to make an offer for 100 percent of Getty Oil's stock. Texaco first contacted the Getty Museum, which, after discussion, agreed to sell its shares to Texaco. Later that evening, Gordon Getty accepted Texaco's offer of $125 per share. On January 6, the Getty Board voted to withdraw its previous counteroffer to Pennzoil and to accept Texaco's offer. Pennzoil later filed suit against Texaco for tortious interference with its contract with the Getty entities. At trial, Texaco argued, among other things, that no contract had existed between Pennzoil and the Getty entities. The jury disagreed, awarding Pennzoil $7.53 billion in actual damages and $3 billion in punitive damages. Texaco appealed.

Source: 729 S.W. 2d 768 (Tex. Ct. App. 1987)

Warren, Justice

Texaco contends that there was insufficient evidence to support the jury's finding that at the end of the Getty Oil board meeting on January 3, the Getty entities intended to bind themselves to an agreement with Pennzoil. Pennzoil contends that the evidence showed that the parties intended to be bound to the terms in the Memorandum of Agreement plus a price term of $110 plus a $5 stub, even though the parties may have contemplated a later, more formal document to memorialize the agreement already reached.

If parties do not intend to be bound to an agreement until it is reduced to writing and signed by both parties, then there is no contract until that event occurs. If there is no understanding that a signed writing is necessary before the parties will be bound, and the parties have agreed upon all substantial terms, then an informal agreement can be binding, even though the parties contemplated evidencing their agreement in a formal document later. It is the parties' expressed intent that controls which rule of contract formation applies. Only the outward expressions of intent are considered—secret or subjective intent is immaterial to the question of whether the parties were bound.

Several factors have been articulated to help determine whether the parties intended to be bound only by a formal, signed writing: (1) whether a party expressly reserved the right to be bound only when a written agreement is signed; (2) whether there was any partial performance by one party that the party disclaiming the contract accepted; (3) whether all essential terms of the alleged contract had been agreed upon; and (4) whether the complexity or magnitude of the transaction was such that a formal, executed writing would normally be expected.

Any intent of the parties not to be bound before signing a formal document is not so clearly expressed in the press release to establish, as a matter of law, that there was no contract at that time. The press release does refer to an agreement "in principle" and states that the "transaction" is subject to execution of a definitive merger agreement. But the release as a whole is worded in indicative terms, not in subjunctive or hypothetical ones. The press release describes what shareholders will receive, what Pennzoil will contribute, that Pennzoil will be granted an option, etc.

We find little relevant partial performance in this case that might show that the parties believed that they were bound by a contract. However, the absence of relevant part performance in this short period of time does not compel the conclusion that no contract existed.

There was sufficient evidence for the jury to conclude that the parties had reached agreement on all essential terms of the transaction with only the mechanics and details left to be supplied by the parties' attorneys. Although there may have been many specific items relating to the transaction agreement draft that had yet to be put in final form, there is sufficient evidence to support a conclusion by the jury that the parties did not consider any of Texaco's asserted "open items" significant obstacles precluding an intent to be bound.

Although the magnitude of the transaction here was such that normally a signed writing would be expected, there was sufficient evidence to support an inference by the jury that expectation was satisfied here initially by the Memorandum of Agreement, signed by a majority of shareholders of Getty Oil and approved by the board with a higher price, and by the transaction agreement in progress that had been intended to memorialize the agreement previously reached.

Judgment for Pennzoil affirmed.

Note: The court's decision was contingent on a reduction in the punitive damages awarded by the jury from $3 billion to $1 billion. Texaco ultimately sought reorganization under the protection of the Bankruptcy Court and the parties finally settled the case for $3 billion.

Acceptance of Ambiguous Offers

Although offerors have the power to specify the manner in which their offers can be accepted by requiring that the offeree make a return promise (a bilateral contract) or perform a specific act (a unilateral contract), often an offer is unclear about which form of acceptance is necessary to create a contract. In such a case, both the Code [2-206(1)(a)] and the *Restatement (Second)*[3] suggest that the offer may be accepted in any manner that is reasonable in light of the circumstances surrounding the offer. Thus, either a promise to perform or performance, if reasonable, creates a contract.

Acceptance by Shipment

The Code specifically elaborates on the rule stated in the preceding section by stating that an order requesting prompt or current shipment of goods may be accepted either by a *prompt promise to ship* or by a *prompt or current shipment* of the goods [2-206(1)(b)]. So, if Ampex Corporation orders 500 IBM personal computers from Marks Office Supply, to be shipped immediately, Marks could accept either by promptly promising to ship the goods or by promptly shipping them. If Marks accepts by shipping, any subsequent attempt by Ampex to revoke the order will be ineffective.

What if Marks did not have 500 IBMs in stock and Marks knew that Ampex desperately needed the goods? Marks might be tempted to ship another brand of computers (that is, *nonconforming goods*—goods different from what the buyer ordered), hoping that Ampex would be forced by its circumstances to accept them because by the time they arrived it would be too late to get the correct goods elsewhere. Marks would argue that by shipping the wrong goods it had made a counteroffer because it had not performed the act requested by Ampex's order. If Ampex accepts the goods, Marks could argue that Ampex has impliedly accepted the counteroffer. If Ampex rejects the goods, Marks would arguably have no liability since it did not accept the order.

The Code prevents such a result by providing that prompt shipment of either conforming goods (what the order asked for) or nonconforming goods (something else) operates as an acceptance of the order [2-206(1)(b)]. This protects buyers such as Ampex because sellers who ship the wrong goods have simultaneously accepted their offers and breached the contract by sending the wrong merchandise.

But what if Marks is an honest seller merely trying to help out a customer that has placed a rush order? Must Marks expose itself to liability for breach of contract in the process? The Code prevents such a result by providing that no contract is created if the seller notifies the buyer within a reasonable time that the shipment of nonconforming goods is intended as an accommodation (an attempt to help the buyer) [2-206(1)(b)]. In this case, the shipment is merely a counteroffer that the buyer is free to accept or reject and the seller's notification gives the buyer the opportunity to seek the goods he needs elsewhere.

Who Can Accept an Offer?

As the masters of their offers, offerees have the right to determine who can bind them to a contract. So, the only person with the legal power to accept an offer and create a contract is the *original offeree*. An attempt to accept by anyone other than the offeree is treated as an offer, because the party attempting to accept is indicating a present intent to contract on the original offer's terms. For example, Price offers to sell his car to Waterhouse for $5,000. Berk learns of the offer, calls Price, and attempts to accept. Berk has made an offer that Price is free to accept or reject.

Communication of Acceptance

Communication Required for Valid Acceptance

To accept an offer for a bilateral contract, the offeree must make the promise requested by the offer. In the Offer chapter, you learned that an offeror must communicate the terms of his proposal to the offeree before an offer results. This is so because communication is a necessary component of the present intent to contract required for the creation of an offer. For similar reasons, it is generally held that an offeree must communicate his intent to be bound by the offer before a contract can be created. To accept an offer for a unilateral contract, however, the offeree must perform the requested act. The traditional contract law rule on this point assumes that the offeror will learn of the offeree's performance and holds that no further notice from the offeree is necessary to create a contract unless the offeror specifically requests notice. The traditional rule can sometimes cause hardship to offerors who may not, in fact, know that the offeree has commenced performance. Neither the Code [section 2-206(2)] nor the *Restatement (Second)* will enforce such a contract against an offeror who has no way of learning of the offeree's performance with reasonable promptness and certainty.[4]

Manner of Communication

The offeror, as the master of the offer, has the power to specify the precise time, place, and manner in which acceptance must be communicated. This is called a *stipulation*. If the offeror stipulates a particular manner of acceptance, the offeree must respond in this way to form a valid acceptance. Suppose Prompt Printing makes an offer to Jackson and the offer states that Jackson must respond by certified mail. If Jackson deviates from the offer's instructions in any significant way, no contract results unless Prompt Printing indicates a willingness to be bound by the deviating acceptance. If, however, the offer merely *suggests* a method or place of communication or is *silent* on such matters, the offerer within a *reasonable time* by *any reasonable means* of communication. So, if Prompt Printing's offer did not *require* any particular manner of accepting the offer, Jackson could accept the offer by any reasonable manner of communication within a reasonable time.

When Is Acceptance Communicated?

Acceptances by Instantaneous Forms of Communication

When the parties are dealing face-to-face, by telephone, or by other means of communication that are virtually instantaneous, there are few problems determining when the acceptance was communicated. As soon as the offered says, "I accept," or words to that effect, a contract is created, assuming that the offer was still in existence at that time.

Acceptances by Noninstantaneous Forms of Communication

Suppose the circumstances under which the offer was made reasonably lead the offeree to believe that acceptance by some noninstantaneous form of communication is acceptable, and the offeree responds by using mail, telegraph, or some other means of communication that creates a time lag between the dispatching of the acceptance and its actual receipt by the offeror. The practical problems involving the timing of acceptance multiply in such transactions. The offeror may be attempting to revoke the offer while the offeree is attempting to accept it. An acceptance may get lost and never be received by the offeror. The time limit for accepting the offer may be rapidly approaching. Was the offer accepted before a revocation was received or before the offer expired? Does a lost acceptance create a contract when it is dispatched, or is it totally ineffective?

Under the so-called "mailbox rule," properly addressed and dispatched acceptances can become effective when they are *dispatched*, even if they are lost and never received by the offeror. The mailbox rule, which is discussed further in the following *Casto v. State Farm Mutual Insurance Co.* case, protects the offeree's reasonable belief that a binding contract was created when the acceptance was dispatched. By the same token, it exposes the offeror to the risk of being bound by an acceptance that she has never received. The offeror, however, has the ability to minimize this risk by stipulating in her offer that she must actually receive the acceptance for it to be effective. Offerors who do this maximize the time that they have to revoke their offers and ensure that they will never be bound by an acceptance that they have not received.

Operation of the Mailbox Rule: Traditional Rules

Under traditional contract law, the mailbox rule makes acceptances effective upon dispatch when the offeree used a manner of communication that was expressly or impliedly **authorized** (invited) by the offeror. Any manner of communication *suggested* by the offeror (e.g., "You may respond by mail") would be *expressly* authorized, resulting in an acceptance sent by the suggested means being effective on dispatch. Unless circumstances indicated to the contrary, a manner of communication *used by the offeror in making the offer* would be *impliedly* authorized (e.g., an offer sent by mail would impliedly authorize an acceptance by mail), as would a manner of communication common in the parties' trade or business (e.g., a trade usage in the parties' business that offers are made by mail and accepted by telegram would authorize an acceptance by telegram). Conversely, an improperly dispatched acceptance or one that was sent by some means of communication that was *nonauthorized* would be effective when *received*, assuming that the offer was still open at that time. This placed on the offeree the risk of the offer being revoked or the acceptance being lost.

Operation of the Mailbox Rule: Modern Rules

Under both the UCC and the *Restatement (Second) of Contracts*, an offer that does not indicate otherwise is considered to invite acceptance by *any reasonable means* of communication, and a properly dispatched acceptance sent by a reasonable means of communication within a reasonable time is effective on dispatch. What is reasonable depends on the circumstances in which the offer was made. These include the speed and reliability of the means used by the offeree, the nature of the transaction (e.g., does the agreement involve goods subject to rapid price fluctuations?), the existence of any trade usage governing the transaction, and the existence of prior dealings between the parties (e.g., has the offeree previously used the mail to accept telegraphed offers from the offeror?). So, under proper circumstances, a mailed response to a telegraphed offer or a telegraphed response to a mailed offer might be considered reasonable and therefore effective on dispatch.

What if an offeree attempts to accept the offer by some means that is *unreasonable* under the circumstances or if the acceptance is not properly addressed or dispatched (e.g., misaddressed or accompanied by insufficient postage)? Modern contract law rejects the traditional rule that such acceptances cannot be effective until received. Under both the Code [1-201(38)] and section 67 of the *Restatement (Second)*, an acceptance sent by an unreasonable means would be effective on dispatch *if* it is received within the time that an acceptance by a reasonable means would normally have arrived. The *Casto* case shows what happens when an improperly dispatched acceptance is not received within the time that a properly dispatched acceptance would have been.

Casto v. State Farm Mutual Insurance Co.

In 1985, State Farm issued Deborah Casto an automobile insurance policy on her Jaguar. Casto also insured a second car, a Porsche, with State Farm. Sometime in September or early October 1987, Casto received two renewal notices, indicating that the next premium was due on October 20, 1987. State Farm sent a notice of cancellation on October 16, indicating that the policy would be canceled on October 29. Casto denied having received this notice. On October 20, Casto placed two checks, one for the Jaguar and one for the Porsche, in two preaddressed envelopes that had been supplied by State Farm. She gave these envelopes to Donald Dick, who mailed them on the same day. The envelope containing the Porsche payment was timely delivered to State Farm, but State Farm never received the Jaguar payment, and that policy was canceled.

Casto was involved in an accident on November 20 while driving the Jaguar. When she made a claim with State Farm, she learned that the policy had been canceled. After the accident, the envelope containing the Jaguar payment was returned to her stamped "Returned for postage." Casto brought this declaratory judgment action seeking a declaration that her insurance policy was in effect as of the date of the accident. The trial court rendered a judgment for State Farm and Casto appealed.

Source: 594 N.E.2d 1004 (Ct. App. Ohio 1991)

Reilly, Presiding Judge

The facts indicate that while the payment was mailed before October 29, it was not received by the insurance company. The issue then is whether the insurance premium is effectively paid on the day it was mailed or the day it is received by the company.

An insurance policy is a contract and the relationship between the insurer and its insured is contractual in nature. The renewal of an insurance policy is generally considered a new contract of insurance to which the requirements of offer and acceptance apply. The well-established general rule of contract formation is that an acceptance transmitted in a form invited by the offer is operative as soon as it is put out of the offeree's possession, regardless of whether it ever reaches the offeror. This is the so-called "mailbox rule" which states that in the absence of any limitation to the contrary in the offer, an acceptance is effective when mailed. One of the parties must bear the risk of loss. As the offeror has the power to condition acceptance of the offer on actual receipt, the courts have uniformly held that, in the absence of language to the contrary, an acceptance is effective when mailed.

To be effective upon mailing, however, the acceptance must be properly dispatched. The offeree must properly address the acceptance and take whatever other precautions as are ordinarily observed in the transmission of similar messages. It is undisputed that State Farm provided Casto with pre-addressed envelopes and thus authorized her to mail her premium payments. Furthermore, the renewal notices contain no language requiring actual receipt before payment is deemed effective. Finally, Casto and Donald Dick testified in their depositions that the Jaguar and Porsche payments were mailed on October 20,1987, nine days before the cancellation date. Their testimony is further supported by the fact that the Porsche payment was actually received by State Farm before the cancellation date. Thus, the only remaining question is whether the payment was properly dispatched.

Casto testified that the check and renewal notice were placed in a pre-addressed and stamped envelope. Donald Dick also testified that both envelopes were stamped when he mailed them. Nevertheless, the envelope did not bear any postage when it was returned to Casto. Casto bore the burden of proving that the envelope was stamped when it was mailed. When the findings of fact leave some material fact undetermined, a reviewing court will presume that the issue of fact was not proved by the party having the burden of proof. We thus presume that the trial court concluded that the envelope was not stamped when mailed, and there is sufficient evidence in the record to support such a finding. As the envelope was not properly dispatched, the payment was not effective upon mailing under the facts of this case.

Judgment affirmed in favor of State Farm.

Stipulated Means of Communication

As we discussed earlier, an offer may stipulate the means of communication that the offeree must use to accept by saying, in effect: "You must accept by mail." An acceptance by the stipulated means of communication is effective on dispatch, just like an acceptance by any other reasonable or authorized means of communication (see Figure 16-2). The difference is that an acceptance by other than the stipulated means does not create a contract because it is an acceptance at variance with the terms of the offer.

FIGURE 16-2
Time of acceptance

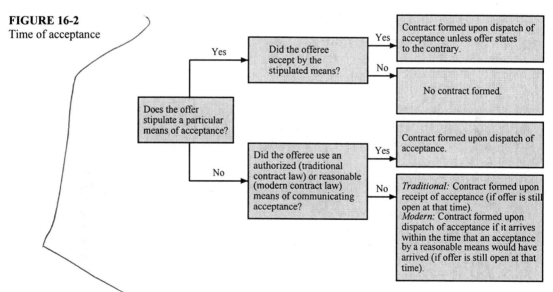

Contradictory Offeree Responses

How do these rules work when the offeree sends mixed signals to the offeror? Suppose Case mails a counteroffer to White, impliedly rejecting an offer that White has made to him, and then, before White receives the rejection, Case mails a letter of acceptance. Is a contract formed? In the last chapter, you learned that Case's counteroffer (that is, rejection) would not be effective to terminate White's offer until White actually *receives* it. If we applied the normal rules of offer and acceptance to these facts, we might conclude that the parties had a contract because Case's acceptance by mail was effective on dispatch. White, however, might receive Case's counteroffer and sell the house to a third party before he receives Case's acceptance. To prevent such an unfair result, most courts hold that when an offeree dispatches an acceptance after first dispatching a rejection, the acceptance does not create a contract unless it is received before the rejection. Therefore, if White receives the counteroffer before he receives the acceptance, no contract results. If, on the other hand, he receives the acceptance before receiving the counteroffer, a contract results.

What is the result if Case had first mailed White an acceptance, then changed his mind and shortly thereafter mailed White a rejection? Applying normal offer and acceptance rules to these facts, we would conclude that Case's acceptance was effective on dispatch and that Case no longer had the power to reject the offer. But the application of these rules would result in unfairness if White received Case's rejection first and relied on it by selling to someone else. In such a situation, Case would be *estopped* from enforcing the contract due to White's reliance.

Concept Review
Contradictory Offeree Responses

Offeree Sends First	Offeree Sends Second	Offeror Receives First	Result
Rejection	Acceptance	Rejection	No contract
Rejection	Acceptance	Acceptance	Contract
Acceptance	Rejection	Rejection	If offeror relied on rejection, offeree is estopped from enforcing the contract
Acceptance	Rejection	Acceptance	Contract

Ethical and Public Policy Concerns

1. It should be apparent to you from the discussion of section 2-207 of the Code, the "Battle of the Forms" section, that the application of that section can sometimes result in a party being held to a contract term to which she has not actually consented. How can this be justified?
2. Compare the ethical standards underlying the traditional contract law approach to the seller who ships nonconforming goods with the ethical standards reflected by section 2-206(1)(b) of the Code.
3. Compare the public policy stances implicit in the different ways in which traditional and modern contract law treat offeree attempts to accept by an nonauthorized or unreasonable means of communication.

Problems and Problem Cases

1. Since 1974, Lone Star Donut Company had placed orders for its sugar requirements with Great Western Sugar Co. (GWS) through a sugar broker. In October 1980, GWS adopted a new policy of requiring a letter agreement for each order. The first such letter was forwarded from GWS to Lone Star by the broker on October 9, 1980. It concluded with the following language:

> This letter is a written confirmation of our agreement, and unless it is signed by the buyer and returned to Great Western within 15 days of the date hereof, the agreement shall be deemed breached by Buyer and automatically terminated. Please sign and return to me the enclosed counterpart of this letter signaling your acceptance of the above agreement.

Lone Star signed and returned this letter. On December 2, Lone Star again ordered sugar. GWS initially neglected to send a letter agreement, finally doing so in late January 1981, in response to prodding by the broker. This letter concluded as follows:

> This letter is a written confirmation of our agreement. Please sign and return to me the enclosed counterpart of this letter signaling your acceptance of the above agreement.

Lone Star, angered over the delay, refused to sign and subsequently refused to purchase sugar. Was a contract formed?

2. First Texas Savings Association promoted a "$5,000 Scoreboard Challenge" contest. Contestants who completed an entry form and deposited it with First Texas were eligible for a random drawing. The winner was to receive an $80 savings account with First Texas, plus four tickets to a Dallas Mavericks home basketball game chosen by First Texas. If the Mavericks held their opponent in the chosen game to 89 or fewer points, the winner was to receive an additional $5,000 money market certificate. In October 1982, Jergins deposited a completed entry form with First Texas. On November 1, 1982, First Texas tried to amend the contest rules by posting notice at its branches that the Mavericks would have to hold their opponent to 85 or fewer points before the contest winner would receive the $5,000. In late December, Jergins was notified that she had won the $80 savings account and tickets to the January 22, 1983, game against the Utah Jazz. The notice contained the revised contest terms. The Mavericks held the Jazz to 88 points. Was Jergins entitled to the $5,000?

3. In April 1973, in response to a request from Mobil Chemical for a bid on a two-sided precoater, Egan Machinery submitted a "quotation" describing the components of the precoater and the details of its operation. The quotation stated a price for the precoater but did not contain conditions of sale. In May 1973, Mobil sent Egan a purchase order for the precoater. The purchase order contained the following language:

> Important—this order expressly limits acceptance to terms stated herein, and any additional or different terms proposed by the seller are rejected unless expressly agreed to in writing.

Egan responded with an order acknowledgment in May 1973, which provided that:

> This order is accepted on the condition that our Standard Conditions of Sale, which are attached hereto and made a part hereof, are accepted by you, notwithstanding any modifying or additive conditions contained on your purchase order. Receipt of this acknowledgment by you without prompt written objection thereto shall constitute an acceptance of these terms and conditions.

One of the terms included in Egan's Standard Conditions required Mobil to indemnify Egan against any liability Egan might incur to persons injured by the precoater if the injury resulted from Mobil's failure to require its employees to follow safety procedures and/or use safety devices while operating it. When a Mobil employee who was injured while operating the precoater later won a $75,000 judgment against Egan, Egan filed suit against Mobil seeking indemnity. Did the indemnity clause become part of the contract?

4. Atwood bought a new pickup truck from Best Buick. When he took it home, his wife objected to the purchase. Atwood returned the car to Best, which agreed to take the truck back as a trade-in on another vehicle. Atwood traded for a new station wagon, which he registered and insured and sought to title in his name. When he took the car home, however, his wife objected to the color of its interior. Atwood returned the car to Best, but refused to accept any of the numerous other vehicles Best made available

to him. He also refused to sign an application that would allow Best to retrieve the title to the car so it could sell it to someone else. Best then told him that unless he removed the car from its premises it would charge him a $5 per day storage fee. The Atwoods later sued Best for the return of the purchase price. Best counterclaimed for the storage fee. Should the Atwoods prevail?

5. Western Tire, Inc., had a lease on a building owned by the Skredes that was due to expire on April 30, 1978. The lease gave Western the right to renew the lease for an additional five-year term if the Skredes were given written notice of Western's intent to renew at least 30 days prior to the expiration date. It also specifically provided that notice would only be effective when it was deposited in a U.S. Post Office by registered or certified mail. On February 27, Western's attorney sent the Skredes a notice of Western's intent to renew by ordinary mail, which the Skredes did not receive until after April 1, 1978. On April 5, 1978, Western's lawyer, discovering his mistake, sent a second notice by certified mail. On April 14, 1978, the Skredes told Western that the lease was canceled. Did they have the right to cancel?

6. On January 16, 1987, Koop, an employee of Professional Search, Inc., called Renner, the director of systems software for Northwest Airlines, to inquire about possible job openings in Renner's department. Koop explained to Renner that if Northwest Airlines hired a candidate recommended by Professional Search, Professional Search would be entitled to charge Northwest Airlines 30 percent of the candidate's starting salary. Renner told Koop that a systems analyst position was open and described the job. Renner also stated that Northwest Airlines was not currently interviewing for that position and that Koop should direct further inquiries to Northwest Airlines's human resources department. Later, Koop and Wawrzyniak discussed Wawrzyniak's desire to be placed as a systems analyst and Wawrzyniak signed a placement contract. On January 20, 1987, Koop sent Wawrzyniak's resume to Renner. Koop later called Renner, who told him the resume "looked good." On February 19, Wawrzyniak filled out an application for a systems position with Northwest Airlines, claiming he heard of the opening through a friend. On April 13, Northwest Airlines hired Wawrzyniak. Professional Search claimed that a placement contract had been formed between it and Northwest Airlines, and sought to recover its $12,000 commission. Will Professional Search prevail?

7. In 1986, Mercy Memorial Hospital decided to open an outpatient family practice clinic in Petersburg. It retained a recruiter to identify a private family practitioner. The recruiter brought the hospital and Dr. Kamalnath together. In June 1986, Iacoangeli, the hospital's director of planning and development, wrote Dr. Kamalnath a letter in which he made an offer to her that proposed terms regarding salary, office rental, line of credit for professional and operational expenses, home relocation, and other matters. Dr. Kamalnath did not accept this written offer. Instead, she suggested various changes and additions, principally an increase in the term of employment to three years and a provision that the hospital handle marketing. On June 30, Iacoangeli sent Dr. Kamalnath a second letter incorporating the longer period of employment, subject to annual performance reviews, and proposing other terms. Iacoangeli also prepared several drafts of a proposed contract, but none of these proved satisfactory to Dr. Kamalnath. Dr. Kamalnath nevertheless moved to Petersburg and began work, although she had no signed contract, the parties still differed as to some contractual duties such as the responsibility for certain major expenses, and the clinic was not yet complete. The Petersburg clinic was not as successful as the parties had hoped. Relations between them deteriorated, and the hospital notified Dr. Kamalnath to vacate the clinic in November 1987. Was there a contract between the hospital and Dr. Kamalnath?

8. On March 30, Cushing, a member of an antinuclear protest group, applied to the New Hampshire adjutant general's office for permission to hold a dance in the Portsmouth armory. On March 31, the adjutant general mailed a signed contract offer agreeing to rent the armory to the group. The agreement required Cushing to accept by signing a copy of the agreement and returning it to the adjutant general within five days after its receipt. On April 3, Cushing received the offer and signed it. At 6:30 P.M. on April 4, Cushing received a call from the adjutant general attempting to revoke the offer. Cushing told the adjutant general that he had signed the contract and placed it in the office outbox on April 3, customary office practice being to collect all mail from outboxes at the end of the day and deposit it in the U.S. mail. On April 6, the adjutant general's office received the signed contract in the mail, dated April 3 and postmarked April 5. Assuming Cushing was telling the truth, did the parties have a contract?

9. Krack Corporation bought steel tubing from Metal-Matic for 10 years. The parties' usual practice was for Krack to send Metal-Matic purchase orders to which Metal-Matic would respond by sending an acknowledgment form and shipping the requested tubing. Metal-Matic's form provided that its acceptance was "expressly made" conditional on Krack's assent to the acknowledgment's terms, which included a clause limiting Metal-Matic's liability for consequential damages due to breach of warranty. Krack sold a cooling unit it had made with Metal-Matic's tubing to Diamond Fruit. The tubing was defective, causing losses to Diamond's fruit. When Diamond sued Krack, Krack sought indemnity from Metal-Matic. Metal-Matic argued that it was not responsible, citing the consequential damages clause in its acknowledgment. Was that clause part of the contract between Krack and Metal-Matic?

10. Soldau was fired by Organon, Inc. He received a letter from Organon offering to pay him double the normal severance pay if he would sign a release giving up all claims against the company. The letter incorporated the proposed release, which Soldau signed, dated, and deposited in a mailbox outside a post office. When he returned home, Soldau found that he had received a check from Organon in the amount of the increased severance pay. He returned to the post office and persuaded a postal employee to open the mailbox and retrieve the release. Soldau cashed Organon's check and subsequently filed an age discrimination suit against Organon. Was Soldau bound by the release?

Endnotes

1. *Restatement (Second) of Contracts* § 50(1) (1981).
2. Chapter 20 discusses this subject in detail.
3. *Restatement (Second) of Contracts* § 30(2) (1981).
4. *Restatement (Second) of Contract* § 54 (2) (1981).

Chapter Seventeen

CONSIDERATION

Introduction

One of the things that separates a contract from an unenforceable social promise is that a contract requires voluntary agreement by two or more parties. Not all agreements, however, are enforceable contracts. At a fairly early point in the development of classical contract law, the common law courts decided not to enforce gratuitous (free) promises. Instead, only promises supported by consideration were enforceable in a court of law. This was consistent with the notion that the purpose of contract law was to enforce freely made bargains. As one 19th century work on contracts put it: "The common law . . . gives effect only to contracts that are founded on the mutual exigencies of men, and does not compel the performance of any merely gratuitous agreements."[1] The concept of consideration distinguishes agreements that the law will enforce from gratuitous promises, which are normally unenforceable. This chapter focuses on the concept of consideration.

The Idea of Consideration

A common definition of **consideration** is *legal value, bargained for and given in exchange for an act or a promise*. Thus, a promise generally cannot be enforced against the person who made it (the *promiser*) unless the person to whom the promise was made (the *promisee*) has given up something of legal value in exchange for the promise. In effect, the requirement of consideration means that a promisee must pay the price that the promiser asked to gain the right to enforce the promisor's promise. So, if the promiser did not ask for anything in exchange for making her promise or if what the promiser asked for did not have legal value (e.g., because it was something to which she was already entitled), her promise is not enforceable against her because it is not supported by consideration. Figure 17-1 graphically illustrates the elements of consideration.

Consider the early case of *Thorne v. Deas*, in which the part owner of a sailing ship named the Sea Nymph promised his co-owners that he would insure the ship for an upcoming voyage.[2] He failed to do so, and when the ship was lost at sea, the court found that he was not liable to his co-owners for breaching his promise to insure the ship. Why? Because his promise was purely gratuitous; he had neither asked for nor received anything in exchange for making it. Therefore, it was unenforceable because it was not supported by consideration.

This early example illustrates two important aspects of the consideration requirement. First, the requirement *tended to limit the scope of a promisor's liability for his promises* by insulating him from liability for gratuitous promises and by protecting him against liability for reliance on such promises. Second, the mechanical application of the requirement *often produced unfair results*. This potential for unfairness has produced considerable dissatisfaction with the consideration concept. As the rest of this chapter indicates, the relative importance of consideration in modern contract law has been somewhat eroded by numerous exceptions to the consideration requirement and by judicial applications of consideration principles designed to produce fair results.

FIGURE 17-1
The elements of
consideration

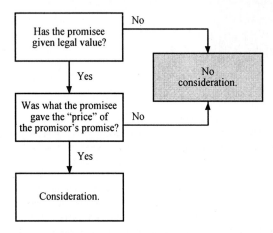

Legal Value

Consideration can be an act in the case of a unilateral contract or a promise in the case of a bilateral contract. An act or a promise can have legal value in one of two ways. If, in exchange for the promisor's promise, the promisee does, or agrees to do, something he had no prior legal duty to do, that provides legal value. If, in exchange for the promisor's promise, the promisee refrains from doing, or agrees not to do, something she has a legal right to do, that also provides legal value. Note that this definition does not require that an act or a promise have monetary (economic) value to amount to consideration. Thus, in a famous 19th-century case, *Hamer v. Sidway*,[3] an uncle's promise to pay his nephew $5,000 if he refrained from using tobacco, drinking, swearing, and playing cards or billiards for money until his 21st birthday was held to be supported by consideration. Indeed, the nephew had refrained from doing any of these acts, even though he may have benefited from so refraining. He had a legal right to indulge in such activities, yet he had refrained from doing so at his uncle's request and in exchange for his uncle's promise. This was all that was required for consideration. *Lyon v. Reames Foods, Inc.*, which appears later in this chapter, elaborates on the different forms that legal value can take.

Adequacy of Consideration

The point that the legal value requirement is not concerned with actual value is further borne out by the fact that the courts generally will not concern themselves with questions regarding the adequacy of the consideration that the promisee gave. This means that as long as the promisee's act or promise satisfies the legal value test, the courts do not ask whether that act or promise was worth what the promiser gave, or promised to give, in return for it. This rule on adequacy of consideration reflects the laissez-faire assumptions underlying classical contract law. Freedom of contract includes the freedom to make bad bargains as well as good ones, so promisers' promises are enforceable if they got what they asked for in exchange for making their promises, even if what they asked for was not nearly so valuable in worldly terms as what they promised in return. Also, a court taking a hands-off stance concerning private contracts would be reluctant to step in and second-guess the parties by setting aside a transaction that both parties at one time considered satisfactory. Finally, the rule against considering the adequacy of consideration can promote certainty and predictability in commercial transactions by denying legal effect to what would otherwise be a possible basis for challenging the enforceability of a contract—the inequality of the exchange.

Several qualifications must be made concerning the general rule on adequacy of consideration. First, if the inadequacy of consideration is apparent on the face of the agreement, most courts conclude that the agreement was a disguised gift rather than an enforceable bargain. Thus, an agreement calling for an unequal exchange of money (e.g., $500 for $1,000) or identical goods (20 business law textbooks for 40 identical business law textbooks) and containing no other terms would probably be unenforceable. Gross inadequacy of consideration may also give rise to an inference of fraud, duress,[4] lack of capacity,[5] unconscionability, or some other independent basis for setting aside a contract. However, inadequacy of consideration, standing alone, is never sufficient to prove lack of true consent or contractual capacity. Although gross inadequacy of consideration is not, by itself, ordinarily a sufficient reason to set aside a contract, the courts may refuse to grant specific performance or other equitable remedies to persons seeking to enforce unfair bargains.

Finally, some agreements recite "$1," or "$1 and other valuable consideration," or some other small amount as consideration for a promise. If no other consideration is actually exchanged, this is called *nominal consideration*. Often, such agreements are attempts to make gratuitous promises look like true bargains by reciting a nonexistent consideration. Most courts refuse to enforce such agreements unless they find that the stated consideration was truly bargained for.

Illusory Promises

For a promise to serve as consideration in a bilateral contract, the promisee must have promised to do, or to refrain from doing, something at the promisor's request. It seems obvious, therefore, that if the promisee's promise is illusory because it really does not bind the promisee to do or refrain from doing anything, such a promise could not serve as consideration. Such agreements are often said to lack the mutuality of obligation required for an agreement to be enforceable. So, a promisee's promise to buy "all the sugar that I want" or to "paint your house if I feel like it" would not be sufficient consideration for a promisor's return promise to sell sugar or hire a painter. In neither case has the promisee given the promiser anything of legal value in exchange for the promisor's promise. Remember, though: So long as the promisee has given legal value, the agreement will be enforceable even though what the promisee gave is worth substantially less than what the promisor promised in return.

Cancellation or Termination Clauses

The fact that an agreement allows one or both of the parties to cancel or terminate their contractual obligations does not necessarily mean that the party (or parties) with the power to cancel has given an illusory promise. Such provisions are a common and necessary part of many business relationships. The central issue in such cases concerns whether a promise subject to cancellation or termination actually represents a binding obligation. A right to cancel or terminate at any time, for any reason, and without any notice would clearly render illusory any other promise by the party possessing such a right. However, limits on the circumstances under which cancellation may occur, such as a dealer's failure to live up to dealership obligations, or the time in which cancellation may occur (such as no cancellations for the first 90 days), or a requirement of advance notice of cancellation (such as a 30-day notice requirement) would all effectively remove a promise from the illusory category. This is so because in each case the party making such a promise has bound himself to do *something* in exchange for the other party's promise.

Of course, some parties to agreements may not want their agreements to amount to binding contracts. For example, a manufacturer selling through a system of independent retail dealers may want to retain maximum flexibility by giving itself a unilateral right to terminate a dealer at any time, for any reason, without notice. Such an "intentional no contract" strategy relies on the fact that the manufacturer's greater bargaining power may allow it to impose such terms on its dealers. This kind of business strategy is very difficult, if not impossible, to pursue today, however, given the numerous "dealer day in court" statutes that past abuses have produced and the fact that many courts have stricken down unilateral cancellation clauses as unconscionable. As you will see in the following *Lyon* case, a party's duty of good faith and fair dealing can limit the right to terminate and prevent its promise from being considered illusory.

Lyon v. Reames Foods, Inc.

William Reames, president and sole shareholder of Reames Foods, recruited and hired Donald Lyon to be a salesperson for the company. Before joining Reames Foods, Lyon had been employed by and was a part owner in the Certified Meat Company. Lyon claims that when Reames approached him about joining the company, he had been concerned about the possibility that Reames might decide to sell the company in the future. Lyon did not want to help build the company's sales over time and then be subject to termination by a new owner after the company was sold. Lyon claimed that he received from Reames and Reames Foods an oral agreement guaranteeing him employment for five years after a change in ownership of the company, but the existence of such an agreement was denied by Reames Foods. Lyon asserted that, in reliance on this oral contract, he sold his ownership interest in the Certified Meat Company, quit his old job, and joined Reames Foods in April 1976.

Lyon attempted to get the terms of the alleged oral contract with Reames Foods reduced to writing, but Reames continually put off his requests. Finally, at a meeting in November 1977, after several discussions between Reames and Lyon, Reames handed to Lyon a copy of a document entitled "Work Agreement." This document, which Lyon claims sets forth the terms of the earlier oral agreement, was typed on Reames Foods's letterhead, and was signed by Reames as president and agent of Reames Foods. The document provided in part that:

it is agreed that in event of the sale of the company . . . we of REAMES FOODS, INC. do guarantee and assure Donald F. Lyon of five (5) years continued employment at a minimum of his current salary effective at such time. . . . Donald Lyon agres that he will, during such period of time, maintain all of his efforts in working for the company and will be employed by no other party during said period of time and said employment may be discontinued at any time if said Donald F. Lyon fails to perform his work in a manner satisfactory to the Board of Directors.

The document was signed by Reames, but was not signed by Lyon. Reames and Reames Foods claim that this document was merely one of many proposals and counterproposals considered by Lyon and Reames, and that it does not amount to an enforceable contract in itself.

Reames sold Reames Foods to the T. Marzetti Company in October 1989. In December 1989, Lyon was terminated. Lyon sued Reames and Reames Foods for breach of contract, among other claims. Lyon sought summary judgment asking the court to determine whether there was an enforceable contract and whether various defenses asserted by the defendants, including lack of consideration, could be maintained.

Source: 1992 U.S. Dist. LEXIS 4184 (U.S. Dist. Ct. Kan. 1992)

Lungstrom, District Judge

It is elementary that, as a general rule, in order for a promise to be legally enforceable as a contract there must be consideration. Consideration can be either a benefit given or to be given to the promisee, a forbearance experienced or to be experienced by the promiser, or mutual promises. Reames Foods contends that the agreement did not require Lyon to give anything of value to Reames Foods in consideration for his alleged employment guarantee. Yet, assuming that an agreement between the parties was reached, the written memorialization, signed by William Reames, requires that Lyon give up his right to work for another employer during the five years that his employment would be guaranteed. If the condition contained in the agreement occurred, i.e., if Reames Foods was sold, Lyon promised to work exclusively for that company in exchange for Reames Foods's promise to assure Lyon of a job for five years. Lyon's promised forbearance would be consideration for Reames Foods's promised employment. In addition, however, Lyon gave up a job and an ownership interest in his former employer in order to join Reames Foods. Therefore, Reames Foods's contention that any alleged agreement was not supported by sufficient consideration is unfounded.

Reames Foods argues that, even if the alleged agreement was supported by consideration, it is unenforceable because it is illusory. According to Reames Foods, it could have terminated Lyon just before a sale of the company was finalized and thereby avoided all liability to him. If a promise is illusory it cannot be sufficient consideration to support a contract. Professor Farnsworth has recognized that promises which allow the promiser to terminate its rights and duties at any time will, without more, have been held to be illusory. He notes, however, that when the promiser retains the power to terminate, but only within a period of time after which it loses this power, the promise is not illusory "if the period expires without either party manifesting an intention not to be bound." E. Farnsworth, Contracts, section 2.14, at 81 (2d ed. 1990). This is exactly the case here. Although Reames Foods may have had the ability to terminate the alleged contract before ownership of the company was transferred, it failed to do so. After this triggering event came and passed without Reames Foods exercising its option to fire Lyon, it became bound to fulfill its obligations under the contract.

Moreover, it also appears that the promise was not illusory from its original making. Lyon argues that Reames Foods was not free to fire him at any time before the company was sold. The court agrees. Iowa law recognizes an implied obligation in all contracts requiring that the party for whom performance will be done will not obstruct, hinder, or delay the other party to the contract from completing his or her obligations under the contract. The current trend among courts is to read such obligations into allegedly illusory promises in order to make them enforceable. Contrary to its assertion, Reames Foods did not possess an unbridled right to terminate Lyon before a sale of the company in order to avoid liability to him. There were sufficient legal constraints on Reames Foods's ability to fire Lyon that this alleged agreement is not illusory.

Reames Foods contends that Lyon never signed [the written document] or otherwise manifested the intention to accept it. It is obvious that genuine issues of fact remain regarding whether the written document delivered to Lyon constitutes an enforceable contract. Resolution should be by the prier of fact, not by the court on a motion for summary judgment. If the prier of fact determines that the parties intended to enter into a contract and that sufficient assent was manifested, the agreement between the parties would be enforceable.

Summary judgment granted in part in favor of Lyon and denied in part.

Note: The case was tried several months later, and the court found in favor of Lyon, awarding him $234,144.82 in damages.

Output and Requirements Contracts

Contracts in which one party to the agreement agrees to buy all of the other party's production of a particular commodity (output contracts) or to supply all of another party's needs for a particular commodity (requirements contracts) are common business transactions that serve legitimate business purposes. They can reduce a seller's selling costs and provide buyers with a secure source of supply. Prior to the enactment of the UCC, however, many common law courts used to refuse to enforce such agreements on the ground that their failure to specify the quantity of goods to be produced or purchased rendered them illusory. The courts also feared that a party to such an agreement might be tempted to exploit the other party. For example, subsequent market conditions could make it profitable for the seller in an output contract or the buyer in a requirements contract to demand that the other party buy or provide more of the particular commodity than the other party had actually intended to buy or sell. The Code legitimizes requirements and output contracts. It addresses the concern about the potential for exploitation by limiting a party's demands to those quantity needs that occur in *good faith* and are not unreasonably disproportionate to any quantity estimate contained in the contract, or to any normal prior output or requirements if no estimate is stated [2-306(1)].

Exclusive Dealing Contracts

When a manufacturer of goods enters an agreement giving a distributor the exclusive right to sell the manufacturer's products in a particular territory, does such an agreement impose sufficient obligations on both parties to meet the legal value test? Put another way, does the distributor have any duty to sell the manufacturer's products and does the manufacturer have any duty to supply any particular number of products? Such agreements are commonly encountered in today's business world, and they can serve the legitimate interests of both parties. The Code recognizes this fact by providing that, unless the parties agree to the contrary, an exclusive dealing contract imposes a duty on the distributor to use her best efforts to sell the goods and imposes a reciprocal duty on the manufacturer to use his best efforts to supply the goods [2-306(2)].

Preexisting Duties

The legal value component of our consideration definition requires that promisees do, or promise to do, something in exchange for a promisor's promise that they had no prior legal duty to do. Thus, as a general rule, performing or agreeing to perform a preexisting duty is not consideration. This seems fair because the promiser in such a case has effectively made a gratuitous promise, since she was already entitled to the promisee's performance.

Preexisting Public Duties

Every member of society has a duty to obey the law and refrain from committing crimes or torts. Therefore, a promisee's promise not to commit such an act can never be consideration. So, Thomas's promise to pay Brown $100 a year in exchange for Brown's promise not to burn Thomas's barn would not be enforceable against Thomas. Since Brown has a preexisting duty not to burn Thomas's barn, his promise lacks legal value.

Similarly, public officials, by virtue of their offices, have a preexisting legal duty to perform their public responsibilities. For example, Smith, the owner of a liquor store, promises to pay Fawcett, a police officer whose beat includes Smith's store, $50 a week to keep an eye on the store while walking her beat. Smith's promise is unenforceable because Fawcett has agreed to do something that she already has a duty to do.

Preexisting Contractual Duties

The most important preexisting duty cases are those involving preexisting *contractual* duties. These cases generally occur when the parties to an existing contract agree to *modify* that contract. As the *Gross* case (which follows shortly) indicates, the general common law rule on contract modification holds that an agreement to modify an existing contract requires some *new consideration* to be binding.

For example, Turner enters into a contract with Acme Construction Company for the construction of a new office building for $350,000. When the construction is partially completed, Acme tells Turner that due to rising labor and materials costs it will stop construction unless Turner agrees to pay an extra $50,000. Turner, having already entered into contracts to lease office space in the new building, promises to pay the extra amount. When the construction is finished, Turner refuses to pay more than $350,000. Is Turner's promise to pay the extra $50,000 enforceable against him? No. All Acme has done in exchange for Turner's promise to pay more is build the building, something that Acme had a preexisting contractual duty to do. Therefore, Acme's performance is not consideration for Turner's promise to pay more.

Although the result in the preceding example seems fair (why should Turner have to pay $400,000 for something he had a right to receive for $350,000?) and is consistent with consideration theory, the application of the preexisting duty rule to contract modifications has generated a great deal of criticism. Plainly, the rule can protect a party to a contract such as Turner from being pressured into paying more because the other party to the contract is trying to take advantage of his situation by demanding an additional amount for performance. However, mechanical application of the rule could also produce unfair results when the parties have freely agreed to a fair modification of their contract. Some critics argue that the purpose of contract modification law should be to enforce freely made modifications of existing contracts and to deny enforcement to coerced modifications. Such critics commonly suggest that general principles such as good faith and unconscionability, rather than technical consideration rules, should be used to police contract modifications.

Other observers argue that most courts in fact apply the preexisting duty rule in a manner calculated to reach fair results, because several exceptions to the rule can be used to enforce a fair modification agreement. For example, any new consideration furnished by the promisee provides sufficient consideration to support a promise to modify an existing contract. So, if Acme had promised to finish construction a week before the completion date called for in the original contract, or had promised to make some change in the original contract specifications such as to install a better grade of carpet, Acme would have done something that it had no legal duty to do in exchange for Turner's new promise. Turner's promise to pay more would then be enforceable because it would be supported by new consideration.

Many courts also enforce an agreement to modify an existing contract if the modification resulted from *unforeseen circumstances* that a party could not reasonably be expected to have foreseen, and which made that party's performance far more difficult than the parties originally anticipated. For example, if Acme had requested the extra payment because abnormal subsurface rock formations made excavation on the construction site far more costly and time-consuming than could have been reasonably expected, many courts would enforce Turner's promise to pay more.

Courts can also enforce fair modification agreements by holding that the parties mutually agreed to terminate their original contract and then entered a new one. Because contracts are created by the will of the parties, they can be terminated in the same fashion. Each party agrees to release the other party from his contractual obligations in exchange for the other party's promise to do the same. Because such a mutual agreement terminates all duties owed under the original agreement, any subsequent agreement by the parties would not be subject to the preexisting duty rule. A court is likely to take this approach, however, only when it is convinced that the modification agreement was fair and free from coercion.

Gross v. Diehl Specialties International

In 1977, Dairy Specialties, Inc. (Dairy), hired George Gross to develop nondairy products for customers allergic to milk and to serve as general manager. The employment contract was for a term of 15 years and provided for annual wages of $14,400 plus cost-of-living increases. It also provided that when 10 percent of Dairy's gross profits exceeded Gross's annual salary, he would receive the difference between the two figures. In addition, Gross would receive a royalty of 1 percent of the selling price of all products Dairy produced using one or more of Gross's inventions or formulae. This royalty increased to 2 percent after the expiration of the agreement, at which time ownership of the inventions and formulae (which were jointly held during the term of the agreement) would revert to Gross.

In 1982, Dairy was bought from its original owner by the Diehl family. The Diehls insisted on renegotiation of Gross's contract with Dairy as a condition of the purchase. Although he was not a party to the sale and received nothing tangible from it, Gross agreed to a new contract that had the same expiration date as the first one but that eliminated his cost-of-living increases, gave Dairy exclusive ownership of his inventions and formulae during and after the term of the agreement, and eliminated his right to royalties after the agreement expired. After the sale, Gross was given additional duties but no additional compensation. In 1984, after a business downturn, Gross was fired. He filed suit, arguing that his termination benefits should be calculated under his original contract. When the trial court ruled in the company's favor, he appealed.

Source: 776 S.W.2d 879 (Mo. Ct. App. 1989)

Smith, Presiding Judge

A modification of a contract constitutes the making of a new contract and such new contract must be supported by consideration. Where a contract has not been fully performed at the time of the new agreement, the substitution of a new provision, resulting in a modification of the obligation of both sides, for a provision in the old contract still unperformed is sufficient consideration for the new contract. A promise to carry out an existing contractual duty does not constitute consideration.

Under the 1982 agreement the company undertook no greater obligations than it already had. Gross on the other hand received less than he had under the original contract. His base pay was reduced back to its 1977 amount despite the provision in the 1977 contract calling for cost of living adjustments. He lost his equal ownership in his formulae during the term of the agreement and his exclusive ownership after the termination of the agreement. He lost all royalties after termination of the agreement. In exchange for nothing, the company acquired exclusive ownership of the formulae during and after the agreement, eliminated royalties after the agreement terminated, and achieved a reduction in Gross's base salary. The company did no more than promise to carry out an already existing contractual duty. There was no consideration for the 1982 agreement.

Judgment reversed in favor of Gross; case remanded for recalculation of damages.

Code Contract Modification

The drafters of the Code sought to avoid many of the problems caused by the consideration requirement by dispensing with it in two important situations: As discussed in the Offer chapter, the Code does not require consideration for firm offers [2-205]. The Code also provides that an agreement to modify a contract for the sale of goods needs *no consideration* to be binding [2-209(1)]. For example, Electronics World orders 200 XYZ televisions at $150 per unit from XYZ Corp. Electronics World later seeks to cancel its order, but XYZ refuses to agree to cancellation. Instead, XYZ seeks to mollify a valued customer by offering to reduce the price to $100 per unit. Electronics World agrees, but when the televisions arrive, XYZ bills Electronics World for $150 per unit. Under classical contract principles, XYZ's promise to reduce the price of the goods would not be enforceable because Electronics World has furnished no new consideration in exchange for XYZ's promise. Under the Code, no new consideration is necessary and the agreement to modify the contract is enforceable.

Several things should be made clear about the operation of this Code rule. First, XYZ had no duty to agree to a modification and could have insisted on payment of $150 per unit. Second, as the following *Roth Steel Products* case illustrates, modification agreements under the Code are still subject to scrutiny under the general Code principles of good faith and unconscionability, so unfair agreements or agreements that are the product of coercion are unlikely to be enforced. Finally, the Code contains two provisions to protect people from fictitious claims that an agreement has been modified. If the original agreement requires any modification to be in writing, an oral modification is unenforceable [2-209(2)]. Regardless of what the original agreement says, if the price of the goods in the modified contract is $500 or more, the modification is unenforceable unless the requirements of the Code's statute of frauds section [2-201] are satisfied [2-209(3)].

Roth Steel Products v. Sharon Steel Corporation

In November 1972, when conditions in the steel industry were highly competitive and the industry was operating at about 70 percent of its capacity, Sharon Steel Corporation agreed to sell Roth Steel Products several types of steel at prices well below Sharon's published book prices for such steel. These prices were to be effective from January 1 until December 31, 1973.

In early 1973, however, several factors changed the market for steel. Federal price controls simultaneously discouraged foreign steel imports and encouraged domestic steel producers to export a substantial portion of their production to avoid domestic price controls, sharply reducing the domestic steel supply. In addition, the steel industry experienced substantial increases in labor, raw material, and energy costs, compelling steel producers to increase prices. The increased domestic demand for steel and the attractive export market caused the entire industry to operate at full capacity; as a consequence, nearly every domestic steel producer experienced substantial delays in delivery.

On March 23, 1973, Sharon notified Roth that it was discontinuing all price discounts. Roth protested, and Sharon agreed to continue to sell at the discount price until June 30, 1973, but refused to sell thereafter unless Roth agreed to pay a modified price that was higher than that agreed to the previous November but still lower than the book prices Sharon was charging other customers. Because Roth was unable to purchase enough steel elsewhere to meet its production requirements, it agreed to pay the increased prices. When a subsequent dispute arose between the parties over late deliveries and unfilled orders by Sharon in 1974, Roth filed a breach of contract suit against Sharon, arguing, among other things, that the 1973 modification agreement was unenforceable. When the trial court ruled in favor of Roth, Sharon appealed.

Source: 705 F.2d 134 (6th Cir. 1983)

Celebrezze, Senior Circuit Judge

The ability of a party to modify a contract which is subject to Article Two of the UCC is broader than common law, primarily because the modification needs no consideration to be binding. [UCC Sec. 2-209(1)]. A party's ability to modify an agreement is limited only by Article Two's general obligation of good faith. In determining whether a particular modification was obtained in good faith, a court must make two distinct inquiries: whether the party's conduct is consistent with "reasonable commercial standards of fair dealing in the trade," and whether the parties were in fact motivated to seek modification by an honest desire to compensate for commercial exigencies.

The first inquiry is relatively straightforward; the party asserting the modification must demonstrate that his decision to seek modification was the result of a factor, such as increased costs, which would cause an ordinary merchant to seek a modification of the contract. The second inquiry, regarding the subjective honesty of the parties, is less clearly defined. Essentially, this requires the party asserting the modification to demonstrate that he was, in fact, motivated by a legitimate commercial reason and that such a reason is not offered merely as a pretext. Moreover, the trier of fact must determine whether the means used to obtain the modification are an impermissible attempt to obtain a modification by extortion or overreaching.

The single most important consideration in determining whether the decision to seek a modification is justified is whether, because of changes in the market or other unforeseeable conditions, performance of the contract has come to involve a loss. In this case, the district court found that Sharon suffered substantial losses by performing the contract as modified. We are convinced that unforeseen economic exigencies existed which would prompt an ordinary merchant to seek a modification to avoid a loss on the contract.

The second part of the analysis, honesty in fact, is pivotal. The district court found that Sharon "threatened not to sell Roth any steel if Roth refused to pay increased prices after July 1, 1973" and, consequently, that Sharon acted wrongfully. We believe that the district court's conclusion that Sharon acted in bad faith by using coercive conduct to extract the price modification is not clearly erroneous. Therefore, we hold that Sharon's attempt to modify the November 1972 contract, in order to compensate for increased costs which made performance come to involve a loss, is ineffective because Sharon did not act in a manner consistent with Article Two's requirement of honesty in fact when it refused to perform its remaining obligations under the contract at 1972 prices.
Judgment affirmed in favor of Roth.

Debt Settlement Agreements

One special variant of the preexisting duty rule that causes considerable confusion occurs when a debtor offers to pay a creditor a sum less than the creditor is demanding in exchange for the creditor's promise to accept the part payment as full payment of the debt. If the creditor later sues for the balance of the debt, is the creditor's promise to take less enforceable? The answer depends on the nature of the debt and on the circumstances of the debtor's payment.

Liquidated Debts

A **liquidated debt** is a debt that is both due and certain; that is, the parties have no good faith dispute about either the existence or the amount of the original debt. If a debtor does nothing more than pay less than an amount he clearly owes, how could this be consideration for a creditor's promise to take less? Such a debtor has actually done less than he had a preexisting legal duty to do—namely, to pay the full amount of the debt. For this reason, the creditor's promise to discharge a liquidated debt for part payment of the debt at or after its due date is *unenforceable* for lack of consideration.

For example, Connor borrows $10,000 from Friendly Finance Company, payable in one year. On the day payment is due, Connor sends Friendly a check for $9,000 marked: "Payment in full for all claims Friendly Finance has against me." Friendly cashes Connor's check, thus impliedly promising to accept it as full payment by cashing it, and later sues Connor for $1,000. Friendly is entitled to the $1,000 because Connor has given no consideration to support Friendly's implied promise to accept $9,000 as full payment.

However, had Connor done something he had no preexisting duty to do in exchange for Friendly's promise to settle for part payment, he could enforce Friendly's promise and avoid paying the $1,000. For example, if Connor had paid early, before the loan contract called for payment, or in a different medium of exchange than that called for in the loan contract (such as $4,000 in cash and a car worth $5,000), he would have given consideration for Friendly's promise to accept early or different payment as full payment.

Unliquidated Debts

A good faith dispute about either the existence or the amount of a debt makes the debt an **unliquidated debt**. The settlement of an unliquidated debt is called an **accord and satisfaction**.[6] When an accord and satisfaction has occurred, the creditor cannot maintain an action to recover the remainder of the debt that he alleges is due. For example, Computer Corner, a retailer, orders 50 personal computers and associated software packages from Computech for $75,000. After receiving the goods, Computer Corner refuses to pay Computech the full $75,000, arguing that some of the computers were defective and that some of the software it received did not conform to its order. Computer Corner sends Computech a check for $60,000 marked: "Payment in full for all goods received from Computech." A creditor in Computech's position obviously faces a real dilemma. If Computech cashes Computer Corner's check, it will be held to have impliedly promised to accept $60,000 as full payment. Computech's promise to accept part payment as full payment would be enforceable because Computer Corner has given consideration to support it: Computer Corner has given up its right to have a court determine the amount it owes Computech. This is something that Computer Corner had no duty to do; by giving up this right and the $60,000 in exchange for Computech's implied promise, the consideration requirement is satisfied. The result in this case is supported not only by consideration theory but also by a strong public policy in favor of encouraging parties to settle their disputes out of court. Who would bother to settle disputed claims out of court if settlement agreements were unenforceable?

Computech could refuse to accept Computer Corner's settlement offer and sue for the full $75,000, but doing so involves several risks. A court may decide that Computer Corner's arguments are valid and award Computech less than $60,000. Even if Computech is successful, it may take years to resolve the case in the courts through the expensive and time-consuming litigation process. In addition, there is always the chance that Computer Corner may file for bankruptcy before any judgment can be collected. Faced with such risks, Computech may feel that it has no practical alternative other than to cash Computer Corner's check.[7]

UCC Section 1-207 and Accord and Satisfaction

In some states, a creditor such as Computech has a third, and much more desirable, alternative course of action to either returning the debtor's full payment check or cashing it and entering an accord and satisfaction. The original version of section 1-207 of the UCC states that:

> A party who with explicit reservation of rights assents to performance in a manner offered by the other party does not thereby prejudice the rights reserved. Such words as "without prejudice," "under protest" or the like are sufficient.

Some state courts have interpreted this language to mean that the Code has changed the common law accord and satisfaction rule by allowing a creditor to accept a full-payment check "under protest" or "without prejudice" without giving up any rights to sue for the balance due under the contract. However, the majority of courts that have considered the issue have held that 1-207 does not supersede accord and satisfaction rules. In addition, a recent revision of 1-207 that has been enacted in a growing number of states specifically provides that 1-207 does not apply to accord and satisfaction.

Composition Agreements

Composition agreements are agreements between a debtor and two or more creditors who agree to accept as full payment a stated percentage of their liquidated claims against the debtor at or after the date on which those claims are payable. Composition agreements are generally enforced by the courts despite the fact that enforcement appears to be contrary to the general rule on part payment of liquidated debts. Many courts have justified enforcing composition agreements on the ground that the creditors' mutual agreement to accept less than the amount due them provides the necessary consideration. The main reason why creditors agree to compositions is that they fear that their failure to do so may force the debtor into bankruptcy proceedings, in which case they might ultimately recover a smaller percentage of their claims than that agreed to in the composition.

Forbearance to Sue

An agreement by a promisee to refrain, or forbear, from pursuing a legal claim against a promiser can be valid consideration to support a return promise—usually to pay a sum of money—by a promiser. The promisee has agreed not to file suit, something that she has a legal right to do, in exchange for the promisor's promise. The courts do not wish to sanction extortion by allowing people to threaten to file spurious claims against others in the hope that those threatened will agree to some payment to avoid the expense or embarrassment associated with defending a lawsuit. On the other hand, we have a strong public policy favoring private settlement of disputes. Therefore, it is generally said that the promisee must have a good faith belief in the validity of his or her claim before forbearance amounts to consideration.

Bargained-for Exchange

Up to this point, we have focused on the legal value component of our consideration definition. But the fact that a promisee's act or promise provides legal value is not, in itself, a sufficient basis for finding that it amounted to consideration. In addition, the promisee's act or promise must have been bargained for and given in exchange for the promisor's promise. In effect, it must be the price that the promiser asked for in exchange for making his promise. Over a hundred years ago, Oliver Wendell Holmes, one of our most renowned jurists, expressed this idea when he said, "It is the essence of a consideration that, by the terms of the agreement, it is given and accepted as the motive or inducement of the promise."[8]

Past Consideration

Past consideration—despite its name—is not consideration at all. Past consideration is an act or other benefit given in the past that was not given in exchange for the promise in question. Because the past act was not given in exchange for the present promise, it cannot be consideration. Consider again the facts of the famous case of *Hamer v. Sidway*, discussed earlier in this chapter. There, an uncle's promise to pay his nephew $5,000 for refraining from smoking, drinking, swearing, and other delightful pastimes until his 21st birthday was supported by consideration because the nephew had given legal value by refraining from participating in the prohibited activities. However, what if the uncle had said to his nephew on the eve of his 21st birthday: "Your mother tells me you've been a good lad and abstained from tobacco, hard drink, foul language, and gambling. Such goodness should be rewarded. Tomorrow, I'll give you a check for $5,000." Should the uncle's promise be enforceable against him? Clearly not, because although his nephew's behavior still passes the legal value test, in this case it was not bargained for and given in exchange for the uncle's promise.

Moral Obligation

As a general rule, promises made to satisfy a preexisting moral obligation are unenforceable for lack of consideration. The fact that a promiser or some member of the promisor's family, for example, has received some benefit from the promisee in the past (e.g., food and lodging, or emergency care) would not constitute consideration for a promisor's promise to pay for that benefit, due to the absence of the bargain element. Some courts find this result distressing and enforce such promises despite the absence of consideration. In addition, a few states have passed statutes making promises to pay for past benefits enforceable if such a promise is contained in a writing that clearly expresses the promisor's intent to be bound.

Concept Review
Consideration

Consideration*	Not Consideration
Doing something you had no preexisting duty to do	Doing something you had a preexisting duty to do
Promising to do something you had no preexisting duty to do	Promising to do something you had a preexisting duty to do
Paying part of a liquidated debt prior to the date the debt is due	Nominal consideration (unless actually bargained for)
Paying a liquidated debt in a different medium of exchange than originally agreed to	Paying part of a liquidated debt at or after the date the debt is due
Agreeing to settle an unliquidated debt	Making an illusory promise
Agreeing not to file suit when you have a good faith belief in your claim's validity	Past consideration

*Assuming bargained for.

Exceptions to the Consideration Requirement

The consideration requirement is a classic example of a traditional contract law rule. It is precise, abstract, and capable of almost mechanical application. It can also, in some instances, result in significant injustice. Modern courts and legislatures have responded to this potential for injustice by carving out numerous exceptions to the requirement of consideration. Some of these exceptions (for example, the Code firm offer and contract modification rules) have already been discussed in this and preceding chapters. In the remaining portion of this chapter, we focus on several other important exceptions to the consideration requirement.

Promissory Estoppel

As discussed in Chapter 14, Introduction to Contracts, the doctrine of promissory estoppel first emerged from attempts by courts around the turn of this century to reach just results in donative (gift) promise cases. Classical contract consideration principles did not recognize a promisee's reliance on a donative promise as a sufficient basis for enforcing the promise against the promiser. Instead, donative promises were unenforceable because they were not supported by consideration. In fact, the essence of a donative promise is that it does not seek or require any bargained-for-exchange. Yet people continued to act in reliance on donative promises, often to their considerable disadvantage.

Refer to the facts of *Thorne v. Deas*, discussed earlier in this chapter. The co-owners of the *Sea Nymph* clearly relied to their injury on their fellow co-owner's promise to get insurance for the ship. Some courts in the early years of this century began to protect such relying promisees by *estopping* promisers from raising the defense that their promises were not supported by consideration. In a wide variety of cases involving gratuitous agency promises (as in *Thorne v. Deas*), promises of bonuses or pensions made to employees, and promises of gifts of land, courts began to use a promisee's detrimental (harmful) reliance on a donative promise as, in effect, a substitute for consideration.

In 1932, the first *Restatement of Contracts* legitimized these cases by expressly recognizing promissory estoppel in section 90. The elements of promissory estoppel were then essentially the same as they are today: a *promise* that the promiser should reasonably expect to induce reliance, *reliance* on the promise by the promisee, and *injustice* to the promisee as a result of that reliance. As the following *Niehaus* case illustrates, promissory estoppel is now widely used as a consideration substitute, not only in donative promise cases but also in cases involving commercial promises contemplating a bargained-for exchange. In fact, although promissory estoppel has expanded far beyond its initial role as a consideration substitute into other areas of contract law, it is probably fair to say that it is still most widely accepted in the consideration context.

Niehaus v. Delaware Valley Medical Center

Patricia Niehaus was an employee of Delaware Valley Medical Center. The medical center distributed an employee handbook that stated that if an employee were granted an approved leave of absence, that employee, at the end of the leave, would be guaranteed the same position or one similar to the position occupied prior to the leave of absence. The handbook also stated, however, that the provisions in the handbook were not to be interpreted as a contract of employment and that either party could terminate the employment relationship at any time. Niehaus made a written request for a nine months' leave, and her request was approved. At the end of her leave, however, Delaware Valley refused to rehire Niehaus for any position. Niehaus sued the medical center for breach of contract and promissory estoppel, and the trial court dismissed her complaint. Niehaus appealed.

Source: 631 A.2d 1314 (Super. Ct. Pa. 1993)

Wicand, Judge

The presumption under Pennsylvania law is that all employment is at will and, therefore, an employee may be discharged for any reason or no reason. The medical center contends in this case that because Niehaus was an employee at will, she could be terminated for any reason or no reason, and that it would be absurd to require a rehiring of Niehaus when she could thereafter be discharged immediately. In any event, suggests the employer, there was no consideration for an agreement to rehire Niehaus following an approved leave of absence. It is argued, therefore, that the provision in the handbook is unenforceable.

In the instant case, whether or not there was consideration, the employer's promise is enforceable under principles of promissory estoppel. "A promise which the promiser should expect to induce action or forbearance on the part of the promisee or a third person and which does induce such action or forbearance is binding if injustice can be avoided only by enforcement of the promise." *Restatement (Second) of Contracts* section 90(1). Where an employer expects, if not demands, that its employees abide by a policy expressed with particularity in an employee handbook, an employee may justifiably rely thereon and expect justifiably that the employer will do the same.

Here, the medical center, by its handbook, had guaranteed its employees that if a leave of absence were requested and approved by the employer, then the employee could return at the end of the leave of absence and would be restored to the same or similar position as that occupied by the employee prior to the leave of absence. Under this policy, the employer had a right to expect a stable work force, where employees would take leave of absence only with the employer's consent and approval. An employee who was granted an approved leave of absence, however, could also rely upon the employer's promise that the employee would be rehired. The employer's promise was not illusory. When the employee was induced in fact to seek and obtain an approved leave of absence without pay on the assurance that she could return to the same or similar employment at the expiration of her leave, enforcement of the promise was essential to avoid injustice.

The medical center argues, however, that a cause of action for breach of contract of employment cannot be based on the provisions of the handbook where other language disclaims an intent to form a contract. In this case, Niehaus was initially employed at will. When the employee requested a leave of absence without pay, the employer could have refused to approve it or, indeed, could have revoked its promise of renewed employment at the end of the leave of absence. This it did not do. Instead, it approved the leave of absence in accordance with its handbook promise. It is this approval which thereupon gave rise to an implied contract and not the mere language in the handbook.

We conclude that the trial court erred when it summarily dismissed Niehaus's amended complaint. The complaint is sufficient to allege a cause of action for breach of a contract to rehire.

Reversed in favor of Niehaus and remanded for further proceedings.

Debts Barred by Statutes of Limitations

Statutes of limitations set an express statutory time limit on a person's ability to pursue any legal claim. A creditor who fails to file suit to collect a debt within the time prescribed by the appropriate statute of limitations loses the right to collect it. Many states, however, enforce a new promise by a debtor to pay such a debt, even though technically such promises are not supported by consideration because the creditor has given nothing in exchange for the new promise. Most states afford debtors some protection in such cases, however, by requiring that the new promise be in writing to be enforceable.

Debts Barred by Bankruptcy Discharge

Once a bankrupt debtor is granted a discharge, creditors no longer have the legal right to collect discharged debts. Most states enforce a new promise by the debtor to pay (reaffirm) the debt regardless of whether the creditor has given any consideration to support it. To reduce creditor attempts to pressure debtors to reaffirm, the Bankruptcy Reform Act of 1978 made it much more difficult for debtors to reaffirm debts discharged in bankruptcy proceedings. The act requires that a reaffirmation promise be made prior to the date of the discharge and gives the debtor the right to revoke his promise within 30 days after it becomes enforceable. This act also requires the Bankruptcy Court to counsel individual (as opposed to corporate) debtors about the legal effects of reaffirmation and requires Bankruptcy Court approval of reaffirmations by individual debtors. In addition, a few states require reaffirmation promises to be in writing to be enforceable.

Charitable Subscriptions

Promises to make gifts for charitable or educational purposes are often enforced, despite the absence of consideration, when the institution or organization to which the promise was made has acted in reliance on the promised gift. This result is usually justified on the basis of either promissory estoppel or public policy.

Ethical and Public Concerns

1. In this chapter, you learned the general rule that the law does not enforce promises that are not supported by consideration. Are there ethical arguments that one could make to support the proposition that people should generally honor their promises to others regardless of whether they are legally required to do so? What might those arguments be? Do any of them help to explain the doctrine of promissory estoppel as an exception to the consideration requirement?
2. Discuss the public policy behind the rule that courts will not inquire into the adequacy of consideration. What social benefits are purchased by such a rule and at what price?
3. Discuss the ethical dimensions of offers by debtors to satisfy a liquidated debt by part payment before the due date. Are such offers ever ethical? What factors would be relevant in determining whether such an offer was ethical?

Problems and Problem Cases

1. Grouse, a recently graduated pharmacist who was working as a retail pharmacist for Richter Drug, applied for a job with Group Health Plan, Inc. Grouse was interviewed at Group Health by Elliott, chief pharmacist, and Shoberg, general manager. On December 4, 1975, Elliott telephoned Grouse at work and offered him a job as a pharmacist at Group Health's St. Louis Park Clinic. Grouse accepted, informing Elliott that he would give Richter two weeks' notice. That afternoon, Grouse received an offer from a Veterans Administration Hospital in Virginia, which he declined because of Group Health's offer. Elliott called back to confirm that Grouse had resigned. Sometime in the next few days, Elliott mentioned to Shoberg that he had hired, or was thinking of hiring, Grouse. Shoberg told him that company hiring requirements included a favorable written reference, a background check, and approval of the general manager. Elliott contacted two faculty members at the University of

Minnesota School of Pharmacy, who declined to give references. He also contacted an internship employer and several pharmacies where Grouse had done relief work. Their responses were that they had not had enough exposure to Grouse's work to form a judgment about his capabilities. Because Elliott was unable to supply a favorable reference for Grouse, Shoberg hired another person to fill the position. On December 15, 1975, Grouse called Group Health and reported that he was free to begin work. Elliott informed Grouse that someone else had been hired. Grouse had difficulty regaining full-time employment and suffered wage loss as a result. Does he have any recourse against Group Health?

2.   Omni Group, Inc., signed an earnest money agreement offering Mr. and Mrs. John Clark $2,000 per acre for a piece of property the Clarks owned, which was thought to contain about 59 acres. The agreement provided that Omni's obligation was subject to receipt of a satisfactory engineer's and architect's feasibility report assessing the property's development potential. The Clarks signed the earnest money agreement, but later refused to proceed with the sale. When Omni filed suit for breach of contract, the Clarks argued that their promise to sell was unenforceable because Omni's promise to buy was illusory due to the fact that it was conditioned on a satisfactory feasibility report. Was Omni's promise illusory?

3.   When Nancy and Gerald Harrington were divorced in 1981, they executed a property settlement agreement giving him ownership of their farm. In return, he agreed to pay her $150,000; a $10,000 down payment and 15 annual payments. He gave her two mortgages on the farm to secure the debt. Gerald paid Nancy the initial $10,000, but was able to pay her only $3,000 in subsequent payments due to financial difficulties. Late in 1981, Gerald asked Nancy to execute satisfactions of the two mortgages so he could obtain refinancing of previous bank loans, which lenders were unwilling to provide as long as the farm was encumbered by the mortgages she held. At that time Nancy and Gerald's son, Ronn, was farming the land with Gerald. Nancy was afraid that Ronn would not inherit the farm because Gerald had remarried and his wife had become pregnant. In exchange for Gerald's promise to will the farm to Ronn, Nancy promised to execute satisfactions of the mortgages and to release Gerald from liability on his debt to her under their original agreement. Gerald subsequently made a will leaving his land to Ronn, but Nancy did not execute satisfactions of the mortgages. Instead, in 1983, she filed a foreclosure suit against Gerald. She asserted that her promise to execute satisfactions of the mortgages was unenforceable for lack of consideration. Is she correct?

4.   In November 1981, C. F. Wooding Co. (Wooding) ordered a number of metal doors and door frames from County Fire Door Corporation (County) for a construction project Wooding was working on. After County was allegedly late in delivering the goods to the work site, Wooding told County that it would only pay $416.88 of the $2,618.88 that County claimed was the balance due because the delays in delivery caused Wooding additional installation expenses. County denied the validity of Wooding's claim and insisted that the full amount was due. Wooding then sent County a check for $416.88. On its face was a notation stating that it was final payment for the project, and on its reverse side the check stated: "By its endorsement, the payee accepts this check in full satisfaction of all claims against the C. F. Wooding Co. arising out of or relating to Purchase Order #3302, dated 11/17/81." County cashed the check, but only after crossing out the conditional language on the reverse side and adding the following language: "This check is accepted under protest and with full reservation of rights to collect the unpaid balance for which this check is

offered in settlement." County filed suit against Wooding for the unpaid balance. In a state that follows the majority view about the effect of UCC section 1-207 on the common law doctrine of accord and satisfaction, can County prevail?

5. Roland and Leslie lived together for four years and had a child together. In June 1983, Roland filed suit to evict Leslie from his house in Duxbury, Massachusetts, and to obtain custody of their child. Leslie then filed a breach of contract action against Roland arguing that she had a right to a share of the property. In September 1983, Leslie and Roland agreed to settle both actions. She and his child were to return to live with him and he was to support them. Roland also promised to pay her legal fees from both actions. Roland and Leslie later separated again, and he refused to pay her legal fees, arguing that his promise was not supported by consideration because Massachusetts does not recognize "palimony" actions by unmarried cohabitants. Is Roland right?

6. Mama Balin, who had suffered two automobile accidents in 1972, hired Norman Kallen, an attorney, to represent her. Kallen did not do much work on the cases and urged Balin to settle for $25,000. She became dissatisfied with his representation, and in 1974 she asked Samuel Delug, another attorney, to take over the cases and get her files from Kallen. Delug wrote and called Kallen several times, but Kallen refused to forward the files or sign a Substitution of Attorney form (things he was obligated to do by the California rules of professional conduct) because he was afraid Balin would not pay him for the work he had done. Only when Delug promised to give him 40 percent of his attorney's fee did Kallen forward the files and sign the form. Delug negotiated a settlement of $810,000, and the attorney's fees amounted to $324,000. When he refused to pay Kallen 40 percent, Kallen filed suit. Is Delug's promise enforceable?

7. The Larabees owned a farm in Dearborn County, Indiana, subject to a life estate held by Mrs. Larabee's mother. In the autumn 1971, the Larabees gave their friends, the Booths, permission to build a summer cottage on the farm. Construction began in the spring of 1972. Shortly thereafter, the Booths asked if they could build a permanent home there, and Mrs. Larabee agreed. In September 1972, she and her husband signed an agreement promising to convey a piece of the farm to the Booths on the expiration of Mrs. Larabee's mother's life estate. The agreement specifically provided that the land was to be conveyed for "no consideration." When the house was completed and Mrs. Larabee's mother had died, however, the Larabees refused to convey the land as promised. Is their promise to convey enforceable?

8. Passander was executive vice president of Spickelmier Industries. Because Spickelmier was facing financial difficulties, a committee of creditors had been formed to oversee its operations. In November 1971, the committee projected a small profit for the year and recommended that bonuses be given to certain key employees if the profit materialized. This recommendation was adopted by Spickelmier's board of directors in late December, and Passander was promised a $1,500 bonus. In January 1972, however, the board's executive committee discovered that the earlier profit estimates had been overly optimistic and that insufficient funds were available to pay the bonuses. Instead of taking the board's recommendation that the bonuses not be paid, the chairman of the board negotiated a compromise whereby one half of the originally specified bonus would be paid as planned, with the balance to be paid when funds were available. Passander accepted the half bonus, and later in the month his contract with Spickelmier was renegotiated to provide for a 25 percent salary increase and guaranteed quarterly bonuses of $500. In June 1972, Passander quit his job, later filing suit against Spickelmier for the remaining half of his 1971 bonus. Can he recover it?

9. Kaufmann was employed by Fiduciary Management, Inc. (FMI). In September 1988, Lanier, president and sole shareholder of FMI, signed and gave a letter to Kaufmann, which stated in part:

   > If your employment is terminated without cause before July 1, 1990, Fiduciary Management, Inc. agrees that within one month of the date on which your full salary ceases to be paid you will receive an additional payment of $150,000.

   The context of this letter was that several projects serviced by FMI were experiencing financial difficulties and Lanier's sons advised him that Kaufmann was distracted, that he may have been considering leaving FMI, and that he needed to focus on his work. The letter was intended to help him focus on his work, presumably by giving him a sense of job security. After receiving the letter, Kaufmann undertook a secret and systematic search for another job. In January 1990, Kaufmann's employment with FMI ceased. He was not paid the $150,000 that had been promised in the letter, and he sued Lanier and FMI to recover the money. Was Lanier's promise to pay $150,000 enforceable?

10. Jensen offered Judy, a resident of Chicago, a position in a company in Los Angeles. Jensen gave Judy an employee handbook, extolled the low turnover of his firm's work force, and told her that there was a "no-cut policy." Jensen told Judy that if she decided to relocate within a year, the job was hers. After deciding to accept the job, Judy called Jensen and informed him. She also told him that she did not know how long it would take to sell her house in Chicago, but Jensen told her to give him a call as soon as she arrived in Los Angeles and said, "We're really looking forward to having you on board." Six months later, Judy and her husband quit their jobs, sold their house in Chicago, and moved to Los Angeles. When Judy called Jensen, however, he said that the position they had discussed was not available and the company had no openings. Was the company's promise to hire Judy enforceable?

11. Tinker Construction had a contract with Scroge to build a factory addition for Scroge by a particular date. The contract contained a penalty clause exacting daily penalties for late performance, and Tinker was working hard to complete the building on time. Because prompt completion of the addition was so important to Scroge, however, Scroge offered Tinker a bonus if it completed the factory addition on time. Scroge also learned that the supplier of parts for machinery that he had contracted for had called and said that it could not deliver the parts on Scroge's schedule for the price it had agreed to. Because there was no other supplier, Scroge promised to pay the requested higher price. The factory addition was completed on time and the parts arrived on time. Scroge then refused to pay both the bonus to Tinker and the higher price for the parts. Were these promises enforceable?

See also "The Stock Option" and "A Bedtime Story."

Endnotes

1.   T. Metcalf, *Principles of the Law of Contracts* (1874), p. 161.
2.   4 Johns. 84 (N.Y. 1809).
3.   27 N.E. 256 (N.Y. Ct. App. 1891).
4.   Fraud and duress are discussed in Chapter 19.
5.   Lack of capacity is discussed in Chapter 18.
6.   Accord and satisfaction is also discussed in Chapter 17.
7.   A new provision of Article 3 of the Uniform Commercial Code, section 3-311, covers accord and satisfaction by use of an instrument such as a "full payment," check. With a few exceptions, the basic provisions of section 3-311 parallel the common law rules regarding accord and satisfaction that are described in this chapter and Chapter 17.
8.   O. W. Holmes, *The Common Law*, p. 239 (1881).

Chapter Eighteen

CAPACITY TO

CONTRACT

Introduction

One of the major justifications for enforcing a contract is that the parties *voluntarily consented* to be bound by it. It follows, then, that a person must have the ability to give consent before he can be legally bound to an agreement. For truly voluntary agreements to exist, this ability to give consent must involve more than the mere physical ability to say yes or shake hands or sign one's name. Rather, the person's maturity and mental ability must be such that it is fair to presume that he is capable of representing his own interests effectively. This concept is embodied in the legal term *capacity*.

Lack of Capacity

Capacity means the ability to incur legal obligations and acquire legal rights. Today, the primary classes of people who are considered to lack capacity are minors (who, in legal terms, are known as *infants*), persons suffering from mental illnesses or defects, and intoxicated persons.[1] Contract law gives them the right to *avoid* (escape) contracts that they enter during incapacity. This rule provides a means of protecting people who, because of mental impairment, intoxication, or youth and inexperience, are disadvantaged in the normal give and take of the bargaining process.

Usually, lack of capacity to contract comes up in court in one of two ways. In some cases, it is asserted by a plaintiff as the basis of a lawsuit for the money or other benefits that he gave the other party under their contract. In others, it arises as a defense to the enforcement of a contract when the defendant is the party who lacked capacity. The responsibility for alleging and proving incapacity is placed on the person who bases his claim or defense on his lack of capacity.

Effect of Lack of Capacity

Normally, a contract in which one or both parties lacks capacity because of infancy, mental impairment, or intoxication is considered to be voidable. People whose capacity is impaired in any of these ways are able to enter a contract and enforce it if they wish, but they also have the right to avoid the contract. There are, however, some individuals whose capacity is so impaired that they do not have the ability to form even a voidable contract. A bargain is considered to be void if, at the time of formation of the bargain, a court had already **adjudicated** (adjudged or decreed) one or more of the parties to be mentally incompetent or one or more of the parties was so impaired that he could not even manifest assent (for example, he was comatose or unconscious).

Minors' Contracts

Minors' Right to Disaffirm

Courts have long recognized that minors are in a vulnerable position in their dealings with adults. Courts granted minors the right to avoid contracts as a means of protecting against their own improvidence and against overreaching by adults. The exercise of this right to avoid a contract is called **disaffirmance**. The right to disaffirm is personal to the minor. That is, only the minor or a legal representative such as a guardian may disaffirm the contract. No formal act or written statement is required to make a valid disaffirmance. Any words or acts that effectively communicate the minor's desire to cancel the contract can constitute disaffirmance.

If, on the other hand, the minor wishes to enforce the contract instead of disaffirming it, the adult party must perform. You can see that the minor's right to disaffirm puts any adult contracting with a minor in an undesirable position: He is bound on the contract unless it is to the minor's advantage to disaffirm it. The right to disaffirm has the effect of discouraging adults from dealing with minors.

Exceptions to the Minor's Right to Disaffirm

Not every contract involving a minor is voidable, however. State law often creates statutory exceptions to the minor's right to disaffirm. These statutes prevent minors from disaffirming such transactions as marriage, agreements to support their children, educational loans, life and medical insurance contracts, contracts for transportation by common carriers, and certain types of contracts approved by a court (such as contracts to employ a child actor).

Period of Minority

At common law, the age of majority was 21. However, the ratification in 1971 of the 26th Amendment to the Constitution giving 18-year-olds the right to vote stimulated a trend toward reducing the age of majority. The age of majority has been lowered by 49 states. In almost all of these states, the age of majority for contracting purposes is now 18.

Emancipation

Emancipation is the termination of a parent's right to control a child and receive services and wages from him. There are no formal requirements for emancipation. It can occur by the parent's express or implied consent or by the occurrence of some events such as the marriage of the child. In most states, the mere fact that a minor is emancipated does *not* give him capacity to contract. A person younger than the legal age of majority is generally held to lack capacity to enter a contract, even if he is married and employed full time.

Time of Disaffirmance

Contracts entered during minority that affect title to *real estate* cannot be disaffirmed until majority. This rule is apparently based on the special importance of real estate and on the need to protect a minor from improvidently disaffirming a transaction (such as a mortgage or conveyance) involving real estate. All other contracts entered during minority may be disaffirmed as soon as the contract is formed. The minor's power to avoid his contracts does not end on the day he reaches the age of majority. It continues for a period of time after he reaches majority.

How long after reaching majority does a person retain the right to disaffirm the contracts he made while a minor? A few states have statutes that prescribe a definite time limit on the power of avoidance. In Oklahoma, for example, a person who wishes to disaffirm a contract must do so within one year after reaching majority.[2] In most states, however, there is no set limit on the time during which a person may disaffirm after reaching majority. In determining whether a person has the right to disaffirm, a major factor that courts consider is whether the adult has rendered performance under the contract or relied on the contract. If the adult has relied on the contract or has given something of value to the minor, the minor must disaffirm within a reasonable time after reaching majority. If he delays longer than a period of time that is considered to be reasonable under the circumstances, he will run the risk of *ratifying* (affirming) the contract. (The concept and consequences of ratification are discussed in the next section.) If the adult has neither performed nor relied on the contract, however, the former minor is likely to be accorded a longer period of time in which to disaffirm, sometimes even years after he has reached majority.

Ratification

Though a person has the right to disaffirm contracts made during minority, this right can be given up after the person reaches the age of majority. When a person who has reached majority indicates that he intends to be bound by a contract that he made while still a minor, he surrenders his right to disaffirm. This act of affirming the contract and surrendering the right to avoid the contract is known as **ratification**. Ratification makes a contract valid from its inception. Because ratification represents the former minor's election to be bound by the contract, he cannot later disaffirm. Ratification can be done effectively only after the minor reaches majority. Otherwise, it would be as voidable as the initial contract. The effect of ratification is illustrated in Figure 18-1.

FIGURE 18-1
Time line showing
effect of ratification

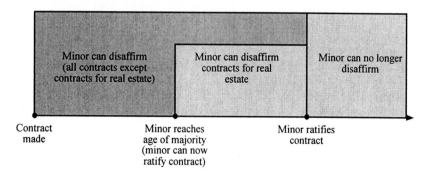

| Contract made | Minor reaches age of majority (minor can now ratify contract) | Minor ratifies contract |

There are no formal requirements for ratification. Any of the former minor's words or acts after reaching majority that indicate with reasonable clarity his intent to be bound by the contract are sufficient. Ratification can be *expressed* in an oral or written statement, or, as is more often the case, it can be *implied* by conduct on the part of the former minor. Naturally, ratification is clearest when the former minor has made some express statement of his intent to be bound. Predicting whether a court will determine that a contract has been ratified is a bit more difficult when the only evidence of the alleged ratification is the conduct of the minor. A former minor's acceptance or retention of benefits given by the other party for an unreasonable time after he has reached majority can constitute ratification. Also, a former minor's continued performance of his part of the contract after reaching majority has been held to imply his intent to ratify the contract.

Duty to Return Consideration upon Disaffirmance

If neither party has performed his part of the contract, the parties' relationship will simply be canceled by the disaffirmance. Since neither party has given anything to the other party, no further adjustments are necessary. But what about the situation where, as is often the case, the minor has paid money to the adult and the adult has given property to the minor? Upon disaffirmance, each party has the duty to return to the other any consideration that the other has given. This means that the minor must return any consideration given to him by the adult that remains in his possession. However, if the minor is unable to return the consideration, most states will still permit him to disaffirm the contract.

The duty to return consideration also means that the minor has the right to recover any consideration he has given to the adult party. He even has the right to recover some property that has been transferred to third parties. One exception to the minor's right to recover property from third parties is found in section 2-403 of the Uniform Commercial Code, however. Under this section, a minor cannot recover *goods* that have been transferred to a good faith purchaser. For example, Simpson, a minor, sells a 1980 Ford to Mort's Car Lot. Mort's then sells the car to Vane, a good faith purchaser. If Simpson disaffirmed the contract with Mort's, he would *not* have the right to recover the Ford from Vane.

Must the Disaffirming Minor Make Restitution?
A Split of Authority

If the consideration given by the adult party has been lost, damaged, destroyed, or simply has depreciated in value, is the minor required to make restitution to the adult for the loss? The traditional rule is that the minor who cannot fully return the consideration that was given to her is *not* obligated to pay the adult for the benefits she has received or to compensate the adult for loss or depreciation of the consideration. Some states still follow this traditional rule. (As you will read in the next section, however, a minor's misrepresentation of age can, even in some of these states, make her responsible for reimbursing the other party upon disaffirmance). The rule that restitution is not required is designed to protect minors by discouraging adults from dealing with them. After all, if an adult knew that he might be able to demand the return of anything that he transferred to a minor, he would have little incentive to refrain from entering into contracts with minors.

The traditional rule, however, can work harsh results for innocent adults who have dealt fairly with minors. It strikes many people as unprincipled that a doctrine intended to protect against unfair exploitation of one class of people can be used to unfairly exploit another class of people. As courts sometimes say, the minor's right to disaffirm was designed to be used as a "shield rather than as a sword." For these reasons, a growing number of states have rejected the traditional rule. The courts and legislatures of these states have adopted rules that require minors who disaffirm their contracts and seek refunds of purchase price to reimburse adults for the use or depreciation of their property. The following case, *Dodson v. Shrader*, follows this approach.

Dodson v. Shrader

Joseph Dodson, age 16, bought a 1984 Chevrolet truck from Burns and Mary Shrader, owners of Shrader's Auto Sales, for $4,900 cash. At the time, Burns Shrader, believing Dodson to be 18 or 19, did not ask Dodson's age, and Dodson did not volunteer it. Dodson drove the truck for about eight months, when he learned from an auto mechanic that there was a burned valve in the engine. Dodson did not have the money for the repairs, so he continued to drive the truck without repair for another month until the engine "blew up" and stopped operating. He parked the car in the front yard of his parents' house. He then contacted the Shraders, rescinding the purchase of the truck and requesting a full refund. The Shraders refused to accept the truck or to give Dodson a refund. Dodson then filed an action seeking to rescind the contract and recover the amount paid for the truck. Before the court could hear the case, a hit-and-run driver struck Dodson's parked truck, damaging its left front fender. At the time of the circuit court trial, the truck was worth only $500. The Shraders argued that Dodson should be responsible for paying the difference between the present value of the truck and the $4,900 purchase price. The trial court found in Dodson's favor, ordering the Shraders to refund the $4,900 purchase price upon delivery of the truck. The Tennessee Court of Appeals affirmed this judgment, and the Shraders appealed.

Source: 824 S.W.2d 545 (Tenn. Sup. Ct. 1992)

O'Brien, Justice

The law on the subject of the protection of infants' rights has been slow to evolve. The underlying purpose of the "infancy doctrine" is to protect minors from their lack of judgment and from squandering their wealth through improvident contracts with crafty adults who would take advantage of them in the marketplace.

There is, however, a modern trend among the states, either by judicial action or by statute, in the approach to the problem of balancing the rights of minors against those of innocent merchants. As a result, two minority rules have developed which allow the other party to a contract with a minor to refund less than the full consideration paid in the event of rescission. The first of these minority rules is called the "Benefit Rule." This rule holds that, upon rescission, recovery of the full purchase price is subject to a deduction for the minor's use of the merchandise. This rule recognizes that the traditional rule in regard to necessaries has been extended so far as to hold an infant bound by his contracts, where he failed to restore what he has received under them to the extent of the benefit actually derived by him from what he has received from the other party to the transaction. The other minority rule holds that the minor's recovery of the full purchase price is subject to a deduction for the minor's "use" of the consideration he or she received under the contract, or for the "depreciation" or "deterioration" of the consideration in his or her possession.

We are impressed by the statement made by the Court of Appeals of Ohio:

> At a time when we see young persons between 18 and 21 years of age demanding and assuming more responsibilities in their daily lives; when we see such persons charged with the responsibility for committing crimes; when we see such persons being sued in tort claims for acts of negligence; when we see such persons subject to military service; when we see such persons engaged in business and acting in almost all other respects as an adult, it seems timely to re-examine the case law pertaining to contractual rights and responsibilities of infants to see if the law as pronounced and applied by the courts should be redefined.

We state the rule to be followed hereafter, in reference to a contract of a minor, to be where the minor has not been overreached in any way, and there has been no undue influence, and the contract is a fair and reasonable one, and the minor has actually paid money on the purchase price, and taken and used the article purchased, that he ought not to be permitted to recover the amount actually paid, without allowing the vendor of the goods reasonable compensation for the use of, depreciation, and willful or negligent damage to the article purchased, while in his hands. If there has been any fraud or imposition on the part of the seller or if the contract is unfair, or any unfair advantage has been taken of the minor inducing him to make the purchase, then the rule does not apply. This rule will fully and fairly protect the minor against injustice or imposition, and at the same time it will be fair to a business person who has dealt with such minor in good faith.

This rule is best adapted to modern conditions under which minors are permitted to, and do in fact, transact a great deal of business for themselves, long before they have reached the age of legal majority. Many young people work and earn money and collect it and spend it oftentimes without any oversight or restriction. The law does not question their right to buy if they have the money to pay for their purchases. It seems intolerably burdensome of everyone concerned if merchants cannot deal with them safely, in a fair and reasonable way. Further, it does not appear consistent with practice of proper moral influence upon young people, tend to encourage honesty and integrity, or lead them to a good and useful business future if they are taught that they can make purchases with their own money, for their own benefit, and after paying for them, and using them until they are worn out and destroyed, go back and compel the vendor to return to them what they have paid upon the purchase price. Such a doctrine can only lead to the corruption of principles and encourage young people in habits of trickery and dishonesty.
Reversed and remanded in favor of the Shraders.

Effect of Misrepresentation of Age

It is not unheard of for a minor to occasionally pretend to be older than he is. The normal rules dealing with the minor's right to disaffirm and his duties upon disaffirmance can be affected by a minor's misrepresentation of his age.[3] Suppose, for example, that Jones, age 17, wants to lease a car from Acme Auto Rentals, but knows that Acme rents only to people who are at least 18. Jones induces Acme to lease a car to him by showing a false identification that represents his age to be 18. Acme relies on the misrepresentation. Jones wrecks the car, attempts to disaffirm the contract, and asks for the return of his money. What is the effect of Jones's misrepresentation? State law is not uniform on this point.

The traditional rule was that a minor's misrepresentation about his age did not affect his right to disaffirm and did not create any obligation to reimburse the adult for damages or pay for benefits received. The theory behind this rule is that one who lacks capacity cannot acquire it merely by claiming to be of legal age. As you can imagine, this traditional approach does not "sit well" with modern courts, at least in those cases in which the adult has dealt with the minor fairly and in good faith, because it creates severe hardship for innocent adults who have relied on minors' misrepresentations of age.

State law today is fairly evenly divided among those states that take the position that the minor who misrepresents his age will be estopped (prevented) from asserting his infancy as a defense and those that will allow a minor to disaffirm regardless of his misrepresentation of age. Among the states that allow disaffirmance despite the minor's misrepresentation, most hold the disaffirming minor responsible for the losses suffered by the adult, either by allowing the adult to counterclaim against the minor for the tort of deceit or by requiring the minor to reimburse the adult for use or depreciation of his property.

Minors' Obligation to Pay Reasonable Value of Necessaries

Though the law regarding minors' contracts is designed to discourage adults from dealing with (and possibly taking advantage of) minors, it would be undesirable for the law to discourage adults from selling minors the items that they need for basic survival. For this reason, disaffirming minors are required to pay the reasonable value of items that have been furnished to them that are classified as **necessaries**. A necessary is something that is essential for the minor's continued existence and general welfare that has not been provided by the minor's parents or guardian. Examples of necessaries include food, clothing, shelter, medical care, tools of the minor's trade, and basic educational or vocational training.

A minor's liability for necessaries supplied to him is **quasi contractual**. That is, the minor is liable for the *reasonable value* of the necessaries that she actually receives. She is not liable for the entire price agreed on if that price exceeds the actual value of the necessaries, and she is not liable for necessaries that she contracted for but did not receive. For example, Joy Jones, a minor, signs a one-year lease for an apartment in Mountain Park at a rent of $300 per month. After living in the apartment for three months, Joy breaks her lease and moves out. Because she is a minor, Joy has the right to disaffirm the lease. If shelter is a necessary in this case, however, she must pay the reasonable value of what she has actually received—three months' rent. If she can establish that the actual value of what she has received is less than $300 per month, she will be bound to pay only that lesser amount. Furthermore, she will not be obligated to pay for the remaining nine months' rent, because she has not received any benefits from the remainder of the lease.

Whether a given item is considered a necessary depends on the facts of a particular case. The minor's age, station in life, and personal circumstances are all relevant to this issue. As is emphasized in the *Webster Street Partnership* case, which follows, an item sold to a minor is not considered a necessary if the minor's parent or guardian has already supplied him with similar items. For this reason, the range of items that will be considered necessaries is broader for married minors and other emancipated minors than it is for unemancipated minors.

Webster Street Partnership v. Sheridan

Webster Street owns real estate in Omaha, Nebraska. On September 18, 1982, Webster Street entered into a written contract to lease an apartment to Matthew Sheridan and Pat Wilwerding for one year at a rental of $250 per month. Although Webster Street did not know this, both Sheridan and Wilwerding were younger than the age of majority (which was 19) when the lease was signed.

Sheridan and Wilwerding paid $150 as a security deposit and rent for the remainder of September and the month of October, for a total of $500. They failed to pay their November rent on time, however, and Webster Street notified them that they would be required to move out unless they paid immediately. Unable to pay rent, Sheridan and Wilwerding moved out of the apartment on November 12. Webster Street later demanded that they pay the expenses it incurred in attempting to rerent the property, rent for the months of November and December (apparently the two months it took to find a new tenant), and assorted damages and fees, amounting to $630.94. Sheridan and Wilwerding refused to pay any of the amount demanded on the ground of minority, and demanded the return of their security deposit. Webster Street then filed this lawsuit. The district court found that the apartment was a necessary and that Sheridan and Wilwerding were liable for the 12 days in November in which they had actually possessed the apartment without paying rent, but that they were entitled to the return of their security deposit. Webster Street appealed from this ruling.

Source: 368 N.W.2d 439 (S. Ct. Neb. 1985)

Krivosha, Chief Justice

The privilege of infancy will not enable an infant to escape liability under all circumstances. For example, it is well established that an infant is liable for the value of necessaries furnished him. Just what are necessaries, however, has no exact definition. The term is flexible and varies according to the facts of each individual case. A number of factors must be considered before a court can conclude whether a particular product or service is a necessary. The articles must be useful and suitable. To be necessaries, the articles must supply the infant's personal needs, either those of his body or those of his mind. However, the term "necessaries" is not confined to merely such things as are required for bare subsistence. What may be considered necessary for one infant may not be necessaries for another infant whose state is different as to rank, social position, fortune, health, or other circumstances. To enable an infant to contract for articles as necessaries, he must have been in actual need of them, and obliged to procure them for himself. They are not necessaries as to him, however necessary they may be in their nature, if he was already supplied with sufficient articles of the kind, or if he had a parent or guardian who was able and willing to supply them. The burden of proof is on the plaintiff to show that the infant was destitute of the articles and had no way of procuring them except by his own contract.

The undisputed testimony is that both tenants were living away from home, apparently with the understanding that they could return home at any time. It would appear that neither Sheridan nor Wilwerding was in need of shelter but, rather, had chosen to voluntarily leave home, with the understanding that they could return whenever they desired. One may at first blush believe that such a rule is unfair. Yet, on further consideration, the wisdom of such a rule is apparent. If landlords may not contract with minors, except at their peril, they may refuse to do so. In that event, minors who voluntarily leave home but who are free to return will be compelled to return to their parents' home—a result which is desirable. We therefore hold that the district court erred in finding that the apartment was a necessary.

Because the rental of the apartment was not a necessary, the minors had the right to avoid the contract, either during their minority or within a reasonable time after reaching their majority. Disaffirmance by an infant completely puts an end to the contract's existence both as to him and as to the adult with whom he contracted. Because the parties then stand as if no contract had ever existed, the infant can recover payments made to the adult, and the adult is entitled to the return of whatever was received by the infant.

The record shows that Wilwerding clearly disaffirmed the contract during his minority. Moreover, when Webster Street ordered the minors out for failure to pay rent and they vacated the premises, Sheridan likewise disaffirmed the contract. The record indicates that Sheridan reached majority on November 5. To suggest that a lapse of 7 days was not disaffirmance within a reasonable time would be foolish. Once disaffirmed, no contract existed between the parties and the minors were entitled to recover all of the moneys which they paid and to be relieved of any further obligation under the contract. The judgment of the district court is therefore reversed and the cause remanded with directions to vacate the judgment in favor of Webster Street and to enter a judgment in favor of Matthew Sheridan and Pat Wilwerding in the amount of $500, representing September rent in the amount of $100, October rent in the amount of $250, and the security deposit in the amount of $150. **Judgment reversed in favor of Sheridan and Wilwerding.**

Capacity of Mentally Impaired Persons

Theory of Incapacity

Like minors, people who suffer from a mental illness or defect are at a disadvantage in their ability to protect their own interests in the bargaining process. Contract law makes their contracts either void or voidable to protect them from the results of their own impaired perceptions and judgment and from others who might take advantage of them.

Test for Mental Incapacity

Incapacity on grounds of mental illness or defect, which is often referred to in cases and texts as "insanity," encompasses a broad range of causes of impaired mental functioning, such as mental illness, brain damage, mental retardation, or senility. The mere fact that a person suffers from some mental illness or defect does not necessarily mean that he lacks capacity to contract, however. He could still have full capacity unless the defect or illness affects the particular transaction in question.

The usual test for mental incapacity is a *cognitive* one; that is, courts ask whether the person had sufficient mental capacity to understand the nature and effect of the contract. Some courts have criticized the traditional test as unscientific because it does not take into account the fact that a person suffering from a mental illness or defect might be unable to *control* his conduct. Section 15 of the *Restatement (Second) of Contracts* provides that a person's contracts are voidable if he is unable to *act* in a reasonable manner in relation to the transaction and the other party has reason to know of his condition. Where the other party has reason to know of the condition of the mentally impaired person, the *Restatement (Second)* standard would provide protection to people who understood the transaction but, because of some mental defect or illness, were unable to exercise appropriate judgment or to control their conduct effectively. This standard is employed by the court in the following case, *Farnum v. Silvano.*

Farnum v. Silvano

Viola Farnum was 90 years old when she sold her real estate in South Yarmouth to Joseph Silvano, age 24. Farnum knew and trusted Silvano because he had done mowing and landscape work on her property. Although the fair market value of Farnum's property was $115,000 at the time of the sale, she agreed to sell it as well as the furniture and other furnishings in the house for $64,900. Silvano had reason to know of the inadequacy of the purchase price. Farnum's nephew had warned Silvano not to proceed with the sale. In addition, Silvano was able to get a mortgage for $65,000 from the bank to finance the purchase.

Farnum's mental competence had begun to fail seriously three years before the sale to Silvano. She began to engage in aberrant conduct such as lamenting not hearing from her sisters, who were dead, and she would wonder where the people upstairs in her house had gone, when there was no upstairs to her house. She offered to sell her house to a neighbor for $35,000. She became abnormally forgetful, locking herself out of her house and breaking into it rather than calling on a neighbor with whom she had left a key. She hid her cat to protect it from "the cops." She would express the desire to return to Cape Cod although she was on Cape Cod. She easily became lost. Her sister and nephew

had to pay her bills and balance her checkbook. She was hospitalized several times during the three-year period preceding the sale to Silvano. Medical tests revealed organic brain disease.

During the transaction in question, Farnum was represented by a lawyer selected and paid by Silvano. That lawyer and a lawyer for the bank that was making a loan to Silvano attended the closing at Farnum's house. At the closing, Farnum was cheerful, engaged in pleasantries, and made instant coffee for those present. After the transaction, however, Farnum insisted to others, including her sister and nephew, that she still owned the property. Six months after the conveyance, Farnum was admitted to the hospital for treatment of dementia and seizure disorder. She was discharged to a nursing home.

Farnum's nephew, who was ultimately appointed her guardian, brought this suit on Farnum's behalf to rescind the sale on the ground of Farnum's mental impairment. The trial judge concluded that Farnum had been "aware of what was going on," and denied the rescission. Farnum appealed.

Source: 540 N.E.2nd 202 (App. Ct. of Mass. 1989)

Kass, Judge

On the basis of a finding that Farnum enjoyed a lucid interval when she conveyed her house to Silvano, for approximately half its market value, a Probate Court judge decided that Farnum had capacity to execute the deed. A different test measures competence to enter into a contract and we, therefore, reverse the judgment.

Competence to enter into a contract presupposes something more than a transient surge of lucidity. It involves not merely comprehension of what is "going on," but an ability to comprehend the nature and quality of the transaction, together with an understanding of its significance and consequences. In the act of entering into a contract there are reciprocal obligations, and it is appropriate, when mental incapacity, as here, is manifest, to require a baseline of reasonableness.

In *Krasner v. Berk*, the court cited with approval the synthesis of those principles now appearing in the *Restatement (Second) of Contracts* section 15(1), which regards as voidable a transaction entered into with a person who, "by reason of mental illness or defect (a) . . . is unable to understand in a reasonable manner the nature and consequences of the transaction, or (b) . . . is unable to act in a reasonable manner in relation to the transaction and the other party has reason to know of [the] condition."

Applied to the case at hand, Farnum could be aware that she was selling her house to Silvano for much less than it was worth, while failing to understand the unreasonableness of doing so at a time when she faced serious cash demands for rent, home care, or nursing care charges. That difference between awareness of the surface of a transaction, i.e., that it was happening, and failure to comprehend the unreasonableness and consequences of the transaction by a mentally impaired person was recognized and discussed in *Ortolere v. Teachers' Retirement Bd.* In the Ortolere case, a teacher who was enrolled in a retirement plan suffered a psychotic break. Her age was sixty, and she also suffered from cerebral arteriosclerosis. While thus afflicted, Grace Ortolere changed her selection of benefit to choose the maximum retirement allowance during her lifetime with nothing payable after her death—this in the face of severely diminished life expectancy and her husband having given up his employment to care for her full time. The court observed that her selection was so unwise and foolhardy that a fact finder might conclude that it was explainable only as a product of psychosis.

We think Farnum did not possess the requisite contextual understanding. She suffered mental disease which had manifested itself in erratic and irrational conduct and was confirmed by diagnostic test. Her physician did not think she was competent to live alone. Relatively soon after the transaction, Farnum's mental deficits grew so grave that it became necessary to hospitalize her. The man to whom she sold her property for less than its value was not a member of her family or someone who had cared for her for long duration. Farnum was not represented by a lawyer who knew her and considered her overall interests as a primary concern. The mission of the lawyer secured by Silvano, and paid by him, was to effect the transaction. As we have observed, Farnum was faced with growing cash demands for her maintenance, and, in her circumstances, it was not rational to part with a major asset for a cut-rate price.

The decisive factor which we think makes Farnum's delivery of her deed to Silvano voidable was his awareness of Farnum's inability to act in a reasonable manner. Silvano knew or had reason to know of Farnum's impaired condition from her conduct, which at the times material caused concern to her relatives, her neighbors, and her physician. Silvano was aware that he was buying the house for about half its value. He had been specifically warned by Farnum's nephew about the unfairness of the transaction and Farnum's mental disability.

Farnum is entitled to rescission of the conveyance.

Judgment reversed in favor of Farnum.

The Effect of Incapacity Caused by Mental Impairment

The contracts of people who are suffering from a mental defect at the time of contracting are usually considered to be *voidable*. In some situations, however, severe mental or physical impairment may prevent a person from even being able to manifest consent. In such a ease, no contract could be formed.

As mentioned at the beginning of this chapter, contract law makes a distinction between a contract involving a person who has been *adjudicated* (judged by a court) incompetent at the time the contract was made and a contract involving a person who was suffering from some mental impairment at the time the contract was entered but whose incompetency was not established until *after* the contract was formed. If a person is under guardianship at the time the contract is formed—that is, if a court has found a person mentally incompetent after holding a hearing on his mental competency and has appointed a guardian for him—the contract is considered *void*. On the other hand, if *after* a contract has been formed, a court finds that the person who manifested consent lacked capacity on grounds of mental illness or defect, the contract is usually considered *voidable* at the election of the party who lacked capacity (or his guardian or personal representative).

The Right to Disaffirm

If a contract is found to be voidable on the ground of mental impairment, the person who lacked capacity at the time the contract was made has the right to disaffirm the contract. A person formerly incapacitated by mental impairment can ratify a contract if he regains his capacity. Thus, if he regains capacity, he must disaffirm the contract unequivocally within a reasonable time, or he will be deemed to have ratified it.

As is true of a disaffirming minor, a person disaffirming on the ground of mental impairment must return any consideration given by the other party that remains in his possession. A person under this type of mental incapacity is liable for the reasonable value of necessaries in the same manner as are minors. Must the incapacitated party reimburse the other party for loss, damage, or depreciation of non-necessaries given to him? This is generally said to depend on whether the contract was basically fair and on whether the other party had reason to be aware of his impairment. If the contract is fair, bargained for in good faith, and the other party had no reasonable cause to know of the incapacity, the contract cannot be disaffirmed unless the other party is placed in *status quo* (the position she was in before the creation of the contract). However, if the other party had reason to know of the incapacity, the incapacitated party is allowed to disaffirm without placing the other party in status quo. This distinction discourages people from attempting to take advantage of mentally impaired people, but it spares those who are dealing in good faith and have no such intent.

Contracts of Intoxicated Persons

Intoxication and Capacity

Intoxication (either from alcohol or the use of drugs) can deprive a person of capacity to contract. The mere fact that a party to a contract had been drinking when the contract was formed would *not* normally affect his capacity to contract, however. Intoxication is a ground for lack of capacity only when it is so extreme that the person is unable to understand the nature of the business at hand. Section 16 of the *Restatement (Second) of Contracts* further provides that intoxication is a ground for lack of capacity only if the *other party has reason to know* that the affected person is so intoxicated that he cannot understand or act reasonably in relation to the transaction.

The rules governing the capacity of intoxicated persons are very similar to those applied to the capacity of people who are mentally impaired. The basic right to disaffirm contracts made during incapacity, the duties upon disaffirmance, and the possibility of ratification upon regaining capacity are the same for an intoxicated person as for a person under a mental impairment. In practice, however, courts traditionally have been less sympathetic with a person who was intoxicated at the time of contracting than with minors or those suffering from a mental impairment. It is rare for a person to actually escape his contractual obligations on the ground of intoxication. A person incapacitated by intoxication at the time of contracting might nevertheless be bound to his contract if he fails to disaffirm in a timely manner.

Ethical and Public Policy Concerns

1. You read that the age of majority for contracting purposes is 18 in almost all states today. We all know that maturity at a given age varies greatly from individual to individual. Does it make sense for the law to *presume* that a person is sufficiently mature to be responsible for his agreements merely because he has reached the age of 18? Would public policy be better served if the maturity of contracting parties were determined on a case-by-case basis in the same way that we now determine the capacity of those who are mentally impaired or intoxicated? Why or why not?
2. In *Dodson v. Shrader*, the court rejected the traditional view that minors who no longer have the consideration in their possession can disaffirm their contracts without reimbursing the adult party for use or depreciation of the adult's property. Which rule, the traditional rule or the rule applied in *Dodson*, makes the most sense? Was Judge O'Brien correct in his remark that the traditional rule is inconsistent with "proper moral influence upon young people?" Discuss.
3. In recent years, there has been growing public concern over alcohol and drug abuse. Through legal developments such as vigorous enforcement of drunken driving laws and the imposition of tort liability on the part of alcohol suppliers, the law encourages moderation in the use of alcohol. Yet, the law also makes it possible for a person who is so intoxicated that he does not appreciate the business at hand to escape his contractual obligations. Is this rule about the capacity of intoxicated persons out of step with sound public policy?

Problems and Problem Cases

1. Smith, age 17, purchased a car from Bobby Floars Toyota, signing an agreement to pay the balance of the purchase price in 30 monthly installments. Ten months after he reached majority (which was 18 in that state), Smith voluntarily returned the car to Floars and stopped making payments. At this point, he had made 11 monthly payments, 10 of which were made after his 18th birthday. Floars sold the car at public auction and sued Smith for the remaining debt. Will Smith be required to pay?
2. Robertson, while a minor, contracted to borrow money from his father for a college education. His father mortgaged his home and took out loans against his life insurance policies to get some of the money he lent to Robertson, who ultimately graduated from dental school. Two years after Robertson's graduation, his father asked him to begin paying back the amount of $30,000 at $400 per month. Robertson agreed to pay $24,000 at $100 per month. He did this for three years before stopping the payments. His father sued for the balance of the debt. Could Robertson disaffirm the contract?

3. Green, age 16, contracted to buy a Camaro from Star Chevrolet. Green lived about six miles from school and one mile from his job, and used the Camaro to go back and forth to school and work. When he did not have the car, he used a car pool to get to school and work. Several months later, the car became inoperable due to a blown head gasket, and Green gave notice of disaffirmance to Star Chevrolet. Star Chevrolet refused to refund the purchase price, claiming, in part, that the car was a necessary. Was it?

4. Clardy had suffered from a manic depressive condition for 15 years, for which he took medication. On April 1, 1989, Clardy first spoke to Shoals Ford about the purchase of a truck and filled out the initial papers. On that same day, while visiting his daughter, he had become agitated and out of control, throwing his medicine into a burning pile of leaves. On April 3, he signed the necessary documents, but was advised that, because of a poor credit rating, a down payment of $10,500 would be required rather than the $5,000 down payment that had been previously discussed. Early in the morning of April 5, Clardy banged on the doors and windows of his daughter's household until he awakened everyone there. He threatened their lives and forced his daughter to write him a check for $500. After Clardy left, his daughter went to her attorney's office and asked that he prepare a petition to have Clardy involuntarily committed. She then called Shoals Ford to notify it that Clardy would be coming in to purchase a particular truck and to tell it of his condition. Clardy's wife also spoke with Shoals Ford's sales representatives and told them that Clardy was not working, that he was ill and would be committed, that "buying sprees" were a symptom of his disease, and that the truck could not be insured. She asked them not to sell the truck to him. Shoals Ford's representative merely stated that if Clardy had the money to buy the truck it was "none of her concern." That same day, Clardy returned to Shoals Ford with the down payment and picked up the truck. Clardy was admitted to the hospital later that night. The psychiatrist who saw him the next day found him to be incompetent and testified that he could not visualize Clardy being otherwise on April 5. A month later, his wife was appointed conservator and guardian for him. She brought an action to set aside the purchase on the ground of lack of capacity and recover the money that Clardy had paid Shoals Ford. Will she win?

5. At a time when the age of majority in Ohio was 21, Lee, age 20, contracted to buy a 1964 Plymouth Fury for $1,552 from Haydocy Pontiac. Lee represented herself to be 21 when entering the contract. She paid for the car by trading in another car worth $150 and financing the balance. Immediately following delivery of the car to her, Lee permitted one John Roberts to take possession of it. Roberts delivered the car to someone else, and it was never recovered. Lee failed to make payments on the car, and Haydocy Pontiac sued her to recover the car or the amount due on the contract. Lee repudiated the contract on the ground that she was a minor at the time of purchase. Can Lee disaffirm the contract without reimbursing Haydocy Pontiac for the value of the car?

6. In 1955, the Probate Court of Franklin County adjudged Beard to be mentally incompetent and appointed a guardian for him. Thereafter, in 1978, a successor guardian was appointed for Beard. On February 22, 1989, while still under guardianship, Beard executed a promissory note for $10,254.60 to Huntington National Bank in order to finance the purchase of a 1987 Nissan pickup truck. The flexible interest rate for the note was to be paid over a five-year period, with monthly installments of $170.91. Beard made only a few payments on the note before dying on July 31, 1989. In the four- or five-year period prior to his death, Beard had several dealings with the bank, including the financing of two other truck purchases. He had maintained a sparkling credit rating, fully repaying his previous loans. Toland was

appointed administrator of Beard's estate. When she learned of the outstanding debt to the bank, she returned the car to the bank. The bank sold it and sought to have the estate pay the outstanding debt left after crediting the proceeds of the car and Beard's payments. Toland rejected the bank's claim, contending that the promissory note was invalid because of Beard's lack of capacity. Is she right?

7. Randy Hyland owed money to the First State Bank of Sinai on two promissory notes that had already become due. The bank agreed to extend the time of payment if Randy's father, Mervin, acted as a cosigner. Mervin had executed approximately 60 promissory notes with the bank and was a good customer. A new note was prepared for Mervin's signature. Buck, the bank employee with whom Randy dealt, knew that Mervin drank, but later testified that he was unaware of any alcohol-related problems. Mervin had been drinking heavily from late summer through the early winter of 1981. During this period, his wife and son managed the farm, and Mervin was weak, unconcerned with family and business matters, uncooperative, and uncommunicative. When he was drinking, he spent most of his time at home, in bed. He was involuntarily committed to hospitals twice during this period. He was released from his first commitment on September 19 and again committed on November 20. Between the periods of his commitments, he did transact some business himself, such as paying for farm goods and services, hauling his grain to storage elevators, and making decisions concerning when grain was to be sold. When Randy brought this note home, Mervin was drunk and in bed. On October 20 or 21, he rose from the bed, walked into the kitchen, and signed the note. Later, Randy returned to the bank with the note, which Mervin had properly signed, and added his own signature. The due date on this note was April 20, 1982. On April 20, the note was unpaid. Buck notified Randy of the overdue note, and on May 5, Randy brought to the bank a blank check signed by Mervin with which the interest on the note was to be paid. Randy filled in the check for the amount of interest owing. No further payments were made on the note, and Randy filed for bankruptcy in June 1982. After unsuccessfully demanding the note's payment from Mervin, the bank ultimately filed suit against Mervin. Mervin asserted incapacity on the ground of intoxication, claiming that he had no recollection of seeing the note, discussing it with his son, or signing it. Can Mervin now avoid the contract?

8. In 1984, when Kavovit was 12 years old, he and his parents entered into a contract with Scott Eden Management whereby Scott Eden became the exclusive personal manager to supervise and promote Kavovit's career in the entertainment industry. This agreement ran from February 8, 1984 to February 8, 1986, with an extension for another three years. It entitled Scott Eden to receive a 15 percent commission on Kavovit's gross compensation. It specifically provided that, with respect to contracts entered by Kavovit during the term of the agreement, Scott Eden was entitled to its "commission from the residuals or royalties of such contracts, the full term of such contracts, including all extensions or renewals thereof, notwithstanding earlier termination of this agreement." In 1986, Kavovit signed an agency contract with the Andreadis Agency, a licensed agent selected by Scott Eden pursuant to industry requirements. Thereafter, Kavovit signed several contracts for his services. The most important contract secured a role for him on "As the World Turns." Income from this contract began in 1987 and continued through 1990 with a possibility of renewal. In February 1989, one week before Kavovit's contract with Scott Eden was to expire, Kavovit's attorney notified Scott Eden that Kavovit was disaffirming the contract on the ground of infancy. Scott Eden sued Kavovit to recover its commissions for Kavovit's performances prior to the date of disaffirmance and its commissions on Kavovit's contracts in the entertainment or promotion fields that were executed during

the term of the agreement between Scott Eden and Kavovit. Must Kavovit pay these commissions even though he disaffirmed the contract?

9. A boy bought an Ernie Banks rookie card for $12 from an inexperienced clerk in a baseball card store owned by Johnson. The card had been marked "1200," and Johnson, who had been away from the store at the time of the sale, had intended the card to be sold for $1,200, not $12. Can Johnson get the card back by asserting the boy's lack of capacity?

Endnotes

1. In times past, married women, convicts, and aliens were also among the classes of persons who lacked capacity to contract. These limitations on capacity have been removed by statute and court rule, however.
2. Okla. Stat. Ann. tit. 15 sec. 18 (1983).
3. You might want to refer back to Chapter 19 to review the elements of misrepresentation.

Chapter Nineteen

REALITY OF

CONSENT

Introduction

In a complex economy that depends on planning for the future, it is crucial that the law can be counted on to enforce contracts. In some situations, however, there are compelling reasons for permitting people to escape or avoid their contracts. An agreement obtained by force, trickery, unfair persuasion, or error is not the product of mutual and voluntary consent. A person who has made an agreement under these circumstances will be able to avoid it, because his consent was not *real*.

This chapter discusses five doctrines that permit people to avoid their contracts because of the absence of real consent: misrepresentation, fraud, mistake, duress, and undue influence. Doctrines that involve similar considerations will be discussed in Chapter 18, Capacity to Contract.

Effect of Doctrines Discussed in this Chapter

Contracts induced by misrepresentation, fraud, duress, mistake, or undue influence are generally considered to be **voidable**. This means that the person whose consent was not real has the power to **rescind** (cancel) the contract. A person who rescinds a contract is entitled to the return of anything he gave the other party. By the same token, he must offer to return anything he has received from the other party.

Necessity for Prompt and Unequivocal Rescission

Suppose Johnson, who recently bought a car from Sims Motors, learns that Sims Motors made fraudulent statements to her to induce her to buy the car . She believes the contract was induced by fraud and wants to rescind it. How does she act to protect her rights? To rescind a contract based on fraud or any of the other doctrines discussed in this chapter, she must act promptly and unequivocally. She must object promptly upon learning the facts that give her the right to rescind and must clearly express her intent to cancel the contract. She must also avoid any behavior that would suggest that she affirms or **ratifies** the contract. (Ratification of a voidable contract means that a person who had the right to rescind has elected not to do so. Ratification ends the right to rescind.) This means that she should avoid unreasonable delay in notifying the other party of her rescission, because unreasonable delay communicates that she has ratified the contract. She should also avoid any conduct that would send a "mixed message," such as continuing to accept benefits from the other party or behaving in any other way that is inconsistent with her expressed intent to rescind.

Misrepresentation and Fraud

Nature of Misrepresentation

A misrepresentation is an assertion that is not in accord with the truth. When a person enters a contract because of his justifiable reliance on a misrepresentation about some important fact, the contract is voidable.

It is not necessary that the misrepresentation be intentionally deceptive. Misrepresentations can be either *innocent* (not intentionally deceptive) or *fraudulent* (made with knowledge of falsity and intent to deceive). A contract may be voidable even if the person making the misrepresentation believes in good faith that what he says is true. Either innocent misrepresentation or fraud gives the complaining party the right to rescind a contract.

Nature of Fraud

Fraud is the type of misrepresentation that is committed knowingly, with the intent to deceive. The legal term for this knowledge of falsity, which distinguishes fraud from innocent misrepresentation, is **scienter**. A person making a misrepresentation would be considered to do so "knowingly" if she knew that her statement was false, if she knew that she did not have a basis for making the statement, or even if she just made the statement without being confident that it was true. The intent to deceive can be inferred from the fact that the defendant knowingly made a misstatement of fact to a person who was likely to rely on it.

As is true for innocent misrepresentation, the contract remedy for fraudulent misrepresentation is rescission. The tort liability of a person who commits fraud is different from that of a person who commits innocent misrepresentation, however. A person who commits fraud may be liable for damages, possibly including punitive damages, for the tort of **deceit**.[1] As you will learn in following sections, innocent misrepresentation and fraud share a common core of elements.

Election of Remedies

In some states, a person injured by fraud cannot rescind the contract and sue for damages for deceit; he must elect (choose) between these remedies. In other states, however, an injured party may pursue both rescission and damage remedies and does not have to elect between them.[2]

Requirements for Rescission on the Ground of Misrepresentation

The fact that one of the parties has made an untrue assertion does not in itself make the contract voidable. Courts do not want to permit people who have exercised poor business judgment or poor common sense to avoid their contractual obligations, nor do they want to grant rescission of a contract when there have been only minor and unintentional misstatements of relatively unimportant details. A drastic remedy such as rescission should be used only when a person has been seriously misled about a fact important to the contract by someone he had the right to rely on. A person seeking to rescind a contract on the ground of innocent or fraudulent misrepresentation must be able to establish each of the following elements:

1   An untrue assertion of fact was made.
2.   The fact asserted was material or the assertion was fraudulent.
3.   The complaining party entered the contract because of his reliance on the assertion.
4.   The reliance of the complaining party was reasonable.

In tort actions in which the plaintiff is seeking to recover damages for deceit, the plaintiff would have to establish *fifth* element: injury. He would have to prove that he had suffered actual economic injury because of his reliance on the fraudulent assertion. In cases in which the injured person seeks only rescission of the contract, however, proof of economic injury is usually not required.

Untrue Assertion of Fact

To have misrepresentation, one of the parties must have made an untrue assertion of fact or engaged in some conduct that is the equivalent of an untrue assertion of fact. The fact asserted must be a *past or existing fact*, as distinguished from a promise or prediction about some future happening.

The **concealment** of a fact through some active conduct intended to prevent the other party from discovering the fact is considered to be the equivalent of an assertion. Like a false statement of fact, concealment can be the basis for a claim of misrepresentation or fraud. For example, if Summers is offering his house for sale and paints the ceilings to conceal the fact that the roof leaks, his active concealment constitutes an assertion of fact. Under some circumstances, **nondisclosure** also can be the equivalent of an assertion of fact. Nondisclosure differs from concealment in that concealment involves the active hiding of a fact, while nondisclosure is the failure to offer information.

Problem Area: Nondisclosure

Suppose you are a prospective home buyer who inspects a house for possible purchase. The seller of the house knows that there is a hidden but serious structural defect in the house that will cost approximately $30,000 to correct, but does not mention this to you. Neither you nor the professional inspector you hire to examine the house for defects observes any evidence of structural defects, and you contract to purchase the house based on your assumption that it is in good condition. You later learn about the existence of this defect. Do you have the right to rescind the contract? The issue raised by this problem is whether the seller's silence about the defect was misrepresentation. In other words, was his nondisclosure the equivalent of an assertion that the structural defect did not exist?

Under traditional contract law, the answer to this question would probably have been no. Under the traditional view of nondisclosure, the circumstances under which the law required disclosure were very limited. (These are the first three circumstances described in the next section.) Mere silence on the part of a contracting party generally did not amount to misrepresentation. One reason for this treatment of nondisclosure was that unlike concealment and outright statements of fact, which are active forms of misconduct, nondisclosure is passive. Fundamentally, though, the traditional view of nondisclosure expressed the highly individualistic philosophy expressed in the well-known phrase *caveat emptor* ("let the buyer beware"): Each contracting party is responsible for taking care of himself and is not his "brother's keeper."

In recent years, however, courts and legislatures have expanded the circumstances under which a person has the duty to take affirmative steps to disclose relevant information. This is consistent with modern contract law's emphasis on influencing ethical standards of conduct and achieving fair results. Some duties of disclosure have been created by statutes, such as the Truth in Lending Act and the federal securities laws, but courts also have been increasingly active in expanding the duty to disclose. In addition to the circumstances in which federal or state statutes would require a contracting party to disclose facts, there are four circumstances in which most courts today require disclosure. In these situations, the person's failure to disclose a fact would be the equivalent of an assertion that the fact did not exist.

1. *Fiduciary relationship.* If a fiduciary relationship (a relationship of trust and confidence) exists between the parties to the contract, a party who knows of an important fact that the other person does not know about would have the duty to disclose it. This makes sense, because a person who has good reason to believe that the other party is looking out for his welfare will not approach the contract with the same degree of vigilance as the person who is dealing at arm's length with a stranger. This sort of duty to disclose would not apply to ordinary contracting parties who are bargaining at arm's length.

2. *Correcting "half-truths."* When a person makes a statement about a situation, he has the duty to disclose any facts that would be necessary to correct a half-truth. For example, Carlson, a car salesperson who is trying to sell a used car, knows that the previous owner of the car used it exclusively for drag racing on Sundays. If Carlson tells a customer that the previous owner of the car "drove it only on Sundays," he would have the legal duty to disclose the additional material fact that the car had been used exclusively for drag racing.

3. *Correcting statements made false by later events.* A person has the duty to disclose information that will be necessary to correct a previous statement that may have been true when made but that has become false because of later events. For example, White, who wants to sell her house, tells a prospective purchaser truthfully that the roof of the house has never leaked. Several days later, the roof leaks after a heavy storm. White has the legal duty to make the disclosure that is necessary to correct her previous statement.

4. *Good faith and fair dealing require disclosure.* In the hypothetical case with which we began this discussion of nondisclosure—the case of the seller who failed to disclose the existence of a hidden structural defect in the house he was selling—the home buyer entered into the contract under the mistaken assumption that the house was free of structural defects. The *Restatement (Second) of Contracts* provides for a duty to disclose that would be applicable in this situation. Under section 161 of the *Restatement (Second)*, a person must disclose facts necessary to correct the other party's mistake about a basic assumption of the contract when nondisclosure amounts to a failure to act in good faith and in accordance with reasonable standards of fair dealing. Most states today apply a duty to disclose along these lines.

Note that this sort of duty to disclose has broader application than the first three circumstances described above because it can apply even when the parties are dealing at arm's length and no partial disclosures have been made. Note also that this duty to disclose is intertwined with concepts of good faith and fair dealing. *The Restatement (Second)* does *not* say that a person who possesses information always has the obligation to educate the other party. Rather, the duty to speak arises only when failing to do so would constitute a failure to behave in a way that is in accord with prevailing concepts of good faith and reasonable standards of dealing. Nondisclosure is most likely to constitute a failure to act reasonably and in good faith when a party has access to information that is not readily available to the other party. In addition, sellers are more likely to be required to disclose information than are buyers.

Transactions involving the sale of real estate are among the most common situations in which this duty to disclose arises. Most states now hold that a seller who knows about a latent (hidden) defect that materially affects the value of the property he is selling has the obligation to speak up about this defect. *Stambovsky v. Ackley*, which follows, involves an interesting application of the duty to disclose in the context of a sale of real estate.

Stambovsky v. Ackley

Jeffrey Stambovsky, a resident of New York City, contracted to purchase a house in the Village of Nyack, New York, from Helen Ackley. The house was widely reputed to be possessed by poltergeists, which Ackley and members of her family had reportedly seen. Ackley did not tell Stambovsky about the poltergeists before he bought the house. When Stambovsky learned of the house's reputation, however, he promptly commenced this action for rescission. The trial court dismissed his complaint, and Stambovsky appealed.

Source: 572 N.Y.S.2d 672 (N.Y. Sup. Ct., App. Div. 1991)

Rubin, Justice

The unusual facts of this case clearly warrant a grant of equitable relief to the buyer who, as a resident of New York City, cannot be expected to have any familiarity with the folklore of the Village of Nyack. Not being a "local," Stambovsky could not readily learn that the home he had contracted to purchase is haunted. Whether the source of the spectral apparitions seen by Ackley are parapsychic or psychogenic, having reported their presence in both a national publication ("Readers' Digest") and the local press (in 1977 and 1982, respectively), Ackley is estopped to deny their existence and, as a matter of law, the house is haunted. More to the point, however, no divination is required to conclude that it is Ackley's promotional efforts in publicizing her close encounters with these spirits which fostered the home's reputation in the community. In 1989, the house was included in a five-home walking tour of Nyack and described in a November 27th newspaper article as a "riverfront Victorian (with ghost)." The impact of the reputation thus created goes to the very essence of the bargain between the parties, greatly impairing both the value of the property and its potential for resale.

[The court discussed the fact that New York law does not recognize a remedy for damages incurred as a result of the seller's mere silence, applying instead the doctrine of caveat emptor. The court then proceeded to discuss the availability of rescission.]

From the perspective of a person in the position of the plaintiff, a very practical problem arises with respect to the discovery of a paranormal phenomenon: "Who you gonna call?" as the title song to the movie "Ghostbusters" asks. Applying the strict rule of caveat emptor to a contract involving a house possessed by poltergeists conjures up visions of a psychic or medium routinely accompanying the structural engineer and Terminix man on an inspection of every home subject to a contract of sale. The doctrine of caveat emptor requires that a buyer act prudently to assess the fitness and value of his purchase. It should be apparent, however, that the most meticulous inspection and the search would not reveal the presence of poltergeists at the premises or unearth the property's ghoulish reputation in the community. Therefore, there is no sound policy reason to deny Stambovsky relief for failing to discover a state of affairs which the most prudent purchaser would not be expected to even contemplate.

Where a condition which has been created by the seller materially impairs the value of the contract and is peculiarly within the knowledge of the seller or unlikely to be discovered by a prudent purchaser exercising due care, nondisclosure constitutes a basis for rescission as a matter of equity. Any other outcome places upon the buyer not merely the obligation to exercise care in his purchase but rather to be omniscient with respect to any fact which may affect the bargain. No practical purpose is served by imposing such a burden upon a purchaser. To the contrary, it encourages predatory business practice and offends the principle that equity will suffer no wrong to be without a remedy.

In the case at bar, Ackley deliberately fostered the public belief that her home was possessed. Having undertaken to inform the public at large, to whom she has no legal relationship, about the supernatural occurrences on her property, she may be said to owe no less a duty to her contract vendee. Application of the remedy of rescission is entirely appropriate to relieve the unwitting purchaser from the consequences of a most unnatural bargain.

Judgment modified in favor of Stambovsky, reinstating his action seeking rescission of the contract.

Problem Area: Statements of Opinion

In holding that only untrue statements of *fact* give a relying person the right to rescind a contract, contract law traditionally has distinguished between assertions of *fact* and assertions of *opinion*. Although it can be difficult to separate fact from opinion, there is an important distinction between a statement that communicates a person's knowledge and a statement that communicates only his uncertain belief about a fact or his personal judgment about such matters as quality or value. The latter sort of statement usually cannot be the basis of a misrepresentation claim because the person to whom such a statement of opinion is made is not justified in relying on it. This is especially true when the statement relates to something about which the parties have relatively equal knowledge and peoples' points of view are likely to differ. In such a case, each party is expected to form his own opinion. A classic example of this sort of statement of opinion is a seller's "puff" (salestalk or general praise of an item being sold), such as "This suit will look terrific on you."

Even when the statement is clearly one of opinion, there are three situations in which the statement of opinion can be the basis of a misrepresentation claim because reliance is justifiable under the circumstances.[3] These include:

1. Relationship of trust and confidence. A person can be justified in relying on a statement of opinion if it is reasonable to do so because of a relationship of trust and confidence between him and the speaker. For example, if Madison, the long-time financial adviser of the elderly Holden, persuades Holden to invest her money in Madison's failing business by telling her that it is a wise investment, Holden would be justified in relying on Madison's statement of opinion.

2. Relying party is unusually susceptible. Reliance on a statement of opinion can be justifiable when the relying party is someone who is particularly susceptible to the particular type of misrepresentation involved. This sort of case would be likely to involve relying parties who are vulnerable to being misled because of some obvious disadvantage such as illiteracy or lack of intelligence or experience.

3. Reliance on person who has superior skill or judgment. Reliance on an assertion of opinion can also be justifiable when the relying party reasonably believes that the person on whose opinion he is relying has superior skill or judgment about the subject matter of the contract. This would apply when the opinion relates to some matter about which superior training or experience is necessary to form the opinion. For example, Buyer, who knows that Salesperson is an experienced auto mechanic, would be justified in relying on Salesperson's statement that a particular used car is "in A-1 condition."

Materiality

If the misrepresentation was innocent, the person seeking to rescind the contract must establish that the fact asserted was **material**. A fact will be considered to be material if it is likely to play a significant role in inducing a reasonable person to enter the contract or if the person asserting the fact knows that the other person is likely to rely on the fact. For example, Rogers, who is trying to sell his car to Ferguson and knows that Ferguson idolizes professional bowlers, tells Ferguson that a professional bowler once rode in the car. Relying on that representation, Ferguson buys the car. Although the fact Rogers asserted might not be important to most people, it would be material here because Rogers knew that his representation would be likely to induce Ferguson to enter the contract.

Even if the fact asserted was not material, the contract may be rescinded if the misrepresentation was *fraudulent*. The rationale for this rule is that a person who fraudulently misrepresents a fact, even one that is not material under the standards previously discussed, should not be able to profit from his intentionally deceptive conduct.

Actual Reliance

Reliance means that a person pursues some course of action because of his faith in an assertion made to him. For misrepresentation to exist, there must have been a causal connection between the assertion and the complaining party's decision to enter the contract. If the complaining party knew that the assertion was false or was not aware that an assertion had been made, there has been no reliance.

Justifiable Reliance

Courts also scrutinize the reasonableness of the behavior of the complaining party by requiring that his reliance be *justifiable*. A person does not act justifiably if he relies on an assertion that is obviously false or not to be taken seriously.

Problem Area: The Relying Party's Failure to Investigate the Accuracy of an Assertion

One problem involving the justifiable reliance element is determining the extent to which the relying party is responsible for investigating the accuracy of the statement on which he relies. Classical contract law held that a person who did not attempt to discover readily discoverable facts was generally not justified in relying on the other party's statements about them. For example, under traditional law, a person would not be entitled to rely on the other party's assertions about facts that are a matter of public record or that could be discovered through a reasonable inspection of available documents or records.

The extent of the responsibility placed on a relying party to conduct an independent investigation has declined in modern contract law, however. For example, section 172 of the *Restatement* states that the complaining party's fault in not knowing or discovering facts before entering the contract does not make his reliance unjustifiable unless the degree of his fault was so extreme as to amount to a failure to act in good faith and in accordance with reasonable standards of fair dealing. Recognizing that the traditional rule operated to encourage misrepresentation, courts in recent years have tended to decrease the responsibility of the relying party and to place a greater degree of accountability on the person who makes the assertion. The case of *Cousineau v. Walker*, which follows, is an excellent example of this trend.

Cousineau v. Walker

Devin and Joan Walker owned property in Eagle River, Alaska. In 1976, they listed the property for sale with a real estate broker. They signed a multiple listing agreement that described the property as having 580 feet of highway frontage and stated, "ENGINEER REPORT SAYS OVER 1 MILLION IN GRAVEL ON PROP." A later listing contract signed with the same broker described the property as having 580 feet of highway frontage, but listed the gravel content as "minimum 80,000 cubic yds of gravel." An appraisal prepared to determine the property's value stated that it did not take any gravel into account but described the ground as "all good gravel base."

Wayne Cousineau, a contractor who was also in the gravel extraction business, became aware of the property when he saw the multiple listing. After visiting the property with his real estate broker and discussing gravel extraction with Mr. Walker, Cousineau offered to purchase the property. He then attempted to determine the lot's road frontage, but was unsuccessful because the property was covered with snow. He was also unsuccessful in obtaining the engineer's report allegedly showing "over

1 million in gravel." Walker admitted at trial that he had never seen a copy of the report, either. Nevertheless, the parties signed and consummated a contract of sale for the purchase price of $385,000. There was no reference to the amount of highway frontage in the purchase agreement.

After the sale was completed; Cousineau began developing the property and removing gravel. Cousineau learned that the description of highway frontage contained in the real estate listing was incorrect when a neighbor threatened to sue him for removing gravel from the neighbor's adjacent lot. A subsequent survey revealed that the highway frontage was 410 feet—not 580 feet, as advertised. At about the same time, the gravel ran out after Cousineau had removed only 6,000 cubic yards.

Cousineau stopped making payments and informed the Walkers of his intention to rescind the contract. Cousineau brought an action against the Walkers, seeking the return of his money. The trial court found for the Walkers, and Cousineau appealed.

Source: 613 P.2d 608 (Alaska Sup. Ct. 1980)

Boochever, Justice

An innocent misrepresentation may be the basis for rescinding a contract. There is no question that the statements made by Walker and his real estate agent in the multiple listing were false.

The bulk of the Walkers' brief is devoted to the argument that Cousineau's unquestioning reliance on Walker and his real estate agent was imprudent and unreasonable. Cousineau failed to obtain and review the engineer's report. He failed to obtain a survey or examine the plat available at the recorder's office. He failed to make calculations that would have revealed the true frontage of the lot. Although the property was covered with snow, the buyer, according to Walker, had ample time to inspect it. The buyer was an experienced businessman who frequently bought and sold real estate. Discrepancies existed in the various property descriptions which should have alerted Cousineau to potential problems. In short, the Walkers urge that the doctrine of *caveat emptor* precludes recovery.

There is a split of authority regarding a buyer's duty to investigate a vendor's fraudulent statements, but the prevailing trend is toward placing a minimal duty on a buyer. The recent draft of the *Restatement of Contracts* allows rescission for an innocent material misrepresentation unless a buyer's fault was so negligent as to amount to "a failure to act in good faith and in accordance with reasonable standards of fair dealing." We conclude that a purchaser of land may rely on material representations made by the seller and is not obligated to ascertain whether such representations are truthful. A buyer of land, relying on an innocent misrepresentation, is barred from recovery only if the buyer's acts in failing to discover defects were wholly irrational, preposterous, or in bad faith.

Although Cousineau's actions may well have exhibited poor judgment for an experienced businessman, they were not so unreasonable or preposterous in view of Walker's description of the property that recovery should be denied.
Judgment reversed in favor of Cousineau.

Concept Review
Misrepresentation and Fraud

	Innocent Misrepresentation	Fraud
Remedy	Rescission	Rescission *and/or* tort action for damages
Elements	1. Untrue assertion of fact (or equivalent)	1 Untrue assertion of fact (or equivalent)
	2. Assertion relates to material fact	2. Assertion made with knowledge of falsity (scienter) and intent to deceive
	3. Actual reliance	3. Actual reliance
	4. Justifiable reliance	4. Justifiable reliance
		5. Economic loss (in a tort action for damages)

Mistake

Nature of Mistake

Anyone who enters a contract does so on the basis of his understanding of the facts that are relevant to the contract. His decision about what he is willing to exchange with the other party is based on this understanding. If the parties are wrong about an important fact, the exchange that they make is likely to be quite different than what they contemplated when they entered the contract, and this difference is due to simple error rather than to any external events such as an increase in market price. For example, Fox contracts to sell to Ward a half-carat stone, which both believe to be a tourmaline, at a price of $65. If they are wrong and the stone is actually a diamond worth at least $2,500, Fox will have suffered an unexpected loss and Ward will have reaped an unexpected gain. The contract would not have been made at a price of $65 if the parties' belief about the nature of the stone had been in accord with the facts. In such cases, the person adversely affected by the mistake can avoid the contract under the doctrine of mistake. The purpose of the doctrine of mistake is to prevent unexpected and unbargained-for losses that result when the parties are mistaken about a fact central to their contract.

What Is a Mistake?

In ordinary conversation, we may use the term *mistake* to mean an error in judgment or an unfortunate act. In contract law, however, a mistake is a *belief* about a fact that is *not in accord with the truth.*[4] The mistake must relate to facts as they exist at the time the contract is created. An erroneous belief or prediction about facts that might occur in the future would not qualify as a mistake.

As in misrepresentation cases, the complaining party in a mistake case enters a contract because of a belief that is at variance with the actual facts. Mistake is unlike misrepresentation, however, in that the erroneous belief is not the result of the other party's untrue statements.

The *Wilkin v. 1st Source Bank* case, which follows, illustrates the concept and effect of mistake in contract law.

Wilkin v. 1st Source Bank

Olga Mestrovic, the widow of internationally known sculptor and artist Ivan Mestrovic, owned a large number of works of art created by her late husband. Mrs. Mestrovic died, leaving a will in which she directed that all the works of art created by her husband were to be sold and the proceeds distributed to surviving members of the Mestrovic family. Mrs. Mestrovic also owned real estate at the time of her death. 1st Source Bank, as the personal representative of Mrs. Mestrovic's estate, entered into a contract to sell this real estate to Terrence and Antoinette Wilkin. The purchase agreement provided that certain personal property on the premises would be sold to the Wilkins, too: specifically, the stove, refrigerator, dishwasher, drapes, curtains, sconces, and French doors in the attic.

After taking possession of the property, the Wilkins complained to the bank that the property was left in a cluttered condition and would require substantial cleaning effort. The trust officer of the bank offered the Wilkins two options: Either the bank would obtain a rubbish removal service to clean the property, or the Wilkins could clean the property and keep any items of personal property they wanted. The Wilkins opted to clean the property themselves. At the time these arrangements were made, neither the bank nor the Wilkins suspected that any works of art remained on the premises.

During the clean-up efforts, the Wilkins found eight drawings apparently created by Ivan Mestrovic. They also found a plaster sculpture of the figure of Christ with three small children. The Wilkins claimed ownership of these works of art by virtue of their agreement with the bank. The probate court ruled that there was no agreement for the purchase of the artwork, and the Wilkins appealed.

Source: 548 N.E.2d 170 (Ind. Ct. App. 1990)

Hoffman, Judge

Mutual assent is a prerequisite to the creation of a contract. Where both parties share a common assumption about a vital fact upon which they based their bargain, and that assumption is false, the transaction may be avoided if because of the mistake a quite different exchange of values occurs from the exchange of values contemplated by the parties. *J. Calarnari & J. Perillo, The Law of Contracts* section 9-26 (1987).

The necessity of mutual assent is illustrated in the classic case of *Sherwood v. Walker* (1887). The owners of a blooded cow indicated to the purchaser that the cow was barren. The purchaser appeared to believe that the cow was barren. Consequently, a bargain was made to sell at a price per pound at which the cow would have brought approximately $80.00. Before delivery, it was discovered that the cow was with calf and that she was, therefore, worth from $750.00 to $1,000.00 The court ruled that the transaction was voidable: "[T]he mistake . . . went to the very nature of the thing. A barren cow is substantially a different creature than a breeding one."

Like the parties in *Sherwood*, the parties in the instant case shared a common presupposition as to the existence of certain facts which proved false. The bank and the Wilkins considered the real estate which the Wilkins had purchased to be cluttered with items of personal property variously characterized as "junk," "stuff," or "trash." Neither party suspected that works of art created by Ivan Mestrovic remained on the premises.

As in *Sherwood*, one party experienced an unexpected, unbargained-for gain while the other experienced an unexpected, unbargained-for loss. Because the bank and the Wilkins did not know that the eight drawings and the plaster sculpture were included in the items of personal property that cluttered the real property, the discovery of those works of art by the Wilkins was unexpected. The resultant gain to the Wilkins and loss to the Bank were not contemplated by the parties when the bank agreed that the Wilkins could clean the premises and keep such personal property as they wished.

The following commentary on *Sherwood* is equally applicable to the case at bar:

"Here the buyer sought to retain a gain that was produced, not by a subsequent change in circumstances, nor by the favorable resolution of known uncertainties when the contract was made, but by the presence of facts quite different from those on which the parties based their bargain." *Palmer, Mistake and Unjust Enrichment* 16-17 (1962).

The probate court properly concluded that there was no agreement for the purchase, sale, or other disposition of the eight drawings and plaster sculpture.

Judgment for 1st Source Bank affirmed.

Mistakes of Law

A number of the older mistake cases state that mistake about a principle of law will not justify rescission. The rationale for this view was that everyone was presumed to know the law. More modern cases, however, have granted relief even when the mistake is an erroneous belief about some aspect of law.

Negligence and the Right to Avoid for Mistake

Although courts sometimes state that relief will not be granted when a person's mistake was caused by his own negligence, they have often granted rescission even when the mistaken party was somewhat negligent. Section 157 of the *Restatement (Second) of Contracts* focuses on the *degree* of a party's negligence in making the mistake. It states that a person's fault in failing to know or discover facts before entering the contract will not bar relief unless his fault amounted to a failure to act in good faith.

Effect of Mistake

The mere fact that the contracting parties have made a mistake is not, standing alone, a sufficient ground for avoidance of the contract. The right to avoid a contract because of mistake depends on several factors that are discussed in following sections. One important factor that affects the right to avoid is whether the mistake was made by just one of the parties (**unilateral mistake**) or by both parties (**mutual mistake**).

Mutual Mistake

A mutual mistake exists when both parties to the contract have erroneous assumptions about the same fact. When *both* parties are mistaken, the resulting contract can be avoided if the three following elements are present:

1. The mistake relates to a basic assumption on which the contract was made.
2. The mistake has a material effect on the agreed-on exchange.
3. The party adversely affected by the mistake does not bear the risk of the mistake.[5]

Mistake about a Basic Assumption

Even if the mistake is mutual, the adversely affected party will not have the right to avoid the contract unless the mistake concerns a basic assumption on which the contract was based. Assumptions about the identity, existence, quality, or quantity of the subject matter of the contract are among the basic assumptions on which contracts typically are founded. It is not necessary that the parties be consciously aware of the assumption; an assumption may be so basic that they take it for granted. For example, if Peterson contracts to buy a house from Tharp, it is likely that both of them assume at the time of contracting that the house is in existence and that it is legally permissible for the house to be used as a residence.

An assumption would not be considered a basic assumption if it concerns a matter that bears an indirect or collateral relationship to the subject matter of the contract. For example, mistakes about matters such as a party's financial ability or market conditions usually would not give rise to avoidance of the contract.

Material Effect on Agreed-On Exchange

It is not enough for a person claiming mistake to show that the exchange is something different from what he expected. He must show that the imbalance caused by the mistake is so severe that it would be unfair for the law to require him to perform the contract. He will have a better chance of establishing this element if he can show not only that the contract is *less* desirable for him because of the mistake, but also that the other party has received an unbargained-for advantage.

Adversely Affected Party Does Not Bear the Risk of Mistake

Even if the first two elements are present, the person who is adversely affected by the mistake cannot avoid the contract if he is considered to bear the risk of mistake.[6] Courts have the power to allocate the risk of a mistake to the adversely affected person whenever it is reasonable under the circumstances to do so.

One situation in which an adversely affected person would bear the risk of mistake is when he has expressly contracted to do so. For example, if Buyer contracted to accept property "as is," he may be considered to have accepted the risk that his assumption about the quality of the property may be erroneous.

The adversely affected party also bears the risk of mistake when he contracts with *conscious awareness* that he is ignorant or has limited information about a fact—in other words, *he knows that he does not know* the true state of affairs about a particular fact, but he binds himself to perform anyway. Suppose someone gives you an old, locked safe. Without trying to open it, you sell it and "all of its contents" to one of your friends for $25. When your friend succeeds in opening the safe, he finds $10,000 in cash. In this case, you would not be able to rescind the contract because, in essence, you gambled on your limited knowledge . . . and lost.

Mutual Mistakes in Drafting Writings

Sometimes, mutual mistake takes the form of erroneous *expression* of an agreement, frequently caused by a clerical error in drafting or typing a contract, deed, or other document. In such cases, the remedy is *reformation* of the writing rather than avoidance of the contract. Reformation means modification of the written instrument to express the agreement that the parties made but failed to express correctly. Suppose Arnold agrees to sell Barber a vacant lot next to Arnold's home. The vacant lot is "Lot 3, block 1;" Arnold's home is on "Lot 2, block 1." The person typing the contract strikes the wrong key, and the contract reads, "Lot 2, block 1." Neither Arnold nor Barber notices this error when they read and sign the contract, yet clearly they did not intend to have Arnold sell the lot on which his house stands. In such a case, a court will reform the contract to conform to Arnold and Barber's true agreement.

Unilateral Mistake

A unilateral mistake exists when only one of the parties makes a mistake about a basic assumption on which he made the contract. For example, Plummer contracts to buy from

Taylor 25 shares of Worthright Enterprises, Inc., mistakenly believing that he is buying 25 shares of the much more valuable Worthwrite Industries. Taylor knows that the contract is for the sale of shares of Worthright. Taylor (the nonmistaken party) is correct in his belief about the identity of the stock he is selling; only Plummer (the mistaken party) is mistaken in his assumption about the identity of the stock. Does Plummer's unilateral mistake give him the right to avoid the contract? Courts are more likely to allow avoidance of a contract when both parties are mistaken than when only one is mistaken. The rationale for this tendency is that in cases of unilateral mistake, at least one party's assumption about the facts was correct, and allowing avoidance disappoints the reasonable expectations of that nonmistaken party.

It is possible to avoid contracts for unilateral mistake, but to do so, proving the elements necessary for mutual mistake is just a starting point. In addition to proving the elements of mistake discussed earlier, a person trying to avoid on the ground of unilateral mistake must show either one of the following:

1. The nonmistaken party caused or had reason to know of the mistake. Courts permit avoidance in cases of unilateral mistake if the nonmistaken party caused the mistake, knew of the mistake, or even if the mistake was so obvious that the nonmistaken party had reason to realize that a mistake had been made.[7] For example, Ace Electrical Company makes an error when preparing a bid that it submits to Gorge General Contracting. If the mistake in Ace's bid was so obvious that Gorge knew about it when it accepted Ace's offer, Ace could avoid the contract even though Ace is the only party who was mistaken. The reasoning behind this rule is that the nonmistaken person could have prevented the loss by acting in good faith and informing the person in error that he had made a mistake. It also reflects the judgment that people should not take advantage of the mistakes of others or

2. It would be unconscionable to enforce the contract. A court could also permit avoidance because of unilateral mistake when the effect of the mistake was such that it would be unconscionable to enforce the contract. To show that it would be unconscionable to enforce the contract, the mistaken party would have to show that the consequences of the mistake were severe enough that it would be unreasonably harsh or oppressive to enforce the contract. In the example above, Ace Electrical Company made an error when preparing a bid that it submits to Gorge General Contracting. Suppose that Gorge had no reason to realize that a mistake had been made, and accepted the bid. Ace might show that it would be unconscionable to enforce the contract by showing that not only will its profit margin not be what Ace contemplated when it made its offer, but also that it would suffer a grave loss by having to perform at the mistaken price.

Concept Review
Avoidance on the Ground of Mistake

	Mutual Mistake	Unilateral Mistake
Description Needed for Avoidance	Both parties mistaken about same fact Elements of mistake: 1. Mistake about basic assumption on which contract was made 2. Material effect on agreed exchange 3. Person adversely affected by mistake does not bear the risk of the mistake	Only one party mistaken about a fact Same elements as mutual mistake *Plus* a. Nonmistaken party caused mistake or had reason to know of mistake *Or* b. Effect of mistake is to make it unconscionable to enforce contract

Duress

Nature of Duress

Duress is wrongful coercion that induces a person to enter or modify a contract. One kind of duress is physical compulsion to enter a contract. For example, Thorp overpowers Grimes, grasps his hand, and forces him to sign a contract. This kind of duress is rare, but when it occurs, a court would find that the contract was *void*. A far more common type of duress occurs when a person is induced to enter a contract by a *threat* of physical, emotional, or economic harm. In these cases, the contract is considered *voidable* at the option of the victimized person. This is the form of duress addressed in this chapter.

The elements of duress have undergone dramatic changes. Classical contract law took a very narrow view of the type of coercion that constituted duress, limiting duress to threats of imprisonment or serious physical harm. Today, however, courts take a much broader view of the types of coercion that will constitute duress. For example, modern courts recognize that threats to a person's economic interests can be duress.

Elements of Duress

To rescind a contract because of duress, one must be able to establish both of the following elements:

1. The contract was induced by an improper threat.
2. The victim had no reasonable alternative but to enter the contract.[8]

Improper Threat

It would not be desirable for courts to hold that every kind of threat constituted duress. If they did, the enforceability of all contracts would be in question, because every contract negotiation involves at least the implied threat that a person will not enter into the transaction unless her demands are met. What degree of wrongfulness, then, is required for a threat to constitute duress? Traditionally, a person would have to threaten to do something she was not legally entitled to do—such as threaten to commit a crime or a tort—for that threat to be duress. Many courts today follow the *Restatement (Second)* position that, to be duress, the threat need not be wrongful or illegal but must be *improper*—that is, improper to use as leverage to induce a contract.

Under some circumstances, threats to institute legal actions can be considered improper threats that will constitute duress. A threat to file either a civil or a criminal suit without a legal basis for doing so would clearly be improper. What of a threat to file a well-founded lawsuit or prosecution? Generally, if there is a good faith dispute over a matter, a person's threat to file a lawsuit to resolve that dispute is not considered to be improper. Otherwise, every person who settled a suit out of court could later claim duress. However, if the threat to sue is made in bad faith and for a purpose unrelated to the issues in the lawsuit, the threat can be considered improper. In one case, for example, duress was found when a husband who was in the process of divorcing his wife threatened to sue for custody of their children—something he had the right to do—unless the wife transferred to him stock that she owned in his company.[9]

The *Restatement (Second)* takes the position that a threat to institute a criminal prosecution is always impermissible pressure to induce a contract, even if the person making the threat has good reason to believe that the other person has committed a crime. It also provides that it is improper for a contracting party to make a threat that would constitute a breach of the duty of good faith and fair dealing under his contract with the person who is the recipient of the threat.[10] This provision is relevant to the many duress cases that arise in the context of coerced modifications of existing contracts or settlements of existing debts.

Victim Had No Reasonable Alternative

The person complaining of duress must be able to prove that the coercive nature of the improper threat was such that he had no reasonable alternative but to enter or modify the contract. Classical contract law applied an objective standard of coercion, which required that the degree of coercion exercised had to be sufficient to overcome the will of a person of ordinary courage. The more modern standard for coercion focuses on the alternatives open to the complaining party. For example, Barry, a traveling salesperson, takes his car to Cheatum Motors for repair. Barry pays Cheatum the full amount previously agreed on for the repair, but Cheatum refuses to return Barry's car to him unless Barry agrees to pay substantially more than the contract price for the repair. Because of his urgent need for the return of his car, Barry agrees to do this. In this case, Barry technically had the alternative of filing a legal action to recover his car. However, this would not be a *reasonable alternative* for someone who needs the car urgently because of the time, expense, and uncertainty involved in pursuing a lawsuit. Thus, Barry could avoid his agreement to pay more money under a theory of duress.

Problem Area: Economic Duress

Today, the doctrine of duress is often applied in a business context. *Economic duress*, or *business compulsion*, are terms commonly used to describe situations in which one person induces the formation or modification of a contract by threatening another person's economic interests. A common coercive strategy is to threaten to breach the contract unless the other party agrees to modify its terms. For example, Moore, who has contracted to sell goods to Stephens, knows that Stephens needs timely delivery of the goods. Moore threatens to withhold delivery unless Stephens agrees to pay a higher price. Another common situation involving economic duress occurs when one of the parties offers a disproportionately small amount of money in settlement of a debt and refuses to pay more. Such a strategy exerts great economic pressure on a creditor who is in a desperate financial situation to accept the settlement because he cannot afford the time and expense of bringing a lawsuit.

Classical contract law did not recognize economic duress because this type of hard bargaining was considered neither improper nor coercive. After all, the victim of the sorts of economic pressure described above had at least the theoretical right to file a lawsuit to enforce his rights under the contract. Modern courts recognize that improper economic pressure can prevent a resulting contract or contract modification from being truly voluntary, and the concept of economic duress is well-accepted today. Even in recent cases, however, it is not always clear how much hard bargaining is tolerated. *Eulrich v. Snap-On Tools Corp.*, which follows, presents an example of hard bargaining that a court found to have gone too far.

Eulrich v. Snap-On Tools Corp.

Snap-On manufactures and sells hand tools to a nationwide network of dealers, each of whom is assigned a marketing territory. The dealers, in turn, resell the tools to professional mechanics. Dan Eulrich, an auto body mechanic who had never before operated a business, entered into a dealership agreement and became a Snap-On dealer in 1986. Eulrich initially invested $22,000 from his savings and promised to pay a balance of $22,500 from the sale of inventory. The dealership agreement included a provision allowing termination of the dealership by either party. It further provided that upon termination, if Snap-On consented, Eulrich could resell to Snap-On any new tools remaining in his possession.

From the very beginning, Eulrich's dealership was not profitable. In early 1987, he tried to get a more profitable territory because his territory was not supporting him, but he was told to work the territory harder. Eulrich's supervisors, Tim Kash and Ray Park, insisted that anyone could succeed as a dealer by following Snap-On's sales program. (However, there was evidence that Snap-On's marketing system was designed to provide a maximum number of potential dealers and profit for Snap-On, while providing inadequate revenue to support dealers. As a result, dealers quickly failed and were replaced by new recruits.) By the spring of 1987, Eulrich was financially ruined and informed Kash and Park that he wanted to exercise his rights under the dealership agreement and terminate his dealership.

Beginning in April, he attempted to get Kash and Park to "check in" his truck, which he understood would allow him to receive a refund for the tools and the equity in his van. He needed this money to pay his household bills because his dealership had depleted his personal finances. Kash and Park repeatedly put off this check-in until June 1. By that time, as they knew, Eulrich was in serious financial difficulty and could not pay his living expenses, a situation that was aggravated by the fact that

Eulrich's wife was ill and required hospitalization but had no medical insurance.

On the day of the check-in, after having worked five or six hours to unload the van under trying circumstances, Kash and Park had Eulrich come into Park's office to "do paperwork." Eulrich was physically tired and emotionally drained. In the office, Kash and Park berated Eulrich for his poor business practices. They also presented Eulrich with a number of documents, none of which had been sent to him in advance to review, and told him to sign them. Kash told Eulrich that he would have to sign the papers before he could get any money. When he asked when he would get a check, Park told him that there would be no checks until the inventory was done and all of the papers were signed. Eulrich signed the papers.

Included in the papers that he signed was a "Termination Agreement," which included an agreement by Snap-On to repurchase Eulrich's tool inventory at current dealer cost. Also included in the document was a release of claims which provided that "each party to this Agreement waives any and all claims it may have against the other arising out of the Dealership terminated by this Agreement. . . ." Eulrich was not aware that a release was included in the Termination Agreement, nor was he aware that he had any legal claims against Snap-On.

Eulrich later filed a lawsuit against Snap-On, Kash, Park, and another Snap-On supervisor to recover damages for fraud, breach of good faith and fair dealing, and breach of contract arising out of the original dealership contract. The defendants asserted that the release barred these claims. Eulrich sought to rescind the release on a number of grounds, including economic duress. The trial judge allowed the rescission and the jury awarded general and punitive damages to Eulrich on his damage claims in the amount of $8,912,000. Snap-On appealed.

Source: 853 p.2d 1350 (Or. Ct. App. 1993)

Riggs, Judge

Eulrich acknowledges that, if the release is not rescinded, all of his claims for damages are barred. He asserts that the release should be rescinded because it was executed under economic duress. The gravamen of a claim of economic duress is that, as a result of some wrongful act by one party, the other party is deprived of free will in entering in the agreement.

Defendants argue that we should look only at their threat not to repurchase the tools and that, because the dealership agreement did not require defendants to buy back Eulrich's tools, there was nothing legally wrongful in that conduct. That inquiry is too narrow. Even if we look only at defendants' acts at the time that the termination agreement was executed, requiring Eulrich to sign the termination agreement in order to receive payment for the tools was a wrongful act. The contract conditioned repurchase of the tools on Snap-On's consent, but defendants' performance of that contract term is subject to the duty of good faith and fair dealing. A threat may be a breach of the duty of good faith and fair dealing under the contract even if the threatened act is not itself a breach of the contract. "In the context of duress, an act or threat is wrongful if it is 'an abuse of the powers of the party making the threat; that is, any threat the purpose of which was not to achieve the end for which the right, power, or privilege was given.'" *Calamari & Perillo, Contracts section 9-3 (3d ed. 1987).* Defendants had no right to abuse their power to consent under the contract by threatening to withhold consent unless Eulrich executed another contract releasing all claims.

In determining whether there was economic duress, a court must consider all surrounding factors and circumstances. Here, there was evidence that defendants' actions, up to the time the termination agreement was signed, were fraudulent and caused Eulrich's economic distress. Defendants knowingly engaged in an ongoing scheme to induce Eulrich into the business, to deny him an adequate sales territory to support his business, to browbeat and demoralize him into believing that the failure of the business was his fault rather than that of the inadequate design of the marketing system, and by depleting all of his financial resources. Defendants knew that their ongoing scheme was causing Eulrich financial distress, resulting in a lack of resources to meet daily household needs and his wife's medical needs. Despite this knowledge, and the provision in the dealer agreement that allowed either party to terminate the agreement on written notification, and despite Eulrich's numerous attempts to return the van and tools for a refund, defendants made Eulrich wait six or seven weeks to terminate the agreement. In the light of all the circumstances leading to the signing of the termination agreement, we conclude that defendants' conduct was wrongful.

Nevertheless, defendants argue that there was no economic duress because Eulrich had reasonable alternatives to signing the release. They contend that, under the dealership agreement, Eulrich had the option of keeping the inventory and selling it outside the dealership, which would have allowed him to recoup his inventory investment, or that he could have refused to sign the agreement, reserving his rights, or could have taken the termination agreement home with him and sought legal advice before he signed it. Under the coercive circumstances present here, those were not reasonable alternatives.

Eulrich had tried in vain for nearly two months to check in his van and tools and obtain the refund that defendants had promised for the tools. During that time, his poor financial situation deteriorated further. Selling Snap-On's product was a losing proposition; it would not have been a reasonable alternative for him to continue that course as a way of recouping his investment. Neither was refusing to sign the termination agreement and seeking a legal remedy a reasonable alternative. By the time defendants finally allowed Eulrich to check in the tools for the promised refund, Eulrich needed money immediately, and defendants knew it. For a legal remedy to be a reasonable alternative, it must be an "immediate and adequate remedy" and [this] is tested by a practical standard that takes into consideration the exigencies of the situation. Refusing to sign defendants' termination agreement and commencing legal action against them was not a reasonable alternative, because such a course would have taken time and Eulrich's financial condition was perilous. Faced with the choice between complying with defendants' demand and receiving the badly needed funds, or refusing to sign and facing financial disaster, Eulrich had no reasonable alternative and thus found himself deprived of the exercise of his free will. Accordingly, we conclude that his agreement to the release was a result of economic duress and that the trial court did not err in allowing the rescission.

Judgment allowing rescission affirmed in favor of Eulrich. [The case was also remanded for the correction of an error in the damages awarded to Eulrich.]

Undue Influence

Nature of Undue Influence

Undue influence is unfair persuasion. Like duress, undue influence involves wrongful pressure exerted on a person during the bargaining process. In undue influence, however, the pressure is exerted through *persuasion* rather than through coercion. The doctrine of undue influence was developed to give relief to persons who are unfairly persuaded to enter a contract while in a position of weakness that makes them particularly vulnerable to being preyed on by those they trust or fear. A large proportion of undue influence cases arise after the death of the person who has been the subject of undue influence, when his relatives seek to set aside that person's contracts or wills.

Determining Undue Influence

All contracts are based on persuasion. There is no precise dividing line between permissible persuasion and impermissible persuasion. Nevertheless, several hallmarks of undue influence cases can be identified. Undue influence cases normally involve both of the following elements:

1. The relationship between the parties is either one of trust and confidence or one in which the person exercising the persuasion dominates the person being persuaded.
2. The persuasion is unfair.[11]

Relation between the Parties

Undue influence cases involve people who, though they have capacity to enter a contract, are in a position of particular vulnerability in relationship to the other party to the contract. This relationship can be one of trust and confidence, in which the person being influenced justifiably believes that the other party is looking out for his interests, or at least that he would not do anything contrary to his welfare. Examples of such relationships would include parent and child, husband and wife, or lawyer and client.

The relationship can also be one in which one of the parties holds dominant psychological power that is not derived from a confidential relationship. For example, Royce, an elderly man, is dependent on his housekeeper, Smith, to care for him. Smith persuades Royce to withdraw most of his life savings from the bank and make an interest-free loan to her. If the persuasion Smith used was unfair, the transaction could be avoided because of undue influence.

Unfair Persuasion

The mere existence of a close or dependent relationship between the parties that results in economic advantage to one of them is not sufficient for undue influence. It must also appear that the weaker person entered the contract because he was subjected to unfair methods of persuasion. In determining this, a court will look at all of the surrounding facts and circumstances. Was the person isolated and rushed into the contract, or did he have access to outsiders for advice and time to consider his alternatives? Was the contract discussed and consummated in the usual time and place that would be expected for such a transaction, or was it discussed or consummated at an unusual time or in an unusual place? Was the contract a reasonably fair one that a person might have entered voluntarily, or was it so lopsided and unfair that one could infer that he probably would not have entered it unless he had been unduly influenced by the other party? The answers to these and similar questions help determine whether the line between permissible and impermissible persuasion has been crossed.

Concept Review
Wrongful Pressure in the Bargaining Process

	Duress	Undue Influence
Nature of Pressure	Coercion	Unfair persuasion of susceptible individual
Elements	1. Contract induced by improper threat 2. Threat leaves party no reasonable alternative but to enter or modify contract	1. Relationship of trust and confidence or dominance 2. Unfair persuasion

Ethical and Public Policy Concerns

1. You read that modern contract law has expanded the circumstances under which a contracting party has the duty to disclose facts material to the contract. Keep in mind that the facts that he is required to disclose would almost always harm his bargaining position—otherwise, he would have been only too happy to have volunteered the information. What are some ethical and public policy justifications for requiring an individual to volunteer information that is contrary to his interests?

2. Do you think the legal rules applied today regarding misrepresentation and duress encourage a higher standard of ethical dealing than did the legal rules applicable under classical contract law?

3. In this chapter, you learned a few of the circumstances under which a contracting party owes a higher duty of conduct to someone with whom she is in a relationship of trust and confidence than she would owe to individuals with whom she stood in an arm's-length relationship. What is the justification for requiring a higher standard of ethical dealing in such relationships? Would you favor the law's imposing the same high standards of conduct in relation to the rest of the world? Why or why not?

Problems and Problem Cases

1. King Chevrolet provided a 1982 Chevrolet Cavalier to one of its salespeople, Stein. During the eight months Stein drove the car, it was repaired or adjusted 10 times. There were repairs to the carburetor, choke, speedometer, door moldings, seat belt buzzer alarm, and spark plugs as well as a complete paint job. Of the 36 demonstrators Stein had driven over the years as a car salesperson, this was the worst. Stein finally complained to the service department about the car, and asked Lewis, King Chevrolet's sales manager, if he could have another demonstrator because his car was so unreliable. Not long afterward, Muzelak, who had purchased her previous car from Lewis, contacted Lewis about buying a new car. Lewis told her that the "right car for her" was the 1982 Chevrolet Cavalier demonstrator that Stein had used. Lewis did tell Muzelak that the car was a demonstrator, but he did not mention any of the previous

repair problems with the car. (Stein later testified that Lewis told him it took someone with his sales ability to "get rid of" that car.) Muzelak bought the car. Over the course of the next eight months, Muzelak's car was in King Chevrolet's service department for repairs 13 times. Some of the problems were never corrected. The car was so unreliable that Muzelak did not drive it after the first eight months of use. Does Muzelak have grounds for an action for fraud?

2.   On May 17, Cobaugh was playing in the East End Open Golf Tournament. When he arrived at the ninth tee, he found a new Chevrolet Beretta, together with signs which proclaimed: "HOLE-IN-ONE Wins this 1988 Chevrolet Beretta GT Courtesy of KLICK-LEWIS Buick Chevy Pontiac $49.00 OVER FACTORY INVOICE in Palmyra." Cobaugh aced the ninth hole and attempted to claim his prize. Klick-Lewis refused to deliver the car, however. Klick-Lewis had offered the car as a prize for a charity golf tournament sponsored by the Hershey-Palmyra Sertoma Club two days earlier and had neglected to remove the car and signs prior to Cobaugh's hole-in-one. Cobaugh sued to compel delivery of the car. Would the doctrine of mistake provide a ground for Klick-Lewis to avoid the contract?

3.   West Branch Land Co. owned a tract of land, which it listed for sale. The listing that was published in the local Multiple Listing Service listing sheet and distributed to all subscribing real estate agencies described the property as being "zoned multi for 35 townhouses" when in fact it was really zoned for only 30. Acleson, a licensed real estate broker, received a copy of the listing and, after calculating the costs per unit on the basis of 35 units, submitted an offer to purchase the property. The parties ultimately contracted for the sale of the property for $65,000. The final contract made no mention of the acreage of the land or of its zoning status. Acleson could have determined the true acreage and zoning status by checking the plat map that was available at the local city planner's office. Almost two years after the sale, Acleson learned that the property was really zoned for only 30 units. Will Acleson's failure to investigate the zoning of the land prevent him from obtaining a remedy for misrepresentation or fraud?

4.   Odorizzi, an elementary school teacher, was arrested on criminal charges involving illegal sexual activity. After having been arrested, questioned by police, booked, and released on bail, and going 40 hours without sleep, he was visited in his home by the superintendent of the school district and the principal of his school. They told him that they were trying to help him and that they had his best interests at heart. They advised him to resign immediately, stating that there was no time to consult an attorney. They said that if he did not resign immediately, the district would dismiss him and publicize the proceedings, but that if he resigned at once, the incident would not be publicized and would not jeopardize his chances of securing employment as a teacher elsewhere. Odorizzi gave them a written letter of resignation, which they accepted. The criminal charges against Odorizzi were later dismissed, and he sought to resume his employment. When the school district refused to reinstate him, Odorizzi attempted to rescind his letter of resignation on several grounds, including undue influence. (He also alleged duress, but the facts of his case did not constitute duress under applicable state law.) Can Odorizzi avoid the contract on the ground of undue influence?

5.   The O'Connors entered into a contract with the Kings in 1986 to lease their townhouse to the Kings with an option to purchase. Prior to leasing the townhouse, Mr. King noticed a crack in a retaining wall near the house's driveway, and Mr. O'Connor showed him an area along the east foundation wall where there was a separation of the earth and foundation. The O'Connors agreed to pay for dirt to be brought in and placed along the east foundation. Both parties believed this would eliminate potential water problems in the basement. At some point prior to the time the Kings leased the

townhouse, water seeped into the basement of the townhouse, but the O'Connors did not tell the Kings about this because there was no apparent water damage. Furthermore, when Ms. King explicitly questioned the O'Connors about the existence of water in the basement, the O'Connors denied any existence of water in the basement. The Kings exercised their option to purchase the townhouse in June of 1987. By the fall of that year, the Kings began experiencing problems with doors sticking and interior walls cracking. They later discovered that the retaining wall crack had widened and that there was water damage in the basement bathroom. When the O'Connors refused their demand to pay for the repairs, the Kings moved out of the townhouse. The O'Connors sued the Kings for breach of contract, and the Kings counterclaimed for rescission of the contract. Can the Kings rescind the contract?

6. Boskett, a part-time coin dealer, paid $450 for a dime purportedly minted in 1916 at Denver and two additional coins of relatively small value. After carefully examining the dime, Beachcomber Coins, a retail coin dealer, bought the coin from Boskett for $500. Beachcomber then received an offer from a third party to purchase the dime for $700, subject to certification of its genuineness from the American Numismatic Society. That organization labeled the coin a counterfeit. Can Beachcomber rescind the contract with Boskett on the ground of mistake?

7. Robert & Wendy Pfister asked Foster & Marshall, a stock brokerage firm, to evaluate some stocks that they owned, including 100 shares of Tracor Computing Corporation. The stock was no longer traded on the New York Stock Exchange. The Pfisters did not know the value of the stock, but they believed it to be of little value. They were surprised when Foster & Marshall told them that the stock was trading at $49.50 under its new name, Continuum Co., Inc., so that the value of the Pfisters' stock was $4,950. They asked Foster & Marshall to recheck the figures and brought their stock certificates in for verification. Based on Foster & Marshall's reassurances that they owned 100 shares of Continuum and that these were worth $4,950, the Pfisters sold the stock to Foster & Marshall. As a result of receiving this money for the stock, the Pfisters made a commitment to build a new home, which before the sale had been a "borderline decision." A year after the transaction, Foster & Marshall discovered that the Tracor Computing stock had been exchanged for Continuum stock at a 10-to-1 ratio and that the Pfisters had owned only 10 shares of Continuum. Foster & Marshall claimed relief under the doctrine of mistake and sued the Pfisters to recover the $4,466.25 it had overpaid them. Will Foster & Marshall win?

8. Mrs. Gossinger slipped and fell on soapy water that had flooded the bathroom floor of the apartment that she and her husband rented from Sutherland, a member of the Apartment Owners Association of the Regency of Ala Wai. She immediately drove herself to the hospital, where the physician examined her, performed tests, and concluded that she had suffered a back strain, which he advised her "would take a long time to heal." He advised her to have a follow-up examination at the beginning of the following week—or sooner if her condition worsened. The next day, the Gossingers wrote to the Association demanding compensation for personal injury and property damage caused by the flooding incident. Three days later, an insurance adjuster for State Farm Insurance Company met with the Gossingers to settle their claims. As a result of the meeting, the Gossingers settled their claims for $1,100 and signed a release that purported to discharge the Association and all other persons who might be liable for her injuries from all liability for any personal injury or property damage resulting from her fall. Approximately one year after signing the release, Mrs. Gossinger's back pain had not subsided. Upon examination by a physician, she was diagnosed as suffering from a herniated disc, requiring surgery and leading to more than $20,000 in medical expenses. The Gossingers filed a negligence suit against

Sutherland and the Association. The Gossingers asserted that the release is invalid because of unilateral or mutual mistake. Was it?

9. Ashton Development hired Rich & Whillock, Inc., to do grading and excavating work on a construction project. The contract specified that removal of any rock encountered would be considered an "extra." After a month's work, Rich & Whillock encountered rock on the project site. Ashton agreed that the rock would have to be blasted and that this would involve extra costs. It directed Rich & Whillock to go ahead with the blasting and bill for the extra cost. Rich & Whillock did so, submitting separate invoices for the regular contract work and the extra blasting work and receiving payment every two weeks. After completing the work, Rich & Whillock submitted a final billing for an additional $72,286.45. This time Ashton refused to pay. Rich & Whillock communicated that it would "go broke" without this final payment because it was a new business with rented equipment and had numerous subcontractors waiting to be paid. Ashton replied that it would pay $50,000 or nothing. Stating, "I have a check for you, and just take it or leave it, this is all you get. If you don't want this, you have got to sue me," Ashton's agent presented Rich & Whillock with an agreement for a final compromise payment of $50,000. Rich & Whillock signed the settlement agreement and received a $25,000 check after communicating that the agreement was "blackmail" and that it was signing the agreement only because it was necessary in order to survive. Rich & Whillock later signed a release form and received a second check for $25,000. Several months afterward, however, Rich & Whillock sued Ashton for breach of contract, maintaining that the settlement agreement and release should not be enforced. Are the settlement agreement and release voidable?

10. Reed purchased a house from King. Neither King nor his real estate agents told Reed before the sale that a woman and her four children had been murdered there 10 years earlier. Reed learned of the gruesome episode from a neighbor after the sale. She sued King and his real estate agents, seeking rescission and damages on the ground that King should have disclosed the history of the house to her. Can Reed rescind the contract?

11. Johnson owned a new baseball card store that had been very busy during its first week of operation. Not wanting to close the store while he went out for dinner, he got a temporary clerk who knew nothing about baseball cards to staff the store in his absence. He instructed the clerk that the prices on the cards were marked, and if anyone wanted to negotiate for the more expensive cards in the glass case, she was to tell them to return and talk to Johnson. While Johnson was out, a boy came in and asked to look at the Ernie Banks rookie card, which was in the glass case. The card was marked "1200." The boy asked whether the card was really worth $12 and the clerk replied, "Yeah, I guess it is" and sold the card to him for $12. When Johnson returned and looked through the sales, he saw that the card had been sold for $12, when its true price was $1,200. Is the contract voidable on the ground of any reality of consent doctrine?

12. As part of an employee benefit plan, Famco gave stock options to its employees. There were two restrictions on the sale of stock to employees, however. First, if the employee terminated employment for any reason, Famco had the right to buy the stock at book value (often less than market value). Second, if an employee wanted to sell the stock while employed, Famco had a right of first refusal. Famco's CEO called a meeting with three employees who had purchased stock. During this meeting, the CEO reminded the employees that if their employment terminated, the company could repurchase the stock at book value. The employees felt that they had to sell their stock

back to Famco or they would lose their jobs, in which case they would have to sell their stock anyway. Two employees agreed to resell the stock to Famco. Were these agreements to sell the stock to Famco voidable?

See also "Car Deals."

Endnotes

1. The tort of deceit is discussed in Chapter 22.
2. Under every state's law, however, a person injured by fraud in a contract for the sale of goods can both rescind the contract and sue for damages. This is made clear by section 2-721 of the Uniform Commercial Code, which specifically states that no election of remedies is required in contracts for the sale of goods.
3. *Restatement (Second) of Contracts* § 169.
4. *Restatement (Second) of Contracts* § 151.
5. *Restatement (Second) of Contracts* § 152.
6. *Restatement (Second) of Contracts* § 154.
7. *Restatement (Second) of Contracts* § 153.
8. *Restatement (Second) of Contracts* § 175.
9. *Link v. Link*, 179 S.E.2d 697 (1971).
10. *Restatement (Second) of Contracts* § 176.
11. *Restatement (Second) of Contracts* § 177.

Chapter Twenty

WRITING

Introduction

Your study of contract law so far has focused on the requirements for the formation of a valid contract. You should be aware, however, that even when all the elements of a valid contract exist, the enforceability of the contract and the nature of the parties' obligations can be greatly affected by the *form* in which the contract is set out and by the *language* that is used to express the agreement. An otherwise valid contract can become unenforceable if it does not comply with the formalities required by state law. A person may be unable to offer evidence about promises and agreements made in preliminary negotiations because the parties later adopted a written contract that did not contain those terms. And, of course, the legal effect of any contract is determined in large part by the way in which a court interprets the language it contains. This chapter discusses the ways in which the enforceability of a contract and the scope of contractual obligations can be affected by the manner in which people express their agreements.

The Statute of Frauds

Despite what many people believe, there is no general requirement that contracts be in writing. In most situations, oral contracts are legally enforceable, assuming that they can be proven. Still, oral contracts are less desirable than written contracts in many ways. They are more easily misunderstood or forgotten than written contracts. They are also more subject to the danger that a person might fabricate terms or fraudulently claim to have made an oral contract where none exists.

In 17th-century England, the dangers inherent in oral contracts were exacerbated by a legal rule that prohibited parties to a lawsuit from testifying in their own cases. Since the parties to an oral contract could not give testimony, the only way they could prove the existence of the contract was through the testimony of third parties. As you might expect, third parties were sometimes persuaded to offer false testimony about the existence of contracts. In an attempt to stop the widespread fraud and perjury that resulted, Parliament enacted the Statute of Frauds in 1677. It required written evidence before certain classes of contracts would be enforced. Although the possibility of fraud exists in every contract, the statute focused on contracts in which the potential for fraud was great or the consequences of fraud were especially serious. The legislatures of American states adopted very similar statutes, also known as statutes of frauds. These statutes, which require certain kinds of contracts to be evidenced by a signed writing, are exceptions to the general rule that oral contracts are enforceable.

Statutes of frauds have produced a great deal of litigation, due in part to the public's ignorance of their provisions. It is difficult to imagine an aspect of contract law that is more practical for businesspeople to know about than the circumstances under which an oral contract will not suffice.

Effect of Failure to Comply with the Statute of Frauds

The statute of frauds applies only to executory contracts. If an oral contract has been completely performed by both parties, the fact that it did not comply with the statute of frauds would not be a ground for rescission of the contract.

What happens if an executory contract is within the statute of frauds but has not been evidenced by the type of writing required by the statute? It is not treated as an illegal contract because the statute of frauds is more of a formal rule than a rule of substantive law. Rather, the contract that fails to comply with the statute of frauds is *unenforceable*. Although the contract will not be enforced, a person who has conferred some benefit on the other party pursuant to the contract can recover the reasonable value of his performance in an action based on *quasi-contract*.

Contracts within the Statute of Frauds

A contract is said to be "within" the statute of frauds if the statute requires that sort of contract to be evidenced by a writing. In almost all states, the following types of contracts are within the statute of frauds:

1. Collateral contracts in which a person promises to perform the obligation of another person.
2. Contracts for the sale of an interest in real estate.
3. Bilateral contracts that cannot be performed within a year from the date of their formation.
4. Contracts for the sale of goods for a price of $500 or more.
5. Contracts in which an executor or administrator promises to be personally liable for the debt of an estate.
6. Contracts in which marriage is the consideration.

Of this list, the first four sorts of contracts have the most significance today, and our discussion will focus primarily on them.

The statutes of frauds of the various states are not uniform. Some states require written evidence of other contracts in addition to those listed above. For example, a number of states require written evidence of contracts to pay a commission for the sale of real estate. Others require written evidence of ratifications of infants' promises or promises to pay debts that have been barred by the statute of limitations or discharged by bankruptcy.

The following discussion examines in greater detail the sorts of contracts that are within most states' statute of frauds.

Collateral Contracts

A **collateral contract** is one in which one person (the *guarantor*) agrees to pay the debt or obligation that a second person (the *principal debtor*) owes to a third person (the *obligee*) if the principal debtor fails to perform. For example, Cohn, who wants to help Davis establish a business, promises First Bank that he will repay the loan that First Bank makes to Davis if Davis fails to pay it. Here, Cohn is the guarantor, Davis is the principal debtor, and First Bank is the obligee. Cohn's promise to First Bank must be in writing to be enforceable.

Figure 20-1 shows that a collateral contract involves at least three parties and at least two promises to perform (a promise by the principal debtor to pay the obligee and a promise by the guarantor to pay the obligee). In a collateral contract, the guarantor promises to pay *only if the principal debtor fails to do so.* As you will read in the following case, *Crozier and Gudsnuk, P.C. v. Valentine,* the essence of the collateral contract is that the debt or obligation is owed primarily by the principal debtor and the guarantor's debt is *secondary.* Thus, not all three-party transactions are collateral contracts.

FIGURE 20-1
Collateral contract

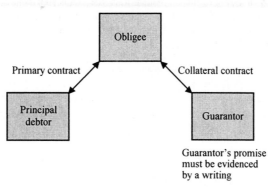

When a person undertakes an obligation that is not conditioned on the default of another person, and the debt is his own rather than that of another person, his obligation is said to be *original*, not collateral. For example, when Timmons calls Johnson Florist Company and says, "Send flowers to Elrod," Timmons is undertaking an obligation to pay *her own*—not someone else's—debt.

Crozier and Gudsnuk, P.C. v. Valentine

Michael Valentine, Jr., an adult over the age of 18, was charged with criminal assault. His parents, Lorraine and Michael Valentine, Sr., contacted the law firm of Crozier and Gudsnuk about representing their son in the criminal action. In October 1990, attorney Barbara DeGennaro, an associate in the law firm, agreed to represent Valentine. The law firm claims that Valentine's parents orally agreed to guarantee payment for the legal fees incurred by their son. Approximately 10 days after DeGennaro had agreed to represent Valentine, Mrs. Valentine paid the firm's retainer by signing a check for $250. The law firm represented Valentine in the criminal assault charge until February 25, 1991, when its representation ended at the request of the Valentines. The law firm claims that the reasonable value of the legal services it performed was $4,200. It brought suit against Valentine's parents to recover the legal fees owed to the firm. It asked the court for a prejudgment attachment of the Valentines' home. A hearing was held on this issue.

Source: 1992 Conn. Super. LEXIS 1179 (Super. Ct. Conn. 1992) No. CV-91-0036504

Jones, Judge

The present case involves an alleged oral contract made between a law firm and the parents of an adult child charged in a criminal action. The Statute of Frauds provides that:

> No civil action may be maintained in the following cases unless the agreement, or a memorandum of the agreement, is made in writing and signed by the party, or the agent of the party, to be charged . . . (2) against any person upon any special promise to answer for the debt, default or miscarriage of another.

The Valentines have raised the Statute of Frauds as a defense, claiming that the oral agreement of guarantee made between the parents and the law firm was a separate, collateral undertaking independent of the law firm's representation of Michael Valentine, Jr. In *Adamowicz v. Stevens*, the court held:

> The statute is not a defense if the promise was an original undertaking. Fundamentally the distinction between a contract which falls within the condemnation of the statute of frauds and one which does not is that the former is a collateral undertaking to answer in case of a default on the part of the obliger in the contract, upon whom still rests the primary liability to perform; whereas, in the latter, the obligation assumed is a primary one that the contract shall be performed.

Further, an undertaking by a party not liable, for the purpose of securing the performance of a duty for which the party for whom the under taking is made continues liable, is a special premise to answer for the debt, default, or miscarriage of another and is within the statute of frauds.

In the present case, only the adult son of the Valentines was legally represented by the law firm. The parents were not charged in any criminal action and received no material benefit from the law firm's representation of Michael Valentine, Jr. If the oral agreement between the parents and the law firm was in fact a separate, collateral undertaking, then the agreement will be within the statute of frauds. From the facts before this court, the parents cannot be seen as principal parties in the legal services agreement between the law firm and their adult son. The record indicates that the oral agreement to guarantee payment for legal fees constitutes a separate and collateral undertaking and as such, it falls within the statute of frauds.

For the foregoing reasons, this Court denies the plaintiff's application for prejudgment remedy. The Court notes in passing that [the statute of frauds] was adopted by the legislature in order to encourage certain contracting parties to put their agreements into writing so as to avoid certain pitfalls.

Plaintiff's application denied in favor of the Valentines.

Exception: Main Purpose or Leading Object Rule

There are some situations in which a contract that is technically collateral is treated like an original contract because the person promising to pay the debt of another does so for the primary purpose of securing some personal benefit. Under the main purpose or leading object rule, no writing is required where the guarantor makes a collateral promise for the main purpose of obtaining some personal economic advantage. When the consideration given in exchange for the collateral promise is something the guarantor seeks primarily for his own benefit rather than for the benefit of the primary debtor, the contract is outside the statute of frauds and does not have to be in writing. Suppose, for example, that Penn is a major creditor of Widgetmart, a retailer. To help keep Widgetmart afloat and increase the chances that Widgetmart will repay the debt it owes him, Penn orally promises Rex Industries, one of the Widgetmart's suppliers, that he will guarantee Widgetmart's payment for goods that Rex sells to Widgetmart. In this situation, Penn's oral agreement could be enforced under the main purpose rule if the court finds that Penn was acting for his own personal financial benefit.

Interest in Land

Any contract that creates or transfers an interest in land is within the statute of frauds. The inclusion of real estate contracts in the statute of frauds reflects the values of an earlier, agrarian society in which land was the primary basis of wealth. Our legal system historically has treated land as being more important than other forms of property. Courts have interpreted the land provision of the statute of frauds broadly to require written evidence of any transaction that will affect the ownership of an interest in land. Thus, a contract to sell or mortgage real estate must be evidenced by a writing, as must an option to purchase real estate or a contract to grant an easement or permit the mining and removal of minerals on land. A lease is also a transfer of an interest in land, but most states' statutes of frauds do not require leases to be in writing unless they are long-term leases, usually those for one year or more. On the other hand, a contract to erect a building or to insure a building would not be within the real estate provision of the statute of frauds because such contracts do not involve the transfer of interests in land.[1]

Exception: Full Performance by the Vendor

An oral contract for the sale of land that has been completely performed by the vendor (seller) is "taken out of the statute of frauds"—that is, is enforceable without a writing. For example, Peterson and Lincoln enter into an oral contract for the sale of Peterson's farm at an agreed-on price, and Peterson, the vendor, delivers a deed to the farm to Lincoln. In this situation, the vendor has completely performed and most states would treat the oral contract as being enforceable.

Exception: Part Performance (Action in Reliance) by the Vendee

When the vendee (purchaser of land) does an act in clear reliance on an oral contract for the sale of land, an equitable doctrine commonly known as the "part performance doctrine" permits the vendee to enforce the contract notwithstanding the fact that it was oral. The part performance doctrine is based on both evidentiary and reliance considerations. The doctrine recognizes that a person's conduct can "speak louder than words" and can indicate the existence of a contract almost as well as a writing can. The part performance doctrine is also based on the desire to avoid the injustice that would otherwise result if the contract were repudiated after the vendee's reliance.

Under section 129 of the *Restatement (Second) of Contracts*, a contract for the transfer of an interest in land can be enforced even without a writing if the person seeking enforcement:

1. Has *reasonably relied* on the contract and on the other party's assent.
2. Has changed his position to such an extent that *enforcement of the contract is the only way to prevent injustice*.

In other words, the vendee must have done some act in reliance on the contract and the nature of the act must be such that restitution (returning his money) would not be an adequate remedy. The part performance doctrine will not permit the vendee to collect damages for breach of contract, but it will permit him to obtain the equitable remedy of **specific performance**, a remedy whereby the court orders the breaching party to perform his contract.[2]

A vendee's reliance on an oral contract could be shown in many ways. Traditionally, many states have required that the vendee pay part or all of the purchase price and either make substantial improvements on the property or take possession of it. For example, Contreras and Miller orally enter into a contract for the sale of Contreras's land. If Miller pays Contreras a substantial part of the purchase price and either takes possession of the land or begins to make improvements on it, the contract would be enforceable without a writing under the part performance doctrine. These are not the only sorts of acts in reliance that would make an oral contract enforceable, however. Under the *Restatement (Second)* approach, if the promise to transfer land is clearly proven or is admitted by the breaching party, it is not necessary that the act of reliance include making payment, taking possession, or making improvements.[3] It still is necessary, however, that the reliance be such that restitution would not be an adequate remedy. For this reason, a vendee's payment of the purchase price, standing alone, is usually *not* sufficient for the part performance doctrine.

Contracts that Cannot Be Performed within One Year

A bilateral, executory contract that cannot be performed within one year from the day on which it comes into existence is within the statute of frauds and must be evidenced by a writing. The apparent purpose of this provision is to guard against the risk of faulty or willfully inaccurate recollection of long-term contracts. Courts have tended to construe it very narrowly.

One aspect of this narrow construction is that most states hold that a contract that has been fully performed by *one* of the parties is "taken out of the statute of frauds" and is enforceable without a writing. For example, Nash enters into an oral contract to perform services for Thomas for 13 months. If Nash has already fully performed his part of the contract, Thomas will be required to pay him the contract price.

In addition, this provision of the statute has been held to apply only when the terms of the contract make it impossible for the contract to be completed within one year. If the contract is for an indefinite period of time, it is not within the statute of frauds. This is true even if, in retrospect, the contract was not completed within a year. Thus, Weinberg's agreement to work for Wolf for an indefinite period of time would not have to be evidenced by a writing, even if Weinberg eventually works for Wolf for many years. As demonstrated by *Hodge v. Evans Financial Corporation*, which follows, the mere fact that performance is unlikely to be completed in one year does not bring the contract within the statute of frauds. In most states, a contract "for life" is not within the statute of frauds because it is possible—since death is an uncertain event—for the contract to be performed within a year. In a few states such as New York, contracts for life are within the statute of frauds.

Hodge v. Evans Financial Corporation

On two occasions in 1980, Albert Hodge met with John Tilley, president and chief operating officer of Evans Financial Corporation, to discuss Hodge's possible employment by Evans. Hodge was 54 years old at that time and was assistant counsel and assistant secretary of Mellon National Corporation and Mellon Bank of Pittsburgh. During these discussions, Tilley asked Hodge what his conditions were for accepting employment with Evans, and Hodge replied, "No. 1, the job must be permanent. Because of my age, I have a great fear about going back into the marketplace again. I want to be here until I retire." Tilley allegedly responded, "I accept that condition."

Regarding his retirement plans, Hodge later testified, "I really questioned whether I was going to go much beyond 65." Hodge subsequently accepted Evans's offer of employment as vice president and general counsel. He moved from Pittsburgh to Washington, D.C., in September 1980 and worked for Evans from that time until he was fired by Tilley on May 7, 1981.

Hodge brought a breach of contract suit against Evans. The case was tried before a jury, which rendered a verdict in favor of Hodge for $175,000. Evans appeals.

Source: 823 F.2d 559 (D.C. Cir. 1987)

Wald, Chief Justice

Evans argues that the oral employment agreement between Evans and Hodge is unenforceable under the statute of frauds. Because the agreement here contemplated long-term employment for a number of years, Evans argues that the statute requires it to have been in writing in order to be enforceable.

Despite its sweeping terms, the one-year provision of the statute has long been construed narrowly and literally. Under prevailing interpretation, the enforceability of a contract under the statute does not depend on the actual course of subsequent events or on the expectations of the parties. Instead, the statute applies only to those contracts whose performance could not possibly or conceivably be completed within one year. The statute of frauds is thus inapplicable if, at the time the contract is formed, any contingent event could complete the terms of the contract within one year.

Hodge argues that, under this interpretation of the statute of frauds, a permanent or lifetime employment contract does not fall within the statute because it is capable of full performance within one year if the employee were to die within the period. Hodge's view of the statute's application to lifetime or permanent employment contracts has, in fact, been accepted by an overwhelming majority of courts and commentators.

The employment contract in this case cannot reasonably be interpreted as a contract for a specified period of time. Hodge unequivocally alleged a contract for permanent employment, not a contract until he reached age sixty-five or for any other stated period of time. The fact that Hodge expected to retire at some point does not mean that his contract could not possibly be performed within one year. All employment contracts of permanent, lifetime, or indefinite duration undoubtedly contemplate retirement; such contracts certainly do not mean that employees are bound to work until the moment they drop dead. Hodge's permanent employment contract with Evans could therefore be fully performed, according to its terms, upon Hodge's retirement or upon his death. Under the conventional view the latter possibility is sufficient to take the contract out of the statute. That Hodge expected to retire before he died is completely irrelevant to this case so long as the contract was legally susceptible of performance within one year. The applicability of the statute of frauds does not depend on the expectations of the parties.

We recognize that the conventional view of the statute is somewhat "legalistic." Yet the statute of frauds itself is widely understood as a formal device that shields promise breakers from the consequences of otherwise enforceable agreements. The conventional, narrowing interpretation overwhelmingly adopted by courts and commentators is designed to mollify the often harsh and unintended consequences of the statute. Here the jury concluded, despite Evans's vigorous defense, that Hodge was promised permanent employment and that he was nonetheless fired without cause. Under the traditional, narrow view of the statute, the statute of frauds does not bar the enforcement of such jury verdicts. **Judgment for Hodge affirmed.**

Computing Time

In determining whether a contract is within the one-year provision, courts begin counting time on the day when the contract comes into existence. If, under the terms of the contract, it is possible to perform it within one year from this date, the contract does not fall within the statute of frauds and does not have to be in writing. If, however, the terms of the contract make it impossible to complete performance of the contract (without breaching it) within one year from the date on which the contract came into existence, the contract falls within the statute and must meet its requirements to be enforceable. Thus, if Hammer Co. and McCrea agree on August 1,1993, that McCrea will work for Hammer Co. for one year, beginning October 1, 1993, the terms of the contract dictate that it is not possible to complete performance until October 1, 1994. Because that date is more than one year from the date on which the contract came into existence, the contract falls within the statute of frauds and must be evidenced by a writing to be enforceable.

Sale of Goods for $500 or More

The original English Statute of Frauds required a writing for contracts for the sale of goods for a price of 10 pounds sterling or more. In the United States today, the writing requirement for the sale of goods is governed by section 2-201 of the Uniform Commercial Code. This section provides that contracts for the sale of goods for the price of $500 or more are not enforceable without a writing or other specified evidence that a contract was made. There are a number of alternative ways of satisfying the requirements of section 2-201. These will be explained later in this chapter.

Modifications of Existing Sales Contracts

Just as some contracts to extend the time for performance fall within the one-year provision of the statute of frauds, agreements to modify existing sales contracts can fall within the statute of frauds if the contract as modified is for a price of $500 or more.[4] UCC section 2-209(3) provides that the requirements of the statute of frauds must be satisfied if the contract as modified is within its provisions. For example, if Carroll and Kestler enter into a contract for the sale of goods at a price of $490, the original contract does *not* fall within the statute of frauds. However, if they later modify the contract by increasing the contract price to $510, the modification falls within the statute of frauds and must meet its requirements to be enforceable.

Promise of Executor or Administrator to Pay a Decedent's Debt Personally

When a person dies, a personal representative is appointed to administer his estate. One of the important tasks of this personal representative, who is called an executor if the person dies leaving a will or an administrator if the person dies without a will, is to pay the debts owed by the decedent. No writing is required when an executor or administrator—acting in his representative capacity—promises to pay the decedent's debts from the funds of the decedent's estate. The statute of frauds requires a writing, however, if the executor, acting in her capacity as a private individual rather than in her representative capacity, promises to pay one of the decedent's debts out of her own (the executor's) funds. For example, Thomas, who has been appointed executor of his Uncle Max's estate, is presented with a bill for $10,500 for medical services rendered to Uncle Max during his last illness by the family doctor, Dr. Barnes. Feeling bad that there are not adequate funds in the estate to compensate Dr. Barnes for his services, Thomas promises to pay Dr. Barnes from his own funds. Thomas's promise would have to be evidenced by a writing to be enforceable.

Contract in which Marriage is the Consideration

The statute of frauds also requires a writing when marriage is the consideration to support a contract. The marriage provision has been interpreted to be inapplicable to agreements that involve only mutual promises to marry. It can apply to any other contract in which one party's promise is given in exchange for marriage or the promise to marry on the part of the other party. This is true whether the promiser is one of the parties to the marriage or a third party. For example, if Hicks promises to deed his ranch to Everett in exchange for Everett's agreement to marry Hicks's son, Everett could not enforce Hicks's promise without written evidence of the promise.

Prenuptial (or antenuptial) agreements present a common contemporary application of the marriage provision of the statute of frauds. These are agreements between couples who contemplate marriage. They usually involve such matters as transfers of property, division of property upon divorce or death, and various lifestyle issues. Assuming that marriage or the promise to marry is the consideration supporting these agreements, they are within the statute of frauds and must be evidenced by a writing.[5]

Concept Review
Contracts within the Statute of Frauds

Provision	Description	Exceptions (situations in which contract does not require a writing)
Marriage	Contracts, other than mutual promises to marry, where marriage is the consideration	—
Year	Bilateral contracts that, *by their terms*, cannot be performed within one year from the date on which the contract was formed	Full (complete) performance by one of the parties
Land	Contracts that create or transfer an ownership interest in real property	1. Full performance by vendor (vendor deeds property to vendees) or 2. "Part performance" doctrine: Vendee relies on oral contract—for example, by: a. Paying substantial part of purchase, and b. Taking possession or making improvements
Executor's Promise	Executor promises to pay estate's debt out of his own funds	—
Sale of Goods at Price of $500 or More (UCC § 2-201)	Contracts for the sale of goods for a contract price of $500 or more; also applies to modifications of contracts for goods where price as modified is $500 or more	See alternative ways of satisfying statute of frauds under UCC
Collateral Contracts, Guaranty	Contracts where promiser promises to pay the debt of another if the primary debtor fails to pay	"Main purpose" or "leading object" exception: Guarantor makes promise primarily for her own economic benefit

Meeting the Requirements of the Statute of Frauds

Nature of the Writing Required

The statutes of frauds of the various states are not uniform in their formal requirements. However, most states require only a *memorandum* of the parties' agreement; they do not require that the entire contract be in writing. The memorandum must provide written evidence that a contract was made, but it need not have been created with the intent that the memorandum itself would be binding. In fact, in some cases, written offers that were accepted orally have been held sufficient to satisfy the writing requirement. As you will see in the following *Putt v. City of Corinth* case, a memorandum may be in any form. Typical examples include letters, telegrams, receipts, or any other writing indicating that the parties had a contract. The memorandum need not be made at the same time the contract comes into being; in fact, the memorandum may be made at any time before suit is filed. If a memorandum of the parties' agreement is lost, its loss and its contents may be proven by oral testimony.

Putt v. City of Corinth

John Putt owned commercial real estate known as the King Tractor Building, which was located in Corinth, Mississippi. Putt had most recently used it to operate a used car business. In the fall of 1984, the Corinth Gas and Water Department, which is an arm of the City of Corinth, was seeking a building suitable for housing its maintenance department and storing equipment and spare parts. Putt learned about this and approached Wayne McGee, department manager, and Dennis Coleman, a department employee, telling them his building was for sale for $100,000. McGee appeared at the regular monthly meeting of the Utilities Commission and reported his conversation with Putt. The commission authorized the inspection of Putt's building and, after receiving a favorable inspection report, authorized commissioner Leland Martin to negotiate a purchase agreement with Putt. There was a metal shed or building on the property that the commission saw no use for. Putt agreed to remove it and reduce the purchase price to $95,000. The parties then reached an agreement for the purchase of the building for $95,000. On March 11, 1985, the commission formally approved the purchase as evidenced by the following minute entry:

WAREHOUSE: Commissioner Martin reported that they had obtained the agreement of John Putt to sell the building on Old Highway 45 (Tate Street) to the City for $95,000.00 with him to retain the shed immediately north of the building. After discussion, the Commission found

that the appraisal by Lou Miller was $100,000.00 and that the shed would be of little value to the Gas and Water Department and that the reasonable market value of the property was $95,000.00 and should be purchased for the use of the Water and Gas Departments. The purchase to be made with funds from the Gas Department and the Water Department to pay rent on the building.

These minutes were signed by the chairman of the commission and attested by the secretary of the commission.

Putt removed the shed from the land and moved his used car business to another location. He also terminated the tenancy of some at-will renters on the property from whom he had been receiving $250 and $450 a month, respectively. He also cleaned up the warehouse in preparation for the closing. A dispute arose between Putt and the City about matters involved in the closing of the sale and the City refused to purchase Putt's property. In July 1985, the City purchased other property. Putt sued the City for breach of contract. The City moved for summary judgment on the ground that the contract did not comply with the statute of frauds, and the trial court granted a summary judgment in favor of the City and dismissed Putt's complaint. Putt appealed.

Source: 579 So. 2d 534 (Sup. Ct. Miss 1991)

Robertson, Justice

People are able to contract for the purchase and sale of real property and have their contracts given effect because the law allows such. As with the other facilities our law affords persons for realizing their wishes, land sales contracts are attended by certain formalities which, if not met, may leave the agreement a nullity and legally unenforceable. As a general rule, Mississippi law does not require that contracts be made in writing. Put otherwise, oral contracts are ordinarily no less enforceable than others.

The legislature has enacted an exception to this general rule, to the end of reducing the risk that persons will be held to contracts they did not make. This exception performs an evidentiary function, and provides, in the present context, that

> An action shall not be brought whereby to charge a defendant . . . upon any contract for the sale of lands . . . unless the promise or agreement upon which such action may be brought, or some memorandum or note thereof; shall be in writing, and signed by the party to be charged therewith.

It is commonly known as the statute of frauds.

What is central to our inquiry today is whether there is in fact an otherwise legally enforceable contract of sale between Putt and the City. Nothing in the statute of frauds requires that the contract itself be in writing. The statute is satisfied so long as there is "some memorandum or note thereof." For the prevention of frauds, the statute merely prescribes the form a part of the evidence must take. Oral testimony regarding the fact is admissible as well. The "memorandum or note" serves but to show a basis for believing that the offered oral evidence rests on a real transaction. *Gulf Refining Company v. Travis* suggests the memorandum "must contain words appropriate to, and indicating an intention thereby, to convey or lease land, must identify the land, [and] set forth the purchase price."

The minutes of the Utilities Commission unmistakably authorized an intent to buy, identify the land, set out the purchase price and otherwise meet *Gulf Reining's* indicia. These minutes are signed by the President and Secretary of the Utilities Commission and were, in fact, approved at a subsequent meeting. We hold that these minutes are a "memorandum or note" satisfying the statute. Beyond this, the present record provides an evidentiary basis upon which we may find that Putt and the City entered a valid and enforceable contract of sale.
Reversed and remanded in favor of Putt.

Contents of the Memorandum

Although there is a general trend away from requiring complete writings to satisfy the statute of frauds, an adequate memorandum must still contain several things. Generally, the essential terms of the contract must be indicated in the memorandum, although states differ in their requirements concerning how specifically the terms must be stated. The identity of the parties must be indicated in some way, and the subject matter of the contract must be identified with reasonable certainty. This last requirement causes particular problems in contracts for the sale of land, since many statutes require a detailed description of the property to be sold.

Contents of Memorandum under the UCC

The standard for determining the sufficiency of the contents of a memorandum is more flexible in cases concerning contracts for the sale of goods. This looser standard is created by the language of UCC section 2-201, which states that the writing must be sufficient to indicate that a contract for sale has been made between the parties, but a writing can be sufficient even if it omits or incorrectly states a term agreed on. However, the memorandum is not enforceable for more than the quantity of goods stated in the memorandum. Thus, a writing that does not indicate the *quantity* of goods to be sold would not satisfy the Code's writing requirement.

Signature Requirement

The memorandum must be signed by the *party to be charged* or his authorized agent. (The party to be charged is the person using the statute of frauds as a defense—generally the defendant unless the statute of frauds is asserted as a defense to a counterclaim.) This means that it is not necessary for purposes of meeting the statute of frauds for both parties' signatures to appear on the document. It is, however, in the best interests of both parties for both signatures to appear on the writing; otherwise, the contract evidenced by the writing is enforceable only against the signing party. Unless the statute expressly provides that the memorandum or contract must be signed at the end, the signature may appear any place on the memorandum. Any writing, mark, initials, stamp, engraving, or other symbol placed or printed on a memorandum will suffice as a signature, as long as the party to be charged intended it to authenticate (indicate the genuineness of) the writing.

Memorandum Consisting of Several Writings

In many situations, the elements required for a memorandum are divided among several documents. For example, Wayman and Allen enter into a contract for the sale of real estate, intending to memorialize their agreement in a formal written document later. While final drafts of a written contract are being prepared, Wayman repudiates the contract. Allen has a copy of an unsigned preliminary draft of the contract that identifies the parties and contains all of the material terms of the parties' agreement, an unsigned note written by Wayman that contains the legal description of the property, and a letter signed by Wayman that refers to the contract and to the other two documents. None of these documents, standing alone, would be sufficient to satisfy the statute of frauds. However, Allen can combine them to meet the requirements of the statute, provided that they all relate to the same agreement. This can be shown by physical attachment, as where the documents are stapled or bound together, or by references in the documents themselves that indicate that they all apply to the same transaction. In some cases, it has also been shown by the fact that the various documents were executed at the same time.

Alternative Means of Satisfying the Statute of Frauds in Sale of Goods Contracts

As you have learned, the basic requirement of the UCC statute of frauds [2-201] is that a contract for the sale of goods for the purchase price of $500 or more must be evidenced by a written memorandum that indicates the existence of the contract, states the quantity of goods to be sold, and is signed by the party to be charged. Recognizing that the underlying purpose of the statute of frauds is to provide more evidence of the existence of a contract than the mere oral testimony of one of the parties, however, the Code also permits the statute of frauds to be satisfied by any of four other types of evidence. These different methods of satisfying the UCC statute of frauds are depicted in Figure 20-2. Under the UCC, then, a contract for the sale of goods for a purchase price of $500 or more for which there is no written memorandum signed by the party to be charged can meet the requirements of the statute of frauds in any of the following ways:

1. *Confirmatory memorandum between merchants.* Suppose Gardner and Roth enter into a contract over the telephone for the sale of goods at a price of $5,000. Gardner then sends a memorandum to Roth confirming the deal they made orally. If Roth receives the memo and does not object to it, it would be fair to say that the parties' conduct provides some evidence that a contract exists. Under some circumstances, the UCC permits such confirmatory memoranda to satisfy the statute of frauds even though the writing is signed by the party who is seeking to enforce the contract rather than the party against whom enforcement is sought [2-201(2)]. This exception applies only when both of the parties to a contract are merchants. Furthermore, the memo must be sent within a reasonable time after the contract is made and must be sufficient to bind the person who sent it if enforcement were sought against him (that is, it must indicate

that a contract was made, state a quantity, and be signed by the sender). If the party against whom enforcement is sought receives the memo, has reason to know its contents, and yet fails to give written notice of objection to the contents of the memo within 10 days after receiving it, the memo can be introduced to meet the requirements of the statute of frauds.

FIGURE 20-2
Satisfying the statute of frauds for a contract for the sale of goods for a price of $500 or more

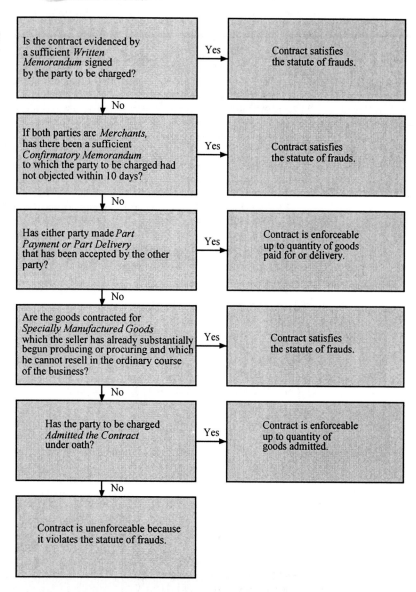

2. *Part payment or part delivery.* Suppose Rice and Cooper enter a contract for the sale of 1,000 units of goods at $1 each. After Rice has paid $600, Cooper refuses to deliver the goods and asserts the statute of frauds as a defense to enforcement of the contract. The Code permits part payment or part delivery to satisfy the statute of frauds, but only

for the quantity of goods that have been delivered or paid for [2-201(3)(c)]. Thus, Cooper would be required to deliver only 600 units rather than the 1,000 units Rice alleges that he agreed to sell.

3   *Admission in pleadings or court.* Another situation in which the UCC statute of frauds can be satisfied without a writing occurs when the party being sued admits the existence of the oral contract in his trial testimony or in any document that he files with the court. For example, Nelson refuses to perform an oral contract he made with Smith for the sale of $2,000 worth of goods, and Smith sues him. If Nelson admits the existence of the oral contract in pleadings or in court proceedings, his admission is sufficient to meet the statute of frauds. This exception is justified by the strong evidence that such an admission provides. After all, what better evidence of a contract can there be than is provided when the party being sued admits under penalty of perjury that a contract exists? When such an admission is made, the statute of frauds is satisfied as to the quantity of goods admitted [2-201(3)(b)]. For example, if Nelson only admits contracting for $1,000 worth of goods, the contract is enforceable only to that extent.

4.   *Specially manufactured goods.* Finally, an oral contract within the UCC statute of frauds can be enforced without a writing in some situations involving the sale of specially manufactured goods. This exception to the writing requirement will apply only if the nature of the specially manufactured goods is such that they are not suitable for sale in the ordinary course of the seller's business. Completely executory oral contracts are not enforceable under this exception. The seller must have made a substantial beginning in manufacturing the goods for the buyer, or must have made commitments for their procurement, before receiving notice that the buyer was repudiating the sale [2-201(3)(a)]. For example, Bennett Co. has an oral contract with Stevenson for the sale of $2,500 worth of calendars imprinted with Bennett Co.'s name and address. If Bennett Co. repudiates the contract before Stevenson has made a substantial beginning in manufacturing the calendars, the contract will be unenforceable under the statute of frauds. If, however, Bennett Co. repudiated the contract after Stevenson had made a substantial beginning, the oral contract would be enforceable. The specially manufactured goods provision is based both on the evidentiary value of the seller's conduct and on the need to avoid the injustice that would otherwise result from the seller's reliance.

Promissory Estoppel and the Statute of Frauds

The statute of frauds, which was created to prevent fraud and perjury, has often been criticized because it can create unjust results. One of the troubling features of the statute is that it can as easily be used to defeat a contract that was actually made as it can to defeat a fictitious agreement. As you have seen, courts and legislatures have created several exceptions to the statute of frauds that reduce the statute's potential for creating unfair results. In recent years, courts in some states have allowed the use of the doctrine of promissory **estoppel**[6] to enable some parties to recover under oral contracts that the statute of frauds would ordinarily render unenforceable.

Courts in these states hold that, when one of the parties would suffer serious losses because of her reliance on an oral contract, the other party is estopped from raising the statute of frauds as a defense. This position has been approved in the *Restatement (Second) of Contracts.* Section 139 of the *Restatement (Second)* provides that a promise that induces action or forbearance can be enforceable notwithstanding the statute of frauds if the reliance was foreseeable to the person making the promise and if injustice can be avoided only by enforcing the promise. The idea behind this section and the cases employing promissory estoppel is that the statute of frauds, which is designed to prevent injustice, should not be allowed to work an injustice. Section 139 and these cases also impliedly recognize the fact that the reliance required by promissory estoppel to some extent provides evidence of the existence of a contract between the parties, since it is unlikely that a person would materially rely on a nonexistent promise.

The use of promissory estoppel as a means of circumventing the statute of frauds is still controversial, however. Many courts fear that enforcing oral contracts on the basis of a party's reliance will essentially negate the statute. In cases involving the UCC statute of frauds, an additional source of concern involves the interpretation of section 2-201. Some courts have construed the provisions listing specific alternative methods of satisfying section 2-201's formal requirements to be exclusive, precluding the creation of any further exceptions by courts.

The Parol Evidence Rule

Explanation of the Rule

In many situations, contracting parties prefer to express their agreements in writing even when they are not required to do so by the statute of frauds. Written contracts rarely come into being without some prior discussions or negotiations between the parties, however. Various promises, proposals, or representations are usually made by one or both of the parties before the execution of a written contract. What happens when one of those prior promises, proposals, or representations is not included in the terms of the written contract? For example, suppose that Jackson wants to buy Stone's house. During the course of negotiations, Stone states that he will pay for any major repairs that the house needs for the first year that Jackson owns it. The written contract that the parties ultimately sign, however, does not say anything about Stone paying for repairs, and, in fact, states that Jackson will take the house "as is." The furnace breaks down three months after the sale, and Stone refuses to pay for its repair. What is the status of Stone's promise to pay for repairs? The basic problem is one of defining the boundaries of the parties' agreement. Are all the promises made in the process of negotiation part of the contract, or do the terms of the written document that the parties signed supersede any preliminary agreements?

The **parol evidence rule** provides the answer to this question. The term *parol evidence* means written or spoken statements that are *not contained in the written contract*. The parol evidence rule provides that, when parties enter a *written contract* that they intend as a complete **integration** (a complete and final statement of their agreement), a court will not permit the use of evidence of *prior* or *contemporaneous* statements to add to, alter, or contradict the terms of the written contract. This rule is based on the presumption that when people enter into a written contract, the best evidence of their agreement is the written contract itself. It also reflects the idea that later expressions of intent are presumed to prevail over earlier expressions of intent. In the hypothetical case involving Stone and Jackson, assuming that they intended the written contract to be the final integration of their agreement, Jackson would not be able to introduce evidence of Stone's promise to pay for repairs. The effect of excluding preliminary promises or statements from consideration is, of course, to confine the parties' contract to the terms of the written agreement. The lesson to be learned from this example is that people who put their agreements in writing should make sure that all the terms of their agreement are included in the writing. The following case, *Slivinsky v. Watkins Johnson Company*, illustrates the application of the parol evidence rule.

Slivinsky v. Watkins-Johnson Company

In July 1984, Sandra Slivinsky applied for a job as a materials scientist with Watkins-Johnson Company, a large aerospace manufacturer. Directly above the signature line on the application she signed was the statement: "I understand that employment by WATKINS-JOHNSON COMPANY is conditional upon . . . execution of an Employment Agreement . . . . I further understand that if I become employed by Watkins-Johnson Company, there will be no agreement, expressed or implied, between the company and me for any specific period of employment, nor for continuing or long-term employment." Over the next several months, Watkins-Johnson contacted Slivinsky's references, requested her transcripts, and set up a series of interviews. Slivinsky claims that at these interviews she was promised "long-term," "indefinite," and "permanent" employment, not dependent on business cycles, and subject to termination only for cause. Finally, Watkins-Johnson made a verbal offer of employment to Slivinsky and she accepted. On January 7, 1985, which was Slivinsky's first day at work, Slivinsky signed the employee agreement that had been referred to in her employment application. Set apart in bold type, the last paragraph of this agreement provided

that there was no express or implied agreement between the parties regarding the duration of her employment and that the employment could be terminated at any time with or without cause.

As a result of the space shuttle *Challenger* disaster in January 1986, Watkins-Johnson experienced significant business losses and government contract cancellations. The management decided that employee cutbacks were essential to cope with the loss of business. Ultimately, 24 employees, including Slivinsky, were selected for the reduction in force program. Watkins-Johnson terminated her employment in June 1986.

Slivinsky brought suit against Watkins-Johnson for breach of the employment contract, asserting that she had been terminated without cause in violation of the parties' express and implied agreement. She also claimed that the reasons given for her termination were pretextual and that she was really fired for other reasons, such as her supervisor disliking her. The trial court granted Watkins-Johnson's motion for summary judgment, and Slivinsky appealed.

Source: 270 Cal. Rptr. 585 (Cal Ct. App. 1990)

Cottle, Associate Justice

Slivinsky claims that the parties' employment agreement includes factors such as oral assurances of job security and Watkins-Johnson's personnel policies and practices not to terminate employees except for good cause. Watkins-Johnson [argues] that it is limited to the parties' express written contract defining the employment as at-will.

The dispositive issue, therefore, is whether we can look beyond the four corners of the parties' written agreements to ascertain the complete agreement of the parties. The answer to that question involves application of the parol evidence rule, a rule of substantive law precluding the introduction of evidence which varies or contradicts the terms of an integrated written instrument. If the parties intended that the Application and Employment Agreement constituted an integration, i.e., the final expression of their agreement with respect to grounds for termination, then those agreements may not be contradicted by evidence of any prior agreement or of a contemporaneous oral agreement. No particular form is required for an integrated agreement. When only part of the agreement is integrated, the parol evidence rule applies to that part.

Applying these standards, we conclude that the contract was integrated with respect to the grounds for termination. Slivinsky's employment application specifically conditioned employment upon execution of an employment agreement. It further provided that if Slivinsky were to become employed by Watkins-Johnson, there "will be no agreement, expressed or implied, . . . for any specific period of employment, nor for continuing or long-term employment." When Slivinsky executed the Employee Agreement, she acknowledged "that there is no agreement, express or implied, between employee and the Company for any specific period of employment, nor for continuing or long-term employment. Employee and the Company each have a right to terminate employment, with or without cause." Reading these documents together, the only reasonable conclusion that can be drawn is that the parties intended that there would be no other agreement regarding termination other than that set forth in the Employee Agreement. Consequently, evidence of an implied agreement which contradicts the terms of the written agreement is not admissible. There cannot be a valid express contract and an implied contract, each embracing the same subject, but requiring different results.

Because we hold that the contract is a contract for employment terminable at will, we do not reach the issues regarding whether good cause existed for Slivinsky's termination based on Watkins-Johnson's decision to reduce its work force. Even if the reduction in force were a pretextual ground for terminating Slivinsky's employment, it would not be actionable with an at-will employment contract unless the employer's motivation for a discharge contravenes some significant public policy principle. No such public policy violation is alleged here.

Judgment for Watkins-Johnson affirmed.

Scope of the Parol Evidence Rule

The parol evidence rule is relevant only in cases in which the parties have expressed their agreement in a written contract. Thus, it would not apply to a case involving an oral contract or to a case in which writings existed that were not intended to embody the final statement of at least part of the parties' contract. The parol evidence rule has been made a part of the law of sales in the Uniform Commercial Code [2-202], so it is applicable to contracts for the sale of goods as well as to contracts governed by the common law of contracts. Furthermore, the rule excludes only evidence of statements made prior to or during the signing of the written contract. It does not apply to statements made after the signing of the contract. Thus, evidence of subsequent statements is freely admissible.

Admissible Parol Evidence

In some situations, evidence of statements made outside the written contract is admissible notwithstanding the parol evidence rule. Parol evidence is permitted in the situations discussed below either because the writing is not the best evidence of the contract or because the evidence is offered, not to contradict the terms of the writing, but to explain the writing or to challenge the underlying contractual obligation that the writing represents.

1. *Additional terms in partially integrated contracts.* In many instances, parties will desire to introduce evidence of statements or agreements that would supplement rather than contradict the written contract. Whether they can do this depends on whether the written contract is characterized as *completely integrated* or *partially integrated*. A completely integrated contract is one that the parties intend as a *complete and exclusive statement* of their entire agreement. A partially integrated contract is one that expresses the parties' final agreement as to some but not all of the terms of their contract. When a contract is only partially integrated, the parties are permitted to use parol evidence to prove the *additional* terms of their agreement. Such evidence cannot, however, be used to contradict the written terms of the contract. To determine whether a contract is completely or partially integrated, a court must determine the parties' intent. A court judges intent by looking at the language of the contract, the apparent completeness of the writing, and all the surrounding

circumstances. It will also consider whether the contract contains a **merger clause** (also known as an **integration clause**). These clauses, which are very common in form contracts and commercial contracts, provide that the written contract is the complete integration of the parties' agreement. They are designed to prevent a party from giving testimony about prior statements or agreements and are generally effective in indicating that the writing was a complete integration. Even though a contract contains a merger clause, parol evidence could be admissible under one of the following exceptions.

2. *Explaining ambiguities.* Parol evidence can be offered to explain an ambiguity in the written contract. Suppose a written contract between Lowen and Matthews provides that Lowen will buy "Matthews's truck," but Matthews has two trucks. The parties could offer evidence of negotiations, statements, and other circumstances preceding the creation of the written contract to identify the truck to which the writing refers. Used in this way, parol evidence helps the court interpret the contract. It does not contradict the written contract.

3. *Circumstances invalidating contract.* Any circumstances that would be relevant to show that a contract is not valid can be proven by parol evidence. For example, evidence that Holden pointed a gun at Dickson and said, "Sign this contract, or I'll kill you," would be admissible to show that the contract was voidable because of duress. Likewise, parol evidence would be admissible to show that a contract was illegal or was induced by fraud, misrepresentation, undue influence, or mistake.

4. *Existence of condition.* It is also permissible to use parol evidence to show that a writing was executed with the understanding that it was not to take effect until the occurrence of a condition (a future, uncertain event that creates a duty to perform). Suppose Farnsworth signs a contract to purchase a car with the agreement that the contract is not to be effective unless and until Farnsworth gets a new job. If the written contract is silent about any conditions that must occur before it becomes effective, Farnsworth could introduce parol evidence to prove the existence of the condition. Such proof merely elaborates on, but does not contradict, the terms of the writing.

5. *Subsequent agreements.* As you read earlier, the parol evidence rule does not forbid parties to introduce proof of *subsequent agreements*. This is true even if the terms of the later agreement cancel, subtract from, or add to the obligations stated in the written contract. The idea here is that when a writing is followed by a later statement or agreement, the writing is no longer the best evidence of the agreement. You should be aware, however, that subsequent modifications of contracts may sometimes be unforceable due to lack of consideration of failure to comply with the statute of frauds. In addition, contracts sometimes expressly provide that modifications must be written. In this situation, an oral modification would be unenforceable.

Concept Review
Parol Evidence Rule

Parol Evidence Rule	Applies when:	Provides that:
	Parties create a writing intended as a final and complete integration of at least part of the parties' contract.	Evidence of statements or promises made before or during the creation of the writing cannot be used to supplement, change, or contradict the terms of the written contract.
But Parol Evidence *Can* Be Used to	1. Prove consistent, additional terms when the contract is *partially integrated*. 2. Explain an ambiguity in the written contract. 3. Prove that the contract is void, voidable, or unenforceable. 4. Prove that the contract was subject to a condition. 5. Prove that the parties subsequently modified the contract or made a new agreement.	

Interpretation of Contracts

Once a court has decided what promises are included in a contract, it is faced with *interpreting* the contract to determine the *meaning* and *legal effect* of the terms used by the parties. Courts have adopted broad, basic standards of interpretation that guide them in the interpretation process.

The court will first attempt to determine the parties' *principal objective*. Every clause will then be determined in the light of this principal objective. Ordinary words will be given their usual meaning and technical words (such as those that have a special meaning in the parties' trade or business) will be given their technical meaning, unless a different meaning was clearly intended.

Guidelines grounded in common sense are also used to determine the relationship of the various terms of the contract. Specific terms that follow general terms are presumed to qualify those general terms. Suppose that a provision that states that the subject of the contract is "guaranteed for one year" is followed by a provision describing the "one-year guarantee against defects in workmanship." Here, it is fair to conclude that the more specific term qualifies the more general term and that the guarantee described in the contract is a guarantee of workmanship only, and not of parts and materials.

Sometimes, there is internal conflict in the terms of an agreement and courts must determine which term should prevail. When the parties use a form contract or some other type of contract that is partially printed and partially handwritten, the handwritten provisions will prevail. If the contract was drafted by one of the parties, any ambiguities will be resolved against the party who drafted the contract.

If both parties to the contract are members of a trade, profession, or community in which certain words are commonly given a particular meaning (this is called a *usage*), the courts will presume that the parties intended the meaning that the usage gives to the terms they use. For example if the word dozen in the bakery business means 13 rather than 12, a contract between two bakers for the purchase of 10 dozen loaves of bread will be presumed to mean 130 loaves of bread rather than 120. Usages can also add provisions to the parties' agreement. If the court finds that a certain practice is a matter of common usage in the parties' trade, it will assume that the parties intended to include that practice in their agreement. If contracting parties are members of the same trade, business, or community but do not intend to be bound by usage, they should specifically say so in their agreement.

Ethical and Public Policy Concerns

1. The statute of frauds requires written evidence of some, but not all, contracts. Is this defensible from a public policy standpoint? Would it be preferable for the law to simply require that all contracts be evidenced by a writing?
2. What ethical problem was the statute of frauds designed to prevent, and what ethical problem does the statute of frauds create? Is the "cure worse than the disease"?
3. Under the law of some states, the doctrine of promissory estoppel permits the enforcement of promises that induce reliance, even when those promises do not comply with the statute of frauds. Should all states adopt this position? What effect would this have on the statute of frauds?
4. For those parties who draft and proffer standardized form contracts, the parol evidence rule can be a powerful ally because it has the effect of limiting the scope of an integrated, written contract to the terms of the writing. Although statements and promises made to a person before he signs a contract might be highly influential in persuading him to enter the contract, the parol evidence rule effectively prevents these

precontract communications from being legally enforceable. Consider also that standardized form contracts are usually drafted for the benefit of and proffered by the more sophisticated and powerful party in a contract (e.g., the insurance company rather than the insured, the automobile dealer rather than the customer, the landlord rather than the tenant). Considering all of this, do you believe that the parol evidence rule promotes ethical behavior?

Problems and Problem Cases

1. Golomb allegedly orally agreed to sell to Lee for $275,000 the Ferrari once owned by King Leopold of Belgium. Golomb ultimately refused to sell the car and Lee sued him. At trial, Golomb denied ever promising to sell the car to Lee. Can Lee enforce this alleged promise?

2. Boyd-Scarp, a building contractor, was building a new home for Rathmann. Rathmann paid Boyd-Scarp for appliances for the new home and Boyd-Scarp contracted with Al Booth's, an appliance supplier, for the purchase of the appliances. Al Booth's had heard that Boyd-Scarp was having financial problems. Before delivering the appliances to the Rathmanns' new home, it contacted Rathmann and asked him to guarantee payment. Al Booth's alleges that Rathmann orally promised to pay for the appliances if Boyd-Scarp failed to pay. Al Booth's then delivered the appliances. BoydScarp became insolvent and did not pay Al Booth's for the appliances. Al Booth's turned to Rathmann for payment. Rathmann asserted the statute of frauds as a defense. Will he be successful in using this defense?

3. In January 1980, Mayer entered into an oral contract of employment with King Cola for a three-year term. Mayer moved from Chattanooga to St. Louis and began working. King Cola paid his moving expenses. In accordance with the parties' negotiations, Mayer awaited a written contract, but none was ever executed. The employment relationship soon began to deteriorate, and after several months King Cola's president told Mayer that he was not going to be given a contract. In May 1980, King Cola discharged Mayer. In a state that does not recognize the doctrine of promissory estoppel as an exception to the statute of frauds, will Mayer be able to enforce the contract?

4. Green owns a lot (Lot S) in the Manomet section of Plymouth, Massachusetts. In July 1980, she advertised it for sale. On July 11 and 12, the Hickeys discussed with Green purchasing Lot S and orally agreed to a sale for $15,000. On July 12, Green accepted the Hickeys' check for $500. Hickey had left the payee line of the deposit check blank, because of uncertainty whether Green or her brother was to receive the check. Hickey asked Green to fill in the appropriate name. Green, however, held the check, did not fill in the payee's name, and neither cashed nor indorsed it. Hickey told Green that his intention was to sell his home and build on the lot he was buying from Green. Relying on the arrangements with Green, the Hickeys advertised their house in newspapers for three days in July. They found a purchaser quickly. Within a short time, they contracted with a purchaser for the sale of their house and accepted the purchaser's deposit check. On the back of this check, above the Hickeys' signatures indorsing the check, was noted: "Deposit on purchase of property at Sachem Rd. and First St., Manomet, Ma. Sale price, $44,000." On July 24, Green told Hickey that she no longer intended to sell her property to him and instead had decided to sell it to someone else for $16,000. Hickey offered to pay Green $16,000 for the lot, but she refused this offer. The Hickeys then filed a complaint against Green seeking specific performance. Green asserted that relief was barred by the statute of frauds. Is this correct?

5. In June 1976, Moore went to First National Bank and requested the president of the bank to allow his sons, Rocky and Mike, to open an account in the name of Texas Continental Express, Inc. Moore promised to bring his own business to the bank and orally agreed to make good any losses that the bank might incur from receiving dishonored checks from Texas Continental. The bank then furnished regular checking account and bank draft services to Texas Continental. Several years later, Texas Continental wrote checks totaling $448,942.05 that were returned for insufficient funds. Texas Continental did not cover the checks, and the bank turned to Moore for payment. When Moore refused to pay, the bank sued him. Does Moore have a good statute of frauds defense?

6. Mark and Barney Brownlee were farmers who, as a partnership doing business as Brownlee Brothers, grew and sold crops. In addition to farming, Barney Brownlee owned a gas station. On July 22, 1983, Barney Brownlee allegedly telephoned Goldkist and, after checking on the current price of soybeans, allegedly agreed to deliver 5,000 bushels of soybeans to Goldkist between August 22 and September 22, at $6.88 per pound. Although no written agreement signed by either of the Brownlees was created, Goldkist did send the Brownlees a written memorandum dated July 22, which confirmed the agreement to sell 5,000 bushels of soybeans on the terms described above. The Brownlees received the memorandum but did not respond to it. They also did not deliver the soybeans, and Goldkist was forced to "cover" the contract (buy soybeans from another source). Goldkist then brought this action to recover its losses arising out of the necessity to cover. The Brownlees asserted as a defense the fact that there was no writing signed by either of them as required by UCC section 2-201. Is this a good argument?

7. Dyer purchased a used Ford from Walt Bennett Ford for $5,895. She signed a written contract, which showed that no taxes were included in the sales price. Dyer contended, however, that the salesperson who negotiated the purchase with her told her both before and after her signing of the contract that the sales tax on the automobile had been paid. The contract Dyer signed contained the following language:

> The above comprises the entire agreement pertaining to this purchase and no other agreement of any kind, verbal understanding, representation, or promise whatsoever will be recognized.

It also stated:

> This contract constitutes the entire agreement between the parties and no modification hereof shall be valid in any event and Buyer expressly waives the right to rely thereon, unless made in writing, signed by Seller.

Later, when Dyer attempted to license the automobile, she discovered that the Arkansas sales tax had not been paid on it. She paid the sales tax and sued Bennett for breach of contract. What result?

8. Starry is a general contractor in the business of asphalt road construction. Murphy was one of its suppliers. In March 1990, a Murphy sales manager orally promised to sell Starry 20,000 tons of asphalt cement oil for $90 per ton. That agreement was confirmed with a written acknowledgment form that specifically stated that causes beyond the control of either party would be an excuse for delay or failure to perform if notice were given promptly. In April 1990, Starry determined that it would need more asphalt cement oil. It contacted Murphy and requested an additional 5,000 tons. Several days later, Murphy's sales manager orally agreed to sell the additional oil on the same terms and conditions as those initially agreed to. Starry neglected to send a

confirmatory memorandum of this oral modification. In August 1990, due to the war in the Persian Gulf, Murphy began experiencing an unprecedented demand for asphalt cement oil. Starry employees became concerned that Murphy might not supply the additional oil and contacted Murphy to request a written confirmation of the modification. Murphy's sales manager allegedly responded, "Don't worry about it. I'll take care of you. I've never cheated you in the past. You are a good customer, and I treat our good customers right." This sales manager, however, was subsequently promoted and replaced by another Murphy employee. In September, the new sales manager informed Starry that because of the oil crisis, Murphy would be forced to allocate its supply. Believing that Murphy would ultimately deliver the additional oil, Starry did not approach other suppliers until late September. At that time, it made arrangements to purchase the additional oil from other suppliers at a higher price. In October 1990, Starry sent a letter to Murphy discussing the agreement between it and Murphy for the sale of 25,000 tons of oil. Murphy was unable to deliver the additional oil and denied that the agreement was ever modified to include an additional 5,000 tons of oil. Starry sued it for breach of contract. Will Starry be able to enforce an agreement to sell the additional quantity of oil?

9. Lovely was living in Ann Arbor, Michigan, and working at two jobs there when Dierkes offered Lovely employment with the Real Food Company in Jackson, Michigan. Dierkes promised Lovely a three-year employment contract, a salary of $400 per week, and a percentage interest in Real Food. He also promised that Lovely would not be discharged without good cause. Lovely relocated his family to Jackson in reliance on Dierkes's promise. He began performing under the agreement and requested several times that Dierkes reduce the contract to writing. Dierkes allegedly assured Lovely that a writing was forthcoming. After two months of employment, Dierkes discharged Lovely. Lovely sued Dierkes and Real Food for breach of contract. Dierkes claims that the contract is unenforceable because of the statute of frauds. Can Lovely enforce this contract?

10. In 1981, Goodman was living in Oklahoma with her husband, who was suffering from a terminal illness. She and her husband traveled to the Connecticut home of her mother, Mayer, to discuss whether Goodman should return to Connecticut. Goodman and Mayer reached an oral agreement providing that Goodman would live in Mayer's house, would make certain refurbishments, and care for Mayer in return for which Mayer would convey the house to Goodman. Goodman also agreed to pay one half the value of the house to her sister, Savoy, upon the death of Goodman's husband. The Goodmans sold their Oklahoma home and moved to Connecticut. They contracted for renovations, which were paid from the proceeds of the Oklahoma house. In September 1981, Goodman and Mayer had an argument, after which the Goodmans vacated Mayer's house at her request. Shortly thereafter, Mayer changed her will, which had left one-half of her estate to each of her two daughters, and disinherited Goodman, leaving her entire estate on her death to Savoy. Mayer sued her mother's estate, claiming the existence of an enforceable oral contract. Will she prevail?

11. Acme Used Cars Sales and Service sold a used car to Jones. Prior to the signing of a written purchase contract, Acme's salesperson told Jones that he "wouldn't find a car like this at any price" and "this car is a crown jewel." However, the purchase order that Jones signed stated that the car was being sold "as is" and that "no warranties or representations concerning the car have been made or given except as contained" in the contract. Jones later discovered that the brakes were defective and needed to be rebuilt. If Jones sued Acme, would the parol evidence rule prevent the admission of testimony about the salesperson's statements?

12. Fred, a jelly manufacturer in Chicago, ordered grapes by telephone for a price of $800 from Gus, a grape grower in California. Gus sent a written purchase order confirmation. He also shipped the grapes, but they were spoiled when they arrived. Would the statute of frauds prevent this contract from being enforced?

    See also "Software Horror Story" and "A Christmas Story."

Endnotes

1. Note, however, that a writing might be required under state insurance statutes.
2. Specific performance is discussed in more detail in Chapter 12.
3. *Restatement (Second) of Contracts* § 129, comment *d*.
4. Modifications of sales contracts are discussed detail in Chapter 17.
5. Note, however, that "nonmarital" agreements between unmarried cohabitants who do not plan marriage are not within the marriage provision of the statute of frauds, even though the agreement may concern the same sorts of matters that are typically covered in a prenuptial agreement.
6. The doctrine of promissory estoppel is discussed in Chapters 14 and 17.

Chapter Twenty-One

PRODUCT LIABILITY

Introduction

Suppose you are the president of a firm making products for sale to the public. One of your concerns would be the company's exposure to civil liability for defects in those products. As president, therefore, you would worry about changes in the law that make such liability more likely or more expensive. In other contexts, however, the same changes might appeal to you. This is especially true if you are harmed by defective products you purchase as a consumer. Such changes might also appeal to you if your firm wants to sue a supplier that has sold it defective products.

Each of these situations involves the law of *product liability*. Product liability law is the body of legal rules governing civil suits for losses resulting from defective goods.[1] After sketching product liability law's historical evolution, this chapter discusses the most important *theories of product liability recovery*. These theories are rules of law allowing plaintiffs to recover for losses resulting from defective goods once they prove certain facts. The second half of the chapter considers certain legal problems that are common to all the theories of recovery but that may be resolved differently from theory to theory.

The Evolution of Product Liability Law

The 19th Century

A century ago, the rules governing suits for defective goods were very much to sellers' and manufacturers' advantage. This was the era of *caveat emptor* (let the buyer beware). In contract suits, there was usually no liability unless the seller had made an express promise to the buyer and the goods did not conform to that promise. Some courts even required that the words *warrant* or *guarantee* accompany the promise before liability would exist. In negligence suits, the maxim of "no liability without fault" was widely accepted, and plaintiffs frequently had difficulty proving negligence because the necessary evidence was under the defendant's control. In both contract and negligence cases, finally, the doctrine of "no liability outside privity of contract" often prevented plaintiffs from recovering against parties with whom they had not directly dealt.[2]

The social and economic conditions that prevailed for much of the 19th century help explain these prodefendant rules. At that time, laissez-faire values strongly influenced public policy and the law. One expression of those values was the belief that sellers and manufacturers should be contractually bound only when they deliberately assumed such liability by actually making a promise to someone with whom they dealt directly. Another factor limiting manufacturers' liability for defective products, some say, was the desire to promote industrialization by preventing potentially crippling damage recoveries against infant industries.

Certain features of the 19th-century economy, however, made that century's product liability rules less hard on plaintiffs than would otherwise have been the case. Chains of distribution tended to be short, so the no-liability-outside-privity defense was not always available. Because goods tended to be simple, buyers could sometimes inspect them for defects. Before the emergence of large corporations late in the 19th century, sellers and buyers were often of relatively equal size, sophistication, and bargaining power. This meant that they could deal on a relatively equal footing.

The 20th Century

Today, many 19th-century social and economic tendencies are conspicuous by their absence. Laissez-faire values do not exercise the influence they did a century ago. Instead, a more protective, interdependent climate has emerged. With the development of a viable industrial economy, there has been less perceived need to protect manufacturers from liability for defective goods. The emergence of long chains of distribution has meant that consumers often do not deal directly with the parties responsible for defects in the products they buy. Because sizable corporations tend to dominate the economy, consumers are less able to bargain equally with such parties in any event. Finally, the growing complexity of goods has made buyer inspections more difficult.

Due to such developments, product liability law has moved from its earlier *caveat emptor* emphasis to a stance of *caveat venditor* (let the seller beware). To protect consumers, modern courts and legislatures intervene in private contracts for the sale of goods and impose liability regardless of fault. As a result, sellers and manufacturers face greater liability and higher damage recoveries for defects in their products. Underlying the shift toward *caveat venditor* is the belief that sellers, manufacturers, and their insurers are best able to bear the economic costs associated with product defects and that they can usually pass on these costs through higher prices. Thus, the economic risk associated with defective products has been effectively spread throughout society, or socialized.

The Current "Crisis" in Product Liability Law

Modern product liability law and its socialization-of-risk strategy have come under increasing attack over the past 15 to 20 years. Such attacks often focus on the difficulty sellers and manufacturers have encountered in obtaining product liability insurance and the increased costs of such insurance. Some observers blame the insurance industry for these problems, while others trace them to the increased liability and greater damage recoveries just discussed. Whatever their origin, the crisis in the liability insurance system has put sellers and manufacturers in a bind. Businesses unwilling or unable to buy expensive product liability insurance run the risk of being crippled by large damage awards unless they self-insure, which itself can be an expensive option today. Firms that purchase insurance, on the other hand, must pay a higher price for it. In either case, the resulting costs may be difficult to completely pass on. In addition, those costs may deter the development and marketing of innovative new products.

For these reasons and others, recent years have witnessed many efforts to scale back the proplaintiff thrust of modern product liability law. This is one aspect of the "tort reform" movement discussed in Chapter 7. However, despite the introduction of several federal reform bills, Congress has yet to make any major changes in product liability law.

As we note later in this chapter, however, tort reform efforts have occasionally been successful in the states.

Theories Of Product Liability Recovery

Technically, some theories of product liability recovery are contractual and some are tort-based. The contract theories involve a product **warranty**—a contractual promise about the nature of the product sold. In warranty cases, plaintiffs claim that the product failed to live up to the seller's promise. In tort cases, on the other hand, plaintiffs usually argue that the defendant was negligent or that strict liability should apply.[3]

Express Warranty

Creating an Express Warranty

UCC section 2-313(1) states that an **express warranty** is created in any of three ways.

1. Any *affirmation of fact or promise* regarding the goods creates an express warranty that the goods will conform to that affirmation. For instance, a computer seller's statement that a particular computer has a certain amount of memory creates an express warranty to that effect.
2. Any *description* of the goods creates an express warranty that the goods will conform to the description. This category includes: (1) statements that goods are of a certain brand, type, or model (e.g., an IBM dot-matrix computer printer); (2) descriptive adjectives characterizing the product (e.g., shatterproof glass); and (3) drawings, blueprints, and technical specifications.
3. A *sample* or *model* of goods to be sold creates an express warranty that the rest of the goods will conform to the sample or model. A sample is an object drawn from an actual collection of goods to be sold, while a model is a replica offered for the buyer's inspection when the goods themselves are unavailable.

The first two kinds of express warranties probably overlap; also, each can be either written or oral. In addition, magic words like warrant or guarantee no longer are needed to create an express warranty.

Value, Opinion, and Sales Talk

Statements of *value* ("This chair would bring you $2,000 at an auction") or *opinion* ("I think that this chair is a genuine antique Louis XIV") do not create an express warranty. The same is true of statements that amount to *sales talk* or *puffery* ("This chair is a good buy"). Of course, no sharp line separates such statements from express warranties. In close cases, a statement is more likely to be an express warranty if it is specific rather than indefinite, if it is stated in the sales contract rather than elsewhere,[4] or if it is unequivocal rather than hedged or qualified. The relative knowledge possessed by the seller and the buyer can also be an important factor. A car salesperson's statement about a used car, for instance, stands a greater chance of being an express warranty where the buyer knows little about cars than where the buyer is another car dealer. The following *Hall Farms* case discusses some of the points made in this paragraph.

The Basis-of-the-Bargain Problem

Under pre-Code law, there was no recovery for breach of an express warranty unless the buyer relied on that warranty in making the purchase. The UCC, however, ambiguously requires that the warranty be *part of the basis of the bargain*. Some courts read the Code's basis-of-the-bargain test as saying that full reliance is necessary. Others only require that the seller's warranty have been a *contributing factor* in the buyer's decision to purchase.

Advertisements

Statements made in advertisements, catalogs, or brochures *may* be express warranties. Such sources, however, are often filled with sales talk. Also, basis-of-the-bargain problems may arise if it is unclear whether or to what degree the statement really induced the buyer to make the purchase. For example, a buyer who reads an advertisement containing an express warranty one month before actually purchasing the product may or may not have been induced to purchase by the express warranty in the advertisement.

Multiple Express Warranties

What happens when the seller gives two or more express warranties and those warranties arguably conflict? UCC section 2-317 says that such warranties should be read as consistent with each other and as cumulative if this is reasonable. If not, the parties' intention controls. In determining that intention: (1) exact or technical specifications defeat a sample, a model, or general descriptive language; and (2) a sample defeats general descriptive language.

Martin Rispens & Son v. Hall Farms, Inc.

Hall Farms, Inc. ordered 40 pounds of Prince Charles watermelon seed from Martin Rispens & Son, a seed dealer. Rispens had obtained the seed from Petoseed Company, Inc., a seed producer. The label on Petoseed's can stated that the seeds are "top quality seeds with high vitality, vigor and germination." Hall Farms germinated the seeds in a greenhouse before transplanting the small watermelon plants to its fields. Although the plants had a few abnormalities, they grew rapidly. By mid-July, however, purple blotches had spread over most of the crop, and by the end of July the crop was ruined. It was later determined that the crop had been destroyed by "watermelon fruit blotch." Hall Farms's lost profits on the crop came to $180,000.

Hall Farms sued Petoseed for, among other things, breach of express warranty. Petoseed moved for summary judgment, but the trial court denied the motion. Petoseed appealed.

Source: 601 N.E.2d 429 (Inc. Ct. App. 1992)

Baker, Judge

An express warranty is created by an affirmation of fact or promise made by the seller to the buyer which relates to the goods and becomes part of the basis of the bargain; it warrants that the goods shall conform to the affirmation or promise. It is not necessary that the seller use formal words such as "warrant" or "guarantee" or that he have a specific intention to make a warranty. On the other hand, an affirmation merely of the value of the goods or a statement purporting to be merely the seller's opinion or commendation of the goods does not create a warranty.

Whether a given representation is a warranty or merely an expression of the seller's opinion is determined in part by considering whether the seller asserts a fact of which the buyer is ignorant, or merely states an opinion or judgment on a matter of which the seller has no special knowledge and on which the buyer may be expected also to have an opinion and to exercise his judgment. Courts must also consider the degree of specificity expressed in the representation.

The label on Petoseed's can stated that the seeds are "top quality seeds with high vitality, vigor and germination." We consider the words "top quality seeds" as a classic example of puffery. The precise meaning of "top quality" is subject to considerably different interpretations.

Petoseed [also] claimed that its seeds possessed "high vitality, vigor and germination." Although reasonable people may differ as to the particular degree of vitality, vigor, and germination meant by the word "high," Petoseed did expressly warrant that its seeds would possess at least a modicum of vitality, vigor, and germination. If this affirmation became a basis of the bargain, an express warranty was created. We need not address this question, however, because even assuming Hall Farms relied on the affirmation, no breach occurred.

"Vitality" is the capacity to live, grow, or develop. "Vigor" is the capacity for natural growth and survival. "Germination" is the beginning of growth or sprouting. Here, there is no dispute that the watermelon seeds sprouted, grew, and developed a normal fruit set. Thus, the seeds conformed to the affirmation on Petoseed's labels; consequently, there was no breach. Partial summary judgment is appropriate when there is no conflict over facts dispositive of a portion of the litigation. Hall Farms may not recover from Petoseed based on an express warranty theory.

Trial court decision denying Petoseed's motion for summary judgment on Hall Farms' express warranty claim reversed.

Implied Warranty of Merchantability

An **implied warrant** is a warranty created by *operation of law* rather than the seller's voluntary express statements. UCC section 2-314(1) creates the Code's **implied warranty of merchantability** by stating that "a warranty that the goods shall be merchantable is implied in a contract for their sale if the seller is a merchant with respect to goods of that kind." This is a clear example of the 20th-century tendency for government to intervene in private contracts to protect allegedly weaker parties.

In an implied warranty of merchantability case, the plaintiff argues that the seller breached the warranty by selling nonmerchantable goods. Under section 2-314, such claims can succeed only where the seller is a *merchant with respect to goods of the kind sold*. A housewife's sale of homemade preserves or a hardware store owner's sale of a used car, for example, do not trigger the implied warranty of merchantability.

UCC section 2-314(2) states that, to be merchantable, goods must at least: (1) pass without objection in the trade; (2) be fit for the ordinary purposes for which such goods are used; (3) be of even kind, quality, and quantity within each unit (case, package, or carton) and among all units; (4) be adequately contained, packaged, and labeled; (5) conform to any promises or statements of fact made on the container or label; and (6) in the case of fungible goods, be of fair average quality. The most important of these requirements is that the goods must be *fit for the ordinary purposes for which such goods are used*. The goods need not be perfect to be fit for their ordinary purposes. Rather, they need only meet the reasonable expectations of the average consumer.

Such broad, flexible tests of merchantability are almost inevitable given the wide range of products sold in the United States today and the varied defects they can present. Still, a few generalizations about merchantability determinations are possible. Goods that fail to function properly or that have harmful side effects generally are not merchantable. A computer that fails to work properly or that destroys the owner's programs, for example, is not fit for the ordinary purposes for which computers are used. In cases involving allergic reactions to drugs or other products, courts frequently find the defendant liable if it was reasonably foreseeable that an appreciable number of consumers would suffer the reaction. As the following *Marriott* case reveals, there is some disagreement about the standard for food products that are alleged to be unmerchantable because they contain harmful objects or substances. Under the *foreign-natural* test, the defendant is liable if the object or substance is "foreign" to the product, but not liable if it is "natural" to that product. Increasingly, however, courts ask whether the food product met the consumer's *reasonable expectations*.

Yong Cha Hong v. Marriott Corporation

Yong Cha Hong bought some take-out fried chicken from a Roy Rogers Family Restaurant owned by the Marriott Corporation. While eating a chicken wing from her order, she bit into an object that she perceived to be a worm. Claiming permanent injuries and great physical and emotional upset from this incident, Hong sued Marriott for $500,000 in federal district court under the implied warranty of merchantability. After introducing an expert's report alleging that the object in the chicken wing was not a worm, Marriott moved for summary judgment. It claimed that the case involved no disputed issues of material fact, and that there was no breach of the implied warranty of merchantability as a matter of law.

Source: 3 UCC Rep. Serv. 2d 83 (D. Md. 1987)

Smalkin, District Judge

It appears that the item encountered by plaintiff was probably not a worm or other parasite, although plaintiff, in her deposition, steadfastly maintains that it was a worm. If it was not a worm (i.e., if the expert analysis is correct), it was either one of the chicken's major blood vessels (the aorta) or its trachea, both of which would appear worm-like (although not meaty like a worm, but hollow). For [present] purposes, the court will assume that the item was not a worm. Precisely how the aorta or trachea wound up in this hapless chicken's wing is a fascinating, but as yet unanswered (and presently immaterial), question.

Does Maryland law provide a breach of warranty remedy for personal injury flowing from an unexpected encounter with an inedible part of the chicken's anatomy in a piece of fast food fried chicken? Marriott contends that there can be no recovery unless the offending item was a foreign object, i.e., not part of the chicken itself.

In many cases that have denied [implied] warranty recovery as a matter of law, the injurious substance was, as in this case, a natural (though inedible) part of the edible item consumed. Thus, in *Shapiro v. Hotel Statler Corp.* (1955), recovery was denied for a fish bone in "Hot Barquette of Seafood Mornay." But in all these cases the natural item was reasonably to be expected in the dish by its very nature, under the prevailing expectation of any reasonable consumer. Indeed, precisely this "reasonable expectation" test has been adopted in a number of cases. The reasonable expectation test has largely displaced the foreign-natural test adverted to by Marriott. This court is confident that Maryland would apply the reasonable expectation rule.

The court cannot conclude that the presence of a trachea or an aorta in a fast food fried chicken wing is so reasonably to be expected as to render it merchantable, as a matter of law. This is not like the situation [in a previous case] involving a one centimeter bone in a

piece of fried fish. Everyone but a fool knows that tiny bones may remain in even the best filets of fish. This case is more like [another decision], where the court held that the issue was for the trier of fact, on a claim arising from a cherry pit in cherry ice cream. Thus, a question is presented that precludes the grant of summary judgment. The jury must determine whether a piece of fast food fried chicken is merchantable if it contains an inedible item of the chicken's anatomy. Of course, the jury will be instructed that the consumer's reasonable expectations form a part of the merchantability concept.
Marriott's motion for summary judgment denied.

Implied Warranty of Fitness

UCC section 2-315's **implied warrant of fitness for a particular purpose** arises where: (1) the seller has reason to know a particular purpose for which the buyer requires the goods, (2) the seller has reason to know that the buyer is relying on the seller's skill or judgment to select suitable goods, and (3) the buyer actually relies on the seller's skill or judgment in purchasing the goods. If these tests are met, there is an implied warranty that the goods will be fit for the buyer's *particular* purpose.

In many fitness warranty cases, buyers effectively put themselves in the seller's hands by making their needs known and saying that they are relying on the seller to select goods that will satisfy those needs. This may happen, for example, where a seller sells a computer system specially manufactured or customized for a buyer's particular needs. But sellers can also be liable where the circumstances reasonably indicate that the buyer has a particular purpose and is relying on the seller to satisfy that purpose, even though the buyer fails to make either explicit. However, buyers may have trouble recovering where they are more expert than the seller, submit specifications for the goods they wish to buy, inspect the goods, actually select them, or insist on a particular brand.

As the following *Dempsey* case makes clear, the implied warranty of fitness clearly differs from the implied warranty of merchantability. The tests for the creation of each warranty are plainly not the same. Under section 2-315, moreover, sellers only warrant that the goods are fit for the buyer's *particular* purposes, not the *ordinary* purposes for which such goods are used. If a 400-pound man asks a department store for a hammock that will support his weight but is sold a hammock that only can support normally sized people, there is a breach of the implied warranty of fitness but no breach of the implied warranty of merchantability. If the hammock cannot support anyone's weight, however, both warranties are breached.

Dempsey v. Rosenthal

Ruby Dempsey purchased a nine-week-old pedigreed male poodle from the American Kennels Pet Stores. She named the poodle Mr. Dunphy. Dempsey later testified that before making the purchase, she told the salesperson that she wanted a dog suitable for breeding purposes. Five days after the sale, she had Mr. Dunphy examined by a veterinarian, who discovered that the poodle had one undescended testicle. This condition did not seriously affect Mr. Dunphy's fertility, but it was a genetic defect that would probably be passed on to any offspring sired. Also, a dog with this condition could not be used as a show dog.

Dempsey demanded a refund from American Kennels, but her demand was denied. She then sued in small claims court, alleging that American Kennels had breached the implied warranty of fitness.

Source: 468 N.Y.S.2d 441 (N.Y. Civ. Ct. 1983)

Saxe, Judge

UCC sections 2-314 and 2-315 make it clear that the warranty of fitness for a particular purpose is narrower, more specific, and more precise than the warranty of merchantability, which involves fitness for the ordinary purposes for which goods are used. The following are the conditions that are not required by the implied warranty of merchantability, but that must be present if a plaintiff is to recover on the basis of the implied warranty of fitness: (1) the seller must have reason to know the buyer's particular purpose, (2) the seller must have reason to know that the buyer is relying on the seller's skill or judgment to furnish appropriate goods, and (3) the buyer must, in fact, rely upon the seller's skill or judgment.

I find that the warranty of fitness for a particular purpose has been breached. Dempsey testified that she specified to the salesperson that she wanted a dog that was suitable for breeding purposes. Although this is disputed by the defendant, the credible testimony supports Dempsey's version of the event. Further, it is reasonable for the seller of a pedigreed dog to assume that the buyer intends to breed it. But it is undisputed by the experts here (for both sides) that Mr. Dunphy was as capable of siring a litter as a male dog with two viable and descended testicles. This, the defendant contends, compels a finding in its favor. I disagree. While it is true that Mr. Dunphy's fertility level may be unaffected, his stud value, because of this hereditary condition (which is likely to be passed on to future generations), is severely diminished.

Judgment for Dempsey.

Negligence

Product liability suits based on the theory of negligence discussed in Chapter 23 usually allege that the seller or manufacturer breached a duty to the plaintiff by failing to eliminate a reasonably foreseeable risk of harm associated with the product.[5] Such suits typically claim one or more of the following: (1) improper *manufacture* of the goods (including improper materials and packaging), (2) improper *inspection*, (3) a failure to provide *adequate warnings* of hazards or defects, and (4) improper *design*.

Improper Manufacture

Negligence suits alleging the manufacturer's improper assembly, materials, or packaging often encounter problems because the evidence needed to prove a breach of duty is under the defendant's control.[6] However, liberal modern discovery rules and the doctrine of *res ipsa loquitur* can help plaintiffs establish a breach in such situations.[7]

Improper Inspection

Manufacturers have a duty to inspect their products for defects that create a reasonably foreseeable risk of harm, if such an inspection would be practicable and effective. As before, *res ipsa loquitur* and modern discovery rules can help plaintiffs prove their case against the manufacturer.

Most courts have held that middlemen such as retailers and wholesalers have a duty to inspect the goods they sell only when they have actual knowledge or reason to know of a defect. In addition, such parties generally have no duty to inspect where this would be unduly difficult, burdensome, or time-consuming. Unless the product defect is obvious, for example, middlemen usually are not liable for failing to inspect goods sold in the manufacturer's original packages or containers.

On the other hand, sellers who prepare, install, or repair the goods they sell ordinarily have a duty to inspect those goods. Examples include restaurants, automobile dealers, and installers of household products. Usually, however, the scope of the inspection need only be consistent with the preparation, installation, or repair work performed. Thus, it is unlikely that such sellers must unearth hidden or latent defects.

If there is a duty to inspect and the inspection reveals a defect, further duties can arise. For example, a seller or manufacturer may be required not to sell the product in its defective state, or at least to give a suitable warning.

Failure to Warn

Sellers and manufacturers have a duty to give an appropriate warning when their products pose a reasonably foreseeable risk of harm. But in determining whether there was a duty to warn and whether the defendant's warning was adequate, courts often consider other factors besides the reasonable foreseeability of the risk. These include the *magnitude or severity* of the likely harm, the *ease or difficulty of providing an appropriate warning*, and the likely *effectiveness of a warning*. As the following Daniell case makes clear, moreover, there is no duty to warn where the risk is *open and obvious*.

Design Defects

Manufacturers have a duty to design their products so as to avoid reasonably foreseeable risks of harm. Like failure-to-warn cases, however, design defect cases frequently involve other factors besides the reasonable foreseeability of harm. As before, one of these factors is the *magnitude or severity* of the foreseeable harm. Three others are *industry practices* at the time the product was manufactured, the *state of the art* (the state of existing scientific and technical knowledge) at that time, and the product's compliance or noncompliance with *government safety regulations*.[8]

Sometimes courts employ *risk-benefit analysis* when weighing these factors. In such analyses, three other factors—the design's *social utility*, the *effectiveness of alternative designs*, and the *cost of safer designs*—may figure in the weighing process. Even where the balancing process indicates that the design was not defective, courts may still require a suitable warning.

Daniell v. Ford Motor Company

Connie Daniell attempted to commit suicide by locking herself inside the trunk of her 1973 Ford LTD. Daniell remained in the trunk for nine days, but survived after finally being rescued. Later, Daniell sued Ford in negligence to recover for her resulting physical and psychological injuries. She contended that the LTD was defectively designed because its trunk did not have an internal release or opening mechanism. She also argued that Ford was liable for negligently failing to warn her that the trunk could not be unlocked from within. Ford moved for summary judgment.

Source: 581 F. Supp. 728 (D.N.M. 1984)

Baldock, District Judge

As a general principle, a design defect is actionable only where the condition of the product is unreasonably dangerous to the user or consumer. Under negligence, a manufacturer has a duty to consider only those risks of injury which are foreseeable. A risk is not foreseeable where a product is used in a manner which could not reasonably be anticipated by the manufacturer and that use is the cause of the plaintiff's injury.

The purposes of an automobile trunk are to transport, stow, and secure the spare tire, luggage, and other goods and to protect those items from the weather. The design features of a trunk make it well near impossible that an adult intentionally would enter the trunk and close the lid. The dimensions of a trunk, the height of its sill and its load floor, and the efforts to first lower the lid and then to engage its latch, are among the design features which encourage closing and latching the trunk lid while standing outside the vehicle. The court holds that the plaintiff's use of the trunk compartment as a means to attempt suicide was an unforeseeable use as a matter of law. Therefore, the manufacturer had no duty to design an internal release or opening mechanism that might have prevented this occurrence.

Nor did the manufacturer have a duty to warn the plaintiff of the danger of her conduct, given the plaintiff's unforeseeable use of the product. Another reason why the manufacturer had no duty to warn the plaintiff of the risk inherent in crawling into an automobile trunk and closing the lid is [that] such a risk is obvious. There is no duty to warn of known dangers. Moreover, the potential efficacy of any warning, given the plaintiff's use of the trunk for a deliberate suicide attempt, is questionable.

Having held that the plaintiff's conception of the manufacturer's duty is in error, the court need not reach the issues of comparative negligence or other defenses such as assumption of risk.

Ford's motion for summary judgment granted; Daniell loses.

Strict Liability

Strict products liability is a relatively recent development. Only in the 1960s did courts begin to impose such liability in significant numbers. The movement toward strict liability received a big boost when the American Law Institute promulgated section 402A of the *Restatement (Second) of Torts* in 1965. By now, the vast majority of the states have adopted some form of strict products liability. The most important reason is the socialization-of-risk strategy discussed earlier. Another common justification for strict products liability is that it stimulates manufacturers to design and build safer products. Strict liability also removes a problem that has long plagued plaintiffs in negligence suits—the need to prove a breach of duty.

Section 402A's Requirements

Because it is the most common version of strict products liability, we limit our discussion of the subject to section 402A. Section 402A provides that a "seller ... engaged in the business of selling" a particular product is liable for physical harm or property damage suffered by the ultimate user or consumer of that product if the product was "in a defective condition unreasonably dangerous to the user or consumer or to his property." This rule applies even though "the seller has exercised all possible care in the preparation and sale of his product." Thus, section 402A states a rule of strict liability that eliminates the plaintiff's need to prove a breach of duty.

However, the liability imposed by section 402A is not absolute, for the section applies only if certain tests are met.

1. The seller must be *engaged in the business of selling the product that harmed the plaintiff.* Thus, section 402A only binds parties who resemble UCC merchants because they regularly sell the product at issue. For example, the section does not apply to a college professor's or a clothing store's sale of a used car.

2. The product must be in a *defective condition* when sold, and also must be *unreasonably dangerous* because of that condition. The usual test of a product's defective condition is whether the product meets the reasonable expectations of the average consumer. An unreasonably dangerous product is one that is dangerous to an extent beyond

the reasonable contemplation of the average consumer. For example, good whiskey is not unreasonably dangerous even though it can cause harm, but whiskey contaminated with a poisonous substance qualifies. However, some courts balance the product's social utility against its danger when determining whether it is unreasonably dangerous.

Due to section 402A's unreasonably dangerous requirement, it covers a smaller range of product defects than the implied warranty of merchantability. A power mower that simply fails to operate, for instance, is not unreasonably dangerous, although it would violate the merchantability standard. Some courts, however, blur the defective condition and unreasonably dangerous requirements, and a few have done away with the latter test.

3. Finally, defendants can avoid section 402A liability where the product was *substantially modified* by the plaintiff or another party after the sale, and the modification contributed to the plaintiff's injury or other loss.

Applications of Section 402A

As the following *Toney* case makes clear, design defect and failure-to-warn suits can be brought under section 402A. Even though section 402A is a strict liability provision, the standards applied in such cases often resemble the negligence standards discussed in the previous section.

Because it applies to sellers, section 402A covers retailers and other middlemen who market goods containing defects that they did not create and may not have been able to discover. Even though such parties often escape negligence liability, some courts have found them liable under section 402A's strict liability rule. However, other states have given middlemen some protection against 402A liability, and/or have required the manufacturer or other responsible party to indemnify them.

What about products (such as some drugs) that have great social utility, but that pose serious risks which cannot be eliminated? Imposing strict liability on such "unavoidably unsafe" products might deter manufacturers from developing and marketing them. Where products of this kind cause harm and a lawsuit follows, many courts follow comment *k* to section 402A. Comment *k* says that unavoidably unsafe products are neither defective nor unreasonably dangerous if they are properly prepared and accompanied by proper directions and a proper warning. For this rule to apply, of course, the product must be genuinely incapable of being made safer.

Toney v. Kawasaki Heavy Industries, Ltd.

Shortly after Billy Toney bought a used Kawasaki 750 motorcycle, he was struck from the side by a truck while riding the motorcycle on a highway. As a result, he suffered severe injuries to his left leg, leading to its eventual amputation. Toney sued Kawasaki in a Mississippi trial court, alleging that the motorcycle was improperly designed because it was not equipped with leg-protection devices, and that Kawasaki improperly failed to warn users about the dangers posed by the absence of such devices. After Kawasaki removed the case to federal district court, the district court granted Kawasaki's motion for summary judgment on Toney's section 402A claim. Toney appealed.

Source: 975 F.2d 162 (5th Cir. 1992)

Jolly, Circuit Judge

To recover under Mississippi product strict liability law, the injured plaintiff must show that the product was "in a defective condition unreasonably dangerous." Mississippi has adopted the objective "consumer expectations" test to determine whether a product is unreasonably dangerous. The plaintiff must establish that the product was dangerous to an extent beyond that which would be contemplated by the ordinary consumer who purchases it, with the ordinary knowledge common to the community as to its characteristics. Furthermore, a product that has an open and obvious danger is not more dangerous than contemplated by the consumer, and hence cannot be unreasonably dangerous.

The ordinary consumer could see that [Toney's] motorcycle had no leg protection and, thus, could fully appreciate the motorcycle's design and its open and obvious dangers. An ordinary consumer would fully appreciate the danger that, if an automobile struck the side of the motorcycle, the rider's leg would be ruinously crushed. The danger of the product thus revealed and appreciated, it was not an unreasonably dangerous product for a manufacturer to market.

Toney next asserts that the district court erred in failing to consider his subjective state of mind in determining whether the danger presented by the design of his motorcycle was patent or latent. He testified that he did not appreciate the danger involved in riding a motorcycle without any leg protection features. Notwithstanding Toney's argument, the Mississippi Supreme Court has adopted an objective test of "consumer expectations" under section 402A. The test is the objective measure of the expectations of the generic consumer who has ordinary knowledge common to the community. The question in product strict liability cases is not whether the product is unreasonably dangerous to a given individual. Modern products are sold by the millions in markets comprising a cross section of the population and therefore are used by people with varying levels of education, experience, and ordinary common sense. The focus in product liability cases is on the product, not the individual purchaser.

District court decision granting Kawasaki's motion for summary judgment affirmed.

Concept Review
Comparing the Major Product Liability Theories—The Basics

Theory	Tort or Contract	Type of Defendant	Nature of Goods Sold	Remarks
Express Warranty	Contract	Seller of goods	Not as warranted by affirmation of fact or promise, description, sample, or model	Exemption for statements of value, opinion, or sales talk
Implied Warranty of Merchantability	Contract	Merchant for goods sold	Not merchantable; usually, not fit for ordinary purposes for which such goods used	Merchantability has other aspects
Implied Warranty of Fitness	Contract	Seller of goods	Not fit for buyer's particular purposes	Seller must have reason to know of buyer's needs and buyer's reliance, and buyer must actually rely
Negligence	Tort	Manufacturer or seller of goods	"Defective" due to improper manufacture, inspection, design, or failure to give suitable warning	Limited inspection duty for middlemen
Section 402A	Tort	Seller engaged in business of selling product sold	Defective and unreasonably dangerous	Strict liability; design defect and failure-to-warn suits possible

Other Theories of Recovery

Warranty of Title

Normally, a seller of goods impliedly warrants that: (1) the title he conveys is good and transfer of that title is rightful, and (2) the goods are free from any lien or security interest of which the buyer lacks knowledge. Thus, a buyer may recover damages against his seller where, for example, the seller has marketed stolen goods or goods that are subject to a third party's security interest. Also, a seller who is a merchant in goods of the kind sold normally warrants that the goods are free of any rightful patent or trademark infringement claim, or any similar claim, by a third party.

The Magnuson-Moss Act

The relevant civil recovery provisions of the federal Magnuson-Moss Warranty Act apply to sales of *consumer products* costing more than *$10 per item*. A consumer product is tangible personal property normally used for personal, family, or household purposes. If a seller gives a *written warranty* for such a product to a *consumer*, the warranty must be designated full or limited. A seller who gives a full warranty promises to: (1) *remedy* any defects in the product and (2) *replace* the product or *refund* its purchase price if, after a reasonable number of attempts, it cannot be repaired.[9] A seller who gives a limited warranty is bound to whatever promises it actually makes. However, neither warranty applies if the seller simply declines to give a written warranty.

Misrepresentation

Section 402B of the *Restatement (Second) of Torts* lets *consumers* recover for *personal injury* resulting from certain *misrepresentations* about goods they have purchased. The misrepresentation must: (1) be made by a party engaged in the business of selling goods of the kind purchased; (2) be made to the public by advertising, labels, or similar means; (3) concern a fact *material* to the goods purchased; and (4) be *actually and justifiably* relied on by the consumer. Suppose the manufacturer of a laxative states in its advertising that the laxative has no adverse side effects if used as directed. Smith, who has been influenced by the advertisements and has no reason to doubt their accuracy, buys a bottle of the laxative. If, after using it according to directions, Smith suffers injury to his digestive system, he can recover from the manufacturer for that injury.

Industrywide Liability

The development we call industrywide liability is a way for plaintiffs to bypass problems of causation that exist where several firms within an industry have manufactured a harmful standardized product, and it is impossible for the plaintiff to prove *which* firm produced the product that injured her. In such cases, each potential defendant can argue that the plaintiff should lose because she cannot show that *its* product caused the harm of which she complains. The usual reasons for the plaintiff's proof problems are the number of firms producing the product and the time lag between exposure to the product and the appearance of the injury. Many of the cases presenting this problem have involved DES (an antimiscarriage drug that has produced various ailments in daughters of the women to whom it was administered) or diseases resulting from long-term exposure to asbestos.

In such cases, some courts continue to deny recovery under traditional causation rules. However, using various theories whose many details are beyond the scope of this text, other courts have made it easier for plaintiffs to recover. Where recovery is allowed, some of these courts have *apportioned* damages among the firms that might have produced the harm-causing product. Typically, the apportionment is based on market share at some chosen time.

Damages in Product Liability Suits

At this point, we begin to consider several problems that are common to each major theory of product liability recovery but that may be resolved differently from theory to theory.[10] The first such problem, the damages obtainable under each theory, strongly influences a plaintiff's strategy in a product liability suit. Here, we describe the major kinds of damages recoverable in products liability cases, along with the theories under which each can be recovered. One lawsuit can involve claims for all these sorts of damages.

1. Basis-of-the-bargain damages. Buyers of defective goods have not received full value for their purchase price. The resulting loss, usually called basis-of-the-bargain damages or direct economic loss, is the value of the goods as promised under the contract, minus the value of the goods actually received.

Where awarded: Basis-of-the-bargain damages are usually *not* recoverable in *negligence* and *strict liability* cases. In *express* and *implied warranty* suits under the UCC, however, basis-of-the-bargain damages are recoverable where there was *privity of contract* (a direct contractual relation) between the plaintiff and the defendant. As discussed in the next section, however, only occasionally will a warranty plaintiff who lacks privity with the defendant obtain basis-of-the-bargain damages. Basis-of-the-bargain recoveries most often occur where an express warranty was made to a remote plaintiff through advertising, brochures, or labels.

2. Consequential damages. Consequential damages include: **personal injury**, **property damage** (damage to the plaintiff's other property), and **indirect economic loss** (e.g., lost profits or lost business reputation) resulting from a product defect. Consequential damages also include **noneconomic loss**—for example, pain and suffering, physical impairment, mental distress, loss of enjoyment of life, loss of companionship or consortium, inconvenience, and disfigurement. Noneconomic loss is usually part of the plaintiff's personal injury claim. Recently, several states have limited noneconomic loss recoveries, typically by imposing a dollar cap on them.

Where awarded: Plaintiffs in *negligence* and strict liability cases normally can recover for personal injury and property damage. Recoveries for foreseeable indirect economic loss are sometimes allowed.

In UCC *express* and *implied warranty* suits where *privity exists* between the plaintiff and the defendant, the plaintiff can recover for: (1) personal injury and property damage, if either proximately resulted from the breach of warranty; and (2) indirect economic loss, if the defendant had reason to know that this was likely. As discussed in the next section, a UCC plaintiff who *lacks privity* with the defendant has a fairly good chance of recovering for personal injury or property damage. But recovery for indirect economic loss is rare because remote sellers usually cannot foresee such losses.

3. Punitive damages. Punitive (or exemplary) damages are intended to punish defendants who have acted in an especially outrageous fashion, and to deter them and others from so acting in the future. Of the various standards for awarding punitive damages, perhaps the most common is the defendant's conscious or reckless disregard for the safety of those likely to be affected by the goods. Examples include concealment of known product hazards, knowing violation of government or industry product safety standards, failure to correct known dangerous defects, and grossly inadequate product testing or quality control procedures.

Due to their perceived frequency, size, and effect on business and the economy, punitive damages have been subjected to state tort reform regulation throughout the 1980s. The approaches taken by these statutes vary. Many set the standards for punitive damage recovery and the plaintiff's burden of proof; some articulate factors courts should consider when ruling on punitive damage awards; and some create special procedures for punitive damage determinations. Also, several states have limited the size of punitive damage recoveries, usually by restricting them to some multiple of the plaintiff's actual damages, or by putting a flat dollar cap on them.

Where awarded: Assuming that the standards just described have been met, punitive damages are recoverable in *negligence* and *strict liability* cases. Due to the traditional rule that punitive damages are not available in contract cases, they are usually not awarded in *express* and *implied warranty* suits.

Figure 21-1 summarizes the plaintiff's chances of recovering the most important kinds of damages in contract and tort cases.

FIGURE 21-1
When the various kinds of damages are recoverable

Type of Damages	Express and Implied Warranty	Negligence and Section 402A
Basis of the Bargain	Within privity: Yes Outside privity: Occasionally	Rarely
Personal Injury and Property Damage	Within privity: If proximate result of breach Outside privity: Fairly good chance	Yes
Indirect Economic Loss	Within privity: If defendant has reason to know this likely Outside privity: Rarely	Sometimes
Punitive Damages	Rarely	Yes, in appropriate cases

The No-Privity Defense

Today, defective products often move through long chains of distribution before reaching the person they harm. This means that a product liability plaintiff often has not dealt directly with the party ultimately responsible for his losses. Figure 21-2 depicts a hypothetical chain of distribution in which goods defectively produced by a manufacturer of component parts move vertically through the manufacturer of a product in which those parts are used, a wholesaler, and a retailer, ultimately reaching the buyer. The defect's consequences may move horizontally as well, affecting members of the buyer's family, guests in his home, and even bystanders. If the buyer or one of these parties suffers loss due to the defect in the component parts, can he successfully sue the component parts manufacturer or any other party in the vertical chain of distribution with whom he did not directly deal?

Because at that time there was no recovery for defective goods without privity of contract between the plaintiff and the defendant, such suits were unlikely to succeed under 19th-century law. In the preceding example, the buyer would have been required to sue his dealer. If the buyer was successful, the retailer might have sued the wholesaler, and so on up the chain. For a variety of reasons (including a middleman's limited negligence liability for failure to inspect), the party ultimately responsible for the defect often escaped liability.

Negligence and Strict Liability Cases

By now, the old no-liability-outside-privity rule has been severely eroded in tort suits. It has little, if any, effect in *strict liability* cases, where even bystanders can recover against remote manufacturers. In *negligence* cases, a plaintiff generally recovers against a remote defendant if the plaintiff's loss was a reasonably foreseeable consequence of the defect. Depending on the circumstances, therefore, bystanders and other distant parties might recover against a manufacturer in negligence as well.

FIGURE 21-2
A hypothetical chain of distribution

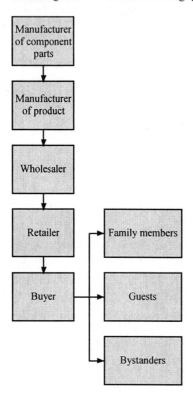

Warranty Cases

The no-privity defense still retains some vitality in UCC cases. Unfortunately, the "law" on this subject is complex and confusing. Under the Code, the privity question is formally governed by section 2-318, which comes in three alternative versions. Section 2-318's language, however, is a questionable guide to the courts' actual behavior in UCC privity cases.

UCC Section 2-318

Alternative A to section 2-318 says that a seller's express or implied warranty runs to natural persons in the family or household of *his* (the seller's) buyer and to guests in his buyer's home if they suffer personal injury and if it was reasonable to expect that they might use, consume, or be affected by the goods sold. On its face, Alternative A does little to undermine the traditional no-privity defense. In Figure 21-2, Alternative A would merely allow the buyer, his family, and guests in his home to sue the *retailer* for their personal injury.

Alternatives B and C go much further. Alternative B extends the seller's express or implied warranty to any natural person who has suffered personal injury, if it was reasonable to expect that this person would use, consume, or be affected by the goods. Alternative C is much the same, but it extends the warranty to any person (not just natural persons) and to those suffering injury in general (not just personal injury). If the reasonable-to-expect test is met, these two provisions should extend the warranty to many remote parties, including bystanders.

Departures from UCC Section 2-318

For various reasons, section 2-318's literal language is of questionable relevance in UCC privity cases. Some states have adopted privity statutes that differ from any version of section 2-318. Also, one of the comments to section 2-318 lets courts extend liability farther than the section expressly permits. Finally, versions B and C are fairly open ended as written. Thus, the plaintiff's ability to recover outside privity in warranty cases varies from state to state and situation to situation. The most important factors affecting resolution of this question include the following:

1. Whether it is *reasonably foreseeable* that a party such as the plaintiff would be harmed by the product defect in question.
2. The *status of the plaintiff.* On the average, consumers and other natural persons fare better outside privity than corporations and other business concerns.
3. The *type of damages* the plaintiff has suffered. In general, remote plaintiffs are: (a) most likely to recover for personal injury, (b) somewhat less likely to recover for property damage, (c) occasionally able to obtain basis-of-the-bargain damages, and (d) rarely able to recover for indirect economic loss. Recall from the previous section that a remote plaintiff is most likely to receive basis-of-the-bargain damages where an express warranty was made to him through advertising, brochures, or labels.

Disclaimers and Remedy Limitations

Introduction

A product liability **disclaimer** is a clause in the sales contract whereby the seller tries to eliminate its *liability* under one or more theories of recovery. A **remedy limitation** is a clause attempting to block recovery of certain kinds of *damages.* Disclaimers attack the plaintiff's theory of recovery; if the disclaimer is effective, no damages of any sort are recoverable under that theory. A successful remedy limitation prevents the plaintiff from recovering certain types of damages but does not attack the plaintiff's theory of recovery. Damages not excluded may still be recovered, because the theory is left intact.

The main justification for enforcing disclaimers and remedy limitations is freedom of contract. Also, because goods accompanied by an effective disclaimer or remedy limitation are apt to be cheaper than other goods, enforcing such clauses gives buyers the flexibility to get a lower price by accepting a greater risk of uncompensated defects. For purchases by ordinary consumers and other unsophisticated buyers, however, these arguments are sometimes illusory. Often, the seller presents the disclaimer or remedy limitation in a standardized, take-it-or-leave-it fashion. In addition, it is doubtful whether many consumers read disclaimers and remedy limitations at the time of purchase or would comprehend them if they were read. As a result, there usually is little or no genuine bargaining over disclaimers or remedy limitations in consumer situations. Instead, they are often effectively dictated by a seller with superior size and organization. These observations, however, are less valid where the buyer is a business entity with the capability to engage in genuine bargaining with sellers.

Because the realities surrounding the sale differ from situation to situation, and because some theories of recovery are more hospitable to contractual limitation than others, the law on product liability disclaimers and remedy limitations is complicated. We begin with a lengthy discussion of implied warranty disclaimers. Then we examine disclaimers of express warranty liability, negligence liability, and strict liability before considering remedy limitations separately.

Implied Warranty Disclaimers

To determine the enforceability of implied warranty disclaimers, we must consider several sets of legal rules.[11] Figure 21-3 structures the steps in this analysis.

FIGURE 21-3
The enforceability of impaired warranty disclaimers

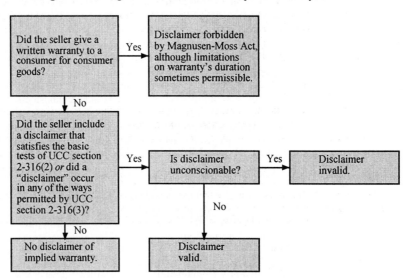

The Basic Tests of UCC Section 2-316(2)

UCC section 2-316(2) apparently makes it easy for sellers to disclaim the implied warranties of merchantability and fitness for a particular purpose. The section states that to exclude or modify the implied warranty of merchantability, a seller must: (1) use the word *merchantability*, and (2) make the disclaimer conspicuous if it is written. To exclude or modify the implied warranty of fitness, a seller must: (1) use a writing, and (2) make the disclaimer conspicuous. A disclaimer is conspicuous if it is written so that a reasonable person ought to have noticed it. Capital letters, larger type, contrasting type, and contrasting colors usually suffice.

Unlike the fitness warranty disclaimer, a disclaimer of the implied warranty of merchantability can be oral. Also, while disclaimers of the latter warranty must always use the word *merchantability*, no special language is needed to disclaim the implied warranty of fitness. For example, a conspicuous written statement that "THERE ARE NO WARRANTIES WHICH EXTEND BEYOND THE DESCRIPTION ON THE FACE HEREOF" disclaims the implied warranty of fitness but not the implied warranty of merchantability.

Other Ways to Disclaim Implied Warranties: UCC Section 2-316(3)

According to UCC section 2-316(3)(a), sellers can also disclaim either implied warranty by using such terms as "with all faults," "as is," and "as they stand." Some courts have held that these terms must be conspicuous to be effective as disclaimers.

UCC section 2-316(3)(b) describes two situations where the buyer's *inspection* of the goods or her *refusal to inspect* can act as a disclaimer. If a buyer examines the goods before the sale and fails to discover a defect that should have been reasonably apparent to her, there can be no implied warranty suit based on that defect. Also, if a seller requests that the buyer examine the goods and the buyer refuses, the buyer cannot base an implied warranty suit on a defect that would have been reasonably apparent had she made the inspection. The definition of a reasonably apparent defect varies with the buyer's expertise. Unless the defect is blatant, ordinary consumers may have little to fear from section 2-316(3)(b).

Finally, UCC section 2-316(3)(c) says that an implied warranty can be excluded or modified by *course of dealing* (the parties' previous conduct), *course of performance* (the parties' previous conduct under the same contract), or *usage of trade* (any practice regularly observed in the trade). For example, if it is accepted in the local cattle trade that buyers who inspect the seller's cattle and reject certain animals must accept all defects in the cattle actually purchased, such buyers cannot mount an implied warranty suit for those defects.

Unconscionable Disclaimers

From the previous discussion, it seems that any seller who retains a competent attorney can escape implied warranty liability at will. In fact, however, a seller's ability to disclaim implied warranties is restricted in various ways. One of these restrictions is the doctrine of **unconscionability** established by UCC section 2-302 and discussed in Chapter 15.

By now, almost all courts apply section 2-302's unconscionability standards to implied warranty disclaimers even though those disclaimers satisfy UCC section 2-316(2). Despite a growing willingness to protect smaller firms that deal with corporate giants, courts still tend to reject unconscionability claims where business parties have contracted in a commercial context. However, implied warranty disclaimers are often declared unconscionable in personal injury suits by ordinary consumers.

The Impact of Magnuson-Moss

The Magnuson-Moss Act creates other important limitations on a seller's ability to disclaim implied warranties. If a seller gives a consumer a full warranty on consumer goods, the seller may not disclaim, modify, or limit the duration of any implied warranty. If a limited warranty is given, the seller may not disclaim or modify any implied warranty but may limit its duration to the duration of the limited warranty if this is done conspicuously and if the limitation is not unconscionable. Presumably, however, a seller can still disclaim by refusing to give a written warranty while placing the disclaimer on some other writing.

Express Warranty Disclaimers

UCC section 2-316(1) says that an express warranty and a disclaimer should be read consistently if possible, but that the disclaimer must yield if such a reading is unreasonable. Because it is normally unreasonable for a seller to exclude with one hand what he has freely and openly promised with the other, it is very difficult to disclaim an express warranty.

Negligence and Strict Liability Disclaimers

Disclaimers of negligence liability and strict liability are usually ineffective in cases involving ordinary consumers. However, some courts enforce such disclaimers where both parties are business entities that: (1) dealt in a commercial setting, (2) had relatively equal bargaining power, (3) bargained the product's specifications, and (4) negotiated the risk of loss from product defects (e.g., the disclaimer itself).

Limitation of Remedies

Due to the expense they can create for sellers, consequential damages are the usual target of remedy limitations. Where a limitation of consequential damages succeeds, buyers of the product may suffer. For example, suppose that Dillman buys a computer system for $20,000 under a contract that excludes consequential damages and limits the buyer's remedies to the repair or replacement of defective parts. Suppose also that the system never works properly, causing Dillman to suffer $10,000 in lost profits. If the remedy limitation is enforceable, Dillman could only have the system replaced or repaired by the seller, and could not recover his $10,000 in consequential damages.

In negligence and strict liability cases, the tests for the enforceability of remedy limitations resemble the previous tests for disclaimers. Under the UCC, however, the standards for remedy limitations differ from those for disclaimers.

UCC section 2-719(3) allows the limitation of consequential damages in express and implied warranty cases, but also states that such a limitation may be unconscionable. The section adds that a limitation of consequential damages is quite likely to be unconscionable where the sale is for *consumer goods* and the plaintiff has suffered *personal injury*. Where the loss is "commercial," however, the limitation may or may not be unconscionable. The meaning of commercial loss is unclear. But in cases where it exists, courts must consider the many factors relevant to unconscionability determinations on a case-by-case basis.

Time Limitations

Traditionally, the main time limits on product liability suits have been the applicable contract and tort statutes of limitations. The usual UCC statute of limitations for express and implied warranty claims is four years after the seller offers the defective goods to the buyer (usually, four years after the sale).[12] In negligence and strict liability cases, the applicable tort statute of limitations is generally shorter. But it only begins to run when the defect was or should have been discovered—often, the time of the injury.

Due in part to tort reform, some states now impose various other limitations on the time within which product liability suits must be brought. Often, these limitations apply only to claims for death, personal injury, and property damage, but they override the states' other time limitations where they do apply. Among these additional time limitations are: (1) special statutes of limitations for product liability cases involving death, personal injury, or property damage (e.g., from one to three years after the time the injury or death occurred or should have been discovered); (2) special time limits for "delayed manifestation" injuries such as those resulting from exposure to asbestos; (3) useful safe life defenses (which prevent plaintiffs from suing once the product's "useful safe life" has passed); and (4) statutes of repose (whose aim is similar). Statutes of repose usually run for a 10- to 12-year period that begins when the product is sold to the first buyer not purchasing for resale—usually an ordinary consumer. In a state with a 10-year statute of repose, for example, such parties cannot recover for injuries that occur more than 10 years after they purchased the product causing the injury. This is true even when the suit is begun quickly enough to satisfy the applicable statute of limitations.

Defenses

Many things—for example, the absence of privity or a valid disclaimer—can be considered defenses to a product liability suit. Here, however, our concern is with product liability defenses that involve the plaintiff's behavior.

The Traditional Defenses

Traditionally, the three main defenses in a product liability suit have been the overlapping trio of product misuse, assumption of risk, and contributory negligence.[13] **Product misuse** (or abnormal use) occurs when the plaintiff uses the product in some unusual, unforeseeable way, and this causes the loss for which she sues. Examples include ignoring the manufacturer's instructions, mishandling the product, and using the product for purposes for which it was not intended. But if the defendant had reason to foresee the misuse and failed to take reasonable precautions against it, there is no defense. Product misuse is usually available in warranty, negligence, and strict liability cases.

Assumption of risk is the plaintiff's voluntary consent to a known danger. It can occur any time the plaintiff willingly exposes herself to a known product hazard—for example, by consuming obviously adulterated food. Like product misuse, assumption of risk ordinarily is a defense in warranty, negligence, and strict liability cases.

Contributory negligence is the plaintiff's failure to act with reasonable, prudent, self-protectiveness. In the product liability context, perhaps the most common example is the simple failure to notice a hazardous product defect. Contributory negligence is clearly a defense in a negligence suit, but courts disagree about whether or when it should be a defense in warranty and strict liability cases.

Comparative Principles

Where they are allowed and proven, the three traditional product liability defenses completely absolve the defendant from liability. Dissatisfaction with this all-or-nothing situation has spurred the increasing use of *comparative* principles in product liability cases.[14] Rather than letting the traditional defenses completely absolve the defendant, courts and legislatures now apportion damages on the basis of relative fault. They do so by requiring that the fact finder establish the plaintiff's and the defendant's percentage shares of the total fault for the injury, and then award the plaintiff his total provable damages times the defendant's percentage share of the fault.

Unsettled questions persist among the states that have adopted comparative principles. First, it is not always clear what kinds of fault will reduce the plaintiff's recovery. However, some state comparative negligence statutes have been read as embracing assumption of risk and product misuse, and state comparative fault statutes usually define fault broadly. Second, comparative principles may assume either the *pure* or the *mixed* forms. In states that use the mixed form, for example, the defendant has a complete defense where the plaintiff is more at fault than the defendant. Finally, there is some uncertainty about the theories of recovery and the types of damage claims to which comparative principles apply.

States v. R. D. Werner Company

Lloyd States was injured after falling from a step ladder at a construction site. He had placed the ladder's front feet (which are on the same side of the ladder as its steps) on a sidewalk, with its rear feet on the surface of an unfinished parking lot that was 6 to 9 inches below the front feet. This was contrary to the manufacturer's instructions for the use of the ladder, which were affixed to it. Then States climbed the ladder, turned on the steps so that his back was to them, and leaned over toward a building. He did so in order to attach a sign to the building with a power wrench while the sign was being held in place by an overhead crane. States pressed against the sign with one hand while using his other hand to apply pressure on the power wrench. As he did so, the ladder moved away from him and he fell.

States sued R. D. Werner Co., the manufacturer of the ladder, in a Colorado trial court under section 402A of the *Restatement (Second) of Torts*. He alleged that a defect in the ladder caused his fall and his injuries. After trial, the jury found for R. D. Werner. States appealed, attacking the trial court's instruction to the jury. The jury had been instructed that: (1) if both a defective product and the plaintiff's conduct contributed to his injury, the plaintiff's recovery must be reduced in proportion to his percentage share of the fault causing the injury; and (2) if the plaintiff's misuse of a product was the sole cause of his injuries, and the alleged product defect played no role in producing them, the seller or manufacturer of that product cannot be liable.

Source: 799 P.2d 427 (Colo. Ct. App. 1990)

Pierce, Judge

Misuse of a product by the injured person is a recognized defense to a section 402A action. Misuse concerns an issue of causation and provides a complete defense to liability, regardless of any defective condition, if an unforeseeable and unintended use of the product, and not the alleged defect, caused the plaintiff's injuries. Plaintiff argues that the concept of comparative [fault] is to be applied to all product liability actions. He asserts that the [second] instruction [stated above] erroneously converts the statutory concept of comparative fault into a recovery bar, rather than a damage diminution remedy.

Section 13-21-406 [of the Colorado Revised Statutes] provides in pertinent part:

Comparative fault as measure of damages.
(1) In any product liability action, the fault of the person suffering the harm, as well as the fault of all others who are parties to the action for causing the harm, shall be compared by the trier of fact in accordance with this section. The fault of the person suffering the harm shall not bar such person . . . from recovering damages, but the award of damages to such person . . . shall be diminished in proportion to the amount of causal fault attributed to the person suffering the harm.

* * * *

(4) The provisions of [Colorado's comparative negligence statute] do not apply to any product liability action.

We interpret section 13-21-406 to mean that once it has been established that the product is defective, if both the defective product and the injured person's conduct contributed to the injury underlying plaintiff's claim, then the plaintiff's recovery must be reduced by a percentage representing the amount of fault attributable to his own conduct. Here, the jury was properly so instructed. Depending on the facts of the case, the injured person's misuse of the product could constitute comparative fault which would reduce the plaintiff's recovery. However, if the misuse is the sole cause of damages, and thus the

alleged defect was not a cause thereof, then the plaintiff cannot recover under [section 402A]. Here, the instruction given to the jury provided that if Lloyd's misuse of the ladder, *rather than a defect*, caused Lloyd's injuries, R. D. Werner could not be held legally responsible for those injuries. The trial court did not err in giving this instruction.
Trial court verdict for R. D. Werner affirmed.

Ethical and Public Policy Concerns

1. As suggested earlier in this chapter, one explanation for the prodefendant thrust of 19th-century product liability law is the courts' desire to protect infant industries by preventing them from suffering potentially crippling damage awards. If this explanation is accurate, it means that those injured by defective products and the survivors of those killed by such products were denied compensation so that the country might be industrialized. Is this right? Should people's rights be sacrificed in this way? In answering this question, assume for the sake of argument that these denials of recovery actually were necessary for industrialization to proceed.

2. Courts are much more likely to find disclaimers and remedy limitations enforceable when the plaintiff is a business firm than when the plaintiff is an ordinary consumer. What is the justification for this difference in treatment?

   One possible way to get around the arguments against enforcing disclaimers and remedy limitations in consumer cases is to enforce them when the seller has used various kinds of "superdisclosure" to make buyers aware of the disclaimer. Possibilities include: positioning the disclaimer or limitation outside the product package, using signs to alert buyers to it, explaining it to buyers, and requiring the buyer to sign separately near a conspicuous disclaimer or limitation. Try to think of some problems with superdisclosure itself and with allowing disclaimers and remedy limitations to be enforced on this basis.

3. Most likely, consumers would pay a somewhat lower price for the products they purchase if the implied warranty of merchantability did not exist. Why is this so? Assuming that it is so, why shouldn't consumers have the choice whether to buy products with the "insurance policy" the warranty provides, or to get a lower price by forgoing this protection? Or would this choice be too difficult for individual sellers and manufacturers to provide? Nonetheless, shouldn't consumers at least know what deal sellers are offering so that they can pick the seller whose terms they prefer? In theory, how does current law make this possible? What would probably *really* be necessary for consumers to get the necessary information? *Hint*: look at the second paragraph of the previous question.

Problems and Problem Cases

1. Allen, a salesperson for an electronics store, is talking to Arnold, a customer, while Arnold picks up a portable TV and puts it on the counter preparatory to buying it. Allen tells Arnold that he "won't have any problems" with the set because he's "buying the best." He also tells Arnold that "I'm sure you'll enjoy your new set." After purchasing the set, taking it home, and plugging it in, Arnold finds that the set does not work. Assuming that Allen has the authority to bind the store, has the store breached an express warranty to Arnold? Assuming that the store is a merchant and has not disclaimed the implied warranty of merchantability, is it liable on that basis?

2. Ewers, who owns a saltwater aquarium with tropical fish, bought several seashells, a piece of coral, and a driftwood branch from the Verona Rock Shop. Just before the purchase, the salesclerk told Ewers that these items were "suitable for saltwater aquariums, if they [are] rinsed." After making the purchase, Ewers took the items home, rinsed them for 20 minutes in a saltwater solution, and put them in his aquarium. Within a week, 17 of his tropical fish died. The "rinsing" required to prevent their deaths is a week-long cleansing process that involves soaking the shells and the coral in boiling water. Suppose that you are Ewers's attorney in his express warranty suit against the shop. Make an argument that the clerk's statement is an express warranty. Make an argument that this warranty was breached.

3. Steven Taterka purchased a 1972 Ford Mustang from a Ford dealer in January 1972. In October 1974, after Taterka had put 75,000 miles on the car and Ford's express warranty had expired, he discovered that the tail-light assembly gaskets on his Mustang had been installed in such a way that water was permitted to enter the tail-light assembly, causing rust to form. Even though the rusting problem was a recurrent one of which Ford was aware, Ford did nothing for Taterka. Is Ford liable to Taterka under the implied warranty of merchantability?

4. Cathy Adelman-Tremblay purchased a "Nailene Nail Kit" at a drugstore. The kit included artificial fingernails, a nail sander file, and a tube of cyanoacrylate liquid glue (also known as Super Glue). After attaching the artificial nails to her fingernails with the glue, Adelman-Tremblay experienced pain and eventually suffered the permanent loss of all of her natural fingernails. The cause of the loss was an allergic reaction called "allergic contact dermatitis."

    The manufacturer of the Nailene kit had sold more than 1 million such kits, and Adelman Tremblay's reaction was the only known adverse reaction to the glue. Also, the relevant medical literature indicated that allergic reactions to the glue were virtually impossible. Nonetheless, a few cases of allergic contact dermatitis from exposure to the glue occurred after Adelman-Tremblay suffered her reaction. Is the manufacturer liable in negligence for failing to warn users of the possibility of such an allergic reaction? Can Adelman-Tremblay recover under the implied warranty of merchantability?

5. Chuck contacts the Bits and Bites Computer Superstore to get a software package suitable for some customized computer program work he is performing for a client. He tells the store's salesperson that he needs a database management system that he can customize at the source code level. However, there is little discussion of his other needs, including the work Chuck is doing for the client. The salesperson recommends a system called "D-Base Hit" for $649, and Chuck relies on the salesperson's judgment in buying that package. As it turns out, D-Base Hit can be modified at the source code level, but it is otherwise unsuitable for the job Chuck is doing. Assuming that Article 2 of the UCC applies, has Bits and Bites breached the implied warranty of fitness for a particular purpose?

6. Gari West used Ovulen-28, a birth control medication manufactured by Searle & Company. She claimed that the Ovulen-28 caused her to develop a hepatic adenoma (a benign liver tumor), which eventually ruptured, causing a life-threatening situation. Assuming that the Ovulen-28 actually caused West's problem, what argument can Searle make to avoid the imposition of strict liability under section 402A? *Hint*: Assume that the Ovulen-28 has considerable social utility and cannot feasibly be made safer than it now is.

7. Curtis Hagans lost the ring finger of his left hand while operating an industrial table saw manufactured by the Oliver Machinery Company. The saw was originally

equipped with a detachable blade guard assembly that would have prevented Hagans's injury had it been attached to the saw while Hagans was working. This assembly was detachable rather than permanently affixed to the saw because many common woodworking functions could not be performed with the assembly in place. Also, the saw exceeded industry safety practices and national and associational safety standards in effect at the time of its manufacture. In addition, few competing manufacturers included blade guards as standard equipment, and none offered a table saw with a permanently affixed blade guard.

Hagans sued Oliver in negligence and under *Restatement (Second) of Torts* section 402A, alleging that the saw was defectively designed because it did not include a permanent blade guard assembly. Did Hagans win? You can assume that injuries of the kind Hagans suffered were foreseeable consequences of manufacturing the saw without a permanent guard, and that Hagans was not careless in his operation of the saw.

8. Floyd Roysden had long smoked Camel and Winston cigarettes, both of which are products of the R. J. Reynolds Tobacco Company. In 1983, Roysden's severe peripheral atherosclerotic vascular disease became so severe that his left leg was amputated below the knee. Some medical evidence links this disease to cigarette smoking. Assuming that they were not improperly manufactured and did not contain any dangerous impurities, were the cigarettes Roysden smoked "defective" under section 402A? Were they "unreasonably dangerous?" Does it matter that there is little public knowledge about the link between cigarette smoking and the specific disease from which Roysden suffered (as opposed to the general health risks cigarette smoking creates)?

9. Joe Kysar purchased a baler built by the Vermeer Manufacturing Company after a Vermeer sales representative told him that the baler in question would produce bales weighing 3,000 pounds. In fact, the baler never produced a 3,000-pound bale. Kysar eventually sued Vermeer in a Wyoming trial court. The court found Vermeer liable under the UCC, but did not specify the exact basis of its holding. As a remedy, it ordered Vermeer to return the purchase price to Kysar, after which Kysar was to return the baler to Vermeer. Assuming that Vermeer breached either an express warranty or the implied warranty of fitness, was this the proper measure of recovery for defective goods under the UCC? Assume for the sake of argument that Kysar suffered no consequential damages of any kind.

10. Arlyn and Rose Spindler were dairy farmers who leased a feed storage silo from Agristor Leasing. The silo was supposed to limit the oxygen reaching the feed and thus to hinder its spoilage. The Spindlers alleged that the silo was defective and that the dairy feed it contained was spoiled as a result. They further alleged that due to the spoilage of the feed, their dairy herd suffered medically and reproductively and their milk production dropped. The Spindlers sued Agristor in negligence and under section 402A for their resulting lost income. What type of damages are they claiming? Under the majority rule, can they recover for such damages in negligence or under section 402A? Would your answer be different if the Spindlers had sued for the damage to the dairy feed itself? Assume for purposes of argument that both section 402A and negligence suits are possible under this equipment lease.

11. Jake, a car salesman, is discussing a particular car with Jones, a customer at Jake's dealership. Jake tells Jones "you won't find a car like this at any price. This car is a crown jewel." Later, Jake says that he bought the car at an auction in Kentucky. Influenced by these statements, Jones buys the car. The bill of sale conspicuously says that the car is being sold "AS IS," and that no warranties or representations concerning

the car have been made or given, except as stated in the bill of sale. Later, Jones discovers that the car's brakes are so defective that the car is unsafe to drive.

Which, if any, of Jake's statements are express warranties? Which, if any, have been breached here? Does the language in the bill of sale disclaim any express warranties that might exist? Does the language in the bill of sale disclaim the implied warranty of merchantability? Assuming that the implied warranty of merchantability has not been disclaimed, is it breached here?

12. Duane Martin, a small farmer, placed an order for cabbage seed with the Joseph Harris Company, a large national producer and distributor of seed. Harris's order form included the following language:

> NOTICE TO BUYER: Joseph Harris Company, Inc. warrants that seeds and plants it sells conform to the label descriptions as required by Federal and State seed laws. IT MAKES NO OTHER WARRANTIES, EXPRESS OR IMPLIED, OF MERCHANTABILITY, FITNESS FOR PURPOSE, OR OTHERWISE, AND IN ANY EVENT ITS LIABILITY FOR BREACH OF ANY WARRANTY OR CONTRACT WITH RESPECT TO SUCH SEEDS OR PLANTS IS LIMITED TO THE PURCHASE PRICE OF SUCH SEEDS OR PLANTS.

All of Harris's competitors used similar clauses in their contracts.

After Martin placed his order, and unknown to Martin, Harris stopped using a cabbage seed treatment that had been effective in preventing a certain cabbage fungus. Later, Martin planted the seed he had ordered from Harris, but a large portion of the resulting crop was destroyed by fungus because the seed did not contain the treatment Harris had previously used. Martin sued Harris for his losses under the implied warranty of merchantability.

Which portion of the notice quoted above is an attempted disclaimer of implied warranty liability, and which is an attempted limitation of remedies? Will the disclaimer language disclaim the implied warranty of merchantability under UCC section 2-316(2)? If Martin had sued under the implied warranty of fitness for a particular purpose, would the disclaimer language disclaim that implied warranty as well? Assuming that the disclaimer and the remedy limitation contained the correct legal boilerplate needed to make them effective, what argument could Martin still make to block their operation? What are his chances of success with this argument?

13. Moulton purchased a 1969 Ford LTD from Hull-Dobbs, a Ford dealer. His sales contracts with Ford and Hull-Dobbs contained valid disclaimers of the implied warranty of merchantability that satisfied UCC section 2-316(2). One year later, while Moulton was driving his car along an interstate highway, the Ford suddenly veered to the right, jumped the guardrail, and fell 26 feet to the street below. The accident was caused by a defect in the car's steering mechanism, and Moulton was seriously injured. Moulton sued Ford under the implied warranty of merchantability. Ford defended on the basis of its disclaimer. Moulton argued that the disclaimer was invalid in a personal injury case under UCC section 2-719(3), which makes the exclusion of consequential damages unconscionable in a case involving consumer goods and personal injury. Did Moulton's argument succeed?

Endnotes

1. This chapter does not discuss the various federal consumer protection laws involving the payment and credit aspects of consumer transactions. Nor does it discuss product safety regulation.

2. Privity of contract is the existence of a direct contractual relationship between two parties. Chapter 1 discusses the gradual demise of the no-liability-outside-privity rule in New York.

3. Negligence and strict liability are discussed in Chapter 23.
4. Parol evidence rule problems can arise in express warranty cases. For example, a seller who used a written sale contract may argue that the rule excludes an alleged oral warranty. For the parol evidence rule, see Chapter 20.
5. Occasionally, such suits may proceed under the theory of *negligence per se* discussed in Chapter 23—for example, where the product violates a consumer product safety regulation or pure food law.
6. Another problem concerns the negligence liability of computer designers and programmers. Some courts have held such parties to a higher standard of care when they develop custom application software, but others reject such claims.
7. Chapter 23 discusses *res ipsa loquitur*.
8. Some states have statutes stating that a product's compliance with state or federal product safety regulations creates a rebuttable presumption that it was not defective. Also, a few states have a statutory state-of-the-art defense.
9. Also, many states have enacted so-called lemon laws that may apply only to motor vehicles, or to various other consumer products as well. The versions applying to motor vehicles generally require the manufacturer to replace the vehicle or refund its purchase price once certain conditions are met. These conditions may include the following: a serious defect covered by warranty, a certain number of unsuccessful attempts at repair or a certain amount of downtime due to attempted repairs, and the manufacturer's failure to show that the defect is curable.
10. We do not consider how these problems are resolved under the warranty of title, the Magnuson-Moss Act, or section 402B.
11. The same rules probably apply where a seller tries to modify an implied warranty or to limit its duration.
12. Also, in express and implied warranty cases, the buyer must notify the seller of the breach within a reasonable time after the buyer discovers or should have discovered it. There is no notice requirement for negligence and strict liability suits.
13. Chapter 23 discusses contributory negligence and assumption of risk.
14. Comparative negligence is discussed in Chapter 23. Some of the newer state statutes, however, speak of comparative *fault*. Although courts and commentators often use the terms *comparative fault* and *comparative negligence* interchangeably, it is not always clear whether comparative negligence embraces forms of fault other than the plaintiff's negligence.

Chapter Twenty-Two

INTENTIONAL TORTS

Introduction

Torts are *private (civil) wrongs* against persons or their property. The basis of tort liability is a breach of a legal duty owed to another person resulting in some legally recognizable harm to that person. The primary aim of tort law is to compensate injured persons for such harms.

Nature and Function of Tort Law

Persons injured by the tortious act of another may file a civil suit for the *actual (compensatory) damages* that they have suffered as a result of a tort. Depending on the facts of the particular case, these damages may be for direct and immediate harms, such as physical injuries, medical expenses, and lost pay and benefits, or for harms as intangible as loss of privacy, injury to reputation, or emotional distress.

In cases where the behavior of the person committing a tort is particularly reprehensible, injured victims may also be able to recover an award of *punitive damages*. Punitive damages are not intended to compensate tort victims for their losses. Instead, they are designed to punish flagrant wrongdoers and to deter them and others from engaging in similar conduct in the future. Accordingly, they are theoretically reserved for only the most egregious forms of wrongdoing. Punitive damages have always been controversial, but they have grown more so in recent years because of the size of some punitive damage awards and the perception that juries are awarding them in cases where they are not justified.

The punishment function of punitive damage awards is obviously similar to the deterrent function in criminal law. Some kinds of behavior can give rise to both criminal and tort liability. For example, a rapist may be criminally liable for rape and also liable for the torts of assault, battery, false imprisonment, and intentional infliction of mental distress. However, since tort suits are civil rather than criminal, the plaintiff's burden of proof in a tort case is the *preponderance of the evidence*, rather than the more stringent beyond a reasonable doubt standard that applies to criminal cases. This means that the greater weight of the evidence introduced at the trial must support the plaintiff's position on every element of the case. Figure 22-1 summarizes the important differences between criminal and tort liability.

FIGURE 22-1	Nature	Criminal	Civil
Crimes and intentional torts	**Elements**	1. Violation of a statute 2. Intent	1. Harm to another person or property 2. Intent
	Actors	Prosecutor versus defendant	Plaintiff (victim) versus defendant (tortfeasor)
	Burden	Prosecutor must establish the defendant's guilt beyond a reasonable doubt	Plaintiff must establish the defendant's liability by a preponderance of the evidence
	Punishment	Fines, imprisonment, execution	Defendant may have to pay the plaintiff compensatory and punitive damages

In tort law, society is engaged in a constant balancing of competing social interests. Excessive protection of some people's physical integrity, for example, may unduly impair other people's freedom of movement. Likewise, undue protection of peace of mind, privacy, and personal reputation may inordinately restrict constitutionally protected freedoms of speech and of the press. Over time, our tort law has demonstrated a tendency to protect an increasingly broad range of personal interests. Some commentators have explained this tendency by saying it demonstrates the courts' growing sensitivity to the nature of life in an increasingly interdependent urban industrialized society. Whatever its origins, this and the next chapter demonstrate that, although the range of the human interests that tort law protects is expanding, the courts have remained mindful of the fact that the protection of any given interest necessarily involves a trade-off in the form of limitations placed on other competing social interests.

Torts are generally classified according to the level of fault exhibited by the wrongdoer's behavior. This chapter deals with **intentional torts**—behavior that indicates either the wrongdoer's conscious desire to cause harm to a legally protected interest or the wrongdoer's knowledge that such harm is substantially certain to result from his actions. The following chapter discusses tort liability founded on principles of *negligence* and *strict liability*, neither of which require proof of any intentional wrongdoing by a defendant.

Interference with Personal Rights

Battery

The tort of *battery* protects a fundamental personal interest—the right to be free from harmful or offensive bodily contacts. Battery is the *intentional, harmful* or *offensive touching of another without his consent*. A contact is *harmful* if it produces any bodily injury. As the following *England* case illustrates, even nonharmful contacts may be considered battery if they are *offensive*—that is, calculated to offend a reasonable sense of personal dignity. Direct contact between a wrongdoer's body and the body of another is not necessary for a battery to result. For example, if Delano throws a rock at Stevens or places a harmful or offensive substance in her food, Delano has committed a battery if Stevens is hit by the rock or if she eats the food. Nor is it necessary that the wrongdoer actually intend to produce the contact if contact in fact results and the wrongdoer's intent was merely to threaten the victim with contact. So, if Delano threatens to shoot Stevens with a gun he mistakenly believes is unloaded, and ends up shooting Stevens, Delano would be liable for battery.

Also, the person who suffers the harmful or offensive touching does not have to be the person whom the wrongdoer intended to injure for liability for battery to occur. Under a general intentional tort concept called the doctrine of *transferred intent*, a wrongdoer who intends to injure one person, but injures another, is nonetheless liable to the person injured, despite the absence of any specific intent to injure him. So, if Walters is hit by the rock thrown at Stevens, or if he eats Stevens's food, Delano would be liable to Walters for battery. Finally, touching anything connected with a person's body in a harmful or offensive manner can also create liability for battery. So, if Johnson snatches Martin's purse, or kicks her dog while she is walking her dog on a leash, he may be liable for battery even though he has not touched her body.

Some of the most interesting battery cases involve the nature of the *consent* that is necessary to avoid liability for battery. As a general rule, consent must be *freely* and *intelligently* given to be a defense to battery. In some cases, consent may be inferred from a person's voluntary participation in an activity. Such consent is ordinarily limited, however, to contacts that are considered a normal consequence of the activity in question. For example, Joe Frazier would be unable to win a battery suit against Muhammad Ali for injuries he suffered during their famous "Thrilla in Manila" title fight. However, the quarterback who is knifed on the 50-yard line during a game has a valid battery claim.

Assault

The tort of **assault** protects the personal interest in freedom from the *apprehension* of battery. Any *attempt* to cause a harmful or offensive contact with another, or any *offer* to cause such a contact, is an assault if it causes a *well-grounded apprehension of imminent (immediate) battery* in the mind of the person threatened with contact. Whether the threatened contact actually occurs is irrelevant.

Because assault is limited to threats of *imminent* battery, threats of *future* battery do not create liability for assault. Likewise, because assault focuses on the apprehension in the mind of the victim, the threats in question must create a reasonable apprehension of battery in the victim's mind. Therefore, threatening words, unaccompanied by any other acts or circumstances indicating an intent to carry out the threat, do not amount to an assault. Finally, the elements of assault require that the victim must actually experience an apprehension of imminent battery before liability results. Therefore, if Markham fires a rifle at Thomas from a great distance and misses him, and Thomas learns of the attempt on his life only at a later date, Markham is not liable to Thomas for the tort of assault.

England v. S & M Foods, Inc.

Betty England worked at a Dairy Queen restaurant owned by S & M Foods in Tallulah, Louisiana. One day while she was at work, her manager, Larry Garley, became upset when several incorrectly prepared hamburgers were returned by a customer. Garley allegedly expressed his dissatisfaction by using profane language and throwing a hamburger that hit England on the leg. England filed a battery suit against Garley and S & M and won a $1,000 judgment. Garley and S & M appealed.

Source: 511 So.2d 1313 (La. Ct. App. 1987)

Jones, Judge

Defendants contend no battery was committed because Garley did not intend to inflict bodily harm upon England. They argue Garley was disgusted about the returned hamburgers anal threw one toward the trash can and it inadvertently splattered on her and

Alcie Rash, another employee. They contend that England's embarrassment was caused as much by her overreaction to the situation as by Garley's conduct.

England said that Garley used profane language when he told her to prepare the hamburgers correctly. She said Garley, while looking straight at her, then threw the hamburger which hit her on the leg. She testified that she argued with Garley about the matter and that several patrons observed the incident which caused her to cry and become emotionally upset.

Rash said that she did not see Garley throw the hamburger, but observed it hit the floor and splatter mayonnaise and mustard on her and England.

A battery is any intentional and unpermitted contact with the plaintiff's person or anything attached to it. In the area of intentional torts, intent means the defendant either desired to bring about the physical results of his act or believed they were substantially certain to follow from what he did. Mental distress and humiliation in connection with a battery are compensable items of damage.

The totality of the evidence provided a substantial basis for the trial judge to conclude Garley must have been substantially certain the hamburger would hit England or splatter on her when he threw it toward her. His contact with her was, therefore, intentional and unpermitted and constituted a battery.
Judgment for England affirmed.

False Imprisonment

The tort of **false imprisonment** protects the personal interest in freedom from *confinement*. False imprisonment is the intentional *confinement of another* for an *appreciable time* (a few minutes is enough) *without his consent*. Confinement may result from physical barriers to the plaintiff's freedom of movement, such as locking a person in a room with no other doors or windows, or the use of physical force or the threat to use physical force against the plaintiff. Confinement also results from the assertion of legal authority to detain the plaintiff, or the detention of the plaintiff's property—for example, a purse containing a large sum of money. Likewise, a threat to harm another, such as the plaintiff's spouse or child, can also be confinement if it prevents the plaintiff from moving.

The confinement required for false imprisonment must be *complete*. Partial confinement of another by blocking her path or by depriving her of one means of escape where several exist, such as locking one door of a building having other, unlocked doors, does not amount to false imprisonment. The fact that a means of escape exists, however, does not render a confinement partial if the plaintiff cannot reasonably be expected to know of its existence. The same is true if it involves some unreasonable risk of harm to the plaintiff, such as walking a tightrope or climbing out of a second-story window, or some affront to his sense of personal dignity (e.g., Jones steals Smith's clothes while Smith is swimming in the nude).

The personal interest in freedom from confinement protected by false imprisonment involves a mental element—knowledge of confinement—as well as a physical element—freedom of movement. Therefore, courts generally hold that the plaintiff must have *knowledge* of his confinement before liability for false imprisonment arises. Similarly, liability for false imprisonment does not arise in cases where the person has *consented* to his confinement. Such consent, however, must be freely given. Consent in the face of an implied or actual threat of force or an assertion of legal authority by the confiner is not freely given.

As the following *Speight* case indicates, many contemporary false imprisonment cases involve shoplifting. The common law held store owners liable for any torts committed while detaining a suspected shoplifter if subsequent investigation revealed that the detainee was innocent of any wrongdoing. In an attempt to accommodate the legitimate interests of store owners in preventing theft of their property, most states have passed statutes giving store owners a *conditional privilege* to stop persons who they reasonably believe are shoplifting. However, the owner must act in a reasonable manner and only detain the suspect for a reasonable length of time. Store owners who act within the scope of such a statute are not liable for any torts committed in the process of detaining a suspected shoplifter.

J. H. Harvey Co. v. Speight

Acting on information that someone had just stolen several cartons of cigarettes from the store, the manager of Harvey's Supermarket stepped outside and approached Speight, who had himself walked out of the store only moments earlier. Upon being asked by the manager if he had anything that did not belong to him, Speight answered, "No, do you want to see?" He then briefly held the sides of his jacket open and let them close, at which point the manager parted the jacket with his hands to see if anything was concealed there. Simultaneously, Speight pointed to another person in the immediate vicinity and said, "I think that is the man you are looking for." The manager then left Speight to pursue this other person. Speight subsequently filed suit against Harvey's for false imprisonment and assault and battery. When a jury awarded him $2,500 in compensatory damages and $30,000 in punitive damages, Harvey's appealed.

Source: 344 S.E.2d 701 (Ga. Ct. App. 1986)

Banke, Chief Judge

Speight testified that the store manager had not been rude to him but stated that he did not consider the manager's conduct in looking inside his jacket as courteous. He admitted that he had invited this search and that the manager had not cursed him nor spoken loudly to him; however, he testified that he felt the manager was angry because of the look in his eyes and the fact that several people had followed the manager out of the store. At trial, Speight testified that the entire encounter had lasted about 45 seconds, whereas during an earlier deposition he had testified that the encounter lasted between 15 and 30 seconds.

According to *Prosser, Law of Torts* (4th ed.), in false imprisonment:

> [T]he imprisonment need not be for more than an appreciable length of time, and . . . it is not necessary that any damage result from it other than the confinement itself, since the ton is complete with even a brief restraint of the plaintiff's freedom. . . . It is essential, however, that the restraint be against the plaintiff's will, and if he agrees of his own free choice to surrender his freedom of motion, as by remaining in a room or accompanying the defendant voluntarily, to clear himself of suspicion or to accommodate the desires of another, rather than yielding to the constraint of a threat, then there is no imprisonment.

Speight's testimony in this case fails to establish any involuntary restraint by Harvey's store manager or employees. Although a person need not make an effort to escape or await application of open force before he can recover, there must be restraint whether by force or fear. With regard to the second count of the complaint, Speight admitted that any touching of his person had been invited by him; and such invitation is inconsistent with the torts of assault and battery. The evidence was consequently insufficient to support any recovery. **Judgment reversed in favor of Harvey's.**

Defamation

The tort of *defamation* protects the individual's interest in his *reputation*. It recognizes the value that society places on reputation, concerning not only the individual's personal dignity but also the value that a good reputation has in the individual's business dealings with others. Defamation is ordinarily defined as the unprivileged *publication of false and defamatory statements* concerning another. A defamatory statement is one that harms the reputation of another by injuring his community's estimation of him or by deterring others from associating or dealing with him. Whether a given statement is defamatory is ordinarily decided by a jury.

Because the primary focus of defamation is to protect the *individual's* right to reputation, an essential element of defamation is that the alleged defamatory statement must be "of and concerning" the plaintiff. That is, the statement must harm the particular plaintiff's reputation. This causes several problems. What about allegedly fictional accounts such as those found in novels and short stories? Do they amount to defamation if the fictional characters bear a substantial resemblance to real persons? Most courts that have dealt with the issue say they do, if a reasonable reader would identify the plaintiff as the subject of the story. Similarly, humorous or satirical accounts do not ordinarily amount to defamation unless a reasonable reader would believe that they purport to describe real events. Likewise, statements of personal opinion traditionally have been thought not to be a proper ground for defamation because they are not statements of fact concerning the plaintiff, unless such statements imply the existence of undisclosed facts that are false and defamatory. Thus, the statement that "Smedley is a lousy governor" would probably not be actionable. But, the statement "I think Irving must be a thief" may be defamatory because a jury may believe that the statement implies that its maker knows facts that justify this opinion.

What about defamatory statements concerning particular groups of persons? The courts generally hold that an individual member of a defamed group cannot recover for damage to her personal reputation unless the group is so small that the statement can reasonably be understood as referring to specific members. This is also true when the circumstances in which the statement is made are such that it is reasonable to conclude that a particular group member is being referred to. So, the statement that "all Germans are thieves," standing alone, would not provide the basis for a defamation suit by any person of German descent. However, if Schmidt, a person of German origin, is being considered for a controller's position in her employer's company and a fellow employee makes the same statement in response to a question concerning Schmidt's qualifications for the job, the statement would probably be a proper basis for a defamation suit.

Finally, the courts have placed some limits on the persons or entities that can suffer injury to reputation. For example, it is generally held that no liability attaches to defamatory statements concerning the dead. Corporations and other business entities have a limited right to reputation and can file suit for defamatory statements that harm them in conducting their business or deter others from dealing with them. As a general rule, statements about a corporation's officers, employees, or shareholders do not amount to defamation of the corporation unless such statements also reflect on the manner in which the corporation conducts its business. Statements concerning the quality of a corporation's products or the quality of its title to land or other property may be the basis of an *injurious falsehood* suit.[1]

Publication

The elements of the tort of defamation require *publication* of a defamatory statement before liability for defamation arises. This requirement can be misleading because, as a general rule, no widespread communication of a defamatory statement is required for publication. Communication of the defamatory statement to *one person* other than the person defamed is ordinarily sufficient for publication. Making a defamatory statement about a person in a personal conversation with him or in a private letter sent to him therefore does not satisfy the publication requirement. In addition, the courts generally hold that one who repeats or republishes a defamatory statement is liable for defamation, regardless of whether he identifies the source of the statement.

Libel and Slander

The courts have divided the tort of defamation into two categories, libel and slander, depending on the medium used to communicate the defamatory statement. **Libel** refers to written or printed defamations or to those that have a physical form, such as a defamatory picture or statue. **Slander** refers to oral defamation. The advent of radio and television initially resulted in some judicial confusion concerning the proper classification of defamatory statements communicated by these new media. Today, the great majority of courts treat broadcast defamations as libel. The distinction between libel and slander is important because the courts have traditionally held that libel, due to its more permanent nature and the seriousness that we tend to attach to the written word, is actionable without any proof of special damage (the loss of anything of monetary value) to the plaintiff. Slander, however, is generally not actionable without proof of special damage, unless the nature of the slanderous statement is so serious that it can be classified as *slander per se*. In slander per se, injury to the plaintiff's reputation is presumed. Four defamatory statements ordinarily qualify for per se treatment: allegations that the plaintiff (1) has committed a crime involving moral turpitude or potential imprisonment, (2) has a loathsome disease (usually a venereal disease or leprosy), (3) is professionally incompetent or guilty of professional misconduct, or (4) is guilty of serious sexual misconduct.

Defamation and the Constitution

Nowhere is the social balancing task of tort law more obvious than in cases of defamation. Overzealous protection of individual reputation could result in an infringement of our constitutionally protected freedoms of speech and of the press, which could thereby inhibit the free flow of information necessary to a free society. In recent years, the Supreme Court has balanced these conflicting social interests in a series of important cases that define the amount of protection the Constitution affords to otherwise defamatory statements. Under the common law, defendants were strictly liable (liable without fault) for defamatory statements. In *New York Times v. Sullivan*, however, the Court held that *public officials* seeking to recover for defamatory statements relating to performance of their official duties must prove *actual malice* (knowledge of falsity or reckless disregard for the truth) on the part of a media defendant to recover any damages.[2] This significant limitation on public officials' right to reputation was justified largely by the public interest in "free and unfettered debate" on important social issues.

For similar reasons, the Court subsequently extended the actual malice test to public figures, persons in the public eye because of their celebrity status or because they have voluntarily involved themselves in matters of public controversy.[3] Then, in *Gertz v. Robert Welch, Inc.*, the Court refused to extend the actual malice test to media defamation of private citizens who involuntarily become involved in matters of public concern.[4] Instead, the Court held that to recover compensatory damages, such persons must prove some degree of fault at least amounting to negligence on the part of the defendant; to recover punitive damages, they must prove actual malice. Most recent was *Dun & Bradstreet, Inc. v. Greenmoss Builders, Inc.,* a case involving a private figure plaintiff—a construction contractor—and defamatory speech about a matter of purely private concern—a false credit report.[5] The Court refused to apply the Gertz standard and upheld a recovery based on the common law strict liability standard.

The amount of protection the Constitution affords to otherwise defamatory statements appears to depend on two factors: whether the plaintiff is a public figure or official or a private person and whether the subject matter of the speech at issue is a matter of public concern or private concern. The Court has yet to speak definitively on the standard that it will apply to cases involving defamatory statements about private matters concerning public figures and officials. Its decisions to date, however, suggest that the Gertz test is likely to be applied to such cases.

Defenses to Defamation

Truth is an absolute defense to defamation. The tort of defamation requires that a statement serving as the basis of a defamation suit be *false* as well as defamatory.

Even where defamatory statements are false, a defense of *privilege* may serve to prevent liability in some cases. The idea of privilege recognizes the fact that, in some circumstances, other social interests may be more important than an individual's right to reputation. Privileges are either *absolute* or *conditional*. Absolute privileges shield the author of a defamatory statement regardless of her knowledge, motive, or intent. Absolutely privileged statements include those made by participants in judicial proceedings, legislators or witnesses in the course of legislative proceedings, certain executive officials in the course of their official duties, and between spouses in private.

Conditional privileges are conditioned on their proper use. One who *abuses* a conditional privilege by making a defamatory statement with the knowledge that it is false, or in reckless disregard of the truth, loses the protection afforded by the privilege. Conditional privileges are abused when the author of a defamatory statement acts with an improper motive, such as a purpose other than protecting the interests justifying the privilege. The author can also exceed the scope of the privilege by communicating the defamation unnecessarily to third persons who do not share his interests. Conditional privileges are often recognized when the author of a defamatory statement acts to protect her own legitimate interests or those of a third person with whom she shares some interest or to whom she owes some duty. Many intracorporate communications enjoy such a conditional privilege.

In recent years, the courts have also begun to recognize a conditional privilege of "fair comment." This privilege protects fair and accurate media reports of defamatory matter in reports or proceedings of official action or originating from public meetings. The privilege is justified by the public's right to know what occurs in such proceedings and meetings. The conditional privilege most important to business, however, is the traditional privilege enjoyed by employers who provide prospective employers with reference letters about former employees. Despite this privilege, employers in recent years have faced a growing number of defamation claims from disgruntled former employees. As a result, many companies, as a matter of policy, refuse to divulge any information about former employees other than to confirm that they did work for the company at one time and the duration of their employment. However, as the following *Lewis* case indicates, even such a policy does not always shield employers from liability.

Lewis v. Equitable Life Assurance Society

Carole Lewis, Mary Smith, Michelle Rafferty, and Suzanne Loizeaux were employed as dental claim approvers in the St. Paul, Minnesota, office of the Equitable Life Assurance Society of the United States. In October 1980, they were sent to assist in Equitable's Pittsburgh office. None of the women had ever traveled on company business before, and they departed for Pittsburgh without being given copies of Equitable's travel expense policies or being told that expense reports would have to be filed. Instead, they were verbally given information on Equitable's daily meal and maid tip allowances and told to keep receipts for hotel bills and airfare. In addition, each was given a $1,400 travel allowance which, having no instruction to the contrary, they spent in full.

When they returned to St. Paul, each of the women received a personal letter from management commending her on her job performance in Pittsburgh. Each was also told for the first time that she would have to submit expense reports detailing her daily expenses in Pittsburgh. This they did, but a dispute subsequently arose over the amount of allowable expenses because Equitable's written guidelines differed from the instructions they had received prior to departure. After first changing their reports with respect to maid tips, they were asked to change their reports again, the net effect of which would have been to obligate each employee to return approximately $200 to Equitable. They refused to do this, arguing that the expenses shown on their reports were honestly incurred, a claim that Equitable never disputed. Subsequently, the women were fired for "gross insubordination."

In seeking new jobs, each woman was asked by prospective employers why she had left Equitable, and each said she had been terminated. When asked in interviews to explain their terminations, each stated that she had been terminated for gross insubordination and attempted to explain the situation. Only one of the women found a new job by being forthright with a prospective employer about her termination from Equitable. The others had various difficulties finding new jobs. They filed a defamation suit against Equitable, and when a jury ruled in their favor, Equitable appealed.

Source: 389 N.W. 2d 876 (Minn. Sup. Ct. 1986)

Amdahl, Chief Justice

In order for a statement to be considered defamatory, it must be communicated to someone other than the plaintiff, it must be false, and it must tend to harm the plaintiff's reputation. Generally, there is no publication where a defendant communicates a statement directly to a plaintiff, who then communicates it to a third person. Plaintiffs themselves informed prospective employers that they had been terminated for gross insubordination. They did so because prospective employers inquired why they had left their previous employment. The question raised is whether a defendant can ever be held liable for defamation when the statement in question was published to a third person only by the plaintiff.

We have not previously been presented with the question of defamation by means of "self-publication." Courts that have considered the question, however, have recognized a narrow exception to the general rule that communication of a defamatory statement to a third person by the person defamed is not actionable. These courts have recognized that if a defamed person was in some way compelled to communicate the defamatory statement to a third person, and if it was foreseeable to the defendant that the defamed person would be so compelled, then the defendant could be held liable for the defamation.

Several courts have specifically recognized this exception for compelled self-publication in the context of employment discharges. The trend of modern authority persuades us that Minnesota law should recognize the doctrine. Compelled self-publication does no more than hold the originator of the defamatory statement liable for damages caused by the statement where the originator knows, or should know, of circumstances whereby the defamed person has no reasonable means of avoiding publication of the statement or avoiding the resulting damages. In such circumstances, the damages are fairly viewed as the direct result of the originator's actions.

The St. Paul office manager admitted that it was foreseeable that plaintiffs would be asked by prospective employers to identify the reason that they were discharged. Their only choice would be to tell them "gross insubordination" or to lie. Fabrication, however, is an unacceptable alternative.

Finding that there was a publication, we next turn to the issue of truth. True statements, however disparaging, are not actionable. The company contends the relevant statement to consider when analyzing the defense of truth is the one that plaintiffs made to their prospective employers, that is, that they had been fired for gross insubordination. Plaintiffs counter that it is the truth or falsity of the underlying statement—that they engaged in gross insubordination—that is relevant.

Requiring that truth as a defense go to the underlying implication of the statement, at least where the statement involves more than a simple allegation, appears to be the better view. Here, the company's charges against plaintiffs went beyond accusations and were conclusory statements that plaintiffs had engaged in gross insubordination. The record amply supports the jury verdict that the charge of gross insubordination was false.

Even though an untrue defamatory statement has been published, the originator of the statement will not be held liable if the statement is published under circumstances that make it conditionally privileged and if privilege is not abused. The doctrine of privileged communication rests upon public policy considerations. The existence of a privilege results from the court's determination that statements made in particular contexts or on certain occasions should be encouraged despite the risk that the statements might be defamatory.

In the context of employment recommendations, the law generally recognizes a qualified privilege between former and prospective employers as long as the statements are made in good faith and for a legitimate purpose. Plaintiffs argue that a self-publication case does not properly fit within the qualified privilege doctrine, but the logic of imposing liability upon a former employer in a self-publication case appears to compel recognition of a qualified privilege. A former employer in a compelled self-publication case may be held liable as if it had actually published the defamatory statement directly to prospective employers. Where an employer would be entitled to a privilege if it had actually published the statement, it makes little sense to deny the privilege where the identical communication is made to identical third parties with the only difference being the mode of publication. Finally, recognition of a qualified privilege seems to be the only effective means of addressing the concern that every time an employer states the reason for discharging an employee it will subject itself to potential liability for defamation. It is in the public interest that information regarding an employee's discharge be readily available to the discharged employee and to prospective employers, and we are concerned that, unless a significant privilege is recognized by the courts, employers will decline to inform employees of reasons for discharges.

This conclusion does not necessarily determine that the company's statements were privileged. A qualified privilege is abused and therefore lost if the plaintiff demonstrates that the defendant acted with actual malice. The jury found that the company's statements were "actuated by actual malice."

Judgment for the plaintiffs affirmed.

Invasion of Privacy

The recognition of a personal *right of privacy* is a relatively recent development in tort law. At present, four distinct behaviors provide a proper basis for an invasion of privacy suit: (1) intrusion on a person's solitude or seclusion, (2) public disclosure of private facts concerning a person, (3) publicity placing a person in a false light in the public eye, and (4) appropriation of a person's name or likeness for commercial purposes. The thread tying these different behaviors together is that they all infringe on a person's "right to be let alone."

Intrusion on Solitude

Any intentional intrusion on the solitude or seclusion of another constitutes an invasion of privacy if that intrusion would be highly offensive to a reasonable individual. The intrusion in question may be physical, such as illegal searches of a person's home or body or the opening of his mail. It may also be a nonphysical intrusion such as tapping his telephone, examining his bank account, or subjecting him to harassing telephone calls. As a general rule, no liability attaches to examining public records concerning a person, or observing or photographing him in a public place, because a person does not have a reasonable expectation of privacy in these instances.

Publicity Concerning Private Facts

Publicizing facts concerning a person's private life can be an invasion of privacy if their publicity would be highly offensive to a reasonable person. The idea is that the public has no legitimate right to know certain aspects of a person's private life. Thus, publicity concerning a person's failure to pay his debts, humiliating illnesses that he has suffered, and details concerning his sex life constitute an invasion of privacy. Truth is *not* a defense to this type of invasion of privacy because the essence of the tort is giving unjustified publicity to purely private matters. Publicity in this context means a widespread dissemination of private details.

This variant of invasion of privacy, similar to the tort of defamation, represents a potential source of conflict with the constitutionally protected freedoms of the press and of speech. The courts have attempted to accommodate these conflicting social interests in several ways. First, no liability ordinarily attaches to publicity concerning matters of public record or of legitimate public interest. Second, public figures and public officials have no right of privacy concerning information that is reasonably related to their public lives.

False Light

Publicity that places a person in a *false light* in the public eye can be an invasion of privacy if that false light would be highly offensive to a reasonable person. This variant of invasion of privacy may in some cases also involve defamation. As in defamation cases, truth is an absolute defense to liability. For liability for invasion of privacy to arise, however, it is not necessary that a person be defamed by the false light in which he is placed. All that is required is unreasonable and highly objectionable publicity attributing to a person characteristics that he does not possess or beliefs that he does not hold. Signing a person's name to a public telegram or letter without her consent or attributing authorship of an inferior scholarly or artistic work to her are examples of this form of invasion of privacy. Because of the overlap between this form of invasion of privacy and defamation and the obvious First Amendment issues at stake, defendants in false light cases enjoy constitutional protection similar to that enjoyed by defamation defendants.

Appropriation of Name or Likeness

Some of the earliest invasion of privacy cases involved the appropriation of a person's name or likeness for commercial purposes without his consent. Liability for invasion of privacy can be created by using a person's name or image in an advertisement to imply his endorsement of a product or service or a nonexistent connection with the person or business placing the ad. This variant of invasion of privacy differs markedly from those previously discussed in that it recognizes the personal property right connected with a person's identity and that he has the exclusive right to its control.

The potential for conflict between this property right and the freedoms of speech and of the press has been illustrated in recent years by cases involving public figures' *right of publicity,* such as the following *White* case. To what extent do public persons have the right to control the use of their names, likenesses, or other matters associated with their identities? For example, should a well-known movie star have the right to prevent the writing of a book about her life or the televising of a docudrama about her? At this point, the scope of a public person's right of publicity varies greatly from state to state; considerable disagreement exists concerning such issues as its duration and inheritability.

Other Limitations

In addition to the various limitations on the right of privacy discussed earlier, two further limits are applicable to invasion of privacy actions. First, with the exception in some states of cases involving the appropriation of a person's name or likeness, the right of privacy is a purely *personal* right. This means that only living individuals whose personal privacy has been invaded can bring suit for invasion of privacy. Therefore, family members of a person exposed to publicity ordinarily cannot maintain an invasion of privacy action unless their personal privacy has also been violated. Second, corporations and other business organizations generally have no personal right of privacy. They do, however, have limited rights associated with the use of their names and identities. These rights are protected by the law of unfair competition.[6]

White v. Samsung Electronics America, Inc.

Samsung Electronics America ran a series of advertisements prepared by David Deutsch Associates, Inc., in a number of national publications. The ads were set in the 21st century and depicted a current item from the popular culture and a Samsung electronic product. The basic message conveyed was that the Samsung products would still be in use at that time in the future. By hypothesizing outrageous future outcomes for the cultural items, the ads created humorous effects.

One of the ads depicted a robot dressed in a wig, gown, and jewelry that Deutsch consciously selected to resemble Vanna White, the hostess of the "Wheel of Fortune"

game show. The robot was posed next to a game board that was instantly recognizable as the Wheel of Fortune set, in a stance for which White is famous. The caption of the ad read: "Longest-running game show. 2012 A.D." Deutsch and Samsung referred to the ad as the "Vanna White" ad. White, who had not consented to the ad, filed suit against Deutsch and Samsung, alleging, among other things, violation of her common law right of publicity. When the district court granted the defendants' summary judgment motion, White appealed.

Source: 971 F.2d 1395 (9th Cir. 1992)

Goodwin, Circuit Judge

In *Eastwood v. Superior Court* (1983), the California Court of Appeal stated that the common law right of publicity cause of action "may be pleaded by alleging (1) the defendant's use of the plaintiff's identity; (2) the appropriation of plaintiff's name or likeness to defendant's advantage, commercially or otherwise; (3) lack of consent; and (4) resulting injury." The district court dismissed White's claim for failure to satisfy *Eastwood's* second prong, reasoning that the defendants had not appropriated White's "name or likeness" with their robot ad. We agree that the robot ad did not make use of White's name or likeness. However, the common law right of publicity is not so confined.

The "name or likeness" formulation referred to in *Eastwood* originated not as an element of the right of publicity cause of action, but as a description of the types of cases in which the cause of action had been recognized. The source of this formulation is Prosser, *Privacy*, 48 Cal. L. Rev. 383 (1960), one of the earliest and most enduring articulations of the right of publicity cause of action. Even though Prosser focused on appropriations of name or likeness in discussing the right of publicity, he noted that "[i]t is not impossible that there might be appropriation of the plaintiff's identity, as by impersonation, without the use of either his name or his likeness." At the time Prosser wrote, he noted, however, that "no such case appears to have arisen."

Since Prosser's early formulation, the case law has borne out his insight that the right of publicity is not limited to the appropriation of name or likeness. In *Motschenbacher v. R. J. Reynolds Tobacco Co.* (1974), the defendant used a photo of the plaintiff's race car in a television commercial. Even though the defendant had not appropriated the plaintiff's name or likeness, this court held that Motschenbacher's right of publicity claim should reach the jury. In *Carson v. Here's Johnny Portable Toilets, Inc.* (1983), the defendant marketed portable toilets under the brand name "Here's Johnny"—Johnny Carson's signature "Tonight Show" introduction—without Carson's permission. The district court dismissed Carson's right of publicity claim because the defendants had not used Carson's "name or likeness." In reversing, the sixth circuit found "the district court's conception of the right of publicity . . . too narrow" and held that the right was implicated because the defendant had appropriated Carson's identity by using the phrase "Here's Johnny."

Although the defendants in these cases avoided the most obvious means of appropriating the plaintiffs' identities, each of their actions directly implicated the commercial interests which the right of publicity is designed to protect. As the Carson court explained:

> The right of publicity has developed to protect the commercial interest of celebrities in their identities. The theory of the right is that a celebrity's identity can be valuable in the promotion of products, and the celebrity has an interest that may be protected from the unauthorized commercial exploitation of that identity. If the celebrity's identity is commercially exploited, there has been an invasion of his right whether or not his "name or likeness" is used.

Motschenbacher and *Carson* teach the impossibility of treating the right of publicity as guarding only against a laundry list of specific means of appropriating identity. A rule which says that the right of publicity can be infringed only through the use of nine different methods of appropriating identity merely challenges the clever advertising strategist to come up with the tenth. If we treated the means of appropriation as dispositive in our analysis of the right of publicity, we would not only weaken the right but effectively eviscerate it. The right would fail to protect those plaintiffs most in need of its protection. The identities of the most popular celebrities are not only the most attractive for advertisers, but also the easiest to evoke without resorting to obvious means such as name, likeness, or voice.

Viewed separately, the individual aspects of the ad in the present case say little. Viewed together, they leave little doubt about the celebrity the ad is meant to depict. Indeed, the defendants themselves referred to their ad as the "Vanna White" ad. We decline Samsung and Deutsch's invitation to permit the evisceration of the right of publicity through means as facile as those in this case. Because White has alleged facts showing that Samsung and Deutsch appropriated her identity, the district court erred by rejecting her right of publicity claim.

Summary judgment reversed in White's favor; case remanded for trial.

Infliction of Emotional Distress

For many years, the courts refused to allow recovery for purely emotional injuries in the absence of some other tort. Thus, victims of such torts as assault, battery, and false imprisonment could recover for the emotional injuries resulting from these torts, but the courts were unwilling to recognize an independent tort of infliction of emotional distress. The reasons for this judicial reluctance included a fear of spurious or trivial claims, concerns about the difficulty in proving purely emotional harms, and uncertainty concerning the proper boundaries of an independent tort of intentional infliction of emotional distress. Recent advances in medical knowledge concerning emotional injuries, however, have helped to overcome some of these judicial impediments. Today, most courts allow recovery for *severe* emotional distress regardless of whether the elements of any other tort are proven.

The courts are not, however, in complete agreement on the elements of this new tort. All courts require that a wrongdoer's conduct must be *outrageous* before liability for emotional distress arises. The *Restatement (Second) of Torts* speaks of conduct "so outrageous in character, and so extreme in degree as to go beyond all possible bounds of decency, and to be regarded as atrocious and utterly intolerable in a civilized community."[7] Some courts, however, still fear fictitious claims and require proof of some bodily harm resulting from the victim's emotional distress. The courts also differ in the extent to which they allow recovery for emotional distress suffered as a result of witnessing outrageous conduct directed at persons other than the plaintiff. The *Restatement (Second) of Torts* suggests that persons be allowed to recover for severe emotional distress resulting from witnessing outrageous behavior toward a member of their immediate family.[8] Where the third person is not a member of the plaintiff's immediate family, the *Restatement (Second)* restricts liability to severe emotional distress that results in some bodily harm.[9] The tendency to expand the circumstances in which recovery for intentional infliction of emotional distress will be allowed is a matter of growing concern for business because, as the *Monsanto* case that follows indicates, recent years have witnessed a growing number of emotional distress claims filed by employees. These include suits by employees who have been discharged or required to take drug tests. Sexual harassment cases have also been a fertile source of emotional distress claims.

White v. Monsanto

Irma White, a church-going woman in her late 40s, worked in the labor pool at Monsanto's refinery. In the spring of 1986, she was assigned to the canning department for several weeks. While there, she and three other employees were told to transfer a chemical from a large container into smaller containers. When they noticed that the large container was marked "hazardous-corrosive," they asked for rubber gloves and goggles. After a supervisor sent for the equipment, White began cleaning up the work area, and one of the other employees went to another area to do some work. The other two employees sat around waiting for the safety equipment, contrary to a work rule requiring employees to busy themselves in such situations.

Someone informed Gary McDermott, the canning department foreman, that the group was idle. McDermott became angry and went to the work station where he launched into a profane tirade at White and the other two workers present, calling them "motherf-----s," accusing them of sitting on their "f-----g asses," and threatening to "show them to the gate." The tirade lasted for about a minute, and then McDermott left the area. White was upset and began to experience pain in her chest, pounding in her head, and had difficulty breathing. The company nurse suggested she see a doctor. Her family physician met her at the hospital where he admitted her, fearing that she was having a heart attack. She was later diagnosed as having had an acute anxiety reaction. White was discharged after three days and returned to work within a week. Monsanto paid her regular wages while she was off work and the company health plan covered her medical expenses. White later sued McDermott and Monsanto for intentional infliction of emotional distress. When a jury awarded her $60,000, Monsanto and McDermott appealed.

Source: 585 So.2d 1205 {La. Sup. Ct. 1991}

Hall, Justice

LSA-R.S. 23:1032 makes worker's compensation an employee's exclusive remedy for a work-related injury caused by a co-employee, except for a suit based on an intentional tort. The particular intentional tort alleged in this case is the intentional infliction of emotional distress. Most states now recognize intentional infliction of emotional distress as an independent tort, not "parasitic" to a physical injury or a traditional tort such as assault, battery, false imprisonment or the like.

The *Restatement (Second) of Torts*, section 46(1) provides:

> One who by extreme and outrageous conduct intentionally or recklessly causes severe emotional distress to another is subject to liability for such emotional distress, and if bodily harm to the other results from it, for such bodily harm.

Several Louisiana court of appeal decisions have recognized and defined the tort, generally in accordance with the *Restatement*. We affirm the viability in Louisiana of a cause of action for intentional infliction of emotional distress with the legal precepts set forth in the *Restatement*. Thus, in order to recover for intentional infliction of emotional distress, a plaintiff must establish (1) that the conduct of the defendant was extreme and outrageous; (2) that the emotional distress suffered by the plaintiff was severe; and (3) that the defendant desired to inflict severe emotional distress or knew that severe emotional distress would be certain or substantially certain to result from his conduct.

The conduct must be so outrageous in character, and so extreme in degree, as to go beyond all possible bounds of decency, and to be regarded as atrocious and utterly intolerable in a civilized community. The extreme and outrageous character of the conduct may arise from an abuse by the actor of a position, or a relation with the other, which gives him actual or apparent authority over the other, or power to affect his interests. Thus, many of the cases have involved circumstances arising in the workplace. A plaintiff's status as an employee may entitle him to a greater degree of protection from insult and outrage by a supervisor with authority over him than if he were a stranger.

On the other hand, conduct which may otherwise be extreme and outrageous may be privileged under the circumstances. Liability does not attach where the actor has done no more than insist upon his legal rights in a permissible way, even though he is aware that such insistence is certain to cause emotional distress. Thus, disciplinary action and conflict in a pressure-packed workplace environment, although calculated to cause some degree of mental anguish, is not ordinarily actionable.

Applying these precepts to the facts of the instant case, we find that White has failed to establish her right to recover from the defendants for an intentional tort. The one-minute outburst of profanity directed at three employees by a supervisor in the course of dressing them down for not working as he thought they should does not amount to such extreme and outrageous conduct as to give rise to recovery for intentional infliction of emotional distress. Such conduct, although crude, rough and uncalled for, was not tortious. The brief, isolated instance of improper behavior by the supervisor who lost his temper was the kind of unpleasant experience persons must expect to endure from time to time. The conduct was not more than a person of ordinary sensibilities can be expected to endure. The tirade was directed to all three employees and not just to White. Although White was a decent person and a diligent employee who would not condone the use of vulgar language and who would be upset at being unjustifiably called down at her place of work, there was no evidence that she was particularly susceptible to emotional distress, or that McDermott had knowledge of any such susceptibility.

The duty here was not to engage in extreme or outrageous conduct intended or calculated to cause severe emotional distress. The duty was not breached because the conduct was not extreme or outrageous to a degree calculated to cause severe emotional distress to a person of ordinary sensibilities and the supervisor did not intend to inflict emotional distress of a severe nature, nor did he believe such a result was substantially certain to follow from his conduct.

Judgment reversed in favor of McDermott and Monsanto.

Misuse of Legal Proceedings

Three intentional tort theories protect persons against the harm that can result from wrongfully instituted legal proceedings. **Malicious prosecution** affords a remedy for the financial and emotional harm, and the injury to reputation, that can result when *criminal* proceedings are wrongfully brought against a person. This tort balances society's interest in efficient enforcement of the criminal law against the individual's interest in freedom from unjustified criminal prosecutions. A plaintiff seeking to recover for malicious prosecution must prove *both* that the defendant *acted maliciously*—that is, without probable cause to believe that an offense had been committed and for an improper purpose—and that the criminal proceedings were *terminated in the plaintiff's favor*. As a general rule, proof that the defendant acted in good faith on the advice of legal counsel, after fully disclosing the relevant facts, conclusively establishes probable cause. Also, proof of the plaintiff's guilt is generally held to be a complete defense to liability, and the issue of his guilt can be retried in the malicious prosecution suit, despite his acquittal in the criminal proceedings. Proof of the plaintiff's innocence, however, cannot support a malicious prosecution action if the criminal proceedings were not terminated in his favor.

The tort of **wrongful use of civil proceedings** is similar to malicious prosecution, but it is designed to protect persons from wrongfully instituted *civil* suits. Its elements are very similar to those of malicious prosecution: It requires proof that the civil proceedings were initiated without probable cause and for an improper purpose and proof that the suit was terminated in favor of the person sued.

The tort of **abuse of process** imposes liability on those who initiate legal proceedings for a primary purpose other than the one for which such proceedings are designed. Abuse of process cases normally involve situations in which the legal proceedings compel the other person to take some action unrelated to the subject of the suit. For example, Rogers wishes to buy Herbert's property, but Herbert refuses to sell. To pressure him into selling, Rogers files a nuisance suit against Herbert, contending that Herbert's activities on his land interfere with Rogers' use and enjoyment of his adjoining property. Rogers may be liable to Herbert for abuse of process despite the fact that he had probable cause to file the suit and regardless of whether he wins the suit.

Deceit (Fraud)

Deceit is the formal name of the tort action for damages that is available to victims of knowing misrepresentation, often called **fraud**. The elements of deceit are a false statement of material fact, knowingly made by the defendant, with the intent to induce reliance by the plaintiff, justifiable reliance by the plaintiff, and harm to the plaintiff due to his reliance. The second element, technically called *scienter*, separates deceit from other forms of misrepresentation. Scienter is present only when the maker of a statement believes it is untrue, doesn't believe it is the truth, or recklessly disregards its truth. So, neither negligent nor innocent misrepresentations can serve as the basis for a deceit action.[10] Because most deceit actions arise in a contractual setting, and because a tort action for deceit is only one of the remedies available to a victim of fraud, a fuller discussion of this topic is deferred until Chapter 19, Reality of Consent.

Interference with Property Rights

Nature of Property Rights

The rights associated with the acquisition and use of property have traditionally occupied an important position in our legal system. Tortious interference with property rights is generally treated as an offense against the right to *possession*. Therefore, where the party entitled to possession is not the same as the owner of the property in question (e.g., a tenant leasing property from its owner), the party entitled to possession is ordinarily the proper person to file suit for interference with his possessory rights. If the interference also results in lasting damage to the property, however, its owner may also have a right to recover for such damage.

Trespass to Land

A person is liable for trespass if he: (1) intentionally and unlawfully enters land in the possession of another, (2) unlawfully remains on such land after entering lawfully, such as a tenant who refuses to move at the end of the lease, (3) unlawfully causes anything to enter such land, or (4) fails to remove anything that he has a duty to remove from such land. In general, no actual harm to the land is required for liability for intentional trespasses, but actual harm is required for liability for reckless or negligent trespasses. Recently, some courts have required plaintiffs to prove actual harm when seeking to recover for trespasses resulting from invisible airborne particulants entering onto their property. Such cases straddle the border between trespass theory and nuisance theory.

It is important to note that a person can be liable for trespass even though the trespass resulted from his mistaken belief that his entry was legally justified. This could arise from a belief that he had a right to possess the land, had the consent of the party entitled to possession, or had some other legal right or privilege entitling him to enter.

Nuisance

Unlawful and unreasonable interferences with another person's right to the use or enjoyment of his land are called *nuisances*. Nuisance suits, unlike trespass actions, do not necessarily involve any physical invasion of a person's property. Noise, vibration, and unpleasant odors are all examples of things that could be nuisances but would not justify a trespass action. In nuisance suits, the courts attempt to balance the competing interests of landowners to use their land as they see fit. Nuisance law recognizes an unfortunate fact of life: to preserve freedom, it must be limited. Put another way, my free use of my property may destroy your enjoyment of yours. For example, should I be able to open a solid waste disposal plant next to your restaurant? The law of nuisance attempts to resolve such perplexing issues.

Trespass to Personal Property

Any intentional intermeddling with personal property in the possession of another is a trespass if it: (1) results in harm to that property (e.g., Franks strikes Goode's dog or throws paint on his car); or (2) deprives the party entitled to possession of its use for an appreciable time (e.g., Franks hides Goode's car and Goode cannot find it for several hours).

Conversion

Conversion is the intentional exercise of dominion or control over another's personal property. To amount to conversion, the defendant's actions must be such a serious interference with another's right to control the property that they justify requiring the defendant to pay damages for the full value of the property. The difference between conversion and trespass to personal property is based on the *degree* of interference with another's property rights. In considering whether an interference with another's property amounts to its conversion, the courts consider such factors as the extent of the harm done to the property, the extent and duration of the interference with the other's right to control the property, and whether the defendant acted in good faith. For example, Sharp goes to Friendly Motors and asks to test-drive a new Ford Thunderbird. If Sharp either wrecks the car, causing major damage, or drives it across the United States, he is probably liable for conversion and obligated to pay Friendly Motors the reasonable value of the car. On the other hand, if Sharp is merely involved in a fender bender, or keeps the car for eight hours, he is probably only liable for trespass. Therefore, he is only obligated to pay damages to compensate Friendly for the loss in value of the car or for its loss of use of the car.

Evolving Concepts of Tort Liability

Recent developments indicate a continuing tendency to expand the scope of tort law as society recognizes an increasing range of personal interests that deserve legal protection. For example, recent cases have recognized the right of fired employees to recover against their employers for a new tort of *wrongful or abusive discharge*. Also, some courts have allowed plaintiffs to recover punitive damages in tort suits arising out of a defendant's bad faith breach of contract, and employee drug-testing programs have spawned a number of claims against employers on intentional tort theories such as defamation, intentional infliction of emotional distress, and invasion of privacy.

Finally, plaintiffs in so-called toxic tort suits, mass actions seeking to recover for a variety of injuries resulting from exposure to toxic substances, are currently attempting to employ novel tort theories to support their claims. Should persons exposed to carcinogenic substances be able to recover for the emotional distress caused by the fear that they may contract cancer in the future? Should employees whose employers knowingly expose them to such substances in the workplace be allowed to sue their employers for damages in tort that would not be recoverable under their state's workers' compensation statute? All of these examples illustrate the dynamic nature of our legal system in general and of tort law in particular. Given the historical development of tort law, one can reasonably expect that as growing technical knowledge or changing social circumstances create the need to protect new personal interests, tort law will evolve to satisfy that need.

Business Torts

Figure 22-2 summarizes the many and varied interests protected by the intentional tort theories we have discussed in this chapter. Today, courts also recognize a variety of tort actions designed to protect various economic interests. Chapter 25, Unfair Competition, discusses these torts in detail.

	Interest	Tort Theory
FIGURE 22-2 Interests protected by tort law	Freedom from harmful or offensive contacts	Battery
	Freedom from apprehension of battery	Assault
	Freedom from confinement	False imprisonment
	Right to reputation	Defamation
	Right of privacy	Invasion of privacy
	Freedom from disagreeable emotions	Intentional infliction of emotional distress
	Freedom from improper criminal proceedings	Malicious prosecution
	Freedom from improper civil proceedings	Wrongful use of civil proceedings and abuse of process
	Possession and enjoyment of personal property	Trespass and conversion
	Possession and enjoyment of real property	Trespass and nuisance
	Freedom from knowing misstatements	Deceit

Ethical and Public Policy Concerns

1. Tort law attempts to protect various individual interests by giving persons whose rights are violated by others the right to sue for money damages. Can monetary awards, however, ever truly compensate persons who have suffered harms such as an invasion of privacy or emotional distress? If not, how do we justify such awards?
2. Safeco Plastics Corporation owns a plant upstream from Morrison's farm. Safeco periodically discharges large amounts of water into the stream, a practice which occasionally results in the flooding of Morrison's property. Assuming that it is cheaper for Safeco to pay damages to Morrison for trespass than it is to take corrective steps to prevent the flooding, is it ethically proper for Safeco to continue to flood Morrison's land?
3. Maxwell is defamed by an article in a local newspaper as a result of careless reporting. When confronted with its error, the paper promptly apologizes and runs an article retracting the defamatory statement. Maxwell has noticed no negative effects from the article, but his lawyer advises him that he would have no trouble proving defamation by the paper and that, as a result, the paper's liability insurance company would probably be eager to settle in the event that Maxwell files suit. Should Maxwell sue?

Problems and Problem Cases

1. While shopping in a Publix Supermarket, Anthony Gatto was accosted by Publix employees who believed that he had shoplifted some paperback books. Gatto alleged that in the process of trying to get the books from him, Harold Stepp, the store manager, touched "either part of my palm or my wrist or my arms." Gatto later filed suit against Publix for assault, battery, and false imprisonment. At trial, Gatto admitted that he was never prevented from leaving and at all times considered himself free to leave the premises. Was the trial court's directed verdict in favor of Publix on all three tort theories correct?
2. In 1985, Ford Motor Company and its ad agency, Young & Rubicam, Inc., ran a series of 19 television commercials aimed at making an emotional connection with Yuppies, bringing back memories of their college days. Seventies pop songs were sung in each commercial, and the agency tried to get the original artists to sing the songs. One of the songs selected was "Do You Want to Dance," a song from a 1973 Bette Midler album. The agency acquired a license from the copyright holder to use the song, but Midler refused to do the commercial. The agency then hired a former backup singer

for Midler to record it, instructing her to "sound as much as possible like the Bette Midler record." After the commercial was aired, a number of people told Midler that it "sounded exactly" like her recording. Midler filed suit against Ford and Young & Rubicam. The trial judge granted summary judgment for the defendants because he believed no legal principle prevented the imitation of Midler's voice. Was the trial judge's decision correct?

3. On April 14, 1984, during the "Saturday Night News" segment of NBC's "Saturday Night Live" program, a skit was presented as the "Fast Frank Feature." A performer was introduced to the audience as Maurice Frank, a tax consultant. The performer bore a noticeable physical resemblance to Maurice Frank, a resident of Westchester County, New York, who was engaged in business as an accountant, tax consultant, and financial planner. The performer proceeded to give "ludicrously inappropriate" tax advice, suggesting, among other things, that viewers claim houseplants as dependents and write off acne medicine under an oil depletion allowance, and guaranteeing that taxpayers who used his service would receive refunds in excess of their earnings. The real Maurice Frank filed a defamation suit against the network. Was he defamed by the skit?

4. In February 1986, Lois Grimsley, a 46-year-old security inspector, unexpectedly gave birth in her home less than two days after doctors had told her that her stomach pains were nothing more than a urinary tract infection and a case of hemorrhoids. A reporter from a local newspaper interviewed Grimsley about the birth, and Grimsley provided details about it and posed for a picture with the child. The story appeared in the local paper the following day, was subsequently picked up by the Associated Press, and also appeared in several other newspapers. In July 1986, a synopsis of the article (including a photo of Grimsley and her son) appeared in the "Hard Times" section of Penthouse magazine (a section that the magazine describes as "a compendium of bizarre, idiotic, lurid, and offtimes witless driblets of information culled from the nation's press") under the heading "Birth of a Hemorrhoid." Grimsley filed suit against Penthouse for defamation, invasion of privacy, and intentional infliction of mental distress. Should her suit succeed?

5. In September 1987, The National Enquirer ran an article reporting Henry Dempsey's harrowing escape from injury or death when he fell out of a small airplane while in flight but clung to the open boarding ladder of the plane, surviving his copilot's landing with only a few scratches. Dempsey had refused to be interviewed for the article, despite repeated attempts by an Enquirer reporter to gain an interview. The reporter allegedly came to his home twice, repeatedly drove past his home for three quarters of an hour after the first refusal, and followed him to a restaurant where she attempted to photograph him and again requested an interview. After the article appeared, Dempsey filed suit against the Enquirer for invasion of privacy and intentional infliction of emotional distress. Should Dempsey's suit succeed?

6. Dorothy Yu, an employee of Northwest Pipeline Corporation, was found to have in her possession a confidential personnel document that she was not authorized to possess. She admitted possession and identified Enser, who worked in the records department, as the source of the document. Both Yu and Enser were terminated for violating Northwest's confidentiality policy. Northwest then informed the Utah Job Services that Yu had been fired for this reason and therefore was ineligible for unemployment compensation. Selected nonsupervisory Northwest employees were also informed of the reasons for Yu's termination. Yu filed a defamation suit against Northwest. Should Northwest's motion for summary judgment be granted?

7. Leta Fay Ford's supervisor at Revlon, Inc., Karl Braun, made numerous sexual advances toward her. At a Revlon picnic on May 3, 1980, Braun grabbed Ford,

restrained her in a chokehold with his right arm, and ran his hand over her breasts, stomach, and crotch. Later in May, Ford began meeting with various members of Revlon management about Braun, who continued to harass her verbally. Revlon failed to act until nine months after Ford's first complaint, when Braun was called in and confronted, and Ford was told that he would be closely monitored. Three months later, Revlon's personnel director submitted a report confirming Ford's charges and recommending that Braun be censured. One month later, Revlon gave Braun a letter of censure. Due to the harassment, Ford developed high blood pressure, a nervous tic in her left eye, chest pains, rapid breathing, and other symptoms of emotional stress. Four months after Braun's censure, she attempted suicide. Later, Ford filed suit against Revlon for intentional infliction of emotional distress. Was the jury correct in ruling in her favor?

8. The Blanks purchased a lot in the Indian Fork subdivision next to a lot owned by Gary Rawson. When Rawson built his home, he located a basketball goal and dog pen immediately next to the property separating the two lots. The Blanks complained to the subdivision developer that Rawson was violating the minimum setback restrictions applicable to the subdivision and were told that Rawson had received permission from the developer to do so. They then filed a nuisance suit against Rawson. At the trial, they alleged that the sound of the basketball hitting the backboard when Rawson's son played was offensive and that when he missed, the ball could come into their yard. They also stated that the dog was a large one and that the pen was not cleaned regularly, with the result that offensive odors continued to reach their property despite the 10-foot privacy fence Rawson had erected between their properties shortly after their complaint against him was filed. Was the trial judge's order forcing Rawson to remove or relocate the goal and the dog pen proper?

9. Moore was receiving treatment for hairy-cell leukemia at a university hospital. After his spleen was removed as part of that treatment, the treating physician and another university employee determined that his cells were unique. Without Moore's knowledge or consent, they applied genetic engineering techniques to his cells, producing a cell line that they patented and marketed very successfully through agreements with a pharmaceutical company and a biotechnology firm. To further their research, they continued to monitor him and take tissue samples from him for almost seven years after his spleen was removed. When Moore discovered the truth, he filed a conversion suit against the university, which moved to dismiss his claim, arguing that he had no property right in his spleen and that, in any event, his cells were worthless without their subsequent modifications to them. Should Moore's suit survive their motion to dismiss?

10. The Bradleys owned land on Vashon Island in King County, Washington, about four miles north of American Smelting and Refining Company's copper smelter in Ruston, Washington. They sued American on trespass and nuisance theories, arguing that invisible arsenic and cadmium particles emitted by American's smelter had been carried by the wind and deposited on their property. American sought summary judgment on the trespass claim on the grounds that the Bradleys had incurred no actual damages. Even assuming that particles of arsenic and cadmium emitted from American's smelter had settled onto the Bradleys' land, American argued that these materials are innocuous in the tiny concentrations in which they actually had been found in the Bradleys' soil. Assuming American's statements are factually correct, should its motion for summary judgment be granted?

Endnotes

1.   Chapter 25 discusses injurious falsehood in detail.
2.   376 U.S. 254 (U.S. Sup. Ct. 1964).
3.   *Curtis Publishing Co. v. Butts*, 388 U.S. 130 (U.S. Sup. Ct. 1967).
4.   418 U.S. 323 (U.S. Sup. Ct. 1974).
5.   472 U.S. 749 (U.S. Sup. Ct. 1985).
6.   Chapter 25 discusses this subject in detail.
7.   *Restatement (Second) of Torts* § 46, comment *d* (1965).
8.   *Restatement (Second) of Torts* § 46(2)(a) (1965).
9.   *Restatement (Second) of Torts* § 46(2)(b) (1965).
10. Chapter 19 discusses this aspect of misrepresentation in detail.

Chapter Twenty-Three

NEGLIGENCE AND

STRICT LIABILITY

Introduction

The Industrial Revolution that changed the face of 19th-century America created serious problems for the law of torts. Railroads, machinery, and other newly developing technologies contributed to a growing number of injuries to persons and their property. These injuries did not fit within the intentional torts framework, however, because most of them were unintended. Some injuries were simply the unavoidable consequences of life in a high-speed, technologically advanced, modern society. Holding infant industries totally responsible for all of the harms they caused could have seriously impeded the process of industrial development. To avoid such a result, new tort rules were needed. In response to these growing social pressures, the courts created the law of negligence.

Elements of Negligence

Negligence focuses on conduct that falls below the legal standards that the law has established to protect members of society against unreasonable risks of harm. Negligence essentially involves an unintentional breach of a legal duty owed to another that results in some legally recognizable injury to the other's person or property. A plaintiff in a negligence suit must prove several things to recover: (1) that the defendant had a *duty* not to injure him, (2) that the defendant *breached* that duty, and (3) that the defendant's breach of duty was the *actual* and *legal (proximate) cause* of his *injury*. To be successful, a plaintiff must also overcome any *defenses* to negligence liability that are raised by the defendant. Most of these defenses involve behavior by the plaintiff that may have originally contributed to his injury.

Duty

The basic idea of negligence is that each member of society has a duty to conduct her affairs in a way that avoids an unreasonable risk of harm to others. The law of negligence holds each of us up to an *objective*, yet *flexible*, standard of conduct—that of a "reasonable person of ordinary prudence in similar circumstances." This standard is objective because the reasonable person is a hypothetical person who is always thoughtful and cautious and never unreasonably endangers others. It is flexible because it allows consideration of all the circumstances surrounding a particular injury. For example, the law does not require the same level of caution and deliberation of a person confronted with an emergency requiring rapid decisions and action as it does of a person in circumstances allowing for calm reflection and deliberate action. Likewise, to a limited extent, the law considers the personal characteristics of the particular defendant whose conduct is being judged. For example, children are generally required to act as a reasonable person of similar age, intelligence, and experience would act under similar circumstances. Persons with physical disabilities are required to act as would a reasonable person with the same disability. Mental deficiencies, however, ordinarily do not relieve a person from the duty to conform to the reasonable person standard.

Special Duties

The question of whether a particular duty exists is entirely a question of law. Does the law recognize a duty of the defendant to protect the interests of this particular plaintiff from harm? Legal duties can originate from several sources. A *contractual relationship* between the plaintiff and the defendant can give rise to a variety of duties that might not exist otherwise. For example, most professional malpractice cases are based on claims that professionals negligently breached professional duties owed to their clients or to third persons who rely on their competent performance of professional tasks.

Other *special relationships* between the parties have long been recognized as the source of special legal duties. For example, common carriers and innkeepers have long been held virtually strictly liable for damaging or losing the property of their customers. In recent years, many courts have extended this duty to include an affirmative duty to protect passengers or guests against the foreseeable wrongful acts of third persons. This has happened despite the fact that the law has long refused to recognize any general duty to aid and protect others from third-party wrongdoing unless a defendant's actions foreseeably increased the risk of such wrongdoing. Some recent decisions have imposed a similar duty on landlords to protect their tenants against the foreseeable criminal acts of others.

The relationship between the parties can also affect the *level* of duty that one person owes to another. For example, the common law has long held that the level of duty that a person in possession of land owes to other persons who enter on the land depends on whether such persons were invitees, licensees, or trespassers. **Invitees** are members of the public who are lawfully on public land, such as a park, swimming pool, or government office; they are also customers, delivery persons, or paying boarders who are on private premises for a purpose connected with the business interests of the possessor of the land. **Licensees** are those whose privilege to enter on the land depends entirely on the possessor's consent. Licensees include persons who are on the land solely for their own purposes, such as someone soliciting money for charity, members of the possessor's household, and social guests. **Trespassers** are persons who enter or remain on another's land without any legal right or privilege to do so.

At common law, a possessor of land owed invitees a duty to exercise reasonable care to keep the premises in reasonably safe condition for their use. He also had a duty to protect invitees against dangerous conditions on the premises that he knew about or reasonably should have discovered, and that they were unlikely to discover. He only owed licensees a duty to warn them of known dangerous conditions that they were unlikely to discover. The possessor of land owed no duty to trespassers to maintain his premises in a safe condition, and only a duty not to willfully and wantonly injure them once their presence was known. As the following *Hopkins* case indicates, recent years have seen a marked tendency to erode these common law distinctions. Many courts no longer distinguish between licensees and invitees, holding that the possessor of land owes the same duties to licensees that he owes to invitees. Also, the courts have made numerous exceptions to the minimal duties that possessors of land owe to trespassers. For example, a higher level of duty is ordinarily owed to trespassers who the possessor of land knows are constantly entering the land (e.g., using a well-worn path across the land) and greater duties are ordinarily owed to protect children if the possessor of land knows that they are likely to trespass.

Finally, *statutes* can create legal duties that can be the source of a negligence action. The doctrine of **negligence per se** provides that one who violates a statute is guilty of negligent conduct if a harm that the statute was designed to prevent results to a person whom the statute was intended to protect. The defendant who has violated a statute may still seek to avoid liability by arguing that his violation was not the legal cause of the plaintiff's injury or by asserting some other general defense to liability, but the statutory violation is generally held to be conclusive evidence of breach of duty.

Hopkins v. Fox & Lazo Realtors

On April 26, 1987, Emily Hopkins accompanied her son and daughter-in-law to an open house in Plainsboro, New Jersey, to which they had been invited by a salesperson employed by Fox & Lazo Realtors. When they first arrived, they were not greeted by a realtor, so they started to tour the house on their own. When they reached the kitchen, they were greeted by a Fox & Lazo representative, who left them free to inspect the house unaccompanied. The house's kitchen led up to a family room that was slightly elevated from the front portion of the house, which also contained a powder room and laundry room. Mrs. Hopkins waited on the upper level in the family room while her family viewed the patio and grounds.

When Mrs. Hopkins heard her son and daughter-in-law reenter the house, she sought to join them in the foyer, where the staircase to the second floor was located. She went down the hallway from the laundry room toward the foyer, unaware that a step led down from the hallway into the foyer. The floors on both levels and the step were covered with the same pattern vinyl, causing Mrs. Hopkins to fail to see the step. She fell, fracturing her ankle. She sued Fox & Lazo, arguing that they had a duty to warn her of any known risks inside the house or any risks that a reasonable inspection would have revealed. When the trial court dismissed her complaint on the ground that the broker had no such duty, she appealed.

Source: 625 A.2d 1110 (N.J. Sup. Ct. 1993)

Handler, Justice

The traditional common law approach to landowner tort liability toward a person who has been injured because of a dangerous condition on private property is predicated on the status of the person on the property at the time of the injury. Historically, the duty of the owner to such a person is gauged by the right of that person to be on the land. Only to the invitee does a landowner owe a duty of reasonable care to guard against any dangerous conditions on his or her property that the owner either knows about or should have discovered.

Initially, we question whether we should resort to the common law doctrine of premises liability to determine if a real-estate broker owes a duty of care to prospective potential purchasers who are inspecting the owner's home on an open-house tour. The rules of the common law embody underlying principles of public policy and perceptions of social values. Because public policy and social values evolve over time, so does the common law. The traditional common law doctrine governing premises liability is no exception. The historical classifications of the degrees of care owing to visitors upon land are undergoing gradual change in favor of a broadening application of a general tort obligation to exercise reasonable care against foreseeable harm to others.

The common law doctrine is rooted in early nineteenth century notions of private property. With the development of a more urbanized, heterogeneous, and complex society, the status of persons in relation to the use of property could no longer be adequately accommodated by traditional classifications of the common law. California was the first jurisdiction to eliminate the common law boundaries between premises-liability classifications in its landmark decision *Rowland v. Christian* (1971). Approximately fourteen jurisdictions have also eliminated the hierarchical scheme defining a landowner's duty toward persons who came on to their land. Many other jurisdictions have eliminated the distinction between licensees and invitees.

The inquiry should be not what common law classification most closely characterizes the relationship of the parties, but whether in the light of the actual relationship between the parties under all of the surrounding circumstances the imposition on the broker of a general duty to exercise reasonable care in preventing foreseeable harm to its open-house customers is fair and just.

A real-estate broker, in many situations, manages or directs an open-house inspection of the premises. The broker is responsible for advertising the open house, posting signs, and ultimately inviting customers onto the premises. A broker frequently suggests conducting such an event to a homeowner. The owner is often absent from the premises for the duration of the open house. In this case, defendant extended a personal invitation to Hopkins and her family. One may reasonably assume in this context that a customer acts on the broker's invitation to come on to the property. The customer may reasonably expect to be able to rely on and use the services proffered by the broker in connection with an examination of the premises.

The broker receives very tangible economic benefits from the relationship with the potential buyers who visit the home. The open house enables the broker to sell the house and earn a commission. Also, an open house presents a broker with an opportunity to meet and cultivate future clients. More generally, the broker can discuss other listings with visitors and thus promote his or her individual business interests. Thus, the economic benefit that a broker obtains from staging an open house extends beyond the potential sale of the particular property. We conclude that implicit in the broker's invitation to customers is some commensurate degree of responsibility for their safety while visiting the premises.

In determining the scope of a broker's duty in these circumstances, one must analyze the extent of the invitation, the risk involved in the activity, and the fairness of imposing a duty to avoid that risk. It is highly foreseeable that visitors to an open house could be injured by dangerous conditions during the course of wandering through an unfamiliar house. In many cases, the customer may reasonably expect that the broker will be familiar with the premises and would rely on the broker's presumed familiarity with the house, including a knowledge of all of its important features and physical characteristics. Nevertheless, not all brokers are actually familiar with all of the houses that they may show to potential buyers. Some brokers will not have had the opportunity to inspect the house before the open house commences.

We thus determine that a broker is under a duty to conduct a reasonable broker's inspection when such an inspection would comport with the customary standards governing the responsibilities and functions of real-estate brokers with respect to open-house tours. Such inspection should consist of an examination of the premises to ascertain the obvious physical characteristics that are material to its salability, as well as those features that a prospective purchaser would routinely examine during a "walk through" of the premises. That inspection would impose on the broker the duty to warn of any such discoverable physical features or conditions of the property that pose a hazard or danger to visitors. That duty, however, would not require the broker to warn against any dangers that are not otherwise known to the broker or would not be revealed during the course of such a reasonable broker's inspection.

As a point of comparison, we underscore the fact that a broker's duty does not replicate the more comprehensive duty owed by homeowners towards their invitees. The home-owner's duty to the business guest will be in most circumstances much broader than a

broker's duty toward the customer. We further emphasize that the existence of a duty by no means resolves the legal dispute between the parties. Although we are satisfied that a sufficient basis exists for finding that a broker has a duty for the safety of its customers who are visitors at an open-house tour, the trier of fact must ultimately determine whether under the circumstances of this case the broker breached a duty to Mrs. Hopkins.
Judgment in favor of Hopkins; case remanded for further proceedings.

Breach

A person is guilty of breach of duty if she exposes another to an *unreasonable, foreseeable* risk of harm. Negligence consists of doing something that a reasonable person would not have done under the circumstances, or failing to do something that a reasonable person would have done under the same circumstances. If a person guards against all foreseeable risks and exercises reasonable care, but harm to others nonetheless occurs, no liability for negligence ordinarily results. For example, if Wilson is carefully driving his car within the speed limit and has a heart attack that causes him to lose control and crash into a car driven by Thomas, Wilson would ordinarily not be liable to Thomas for his injuries. As another member of the public using the highways, Wilson owed Thomas a duty to exercise reasonable care while driving. However, the accident was not the result of any breach of that duty because it was unforeseeable. If, on the other hand, Wilson's doctor had advised him that he had a heart condition that made driving dangerous, his failure to heed his doctor's warning would probably amount to a breach of duty because he was plainly exposing others to a foreseeable risk of harm by driving.

Of course, many behaviors involve some risk of harm to others, but the risk must be an *unreasonable* one before that behavior amounts to a breach of duty. In deciding the reasonableness of the risk, the courts balance the social utility of a person's conduct and the ease of avoiding or minimizing the risk against the likelihood that harm will result and the probable seriousness of that harm. As the risk of serious harm to others increases, so does the duty to take steps to avoid that harm. The following *Culli* case illustrates the steps a court follows in deciding whether a business has breached its duty to an invitee.

Culli v. Marathon Petroleum Co.

On Saturday, August 4, 1984, Elizabeth Culli stopped at a 24-hour self-service gas station operated by Marathon Petroleum in Mt. Vernon, Illinois. She filled her gas tank and then picked up five eight-pack cartons of soda that were featured as part of a special soda sale the station was running that day. After paying for the gas, she headed back toward her car. Before she reached her car, however, she slipped and fell on what an ambulance attendant who was called to the scene later described as a "clearish" slippery substance in a pool approximately 8 to 10 inches in width and length. Culli suffered a compound fracture of her ankle and had to use a wheelchair and walker for several months thereafter.

At the trial of her suit against Marathon, the evidence indicated that the station was typically staffed by one person, who would primarily stay inside and run the cash register and was also responsible for replenishing supplies of the other items sold at the station, such as milk, candy, hot food, and sandwiches. The station lot was normally swept once a day during the night shift, but the attendant on duty the evening prior to the accident could not recall whether or not he had swept that night. There was also testimony that spills in general occurred once or twice each day, and that one employee had asked the station manager to hire more help because the station was understaffed, a request that he relayed to his superiors but which went unheeded. When a jury awarded Culli $87,500, Marathon appealed.

Source: 862 F.2d 119 (7th Cir. 1988)

Will, Senior District Judge

The defendant owed the plaintiff invitee the duty of maintaining its property in a reasonably safe condition. This includes a duty to inspect and repair dangerous conditions on the property or give adequate warnings to prevent injury. To be liable, Marathon must have had actual or constructive notice of the dangerous condition. Both parties agree that Marathon did not have actual notice.

Constructive notice can be established under Illinois law under two alternative theories: (1) the dangerous condition existed for a sufficient amount of time so that it would have been discovered by the exercise of ordinary care, or (2) the dangerous condition was part of a pattern of conduct or a recurring incident.

In *Hresil v. Sears, Roebuck & Co.* (1980), plaintiff sought damages for injuries she suffered when she slipped on a "gob" of phlegm in the defendant's self-service store. At the time of her accident, there were few customers in the store and, due to the inactivity in the store at the place where she fell, the foreign substance could have been on the floor for at least 10 minutes. The court found that, as a matter of law, 10 minutes was not long enough to give Sears constructive notice of the gob, and "to charge the store with constructive notice would place upon the store the unfair requirement of the constant patrolling of its aisles."

Because of the lack of testimony establishing how long the substance in this case was present, we do not know if it was present for a period of time which would have placed Marathon on constructive notice of it. It could have been present for a few minutes or several hours. Under the first constructive notice theory evidence establishing how long the particular substance was present is necessary.

Under the second constructive notice theory what is needed is a pattern of dangerous conditions which were not attended to within a reasonable time. There was substantial evidence presented at trial establishing that there were spills on a daily basis in the pump area and that the volume of sales on the day in question made it unreasonable for Marathon to sweep the lot only at night and operate for most of the day with only one attendant who was primarily confined to the cash register. The evidence is sufficient to support the jury's verdict that Marathon's maintenance of its property was unreasonable and proximately caused Culli's injury.

Judgment for Culli affirmed.

Causation

Even if a person breaches a duty that he owes to another person, no liability for negligence results unless the breach of duty was the *actual cause*, or the cause in fact, of injury to the other person. To determine the existence of actual cause, many courts employ a *but for* test: A defendant's conduct is the actual cause of a plaintiff's injury if that injury would not have occurred *but for* the defendant's breach of duty. In some cases, however, a person's negligent conduct may combine with the negligent conduct of another to cause a plaintiff's injury. For example, on a windy day, Allen negligently starts a fire by using gasoline to start his charcoal grill. The fire started by Allen spreads and joins forces with another fire started by Baker, who was burning brush on his property but who failed to take any precautions to prevent the fire from spreading. The combined fires burn Clark's home to the ground. Clark sues both Allen and Baker for negligence. In such a case, the court would ask whether each defendant's conduct was a *substantial factor* in bringing about Clark's loss. If the evidence indicates that Clark's house would have been destroyed by either fire in the absence of the other, both Allen and Baker are liable for Clark's loss.

Proximate Cause

Holding persons guilty of negligent conduct responsible for all of the harms that actually result from their negligence could, in some cases, expose them to potentially catastrophic liability. Although the law has long said that those who are guilty of intentional wrongdoing are liable for all of the direct consequences of their acts, however bizarre or unforeseeable, the courts have also recognized that a person who was merely negligent should not necessarily be responsible for every injury actually caused by her negligence. This idea of placing some legal limit on a negligent defendant's liability for the consequences of her actions is called **proximate cause**. Courts often say that a negligent defendant is liable only for the *proximate* results of her conduct. Thus, although a defendant's conduct may have been the *actual cause* of a particular plaintiff's injury, she is liable only if her conduct was also the *proximate (legal) cause* of that injury.

The courts have not, however, reached any substantial agreement on the test that should be employed for proximate cause. In reality, the proximate cause question is one of social policy. In deciding which test to adopt, a court must weigh the possibility that negligent persons can be exposed to catastrophic liability by a lenient test for proximate cause against the fact that a restrictive test inevitably prevents some innocent victims from recovering any compensation for their losses. Courts have responded in a variety of ways to this difficult choice.

Some courts have said that a negligent person is liable only for the "natural and probable consequences" of his actions. Others have limited a negligent person's liability for unforeseeable injuries by saying that he is liable only to plaintiffs who are within the "scope of the foreseeable risk." Thus, such courts hold that if the defendant could not have reasonably foreseen *some* injury to the plaintiff as a result of his actions, he is not liable to the plaintiff for any injury that in fact results from his negligence. Although this rule is often characterized as a rule of causation, in reality it is a rule limiting the defendant's *duty*, because courts adopting the rule hold that a defendant owes *no duty* to those to whom he cannot foresee any injury. On the other hand, such courts commonly hold that a defendant may be liable even for unforeseeable injuries to persons whom he has exposed to a foreseeable risk of harm.[1] The *Restatement (Second) of Torts* suggests that a defendant's negligence is not the legal cause of a plaintiff's injury if, looking back after the harm, it appears "highly extraordinary" to the court that the defendant's negligence should have brought about the plaintiff's injury.[2]

In the following *Republic of France* case, the defendant is able to avoid tremendous liability for the actual consequences of its negligence because the court refuses to hold it legally responsible due to the unforeseeable nature of those consequences.

Republic of France v. United States

On April 16, 1947, the SS *Grandchamp*, a cargo ship owned by the Republic of France and operated by the French Line, which was also 80 percent owned by the Republic of France, was loading a cargo of Fertilizer Grade Ammonium Nitrate (FGAN) at Texas City, Texas. A fire began on board the ship, apparently as a result of a cigarette or match carelessly discarded by a longshoreman in one of the ship's holds. Despite attempts to put it out, the fire spread quickly. A little over an hour after the fire was first discovered, the *Grandchamp* exploded with tremendous force. Fire and burning debris spread throughout the waterfront, touching off accompanying fires and explosions in other ships, refineries, gasoline storage tanks, and chemical plants that were not brought under complete control for days. When the conflagration was over, 500 people had been killed and more than 3,000 had been injured.

The evidence indicated that despite the fact that ammonium nitrate was known throughout the transportation

continued

industry as an oxidizing agent and as a fire hazard, no one aboard the *Grandchamp* made any attempt to prevent smoking in the ship's holds. Numerous lawsuits were filed after the incident, many of them against the United States because the FGAN had been manufactured in army ordnance plants. After the United States was found not liable, Congress passed the Texas City Relief Act in 1955. The act left insurance underwriters to bear their own losses but allowed those with uninsured claims to recover up to $25,000 per claim. The U.S. government paid out approximately $16 million to victims of the disaster, obtaining in return assignments of their claims for death, personal injuries, and property damage totaling approximately $70 million. The U.S. government sought to recover the full $70 million. The Republic of France and the French Line argued that they should not be liable for claims arising out of the explosion because FGAN was not known to be capable of exploding under such circumstances. When the trial court rejected their petition for limitation of liability, they appealed.

Source: 290 F.2d 395 (5th Cir. 1961)

Rives, Circuit Judge

In Texas, as elsewhere, not only proximate causal connection but also the very existence of a duty depends upon reasonable foreseeability of consequences. The test of whether a negligent act or omission is a proximate cause of an injury is whether the wrongdoer might by the exercise of ordinary care have foreseen that *some similar injury* might result from the negligence.

The United States argues with much force that the district court found that fault or negligence of the owners caused the fire and permitted it to increase in intensity, and that the fire caused the disastrous explosion. It insists that causal connection is sufficient. The fallacy in that chain of argument is that it is only the operation of natural forces theretofore recognized as normal which one is charged with foreseeing.

The district court found it "undoubtedly true that the force and devastating effects of this explosion shocked and surprised the scientific field as well as the transportation industry." The court further found as to ammonium nitrate, which constituted approximately 95 percent of the FGAN, and which, with the benefit of hindsight, we now know to be the explosive part of the mixture:

> Despite its use as a principal ingredient of high explosives, at the time of the disaster ammonium nitrate was not, and is not now, classified as an "explosive" for transportation purposes by the Interstate Commerce Commission or the Coast Guard. This is true because it was considered that to cause the detonation of ammonium nitrate, an initial shock or "booster" of considerable magnitude was required. The chances of such an initial or booster detonation being encountered in normal conditions of transportation has always been considered so remote as to be negligible.

Substantially all of the evidence is to the effect that the explosion, as distinguished from the fire, could not reasonably have been foreseen.

It would be ironic indeed if the United States were permitted to impose liability for these claims on the Republic of France and the French Line by claiming now that, unlike the officials and employees of the United States, the officials and employees of the French Government and the master of the *Grandchamp* should have known that FGAN was a dangerous explosive and that an explosion from fire should reasonably have been anticipated. **Judgment reversed in favor of the Republic of France.**

Superseding Causes

In some cases, an *intervening force* occurring after a defendant's negligence may play a significant role in bringing about a particular plaintiff's injury. For example, a high wind may spring up that causes a fire set by Davis to spread and damage Parker's property, or after Davis negligently runs Parker down with his car, a thief may steal Parker's wallet while he is lying unconscious in the street. Such cases present difficult problems for the courts, which must decide when an intervening force should relieve a negligent defendant from liability. As the following *Rowe* case indicates, if the intervening force is a *foreseeable* one, either because it frequently occurs in the ordinary course of human events or because the defendant's negligence substantially increases the risk of its occurrence, it will *not* relieve the defendant from liability. So, in the first example given above, if high winds are a reasonably common occurrence in the locality in question, Davis may be liable for the damage to Parker's property even though his fire would not have spread that far under the wind conditions that existed when he started it. Likewise, in our second example, Davis may be responsible for the theft of Parker's wallet if the theft is foreseeable, given the time and location of the accident.

On the other hand, if the intervening force that contributes to the plaintiff's injury is unforeseeable, most courts hold that it is a **superseding** or **intervening cause** that absolves the defendant of any liability for negligence. For example, Dalton negligently starts a fire that causes injury to several persons. The driver of an ambulance summoned to the scene to aid the injured has been drinking on duty and, as a result, loses control of his ambulance and runs up onto a sidewalk, injuring several pedestrians. Most courts would not hold Dalton responsible for the pedestrians' injuries. One important exception to this general rule, however, concerns intervening forces that produce a harm *identical to the harm risked by the defendant's negligence*. For example, the owners of a concert hall fail to install the number of emergency exits required by law for the protection of patrons. A negligently operated aircraft crashes into the hall during a concert, and many patrons are burned to death in the ensuing fire because the few available exits are jammed by panicked patrons trying to escape. Most courts would probably find that the owners of the hall were liable for the patrons' deaths.

Rowe v. State Bank of Lombard

In the early morning hours of April 24, 1978, Lori Rowe and Bonnie Serpico were shot by an intruder while working at the offices of their employer, J-Mar Enterprises, in the Glen Hill Office Park in Glen Ellyn, Illinois. Serpico died and Rowe was seriously injured. The intruder was later identified as James Free, a former construction laborer for the park's developer. Free was arrested, convicted, and sentenced to death.

Rowe's and Serpico's estates filed suit against the Paramount Group, Inc., the beneficial owner and manager of the office park; Todd Fennessey, Paramount's managing agent; and the State Bank of Lombard, which held title to the property and served as

trustee. The complaint alleged that the defendants were negligent for failing to warn tenants that master keys to the complex were outstanding and unaccounted for; failing to properly maintain the locks and doors on J-Mar's offices; failing to warn of numerous criminal incidents that had been reported at the park; and failing to provide adequate security on the premises. The trial court granted the defendants' motion for summary judgment on the ground that they had no duty as a matter of law to protect Rowe and Serpico from the criminal actions of Free.

Source: 531 N.E.2d 1358 (Ill. Sup. Ct. 1988)

Ward, Justice

Generally, there is no duty requiring a landowner to protect others from criminal activity by third persons on his property absent a "special relationship" between the parties. A special relationship has been recognized where the parties are in a position of innkeeper and guest, or business invitor and invitee, but this court has repeatedly held that the simple relationship between a landlord and tenant, or a landlord and those on the premises with the tenant's consent, is not a "special" one imposing a duty to protect against the criminal acts of others. Although there are courts that have placed a duty upon a landlord to protect tenants from foreseeable criminal acts committed by third parties on the premises, the overwhelming majority of courts have not.

A landlord may be held liable for the criminal acts of third parties when it voluntarily undertakes to provide security measures, but performs the undertaking negligently, if the negligence is the proximate cause of injury to the plaintiff. The plaintiffs have not shown that Paramount or Fennessey did anything which can be reasonably considered as a voluntary assumption of protecting Rowe and Serpico from the criminal acts of third persons on the premises. On the contrary, in the lease Paramount specifically disclaims responsibility for protecting its tenants or their property from criminal acts.

There is no evidence in the record that Paramount or its agents were negligent in failing to maintain proper control over the master keys which possibly enabled Free to gain access to a key. They were aware, nonetheless, of the risk posed by the outstanding master keys, having been informed that keys were outstanding and that they were unaccounted for. Under these circumstances we consider that they had a duty either to warn those rightfully on the premises of the danger or to take reasonable precautions to prevent foreseeable unauthorized entries by those with a master key. Having failed to do so, they breached their duty and can be held responsible for the reasonably foreseeable criminal acts of third persons which are proximately caused by their negligence.

Paramount and Fennessey argue that even if they were negligent the criminal acts constituted an "independent intervening cause" of the plaintiff's injuries. Generally, where between the defendant's negligence and the plaintiff's injury an independent, illegal act of a third person has intervened which causes the plaintiff's injury, and without which it would not have occurred, the criminal act is a superseding cause of injury relieving the originally negligent party of liability. There is an exception where the defendant's acts or omissions create a condition conducive to a foreseeable intervening criminal act. If the criminal act is reasonably foreseeable at the time of the negligence, the causal chain is not necessarily broken by the intervention of such an act.

From the record it is a reasonable inference that Free's entry into J-Mar's office was facilitated by the failure to take precautions to guard against unauthorized entries by those with master keys. It is Paramount and Fennessey's contention that although they might have had notice that master keys were outstanding, it was not foreseeable that an individual would use one and enter a tenant's office and assault those present, particularly in light of the fact that there had not been any violent crimes at the office park in the past. On the record the contention is not convincing. There were 17 incidents of criminal activity at the complex in the preceding two years. Though most were minor thefts from the parking lot area, several of the incidents involved burglaries from offices where there were no signs of forced entry. Even though there had not been previous crimes of violence at the office park, where a plaintiff's injury results from the same risk, the existence of which required the exercise of greater care, unforeseeability of what exactly could develop and the extent of the injury or loss will not limit liability. Under the circumstances here the crimes were within the scope of the foreseeable risk created by the inadequate control of the master keys.

Providing adequate security measures would have been relatively inexpensive. The office space in the park could have been secured simply by "rekeying" the locks, which would cost $2,500. The risk of unauthorized entry could also have been avoided by notifying those on the premises of the danger. In light of the risks created, it would not have been an unreasonable burden for Paramount to assume. The circumstances here create a triable issue of fact as to whether the danger of criminal conduct by individuals possessing passkeys was sufficiently probable and predictable to create a duty upon the defendants to take reasonable precautionary measures, and whether their failure to do so was a proximate cause of the plaintiffs' damages. The trial court erred in granting Paramount and Fennessey summary judgment.

Judgment reversed in favor of Rowe and Serpico; case remanded for trial.

Generally Accepted Causation Rules

Whatever test for proximate cause a court says it adopts, most courts generally agree on certain basic principles of causation. One such basic principle is that persons guilty of negligence "take their victims as they find them." This means that a negligent defendant is liable for the full extent of his victim's injuries even if those injuries are aggravated by some preexisting physical characteristic of the victim. Similarly, negligent defendants are normally held liable for diseases contracted by their victims while in a weakened state caused by their injuries. They are *jointly* liable—along with the attending physician—for negligent medical care that their victims receive for their injuries.

Negligent defendants are also commonly held responsible for injuries sustained by persons seeking to avoid being injured by the defendant's negligence. For example, Peters swerves to avoid being hit by Denning's negligently driven car and in the process loses control of her own car and is injured. Denning is liable for Peters' injuries. Finally, it is commonly said that "danger invites rescue." This means that negligent persons are liable to those injured in attempting to rescue the victims of their negligence. One corollary of this rescue rule is that the claim of a would-be rescuer ordinarily is not defeated by contributory fault on the part of the rescuer so long as he is not reckless in making the rescue attempt.

Res Ipsa Loquitur

In some cases, negligence may be difficult to prove because the defendant has superior knowledge of the circumstances surrounding the plaintiff's injury. Thus, it may not be in the defendant's best interests to disclose those circumstances if they point to liability on his part. The classic example of this is *Byrne v. Boadle*, where a pedestrian was hit on the head by a barrel of flour that fell from a warehouse owned by the defendant.[3] The victim had no way of knowing what caused the barrel to fall; he merely knew he had been injured. The only persons likely to know the relevant facts were the owners of the warehouse and their employees, but the odds were that they were the ones responsible for the accident. The English court observed: "A barrel could not roll out of a warehouse without some negligence" and held that it was up to the defendant owner to show that he was not at fault. Out of this case grew the doctrine of ***res ipsa loquitur*** ("the thing speaks for itself"). *Res ipsa* applies when: (1) the defendant has *exclusive control* of the instrumentality of harm (and therefore probable knowledge of, and responsibility for, the cause of the harm), (2) the harm that occurred *would not ordinarily occur* in the absence of negligence, and (3) the plaintiff was in no way responsible for his own injury. When these elements are present, most states hold that an *inference* may arise that the defendant was negligent and that her negligence was the cause of the plaintiff's injury. Practically speaking, this may force the defendant to come forward with evidence to rebut the inference that she is responsible. If she fails to do so, a court or jury *may* choose to impose liability on her. Some courts, however, give *res ipsa* much greater effect, holding that it creates a *presumption* of negligence that requires a directed verdict for the plaintiff in the absence of proof by the defendant rebutting the presumption.

Injury

The plaintiff in a negligence case must prove not only that the defendant breached a duty owed to the plaintiff and that the breach of duty was the legal cause of her injury, but also that the resulting injury was to an interest that the law seeks to protect. Ordinarily, purely physical injuries to a person or her property present no problem in this respect because the law has long protected such interests. Serious problems arise, however, when injuries are purely *emotional* in nature. With Intentional Torts, the law has long demonstrated a considerable reluctance to afford recovery for purely emotional harms. The courts' reluctance is due, among other things, to the danger of spurious claims and the difficulty inherent in placing a monetary value on emotional injuries. Given our great reluctance to impose liability for purely emotional harms caused by intentional wrongs, one might correctly assume that an even greater reluctance would exist when the conduct producing an emotional injury was merely negligent.

Negligent Infliction of Emotional Distress

Until fairly recently, most courts would not allow a plaintiff to recover for emotional injuries resulting from a defendant's negligent behavior in the absence of some impact or contact with the plaintiff's person. Today, many courts have abandoned the impact rule and allow recovery for foreseeable emotional injuries standing alone. A large number of such courts, however, still require, as a precondition of recovery, proof that some serious physical injury or symptoms resulted from the plaintiff's emotional distress. Nonetheless, a growing number of courts have dispensed with the injury requirement where the plaintiff has suffered serious emotional distress as a foreseeable consequence of the defendant's negligent conduct.

Third-Party Emotional Distress

In recent years, more and more negligence cases have involved claims by third persons for emotional injuries that they suffered by witnessing a negligently caused harm to another person, usually a spouse or child. For example, Mr. Porter has a heart attack after seeing Mrs. Porter run down by a car negligently driven by Denton. Is Denton liable for Mr. Porter's injury? Until fairly recently, most courts would have denied Mr. Porter any recovery on the ground that he had suffered no impact as a result of Denton's negligence. In recent years, however, many courts have abandoned the impact rule in third-party cases in favor of the "zone of danger" test. This test allows third parties who are themselves in the zone of danger created by a defendant's negligence to recover for emotional injuries resulting from the threat of harm to them, regardless of whether any impact ever occurred. Courts following this rule would, therefore, allow Mr. Porter to recover if he was close enough to his wife to be in danger of being hit by Denton's car. Some courts would insist, in addition, that Mr. Porter prove that he suffered some physical injury as a result of his emotional distress.

Today, some courts have abandoned the zone of danger requirement entirely and allow recovery for emotional injuries suffered by third parties, regardless of whether there was any threat of injury to them. However, most courts that have taken this step still attempt to limit recovery in a variety of ways. For example, such courts commonly require that a close personal relationship exist between the third-party plaintiff and the direct victim of the defendant's negligence and that the third party's emotional distress result from actually witnessing the injury to the direct victim. Also, they commonly impose a requirement that the third party demonstrate some physical "injury" resulting from his emotional distress.

This area of the law is undergoing rapid development, however, and some recent cases may be found that dispense with the injury requirement or allow recovery for emotional distress suffered as a result of seeing the direct victim in an injured state shortly after the injury occurred.

Defenses to Negligence

The common law traditionally recognized two defenses to negligence: **contributory negligence** and **assumption of risk**. Both of these defenses are based on the idea of *contributory fault*: If a plaintiff's own behavior contributed in some way to his injury, this fact should relieve the defendant from liability. As the following paragraphs indicate, however, the contributory fault idea often produced harsh results, and recent years have witnessed a significant erosion of its impact in negligence cases.

Contributory Negligence

The doctrine of **contributory negligence** provides that plaintiffs who *fail to exercise reasonable care for their own safety* are totally barred from any recovery if their contributory negligence is a *substantial factor* in producing their injury. So, if Parker steps into the path of Dworkin's speeding car without first checking to see whether any cars are coming, Parker would be denied any recovery against Dworkin because of the clear causal relationship between his injury and his failure to exercise reasonable care for his own safety. On the other hand, if Parker is injured one night when his speeding car crashes into a large, unmarked hole in the street caused by a city street repair project, and the facts indicate that the accident would have occurred even if Parker had been driving at a legal speed, he is not barred from recovering damages from the city for its negligence.

In some cases, a contributorily negligent plaintiff may be able to overcome an otherwise valid contributory negligence defense by arguing that the defendant had the **last clear chance** to avoid harm. The doctrine of last clear chance focuses on who was *last* at fault *in time*. Therefore, if, despite the plaintiff's contributory negligence, the harm could have been avoided if the defendant had exercised reasonable care, the defendant's *superior opportunity* to avoid the accident makes him more at fault. For example, Durban pulls into the path of Preston's speeding car without looking, causing an accident. When Preston files suit to recover for the damage, Durban argues that the fact that Preston was speeding amounts to contributory negligence. If Preston can convince the court that the accident could have been avoided if Durban had looked before pulling onto the highway, she has a good chance of overcoming Durban's contributory negligence defense.

Comparative Negligence

Contributory negligence can sometimes produce harsh results because it may operate to prevent slightly negligent persons from recovering any compensation for their losses. In reaction to this potential unfairness, most of the states have adopted **comparative negligence** systems either by statute or by judicial decision. The details of these systems vary by state, but the principle underlying them is essentially the same: Courts seek to determine the *relative fault* of the parties to a negligence action and to award damages in proportion to the degree of fault determined. For a simple example, assume that Dunne negligently injures Porter and Porter suffers $10,000 in damages. A jury, however, determines that Porter was 20 percent at fault. Under a comparative negligence system, Porter could recover only $8,000 from Dunne. But what if Porter is determined to be 60 percent at fault? Here, the results vary depending on whether the state in question has adopted a pure or a minced comparative fault system. Under a pure comparative fault system, plaintiffs are allowed to recover a portion of their damages even if they are more at fault than the defendant, so Porter could recover $4,000. Under a mixed system, plaintiffs who are as much at fault as, or, in some states, more at fault than, the defendant are denied any recovery. Such a state refuses Porter any recovery, just as though contributory negligence principles still applied (see, for example, Figure 23-1).

FIGURE 23-1
Plaintiff's recovery under contributory and comparative negligence systems

Plaintiff's Relative Fault	Contributory Negligence	Comparative Negligence (Pure)	Comparative Negligence (Mixed)
0%	100%	100%	100%
10	0	90	90
60	0	40	0
90	0	10	0

The full extent of the impact that comparative fault systems will have on tort law is as yet undetermined. What is clear, however, is that comparative fault is affecting other tort doctrines besides contributory negligence. For example, as the following *Roggow* case indicates, many comparative negligence states have discarded the doctrine of last clear chance. In addition, some states now apply comparative fault principles to recklessness and strict liability cases, as well as to negligence cases.

Roggow v. Mineral Processing Corp.

Charles Roggow, a long-distance truck driver out of Buffalo, New York, made a delivery of scrap aluminum to a processing plant located in Needmore, Indiana, and owned by Mineral Processing Corporation—Needmore Division (Needmore). After making delivery, Roggow was to pick up an unloaded trailer. Because Needmore's employees had failed to secure the header bar of the trailer (the part that secures the sides of the trailer to prevent damaging vibration), Roggow had to fasten the bar before leaving Needmore's plant. The bar had to be set in place at the very top of the trailer, but Needmore had no ladder available for Roggow's use. Consequently, Tracy Phillips, a Needmore employee, offered to assist Roggow by placing him in the bucket of a highloader and raising him high enough to set the bar in place.

Roggow accepted the offer and succeeded in fastening the header bar, but as Phillips was lowering him to the ground, Phillips's sleeve caught the highloader's dump lever, causing the bucket to overturn and dump Roggow approximately 9 feet onto a concrete floor. As a result of the fall, Roggow fractured both wrists and suffered two compressed vertebrae. He filed suit against Needmore. The jury found Roggow's damages to be $80,000 but reduced his award to $48,000 because they found him to be 40 percent at fault. Roggow filed a motion for a new trial, arguing, among other things, that the trial court erred in refusing to instruct the jury on the doctrine of last clear chance.

Source: 698 F. Sup. 1441 (S.D. Ind. 1988)

Endsley, U.S. Magistrate

This matter was tried under Indiana's Comparative Fault Act (the Act). Prior to the enactment of comparative fault, Indiana followed the common law rule of contributory negligence. This antiquated "all-or-nothing" rule totally bars a plaintiff from recovering damages for injuries if he is guilty of negligence, albeit slight. During the twentieth century, common law doctrines were developed to alleviate the harsh results of contributory negligence. Last clear chance was one of those doctrines. Roggow now invites the Court to determine the applicability of this exception to contributory negligence under the Act even though the statute is silent, and no Indiana court of review has yet passed on these issues.

Because no Indiana court has addressed this issue, this federal court must determine how the highest court in Indiana would decide this issue if it were presented with the question. Under the Act, assumption of risk is not available as an absolute defense for the defendant. Specifically, "assumption of risk not constituting an enforceable express consent" is a factor to be considered by the fact finder when weighing the fault attributable to the individual actors. Similarly, by its definition in the Act, "fault" necessarily includes the factors which make up last clear chance. The Indiana legislature defined fault as "any act or omission that is negligent, willful, wanton, or reckless toward the person or property of the actor or others." Consequently, just as assumed risk is no longer available to completely excuse the negligence of the defendant, so too, this Court believes, is the doctrine of last clear chance no longer available to completely excuse the negligence of the plaintiff. This conclusion is in accord with the holdings and statutes of a majority of states which have addressed the issue. Consequently, failure to give Roggow's tendered instruction was not error in this case.

Motion for new trial denied.

Assumption of Risk

In some cases, a plaintiff has *voluntarily* exposed herself to a *known danger* created by the defendant's negligence. Such plaintiffs are said to have *assumed the risk* of their injury and ordinarily are denied any recovery for it. The idea here is that the plaintiff *impliedly* consented to accept the risk, thereby relieving the defendant of the duty to protect him against it. For example, Stevens voluntarily goes for a ride in Markley's car, even though Markley has told him that her brakes are not working properly. Stevens has assumed the risk of injury as a result of the car's defective brakes. A person must fully understand the nature and extent of the risk, however, to be held to have assumed it. A plaintiff can also assume the risk of injury *expressly* by entering a contract containing a provision purporting to relieve the defendant of a duty of care that he would otherwise owe to the plaintiff. Such contract provisions are called *exculpatory clauses.* As the *Roggow* case indicated, some states that have adopted comparative negligence systems have done away with the assumption of risk defense in negligence cases and treat all forms of contributory fault under their comparative negligence scheme. The following *Hull* case, however, proves that assumption of risk remains a viable defense in some jurisdictions.

Hull v. Merck & Co., Inc.

On September 4, 1980, Augusta Fiberglass Coatings (AFC) began replacing fiberglass sewer lines at three adjacent Albany, Georgia, chemical plants operated by Merck & Co., Inc. The lines delivered waste chemicals into a 1 million gallon neutralizing pool. Merck warned AFC that it intended to continue in operation throughout the replacement activity and that bypass pipes and various safety equipment would be necessary to the work. AFC relayed Merck's warnings to its employees and provided them with rubber boots, pants, coats, and gloves, as well as goggles and masks.

Jim Dale Hull was AFC's supervisor on the job at Merck. Although Hull had long experience working with chemicals, he quit wearing any of the safety gear after a few days on the job. Hull spent four hours each day in the trench dug to expose the pipelines. He regularly breathed gases and allowed liquid to spill on his clothing and body. He noted at the time that the chemical fumes in and around the pipes were a health hazard. On September 22, 1980, Hull stuck his head inside a 20-inch connecting pipe which, due to an accidental spill in the factories, contained an 80 to 85 percent solution of toluene, rather than the 2 percent solution the pipes were supposed to carry. He became dizzy and nauseous and was given oxygen at the plant infirmary.

continued

Within a year after completion of the Merck contract, Hull suffered bone marrow depression, followed by leukemia. Hull sued Merck for $2.5 million plus punitive damages, alleging that: (1) Merck had negligently failed to disclose the nature and health dangers of the waste chemicals carried by the pipelines; (2) Merck had negligently failed to inform him adequately of the necessity for wearing protective gear during construction; (3) the inter- mittent discharge without warning of high-concentration spills into the pipelines resulted from the negligent operation of the factories; and (4) Merck's decision to continue plant operations and consequently the flow of waste chemicals during the pipeline replacement project amounted to negligence. After being charged by the trial judge that assumption of risk on Hull's part would bar his recovery under Georgia's comparative fault law, the jury ruled in favor of Merck. Hull appealed.

Source: 758 F.2d 1474 (11th Cir. 1985)

Per Curiam

Under Georgia law, a plaintiff assumes the risk when he "deliberately chooses an obviously perilous course of conduct and fully appreciates the danger involved." The plaintiff must do so voluntarily, "without restriction from his freedom of choice either by the circumstances or by coercion." Georgia typically applies assumption of risk to situations where the plaintiff races to beat a train at a crossing, drag races, or walks onto a pond covered with thin ice. Although assumption of the risk presupposes awareness of the nature and extent of the threat posed, perfect knowledge is not necessary. But Georgia law offers little guidance as to the depth of knowledge a plaintiff must possess to assume the sometimes very subtle risks posed by chemical exposure.

There was ample evidence to justify the charge in this case, especially as it pertained to Hull's allegation that Merck negligently decided to operate the factories during the replacement of the pipelines. Hull knew before he ever entered the plant grounds that Merck and AFC planned for operations to continue, with waste chemicals to be expelled via a bypass system of hoses assembled by AFC workers. Although Hull might or might not have had knowledge of any specific carcinogenic risk posed by toluene, he knew from long experience that the handling of waste chemicals warranted protective measures, and that coping with a continued flow of waste warranted an even greater degree of caution.

He also knew Merck and AFC were supplying adequate safety gear, which he used only for the first few days, but which many of his coworkers wore throughout the project without hampering their work. The gear remained available for his use at all times. He testified that while he was working he concluded the fumes were dangerous to good health. Finally, his severe exposure on September 22, 1980, forcefully brought home the risk posed by Merck's operations, yet he voluntarily remained, exposing himself for another month or more. The evidence at the trial left the jury free to conclude that Hull's leukemia was caused by post-September 22nd exposure, and Hull's remaining after that date might be construed as a knowing assumption of all four of the risks arising from Merck's alleged negligence. In any case, there was more than enough evidence to warrant the jury finding that Hull assumed the risk posed by working around a continuing flow of waste chemicals during the replacement of the pipes.

Judgment for Merck affirmed.

Figure 23-2 shows all of the elements of a successful negligence case.

Strict Liability

Introduction

In addition to intentional wrongdoing and negligence, the third fundamental basis of tort liability is **strict liability**. Strict liability means that defendants who participate in certain harm-producing activities may be held *strictly liable* for any harm that results to others, even though they did not intend to cause the harm and did everything in their power to prevent it. Also, defendants in strict liability cases traditionally have fewer defenses to liability than do defendants in negligence cases. This is because most courts hold that contributory negligence is *not* a defense to strict liability, although assumption of risk is a good defense. The imposition of strict liability represents a social policy decision that the risk associated with an activity should be borne by those who pursue it, rather than by wholly innocent persons who are exposed to that risk.

FIGURE 23-2
Elements of negligence

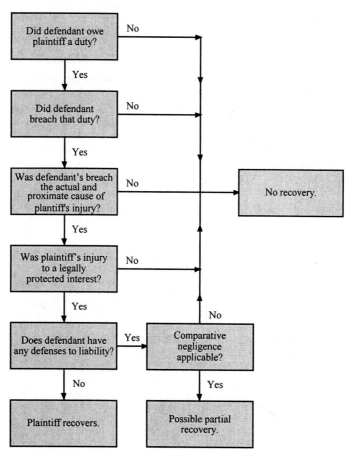

Such liability has been justified either by the defendant's voluntary decision to engage in a particularly risky activity or, more recently, by the defendant's superior ability to bear losses. Thus, corporations are often said to be superior to individuals as risk bearers due to their ability to pass the costs of liability on to consumers in the form of higher prices for goods or services. The owners of trespassing livestock and the keepers of naturally dangerous wild animals were among the first classes of defendants on whom the courts imposed strict liability. Today, the two most important activities subject to judicially imposed strict liability are *abnormally dangerous (or ultrahazardous) activities and the manufacture or sale of defective and unreasonably dangerous products.* Chapter 21, Product Liability, discusses the product liability dimension of strict liability in detail.

Abnormally Dangerous Activities

Abnormally dangerous activities are activities that *necessarily involve a risk of harm to others that cannot be eliminated by the exercise of reasonable care*. Activities that have been classed as abnormally dangerous include blasting, crop dusting, stunt flying, and, in one case, the transportation of large quantities of gasoline by truck. The following Klein case discusses the numerous factors that courts must consider before deciding whether a particular activity should be classified as abnormally dangerous.

Klein v. Pyrodyne Corporation

Pyrodyne Corporation was hired to display the fireworks at the Western Washington State Fairgrounds in Puyallup, Washington, on July 4, 1987. During the display, one of the 6-inch mortars was knocked into a horizontal position, from which position a rocket inside ignited and flew 500 feet parallel to the earth, exploding near the crowd of onlookers. Danny and Marion Klein were injured by the explosion. They filed a strict liability suit against Pyrodyne, arguing that Pyrodyne failed to carry out a number of the statutory and regulatory requirements in preparing for

and setting off the fireworks. Pyrodyne argued that the accident was caused by a rocket detonating in its mortar tube without ever leaving the ground, causing another rocket to be knocked over, ignited, and set off horizontally. Pyrodyne moved for summary judgment on the ground that negligence principles should be applied to the case. When the trial court denied its motion and found it strictly liable, Pyrodyne appealed.

Source: 810 P.2d 917 (Wash. Sup. Ct. 1991)

Guy, Justice

The modern doctrine of strict liability for abnormally dangerous activities derives from *Rylands v. Fletcher* (Eng. 1866), in which the defendant's reservoir flooded mine shafts on the plaintiff's adjoining land. *Rylands v. Fletcher* has come to stand for the rule that "the defendant will be liable when he damages another by a thing or activity unduly dangerous and inappropriate to the place where it is maintained, in the light of the character of that place and its surroundings." *Prosser and Keeton on Torts* (1984).

The basic principle of *Rylands v. Fletcher* has been accepted by the *Restatement (Second) of Torts* (1977). Section 519 of the *Restatement* provides that any party carrying on an "abnormally dangerous activity" is strictly liable for the ensuing damages. Section 520 of the *Restatement* lists six factors that are to be considered in determining whether an activity is "abnormally dangerous":

a.   existence of a high degree of risk of some harm to the person, land or chattels of others;
b.   likelihood that the harm that results from it will be great;
c.   inability to eliminate the risk by the exercise of reasonable care;
d.   extent to which the activity is not a matter of common usage;
e.   inappropriateness of the activity to the place where it is carried on; and
f.   extent to which its value to the community is outweighed by its dangerous attributes.

The comments to section 520 explain how these factors should be evaluated:

> Any one of them is not necessarily sufficient of itself in a particular case, and ordinarily several of them will be required for strict liability. On the other hand, it is not necessary that each of

them be present, especially if others weigh heavily. The essential question is whether the risk created is so unusual, either because of its magnitude or because of the circumstances surrounding it, as to justify the imposition of strict liability for the harm that results from it, even though it is carried on with all reasonable care.

We find that the factors stated in clauses (a), (b), and (c) are all present in the case of fireworks displays. Any time a person ignites rockets with the intention of sending them aloft to explode in the presence of large crowds of people, a high risk of serious personal injury or property damage is created. That risk arises because of the possibility that a rocket will malfunction or be misdirected. Furthermore, no matter how much care pyrotechnicians exercise, they cannot entirely eliminate the high risk inherent in setting off powerful explosives near crowds.

Pyrodyne argues that the factor stated in clause (d) is not met because fireworks are a common way to celebrate the 4th of July. Although fireworks are frequently and regularly enjoyed by the public, few persons set off special fireworks displays. Indeed, anyone wishing to do so must first obtain a license.

The Puyallup Fairgrounds is an appropriate place for the fireworks show because the audience can be seated at a reasonable distance from the display. Therefore, the clause (e) factor is not present in this case. The factor in clause (f) requires analysis of the extent to which the value of the fireworks to the community outweighs its dangerous attributes. This country has a long-standing tradition of fireworks on the 4th of July. That tradition suggests that we have decided that the value of fireworks on the day celebrating our national independence and unity outweighs the risks of injuries and damage.

In sum, we find that setting off public fireworks displays satisfies four of the six conditions under the *Restatement* test. We therefore hold that conducting public fireworks displays is an abnormally dangerous activity justifying the imposition of strict liability. **Judgment for the Kleins affirmed.**

Statutory Strict Liability

Strict liability is not an exclusive creation of the courts. Strict liability principles are also embodied in modern legislation. The most important examples of this phenomenon are the *Workers' Compensation Acts* passed by most states in the early decades of this century. Such statutes allow employees to recover statutorily limited amounts from their employers despite the absence of any fault on the part of the employer or the presence of contributory fault on the part of the employee. Employers participate in a compulsory liability insurance system and are expected to pass the costs of the system on to consumers, who then become the ultimate bearers of the human costs of industrial production. Other examples of statutory strict liability include the Dram Shop statutes of some states, which impose liability on sellers of alcoholic beverages without proof of any negligence when third parties are harmed due to a buyer's intoxication. Also included is the statutory liability without proof of fault that some states impose on the operators of aircraft for ground damage resulting from aviation accidents.

Tort Reform

By 1990, most states had enacted some form of tort reform legislation. The primary beneficiaries of such legislation were physicians, local governments, and manufacturers. The main driving force behind the tort reform movement is the "crisis" in the liability insurance system. In recent years, the insurance system has been characterized by outright refusals of coverage, reductions in coverage, and dramatically escalating premiums when coverage remains available. The supporters of tort reform argue that the main factors underlying the insurance crisis are the trend toward strict liability for various harms and escalating damage awards. Observers often attribute this latter factor to the increased frequency with which punitive damages are awarded and to a tendency toward more frequent damage awards for noneconomic harms such as pain and suffering in tort cases.

Tort reform advocates also argue that large jury awards contribute to inflation because, where market conditions permit, those who initially bear the cost of liability insurance will pass such costs on to their customers in the form of higher prices. Supporters of tort reform also argue that the threat of huge jury awards impedes the development of new products and technologies.

States have enacted a variety of devices in the name of tort reform. Statutes that limit the amounts recoverable for noneconomic harms are now fairly common, as are statutes that limit the liability of social hosts or businesses for the damage caused by intoxicated persons to whom they serve alcohol. Local governments in many states now enjoy statutory limits on their liability for negligence, affording them partial relief from the negligence claims for improper maintenance of streets and traffic signals; such claims now routinely accompany many automobile accident cases. Likewise, physicians in a number of states have received some relief from spiraling liability costs by reform devices such as caps on the amount recoverable in liability suits and mandatory pretrial mediation of all claims over a prescribed threshold. Finally, statutory ceilings on punitive damage awards or rules making such damages more difficult to recover are also common reform measures.

Critics of the tort reform movement argue that the liability insurance crisis is largely the fault of the insurance industry. Some have argued that insurers have manufactured the crisis to get unjustified premium increases and to divert attention from insurer mismanagement of invested premium income. Others argue that insurers are raising premiums to offset income losses resulting from the drop in interest rates in recent years. Whatever the truth of such allegations, it is becoming increasingly common for state legislatures to couple tort reform legislation with increased regulation of insurers, something that is understandably dulling the insurance industry's enthusiasm for tort reform. For example, Florida forced a rate rollback as a price of tort reform. Other common reform devices include requiring prior approval of rate increases and placing closer restraints on insurer policy cancellation and nonrenewal practices.

The battle for tort reform is far from over, however. Tort reform opponents who lost the fight against tort reform in the legislature have continued it in the courts. Thus, tort reform statutes have been challenged by arguments that statutes capping damage awards violate state constitutional provisions guaranteeing jury trials because they limit jury discretion in setting damages, and by arguments that reform measures targeted at certain types of cases (e.g., medical malpractice cases) violate equal protection guaranties by unjustifiably discriminating against plaintiffs in such cases. Such challenges have succeeded in some states and have been rebuffed in others. Whatever the outcome of the current struggle, the tort reform debate highlights the perennial dilemma facing tort law—how to fashion a system adequately compensating the victims of civil wrongs in an economically efficient manner that does not impose undue burdens on business or society as a whole.

Ethical and Public Policy Concerns

1.   In the famous *Palsgraf* case cited in footnote 1 in this chapter, the plaintiff was injured
     when a late-boarding train passenger dropped a package of fireworks he was carrying

as he attempted to board a train that was pulling out of the station. Two employees of the railroad were trying to help him board, one pulling and one pushing. The package was jostled loose and exploded on impact. The concussion from the explosion caused some scales to fall on the victim, who was standing several feet away from the action. The defendant railroad escaped liability to the victim because the court found it had no duty to her because its employees could not reasonably have foreseen that they were endangering her by their actions. Yet, plainly the harm to her would not have occurred had the railroad's employees refused to allow the passenger to try to board a moving train. Even if the railroad had no legal duty to Palsgraf, did it have any ethical duty to her?

2. Implicit in the idea of proximate cause is the fact that a negligent defendant can be the actual cause of some plaintiffs' injuries but avoid any liability for those injuries because his negligence was not the proximate cause of such injuries. Is the doctrine of proximate cause ethically justifiable?

3. While the doctrine of proximate cause allows defendants to avoid responsibility for some consequences of their negligence, the doctrine of strict liability imposes liability on persons who participate in abnormally dangerous activities even though they exercised all possible care to avoid injuring anyone. Can such liability be ethically justified?

Problems and Problem Cases

1. On September 5, 1984, the Citizens for Bob Olexo Campaign Committee rented three tanks of helium from James Dawes Company. The helium was to be used to fill balloons that were to be handed out to the public during the Belmont County Fair. Although the agreement with Dawes called for the Committee to return the used cylinders, they were left at the fairgrounds leaning up against a commercial building. On September 28, Philip C. Jeffers III, age 14, attended a football game at the fairgrounds, where he and some friends discovered the tanks. Despite the warning on the tanks, which stated "CAUTION! HIGH PRESSURE GAS. CAN CAUSE RAPID SUFFOCATION," Jeffers inhaled some helium from one of the tanks, collapsed, and died. Jeffers' father sued the Dawes Company, which moved for a summary judgment on a number of grounds, among which was the argument that it owed no duty to Jeffers. Should Dawes' motion be granted?

2. On August 7, 1981, a young man abducted R.M.V., age 10, from the sidewalk in front of her home and dragged her across the street to a vacant apartment at the Chalmette Apartments. He raped her, put her in the closet, told her not to leave, and disappeared. The apartment in question was described by the police officer called to the scene as "empty, filthy, dirty, and full of debris." Glass was broken from its windows and the front door was off its hinges. In the two years prior to the attack on R.M.V., Dallas police had investigated numerous crimes committed at the Chalmette Apartments complex, including 1 attempted murder, 2 robberies, 2 aggravated assaults, 16 apartment burglaries, 4 vehicle burglaries, 4 cases of theft, and 5 cases of criminal mischief. A Dallas City Ordinance established minimum standards for property owners, requiring them, among other things, to "keep the doors and windows of a vacant structure or vacant portion of a structure securely closed to prevent unauthorized entry." Gaile Nixon, R.M.V.'s mother, filed a negligence suit against the Chalmette's owner and Mr. Property Management Company, Inc., the manager of the complex. Were the defendants correct in arguing that they owed no duty to R.M.V.?

3. On September 3, 1984, Valerie Jones, a lab technician at Kelco's chemical plant in Okmulgee, Oklahoma, stole a cupful of sulfuric acid from the plant. After work, she drove to the home of her sister-in-law, Gwendolyn Henry. After a brief verbal altercation with Henry over the fact that Henry, who had been babysitting Jones' 2-year-old son, had trimmed the child's hair, she threw the acid in Henry's face. Henry suffered severe and permanent injuries, and Jones was ultimately sentenced to 7 years in prison for the attack. Henry filed a negligence suit against Kelco, and a jury awarded her $450,000. Kelco appealed, arguing that it owed no duty to Henry and that, in any event, Jones's act was an intervening cause that relieved it of liability. The evidence at trial indicated that Jones had been a model employee who had to have access to the chemical storage area to perform her duties. Should the jury's verdict be reversed?

4. On August 12, 1980, while riding her bike in the residential area near her home. Fourteen-year-old Mumtaz Mazzagatti was struck and fatally injured by a car driven by Ricky Everingham. At the time of the accident her mother, Jane Mazzagatti, was at work, approximately one mile away. She received a telephone call immediately after the collision informing her that her daughter had been involved in an automobile accident. She arrived on the scene a few minutes later and saw her daughter lying in the road. She later filed a negligent infliction of emotional distress suit against Everingham. In her complaint she alleged that she "became hysterical, unnerved, and emotionally shattered" at the sight of her injured daughter, that as a result of the observation she suffered shock to her nervous system, and grievous mental pain and suffering, resulting in severe depression and an acute nervous condition. Was the trial court's decision to grant a summary judgment in favor of Everingham justified?

5. In July 1980, Higgins and some friends went to a night baseball game at Comiskey Park in Chicago. Near the end of the game, Higgins went to the men's room. On his way back to his seat, he walked down a corridor that ran past a concession stand. As he passed the stand, the door to the front of the stand (a 4- by 6-foot sheet of plywood attached to the top of the stand and hooked to an eyelet in the ceiling when opened) fell from its open position and struck him on the head, causing permanent head and neck injuries. None of the eyewitnesses to the incident saw anyone touch either the door or the hook securing it or do anything that might have caused the door to fall. There was, however, testimony that, just before the door fell, the crowd in the stadium was screaming and stamping, and that one "could feel the place tremble." Higgins filed suit against the Chicago White Sox, owners of the stadium, arguing that *res ipsa loquitur* should be applied to the case. Was he right?

6. At 6:45 A.M. on July 25, 1982, Simone Waters was walking on a public street where she was accosted by a knife-wielding man who forced her to walk with him to a building around the corner. Once inside the building, which was unlocked, the man forced her to the roof and, after taking her money, sodomized her. The building was owned by the New York Housing Authority. The evidence at the trial indicated that the front door locks on the building had been either broken or missing for at least two years before. Simone was attacked, that several tenants had complained about the condition over that two-year period, and that there had been at least five criminal incidents in the building involving outsiders. The Housing Authority argued that it owed no duty to Waters to protect her against the criminal acts of third persons. Was the trial court's decision to grant a summary judgment in favor of the Housing Authority correct?

7. Jenkins, an employee of Acme Paper Stock Company, was riding on a freight elevator in Acme's plant when the elevator cable broke. As a result, the hoist motor fell on Jenkins, fatally injuring him. The hoist motor and lifting cables had been installed by Edwards Transfer Company. The evidence at trial indicated that Edwards used steel

cables to mount the hoist from an I-beam that ran along the ceiling of Acme's plant, but failed to use "softeners" to protect the cables against the sharp edges of the beam. The evidence also indicated that Acme had warned employees that the elevator was only to be used for freight and was not safe for use as a personnel elevator and that Jenkins himself had told an Edwards employee prior to the accident that the hoist was improperly secured. Jenkins' heirs filed a negligence suit against Edwards. The trial judge refused to instruct the jury on contributory negligence on the ground that Jenkins could not reasonably have foreseen that he could be injured by the falling hoist motor. Was this refusal proper?

8. On April 25, 1984, Allen Beckett, a fourth-year player on his high school baseball team, was injured when he collided with another player during outfielder practice. The accident occurred after the coach conducting the practice hit a fly ball to Beckett. Beckett called for the ball, but the wind was blowing so hard that neither the coach nor the other players heard him. The coach called for another player to catch the ball, and that player and Beckett collided head-on. Beckett's jaw was broken, and he filed suit against the school, arguing that it had failed to warn him of the danger of such collisions, failed to adequately supervise the practice, and had conducted the practice in an unreasonably dangerous manner. At one point in his testimony, Beckett denied that he had ever heard of baseball players colliding and said that he had no knowledge of any accidents happening on baseball fields. Under cross-examination, however, he admitted that his coaches had repeatedly stressed communication among players to avoid accidents, that it was possible on such a windy day for his voice to have gotten lost in the wind, and that the same type of thing could have happened in a game. Was the trial court summary judgment in favor of the school proper?

9. Lee Ann Laird, age 12, was injured when her bicycle was hit by a car driven by Larry Kostman. Lee Ann was in the process of pulling into the street from a driveway, and she emerged from behind a van parked at the curb. At the trial, Kostman testified that he hit his brakes as soon as he saw the bicycle. His passenger testified that Laird "came out of nowhere," and that he didn't see her until the moment of impact. Laird testified that she saw Kostman's car turn onto the street from an intersection more than 200 feet from the point of impact, that no more than two feet of her bicycle extended into the street from behind the parked van, and that when she tried to move the bike back to avoid the collision, the brakes locked. After the trial judge refused to instruct the jury on the doctrine of last clear chance, the jury ruled in favor of Kostman. Was the trial judge's refusal proper?

10. On January 9, 1979, a railroad car leased by American Cyanamid (American) and containing 20,000 gallons of acrylonitrile manufactured by American began leaking. At the time, the car was sitting just south of Chicago in the Blue Island yard of the Indiana Harbor Belt Railroad (Indiana) awaiting switching to Conrail for delivery to its final destination. Indiana's employees stopped the leak but were uncertain about how much of the car's contents had escaped. Because acrylonitrile is flammable, highly toxic, and possibly carcinogenic, Illinois authorities ordered homes near the yard temporarily evacuated. Later, it was discovered that only about a quarter of the car's contents had leaked, but the Illinois Department of Environmental Protection, fearing that the soil and water had been contaminated, ordered Indiana to take decontamination measures costing $981,000. Indiana filed suit against American on negligence and strict liability theories seeking to recover its expenses. Evidence introduced at the trial included a list of 125 hazardous materials that are shipped in highest volume on the nation's railroads. Acrylonitrile was the 53rd most hazardous on the list. Was the trial court's entry of summary judgment for Indiana on the strict liability claim proper?

Endnotes

1.   The most famous case adopting this approach is *Palsgraf v. Long Island Railroad Co.*, 12 N.E. 99 (N.Y. Ct. App. 1928).
2.   *Restatement (Second) of Torts* § 435(2) (1965).
3.   2 H. & C. 722 (Eng. 1863).

Chapter Twenty-Four

THIRD-PARTY RELATIONS
OF THE PRINCIPAL

AND THE AGENT

Introduction

By letting principals contract through their agents and thereby multiply their dealings, agency law stimulates business activity. For this process to succeed, there must be rules for determining when the principal and the agent are liable on the agent's contracts. Principals need to predict and control their liability on agreements their agents make. Also, third parties need assurance that such agreements really bind the principal. Furthermore, both agents and third parties have an interest in knowing when an agent is bound on these contracts. The first half of this chapter discusses the principal's and the agent's contract liability.

While acting on the principal's behalf agents sometimes harm third parties in various ways. Normally, this makes the agent liable to the injured party in tort. Sometimes, moreover, a principal is liable for his agent's torts. Because tort judgments can be expensive, the rules for determining the principal's and the agent's tort liability are of great concern to principals, their agents, and third parties. Thus, we examine these subjects in this chapter's second half.

Contract Liability of the Principal

A principal is normally liable on a contract made by his agent if the agent had **express, implied, or apparent authority** to make the contract. Occasionally, however, a principal's contract liability may be affected by other factors. Even where the agent lacked authority to contract, moreover, a principal may bind herself by later **ratifying** the agent's contract.

Express Authority

Express authority is created by a principal's *words* to his agent, whether written or oral. Thus, an agent has express authority to bind her principal to a particular contract if the principal clearly told the agent that she could make that contract on the principal's behalf. For example, suppose that Payne instructs his agent Andrews to contract to sell a specific antique chair for $400 or more. If Andrews contracts to sell the chair to Tucker for $425, Payne is liable to Tucker on the basis of Andrews's express authority. However, Andrews would not have express authority to sell the chair for $375, or to sell a different chair.

Implied Authority

Often, it is difficult or impossible for a principal to specify his agent's authority completely and precisely. Thus, agents also can bind their principals on the basis of the agent's **implied authority**. An agent generally has implied authority to do whatever it is reasonable to assume that his principal wanted him to do, in light of the principal's express statements and the surrounding circumstances. Relevant factors include the principal's express statements, the nature of the agency, the acts reasonably necessary to carry on the agency business, the acts customarily done when conducting that business, and the relations between principal and agent.

Implied authority often derives from a grant of express authority or some other express statement by the principal. Ordinarily, an agent has implied authority to make those contracts that are reasonably necessary for conducting the business he has been expressly authorized to perform, or that are customarily made in conducting that business. Implied authority, however, cannot conflict with the principal's express statements. Thus, there is no implied authority to contract where a principal has limited her agent's authority by express statement or clear implication and the contract would conflict with that limitation.

On occasion, implied authority may exist even though there is no relevant grant of express authority. Here, courts generally derive implied authority from the nature of the agency business, the relations between principal and agent, customs in the trade, and other facts and circumstances. For example, there may be implied authority to make a certain contract if the agent has made similar past contracts with the principal's knowledge and without his objection.

Examples of Implied Authority

Courts have created general rules or presumptions for determining the implied authority of certain agents in certain situations. For example:

1. An agent hired to *manage a business* normally has implied authority to make those contracts that are reasonably necessary for conducting the business or that are customary in the business. These include contracts for obtaining equipment and supplies, making repairs, employing employees, and selling goods or services. However, a manager has no power to borrow money or issue negotiable instruments in the principal's name unless the principal is a banking or financial concern regularly performing such activities.
2. An agent given *full control over real property* has implied authority to contract for repairs and insurance, and may rent the property if this is customary. But such an agent may not sell the property or allow any third-party liens or other interests to be taken on it.
3. Agents appointed to *sell the principal's goods* may have implied authority to make customary warranties on those goods. In states that still recognize the distinction, the *general agent* is more likely to have such authority than a *special agent*.

Apparent Authority

Apparent authority arises when the *principal's behavior* causes a third party to form a *reasonable belief* that the agent is authorized to act in a certain way. Principals can give their agents apparent authority through the statements they make, or tell their agents to make, to third parties, and through the actions they knowingly allow their agents to take.

Background factors such as trade customs and established business practices often determine whether it is reasonable for the third party to believe such manifestations of authority. For instance, if a principal appoints his agent to a position such as general manager that customarily involves the power to make certain contracts, the agent normally has apparent authority to make those contracts. Here, the principal's behavior in appointing the agent to the position, as reasonably interpreted in light of business customs, creates apparent authority in the agent. This is true even if the principal expressly told the agent not to make such contracts, so long as this limitation remains unknown to the third party. Because agents cannot give themselves apparent authority, however, there would be no such authority if an agent falsely told third parties that he had been promoted to general manager without the principal's knowledge or permission.

Established business customs can help create apparent authority in other ways as well. For example, an agent can often bind his principal to forbidden promises that customarily accompany contracts the agent actually is authorized to complete, if the third party is unaware that the promises were forbidden. In states that still recognize the distinction, general agents are more likely to have this kind of apparent authority than are special agents. Suppose that Perry employs Arthur as general sales agent for his manufacturing business. Certain warranties customarily accompany the products Perry sells, and agents like Arthur are ordinarily empowered to give these warranties. But Perry tells Arthur not to make any such warranties to buyers, thus cutting off Arthur's express and implied authority. Despite Perry's orders, however, Arthur makes the usual warranties in a sale to Thomas, who is familiar with customs in the trade. If Thomas did not know about the limitation on Arthur's authority, Perry is bound by Arthur's warranties.

Finally, apparent authority may exist where a principal has, to the knowledge of a third person, permitted his agent to make contracts that the agent was expressly forbidden to make. Suppose Potter has told Abram, the manager of his business, to hire loaders for his trucks for no more than one day at a time. No one else knows about this limitation on Abram's actual authority. With Potter's knowledge and without his objection, however, Abram frequently has employed loaders by the week. Then Abram agrees to employ Trapp as a loader for a week. If Trapp knew about the earlier employment by the week, Potter would be bound to the one-week employment contract on the basis of Abram's apparent authority.

Other Factors Affecting a Principal's Contract Liability

Agent's Notification and Knowledge

Sometimes the general agency rules regarding *notification* and *knowledge* affect a principal's contract liability. If a third party gives proper notification to an agent with actual or apparent authority to receive it, the principal is bound as if the notification had been given directly to him. For example, where a contract between Phillips and Thomas made by Phillips's agent Anderson contains a clause allowing Thomas to cancel if she notifies Phillips, she can cancel by notifying Anderson if Anderson has actual or apparent authority to receive the notification. Similarly, notification *to* a third party *by* an agent with the necessary authority is considered notification by the principal.

In certain circumstances, an agent's knowledge of certain facts is imputed to the principal. This means that the principal's rights and liabilities are what they would have been if the principal had known what the agent knew. Generally, an agent's knowledge is imputed to a principal when it is relevant to activities that the agent is authorized to undertake, or when the agent is under a duty to disclose the knowledge to the principal. Suppose that Ames contracts with Timmons on Pike's behalf, knowing that Timmons is completely mistaken about a matter material to the contract. Even though Pike knew nothing about Timmons's unilateral mistake, Timmons probably can avoid his contract with Pike.[1]

Incapacity of Principal or Agent

A principal who lacks capacity at the time an agency is formed may usually avoid the agency, and a principal's permanent loss of capacity after the agency's formation terminates the agency. Where the agency continues to exist, is a minor or a person of limited mental capacity bound on contracts made by his agent? Subject to the exceptions discussed in Chapter 18, such contracts are voidable at the principal's option. These contracts would normally be voidable if made by the principal himself, and it is difficult to see why acting through an agent should increase the principal's capacity.

Like the principal, an agent can avoid the agency agreement if she lacks capacity at the time it is formed. Where the agency survives, however, the agent's incapacity usually does *not* affect the contract liability of a principal who has capacity. Just as an agent cannot increase the principal's capacity, neither can she diminish it. However, the principal may sometimes escape liability where an agent's incapacity is so extreme that the agent cannot receive or convey ideas, or cannot follow the principal's instructions.

Ratification

Ratification is a process whereby a principal binds himself to an unauthorized act done by an agent of by a person purporting to act as an agent. Ratification relates back to the time when the act was performed. For contracts, its effect is to bind the principal as if the agent had possessed authority at the time the contract was made.

Conduct Amounting to Ratification

Ratification can be express or implied. An *express ratification* occurs when the principal communicates an intent to ratify by written or oral words to that effect. *Implied ratification* arises when the principal's behavior evidences an intent to ratify. Part performance of the agent's contract by a principal or a principal's acceptance of benefits under the contract may work an implied ratification. Sometimes even a principal's silence, acquiescence, or failure to repudiate the transaction may constitute ratification. This can occur where the principal would be expected to object if he did not consent to the contract, the principal's silence leads the third party to believe that he does consent, and the principal is aware of all relevant facts.

Additional Requirements

Even if a principal's words or behavior indicate an intent to ratify, other requirements must be met before ratification occurs. These requirements have been variously stated; the following list is typical.

1. The act ratified must be one that was *valid* at the time it was performed. For example, an agent's illegal contract cannot be made binding by the principal's subsequent ratification. However, a contract that was voidable when made due to the principal's incapacity may be ratified by a principal who has later attained or regained capacity.

2. The principal must have been *in existence* at the time the agent acted. However, corporations may bind themselves to their promoters' preincorporation contracts by adopting such contracts.
3. When the act to be ratified occurred, the agent must have indicated to the third party that she was acting for *a* principal and not for herself. But the agent need not have disclosed the principal's identity.
4. The principal must be *legally competent* at the time of ratification. For instance, an insane principal cannot ratify.
5. The principal must have *knowledge* of all material facts regarding the prior act or contract at the time it is ratified. Here, an agent's knowledge is not imputed to the principal. In the following *Adams* case, the principal did not ratify because it lacked sufficient knowledge.
6. The principal must ratify the *entire* act or contract. He cannot ratify the beneficial parts of a contract and reject those that are detrimental.
7. In ratifying, the principal must use the *same formalities* required to give the agent authority to execute the transaction. Few formalities are normally needed to give an agent authority. But where the original agency contract requires a writing, ratification likewise must be written.

Intervening Events

Certain events occurring after an agent's contract but before the principal's ratification may cut off the principal's power to ratify. These include: (1) the third party's *withdrawal* from the contract; (2) the third party's *death* or *loss of capacity*; (3) the principal's *failure to ratify within a reasonable time* (assuming that the principal's silence did not already work a ratification); and (4) *changed circumstances* (especially where the change places a greater burden on the third party than he assumed when the contract was made).

Adams v. Louisiana Coca-Cola Bottling Co.

Rosia Adams, an employee at a Jefferson Parish School Board warehouse, was injured when she slipped on a wet floor at the warehouse. The floor was wet because it had been mopped to clean a spill from a malfunctioning Coca-Cola vending machine leased to the school board by the Louisiana Coca-Cola Bottling Company (Coca-Cola). A warehouse inventory clerk signed the lease on behalf of the school board.

Adams sued Coca-Cola for her injuries. Coca-Cola then filed a third-party action against the school board, alleging that under the terms of the lease the school board was required to indemnify and insure Coca-Cola against injuries to employees like Adams. After trial, Adams obtained a jury verdict against Coca-Cola, and the trial judge dismissed Coca-Cola's claim against the school board. Coca-Cola then appealed the trial judge's decision dismissing its claim against the school board.

Source: 531 So. 2d 501 (La. Ct. App. 1988)

Ciaccio, Judge

The question is whether the school board is obligated under the lease. The clerk who signed the lease did not have express authority to do so. Whether he had implied authority, the other component of actual authority, is determined by inference from the circumstances, purposes, and nature of the agency. An agent is invested with the implied authority to do all those things necessary or incidental to the accomplishment of the purpose of the agency.

Coca-Cola argues that the clerk was empowered with general authority to operate the warehouse. Such a mandate confers only a power of administration. The proof does not establish any particular circumstances, purposes, or nature of the agency beyond receiving and inventorying goods delivered to the warehouse. We do not find therein any implied authority to agree to indemnify and insure the lessor of a vending machine placed on the premises.

For apparent authority to apply, the principal must first act to manifest the agent's authority to [a] third party. Second, the third party must rely reasonably on the manifested authority of the agent. In support of its argument for the clerk's apparent authority to execute this lease on behalf of the board, Coca-Cola relies on the following facts. The clerk has worked for the school board for twenty years. During this time he has always handled soft drink vending machines on the premises. Either he or another school board employee initially contacted Coca-Cola to have a machine installed at the warehouse. The school board's representative admitted that employees all over the school board system were signing similar leases. He also admitted that some of the seven thousand school board employees have previously bound the school board without formal authorization.

There is no indication that the school board acted to manifest authority for the clerk to execute this lease. There is no evidence that the school board knew of the lease, much less its provisions. The board's role was passive; it apparently paid no attention to the vending machines on its premises. We do not find that this passiveness manifested authority in its employees to agree to indemnify and insure the lessor of these machines.

Further, we find unreasonable any reliance by Coca-Cola upon any perception of authority in the clerk. Coca-Cola did not inquire into the nature and extent of the clerk's authority. Agreeing to indemnify and insure Coca-Cola as lessor requires greater authority than one would reasonably perceive to be vested in an inventory clerk.

Coca-Cola finally argues that the school board ratified the lease by permitting the machine to remain at the warehouse, permitting another machine to be placed there, and [later] permitting over one hundred other machines to be placed at various other school board locations under similar lease conditions. There is no indication that the school board was aware that the machines were being leased, that the leases were being executed in its name, or that the leases contained onerous provisions that the board indemnify and insure Coca-Cola as lessor. We do not find the board's permitting the presence of the machines to be a ratification of the lease provisions connected by Coca-Cola.

Judgment in favor of the school board on Coca-Cola's third-party claim affirmed.

Contracts Made by Subagents

The rules governing a principal's liability for her agent's contracts generally apply to contracts made by her subagents. If an agent has authorized his subagent to make a certain contract and this authorization is within the authority granted the agent by his principal, the principal is bound to the subagent's contract. Suppose that Peters employs the Ajax Company to sell certain personal property while she is out of the country, with the understanding that one of Ajax's agents will handle the sale from start to finish. If Ajax authorizes its agent Sampson (Peters's subagent) to contract to sell the property and Sampson does so, Peters is bound to the contract.

Because the relationship between agent and subagent closely resembles the relationship between principal and agent, a subagent acting within the authority conferred by her principal (the agent) can bind the *agent* in contract. Finally, although the authorities do not clearly address the subject, both the principal and the agent can probably ratify the contracts of subagents.

Contract Liability of the Agent

An *agent's* liability on contracts he makes for the principal usually depends on a different set of factors than the factors determining the principal's liability.[2] The most important of these variables is the *nature of the principal*. Thus, this section first examines the liability of agents who contract for several distinct kinds of principals. Then it discusses two ways that an agent can be bound after contracting for almost any type of principal—by agreeing to be liable, or by contracting without the necessary authority.

The Nature of the Principal

Disclosed Principal

A principal is disclosed if a third party knows or has reason to know: (1) that the agent is acting for a principal, and (2) the principal's identity. Unless he agrees otherwise, an agent who represents a disclosed principal is *not liable* on authorized contracts made for such a principal. Suppose that Adkins, a sales agent for Parker, calls on Thompson and presents a business card clearly identifying her as Parker's agent. If Adkins contracts to sell Parker's goods to Thompson with authority to do so, Adkins is not bound because Parker is a disclosed principal. This rule is usually consistent with the third party's intentions; for example, Thompson probably intended to contract only with Parker. In the following *Cahn* case, the agents were bound even though they contracted for a disclosed principal, because they had impliedly agreed to be bound.

Partially Disclosed Principal

A principal is **partially disclosed** if the third party: (1) knows or has reason to know that the agent is acting for *a* principal, but (2) lacks knowledge or reason to know the principal's *identity*. This can occur where an agent simply neglects to disclose his principal's identity. Also, a principal may tell her agent to keep her (the principal's) identity secret to preserve her bargaining position.

Among the factors affecting anyone's decision to contract are the integrity, reliability, and creditworthiness of the other party to the contract. Where the principal is partially disclosed, the third party ordinarily cannot judge these matters. As a result, he usually depends on the agent's reliability to some degree. For this reason, and to give the third party additional protection, an agent is liable on contracts made for a partially disclosed principal unless the parties agree otherwise.

Undisclosed Principal

A principal is **undisclosed** where the third party lacks knowledge or reason to know *both* the principal's existence and the principal's identity. This can occur where a principal judges that he will get a better deal if his existence and identity remain secret, or where the agent simply neglects to make adequate disclosure.

A third party who deals with an agent for an undisclosed principal obviously cannot assess the principal's reliability, integrity, and creditworthiness. Indeed, here the third party reasonably believes that the *agent* is the other party to the contract. Thus, an agent is liable on contracts made for an undisclosed principal.

Cahn v. Fisher

H. Richmond Fisher and Francis Smith, two attorneys, ordered three deposition transcripts from Harry Cahn and Conrad Blain, two court reporters. The attorneys did so as part of some litigation work they were performing for two clients. Fisher and Smith did not tell Cahn and Blain that they were acting on their clients' behalf when ordering the transcripts; nor did they specifically identify their clients to the court reporters. Presumably, however, the depositions contained a caption identifying those clients and suggesting that Fisher and Smith were acting in a representative capacity.

After the lawyers placed their order with Cahn and Blain, their clients went bankrupt. Thus, they did not pay the reporters' $579.95 bill for the transcripts. Cahn and Blain then sued Fisher and Smith for this amount. Later, they moved for summary judgment. Included in their summary judgment motion was another court reporter's affidavit stating that it was the "custom and usage" of local court reporters to bill and extend credit to lawyers rather than their clients. The trial court granted the reporters' summary judgment motion, and the lawyers appealed.

Source: 805 P.2d 1040 (Ariz. Ct. App. 1991)

Lankford, Judge

The lawyers argue that agency law protects an agent from liability on a contract entered into on behalf of a disclosed principal. Unless otherwise agreed, a person making or purporting to make a contract with another as agent for a disclosed principal does not become a party to the contract. Disclosure of the principal requires that the agent give the other party both notice that the agent is acting for a principal and the principal's identity. Reasonable inferences can be drawn that the court reporters were aware that the lawyers were ordering the transcripts not for themselves but on behalf of their clients, and that the reporters were aware of the clients' identities. Under these circumstances, agency law precludes a judgment resting on the theory that lawyers are generally liable on a contract with court reporters.

While the lawyers ordinarily would not be bound under agency law to a contract entered into on behalf of their disclosed principals, the parties were certainly free to agree otherwise. In this case, the court reporters attempted to show that "custom and usage" between court reporters and lawyers is that the lawyers are directly liable for the reporters' fees. Court reporters might also be able to establish such liability by proof of a course of dealing between the parties. The lawyers argued below that the affidavit offered by the reporters was insufficient to show custom and usage. However, they abandoned that argument on appeal and we therefore decline to consider the sufficiency of the affidavit. [This] evidence of custom and usage was uncontroverted. It showed that the parties' understanding was that the lawyers would be responsible for paying the reporters. This evidence fully sustains the [trial] court's entry of summary judgment against the lawyers. **Judgment for Cahn and Blain affirmed.**

Nonexistent Principal

In the absence of an agreement to the contrary, an agent who purports to act for a legally nonexistent principal such as an unincorporated association is personally liable. This is true even where the third party knows that the principal is nonexistent.

Principal Lacking Capacity

As stated earlier, a principal who lacks contractual capacity due to insanity or infancy can avoid contracts made by his agent. In this case, the *agent* also escapes liability unless:

(1) she misrepresents the capacity of her principal, or (2) she has reason to believe that the third party is unaware of the principal's incapacity and she fails to disclose this. Also, unless the parties agree otherwise, an agent is liable on contracts made for a *wholly incompetent* principal such as a person who has been adjudicated insane.

Liability of Agent by Agreement

An agent may bind herself on contracts she makes for a principal by *expressly or impliedly agreeing* to be liable. This is true regardless of the principal's nature. An agent may expressly bind herself by: (1) making the contract in her own name rather than in the principal's name, (2) joining the principal as an obliger on the contract, or (3) acting as surety or guarantor for the principal.

Problems of contract interpretation can arise when it is claimed that an agent has expressly promised to be bound. The two most important factors affecting the agent's liability are the wording of the contract and the way the agent has signed it. An agent who wishes to avoid liability should make no express promises in her own name and should try to ensure that the agreement only obligates the principal. In addition, the agent should use a signature form that clearly identifies the principal and indicates the agent's representative capacity—for example, "Parker, by Adkins," or "Adkins, for Parker." Simply adding the word "agent" when signing her name (Adkins, Agent) or signing without any indication of her status (Adkins) could subject the agent to liability. Sometimes, as in the following Wired Music case, the body of the agreement suggests one result and the signature form another. Here, and generally, oral evidence or other extrinsic evidence of the parties' understanding may help resolve the uncertainty.[3]

Wired Music, Inc. v. Great River Steamboat Co.

A sales representative of Wired Music, Inc., sold Frank Pierson, president of the Great River Steamboat Company, a five-year Muzak Program Service for a riverboat and restaurant owned by Great River. Pierson signed a form contract drafted by Wired Music in the following manner:

By /s/ Frank C. Pierson, Pres.

Title

The Great River Steamboat Co.

~~Port of St. Louis Investments, Inc.~~

For the Corporation

In signing, Pierson crossed out "Port of St. Louis Investments, Inc.," which had been incorrectly listed as the name of the corporation, and inserted the proper name. The contract included the following clause arguably making Pierson a surety or guarantor for Great River: "The individual signing this agreement for the subscriber guarantees that all of the above provisions shall be complied with."

Great River made approximately four payments under the contract and then ceased to pay. Wired Music brought an action for contract damages against Pierson personally. The trial court ruled in Pierson's favor, and Wired Music appealed.

Source: 554 S.W.2d 466 (Mo. Ct. App. 1977)

Gunn, Judge

The general rule regarding liability incurred by an individual who signs an instrument on behalf of another party is: where the principal is disclosed and the capacity in which the individual signs is evident, e.g., president, secretary, agent, the liability is the principal's and not that of the individual signing for the principal. Of course, where the circumstances surrounding the transaction disclose a mutual intention to impose personal responsibility on the individual executing the agreement, the individual may be personally liable even though the form of the signature is that of the agent.

The determinative issue here is whether, in view of the form of the signature to the agreement, the language of the so-called guaranty clause is sufficient to manifest a clear and explicit intent by Pierson to assume a personal guaranty contract. We hold that standing alone it does not. The contract language imposing a personal obligation is inconsistent with the form of execution, which positively limited Pierson's participation to his official corporate capacity and not as an individual. Such inconsistency creates at least a latent ambiguity which permits the admission of parol evidence to explain the true intent of the parties.

Pierson has stressed that he neglected to read the contract prior to its signing. One who signs a contract is presumed to have known its contents and accepted its terms. Thus, Pierson's failure to examine the terms of the instrument would afford no defense to the corporation regarding its obligations under the contract, as his signature was sufficient to bind the corporation. Such neglect is a relevant circumstance, however, in ascertaining Pierson's intent to assume personal liability, as his personal signature appeared nowhere on the instrument. Without knowledge of the guaranty clause he could not have possessed the requisite intent to assume obligations under it. The record is destitute of any indication that Pierson was ever made aware of potential personal liability under the guaranty clause, and he steadfastly denied any such knowledge. Wired Music drafted the contract, and its agents procured Pierson's corporate signature without explanation of or bargaining over its terms. Under these circumstances we find that there was an absence of the meeting of the minds as to the nature and the extent of the personal obligations imposed, essential to the formation of a binding guaranty.

Judgment for Pierson affirmed.

Agent's Liability on Unauthorized Contracts

An agent may also become liable to a third party if he contracts for the principal while *lacking authority* to do so. Here, the principal is not bound, and it is arguably unfair to leave the third party without any recovery. Thus, an agent is normally bound on the theory that he made an implied warranty of his authority to contract.[4] This liability exists regardless of whether the agent is otherwise bound to the third party.

To illustrate, suppose that Allen is a salesperson for Prine, a seller of furs. Allen has actual authority to receive offers for the sale of Prine's furs, but not to make contracts of sale, which must be approved by Prine himself. Prine has long followed this practice, and it is customary in the markets where his agents work. Representing himself as Prine's agent but saying nothing about his authority, Allen contracts to sell Prine's furs to Thatcher on Prine's behalf. Thatcher, who should have known better, honestly believes that Allen has authority to contract to sell Prine's furs. Prine is not liable on Allen's contract because Allen lacked actual or apparent authority to bind him. But Allen is liable to Thatcher for breaching his implied warranty of authority.

However, an agent is *not* liable for making an unauthorized contract if:

1.   The third party *actually knows* that the agent lacks authority. However, note from the Allen-Prine example that the agent is still liable where the third party only had *reason to know* that authority was lacking.

2.   The principal subsequently *ratifies* the contract. Here, the principal is bound and the agent is discharged. Because ratification relates back to the time the contract was made, the relation of the parties is the same as if the agent had possessed authority in the first place.
3.   The agent adequately *notifies* the third party that he does not warrant his authority to contract.

Contract Suits Against Principal and Agent

Figure 24-1 sketches the most important situations where the principal, the agent, or both are liable due to the agent's contracts. As it suggests, a third party usually has *someone* to sue if neither the principal nor the agent performs.

FIGURE 24-1
Contract liability of principal and agent: the major possibilities

	Actual	Apparent	None
		Agent's Authority	
Principal	**Actual**	**Apparent**	**None**
Disclosed	P liable; A not liable unless agreement	P liable; A not liable unless agreement	P not liable; A usually liable
Partially Disclosed	P liable; A liable	P liable; A liable	P not liable; A liable
Undisclosed	P liable; A liable	Impossible	P not liable; A liable

Without ratification, a principal is not liable on contracts made by an agent who lacks authority. Here, though, the agent is usually bound under an implied warranty of authority. In addition, the agent is bound on the contract where the principal was partially disclosed, undisclosed, or legally nonexistent.[5] Authorized contracts for a disclosed principal do not bind an agent unless he has agreed to be bound. But here the agent's actual or apparent authority binds the principal.

As Figure 24-1 further illustrates, in certain situations both the principal and the agent are liable on a contract made by the agent. This can occur where an agent with appropriate authority contracts on behalf of a partially disclosed or undisclosed principal. Also, an agent can bind himself by express or implied agreement in situations where the principal is also bound. In such cases, which party is ultimately responsible to the third person? The complicated rules governing this question vary from situation to situation. Due to their complexity and variety, they are beyond the scope of this text.

Tort Liability of the Principal

A principal's liability for her agent's torts involves four distinct subjects, which we consider in turn.[6]

Respondeat Superior Liability

Under the doctrine of ***respondeat superior*** (let the master answer), a principal who is an **employer** is liable for torts committed by agents who are **employees** and who commit the tort while acting within the **scope of their employment**. This doctrine applies to an employee's negligence, recklessness, or intentional torts. The most important of these factors is a principal's right to control the physical details of an agent's work.

Respondeat superior is a rule of *imputed* or *vicarious* liability because it bases an employer's liability on his relationship with the employee rather than his own fault. This imputation of liability reflects the following beliefs: (1) that the economic burdens of employee torts can best be borne by employers; (2) that employers can often protect themselves against such burdens by self-insuring or purchasing insurance; and (3) that the resulting costs can frequently be passed on to consumers, thus "socializing" the economic risk posed by employee torts. *Respondeat superior* also motivates employers to ensure that their employees avoid tortious behavior. Because they typically control the physical details of the work, employers are fairly well positioned to do so.

Scope of Employment

Respondeat superior's scope-of-employment requirement has been stated in many ways and is notoriously ambiguous. In the past, for example, some courts considering this question asked whether the employee was on a "frolic" of his own, or merely made a "detour" from his assigned activity. According to the *Restatement*,[7] an employee's conduct is within the scope of his employment if it meets *each* of the following four tests:

1.   It was of the *kind* that the employee was employed to perform. To meet this test, an employee's conduct need only be of the same general nature as work expressly authorized, or be incidental to its performance. For instance, the following *Gatzke* case treats on-the-job smoking as an act incidental to an employee's authorized work. But an employee hired only to care for his employer's horses is probably not within the scope of employment if he paints the employer's house without the employer's authorization.

     Even criminal conduct may occasionally be within the scope of employment. Here, the test seems to be whether the employer could reasonably anticipate the criminal behavior in question. Thus, a delivery driver who exceeds the speed limit while on a rush job is probably covered, but a driver who shoots another driver after a traffic altercation almost certainly is not.

2.   It occurred substantially within the authorized *time* period. This is simply the employee's assigned time of work. Beyond this, there is an extra period of time during which the employment may continue. For instance, a security guard whose regular quitting time is 5:00 probably meets the time test if he unjustifiably injures an intruder at 5:15. Doing the same thing three hours later, however, would put the guard outside the scope of employment.

3.   It occurred substantially within the *location* authorized by the employer. This includes locations not unreasonably distant from the authorized location. For example, a salesperson told to limit her activities to New York City probably would satisfy the location requirement while pursuing the employer's business in suburbs just outside the city limits but not while pursuing the same business in Philadelphia. Generally, the smaller the authorized area of activity, the smaller the departure from that area needed to put the employee outside the scope of employment. For example, consider the different physical distance limitations that should apply to a factory worker and a traveling salesperson.

4.   It was motivated *at least in part* by the *purpose* of serving the employer. This test is met where the employee's conduct was motivated *to any appreciable extent* by the desire to serve the employer. Thus, an employee's tort may be within the scope of employment even if the motives for committing it were partly personal. For example, suppose that a delivery employee is behind schedule and for that reason has an

accident while speeding to make a delivery in his employer's truck. The employee would be within the scope of employment even if another reason for his speeding was to impress a friend who was riding with him.

In the following *Gatzle* case, all four *Restatement* tests were met and the employer was liable. In applying those tests, was the court influenced by a desire to see the plaintiff recover?

Edgewater Motels, Inc. v. Gatzke

A. J. Gatzke, a district manager for the Walgreen Company, spent several weeks in Duluth, Minnesota, supervising the opening of a new Walgreen restaurant there. He remained at the restaurant approximately 17 hours a day, and he was on call 24 hours a day to handle problems arising in other Walgreen restaurants in the district. While in Duluth, he lived at the Edgewater Motel at Walgreen's expense. After some heavy drinking late one night, Gatzke returned to his motel room and spent some time at a desk filling out an expense account required by his employer. Gatzke was a heavy smoker, and he testified that he probably smoked a cigarette while completing the expense account. Shortly after Gatzke went to bed, a fire broke out in his motel room. Gatzke escaped, but fire damage to the motel totaled over $330,000. An expert witness testified that the fire was caused by a burning cigarette or a match and that it started in or near a wastebasket located beside the desk at which Gatzke worked.

Edgewater sued Walgreen for Gatzke's negligence. The jury found for Edgewater, in the process concluding that Gatzke acted within the scope of his employment when he filled out the form and disposed of the cigarette. The trial court, however, granted Walgreen's motion for judgment notwithstanding the verdict. Edgewater appealed. The question for the appellate court was whether Gatzke's negligent conduct occurred within the scope of his employment.

Source: 277 N.W.2d 11 (Minn. Sup. Ct. 1979)

Scott, Justice

Gatzke's negligent smoking of a cigarette was a direct cause of the damages sustained by Edgewater. The question is whether the facts reasonably support the imposition of vicarious liability on Walgreen's for the conceded negligent act of its employee.

For an employer to be held vicariously liable for an employee's negligent conduct, the employee's wrongful act must be committed within the scope of his employment. To support [such] a finding, it must be shown that his conduct was, to some degree, in furtherance of the interests of his employer. This principle is recognized by *Restatement (Second) of Agency* section 235, which states: "An act of a servant is not within the scope of employment if it is done with no intention to perform it as a part of or incident to a service on account of which he is employed." Other factors to be considered in the scope-of-employment determination are whether the conduct is of the kind that the employee is authorized to perform and whether the act occurs substantially within authorized time and space restrictions.

The question is whether an employee's smoking of a cigarette can constitute conduct within his scope of employment. The courts which have considered the question have not agreed on its resolution. A number of courts have ruled that the act of smoking, even when done simultaneously with work-related activity, is not within the employee's scope of employment because it is a matter personal to the employee which is not done in furtherance of the employer's interest. Other courts have reasoned that the smoking of a cigarette, if done while engaged in the business of the employer, is within an employee's scope of employment because it is a minor deviation from the employee's work-related activities, and thus merely incidental to employment. We agree with this analysis and hold that an employer can be vicariously liable for an employee's negligent smoking of a cigarette if he was otherwise acting in the scope of his employment at the time of the negligent act.

Thus, we must next determine whether Gatzke was otherwise in the scope of his employment at the time of his negligent act. Even assuming that Gatzke was outside the scope of his employment while he was at the bar, Gatzke resumed his employment activities after he returned to his motel room and filled out his expense account. The expense account was completed so that Gatzke could be reimbursed by Walgreen's for his work-related expenses. In this sense, Gatzke is performing an act for his own personal benefit. However, the completion of the expense account also furthers the employer's business in that it provides detailed documentation of business expenses so that they are properly deductible for tax purposes. In this light, the filling out of the expense form can be viewed as serving a dual purpose: that of furthering Gatzke's personal interests and promoting his employer's business purposes. Accordingly, the completion of the expense account is an act done in furtherance of the employer's business purposes.

Additionally, the record indicates that Gatzke was an executive type of employee who had no set working hours. He considered himself a 24-hour-a-day man; his room at the Edgewater Motel was his "office away from home." It [is] therefore reasonable to determine that the filling out of his expense account was done within authorized time and space limits of his employment.
Judgment reversed in favor of Edgewater.

Direct Liability

As the following *Victory Tabernacle* case makes clear, a principal's **direct liability** for an agent's torts differs considerably from *respondeat superior* liability. Here, the principal *himself* is at fault, and there is no need to impute liability to him. Also, no scope-of-employment requirement exists in direct liability cases, and the agent need not be an employee. Of course, a principal might incur both direct liability and *respondeat superior* liability in cases where due to the principal's fault, an employee commits a tort within the scope of her employment.

A principal is directly liable for an agent's tortious conduct if the principal *directs* that conduct and *intends* that it occur. In such cases, the *agent's* behavior might be intentional, reckless, or negligent. For instance, if Petty tells his agent Able to beat up Tabler and Able does so, Petty is directly liable to Tabler. Petty also would be liable for harm to third parties that results from his telling Able to do construction work in a negligent, substandard fashion.

The typical direct liability case, however, involves harm caused by the principal's *negligence* regarding the agent. Examples of direct liability for negligence include: (1) giving the agent improper or unclear instructions; (2) failing to make and enforce appropriate regulations to govern the agent's conduct; (3) hiring an unsuitable agent; (4) failing to discharge an unsuitable agent; (5) furnishing an agent with improper tools, instruments, or materials; and (6) carelessly supervising an agent.

J. v. Victory Tabernacle Baptist Church

A woman sued the Victory Tabernacle Baptist Church, alleging that due to its negligence her 10-year-old daughter had been repeatedly raped and sexually assaulted by a church employee. The plaintiff's complaint claimed that when the church hired the employee, it knew or should have known that he had recently been convicted of aggravated sexual assault on a young girl, that he was on probation for this offense, and that a condition of his probation was that he not be involved with children. Despite all this, the complaint continued, the employee's

duties allowed him to freely come into contact with children, including the plaintiff's daughter, and he was given keys enabling him to lock and unlock all the church's doors.

The complaint alleged (among other things) negligent hiring on the church's part. The church filed a demurrer to the complaint, and the trial court sustained the demurrer. The plaintiff appealed this decision, and the case reached the Virginia Supreme Court.

Source: 372 S.E.2d 391 (Va. Sup. Ct. 1988)

Thomas, Justice

We decide only whether the allegations of negligent hiring state a cause of action in Virginia. Victory Baptist argues that the trial court properly sustained the demurrer on [this] question because plaintiff failed to allege that the harm to the victim was caused by negligence on the part of the employee. According to this argument, the negligent hiring cause of action requires that the negligently hired individual negligently injured the plaintiff. We disagree. The very thing that allegedly should have been foreseen in this case is that the employee would commit a violent act upon a child. To say that a negligently hired employee who acts willfully or criminally thus relieves his employer of liability for negligent hiring when willful or criminal conduct is precisely what the employer should have foreseen would rob the tort of vitality.

Victory Baptist also argues that the [plaintiff's] allegations do not establish a sufficient nexus among the employer's breach of duty, the employee's conduct, and the employee's employment. In oral argument, counsel explained that there were no allegations that the employee was engaged in the church's business when the child was injured—no allegation, for example, that the employee was on duty for the church at the time the girl was raped. Counsel then made clear that what he was complaining about was that there were no allegations to bring the employee's conduct within the scope of his employment.

This argument demonstrates that Victory Baptist is confusing the doctrine of *respondeat superior* with the tort of negligent hiring. This distinction was succinctly stated in a recent law review article:

> Under respondeat superior, an employer is vicariously liable for an employee's tortious acts committed within the scope of employment. In contrast, negligent hiring is a doctrine of primary liability; the employer is principally liable for negligently placing an unfit person in an employment situation involving an unreasonable risk of harm to others. Negligent hiring, therefore, enables plaintiffs to recover in situations where respondeat superior's scope of employment limitation previously protected employers from liability.

Thus, Victory Baptist's contention is misplaced.

In our opinion, the [complaint] was fully sufficient to state a claim of negligent hiring, and thus it was error for the trial court to sustain the demurrer on that issue.

Judgment for the church on the negligent hiring claim reversed. Case remanded for trial consistent with the Supreme Court's opinion.

Liability for Torts of Independent Contractors

A principal ordinarily is *not* liable for torts committed by **independent contractors**. As compared with employees, independent contractors are more likely to have the size and resources to insure against tort liability and to pass on the resulting costs themselves. Sometimes, therefore, the risk can still be socialized if only the independent contractor is held responsible. Because the principal does not control the manner in which an independent contractor's work is performed, moreover, he has less ability to prevent a contractor's torts than an employer has to prevent an employee's torts. Thus, imposing liability on principals for the torts of independent contractors may do little to eliminate the contractor's torts.

However, the rule that principals are not liable for torts committed by independent contractors has exceptions. For example:

1. A principal can be *directly* liable for tortious behavior connected with the retention of an independent contractor. One example is the hiring of a dangerously incompetent independent contractor.
2. A principal is liable for harm resulting from the independent contractor's failure to perform a *nondelegable duty.* A nondelegable duty is a duty whose proper performance is so important that a principal cannot avoid liability by contracting it away. Examples include a carrier's duty to transport its passengers safely, a municipality's duty to keep its streets in repair, a railroad's duty to maintain safe crossings, and a landlord's duties to make repairs and to use care in doing so. Thus, a landlord who retains an independent contractor to repair the stairs in an apartment building is liable for injuries caused by the contractor's failure to repair the stairs properly.
3. A principal is liable for an independent contractor's negligent failure to take the special precautions needed to conduct certain *highly dangerous* or *inherently dangerous* activities.[8] Examples of such activities include excavations in publicly traveled areas, the clearing of land by fire, the construction of a dam, and the demolition of a building. For example, a contractor engaged in demolishing a building presumably has duties to warn pedestrians and to keep them at a safe distance. If injury results from the independent contractor's failure to meet these duties, the principal is liable.

Liability for Agent's Misrepresentations

A principal's liability for misrepresentations made by agents to third parties involves both contract and tort principles.[9] A principal is *directly* liable for misrepresentations made by her agent during authorized transactions if she *intended* that the agent make the misrepresentations. In some states, a principal may also be directly liable if she *negligently* allows the agent to make misrepresentations.

Even where a principal is not directly at fault, she may be liable for an agent's misrepresentations if the agent had *actual or apparent authority to make true statements on the subject.* Suppose that an agent to sell farmland falsely states that a stream on the land has never flooded the property when in fact it does so almost every year, and that this statement induces a third party to buy the land. The principal is directly liable if she intended that the agent make this false statement. Even if the principal is personally blameless, she is liable if the agent had actual or apparent authority to make true statements about the spring.

If the agent intended to make the misrepresentation, or if the principal intended that the agent make it, the third party can recover in tort for the losses that result. In some states, a third party may also recover in tort for misrepresentations resulting from the principal's or the agent's negligence. In either case, the third party can elect to rescind the transaction instead of pursuing a tort suit.

Exculpatory Clauses

Both honest and dishonest principals may try to escape liability for an agent's misrepresentations by including an exculpatory clause in contracts the agent makes with third parties. Such clauses typically state that the agent only has authority to make the representations contained in the contract and that only those representations bind the principal. Exculpatory clauses do not protect a principal who intends or expects that an agent will make false statements. Otherwise, though, they insulate the principal from *tort* liability if the agent misrepresents. But the third party still may *rescind* the transaction, because it would be unjust to let the principal benefit from the transaction while disclaiming responsibility for it.

Concept Review
An Outline of the Principal's Tort Liability

Respondeat Superior	1. Agent must be an employee, *and* 2. Employee must act within scope of employment while committing tort
Direct Liability	1. Principal intends and directs agent's intentional tort, recklessness, or negligence, *or* 2. Principal is negligent regarding agent
Torts of Independent Contractors	1. Principal generally is *not* liable 2. Exceptions for direct liability, highly dangerous activities, and nondelegable duties
Misrepresentation	1. Direct liability 2. Vicarious liability where agent had authority to make true statements on the subject of the misrepresentation 3. An exculpatory clause may eliminate the principal's tort liability, but the third party still can rescind
Torts of Subagents	The preceding rules govern the principal's liability, but their application varies

Tort Liability of the Agent

Agents are usually liable for their own torts.[10] Normally, they are not absolved from liability just because they acted at the principal's command. However, there are exceptions to this generalization.

1. An agent can escape liability if she is *exercising a privilege of the principal.* Suppose that Tingle grants Parkham a right-of-way to transport his farm products over a private road crossing Tingle's land. Parkham's agent Adams would not be liable in trespass for driving across Tingle's land to transport farm products if she did so at Parkham's command. However, an agent must not exceed the scope of the privilege and must act for the purpose for which the privilege was given. Thus, Adams would not be protected if she took her Jeep on a midnight joyride across Tingle's land. Also, the privilege given the agent must be delegable in the first place. If Tingle had given the easement to Parkham exclusively, Adams would not be privileged to drive across Tingle's land.

2. A principal who is *privileged to take certain actions in defense of his person or property* may often authorize an agent to do the same. In such cases, the agent escapes liability if the principal could have done so. For example, a properly authorized agent may use force to protect the life or property of his principal if the principal could have done the same.

3. An agent who makes *misrepresentations* while conducting the principal's business is not liable in tort unless he either *knew or had reason to know* their falsity. Suppose Parker authorizes Arnold to sell his house, falsely telling Arnold that the house is fully insulated. Arnold does not know that the statement is false, and could not discover its falsity through a reasonable inspection. If Arnold tells Thomas that the house is fully insulated and Thomas relies on this statement in purchasing the house, Parker is directly liable to Thomas, but Arnold is not liable.

4. An agent is not liable for injuries to third persons caused by *defective tools or instrumentalities* furnished by the principal unless the agent had actual knowledge or reason to know of the defect.

Tort Suits Against Principal and Agent

Both principal and agent are sometimes liable for an agent's torts. Here, the parties are *jointly and severally* liable. This means that a third party may join the principal and the agent in one suit and get a judgment against each, or may sue either or both individually and get a judgment against either or both. However, once a third party actually collects in full from either the principal or the agent, no further recovery is possible.

In some cases, therefore, either the principal or the agent has to satisfy the judgment alone despite the other party's liability. Here, the other party is sometimes required to *indemnify* the party who has satisfied the judgment. For example, sometimes a principal is required to indemnify an agent for tort liability the agent incurs. On the other hand, some torts committed by agents may involve a breach of duty to their principal, and the principal may be able to recover from an agent on this basis.

Ethical and Public Policy Concerns

1. One of the justifications for *respondeat superior* is that employers are in a relatively good position to absorb the liability of employee torts, to insure against such liability, and to pass on the resulting costs. What are the advantages and disadvantages of applying this reasoning to make principals liable for all torts committed by *independent contractors* within the scope of their employment?

2. If the purposes underlying *respondeat superior* are sound ones, why limit the doctrine to employee torts committed within the scope of employment? In other words, why not make employers liable for *all* torts committed by their employees?

3. Agents who make unauthorized contracts are not liable if the principal later ratifies the contract. The official justification for this rule is that, because ratification relates back to the time the unauthorized contract was made, the relations of the parties are the same as if the agent had originally had authority. However, there is another, much more down-to-earth, justification for this rule. What is it?

Problems and Problem Cases

1. The Capital Dredge and Dock Corporation sued the city of Detroit for damages associated with certain construction work it had been performing for the city. One of the city's defenses was that Capital had released the city from liability on some of Capital's present claims during earlier, related litigation between Capital and the city. The releases were part of a settlement document signed by Capital Dredge's attorney, Alteri. Capital Dredge had held Alteri out as having authority to represent it in the relevant litigation, and this included authority to negotiate a settlement. However, unknown to the city, Capital Dredge had also specifically told Alteri not to compromise some of the claims he later settled. Under these circumstances, could Alteri have had implied authority to settle the claims in question? Could he have had apparent authority to do so?

2. Jeff Hartman, a hauler of hay, contracted to purchase Larry Draper's entire 1988 alfalfa hay crop. According to that contract, Hartman had to pay in advance for any hay taken from Draper's farm. Later, Hartman approached Cecil Hilt about buying some of the hay crop Hartman had purchased. Hartman told Hilt that the hay was from Draper's farm, but he did not say that he was acting as Draper's agent. Nonetheless, Hilt believed that Hartman was acting on Draper's behalf. On July 5, 1988, Hilt agreed to buy 400 tons of hay at $60 per ton. As part of the deal, he wrote a $3,000 check payable to Draper as a deposit. Hartman then gave the check to Draper, who indorsed and cashed it.

   Much later, Hartman found himself unable to produce the money needed to get Hilt's hay from Draper. Draper eventually sold the hay to another party, and Hilt sued Draper for breach of contract. Assuming for the sake of argument that Hartman was Draper's agent, did Hartman have apparent authority to bind Draper to the deal with Hilt?

3. Roma Funk, who co-owned a piece of land along with her seven brothers and sisters, contracted to sell the land to her neighbors. It was unclear whether Funk had authority to sell the land on behalf of her siblings. For certain, there was no writing giving her such authority. Funk's siblings eventually backed out of the deal, and the buyers sued for specific performance. They argued that Funk's siblings had ratified her contract by failing to come forward and repudiate it. Can a contract ever be ratified in this way? Regardless of your answer to this question, there is another reason why Funk's siblings could not have ratified this particular contract. What is it? Assume that in this state an agent who executes an agreement conveying an interest in land on behalf of his principal must be authorized in writing.

4. Seascape Restaurants, Inc., operated a restaurant called The Magic Moment. Jeff Rosenberg was one-third owner and president of Seascape. Van D. Costas, the president of Van D. Costas, Inc., contracted to construct a "magical entrance" to the Magic Moment. Jeff Rosenberg signed the contract on a line under which appeared the words "Jeff Rosenberg, the Magic Moment." The contract did not refer to Seascape, and Costas knew nothing of Seascape's existence. After a dispute over performance of the contract, Costas sued Rosenberg for breach of contract. Is Rosenberg personally liable to Costas?

5. Dale F. Everett did business as the Dale F. Everett Company, Inc. (the Company). He also formed a retail business known as The Clubhouse, which had no legal status aside from its registration as a trade name for the Company. Everett contracted with James Smith for $8,424 of advertising time. Everett signed his contract with Smith as follows: "THE CLUBHOUSE, Client, By Dale F. Everett." Smith later sent billing

statements for the ads to "The Clubhouse, Inc." Everett never paid Smith the $8,424, and Smith sued Everett personally. Is Everett personally liable on the contract with Smith?

6.   Mr. Martin, the president of Martin Manufacturing, was talking with Arnold, a new traveling salesman, about Arnold's first week on the road. Arnold told Martin that he hit one of Martin's customers in the customer's store, causing the customer some physical harm. The blow came after Arnold and the customer got into an argument, during which the customer ordered Arnold out of his store. In striking the customer, Arnold was motivated at least in part by a feeling that no Martin employee should have to endure such disrespect.

Shortly after this, Martin also learned from Arnold that Arnold had gotten into an accident while driving a company van. The accident came after Arnold negligently ran a stop sign while thinking about the fight. The driver of the other car was seriously injured in the accident.

Assuming that Arnold is an employee, is Martin liable to the customer for any battery Arnold committed, and to the driver of the car for Arnold's negligence?

7.   Redford had been a backhoe operator for five years. Although he had worked for other sign companies, he had spent 90 percent of his time during the past three years working for Tube Art Display, Inc. Redford generally dug holes exactly as directed by the sign company employing him. He did, however, pay his own business taxes, and he did not participate in any of the fringe benefits available to Tube Art employees.

Tube Art obtained a permit to install a sign in the parking lot of a combination commercial and apartment building. Telling Redford how to proceed, Tube Art's service manager laid out the exact location of a 4 × 4-foot square on the asphalt surface with yellow paint and directed that the hole be 6 feet deep. After Redford began the job, he struck a small natural gas pipeline with the backhoe. He examined the pipe, and, finding no indication of a leak or break, concluded that the line was not in use and left the worksite. Later, an explosion and fire occurred in the building serviced by the line. As a result, a business owned by Massey was destroyed. Massey sued Tube Art for Redford's negligence under the doctrine of respondeat superior. Will Massey recover? Assume that Redford was negligent.

8.   John Hondzinski delivered newspapers in his own car for a newspaper called the News Herald. Under the contract between Hondzinski and the News Herald, Hondzinski was obligated to pick up and promptly deliver newspapers provided by the News Herald, but the means and the routes for doing so were within Hondzinski's control. While making deliveries for the News Herald one day, Hondzinski negligently allowed his car to collide with a car driven by Peter Janice. Janice sued the News Herald for Hondzinski's negligence. Can Janice recover against the News Herald under the doctrine of respondeat superior? Why or why not?

9.   William Smith was employed by P&M Heating and Air Conditioning, Inc., as a service technician. Smith normally worked a 40-hour week. P&M provided Smith with a service van containing the tools he used in his work. P&M allowed Smith to drive his van home after work, keep it there overnight, call in to P&M to receive his first job assignment each morning, and travel to that assignment in the van.

On July 23, 1986, Smith worked a normal eight-hour day, finishing at 4:00 P.M. After Smith drove the van home and had dinner, his stepdaughter called to tell him that she was having problems with her home air-conditioning unit. As a favor to his stepdaughter, Smith, accompanied by his wife, drove the van to the stepdaughter's home to check out the unit. He did not tell P&M about this work, he did not fill out a customer receipt or any other paperwork for it, and P&M apparently never billed his stepdaughter for it. Smith finished working on his stepdaughter's unit about

10:45 P.M. After that, he took a swim in her pool. About midnight, Smith and his wife left for home. At about 1:00 A.M., the P&M van driven by Smith collided with a vehicle driven by Anthony S. Giannoble, killing Giannoble.

Assuming that the collision was due to Smith's negligence, is P&M liable to Giannoble's estate for that negligence? Assume that Smith was an employee of P&M.

10. Susie Mae Woodson's husband was killed due to a cave-in at a construction site where he was laying sewer pipe in a trench dug by an independent contractor of Davidson & Jones, Inc. (D&J). The trench in which Mr. Woodson was working had not been braced or shored to prevent a cave-in, and this was a violation of federal occupational safety regulations. Mrs. Woodson sued D&J for the independent contractor's negligence. Will she recover? Assume that D&J was not in any way directly liable regarding the independent contractor.

11. Edward J. Opatz maintained an investment account with John G. Kinnard and Company. Byron Jensen, a Kinnard broker, handled Opatz's account. In January 1985, Jensen told Opatz that he would buy three fourths of a $24,000 investment unit if Opatz would buy the remaining fourth. Relying on this statement and believing that the transaction was within Jensen's authority, Opatz gave Jensen a $6,000 check payable to Jensen. One week later, Jensen admitted to Opatz that he had never purchased the unit, and gave Opatz a personal check for $6,000. Still later, the check bounced and Jensen disappeared. Is Kinnard liable to Opatz for the $6,000? Assume that: (1) Jensen's statement that he would invest the $6,000 was actionable fraud, (2) Kinnard was not directly liable for Jensen's behavior, and (3) Kinnard did not expressly or impliedly authorize Jensen's statements to Opatz.

Endnotes

1. Unilateral mistake is discussed in Chapter 19.
2. The rules stated here should generally govern the contract liability of subagents as well as agents. See *Restatement (Second) of Agency* § 361 (1959).
3. However, the introduction of such evidence may be blocked by the parol evidence rule. See Chapter 20.
4. An agent who intentionally misrepresents his authority also may be liable to the third party in tort. In addition, some states may allow tort liability for negligent misrepresentations. Where the third party has a tort suit, he may often elect to recover damages or to rescind the contract.
5. Note, however, that it is impossible for an agent for an undisclosed principal to have apparent authority. Apparent authority exists when the principal's communications to the third party cause that party to reasonably believe that the agent has authority to contract for another. How can this occur when the principal is undisclosed?
6. In addition to the various forms of tort liability discussed in this section, a principal can also *ratify* an agent's torts. Furthermore, the *Restatement* says that the rules governing a principals liability for an agents torts generally control a principal's liability for the torts of *subagents*. *Restatement (Second) of Agency* § 255 (1959).
7. *Restatement (Second) of Agency* § 228(1) (1959). This section adds that if an employee intentionally uses force on another, this must have been "not unexpectable" by the employer to be within the scope of employment.
8. The range of activities considered "highly dangerous" or "inherently dangerous" is probably greater than the range of activities considered "ultrahazardous" or "abnormally dangerous" for strict liability purposes. On the latter activities, see Chapter 23.
9. On fraud and misrepresentation in the tort and contract contexts, see Chapters 19 and 22.
10. The rules stated in the previous section generally govern an agents liability for torts committed by his subagents. *Restatement (Second) of Agency* § 362 (1959).

Chapter Twenty-Five

UNFAIR COMPETITION

Introduction

This chapter discusses certain legal rules that limit free competition by allowing civil recoveries for abuses of that freedom. These abuses are: (1) patent, copyright, and trademark infringement; (2) the misappropriation of trade secrets; (3) the intentional torts of injurious falsehood, interference with contractual relations, and interference with prospective advantage; and (4) the many forms of unfair competition attacked by section 43(a) of the Lanham Act. Indeed, the term unfair competition describes the whole chapter. In general, competition is deemed unfair because: (1) it discourages creative endeavor by robbing creative people of the fruits of their innovations, or (2) it renders commercial life too uncivilized and indecent for the law to tolerate.

Patent, Copyright, and Trademark Infringement

Patents

A patent can be regarded as an agreement between an inventor and the federal government. Under that agreement, the inventor gets the exclusive right to make, use, and sell his invention, in return for making the invention public by giving the government certain information about it. The patent holder's (or **patentee's**) monopoly encourages the creation and disclosure of inventions by stopping third parties from appropriating them once they become public. However, third parties may develop the invention in ways that do not interfere with the patentee's rights.

What Is Patentable?

An inventor may patent: (1) a *process* (as described in the following *Diamond* case), (2) a *machine*, (3) a *manufacture* or product, (4) a *composition of matter* (a combination of elements with qualities not present in the elements taken individually, such as a new chemical compound), (5) an *improvement* of any of the above, (6) an *ornamental design* for a product, and (7) a *plant* produced by asexual reproduction. Naturally occurring things (e.g., a new wild plant) and new business methods (e.g., an innovative accounting technique) are not patentable. In addition, as *Diamond* states, abstract ideas, scientific laws, and other mental concepts are not patentable, although their practical applications often are. As *Diamond* also reveals, a computer program may be patentable if it is part of a patentable process. However, it is unclear whether a program that stands alone and that is not part of a patentable process is patentable.[1]

Even though an invention fits within one of the above categories, it is not patentable if it lacks novelty, is obvious, has no utility, was not created by the patent applicant, or was abandoned by him.[2] One example of the *novelty* requirement is the rule that no patent should be issued where *before the invention's creation* it has been: (1) known or used in the United States, (2) patented in the United States or a foreign country, or (3) described in a printed publication in the United States or a foreign country. Another example is the requirement that no patent should be issued if more than one year before the *patent application* the invention was: (1) patented in the United States or a foreign country, (2) described in a printed publication in the United States or a foreign country, or (3) in public use or on sale in the United States. Also there can be no patent if the invention would have been *obvious* to a person having ordinary skill in the area. Furthermore, a patentable invention must have *utility*, or usefulness. Finally, there can be no patent if the party seeking it did not create the invention in question, or if she abandoned the invention. *Creation* problems frequently arise where several people allegedly contributed to the invention. *Abandonment* can be by express statement, such as publicly devoting an invention to humanity, or by implication from conduct, such as delaying for an unreasonable length of time before making a patent application.

Obtaining a Patent

The Patent and Trademark Office of the Department of Commerce handles patent applications. The application must include a *specification* describing the invention with sufficient detail and clarity to enable any person skilled in the area to make and use it. The application must also contain a drawing where this is necessary for understanding the subject matter to be patented. The Patent Office then determines whether the invention meets the various tests for patentability. If the application is rejected, the applicant may resubmit it. Once any of the applicant's claims has been twice rejected, the applicant may appeal to the Office's Board of Patent Appeals and Interferences. Subsequent appeals to the federal courts also are possible.

Diamond v. Diehr

Diehr and Lutton attempted to obtain a patent covering a process for molding raw, uncured synthetic rubber into cured precision products. The process used a mold for shaping the uncured rubber under heat and pressure and then curing it in the mold. Previous efforts at curing and molding synthetic rubber had suffered from an inability to measure the temperature inside the molding press and thus to determine a precise curing time. Diehr and Lutton's invention involved a process for constantly measuring the temperature inside the mold, feeding this information to a computer that constantly recalculated the curing time, and enabling the computer to signal the molding press to open at the correct instant.

The patent examiner rejected Diehr and Lutton's patent application. The Patent and Trademark Office Board of Appeals (now the Board of Patent Appeals and Interferences) agreed with the examiner, but the now-defunct Court of Customs and Patent Appeals reversed. The patent office appealed to the U.S. Supreme Court.

Source: 450 U.S. 175 (U.S. Sup. Ct. 1981)

Rehnquist, Justice

In defining the nature of a patentable process, this Court has stated:

A process is a mode of treatment of certain materials to produce a given result. It is an act, or a series of acts, performed upon the subject matter to be transformed and reduced to a different state or thing. If new and useful, it is just as patentable as is a piece of machinery. The machinery pointed out as suitable to perform the process may or may not be new or patentable; whilst the process itself may be altogether new and produce an entirely new result.

Recently, we repeated the above definition, adding:

Transformation and reduction of an article to a different state or thing is the clue to the patentability of a process claim that does not include particular machines.

That Diehr and Lutton's claims involve the transformation of an article, raw uncured synthetic rubber, into a different state or thing cannot be disputed. Industrial processes such as this have historically been eligible to receive the protection of our patent laws.

Excluded from patent protection are laws of nature, physical phenomena, and abstract ideas. Only last Term, we explained:

A new mineral discovered in the earth or a new plant found in the wild is not patentable subject matter. Likewise, Einstein could not patent his celebrated law that $E = mc^2$; nor could Newton have patented the law of gravity. Such discoveries are manifestations of nature, free to all men and reserved exclusively to none.

Diehr and Lutton do not seek to patent a mathematical formula. Instead, they seek patent protection for a process of curing synthetic rubber. Their process employs a well-known mathematical equation, but they do not seek to preempt the use of that equation. They seek only to foreclose from others the use of that equation in conjunction with all the other steps in their process. It is now a commonplace that an *application* of a law of nature or mathematical formula to a known structure or process may be deserving of patent protection.

It may later be determined that the process is not deserving of patent protection because it fails to satisfy the statutory conditions of novelty or nonobviousness. A rejection on either of these grounds does not affect the determination that Diehr and Lutton's claims recited subject matter which was eligible for patent protection.
Judgment for Diehr and Lutton affirmed.

Ownership and Transfer of Patent Rights

A patent normally gives the patentee exclusive rights to make, use, and sell the patented invention for a 17-year period. Design patents, however, extend for only 14 years. The patentee can transfer title to all or part of his patent rights by *assigning* them, or may retain title and *license* them.

Usually, the party who created the invention is the patent holder. But what happens when the creator of the invention is an employee and her employer seeks rights in her invention? If the invention was developed by an employee *hired to do inventive or creative work*, she must use the invention solely for the employer's benefit and must assign any patents she obtains to the employer. But if the employee was hired for purposes *other than invention or creation*, she owns any patent she acquires. Regardless of the purpose for which the employee was hired, finally, the *shop right* doctrine gives the employer a nonexclusive, royalty-free *license* to use the employee's invention if it was created on company time and through company facilities. Any patent the employee might retain is still effective against parties other than the employer.

Patent Infringement

A *direct* patent infringement occurs when a party makes, uses, or sells a patented invention without the patentee's authorization. It is easy to establish a direct infringement where the subject matter made, used, or sold clearly is within the language of a successful patent application. Courts also find direct infringement where this subject matter is *substantially equivalent* to the protected invention. Here, the test is whether the alleged offender's subject matter performs substantially the same function as the protected invention in substantially the same way to produce substantially the same result.

Also, one who *actively induces* another's infringement of a patent is liable as an infringer if he knows and intends that the infringement occur. For example, if Isaac directly infringes Pinder's patent on a machine and Dailey knowingly sells Isaac an instruction manual for the machine, Daily may be liable as an infringer. Finally, if one knowingly sells a direct patent infringer a component of a patented invention or something useful in employing a patented process, the seller may be liable for *contributory infringement*. Here, the thing sold must be a material part of the invention and must not be a staple article of commerce with some other significant use. For example, suppose that Ireland directly infringes Potter's patent for a radio by selling virtually identical radios. If Davis sells Ireland sophisticated circuitry for the radios with knowledge of Ireland's infringement, Davis may be liable for contributory infringement if the circuitry is an important component of the radios and has no other significant uses.

The basic recovery for patent infringement is damages adequate to compensate for the infringement, plus court costs and interest. The damages cannot be less than a reasonable royalty for the use made of the invention by the infringer. Also, the court may in its discretion award damages of up to three times those actually suffered. Finally, injunctive relief is sometimes available, and attorney's fees may be awarded in exceptional cases.

Defenses to Patent Infringement

One defense to a patent infringement suit is that the subject matter of the alleged infringement is neither within the literal scope of the patent nor substantially equivalent to the patented invention. Also, the alleged infringer may defend by attacking the validity of the patent. Despite their approval by the Patent and Trademark Office, many patents are declared invalid when challenged in court.

Further, the defendant can sometimes assert that the patentee has committed *patent misuse*. This is behavior that unjustifiably exploits the patent monopoly. For example, the patentee may require the purchaser of a license on his patent to buy his unpatented goods, or may tie the obtaining of a license on one of his patented inventions to the purchase of a license on another.[3] One who refuses the patentee's terms and later infringes the patent may escape liability by arguing that the patentee misused his monopoly position.

Copyrights

Copyright law gives creative people certain exclusive rights to their intellectual endeavors. Thus, it prevents others from using their work, gives them an incentive to innovate, and thereby benefits society. But copyright law also tries to balance these purposes against the equally compelling public interest in the free movement of ideas, information, and commerce. It does so mainly by limiting the intellectual products it protects and by allowing the fair use defense described later.

Coverage

Federal copyright law protects a wide range of creative works, including books, periodical articles, dramatic and musical compositions, works of art, motion pictures, sound recordings, lectures, computer programs, and architectural plans. To merit copyright protection, such works must be *fixed*—set out in a tangible medium of expression from which they can be perceived, reproduced, or communicated. They also must be *original* (the author's own work), but unlike the inventions protected by patent law, they need not be novel.

Copyright protection does not extend to ideas, procedures, processes, systems, methods of operation, concepts, principles, or discoveries *as such*. However, it may protect the *form in which they are expressed*. The story line of a play, for instance, probably is protected, but the ideas, themes, or messages underlying it probably are not. Although there is no copyright in facts as such, nonfiction works and compilations of fact are protectible if their creation involved originality. The following *Narell* case discusses the protection of phrases and expressions within a copyrighted work.

Computer programs involve their own special problems. It is fairly well settled that copyright law protects a program's *object code* (program instructions that are machine-readable but not intelligible to humans) and *source code* (instructions intelligible to humans). But there is less agreement about the copyrightability of a program's nonliteral elements such as its organization, its structure, and its presentation of information on the screen. Most of the courts that have considered the issue hold that nonliteral elements can be protected by copyright law, but courts differ about the extent of this protection.

Creation and Notice

A copyright comes into existence upon the creation and fixing of a protected work. For works created in 1978 and thereafter, the copyright usually lasts for *the life of the author plus 70 years*. Although a copyright owner may register the copyright with the Copyright Office of the Library of Congress, registration is not necessary for the copyright to exist. However, registration often *is* necessary before the owner can begin a suit for copyright infringement.

Even though it is not required, copyright owners often provide *notice* of the copyright. Federal law authorizes various forms of notice for different copyrighted works. A book, for example, might include the term *Copyright*, the year of its first publication, and the name of the copyright owner in a location likely to give reasonable notice to readers.

Ownership Rights

A copyright owner has exclusive rights to: (1) reproduce the copyrighted work, (2) prepare derivative works based on it (e.g., a movie version of a novel), (3) distribute copies of the work by sale or otherwise, and (4) perform or display it publicly. Copyright ownership initially resides in the creator of the copyrighted work, but the copyright may be transferred to another party. Also, the owner may individually transfer each of the listed rights, or a portion of each, without losing ownership of the remaining rights. Most transfers of copyright ownership require a writing signed by the owner or his agent. The owner may also retain ownership while licensing the copyrighted work or a portion of it.

Infringement

Those who violate any of the copyright owner's exclusive rights may be liable for *copyright infringement*. Infringement is easily proven where direct evidence of copying exists;

verbatim copying of protected material is an example. But as *Narell* states, infringement usually is proven by showing that the defendant had *access* to the copyrighted work and that there is *substantial similarity* between that work and the allegedly infringing work. Access can be proven circumstantially—for example, by wide circulation of the copyrighted work. Determining substantial similarity necessarily involves discretionary case-by-case judgments.

The basic recovery for copyright infringement is the owner's actual damages plus the profits received by the infringer. However, the plaintiff may elect to receive statutory damages—which fall within certain defined ranges—in lieu of the basic remedy. Injunctive relief, awards of costs and attorney's fees, and criminal penalties are possible in certain cases.

The Fair Use Defense

The fair use defense to a copyright infringement suit requires the weighing of several factors whose application varies from case to case. These factors are: (1) the purpose and character of the use, (2) the nature of the copyrighted work, (3) the amount and substantiality of the portion used in relation to the copyrighted work as a whole, and (4) the effect of the use on the potential market for the copyrighted work or on its value. *Narell* discusses and applies these factors.

Narell v. Freeman

Irena Narell wrote a social history of the Bay Area Jewish community entitled *Our City: The Jews of San Francisco*. After its publication in 1981, her book sold fewer than 5,000 copies. In 1986, Narell repurchased the copyright and the remaining inventory from the publisher.

Illusions of Love, a novel by Cynthia Freeman, was published in hardcover in 1984 and in paperback in 1986, selling approximately 1 million copies. *Illusions* told a fictional story about the heir of a large, wealthy Jewish family who had to choose between his family and a lover from a vastly different background. Freeman consulted and used *Our City* in writing *Illusions*, and portions of *Illusions* were based on historical events described in *Our City*. Also, *Illusions* contained several instances of verbatim copying from *Our City*; these totaled about 300 words. On several more occasions, Freeman paraphrased passages from Narell's book.

Narell sued Freeman and her publishers for copyright infringement in federal district court. The court granted the defendants' motion for summary judgment and Narell appealed.

Source: 872 F.2d 907 (9th Cir. 1989)

Farris, Circuit Judge

To establish a successful copyright infringement claim, Narell must show that she owns the copyright and that Freeman copied protected elements of the work. Because in most copyright cases direct evidence of copying is not available, a plaintiff may establish copying by showing that the infringer had access to the work and that the two works are substantially similar. Narell's ownership of the copyright and Freeman's access to Narell's work are not in dispute.

The [first] question is whether Freeman's admitted takings—several instances of identical phrases and the more numerous paraphrases—were of protected material. Copyright law protects only an author's expression. Facts and ideas within a work are not protected. Freeman largely took unprotected factual information from *Our City*.

Freeman did copy a few phrases from Narell. Ordinary phrases [and] phrases and expressions conveying an idea typically expressed in a limited number of stereotyped fashions are not subject to copyright protection. Most of the phrases Freeman copied are commonly-used expressions, such as describing a muddy street as a "cow path." The appropriation of expressive elements is minimal. The more numerous paraphrasings cited by Narell [also] cannot be said to take the expressive elements of her work. Instead, unprotected factual details are taken, although in some cases commonly-used expressions are echoed, such as "mosquitos ravished his flesh" versus "mosquitos feasted on his flesh." Freeman's borrowings did not take a sequence of creative expression, as opposed to an ordinary phrase, and therefore were not infringing.

The arguments of the parties and the decision of the district court focused on the issues of substantial similarity and fair use. Viewed as a whole, the two works have slight resemblance to each other. *Illusions* is a romantic novel. *Our City* is a historical treatment of the Bay Area Jewish community. The similarities between the two works are neither quantitatively nor qualitatively significant. Quantitatively insignificant infringement may be substantial only if the material is qualitatively important to either work. The passages at issue are a small part of Narell's book. The material taken is not qualitatively important to either book. Because of the fundamental differences between the works and the insubstantial nature of the copied passages, no reasonable reader could conclude that the works are substantially similar.

The doctrine of fair use allows [one] to use copyrighted material in a reasonable manner without the consent of the copyright owner. The copyright act sets out four factors for evaluating whether a use is a fair use.

Purpose and Character of the Use—The first factor strongly weighs against Freeman, because commercial use of copyrighted material is presumptively unfair. Freeman's use is admittedly commercial.

Nature of the Copyrighted Work—The scope of permissible fair use is greater with an informational work than a creative work. Although this factor weighs slightly in Freeman's favor, Narell's work contains enough creative expression that any use of it is not presumptively fair.

Amount and Substantiality of Portions Used—This factor essentially repeats the analysis of the substantial similarity test. As explained above, no reasonable juror could conclude that *Illusions* is substantially similar to *Our City*. This factor weighs strongly in Freeman's favor.

Effect on the Market—This is the single most important element of fair use. The publication of *Illusions* has not had, and is not likely to have, any effect on the value or marketability of *Our City*. The works are directed to fundamentally different purposes. Readers interested in Narell's book are highly unlikely to find historical romance novels an acceptable substitute.

In sum, the first factor weighs strongly in Narell's favor and the second factor slightly favors Freeman. However, the third and final factors strongly favor Freeman. Because of the predominant role of the market factor, the district court's grant of summary judgment on the fair use defense should be affirmed.

Summary judgment for Freeman affirmed.

Trademarks

Trademarks help purchasers identify favored products and services. For this reason, they also give sellers and manufacturers an incentive to innovate and to strive for quality. However, both these ends would be defeated if competitors were free to appropriate each other's trademarks. Thus, the federal Lanham Act protects trademark owners against certain uses of their marks by third parties.[4]

Protected Marks

The Lanham Act recognizes four kinds of marks. It defines a **trademark** as any word, name, symbol, device, or combination thereof used by a manufacturer or seller to identify its products and to distinguish them from the products of competitors. On occasion, federal trademark protection has been extended to colors, pictures, label and package designs, slogans, sounds, arrangements of numbers and/or letters (e.g., "7-Eleven"), and shapes of goods or their containers (e.g., Coca-Cola bottles). **Service marks** resemble trademarks but identify and distinguish services.

    Certification marks certify the origin, materials, quality, method of manufacture, and other aspects of goods and services. Here, the user of the mark and its owner are distinct parties. A retailer, for example, may sell products bearing the Good Housekeeping Seal of Approval. **Collective marks** are trademarks or service marks used by organizations to identify themselves as the source of goods or services. Trade union and trade association marks fall into this category. Although all four kinds of marks receive federal protection, this chapter focuses on trademarks and service marks, using the terms *mark* or *trademark* to refer to both.

Distinctiveness

Because their purpose is to help consumers identify products and services, trademarks must be *distinctive* to merit maximum Lanham Act protection. Marks fall into four general categories of distinctiveness:

1. *Arbitrary or fanciful marks.* These marks are the most distinctive—and the most likely to be protected—because they do not describe or suggest the qualities of the product or service they identify. The "Exxon" trademark is an example.
2. *Suggestive marks.* These marks convey the nature of a product or service only through imagination, thought, and perception. A "Dietene" trademark for a dietary food supplement is an example. Although not as secure as arbitrary or fanciful marks, suggestive marks still are good candidates for protection.
3. *Descriptive marks.* These marks directly describe the product or service they identify—for example, "Exquisite" wearing apparel. Descriptive marks usually are not protected unless they acquire a *secondary meaning*. This occurs when their identification with particular goods or services has become firmly established in the minds of a substantial number of buyers. Among the factors considered in secondary meaning determinations are the length of time the mark has been used, the volume of sales associated with that use, and the nature of the advertising employing the mark. When applied to a package delivery service, for instance, the term *overnight* is usually just descriptive and thus not protectible. But it may come to deserve trademark protection through long use by a single firm that advertised it extensively and made many sales while doing so.
4. *Generic marks.* Generic marks (e.g., "diamond" or "truck") simply refer to the general class of which the particular product or service is one example. Because any seller has the right to call a product or service by its common name, generic marks are quite unlikely to receive Lanham Act protection.

Federal Registration

Once the seller of a product or service uses a mark in commerce or forms a bona fide intention to do so, she may try to register the mark with the U.S. Patent and Trademark Office. The office reviews applications for distinctiveness. Its decision to deny or grant the application may normally be contested either by the applicant or by a party who feels that he would be injured by registration of the mark. Such challenges may eventually reach the federal courts.

Trademarks of sufficient distinctiveness are placed on the Principal Register of the Patent and Trademark Office. A mark's inclusion in the Principal Register: (1) is prima facie evidence of the mark's ownership, validity, and registration (which is useful in trademark infringement suits); (2) gives nationwide constructive notice of the owner's claim of ownership (thus eliminating the need to show that the defendant in an infringement suit had notice of the mark); and (3) helps make the mark incontestable after five years (as described later).

Regardless of their distinctiveness, however, some kinds of marks are denied placement on the Principal Register. Examples include marks that: (1) consist of the flags or other insignia of governments; (2) consist of the name, portrait, or signature of a living person; (3) are immoral, deceptive, or scandalous; or (4) are likely to cause confusion or deceive because they resemble a mark previously registered or used in the United States. Certain other marks are not placed on the Principal Register unless they have acquired a secondary meaning. Examples include marks that: (1) are deceptively misdescriptive (such as "Dura-Skin" plastic gloves); (2) are geographically descriptive (e.g., "Nationwide" Life Insurance); or (3) are primarily a surname (because everyone should have the right to use his own name in connection with his business).

Transfer of Rights

Due to the purposes underlying trademark law, transferring trademark rights is more difficult than transferring copyright or patent interests. A trademark owner may license the use of the mark, but only if the licensee is a related company through which the owner can control the nature and quality of the goods or services identified by the mark. An uncontrolled "naked license" would allow the sale of goods or services bearing the mark but lacking the qualities formerly associated with it, and could confuse purchasers. Trademark rights may also be assigned or sold, but only along with the sale of the goodwill of the business originally using the mark.

Losing Federal Trademark Protection

Federal registration of a trademark lasts for 10 years, with renewals for additional 10-year periods possible. However, trademark protection may be lost before the period expires. The government must cancel a registration six years after its date, unless the registrant files with the Patent and Trademark Office an affidavit detailing that the mark is in use or explaining its nonuse and does so within the fifth and sixth years following the registration date.

Also, any person who believes that he is or will be damaged by a mark's registration may petition the Patent and Trademark Office to cancel that registration. Normally, the petition must be filed within five years of the mark's registration or the mark becomes *incontestable* as regards goods or services with which it has continuously been used for five consecutive years after the registration.[5] A mark's incontestability means that the permissible grounds for canceling its registration are limited. Even an incontestable mark, however, may be canceled *at any time* if, among other things, it was obtained by fraud, has been abandoned, or has become the generic name for the goods or services it identifies. *Abandonment* can occur through an express statement or agreement to abandon, through the mark's losing its significance as an indication of origin, or through the owner's failure to use it. A mark acquires a *generic meaning* when it comes to refer to a class of products or services rather than a particular product or service. For example, this has happened to such once-protected marks as aspirin and cellophane.

Trademark Infringement

A registered trademark is infringed when, without the registrant's consent, another party uses a substantially similar mark in connection with the advertisement or sale of goods or services and this is likely to cause confusion, mistake, or deception regarding their origin. The following *Nikon* case discusses many of the factors courts sift and weigh when determining whether the use is likely to cause confusion, mistake, or deception. A trademark owner who wins an infringement suit can obtain an injunction against uses of the mark that are likely to cause confusion. In certain circumstances, the owner can also obtain money damages for provable injury resulting from the infringement and for profits realized by the defendant from the sale of infringing products or services.

Nikon, Inc. v. Ikon Corp.

In 1986, Jack Elo founded Ikon Photographic Corporation (IPC) to market inexpensive 35 mm and 110 mm pocket cameras. Later, IPC applied to register the "Ikon" trademark and its logo but failed to get it on the Principal Register. Still later, IPC managed to register a separate "Ikon" mark with a stylized "I" logo. Eventually, Nikon, Inc., sued IPC for infringement of its "Nikon" trademark in federal district court. Nikon mainly manufactures more expensive and complicated cameras than those made by IPC, but it also had been making point-and-shoot cameras similar to IPC's offerings. After the court found IPC liable and issued an injunction recalling all of its outstanding products and enjoining it from using the "Ikon" mark, IPC appealed.

Source: 987 F.2d 91 (2d Cir. 1993)

Timbers, Circuit Judge

On this appeal from a permanent injunction, our function is limited to a review for abuse of discretion. Abuse of discretion can be found if the district court relied on a clearly erroneous finding of fact or incorrectly applied the law. The Lanham Act prohibits trademark infringement. The key issue in [such] cases is whether an appreciable number of consumers are likely to be misled or confused about the source of the product in question. It is well settled that in cases involving a claim under the Lanham Act the trier of fact must consider and balance [certain] factors to determine the likelihood of confusion. This list, however, is not exhaustive, nor is any one factor determinative.

1. *Strength of the Nikon Mark.* There is no dispute over the strength of the Nikon mark. It deserves broad protection against infringement.

2. *Similarity Between the Marks.* Although one of IPC's marks uses a stylized "I" and is not visually very similar to the Nikon mark, the stylized "I" is not used on all of IPC's cameras or packaging. In several contexts, therefore, the marks are similar. Further, the

sounds of both marks are extremely similar, differing by only one letter. That letter is easily obscured in statements such as "This is an Ikon," and "This is a Nikon." There [also] was similarity in the appearance of the cameras.

3. *Proximity of the Products.* This factor focuses on whether the products compete. If the products serve the same purposes, fall within the same class, or are used for similar purposes, the likelihood of confusion is greater. While the parties have cameras at the opposite ends of the spectrum, there is a substantial overlap of Nikon's low-end cameras with IPC's high-end cameras. These lines produce a substantial percentage of the respective companies' sales. Further, both Nikon and IPC market these products through similar channels of trade and to similar types of customers.

4. *Bridging the Gap.* While this factor turns on the likelihood of whether the senior user will enter the market of the junior user, the court was correct in finding that, if there already is an overlap in the market, the likelihood of confusion is greater. There [indeed] already is a market overlap, increasing the likelihood of confusion.

5. *Sophistication of Consumers.* The more sophisticated and careful the average consumer of a product, the less likely it is that similarities in trademarks will result in confusion concerning the source of the product. Although the purchasers of Nikon's upper-end cameras generally are sophisticated in this area, the purchasers of the lower-end line often are amateur photographers, not unlike the purchasers of IPC cameras. While purchasers of these cameras are not impulsive, less sophisticated consumers could be confused about an affiliation between the products.

6. *Quality of Junior User's Product.* We have taken two approaches about the quality of the junior user's product: (1) an inferior quality product injures the senior user's reputation because people may think they come from the same source, or (2) a product of equal quality promotes confusion that they come from the same source. While IPC's quality is good for its price, IPC does not have the same quality controls as Nikon. This factor [weighs] in favor of Nikon.

7. *Actual Confusion.* [There is] very limited evidence to support a claim of actual confusion. Thus, this factor [tips] toward IPC.

8. *Bad Faith.* IPC claims the name "Ikon" was chosen after Elo saw this spelling of the word in an encyclopedia and thought it would be familiar because of the pictorial religious connotations associated with it. Elo's twenty years of experience in the camera business make it unlikely that he did not realize there was a significant resemblance between this name and Nikon. There also is evidence that he rejected the advice of his counsel to adopt a mark with a word other than Ikon as the dominant part. Elo did not disclose to his counsel his intent to market 35 mm cameras similar to Nikon's. There [is] sufficient evidence that IPC acted in bad faith.

9. *Balancing the Factors.* Each factor, with the exception of actual confusion, weighs heavily in favor of Nikon. We hold that the situation taken as a whole clearly tips in favor of Nikon and supports the finding of a likelihood of confusion and trademark infringement. **District court judgment in Nikon's favor affirmed.**

Concept Review
The Three Forms of Intellectual Property Compared

	Patent	Copyright	Trademark
What Is Protected?	Process, machine, product, composition of matter, improvement, ornamental design, plant produced by asexual reproduction, if *novel*, *nonobvious*, and *useful*	Wide range of creative works that are *fixed* and *original*	Trademarks, service marks, certification marks, and collective marks of sufficient distinctiveness
Registration Needed?	Yes	Although copyright exists in the absence of registration, registration often necessary for infringement suit	Necessary for infringement suit under Lanham Act section 32(1). Unregistered marks protected under Lanham Act section 43(a).
Duration	17 years (14 years for design patents)	Life of author plus 50 years	10 years, with 10-year renewals possible
Transferability	By assignment or license	By assignment or license	Limited
How Infringed	Making, using, or selling patented invention or its substantial equivalent	Violation of owner's exclusive rights to reproduce, prepare derivative works, distribute copies, perform, or display. But *fair use* defense available.	Use of mark in connection with advertisement or sale that is likely to cause confusion, mistake, or deception regarding origin

Trade Secrets

The law provides at least two means of protecting creative inventions. Owners of such inventions may go public and obtain monopoly patent rights. Or they may keep the invention secret and rely on trade secrets law to protect it. Figure 25-1 sketches some of the advantages and disadvantages of each alternative.

FIGURE 25-1

Patent and trade secrets protection compared

Factor	Patent Law	Trade Secrets Law
Range of Protected Matter?	Probably narrower than trade secrets law	Probably broader than patent law
Need to Register?	Yes	No
Burden of Maintaining Secrecy?	No	Yes
Duration	Usually 17 years	So long as secrecy maintained?
Transferability	Fairly easy	Fairly easy
Ability to Keep Knowledge Secret?	No	Yes, if secrecy really maintained
Effective Monopoly over Protected Matter?	Yes	No, because discovery/use by proper means is permissible

The policies underlying patent protection and trade secrets protection differ. The general aim of patent law is to encourage the creation and disclosure of inventions by granting the patentee a temporary monopoly in the patented invention in exchange for his making it public. Trade secrets, however, are nonpublic by definition. Although protecting trade secrets may stimulate creative activity, it also keeps the information from becoming public knowledge. Thus, the main justification for trade secrets protection is simply to preserve certain standards of commercial morality.

Definition of a Trade Secret

A trade secret can be defined as any secret formula, pattern, process, program, device, method, technique, or compilation of information that is used in the owner's business and that gives its owner an advantage over competitors who do not know it or use it.[6] Examples include chemical formulas, computer software, manufacturing processes, designs for machines, and customer lists. To be protectible, a trade secret must usually have sufficient value or originality to provide an actual or potential competitive advantage. But it need not possess the novelty required for patent protection.

The following *Mason* case considers some factors courts may examine when determining whether a trade *secret* exists. As several of those factors suggest, a trade secret must actually be secret. A substantial measure of secrecy is necessary, but it need not be absolute. Thus, information that becomes public knowledge or becomes generally known in the industry cannot be a trade secret. Also, information that is reasonably discoverable by proper means may not be protected. "Proper means" include independent invention of the secret, observation of a publicly displayed product, the owner's advertising, published literature, product analysis, and reverse engineering (starting with a legitimately acquired product and working backward to discover how it was developed).

In addition, a firm claiming a trade secret must usually show that it took *reasonable measures to assure secrecy*. Examples include advising employees about the secret's secrecy, limiting access to the secret on a need-to-know basis, requiring those given access to sign a nondisclosure agreement, disclosing the secret only on a confidential basis, and controlling access to an office or plant. Computer software licensing agreements commonly forbid the licensee to copy the program except for backup and archival purposes, require the licensee and its employees to sign confidentiality agreements, require those employees to use the program only in the course of their jobs, and require the licensee to use the program only in a central processing unit. Because the owner must only make *reasonable* efforts to ensure secrecy, however, she need not adopt extreme measures to block every ingenious form of industrial espionage.

Ownership and Transfer of Trade Secrets

The owner of a trade secret is usually the person who developed it or the business under whose auspices it was generated. But establishing the ownership of a trade secret can pose problems where an employee develops a secret in the course of her employment. In such cases, courts often find the *employer* to be the owner if: (1) the employee was hired to do creative work related to the secret, (2) the employee agreed not to divulge or use trade secrets, or (3) other employees contributed to the development of the secret. Even where the employee owns the secret, the employer still may obtain a royalty-free license to use it through the shop right doctrine discussed in the section on patents.

The owner of a trade secret can transfer rights in the secret to third parties. This can occur by assignment (in which case the owner loses title) or by license (in which case the owner retains title but allows the transferee certain uses of the secret).

Misappropriation of Trade Secrets

Misappropriation of a trade secret can occur in various ways, most of which involve disclosure or use of the secret. For example, misappropriation liability occurs when the secret is disclosed or used by one who did one of the following:

1. Acquired it by *improper means*. Improper means include theft, trespass, wiretapping, spying, bugging, bribery, fraud, impersonation, and eavesdropping.
2. Acquired it from a party who is *known or should be known* to have obtained it by improper means. For example, a free-lance industrial spy might obtain one firm's trade secrets by improper means and sell them to the firm's competitors. If those competitors know or have reason to know that the spy obtained the secrets by improper means, they are liable for misappropriation along with the spy.
3. *Breached a duty of confidentiality regarding the secret.* Where an employer owns a trade secret, for example, an employee is generally bound not to use or disclose it during his employment or thereafter.[7] The employee may, however, utilize general knowledge and skills acquired during her employment.

Remedies for misappropriation of a trade secret include damages, which might involve both the actual loss caused by the misappropriation and/or the defendant's unjust enrichment. In some states, punitive damages are awarded for willful and malicious misappropriations. Also, an injunction may be issued against actual or threatened misappropriations.

Mason v. Jack Daniel Distillery

Tony Mason created a mixed drink that he named "Lynchburg Lemonade." The drink consisted of Jack Daniel's whiskey, Triple Sec, sweet and sour mix, and 7-Up. Mason served the drink at his restaurant and lounge, where it became very popular. Later, Winston Randle, a sales representative for Jack Daniel Distillery, drank Lynchburg Lemonade while in Mason's restaurant and lounge. Although the source of his information is unclear, he also learned the recipe for the drink at this time. Randle informed his superiors about Lynchburg Lemonade and its recipe, and about one year later Jack Daniel was developing a national promotion campaign for the drink.

Mason, who never received any compensation for this use of Lynchburg Lemonade, sued Jack Daniel and Winston for misappropriation of a trade secret. Mason won a trial court jury verdict, and the defendants appealed the trial court's refusal to grant their motion for a directed verdict.

Source: 518 So. 2d 130 (Ala. Civ. App. 1987)

Holmes, Judge

The defendants contend that Mason's recipe for Lynchburg Lemonade was not a trade secret. The *Restatement* provides in pertinent part:

> A trade secret may consist of any formula, pattern, device, or compilation of information which is used in one's business, and which gives him an opportunity to obtain an advantage over competitors who do not know or use it. . . .
>
> An exact definition of a trade secret is not possible. Some factors to be considered in determining whether given information is one's trade secret are: (1) the extent to which the information is known outside of his business; (2) the extent to which it is known by employees and others involved in his business; (3) the extent of measures taken by him to guard the secrecy

of his information; (4) the value of the information to him and to his competitors; (5) the amount of effort or money expended by him in developing the information; (6) the ease or difficulty with which the information could be properly acquired or duplicated by others.

Applying these factors to this case, we find that some support and some negate the conclusion that Lynchburg Lemonade was Mason's trade secret.

Mason apparently spent little time, effort, or money in concocting the recipe for Lynchburg Lemonade. He seems to have created the beverage one evening to ease a sore throat. However, he put much effort into making the beverage an exclusive specialty of his restaurant and lounge. Mason testified that Lynchburg Lemonade comprised about a third of his total sales of alcoholic drinks. Obviously, the exclusive sale of Lynchburg Lemonade was of great value to Mason. The beverage could also have been valuable to his competitors in the area.

Mason [also] testified that he told only a few of his employees the recipe. He stated that each one was specifically instructed not to tell anyone the recipe. To prevent customers from learning the recipe, the beverage was mixed in the back of the restaurant and lounge. Mason's efforts to keep the recipe a secret were apparently successful until Randle learned the recipe. It appears that one could not order a Lynchburg Lemonade in any establishment other than that of the plaintiff. Absolute secrecy is not required for the recipe to constitute a trade secret—a substantial element of secrecy is all that is necessary.

The defendants contend that Mason's recipe was not a trade secret because it could be easily duplicated by others. The defendants' [expert] testimony characterized Lynchburg Lemonade as a member of the Collins family of drinks, of which there are dozens, if not hundreds, with essentially the same elements. At least one witness testified that he could duplicate the recipe after tasting a Lynchburg Lemonade. Certainly, this testimony is a strong factor against the conclusion that Mason's recipe was a trade secret. We do not think, however, that this evidence in and of itself could prevent such a conclusion. Rather, this evidence should be weighed and considered along with the evidence tending to show the existence of a trade secret. Courts have protected information as a trade secret despite evidence that it could easily be duplicated by others competent in the given field.

A motion for directed verdict should not be granted if there is a scintilla of evidence supporting an element essential to the plaintiff's claim. Our review of the record indicates that Mason did present a scintilla of evidence that his recipe, or formula, for Lynchburg Lemonade was a trade secret.

Trial court's refusal to grant the defendant's motion for a directed verdict affirmed.

Commercial Torts

In addition to the intentional torts discussed in Chapter 22, certain other intentional torts involve business or commercial competition. Like the rules discussed thus far in this chapter, they are means by which the law polices commercial life. These torts may help promote innovation by protecting creative businesses against certain competitive abuses. But their main aim is simply to uphold certain minimum standards of commercial morality.

Injurious Falsehood

Injurious falsehood also goes by names such as product disparagement, slander of title, and trade libel. This tort involves the publication of false statements that disparage another's business, property, or title to property, and thus harm her economic interests. One common kind of injurious falsehood involves false statements that disparage either a person's *property rights* in land, things, or intangibles, or their *quality*. The property rights in question include virtually all legally protected property interests that can be sold; examples include leases, mineral rights, trademarks, copyrights, and corporate stock. As the following *Atlas* case indicates, injurious falsehood also includes false statements that harm another's economic interests even though they do not disparage property or property rights as such.

Elements and Damages

In injurious falsehood cases, the plaintiff must prove that the defendant made a statement of the sort just described, the statement's falsity, and its communication to a third party. The degree of fault required for liability is unclear. Sources often say that the standard is malice, but formulations of this differ. The *Restatement* requires either knowledge that the statement is false, or reckless disregard as to its truth or falsity. There is usually no liability for false statements that are made negligently and in good faith.

The plaintiff must also prove that the false statement played a substantial part in causing him to suffer *special damages*. These may include: losses resulting from the diminished value of disparaged property, the expense of measures for counteracting the false statement (e.g., advertising or litigation expenses), losses resulting from the breach of an existing contract by a third party, and the loss of prospective business. In cases involving the loss of prospective business, the plaintiff is usually required to show that some specific person or persons refused to buy because of the disparagement. But as *Atlas* states, this rule is often relaxed where these losses are difficult to prove.

The special damages that the plaintiff is required to prove are his usual—and virtually his only—remedy in injurious falsehood cases. Damages for personal injury or emotional distress, for instance, are generally not recoverable. However, punitive damages and injunctive relief are sometimes obtainable.

Injurious Falsehood and Defamation

Injurious falsehood may or may not overlap with the tort of defamation discussed in Chapter 22. Statements impugning a businessperson's character or conduct are probably only defamatory. If the false statement is limited to the plaintiff's business, property, or property rights, on the other hand, his normal claim is for injurious falsehood. Both claims are possible where the injurious falsehood implies something about the plaintiff's character and affects his overall reputation. An example is a defendant's false allegation that the plaintiff knowingly sells dangerous products to children.

Defamation law's absolute and conditional privileges generally apply in injurious falsehood cases.[8] Certain other privileges protect defendants who are sued for injurious falsehood. For example, a rival claimant may in good faith disparage another's property rights by asserting his own competing rights. Similarly, one may make a good faith allegation that a competitor is infringing one's patent, copyright, or trademark. Finally, a person may sometimes make unfavorable comparisons between her own property and that of a competitor. This privilege is generally limited to sales talk asserting the superiority of one's property and does not cover unfavorable statements about a competitor's property.

Charles Atlas, Ltd. v. Time-Life Books, Inc.

Time-Life Books published a book entitled *Exercising for Fitness*. The book contained a reproduction of the famous Charles Atlas advertisement in which a 97-pound weakling uses Atlas's Dynamic Tension body-building program to become a real man after a bully kicks sand in his face and the face of his girlfriend. The caption accompanying the reproduction told the book's readers that Atlas's program is a system of isometric exercises. On the same page, the book warned readers about the extreme dangers of isometric exercises.

Charles Atlas, Ltd. sued Time-Life in federal district court for product disparagement (injurious falsehood). It basically alleged that the book's caption was false because Atlas's method was not isometric, and that this falsehood, coupled with the warning about the dangers of isometric exercises, caused it to suffer economic loss. Time-Life moved to dismiss Atlas's complaint. The question before the court was whether the facts in the complaint were sufficient to state a claim upon which relief could be granted.

Source: 570 F. Supp. 150 (S.D.N.Y. 1983)

Goettel, District Judge

This court cannot say as a matter of law that the alleged misstatements are not reasonably susceptible to a defamatory meaning and that no reasonable reader could conclude that the statements [concern] the plaintiff's product. When the caption is read in conjunction with the text, a reasonable reader could conclude that Atlas markets an isometric exercise program, that isometric exercises are dangerous, and that therefore Atlas's exercise program is dangerous. Whether the trier of fact will conclude that a defamatory connotation was indeed conveyed will have to await trial.

Malice is pleaded adequately. It is extremely questionable whether the plaintiff must show common-law malice to state a claim for product disparagement. Rather, it appears that the plaintiff must show knowledge of the alleged false statement or reckless disregard as to the truth of the statement [citing the *Restatement*]. Atlas alleges that the allegedly false statements were known by Time-Life to be false when they were made, or were made with recklessness, malice, and intent to injure Atlas.

Finally, Atlas has pleaded special damages adequately. According to Atlas, the alleged disparagement has caused it to lose $30,323 in sales and revenues and to expend $14,000 in special advertising expenses and $16,687 in legal expenses to counteract the alleged disparagement. Special damage is the pecuniary loss resulting directly from the effect of a defendant's allegedly wrongful conduct. Among the losses deemed to constitute special damages are the expenses necessary to counteract the alleged wrongful conduct. Thus, Atlas can recover at least the special advertising expenses incurred to counteract the alleged product disparagement, and the pleading of these expenses is sufficient to support the claim at this stage of the litigation.

Loss of sales is also a proper item of special damages. However, Time-Life argues that Atlas has failed to plead this adequately because it has failed to identify lost customers. Adopting such a rule would be grossly unfair in this case. Atlas sells only through mail orders. It is, therefore, virtually impossible to identify those who did not order Atlas's product because of *Exercising for Fitness*. As Dean Prosser has noted: "[A] more liberal rule has been applied, requiring the plaintiff to be particular only where it is reasonable to expect him to do so. It is probably still the law everywhere that he must either offer the names of those who have failed to purchase or explain why it is impossible for him to do so; but where he cannot, the matter is dealt with by analogy to the proof of lost profits resulting from breach of contract."

Whether legal fees expended to prosecute a claim for product disparagement can be recovered as an item of special damages is an interesting issue. It can be argued that the expenses incurred in bringing the lawsuit are similar to other expenses necessary to counteract the alleged wrongful conduct. Be that as it may, the court need not resolve the question at this time because it has already determined that Atlas has stated a claim for product disparagement.

Time-Life's motion to dismiss denied; Atlas's case continues.

Interference with Contractual Relations

In a suit for intentional interference with contractual relations, one party to a contract claims that the defendant's interference with the other party's performance of the contract wrongly caused the plaintiff to lose the benefit of that performance. One can interfere with the performance of a contract by causing a party to repudiate it, or by wholly or partly preventing that party's performance. The means of interference can range from mere persuasion to threatened or actual violence. The agreement whose performance is checked, however, must be an *existing* contract. This includes contracts that are voidable, unenforceable, or subject to contract defenses, but *not* void bargains, contracts that are illegal on public policy grounds, or contracts to marry. Finally, the defendant must have *intended* to cause the breach; there is usually no liability for negligent contract interferences.

Even if the plaintiff proves these threshold requirements, the defendant is liable only if his behavior was *improper*. The following RAN case lists the factors the Restatement uses to decide this question. Despite the flexible, case-by-case nature of such determinations, a few generalizations about improper interference are possible.

1. Where the contract's performance was blocked by such clearly improper means as threats of physical violence, misrepresentations, defamatory statements, bribery, harassment, or bad-faith civil or criminal actions, the defendant usually is liable. Liability is also likely where the interference was motivated *solely* by malice, spite, or a simple desire to meddle.

2. If his means and motives are legitimate, a defendant generally escapes liability when his contract interference is in the *public interest*—for example, when he informs an airport that an air traffic controller is a habitual user of hallucinogenic drugs. The same is true where the defendant acts to *protect a person for whose welfare she is responsible*—for example, where a mother induces a private school to discharge a diseased student who could infect her children.

3. A contract interference resulting from the defendant's good faith effort to protect her own *existing* legal or economic interests usually does not create liability so long as appropriate means are used. For example, a landowner can probably induce his tenant to breach a sublease to a party whose business detracts from the land's value. However, business parties generally cannot interfere with existing contract rights merely to further some *prospective* competitive advantage. For example, a seller cannot entice its competitors' customers to break existing contracts with those competitors. Is the *RAN* case completely consistent with these rules?

4. Finally, competitors are unlikely to incur liability where, as is still often true of employment contracts, the agreement interfered with is *terminable at will*. The reason is that in such cases, the plaintiff has only an expectancy that the contract will continue, and not a right to have it continued. Thus, a firm that hires away its competitors' at-will employees usually escapes liability.

The basic measure of damages for intentional interference with contractual relations is the value of the lost contract performance. Some courts also award compensatory damages reasonably linked to the interference (including emotional distress and damage to reputation). Sometimes the plaintiff may obtain an injunction prohibiting further interferences.

Interference with Prospective Advantage

The rules and remedies for intentional interference with prospective advantage parallel those for interference with contractual relations. The main difference is that the former tort involves interferences with *prospective* relations rather than existing contracts. The protected future relations are mainly potential contractual relations of a business or commercial sort. Liability for interference with such relations requires intent; negligence usually does not suffice.

The "improper interference" factors weighed in interference-with-contract cases generally apply to interference with prospective advantage as well. One difference, however, is that interference with prospective advantage can be justified if: (1) the plaintiff and the defendant are in competition for the prospective relation with which the defendant interferes; (2) the defendant's purpose is at least partly competitive; (3) the defendant does not use such improper means as physical threats, misrepresentations, and bad faith lawsuits; and (4) the defendant's behavior does not create an unlawful restraint of trade under the antitrust laws or other regulations. Thus, a competitor ordinarily can win customers by offering lower prices and attract suppliers by offering higher prices. Unless this is otherwise illegal, he can also refuse to deal with suppliers or buyers who also deal with his competitors.

Ran Corporation v. Hudesman

David Hudesman leased commercial property housing the Red Dog Saloon to Don Harris, the saloon's owner and operator. The lease said that Harris could assign it to any subtenant or assignee who was financially responsible and would properly care for the premises. It also required that Hudesman consent to such an assignment, but added that this consent could not be withheld unreasonably. After Harris decided to relocate his business, he was contacted by Richard Stone, president of the RAN Corporation. Stone wanted to use the property for an artifacts gallery. Harris and Stone agreed that Harris would assign the lease for $15,000, conditional on Hudesman's approval.

About this time, a politically influential man named Jerry Reinwand contacted Hudesman about the property. In exchange for Reinwand's promise to help Hudesman secure government leases for a large building Hudesman owned, Hudesman promised Reinwand that if Harris

relocated his business, Reinwand would be assigned the property. Then Hudesman told Harris that he would not consent to Harris's assignment of the lease to RAN, and that Harris would be "looking at litigation" if he tried to assign the lease to Stone. Thus, Harris told Stone that the deal was off, returned his $15,000 deposit, and assigned the lease to Reinwand for $15,000.

RAN then sued for an injunction to invalidate Reinwand's lease and to enforce its assignment contract with Harris, and also for damages. After RAN settled with several defendants, its main remaining claims were interference with contractual relations and interference with prospective advantage claims against Hudesman. Both parties then moved for summary judgment, and the trial court held for Hudesman. RAN appealed.

Source: 823 P.2d 646 (Alaska Sup. Ct. 1991)

Matthews, Justice

The elements of intentional interference with contractual relations are: (1) a contract existed, (2) the defendant knew of the contract and intended to induce a breach, (3) the contract was breached, (4) the defendant's wrongful conduct engendered the breach, (5) the breach caused the plaintiff's damages, and (6) the defendant's conduct was not privileged or justified. The fourth, fifth, and sixth elements also apply to the related tort of intentional interference with prospective economic advantage. As our analysis applies equally to either tort, we will refer to them collectively.

The sixth element is troublingly vague. The *Restatement (Second) of Torts* section 767 speaks not in terms of "privilege," but requires that the actor's conduct not be "improper." Other authorities used the catch word "malice." Regardless of the phrase used, the critical question is what conduct is not "privileged" or "improper" or "malicious." The *Restatement* lists seven factors for consideration: (1) the nature of the actor's conduct, (2) the actor's motive, (3) the interests of the other with which the actor's conduct interferes, (4) the interests sought to be advanced by the actor, (5) the social interests in protecting the freedom of action of the actor and the contractual interests of the other, (6) the proximity or remoteness of the actor's conduct to the interference, and (7) the relations between the parties. While these factors are relevant in some or all incarnations of the interference tort, they are hard to apply in any sort of predictive way.

Instead of relying on the *Restatement* factors, we [have] adopted a test of privilege which hold[s] that where an actor has a direct financial interest, he is privileged to interfere with a contract for economic reasons, but not where he is motivated by spite, malice, or some other improper motive. In our view, this rule applies to this case. A number of other cases have recognized that a landlord has a sufficient interest to interfere with a prospective or actual lease assignment. The right to intervene has also been recognized in the analogous setting of transfers of distributorships.

It seems beyond reasonable argument that an owner of property has a financial interest in the assignment of a lease of the property he owns. An effective lease assignment makes the assignee the tenant of the owner. The tenant has an obligation to pay rent directly to the owner, and the use, or abuse, of the property by the assignee may affect its value to the owner. Further, the owner may know of another potential assignee who will pay more rent than the prospective assignee. Moreover, the owner may wish to terminate the lease based on knowledge of a more profitable use for the property.

Since Hudesman had a direct financial interest in the proposed assignment of the lease, the essential question in determining if interference is justified is whether Hudesman's conduct is motivated by a desire to protect his economic interest, or whether it is motivated by spite, malice, or some other improper objective. As there is no evidence of spite, malice, or other improper objective—Hudesman did not even know RAN Corporation's principals—and since it is clear that Hudesman refused to approve the assignment because he believed that he would receive a greater economic benefit from a tenancy by Reinwand, the interference was justified.

Hudesman's threat of litigation does not seem relevant to RAN's claim for interference. RAN's assignment agreement with Harris was explicitly conditional on Hudesman's approval. When Hudesman disapproved of the assignment, the interference was complete. Hudesman's disapproval may have been a breach of the Hudesman/Harris lease, but it was privileged from a tort standpoint because of Hudesman's preexisting interest as a property owner-lessor. The threat of litigation may, at worst, have been another breach of the Hudesman/Harris lease. However, it too was not tortious and it was, in any case, superfluous to the interference, because RAN's prospective economic relationship was terminated by Hudesman's disapproval, not by his threat to sue.

Lower court judgment in favor of Hudesman affirmed.

Lanham Act Section 43(a)

Section 43(a) of the Lanham Act basically creates a federal law of unfair competition. Section 43(a) is not a consumer remedy; it is normally available only to commercial parties, who usually are the defendant's competitors. The section creates civil liability for a wide range of false, misleading, confusing, or deceptive descriptions of fact made in connection with goods or services. Section 43(a)'s many applications include:

1. *Common law tort suits for "palming off" or "passing off."* This tort involves false representations that are likely to induce third parties to believe that the defendant's goods or services are those of the plaintiff. Such representations include imitations of the plaintiff's trademarks, trade names, packages, labels, containers, employee uniforms, and place of business.

2. *Trade dress infringement claims.* These claims resemble palming-off claims. A product's trade dress is its overall appearance and sales image. Section 43(a) prohibits a party from passing off its goods or services as those of a competitor by employing a substantially similar trade dress that is likely to confuse consumers as to the source of its products or services. For example, a competitor that sells antifreeze in jugs that are similar in size, shape, and color to a well-known competitor's jugs may face section 43(a) liability.

3. *The infringement of both registered and unregistered trademarks.*

4. *Some cases involving a form of invasion of privacy discussed in Chapter 22—the appropriation of another's name or likeness for commercial purposes.*

5. *Commercial advertising that misrepresents the nature of goods or services.* This important application of section 43(a) includes ads that misrepresent the nature or origin of either the *advertiser's* products and services or a *competitor's* products and services. As the following Castrol case asserts, this includes ads that are likely to deceive buyers even if they are not clearly false on their face. Section 43(a) probably applies to ads containing certain deceptive *omissions* as well.

Castrol, Inc. v. Quaker State Corp.

A Quaker State Corporation television commercial asserted that "tests prove" that: "At startup Quaker State 10W-30 protects better than any other leading 10W-30 motor oil." The commercial also depicted an engine, superimposed over which were bottles of Quaker State oil and four competing motor oils, including Castrol GTX 10W-30. Nearby was a bar graph displaying the superior speed with which Quaker State oil flowed to engine components once the engine is started.

Castrol, Inc., sued Quaker State for false advertising under Lanham Act section 43(a). As part of that suit, it sought a preliminary injunction against Quaker State's airing the commercial. The evidence at trial indicated that while Quaker State's oil indeed did reach engine parts faster than its competitors at start-up, this had no discernible effect on engine wear. The apparent reason is that the "residual oil" remaining from prior engine starts protects the engine until new oil arrives. The district court granted Castrol's requested preliminary injunction, and Quaker State appealed.

Source: 977 F.2d 57 (2d Cir. 1992)

Walker, Circuit Judge

A party seeking preliminary injunctive relief must show: (a) that it will suffer irreparable harm if relief is denied, and (b) either (1) a likelihood of success on the merits or (2) sufficiently serious questions going to the merits to make them fair ground for litigation and a balance of hardships tipping decidedly in plaintiff's favor. We presume irreparable harm where plaintiff demonstrates a likelihood of success in showing literally false defendant's comparative advertisement which mentions plaintiff's product by name.

To succeed under section 43(a), a plaintiff must demonstrate that an advertisement is either literally false, or that an advertisement, though literally true, is likely to mislead and confuse consumers. Where the advertising claim is shown to be literally false, the court may enjoin the use of the claim without reference to the advertisement's impact on the buying public. Here, Castrol contends that the challenged advertisement is literally false. It bears the burden of proving this to a "likelihood of success" standard.

Plaintiff bears a different burden in proving literally false the advertised claim that tests prove defendant's product superior, than it does in proving the falsity of a superiority claim which makes no mention of tests. Where the defendant's advertisement claims that its product is superior, plaintiff must affirmatively prove defendant's product equal or inferior. Where, as in the current case, defendant's ad represents that tests or studies prove its product superior, plaintiff satisfies its burden by showing that the tests did not establish the proposition for which they were cited. A plaintiff can meet this burden by demonstrating that the tests were not sufficiently reliable to permit a conclusion that the product is superior. If the plaintiff can show that the tests, even if reliable, do not establish the proposition asserted by the defendant, the plaintiff [also] has met its burden. The district court held that Castrol had met this latter burden. We will reverse the district court's order of preliminary injunctive relief only upon a showing that it abused its discretion, which may occur when a court bases its decision on clearly erroneous findings of fact or on errors as to applicable law.

Quaker State asserts that the district court's factual findings as to the role of residual oil are clearly erroneous. We disagree. If the district court's account of the evidence is plausible in light of the record viewed in its entirety, the court of appeals may not reverse it even though convinced that had it been sitting as the trier of fact, it would have weighed the evidence differently. We owe particularly strong deference where the district court premises its findings on credibility determinations. In this case, the district court heard five days of expert testimony. Its credibility determinations in favor of Castrol's experts support its finding that residual oil holds the fort. This finding also receives support from [a] videotape of residual oil in the engine and [the tests'] failure to demonstrate reduced engine wear. Nothing in the record convincingly contradicts the district court's conclusion.

District court preliminary injunction against Quaker State affirmed.

Ethical and Public Policy Concerns

1. An ethical theory known as *utilitarianism* says that the test for the moral worth of actions is their ability to produce the greatest degree of aggregate net satisfaction throughout society. Some utilitarians say that satisfaction is maximized when people are best able to realize their individual preferences. Some say that one measure of satisfaction is the creation of economic wealth. Look at the purposes said to underlie trademark law. Are these generally utilitarian? Why or why not?

2. Legal reasoning is sometimes deductive or syllogistic. In such cases, the court states a general rule as a major premise, treats the facts as a minor premise, and applies the rule to the facts to generate a result. But another style of legal reasoning called *factor-based balancing* proceeds differently. In cases of this kind, the court states various factors that are relevant to its decision and decides by weighing these factors against one another under the facts before it. Which cases in this chapter use this method in whole or in part? Based on those cases, what is good about this style of legal reasoning? Are sensible decisions possible in any other way? On the other hand, what is bad about this decision-making process? In answering this last question, consider whether or how well this process enables business parties to predict the legal consequences of their behavior.

3. Take another look at the *Narell* case earlier in the chapter. Even though Narell's copyright infringement suit failed, isn't Freeman morally obligated to give Narell *something* for the portions of Narell's book that Freeman used? After all, this material probably helped sell Freeman's book. On the other hand, what would be likely to happen if everyone in a similar situation has such a moral obligation and acts on it? Would this result be consistent with the purposes underlying copyright law? *Hint:* If Freeman had to pay Narell for what ever she used, would Freeman be likely to use Narell's information? Who loses out if Freeman doesn't use that information in her book?

Problem Cases

1. Huey J. Rivet patented an "amphibious marsh craft" for hauling loads and laying pipeline in swamps. Rivet's model could "walk" over stumps for extended periods while carrying heavy loads. Later, Robert Wilson, who had once worked for Rivet as a welder, began marketing a similar craft. The craft sold by Wilson differed from the craft described in the specification accompanying Rivet's patent application in several respects. Overall, though, the Wilson boat performed much the same functions about as effectively as the Rivet craft, and used much the same engineering techniques and concepts to do so. Has Wilson infringed Rivet's patent?

2. Lorna Nelson, half-sister of the rock star Prince, sued Prince for copyright infringement. She alleged that Prince's hit "U Got the look" infringed her copyrighted song "What's Cooking in this Book." Lorna's song, to which Prince had access, had six verses totaling 35 lines and 176 words. "U Got the look" had eight verses totaling 47 lines and 242 words. The alleged infringements concerned the following verses and words from the two songs:

    a. *Lorna's verse 2:* "I glanced up and saw you, a smile so pretty." *Prince's verses 2 and 7:* "I woke up, I've never seen such a pretty girl."
    b. *Lorna's verse 3:* "Makeup was rolling down my face." *Prince's verse 5:* "A whole hour just to make up your face."
    c. *Lorna's verse 6:* "What's cooking in this book, what's cooking in ..." *Prince's verses 4 and 6:* "U sho 'nuf do be cooking in my book."
    d. *Lorna's verses 1 and 6:* "Take a look, Take another look." *Prince's verses 1 and 7:* "U got the look."

    The main issue in the case was whether there was substantial similarity between the lyrics just quoted. Although you cannot answer this question from the chapter, do you think that these lyrics are sufficiently similar to justify imposing liability on Prince?

3. In 1970-71, James Doran, a student at Iowa State University, helped produce a 28-minute film biography of Dan Gable, an Iowa State wrestler who eventually won a gold medal at the 1972 Olympics. Iowa State obtained a valid statutory copyright to the film. In 1972, when Doran was employed by the American Broadcasting Company, he helped arrange for ABC to use a 2½-minute segment of the film for the network's broadcasts of the 1972 Olympics. He did so without Iowa State's knowledge or consent. Is the fact that ABC only used about 9 percent of the film sufficient by itself to give ABC a fair use defense in a copyright infringement suit by Iowa State?

4. Accuride International, Inc., is a wholly owned subsidiary of Standard Precision, Inc., a leading producer of drawer slide mechanisms. Standard Precision and Accuride market drawer slide mechanisms under the "ACCURIDE" trademark. Is this mark arbitrary or fanciful, suggestive, descriptive, or generic?

5. Levi Strauss & Co. makes Levi jeans. Each pair of Levi jeans has a striking and original back pocket stitching pattern consisting of two intersecting arcs that roughly bisect both pockets. In terms of distinctiveness, what kind of trademark is this? Should such a mark receive strong protection or relatively little protection if Levi Strauss sues another jeans manufacturer for trademark infringement?

6. E. I. du Pont de Nemours & Co., was building a plant to develop a highly secret unpatented process for producing methanol. During the construction, some of its trade secrets were exposed to view from the air because the plant in which they were contained did not yet have a roof. These secrets were photographed from an airplane by two photographers who were hired by persons unknown to take pictures of the new construction. Did this action amount to a misappropriation of Du Pont's trade secrets?

7. Frank and Frances Gardner sued Sailboat Key, Inc., to prevent it from constructing certain improvements pursuant to building permits issued by the city of Miami. Sailboat Key later sued the Gardners for injurious falsehood. It alleged that false statements contained in the Gardners' pleadings in the earlier case caused it to lose its interest in the land where the construction was to occur because it could not obtain financing. The Gardners claimed that defamation law's absolute privilege for statements made in the course of judicial proceedings also applied to this injurious falsehood action, and thus protected them from liability. Are the Gardners correct?

8. Joanna Wells and Paula Snyder visited the Brownsville Golden Age Nursing Home in connection with their interest in placing a relative in a nursing home. Appalled at the conditions they found there, Wells and Snyder communicated their concerns to a variety of sources, including the governor of Pennsylvania, President Ronald Reagan, CBS News, and the television show "60 Minutes." Their various communications eventually caused Golden Age to lose its state operating license due to various violations of state regulations. Golden Age sued Wells and Snyder for intentional interference with its contractual relations. Did Golden Age win? Why or why not?

9. The New Mexico and Arizona Land Company owned a sizable tract of land in Arizona. It leased a portion of this land, which contained water for grazing, to the Bar J Bar Cattle Company. New Mexico had the right to cancel the lease upon 30 days' notice once it sold the land. Malcolm Pace, who owned a ranch adjoining the Bar J Bar ranch and wanted its water rights, bought the land leased by Bar J Bar from New Mexico. Shortly thereafter, New Mexico gave Bar J Bar 30 days' notice of termination. Bar J Bar sued Pace for intentional interference with contractual relations. One feature of the Bar J Bar lease weakens its chances of recovery against Pace. What is that feature of the lease? *Hint:* The answer requires that you make an analogy to a subject discussed in this chapter's discussion of intentional interference with contractual relations.

10. After retiring from professional football, ex-Notre Dame and Green Bay Packer star Paul Hornung began a career as a television sports announcer. From the mid-1960s until 1980, he worked as a play-by-play announcer and color commentator at both college and professional games. In 1981 or 1982, the Atlanta television station WTBS contracted with the NCAA to telecast 19 college football games during the 1982 and 1983 seasons. The contract gave the NCAA the right to approve or disapprove any announcer or color commentator used on the broadcasts. When WTBS proposed Hornung as a color analyst for the games, the NCAA rejected him. The stated reasons for Hornung's rejection were his close association with professional football, his suspension for gambling while an NFL player, and his participation in Miller Lite beer commercials. The NCAA, however, itself accepted advertising revenue from the Miller Brewing Company.

    Hornung sued the NCAA for intentional interference with prospective advantage. Did he win? Why or why not?

11. Tracy-Locke, Inc., the ad agency for FritoLay, Inc., used a 1976 Tom Waits song called "Step Right Up" in an advertisement for a new Frito-Lay product called "SalsaRio Doritas." Tracy-Locke got Stephen Carter, a professional singer and musician, to sing "Step Right Up" in the commercial. Carter did a near-perfect imitation of Waits's distinctive singing voice and style. After the ad containing Carter's imitation was disseminated to the public, Waits found out about it. As a result, he wanted to sue Frito-Lay. Of the various statutory provisions and common law rules discussed in this chapter, which is Waits's best bet?

Endnotes

1. As discussed later in this chapter, however, computer programs do get copyright and trade secrets protection.
2. Plant and design patents are subject to slightly different requirements than those stated here.
3. Some forms of patent misuse may be antitrust violations. Chapter 31 discusses the interaction between patent law and antitrust law.
4. In addition, the owner of a trademark may enjoy legal protection under common law trademark doctrines and state trademark statutes.
5. The Lanham Act's incontestability provision also imposes on the owner an affidavit requirement resembling the cancellation affidavit requirement just stated.
6. This definition comes mainly from *Restatement of Torts* section 757, comment b (1939), with some additions from *Uniform Trade Secrets Act* section 1(4) (1985). Many states have adopted the Uniform Trade secrets Act (UTSA) in some form. The discussion in this chapter is a composite of the *Restatement's* and the UTSA's rules.
7. This is an application of the agent's duty of loyalty, which is discussed in Chapter 24.
8. Chapter 25 discusses those privileges.

Chapter Twenty-Six

WHY GOVERNMENTS

ARE NEEDED

We hold these truths to be self-evident, that all men are created equal, that they are endowed by their Creator with certain unalienable Rights, that among these are Life, Liberty, and the pursuit of Happiness. That to secure these rights, Governments are instituted among men deriving their just powers from the consent of the Governed.

Declaration of Independence

We the people of the United States, in Order to form a more perfect Union, establish Justice, insure domestic Tranquillity, provide for the common defense, promote the general Welfare, and secure the Blessings of Liberty to ourselves and our Posterity, do ordain and establish this Constitution for the United States of America.

Constitution of the United States

Introduction

Public policies come from governments, but why are governments needed? This question acquires great significance as governments throughout the world grow increasingly. They have expanded what they do, taken on new tasks, and run up huge deficits. In 1995, it was estimated that in 10 years the U.S. government deficit would increase from 2.3 percent of the gross domestic product (GDP) to 3.6 percent. The main reason for this increase was growth in entitlement spending (e.g., Social Security, Medicare, and Medicaid). Discretionary spending was projected to grow by 2 percent per year, while spending on entitlements was forecast to increase by 7 percent (see Case 10-A on the Contract with America at the end of this chapter).

Government deficits have seriously affected many nations in the world. They hurt national economies. With governments competing with businesses and consumers for scarce investment capital, interest rates soar. Credit becomes less available. Without foreign investment, government borrowing crowds out private investment. The problem of spiraling deficits raises the question: What is the appropriate role of government?[1] What activities should government carry out? More important, perhaps, what activities can it cease carrying out? What activities can be cut?

The founding documents of the United States provide alternate perspectives. The Declaration of Independence stresses that the main goal of government is to protect liberty, while the Constitution proposes that the main goal is to promote the common welfare. Adam Smith, writing in the same period, held that people should have the liberty to pursue

Business and Society, Second Edition, by Alfred A. Marcus. © Irwin/McGraw-Hill, The McGraw-Hill Companies, 1993, 1996.

their economic interests so long as there was a corresponding improvement in the social good.[2] If this liberty did not improve society, then government intervention was justified.

Many economists after Smith have debated the question of why government is needed. They usually start with the premise that markets are a superior means to organize production; governments are needed only to correct defects in the functioning of markets. Most economists agree that governments perform critical functions that cannot be performed adequately by markets (e.g., providing police protection, administering justice, and preventing pollution), but they do not agree that governments should be involved in the redistribution of income or take actions to smooth the business cycle. Economists also acknowledge that government actions are not always called for in the face of market defects. The gains from correcting the defects have to be weighed against the costs of administering the government programs. In this chapter, the arguments about why government is needed made by classic liberal, contemporary liberal, and neoconservative economists are compared.

The Need for Government

For business managers, hounded by unnecessary regulation and red tape, the question of why governments are needed is of real concern. The founders of the American republic did not question the need for government, but they were divided about why. The Declaration of Independence starts with the individual's right to life, liberty, and the pursuit of happiness, which government must protect. If government does not live up to its obligations, the people have the right "to alter or to abolish it" and to institute a new government. In contrast, the framers of the Constitution start with collective interests ("We the people"), which state that government should promote justice, order, and the general welfare, and to provide for the common defense.

These great documents reveal an enduring tension among Americans about why governments exist. Some people start from the premise that individual rights are paramount and governments exist to protect liberty, while others start from the premise that collective welfare is paramount and governments exist to further justice. Almost all U.S. politicians are pragmatic; to reach solutions to problems they draw upon arguments from both schools of thought.

In Economic Theory

consumer sovereignty
Rule by consumers, or decentralized decision making in the market, rather than centralized control by the government.

While politicians are pragmatic about the role of government, economists offer the strongest body of theory on that role. Economists generally prefer **consumer sovereignty**, or decentralized decision making by consumers in the marketplace, to the centralized control of the government. This preference is based on the efficiency advantages of markets, but it is broader than that and includes economic and technological progress, a rising standard of living, social mobility, and political freedom.[3]

Markets have a number of efficiency advantages. First, they tend to achieve particular purposes at lower costs than government, or they accomplish these purposes better for the same costs. In this way, markets outperform government in static efficiency terms. However, they also outperform it in terms of dynamic efficiency; that is, they are better than government at promoting new technologies, improving product quality, and creating new products.[4] Finally, markets outperform government by stimulating organizational improvements, increasing worker and management motivation, and enhancing business decision making.[5]

Market Defects

One of the main proofs of markets outperforming government is illustrated by the newly industrialized economies of Asia, which are in striking contrast to the state-centered economies of the old Communist bloc countries. Nonetheless, almost all economists admit that markets are not perfect and have certain defects or shortcomings that should be corrected by government action (see Figure 26-1). For instance, economic efficiency requires competitive factor and product markets; that is, there must be full market knowledge, full market power by existing producers and consumers, and no obstacles to the free entry of new market participants. These conditions are seldom completely met by markets.[6] Another market defect is the possible inadequate protection of future rights and interests. Government intervention may be justified because private and public perspectives on the valuation of the present and future differ.

FIGURE 26-1
Why governments are needed

The Declaration of Independence:	To preserve liberty.
The Constitution:	To promote the common welfare.
Economic Theory:	To provide for public goods.
	To handle market defects, for example:
	Entry barriers.
	Insufficient consumer knowledge.
	Insufficient consumer power.
	Insufficient protection of future interests.
	To deal with spillovers and externalities.

Public Goods

public goods
Broadly shared commodities that people tend to demand in quantities that private markets cannot provide.

Economists admit that even if markets are operating according to theory, they do not provide certain types of public goods that are needed collectively and not individually. **Public goods** are broadly shared commodities that people tend to demand in quantities that private markets cannot provide. Such goods would not be provided in sufficient quantities were it not for government intervention. For instance, when a given air quality improvement is achieved, the resulting gain is available to everyone. Those who pay for the benefit cannot exclude others from enjoying it. This condition also applies to other public goods, such as national defense, police protection, national parks, and highways. The private market incentive to provide public goods is deficient, even if the preference for them is high.

Spillovers and Externalities

Private market activities also create so-called spillovers or externalities. A positive spillover or externality exists when a producer cannot appropriate all the benefits of the activities it has undertaken. An example would be research and development that yields benefits to society (e.g., employment in subsidiary industries) that the producer cannot capture. Thus, the producer's incentive is to underinvest in the activity unless government subsidizes it. With positive externalities, too little of the good in question is produced; with negative ones too much is made. Negative externalities such as air pollution occur when the producer cannot be charged all the costs. Since the external costs do not enter the calculations the producer makes, the producer manufactures more of the good than is socially beneficial. With both positive and negative externalities, market outcomes need correction to be efficient.

Other Market Defects

Many economists accept that two additional market defects exist. First, to correct for apparent instabilities in the business cycle, the government can implement a variety of fiscal and monetary policies. By themselves, markets may not guarantee a high level of employment, price stability, and a socially desired rate of growth. While Milton Friedman accepts the earlier justifications for government intervention, he contests these premises.[7]

Second, market outcomes may violate cherished values about equality and justice. In the market, a person's distribution of goods depends on factor endowments (e.g., skill and inherited wealth) and the relative prices they command. Society, however, may consider this distribution neither fair nor just. Thus, government may redistribute income through the tax code or the alteration of inheritance laws.

Libertarians reject this argument for two reasons. First, they claim on moral grounds that what someone earns belongs to the person and government has no right to take it away. Second, they argue on practical grounds that if government routinely redistributes income, then the incentive to earn will decline. If this acquisitive instinct diminishes, society is worse off because the economy will not grow as fast.[8]

Imperfect Governments

Where a rationale exists for government involvement, it does not necessarily follow that the government is capable of effectively addressing the problem. While markets are imperfect, governments too have shortcomings, and their ability to correct market imperfections is limited.[9]

In each instance of a market defect, it is necessary to weigh whether the proposed government action would make things better. A helter-skelter approach, where the government tries to correct all that is wrong with markets without first making a careful analysis, is as dangerous to the economy as the defects. The many unintended consequences of this approach tend to complicate matters and make the situation worse rather than better. In the next section, three views of the appropriate role for government—the classic liberal, contemporary liberal, and neoconservative—are summarized and contrasted.

The Classic Liberal View

The best representative of this school is Milton Friedman. His 1962 book, *Capitalism and Freedom*, considered extreme in the 1960s, nearly became the standard wisdom during the Reagan years. Friedman views himself as a classic liberal, not a conservative, because his starting point, like that of Adam Smith, is in opposition to traditional societies that restricted individual liberty.

In traditional societies, people's ability to influence their future is affected by the group to which they belong and the beneficence of the ruling authorities. The modern revolutions that ushered in capitalism stripped away the importance of inherited categories such as peasant and aristocrat, Christian and Jew, or Caucasian and Hispanic. Market economies gave people the right to make transactions without being limited by these restrictions. States became governed by the rule of law rather than the arbitrary whims of kings and nobles.

Friedman has written that "an impersonal market separates economic activities from political views and protects men from being discriminated against in their economic activities for reasons that are irrelevant to their productivity."[10] No government body, no matter what higher purpose it appeals to, should stand in the way of economic liberty. The emancipation of individual talent, energy, and initiative is critical to achieving the economic growth that is synonymous with modern societies.

Friedman believes that a market system provides this freedom for the individual. In a market, people do business with one another, not because of some group to which they belong, but because they offer each other a good or service that is of high quality, low price, or has some other desirable feature.

If forced to choose, Friedman's primary allegiance is to the individual freedom that the market provides, even above economic prosperity. Since individual freedom is his primary value, Friedman's position has been labeled libertarian to distinguish it from economists who defend markets on utilitarian grounds (i.e., they yield prosperity). Markets are a superior means of social organization because they allow for voluntary cooperation based on free discussion, which is the purpose of a liberal society (see Figure 26-2).

FIGURE 26-2
The classic liberal view

Markets are superior because they promote liberty:
    Grant right to make transactions as individuals.
    Permit free discussion/voluntary cooperation.
    Not binding on those not subject to transactions (unlike government).

Governments needed when markets are not practical:
    To protect people and the nation from coercion: "civil order."
    To resolve disputes between conflicting parties: "rule maker and umpire."
    To protect consumers from excessive market power: "technical monopoly."
    To protect individuals from the actions of others: "neighborhood effects."
    To act for those incapable or incompetent to act for themselves: "paternalism."

Governments in pursuing above should not restrict freedom of entry:
    Retards technological innovation.

Governments should limit themselves to areas of technical competence:
    Even with obvious market defect like pollution.

Democratically elected governments, according to Friedman, have deficiencies that markets do not have. For instance, when a democratically elected government makes a decision passed by a majority, all citizens have to obey, even those who oppose the measure. Once made, the decision is binding on everyone. In contrast, each person in the market decides if and how much of a particular good or service to acquire. Each chooses whether to buy, sell, or stay out of the market altogether. The individual makes this choice without being bound by the community's interests as represented by the will of a political majority.[11]

A political decision about national defense spending compels all citizens to conform to its mandate. No longer is each citizen in a position to weigh the evidence and choose how much national defense the person might need or want. However, Friedman recognizes that in the case of indivisible matters such as "protection of the individual and the nation from coercion," reliance on the market is not practical.[12] If each person or group chose the type of protection it wanted (its own weapons and weapon systems, private armies, and security forces), anarchy would result similar to that in Beirut during the 1970s and 1980s or Somalia in the early 1990s.

No settled society is possible under such conditions, nor can the orderly selling and buying necessary for the exercise of free choice in a market exist. So classic liberals accept the cost of relying on government to preserve civil order even if it strains the social fabric. Since the cost exists, reliance on government should be limited to the issues where people have common views and no alternatives are feasible. For example, nearly all people agree about the need for police that guarantee civil order and armies for external defense.

Appropriate Areas for Government

Thus, classic liberals accept that government has an appropriate role to play in certain areas. Besides domestic order and defense, it has an appropriate role as *rule maker and umpire*.[13] The interactions that take place in a market are like a game where the players have to respect the rules. These rules have to be interpreted, enforced, and modified. When individuals have disputes, someone has to resolve them. A judicial system is needed.

Rule Maker and Umpire

People's freedoms come into conflict. One person's right to live, for instance, comes into conflict with another's desire to kill. The government has to guarantee that the freedom to maintain life takes precedence. The government also must be the arbiter between the freedom to combine and the freedom to compete. The European tradition has favored the freedom to combine, while the United States has inclined toward the freedom to compete. In Europe, competitors have had the right to fix prices, divide up markets, and take other actions to keep out potential competitors. In the United States, they have been restricted from doing so and have had to compete by selling better products.

Another case where freedoms conflict concerns the definition of property rights. For instance, does title to a piece of property give owners the right to the minerals in the ground below it or control over what goes on in the air above it? Can owners charge a nuisance price for noise if someone flies an airplane above their property, or must the owners pay the airplane pilots to stop them from making the noise? These are the kinds of questions the judicial system attempts to resolve.

Friedman includes the government's constitutional responsibility "to coin money" and maintain a monetary system as part of the responsibility to be a rule maker and umpire.[14] Friedman does not favor using monetary policies to stabilize economic activity. According to Friedman, the government should increase the money supply in accord with the historic growth rate of the economy (about 3 percent per year), and should not have discretionary authority to adjust the money supply to stimulate or suppress economic activity. As rule-maker and umpire, the government should be neutral.

Correct Market Defects

technical monopoly
The capacity of a company, because of its proficiency, to drive all competitors from the market.

Classic liberals also believe that it is appropriate for government to correct market defects.[15] One of these defects is **technical monopoly**, that is, a company can gain near complete dominance because it is technically more proficient than its competitors. It might legitimately acquire some advantage—economies of scale or scope—that drive virtually all its competitors from the market. The government faces a difficult dilemma because technical monopoly reduces the choices that consumers have in the market. The dominant firm, if no substitutes exist for what it sells, can use its monopoly power to withhold the products from the market and arbitrarily raise their prices.

In many industries, it is possible for firms to gain market dominance via some type of technical advantage. In such industries as electric utilities, the argument that technical monopolies exist has been used to justify regulating utility prices and entry to the industry. Prices are regulated to prevent the monopolist from gaining unfair advantage over consumers. In exchange for limitations on the monopolist's profits, it is guaranteed entry restrictions. No firm can challenge its position, as the government does not let potential challengers compete with the dominant firm.

The United States has favored regulation to deal with technical monopoly. Many European nations, on the other hand, consider public ownership as the answer to this problem. Friedman offers a third alliterative: Allow the monopoly to exist without government controls.[16] As long as the government does not enforce entry restrictions, the monopolist must always be on guard against the threat of technological challenge from a latent rival. If regulation were in place, it would not have to face this challenge. Entry barriers make its markets uncontestable, but they also shield it from technological change that can benefit the public. Free markets work when a firm has gained uncontested dominance through technical means, so long as rivals are not excluded entry into the market through regulation. Friedman's point is that technological stagnation is likely with public regulation.

neighborhood effect
Negative by-products for society created as a result of a transaction between two parties who themselves may be better off.

Another type of market defect that classic liberals recognize is a **neighborhood effect**. The premise of a free market is that when two people voluntarily make a deal, society as a whole will become richer from the aggregation of many such deals. However, what happens if the transactions cause a by-product (e.g., hazardous waste) that society has to clean up? The parties to the transaction may be better off, but society as a whole has to pay the costs.

Friedman's answer to the neighborhood effect is simple: Society must charge the parties to the deal the costs of the cleanup because they are responsible. Whatever damage they generate has to be internalized in the price. By doing so, the market defect (i.e., the price of pollution, which is not counted in the transaction) is corrected. The market price then reflects the true social costs of the deal and the parties have to adjust accordingly. Thus, only deals in the social interest, will be consummated.[17]

To solve this dilemma, however, the U.S. government does not generally supplement the price system, but it regulates the polluter. Friedman maintains that whenever government intervenes in business activity, there is a cost in reduced freedom. He also questions whether government, even by imposing a tax or charge on the polluting parties, is able to determine what damage has been caused or what the monetary value of the damage is. When pollution is involved, the damage is often long term (increased sickness and disease) and intangible (reduced visibility). To collect, the government would have to set up a burdensome administrative apparatus.

Paternalism

A final area where government intervention is appropriate, according to Friedman, is to act on *paternalistic* grounds for those who are incapable or incompetent to act for themselves.[18] The word *paternalism* is an anachronism: remember, Friedman wrote his book in 1962. However, his argument still has merit. Markets demand a high level of capability and competence. People have to be able to reason about their self-interest, absorb information pertaining to it, and then successfully make transactions that make them better off. Not everybody is up to this task. Thus, Friedman provides the rationale for welfare state activities that protect people who are otherwise unable to care for themselves (for example, children, handicapped, and the mentally ill).

The classic liberals' rationales for government activities, even with these qualifications, are extensive. The government has a role to play in defending the nation, providing for law and order, defining property rights, adjudicating disputes, enforcing contracts, preserving competition, establishing a monetary framework, countering technical monopolies and neighborhood effects, and supplementing private charity by helping people who cannot otherwise help themselves. The list of appropriate government functions is quite large, but not as large as the actual list of programs that the government of the United States carries out. (See Figure 26-3).[19]

FIGURE 26-3
Federal government actions that classic liberals cannot justify

Price supports for agriculture.
Tariffs on imports or restrictions on exports.
Rent controls.
Wage and price controls.
Minimum wages.
Maximum interest rates.
Detailed regulations of particular industries.
Mandatory social security, old-age, and retirement programs.
Occupational licensing.
Public housing.
Military conscription.
The creation and maintenance of national parks.
The public delivery of mail.
Publicly owned and operated toll roads.

The Contemporary Liberal View

A good representative of the contemporary liberal school is the Harvard economist Richard Musgrave who, with his wife Peggy Musgrave, has written extensively on public finance. Contemporary liberals like the Musgraves also have a preference for decentralized decision making and individual choice by consumers in the marketplace. Their justifications for government activity rest on a variety of market imperfections with which classic liberals would agree.[20]

1. *Uncompetitive factor and product markets.* Free entry, full market knowledge, and market power on the part of producers and consumers are needed. Government assures competition and expands producer and consumer knowledge. Thus, it endeavors to prevent monopoly and require that warning labels be attached to products such as cigarettes.

2. *Public goods.* Government should provide such public goods as national defense, education, roads, and canals. Such goods would not be provided in ample quantities were it not for government intervention. The providers could not appropriate sufficient benefits for themselves to justify creating the amount demanded by the public.

Contemporary liberals differ from classic liberals in adding the following justifications to their list (see Figure 26-4):

3. *Justice and equality*. These cherished values may be violated by the market. Thus, government has to make adjustments in the distribution of income by means of the tax systems and other means such as the laws of inheritance.
4. *Employment, price stability, and growth*. The market system may not guarantee a high level of employment, price stability, and a socially desired rate of growth without government intervention. To correct instability in the business cycle, the government can use fiscal (budgetary) and monetary policies.

FIGURE 26-4
The contemporary
liberal view

Governments needed to deal with market defects:
  Uncompetitive factor and product markets.
  Public goods.
  Justice and equality.
  Employment, price stability, and growth.

Even contemporary liberals, despite their commitment to a larger role for government, admit that governments can err and be inefficient in attempting to remedy market defects.

Three Functions

Contemporary liberals divide the appropriate functions of government into three categories: allocation, distribution, and stabilization. Conflicts can exist among these functions and resolving them is a major challenge that governments face.

Allocation

Both classic and contemporary liberals accept nearly the same position regarding allocation of public goods. All members of society, not just those who purchase the good, enjoy the benefits. The private market incentive for providing such public goods as national defense or police protection is not great, even if the preference for them is high. Therefore, government intervenes; in this instance, voting by ballot replaces free market decision making.

A distinction, however, must be made between public provision of goods and public production. While the public provision of goods is relatively high (at least 20 percent) in all countries in the world—both those with large public and those with large private sectors—in only a few countries is there a large degree of public production. The United States is roughly equivalent to other countries in the world with regard to the provision of public goods, but ranks low in public production (only 12 percent). Most public goods (e.g., weapons and weapons systems) in the United States are purchased from the private sector (i.e., the defense industry).[21]

Distribution

distribution
Government alteration of
society's income toward
greater equality.

Contemporary liberals accept but classic liberals reject **distribution** as a government function. Unlike classic liberals, contemporary liberals argue that some alteration in the pattern of inequality is necessary. Contemporary liberals are critical of the tenet of welfare economics, the Pareto rule, that holds that a change in economic conditions improves the welfare of society when it makes the situation of Person A better without Persons B or C becoming worse off. Someone gains, but no one loses. However, this may mean that excessive concentrations of wealth exist at the top of the scale and inadequate incomes exist at the lower end. The blight of poverty then affects nearly everyone as it spawns crime, drug addiction, and numerous other social problems. Thus, contemporary liberals call for tax transfers that tax the wealthiest to subsidize low-income people. The cost is in deadweight losses that arise from the inefficiencies of administering government programs. Another cost is reduced efficiency for the economy as a whole as the wealthy may choose leisure over work.

Stabilization

stabilization
Government control over budgets and monetary policy is used to maintain high levels of growth and employment and low levels of inflation.

Another government function over which contemporary and classic liberals disagree is **stabilization**. There are substantial fluctuations in the business cycle; contemporary liberals believe that it is the role of government to try to control these cycles.[22] Unemployment and inflation may plague society unless government acts to change the level of aggregate demand by means of taxation and consumption. Of course, government, by making mistakes, could cause destabilization. This is the essence of Friedman's main critique of macroeconomic policies.

Moreover, economies do not operate in isolation but are linked to other economies by means of trade and capital flows. These flows have been increasing rapidly in the post World War II period. They make it difficult for any single national government to control its economy by means of macroeconomic stabilization. International cooperation is needed but difficult to achieve. Still, there is agreement in most countries in the world to stabilize the business cycle by means of monetary and fiscal policies.

The Neoconservative View

neoconservatives
Economic view that considers government shortcomings before advocating that government act to correct market defects.

Many people who formerly were contemporary liberals became neoconservatives after the failure of government programs such as the War on Poverty and the Vietnam War. The views of neoconservatives have been elegantly summarized by Rand Institute economist Charles Wolf, Jr.[23] Classic and contemporary liberals admit that government failure is possible. **Neoconservatives** emphasize this possibility. They ask that the shortcomings of the government be compared with the shortcomings of the market before proposals to remedy market defects are carried out (see Figure 26-5).

FIGURE 26-5
The neoconservative view

Compare government shortcomings with market shortcomings:
Government exclusive provider.
Uncertain technology for providing goods.
Unanticipated results.

The analysis of government failures should be expanded to include the following:

1. Government is often the exclusive provider of public goods and has near monopoly status.
2. Uncertainty surrounds the means of providing public goods (e.g., on education, what constitutes good teaching; on defense, what is needed to guarantee national security).

3.   The unanticipated results of government activities (e.g., good intentions to provide for the poor may result in welfare dependence).

Neoconservatives judge markets and governments on the basis of efficiency and equity. In their emphasis on equity they resemble contemporary liberals. They have looked very closely at the definitions of equity. Rawlsian notions of equity favor the lot of the least advantaged in society before the lot of the most advantaged. (Marx would distribute to each person according to the person's needs and demand from each according to the person's abilities.) Neoconservatives favor equality of opportunity over that of outcome.

Neoconservatives accept public goods arguments for government intervention. There may be positive externalities from government investment in research and development—benefits not appropriable by firms operating in the private market.[24] Another case of under-investment, if only private market forces are operating, is philanthropy, where the benefits are available to society at large (less crime, drug addiction, and fewer social problems) but the costs are borne exclusively by the donor.

In some cases of traditionally labeled "market failure," neoconservatives are skeptical of why government should be involved. Their arguments about technical monopoly, for instance, are similar to those made by Milton Friedman. So-called technical monopoly situations may not require government intervention if there are contestable markets. If new entrants can challenge the monopoly, its status is temporary. If a firm has to be constantly on guard against this situation, it cannot exploit consumers.

Acceptable Government Involvement

Neoconservatives accept a broad range of government involvement. First, government action is justified in providing regulatory services in such areas as the environment (where there are externalities), food and drug controls (where consumers lack information), and radio and television licensing (where there otherwise would be a monopoly). Second, it is justified in producing pure public goods such as national defense, police protection, and the administration of justice. These goods cannot be provided by the private sector. Third, the government is justified in producing quasi-public goods such as education, postal services, and health research. These goods may also be provided by the private sector (so there is some competition), but not in the quantities required by the public. Finally, some transfer programs such as social security and welfare are justified.

Neoconservatives believe that in theory these activities are justified, but in practice these offerings have proliferated too greatly. Wolf, for instance, argues that demand for government intervention is inflated for a variety of reasons (see Figure 26-6).[25]

FIGURE 26-6
Reasons that demand for government programs is inflated

- Increased public awareness of market shortcomings.
- Less tolerance for these shortcomings.
- Greater degree of political organization and enfranchisement.
- The rewards to legislators and government officials to publicize problems and find solutions.
- Legislators' need to show that they are taking dramatic actions so that they will be reelected.
- The decoupling of burdens and benefits.

Decoupling of Burdens and Benefits

To explain government growth, neoconservatives emphasize the decoupling of burdens and benefits. Decoupling explains why some programs like gun control are so difficult to pass. The public that would benefit is large and dispersed, while those that would bear the burden—the gun lobby—are concentrated and well organized. On the other hand, some programs help specific groups, while the burden is widely dispersed throughout the public. The specific groups have a large incentive to organize and to appropriate the benefit, while the broad public, where each person may lose only a few dollars, has little incentive to organize and to oppose the program. Thus, farmers and retirees are formidable political blocs capable of winning substantial gains through the political process because of the decoupling of burdens and benefits. These two types of decoupling the neoconservatives call **microdecoupling**.

microdecoupling
The dominance of small, concentrated special interest groups in politics over the larger, dispersed and less well-organized majority.

Another type of decoupling occurs when the vast majority enjoys the benefits of government programs, such as progressive taxation (because the vast majority is relatively poor), while a small minority bear the burden (the small but wealthy minority that provides most of the tax base). As long as political power is based on majority rule, there is a danger of the majority exploiting a minority in a democracy. This type of decoupling the neoconservatives call *macrodecoupling*.[26]

Government Incapacity

Neoconservatives also stress the incapacity of government to effectively manage programs that have been created. Conditions such as the following lead to ineffective management:

1. Without competition, it is hard for the government to provide services at adequate levels of efficiency and quality.
2. It is difficult to define and measure the output of government programs.
3. There is no bottom-line termination mechanism.

In a market, costs are linked to prices by consumers who decide what to buy. In government, revenues come from taxes linked only indirectly to services. Taxpayers do not directly obtain goods or services for tax dollars. They express their will by voting. Politicians support programs they oppose, but they also vote for programs that taxpayers favored. The taxpayers cannot unbundle their support for politicians in the same way they unbundle their decisions to buy goods and services in the market.

The result is that government agencies have less need than businesses to be precise about their actions. The standards they use can be vague. Private internal goals may dominate and take precedence over public goals.

Additional problems affect the supply of government services. First, the systems that government is attempting to influence are very complex. Efforts to correct market failures in one area may create unanticipated consequences in another. In addition, although inequality of income is less of a problem, inequality of power and privilege among government officials can be problematic. When one group has the right to command and coerce another, abuses are likely.[27]

Traditional Conservatives

Although not a major part of present-day economic thought, another increasingly important group is traditional conservatives. They do not share the individualistic premises of the economists, do not value individual freedom as the highest good, and do not see free markets, inviolable property rights, and limited governments as the means to assure that freedom. Rather, they follow in the footsteps of Edmund Burke, the 18th-century British philosopher, who was a critic of the French Revolution and individual rights. The traditional conservatives argue that institutions like the family, church, and state are important in stabilizing the social order. These collective institutions, which help protect the delicate fabric of society and promote law and order, come before individual rights and liberties.

The Fusionist Conservative Coalition

The fusionist conservative coalition of the modern Republican party, which elected Ronald Reagan and George Bush, appealed to both classic liberals and traditional conservatives. Reagan, as a representative of this coalition, showed his hostility to big government and favored market forces. At the same time, he supported large increases in defense expenditures and maintained that the family and church should be relied upon to mitigate social problems. The eclectic forces brought together in the Republican coalition helps explain its inconsistencies on an issue like abortion, which classic liberals permit and traditional conservatives prohibit.

If their viewpoints are so different, how could classic liberals and traditional conservatives find a common home in the Republican party? An important reason is that they both vigorously opposed communism, the classic liberals for communism's repressing individual rights and markets, and the traditional conservatives for communism's atheism and its opposition to organized religions.[28] The demise of worldwide communism may spell the end of the coalition as religious elements threaten to dominate it.

Government in Practice

Government policies are not crafted by economic theoreticians but by politicians, and fathoming what politicians do and why they do it is a complicated matter. The deliberations that determine political outcomes are influenced by the constitutional system of checks and balances instituted by the founders of the American republic. The founders imagined a large country with diverse interests. Fearful of a powerful majority, they tried to create a system where no faction could dominate. The participants in political controversies, therefore, are wide-ranging and diverse. They include citizens, interest groups, corporations, trade associations, environmental organizations, federal bureaucrats, and the media. Different professional groups—scientists, physicians, engineers, and lawyers—provide expert opinion. Sages, seers, and pundits testify in front of congressional committees, appear on talk shows, and write columns for newspapers. Policy is affected by factual information, theory, beliefs, values, attitudes, conjectures, statistics, and anecdotes. When economists are consulted, it is simply as part of this process.

Among economists there is a broad consensus that, all things being equal, markets are superior to government in achieving efficient outcomes. There is consensus about market defects that justify government intervention to guarantee market efficiency. However, when it comes to applying principles, economists disagree.

Why Governments Have Grown

Governments have grown for many reasons, most of them not because of matters of economic principle. To get a sense of the magnitude of this growth, it is useful to compare

1929 statistics with current ones. In 1929, there were 68,000 civilian federal employees in Washington, and 500,000 federal civil servants in the nation, of whom 300,000 worked for the Post Office.[29] Nonetheless, the federal government was smaller than companies such as United States Steel, General Motors, and Standard Oil. By 1940, however, there were a million federal employees, and by 1970 nearly three million. To this day, the government surpasses most corporations in the number of employees.

Theories on why government has grown are plentiful.[30]

Economic Development

In undeveloped nations, taxes and social security contributions typically account for a much lower percentage of gross national product (GNP) than in developed nations. The "law of increasing state activity" attributes growth in government to the complex social changes associated with industrialization.

Party Politics

Whether a nation's government is controlled by left-wing or right-wing political parties provides a strong key to the relative degree of change in government spending. There is a strong positive correlation between the size of increases in the public sector and the degree to which left-wing parties dominate.

Voting

Alexis de Tocqueville, in his classic formulation, attributes the expansion of government expenditures to the spread of the franchise and an increase in economic equality.[31] As the franchise is extended, the income of the median voter declines. The median voter is able to redistribute income.

The Supply of Revenues

Economic development, party politics, and voting are demand-side theories. Other theories focus on the supply side, explaining government growth in terms of the public revenues that can be sustained through taxation. The bracket creep explanation of government growth, for example, holds that a progressive income tax, with inflation and unindexed brackets, moves taxpayers into higher marginal brackets and leads to increased revenues and a real increase in public expenditures. Decreases in self-employment lead to increases in taxable earnings, as employees who work for others are less able to underreport their income than are the self-employed.

Legislative Decision Making

Other explanations for increased government expenditures focus on institutions. For example, in a simplified world, legislators are likely to favor all bills benefiting their own districts. When the costs of such bills are allocated across all districts, legislators will agree to pass all bills so long as the ones that benefit their own districts are supported.

Bureaucratic Process

Another theory is that the size and the structure of the budget are the inadvertent result of bureaucratic drift.[32] How bureaucrats solve year-to-year problems influences the problems and sets of solutions available in subsequent years. Short-sighted yearly decisions lead to cumulative long-term problems.

The size and scope of governments in countries with different systems vary a great deal. The United States is behind many other countries in total taxes as a percentage of GNP. The relative size of the government sector is lower in the United States than in any other major developed country except Japan. No theory provides definitive guidance about what the size and scope of government should take in countries with different social, political, and cultural systems.

Conclusions

Economic theory is one of the main foundations for contemporary ideology about the state. Economists believe that markets are the superior means for organizing a nation's economic life; their preference is for a minimal state. Most believe that the individual consumer should be sovereign. Economists contrast consumer sovereignty with rule by government. Consumers should govern because individuals are best able to judge their needs and preferences through the transactions they make in the marketplace. Through the invisible hand of the marketplace, society prospers. Reflective of those marketplace transactions are the laws of supply and demand, which move the goods of a society to their most productive uses. No central planning agency of government can achieve with the same wisdom and foresight what freely cooperating consumers accomplish on their own.

Economists, however, are not anarchists about government. Most economists accept that government should play an important role: provide for the common defense, establish domestic order, make laws and settle disputes, regulate unfair business practices, protect citizens from monopoly and the undesired side effects (externalities) of market activities, and provide them with some of the collective goods (e.g., highways) they seek but which their voluntary behavior does not provide. The question is not so much one of permitting or not permitting government activity, but of determining the proper mix of government and markets in a well-functioning system.

Even though economists share a preference for markets and recognize that government has a role to play in correcting market defects, they divide with regard to the following points:

1. Classic liberals emphasize individual liberty and believe that big government is the gravest threat. They prefer a minimal state in which the functions and size of government are severely limited. Every infringement by government on individual rights is to be avoided.
2. Contemporary liberals begin with community values, such as justice and the common welfare, instead of individual happiness. To promote community goals, they accept that the government should try to smooth the business cycle and that its programs should redistribute income from the wealthy to the less advantaged (see the special feature, "On Property and Poverty"). In this way, all people are on a more equal footing in the competition that goes on in the marketplace.
3. Neoconservatives are skeptical of the government's abilities to achieve public goals. They emphasize that whenever the government acts, unanticipated side effects that run counter to what the government intends can occur. Thus, in trying to provide for aid to the disadvantaged, the government may stifle individual initiative. While its aims are noble, the government's capabilities to remake society are limited.

On Property and Poverty

It is interesting to note that classic liberals and contemporary liberals both can appeal to John Locke's views on property. Locke believed that property was the result of people's hard work, applied skills, and unusual talent and that therefore they were entitled to the fruits of their labor. On the other hand, he felt that no person should own more property than that person could properly use. According to this "spoilage principle," the government had the right to redistribute any excess.

With regard to poverty, the classic liberal would like to see problems like poverty solved by the voluntary actions of private charities and social welfare agencies, but recognizes that government might have to play a role. The contemporary liberal stresses that in an increasingly interdependent society, it is impossible for people to participate in the economy in isolation from each other.

Whenever voluntary deals are made, they are likely to affect others who are not immediate parties to the deals. The right to freedom, moreover, is not sufficient if one does not also possess the means, that is, the resources and educational attainments, to express that freedom. Thus, government must give the disadvantaged a place to start in life so that they can catch up with the more advantaged.

All three ideologies agree that unless the problems of the disadvantaged are addressed, society will face more crime, social conflict, and discord, which will hurt everyone. The neoconservatives simply emphasize that there may be little that government can effectively do in this area.

Source: P. Navarro, *The Policy Game* (New York: John Wiley, 1984).

Discussion Questions

1. Compare the views expressed in the Declaration of Independence and the Constitution concerning why government is needed. Are these views really so different?
2. Why do economists prefer markets to governments?
3. What is a market defect? Give some examples.
4. What is a spillover? Give an example of a positive and a negative spillover.
5. Are governments perfect? If so, what difference does it make?
6. Friedman cites the benefits of an "impersonal market." What are they?
7. What is wrong with democracy, according to Friedman? Why are markets superior?
8. Why can't the armed forces be privatized? Why can't the police be privatized? Would the justice system work better if it were privatized? Would jails and schools be better run if they were privatized? Isn't Friedman really a big government liberal?
9. What do you think about Friedman's argument about contestable markets (freedom of entry) in the case of technical monopoly?
10. Do you think pollution taxes are a good idea? Why or why not?
11. Why doesn't Friedman's paternalism argument justify social security?
12. What is a public good? Why does the government have to intervene to provide it?
13. How do the views of contemporary liberals differ from the views of classic liberals like Friedman?
14. How do the views of neoconservatives differ from the views of classic liberals like Friedman?
15. How do the views of neoconservatives differ from the views of contemporary liberals?
16. What is microdecoupling? What is macrodecoupling?
17. Why is government not better at providing goods and services to the public? Why is it not more efficient?
18. What is the fusionist conservative coalition?
19. What are some reasons for the growth of government?

Endnotes

1. Jonathan Rauch, "The Long Good-Bye," *National Journal*, Feb. 22, 1992, pp. 438-41.
2. Dennis Collins, "Adam Smith's Social Contract," *Business and Professional Ethics* 7, pp. 119-46.

3. M. Friedman and R. Friedman, *Free to Choose: A Personal Statement* (New York: Avon Books, 1980).

4. "Dear Landlord," *The Economist*, February 9, 1991, pp. 75-76 (a review of "Directly Unproductive Profit-seeking Activities," by J. Bhagwati, in *Journal of Political Economy*, 1982, p. 90); C. Wolf, Jr., *Markets or Governments: Choosing between Imperfect Alternatives* (Cambridge, Mass.: MIT Press, 1988).

5. H. Leibenstein, "A Branch of Economics Is Missing: Micro-Micro Theory," *Journal of Economic Literature* 17 (1979), pp. 477-502.

6. R. Musgrave and P. Musgrave, "Fiscal Functions: An Overview," in *The Politics of American Economic Policy Making*, ed. R. Peretz (Armonk, N.Y.: M. E. Sharpe, 1987), pp. 3-22.

7. M. Friedman, *Capitalism and Freedom* (Chicago: University of Chicago Press, 1962).

8. G. Gilder, *Wealth and Poverty* (New York: Basic Books, 1981).

9. Wolf, *Markets or Governments*.

10. Cited by P. Navarro, *The Policy Game* (New York: John Wiley, 1984).

11. Friedman, *Capitalism and Freedom*.

12. Ibid., p. 23.

13. Ibid.

14. Ibid.

15. Ibid.

16. Ibid.

17. Ibid.

18. Ibid., pp. 31-32.

19. Ibid.

20. R. Musgrave and P. Musgrave, "Fiscal Functions: An Overview from Musgrave and Musgrave," *Public Finance in Theory and Practice*, 4th ed. (New York: New York University Press, 1984), pp. 3-22.

21. Ibid.

22. Ibid.

23. Wolf, *Markets or Governments*.

24. Ibid.

25. Ibid.

26. Ibid.

27. Wolf, *Markets or Governments*; Richard Rose, "What if Anything Is Wrong with Big Government?" *Journal of Public Policy*, 1981, pp. 5-37.

28. Wolf, *Markets or Governments*.

29. B. D. Porter, "Parkinson's Law Revisited: War and the Growth of American Government," *The Public Interest*, Summer 1980.

30. Patrick Larkey et al., "Theorizing about the Growth of Government: A Research Assessment," *Journal of Public Policy* 1, pt. 2 (May 1981), p. 167; D. R. Cameron, "The Expansion of the Public Economy: A Comparative Analysis," *American Political Science Review* 72 (1978), pp. 1243-61; J. B. Kau and P. H. Rubin, "The Size of Government," *Public Choice* 37, no. 2 (1981), pp. 261-74; A. Meltzer and S. Richard, "A Rational Theory of the Size of Government," *Journal of Political Economy* 89, no. 5 (Oct. 1981), pp. 914-27; A. T. Peacock and J. Wiseman, *The Growth of Public Expenditures in the United States*, (Princeton, N.J.: Princeton University Press, 1961), as cited by R. Larkey et al., "Theorizing about the Growth of Government," p. 167.

31. Alexis de Tocqueville, *Democracy in America* (Oxford: Oxford World Classics, 1835).

32. C. E. Lindblom, "The Science of 'Muddling Through,'" in H. I. Ansoff, ed., *Business Strategy* (New York: Penguin Books, 1977), pp. 41-60.

Chapter Twenty-Seven

GOVERNMENT SUPPORT FOR INDUSTRY

COMPETITIVENESS

Laissez-faire should be the general practice; every departure from it, unless required by some great good, is a certain evil.

John Stuart Mill

While America's commitments steadily increased after 1945, its share of world manufacturing and of world gross national product began to decline, at first rather slowly, and then with increasing speed ... there is the country's industrial decline relative to overall world production, not only in older manufacturers, such as textiles, iron and steel, shipbuilding, and basic chemicals, but also ... in robotics, aerospace technology, automobiles, machine tools, and computers ... The uncompetitiveness of U.S. industrial products abroad ... have ... produced staggering deficits in visible trade ...

Paul Kennedy, "The (Relative) Decline of America"[1]

Introduction

This chapter examines the recent performance of the U.S. economy and the role of government in promoting competitiveness. It will show that by changing the size and structure of markets and the costs of doing business, government has affected businesses in many ways. Post-World War II policies were influenced by business cycle management and the growth of social regulation (e.g. occupational safety, pollution control, and affirmative action). These were followed by a wave of deregulation of controlled industries (e.g., airlines and banks). The current debate is whether the United States should have policies, like those in Japan and the European countries, that promote industry competitiveness. U.S. political traditions, however, differ from those in other countries. This chapter will look at the debate about government's role in promoting industry competitiveness.

The Performance of the U.S. Economy

The Japanese, along with other international rivals, are supposed to be eroding U.S. economic strength. Critiques of U.S. economic performance include the following:

"paper entrepreneurs"
U.S. managers are charged with being experts in financial manipulation but lacking in knowledge and skills of basic technologies and production.

- Having been hurt by declining mathematical scores among students, a glut of attorneys, and a shortage of machinists and skilled laborers, the productivity of U.S. manufacturing has fallen seriously behind that of other nations.[2]
- Too many American managers lack hands-on knowledge of technologies and production. They are experts in the arts of financial manipulation, mere **"paper entrepreneurs,"** who have no understanding of what happens on the factory floor.[3]

- American manufacturing is held back by a proliferation of rules and unnecessary control systems. It is well suited to making mass items in a predictable and routinized fashion, but it is not well suited to flexible manufacturing that involves skilled labor and rapidly changing technologies in knowledge intensive industries.[4]

Some believe that "U.S. industry's loss of competitiveness ... has been nothing short of an economic disaster."[5] It is no longer true that each generation of Americans can look forward to more comfortable conditions than its predecessors.

This dim view of U.S. economic prospects, however, is not shared by everyone.[6] Some feel that a relative decline of the United States was inevitable, natural, and indeed beneficial; certainly, it is not something about which to be alarmed. The easy superiority achieved by Americans after World War II was not sustainable. Indeed, U.S. intentions have been to help other nations achieve greater equality with the United States because it needed strong trading partners.[7] Through programs such as the Marshall Plan and the promotion of free trade, the United States contributed to the recovery of the Western European and Japanese economies.

How Well Has the U.S. Economy Been Doing?

A report issued in 1985 by President Reagan's Commission on Industrial Competitiveness claimed that the nation's ability to compete internationally was facing "unprecedented" challenges from abroad. U.S. world leadership and the ability to provide Americans with the standard of living and opportunities to which they aspired were at stake.[8] Contrary to these views, another report stated that with the exception of selected industries, the U.S. economy remained competitive with the economies of Japan and Western Europe.[9]

Signs of Decline

The signs of declining competitiveness were U.S. growth rates, which had fallen behind those of its international rivals (see Figure 27-1),[10] and major trade deficits. By 1986, the current account (trade) deficit had reached $160 billion. In a host of critical industries from automobiles to textile machinery, imports increased as a percentage of the domestic market. New industries, moreover, were not springing up to replace the old and annual productivity increases had been falling, which did not portend well for the future.

Continued Strength in the Economy

In some areas, the U.S. economy showed surprising strength (see Figure 27-2).[11] Living standards remained equal to or above those in Western Europe and Japan. Social mobility was high. Almost half of the top 25 percent of earners in the United States fell from that position every seven years, and nearly half of the bottom 25 percent moved up. Compared with the economies of Europe and Japan, the U.S. economy was a powerful job creator. It absorbed the baby-boom generation and nearly 12 million legal and illegal immigrants, and created over 22 million jobs during the 1970s. The European economies, in contrast, had net job losses and high rates of unemployment. From 1960 to 1980, 30 million new jobs were created in the United States, but only 7.5 million in Japan and 2.5 million in Western Europe. U.S. unemployment rates fell behind those of most of its international competitors between 1985 and 1995. The exception was Japan, which had very low participation by women in the workforce.

FIGURE 27-1

Evidence of declining
U.S. competitiveness[11]

Growth in GNP per Employed Person (%)

	1960-73	1974-78
U.S.	1.8%	.1%
Germany	4.7	3.0
France	4.5	3.0
U.K.	3.2	.8
Japan	8.9	3.2

U.S. Trade Gap

Exports as Percentage of GNP		Imports as Percentage of GNP		Trade Gap as Percentage of GNP	
1970	1980	1970	1980	1970	1980
9.3%	19%	9.3%	22.0%	0	3.0%

Weakened Industries:
Imports as a Percentage of the U.S. Domestic Market

	1960	1980
Automobiles	4.1%	27.0%
Consumer electronics	5.6	50.6
Cutlery	8.2	90.0
Steel	4.2	14.0
Machine tools	3.2	28.0
Textile machinery	6.6	45.5

Declines in U.S. Productivity Growth

	Average Annual Increase
1948-65	3.2%
1965-73	2.4
1973-78	1.1

FIGURE 27-2

Evidence of U.S.
economic strength

Per Capita Purchasing Power, 1992 (in U.S. $)

U.S.	$23,400
Japan	19,800
Canada	19,600
France	18,900
Germany	17,400
U.K.	15,900

Unemployment Rates in Major Industrialized Nations[12] (as a percent of total workforce)

	1995	1990	1985	1980	1970	1960
Japan	2.9%	2.1%	2.6%	2.0%	1.2%	1.7%
U.S.	5.4	5.5	7.2	7.1	4.9	5.5
U.K.	8.6	5.9	11.2	7.0	3.1	2.2
Germany	8.2	7.1	7.2	6.4	.5	1.1
Canada	9.6	8.1	10.5	7.5	5.7	6.5
France	12.6	10.2	10.4	6.4	2.5	1.5

Productivity Trends

According to the economist Paul Krugman, the most important indicator of competitive strength was productivity: "Productivity isn't everything, but in the long run it is almost everything."[13] In this area, the United States still held an absolute edge. In 1990, the average U.S. worker produced $45,000 in goods and services as opposed to $38,000 for the average German worker and $35,000 for the average Japanese worker. However, U.S. productivity growth averaged just 0.9 percent per year during 1973-1992, after averaging 3 percent per year from 1937 to 1972. Between 1972 and 1990, Japanese productivity grew at an annual rate of 3 percent and German productivity at an annual rate of 1.6 percent while U.S. productivity grew at only 0.5 percent per year. If these trends continued, Japan and Germany would overtake the United States in productivity.[14]

It is important to note that U.S. productivity gains often were achieved through curtailing wages and downsizing companies, while in Germany and Japan they were achieved by investment in new plant and equipment and in worker skills.[15] German and Japanese companies were constrained from pursuing low wages and layoffs by unions, social policies, and regulation. Managers in those countries could not hire, fire, and redeploy their workforces as readily as U.S. managers. They had to invest in new plant and equipment, education, training, and innovation. U.S. investment from 1987 to 1992 was the lowest among the Group of 7 nations.[16] At 10.7 percent of GDP in 1991, it represented only one-half the investment of Japan. Unsurprisingly, the typical machine tool in the United States was seven years older than that in Japan.

Service Sector Jobs

Millions of new jobs had been created in the U.S. service sector, which employed nearly 80 percent of U.S. workers. Labor-intensive jobs in this sector, such as health care and fast foods, were expanding. In contrast, manufacturing employment in the United States contracted from 26.4 percent of total employment in 1960 to under 20 percent in 1980.[17]

To thrive, many service industries such as finance, process engineering, and consulting, depended on a strong manufacturing base to create demand for what they had to offer. Historically, productivity growth had been most rapid in manufacturing. Technological progress was achieved through automation and economies of scale. On the other hand, the nation's largest sector, the service industries, depended on personal relations (e.g., medicine or hairstyling) where productivity growth remained sluggish because it was difficult to introduce gains. Though output in the service sector was hard to measure, the data suggested weak growth during the 1980s, only 0.7 percent annual increases in productivity compared with 3.8 percent in manufacturing.[18]

Service Sector Cutbacks During the Recession

The recession at the outset of the 1990s led to large layoffs in the service industries. Downsizing was common in banks, department stores, advertising agencies, and airlines, where cuts were made among middle managers, loan officers, and sales personnel. White-collar workers lost 41 percent of the jobs during the recession, the highest proportion on record. With growing global competition and the deregulation of telecommunications, transportation, banking, and insurance, these trends were likely to continue.[19]

core staffing
A company retains only a nucleus of permanent workers and contracts out the remaining jobs to temporary workers, part-time workers, and consultants.

Many service firms were moving toward a concept of **core staffing**, where the company retained only a shrinking nucleus of permanent workers and contracted out the remaining jobs to temporary workers, part-time workers, and consultants. Companies found it increasingly difficult to add full-time workers because of the cost of worker benefits (e.g., unemployment, health insurance, workers compensation and social security).

Many service companies also started to rethink the way they did their work. Work redesign, lean production, and total quality management were the rule. The Bank of Boston, for instance, changed the way it processed securities by consolidating the activity at a single location instead of 11 and reducing the number of computer systems from six to two.

Trade Imbalances

Service industries such as medical care, education, transportation, and government offered few opportunities for export. The country's merchandise trade balance, which in 1971 became negative for the first time in this century, continued along a negative path to reach record low levels (see Figure 27-3). The United States had a negative trade balance of $158.9 billion in 1990. Among its major rivals, only the United Kingdom had a similar negative balance. Other rivals had positive balances: Japan, $145.2 billion; Germany, $43.6 billion; France, $16.2 billion; and Canada, $9.2 billion.[20] The United States remained the world's leader in per capita purchasing power, but it trailed Japan in per capita GNP, largely because the GNP adjusts for the flow of money into a national economy from positive trade balances and resulting currency strength.

FIGURE 27-3
Trade balances and GNP per capital:[21] (U.S. $ billions)

	United States	United Kingdom	France	Canada	Japan	Germany
Trade balance	$-122.3	$-37.6	$-17.8	$ 6.8	$ 52.2	$ 65.2
Imports	516.2	222.8	234.4	124.8	235.4	354.8
Exports	393.9	185.2	216.6	131.7	287.6	420.0
GNP per Capita (U.S. $ thousands)	21.0	14.3	20.1	16.8	22.9	19.5

Manufacturing

U.S. decline was evident in capital-intensive manufacturing industries such as automobiles, steel, electronics, and home appliances. In these industries, improvement in productivity depends on capital investment; however, U.S. capital formation per employed person in the United States was down.[22]

Investment

Investment depends on savings, but U.S. savings rates also lagged behind other countries (see Figure 27-4). Capital costs in the United States, therefore, were higher. The weighted average of debt and equity costs after taxes during the 1980s was about 5.5 percent in the United States, 4 percent in West Germany, 3.5 percent in Great Britain, and 3 percent in Japan. Given Japan's advantage in capital costs, it was no surprise that its annual gross investment per factory worker was higher than that of the United States. This gap widened from a 40 percent lead during 1972-1982 to an 85 percent lead from 1982 to 1986.[23]

American businesses, like those in the United Kingdom, depended more heavily on equity financing than businesses in Japan or Germany. Equity holders assumed a part-ownership position—and the additional risks entailed—because they expected higher returns. This expectation put pressure on managers to produce short-term profits, and thus prevented as much investment in labor-saving equipment as the foreign rivals of the United States. Though productivity growth in the United States improved somewhat between 1986 and 1989, it still lagged behind that of other nations.

FIGURE 27-4
Personal savings as share of disposable personal income

	United States	United Kingdom	France	Canada	Japan	Germany
1960	6.2	6.6	15.2	3.9	17.4	8.6
1970	8.3	9.2	18.7	5.6	18.2	13.8
1980	7.3	13.5	17.6	13.6	17.9	12.7
1985	4.5	9.7	14.0	13.3	16.0	11.4
1990	4.6	8.7	12.8	10.8	15.9	13.7

High Capital Costs

High capital costs meant that U.S. managers had to be extremely careful about the types of investments they made. They had to be able to demonstrate on a project-by-project basis that they could maximize returns or the projects would not be approved. The discount rate estimates used in cost projections made projects that promised big, immediate paybacks the favorites over long-term projects that promised gradual, less spectacular returns.

Dow Chemical estimated that its international competitors, which controlled 32 percent of the chemical market, paid three percentage points less for borrowed money and six points less for equity financing.[24] Dow's long-term spending had to be concentrated on a select group of technologies including engineering thermoplastics and pharmaceuticals, which were in related areas that complemented each other. Dow could wait only five years for these investments to start to pay off.

High-Tech Weakness

Weakness in manufacturing did not pose a serious threat if the United States continued to hold the lead in high technology, but the U.S. advantage in this area also deteriorated. The country lost market share in such high-tech industries as semiconductors, scientific and medical equipment, robotics, advanced fiber optics, and composite materials. The level of American inventions remained high, but the commercialization of new ideas into competitive products fell behind that of other nations.

High capital costs plagued computer giants like Control Data and Cray Research, which had to alter or abandon long-term plans to develop U.S. supercomputer technology. Although Control Data had invested $350 million in supercomputers, its bankers and shareholders were unwilling to spend at least $150 million more to wait for a possible payback. Cray Research also needed up to $200 million to complete its supercomputer projects; it even created a separate company for the venture called Cray Computer Corporation headed by Cray's founder, Seymour Cray, but Cray Computer did not last. In 1995, it filed for Chapter 11 protection under the Federal Bankruptcy Act.[25] This financial turbulence in the American computer industry put Japan's Hitachi, Fujitsu, and NEC, computer giants with no such problems, in a position to gain dominance in an important technology.

High capital costs have hurt technological development in particularly critical areas such as semiconductors, which are components to many other products. DRAMs are the semiconductor memory chip used in products from digital watches to supercomputers. The Japanese were able to gain control of a large percentage of this market, in part because they had lower capital costs that enabled them to continue to make high levels of investment even during downturns in the business cycle, something that no American manufacturer was able to do. While U.S. companies relied on the equity market to fund development and early manufacturing, the Japanese companies borrowed at one-quarter of the cost.[26]

U.S. companies hoped to overcome this disadvantage by forming a new joint venture. Called U.S. Memories, it included Intel, National Semiconductor, Advanced Micro Devices, LSI Logic, IBM, Digital Equipment Corporation (DEC), and Hewlett-Packard.[27] U.S. Memories tried to raise $1 billion in capital, half in equity from the member companies and the rest in debt. IBM, DEC, and Hewlett-Packard would be major consumers of the output of the new company, which would reduce much of the risk that chip makers standing alone previously faced (see Case 27-A on U.S. Memories at the end of this chapter).

Sometimes the rights to promising technologies were sold to overseas concerns because U.S. companies could not afford the development costs. In the late 1980s Allied-Signal Corporation's Bendix Electronics Groups became an innovator in the development of engine sensors and antilock brakes. However, to fully exploit these technologies the company would have to make a five-year investment of $1 billion. The German electronics giant Siemens was more willing and able to tolerate this expense. It purchased Bendix from Allied-Signal. Siemens' goals for the company were driven less by its monthly cash flow and more by what Bendix was doing to become a global leader in the technological areas in which it excels.[28]

The Call for Policies to Aid U.S. Industries

It could be argued that in a world of increasing international economic competition, the U.S. government had to take a more active role in enhancing the competitiveness of U.S. business. The best example was the Japanese government and its powerful Ministry of Trade and Industry (MITI), which played a role in that country's success.

Governments in other nations of the world routinely stimulated specific industries to promote exports (e.g., South Korea and textiles) and protect industries in decline (e.g., Germany and automobiles). They engaged in national planning or created complex systems of tariffs and subsidies that distorted free markets. They also tried to win an advantage in international trade by pegging their currencies to the dollar in a way that lowered export or import prices.

Another way government planners sought to gain a national advantage was by manipulating capital markets to encourage savings. If the flow of capital across international boundaries was restricted, the people in a country had to accept low rates of return, but industries benefited from low interest rates that stimulated investment and the modernization of industrial facilities. Governments then could use their influence on the financial system to direct investments toward industries they favored.

U.S. firms, it was argued, simply could not compete against subsidized and protected foreign firms unless the U.S. government had similar policies. Advocates of government assistance to industries argued that it was appropriate for the U.S. government to do the same as foreign governments. U.S. government officials should focus on the **sunrise industries** of tomorrow (e.g., biotechnology) and help ease the nation out of the **sunset industries** of yesterday (e.g., smokestack industries such as steel and coal).

Whereas, the opponents of these policies maintained that government officials were incapable of making these important decisions and that the market was better able to decide which industries had long-term potential, the advocates argued that the government had no

sunrise and sunset industries
The U.S. government should encourage the industries of tomorrow and phase out industries with no economic future.

choice but to become involved. They pointed to the many areas where the U.S. government already was involved in influencing the competitiveness of U.S. business (e.g., a host of federal rules and regulations that distort the operations of a free market). At a minimum, more coordinated government policy making was necessary.

The Government's Role in U.S. Economic Development

The United States started as a separate nation in 1776, the same year that *The Wealth of Nations* was published. Its author, Adam Smith, warned against a system of industrial policies that endeavors

> either by extraordinary encouragements to draw towards a particular species of industry a greater share of the capital of the society than what would naturally go to it; or, by extraordinary restraints to force from a particular species of industry some share of the capital that would otherwise be employed in it.[29]

Thomas Jefferson envisioned a nation of small proprietors and farmers, each with the liberty to conduct their own affairs as they saw fit.[30] The Federalists opposed Jefferson by promoting a vision of a strong central government that would play an active role in the nation's economic development. Alexander Hamilton, the Federalists' leader, believed that dispersed power would disrupt commerce and prevent the nation from making economic progress. Concentrating power in national institutions like a national bank would help further economic development. The easing of credit by the bank would stimulate commerce.

Since Hamilton's time, the federal government assisted in the building of railroads, canals, and harbors. It created roads and highways. It employed public funds to construct airports. It placed, at certain periods, high import taxes on products brought into the United States to protect American business. The 1896 Republican party platform advocated protectionism as the bulwark of American industrial independence and the foundation of U.S. development and prosperity.

Today, the federal government extends loans to the private sector with the Small Business Administration and the Federal Home Loan Bank system. In times of trouble, particular companies (e.g., Lockheed and Chrysler) have received government loans to bail them out. In addition, agriculture has been the recipient of a well-developed price support system. In addition, the U.S. government provides weather information and other navigational aids to the airline industry. Had it not been for the government, many businesses could not have started, would have failed, or would have been less profitable.

Assisting and Constraining Business

In the United States, a broad array of policies both assist and constrain business. They change the size of markets, the structure of markets, and the costs of doing business in an industry.[31] Government shifts the rules affecting commerce, but it also influences businesses more directly, simply by changing its purchases, since nearly a quarter of the nation's product is consumed by government.

The Size of Markets

Government's direct impacts come from the purchase of products or services (e.g., the defense industry). Indirect effects occur through policies that affect complements or substitutes for the products an industry sells. For the automobile industry, a critical complement is gasoline, whose price is affected by government policies. Highways are also affected by government policies. A substitute for auto travel is mass transit, which depends heavily on federal subsidies.

The Structure of Markets

The markets businesses serve are affected by the government. The patent system rewards innovation by granting a temporary monopoly, which is, in effect, a legal barrier to entry. Public regulation of gas and electric utilities has prevented competition and denied freedom of entry. Trade protection and antitrust actions have favored one industry over another. The extent of competition and the type of competition in an industry are influenced by government policies.

The Costs of Doing Business

Government policies also affect the costs of doing business. They vary the costs of inputs (e.g., raw materials, labor, and capital), thereby changing the overall cost structure. For instance, in addition to increasing the costs of all companies that rely on pollution-producing technologies, pollution requirements impact competitors—with different plant and equipment configurations—differently. In so doing, they create competitive advantage for some firms and competitive disadvantage for others. In contrast, government subsidies lower the cost structure in industries by reducing capital and other costs. Indirect subsidies, such as accelerated depreciation and tax credits, abound in the tax codes. Subsidies affect industries differently, favoring some industries over others. Likewise, government aid to education or sponsorship of R&D lowers the costs of firms and industries that require this aid.

Government policies have a large role to play in directing free-market forces. Michael Porter's model of business strategy identifies five forces that should be analyzed: rivalry among firms in an industry, the threat of new entrants, the threat of substitute products or services, the bargaining power of suppliers, and the bargaining power of buyers. The impact of these forces determines the ultimate profit potential of an industry. However, without a diagnosis of government policy, this analysis is incomplete.[32]

The Amount and Type of Involvement

Some commentators argue that from the American Revolution until about 1929, government involvement in the U.S. economy was minimal. U.S. businesses enjoyed relatively little interference and, as a consequence, flourished.[33] The reality, however, is that government involvement in the U.S. economy has always been significant.

It also has been controversial. Politicians were divided about how much involvement and what type of involvement the United States should encourage.[34] Some politicians cherished the competitive system and its individual freedom and feared a powerful state. Others welcomed concentrated state power. They believed the exercise of state power was essential for economic growth.

First Stirrings of Regulation

At about the time that the federal government passed the first national regulatory legislation, the 1887 Interstate Commerce Act (initially targeting price fixing and other abuses in the railroad industry), it also passed the Sherman Antitrust Act (1890), which was designed to prevent monopoly and promote free markets (see Figure 27-5). During the 1912 national elections, Theodore Roosevelt's Progressive party argued for centralized policies. Roosevelt hoped that the government would establish national regulation and have the power to control most aspects of commerce. It would fix prices. It would force companies to publish detailed accounts of their transactions, control security issuance, and investigate business activities. It also would control hours, wages, and the other conditions of labor.

FIGURE 27-5
A history of U.S.
government
involvement in
economic activities

1887	Interstate Commerce Act
1890	Sherman Antitrust Act
1914	Clayton Act and Federal Trade Commission Act
1917	World War I: War Industries Board
1929-1933	Hoover presidency: Associationalist Policies
1933	National Industrial Recovery Act
1935	National Recovery Administration (found unconstitutional)
Late 1930s	New Deal: Selective regulation of key industries (e.g., airlines, communication, power)
1948	Employment Act
Early 1970s	Growth of new social regulation (e.g., EPA, OSHA, EEOC)
Late 1970s	Demise of Old Economic Regulation (e.g., airlines, trucking, banking)
1980s	Debate about industrial policies

In opposition to Roosevelt stood the Democratic party of Woodrow Wilson, which continued to adhere to its Jeffersonian origins. Wilson argued that it was not appropriate for government to try to dictate to businesses.

Influential political commentators like Walter Lippman criticized Wilson's ideas as appealing to the "planless scramble of little profiteers." Lippman favored big business over entrepreneurs. According to Lippman, the country did not need antitrust policies that would break up industries and restore the economy to "primitive competitive-like conditions."[35]

The controversy between Wilson and Roosevelt focused on the purposes the nation's antitrust legislation would serve. In 1914, the Clayton Act and the Federal Trade Commission Act were offered as extensions to the Sherman Act. Under Wilson's economic program, called the **New Freedom**, the purpose of these laws would be to specify which business practices were unfair and uncompetitive and to give a new antitrust commission wide powers to investigate and prosecute.

New Freedom
Woodrow Wilson's
program to promote
individual freedom by
enhancing antitrust
protection and increasing
investigation of unfair
business practices.

A Stronger Federal Role

This battle was won by Wilson, but the proponents of a stronger federal role had other chances to implement the policies they favored. During World War I, the War Industries Board (WIB) gained sweeping control over the national economy. Headed by financier Bernard Baruch, its purpose was to give business leaders the chance to benefit from "combination, cooperation, and common action with their natural competitors."[36]

This philosophy of business combination later flourished under the leadership of Secretary of Commerce, and later President, Herbert Hoover. Hoover encouraged businesses under his theme of associationalism to form trade and professional societies that would work in close cooperation with government. He used the FTC to implement his associationalist ideas. Business leaders would meet, ostensibly for the purpose of outlawing or suppressing unscrupulous forms of business practice. In reality, the codes devised under FTC authority often fostered collusion in fixing prices and restricting output. They failed to protect consumer interests. Ironically, Hoover associationalism became the model for

associationalism
Formation of business
trade and professional
alliances that work closely
with government to pursue
common economic goals.

postwar European reconstruction in Europe. French statesman Jean Monnet (the founder of the Common Market) called it "indicative planning" and tried to apply it throughout the European Community.

Planning under the New Deal

During the Great Depression, another effort to engage in business planning took place in the United States. The New Deal of Franklin Roosevelt was skeptical of the individualism of the past, which it blamed for the country's distress. It therefore sought increased collective action to turn around the nation's ailing economy.

One of the first initiatives of the New Deal was the National Industrial Recovery Act, which Congress passed in 1933. Under this legislation, the federal government set up the National Recovery Administration (NRA). It established industry codes that covered output, prices, wages, working conditions, investment, and trade practices. By 1934, the NRA had written 450 codes that extended to 5 million companies and 23 million employees.[37]

Although consumer and labor interests were represented on the NRA, business was the dominant group. Through its powerful trade associations, it was able to cast the NRA codes as it wanted. Labor was given increased wages in exchange for industry's right to raise prices and restrict output. Consumers received the promise of economic recovery. Small business was also underrepresented on the NRA and complained bitterly.

In 1935, the Supreme Court declared the NRA unconstitutional, effectively abolishing it. Supreme Court judges Louis Brandeis, a former adviser to Woodrow Wilson, and Felix Frankfurter opposed consolidated state power. They did not want the party of Jefferson to suppress the individualism for which it always had stood.[38]

Regulating Particular Sectors

With the passing of the NRA, the New Deal lost its capacity to comprehensively regulate economic activity. It regulated prices and entry in particular sectors instead. Separate regulatory agencies were established in a number of important emerging industries. In effect, protection against competition was afforded to the high-tech, infant industries of the period: aviation (Civil Aeronautics Board), communications (Federal Communications Commission), and natural gas (Federal Power Commission).

The deregulation movement of the late 1970s terminated the protection of these industries. They were now mature, and the agencies that had been set up during the New Deal to promote them stifled innovation and prevented dynamic adaptation to new competitive conditions.[39]

Business Cycle Management

After World War II, the government was expected to play an active role in smoothing the business cycle. Through the use of fiscal and monetary policies it could gain effective control over rates of growth, employment, and prices and prevent another depression.

The Council of Economic Advisers (CEA) was created to assist the president in devising appropriate macroeconomic policies to influence overall economic activity. The Employment Act of 1948 gave the federal government the responsibility to maintain economic growth, keep employment up, and assure that price levels were stable. President Kennedy's tax cuts, inspired by CEA director Walter Heller, helped start the longest continuous period of growth in American history.

When Richard Nixon assumed the presidency, economists believed the basic economic problem—business cycle instability—had been solved.[40] They felt that the "level of misery" in society, that is, the combined unemployment and inflation rates, was constant. Thus, fiscal and monetary policy tools simply gave partisan administrations a choice between tolerating more unemployment or more inflation: tight-money Republicans tolerated more unemployment while Democrats had to worry about a working-class constituency and favored less unemployment.[41] In 1970, no one anticipated that both the unemployment rate and the inflation rate could increase simultaneously, or that the economy again would get so out of control.

The New Social Regulation

Another government activity that gained ground in the post-World War II period was protecting people from unintended by-products of business activities, including environmental degradation, erosion of health, and exclusion of minorities. A new type of regulation, called social regulation, rose in importance (see Figure 27-6). It was far less acceptable to business than the old economic regulation, because it often involved government control over production and the quality of goods and services, not just government control over prices and entry.[42]

FIGURE 27-6
Selected federal
regulatory agencies

New Social	Old Economic
1964: Equal Employment Opportunity Commission (EEOC)	1887: Interstate Commerce Commission (ICC)
1970: Environmental Protection Agency (EPA)	1920: Federal Power Commission (FPC)
1970: Occupational Safety and Health Administration (OSHA)	1933: Federal Deposit Insurance Corporation (FDIC)
1972: Consumer Product Safety Commission (CPSC)	1943: Federal Communications Commission (FCC)

The new social regulation differed from earlier regulation in two other ways. First, the new agencies often had lengthy, specific laws rather than vague statutes. The Environmental Protection Agency (EPA), for example, had precise pollution reduction targets and timetables, which allowed little room for discretion. In contrast, the Federal Trade Commission, which had no specific timetable for eliminating unfair methods of competition, had great latitude for discretionary behavior. In addition, the new agencies were often organized along functional lines. The EPA, for example, regulated the pollution of all firms, unlike the FCC or the ICC, which were limited to a particular industry. The new agencies, as a result, were less likely to have sympathy with those they regulated. They were more resistant to domination by forces within a single industry.

According to Murray Weidenbaum, who served in the Reagan administration as head of the CEA, these changes signified a "second managerial revolution." The first revolution had involved a shift in decision-making power from the formal owners of business corporations to professional managers. The second revolution shifted power from corporate management to government planners and regulators, who influenced and controlled key managerial tasks. The distinction between private power and public power was becoming "increasingly blurred."[43]

Growth in the new social regulation, however, must not be confused with government growth in general.[44] It constitutes less than 3 percent of all federal spending and employment.

Defense expenditures, entitlements, transfers to state and local governments, and interest payments on the federal debt dwarf the amount of money spent on regulation.

Government Support for Industries in Other Nations

Today, the debate about government's role concerns industrial policies, which are meant to improve a country's international competitive position by fostering the growth of "strategic" industries.[45] These policies rely on the government to offer incentives and impose constraints. Incentives cause transactions that would not occur if market forces alone were operating. Constraints prevent deals that would take place if these forces operated by themselves. The proponents of industrial policies argue that the American economy, which has been threatened by energy shortages, inflation, unemployment, and economic stagnation, is in decline. The Japanese, along with other international rivals, support their industries. Therefore, the United States has no choice but to do so also.

General or nonselective industrial policies, which can be distinguished from sector-specific industrial policies, are available to all industries. An example of a sector-specific policy is the government's long-term effort to shape the development of American agriculture through production quotas, prices, and income policies. Another example is its use of price controls, taxes, direct regulation, and research and development to shape energy development. On the other hand, the bailouts of Lockheed, Boeing, Continental Illinois, and other companies, are examples of short-term, firm-specific policies.

These policies raise two separate but related issues: the economic issue of whether it is possible in the United States to select strategic sectors that are worth promoting, and the political issue of whether it is possible to administer a national policy designed to help these sectors.

Have Government Policies Helped Industries in Other Nations?

Opponents of industrial policies maintain that the extent to which they have actually helped economic development in other countries is exaggerated.[46] For instance, in Japan, MITI tried but failed to coordinate firm behavior in industries such as cotton spinning, automobiles, and computers. These industries remain intensely competitive despite efforts by MITI to limit competition. It is even possible that MITI's policies inadvertently spurred competition as firms entered the market in anticipation of earning cartel-like profits.

In industries where Japan had the most domestic competitors (e.g., pocket calculators) it was the most successful. In industries where MITI was active (e.g., shipbuilding), Japan confronted overcapacity. MITI helped downsize these industries.

In the early stages of industrialization, when a nation is building heavy industry and infrastructure, centrally coordinated industrial policies may be effective, but in later stages, when a nation is involved in worldwide competition in high-tech areas such as integrated circuits and microprocessors, relying on government-coordinated industrial policies may be a disadvantage. In this stage, industries must be prepared for rapid change. They have to be sensitive to market signals and cannot take orders from slow-moving government bureaucracies whose orientation is as much political as economic.

Industrial Policy Making in France

The French government takes an active role in planning industrial policy. Its indicative planning model, borrowed from Hoover's associationalism, had as its purpose to "construct a series of national champions" that would compete in international markets.[47] The French believed strongly that those policies were needed because the scale and efficiency of French industry were not adequate for world competition. A group of elite civil servants, trained in the most prestigious institutions of higher learning in France, implemented the policies. Insulated from political pressures, their mission was to regulate competitive forces without input from trade unions, consumer groups, small businesses, or farmers, all of which were excluded from their forums.

French industrial policies came together in national plans after World War II, when the French economy, along with that of other nations, flourished. The fifth and sixth plans, formulated in 1968 and 1970, involved comprehensive efforts at resource allocation, including incomes policies for labor and specific investments for business, but they were not completely implemented. Neither business, government, nor labor was willing to cooperate fully. Notable flops were the plans to build an internationally competitive computer industry and a commercially viable supersonic aircraft, the Concorde, in cooperation with Great Britain.

U.S. Policies Affecting Industry

Critics have argued that American industries suffered because the policies of the U.S. government were inconsistent and lacked order. There was little overall coordination or sense of purpose.[48] For instance:

- Import restrictions mainly aided the steel, textiles and apparel, and motor vehicle industries.
- Federally subsided loans mainly helped the home construction industry and agriculture.
- The federal government financed roughly one-half of U.S. research and development (R&D), but much of it went to defense-related businesses and a high proportion to the aerospace industry.

The patchwork of federal policies, created incrementally over time in response to specific contingencies, reflected the influence of lobbyists and special-interest groups.

Outcomes of the policy-making process were unstable. What one Congress or administration did was undone by another. Laws were amended and reamended in rapid succession. Changes in party, administration, and intellectual fashion brought new policies to the forefront; with them came new conditions with which business managers had to contend. For example, regular overhauls of the tax system meant that business managers could not be certain that today's tax policies would remain in place tomorrow. The investments they made might not pay off when the political environment was different.[49]

Government Responsibility for Declining Competitiveness

According to the critics, government's responsibility for declining competitiveness was in two main areas:[50]

Contradictory, Stop-and-Go Macroeconomic Policies

stop-and-go macroeconomic policies Alternating stimulatory and deflationary policies used by the government to deal with stagflation (high unemployment and inflation).

President Lyndon Johnson's guns-and-butter spending policies were not matched by tax increases. He conducted the War on Poverty at the same time that the United States was engaged in the Vietnam War. Strong inflationary pressures already were present at the time of the 1973 Arab oil embargo. The transfer of huge amounts of money to oil-exporting nations weakened the economy further.

The efforts by presidents Nixon, Ford, and Carter to deal simultaneously with high inflation and unemployment—stagflation—were largely ineffective. Existing macroeconomic theory was not designed to cope with these conditions. It had good remedies for only one problem at a time. With both problems present, successive administrations waffled between stimulatory policies to end the recessionary conditions and deflationary policies to put a brake on high prices.

President Reagan took new initiatives. He cut taxes to spur consumer spending and increased government spending on defense. The Federal Reserve Bank, under the leadership of Paul Volcker, tightly controlled the money supply, bringing the rapidly accelerating inflation of the late 1970s to a halt. The cost, however, was a massive recession; weak economic growth quickly depleted government revenues.

The combined effects of these policies yielded a federal debt that nearly doubled. The interest payments on the debt accelerated. Government demand for money to finance the deficit crowded out private investment, which in turn hurt lagging U.S. competitiveness.

With the demand for money high, U.S. interest rates were greater than interest rates in other nations. Foreign money was attracted to the United States, raising the value of the dollar. With the dollar highly valued, American manufacturers had difficulty selling their goods abroad and foreign producers found it easy to sell their goods in the United States.

Inconsistent Industrial Policies and Ineffective Trade Policies

Macroeconomic difficulties took place at the same time that the government failed to develop consistent industrial or effective trade policies. To many people in the business community, federal tax, credit, spending, and trade policies were inefficient, random, and confusing. The tax system, for instance, rewarded real estate investments but discriminated against investments in manufacturing. The assistance provided to the chemical and aerospace industries was greater than that given to paper products and pharmaceuticals. The reasons for the differences were not apparent; federal policies neither created an "even playing field" nor did they marshal resources in an effective manner to assist targeted growth industries.

Business Responsibility for Declining Competitiveness

These arguments about government's responsibility for lagging American competitiveness were matched by arguments placing the responsibility squarely on business.[51]

- American managers had a short-term time horizon, where the emphasis was almost exclusively on return on investment and share price increases rather than market share and new products (see Figure 27-7).
- They did not pay sufficient attention to product quality and costs.
- They were bureaucratic and indecisive, and slow in introducing new technologies, manufacturing processes, and products.
- They were more interested in financial manipulation and short-term cost reductions than in achieving long-term competitiveness and market share.
- They set high return-on-investment (ROI) targets, so that many potentially worthy projects were not undertaken.
- Their preoccupation with selling and buying assets kept them from focusing on production; and caused unnecessary labor-management friction.
- Their investments in real estate and commerce, speculative activities, and interest in takeovers sacrificed long-term competitiveness and markets for short-term.

FIGURE 27-7	**U.S. Managers**	**Japanese Managers**
Corporate objectives: U.S. and Japanese managers[52]	1. Return on investment 2. Share price increase 3. Market share 4. Product portfolio	1. Market share 2. Return on investment 3. New products 4. Rationalize production and distribution

Critics maintained that foreign managers had different goals and time frames (compare the order of priorities of U.S. and Japanese managers in Figure 27-7). The goals and timetables of foreign managers matched those of their governments. While U.S. managers sought short-term profitability and shareholder wealth maximization, foreign managers pursued long-term growth, competitive viability, and stable employment, precisely the goals needed for sustained success in the international marketplace.

Why Carrying Out Policies to Assist U.S. Industries is Difficult

The critics missed an important point about why it is difficult to effectively carry out policies to assist industries in the United States. National crises, like war, may be able to temporarily unify the American people, but the Constitutional system is built on checks and balances and divided power.

The American Political Tradition

Three characteristics of the American system make it difficult to carry out industrial policies:

1. *A profusion of interest groups.* The founders of the American republic embraced the idea that numerous interests should exist. Diversity reflects the different backgrounds of the American people and the dynamic character of U.S. society: The existence of many interests dilutes the strength of any particular one. Indeed, no single organization represents business or labor in the United States as it does in other countries. Thus, policies favored by one business group are likely to be opposed by another business group.

2. *The accessibility of political institutions.* No one ever seems to permanently lose a political battle in the United States. Frustrated interests always have appeal to other governmental units. State and local governments exist alongside the federal government. The three branches of the federal government are not unified in any coherent and logical way. The executive branch has departments that represent diverse interests—business and labor, environmentalists and developers, and so on. Congress is divided into numerous committees and subcommittees. Even after it has enacted a law, there is no assurance that the law can be effectively carried out because the bureaucracy, which is charged with implementing the legislation, must face an array of competing interests.

3. *The absence of a neutral administrative elite.* No trusted, professionally based, neutral civil service exists in the United States on the scale that it exists in such European nations as France or Great Britain. The U.S. bureaucracy, particularly at its upper reaches where the appointments are almost all political, is more partisan. An impartial bureaucracy is needed to make industrial policy decisions.

These obstacles do not mean that industrial policies cannot be carried out in the United States. They simply mean that the U.S. political system has not been designed to make it easy to do so. An enduring sense of national peril would be necessary if private groups were to permit the government to exercise the kind of authority needed to carry out industrial policies effectively.

The Need Still Exists

The proponents of industrial policies grant that these obstacles exist. Nevertheless, they hold that industrial policies are still necessary.[53] They point to four reasons:

1. The federal government already is extensively involved in making these policies. It is playing a role in a variety of ways, but the role it is playing is inadvertent and lacks coherence. For instance, the U.S. tax code favors some industries over others. Federal R&D constitutes nearly half the R&D conducted but federal R&D policies lack clear priorities and were formulated without careful consideration of their overall effects. At a minimum, the U.S. government should coordinate the many policies it already has.
2. The nature of international competition is such that other nations are providing assistance to their industries through subsidies, favorable exchange rates, low-interest loans, and in other ways. Thus, the U.S. government also needs to provide help.
3. When industries ask for trade relief, the government needs to have criteria to evaluate the claims. It cannot engage in ad hoc policy making. In exchange for the relief it grants, it must demand concessions that will force industries to modernize and compel them to reduce excess capacity, invest in new plant and equipment, lower wages, and change work rules.
4. As some industries lose competitiveness and others gain competitiveness, the government should play a role in easing the transition. It should follow the lead of Japan, which provides for the retraining of displaced workers who might otherwise have trouble finding new jobs.

Institutional Arrangements to Implement These Policies

The proponents of industrial policies believe that institutional arrangements have to be created to implement these policies. They imagine a Council on Industrial Competitiveness in the White House, which would function like the Council of Economic Advisers. Just as the CEA coordinates the federal government's macroeconomic decisions, the Council on Industrial Competitiveness would coordinate the microeconomic decisions.

For proponents of industrial policies, federal government involvement in macroeconomic matters is insufficient. Since the government is already involved in microeconomics, proponents say, it should be more careful about what it is doing. Given the realities of international competition, it has to coordinate its efforts.

Opponents of industrial policies believe that additional government bureaucracies are unnecessary and unwarranted, that they extend the scope of government far beyond what can be defended in economic theory. Even if coordinated industrial policies have facilitated economic growth in other nations, they would not necessarily succeed in the United States with its special political traditions.

In carrying out industrial policies, four problems stand out:

*   Changing market perceptions about the relative costs and benefits of a policy.
*   Division within government (e.g., between prodevelopment and antidevelopment forces or between politicians with different views of the proper role of government).

- Industry disagreement (e.g., whether a program should exist and how extensive it should be).
- Lack of consensus about the appropriate means to achieve policy goals.

These factors suggest difficulties likely to affect any effort to initiate and carry out long-term, strongly interventionist industrial policies.

An Agenda to Restore U.S. Competitiveness

Some things that the United States might consider doing to help restore its competitiveness include increasing savings and investment while keeping consumption at a fixed share of the GNP and cutting military expenditures by eliminating the causes of war.[54] Like Great Britain before it, the United States is finding it difficult to combine high domestic consumption with substantial military commitments. A number of other suggestions are:[55]

- Open foreign markets to U.S. exports.
- Provide managers with the incentive to take a long-term perspective.
- Elevate technically sophisticated individuals to top management positions.
- Remove incentives for financial manipulation and paper profits.
- Raise educational standards.
- Strengthen incentives for environmental protection and energy conservation.
- Reform the system of product liability.

Conclusions

This chapter has looked at arguments that the U.S. economy is in decline. It has examined how well the country is doing compared with its major international rivals, stressed the issue of productivity, discussed the decline in services and manufacturing, and noted weaknesses in high-tech areas such as supercomputers and semiconductors.

The U.S. government has provided practical assistance to American businesses in many ways. Its policies affect the size and structure of markets and the costs of doing business. Government policies are of strategic importance to all firms.

Among the most important changes in the role of government in the post-World War II period has been its involvement in fiscal policy management, its expanded role in social regulation, and its diminished role in economic regulation. In the 1980s, the debate about government shifted: Given the realities of the new international competition, what should it do? Proponents of industrial policies maintained that the U.S. government should play an active role. Opponents held that the U.S. government was incapable of playing a larger role. This chapter ends with several suggestions to enhance U.S. competitiveness.

Discussion Questions

1. What are some of the trends in the U.S. economy? How strong is the U.S. economy? What are some of its weaknesses?
2. Give some examples of what governments do to promote business. Should the United States carry out similar policies?
3. How would you distinguish the views of Jefferson and Hamilton on the role of government in economic development? Has the United States evolved in a more Jeffersonian or more Hamiltonian direction?
4. Give examples of the way the U.S. government influences business. What strategic importance do these influences have?
5. Describe the controversy surrounding the passage of the 1914 FTC Act.
6. Explain why you would or would not agree with the statement that the Democrats always have been the party of big government and the Republicans always have been the party of small government.

7. What was the NRA? What was it designed to accomplish? Why was it declared unconstitutional ?
8. Distinguish between the new social regulation and the old economic regulation.
9. Discuss the major innovations in U.S. government policy toward industry after World War II.
10. To what degree is the U.S. government responsible for declining U.S. competitiveness?
11. To what extent is business responsible for declining U.S. competitiveness?
12. Why is it so difficult to formulate policies to aid the competitiveness of U.S. industries?
13. What can the United States do to enhance its competitiveness? What policies should a major business group like the Business Roundtable propose to the U.S. government ?
14. In your opinion, should the United States have industrial policies? If yes, what kind of industrial policies should it have?

Endnotes

1. Paul Kennedy, "The (Relative) Decline of America," *Atlantic*, August 1987, pp. 29-38; P. Kennedy, *The Rise and Fall of the Great Powers* (New York: Vintage Books, 1987).
2. P. G. Peterson, "The Morning After," *Atlantic* 260 (1987), pp. 43-69.
3. L. C. Thurow, "How to Get Out of The Economic Rut," *New York Review of Books*, February 14, 1985, pp. 9-10.
4. "U.S. Competitiveness in Manufacturing," Case No. 9-386-133, Harvard Business School, 1986.
5. *The Reindustrialization of America* (New York: McGraw-Hill, 1982); I. M. Destler, *American Trade Politics: System under Stress* (Washington, D.C.: Institute for International Economics, 1986).
6. R. Z. Lawrence, *Can America Compete?* (Washington, D.C.: Brookings Institution, 1984); J. S. Nye, *Bound to Lead* (New York: Basic Books, 1990); J. E. Schwarz, *America's Hidden Success: A Reassessment of Public Policy from Kennedy to Reagan* (New York: W. W. Norton, 1988); J. E. Schwarz and T. J. Volgy, "The Myth of America's Economic Decline," *Harvard Business Review*, Sept.-Oct. 1985, p. 101.
7. D. B. Yoke, "Note on Free Trade and Protectionism," Working Paper no. 383-174, Harvard Business School, 1983.
8. President's Commission on Industrial Competitiveness, *Global Competition: The New Reality*, vol. I (Washington, D.C.: U.S. Government Printing Office, 1985).
9. "U.S. Competitiveness in Manufacturing," Case 9-386-133, Harvard Business School, 1986; New York Stock Exchange, Office of Economic Research, *U.S. International Competitiveness: Perception and Reality*, August 1984.
10. Robert Reich, "Making Industrial Policy," *Foreign Affairs*, Spring 1982, pp. 852-82.
11. Ibid.
12. Central Intelligence Agency, *Handbook of Economic Statistics*, (Washington, D.C.: U.S. Government Printing Office, 1991), p. 11.
13. "Can America Compete?" *Business Week*, Aug. 6, 1990, p. 14.
14. Thomas Steward, "U.S. Productivity," *Fortune*, Oct. 19, 1992, pp. 54-57.
15. Andrew Kupfer, "How American Industry Stacks Up," *Fortune*, March 9, 1992, pp. 30-46.
16. "America's Investment Famine," *The Economist*, June 27, 1992, pp. 89-90.
17. E. F. Denison, *Trends in American Economic Growth, 1929-1982* (Washington, D.C.: Brookings Institution, 1985); "U S. Competitiveness in Manufacturing," Case no. 9-386-133, Harvard Business School, 1986; Council of Economic Advisers, *Economic Report of the President*, 1984.
18. "Why Services Are Different," *The Economist*, July 18, 1992, p. 67.
19. *The Economist.*
20. *The Economist.*
21. Central Intelligence Agency, *Handbook of Economic Statistics.*
22. Louis Richman, "How Capital Costs Cripple America," *Fortune*, Aug. 14, 1989, pp. 50-54.
23. "U.S. Competitiveness in Manufacturing," Harvard Business School; C. Rappoport, "Why Japan Keeps Winning," *Fortune* 124 (1991), pp. 76-88.
24. Rappoport, "Why Japan Keeps Winning," pp. 76-88.
25. Ibid.
26. W. Ouchi, *The M-Form Society: How American Teamwork Can Recapture the Competitive Edge* (Reading, Mass.: Addison-Wesley, 1984).
27. Michael Hawthorne, "High Technology Economic Policy: Some Thoughts on Sematech," paper presented at the Annual Meeting of the American Political Science Association, Sept. 1991.
28. Rappoport, "Why Japan Keeps Winning."
29. Adam Smith, *The Wealth of Nations* (New York: Modern Library, 1965), p. 650.
30. K. Prewitt and S. Verba, *An Introduction to American Government* (New York: Harper & Row, 1974).

31. J. Gale, R. A. Buchholz, and A. A. Marcus, *Achieving Competitive Advantage through the Political Process: Business Strategy and Legitimacy*, Discussion Paper No. 75, The Strategic Management Research Center, The University of Minnesota, 1987; J. Gale and R. A. Buchholz, "The Political Pursuit of Competitive Advantage: What Business Can Gain from Government," in *Business Strategy and Public Policy*, ed. A. A. Marcus, A. M. Kaufman, and D. R. Beam (Westport, Conn.: Greenwood Press, 1987), pp. 31-41.

32. M. E. Porter, "The Competitive Advantage of Nations," *Harvard Business Review*, March-April 1990, p. 28.

33. M. Friedman and R. Friedman, *Free to Choose: A Personal Statement* (New York: Avon Books, 1980).

34. A. Kaufman, L. S. Zacharias, and A. Marcus, "Managers United for Corporate Rivalry: A History of Managerial Collective Action," *Journal of Policy History* 2 (1990), pp. 56-97; T. K. McCraw, "Mercantilism and the Market: Antecedents of American Industrial Policy," in *The Politics of Industrial Policy*, ed. C. E. Barfield and W. A. Schammbra (Washington, D.C.: American Enterprise Institute, 1986), pp. 33-62; J. C. Miller, T. E Walcott, W. E. Kovacic, and J. A. Rabkin, "Industrial Policy: Reindustrialization through Competition or Coordinated Action?" *Yale Journal on Regulation* 2 (1984), pp. 1-37.

35. Cited in Miller et al., "Industrial Policy."

36. Ibid., p. 124.

37. Kaufman et al., "Managers United for Corporate Rivalry"; Miller, et al., "Industrial Policy."

38. T. K. McCraw, *Prophets of Regulation: Charles Frances Adams, Louis D. Brandeis, James M. Landis, Alfred E. Kahn* (Cambridge, Mass.: Harvard University Press, 1984)

39. A. Marcus, "Business Demand for Regulation: An Exploration of the Stigler Hypothesis," *Research in Corporate Social Performance and Policy* 7 (1985), pp. 25-46; A. Marcus, "Airline Deregulation, Business Strategy, and Regulatory Theory," in *Public Policy and Economic Institutions* (Greenwich, Conn.: JAI Press, 1990); A. Marcus, "Airline Deregulation: Why the Supporters Lost Out," *Long Range Planning* 20, no. 1 (1987), pp. 90-98; B. Mitnick, *The Political Economy of Regulation* (New York: Columbia University Press, 1980).

40. J. D. Gwartney and R. L. Stroup, *Economics: Private and Public Choice* (New York: Harcourt Brace Jovanovich, 1987).

41. A. Marcus and B. Mevorach, "Planning for the U.S. Political Cycle," *Long Range Planning* 21 (1988), pp. 50-56; P. Young, A. Marcus, R. S. Koot, and B. Mevorach, "Improved Business Planning through an Awareness of Political Cycles," *Journal of Forecasting* 9 (1990), pp. 37-52.

42. W. Lilley and J. C. Miller, "The New Social Regulation," *Public Interest*, Spring 1977, pp. 49-62; P. Weaver, "Regulation, Social Policy, and Class Conflict," *Public Interest*, Winter 1978, pp. 45-64; A. A. Marcus, *The Adversary Economy: Business Responses to Changing Government Requirements* (Westport, Conn.: Quorum Books, 1984).

43. M. L. Weidenbaum, "The Future of Business/Government Relations in the United States," in *The Future of Business: Global Issues in the 80s and 90s*, ed. M. Ways (New York: Pergamon Press, 1979), pp. 48-76.

44. A. A. Marcus, *The Adversary Economy: Business Responses to Changing Government Requirements* (Westport, Conn.: Quorum Books, 1984).

45. E G. Adams and C. A. Bollins, "Meaning of Industrial Policy," in F. G. Adams and L. R. Klein, eds., *Industrial Policies for Growth and Competitiveness* (Lexington, Mass.: D.C. Heath, 1983); C. S. Allen, and H. Rishikoff, "Tale Thrice Told: A Review of Industrial Policy Proposals," *Journal of Policy Analysis and Management*, 1985, p. 4; J. L. Badaracco and D. B. Yoffie, "'Industrial Policy': It Can't Happen Here," *Harvard Business Review*, November-December 1983, pp. 97-105; C. E. Barfield and W. A. Schammbra, eds., *The Politics of Industrial Policy* (U.S.A.: American Enterprise Institute, 1986), pp. 187-205; A. T. Denzau, *Will an 'Industrial Policy' Work for the United States?* formal publication No. 57, Center for the Study of American Business, Washington University, 1983; A. A. Marcus and A. M. Kaufman, "Why It Is Difficult to Implement Industrial Policies: Lessons from the Synfuels Experience," *California Management Review* 28 (1986), pp. 98-114; P. Norton, "A Reader's Guide to Industrial Policy," in *The Politics of American Economic Policy Making*, ed. P. Peretz (Armonk, NY: M. E. Sharpe, 1987), pp. 126-27; K. Phillips, *Staying on Top: The Business Case for a National Industrial Strategy* (New York: Random House, 1984); C. L. Schultze, "Industrial Policy: A Solution in Search of a Problem," *California Management Review* 25 (1983), pp. 5-15.

46. G. Gilder, "A Supply-Side Economics of the Left," *Public Interest*, Summer 1983, pp. 29-43; A. Etzioni, "The MITIzation of America," *Public Interest*, Summer 1983, pp. 44-51.

47. S. S. Cohen, S. Halimi, and J. Zysman, "Institutions, Politics, and Industrial Policy in France," in *The Politics of Industrial Policy*, ed. C. E. Barfield and W. A. Schammbra (Washington, D.C.: American Enterprise Institute, 1986), pp. 106-27; D. C. Mueller, ed., *The Political Economy of Growth* (New Haven: Conn.: Yale University Press, 1983).

48. R. Reich, "An Industrial Policy of the Right," *Public Interest*, Fall 1983, pp. 3-17; R. B. Reich, *The Next American Frontier: A Provocative Program for Economic Renewal*, (Harrisonburg, Va.: R. R. Donnelley, 1983).

49. A. A. Marcus, "Policy Uncertainty and Technological Innovation," *Academy of Management Review* 6 (1981), pp. 443-48.

50. U.S. House of Representatives, Committee on Banking, Finance and Urban Affairs, Industrial Competitiveness Act, April 1984; "U.S. Competitiveness in Manufacturing," Case No. 9-386-33, Harvard Business School, 1986.

51. Denison, *Trends in American Economic Growth*; C. W. L. Hill, M. A. Hitt, and R. E. Hoskisson, "Declining U.S. Competitiveness: Reflections on a Crisis," *The Academy of Management Executive* 2 (1988), pp. 51-60; U.S. House of Representatives, Committee on Banking, Finance and Urban Affairs, Industrial Competitiveness Act, April 1984; "U.S. Competitiveness in Manufacturing," Harvard Business School; Robert Reich, "The Next American Frontier," *Atlantic Monthly*, 1983, pp. 53-57.
52. George Cabot Lodge, *Comparative Business Government Relations* (Englewood Cliffs, N.J.: Prentice Hall, 1990), p.26.
53. S. E. Eizenstat, "Reindustrialization through Coordination or Chaos ?" *Yale Journal on Regulation* 2 (1984), pp. 39-51.
54. R. Rosecrance, *America's Economic Resurgence: A Bold New Strategy* (New York: Harper & Row, 1990).
55. Compare with Michael Porter, *The Competitive Advantage of Nations* (New York: Free Press, 1990).

Case 27-A: U.S. Memories: Global Competition in the Semiconductor Industry[1]

The way I describe it is, we finally after a lot of years of bickering with one another found a common motivator. It was called fear ... The CEOs discovered they were in deep trouble. They honestly understood that it was not likely that they could turn [the U.S. DRAM industry] around on their own and that something needed to be done or they would have difficulty surviving as companies.

Sanford Kane, CEO, U.S. Memories, April 1992

It was late Friday afternoon on a sunny July day in Cupertino, California, in 1989. John Smith resumed to his office at Apple Computer after a long management team meeting to find a thick envelope with a business plan for a new semiconductor manufacturing consortium called U.S. Memories. The president of Apple was asking John to evaluate the plan and present his recommendations to the board. John had to decide whether or not Apple should join seven other firms, including IBM, Hewlett-Packard (HP), and Digital Equipment Corporation (DEC), and become a member of U.S. Memories.

U.S. Memories' goal was to become a major DRAM (pronounced *DEE-Ram*) producer. DRAMs, or dynamic random access memory chips, are the most common type of semiconductor chip, representing approximately 14 percent of the total market. For the past two years, these memory chips had been extremely expensive and difficult to obtain. DRAM prices began to rise in mid-1987 after a series of trade disputes between the United States and Japan. These disputes culminated in the 1986 U.S.-Japanese Semiconductor Trade Agreement (SCTA), which was followed by the imposition of sanctions on Japanese semiconductor manufacturers for failure to comply with the agreement.

During this time, semiconductor and computer systems manufacturers, numerous politicians, and policy makers were extremely concerned that Japanese firms produced approximately 90 percent of the world's DRAMs. U.S. Memories principal goal was to assure a stable, American-made supply of DRAMs for its member companies. In addition, the consortium sought to double the world market share of American DRAM producers and to restore domestic DRAM production.

Smith knew Apple had lost a lot of money buying DRAMs in 1988 and 1989 when prices were high and supplies tight. Though the idea of a stable, domestic DRAM supply was indeed attractive, Smith needed to carefully evaluate the proposed venture.

Buying DRAMS

In 1984, world chip consumption began to slow; the next year demand for DRAMs collapsed. Chip makers were hit with tremendous losses due to excess capacity. They responded by cutting prices. Aggregate DRAM prices per bit fell by nearly 80 percent. Unable to compete in the face of overcapacity and rapidly falling prices, U.S. DRAM manufacturers pressured the government for trade protection against Japanese rivals. The government responded with the Semiconductor Trade Agreement and imposition of trade sanctions. These sanctions came shortly after DRAM prices had bottomed out. During the next two years, DRAM prices surged to unprecedented levels. Price increases and tight supplies had not been experienced before by computer systems manufacturers.

Apple and the other systems manufacturers were extremely concerned about the volatile DRAM market conditions of the late 1980s. A combination of unique events made DRAM market signals difficult to interpret. First, there was the almost complete shift in global market share from the United States to Japan. This brought with it considerable suspicion and mistrust of Japanese firms by U.S. manufacturers. Second, the introduction of the 1 Mb chip in 1986 brought new technological challenges for semiconductor manufacturers, as the use of new materials in the production process made initial reject rates as high as 90 to 95 percent in some cases. Chip prices stayed high longer than usual in the early stage of this generation because new manufacturing systems had to be developed. Third, higher DRAM prices after 1987 were partly the result of an upsurge in demand for personal computers and workstations packed with as much as four times the memory of previous models. The increased demand for personal computers drove up demand for chips, but DRAM suppliers had cut their production in response to the soft demand of 1984-1985. This meant that demand outstripped supply for a short period while chip makers rushed to increase capacity. Moreover, a short supply of older generation chips, such as the 256K, was in part caused by manufacturers shifting too much capacity too quickly to the newer generation chips. Finally, the sanctions levied against Japan for failure to comply with the SCTA added yet another element of uncertainty to the price surge of 1987.

In addition to high prices and tight supplies, rumors began to surface in the industry that some Japanese chip manufacturers had begun using controversial "tying practices," that is, pressuring U.S. DRAM consumers to buy other unwanted products as a precondition for being allowed to purchase DRAMs.[2] The Semiconductor Industry Association (SIA) charged that Japanese firms were using the SCTA and trade sanctions as a convenient cover for their coordinated attack on the U.S. computer manufacturing industry. Indeed, Apple Computer and other U.S. computer systems manufacturers depended on Japanese firms for their DRAM supplies. The vertically integrated Japanese DRAM manufacturers, however, competed directly with Apple in downstream computer markets. This strange dependence was uncomfortable at best and a serious strategic threat at worst.

In the past, Apple had been accustomed to regular price and supply cycles over each chip generation and maintained a policy of buying its chips from a wide range of suppliers from around the world. The turbulent DRAM market conditions of 1987-1989 had eroded Apple's leverage with its chip suppliers. Apple had lost money buying expensive DRAMs for two years in a row. It was unclear whether high DRAM prices and tight supplies were transitory phenomena or permanent structural changes in the international semiconductor industry. If permanent structural changes were indeed occurring, perhaps a stronger domestic industry would be the answer to the problems Apple faced.

By 1989, all but three U.S. companies (Micron, Texas Instruments, and Motorola) had left the DRAM business, and those remaining did not have nearly the capacity to satisfy the DRAM needs of Apple and other U.S. systems manufacturers. If the unprecedented price surge and tight supplies were the result of a calculated attack by Japanese firms, management would need to take some action to secure a stable supply of DRAMs.

Concerns about the Domestic DRAM Industry

The volatile state of the DRAM market in the late 1980s reinforced the need for domestically owned production capabilities. Industrial policy advocates and large computer systems manufacturers such as IBM emphasized the need to protect and nurture vital domestic industries such as DRAMs. The loss of these industries would be detrimental for the following reasons:

1. Users of DRAMs became dependent on foreign suppliers.
2. Semiconductor equipment manufacturers—companies providing machines and materials used in making DRAMs and other semiconductors—had their customer base weakened.
3. Spillovers resulting from the design and production of DRAMs, such as the diffusion of technological know-how, were not realized.
4. National security could be jeopardized.

U.S. Memories was meant to be an important first step in restoring the domestic DRAM industry through active industry and government intervention.

DRAM Users

By the late 1980s, computer systems manufacturers faced technological dependence on foreign firms that were their direct competitors in many downstream markets. Japan's main DRAM manufacturers—NEC, Mitsubishi, Fujitsu, Hitachi, Toshiba, and Oki—were vertically integrated into downstream products such as computer systems, laser printers, and business machines. U.S. computer systems manufacturers such as IBM, HP, and DEC competed with them in many markets and relied on them for DRAMs. Japanese firms had captured more than 80 percent of the worldwide DRAM market and more than go percent of the most advanced 1 Mb DRAM market by 1987. With only three domestic DRAM manufacturers remaining, U.S. computer makers had few domestic supply options.

U.S. systems manufacturers were hurt by escalating DRAM prices that raised their production costs. For example, the price of 256K DRAMs was $1.99 in late 1986. This price rose to as much as $3.50 in late 1988. Faced with rising costs, computer systems manufacturers had to increase prices, difficult for systems manufacturers since demand for computers is highly price-elastic. A small price increase leads to a much larger decline in demand. Price hikes and supply interruptions caused several U.S. computer systems manufacturers to ration memory chips and to delay the introduction of new products. In a business like computers, where R&D and innovation are vital to survival, such delays seriously weakened competitiveness.

Higher costs hurt the competitive position of U.S. computer systems manufacturers in both domestic and global markets. This provided Japanese systems manufacturers, who made their own DRAMs, with the opportunity to penetrate computer markets in which U.S. firms had held a dominant position.

Semiconductor Equipment Manufacturers

Supporters of U.S. Memories warned that the failure of the U.S. DRAM industry would weaken the semiconductor materials and equipment manufacturing industry. IBM was particularly concerned about this issue. Even though it made most of the DRAMs it needed, IBM did not make the equipment used to manufacture DRAMs. IBM worried that unless U.S. semiconductor firms produced enough memory chips to keep U.S. equipment makers healthy, these firms would fall into Japanese hands or go out of business due to the erosion of their domestic customer base. That could leave IBM and other U.S. firms dependent on Japanese companies for critical semiconductor process technologies.

Spillovers

Another consideration associated with a domestic DRAM industry is the preservation of skills and know-how obtained from producing these chips. DRAMs are considered technology drivers, that is, high-volume products that allow a firm to hone its manufacturing skills and improve its production processes. Since DRAMs are produced in such large volumes, firms have a continuous opportunity to learn about and improve their complex production technologies. This valuable knowledge can drive innovation and improvements in more sophisticated, higher-margin chips like microprocessors.

In addition to the spillovers created in the manufacturing process, domestic production created human capital benefits. DRAM production required trained engineers, technicians, and designers. When they left these companies, they started new businesses or went to other firms, taking with them and diffusing their know-how and expertise.

National Security

The loss of semiconductor manufacturing know-how also concerned defense planners. With components playing an increasingly important role in advanced weapons systems, these developments posed the risk of losing access to essential know-how. Depending solely on foreign firms for sourcing of military components was an added concern.

The Birth of U.S. Memories

The idea for U.S. Memories was born out of the conviction on the part of the U.S. electronics industry that the presence of U.S. companies in the worldwide DRAM market was critical. When it became clear in early 1989 that no single U.S. semiconductor company could take on that challenge alone, the concept of a collective effort was developed.

The collective effort resulted in U.S. Memories, a joint venture of U.S. semiconductor manufacturers and electronics systems manufacturers. The reason for U.S. Memories was to provide its investors and others with a large, stable, and assured supply of DRAMs while providing a real return on investment. U.S. Memories intended to become a long-term, leading player in the industry.

On June 21, 1989, the Semiconductor Industry Association (SIA) announced the formation of U.S. Memories. The new company was to be an independent, for-profit, self-sustaining corporation with initial funds provided by its semiconductor and computer systems members. For computer systems manufacturers (IBM, HP, and DEC), joining the consortium meant a reliable supply of DRAMs and technological independence from Japanese competitors. For semiconductor manufacturers (Intel, National Semiconductor, LSI Logic, and Advanced Micro Devices), many of whom had exited the DRAM market several years earlier, joining U.S. Memories meant being able to offer their customers a complete line of chips. This would reduce their vulnerability to Japanese chip makers. Selling a broader product line was considered a marketing advantage because it enlarged the chip maker's customer base and allowed "one-stop shopping."

In addition to U.S. Memories' seven original members, more participants were needed to finance the venture. The up-front capital costs to start production were enormous; having more members meant that those costs could be spread out over a larger base of investors. Even with a larger membership base, the initial equity investment per member would be large: at the very least, a total equity investment of $100 million. If additional members could not be persuaded to join, U.S. Memories would have trouble getting off the ground. With this in mind, U.S. Memories' CEO Sandy Kane—a charismatic and persuasive 27-year IBM veteran—launched a bold effort to attract other members such as AT&T, Compaq, Apple,

Sun, and Tandy. Because the addition of more members would increase administrative costs, the corporation required members to take at least a 1 percent equity position. This meant that only larger companies could afford to join, and smaller companies would not be considered for potential membership.

All consortium members would be required to buy a share of the output of U.S. Memories and would have the option of purchasing additional output if desired. U.S. Memories would begin by manufacturing 4 Mb DRAMs, the newest technology licensed from IBM.

Sandy Kane believed that it was vital to secure the necessary funds and build the new plant as quickly as possible; the rapid pace of technological change made early production of 4 Mb DRAMs essential. This would enable U.S. Memories to move down the learning curve, increase yields, lower costs, and gain market share. Conversely, any delays in launching the venture could result in competitive disadvantage. If Japanese firms began production earlier than U.S. Memories, they would benefit from moving down the learning curve first and would capture market share at the expense of U.S. Memories. Furthermore, Kane wanted to preserve the sense of excitement and momentum that accompanied the announcement of the creation of U.S. Memories. Computer and semiconductor industry executives, journalists, and politicians watched the progress of the venture with great interest.

The original business plan required a $1 billion investment—50 percent equity-financed by member companies and 50 percent debt-financed, for which Kane hoped to secure low-interest government-guaranteed loans. Member companies also would purchase collectively at least 50 percent of U.S. Memories' output with the remaining output be offered first to members and then sold on the open market. Consortium members were guaranteed their committed chip allotment at no more than competitive market prices.

Four semiconductor manufacturing facilities (fabs) would be built over approximately four years. The first three fabs would produce 4 Mb chips at different stages of the generation life cycle. Plants would be built and commence production in a staggered process, and each would be shut down in the same fashion to retool for the next generation. The fourth plant, the last to be built, would produce only 16 Mb chips, the next DRAM generation.

The four-fab plan was extremely risky. Since the fabs were to be constructed in a staggered process over the course of the 4 Mb generation, timing was crucial. Even a one-month delay could make the difference between success or failure. If the second or third fab commenced production too late relative to the market introduction of the 16 Mb generation, much of the output of these plants would be superfluous.

Member companies complained about the output share they were required to purchase. Until the late 1980s, systems manufacturers had enjoyed considerable leverage over their suppliers and chafed at the idea of being committed to buy a fixed share from U.S. Memories. This aspect of the business plan was vital to the success of U.S. Memories, however, since it would save marketing expenses and buffer the consortium from fluctuations in demand. In the DRAM industry, which was frequently beset by overcapacity and cyclical demand patterns, the assurance of a stable customer base would be a great advantage.

After receiving much criticism on the business plan from members and prospective members, Kane was forced to make modifications. A wait-and-see approach was taken with respect to the second fab, and the third fab was to be eliminated altogether. Depending upon the success of Fab 1 and general market conditions, members would decide whether to construct Fab 2. Cost and timing considerations led to almost universal agreement on eliminating Fab 3. Rather than having four manufacturing facilities as originally planned, U.S. Memories would eventually have only two or three.

The second modification to the business plan involved increasing the output members were required to buy. Initially, members had to buy an output share equal to half of their committed investment percentage. This meant that if a member had a 10 percent investment commitment, it would have to purchase 5 percent of the output. The revised plan asked members to buy an output percentage up to their investment percentage. If a member's investment commitment was 10 percent, it would now be required to buy a 5 to 10 percent share of output. Finally, the initial equity requirement was reduced from $500 million to $100 million and the debt/equity ratio would be changed from 50-50 to 60-40.

Considerations and Recommendations

In deciding whether to join the consortium, Apple Computer had many issues to consider. First, the capital requirement was significant, and the rate of return on the investment in U.S. Memories was low—much lower than what could be obtained through alternative investments. But, as Kane made clear, an investment in U.S. Memories was not principally a financial investment. Acquiring a stable supply of DRAMs was potentially a strategic investment in Apple's long-term survival.

The Market

On the other hand, if the price and supply conditions in the market were simply a "temporary blip" as opposed to real structural market changes, then the advice of T. J. Rodgers—the flamboyant CEO of Cypress Semiconductor who was an ardent opponent of U.S. Memories—"be brave, do nothing" would have been warranted. In this case, the best strategy would be to ride out the rough DRAM market conditions and to wait for supplies to loosen up and for prices to fall.

Relations with Japanese Suppliers

Another consideration in joining U.S. Memories involved Apple's relationships with its Japanese suppliers. If Apple announced its decision to join the consortium, it would have to wait two years for U.S. Memories to start production to buy its share of DRAMs. During this time, it would still be dependent on its Japanese suppliers. DRAMs were already difficult to obtain. If its present suppliers learned that Apple intended to cut them off in the future, they could retaliate. On the other hand, if its present suppliers were currently holding back on DRAM supplies in order to erode Apple's position in the computer market, Apple had to do something to stay competitive.

Viability of U.S. Memories

Apple also needed to assess the viability of U.S. Memories itself. At the time the consortium was formed, the only remaining American DRAM producers were Texas Instruments (TI), Micron, and Motorola, which had a combined global market share of 10 to 15 percent in 1988. One of the objectives of U.S. Memories was to double the worldwide market share of U.S. DRAM producers. It was assumed this could be done without hurting existing U.S. firms and that U.S. Memories would only take market share away from Japanese manufacturers. This assumption was challenged by TI, Micron, Motorola, and by T. J. Rodgers. Existing DRAM manufacturers reflected the controversy. James Peterman, vice president of the Semiconductor Group at Texas Instruments said that while U.S. Memories represents a welcome initiative, "We don't really see any way we can participate. [The new consortium will manufacture DRAMs, and] that's what our business is. We have to view it as a competitor. We have a lot invested in this business—not only assets, but in the tough times we had in 1985-86 when we lost money."

Government Support

A related issue involved the types of government support U.S. Memories hoped to get. First, the founders of U.S. Memories hoped that the Semiconductor Trade Agreement (SCTA), due to expire in 1991, would be extended. To be price competitive, U.S. Memories was counting on maintaining the controversial system of fair market values (FMVs) that had been established to prevent dumping by Japanese firms. FMVs allowed firms like TI, Micron, and Motorola (along with all the Japanese DRAM producers) to reap huge profits from DRAM production in the late 1980s.[3] At the same time, the FMVs proved extremely damaging to Apple and other systems manufacturers who found themselves suddenly faced with significantly higher DRAM prices. This situation was paradoxical: on the one hand, the FMVs were a form of trade protection that U.S. Memories needed to be viable; on the other hand, they raised the price of DRAMs to the detriment of the U.S. systems manufacturers, some of whom were members of U.S. Memories. These price increases put U.S. computer systems manufacturers at a competitive disadvantage vis-á-vis their Japanese competitors.

The second type of government support U.S. Memories required was an exemption from antitrust laws. Although U.S. Memories did not appear to be in violation of federal antitrust laws, it could still be sued by a third party (e.g., another semiconductor manufacturer). According to existing antitrust law, firms participating in anticompetitive activities that harm other firms are liable for treble damages—three times their profits. If some members were unable to pay their share, the remaining members would have to assume the additional burden. In an extreme case, a single member could be liable for the entire amount of the treble damages.

Finally, U.S. Memories hoped to receive a $500 million low-interest government-guaranteed loan as a source of debt capital. This was a great point of contention for opponents of U.S. Memories. Presumably, the low-interest government loan would level the financial playing field with respect to Japanese chip makers. However, it would also give U.S. Memories an advantage over domestic chip makers such as the small, entrepreneurial firm of Micron Technologies, which did not have access to government loans of the type U.S. Memories hoped to receive. With access to cheaper capital, U.S. Memories would have a competitive edge over other domestic firms and could potentially pose a threat to domestic as well as foreign competition.

What Should Apple Do?

To answer the question of what Apple should do—Should it become a member of U.S. Memories or not—certain factors had to be reviewed: (1) What is a DRAM? (2) What is the market for DRAMs? (3) What is the state of U.S.-Japan trade relations? (4) What is the composition of the U.S. computer systems' industry? (5) How has cooperation worked in the past in this industry? (6) What were Apple's interests?

1. *What Is a DRAM?*

Dynamic random access memory chips, or DRAMs, are the most common type of semiconductor chip. Invented by Intel in 1971, DRAMs have the paradoxical property of being both technologically sophisticated and a common commodity. Their status as a commodity has earned DRAMs the nickname of "jellybeans" by semiconductor manufacturers. DRAMs are almost perfectly standardized from one to another and require little specialized marketing and distribution. Price is the primary criterion that systems makers use to choose one DRAM over another. DRAMs are distributed in several ways. Most of the larger systems manufacturers buy DRAMs directly from chip makers. Smaller DRAM customers often buy through distributors, who purchase chips from DRAM makers.

The most common use of DRAMs is in computer systems; they form the backbone of a computer's random access memory (RAM). This memory controls "short-term" computer operations such as what types of software applications to use; how many applications can be open at the same time, and the speed with which a computer is able to process applications currently in use. Random access memory is different from the type of memory that governs the storage size of a computer's hard disk. The two types of memories—random access and storage—are roughly analogous to short- and long-term memory.

An important attribute of DRAMs is their historic position as technology drivers. The mass production of these highly complex devices generates "learning" about complex production processes that can be applied to a much wider range of other device types produced by a company in lower volume. Such high-complexity, high-volume technology drivers are widely viewed as a prerequisite to remaining competitive in semiconductors over the long term. Since low manufacturing costs are crucial to success in DRAM production, chip makers seeking to lower their costs do so through increased yields and improved manufacturing. The emphasis on manufacturing creates skills and knowledge in production processes which can spill over onto many other higher-value semiconductor products such as microprocessors. It is precisely for these reasons that Japanese companies and industrial policymakers believed that Japan's initial entry into the semiconductor industry should begin with DRAM production.

DRAMs come in generations, occurring at intervals of approximately three to four years. A new generation will have four times the memory capacity of the one it replaces, and will often require radically different manufacturing processes from the previous generation. Tremendous expense is involved in retooling plants for a new chip generation; in extreme cases, entirely new plants may have to be constructed. From the standpoint of the computer systems manufacturers, switching costs are fairly low across DRAM generations because computers, unlike microprocessors, do not need to be assembled with the latest DRAM technology. Increasing the amount of older DRAMs in a PC has roughly the same effect as using a DRAM with a higher memory capacity. Thus, systems manufacturers have the luxury of waiting until prices drop and technologies standardize to switch to the new generation.

When a new generation is introduced, unfamiliarity with the new manufacturing processes will frequently result in low yields and extremely high chip prices. At this stage in the life cycle of a new chip, computer systems manufacturers continue to purchase the previous chip generations. They do not buy the new chip until the price per bit on the two generations roughly equalizes. The point at which systems manufacturers adopt the new generation chip is referred to as the "crossover." Since the new generation will have four times the bit capacity as the one it replaces, the crossover will occur when the new chip costs approximately four times the price of the older one. At this price level, the permit price for the old and new chips are equal.

Because of short product life cycles and extremely high up-front R&D costs in developing new chip generations, margins on DRAM production are low to nonexistent. Since demand for DRAMs is extremely price sensitive, chip makers will often use forward pricing on a new generation to encourage early crossover This type of pricing strategy is common in industries where economies of scale in production are important. Firms that use forward pricing set initial prices below costs in order to move down the reaming curve in production. This allows chip makers to produce and sell greater volumes than would be possible if they priced DRAMs at or above cost. Large-volume production enables chip makers to lower their costs and gain market share.

For systems manufacturers, the most unpredictable aspect of buying DRAMs is the cyclical nature of DRAM prices and supplies. As mentioned previously, chip supplies may be tight and chip prices high in the early stages in a new chip generation. When the crossover occurs, systems makers will frequently order higher-priced chips from their suppliers or distributors in order to assure a supply of the new generation chip. In response to orders from customers and distributors, chip makers will increase capacity and flood the market with DRAMs. Because the price of DRAMs is still falling at this stage, systems makers may cancel the orders they made when prices were higher and demand lower prices from their suppliers. Systems manufacturers may also cancel orders if demand for computers slows. After flooding the market, chip makers will be left with excess capacity. They are often forced to sell DRAMs at below cost. To avoid incurring further losses, chip makers will cut production.[4]

2. *The DRAM Market*

Since its invention by Intel in 1971, the DRAM market has had a turbulent history. Throughout the 1970s, DRAM manufacture was dominated by U.S. firms, which were the unrivaled leaders in technology, engineering, and manufacturing of all semiconductor products.

At approximately the same time as the invention of the DRAM came the invention, also by Intel, of the microprocessor. The semiconductor industry would thereafter be split into high-volume commodity chips such as DRAMs and EPROMs (erasable programmable read-only memory) and lower-volume, more technologically advanced chips such as microprocessors. As chip technology became increasingly sophisticated, U.S. firms began concentrating on higher-end chips at the expense of commodity chips. Short product life cycles for memory chips brought smaller returns and necessitated enormous R&D expenditures.

The late 1970s was perhaps the most eventful period in the history of the semiconductor industry. Price competition was intensifying, and the industry began to experience cyclical demand swings which, combined with the proliferation of small, upstart semiconductor firms, would lay the groundwork for the stormy and antagonistic relationship between semiconductor producers (called the "cowboys" of Silicon Valley by computer makers) and systems manufacturers. This buyer-supplier ill-will would characterize the U.S. industry for many years to come.

The mid-1970s also brought increasing industry globalization as U.S. firms moved more of their operations offshore, European firms began to enter the market, and Japanese firms emerged as world-class competitors. Japanese competition caused the market share of U.S. firms to decline rapidly. From 1974 to 1988, U.S. firms lost market share at about 6 percentage points per year. By 1989, only three U.S. firms continued to make DRAMs, and most of their production was located offshore. As the dynamic memory market matured, Japanese DRAM manufacturers commanded increasingly larger shares of the global market with each successive chip generation, peaking at close to 90 percent of the advanced IBM market in late 1989.

Although Japan's domination of the DRAM market seemed only to be increasing throughout the 1970s and 1980s, industry globalization continued to bring new players into the market. By the late 1980s, firms from Korea (Samsung and Hyundai) were growing rapidly and were among the largest DRAM manufacturers in the world. Additionally, the governments of Hong Kong and Taiwan were making commitments to manufacture DRAMs as a part of their industrial policies.

3. *U.S.-Japanese Semiconductor Trade Issues*

Industry globalization, low chip prices, and declining U.S. market share in DRAMs brought inevitable trade frictions between the United States and Japan. U.S. firms contended that Japan made it difficult for them to enter the Japanese semiconductor market and accused Japanese semiconductor manufacturers of dumping in the United States and the markets of other countries. A series of dumping complaints culminated in 1986 with the U.S.-Japan Semiconductor Trade Agreement (SCTA). The three objectives of the SCTA were to open the Japanese market to foreign semiconductor manufacturers, to prevent Japanese semiconductor manufacturers from dumping chips in the United States, and to prevent Japanese semiconductor manufacturers from dumping chips in third country markets.

Dumping, or selling goods at less than their fair value, was made illegal in the United States in 1921 with the passage of the Antidumping Act. This act provides for a duty to be imposed on certain imported foreign merchandise to make it unprofitable for foreign manufacturers to sell goods on U.S. markets at prices below cost. The Department of Treasury must inform the International Trade Commission (ITC) that goods are being sold in the United States at less than their fair market value.

To determine dumping, the Department of Commerce constructs quarterly fair market values (FMVs) for DRAMs with a formula made up of the sum of the following parts:

1. Material costs, including some R&D for materials.
2. Fabrication costs.
3. General sales and administrative expenses, including some R&D for other purposes (not less than 10 percent of the above two costs).
4. Profit (not less than 8 percent of the above two costs).

This formula is applied on a company-by-company basis using proprietary cost information to determine the minimum price of each company's products. Real-time fabrication cost data is used in determining FMVs.

As discussed earlier, semiconductor prices tend to fall rapidly as firms move down the learning curve within a given chip generation. This rapid price decline, combined with tremendous up-front R&D costs and the use of forward pricing, makes the determination of a "fair" price at any given point on the life cycle extremely difficult. For this reason, the system of FMVs is highly controversial in the semiconductor industry.

Despite the SCTA, chip prices remained low through 1986, and American DRAM manufacturers were unable to gain access to the Japanese market. This prompted the Reagan administration to impose sanctions on Japan in March 1987. Following the imposition of sanctions, chip prices began an unprecedented surge.

4. *The Computer Systems Industry*

In 1989, computer systems manufacturing was an estimated $250 billion a year industry worldwide. In the United States alone, revenues totaled $150 billion a year, making it the third largest industry after automobiles and petroleum.

Historically, the computer manufacturing industry had been segmented into three broad product classifications: mainframes, minicomputers, and microcomputers. Mainframe computers, usually priced between $500,000 and $14 million, are centrally located computers designed to handle the large-scale computing needs of up to 128 concurrent users. These computer systems are typically accompanied by custom software applications which are tailored to meet the data-processing demands of an entire organization. IBM has dominated the mainframe market for the past 30 years and held 70 percent of the $30 billion worldwide market in 1989.

Minicomputers are smaller, somewhat more decentralized versions of mainframes. These computer systems, capable of supporting 64 concurrent users, are aimed at satisfying the information processing needs of small organizations or large departments. These computers range in price from $100,000 to $500,000. DEC, the traditional leader of the minicomputer market, has recently been challenged by IBM.

Microcomputers were initially designed as single-user, stand-alone systems aimed at satisfying an individual's unique computing needs. It was not until the late 1970s, when Intel introduced its 8088 microprocessor, these desktop computer systems became widely available. The 8088 microprocessor was eventually replaced by the 80286 ("286") chip which fueled the popular IBM PC AT computers.

By the mid-1980s, more powerful and less expensive semiconductors and microprocessors radically altered the structure of the global computer industry. The long-standing distinctions between the three major industry classifications became less clear as computer makers were increasingly able to build machines with superior price/performance capabilities. Furthermore, advances in hardware, software, and peripheral systems eventually led to the creation of new types of computers like PCs and workstations which were less easily classified. These product innovations put mainframe and minicomputer manufacturers into competition with PC and workstation manufacturers who were capable of putting more affordable computing power into smaller machines.

The 1980s ushered in other significant structural changes in the global computer industry. In the early 1980s, hardware manufacturers were able to sell nearly all the goods they could produce. The industry reaped enormous profits regardless of economic conditions. All of this changed in the mid-1980s when markets had become saturated. Buyers had purchased enough hardware and only needed to replace computer equipment as it became worn-out. Demand for computers became increasingly sensitive to price, and firms could no longer increase their revenues and earnings regardless of economic conditions. In 1985, a severe downturn hit the entire industry and threatened the survival of many firms.

Further structural changes resulted from buyer demands for open systems that were completely compatible with each other. Compatibility of systems made computers more standardized and lowered barriers to entry; this forced manufacturers to shift the focus of competition from differentiated product features to price, and industry profit margins declined. To cope with the new competitive environment, computer manufacturers concentrated on shortening the transition between design and manufacture, and attempted to locate low-cost sources of reliable components.

Increasingly, competition in the computer industry became a race to reduce the time to market. Since barriers to entry by way of imitation decrease rapidly after a new product's introduction, profit margins are highest at the beginning of the product's life cycle. Companies that beat rivals to market with a new product stood to gain considerably more than their slower competitors.

The trend towards open systems also resulted in a proliferation of computer manufacturers, many from Japan and South Korea, which took advantage of the freely available technological know-how. By 1988, more than 200 companies manufactured IBM-compatible PC clones in a fiercely competitive product market.

The rise of Japanese companies as major players in the computer industry caused further structural change. Bolstered into action by a large industry-government cooperative venture during the late 1970s, Japanese companies made staggering advances into semiconductors and computers. The four largest Japanese computer producers—Fujitsu, NEC, Hitachi, and Toshiba—are also the largest semiconductor makers. By 1982, Japan reached parity with the United States in bilateral computer trade, and it achieved a surplus of more than $4 billion in 1987. At the same time, the share of U.S. firms in the Japanese market steadily declined.

5. *Cooperation between the Computer and Semiconductor Industries*

Despite the difficult relations between semiconductor manufacturers and computer systems makers, the two industries have a long history of cooperation in both the United States and Japan. Indeed, the kind of multifirm cooperative venture after which U.S. Memories had been modeled had existed for more than six years in the United States and dated back to the 1970s in Japan. Many of these consortia involved cooperative research rather than production, since it was believed that technological economies of scope existed across the computer and semiconductor industries. Most of the well-known U.S. ventures such as the Microelectronics and Computer Technology Corporation (MCC), Sematech, and the Semiconductor Research Corporation involved many of the same companies that eventually became members of U.S. Memories.

MCC

The Microelectronics and Computer Technology Corporation (MCC) was founded in 1983 by 10 computer systems and semiconductor manufacturers. Conceived as a response to Japan's Fifth Generation Computer Project, MCC was the first research consortium of its kind in the United States. Its goal was to conduct cooperative research in four main areas—advanced computer architecture, computer-aided design, computer software technology, and microcircuitry—and to pioneer the technologies necessary to keep the United States ahead in the global computer race. Since many firms with varied skills can pool both their knowledge and financial resources, cooperative research consortia like MCC were believed to be an important component of success in technology industries like computers and semiconductors and had been widely used in Japan. Moreover, since 1984 cooperative research consortia have been permitted under U.S. antitrust laws and do not face the same potential scrutiny as multifirm production ventures.

Six years after its inception, MCC's record was mixed. It had serious problems from the beginning such as the refusal of IBM—the dominant force in the computer industry—to join due to worries about giving away trade secrets. Many of the companies that did join had similar fears about secrecy and either remained suspicious of each other or were reluctant to provide any proprietary data to benefit cooperative research projects. Because many of the research projects undertaken by MCC were at least a decade away from product development, member companies were generally dissatisfied with the return that they got on their financial contributions to the consortium. In spite of these problems, however, MCC did produce numerous practical successes in a diverse range of areas such as integrated circuits (semiconductors) and artificial intelligence. If member companies did gain access to MCC technologies, it often proved to be worth their while. Even T. J. Rodgers, ardent critic of U.S. Memories, was one of the technology beneficiaries.

Sematech

Started four years after MCC, Sematech was also conceived as a response to a Japanese alliance—the Very Large Scale Integration (VLSI) project which promoted leading-edge research in DRAM technology. Unlike MCC, Sematech was able to recruit most of the leading companies in both semiconductor and computer systems manufacture including IBM, AT&T, Intel and Motorola. Fourteen companies joined at the outset, almost all of which were large due to the high ticket price of membership. Another key difference between Sematech and MCC was the Defense Department (DOD) participation in the former. Indeed, since its inception, Sematech has received hundreds of millions of dollars from DOD appropriations, which has attracted severe criticism from nonmember firms. Small companies that could not afford to join accuse large companies of ganging up together with government support to create a "Club of Big Boys" to hurt smaller, more innovative rivals. In one instance, Sematech was even accused of holding back technology from other American manufacturers who were not members of the consortium.

Sematech learned much from MCC's mistakes. Its goals were clearer and its research was less abstract. Its stated objective was to provide U.S. chipmakers with "domestic capability for world leadership in manufacturing," and to make Sematech the "manufacturing driver." In spite of its focus on manufacturing, Sematech would not actually manufacture anything. It hoped instead to create the same technologies that Japanese companies obtain naturally by doing high-volume manufacturing. These goals met with mixed success and were later redirected toward supporting the semiconductor equipment manufacturing industry.

Like MCC, Sematech's overall record has been varied. Some members were dissatisfied with the way Sematech's resources were being allocated and with the types of research being undertaken. Several companies ultimately quit. Some companies like Texas Instruments objected to Sematech's initial goal of focusing on DRAM manufacturing, fearing it would compete with their own DRAM business. Others, like Intel, remained strong supporters: "we [at Intel] think the success of Sematech is critical to the success of America's high-technology sector."

Multinational Joint Ventures

In addition to the multifirm ventures in the United States, some semiconductor and computer systems manufacturers formed multinational joint ventures involving, in some cases, research. In others, the intent was to secure DRAM supplies. Texas Instruments, one of three U.S. DRAM makers, launched such a venture with Acer, a Taiwanese computer maker. In return for an up-front investment from Acer, Texas Instruments agreed to build a DRAM manufacturing plant in Taipei. The output of the new plant would be split between the two partners.

6. Apple Computer, Inc.

Founded in a California garage in the mid-1970s, Apple Computer began as one of the most revolutionary companies in the United States. Its initial product was the company's entire reason for being—the Macintosh computer, which set a new standard for user friendliness. Known for its graphical user interface that represented information with icons and symbols, its consistency of use across different software applications, and its introduction of the mouse, the Macintosh offered high-end graphics capabilities in desktop publishing applications.

Apple's founders, Steven Jobs and Steve Wozniak, also revolutionized a uniquely Californian atmosphere at the new company. In return for their devotion, enthusiasm, and willingness to put in frequent work weeks of up to 90 hours, employees were rewarded with a casual but stimulating environment that fostered creativity and respect. This environment was a great source of pride to Apple's founders who rebelled against the ossified culture of larger, established rivals like IBM.

Apple's culture did not come without a price, however. Its innovative products required large and continuous investment in R&D, but the original company engineers and executives refused to be burdened by thinking about money. Moreover, the company had been so "stuck" on the Macintosh product that it did not really forge plans for its future direction. Finally, its casual corporate environment frequently resulted in considerable inefficiencies.

By 1985, Apple was no longer the small company it once was. It was hit hard by the downturn in the computer market in the mid-1980s and was forced to lay off 20 percent of its workforce. Amid these changes, Apple brought in John Sculley, president and CEO of Pepsi-Cola, to craft a new direction for the company.

Apple's initial marketing strategy had differed from that of its rivals. Instead of focusing on systems managers at large corporations and government institutions, Apple's sales staff pitched the Macintosh to ordinary individuals in corporations and to the educational market. By 1988 Apple had captured 12 percent of the office and professional market sector.

Sculley ushered in a more mainstream corporate environment along with a host of strategic and marketing changes. In the future, Apple would concentrate more on high-end business machine sales and its new products would be less revolutionary. To meet this objective, Apple introduced the second-generation Macintoshes in 1987. The company would expand the efforts to make its systems "talk" to other computers, such as IBM PCs and DEC systems, and strengthen its established position in office networking, the computing wave of the future. Finally, Apple hoped to increase its presence in computer peripheral products and software.

Following the downturn of the mid-1980s, Apple's performance was stellar. Its profits increased 41 percent in 1987 and 84 percent in 1988 ($400.3 million on revenues of $4.1 billion). Its 1988 ROE was 40 percent, nearly three times that of IBM. Corporate goals were to reach a 20 percent share of the business PC market in the next few years and to double the company's revenue to $10 billion by the early 1990s. At the upper management level, however, infighting ensued and many of the original Apple members, including Steven Jobs, left the company.

In mid-1989, Apple faced two important threats to its position. First, IBM had teamed up with Microsoft, to give IBM's new PS/2 line of computers the same easy-to-use graphics that were the Mac's biggest selling point. While experts still believed the PS/2 to be inferior to the Mac in ease of use, the gap was narrowing. Apple had to do something more striking to forge to the lead.

The second threat to Apple was the DRAM crisis and the mistakes Apple had made in responding to it. Rather than cut production of Macintoshes, Apple bought chips on the spot market at twice the normal price. Instead of swallowing its higher costs, Apple increased the price of its Macs by as much as $800 at a time when computers were getting cheaper. Sales fell off sharply. The increased costs of memory components adversely affected the company's operating results during the second half of 1988, resulting in a 51.5 percent gross margin decline in the third quarter and 49.2 percent in the fourth quarter. The impact of higher DRAM costs continued during the first half of 1989, as the gross margin further declined to 49.1 percent in the first quarter and 46.2 percent in the second quarter. To make matters worse, Apple led Wall Street to believe that its earnings would come to about $.65 per share, but in January 1989 it announced that they would be closer to $.35 per share. The market reacted violently and nearly 10 percent of Apple shares were sold that day—the biggest one-day sell-off in Nasdaq history, and Apple's market value fell by 10 percent in one day alone.

Apple's annual reports reflected the severity of the DRAM crisis:

1988
In 1988, gross margin was positively affected by improved operating efficiencies related to increased sales volumes, by increased sales of higher-margin products as a proportion of net sales, and by the overall favorable effect of foreign currency exchange rates on revenues earned overseas. These favorable effects, however, were offset by the increasing cost of certain key purchased part components, particularly DRAMs, of which a worldwide shortage continues to

exist ... The continuing industry wide shortage of DRAM devices has resulted in increased prices for these components. This situation may have an adverse impact on gross margin, to the extent the Company is unable to procure DRAMs at relatively favorable prices.

1989

The most significant factor affecting Apple profits was pressure on our gross margin caused by our increased cost of goods—most notably the DRAM ... It was a product cost increase that the U.S. computer market did not absorb.

Discussion Questions

1. What are the dominant economic characteristics of the DRAM industry?
2. What are the forces driving change in the DRAM industry?
3. What is competition like in the DRAM industry? Is this industry attractive?
4. What should Apple Computer do? Should it become a member of U.S. Memories or not? Discuss the arguments for and against joining U.S. Memories.
5. If Apple does not join U.S. Memories, what alternatives does it have for obtaining DRAMS?
6. Should U.S. industries in advanced technological areas combine in associations like U.S. Memories, and should they be encouraged to do so by the U.S. government to meet foreign competitive challenges?

Endnotes

1. This case was prepared by Susan Feinberg, Bill McEvily, and Stefanie Lenway.
2. Rumors of tying practices appeared in the press, in SIA publications, and in interviews with Sandy Kane, Andy Procassini (president of the Semiconductor Industry Association), and Craig Stacey (manager of All American SemiConductors, a semiconductor distributor). Stacey recalled that in the late 1980s, DRAM manufacturers were asking their distributors to sell memory chips in "packages" with more advanced chips. Stacey considered this packaging of chips extremely unusual.
3. After the imposition of sanctions against Japan in mid-1987, U.S. semiconductor firms experienced profits for two reasons. First, an unprecedented chip shortage led to higher DRAM prices. Second, the SCTA called for Japanese DRAM manufacturers to raise prices on DRAMs to the fair market value. American DRAM manufacturers also benefited from these price increases. For example, Micron Technologies, of Boise, Idaho, which lost $34 million in 1986 and $23 million in 1987, earned $98 million in 1988!
4. An extreme example of this "futures-like" aspect of the DRAM market was described by Craig Stacey, a semiconductor distributor. Stacey had sold DRAMs to a customer at the prevailing marker price. Several days later the market price fell, and the customer attempted to return the chips and repurchase them at the lower market price. Semiconductor distributors who purchase DRAMs when the price is declining are often forced to sell them at prices below costs. Distributors try to avoid this situation by maintaining small inventories.

Chapter Twenty-Eight

BENEFITING FROM PUBLIC POLICIES:

INTERNATIONAL TRADE

International Trade

We simply knew we could not leave Japanese competitors the isolation in Japan, while they prospected in our home market. We set about using very commercial and political means to influence change ...

Robert Galvin, former CEO of Motorola[1]

Introduction

This chapter introduces you to the importance of government in affecting the fortunes of companies, and it provides examples showing how this is done. It explores the differences between responding to market demands and responding to public policies. It presents a strategic approach to managing the corporation's relations with government.

This chapter also introduces the topic of global competition, focusing on trade policy, explaining David Ricardo's principle of comparative advantage, tracing the evolution of U.S. trade policy, and describing how the General Agreement for Trade and Tariffs (GATT) works. The chapter concludes with a discussion of the comparative strengths and weaknesses of four major world economic powers: Germany, Japan, the United Kingdom (U.K.), and the United States.

The Impact of Public Policy

In theory, businesses compete in unfettered free markets as privately owned, profit-maximizing entities. In reality, they are affected by public policies forged by government at home and countries throughout the globe where they operate. An example is Levi Strauss & Company, the privately owned apparel company, which expanded internationally in the 1980s to serve new markets and buy products from additional suppliers.[2] Buying certain foreign-made products subjected Levi Strauss to criticism from activist groups, which claimed that working conditions in factories outside the United States depended on child labor and a prison workforce, and that poor plant safety and environmental conditions were common. The activists uncovered human rights violations in many of the foreign plants.

The values and image of Levi Strauss were at stake. It sent audit teams to make a detailed assessment of its suppliers. After being visited by auditors, 30 percent of the suppliers agreed to improvements, but 5 percent refused to make changes and no longer work for Levi Strauss. On its own, the company decided to end all arrangements with Burmese suppliers, and it chose to exit China by 1995.

The decision to leave China was a painful one. Levi Strauss could no longer rely on a cheap, highly skilled work force. It would be precluded from selling to an immense market in the world's most rapidly growing economy. But Levi Strauss did not feel comfortable with Chinese policies, and it believed it had no choice but to pull out.

Government Effects on Business

Governments set the tone for business operations throughout the world. They provide a fundamental framework that determines what businesses can and cannot do. Firms strive for sustainable competitive advantage based on superior products, constant innovation, and the creation of assets that cannot be imitated by their competitors. Their success depends on national endowments—capital, labor, and natural resources.[3] It also depends on intense domestic rivalry, sophisticated buyers, and the clustering of firms. Universities, financial institutions, and suppliers concentrate in areas of economic excellence such as the Silicon Valley. A number of factors that make for a company's success are influenced by government.[4]

Government plays an enormous role in determining how well a company does. Among the influences government has are:

infant industry protection
Protective tariffs to keep out foreign competitors so that new industries can get started.

1. Research and development (R&D) programs, which help make innovation possible. The aerospace and semiconductor industries in the United States owe a heavy debt to the U.S. government for the research it financed.
2. Infant industry protection, which includes special subsidies to industries in their early stages, allowing them to achieve the economies of scale they need to become world-class competitors.
3. Help in reviving declining industries.
4. Aiding labor market mobility by retraining workers.
5. Supporting the start-up of small businesses that cannot obtain backing from private capital markets because of the risk involved.
6. Vigorous enforcement of antitrust and consumer protection laws to ensure that competitive market conditions exist for business development.
7. Tough laws that challenge businesses to come up with creative ways to solve environmental and occupational safety and health problems.
8. Competition among local governments for businesses to locate in their region to stimulate job creation and expand the tax base.
9. Providing subsidies ranging from loan guarantees to tax breaks.

Managers have to know how to maneuver through a host of government-related issues. The effects of government on business strategy and performance range from tax policies and subsidies to regulations on prices, products, and profits. Government can control entry into the market through licenses, permits, charters, concessions, patents, and franchises. It can structure markets through trade and antitrust policies, and it may directly compete with firms through public enterprise.

Federal, state, and local governments also aid businesses by providing the necessary infrastructure. They build roads, bridges, dams, airports, and railways. They finance police protection, public education, public parks, libraries, and the justice system. They purchase goods and services from business, including weapons, office furniture, computer software, and economic and policy analyses. Government policies influence business conditions from interest rates to growth rates, unemployment, and prices.

Rapid changes in government policies at home and abroad in recent years have made businesses increasingly subject to a climate of uncertainty. This integration of public policy and business strategy around issues such as global competitiveness corresponds to a growing merger between government and the economy through many types of policies—macroeconomic, national security, trade, and regulation—that meaningfully affect a firm's performance and operations.[5]

Reconciling Business and Political Interests

For any business to succeed, it is critical that management have the capacity to understand the origins and impacts of public policies. Business actions must be consistent with the institutional rules and arrangements that governments establish as well as the competitive conditions in the marketplace. Managers must be able to integrate and reconcile their business and political interests.

United Airlines quickly learned this lesson. In the debates leading up to the deregulation of the airline industry, United vigorously supported lifting market controls. However, it was less prepared than its competitor American in dealing with the challenges of an open market. American Airlines, whose CEO Robert Crandall led the charge against deregulation, was more successful in making innovations in the immediate postderegulation period with its frequent flier mileage program and a renegotiated contract with the airline pilots' union. Its responses to deregulation enabled American to take market share from United.[6]

Responses to government, unlike the market where the price system dominates, require a different set of skills. Managers have to take into account voting, majority rule, and due process in democratic societies. They need strategies to influence public opinion, interest groups, administrative bodies, legislatures, the courts, and the media as much as strategies to guide their interactions with customers, suppliers, and competitors. For company strategies to be effective, they must be consonant not only with the firm's internal competencies and competitive strengths, but they also must conform to public policies.

Issues, Interests, Information, and Institutions

To manage corporate public affairs, managers must pay attention to issues, interests, information, and institutions.[7] Issues are disputes moving toward resolution. How they are settled has the potential to benefit or hurt a firm. The firm's actions will influence how the dispute is decided. An example of an important issue was the court's decision to break up AT&T following an antitrust suit against this corporate giant.

Many interest groups have a stake in an issue, and they mobilize to affect the decision making process. Businesses themselves lobby, make political contributions, and present their cases before the courts and administrative agencies. Trade associations conduct some of this activity. Today many companies have set up their own political offices in Washington, D.C., and in state capitals. They also have established full-time staffs at corporate headquarters to analyze emerging issues and manage their political activities. In addition, firms rely on law firms, lobbyists, and other specialized intermediaries to speak for them.

Sometimes, issues lead to conflicts between different businesses. At other times, the conflicts involve corporations and environmentalists, labor unions, women, ethnic and racial minorities, and consumers. The media plays a key role in defining the issues and presenting different points of view.

All interests bring the information they know to bear. Companies, for instance, run full-page ads in major newspapers, testify in Congress, sponsor specialized studies and reports, and try to influence public opinion. Their capacity to articulate and advance positions using available information is a critical resource in their ability to achieve their goals.

Institutions are the bodies that make public policy and have the right to take binding action. In the United States, they are the executive, legislative, and judicial branches of government, which exist at all levels of government from the states to the national government. The complex sharing of power among different branches of government is illustrated by the Federal Communications Commission (FCC). Congress has given it broad authority over the telecommunications industry, but it is the president who selects the commissioners who serve on the FCC. The commissioners are appointed to staggered terms, so that no president has complete control over them. FCC decisions have local impact; for example, the right to operate a television station. Its decisions also are subject to judicial appeal. The courts, which interpret statutes passed by Congress, can overturn and modify commission rulings. Congress itself continually revises these statutes with new amendments.

The diversity of institutions means that affected businesses have access to different layers of government. Losers might hope to win the battle the next time the issue is brought up in a different context. Also, though an issue is on the agenda, public policy making bodies can refuse to act. Without consensus, stalemate can prevail for substantial periods of time. The best recent example is U.S. health care reform, where no action was taken despite long debate.

Coping with Public Policies

issues management
The process by which corporations identify, evaluate, and respond to emerging issues.

Issues management is the process by which corporations identify, evaluate, and respond to emerging issues. In engaging in this activity, managers should ask the following questions:

- How will an issue influence the profitability and productivity of the company?
- How will an issue affect competitive conditions in the industry?
- What is likely to determine the outcome?
- How can the company exert its influence?
- How must the company adapt to changes that the issue is likely to bring into being?
- In what ways will the company have to modify its business practices and structure?

The growing connection between public and private policies has led many firms to reexamine how they manage issues. Companies increasingly are trying to transform public policy constraints into opportunities for gain. The firm's ability to manage its relationships with public policy making bodies can be an important strategic advantage.[8]

A Strategic Orientation

Businesses have many choices in their response to public policies. They can fight all the way and do only what is required, or they can be progressive and take a leadership role. Their responses can be reactive and defensive or accommodative and proactive.

A company with a proactive orientation will try to identify the competitive impacts of alternative public policies. Public policies can have different effects on firms within an industry. Larger and more efficient firms may have low costs because of economies of scale. Smaller, recent entrants to a market may have low costs because of their flexibility and ability to make rapid progress on the learning curve. In either situation, the low cost position provides opportunities for gain. Competitors might have to cope with changes in public policies at a later time and with more bother, greater expense, and a famished image.

opportunism
The effort to transform public policy constraints into opportunities for gain.

Opportunism is the effort to transform public policy constraints into opportunities for gain. For instance, 3M has created a highly successful Pollution Prevention Pays (3P) program in response to growing environmental regulations. Honda developed the revolutionary CVCC engine in response to air pollution requirements.

Opportunism usually is a thought-out, long-term strategy that is part of overall business practice. An opportunistic firm follows up its awareness of the competitive implications of policy changes by anticipating how the issue is likely to develop. The firm plans its responses to expected events, but it must also consider unlikely contingencies.

The Stages of Issues Management

The stages in managing an issue are (1) formation—issue identification, analysis, development of a range of responses, and selection of a specific response; (2) development of an implementation plan; and (3) assessment of the results. Relevant questions at different stages in issues development are:

Formation
1. How do coalitions and movements for political change come into existence? How do they get issues on the public agenda?
2. How do businesses, public interest associations, and others influence government decision making?
3. How is legislation transformed into government programs?

Implementation
1. How do government officials interpret and administer government programs?
2. How do they respond to the pressures from external parties?
3. What effect do government programs have on external groups and interests?

Evaluation
1. What coalitions have formed in favor of or in opposition to policy innovation?
2. What obstacles hinder the institutionalization of policy changes?
3. What actions can be taken to overcome these obstacles?

Collective action is only one choice open to companies pursuing their interests. The decision to work together with other firms, like other business decisions, is subject to the test of profit potential. Because participation in a group imposes costs on the members, the firm will weigh these costs against the benefits of participation.

anticipatory strategy
A company's effort to improve its competitive position and increase public support by responding early to public issues.

As a general rule, an **anticipatory strategy** is preferable to a reactive one. An organization that anticipates public expectations will have more options. It can improve its competitive position and increase public support while still meeting profit and performance goals expeditiously. However, foot-dragging or stonewalling is reasonable in some cases. Therefore, strategic analysis is needed.

Legitimacy and Advantage

legitimacy
The extent to which a corporations purposes, and methods mesh with those of society.

Though corporate advantage is a prime objective of public affairs participation, legitimacy is also important. **Legitimacy** is the extent to which a corporation's goals, purposes, and methods mesh with those of society. Managers find that legitimacy is a difficult problem because of its intangible and subjective qualities. The values held by society are fluid and diverse; at any point in time, managers might be able to find some subgroup that espouses values consistent with corporate activities. Therefore, managers have the option to conform to society's values, to change these values, or to align themselves with a subgroup that holds a minority viewpoint.

Business success in influencing politicians depends on building coalitions within the context of emerging and ongoing social and political movements. The influence a business exerts is a result of its ability to fuse its demands with a program that has wider appeal. In politics, beliefs are as important as interests, and positions must be justified in terms other than mere self-interest. The pursuit of advantage has to be tempered by a concern for legitimacy.

Real-World Example

Monsanto: Competitive Cooperation

Monsanto has tried to develop a strategic approach to public policy. The company calls the approach *competitive cooperation*, competitive because issues management has a material impact on the company's competitiveness measured by the achievement of corporate goals; and cooperative because diverse issue agendas require issue-by-issue coalition building, even with traditional adversaries (e.g., environmentalists).[9]

Monsanto has changed from a capital-intensive, largely chemical commodity company into a firm that concentrates on proprietary, patented products. In doing so, the company has tried to harness issues management to assist it directly in the pursuit of its strategic goals. To reduce the likelihood of surprise, elaborate scanning systems have been installed to identify and list emerging issues that might affect the firm. Monsanto also has established an Issue Identification Committee, made up of 13 key and senior managers, which has identified 10 broad areas of concern, including global competitive challenges, the management of technology, and the management of multinational business. Hundreds of publications are read and thousands of clippings assembled to make managers aware of external social and political trends in a new and more comprehensive way.

A high-level Emerging Issues Committee has been formed to focus attention on these issues. Richard Mahoney, Monsanto's CEO, wanted to be sure that senior executives were making the best use of their time with public issues. Mahoney set up a process that determined the priority of issues of greatest concern to the company and about which it could have greatest influence. To narrow the list of issues, he advised that the effects of a particular issue on the company's assets and business direction should determine its place on the list.

Cataloging the universe of issues facing Monsanto led to the creation of a regularly updated Public Issues Book with summaries of 170 different issues. The company evaluated and sorted these issues on a division-by-division basis to provide managers with issues that were key to their operations. The Executive Management Committee reviewed the list. Its highest priorities were fair trade, biotechnology regulation, intellectual property rights, agricultural policy, and hazardous waste policy. Fair trade was in the foremost position because Monsanto does business in more than 100 countries. A high-level executive was assigned to each issue and a detailed action plan drawn up. For each issue, the company outlined specific objectives and action steps. It routinely checks performance against the plans and has responsible executives provide the Executive Management Committee with periodic reports.

Trade Policy

The issue of trade policy has become a top priority at many companies. Let us look at two examples.

Toys 'R' Us versus LSRSL[10]

To gain entry to the Japanese market, Toys 'R' Us, the U.S. toy discount retailer, had to fight Japan's Large-Scale Retail Store Law (LSRSL), which gives local (i.e., Japanese) retailers the right to review, comment on, and oppose the building of any new large store. The stated purpose of the LSRSL is to control the retail activities of large stores, secure business opportunities for local retailers, and provide sound development of the retail trade without hampering the benefits to consumers. The law applies to establishing and extending buildings for a retail business whose size exceeds 500 square meters. In principle, it allows large stores to open a business only upon giving notification to the Ministry of International Trade and Industry (MITI), which must then review each application. If MITI believes that the activity of the large store may damage local small retailers, it can advise the applicant to postpone opening the store and to reduce its business space.

The LSRSL was a formidable barrier to the entry of Toys 'R' Us into the Japanese market. To overcome this barrier, the company first formed a joint venture with McDonald's to obtain that company's expertise about the Japanese regulatory system and store location policies. Next, Toys 'R' Us petitioned the U.S. government for assistance. It wanted the government to make the toy firm's difficulties an international trade issue and to pressure the Japanese to loosen up their administration of the LSRSL. The Japanese promised to revise the law to make it easier for U.S. discounters to establish themselves in Japan. In 1991, Toys 'R' Us finally opened its first Japanese outlet. Without U.S. government assistance, however, it is unlikely that the company would have successfully resolved the matter as soon as it did.

CEMEX[11]

Another example is Cementos Mexicanos (CEMEX), the largest North American cement producer. In the 1980s, the Mexican company tried to enter the U.S. market. Almost immediately, U.S. producers and labor unions filed an antidumping petition with the U.S. International Trade Commission (ITC), claiming that they had been injured by imports. The ITC decided in favor of the U.S. manufacturers and imposed a 58 percent duty on the Mexican imports.

CEMEX appealed to the U.S. Court of International Trade (CIT) and the U.S. Court of Appeals, but it lost in both instances. It then petitioned through the General Agreement on Trade and Tariffs (GATT), which decided in favor of CEMEX, but the U.S. government, which has the right to withhold its approval of a GATT ruling, refused to go along. CEMEX was forced to restrict its entry into the U.S. market to states like Arizona and California, where cement prices are high, and to keep out of Florida where prices are low because of the way the ITA computes dumping margins.

International trade issues have come to dominate corporate politics to a far greater extent than in the past. It is worth delving deeper into this matter because corporate public affairs managers have to increasingly grapple with this type of complicated issue.

Free Trade

If the United States is falling behind in international commerce, to what extent should it move away from its traditional commitment to free trade? To what extent should it remain committed to these policies? Adam Smith argued that free trade stimulated competition and provided opportunities for countries to specialize and to achieve economies of scale. Countries would produce what they were best at making and trade for the rest. However, what if a country's economy was weak? What if it was not good at making anything and had no absolute advantage in any area? To understand this situation David Ricardo, the early 19th-century British economist, formulated the principle of **comparative advantage**, perhaps one of the most powerful in economics.[12]   Comparative advantage says that countries should specialize in producing the goods they make best and import other goods.

comparative advantage
David Ricardo's principle of international trade, which states that countries should specialize in producing goods it makes best and import other goods.

If it takes 10 hours of labor to make a gallon of wine and 20 hours to make a pound of cheese in Greece and it takes 60 hours of labor to make a gallon of wine and 30 hours to make a pound of cheese in Turkey, Greece is more productive than Turkey in both commodities.   It has the *absolute* advantage in wine and cheese, but its *comparative* advantage is in wine while Turkey's *comparative* advantage is in cheese. It makes sense for Greece to specialize in wine production and for Turkey to specialize in cheese production. The two countries should trade with each other because both will be better off; however, since Greek workers in this instance are more efficient than Turkish workers, they will earn more income.

Trade does not make earnings across countries equal when productivity differs, it simply makes both countries better off than they otherwise would be. Tariffs and quotas, on the other hand, reward inefficient domestic producers and make goods more expensive (and less plentiful) for domestic consumers. The economy has less reason to be innovative. Consumers in economies insulated from international competition have to pay higher prices for lower-quality goods and services.

Smoot-Harley and Its Aftermath

In 1930, the U.S. Congress passed the Smoot-Harley Tariff Act, which established the highest general tariff rate structure in U.S. history. Country after country retaliated, world trade stagnated, and the Great Depression, already underway, deepened and became global.[13]   Why did the U.S. Congress ignore the warnings of experts? Why did it raise tariffs to unprecedented levels? The power of special interests seeking import protection dominated the legislative process. Though most people benefit from international trade, the firms and industries whose home markets will be diminished suffer. They are concentrated, organized, and capable of pressing their interests in the political arena. In contrast, the broad mass of consumers who benefit from foreign trade is diffuse and its interest in any particular trade issue is usually slight. For free trade to have a chance, antiprotectionist counterweights must be in place.

The process of creating these counterweights started in 1934 when Congress passed the Reciprocal Trade Agreements Act. This act authorized the president to negotiate and implement tariff-cutting pacts with other countries. The law had an effect. By 1942, U.S. exports resumed to their predepression levels.   After a long history of passing comprehensive tariff bills, Congress, with some exceptions, stopped making product-specific trade law. It relinquished that task to the executive branch.[14]

GATT

Since 1947, the world has benefited from the General Agreement on Tariffs and Trade (GATT), which has promoted free trade. Its secretariat monitors the trade policies of 117 member nations. Originally composed of 23 countries, the GATT's purpose was to fight against the legacy of protectionism, which had severely hurt the world economy in the period between the two world wars and had made the Great Depression worse.[15]

The GATT works on the basis of three principles. The first is *reciprocity*; if a country lowers its tariffs against another country's exports, the other country is expected in turn to lower its tariffs. The second principle is *nondiscrimination*, by which no country should grant favorable trade treatment to another country or groups of countries. The third principle is *transparency*: Countries replace nontariff barriers such as import quotas with tariffs, and then make these tariffs binding by promising not to raise them.[16]

Between 1948 and 1973, the GATT was very successful. The growth rate in international commerce went up 7 percent each year after 1948 after having grown at a rate of only .5 percent per year between 1913 and 1948. From 1950 to 1980, the sum of imports and exports rose from 8.4 percent of the U.S. GNP to 21.1 percent. The increase for West Germany (Germany was not united until 1990) went from 25.4 percent to 57.3 percent and for Japan from 20.1 percent to 31.2 percent.[17]

Today, more than 70 percent of U.S. products and services are in markets where they face foreign competition. The largest increases in world trade followed the so-called Kennedy Round of negotiations that lasted from 1963 to 1967. Cuts of 50 percent and more were made on more than two-thirds of the products of industrial countries. Between 1969 and 1973, world exports more than doubled.[18]

Unfortunately, the result of this burgeoning trade was a call for protectionism. Specific sectors of the economy had trouble adjusting to the new competition. Under the GATT, however, countries were restricted in what they could do. Only developing countries and advanced nations with severe balance-of-trade problems could use quotas. A country had to consult with other GATT nations before raising a tariff and it had to provide affected nations with compensation. Countervailing duties were allowed only if imported goods had been subsidized. Special duties were sanctioned only if charges of dumping could be proved; that is, an importer had to sell goods at below cost.

Because of these restrictions, countries resorted to more subtle forms of trade protection: voluntary export restraints (bilateral quotas), public subsidies, and nationalistic procurement policies. The Tokyo Round of GATT talks, which lasted from 1973 to 1979, was successful in lowering tariffs (the weighted average tariff rate went down from 7 percent to 4.67 percent), but it was unsuccessful in eliminating ambiguities in the treatment of nontariff barriers.[19] The 1990 round of GATT negotiations—the Uruguay Round—was extremely complicated and very hotly contested. However, new agreements were reached to lower agricultural trade barriers and to deal with questions of intellectual property and services.

Against Free Trade

Throughout the world, a new nationalism has surfaced and, with it, arguments against free trade and for protectionism have gained momentum. Briefly, these arguments consist of the following:

1. National security reasons justify the violation of free trade principles. A country needs certain vital industries in case of war.

2. Violating free trade principles for the sake of job protection is justified. Low wages provide the developing countries with an unfair trade advantage that robs the developed countries of jobs. Much of international trade is in the form of intrafirm transactions wherein a company exports manufacturing to low-wage countries.

3. Some countries create unfair trade advantages. They do so by means of tax incentives and selected subsidies to companies, such as government-sponsored R&D, preferential loans, and giving companies the freedom to collude. Foreign companies that cannot compete with the subsidized companies should be allowed to violate free trade principles to put themselves in a better position to compete.

4. During the infant industry stage, special subsidies and protection in various forms from import restrictions to reduced tax are appropriate, provided they are removed when the industry gains strength and matures. Infant industry protection has long been accepted in international trade theory: To build comparative advantage in particular industries, a country may have to protect them when they are young.

5. It might be justifiable to violate free trade principles to obtain more favorable terms of trade. Threatening a country with a tariff can help open the country's markets to foreign goods.[20]

Trade wars, whereby countries retaliate against the protectionism of other countries, are extremely damaging to the world economy, however. A severe decline in world trade would hurt everyone except special interests.

Remedies for Firms Harmed by Foreign Competition

The U.S. government has established a number of remedies for firms and industries that allege they have been harmed by imports.[21] The main components of U.S. trade law can be found in the 1974 Trade Act. The remedies available to businesses are:

- Offsetting duties in special cases
- Antidumping measures
- Temporary relief (the escape clause)
- Trade adjustment assistance
- Deals in special cases (voluntary export restrictions and orderly marketing arrangements).

In 1897, Congress allowed the imposition of special offsetting duties if it found that foreign governments were unduly subsidizing exports. The 1921 Anti-dumping Act permitted similar measures if foreign sellers were unloading goods in the U.S. market at prices below those in their home market. In a 1943 agreement with Mexico, the U.S. government drew on precedents to establish an "escape clause," which allowed an affected industry to appeal for temporary relief if it could prove injury from the results of U.S. trade policies.

The 1962 Trade Expansion Act brought major revision and codification of the escape clause. It also introduced the idea of trade adjustment assistance as an alternative or supplement to tariff relief. Workers and companies adversely affected by imports could seek government financial, technical, and retraining assistance.

Under a special section of the 1956 Agricultural Act, the president had the authority to negotiate bilateral export limitation agreements with foreign governments on textiles or textile products. Presidents Eisenhower, Kennedy, and Nixon used this authority to get deals for voluntary export restraints (VERs) on textiles. The idea of establishing VERs and orderly marketing arrangements (OMAs) was extended to automobiles and steel.

Between 1979 and 1980, the foreign share of the new-car market in the United States increased from 17 percent to over 25 percent; the 1982 agreement limited the Japanese to no more than 25 percent of the U.S. market. To get around the limitation, the Japanese automakers increased their export of luxury models to the U.S. market and raised prices. They also made investments in U.S. car manufacturing facilities not covered by the agreement. Though it increased employment in the U.S. automobile industry by 55,000 in the early 1980s, the auto agreement with Japan raised the prices paid by consumers an estimated 4.4 percent. U.S. automakers benefited by $2.6 billion and those in Japan benefited by $2.2 billion.

A similar agreement was negotiated between the U.S. government and each country supplying steel to the United States. In 1984, the U.S. government set the limit on steel imports to the U.S. at about 20 percent through the use of VERs. Again, the costs to consumers has been very high. Industrial users of steel have had to pay higher costs, which they have passed on to consumers. To get around the quotas, foreign steel manufacturers have entered specialty steel markets not covered by the agreement. This prompted U.S. specialty steel makers to petition the U.S. government for relief.

These special deals were used because they circumvented national and international rules. They got around national rules because the U.S. government did not have to prove injury or limit the duration of protection. They avoided GATT requirements that permit other nations to impose equivalent trade restrictions unless the United States offers compensation in the form of offsetting tariff reductions.

The Omnibus Trade Act of 1988

Under the Omnibus Trade and Competitiveness Act of 1988, the U.S. government became even more vigilant in trying to remove nontariff barriers.[22] The act strengthened U.S. trade negotiators' leverage and gave the government negotiating authority for the Uruguay Round of trade talks. The act also required notification of plant closings and expanded assistance to workers who lose their jobs.

Super 301 provision
Gives the U.S. government the right to name priority unfair trading practices and countries.

Under the **Super 301 provision** of the act, the U.S. government had the right to name "priority" unfair trading practices and "priority" unfair trading countries. When this is done, a 12- to-18-month period of negotiations takes place to remove the cited nation's trade barriers. In 1989, Japan was cited for exclusionary government procurement practices for supercomputers and satellites and for technical barriers preventing forest product imports. Brazil was cited for quantitative import restrictions and India for trade-related investment barriers and for closure of its insurance market to foreign firms.

The Super 301 provision opened the door for U.S. businesses to present cases against Japan. In 1990, Allied-Signal maintained that Japan put together a business combination to develop and market a product to compete with Allied-Signal's amorphous metal alloys. It also claimed that the Japanese government tried to keep Japanese firms from purchasing its alloys and that Japan held up an Allied-Signal patent application for 11 years before approving it. To relieve the tension in U.S.-Japan relations, the chief U.S. trade representative reached an agreement with Japan in which Allied-Signal withdrew its complaint and Japan agreed that its utilities could buy transformers that use Allied-Signal's metals.[23]

Exporting Mechanics

In addition to negotiating trade agreements for U.S. companies, the American government provides numerous other types of trade assistance. The export market is far more complicated than producing and selling for the domestic market.[24] The Department of Commerce has 47 local U.S. offices that provide information about trade and investment opportunities abroad, foreign markets, and financing and insurance, tax advantages, trade exhibitions, documentation, and licensing and import requirements. Most its offices have a business library and lists of people who are experienced in exporting. Many state governments have similar offices..

The Business Counseling Section of the International Trade Administration also provides advice to exporters. Programs in the Export-Import Bank and Overseas Private Investment Corporation offer information about political conditions in various countries. The State Department, an additional source of information, works with large commercial banks and industry trade associations.

In selecting a foreign market, a prospective exporter can study the *Foreign Trade Report* published by the Bureau of the Census. It includes statistical records of the merchandise shipped from the United States to foreign countries. *Overseas Business Reports* provides details on marketing strategies for individual countries. U.S. embassies and consulates prepare *Foreign Economic Trends* with country-by-country data on business conditions. International economic indicators, demographic data, and market share reports can be obtained from other government reports. For a nominal annual subscription fee, TOPS (the Trade Opportunities Program) will make matches between individual firms and particular business opportunities.

Developing an export marketing strategy involves deciding what is unique about the product and how it will stand up to the foreign competition. The product may have to be modified for the foreign market. The quality image is important because American products have slipped in recent years. Questions about production capacity, promotion and advertising, training and translation, distribution, and customer service should be considered. For instance, to what extent will the product have to be disassembled for shipping? All of these questions bear on the final price of the product.

The U.S. producer can sell the good directly overseas or rely on an intermediary for both sales and shipping. There are many types of intermediaries. Foreign firms often use commission agents to find foreign products they need. Country-controlled buying agents fulfill the same function. Export management companies, on the other hand, purchase U.S. goods for sale abroad, and the manufacturer usually bears the risk. To enhance the practicality of exports by small- and medium-sized companies, joint trading companies may be established. It is also possible to rely upon conventional sales representatives, wholesale outlets, and government purchasing agents. In making all of these decisions, business people will find government agencies useful.

Though one hears a great deal about U.S. trade deficits, much less is heard about exports. The United States is the world's largest exporter. Its exports valued at more than $500 billion per year outdistance both Germany and Japan, the world's number two and number three exporters. Boeing is the largest exporting company, but most of the increase in U.S. exports in recent years has come from small- and medium-size businesses.

Comparing National Strengths and Weaknesses

Trade theory holds that each economy in the world builds up unique advantages and disadvantages and that by means of mutually beneficial transactions everyone benefits. For the world to prosper, there should be a division of labor among the world's major trading partners. In what follows, some of the advantages and disadvantages of four major industrial nations—Germany, Japan, the United Kingdom, and the United States—are compared (see Figure 28-1).[25]

FIGURE 28-1
Strengths of national
economies

Germany	Japan	United Kingdom	United States	
chemicals	electronics	services	computers	defense
plastics	equipment	consumer goods	software	aerospace
machinery	steel	publishing	biotech	health care
printing	transportation	advertising	consumer goods	entertainment
optical	office computing	luxury items	forest products	leisure
	cameras	leisure	agriculture	
		consulting		

Germany

The particular strengths of the German economy are in chemicals, plastics, machinery, printing, and optical products. The economy is adept at complex production processes that require a high degree of precision. There is strong domestic rivalry for prestige in science and technology. A pragmatic, technical management aims to master and dominate sophisticated market segments. It puts a stress on quality, premium high performance products that command high prices. The Germans try to compete based on quality and differentiation, not on cost.

Germany has a large domestic market, sophisticated buyers, and an international orientation among its companies. Banks hold shares in companies and bank executives serve on company boards. To a greater extent than in the United States or the United Kingdom, ownership is in private hands. The firms tend to be small, hierarchical, well disciplined, and owner-managed. For all these reasons, German firms have a long-term perspective; they are not as preoccupied with quarterly profits.

These advantages have not prevented major declines in the steel, coal, shipbuilding, and apparel industries. Germany has relatively few natural resources, with the exception of coal and coke, and domestic markets are saturated in many areas. The government imposes tough product standards and has demanding environmental laws. Consumers are sophisticated, but also cautious and conservative and not easily swayed by image marketing. In any event, television and radio advertising on the public media in Germany is limited. A product does not make rapid headway if intangible brand name and mass communication is critical to its success.

German businesses have not been strong in consumer products. In business services, they have been held back by high wages. Public ownership and regulation have inhibited innovation in telecommunications, transportation, and electric power. Management education is weak, electronics and computer industries have failed to flourish, and the pace of small business formation has been slow. Finally, group decision making has retarded innovation, and a creeping financial orientation in addition to poorly developed risk capital markets have prevented further progress.

Germany has faced a huge burden in integrating the formerly Communist East. Employment and environmental difficulties could hold the unified Germany back.

Japan

Japanese strengths are in electronic products, heavy equipment, steel- and transportation-related industries, autos, office machines, computing equipment, and cameras. Although Japanese companies have R&D programs, they do much of their technology sourcing abroad. Project teams are able to bring new products into production very quickly. The emphasis on product quality remains great even though Japan has long ago overcome the image of producing cheap goods.

The dynamism of the Japanese economy has been promoted by intense domestic rivalry, demanding buyers, cooperative suppliers, rapid upgrading of technology, and an international orientation. Savings and investment are high and capital investment strong. Investment has been aimed at creating large, efficient facilities with the latest technology. Since World War II, the Japanese approach has been to scrap old production facilities and build new ones rather than make incremental adjustments.

Sophisticated domestic buyers insist on the latest model of car, electronic product, or camera with the most up-to-date features. Japanese companies have been aware the presentation and packaging is an important part of sales, and the mass media and advertising business are well developed.

Japanese companies expect a great deal from their suppliers. World-class suppliers have developed cooperative long-term relationships with Japanese companies. The flow of information is very important. Trading companies help exporters penetrate foreign markets. Distribution channels, however, are dominated by diverse and highly fragmented outlets, not the uniform mass-marketing channels such as supermarkets and discount chains that dominate in the United States.

The goals of Japanese business usually are defined in term of market share. Companies try to maintain employment, achieve economies of scale, and outdo rivals. A considerable amount of public information is available on the economy, as is production and market share information.

Still, the Japanese economy has weaknesses in some areas. It lags behind foreign competition in chemicals, plastics, food and beverages, and personal consumer products. Japan has a paucity of raw materials, and labor is in short supply and very expensive.

United Kingdom (U.K.)

The strengths of British industry are in services, consumer goods, and trading. The country has a large capital pool and a favorable geographic location; its economy has a cost advantage in advanced human resources, which provide it with an important edge in consulting, publishing, and advertising. Certainly it has not hurt the U.K. to have English as the international language of business. Great Britain is a leading maker of luxury and leisure goods and entertainment.

British industries are recognized internationally by their brand names (e.g., Schweppes "bitter lemon"), and they have competed well in many areas, including consumer packaged goods, alcoholic beverages, food, confectionery products, personal products, household furniture, insurance, auctioneering, money management, pharmaceuticals, and entertainment and leisure. Gains in petroleum and petroleum-related products were made with the discovery of North Sea oil.

British disadvantages are a lack of domestic rivalry and a downward slide in living standards that have eroded domestic demand. Many exports are to Commonwealth members, which are chiefly underdeveloped countries with low-income buyers. While many parts of the economy have been successful, the core manufacturing areas in the north and Midlands have been declining for a long period of time and show few signs of revival. The U.K. has had to rely heavily on foreign inputs and machinery for its industry. Losses have been greater than gains, and few positions exist where industry is unusually strong.

Investors often are short-term institutional buyers whose major concern is share price appreciation and dividends. There has been an explosion of acquisitions and takeovers. British companies appear to be merging rather than competing. Managers frequently lack the strong profit motivation or market share orientation found in the United States.

The U.K. seemed to have fallen into a comfortable pattern of slow decay. Widespread state ownership and regulation following World War II retarded dynamism and innovation and contributed to the stodgy attitude and dependency on protocol, form, and bureaucracy in companies. Government-directed intervention in the form of subsidies, consolidation, and protection did not work. And labor unions were no help to Britain moving ahead. Notable failures occurred after the government encouraged mergers to create world-class companies in steel, autos, machine tools, and computers. The government's choices of promising technologies led to few commercial successes. The alteration of power between Conservative and Labour parties brought on sharp policy reversals on matters such as government ownership. The United Kingdom was in a downward cycle, so that it became very hard to turn the economy around, but trends in the 1990s have been better.

The United States

The U.S. economy is strong in computers, packaged software, biotechnology, consumer goods, and services; however, 15 of the top 25 U.S. industries are natural resource-based, which reflects their relative abundance in the country. Despite increasing cutbacks, the United States has a commanding position in defense, aerospace, and related fields that are affected by government spending, and it remains strong in health care, entertainment and leisure, and consumer and business services.

The United States has many remaining advantages: scientific research, especially in the fundamental disciplines; the media, chain stores, and modern marketing; and financial services and money management capabilities. The country remains a good place to start new businesses. The average productivity of the workforce is as high as any other nation, but real wages are declining.

Broad segments of U.S. industry (e.g., autos, machine tools, semiconductors, consumer electronics), however, have been losing competitive advantage. The United States has very large trade deficits, weak and uneven productivity growth, and low rates of business investment. It has been slow to adopt new process technologies, upgrade its facilities, and introduce new products and features. Its science and technology are superb, but these have lagged in converting into competitive industries. Relatively low wages and high employee availability have lowered the pressure to automate. Manufacturers have been making mass-produced standardized disposable goods for a large domestic market where consumers have had an insatiable demand for credit. Goods are often made with compromises in product design, quality, and service. The relationship between producers and suppliers has been competitive and at arms' length.

Companies have become easy targets for takeovers, so management has tried to head them off by boosting short-term earnings and restructuring in a way that has not always been in the long-term interests of the company. Mergers and alliances have been carried out to create stock market excitement, but relatively little capital has gone into new plants, products, and technology. Unrelated diversification and downsizing undermine competitiveness. Companies seek government protection to deal with the competition, claiming that foreign competitors are engaged in uncompetitive acts such as dumping.

Conclusions

In a global competitive environment, close ties between business and government mean that the issues management function takes on increasing importance. The process by which a corporation identifies, evaluates, and responds to emerging political, social, and economic trends that affect it significantly is critical for its long-term success. Issues management has special importance for firms involved in global commerce, as the examples show.

The viability of the firm is supposed to depend on its ability to produce at low cost and meet market demand. However, firms often seek relief from the pressures of a competitive market. They act opportunistically toward public policy, trying to obtain government subsidies, entry restrictions, protection from new products and technologies, and prices that guarantee profits. Government policies protect many firms from the market's judgment. Whatever the merits or demerits of a public policy from a broad social perspective, it is likely to create individual competitive winners and losers. Armed with competitive analysis, firms are able to participate more effectively in the public policy process.

Discussion Questions

1. Provide some example of government effects on business.
2. What are some of the differences between responding to market demands and responding to public policies?
3. Define what is meant by issues, interests, information, and institutions. Why are they important?
4. What is issues management? What is a strategic approach to issues management?
5. What are the different stages in issues management? What kinds of questions are relevant at the different stages?
6. What is meant by corporate legitimacy? Why is it important?
7. Describe and assess Monsanto's issues management program.
8. Why has trade policy become a top priority at many companies? Give some examples.
9. Explain David Ricardo's principle of comparative advantage.
10. Provide a description of how U.S. trade policy has evolved since the Smoot-Hawley Act.
11. What is the GATT? How does it work?
12. What are some of the arguments against free trade? Assess these arguments.
13. What remedies do U.S. firms have against alleged harm by unfair foreign competition?
14. Describe the purpose and major provisions of the 1988 Omnibus Trade Act.
15. Describe some of the assistance the federal government provides for exports.
16. Compare the economic strengths and weaknesses of Germany, Japan, the United Kingdom, and the United States.

Endnotes

1. John Coleman, "Motorola's Japan Strategy," Harvard Business School Case, April 1987.
2. David Baron, "Integrated Strategy: Market and Non-Market Components," Stanford Graduate School of Business paper, May 11, 1994.
3. M. Porter, "The Competitive Advantage of Nations," *Harvard Business Review*, 1990, pp. 73-93.
4. Willis Emmons, "Public Policy and the Manager," Harvard Business School Case, Sept. 2, 1993.
5. Alfred Marcus, Allen Kaufman, and David Beam, eds., *Business Strategy and Public Policy* (Westport, Conn.: Greenwood Press, 1987).
6. Alfred Marcus, "Airline Deregulation, Business Strategy, and Regulatory Theory," in *Public Policy and Economic Institutions* (Greenwich, Conn.: JAI Press, 1991), pp. 325-350.
7. Baron, "Integrated Strategy."
8. Alfred Marcus, *The Adversary Economy* (Westport, Conn.: Greenwood Press, 1984).
9. Steve Littlejohn, "Competition and Cooperation," in Marcus, Kaufman, and Beam, eds., *Business Strategy and Public Policy*, pp. 19-31.
10. "Guess Who's Selling Barbies in Japan Now?" *Business Week*, Dec. 9, 1991, pp. 72-73; see also Baron, "Integrated Strategy."
11. Baron, "Integrated Strategy."
12. J. D. Gwartney and R. L. Stroup, *Economics: Private and Public Choice* (San Diego: Harcourt Brace Jovanovich, 1987); D. B. Yoffie, *Note on Free Trade and Protectionism*, Working Paper 383-174, Harvard Business School, 1983; D. B. Yoffie and J. W. Rosenblum, "Zenith and the Color Television Fight," Case No. 383-070, Harvard Business School, 1982; D. B. Yoffie and J. K. Austin, "Textiles and the Multi-Fiber Arrangement," Case No. 383-164, Harvard Business School, 1983.
13. Stephanie Lenway, *The Politics of U.S. International Trade* (Marshfield, Mass.: Pitman, 1985).
14. David Baron, *Business and Its Environment* (Englewood Cliffs, N.J.: Prentice Hall, 1993); see also Destler, 1986; and Lenway, *The Politics of U.S. International Trade*.
15. "Jousting for Advantage," *The Economist*, September 22, 1990; N. Vousden, *The Economics of Trade Protection* (New York: Cambridge University Press, 1990).

16. Ibid.
17. Yoffie, *Note on Free Trade and Protectionism.*
18. Ibid.
19. Ibid.
20. Ibid.
21. Destler, 1986.
22. J. S. Lublin, "U.S. Food Firms Find Europe's Huge Market Hardly a Piece of Cake," The *Wall Street Journal*, May 15, 1990, p. A1; B. Stokes, "Off and Running," *National Journal*, June 17, 1989, pp. 1562-66.
23. Baron, *Business and Its Environment.*
24. M. L. Whicker and R. A. Morre, "Policies to Build a More Competitive America," Paper presented at the American Political Science Association Annual Meetings, 1987
25. M. Porter, *The Competitive Advantage of Nations* (New York: Free Press, 1990); J. Chipman, "On the Concept of International Competitiveness," Discussion Paper 118, Strategic Management Research Center, University of Minnesota, 1989; R. T. Kudrle, "Business-Government' Relations Abroad: What's Important for the U.S.?" Discussion Paper 81, Strategic Management Research Center, University of Minnesota, 1987; S. A. Lenway, "Between War and Commerce: Economic Sanctions as a Tool of Statecraft," *International Organization* 42 (1988), pp. 397-426; J. A. Limprecht and R. H. Hayes, "Germany's World-Class Manufacturers," *Harvard Business Review*, Nov.-Dec. 1982, pp. 106-114; P. S. Nivola, "More Like Them? The Political Feasibility of Strategic Trade Policy," paper prepared for the Annual Meeting of the American Political Science Association, San Francisco, Aug. 30-Sept. 2, 1990; M. Porter, "The Competitive Advantage of Nations," *Harvard Business Review*, March-April 1990 pp. 73-93; "The New Germany: The Spontaneous Union," *The Economist*, June 30, 1990; "Two Germanys United Would Pose Challenge to Other Economies," The *Wall Street Journal*, Nov. 13, 1989, p. A1; "West Germany: Heading for Unity," *The Economist*, Oct. 38-Nov. 3 1989.

Chapter Twenty-Nine

GLOBAL COMPETITION

Since 1973, economic growth in Western countries has slowed in terms of all relevant measuring rods. The phenomenon has been strikingly general, persistent, and large.

Angus Maddison, "Growth and Slowdown in Advanced Capitalist Economies"[1]

Introduction

What accounts for differences in the economic performance of nations? Economic theory stresses labor and capital. Consumers and markets also are important as the examples of the formerly centrally planned economies of the Soviet Union and Eastern Europe show. France, South Korea, and Taiwan demonstrate the importance of international market exposure. The ability to incorporate the latest technology into high-quality low-cost goods also plays a role. The United States, strong in product innovation, has lagged behind in production capabilities. Product innovation has to be matched by production strength. The Japanese lag behind in introducing new products, but excel at making products others have originated.

Differences between the U.S. and Japanese economies are discussed in this chapter. The British sociologist Ronald Dore argues that the U.S. economy is built on a contract model that emphasizes individual rights, while the Japanese economy is built on a community model that emphasizes loyalty and long-term attachments. The continued success of Japan is questioned by some who see a "hollowing out" as Japan becomes more involved in finance and investment abroad than manufacturing at home. Reasons for Japan's recent economic problems are given. The prospects for the European Union (EU) are discussed, with an emphasis placed on Germany's pivotal role, along with the challenges the EU faces in dealing with the former communist countries of Central and Eastern Europe.

This chapter concludes with a discussion of the comparative place of the United States in the world economy. It provides evidence for a U.S. comeback and gives some reasons why it is taking place. In exploring these matters, the focus is placed on the reasons for the varying economic performance of nations.

Economic Competitiveness

From 1580 to 1820, the Netherlands was the world's economic leader; its average annual growth in domestic product (GDP) per worker was .2 percent. From 1820 to 1890, the United Kingdom (U.K.) was the leader with an average annual growth in GDP per worker of 1.2 percent. The United States took over the leadership from 1890 to 1989, when its average annual increase in GDP per worker was 2.2 percent. By 1990, Japan had surpassed the United States; from 1950 to 1990, its average annual growth rate had averaged 7.7 percent, while the U.S. average was 1.9 percent. The average annual income per Japanese worker in 1950 was $1,230; in 1990 it was $23,970, an economic performance unsurpassed by that of any other nation since the end of World War II.[2]

All nations in the world increased their economic welfare in the postwar period. In general, however, countries initially rich had greater increases in wealth than countries initially poor. Countries like Japan were the world's development miracles, but other countries were development disasters (see Figure 29-1). Differences in the distribution of wealth among nations did not change much between 1960 and 1985. The wealthiest countries remained 29 times richer than the poorest. The United States, the wealthiest country in the world in 1985, had a per capita income 43.3 times greater than the per capita income of the poorest country, Ethiopia.[3]

FIGURE 29-1
Statistics on selected developing nations, 1990

	GDP (% real growth)	Per Capita Purchasing Power ($)	Population (millions)
Thailand	10.0	1,410	56.6
South Korea	9.0	5,560	42.8
Singapore	8.3	12,810	2.7
Taiwan	5.2	7,390	20.4
Pakistan	5.0	380	114.6
India	4.5	300	852.7
Zimbabwe	4.2	550	10.4
Mexico	3.9	2,650	88.0
Columbia	3.7	1,300	33.1
Hong Kong	2.5	11,000	5.8
Philippines	2.5	700	64.4
Egypt	1.0	700	53.2
Zaire	–2.0	190	36.6
Argentina	–3.5	2,560	32.3
Brazil	–4.6	2,560	152.5

Source: Adapted from Directorate of Intelligence, Central Intelligence Agency, *Handbook of Economic Statistics* (Washington, D.C.: U.S. Government Printing Office, 1991), p.30.

Since the end of World War II, the pace of economic change in the world accelerated. Starting in 1780, it took the United Kingdom 58 years to double its real income per person. Beginning in 1839, the United States accomplished this feat in 47 years. Postwar Japan did the same in only 34 years. South Korea doubled its wealth in 11 years since 1966, and China did so in less than 10 years starting in 1985.[4] With rapid communication and diffusion of technologies, catching up was taking less time than it had in the last century.

The next 30 years offered unprecedented opportunity for many nations, as they adopted market-friendly economic reforms and linked their economies to the rest of the world through trade and investment. Though the outlook for Russia and much of Africa remained troubled, many people living in Asia, Latin America, and Eastern Europe had the potential to enjoy much higher living standards.[5] If China, India, and Indonesia were to have average annual growth rates of 6 percent, by the year 2010, they would have 700 million consumers with living standards comparable to those of present-day Spain. The resurgence of India and China reflect a return to the past, because for most of history these nations had the world's largest economies. As late as 1830, more than 60 percent of the world's manufacturing output was centered in these nations. Their rapid growth could have an immensely positive effect on the world economy, stimulating the economic growth of all nations and providing many opportunities for market development and investment.

The Post-1973 Slowdown

Though the future looked bright, the Arab oil embargo of 1973 had inaugurated a slowdown in world economic growth; average annual growth during 1973-1985 was only 1.4 percent compared with 2.9 percent during 1960-1973. As economic growth leveled off, many nations had difficulties they had not experienced previously. The U.S. decline in average annual growth from 3.7 to 2.3 percent was not exceptional. Japan could not be happy with a mere 3.8 percent average annual growth rate after having enjoyed rates of more than 10 percent during the 1960s.[6] Japan's percent decline during the 1970s was the greatest among industrialized nations (see Figure 29-2).

FIGURE 29-2

Average annual growth rates in major industrial nations

	Real Gross National Product per Capita			
	1961-70	1971-80	1981-85	1986-90
Japan	9.4	3.4	3.2	5.1
France	4.4	3.0	1.0	2.4
West Germany	3.6	2.6	1.3	2.8
Canada	3.3	3.3	1.9	2.3
United States	2.5	1.7	1.8	2.0
United Kingdom	2.2	1.8	1.7	2.4

Source: Adapted from Directorate of Intelligence, Central Intelligence Agency, *Handbook of Economic Statistics* (Washington, D.C.: U.S. Government Printing Office, 1991), p. 59.

Many factors contributed to the post-1973 slowdown: the oil price shocks of 1973-1974 and 1979-1980, the movement from a fixed to a floating monetary system, and worldwide recessions in 1974-1975 and 1980-1981. Perhaps, the rate of growth in the period after World War II simply was unusual, and the world was regressing toward a more normal and sustainable growth rate.

The reasons for the post 1973 slowdown were not readily apparent nor was it clear why some countries and some regions of the world fared better than others. The extent to which government contributed to country performance also was uncertain. In any case, with the slowdown came changes in relative competitive advantage. Among developing nations, some performed better than others.[7] The gap between the United States and other countries was shrinking. So-called follower nations were catching up with the leader.

Labor and Capital

Economists use labor and capital productivity to account for differences in national growth rates (see Figure 29-3).[8] Labor input consists of weekly working hours while capital input equals increments in investment less depreciation. Labor input can be augmented by improvements in educational quality and work intensity that partially offset a decline in working hours.

FIGURE 29-3
The contribution
of labor, capital,
and technology
to economic growth

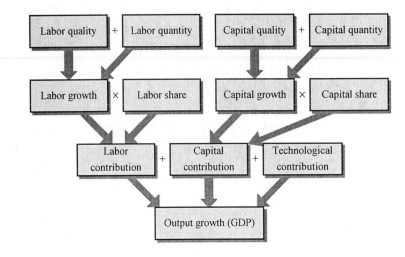

The average Japanese worker, for instance, continued to work more hours per year (2,149) than the average West German (1,676), American (1,632), French (1,554), or British (1,518) worker.[9] The main reason for this difference was that the Japanese work week was six days, while employees in other countries worked only five days. Other differences had to do with vacation, sick time, and lost time due to occupational accidents, strikes, and so forth.

Educational Quality and National Competitiveness

Differences in the educational quality of the workforce also played a role in national competitiveness.[10] Germany, for instance, has long been noted for its highly skilled workforce and its high-quality scientific and technical education and specialized training. It had a distinctive industrial apprenticeship system that was unmatched by most countries. Along with its world-class research capabilities and good management-labor relations, these qualities resulted in high labor productivity.

Japanese workers also were known for their skills in subjects such as mathematics, and for their discipline, willingness to work hard, and group orientation. Japan had a large pool of well-trained engineers and its in-house company training programs were excellent. Japan's strengths in elementary and secondary education, private tutoring, and company training more than compensated for weaknesses in its colleges and universities.

The United Kingdom had a truly outstanding upper tier of people who were noted for their creativity, inventiveness, and independent thinking and for their capabilities in pure scientific research. However, the overall workforce was poorly skilled and poorly motivated. The educational system lagged behind that of other countries, with access to the best education primarily only to the elite. Technical colleges had a very low status and industry had no well-developed apprenticeship system. Humanities and pure science were valued above practical pursuits like engineering. Managers generally had their origins in the lower middle class and frequently lacked higher education; company training, which was not particularly strong, did not compensate. A high degree of labor-management antagonism existed, breeding narrow definitions of responsibility and an unwillingness to change traditional practices.

The eroding quality of human resources in the United States long has been a topic of discussion.[11] The country possessed very high quality schools at the top, but the standards of the average German university were higher than the standards of the average American university, and the percentage of students with technical majors in U.S. universities was lower. Public elementary and high schools had low educational standards and weak discipline and provided poor training in the sciences, mathematics, and languages compared with many other countries (see Figure 29-4).

FIGURE 29-4
Education expenditures in industrialized countries, 1985

	As a Percentage of Gross Domestic Product		
	K-12	**Higher Education**	**All Levels**
Canada	4.0	1.8	6.3
France	3.9	0.7	5.5
United States	3.8	2.5	6.2
Japan	3.1	1.0	4.8
United Kingdom	2.3	0.9	4.8
West Germany	2.2	0.9	4.1

Source: Adapted from United Nations Educational, Scientific, and Cultural Organization, *Statistical Yearbook* (Paris: UNESCO, 1988).

Though spending was high, American schools were weak. Their weakness often was cited as being a major reason for declining U.S. competitiveness. Functional illiteracy was said to exist among a high proportion of the workforce. Neither a significant apprenticeship system nor a well-developed vocational school system existed to compensate for this weakness. Recommendations for improvement ranged from better teacher training to providing prenatal and preschool programs for disadvantaged youngsters. A key element in providing an effective workforce in the future was to properly educate children from low-income families. Educationally disadvantaged youth, who constituted more than a third of the country's young people, were more than three times as likely to drop out of school as students from middle- and high-income families.[12]

Capital Augmentation

A country's capital as well as its labor had to be improved if its economy was to grow. Capital could be augmented by replacing older factories, machines, buildings, and equipment with newer ones. New capital would embody the fruits of technical progress (e.g., investments in R&D); thus, investing in new factories and machines should be the surest way to realize economic gains.[13] Some augmentation of capital also is achieved by employees from the experience and knowledge they gain on the job and from recombining and retrofitting existing capital rather than replacing it.

Beyond Capital: The Importance of Markets

Analyses done on developing countries show that capital accumulation (measured by investment to GDP) is the most significant reason for economic development.[14] However, economists recognize that emphasizing capital without paying attention to markets is insufficient. For instance, Porter has emphasized the importance of markets by noting that Japanese demand for compact, portable, quiet, light, multifunctional products comes from the crowded living conditions and small plants, offices, and warehouses that exist in that country. These conditions have led to innovations in the use of materials, energy, and logistics. They have resulted in the production of compact and space-efficient goods and innovations in short production lines, the avoidance of unnecessary storage space and inventory, and combined production operations. Pioneering in space-saving and just-in-time production has been necessary to meet the demands of sophisticated home buyers who have limited room.[15] **Sophisticated domestic consumers** who are quality conscious can force a nation's firms to be more innovative and to produce to more exacting standards, generating competitive advantage when those firms face global markets.

sophisticated domestic consumers
Buyers who force a nation's firms to be more innovative and produce to more exacting standards, thereby increasing competitive advantage.

Centrally Planned Economies

Centrally planned economies like the former Soviet bloc nations were not subject to this kind of market discipline (see Figure 29-5). Although they possessed attributes needed for economic growth, including a well-educated workforce, technically trained and guaranteed life-time employment, and a government bureaucracy with a long-term planning horizon and a willingness to sacrifice today's consumption for tomorrow's growth, their economic performance was so dismal during the 1980s that it pushed them into a massive crisis.

FIGURE 29-5
Average annual growth rates of formerly centrally planned economies

Real Gross National Product per Capita

	1961-70	1971-80	1981-85	1986-90	Population	Per Capita Purchasing Power ($)
Soviet Union	3.5	1.5	0.9	0.2	290.9	9,140
Czechoslovakia	2.4	2.3	1.0	0.5	15.7	8,100
Hungary	3.1	2.5	0.6	−0.2	10.6	6,100
Poland	3.3	3.0	1.0	−1.8	37.8	4,400
Romania	4.2	3.5	−0.6	−3.3	23.3	3,200

Source: Adapted from Directorate of Intelligence, Central Intelligence Agency, *Handbook of Economic Statistics* (Washington, D.C.: U.S. Government Printing Office, 1991), pp. 29, 38.

These nations were closed economies, which were not exposed to world economic conditions. They built up their human and physical capital without responding to market demand. Their workforces were generally skilled and capable; human resources were not a major problem. Their leaders made long-term capital commitments; indeed, they had sacrificed the present for the future and forced people to save by literally confiscating their possessions. But the lack of innovative activity and the tendency of the system to produce low-quality goods that fell far short of world standards and consumer needs severely hindered development.[16]

The former Soviet bloc nations were battered by their inability to compete successfully in increasingly competitive world markets. The problem of quality in their goods had a number of dimensions: (1) an abundance of low-quality goods that consumers were forced to accept because there were no alternatives; (2) goods that were several generations behind those available in the rest of the world; and (3) low-quality services (e.g., in retailing and transportation) upon which manufacturers and consumers rely.

In a centrally planned economy, planners, not producers or consumers, made the important decisions. The planners could not always anticipate what producers or consumers wanted. Producers experienced serious bottlenecks in making goods, and consumers endured shortages in the goods they valued. While store shelves remained full of goods they shunned, there were long waiting lines for the goods they wanted.

The socialist ideology also hindered development. Its dedication to income equality and job security took away incentives people need to excel.[17] Since few opportunities were open and the chances of advancement were limited, people made few serious efforts to succeed. Apathy reigned among workers and dissatisfaction was high.

A final problem was the desire of central planners to maintain price stability.[18] Prices were not used to adjust the economy to changing competitive conditions. Market signals needed to bring change into motion were missing. The system was static, rigid, and closed to competitive forces emanating from domestic consumers and the world economy.

International Market Exposure

In contrast to the former Soviet bloc nations, the economic successes of such nations as France, South Korea, and Taiwan were built upon exposure to international market conditions and consumer demand. The experience of these countries, however different, shows the importance of such exposure.

France

Contrary to the myth that French economic development is mainly a result of central planning, the underpinnings of French success are in its international market exposure.[19] The strategy France employed after World War I, political isolation and economic exploitation of its traditional adversary Germany, had failed.

France's goal after World War II was instead to integrate as much as possible with its European neighbors to prevent war and to enhance its own prosperity and that of all of Europe. France became a charter member of the General Agreement on Tariffs and Trade (GATT) in 1947 (see Chapter 28). In 1948, it joined the Organization for European Economic Cooperation (OEEC). It was committed in principle, if not always in practice, to the doctrine of free trade. The OEEC had great trouble at first in liberalizing trade, and some of the earliest problems, such as the timing of compliance for the loosening of quotas, involved France.

Nonetheless, in 1950 France called for the creation of a European common market for coal and steel. The Treaty of Paris established the European Coal and Steel Community, six of whose members then agreed in 1957 to extend the scope of their agreement into the European Economic Community (EEC), which became known as the Common Market. The EEC prohibited tariffs, quotas, and subsidies that restricted or distorted trade between member states. The Common Market now has 12 members and since 1994 has been called the European Union.

Meanwhile, France lost its colonies and focused more on developed nations. The share of exports that France's former colonies absorbed declined from 42 percent in 1952 to about 10 percent in 1962, when most of them had achieved independence.[20]

The French, like the rest of the EEC nations, became heavily exposed to foreign direct investment. It served to increase the competitive vigor of the markets in which French companies competed. Overall, it is probable that the salutary effects of international exposure rather than government planning largely explain French success in the post-World War II period.

South Korea

South Korea's growth also has involved exposure to international markets stimulated by the government's strong proexport policies and by the economy's ability to take over Japanese markets as the yen appreciated.[21]   After the Korean War ended, South Korea tried to compete with Japan as a low-cost producer; it relied on its low labor rates to enter the world cotton textile market. However, it lacked certain Japanese advantages—group control over industry, large manufacturing units, shipping subsidies and low transportation costs, bulk purchases of raw materials, and efficient marketing of finished products. In addition, low wage rates imposed domestic costs in the form of low consumer spending, purchasing power, and productivity.

Currency manipulation did not provide a way out of this dilemma. Devaluations, which were intended to make South Korean exports cheaper and increase sales abroad, instead made the raw materials and capital goods South Korea needed more expensive. Exchange rate fluctuations, other than accounting for increased volatility, appear to have had little impact on real economic growth and national competitiveness. The cure for South Korea's problem was productivity growth, not devaluation.

To achieve this growth, the South Korean government imposed itself on the economy. It assumed control over the private sector with the purpose of expanding exports significantly. First, it used the Law for Dealing with Illicit Wealth Accumulation to confiscate assets from profiteers. Then it forged alliances with these profiteers and provided them with the incentives to become legitimate businesses so long as they were willing to lay the groundwork for export-led growth.

The government provided the newly formed firms with incentives to offset some of Japan's advantages. Barriers were imposed on imports and firms were allowed to inflate their returns on domestic sales. The government nationalized the banks, and it offered long-term capital at favorable rates to targeted firms and industries willing to invest heavily in foreign trade. A strong interventionist state made exports a compulsion rather than a choice for South Korean companies.[22]

Other factors helped. Inflows of foreign credit came to South Korea from financial institutions like the World Bank and International Monetary Fund. South Korea, located on the border of the Communist world, was considered a strategic asset. The loans allowed South Korea to purchase modern plant and equipment. Learning by doing aided in the rapid productivity enhancements. Synthetic fibers reduced the need for expensive imported raw materials. When Japan's wage levels rose, South Korea was ready to take Japan's place as a low-cost producer of textiles.

The emphasis on export-led growth means that no other industrial power, including Japan, has such a high dependence on foreign trade as South Korea. Only Hong Kong, Singapore, and Taiwan are comparable.[23]

The government-orchestrated strategy of exported growth helped make the South Korean economy strong in an extremely short period of time. The South Korean story illustrates how important an emphasis on export-led growth can be. Investments, however, must be based on the existence of a market for the manufactured goods. The South Korean example goes against the argument that central planning can have little effect on strengthening a country's export potential.

Comparing Taiwan's and South Korea's Paths to Prosperity

Both Taiwan and South Korea made enormous strides in the post-World War II period. The progress they achieved is instructive because it can be directly compared to the backwardness of their Communist neighbors, the People's Republic of China and North Korea, both of which started at similar levels but did not go nearly as far.

Social welfare and equality in both Taiwan and South Korea are at all-time highs. The unemployment rate in Taiwan is consistently below 2 percent. In South Korea it has not exceeded 4 percent in the last 20 years.[24]

Both countries have few resources, little arable land, and high population densities. Both have pursued export-led growth policies, but they have done so in different ways. Taiwan has been less aggressive in protecting domestic industry. The South Korean government has been more interventionist in rewarding companies for some activities and punishing them for others.

Taiwan has relied more on the free market and a highly educated, technically trained (more than a third of Taiwanese students in higher education study engineering), and enterprising workforce. It has let interest rates rise to their market level, encouraging savings and investment and creating a very atomized industrial structure. Taiwan's companies are financed through equity markets; they are lightly leveraged and small. In 1981, more than 80 percent of the country's firms had fewer than 20 employees.[25]

In comparison, South Korea's companies are highly concentrated and very heavily leveraged. They have received low-interest loans from government planners. Some of these firms grew into the South Korean giants known as the *chaebol*. In 1984, the sales of the top 10 *chaebol* represented about two-thirds of South Korea's GNP (see Figure 29-6).

FIGURE 29-6
South Korea's
Chaebol, 1990

	Sales (in billions $)	Net Profit (in millions $)
Samsung	$35.6	$348
Hyundai	31.8	445
Lucky-Goldstar	22.8	308
Daewoo	15.8	217
Sunkyong	10.6	90
Ssangyung	7.2	159
Kia	6.1	100
Lotte	4.9	142

Source: Adapted from *The Economist*, June 8, 1991, p 76.

There is much controversy about which country's economy will be stronger in the future. While the South Korean *chaebol* have some admirable strengths, including people, persistence, agility, and financial clout, they also have notable weaknesses including bureaucracy, lack of focus, and lack of creativity.

Technology

Global market exposure was an important factor in spurring economic growth. Another important factor was technology.[26] Expanded markets were insufficient if the goods produced did not incorporate the latest in technology. High-quality, low-cost goods required technological innovation.

The Austrian economist Joseph Schumpeter argued that new capital replaces old capital in waves ("creative destruction") as particular sectors (e.g., textiles, steel, railroads, automotive, chemicals, pharmaceuticals, telecommunications, computers, biotechnology) dominate the world economy at certain intervals. Thus, technical change and the ability to generate innovations are critical for economic growth.[27]

R&D spending by corporations is an important part of this process. U.S. companies lost market share in 12 of 15 critical industries from 1960 to 1986. This drop in market share is connected to lower R&D spending by American firms. Corporate R&D, not government-sponsored R&D, spurs competitiveness, and U.S. firms fund R&D at a rate lower than firms in other countries. The large, diversified American company, organized into separate profit centers and dominated by professional managers, is likely to be risk-averse and invest less heavily in R&D than firms that are functionally organized and operating to maximize returns to investors.[28]

Product versus Process

When a group of Europeans rated the 50 best people in the world in nine technologies, U.S. scientists and engineers rated best in five instances, they were tied for first twice, and they were second twice. However, Japan was number two in every case where the United States was number one, and it was number one in the two cases where the United States was number two.[29] The gap between the United States and countries such as Japan has been narrowing. More U.S. patents were going to foreigners, especially the Japanese, than ever before.

While the United States was spending about the same on R&D as a percentage of GNP as Japan and West Germany—about 2.7 to 2.8 percent—only 1.7 to 1.8 percent of U.S. spending was for civilian research and development.[30] The United States spent a much higher percentage of its GNP on defense (see Figure 29-7). Virtually all Japanese and West German spending was on civilian research and development. Military spin-offs to the commercial sector, once common (e.g., the jet aircraft), had become infrequent. Instead, the U.S. commercial sector often developed technologies that were "spun into" the military (e.g., the semiconductor).

FIGURE 29-7
Defense expenditures
of major
industrialized nations

	As a Percentage of GNP			
	1965	1975	1985	1988
United States	7.2	5.6	6.5	6.1
United Kingdom	5.9	4.9	5.2	4.3
France	5.2	3.8	4.0	3.9
Canada	3.0	1.9	2.2	2.1
West Germany	4.3	3.6	3.2	2.9
Japan	1.0	0.9	1.0	1.0

Source: Adapted from Directorate of Intelligence, Central Intelligence Agency, *Handbook of Economic Statistics* (Washington, D.C.: U.S. Government Printing Office, 1991), pp. 29, 38.

The Japanese in particular excelled at process technologies (e.g., robotics). The U.S. decline in this area was directly related to the slump in productivity growth.[31] U.S. managers have thought that the highest returns on investment came from new products, not from building old products better. First-rate people went into new-product development, not process technologies. However, the Japanese discovered that it was unnecessary to invent new products. By manufacturing existing products cheaper and better than the people who invented them, they could capture the profits.

Americans, for instance, invented the video recorder, but could manufacture it only at a unit cost of $100,000. The Japanese lowered the costs of manufacturing so that they could sell VCRs at a unit cost of $300. No VCRs are now manufactured in the United States. Instead, the Japanese have made enormous profits selling this product to Americans.

The Japanese approach to managing the R&D process involved the deliberate creation of excess information and its sharing by different groups that were linked horizontally and vertically in the firm and outside it. Project teams in Japan had cross-sectional diversity, which was supposed to produce ideas of higher quality and quantity. Every member involved in a project was given a part in creating or suggesting solutions to problems regardless of the position they held in the organization. Vendors and subcontractors also were consulted about project needs. Different phases in project development were overlapped to speed entry into the market and gain rapid information from consumers. The Japanese aim was to gain insights from consumers about product improvements while at the same time maintaining their existing customer loyalty.[32]

The Japanese Economy

Managers, politicians, academicians, and others have been fascinated by the growth of the Japanese economy. Much has been written to explain this success and to show how the factors behind it can be transferred to other countries.[33] As analyses of the Japanese economy proliferated, however, there was a tendency for writers to find in Japan what they already valued. Few analysts saw the Japanese economic miracle as an aggregate, focusing instead on a particular area. Thus, Japanese success was variously attributed to low defense spending, easy access to capital, a high educational level, low levels of unionization, labor management cooperation, lifetime employment, decision making by consensus, quality circles, industrial policies, trade protection, or any of a number of other factors. In the discussion that follows, three features of the Japanese economy will be stressed: a high level of savings and investment, a high level of equity held by banks, and the importance of business alliances in the Japanese economic system.

High Levels of Savings and Investment

Japanese firms enjoyed a competitive advantage over U.S. firms because they could secure funds at low rates of interest. What made this possible was that Japan had an excess of savings over investment. Individuals were encouraged to save through many means, including tax incentives, and they paid no taxes on capital gains (up to a certain high amount) and interest on savings. Unlike Americans, however, the Japanese had to save money to buy a house because there were no tax deductions for the interest on mortgage payments. They also had to save for old age, since Japanese social security benefits were small by U.S. standards.

Since the Japanese government was averse to running fiscal deficits, the bulk of the savings was invested in industry. The Bank of Japan and the Ministry of Finance played an important role in this process. The government was able to direct capital flows into industries targeted for development, and industry received numerous tax incentives and depreciation allowances to encourage investment and export.

Comparative studies of U.S. and Japanese firms in the semiconductor business showed significantly lower costs of debt financing in Japan.[34] During the mid-1970s recession, U.S. semiconductor manufacturers were forced to cut back on capital spending, but NEC, Hitachi, and Toshiba did not face the same constraint. They continued to invest heavily in new production capacity, so that when the recession ended they had the capacity to supply a growing market. Since the mid-1980s, however, the situation for Japanese firms changed somewhat as companies used substantial cash inflows to lower their debt burdens and to invest heavily in equities.

Equity Held by Banks

Japanese banks were permitted to hold equity in companies. U.S. banks have not been allowed to do so; the Glass-Steagall Act of 1933 separated the activities of trust departments and commercial banking. In the United States, banks legally must have an arm's length relationship with the companies to whom they lend money. They have not been allowed to take an active role in managing a company's affairs under pain of losing their legal status of lender and becoming a shareholder with all the limitations that entails (the last to be paid back in case of bankruptcy).

Japanese banks can assume managerial responsibilities, including not only the rescheduling of loan payments and the granting of emergency loans but also taking active control by extending advice about which assets to liquidate, business opportunities to pursue, managers to hire or fire, and reorganizations to be carried out.[35] However, the control of a company's policy and the selection of managers was not a function that banks readily aggrandized. The threat of extensive intervention existed only when a company found itself in very serious financial difficulty.

Some analysts have argued that the close ties between Japanese firms and banks meant that the former could obtain loans at a higher debt to equity ratio than U.S. firms. Banks made large loans at low interest rates because they had more power and regularly obtained good information on how a company's divisions were doing. They relied less on annual accounting data and more on their intimate knowledge of the firm's management, customers, and progress in product development. However, some analysts disputed the significance of the good information ties and resultant high debt to equity ratio. They claimed that most loans were secured by assets (e.g., property), and that accounting practices in Japan were more conservative than in the United States.[36]

As world capital markets became more open, Japanese savers were attracted by higher rates of return outside Japan. They purchased large amounts of assets (e.g., real estate and U.S. Treasury bonds) on international markets. Similarly, foreign firms were attracted by the low rates of interest offered by Japanese and sought to obtain loans from them. Thus, Japanese banks have become the largest in the world and, with the free flow of capital across international boundaries, the distinctive advantages of Japan's banking system have receded.

Business Alliances

kereitsu
An interlocking group of Japanese banks, insurance companies, and manufacturers in which controlling interests of stock are held by management and other members of the enterprise group.

Company ownership in Japan also has been more concentrated than in the United States. In a sample of 585 U.S. companies, only about half had individuals who owned 5 percent or more of the shares of stock. In a sample of 585 Japanese firms, all but six had a single shareholder with this kind of holding. Whereas the large owner in the United States was likely to be a founding family, in Japan it was likely to be an interlocking group of banks, insurance companies, and manufacturing concerns called a **kereitsu**. Typically, about 20 to 30 percent of the common stock was controlled by the *kereitsu* with the understanding that these long-term holdings were not to be traded. As a result, only about 25 percent of the shares listed on the Tokyo Stock Exchange were available for trading; takeovers and other types of corporate restructuring were extremely rare.[37]

Kereitsu evolved out of a system of longstanding cooperation among Japanese firms that distinguished them from U.S. firms. Believing that funds and managerial skills were limited the kereitsus pooled resources. A corporation lacking experience overseas and needing natural resources from abroad would join the group. The Mitsubishi Bank, for instance, owned significant portions of Mitsubishi Trust Bank, Tokyo Marine, Mitsubishi

Heavy Industries, Mitsubishi Corporation (the trading company), Mitsubishi Electric, Asahi Glass, Kirin Beer, Mitsubishi Chemical, and NYK. These companies in turn owned more than a quarter of Mitsubishi Bank's stock.[38]

zaibatsu
Pre-World War II Japanese business alliances often family controlled, which were pyramid-like structures that held other businesses, subsidiaries, and affiliated firms.

Earlier enterprise groups were called *zaibatsu*. They were pyramid-like structures, run by autocratic leaders, in which a family-held business in turn controlled other businesses, which also controlled subsidiaries and affiliated firms. After World War II, the *zaibatsu* were reconstituted and renamed *keiretsu*. The dominant ones are Mitsui, Mitsubishi, and Sumitomo and the Fuji, Sanawa, and Dai-ichi Kang banks.

The *zaibatsu* derived their power from their commercial might. They were large trading companies particularly good at helping Japanese businesses penetrate foreign markets. Today's *keiretsu* obtain their power from the financial clout of the large banks and insurance companies around which other companies are organized. Member companies in the *keiretsu* have much more independence than the *zaibatsu*. They carry on much less of their commerce (typically less than 30 percent) with other members of the *keiretsu*. Goods are bought from nonmember companies when they are offered at lower prices.

Still, members of the *keiretsu* are highly interconnected. They own each other's stock, which contributes to the stabilization of stock prices, have various kinds of financial relations, and sometimes share or exchange top managers. The easy availability of funding during Japan's rapid economic growth was advantageous to *keiretsu* members. The sharing of managerial know-how helped an economy in which employees did not move from firm to firm. Companies could obtain information about technology and markets that otherwise might not be available to them.

Cooperative ventures primarily were in importing energy resources, introducing new technologies, launching new businesses, and the export of large projects. However, high technology companies just starting up generally found the *keiretsu* stifling and did not become heavily involved with them. The *keiretsu* mainly have large, capital-intensive businesses that rely on substantial economies of scale. Such cooperation among American firms is prohibited by antitrust laws.[39]

A Hollowing Out

hollowing out
Process by which a country achieves manufacturing superiority and becomes more involved in finance, investment, and manufacturing abroad, but faces the possibility of losing its capacity for domestic productivity gains.

Is Japan going through a predictable cycle of decline with the **hollowing out** of its industry whereby the country engages more in finance, investment, and manufacturing abroad and produces less at home? Its mercantile period lasted from 1945 to 1980, during which the government promoted exports, restricted imports, and manipulated incentives for the formation and use of capital. The Japanese focused initially on labor intensive, low-technology industries such as textiles. The dominance of heavy industry like steel was next, followed by high value-added products such as electronics. Japanese successes yielded very large current account surpluses that provided it with the means to make the transition from an industrial economy concentrating on trade to an investment-oriented economy.[40]

Though the Japanese were able to consume more, they did not do so. They maintained their frugal saving habits, which provided them with even more funds for foreign investment. Early Japanese investments were in low-tech industries and raw material sources in Asia and elsewhere. Japanese foreign direct investment then moved to manufacturing. Foreign direct investment in raw materials declined from 60 percent in 1980 to 28 percent in 1985. Total foreign investment was up from $0.4 billion in 1960 to $38.5 billion in 1985, paralleling the rise in Japan's trade surplus. Much of the new investment was destined for manufacturing in the United States and Asian nations.[41]

With U.S. trade restrictions in place, the only alternative the Japanese had for an expanding market share in the United States was to expand their manufacturing base in that country. With labor costs reaching levels near to those of the United States and Europe, the Japanese also had to rely on low-cost Asian manufacturing. This investment in manufacturing abroad led to declines in domestic productivity growth. The existence of an easy income source abroad distracted industrial producers from the dynamic and innovative pursuit of productivity at home. When production experience moved overseas, organizational learning, which was often tacit, was not easily transferred back to Japan. As a consequence, Japan was losing some of its manufacturing excellence.[42]

Bursting of the Bubble

In 1989, the Tokyo Stock Exchange was valued at $3.6 trillion, three times the value of all listed U.S. companies on the New York Stock Exchange. Land prices in Tokyo were so high that the grounds of the Imperial Palace were reputed to be worth more than all the land in California.[43] In 1982, the Japanese yen fell to record low levels compared with the dollar. The U.S. trade deficit swelled and the industrial nations of the world started a campaign to bring down the value of the dollar. To slow the process, the Bank of Japan drove up the money supply, making credit cheap and easily available. Manufacturing firms borrowed not only to acquire new capital but to buy assets in other companies and to invest abroad. These conditions led to a speculative bubble; borrowers expected that land and equity values would keep rising, so they used rising asset values as collateral to borrow more. Property values skyrocketed, and the average family could no longer afford a simple apartment. Speculators made vast amounts of money, threatening the egalitarian character of Japanese society.

Meanwhile, the Japanese government began to fear inflation. Labor shortages were common and foreign workers were recruited to work in Japanese factories. The Bank of Japan, under veteran bureaucrat Yasushi Mieno, believed that the situation was intolerable. To restore Japan's social cohesion and stop inflation, he tightened monetary policy. He also intended to limit the use of foreign workers, punish speculators, and make property more affordable for the typical family.

The result of the Bank of Japan's policies was a collapse in asset prices, a massive contraction in household and corporate wealth, and a fall in demand that drove many businesses to bankruptcy. Banks suffered because the land and equity they held as collateral were now worth less than the loans extended against them. People feared that the bad debts would bring down the banking system. Japan's banks, the world's largest, had little money to loan to the rest of the world, which contributed to the worldwide recession of the early 1990s.

The Japanese economy, however, continued to be cushioned from the worst of this economic shock by a widening trade surplus with the United States. This occurred despite the growing value of the yen. Also, Japan continued to have relatively large government budget surpluses, which it could use to stimulate the economy. The controversy over how to stimulate the economy (tax cuts or increased public spending), however, helped to end political stability and contributed to the downfall of the Liberal Democratic party.[44]

Effects on the Automobile Industry

Japan's automakers suffered under these changing conditions. In 1980, they exceeded U.S. manufacturers in worldwide production and started to dominate the world industry with their manufacturing and product development skills. They changed the domain of competition with high productivity, low-cost production, quality workmanship, and rapid product change and technological innovation. While U.S. and European firms took an average of 65 months to introduce a new car, Japanese manufacturers could do so every

42 months. They relied on close ties with their suppliers and relatively independent project teams in contrast to in-house suppliers and functional departments.[45]

By the early 1990s, however, Japanese society was in gridlock. The production system was not working well in congested urban areas where poor roads and massive pollution existed. A shortage of well-trained blue-collar workers who could be given broad responsibilities made it less easy to do rapid setups and frequent product changes, and inadequately trained foreign workers introduced quality problems. With so many model changes, automotive recycling became an issue. Only so many old cars could be sold to the rest of Asia.

The weakness of Japanese banks and the stock market collapse also contributed to the problems of the auto companies. The bursting of the bubble meant that money was not as available to finance rapid model changes. Japanese companies had to become more like companies in other countries—focused more on profit and less on growth. In any case, the best U.S. plants had successfully copied Japanese methods. They now were achieving near parity in efficiency and quality. Competitive domains in the industry were shifting to materials, innovative products, skillful overseas management, and styling. Whether the Japanese companies would be able to maintain dominance was uncertain.

Other Problems

Japan had several other problems with which to contend:

1. Consumers were aware that despite their wealth they did not enjoy comparable living standards with Americans. Over time, the Japanese would be more likely to consume and less inclined to save.
2. Japan's population was aging, which was also likely to suppress savings. The cost of capital could go up, interest rates rise, and investment might fall.
3. The political consensus was breaking down. The Liberal Democratic party lost power because of corruption and a failing economy.
4. As Japan lost the advantage of catching up, its skill in adopting foreign technology could no longer be the main engine of its growth. It had to be creative.

All these factors put new strains on the distinctive form of capitalism that had served Japan so well in the past.

_____
Special Feature
_____

The Community Model

Ronald Dore, the British sociologist, who lived for long periods of time in Japan and wrote extensively about Japanese society, argues that a sense of fairness explains Japan's success. He believes that Japanese capitalism is practiced according to a "community model" which distinguishes it from the "company law" model of capitalism in the United States and the United Kingdom. In the community model, managers are senior members in the firm, and shareholders are one of many stakeholder groups that have to be satisfied. In the company law model, on the other hand, the firm is the property of shareholders, and managers act as their agents seeking to maximize shareholder wealth and to minimize expenses.

For the community model to flourish, the participants must feel that the system is fair. They must practice "restraint in the use of market power" out of consideration for the interests of their bargaining partners and adversaries. This sense of fairness is fostered by many elements:[46]

continued

1. Government:
   a. *The size of government in Japan is relatively small.* Both the United States and United Kingdom absorb more of national income in taxes than does Japan. The U.S. tax code is more burdensome than Japan's.
   b. *The Japanese value and honor public service.* Government ministries are able to recruit some of Japan's most talented people into the civil service, which is considered a prestige career. Ministries like MITI thus have the respect of the business community. The official economic White Papers and "Visions" that it issues are influential in mobilizing and unifying public opinion on economic issues.
   c. *By contrast, the Japanese do not much honor politicians, whose role in running the economy is small.* This eliminates, for the most part, destabilizing swings in policy caused by changes in party control of government. The *Liberal Democratic party* maintained power for over 30 years. Politicians have less economic influence than ministry officials.

2. Labor:
   a. *The Japanese work not only hard, but well.* Although yearly working hours are greater than in the United States or Britain, the crucial difference behind product quality and innovation in Japan is that the Japanese managers and engineers work well together. Institutional and cultural characteristics account for their dedication to hard work in teams.
   b. *The Japanese are well educated.* The educational quality of the workforce is high: over 90 percent of each age group stays in school until the age of 18, 40 percent go on to college and 50 percent of all master's degrees are in engineering.[47]
   c. *The Japanese work cooperatively in large corporations.* Decision-making processes emphasize widespread and slow consultation and diffusion of responsibility, yet swift execution of agreed decisions. Decisions may take longer to make, but implementation proceeds rapidly because of the commitment earned during the decision-making process. Specific features of the employment system—lifetime employment as the norm, representation of employee interests, and predictable tracks of promotion by merit with minimum seniority thresholds—are thought to foster cooperation.
   d. *The Japanese maintain a constant emphasis on quality.* Since Japan became aware in the mid-1990s that the rest of the world perceived its goods as shoddy, its view has been that quality improvement is a constant battle. While American managers blame workers for quality gaps and have relied on end-of-the-line inspections to eliminate defects, Japanese firms stress process improvements and the constant redesigning and upgrading of products to enhance quality.[48]
   e. *Japanese workers have a sense of ownership.* The Japanese payment system is based on bonuses to employees for profitability gains rather than straight salaries that are paid regardless of how well the firm has done. Japanese workers therefore feel a sense of ownership in the businesses that employ them.
   f. *Japan has an effective form of union-management relations.* All Japanese companies conclude bargaining arrangements with unions at the same time. Pay raises start at the same date (April 1).

3. Capital:
   a. *Japan has a high savings rate and low interest rates, and corporate investment is very high.* Japanese culture values prudence and a willingness to defer gratification. Its weak natural-resource position also has contributed to the high savings rate.
   b. *Equity often is held by banks that finance the loans.* As discussed, a high proportion of corporate capital has been in the form of bank loans rather than equity. Creditors and owners are not separate as in the United States. The close working relationships between banks and corporations foster long-term relationships. They allow Japan to have a managerial, production-oriented capitalism, not a shareholder dominated form of capitalism.
   c. *Japanese corporations are good at forming alliances with each other.* Also, as discussed, Japan has an impressive array of industry associations that foster close cooperation between corporations.

Toward a Single European Market

With Japan hurting, would Europe, with its tremendous potential, be able to fill the void? In 1985, the European Economic Community made the decision to create a single market by 1992. Its reasons were that continuing fragmentation harmed consumers and prevented businesses from effectively competing against the United States and Japan.[49]

The problems with fragmentation were numerous:

1. European companies had to have additional engineers on staff to design products for the different standards that prevailed in each European country. Philips Industries, for instance, employed an additional 70 engineers to make the seven types of television sets needed for different European countries. The cost to Philips was over $20 million a year.
2. Long truck lines at European borders meant that truckers had to wait an average of 80 minutes before the paper work was cleared. These delays cost the European economy an estimated $10 billion a year.

The all-European market was designed to:

- Harmonize regulations and standards.
- Liberalize the movement of capital, people, and services.

There would be baseline essential standards in such areas as health, safety, and environmental protection; deregulation of the transportation and insurance industries; and mutual recognition of professional qualifications. Some border controls would have to continue to check for narcotics, terrorism, and illegal immigration. No one expected to achieve the goal of equalizing taxes, and differences in value-added and excise taxes would remain because high-tax countries would lose too much money and low-tax countries would have to raise taxes if tax rates were harmonized. Many high-tech businesses in the United States were concerned about the implications of a possible "fortress-like" Europe, which would impose specific conditions that U.S. firms would find hard to accept.

Planned Expansion of the European Union

Treaty of Maastricht
Set the terms for the creation of a single European government, where all European nations would have a common currency, foreign and defense policies, and citizenship.

The European Community aimed to expand beyond the 12 member states it had in 1985. These nations were Belgium, Denmark, France, Germany, Greece, Ireland, Italy, Luxembourg, Netherlands, Portugal, Spain, and the United Kingdom. They encompassed 350 million people. The European Community wanted to add 13 more countries so that it would have a market of more than 450 million people by the year 2000. When the European Community officially became the European Union (EU), after its member nations ratified the **Treaty of Maastricht**, it first chose new members from the countries in the European Free Trade Association—Austria, Finland, Iceland, Liechtenstein, Norway, Sweden, and Switzerland. With 35 million people, these countries had the world's most affluent consumers. Following the breakup of the Soviet bloc, the East European countries were eager to join the EU. While the EU had special trading arrangements with some of these countries—the Czech Republic, Hungary, Poland, and Slovakia—it refused to consider them for full membership until the end of the century.

The EU realized that Central and Eastern Europe could be an important growth market in the future, adding as much as 1 to 2 percent to the EU's growth rates, but it was reluctant to open up its markets rapidly, because these nations had cheap labor and inexpensive agricultural products, with which the EU nations would have trouble competing. For instance, an average Czech factory worker earned $2,500 a year in 1990, while an average German worker took home $23,000. An engineer in Hungary was paid $7,000 that year, while one in the EU received more than $50,000. The production of milk in Central Europe cost half what it cost in the EU. Potatoes produced in Central Europe were one-third as expensive as potatoes produced in the EU. In sum, the EU feared immediate entry of the former Soviet bloc nations because its own workers and farmers would be threatened.

Germany's Pivotal Role

A newly united Germany was expected to play the pivotal role in developing ties with Central European countries. Germany had invested more in these nations than any other country. However, the bulk of its investments were used to meet the challenges of reunification. The unification of West Germany and East Germany proved to be more complex and time-consuming than anyone imagined. Germany's public debt jumped to 33 percent of GNP between 1991 and 1994, peaking at 59 percent of GNP.[50]

The Germans feared runaway inflation because it had helped destroy the fledgling democracy of the Weimar Republic in the 1920s and made it possible for extremists like Hitler to rise to power. But the Deutsche Bank, under the leadership of Hans Tietmeyer, kept interest rates high to prevent inflation from getting out of control. With the currencies of the EU linked, Germany's policy depressed economic growth throughout the European Union and created tensions among the European nations.

As tensions rose and the economies of the former Communist bloc countries stalled, a vast migration of people to Germany took place. Capital that Germany might have spent in the East was diverted toward paying for the absorption of millions of new immigrants. Many ethnic Germans living in Poland, Yugoslavia, Romania, and Russia exercised their right under Germany's constitution to return to Germany. Germany also accepted many non-German political and economic refugees from the former Soviet bloc. It provided them with housing, training, and welfare, raising government deficits even further. The large numbers of immigrants created social tensions in Germany. The neo-Nazi revival, racism, and riots threatened the country's political stability.

Despite these challenges, the German economy remained strong. Its pluses were its high level of investment, quality of life, and the peculiar form of capitalism, called *Mitbestimmung* **(codetermination)**, that had evolved. This form of capitalism allowed for a great deal of worker participation, by which workers had extensive consultative powers. Company boards in Germany were run almost like constitutional democracies with trade unions playing a substantial role.

Mitbestimmung (codetermination)
The extensive consultative powers that German workers and trade unions have on the boards of major corporations.

Like the Japanese, the Germans had created an alternative form of capitalism. Germany's was based on the idea that completely free markets were damaging when they extended to workers competing for jobs in the labor market. Workers should not be treated like goods that customers bought in consumer markets. While the German system provided for great continuity and stability, it also had its negatives. One of them was immobility in the labor market. Another was overregulation; there was a regulation for nearly everything in Germany. The German system was both heavy-handed (because of so many regulations) and expensive. Social insurance for the unemployed, by U.S. standards, provided extremely generous benefits. For the employed, wages were high and holidays were long. An employer could not easily lay off its workers.

Capital markets were as rigid as labor markets. It was hard to start a new business in Germany. The expansion of the welfare state, the resistance to change, and the veto power of affected interests made it difficult for the German economy to adjust to new conditions.

Germany could not easily compete globally on the basis of providing low-cost goods. With the type of capitalism it had created, its comparative advantage was high-cost, precision-built, value-added products.

Germany had a secure place, along with the United States and Japan, as one of the world's economic superpowers. Some nations in the EU, however, expressed bitterness toward Germany. They resented its anti-inflation stand, which held back their own growth and prolonged the European recession.

Central and Eastern European Privatization

With credit in Germany in tight supply, there was not enough cash for investment in Central and Eastern Europe. Unlike the fast-growing economies of Asia, the likelihood was slim that the nations of this area could pay for their own development through high domestic savings and strong export growth. Economic growth was slow after years of decline, and hopes faded for a quick transition to fully functioning market economies.

No precedent existed for the vast privatization programs of the Central and Eastern European economies. The building of full market economies with their many rules and institutions was an immense undertaking. A whole new system had to be created: property and contract laws, accounting and bankruptcy rules, administrative bodies and courts to enforce these rules, labor laws and tax codes, and banks and financial institutions.[51]

big bang approach
The attempt by some former Communist countries to hand over their economy at once to private investors.

Poland tried the "**big bang**" **approach** of privatizing all at once: by 1991, more than 40 percent of its economy had been turned over to private hands. However, in the Czech Republic, while government officials allowed 85 percent of prices to be set by market conditions, private business constituted only 2 percent of GDP in 1991. In Hungary, only about 33 percent of the economy was in private hands. In Romania and Bulgaria, progress in freeing prices and creating a private sector was very slow.

Many of the formerly state-owned firms in Central and Eastern Europe were worthless. They had been propped up by low oil prices, caused massive pollution, and consumed more than they produced. No one wanted to buy or own them. It was estimated that up to 25 percent of the businesses in these nations had no real value.

Downturn in the European Union's Popularity

The difficulties Europe was experiencing, especially in integrating formerly Communist Central and Eastern Europe put a strain on the EU. In the early 1990s, the popularity of the EU declined and new tensions came to the surface. The United Kingdom expressed its dissatisfaction with EU social policies such as granting part-time workers the same benefits as full-time workers and providing full-time workers four weeks of guaranteed vacation. Poor nations like Spain and Greece pressured the rich nations for more subsidies. The rich nations lacked funds because of their high unemployment. The Norwegians, when given the chance to join the EU, voted against it.

Big countries had more votes in the EU Council of Ministers, which functions like a legislature (the European Parliament is largely symbolic). Small countries were protected by a system of weighted voting. With additional states joining the EU, there was a great deal of discussion about redefining voting rules.

Many Europeans resented the EU's civil servants, who were perceived as technocrats far removed from popular needs and aspirations. The Maastricht Treaty, which was supposed to create for Europe a single government with a common foreign and defense policy, a common currency (the ecu), and a common citizenship, was in trouble. Europeans in favor of the EU, however, were optimistic that in the long run and despite setbacks, the gains that the EU had brought to member countries would be expanded. While not realizing all the goals its leaders had set for it, the EU would remain a very important force.

The United States' Renewal

Compared with Europe and Japan, to what extent was the United States in a serious and irreversible decline.[52] First, the United States continued to have advantages other countries did not have. Its military prowess could be matched by no other country. It remained an immigrant country that was constantly being revitalized by the entrepreneurial talents and energies of its newcomers (see Figure 29-8).

FIGURE 29-8
A comparison of immigrant skills with those of U.S. population, 1988

	Immigrants Entering U.S. (percentage)	U.S. Population (percentage)
College education	22.7%	19.9%
Engineers	2.9	1.5
Teachers	3.4	3.8
Medical doctors	0.6	0.5
Skilled blue-collar workers	10.2	12.1

Source: Council on Competitiveness, based on data from Immigration and Naturalization Service, Labor Department, and Census Bureau.

Japan, the world's second largest economy, was tied to the U.S. economy, its major overseas market. If the United States declined, Japan would suffer. It was in Japan's interest to see continued American prosperity. Europe's resources were impressive—twice that of Japan's. The continent played a larger role in world trade than Japan, and its armed forces, if combined, outnumbered those of the United States. However, the issue of political cohesiveness remained a stumbling point. Moreover, the immobility of labor and capital showed the European economy to be less dynamic than the U.S. economy. In the early 1990s, there were signs of renewed American competitiveness, while the economies of Japan and Europe were struggling.

To a greater extent than either Japan or Germany, the United States in the 1990s was growing faster, creating more jobs, and keeping inflation in check. It still held an absolute lead in productivity and was making gains there, too. In the postwar period, it was unusual to see the United States outperforming Japan and Germany in GNP growth and productivity improvement.[53]

Exploring the reasons for the renewed U.S. competitiveness requires consideration of the role of: capital, technology, and labor; management and organization innovations; environmental standards and energy prices; and new government policies.

Fluid Capital

In a period of vast global transformation, countries with fluid capital like the United States and the United Kingdom were outperforming countries with systems of dedicated capital like Germany and Japan. Fluid capital was transient and transaction driven; it involved outside owners, fragmented stakes, and a relatively limited flow of information. Dedicated capital, in contrast, was relationship driven; it involved significant stakes with great owner influence, inside information, and extensive information flow.

Throughout the 1980s, the conventional wisdom was that dedicated capital was superior to fluid capital. A reliance on fluid capital was frequently given as a reason for the comparative economic decline of the United States. However, fluid capital provides benefits that may be better suited to the dynamic economic changes of the 1990s. For example, it has allowed businesspeople to enter new fields and to recognize and exploit emerging opportunities. In systems of dedicated capital, businesspeople are more apt to stick with an investment through ups and down in order to realize a long-term gain. On the other hand, small business growth in the United States has been phenomenal even as large business downsized and reduced its workforce.

Technology

In technology, the United States had the lead in the number of personal computers per worker but it had not translated this advantage into productivity gains because, most economists believed, organizational adjustments had not been made and workers were not adept at using the software that was available. New studies, however, indicated that the U.S. lead in computers per worker was beginning to pay off.

While the United States showed weakness in process technology, it had an enormous capacity to introduce new products. In a period of rapid economic transformation, this capacity was more important than a capacity to manufacture existing products more cheaply. U.S. creativity produced gains because of the transition to new products and technologies.

Labor

The gap between the performance of U.S. students and those of other nations on standardized tests was going up. Nonetheless, the United States remained a haven (through immigration) for talented scientists and technical workers from around the world (the "brain drain"), which compensated for a relatively weak educational system. Moreover, it might not be the competence and intelligence of the workforce that makes a difference, but the variety and diversity of talents and skills that the workforce brings to bear on its tasks. In workforce variety and diversity, the United States had a clear lead over its major rivals.

Management and Organization

Management also was important. Around 1900, Russia, Australia, and Argentina were the equal of the United States in raw materials per capita. A highly educated and trained workforce, innovative and capable of technical invention was found to a greater extent in Great Britain and Germany. What the United States did possess that no other country had—and that helped assure its economic ascendancy—was the large modern corporation. The separation of management from ownership in the corporation, the capacity to raise vast funds of money and to serve large markets, with a managerial system run by a professional, educated managerial class divided into functional areas of expertise (e.g., marketing, finance, production, etc.) was unique.[54]

Starting in the 1980s, the United States borrowed various aspects of the Japanese system (e.g., just-in-time inventory systems, quality circles, defect-free production).[55] The massive experimentation in new managerial forms that was taking place (e.g., corporate reengineering) was purely American, and other countries were trying to catch up. This willingness to experiment and adjust to new conditions was lacking in other capitalist nations (Germany and Japan) that were more frozen in their old managerial and organizational forms.

Environmental Standards and Energy Prices

Exacting environmental standards in the United States also forced innovations in the use of raw materials and the elimination of waste, which may have had positive effects on productivity. U.S. environmental pressures had the potential to be "good for business" because they:

- Spurred technological change such as the reformulation of fuels and new designs for zero-emission vehicles.
- Stimulated the growth of an environmental protection business sector made up of consultants, products, recyclers, and nonprofit specialty firms.
- Helped build an industry devoted to the export of environmental products and services.
- Motivated the reduction of waste (e.g., pollution prevention), which in turn increased business efficiency.
- Gave an advantage to those companies that advertised environmental friendliness as a product attribute.

Ultra-low U.S. fossil-fuel prices also may have provided a temporary advantage. The price of energy in the rest of the world was approximately four times that in the United States (primarily owing to taxes). In the short run, low cost energy provided U.S. businesses with lower costs in the U.S. market. In the long run, this advantage might dissipate as U.S. companies lagged in introducing the efficiency enhancing changes that high-price energy demands.

Government Policies

The U.S. government actually was more successful than many foreign governments in keeping its budget deficit in check. It also started to move from an emphasis on basic R&D to one of commercial application (e.g., the transformation of the Defense Advanced Research Program into a commercial program). It began to convert its extensive laboratory systems—20 percent of all U.S. scientists and technical employees work in government labs—to commercial uses. Under the Omnibus Competitiveness Act of 1988, the Commerce Department set up an advanced technology program of direct government funding for a select group of technologies that showed commercial promise. This department also had a program of assistance to small and midsized businesses with the purpose of manufacturing for commercial use some of the advanced technologies developed in government labs. This federal program was matched by numerous local and state government assistance programs designed to protect and create jobs. Finally, the government stretched its laws to permit Japanese-like business alliances in many fields.

Understanding Comparative Economic Performance

In sum, to understand the comparative economic performance of nations, many factors have to be considered:

1. *The catch-up phenomenon.* Other countries started to catch up with the United States. They copied U.S. technology and improved upon it without having to bear the large initial costs associated with its development. Thus, they enjoyed the opportunities of backwardness, which began to wither away as the economies of the United States and other countries converged.

2. *The foreign trade bonus.* Loosening of foreign trade restrictions gave other nations in the world the advantages of a huge world marketplace, which the United States had enjoyed on a more exclusive basis. Large markets meant economies of scale and efficiencies that could not otherwise be realized.

3. *Government policies.* Other nations used government policies to advance their economic interests. These policies might be inwardly oriented and protective of domestic industries, however inefficient they were, or outwardly oriented and export-led, fully exposing economies to world economic competition. They could be used to raise savings, lower interest rates, and increase investment. They could be employed, alternatively, to devalue and appreciate the domestic currency to make domestic goods cheaper on international markets or to make imported raw materials and capital cheaper. Political stability and the social solidarity that governments created also were important. For example, it was hard to imagine rapid economic development in the nations of the Middle East because of the civil discord and political tension that prevailed.

What Managers Can Do

Economic growth and international competitiveness were complex phenomena composed of many elements, and only some factors were under direct managerial control. What could managers do to advance their companies' interests?

This question has to be focused on the kinds of matters managers are best able to address:[56]

- Facilitating innovation through research and development.
- Aligning ownership patterns to take a long-term view.
- Forging alliances so as to combine different firms' strengths.
- Instilling an awareness of product quality and safety among employees.
- Changing organization structures to acknowledge different international market conditions.
- Diversifying their companies with long-run competitiveness in mind.
- Generating employee commitment to improved productivity.
- Effectively managing business cycle changes.
- Effectively managing the political risk of operating in different conditions throughout the world.

A more inclusive list of some of the elements involved in enhancing a nation's economic performance is provided in the special feature that follows.

Special Feature

Elements that Enhance a Nation's Economic Performance

---

1. Labor productivity:
   a. Value of leisure time.
   b. Work intensity.
   c. Educational quality.
   d. Experience and knowledge gained on the job (learning by doing).
   e. Employment contracts (short-term versus lifetime).
   f. Payment schemes (straight salary versus salary + bonus).
   g. Unions and relative wages.
   h. The work ethic.

continued
   i.   Cultural factors (e.g., Confucianism/the Protestant ethic).
2. Capital accumulation and innovation:
   a.   Extent of investment increments.
   b.   Age of capital:
      (1) Replacement of old with new (modernization).
      (2) Investment in short-lived versus durable.
      (3) Recombination and retrofitting of existing capital.
   c.   Ability to innovate in use of capital:
      (1) R&D spending in the firm.
      (2) R&D spending in society as a whole.
      (3) Extent of engineers in the population.
      (4) Technical education.
      (5) Ability to exploit scale economies from large-scale projects.
      (6) Development of an entrepreneurial/managerial class with the requisite motivations and skills to start projects and sustain economic development.
   d.   Risk-taking propensities in population (e.g., availability of venture capital opportunities).
   e.   Requisite flexibility in use of capital: capability of managers to shift resources to most profitable applications:
      (1) Skill development among managers.
      (2) Training and awareness.
3. The cost of capital:
   a.   Ability of firms to generate retained earnings.
   b.   Savings.
      (1) Government programs to expand savings.
      (2) Individual propensity in population to delay gratification.
   c.   Debt:
      (1) Availability and use of domestic financing and government saving.
      (2) Availability and use of foreign financing, foreign aid, and assistance from the World Bank and IMF.
      (3) Conditions imposed by banks in financing and refinancing loans.
      (4) Types of financial institutions (bank/nonbank):
         (a) Expansion of these institutions.
         (b) Their soundness.
         (c) Government ownership and direction.
         (d) Legal climate for lending.
         (e) Acceptance of equity ownership by banks.

   d.   Equity market and bond market development: pressures exerted by these markets for short-term payoffs.
   e.   Return on investment (actual/expected) needed for loans and capital market investment.
4. Resource/sectoral factors:
   a.   Energy intensity.
   b.   Natural resource intensity.
   c.   Sectoral elements (industrial versus service sector versus specialization in primary and secondary products).
   d.   Emphasis on labor-intensive or capital-intensive industries.
5. Government factors:
   a.   Industrial policies:
      (1) Inward orientation or export-led.
      (2) Aggressive/nonaggressive.
      (3) Sector-specific/neutral.
      (4) Responsiveness to market signals/nonresponsiveness.
      (5) Government control of financial sector (e.g., benefits offered exporters).
      (6) Government control of trade policy and other instruments.
         (a) Import barriers.
         (b) Import substitution targets.
   b.   Extent and type of government regulation.
   c.   Government commitment to private sector and extent of privatization.
   d.   Extent and type of government ownership.
   e.   Ratio of government expenditures to GDP.
   f.   Extent of government deficits.
   g.   Willingness to use deficits for countercyclical purposes.
   h.   Political stability:
      (1) Social solidarity/political cohesion.
      (2) Distribution of income.
      (3) Extent of democratization.
   i.   Skills of economic policymakers (e.g., existence of people with perception, artfulness, imagination, and skill in leadership class and bureaucracy).
6. World market orientation of firm and economy of which firm is a part:
   a.   Closed/open character of economy.
   b.   Government protection of infant industries/promotion of exports.
   c.   Knowledge of foreign markets and language capabilities among managers needed to enter foreign markets.
   d.   Extent of involvements in foreign markets:
      (1) Import intensive (raw materials).

continued

        (2) Export intensive (finished products).
- e. Imitation capabilities:
  - (1) Introduction of foreign technology.
  - (2) Absorption of foreign know-how.

        (3) Abilities to take over markets opened by others.
- f. Exchange rate influences:
  - (1) Availability of foreign exchange.
  - (2) Competitive devaluations/inflation.

Conclusions

This chapter has argued that when considering rates of growth among countries in the world, examining only labor and capital is insufficient. A host of other factors are important. This chapter focused on international market exposure, technological innovation, and a sense of fairness that is reinforced by other conditions in the economy. Specific country examples have been given to illustrate how these elements play a role in economic development. The strengths and weaknesses of the world's major economic powers have been compared.

Some reasons for the revival of the U.S. economy in the mid-1990s have been suggested. To what extent will the United States continue to perform well? There is good reason to believe that the fluid capital system in place in the United States can outperform the dedicated capital system in place in Japan and Germany, because fluid capital is more capable of redeploying assets and adjusting to change. The American penchant for experimentation is helping the United States to retake the lead. U.S. managers move from one management fad to the next at a dizzying pace. This innovation frenzy is a powerful contributor to unfreezing systems no longer workable in a world of change. In many ways, the U.S. system is more flexible than the systems of its global competitors, a factor that needs to be better incorporated into theories of comparative economic performance.

Discussion Questions

1.   How have different national economies evolved historically?
2.   What happened to the world economy after 1973?
3.   What role do labor and capital play in economic development?
4.   How can labor's input be augmented?
5.   What role does educational quality play in national competitiveness?
6.   Why aren't labor and capital sufficient to explain economic growth? What other factors have to be considered?
7.   Why did the formerly socialist economies of Central and Eastern Europe fall apart?
8.   What has to be done now to get these economies to work?
9.   What explains the success of the French economy in the post-World War II period?
10. What explains the success of the South Korean economy?
11. Compare the South Korean and Taiwanese economies.
12. What role does technology play in economic development?
13. What is the difference between product innovation and process innovation? Which country (the U.S. or Japan) excels at product innovation? Which country excels at process innovation? Why do these differences exist?
14. What theme does sociologist Ronald Dore use to explain Japanese economic success? Do you agree with his analysis? Why or why not?
15. What is the future of Japan's economy? Is hollowing out going to have a negative effect? Why or why not?
16. Why did the Japanese bubble burst?
17. How have changes in the Japanese economy affected the Japanese automobile industry?
18. What are some of the factors retarding European integration? Discuss.
19. What factors have hindered privatization of the Central and Eastern European economies? Discuss the strengths and weaknesses of these economies.
20. What unique advantages does the United States bring to global competition? What disadvantages? Should one be optimistic or pessimistic about the future of the U.S. economy? Why?
21. What should managers do to make their companies more competitive? What are your recommendations?

Endnotes

1.   A. Maddison, "Growth and Slowdown in Advanced Capitalist Economies," *Journal of Economic Literature*, 1987, p. 649; R. L. Bartley, "The Great International Growth Slowdown," *The Wall Street Journal*, July 10, 1990, p. A18, 30; G. Bombach, Postwar Economic Growth Revisited (New York: North-Holland, 1985).

2.   Stephen Parente, "Changes in the Wealth of Nations," Federal Reserve Bank of Minneapolis, 1993, pp. 3-16; Richard Kirkland, "What if Japan Triumphs?" *Fortune*, May 18, 1992, pp. 60-67; CIA, Directorate of Intelligence, *Handbook of Economic Statistics:* (Washington, D.C. U.S. Government Printing Office, 1991), p. 30.

3.   Wealth disparities among nations were much larger than wealth disparities among U.S. states. Connecticut, the richest state, was 1.8 times wealthier than Mississippi, the poorest. The disparities among U.S. workers, on the other hand, matched the disparities among nations; incomes of the highest paid U.S. workers were about 30 times the incomes of the lowest paid.

4.   Michael Porter, "The Competitive Advantage of Nations," *Harvard Business Review*, 1990, pp. 73-93; "Asia: A Billion Consumers," *Economist*, 1993, pp. 3-22; "When China Wakes," *Economist*, 1992, pp. 3-18; "Indonesia: The Long March," *Economist*, 1993, pp. 3-18.

5.   "Helping Russia," *Economist*, Dec. 21, 1992-Jan. 3, 1993, pp. 101-104; Louis Kraar, "Korea's Tigers Keep Roaring," *Fortune*, May 4, 1992, pp. 108-10.

6.   Maddison, "Growth and Slowdown in Advanced Capitalist Economies," pp. 649-98; *World Development Report 1987* (New York: Oxford University Press, 1987).

7.   K. Dervis and R Petri, "The Macroeconomics of Successful Development," *NBER Macroeconomics Annual*, 1987, pp. 211-62.

8.   K. Choi, *Theories of Comparative Economic Growth* (Ames, Ia.: Iowa State University Press, 1983); Maddison, "Growth and Slowdown in Advanced Capitalist Economies."

9.   Maddison, "Growth and Slowdown in Advanced Capitalist Economies."

10. G. S. Becker, *Human Capital: A Theoretical and Empirical Analysis, with Special Reference to Education*, 2nd ed. (Chicago: University of Chicago Press, 1975); M. Porter, *The Competitive Advantage of Nations* (New York: Free Press, 1990), pp. 69-131; M. Porter, "Determinants of National Competitive Advantage," *The Competitive Advantage of Nations*, (New York: Free Press, 1990), pp. 69-131. "Education: Trying Harder," *Economist*, 1993, pp. 3-18. J. Pencavel, "The Contributions of Higher Education to Economic Growth and Productivity," Stanford Center for Economic Policy Research, 1990, pp. 1-48; R. Sturm, "How Do Education and Training Affect a Country's Economic Performance" (Santa Monica, Calif.: Rand Institute, 1933); A. Heidenheimer, "Aligning Global and Parochial Concerns in Education Policy," Washington University Department of Political Science, 1990; Clark Kerr, "Education and the Decline of the American Economy: Guilty or Not?" University of Minnesota Industrial Relations Center Distinguished Lecture, 1989.

11. "Human Capital: The Decline of America's Work Force," *Business Week*, September 19, 1988; Kerr, "Education and the Decline of the American Economy."

12. "Human Capital."

13. Maddison, "Growth and Slowdown in Advanced Capitalist Economies."

14. Dervis and Petri, "The Macroeconomics of Successful Development"; Yuan-li Wu and Hungchao Tai, "Economic Performance in Five East Asian Countries," in *Confucianism and Economic Development* (Washington, D.C.: Washington Institute, 1989), pp. 38-55.

15. Porter, "Determinants of National Competitive Advantage."

16. P. Gumbel, "How Gorbachev's Plan Has Left Soviet Union without Much Soap," The *Wall Street Journal*, November 20, 1989, p. AI; E. A. Hewett, ea., *Reforming the Soviet Economy: Equality versus Efficiency* (Washington, D.C.: Brookings Institution, 1988); E. A. Hewett, "Soviet Economic Performance: Strengths and Weaknesses," in *Reforming the Soviet Economy*, ed. E. A. Hewett (Washington, D.C.: Brookings Institution, 1988), pp. 31-94.

17. Hewett, "Soviet Economic Performance."

18. Ibid.

19. W. J. Adams, "A New International Environment," in *Restructuring the French Economy*, ed. W. J. Adams (Washington, D.C.: Brookings Institution, 1989), pp. 120-206.

20. Adams, *Restructuring the French Economy*.

21. A. H. Amsden, *Asia's Next Giant: South Korea and Late Industrialization* (New York: Oxford University Press, 1989), pp. 55-79.

22. Ibid.

23. Ibid.

24. "Taiwan and Korea: Two Paths to Prosperity," *Economist*, July 14, 1990, pp. 22-29; E. Hartfield, "The Divergent Economic Development of China and Japan," in *Confucianism and Economic Development* (Washington, D.C.: Washington Institute, 1989), pp. 92-115; Porter, "Determinants of National Competitive Advantage."

25. "Taiwan and Korea: Two Paths to Prosperity."

26. Lester Thurow, "An American Game Plan," *MIT Management*, Spring 1992, pp. 33-48.

27. Porter, "Determinants of National Competitive Advantage."

28. L. G. Franko, "Global Corporate Competition: Who's Winning, Who's Losing, and the R&D Factor as One Reason Why," *Strategic Management Journal* 10 (1989), pp. 449-74; C L. Hill and A. A. Snell, "External Control, Corporate Strategy, and Firm Performance in Research Intensive Industries," *Strategic Management Journal* 9 (1988), pp. 577-90; R. E. Hoskisson and M. A. Hitt, "Strategic Control Systems and Relative R&D Investment in Large Multiproduct Firms," *Strategic Management Journal* 9 (1988), pp. 605-21.

29. R. H. Hayes and W. J. Abernathy, "Managing Our Way to Economic Decline," *Harvard Business Review*, July-Aug. 1980; L. C. Thurow, *Technology Leadership and Industrial Competitiveness* (Minneapolis: Center for the Development of Technological Leadership, University of Minnesota, 1988).

30. Ibid.

31. Thurow, *Technology Leadership and Industrial Competitiveness*.

32. Nonaka, "Redundant, Overlapping Organization," pp. 27-38.

33. J. C. Abegglen and G. Stalk, *Kaisha: The Japanese Corporation* (New York: Basic Books, 1985); A. Murray and U. C. Lehner, "U.S., Japan Struggle to Redefine Relations as Resentment Grows," The *Wall Street Journal*, June 13, 1990, p. A1; R. T. Pascale and A. G. Athos, *The Art of Japanese Management: Applications for American Executives* (New York: Simon and Schuster, 1981); D. Garvin, "Quality Problems, Policies, and Attitudes in the U.S. and Japan: An Exploratory Study," *AMJ*, Dec. 1986, pp. 653-74; D. Encarnation, "Cross-investment: A Second Front of Economic Rivalry," *California Management Review*, Winter 1987, pp. 20-49; D. Dunphy, "Convergence/Divergence: A Temporal Review of the Japanese Enterprise and Its Management," *AMR*, July 1987, pp. 445-59; M. Olson, *The Rise and Decline of Nations*, 1982.

34. W. Ouchi, *The M-form Society: How American Teamwork Can Recapture the Competitive Edge* (Reading, Mass.: Addison-Wesley, 1984).

35. Ibid.

36. Abegglen and Stalk, *Kaisha: The Japanese Corporation*; "Japan's Troublesome Imports," *Economist*, Jan. 11, 1992, p. 61; Abegglen and Stalk, *Kaisha*.

37. "Capitalism: In Triumph, in Flux," *Economist*, May 5, 1990, special section, "Punters or Proprietors?" p. 6.

38. Lester Thurow, ed., *The Management Challenge: Japanese Views* (Cambridge, Mass.: MIT Press, 1985); R. Sheard, "The Economics of Interlocking Shareholding in Japan," Stanford Center for Economic Policy Research, 1991, pp. 1-44.

39. R. Komiya, "Structural and Behavioristic Characteristics of the Japanese Firm" [in Japanese in *Gendia Chugoku Keizei: Nicchu no Hikaku Kosatsu (The Contemporary Chinese Economy: A Comparative Study of China and Japan)*] (Tokyo: University of Tokyo Press, 1989), pp. 97-145; M. Aoki, "Toward an Economic Model of the Japanese Firm," *Journal of Economic Literature* 28 (1990), 1-27; 5.63; W. C. Kester, "Capital and Ownership Structure: A Comparison of U.S. and Japanese Manufacturing Corporations," in A. M. Spence, ed., *International Competitiveness* (Cambridge, Mass.: Ballinger, 1988).

40. E. J. Lincoln, *Japan: Facing Economic Maturity* (Washington, D.C.: Brookings Institution, 1988); Maddison, "Growth and Slowdown in Advanced Capitalist Economies," pp. 649-98; Young Kwan Yoon, *The Irony of Plenty: Japanese Foreign Direct Investment and Productivity*, APSA paper, 1987, pp. 1-36; G. S. Hansen and B. Wernerfelt, "Determinants of Firm Performance: The Relative Importance of Economic and Organizational Factors," *Strategic Management Journal* 10 (1989), pp. 399-411; W.S. Kim and E. Lyn, "FDI Theories and the Performance of Foreign Multinationals Operating in the U.S.," *Journal of International Business*, 1990, pp. 41-54; K. Miller and R Bromiley, "Strategic Risk and Corporate Performance," *Academy of Management Journal* 33 (1990), pp. 756-79.

41. Yoon, *The Irony of Plenty*; K. Gartrell, "Innovation, Industry Specialization, and Shareholder Wealth," *California Management Review*, 1990, pp. 87-101; J. E. Butler, "Theories of Technological Innovation as Useful Tools for Corporate Strategy," *Strategic Management Journal* 9 (1988), pp. 15-29; B. Mascarenhas, "Domains of State-Owned, Privately Held, and Publicly Traded Firms in International Competition," *Administrative Science Quarterly* 34 (1989), pp. 582-97; R. Osborn and C. C. Baughn, "Forms of Interorganizational Governance for Multinational Alliances," *Academy of Management Journal* 33 (1990), pp. 503-19.

42. Yoon, *The Irony of Plenty*; R. Bromiley and A. Marcus, "The Deterrent to Dubious Corporate Behavior: Profitability, Probability, and Safety Recalls," *Strategic Management Journal*, 1989, pp. 233-50; N. Rose, "Profitability and Product Quality: Economic Determinants of Airline Safety Performance," *JPE*, 1990, pp. 943-61.

43. "Japanese Finance," *Economist*, May 30, 1992, p.84.

44. Andrew Pollack, "Japanese Deficit to Grow Sharply," *New York Times*, Feb. 20, 1995, p. C1.

45. M. Cusumano, "The Limits of Lean," *Sloan Management Review*, 1994, pp. 27-33.

46. R. Dore, *Taking Japan Seriously* (Stanford, Calif.: Stanford University Press, 1987).

47. Ibid.

48. R. E. Cole, "U.S. Quality Improvement in the Auto Industry: Close but No Cigar," *California Management Review*, 1989, pp. 71-85.

49. "Europe: The Deal Is Done," *Economist*, Dec. 14, 1991, pp. 51-52; Shawn Tully, "Europe 1992," *Fortune*, Aug. 24, 1992, pp. 135-42; Shawn Tully, "Now the New Europe," *Fortune*, Dec. 2, 1991, pp. 136-56; "The Business of Europe," *Economist*, Dec. 7, 199 , pp. 63-64; "What Are the Costs and Benefits of an Enlarged European Community?" *Economist*, Oct. 17, 1992, p. 75; "Europe's Two Trade Areas," *Economist*, Oct. 26, 1991, pp. 81-82; Commission of the European Communities, *The Competitiveness of the Community Industry* (Luxembourg, 1982); "The European Community: An Expanding Universe," *Economist*, July 7, 1990.

50. Carla Rapoport, "Why Germany Will Lead Europe," *Fortune*, Sept. 21, 1992, pp. 149-54; Paul Hofheinz, "How Germany Is Attacking Recession," *Fortune*, June 14, 1993, pp. 132-34; "Germany: The Shock of Unity," *Economist*, May 23, 1992, special report; "Is Germany's Treuhandanstalt a Good Thing?" *Economist*, March 21, 1992, p. 71; Craig Whitnew, "Bonn Politicians Vow a Crackdown Against Violence," *The New York Times*, Oct. 9, 1992, pp. 1, A7.

51. "Pioneers of Capitalism," *Economist*, April 4, 1992, pp. 79-80; "Business in Eastern Europe," *Economist*, Sept. 21, 1991, special report; "Eastern Europe: The Old World's New World," *Economist*, 1993, pp. 3-22; "Poland: Souls in a New Machine," *Economist*, 1994, pp. 3-22; N. Healey, "The Transition Economies of Central and Eastern Europe," *Columbia Journal of World Business*, 1994, pp. 62-72; A. Shama, "Management Under Fire: The Transformation of Managers in the Soviet Union and Eastern Europe," *Executive*, 1993, pp. 22-36; "Russia: The Sixth Wave," *Economist*, 1992, pp. 30-36; "Ukraine: The Birth and Possible Death of a Country," *Economist*, 1994, pp. 1-10; D. Rondinelli and M. Fellenz, "Privatization and Private Enterprise in Hungary: An Assessment of Market Reform Policies," *Business and the Contemporary World*, 1993, pp. 75-88; K. Obloj and M. Kostera, "Polish Privatization Program," *Industrial and Environmental Crisis Quarterly*, 1993, pp. 7-22; R. Rottenburg, "From Socialist Realism to Postmodern Ambiguity: East German Companies in Transition," *Industrial and Environmental Crisis Quarterly*, 1993, pp. 71-92; D. Holt, D. Ralston, and R. Terpstra, "Constraints on Capitalism in Russia: The Managerial Psyche," *California Management Review*, 1994, pp. 124-42; M. King, "The Challenge of Accounting in Eastern Europe," *Business and the Contemporary World*, 1994, pp. 112-22.

52. J. S. Nye, *Bound to Lead* (New York: Basic Books, 1990); J. E. Schwarz, *America's Hidden Success: A Reassessment of Public Policy from Kennedy to Reagan* (New York: W. W. Norton, 1988); J. E. Schwarz, and T. J. Volgy, "The Myth of America's Economic Decline," *Harvard Business Review*, Sept.-Oct. 1985, p. 101; J. Erceg and T. Bernard, "Productivity, Costs, and International Competitiveness," Federal Reserve Bank of Cleveland, November 15, 1988.

53. Alfred Marcus, "Explaining the Renewed Competitiveness of the U.S. Economy," *Business and the Contemporary World*, 1994, pp. 29-34; Sylvia Nasar, "The American Economy, Back on Top," *New York Times Business*, Feb. 27, 1994, p. 1, 6.

54. Alfred Chandler, "Organizational Capabilities and Industrial Restructuring," Harvard Business School, 1992.

55. Jeremy Main, "How to Steal the Best Ideas Around," *Fortune*, Oct. 19, 1992, pp. 102-6.

56. W. G. Egelhoff, "Strategy and Structure in Multinational Corporations," *Strategic Management Journal* 9 ('988), pp. 1-14; S. Ghoshal and N. Nohria, "Internal Differentiation within Multinational Organizations," *Strategic Management Journal* 10 (1989), pp. 323-37; J. M. Geringer, R. W. Beamish, and R. C. deCosta, "Diversification Strategy and Internationalization: Implications for MNE Performance," *Strategic Management Journal* 10 (1989), pp. 109-19; W. C. Kim, R. Hwang, and W. R. Burgers, "Global Diversification Strategy and Corporate Profit Performance," *Strategic Management Journal* 10 (1989), pp. 45-57; R. C. Earley, "Social Loafing and Collectivism," *Administrative Science Quarterly* 34 (1989), pp. 565-81; I. Harpaz, "The Importance of Work Goals: An International Perspective," *Journal of International Business*, 1990, pp. 75-93; B. Mascarenhas and D. A. Aaker, "Strategy over the Business Cycle," *Strategic Management Journal* 10 (1989), pp. 199-210; C. Y. Kwok and L. D. Brooks, "Examining Event Study Methodologies in Foreign Exchange Markets," *Journal of International Business*, 1990, pp. 189-224; R. Johnson, V. Srinivasan, and R. Bolster, "Sovereign Debt Ratings: A Judgmental Model Based on the Analytic Hierarchy Process," *Journal of International Business*, 1990, pp. 95-117.

Chapter Thirty

ANTI-TRUST: THE

SHERMAN ACT

Introduction

The post-Civil War emergence and growth of large industrial combines and trusts significantly altered the business environment of earlier years. A major feature of this economic phenomenon was the tendency of various large business entities to acquire dominant positions in their industries by buying up smaller competitors or engaging in practices aimed at driving smaller competitors out of business. This behavior led to public demands for legislation to preserve competitive market structures and prevent the accumulation of great economic power in the hands of a few firms.

Although the common law had long held that contracts unreasonably restraining trade violated public policy, courts could implement this rule only by refusing to enforce such a contract if one of the parties objected to it. Legislation was therefore necessary to give the courts greater power to deal with the problem of anticompetitive practices. Congress responded in 1890 with the Sherman Act. It supplemented this response by enacting the Clayton Act in 1914 and the Robinson-Patman Act in 1936.

Preservation of Competition

In enacting the antitrust statutes, Congress adopted a public policy in favor of preserving and promoting free competition as the most efficient means of allocating social resources. The Supreme Court summarized the rationale for this faith in competition's positive effects when it said:

> Basic to faith that a free economy best promotes the public weal is that goods must stand the cold test of competition; that the public, acting through the market's impersonal judgment, shall allocate the nation's resources and thus direct the course its economic development will take.[1]

Congress thus presumed, in enacting the antitrust statutes, that competition was more likely to exist in an industrial structure characterized by a large number of competing firms than in concentrated industries dominated by a few large competitors. As Judge Learned Hand observed:

Business Law and the Regulatory Environment, Ninth Edition, by Michael B. Metzger, Jane P. Mallor, A. James Barnes, Thomas Bowers, Michael J. Phillips, Arlen Langvardt. © Irwin/McGraw-Hill, The McGraw-Hill Companies, 1946, 1951, 1955, 1959, 1963, 1966, 1970, 1974, 1978, 1982, 1986, 1989, 1992, 1995.

Many people believe that possession of an unchallenged economic power deadens initiative, discourages thrift, and depresses energy; that immunity from competition is a narcotic, and rivalry is a stimulant, to industrial progress; that the spur of constant stress is necessary to counteract an inevitable disposition to let well enough alone.[2]

Despite this longstanding policy in favor of competitive market structures, the antitrust laws have not been very successful in halting the trend toward concentration in American industry. The market structure in many important industries today is highly *oligopolistic*, with the bulk of production accounted for by a few dominant firms. Traditional antitrust concepts are often difficult to apply to the behavior of firms in these highly concentrated markets. Recent years have witnessed the emergence of new ideas that challenge various longstanding antitrust policy assumptions.

The Antitrust Policy Debate

Antitrust enforcement necessarily reflects fundamental public policy judgments about the economic activities to be allowed and the industrial structure best suited to foster desirable economic activity. Given the importance of such judgments to the future of the American economy, it is not surprising that antitrust policy spurs vigorous public debate.

Chicago School Theories

In recent years, traditional antitrust assumptions have faced a highly effective challenge from commentators and courts advocating the application of microeconomic theory to antitrust enforcement. These new methods of antitrust analysis are commonly called **Chicago School theories** because many of their major premises were advanced by scholars associated with the University of Chicago.

Chicago School advocates tend to view *economic efficiency* as the primary, if not the sole, goal of antitrust enforcement. They are far less concerned with the supposed effects of industrial concentration than are traditional antitrust thinkers. Even highly concentrated industries, they argue, may engage in significant forms of nonprice competition, such as competition in advertising, styling, and warranties. They also point out that concentration in a particular industry does not necessarily preclude *interindustry competition* among related industries. For example, a highly concentrated glass container industry may still face significant competition from the makers of metal, plastic, and fiberboard containers. Chicago School advocates are also quick to point out that many markets today are international in scope, so that highly concentrated domestic industries such as automobiles, steel, and electronics may nonetheless face effective foreign competition. In fact, they argue that the technological developments necessary for American industry to compete more effectively in international markets may require the great capital resources that result from concentration in domestic industry.

According to the Chicago School viewpoint, the traditional antitrust focus on the structure of industry has improperly emphasized protecting *competitors* rather than protecting *competition*. Chicago School theorists argue that the primary thrust of antitrust policy should involve *anticonspiracy* efforts rather than *anticoncentration* efforts. In addition, most of these theorists take a rather lenient view toward various vertically imposed restrictions on price and distribution that have been traditionally seen as undesirable, because they believe that such restrictions can promote efficiencies in distribution. Thus, they tend to be more tolerant of attempts by manufacturers to control resale prices and establish exclusive distribution systems for their products.

Traditional Antitrust Theories

Traditional antitrust thinkers, however, contend that although economic efficiency is *an* important goal of antitrust enforcement, antitrust policy has historically embraced *political* as well as economic values. Concentrated economic power, they argue, is undesirable for a variety of noneconomic reasons. It may lead to antidemocratic concentrations of political power. Moreover, it may stimulate greater governmental intrusions into the economy in the same way that the post-Civil War activities of the trusts led to the passage of the antitrust laws. According to the traditional view, lessening concentration enhances individual freedom by reducing the barriers to entry that confront would-be competitors and by ensuring broader input into economic decisions having important social consequences. Judge Learned Hand summed up this perspective on antitrust policy:

> Great industrial consolidations are inherently undesirable, regardless of their economic results. Throughout the history of [sections 1 and 2 of the Sherman Act] it has been constantly assumed that one of their purposes was to perpetuate and preserve, for its own sake and in spite of possible cost, an organization of industry in small units which can effectively compete with each other.[3]

Effect of Chicago School Notions

Chicago School notions, however, have had a significant impact on the course of antitrust enforcement in recent years. The Supreme Court and many of President Reagan's appointees to the lower federal courts have given credence to Chicago School economic arguments in many cases. Some of President Reagan's appointees to the Department of Justice and the Federal Trade Commission were sympathetic to Chicago School policy views. The Bush administration's agency appointees appeared to be somewhat more inclined toward government enforcement of the antitrust laws than their Reagan administration predecessors had been. Public positions taken by Department of Justice of officials during the early portion of the Clinton administration (when this book went to press) revealed the likelihood of a stepped-up government role in policing the marketplace for probable antitrust violations. Nevertheless, the presence on the federal bench of so many judges embracing Chicago School ideas means that those views are likely to continue to have an impact on the shape of antitrust law for the foreseeable future.

Jurisdiction, Types of Antitrust Cases, and Standing

Jurisdiction

The Sherman Act outlaws monopolization and agreements in restraint of trade. Because the federal government's power to regulate business originates in the Commerce Clause of the U.S. Constitution, the federal antitrust laws apply only to behavior having some significant impact on *interstate* or *foreign* commerce. Given the interdependent nature of our national economy, it is normally fairly easy to demonstrate that a challenged activity either involves interstate commerce (the "in commerce" jurisdiction test) or has a substantial effect on interstate commerce (the "effect on commerce" jurisdiction test). Various cases indicate that a business activity may have a substantial effect on interstate commerce even though the activity occurs solely within the borders of one state. Activities that are purely *intrastate* in their effects, however, are outside the scope of federal antitrust jurisdiction and must be challenged under state law.

The federal antitrust statutes have been extensively applied to activities affecting the international commerce of the United States. The activities of American firms operating outside U.S. borders may be attacked under our antitrust laws if those activities have an intended effect on our foreign commerce. Likewise, foreign firms "continuously engaged" in our domestic commerce are subject to federal antitrust jurisdiction. Determining the full extent of the extraterritorial reach of our antitrust laws often involves courts in difficult questions of antitrust exemptions and immunities. The extraterritorial reach issue also suggests a troubling political prospect: Aggressive expansion of antitrust law's applicability may create tension between our antitrust policy and our foreign policy in general.

Types of Cases and the Role of Pretrial Settlements

Sherman Act violations may give rise to criminal prosecutions and civil litigation instituted by the federal government (through the Department of Justice), as well as to civil suits filed by private parties. A significant percentage of the antitrust cases brought by the Department of Justice are settled without trial through the use of *nolo contendere* pleas in criminal cases and *consent decrees* in civil cases. A defendant who pleads nolo contendere technically has not admitted guilt. The sentencing court, however, is free to impose the same penalty that would be appropriate in the case of a guilty plea or a conviction at trial. Consent decrees involve a defendant's consent to remedial measures aimed at remedying the competitive harm resulting from his actions. Because neither a nolo plea nor a consent decree is admissible as proof of a violation of the Sherman Act in a later civil suit filed by a private plaintiff, both of these devices are often attractive to antitrust defendants.

Criminal Prosecutions

Individuals criminally convicted of Sherman Act violations may receive a fine of up to $350,000 per violation and/or a term of imprisonment of up to three years. Corporations convicted of violating the Sherman Act may be fined up to $10 million per violation. Before an individual may be found criminally responsible under the Sherman Act, however, the government must prove an *anticompetitive* effect flowing from the challenged activity, as well as *criminal intent* on the defendant's part. The level of criminal intent required for a violation is a "knowledge of [the challenged activity's] probable consequences" rather than a specific intent to violate the antitrust laws.[4] Civil violations of the antitrust laws may be proved, however, by evidence of either an unlawful purpose or an anticompetitive effect.

Civil Litigation

The federal courts have broad injunctive powers to remedy civil antitrust violations. Courts may order convicted defendants to *divest* themselves of the stock or assets of acquired companies, to *divorce* themselves from a functional level of their operations (e.g., ordering a manufacturer to sell its captive retail outlets), to refrain from particular conduct in the future, and to cancel existing contracts. In extreme cases, courts may also enter a *dissolution decree* ordering a defendant to liquidate its assets and cease business operations. Private individuals and the federal Department of Justice may seek such injunctive relief regarding antitrust violations.

Treble Damages for Private Plaintiffs

Section 4 of the Clayton Act gives private parties a significant incentive to enforce the antitrust laws by providing that private plaintiffs injured by Sherman Act or Clayton Act violations are entitled to recover *treble damages* plus court costs and attorney's fees from the defendant. This means that once antitrust plaintiffs have demonstrated the amount of their actual losses (such as lost profits or increased costs) resulting from the challenged violation, this amount is tripled. The potential for treble damage liability plainly presents a significant deterrent threat to potential antitrust violators. For example, a famous antitrust case against General Electric Company and several other electrical equipment manufacturers resulted in treble damage awards in excess of $200 million. Some Chicago School critics have argued unsuccessfully that treble damages should be allowed only for per se antitrust violations, with plaintiffs who prove *"rule of reason"* violations being limited to recovering actual damages. (Per se and rule of reason violations are discussed later in this chapter.)

Standing

Private plaintiffs seeking to enforce the antitrust laws must first demonstrate that they have **standing** to sue. This means that they must show a *direct antitrust injury* as a result of the challenged behavior. An antitrust injury results from the unlawful aspects of the challenged behavior and is of the sort Congress sought to prevent by enacting the antitrust laws. For example, in *Brunswick Corp. v. Pueblo Bowl-o-Mat, Inc.*,[5] the operator of a chain of bowling centers (Pueblo) challenged a bowling equipment manufacturer's (Brunswick's) acquisition of various competing bowling centers that had defaulted on payments owed to Brunswick for equipment purchases. In essence, Pueblo asserted that if Brunswick had not acquired them, the failing bowling centers would have gone out of business—in which event Pueblo's profits presumably would have increased. The Supreme Court rejected Pueblo's claim because Pueblo's supposed losses flowed from Brunswick's having *preserved* competition by acquiring the failing centers. Allowing recovery for such losses would be contrary to the antitrust purpose of *promoting* competition. The antitrust injury requirement also plays a major role in the *Atlantic Richfield* case, which appears later in the chapter.

Importance of Direct Injury

Proof that an antitrust injury is direct is critical because the Supreme Court has held that *indirect purchasers* lack standing to sue for antitrust violations. In *Illinois Brick Co. v. State of Illinois*,[6] the state of Illinois and several other governmental entities sought treble damages from concrete block suppliers who, they alleged, were guilty of illegally fixing the price of the block used in the construction of public buildings. The plaintiffs acknowledged that the builders hired to construct the buildings in question had actually paid the inflated prices for the blocks, but argued that these illegal costs probably had been passed on to them in the form of higher prices for building construction. The Supreme Court refused to allow recovery, however, holding that granting standing to indirect purchasers would create a risk of "duplicative recoveries" by purchasers at various levels in a product's chain of distribution. The Court also observed that affording standing to indirect purchasers would lead to difficult problems of tracing competitive injuries through several levels of distribution and assessing the extent of an indirect purchaser's actual losses.

A number of state legislatures responded to *Illinois Brick* by enacting statutes allowing indirect purchasers to sue under state antitrust statutes. The Supreme Court has held that the *Illinois Brick* holding does not preempt such statutes.[7]

Section 1—Restraints of Trade

Concerted Action

Section 1 of the Sherman Act states that "[e]very contract, combination in the form of trust or otherwise, or conspiracy, in restraint of trade or commerce among the several states, or with foreign nations is declared to be illegal." A **contract** is any agreement, express or implied, between *two or more* persons or business entities to restrain competition; a **combination** is a continuing *partnership* in restraint of trade; a **conspiracy** occurs when *two or more* persons or business entities join for the purpose of restraining trade.

The above statutory language makes obvious the conclusion that section 1 of the Sherman Act is aimed at **concerted action** (i.e., *joint action*) in restraint of trade. *Purely unilateral action* by a competitor, on the other hand, cannot violate section 1. This statutory section reflects a basic public policy that businesspersons should make important competitive decisions on their own, rather than in conjunction with competitors. In his famous book *The Wealth of Nations* (1776), Adam Smith acknowledged both the danger to competition posed by concerted action and the tendencies of competitors to engage in such action. Smith observed that "[p]eople of the same trade seldom meet together, even for merriment and diversion, [without] the conversation end[ing] in a conspiracy against the public, or in some contrivance to raise prices."

Problems Posed by Concerted Action Requirement

Section 1's concerted action requirement poses two major problems. First, how separate must two business entities be before their joint activities are subject to the act's prohibitions? For example, it has long been held that a corporation cannot conspire with itself or its employees and that a corporation's employees cannot be guilty of a conspiracy in the absence of some independent party. What about conspiracies, however, among related corporate entities? In decisions more than 40 years ago, the Supreme Court appeared to hold that a corporation could violate the Sherman Act by conspiring with a wholly owned subsidiary. More recently, however, in *Copperweld Corp. v. Independence Tube Corp.*,[8] the Court repudiated the "intra-enterprise conspiracy doctrine." The Court held that a parent company is legally incapable of conspiring with a wholly owned subsidiary for Sherman Act purposes, because an agreement between parent and subsidiary does not create the risk to competition that results when two independent entities act in concert. It remains to be seen whether this approach extends to corporate subsidiaries and affiliates that are not wholly owned. *Copperweld's* logic would appear, however, to cover any subsidiary in which the parent firm has a controlling interest.

A second—and more difficult—problem frequently accompanies attempts to enforce section 1. This problem arises when courts are asked to *infer* (from the relevant circumstances) the existence of an agreement or conspiracy to restrain trade despite the lack of any *overt* agreement by the parties. Should parallel pricing behavior by several firms be enough, for instance, to justify the inference that a price-fixing conspiracy exists? Courts have consistently held that proof of pure "*conscious parallelism*," standing alone, is **not** enough to establish a section 1 violation. Other evidence must be presented to show that the defendants' actions stemmed from an **agreement**, *express or implied*, rather than from independent business decisions. It therefore becomes quite difficult to attack *oligopolies* (a few large firms sharing one market) under section 1, because such firms may independently elect to follow the pricing policies of the industry "price leader" rather than risk their large market shares by engaging in vigorous price competition.

Per Se Analysis

Although section 1's language condemns "every" contract, combination, and conspiracy in restraint of trade, the Supreme Court has long held that the Sherman Act applies only to behavior that *unreasonably* restrains competition. In addition, the Court has developed two fundamentally different approaches to analyzing behavior challenged under section 1. According to the Court, some actions always have a negative effect on competition—an effect that cannot be excused or justified. Such actions are classified as **per se** unlawful. If a particular behavior falls under the per se heading, it is conclusively presumed to violate section 1. Per se rules are thought to provide reliable guidance to business. They also simplify otherwise lengthy antitrust litigation, because if per se unlawful behavior is proven, the defendant cannot assert any supposed justifications in an attempt to avoid liability.

Per se rules, however, are frequently criticized on the ground that they tend to oversimplify complex economic realities. Recent decisions indicate that for *some* economic activities, the Supreme Court is moving away from per se rules and instead adopting "rule of reason" analysis. This trend is consistent with the Court's increased inclination to consider new economic theories that seek to justify behavior previously held to be per se unlawful.

"Rule of Reason" Analysis

Behavior not classified as per se unlawful is judged under the "**rule of reason**." This approach requires a detailed inquiry into the actual competitive effects of the defendant's actions and includes consideration of any justifications that the defendant may advance. If the court concludes that the challenged activity had a significant anticompetitive effect that was not offset by any positive effect on competition or other social benefit such as enhanced economic efficiency, the activity will be held to violate section 1. On the other hand, if the court concludes that the justifications advanced by the defendant outweigh the harm to competition resulting from the defendant's activity, there is no section 1 violation.

The following subsections of the chapter examine some of the behaviors held to violate section 1 of the Sherman Act. The legal treatment (per se or rule of reason) given to the respective behaviors is also considered.

Horizontal Price-Fixing

An essential attribute of a free market is that the price of goods and services is determined by the free play of the impersonal forces of the marketplace. Attempts by competitors to interfere with market forces and control prices—called **horizontal price-fixing**—have long been held per se unlawful under section 1. Price-fixing may take the form of direct agreements among competitors about the price at which they sell or buy a particular product or service. It may also be accomplished by agreements on the quantity of goods to be produced, offered for sale, or bought. In one famous case, an agreement by major oil refiners to purchase and store the excess production of small independent refiners was held to amount to price-fixing because the purpose of the agreement was to affect the market price for gasoline by artificially limiting the available supply.[9]

Some commentators have suggested that agreements among competitors to fix *maximum* prices should be treated under a rule of reason approach rather than the harsher per se standard because, in some instances, such agreements may result in savings to consumers. In addition, lower courts have occasionally sought to craft exceptions to the rule that horizontal price-fixing triggers per se treatment. It is important to note, however, that the Supreme Court continues to adhere to the longstanding rule of per se illegality for any form of horizontal price-fixing. In the *Denny's Marina* case, which follows, a federal court of appeals overturned a district court's attempt to limit the applicability of the per se rule in the horizontal price-fixing context.

Denny's Marina, Inc. v. Renfro Productions, Inc.

Denny's Marina, Inc. filed an antitrust action, described more fully below, against various defendants: the "Renfro Defendants" (Renfro Productions, Inc., Indianapolis Boat, Sport, and Travel Show, Inc., and individuals connected with those firms); "CIMDA" (the Central Indiana Marine Dealers Association); and the "Dealer Defendants" (various boat dealers who competed with Denny's in the sale of fishing boats, motors, trailers, and marine accessories in the central Indiana market). The Renfro Defendants operate two boat shows each year, one in the spring and one in the fall, at the Indiana State Fairgrounds. The spring show has occurred annually for more than 30 years and is one of the top three boat shows in the United States. It attracts between 160,000 and 191,000 consumers each year. The fall show is a smaller operation that has occurred each year since 1987. Numerous boat dealers participate in the two shows.

Denny's participated in the fall show in 1988, 1989, and 1990. It participated in the spring show in 1989 and 1990. According to allegations made by Denny's in its antitrust complaint, Denny's was quite successful at each of these shows, apparently because it urged customers to shop the other dealers and then return to Denny's for a lower price. After the 1989 spring show, some of the Dealer Defendants began to complain (according to Denny's) to the Renfro Defendants about the sales methods used by Denny's. In addition, Denny's alleged, the Dealer Defendants spent a significant part of a CIMDA meeting venting frustration about similar sales tactics used by Denny's at the 1990 spring show. Denny's also asserted that the Dealer Defendants' complaints to the Renfro Defendants escalated, and that as a result, the Renfro Defendants informed Denny's after the 1990 fall show that Denny's could no longer participate in the boat shows.

Denny's claimed that the above-described conduct of the defendants amounted to a conspiracy, prohibited by Sherman Act section 1, to exclude Denny's from participating in the boat shows because its policy was to "meet or beat" its competitors' prices at the shows. When the district court granted the defendants' motions for sublunary judgment, Denny's appealed to the Seventh Circuit Court of Appeals.

Source: 8 F.3d 1217 (7th Cir. 1993)

Cummings, Circuit Judge

Because summary judgment was granted to the defendants, the facts alleged by Denny's and any inferences therefrom must be construed in its favor. Summary judgment will be denied if a reasonable jury could return a verdict for the plaintiff.

A successful claim under Section 1 of the Sherman Act requires proof of three elements: (1) a contract, combination, or conspiracy; (2) a resultant unreasonable restraint of trade in the relevant market; and (3) an accompanying injury. The district court noted that [for purposes of a ruling on their summary judgment motions] defendants do not dispute the first and third elements of proof. Hence the parties' only argument is whether Denny's has made a sufficient showing of the second element, unreasonable restraint of trade, to withstand defendants' motions for summary judgment.

There are two standards for evaluating whether an alleged restraint of trade is unreasonable: the rule of reason and the per se rule. The nature of the restraint determines which rule will be applied. Because the restraint alleged by Denny's constitutes a horizontal price-fixing conspiracy, it is per se an unreasonable restraint of trade [under a long line of Supreme Court decisions]. The conspiracy in this case was horizontal because it ... consisted of Denny's competitors and their association. That the conspiracy was joined by the operators of the ... boat shows does not transform it into a vertical agreement.

Likewise, the conspiracy was to fix prices. Price-fixing agreements need not include "explicit agreement on prices to be charged or that one party have the right to be consulted about the other's prices." *Palmer v. BRG of Georgia, Inc.* (1990). "Under the Sherman Act a combination formed for the purpose and with the effect of raising, depressing, fixing, pegging, or stabilizing the price of a commodity in interstate or foreign commerce is illegal per se." *United States v. Socony Vacuum-Oil Co.* (1940). Concerted action by dealers to protect themselves from price competition by discounters constitutes horizontal price-fixing. Hence the actions of the Dealer Defendants and CIMDA, joined by the Renfro Defendants, to prevent Denny's from participating in the boat shows constitutes a horizontal price-fixing conspiracy notwithstanding the apparent lack of an explicit agreement to set prices.

So far, the position of this court is similar to that of the court below. Nevertheless, having essentially found that Denny's had adduced sufficient evidence of a horizontal price-fixing conspiracy to withstand a motion for summary judgment, the court below refused to apply the per se rule that would allow it to conclude that there had been an unreasonable restraint of trade in the relevant market. Instead, before it would apply the per se rule the court required Denny's to demonstrate a substantial potential for impact on competition in the central Indiana market as a whole. Such an exception to the per se rule against price-fixing is unwarranted by cited precedent ... [and] would effectively require plaintiffs to make a rule of reason demonstration in order to invoke the per se rule! [In cases governed by the rule of reason], both parties are likely to present extensive economic analysis of the relevant market. It is in part to avoid such excessive costs of litigation that the per se rule is applied in cases where the anti-competitive effect of certain practices may be presumed.

As far back as 1940, it has been clear that horizontal price-fixing is illegal per se without requiring a showing of actual or likely impact on a market. *See Socony-Vacuum Oil.* This is because joint action by competitors to suppress price-cutting has the requisite "substantial potential for impact on competition" to warrant per se treatment. *Federal Trade Commission v. Superior Court Trial Lawyers Association* (1990). The district court would require Denny's to demonstrate a particular potential for impact on the market, when one of the purposes of the per se rule is that in cases like this such a potential is so well-established as not to require individualized showings. The pernicious effects are conclusively presumed.

Since Denny's presented enough evidence for a court and jury to conclude that the defendants engaged in [per se behavior consisting of] a horizontal conspiracy to suppress price competition at boat shows, ... the district court's grant of summary judgment to the defendants [was erroneous].

Summary judgment for defendants reversed in favor of Denny's; case remanded for trial.

Vertical Price-Fixing

Attempts by manufacturers to control the resale price of their products may also fall within the scope of section 1. This behavior, called **vertical price-fixing** or *resale price maintenance*, has long been held to be per se illegal. Manufacturers may lawfully state suggested retail price for their products, because such an action is purely unilateral in and does not involve the concerted action necessary for a violation of section ·

illegality is present, however, whenever there is a manufacturer-dealer *agreement* (express or implied) obligating the dealer to resell at a price dictated by the manufacturer. The latter scenario involves prohibited *concerted action*.

Consignment Sales

The section 1 emphasis on concerted action provides the basis for two indirect methods that some manufacturers may lawfully be able to use to control resale prices: *consignment sales* and *unilateral refusals to deal*. Consignments are agreements in which an owner of goods (the consignor) delivers them to another who is to act as the owner's agent in selling them (the consignee). Because the consignee is effectively the consignor's agent in selling the goods, and because the owners of goods generally have the right to determine the price at which their goods are sold, an early Supreme Court decision established that consignment sales were not covered by Section 1.[10]

More recent cases, however, have cast some doubt on the legality of resale price maintenance achieved by consignment dealing.[11] Consignment selling systems whose primary purpose is resale price maintenance may be held unlawful if they result in restraining price competition among a large number of consignees who would otherwise be in competition with one another. This is especially likely to be true in cases where the consignor has sufficient economic power over his consignees to permit him to refuse to deal with them on any basis other than a consignment. Finally, to have any hope of avoiding liability, the arrangement in question must be a true consignment. The consignor must retain title to the goods and bear the risk of loss of the goods while they are in the consignee's hands. In addition, the consignee must have the right to return unsold goods.

Unilateral Refusals to Deal

In *United States v. Colgate & Co.*,[12] the Supreme Court held that a manufacturer could *unilaterally refuse to deal* with dealers who failed to follow its suggested resale prices. The rationale underlying this holding was that a single firm may deal or not deal with whomever it chooses without violating section 1, because unilateral action is not the concerted action prohibited by the statute. Subsequent cases, however, have narrowly construed the "*Colgate* doctrine." Manufacturers probably will be held to have violated section 1 if they enlist the aid of dealers who are not price-cutting to help enforce their (the manufacturers') pricing policies, or if they engage in other joint action to further those policies.

Future of Per Se Illegality

Recent events have cast doubt on the long-term future of the rule of per se illegality for all resale price maintenance agreements. Chicago School theorists argue that many of the same reasons that led the Supreme Court to extend rule of reason treatment to vertically imposed *n*price restraints on distribution (see the *Sylvania* case, set forth later in this chapter) are ally applicable to vertical pricefixing agreements. In particular, these critics argue that cal restrictions limiting the maximum price at which a dealer can resell may prevent s with dominant market positions from exploiting consumers through price-gouging. *lantic Richfield* case, which follows, contains hints that the Supreme Court may be to reconsider the per se rule for vertically imposed maximum price restraints.

Atlantic Richfield Co. v. USA Petroleum Co.

Atlantic Richfield (ARCO) is an integrated oil company that sells gasoline to consumers both directly through its own stations and indirectly through ARCO-brand dealers. USA is an independent retail marketer of gasoline which, like other independents, buys gasoline from major petroleum companies for resale under its own brand name. USA competes directly with ARCO dealers at the retail level. Its outlets typically are low-overhead, high-volume "discount" stations that charge less than stations selling equivalent quality gasoline under major brand names.

In early 1982, ARCO adopted a new marketing strategy in order to compete more effectively with independents such as USA. ARCO encouraged its dealers to match the retail gasoline prices offered by independents in various ways, making available to its dealers and distributors short-term discounts and reducing its dealers' costs by, for example, eliminating credit card sales. ARCO's strategy increased its sales and market share. When USA's sales dropped, it sued ARCO, charging that ARCO and its dealers were engaged in a per se illegal vertical price-fixing scheme.

The district court granted ARCO a summary judgment, holding that USA had not shown an antitrust injury resulting from ARCO's actions. When the Ninth Circuit Court of Appeals reversed, ARCO appealed.

Source: 495 U.S. 328 (U.S. Sup. Ct. 1990)

Brennan, Justice

A private plaintiff may not recover damages under section 4 of the Clayton Act merely by showing injury causally linked to an illegal presence in the market. Instead, a plaintiff must prove the existence of *antitrust* injury, injury of the type the antitrust laws were intended to prevent that flows from that which makes defendants' acts unlawful. Injury, although causally related to an antitrust violation, nevertheless will not qualify as "antitrust injury" unless it is attributable to an anticompetitive aspect of the practice under scrutiny, since it is inimical to the antitrust laws to award damages for losses stemming from continued competition.

In *Albrecht v. Herald Co.* (1968) we found that a vertical, maximum price-fixing scheme was unlawful per se under section 1 of the Sherman Act. We assume, *arguendo*, that *Albrecht* correctly held that vertical, maximum price-fixing is subject to the *per se* rule.

In holding such a vertical agreement illegal, we analyzed the manner in which it might restrain competition by dealers. First, we noted that such a scheme, by substituting the perhaps erroneous judgment of a seller for the forces of the competitive market, may severely intrude upon the ability of buyers to compete and survive in that market. We further explained that maximum prices may be fixed too low for the dealer to furnish services essential to the value which goods have for the consumer or to furnish services and conveniences which consumers desire and for which they are willing to pay. By limiting the ability of small dealers to engage in nonprice competition, a maximum price-fixing agreement might channel distribution through a few large or specifically advantaged dealers. Finally, we observed that if the actual price charged under a maximum price scheme is nearly always the fixed maximum price, which is increasingly likely as the maximum price approaches the actual cost of the dealer, the scheme tends to acquire all the attributes of an arrangement fixing minimum prices.

USA alleges that it has suffered losses as a result of competition with firms following a vertical, maximum price-fixing agreement. But in *Albrecht* we held such an agreement *per se* unlawful because of its potential effects on dealers and consumers, not because of its effect on *competitors*. USA's asserted injury does not resemble any of the potential dangers described in *Albrecht*. For example, if a vertical agreement fixes maximum prices too low for the dealer to furnish services desired by consumers, or in such a way as to channel business to large distributors, then a firm dealing in a competing brand would not be harmed. USA was *benefited* rather than harmed if ARCO's pricing policies restricted ARCO sales to a few large dealers or prevented ARCO's dealers from offering services desired by consumers such as credit card sales. Even if the maximum price agreement ultimately had acquired all of the attributes of a minimum price-fixing scheme, USA still would not have suffered antitrust injury because higher ARCO prices would have worked to USA's advantage.

USA argues that even if it was not harmed by any of the anticompetitive effects identified in *Albrecht*, it nonetheless suffered antitrust injury because of the low prices produced by the vertical restraint. We disagree. When a firm, or even a group of firms adhering to a vertical agreement, lowers prices but maintains them above predatory levels, the business lost by rivals cannot be viewed as an "anticompetitive" consequence of the claimed violation. A firm complaining about the harm it suffers from nonpredatory price competition "is really claiming that it [is] unable to raise prices." Blair & Harrison, Rethinking Antitrust Injury, 42 Vand. L. Rev. 1539, 1554(1989). This is not *antitrust* injury; indeed, cutting prices in order to increase business often is the very essence of competition. The antitrust laws were enacted for the protection of *competition*, not *competitors*. To hold that the antitrust laws protect competitors from the loss of profits due to nonpredatory price competition would, in effect, render illegal any decision by a firm to cut prices in order to increase market share.

We also reject USA's suggestion that no antitrust injury need be shown where a *per se* violation is involved. The *per se* rule is a method of determining whether section 1 of the Sherman Act has been violated, but it does not indicate whether a private plaintiff has suffered antitrust injury and thus whether he may recover damages under section 4 of the Clayton Act. *Per se* and rule-of-reason analysis are but two methods of determining whether a restraint is "unreasonable," i.e., whether its anticompetitive effects outweigh its procompetitive effects. The *per se* rule is a presumption of unreasonableness based on business certainty and litigation efficiency. It represents a long-standing judgment that the prohibited practices by their nature have a substantial potential for impact on competition.

The purpose of the antitrust injury requirement is different. It ensures that the harm claimed by the plaintiff corresponds to the rationale for finding a violation in the first place, and it prevents losses that stem from competition from supporting suits by private plaintiffs for either damages or equitable relief. Actions *per se* unlawful under the antitrust laws may nonetheless have *some* procompetitive effects, and private parties might suffer losses therefrom.

When a manufacturer provides a dealer an exclusive area within which to distribute a product, the manufacturer's decision to fix a maximum resale price may actually protect consumers against exploitation by the dealer acting as a local monopolist. The manufacturer acts not out of altruism, of course, but out of a desire to increase its own sales—whereas the dealer's incentive, like that of any monopolist, is to reduce output and increase price. Vertical, maximum pricefixing thus may have procompetitive interbrand effects even if it is *per se* illegal because of its potential effects on dealers and consumers. The procompetitive potential of a vertical maximum price restraint is more evident now than it was when *Albrecht* was decided, because exclusive territorial arrangements and other nonprice restrictions were unlawful *per se* in 1968. These agreements are currently subject only to rule-of-reason scrutiny, making monopolistic behavior by dealers more likely.

Insofar as the *per se* rule permits the prohibition of efficient practices in the name of simplicity, the need for the antitrust injury requirement is underscored. "[P]rocompetitive or efficiency-enhancing aspects of practices that nominally violate the antitrust laws may cause serious harm to individuals, but this kind of harm is the essence of competition and should play no role in the definition of antitrust damages." Page, The Scope of Liability for Antitrust Violations, 37 Stan. L. Rev. 1445, 1460 (1985). We decline to dilute the antitrust injury requirement here because we find that there is no need to encourage private enforcement by competitors of the rule against vertical, maximum price-fixing. If such a scheme causes the anticompetitive consequences detailed in *Albrecht*, consumers and the manufacturer's own dealers may bring suit.

Judgment reversed in favor of ARCO.

Horizontal Divisions of Markets

It has traditionally been said that **horizontal division of markets** agreements—those agreements among competing firms to divide up the available market by assigning one another certain exclusive territories or certain customers—are illegal per se. Such agreements plainly represent agreements not to compete. They result in each firm being isolated from competition in the affected market.

More than 20 years ago, in *United States v. Topco Associates, Inc.*,[13] the Supreme Court reaffirmed this longstanding principle by striking down a horizontal division of markets agreement among members of a cooperative association of local and regional supermarket chains. The *Topco* decision was widely criticized, however, on the ground that its per se approach ignored an arguably important point—that the defendants' joint activities in promoting Topco brand products were aimed at enabling them to compete more effectively with national supermarket chains. Critics argued that when such horizontal restraints were ancillary to *procompetitive* behavior, they should be judged under the rule of reason.

Naked Restraints and Ancillary Restraints

Such criticism evidently has had an impact. Several recent decisions by lower federal courts have distinguished between "naked" horizontal restraints (those having no other purpose or effect except restraining competition) and "ancillary" horizontal restraints (those constituting a necessary part of a larger joint undertaking serving procompetitive ends).[14] Although these courts continue to apply the per se rule to naked horizontal restraints, they give rule-of-reason treatment to ancillary restraints. In determining whether ancillary restraints are lawful under the rule of reason, courts weigh the harm to competition resulting from such restraints against the alleged offsetting benefits to competition. One factor likely to be of substantial importance in this weighing process is the market strength of the defendants. The idea here is that if an agreement restrains competition among firms lacking market power because they face strong competition from other firms not subject to the agreement, consumers are unlikely to be harmed. This is because the existence of competition limits the ability of the agreeing firms to exploit their agreement by raising prices.

Whether the Supreme Court ultimately will endorse such departures from *Topco* remains to be seen. However, the Court's post-*Topco* tendency to discard per se rules in favor of a rule of reason approach in other areas suggests that *Topco*'s critics may ultimately prevail with their arguments.

Vertical Restraints on Distribution

Vertical restraints on distribution (or *vertical nonprice restraints*) also fall within the scope of the Sherman Act. A manufacturer has always had the power to *unilaterally* assign exclusive territories to its dealers or to limit the dealerships it grants in a particular geographic area. However, manufacturers may run afoul of section 1 by causing dealers to *agree* not to sell outside their dealership territories or by placing other restrictions on their dealers' right to resell their products.

In *United States v. Arnold, Schwinn & Co.*,[15] a 1967 decision, the Supreme Court held that vertical restraints on distribution were per se illegal when applied to goods that the manufacturer had sold to its dealers (consignment sales being treated under the rule of reason). A decade later, however, the Court changed course. In the *Sylvania* case, which follows shortly, the Court abandoned the per se rule in favor of a rule of reason approach to most vertical restraints on distribution. The Court accepted many Chicago School arguments concerning the potential *economic efficiencies* that could result from vertical restraints on distribution. Most notably, such restraints were alleged to offer a chance for increased *interbrand* competition among the product lines of competing manufacturers at the admitted cost of restraining *intrabrand* competition among dealers in a particular manufacturer's product.

Subsequent decisions on the legality of vertical restraints on distribution have emphasized the importance of the market share of the manufacturer imposing the restraints. Restraints imposed by manufacturers with large market shares are more likely to be found unlawful under the rule of reason because the resultant harm to intrabrand competition is unlikely to be offset by significant positive effects on interbrand competition.

Continental T.V., Inc. v. GTE Sylvania, Inc.

In the early 1950s, Sylvania's share of the national TV market had declined to about 1 percent. In an attempt to remedy this situation, Sylvania phased out all wholesalers and limited the retail franchises that it granted for a given area. Sylvania also required that each franchisee sell Sylvania products only from the sales location described in its franchise. This strategy apparently contributed to increasing sales by Sylvania, but it led to friction with some dealers when Sylvania shuffled sales location areas and refused to grant requests for expansion of some sales areas.

Continental, a Sylvania dealer, became unhappy when Sylvania franchised another dealer in part of Continental's market and then refused Continental's request for permission to expand into another market area. As the dispute developed, Sylvania reduced Continental's credit line.

In response, Continental withheld all payments owed to the finance company that handled all credit arrangements between Sylvania and its retailers. Shortly thereafter, Sylvania terminated Continental's franchise and the finance company filed suit to recover payments due on merchandise purchased by Continental. Continental cross-claimed against Sylvania, arguing that Sylvania's location restriction was a per se violation of section 1 of the Sherman Act. The jury agreed and awarded Continental $1.7 million in treble damages. The Ninth Circuit Court of Appeals reversed, holding that Sylvania's location restriction should be judged under the rule of reason because it presented less of a threat to competition than did the restrictions held per se illegal in the *Schwinn* case. Continental appealed.

Source: 433 U.S. 36 (U.S. Sup. Ct. 1977)

Powell, Justice

Vertical restrictions reduce intrabrand competition by limiting the number of sellers of a particular product competing for the business of a given group of buyers. Location restrictions have this effect because of practical constraints on the effective marketing area of retail outlets. Although intrabrand competition may be reduced, the ability of retailers to exploit the resulting market may be limited both by the ability of consumers to travel to other franchised locations and, perhaps more importantly, to purchase the competing products of other manufacturers. None of these key variables, however, is affected by the form of the transaction by which a manufacturer conveys his products to the retailers.

Vertical restrictions promote interbrand competition by allowing the manufacturer to achieve certain efficiencies in the distribution of his products. New manufacturers and manufacturers entering new markets can use the restrictions in order to induce competent and aggressive retailers to make the kind of investment of capital and labor that is often required in the distribution of products unknown to the consumer. Established manufacturers can use them to induce retailers to engage in promotional activities or to provide service and repair facilities necessary to the efficient marketing of their products. Service and repair are vital for many products, such as automobiles and major household appliances. The availability and quality of such services affect a manufacturer's goodwill and the competitiveness of his product. Because of market imperfections such as the so-called free rider effect, these services might not be provided by retailers in a purely competitive situation, despite the fact that each retailer's benefit would be greater if all provided services than if none did.

Economists also have argued that manufacturers have an economic interest in maintaining as much intrabrand competition as is consistent with the efficient distribution of their products. Although the view that the manufacturer's interest necessarily corresponds with that of the public is not universally shared, even the leading critic of vertical restrictions concedes that *Schwinn*'s distinction between sale and nonsale transactions is essentially unrelated to any relevant economic impact.

We revert to the standard articulated in *Northern Pac. R. Co.* for determining whether vertical restrictions must be "conclusively presumed to be unreasonable and therefore illegal without elaborate inquiry as to the precise harm they have caused or the business excuse for their use." Such restrictions, in varying forms, are widely used in our free market economy. There is substantial scholarly and judicial authority supporting their economic utility. There is relatively no showing in this case, either generally or with respect to Sylvania's agreements, that vertical restrictions have or are likely to have a "pernicious effect on competition" or that they "lack any redeeming virtue." Accordingly, the *per se* rule stated in *Schwinn* must be overruled. In so holding we do not foreclose the possibility that particular applications of vertical restrictions might justify *per se* prohibition under *Northern Pac. R. Co.* But we do make clear that departure from the rule of reason standard must be based upon demonstrable economic effect rather than—as in *Schwinn*—upon formalistic line drawing.
Judgment for Sylvania affirmed.

Group Boycotts and Concerted Refusals to Deal

Under the *Colgate* doctrine, a single firm may lawfully refuse to deal with certain firms. The same is not true, however, of *agreements* by two or more business entities to refuse to deal with others, to deal with others only on certain terms and conditions, or to coerce suppliers or customers not to deal with one of their competitors. Such agreements are *joint* restraints on trade. Historically, they have been per se unlawful under section 1. For example, when a trade association of garment manufacturers agreed not to sell to retailers that sold clothing or fabrics with designs pirated from legitimate manufacturers, the agreement was held to be a per se violation of the Sherman Act.[16]

Vertical Boycotts

Recent antitrust developments, however, indicate that not all concerted refusals to deal will receive per se analysis. If a manufacturer terminated a distributor in response to complaints from other distributors that the terminated distributor was selling to customers outside its prescribed sales territory, the manufacturer will be held to have violated section 1 only if the termination resulted in a significant harm to competition. This result follows logically from the *Sylvania* decision. If vertical restraints on distribution are judged under the rule of reason (as established in *Sylvania*), the same standard should apply to a vertical boycott designed to enforce such restraints.

Even distributors claiming to have been terminated as part of a per se illegal vertical price-fixing scheme have found recovery increasingly difficult to obtain in recent years. In *Monsanto v. Spray-Rite Service Corp.*,[17] a manufacturer had terminated a discounting distributor after receiving complaints from its other distributors. The Supreme Court held that these facts would not trigger per se liability for vertical price-fixing in the absence of additional evidence tending to exclude the possibility that the manufacturer and the nonterminated distributors acted independently. More recently, in *Business Electronics Corp. v. Sharp Electronics Corp.*,[18] the Court held that even proof of a conspiracy between a manufacturer and nonterminated distributors to terminate a price-cutter would not trigger per se liability unless it was accompanied by proof that the manufacturer and nonterminated dealers were also engaged in a vertical price-fixing conspiracy. *Monsanto* and *Sharp* have generated a substantial controversy, as well as proposals for legislation overruling them and codifying the per se rule for vertical price-fixing. As of the time this book went to press, no such legislation had been enacted.

Horizontal Boycotts

It also appears that the Supreme Court is willing to relax the per se rule for some *horizontal* boycotts. For instance, in *Northwest Wholesale Stationers, Inc. v. Pacific Stationery & Printing Co.*, members of an office supply retailers' purchasing cooperative had expelled a member retailer that engaged in some wholesale operations in addition to retail activities. The Court held that rule of reason treatment should be extended to the alleged boycott at issue, but declined to eliminate the per se rule for all horizontal boycotts. The Court has offered only general guidance for determining which horizontal boycotts trigger rule of reason analysis and which ones amount to per se violations. The appropriate legal treatment in a given case is therefore difficult to predict. Future decisions may resolve the uncertainty.

Tying Agreements

Tying agreements occur when a seller refuses to sell a buyer a certain product (the *tying product*) unless the buyer also agrees to purchase a different product (the *tied product*) from the seller. For example, a fertilizer manufacturer refuses to sell its dealers fertilizer (the tying product) unless they also agree to buy its line of pesticides (the tied product). The potential anticompetitive effect of a tying agreement is that the seller's competitors in the sale of the tied product may be foreclosed from competing with the seller for sales to customers that have entered into tying agreements with the seller. To the extent that tying agreements are coercively imposed, they also deprive buyers of the freedom to make independent decisions concerning their purchases of the tied product. Tying agreements may be challenged under both section 1 of the Sherman Act and section 3 of the Clayton Act.[19]

Elements of Prohibited Tying Agreements

Tying agreements are often said to be per se illegal under section 1. However, because a tying agreement must meet certain criteria before it is subjected to per se analysis, and because evidence of certain justifications is sometimes considered in tying cases, the rule against tying agreements is at best a "soft" per se rule. Before a challenged tying agreement is held to violate section 1, these must be demonstrated: (1) the agreement involves *two* separate and distinct items rather than integrated components of a larger product, service, or system of doing business; (2) the tying product cannot be purchased unless the tied product is also purchased; (3) the seller has sufficient economic power in the market for the tying product (such as a patent or a large market share) to appreciably restrain competition in the tied product market; and (4) a "not insubstantial" amount of commerce in the tied product is affected by the seller's tying agreements.[20] The following *Eastman Kodak* case contains a discussion of the elements of prohibited tying arrangements, with a focus on the third element: *market power as to the tying product.*

Eastman Kodak Co. v. Image Technical Services, Inc.

Eastman Kodak Co. (Kodak) manufactures and sells photocopiers and micrographic equipment. In addition, Kodak provides customers with service and replacement parts for its equipment. Kodak produces some of the parts itself. The other parts are made to order for Kodak by independent original equipment manufacturers (OEMs). Rather than selling a complete system of original equipment, lifetime parts, and lifetime service for a single price, Kodak furnishes service after an initial warranty period either through annual service contracts or on a per-call basis. Kodak provides between 80 and 95 percent of the service for Kodak machines.

In the early 1980s, independent service organizations (ISOs) began repairing and servicing Kodak equipment, as well as selling parts for it. ISOs kept an inventory of parts, purchased either from Kodak or from other sources (primarily OEMs). In 1985, Kodak adopted policies designed to limit ISOs' access to parts and to make it more difficult for ISOs to compete with Kodak in servicing Kodak equipment. Kodak began selling replacement parts only to Kodak equipment buyers who used Kodak service or repaired their own machines (i.e., buyers who

did not use ISOs for service). In addition, Kodak sought to limit ISO access to other sources of Kodak parts by working out agreements with OEMs that they would sell parts for Kodak equipment to no one other than Kodak, and by pressuring Kodak equipment owners and independent parts distributors not to sell Kodak parts to ISOs.

Eighteen ISOs sued Kodak, claiming that these policies amounted to (1) unlawful tying of the sale of service for Kodak machines to the sale of parts (in violation of Sherman Act Section 1), and (2) monopolization or attempted monopolization of the sale of service for Kodak machines (in violation of Sherman Act Section 2). The U.S. District Court granted summary judgment in favor of Kodak on each of these claims. The Ninth Circuit Court of Appeals reversed, holding that summary judgment was inappropriate because there were genuine issues of material fact regarding the ISOs' claims. The Supreme Court granted Kodak's petition for a writ of certiorari.

Source: 112 S. Ct. 2072 (U.S. Sup. Ct. 1992)

Blackmun, Justice

Because this case comes to us on Kodak's motion for summary judgment, the evidence of the ISOs is to be believed, and all justifiable inferences are to be drawn in the ISOs' favor [for purposes of determining whether Kodak is entitled to summary judgment or whether a trial is instead necessary].

A tying arrangement is "an agreement by a party to sell one product but only on the condition that the buyer also purchases a different (or tied) product, or at least agrees that he will not purchase that product from any other supplier." *Northern Pacific Railway Co. v. United States* (1958). Such an arrangement violates Section 1 of the Sherman Act if the seller has "appreciable economic power" in the tying product market and if the arrangement affects a substantial volume of commerce in the tied market. *Fortner Enterprises, Inc. v.*

U.S. Steel Corp. (1969). Kodak did not dispute that its arrangement affects a substantial volume of interstate commerce. It, however, did challenge whether its activities constituted a "tying arrangement" and whether Kodak exercised "appreciable economic power" in the tying market.

For the ISOs to defeat [Kodak's] motion for summary judgment, ... a reasonable trier of fact must be able to find, first, that service and parts are two distinct products, and second, that Kodak has tied the sale of the two products. For service and parts to be considered two distinct products, there must be sufficient consumer demand so that it is efficient for a firm to provide service separately from parts. Evidence in the record indicates that service and parts have been sold separately in the past and still are sold separately to self-service equipment owners. Kodak insists that because there is no demand for parts separate from service, there cannot be separate markets for service and parts. By that logic, we would be forced to conclude that there can never be separate markets, for example, for cameras and film, computers and software, or automobiles and tires. That is an assumption we are unwilling to make.

Kodak's assertion also appears to be incorrect as a factual matter. At least some consumers would purchase service without parts, because some service does not require parts, and some consumers, those who self-service for example, would purchase parts without service. Enough doubt is cast on Kodak's claim of a unified market that it should be resolved by the trier of fact. [T]he ISOs have [also] presented sufficient evidence of a tie between service and parts. The record indicates that Kodak would sell parts to third parties only if they agreed not to buy service from ISOs.

[We now] consider the other necessary feature of an illegal tying arrangement: appreciable economic power in the tying market. Market power is the power "to force a purchaser to do something that he would not do in a competitive market." *Jefferson Parish Hospital Dist. No. 2 v. Hyde* (1984). The existence of such power ordinarily is inferred from the seller's possession of a predominant share of the market.

The ISOs contend that Kodak has more than sufficient power in the parts market to force unwanted purchases of the tied market, service. The ISOs [assert or] provide evidence that certain parts are available exclusively through Kodak, ... that Kodak has control over the availability of parts it does not manufacture, [and that Kodak has both] prohibited independent manufacturers from selling Kodak parts to ISOs [and] pressured Kodak equipment owners and independent parts distributors to deny ISOs the purchase of Kodak parts. The ISOs also allege that Kodak's control over the parts market has excluded service competition, boosted service prices, and forced unwilling consumption of Kodak service. [They] offer evidence that consumers have switched to Kodak service even though they preferred ISO service, that Kodak service was of higher price and lower quality than the preferred ISO service, and that ISOs were driven out of business by Kodak's policies. Under our prior precedents, this evidence would be sufficient to entitle the ISOs to a trial on their claim of market power.

Kodak counters that even if it concedes monopoly *share* of the relevant parts market, it cannot actually exercise the necessary market *power* for a Sherman Act violation. This is so, according to Kodak, because competition exists in the equipment market. Kodak argues that it could not have the ability to raise prices of service and parts above the level that would be charged in a competitive market because any increase in profits from a higher price in the aftermarkets at least would be offset by a corresponding loss in profits from lower equipment sales as consumers began purchasing equipment with more attractive service costs. Kodak does not present any actual data on the equipment, service, or parts markets. Instead, it urges the adoption of a substantive legal rule that equipment competition precludes any finding of monopoly power in derivative aftermarkets. Legal presumptions that rest on formalistic distinctions rather than actual market realities are generally disfavored in antitrust law. This Court has preferred to resolve antitrust claims on a case-by-case basis, focusing on the particular facts disclosed by the record ... and the economic reality of the market at issue.

Even if Kodak could not raise the price of service and parts one cent without losing equipment sales, that fact would not disprove market power in the aftermarkets. Kodak's [theory] is based on the false dichotomy that there are only two prices that can be charged [for parts and service]—a competitive price or a ruinous one. But there could easily be a middle, optimum price at which the increased revenues from the high-priced sales of service and parts would more than compensate for the lower revenues from lost equipment sales. [Contrary to the assertion in Kodak's brief], there is no immutable physical law—no "basic economic reality"—insisting that competition in the equipment market cannot coexist with market power in the aftermarkets.

[Kodak also overlooks] the existence of significant information and switching costs. These costs could create a less responsive connection between service and parts prices and equipment sales. For the service-market price to affect equipment demand, consumers must inform themselves of the total cost of the "package"—equipment, service, and parts—at the time of purchase; that is, consumers must engage in accurate lifecycle pricing. The necessary information would include data on price, quality, and availability of parts needed to operate, upgrade, or enhance the initial equipment, as well as service and repair costs, including estimates of breakdown frequency, nature of repairs, price of service and parts, length of "down-time," and losses incurred from down-time. Much of this information is difficult—some of it impossible—to acquire at the time of purchase.

Moreover, even if consumers were capable of acquiring and processing the complex body of information, they may choose not to do so. Acquiring the information is expensive. [Consumers] may not find it cost-efficient to compile the information. [It therefore] makes little sense to assume, in the absence of any evidentiary support, that equipment-purchasing decisions are based on an accurate assessment of the total cost of equipment, service, and parts over the lifetime of the machine.

A second factor undermining Kodak's claim that supracompetitive prices in the service market lead to ruinous losses in equipment sales is the cost to current owners of switching to a different product. If the cost of switching is high, consumers who already have purchased the equipment, and are thus "locked-in," will tolerate some level of service price increases before changing equipment brands. Under this scenario, a seller profitably could maintain supracompetitive prices in the aftermarket if the switching costs were high relative to the increase in service prices, and the number of locked in customers were high relative to the number of new purchasers. Respondents have offered evidence that the heavy initial outlay for Kodak equipment, combined with the required support material that works only with Kodak equipment, makes switching costs very high for existing Kodak customers.

We conclude, then, that Kodak has failed to demonstrate that the ISOs' inference of market power in the service and parts markets is unreasonable. It is clearly reasonable to infer that Kodak has market power to raise prices and drive out competition in the aftermarkets, since the ISOs offer direct evidence that Kodak did so. It is also plausible ... to infer that Kodak chose to gain immediate profits by exerting that market power where locked-in customers [and] high information costs ... limited and perhaps eliminated any long-term loss.

In this case, ... the balance tips against [granting Kodak's request for] summary judgment.

Denial of Kodak's motion for summary judgment affirmed in favor of the ISOs; case remanded for further proceedings.

Note: In another portion of the opinion not set forth here, the Court held that Kodak was not entitled to summary judgment on the ISOs' Sherman Act section 2 claim.

Possible Justifications for Tying Agreements

The first two of the above elements have been particularly significant in recent cases involving alleged tying agreements among franchisers and their franchised dealers. For example, a suit by a McDonald's franchisee alleged that McDonald's violated section 1 by requiring franchisees to lease their stores from McDonald's as a condition of acquiring a McDonald's franchise. The Eighth Circuit Court of Appeals rejected the franchisee's claim, however, holding that no tying agreement was involved. Instead, the franchise and the lease were integral components of a well-thought-out system of doing business.[21]

The lower federal courts have recognized two other possible justifications for tying agreements. First, tying arrangements that are instrumental in launching a new competitor with an otherwise uncertain future may be lawful until the new business has established itself in the marketplace. The logic of this "new business" exception is obvious: If a tying agreement enables a fledgling firm to become a viable competitor, the agreement's net effect on competition is positive. Second, some courts have recognized that tying agreements sometimes may be necessary to protect the reputation of the seller's product line. For example, one of the seller's products functions properly only if used in conjunction with another of its products. To qualify for this exception, however, the seller must convince the court that a tying arrangement is the only viable means to protect its goodwill.

Chicago School Views on Tying Agreements

Chicago School thinkers have long criticized the traditional judicial approach to tying agreements because they do not believe that most tie-ins result in any significant economic harm. They argue that sellers who try to impose a tie-in in competitive markets gain no increased profits as a result. This is so because instead of participating in a tying agreement, buyers may turn to substitutes for the tying product or may purchase the tying product from competing sellers. The net effect of a tie-in may therefore be that any increase in the seller's sales in the tied product is offset by a loss in sales of the tying product. Only when the seller has substantial power in the tying product market is there potential that a tie-in may be used to increase the seller's power in the tied product market. However, even when the seller has such market power in the tying product, Chicago School thinkers argue that no harm to competition is likely to result if the seller faces strong competition in the tied product market. For these and other reasons, Chicago School thinkers favor a rule of reason approach to all tying agreements. A majority of the Supreme Court has yet to accept these arguments. Some Justices, however, appear willing to do so. If other members of the Court are similarly persuaded in the future, a substantial change in the legal criteria applied to tying agreements will be the likely result.

Reciprocal Dealing Agreements

Under a **reciprocal dealing agreement**, a buyer attempts to exploit its purchasing power by conditioning its purchases from suppliers on reciprocal purchases of some product or service offered for sale by the buyer. For example, an oil company with a chain of wholly owned gas stations refuses to purchase the tires it sells in those stations unless the tire manufacturer (the would-be supplier of the tires) agrees to purchase, from the oil company, the petrochemicals used in the tire manufacturing process. Reciprocal dealing agreements are quite similar in motivation and effect to tying agreements. Courts therefore tend to treat them in a similar fashion. In seeking to impose the reciprocal dealing agreement on the tire manufacturer, the oil company is attempting to gain a competitive advantage over its competitors in the petrochemical market. A court judging the legality of such an agreement would examine the oil company's economic power as a purchaser of tires and the dollar amount of petrochemical sales involved.

Exclusive Dealing Agreements

Exclusive dealing agreements require buyers of a particular product or service to purchase that product or service exclusively from a particular seller. For example, Standard Lawnmower Corporation requires its retail dealers to sell only Standard brand mowers. A common variation of an exclusive dealing agreement is the *requirements contract*, under which the buyer of a particular product agrees to purchase all of its requirements for that product from a particular supplier. For example, a candy manufacturer agrees to buy all of its sugar requirements from one sugar refiner. Exclusive dealing contracts present a threat to competition similar to that involved in tying contracts—they may reduce interbrand competition by foreclosing a seller's competitors from the opportunity to compete for sales to its customers. Unlike tying contracts, however, exclusive dealing agreements may sometimes enhance efficiencies in distribution and stimulate interbrand competition. Exclusive dealing agreements reduce a manufacturer's sales costs and provide dealers with a secure source of supply. They may also encourage dealer efforts to market the manufacturer's products more effectively, because a dealer selling only one product line has a greater stake in the success of that line than does a dealer who sells the products of several competing manufacturers.

Because many exclusive dealing agreements involve commodities, they may also be challenged under section 3 of the Clayton Act. The legal tests applicable to exclusive dealing agreements under both acts are identical.

Joint Ventures by Competitors

A **joint venture** is a combined effort by two or more business entities for a limited purpose such as research. Because joint ventures may yield enhanced efficiencies by integrating the resources of more than one firm, they are commonly judged under the rule of reason. Under this approach, courts tend to ask whether any competitive restraints that are incidental to the venture are necessary to accomplish its lawful objectives and, if so, whether those restraints are offset by the venture's positive effects. Joint ventures whose primary purpose is illegal per se, however, have often been given per se treatment. An example of such a case would be two competing firms that form a joint sales agency and authorize it to fix the price of their products.

National Cooperative Research and Production Act

Antitrust critics have long argued that the threat of antitrust prosecution seriously inhibits the formation of joint research and development ventures, and that American firms are placed at a competitive disadvantage in world markets as a result. Such arguments have enjoyed more acceptance during roughly the past decade, given concerns about the American economy's performance. In 1984, Congress passed the National Cooperative Research Act (NCRA). This act applies to "*joint research and development ventures*" (JRDVs), which are broadly defined to include basic and applied research and joint activities in the licensing of technologies developed by such research. The NCRA requires the application of a reasonableness standard, rather than a per se rule, when a JRDV's legality is determined. It also requires firms contemplating a JRDV to provide the

Department of Justice and the Federal Trade Commission with advance notice of their intent to do so. The NCRA provides that only actual (not treble) damages may be recovered for losses flowing from a JRDV ultimately found to be in violation of section 1. In addition, the NCRA contains a provision allowing the parties to a challenged JRDV to recover attorney's fees from an unsuccessful challenger if the suit is shown to be "frivolous, unreasonable, without foundation, or in bad faith." Congress amended the statute in 1993 to extend its application to joint *production* ventures. In doing so, Congress renamed the statute the National Cooperative Research and Production Act.

Figure 30-1 summarizes the judicial treatment of potentially illegal practices under section 1 of the Sherman Act.

FIGURE 30-1
Potentially illegal practices and their treatment under Sherman Act

	Judicial Treatment	
Potentially Illegal Practice	**Per Se**	**Rule of Reason**
Horizontal price-fixing	*	
Vertical price-fixing	*?	
Horizontal division of markets	*?	*?
Vertical division of markets		*
Horizontal boycotts	*	*
Vertical boycotts	*	*
Tying agreements	*?	*
Reciprocal dealing agreements	*?	*
Exclusive dealing agreements		*
Joint ventures	*	*

Note: an entry with an * in both columns means the facts of the individual case determine the treatment. A ? indicates that future treatment is in question.

Section 2—Monopolization

Introduction

Firms that acquire **monopoly power** in a given market have defeated the antitrust laws' objective of promoting competitive market structures. Monopolists, by definition, have the power to fix prices unilaterally because they have no effective competition. Section 2 of the Sherman Act was designed to prevent the formation of monopoly power. It provides: "Every person who shall monopolize, or attempt to monopolize, or combine or conspire with any other person to monopolize any part of trade or commerce among the several states, or with foreign nations shall be deemed guilty of a felony." Section 2 does not, however, outlaw monopolies. Instead, it outlaws the act of "*monopolizing*." Under section 2 a *single firm* can be guilty of "monopolizing" or "attempting to monopolize" a part of trade or commerce. The proof of joint action required for violations of section 1 is required only when two or more firms are charged with a conspiracy to monopolize under section 2.

Monopolization

Monopolization is "the willful acquisition or maintenance of monopoly power in a relevant market as opposed to growth as a consequence of superior product, business acumen, or historical accident."[22] This means that to be guilty of monopolization, a defendant must have possessed not only monopoly power but also an **intent to monopolize**.

Monopoly Power

Monopoly power is usually defined for antitrust purposes as the power to *fix prices* or *exclude competitors* in a given market. Such power is generally inferred from the fact that a firm has captured a predominant share of the relevant market. Although the exact percentage share necessary to support an inference of monopoly power remains unclear and courts often look at other economic factors (such as the existence in the industry of barriers to the entry of new competitors), market shares in excess of 70 percent have historically justified an inference of monopoly power.

Before a court can determine a defendant's market share, it must first define the **relevant market**. This is a crucial issue in section 2 cases because a broad definition of the relevant market normally results in a smaller market share for the defendant and a resulting reduction in the likelihood that the defendant will be found to possess monopoly power. The two components of a relevant market determination are the relevant **geographic market** and the relevant **product market**.

Economic realities prevailing in the industry determine the relevant geographic market. In which parts of the country can the defendant effectively compete with other firms in the sale of the product in question? To whom may buyers turn for alternative sources of supply? Factors such as transportation costs may also play a critical role in relevant market determinations. Thus, the relevant market for coal may be regional in nature, but the relevant market for transistors may be national in scope.

The relevant product market is composed of those products meeting the *functional interchangeability* test, which identifies the products "reasonably interchangeable by consumers for the same purposes." This test recognizes that a firm's ability to fix the price for its products is limited by the availability of competing products that buyers view as acceptable substitutes. In a famous antitrust case, for example, Du Pont was charged with monopolizing the national market for cellophane because it had a 75 percent share. The Supreme Court concluded, however, that the relevant market was all "flexible wrapping materials," including aluminum foil, waxed paper, and polyethylene. Du Pont's 20 percent share of that product market was far too small to amount to monopoly power.[23]

May a *single brand* of a product or service ever be a relevant market for section 2 purposes? Although most section 2 cases would logically be expected to involve product markets consisting of more than one brand of a given type of product (and perhaps other products that are reasonably interchangeable for the same purposes), the Supreme Court refused to rule, in the *Eastman Kodak* case, that a single brand cannot be a relevant market. (*Eastman Kodak* involved claims under sections 1 and 2 of the Sherman Act. The case's major facts and the section 1 aspect of the Court's opinion were set forth in this chapter's discussion of tying arrangements.) Because *Eastman Kodak* dealt with allegedly anticompetitive practices regarding parts and service for Kodak equipment, the Court observed that "[t]he relevant market for antitrust purposes is determined by the choices available to Kodak equipment owners." The Court concluded that "[b]ecause service and parts for Kodak equipment are not interchangeable with other manufacturers' service and parts, the relevant market from the Kodak-equipment owner's perspective is composed of only those companies that service Kodak machines." According to the Court, "prior cases support the proposition that in some instances one brand of a product can constitute a separate market." Evidence that Kodak controlled nearly 100 percent of the parts market and 80 to 95 percent of the service market for Kodak brand equipment was held to be sufficient evidence of monopoly power for purposes of the Court's ruling that Kodak was not entitled to summary judgment on the plaintiffs' section 2 claim against it.

Intent to Monopolize

Proof of monopoly power standing alone, however, is never sufficient to prove a violation of Section 2. The defendant's **intent to monopolize** must also be shown. Early cases under section 2 required evidence that the defendant either acquired monopoly power by predatory or coercive means that violated antitrust rules (e.g., price-fixing or discriminatory pricing) or abused monopoly power in some way after acquiring it (such as by engaging in price-gouging). Contemporary courts focus on how the defendant acquired monopoly power. If the defendant *intentionally acquired it* or *attempted to maintain it* after acquiring it, the defendant possessed an intent to monopolize. Defendants are not in violation of section 2, however, if their monopoly power resulted from the superiority of their products or business decisions, or from historical accident (e.g., the owner of a professional sports franchise in an area too small to support a competing franchise).

Purposeful acquisition or maintenance of monopoly power may be demonstrated in various ways. A famous monopolization case involved Alcoa, which had a 90 percent market share of the American market for virgin aluminum ingot. Alcoa was found guilty of purposefully maintaining its monopoly power by acquiring every new opportunity relating to the production or marketing of aluminum, thereby excluding potential competitors.[24] As the *Grinnell* case indicates, firms that develop monopoly power by acquiring ownership or control of their competitors are very likely to be held to have demonstrated an intent to monopolize.

United States v. Grinnell Corp

Grinnell manufactured plumbing supplies and fire sprinkler systems. It also owned 76 percent of the stock of ADT, 89 percent of the stock of AFA, and 100 percent of the stock of Holmes. ADT provided both burglary and fire protection services; Holmes provided burglary services alone; AFA supplied only fire protection service. Each offered a central station service under which hazard-detecting devices installed on the protected premises automatically transmitted an electrical signal to a central station. There were other forms of protective services. The record indicated, however, that subscribers to an accredited central station service (i.e., one approved by the insurance underwriters) received reductions in their insurance premiums substantially greater than the reductions received by the users of other protection services. In 1961, ADT, Holmes, and AFA were the three largest central station service companies in terms of revenue, with about 87 percent of the business.

In 1907, Grinnell and the other defendants entered into a series of agreements that allocated the major cities and markets for central station alarm services in the United States. Each defendant agreed not to compete outside the market areas allocated. Over the years, the defendants bought 30 other companies providing burglar or fire alarm services. After Grinnell acquired control of the other defendants, the latter continued in their attempts to acquire central station companies. Offers were made to at least eight companies between 1955 and 1961, including four of the five largest remaining companies in the business. When the present suit was filed, each of those defendants had outstanding an offer to purchase one of the four largest nondefendant companies.

Over the years, ADT reduced its minimum basic rates to meet competition and renewed contracts at substantially increased rates in cities where it had a monopoly of accredited central station service. ADT threatened retaliation against firms that contemplated inaugurating central station service.

The government filed suit against Grinnell under section 2 of the Sherman Act, asking that Grinnell be forced to divest itself of ADT, Holmes, and AFA and that other injunctive relief be granted. The district court ruled in favor of the government. Grinnell appealed.

Source: 384 U.S. 563 (U.S. Sup. Ct. 1966)

Douglas, Justice

The offense of monopolization under Section 2 of the Sherman Act has two elements: (1) the possession of monopoly power in the relevant market and (2) the willful acquisition or maintenance of that power as distinguished from growth or development as a consequence of a superior product, business acumen, or historic accident. This second ingredient presents no major problem here, as what was done in building the empire was done plainly and explicitly for a single purpose. In *United States v. E. I. du Pont de Nemours & Co.*, we defined monopoly power as "the power to control prices or exclude competition." The existence of such power ordinarily may be inferred from the predominant share of the market. In *American Tobacco Co. v. United States*, we said that "over two thirds of the entire domestic field of cigarettes, and over 80 percent of the field of comparable cigarettes" constituted "a substantial monopoly." In *United States v. Aluminum Co. of America*, 90 percent of the market constituted monopoly power. In the present case, 87 percent of the accredited central station service business leaves no doubt that these defendants have monopoly power—power which they did not hesitate to wield—if that business is the relevant market. The only remaining question therefore is, what is the relevant market?

A product may be of such a character that substitute products must also be considered, as customers may turn to them if there is a slight increase in the price of the main product. That is the teaching of the *Du Pont* case, that commodities reasonably interchangeable make up that "part" of trade or commerce which Section 2 protects against monopoly power. The District Court treated the entire accredited central station service business as a single market and it was justified in so doing. Grinnell argues that the different central station services offered are so diverse that they cannot under *Du Pont* be lumped together to make up the relevant market. For example, burglar alarm services are not interchangeable with fire alarm services. It further urges that *Du Pont* requires that protective services other than those of the central station variety be included in the market definition.

We see no barrier to combining in a single market a number of different products or services where that combination reflects commercial realities. There is here a single basic service—the protection of property through use of a central service station—that must be compared with all other forms of property protection. There are, to be sure, substitutes for the accredited central station service. But none of them appears to operate on the same level as the central station service so as to meet the interchangeability test. What Grinnell overlooks is that the high degree of differentiation between central station protection and the other forms means that for many customers, only central station protection will do.

As the District Court found, the relevant market for determining whether the defendants have monopoly power is not the several local areas which the individual stations serve, but the broader national market that reflects the reality of the way in which they built and conduct their business. We have said enough about the great hold that the defendants have on this market. The percentage is so high as to justify the finding of monopoly. And this monopoly was achieved in large part by unlawful and exclusionary practices. The agreements that pre-empted for each company a segment of the market where it was free of competition of the others were one device. Pricing practices that contained competitors were another. The acquisitions by Grinnell of ADT, AFA, and Holmes were still another. Its control of the three other defendants eliminated any possibility of an outbreak of competition that might have occurred when the 1907 agreements terminated. By those acquisitions it perfected the monopoly power to exclude competitors and fix prices.

Judgment for the government affirmed.

Attempted Monopolization

Firms that have not yet attained monopoly power may nonetheless be liable for an **attempt to monopolize** in violation of section 2 if they are dangerously close to acquiring monopoly power and are employing methods likely to result in monopoly power if left unchecked. The *Spectrum Sports* case (which follows shortly) reveals that as part of the required proof of a dangerous probability that monopoly power will be acquired, plaintiffs in attempted monopolization cases must furnish proof of the relevant market—as in monopolization cases. Unlike monopolization cases, however, attempt cases also require proof that the defendant possessed a specific intent to acquire monopoly power through anticompetitive means.

A controversial issue that surfaces in many attempted monopolization cases concerns the role that *predatory pricing* may play in proving an intent to monopolize. The Supreme Court has recently defined predatory pricing as "pricing below an appropriate measure of cost for the purpose of eliminating competitors in the short run and reducing competition in the long run."[25] What constitutes "an appropriate measure of cost" in predatory pricing cases has long been a subject of debate among antitrust scholars. The Supreme Court has declined to resolve this debate definitively. What the Court's recent opinions do tell us is that the Court is likely to take a skeptical view of predatory pricing claims in the future. The Court has described predatory pricing schemes as "rarely tried, and even more rarely successful."[26] As part of this characterization of predatory pricing schemes, the Court indicated that it agrees with those economists who have argued that predatory pricing is often economically irrational because, to be successful, the predator must maintain monopoly power long enough after it has driven its competitors out of business to recoup the profits it lost through predatory pricing. The predator would be able to sustain monopoly power only if high barriers to entry prevented new competitors from being drawn into the market by the supracompetitive prices the predator would have to charge in order to recoup its losses.

Conspiracy to Monopolize

When two or more business entities **conspire to monopolize** a relevant market, section 2 may be violated. This portion of section 2, however, largely overlaps section 1, because it is difficult to conceive of a conspiracy to monopolize that would not also amount to a conspiracy in restraint of trade. The lower federal courts have differed on the elements necessary to prove a conspiracy to monopolize. In addition to requiring proof of the existence of a conspiracy, some courts insist on proof of the relevant market, a specific intent to acquire monopoly power, and overt action in furtherance of the conspiracy. Other courts do not require extensive proof of the relevant market. According to these courts, a violation is established through proof that the defendants conspired to exclude competitors from, or acquire control over prices in, some significant area of commerce. The Supreme Court's *Spectrum Sports* decision, however, would seem to cast doubt on the validity of an approach that deemphasizes the requirement of proof of the relevant market.

Figure 30-2 summarizes the elements of section 2 offenses.

FIGURE 30-2
Elements of section 2 offenses

Offense	Monopoly Power	Intent to Monopolize	Concerted Action
Monopolization	Required	Required	Not required
Attempted monopolization	"Dangerously close"	Specific intent required	Not required
Conspiracy to monopolize	Not required	Specific intent required	Required

---

Spectrum Sports, Inc. v. McQuillan

Sorbothane is a patented elastic polymer whose shock-absorbing characteristics make it useful in a variety of medical, athletic, and equestrian products. BTR, Inc. owns the patent rights to sorbothane. Prior to 1982, a BTR subsidiary, Hamilton-Kent Manufacturing Co. (H-K) produced and distributed sorbothane for BTR. Another BTR subsidiary, Sorbothane, Inc. (SI), was formed in 1982 to replace H-K as the manufacturer of sorbothane and holder of distribution rights regarding it.

H-K and Shirley and Larry McQuillan signed a letter of intent in 1980. This letter of intent granted the McQuillans, who were designing a horseshoe pad that used sorbothane, exclusive rights to purchase sorbothane for use in equestrian products. In 1981, H-K established five regional distributorships for sorbothane. The McQuillans were chosen as distributors of all sorbothane products, including medical products and shoe inserts, for the Southwest. Spectrum Sports, Inc., was selected as distributor for another region of the country. Spectrum's co-owner, Kenneth Leighton, Jr., was the son of Kenneth Leighton, Sr., the president of H-K and later the president of SI.

In January 1982, H-K shifted responsibility for selling medical products from five regional distributors to a single national distributor. Three months later, H-K told the McQuillans that it wanted them to relinquish their athletic shoe distributorship as a condition of being able to retain the right to develop and distribute equestrian products. In May 1982, SI (having succeeded H-K in handling the sorbothane business for BTR) made the same demand to the McQuillans. At a meeting scheduled to discuss a possible sale of the McQuillans' athletic shoe distributorship to Spectrum, Shirley McQuillan was told by Leighton, Jr., that if the McQuillans did not come to agreement with Spectrum, they would be "looking for work." The McQuillans refused to sell and continued to distribute athletic shoe inserts.

Leighton, Sr., informed the McQuillans during the fall of 1982 that another firm had been appointed as the national equestrian distributor, and that the McQuillans were "no longer involved in equestrian products." In January 1983, SI began marketing, through a national distributor, a sorbothane horseshoe pad that, according to the McQuillans, was indistinguishable from the one they had designed. SI named Spectrum as the national distributor of sorbothane athletic shoe inserts in August 1983. At roughly the same time, SI informed the McQuillans that it would no longer accept their sorbothane orders. With the McQuillans thus being unable to obtain sorbothane, their business failed.

The McQuillans sued the other parties referred to above on various legal theories, including a claim of attempted monopolization in violation of section 2 of the Sherman Act. The jury returned a $1,743,000 verdict in favor of the McQuillans on the section 2 count. The district court trebled the jury's compensatory damages award. After the Ninth Circuit Court of Appeals affirmed, the Supreme Court granted the petition for a writ of certiorari filed by Spectrum and Leighton, Jr.

Source: 113 S. Ct. 884 (U.S. Sup. Ct. 1993)

White, Justice

On the Section 2 issue ... present here, the Court of Appeals ... rejected [the] argument that attempted monopolization had not been established because the McQuillans had failed to prove that [the defendants] had a specific intent to monopolize a relevant market. The court also held that in order to show that [an] attempt to monopolize was likely to succeed, it was not necessary to present evidence of the relevant market or of the defendants' market power. In so doing, the Ninth Circuit relied on *Lessig v. Tidewater Oil Co.* (1964) [a Ninth Circuit decision] and its progeny. The Court of Appeals noted that these cases, in dealing with attempt to monopolize claims, had ruled that if evidence of unfair or predatory conduct is presented, [such evidence will also] satisfy both the specific intent and dangerous probability elements of the offense, without any proof of relevant market or the defendant's market power. The court went on to find [that the defendants] engaged in unfair or predatory conduct, [that the jury could therefore infer that the defendants] had the specific intent and the dangerous probability of success, [and that the McQuillans] did not have to prove [the] relevant market or the defendants' market power.

The decision below, and the *Lessig* line of decisions on which it relies, conflicts with holdings of courts in other circuits that proving an attempt to monopolize requires proof of a dangerous probability of monopolization of a relevant market. We granted certiorari to resolve this conflict.

Section 2 does not define the elements of the offense of attempted monopolization. Nor is there much guidance to be had in the scant legislative history of that provision. The legislative history does indicate that much of the interpretation of the necessarily broad principles of the Act was to be left for the courts in particular cases.

This Court first addressed the meaning of attempt to monopolize under Section 2 in *Swift & Co. v. United States* (1905). The Court's opinion [set forth the elements of intent to bring about a monopoly and a dangerous probability that a monopoly would occur]. The Court went on to explain, however, that not every act done with intent to produce an unlawful result constitutes an attempt: "It is a question of proximity and degree." *Swift* thus indicated that intent is necessary, but alone is not sufficient, to establish the dangerous probability of success that is the object of Section 2's prohibition of attempts.

The Court's decisions since *Swift* have reflected the view that the plaintiff charging attempted monopolization must prove a dangerous probability of actual monopolization, which has generally required a definition of the relevant market and examination of market power. In *Walker Process Equipment, Inc. v. Food Machinery & Chemical Corp.* (1965), we found that enforcement of a fraudulently obtained patent claim could violate the Sherman Act. We stated that, to establish monopolization or attempt to monopolize under Section 2 ..., it would be necessary to appraise the exclusionary power of the illegal patent claim in terms of the relevant market for the product involved. The reason was that "without a definition of that market there is no way to measure ability to lessen or destroy competition." Similarly, this Court reaffirmed in *Copperweld Corp. v. Independence Tube Corp.* (1984) that ... the conduct of a single firm [violates Section 2] "only when it threatens actual monopolization."

The Courts of Appeals other than the Ninth Circuit have followed this approach. Consistent with our cases, it is generally required that to demonstrate attempted monopolization a plaintiff must prove (1) that the defendant has engaged in predatory or anticompetitive conduct with (2) a specific intent to monopolize and (3) a dangerous probability of achieving monopoly power. In order to determine whether there is a dangerous probability of monopolization, courts have found it necessary to consider the relevant market and the defendant's ability to lessen or destroy competition in that market.

Notwithstanding the array of authority contrary to *Lessig*, the Court of Appeals in this case reaffirmed its prior holdings. We are not at all inclined to embrace *Lessig*'s interpretation of Section 2, for there is little if any support for it in the statute or the case law, and the notion that proof of unfair or predatory conduct alone is sufficient to make out the offense of attempted monopolization is contrary to the purpose and policy of the Sherman Act. The purpose of the Act is not to protect business from the working of the market; it is to protect the public from the failure of the market. The law directs itself not against conduct which is competitive, even severely so, but against conduct which unfairly tends to destroy competition itself. It does so not out of solicitude for private concerns but out of concern for the public interest.

Thus, this Court and other courts have been careful to avoid constructions of Section 2 which might chill competition, rather than foster it. It is sometimes difficult to distinguish robust competition from conduct with long-term anticompetitive effects; moreover, single-firm activity is unlike concerted activity covered by Section 1, which inherently is fraught with anticompetitive risk. For these reasons, Section 2 makes the conduct of a single firm unlawful only when it actually monopolizes or dangerously threatens to do so.

The concern that Section 2 might be applied so as to further anticompetitive ends is plainly not met by inquiring only whether the defendant had engaged in "unfair" or "predatory" tactics. Such conduct may be sufficient to prove the necessary intent to monopolize, which is something more than an intent to compete vigorously, but demonstrating the dangerous probability of monopolization in an attempt case also requires inquiry into the relevant product and geographic market and the defendant's economic power in that market.

Judgment reversed in favor of Spectrum and Leighton; case remanded for further proceedings consistent with Supreme Court's opinion.

Ethical and Public Policy Concerns

1. Early in this chapter, you read Judge Learned Hand's statement that "[g]reat industrial consolidations are inherently undesirable, regardless of their economic results." Yet you also learned that Chicago School antitrust thinkers, who have very different notions about the effects of industrial concentration, have had an important influence on antitrust policy in recent years. Identify two aspects of the current global business environment that might make today's American policymakers less willing than Judge Hand to "perpetuate and preserve, for its own sake and in spite of possible cost, an organization of industry in small units which can effectively compete with each other."

2. Some of the cases in this chapter recite the statement that antitrust was designed to protect competition, not competitors. How is this statement consistent with the ethical justification of markets as the most efficient form of economic organization? Consider the case of a competitor who is driven out of business by another competitor's ultimately unsuccessful predatory pricing efforts (unsuccessful because the predator could not maintain monopoly power long enough to recoup the profits lost through predatory pricing). Although competition may not suffer in such a case, does such a competitor have any *ethical* claim to compensation? What public policy argument could be made in favor of compensation?

3. Tying arrangements that do not satisfy the criteria for per se illegality explained earlier in this chapter are judged under the rule of reason. This means that they will be judged lawful unless evidence demonstrates that they unreasonably restrain competition. Is there an *ethical* basis for arguing a seller's imposition of a tie-in is wrong, regardless of its effect on competition?

Problems and Problem Cases

1. Syufy Enterprises, a motion picture exhibitor operating theaters in four states, entered the Las Vegas first-run movie exhibition market in 1981 by opening a six-screen cinema complex. Before Syufy's entry there were 17 first-run theaters in Las Vegas. This situation produced intensive bidding among theater owners regarding first-run film exhibition rights because there were often not enough such films to fill all 17 screens. This meant owners paid substantially more for the right to exhibit such films than they paid in other comparable markets. To reduce this competition, Syufy bought out the owners of six Las Vegas theaters. In late July 1984, Syufy submitted successful bids for the right to show the movie *The Cotton Club* during the Christmas season in Las Vegas and several other locations. On October 18, 1984, Syufy bought

out Cragin, the owner of the remaining first-run theaters in Las Vegas. On October 23, 1984, after seeing the first trade screening of *The Cotton Club*, Syufy canceled the guarantees included in its bids for *The Cotton Club*. Syufy maintained that the movie was not as good as its distributor, Orion Pictures, had represented it to be, and that contrary to Orion's representations, a viewable version of the film had been available when the blind bids for exhibition rights were solicited. Orion filed suit against Syufy for breach of contract and for monopolizing and attempting to monopolize the Las Vegas market. Orion sought to recover the difference between the amount guaranteed in its contracts with Syufy and the amount it actually earned renting the film to other theaters. Was it proper for the district court to direct a verdict in Syufy's favor on the Sherman Act claims on the ground that Orion had failed to show an antitrust injury?

2.   Co-Operative Theatres (Co-op), a Cleveland area movie theater booking agent, began seeking customers in southern Ohio. Shortly thereafter, Tri-State Theatre Services (Tri-State), a Cincinnati booking agent, began to solicit business in the Cleveland area. Later, however, Co-op and Tri-State allegedly entered into an agreement not to solicit each other's customers. The Justice Department prosecuted them for agreeing to restrain trade in violation of section 1 of the Sherman Act. Under a government grant of immunity, Tri-State's vice president testified that Co-op's vice president had approached him at a trade convention and threatened to start taking Tri-State's accounts if Tri-State did not stop calling on Co-op's accounts. He also testified that at a luncheon meeting he attended with officials from both firms, the presidents of both firms said that it would be in the interests of both firms to stop calling on each other's accounts. Several Co-op customers testified that Tri-State had refused to accept their business because of the agreement with Co-op. The trial court found both firms guilty of a per se violation of the Sherman Act, rejecting their argument that the rule of reason should have been applied and refusing to allow them to introduce evidence that the agreement did not have a significant anticompetitive effect. Should the rule of reason have been applied?

3.   Advanced Health-Care Services (ACHS), a supplier of durable medical equipment (DME) such as wheelchairs, hospital beds, walkers, crutches, and other equipment used by persons convalescing at home after hospitalization, filed a Sherman Act suit against Radford Community Hospital and Radford's holding company owner, Southwest Virginia Health Services Corporation (Southwest). ACHS's complaint alleged, among other things, that Radford, which provided acute health care services to approximately 75 percent of the residents of the greater Radford, Virginia, region, had conspired with another wholly owned subsidiary of Southwest's to prevent Radford patients from dealing with ACHS and to induce them to purchase DME from the Southwest subsidiary instead. ACHS argued that Radford and Southwest were guilty of conspiring to restrain trade in violation of Sherman Act section 1, and of monopolization and conspiracy to monopolize in violation of Sherman Act section 2. Was the district court's summary dismissal of all of ACHS's claims proper?

4.   The Maricopa Foundation for Medical Care was a nonprofit organization established by the Maricopa County Medical Society to promote fee-for-service medicine. Roughly 70 percent of the physicians in Maricopa County belonged to the foundation. The foundation's trustees set maximum fees that members could charge for medical services provided to policyholders of approved medical insurance plans. To obtain the foundation's approval, insurers had to agree to pay the fees of member physicians up to the prescribed maximum. Member physicians were free to charge less than the prescribed maximum, but had to agree not to seek additional payments in excess of the maximum from insured patients. The Arizona attorney general filed suit for injunctive relief against the Maricopa County Medical Society and the foundation, arguing that

the fee agreement constituted per se illegal horizontal price-fixing. The district court denied the state's motion for a partial summary judgment. The Ninth Circuit Court of Appeals affirmed on the ground that the per se rule was not applicable to the case. Was the Ninth Circuit correct?

5. In 1986, Market Force, Inc. (MFI), began operating in the Milwaukee real estate market as a buyer's broker. MFI and prospective home buyers entered into exclusive contracts providing that MFI would receive a fee equal to 40 percent of the sales commission if it located a house that the buyer ultimately purchased. This 40 percent commission was the same commission selling brokers (those who ultimately produced a buyer, but whose duty of loyalty was to the seller) earned when they sold property placed on the local multiple listing service (MLS) by other brokers. MFI's contracts anticipated that the buyer would ask the listing broker (the one who had listed the property for sale on behalf of its owners and who received 60 percent of the commission when the property was sold) to pay MFI the commission at the time of the sale. If the listing broker agreed to do so, the buyer had no further obligation to MFI. For some time after MFI began operations, other real estate firms treated it inconsistently; some paid the full 40 percent commission but others paid nothing. In the fall of 1987, Wauwatosa Realty Co. and Coldwell Banker, the top two firms listing high-quality homes in Milwaukee, issued formal policies on splitting commissions with buyer's brokers. Wauwatosa said it would pay 20 percent of the selling agent's 40 percent commission. Coldwell Banker said it would pay 20 percent of the total sales commission. Several other real estate firms followed suit, setting their rates at 10 or 20 percent of the total sales commission, with the result that firms accounting for 31 percent of the annual listings of the MLS adopted policies and disseminated them to other MLS members. MFI filed suit against the brokers who had announced policies, arguing that they had conspired to restrain trade in violation of section 1 of the Sherman Act. At trial, the defendants introduced evidence of numerous business justifications for their policies and argued that their knowingly having adopted similar policies was not enough, standing alone, to justify a conclusion that the Sherman Act was violated. Was this argument correct?

6. When Triple-A Baseball Club Associates was in the process of building the Old Orchard Beach Ballpark, both Gemini Concerts, Inc., and Don Law Co., Inc., expressed interest in promoting concerts at the ballpark. Triple-A, however, had neither the time nor money to make the facility suitable for concerts. Gemini eventually ceased its efforts to use the facility. Law, however, persisted. After several years of discussions, Law and Triple-A signed an agreement giving Law the exclusive right to promote concerts at the ballpark for two years, with an option to renew for another five years. In return, Law paid for many of the capital improvements necessary to equip the ballpark for concerts and shared with Triple-A the cost of others. Gemini filed suit against Triple-A and Law, arguing that their exclusive dealing contract violated section 1 of the Sherman Act. Should the trial court grant the restraining order requested by Gemini?

7. Concerned that its dealers might not have sufficient spare parts to make repairs on recently purchased Subaru cars, Subaru of America (SOA) decided in 1973 to require its dealers to keep certain spare parts kits on hand. Grappone, Inc., a New Hampshire Subaru dealer, also had AMC, Pontiac, Jeep, Toyota, and Peugot franchises. Grappone acquired its cars from Subaru of New England, Inc. (SNE), a regional Subaru distributor. Grappone objected when told by SNE that it needed to purchase two "dealer's kits" containing 88 parts for 1974 cars and two "supplemental kits" containing 44 parts each (the total number of different Subaru parts being somewhere between 4,000 and 5,000). SNE refused to give Grappone its 1974 car allotment until

Grappone bought the kits. Grappone went 10 months without cars; it then agreed to take the kits. Grappone later sued SNE, arguing that SNE violated section 1 of the Sherman Act by tying the sale of the parts kits to the sale of cars. The evidence introduced at trial indicated that Subaru's national market share was under 1 percent and that its share of the New Hampshire market was 3.4 percent. Was the trial court correct in granting judgment in favor of Grappone?

8. McClain and others brought a private antitrust action under the Sherman Act against the Real Estate Board of New Orleans. They alleged pricefixing by means of fixed commission rates, fee splitting, and suppression of market information useful to buyers. The trial court granted the board's motion for dismissal on the ground that real estate brokerage activities were wholly local in nature and therefore lacked the effect on interstate commerce necessary to invoke the Sherman Act. Was the trial court correct?

9. In mid-1982, Indiana Grocery (Indiana) owned 28 supermarkets in the Indianapolis area and sold about 13 percent of the area's groceries. Indiana bought Preston-Safeway in 1985. After 1986, all of Indiana's Indianapolis stores operated under the Preston-Safeway name. The Kroger Company (Kroger) operates over 1,400 supermarkets throughout the United States. In 1983, Kroger operated 32 stores in the Indianapolis area and sold about 28 percent of the area's groceries. Super Valu Stores, Inc., is primarily a grocery wholesaler. Since 1980, however, it has owned and franchised "Cub" retail food stores in various states. Cub stores, which are substantially larger than conventional supermarkets, offer a low level of services to customers in exchange for prices that normally are 6 to 10 percent lower than those of conventional stores. Between 1983 and 1986, four Cub stores were opened in the Indianapolis area. This ushered in a period of intense price competition as Kroger and others, realizing that gains by Cub would come at their expense, sought to compete. Cub had captured a 15 percent share of Indianapolis retail grocery sales by early 1985. Nevertheless, as of 1987, Kroger (with 33 stores), Marsh (with 30), Indiana (with 24), O'Malia (with 9), Mr. D's (with 5), Aldi (with 5), and 7-Eleven (with 4), all remained in the Indianapolis market, as did other firms operating approximately 38 more supermarkets. Indiana filed suit in 1985 against Kroger. Indiana asserted, among other things, that Kroger used predatory pricing as a means of attempting to monopolize the Indianapolis retail grocery market. The district court granted summary judgment in Kroger's favor. Was the district court correct in doing so?

10. In July 1977, anesthesiologist Edwin G. Hyde applied for admission to the medical staff of East Jefferson Hospital in New Orleans. The credentials committee and the medical staff executive committee recommended approval, but the hospital board denied the application because the hospital was a party to a contract providing that all anesthesiological services required by the hospital's patients would be performed by Roux & Associates, a professional medical corporation. Hyde filed suit against the board, arguing that the contract violated section 1 of the Sherman Act. The district court ruled in favor of the board, finding that the anticompetitive effects of the contract were minimal and outweighed by the benefits of improved patient care. It noted that there were at least 20 hospitals in the New Orleans metropolitan area and that about 70 percent of the patients residing in Jefferson Parish went to hospitals other than East Jefferson. It therefore concluded that East Jefferson lacked any significant market power and could not use the contract for anticompetitive ends. The Fifth Circuit Court of Appeals reversed, holding that the relevant market was the East Bank Jefferson Parish rather than the New Orleans metropolitan area. The court therefore concluded that because 30 percent of the parish residents used East Jefferson and "patients tend to choose hospitals by location rather than price or quality," East Jefferson possessed

sufficient market power to make the contract a per se illegal tying contract. Was the Fifth Circuit correct?

11. Häagen-Dazs was the first "super premium" ice cream manufacturer to achieve national distribution. Häagen-Dazs refused to sell its products to any distributor who also sold a comparable, competing ice cream brand. Two Count had been a Häagen-Dazs distributor in the San Francisco area since 1976. In 1985, Two Count agreed to become a distributor (in addition to being a Häagen-Dazs distributor) for Double Rainbow, another "super premium" ice cream manufacturer. When informed of this agreement, Häagen-Dazs terminated Two Count's distributorship. Two Count and Double Rainbow subsequently sued Häagen-Dazs, arguing, among other things, that Häagen-Dazs was guilty of monopolizing, or attempting to monopolize, the "super premium" ice cream market. At trial, Häagen-Dazs introduced uncontroverted evidence indicating that all grades of ice cream compete with one another for customer preference and space in retailers' freezers. Häagen-Dazs's share of the San Francisco ice cream market was 4 to 5 percent. Its national market share was in the same range. Should the trial court have granted Häagen-Dazs's motion for summary judgment on the section 2 claims?

Endnotes

1. *Times-Picayune Co. v. United States*, 345 U.S. 594 (U.S. Sup. Ct. 1953).
2. *United States v. Aluminum Co. of America, Inc.*, 148 E2d 416 (2d Cir. 1945).
3. *United States v. Aluminum Co. of America, Inc.*, 148 F.2d 416 (2d Cir. 1945).
4. *United States v. U.S. Gypsum Co.*, 438 U.S. 422 (U.S. Sup. Ct. 1978).
5. 429 U.S. 477 (U.S. Sup. Ct. 1977).
6. 431 U.S. 720 (U.S. Sup. Ct. 1977).
7. *California v. ARC America Corp.*, 490 U.S. 93 (U.S. Sup. Ct. 1989).
8. 467 U.S. 752 (U.S. Sup. Ct. 1984).
9. *United States v. Socony-Vacuum Oil Co.*, 310 U.S. 150 (U.S. Sup. Ct. 1940).
10. *United States v. General Electric Co.*, 272 U.S. 476 (U.S. Sup. Ct. 1926).
11. See, for instance, *Simpson v. Union Oil Co. of California*, 377 U.S. 13 (U.S. Sup. Ct. 1964).
12. 250 U.S. 300 (U.S. Sup. Ct. 1919).
13. 405 U.S. 596 (U.S. Sup. Ct. 1972).
14. See, for example, *Polk Bros. v. Forest City Enterprises*, 776 F.2d 185 (7th Cir. 1985). In this case, two retailers were constructing a new building that they were to share. An agreement by the retailers not to compete in the sale of certain product lines was upheld as ancillary to their agreement to develop the joint facility.
15. 338 U.S. 365 (U.S. Sup. Ct. 1967).
16. *Fashion Originators' Guild v. FTC*, 312 U.S. 457 (U.S. Sup. Ct. 1941).
17. 465 U.S. 752 (U.S. Sup. Ct. 1984).
18. 485 U.S. 108 (U.S. Sup. Ct. 1988).
19. Section 3 of the Clayton Act applies, however, only when both the tying and the tied products are commodities.
20. *U.S. Steel Corp. v. Fortner Enterprises, Inc.*, 429 U.S. 610 (U.S. Sup. Ct. 1977).
21. *Principe v. McDonald's Corp.*, 631 F.2d 303 (4th Cir. 1980).
22. *United States v. Grinnell Corp.*, 384 U.S. 563 (U.S. Sup. Ct. 1966).
23. *United States v. E. I. du Pont de Nemours & Co.*, 351 U.S. 377 (U.S. Sup. Ct. 1956).
24. *United States v. Aluminum Co. of America, Inc.*, 148 F.2d 416 (2d Cir. 1945).
25. *Cargill, Inc. & Excel Corp. v. Monfort of Colorado, Inc.*, 479 U.S. 484 (U.S. Sup. Ct. 1986).
26. *Matsushita Electric Industrial Co., Ltd. v. Zenith Radio Corp.*, 475 U.S. 574 (U.S. Sup. Ct. 1986).

Chapter Thirty-One

THE CLAYTON ACT, THE ROBINSON-PATMAN ACT, AND ANTITRUST EXEMPTIONS AND IMMUNITIES

Introduction

Concentration in the American economy continued despite the 1890 enactment of the Sherman Act. Early restrictive judicial interpretations of section 2 of the Sherman Act limited its effectiveness against many monopolists. Critics therefore sought legislation to thwart would-be monopolists before they achieved full-blown restraint of trade or monopoly power. In 1914, Congress responded by passing the Clayton Act.

Congress envisioned the Clayton Act as a vehicle for attacking some of the specific practices that monopolists had historically employed to acquire monopoly power. These practices included tying and exclusive dealing arrangements designed to squeeze competitors out of the market, mergers and acquisitions aimed at reducing competition through the elimination of competitors, interlocking corporate directorates designed to reduce competition by placing competitors under common leadership, and predatory or discriminatory pricing designed to force competitors out of business. Each of these practices will be discussed in the following pages.

In view of the congressional intent that the Clayton Act serve as a preventive measure, only a probability of a significant anticompetitive effect must be shown for most Clayton Act violations. Because the Clayton Act focuses on probable harms to competition, there are no criminal penalties for violating its provisions. Private plaintiffs, however, may sue for treble damages or injunctive relief if they are injured, or threatened with injury, by another party's violation of the statute. The Justice Department and the Federal Trade Commission (FTC) share responsibility for enforcing the Clayton Act. Each has the authority to seek injunctive relief to prevent or remedy violations of the statute. In addition, the FTC has the power to enforce the Clayton Act through the use of cease and desist orders.

Clayton Act Section 3

Section 3 of the Clayton Act makes it unlawful for any person engaged in interstate commerce to *lease or sell commodities*, or to *fix a price for commodities*, on the *condition, agreement, or understanding* that the lessee or buyer of the commodities will not use or deal in the commodities of the lessor's or seller's competitors, if the effect of doing so *may be* to *substantially lessen competition* or *tend to create a monopoly* in any line of commerce. Section 3 primarily targets two potentially anticompetitive behaviors: **tying agreements** and **exclusive dealings agreements**. As you learned in the preceding chapter, both of theses types of contracts may amount to restraints of trade in violation of Sherman Act section 1. The language of section 3, however, contains limitations on the Clayton Act's application to such agreements.

A major limitation is that section 3 applies only to those tying agreements and exclusive dealing contracts involving *commodities*. Any such agreements involving services, real estate, or intangibles must therefore be attacked under the Sherman Act. In addition, section 3 applies only when there has been a *lease or sale* of commodities. It thus does not apply to true consignment agreements, because no sale or lease occurs in a consignment. Although section 3 speaks of sales and leases on the "condition, agreement, or understanding" that the buyer or lessee not deal in the commodities of the seller's or lessor's competitors, no formal agreement is required. Whenever a seller or lessor uses its economic power to prevent its customers from dealing with its competitors, potential Clayton Act concerns are triggered.

Tying Agreements

Many *tying agreements* plainly fall within at least the first portion of the relevant section 3 language. Any agreement that requires a buyer to purchase one product (the *tied product*) from a seller as a condition of purchasing another product (the *tying product*) from the same seller necessarily prevents the buyer from purchasing the tied product from the seller's competitors.

Only tying agreements that may "*substantially lessen competition or tend to create a monopoly*," however, violate section 3. The lower federal courts are not in complete agreement on the nature of the proof necessary to demonstrate such a probable anticompetitive effect. More than 40 years ago, the Supreme Court appeared to indicate that a tying agreement would violate the Clayton Act if the seller either had monopoly power over the tying product or restrained a substantial volume of commerce in the tied product.[1]

As the *Mozart* case (which follows shortly) indicates, however, many lower federal courts today require essentially the same elements of proof for a Clayton Act violation that they require for a violation of the Sherman Act: the challenged agreement must involve *two separate products, sale of the tying product must be conditioned* on an accompanying sale of the tied product, the seller must have *sufficient economic power in the market for the tying product* to appreciably restrain competition in the tied product market, and the seller's tying arrangements must restrain a "*not insubstantial" amount of commerce in the tied product market*. A few courts continue to apply a less demanding standard for Clayton Act tying liability by dispensing with proof of the seller's economic power in the market for the tying product as long as the seller's tying arrangements involve a "not insubstantial" amount of commerce in the tied product. The *Mozart* case also reveals that defenses to tying liability under the Sherman Act are also applicable to tying claims brought under the Clayton Act.

Mozart Co. v. Mercedes-Benz of North America, Inc.

Mercedes-Benz of North America (MBNA), the exclusive U.S. distributor of Mercedes-Benz (Mercedes) automobiles, is a wholly owned subsidiary of Daimler-Benz Aktiengesellschaft (DBAG), the manufacturer of Mercedes automobiles. MBNA required the approximately 400 franchised Mercedes dealers to agree not to sell or use (in the repair or servicing of Mercedes automobiles) any parts other than genuine Mercedes parts. Mozart, a wholesale automotive parts distributor, filed an antitrust suit against MBNA. Mozart alleged, among other things, that MBNA had violated both section 1 of the Sherman Act and section 3 of the Clayton Act by tying the sale of Mercedes parts to the sale of Mercedes automobiles. When the trial court ruled in favor of MBNA, Mozart appealed.

Source: 833 F.2d 1342 (9th Cir. 1987)

Sneed, Circuit Judge

In *Jefferson Parish Hospital v. Hyde* (1984), a bare majority reaffirmed the per se rule against tying. The majority opinion concluded that it was "far too late in the history of our antitrust jurisprudence to question the proposition that certain tying arrangements pose an unacceptable risk of stifling competition." Three elements are necessary to establish a per se illegal tying arrangement: (1) a tie-in between two distinct products or services; (2) sufficient economic power in the tying product to impose significant restrictions in the tied product market; and (3) an effect on a non-insubstantial volume of commerce in the tied product market.

The district court determined as a matter of law that the Mercedes passenger car and its replacement parts were separate products tied together by the terms of the MBNA dealer agreement, and that the tying arrangement affected a substantial amount of interstate commerce. The market power issue was submitted to the jury, which found that MBNA possessed the requisite power in the tying product, the Mercedes passenger car.

The instructions employed in submitting this issue to the jury were flawed, however. That flaw pertained to the "market power" that the defendant must possess in the tying product to justify the invocation of the per se standard. The required market power must be sufficient to "force a purchaser to do something he would not do in a competitive market." Such "forcing" is the equivalent of increasing the price of the tying product to increase profits.

In *Hyde*, the Court identified three sources of market power. First, when the government has granted the seller a patent or similar monopoly over a product, it is fair to presume that the inability to buy the product elsewhere gives the seller market power. The second is when the seller's share of the market is high. The third is when the seller offers a unique product that competitors are not able to offer. Mozart's theory of this case is that the Mercedes automobile is sufficiently unique to confer economic power on MBNA in the tying product.

The jury was instructed that "[a] prestigious and desirable trademark can be persuasive evidence of economic power." First, a prestigious trademark is not itself persuasive evidence of economic power. It is true that we have previously held that copyright protection may be evidence of market power because it creates barriers to entry for competitors in the tying market. *Digidyne Corp. v. Data General Corp.* (1984). However, unlike a patent or copyright, which is designed to protect the uniqueness of the product itself, a trademark protects only the name or symbol of the product. Market power, if any, is derived from the product, not from the name or symbol as such.

Second, the court's instructions indicate that somehow market power can be proven from the uniqueness of the Mercedes automobile. The difficulty with this is that while many individual purchasers undoubtedly regard a Mercedes as unique, it is by no means clear that dealers view the Mercedes in the same manner. The critical issue is whether MBNA possesses the market power to force dealers to purchase the tied product rather than acquire the franchise to sell a different automobile. Obviously there are costs of surrendering one franchise and acquiring another, but these are costs unrelated to the market power of a unique automobile. These costs will enable the car maker to extract concessions from the dealer, but this power is related to the franchise method of doing business, not to the possible uniqueness of the car.

However, we do not find that the flawed instructions necessitate a reversal of the judgment. The instructions were more favorable to Mozart than would be a proper recasting. This brings us to the heart of this case, whether the tying arrangement was justified by business necessity. A tie-in does not violate the antitrust laws if implemented for a legitimate purpose and if no less restrictive alternative is available. The defendant bears the burden of showing that the case falls within the contours of this affirmative defense.

The justification asserted by MBNA is that the tying arrangement is necessary to assure quality control and to protect its goodwill. The difficulty confronting MBNA is the problem of "freeriding" by Mercedes dealers. To MBNA it is crucial that a dealer offer standardized products. Only then can customers confidently rely on the Mercedes name. Franchisees, on the other hand, experience a conflict of interest. True, they wish to maintain the goodwill of MBNA, but some will yield to avarice and increase their profits by supplying inferior products while continuing to attract customers at the expense of dealers who conform to quality standards. The cost of these transgressions will be borne by all franchisees in the form of decreased future demand. Although a consumer may realize that a particular franchisee "cut a corner," the adverse reaction of consumers as a group is not confined to that particular franchisee because they are appropriately reacting to the poor job of policing done by the franchiser.

Substantial evidence exists to support MBNA's claim that the tie-in was used to assure quality control. MBNA purchases approximately 80% of its replacement parts from DBAG. Of those parts half are manufactured by DBAG itself, and half are acquired from other original equipment manufacturers (OEMs). These OEMs produce the parts according to DBAG specifications. A selection of each shipment of OEM parts, which has already passed through one round of inspection, is tested a second time by DBAG. If any of the test parts is deficient, the whole lot is rejected. The remaining 20% of the replacement parts purchased by MBNA come directly from OEMs that have met DBAG's standards. Mozart purchased most of the parts it sold from OEMs in the United States.

MBNA introduced evidence showing that DBAG's strict testing standards helped to assure the high quality of replacement parts. MBNA maintains an excellent reputation in the automobile industry for reliable service and quality replacement parts. In fact, 75% of Mercedes automobile owners are repeat purchasers, and over one third of the owners return to the dealer for service and repairs. There was considerable testimony by dealers and employees of MBNA about the inferiority of parts supplied by independent jobbers. Although Mozart introduced evidence to the contrary, the jury was entitled to make credibility determinations in favor of MBNA.

Mozart insists that MBNA could have furnished manufacturing specifications for replacement parts, and that such specifications would eliminate the need for a tie-in. The jury rejected this contention. Mozart is right, of course, when it insists that MBNA could have furnished design specifications for Mercedes replacement parts. That alone, however, does not eliminate the business justification defense. MBNA offered evidence that DBAG's vigorous testing programs could not be replicated by individual dealerships. The evidence further indicates the impracticality of Mozart's suggestion that MBNA could have inspected all replacement products furnished to independents. There was evidence from which the jury could find that the cost of such an undertaking would be prohibitive. We do not believe MBNA was required to make extreme steps to protect its legitimate interest in assuring public confidence in the quality of its trademarked product.

The elements for establishing a Sherman Act section 1 claim and a Clayton Act section 3 claim are virtually the same. There is no reason for allowing a business justification for a section 1 claim and not for a section 3 claim. Courts permit a business justification defense to tying claims because of a frank recognition that a package transaction with substantial justifications and few harmful effects should not be condemned. That recognition applies with equal force to the Sherman Act and the Clayton Act. The section 3 claim falls with the section 1 claim.

Judgment for MBNA affirmed.

Exclusive Dealing Agreements

Exclusive dealing agreement clearly falls under the initial portion of the relevant section 3 language because buyers who agree to handle one seller's product exclusively, or to purchase all of their requirements for a particular commodity from one seller, are by definition agreeing not to purchase similar items from the seller's competitors. As with tying agreements, however, not all exclusive dealing agreements are unlawful. Section 3 outlaws only those agreements that may "substantially lessen competition or tend to create a monopoly."

Exclusive dealing agreements initially were treated in much the same way as tying agreements. Courts looked at the dollar amount of commerce involved and declared illegal those agreements involving a "not insubstantial" amount of commerce. This *quantitative substantiality* test was employed, for example, by the Supreme Court in *Standard Oil Co. v. United States*.[2] Standard Oil was the largest refiner and supplier of gasoline in several western states, holding approximately 14 percent of the retail market. Roughly half of these sales were made by retail outlets owned by Standard. The other half were made by independent dealers who had entered into exclusive dealing contracts with Standard. Standard's six major competitors had entered into similar contracts with their own independent dealers. The Court recognized that exclusive dealing contracts, unlike tying agreements, could benefit both buyers and sellers, but declared Standard's contracts illegal on the ground that nearly $58 million in commerce was involved.

The Court's decision in the *Standard Oil* case provoked considerable criticism. In *Tampa Electric Co. v. Nashville Coal Co.*, however, the Court applied a broader *qualitative substantiality* test to gauge the legality of a long-term requirements contract for the sale of coal to an electric utility.[3] In *Tampa Electric*, the Court looked at the "area of effective competition," which was the total market for coal in the geographic region from which the utility could reasonably purchase its coal needs. The Court then examined the percentage of this region's total coal sales accounted for by the challenged contract. Because that percentage share was less than 1 percent of the region's total coal sales, the Court upheld the agreement even though it represented more than $100 million in coal sales.

Tampa Electric, however, is distinguishable from *Standard Oil*, which, in any event, the Court has not overruled. Unlike *Standard Oil*, *Tampa Electric* involved parties with relatively equal bargaining power and an individual agreement, rather than an industrywide practice. In addition, there were obvious reasons why an electric utility such as Tampa Electric might want to lock in its coal costs by using a long-term requirements contract. Although lower court opinions employing each test may be found, the *qualitative* approach employed in *Tampa Electric* is the one more likely to be employed by the current Court.

Clayton Act Section 7

Introduction

Section 7 of the Clayton Act was designed to attack merger term used broadly in this chapter to refer to the acquisition of one company by another. Our historical experience indicates that one way in which monopolists acquired monopoly power was by acquiring control of their competitors. Section 7 prohibits any party engaged in commerce or in any activity affecting commerce from *acquiring the stock or assets* of another such party if the effect, in *any line of commerce* or *any activity affecting commerce* in any section of the country, *may be* to *substantially lessen competition* or *tend to create a monopoly*. Rather than adopting the Sherman Act section 2 approach of waiting until a would-be monopolist has acquired monopoly power or is dangerously close to doing so, section 7 attempts to "nip monopolies in the bud" by barring mergers that *may* have an anticompetitive effect.

Although section 7 is plainly an anticoncentration device, it has also been used (as the following text indicates) to attack mergers that have had no direct effect on concentration in a particular industry. As such, its future evolution is in doubt, given the influence of Chicago School economic theories on contemporary antitrust law and the more tolerant stance those theories take toward mergers. During the 1980s, the Justice Department signaled a more permissive approach to merger activity than the government had previously adopted. During roughly the first year of the Clinton presidency (the approximate time this book went to press), however, Justice Department officials offered hints of increased government scrutiny of mergers in some industries, though not necessarily on an across-the-board basis. It remains to be seen whether the Clinton administration will in fact pursue a stepped-up enforcement policy regarding mergers. Regardless of the enforcement approach chosen by the federal government, it should be remembered that private enforcement of section 7 is also possible.

Predictions regarding section 7's ultimate judicial treatment are complicated considerably by the fact that many of the important merger cases in recent years have been settled out of court. This leaves interested observers of antitrust policy with few definitive expressions of the Supreme Court's current thinking on many merger issues. Most of the available indications, however, point to potentially significant revisions of merger policy in the years to come.

Relevant Market Determination

Regardless of the treatment section 7 ultimately receives in the courts, determining the **relevant market** affected by a merger is likely to remain a crucial component of any section 7 case. Before a court can determine whether a particular merger will have the *probable* anticompetitive effect required by the Clayton Act, it must first determine the *line of commerce* (or *relevant product market*) and the *section of the country* (or *relevant geographic market*) that are likely to be affected by the merger. If the court adopts a broad relevant market definition, this will usually enhance the government's or private plaintiff's difficulty in demonstrating a probable anticompetitive effect flowing from a challenged merger.

Relevant Product Market

"Line of commerce" determinations under the Clayton Act have traditionally employed *functional interchangeability* tests similar to those employed in relevant product market determinations under section 2 of the Sherman Act. Which products do the acquired and acquiring firms manufacture (assuming a merger between competitors), and which products are reasonably interchangeable by consumers to serve the same purposes? The federal government's merger guidelines indicate that the relevant market includes those products that consumers view as good substitutes at prevailing prices. The guidelines also state that the relevant market includes any products that a significant percentage of current customers would shift to in the event of a "small, but significant and non-transitory increase" in price of the products of the merged firms.

Relevant Geographic Market

To determine a particular merger's probable anticompetitive effect on a section of the country, courts have traditionally asked where the effects of the merger will be "direct and immediate."[4] This means that the relevant geographic market may not be as broad as the markets in which the acquiring and acquired firms actually operate or, in the case of a merger between competitors, the markets in which they actually compete. The focus of the relevant market inquiry is on those sections of the country in which competition is most likely to be injured by the merger. As a result, the relevant geographic market in a given case could be drawn as narrowly as one metropolitan area or as broadly as the entire nation. All that is necessary to satisfy this aspect of section 7 is proof that the challenged merger might have a significant negative effect on competition in any economically significant geographic market.

The federal government's merger guidelines adopt a somewhat different approach to determining the relevant geographic market. They define the relevant geographic market as the geographic area in which a sole supplier of the product in question could profitably raise its price without causing outside suppliers to begin selling in the area. The guidelines contemplate beginning with the existing markets in which the parties to a merger compete, and then adding the markets of those suppliers that would enter the market in response to a "small, but significant and non-transitory increase" in price.

Horizontal Mergers

The analytical approach employed to gauge a merger's probable effect on competition varies according to the nature of the merger in question. **Horizontal mergers**—mergers among firms competing in the same product and geographic markets—have traditionally been subjected to the most rigorous scrutiny because they clearly lead to increased concentration in the relevant market.

Market Share of Resulting Firm

To determine the legality of such a merger, courts look at the *market share of the resulting firm*. In *United States v. Philadelphia National Bank*, the Supreme Court indicated that a horizontal merger producing a firm with an "undue percentage share" of the relevant market (33 percent in that case) and resulting in a "significant increase in concentration" of the firms in that market would be presumed illegal, absent convincing evidence that the merger would not have an anticompetitive effect.[5]

In the past, mergers involving firms with smaller market shares than those involved in *Philadelphia National Bank* were also enjoined if other economic or historical factors pointed toward a probable anticompetitive effect. Some of the factors that courts have traditionally considered relevant include:

1. *A trend toward concentration in the relevant market:* Has the number of competing firms decreased over time?
2. *The competitive position of the merging firms:* Are the defendants dominant firms despite their relatively small market shares?
3. *A past history of acquisitions by the acquiring firm:* Are we dealing with a would-be empire builder?
4. *The nature of the acquired firm:* Is it an aggressive, innovative competitor despite its small market share?

Recent Assessments of Merger Effects

Recent developments, however, indicate that the courts and federal antitrust enforcement agencies have become increasingly less willing to presume that anticompetitive effects will necessarily result from a merger that produces a firm with a relatively large market share. Instead, a more detailed inquiry is made into the nature of the relevant market and of the merging firms in order to ascertain the likelihood of a probable harm to competition as a result of a challenged merger. The federal government's horizontal merger guidelines indicate that when regulators assess a merger's probable effect, the focus is on the existing concentration in the relevant market, the increase in concentration as a result of the proposed merger, and other nonmarket share factors. The more concentrated the existing market and the greater the increase in concentration that would result from the proposed merger, the more likely the merger is to be challenged by the government.

The nonmarket share factors considered by federal regulators are more traditional. They include: the existence of barriers to the entry of new competitors into the relevant market, the prior conduct of the merging firms, and the probable future competitive strength of the acquired firm. The last factor is particularly important because courts have acknowledged that a firm's current market share may not reflect its ability to compete in the future. For example, courts have long recognized a "failing company" justification for some mergers. If the acquired firm is a failing company and no other purchasers are interested in acquiring it, its acquisition by a competitor may be lawful under section 7. Similarly, if an acquired firm has financial problems that reflect some underlying structural weakness, or if it lacks new technologies that are necessary to compete effectively in the future, its current market share may overstate its future competitive importance.

Finally, given the increased weight being assigned to economic arguments in antitrust cases, two other merger justifications may be granted greater credence in the future. Some lower federal courts have recognized the notion that a merger between two small companies may be justifiable, despite the resulting statistical increase in concentration, if the merger enables them to compete more effectively with larger competitors. In a somewhat similar vein, some commentators have argued that mergers resulting in enhanced economic efficiencies should sometimes be allowed even though they may have some anticompetitive impact. Though Courts have not been very receptive to efficiency arguments in the past, the government's horizontal merger guidelines are flexible enough to allow the Justice Department and FTC to consider efficiency claims in deciding whether to challenge a merger.

United States v. Waste Management, Inc.

Waste Management, Inc. (WMI), a company in the solid waste disposal business, acquired the stock of EMW Ventures, Inc. EMW was a diversified holding company, one of whose subsidiaries was Waste Resources. WMI and Waste Resources each had subsidiaries operating in or near Dallas, Texas. The government challenged the merger, arguing that it violated section 7 of the Clayton Act. The trial court (Judge Griesa) agreed, defining the relevant market as including all forms of trash collection (except at single-family or multiple-family residences or small apartment complexes) in Dallas County plus a small fringe area. The combined WMI and Waste Resources subsidiaries had 48.8 percent of the market so defined. The trial court found this market share presumptively illegal. WMI appealed.

Source: 743 F.2d 976 (2d Cir. 1984)

Winter, Circuit Judge

A post-merger market share of 48.8% is sufficient to establish prima facie illegality under *United States v. Philadelphia National Bank*. That decision held that large market shares are a convenient proxy for appraising the danger of monopoly power resulting from a horizontal merger. Under its rationale, a merger resulting in a large market share is presumptively illegal, rebuttable only by a demonstration that the merger will not have anticompetitive effects. Thus, in *United States v. General Dynamics Corp.* (1974), the Court upheld a merger of two leading coal producers because substantially all of the production of one firm was tied up in long-term contracts and its reserves were insubstantial. Since that firm's future ability to compete was negligible, the Court reasoned that its disappearance as an independent competitor could not affect the market.

WMI does not claim that 48.8% is too small a share to trigger the *Philadelphia National Bank* presumption. Rather, it argues that the presumption is rebutted by the fact that competitors can enter the Dallas waste hauling market with such ease that the finding of a 48.8% market share does not accurately reflect market power. WMI argues that it is unable to raise prices over the competitive level because new firms would quickly enter the market and undercut them.

The Supreme Court has never directly held that ease of entry may rebut a showing of *prima facie* illegality under *Philadelphia National Bank*. However, on several occasions it has held that appraisal of the impact of a proposed merger upon competition must take into account potential competition from firms not presently active in the relevant product and geographic markets. Moreover, under *General Dynamics*, a substantial existing market share is insufficient to void a merger where that share is misleading as to actual future competitive effect. In that case, long-term contracts and declining reserves negated the inference of market power drawn from the existing market share. In the present case, a market definition artificially restricted to existing firms competing at one moment may yield market share statistics that are not an accurate proxy for market power when substantial potential competition able to respond quickly to price increases exists.

Finally, the *Merger Guidelines* issued by the government itself not only recognize the economic principle that ease of entry is relevant to appraising the impact upon competition of a merger but also state that it may override all other factors. Where entry is "so easy that existing competitors could not succeed in raising prices for any significant period of time," the government has announced that it will usually not challenge a merger.

Turning to the evidence in this case, we believe that entry into the relevant product and geographic market by new firms or by existing firms in the Fort Worth area is so easy that any anticompetitive impact of the merger before us would be eliminated more quickly by such competition than by litigation. Judge Griesa specifically found that individuals operating out of their homes can acquire trucks and some containers and compete successfully "with any other company." His conclusion that "there is no showing of any circumstances, related to ease of entry or the trend of the business, which promises in and of itself to materially erode the [defendants'] competitive strength" is consistent with our decision. They may well retain their present market share. However, in view of the findings as to ease of entry, that share can be retained only by competitive pricing. Ease of entry constrains not only WMI, but every firm in the market. Should WMI attempt to exercise market power by raising prices, none of its small competitors would be able to follow the price increases because of the ease with which new competitors would appear. WMI would then face lower prices charged by all existing competitors as well as entry by new ones, a condition fatal to its economic prospects if not rectified.

Judgment reversed in favor of Waste Management, Inc.

Vertical Mergers

A **vertical merger** is a merger between firms that previously had, or could have had, a supplier-customer relationship. For example, a manufacturer may seek to vertically integrate its operations by acquiring a company that controls retail outlets at which the manufacturer's products could be sold. Alternatively, the manufacturer could vertically merge by acquiring a company that makes a product the manufacturer regularly uses in its production processes. Vertical mergers, unlike horizontal mergers, do not directly result in an increase in concentration. Nonetheless, they traditionally have been thought to threaten competition in various ways.

Foreclosing Competitors in Relevant Market

First, vertical mergers may *foreclose competitors* from a share of the relevant market. For example, if a major customer for a particular product acquires a captive supplier of that product, the competitors of the acquired firm are thereafter foreclosed from competing with it for sales to the acquiring firm. Similarly, if a manufacturer acquires a captive retail outlet for its products, the manufacturer's competitors are foreclosed from competing for sales to that retail outlet. A vertical merger in the latter case may also result in reduced competition at the retail level. For instance, a shoe manufacturer acquires a retail shoe store chain that carries the brands of several competing manufacturers and has a dominant share of the retail market in certain geographic areas. If the retail chain carries only the acquiring manufacturer's brands after the merger occurs, competition among the acquiring manufacturer and its competitors is reduced in the retail market for shoes.

Creation of Increased Market Entry Barriers

A second way in which vertical mergers threaten competition is that they may lead to *increased barriers to market entry* for new competitors. For example, if a major purchaser of a product acquires a captive supplier of that product, potential producers of the product may be discouraged from commencing production due to the merger-related contraction of the market for the product.

Elimination of Potential Competition in Acquired Firm's Market

In addition, some vertical mergers threaten competition by *eliminating potential competition* in one of two ways. First, an acquiring firm may be perceived by existing competitors in the acquired firm's market as a likely potential entrant into that market. The threat of such a potential entrant "waiting in the wings" may moderate the behavior of existing competitors because they fear that pursuing pricing policies which exploit their current market position might cause the potential entrant to react by entering the market. The acquiring firm's entry into the market by the acquisition of an existing competitor means the end of its moderating influence as a potential entrant. Second, a vertical merger may deprive the market of the potential benefits that would have resulted if the acquiring firm had entered the market in a more competitive manner, such as by creating its own entrant into the market through internal expansion or by making a toehold acquisition of a small existing competitor and subsequently building it into a more significant competitor.

Historically, courts seeking to determine the legality of vertical mergers have tended to look at the *share of the relevant market foreclosed to competition.* If a more than insignificant market share is foreclosed to competition, courts consider other economic and historical factors. Factors viewed as aggravating the anticompetitive potential of a vertical merger include: a trend toward concentration or vertical integration in the industry, a past history of vertical integration in the industry, a past history of vertical acquisitions by the acquiring company, and significant barriers to entry resulting from the merger. This approach to determining the legality of vertical mergers has been criticized by some commentators. These critics argue that vertical integration may yield certain efficiencies of distribution and that vertical integration by merger may be more economically efficient than vertical integration by internal expansion. The Justice Department generally affords greater weight to efficiency arguments in cases involving vertical mergers than in cases involving horizontal mergers. The department generally applies the same criteria to all nonhorizontal mergers. We discuss these criteria in the following section.

Conglomerate Mergers

A **conglomerate merger** is a merger between two firms that neither compete with each other (because they do business in different product or geographic markets) nor have a supplier-customer relationship with each other. Conglomerate mergers may be either *market extension* mergers or *product extension* mergers. In a market extension merger, the acquiring firm expands into a new geographic market by purchasing a firm already doing business in that market. For example, a conglomerate that owns an east coast grocery chain buys a west coast grocery chain. In a product extension merger, the acquiring firm diversifies its operations by purchasing a company in a new product market. For example, a conglomerate with interests in the aerospace and electronics industries purchases a department store chain.

There is considerable disagreement over the economic effects of conglomerate acquisitions. As later discussion will reveal, conglomerate mergers have been attacked with some degree of success under section 7 if they involve **potential reciprocity**, serve to **eliminate potential competition**, or give an acquired firm an **unfair advantage** over its competitors. Nevertheless, there is significant sentiment that the Clayton Act is not well suited to dealing with conglomerate mergers. This realization has produced calls for specific legislation on the subject. Such legislation is probably desirable if we ultimately conclude that conglomerate merger activity is a proper subject for regulation.

Potential Reciprocity

Conglomerate mergers that involve *potential reciprocity* are among those sometimes held to be prohibited by section 7. A conglomerate merger may create a risk of potential reciprocity if the acquired firm produces a product regularly purchased by the acquiring firm's suppliers. Such suppliers, eager to continue their relationship with the acquiring firm, may thereafter purchase the acquired firm's products rather than those of its competitors.

Elimination of Potential Competition

Some conglomerate mergers may result in *elimination of potential competition* in ways similar to vertical mergers, and thus may be vulnerable to attack under section 7. If existing competitors perceive the acquiring company as a potential entrant in the acquired company's market, the acquiring company's entry by means of a conglomerate acquisition may result in the loss of the moderating influence that it had while waiting in the wings. In addition, when the acquiring company actually enters the new market by acquiring a well-established competitor rather than by starting a new competitor through internal expansion (a *de novo* entry) or by making a toehold acquisition, the market is deprived of the potential for increased competition flowing from the reduction in concentration that would have accompanied either of the latter strategies.

Relevant Supreme Court decisions suggest, however, that a high degree of proof is required before either of these potential competition arguments will be accepted. Arguments that a conglomerate merger eliminated a *perceived potential entrant* must be accompanied by proof that existing competitors actually perceived the acquiring firm as a potential entrant.[6] Arguments that a conglomerate acquisition eliminated an actual potential entrant (and thereby deprived the market of the benefits of reduced concentration) must be accompanied by evidence that the acquiring firm had the ability to enter the market by internal expansion or a toehold acquisition and that doing so would have ultimately yielded a substantial reduction in concentration.[7]

Unfair Advantage to Acquired Firm

Finally, conglomerate mergers may violate section 7 in certain instances when the acquired firm obtains an unfair advantage over its competitors. When a large firm acquires a firm that already enjoys a significant position in its market, the acquired firm may gain an *unfair advantage* over its competitors through its ability to draw on the greater resources and expertise of its new owner. This advantage may entrench the acquired firm in its market by deterring existing competitors from actively competing with it for market share and by causing other potential competitors to be reluctant to enter the market after the acquisition.

Virtually all of the important recent conglomerate merger cases have been settled out of court. As a result, we do not have a clear indication of the Supreme Court's current thinking on conglomerate merger issues. In recent years, the Justice Department has taken the position that the primary theories to be used by the department in attacking all *nonhorizontal* mergers are the *elimination of perceived and actual potential competition* theories. In employing these analytical tools, the department also considers other economic factors. These include: (1) the degree of concentration in the acquired firm's market; (2) the existence of barriers to entry into the market and the presence or absence of other firms with a comparable ability to enter; and (3) the market share of the acquired firm (with challenges being unlikely if this is 5 percent or less and likely if it is 20 percent or more). It remains to be seen whether the Supreme Court will accept this more restrictive view of the scope of section 7.

Figure 31-1 summarizes the types of mergers covered by section 7.

FIGURE 31-1
Types of mergers covered by section 7

Category	Description	Example
Horizontal	Between competitors	One automobile manufacturer merges with another automobile manufacturer
Vertical	Between a supplier and its customer	An oil producer merges with an oil refiner
Conglomerate	Between two largely unrelated businesses	A candy company merges with a greeting card company

Tenneco, Inc. v. FTC

In 1975, Tenneco, Inc., was the 15th largest industrial corporation in America. Tenneco's Walker Manufacturing Division produced and distributed a wide variety of automotive parts, the most important of which were exhaust system parts. Walker was the nation's leading seller of exhaust system parts in 1975 and 1976. Tenneco acquired control of Monroe Auto Equipment Company, a leading manufacturer of automotive shock absorbers. Monroe was the number two firm in the national market for replacement shock absorbers. Monroe and Gabriel, the industry leader, accounted for over 77 percent of replacement shock absorber sales in 1976. General Motors and Questor Corporation, the third and fourth largest firms, controlled another 15 percent of the market.

continued

The replacement shock absorber market exhibited significant barriers to the entry of new competitors. Economies of scale in the industry dictated manufacturing plants of substantial size. Furthermore, the nature of the industry required would-be entrants to acquire significant new technologies and marketing skills unique to the

industry. The Federal Trade Commission (Commission) concluded that Tenneco's acquisition of Monroe violated section 7 of the Clayton Act by eliminating both perceived and actual potential competition in the replacement shock absorber market. The Commission therefore ordered Tenneco to divest itself of Monroe. Tenneco appealed.

Source: 689 F.2d 346 (2d Cir. 1982)

Meskill, Circuit Judge

The Supreme Court has described the theory of perceived potential competition, which it has approved for application to cases brought under Section 7 of the Clayton Act, as the principal focus of the potential competition doctrine. The Court has recognized that:

> A market extension merger may be unlawful if the target market is substantially concentrated, if the acquiring firm has the characteristics, capabilities, and economic incentive to render it a perceived potential *de novo* entrant, and if the acquiring firm's presence on the fringe of the target market in fact tempered oligopolistic behavior on the part of existing participants in that market. *United States v. Marine Bancorporation, Inc.* (1974).

The actual potential competition theory, which has yet to receive sanction from the Supreme Court, would

> proscribe a market extension merger solely on the ground that such a merger eliminates the prospect for long-term Reconcentration of an oligopolistic market that in theory might result if the acquiring firm were forbidden to enter except through a *de novo* undertaking or through the acquisition of a small existing entrant.

We reject the Commission's finding that Tenneco was an actual potential entrant likely to increase competition in the market for replacement shock absorbers. Tenneco was actively considering entry into the market and was pursuing all leads to that end at least since the late 1960s or early 1970s. Moreover, Tenneco clearly possessed adequate financial resources to make the large initial investment needed to attempt to penetrate the market. The record, however, is deficient in evidence that there were viable toehold options available to Tenneco or that Tenneco would have entered the market *de novo*.

The Commission conceded that Tenneco never expressed any interest in entering the market for replacement shock absorbers "on a completely *de novo* basis." However, the Commission found that Tenneco had expressed interest in entering the market essentially *de nova*, building the required production facilities from scratch and acquiring the necessary technology via a license from an established foreign shock absorber producer. The Commission concluded that Tenneco would likely have done so absent its acquisition of Monroe.

The Commission's reasoning is flawed. It ignores Tenneco's decision not to enter the market during the 1960s and early 1970s, a period of high profitability for shock absorber manufacturers, because of anticipated inadequate earnings during early years. The record is devoid of evidentiary support for the Commission's assertion that in the period relevant to this case, when industry earnings were in decline, Tenneco would have been willing to suffer the "cost disadvantage" inherent in the building of an efficient scale plant that would remain underutilized "for a number of years."

The Commission's Conclusion that Tenneco would likely have entered the replacement shock absorber market through toehold acquisition is similarly flawed. The Commission identified Armstrong Patents, Ltd. ("Armstrong"), a British shock absorber manufacturer, DeCarbon Shock Absorber Co. ("DeCarbon"), a French company, and Blackstone Manufacturing Corp. ("Blackstone"), a small United States producer of shock absorbers, as potential toeholds. However, Tenneco in fact negotiated unsuccessfully with Armstrong and DeCarbon. Armstrong management indicated that Tenneco would have to offer a 100 percent premium over the market price of its stock to generate its interest. Tenneco's negotiations with DeCarbon, which were conducted through an independent broker, were equally fruitless. DeCarbon had asked a selling price of 100 times its earnings.

As for Blackstone, the Commission itself described that company as "a small, struggling domestic firm burdened with aged equipment, a less than complete product line, declining market share and a mediocre reputation." Since 1974 Blackstone had unsuccessfully sought a buyer for its business, soliciting, among others, Midas International Corp., which operates a chain of muffler installation shops, and Questor. Nevertheless, the Commission remarkably concluded that Blackstone "would have served as a viable method of toehold entry."

We also conclude that the record contains inadequate evidence to support the Commission's conclusion that Tenneco's acquisition of Monroe violated Section 7 by eliminating Tenneco as a perceived potential competitor in the market for replacement shock absorbers. There is abundant evidence that the oligopolists in the market for replacement shock absorbers perceived Tenneco as a potential entrant. Industry executives testified that they considered Tenneco one of very few manufacturers with both the incentive and the capability to enter the market. This perception was based on Tenneco's financial strength and on the compatibility of shock absorbers with exhaust system parts produced by Tenneco's Walker Division.

However, the Commission's conclusion that the perception of Tenneco as a potential entrant actually tempered the conduct of oligopolists in the market must also be supported by substantial evidence. It is not. Tenneco argued that in the years immediately preceding its acquisition of Monroe the market for replacement shock absorbers had become highly competitive. The Commission apparently agrees with this assessment. The rate of increase in advertised retail prices for shock absorbers fell significantly behind inflation, and mass merchandisers such as Sears, Roebuck replaced traditional wholesale distributors as the leading purchasers of replacement shock absorbers from manufacturers. Sears's retail prices for shock absorbers were frequently below the prices that manufacturers charged wholesale distributors, who were several levels above the retail customer in the traditional chain of distribution.

The advent of increased sales by mass merchandisers coincided with aggressive competition among shock absorber manufacturers. Manufacturers offered substantial discounts off their circulated price sheets to traditional wholesalers and implemented "stocklifting," a practice in which a manufacturer buys a wholesaler's inventory of a competing manufacturer's product and replaces it with his own product.

While agreeing that competitive activity increased dramatically in the mid-1970s, the Commission stated:

> We disagree with [Tenneco] over the cause of that new competitive vigor. In brief, we find that the source of the improved economic performance lay in industry fears that Tenneco was likely to attempt entry—an actual "edge effect"—rather than in the buyer power supposedly asserted by mass merchants against their suppliers.

The Commission's hypothesis depends almost entirely on inferences drawn from the activity of Maremont [Gabriel's owner]. We have no doubt that direct evidence of an "edge effect" is not required to support a Commission finding of a Section 7 violation. In this case, however, direct evidence concerning Tenneco's "edge effect" on Maremont was elicited by the Commission, though it does not support the Commission's conclusion. During the testimony of Byron Pond, Senior Vice-President and Director of Maremont, the following colloquy occurred:

> *Q*: [by Commission Counsel]: Did the presence of Walker, IPC or Midas and/or TRW as likely potential entrants into the shock absorber market, have any effect on Maremont's decisions, business decisions?
> *A*: [by Mr. Pond]: I don't think that we looked specifically at competitors on a periodic basis or potential competitors in developing our strategy. I think we developed our strategy and approach to the business based on how we perceive it and how we perceived the opportunities.

Mr. Pond's testimony constitutes direct evidence that Tenneco had no direct effect on Maremont's business decisions or competitive activity. In the face of this contrary and unchallenged direct evidence, the substantiality of circumstantial evidence arguably suggesting an "edge effect" vanishes. Accordingly, we hold that the Commission's finding that Maremont's actions were probably taken in response to its desire to dissuade Tenneco from entering the market is unsupported by substantial evidence in the record. **Commission order set aside in favor of Tenneco.**

Clayton Act Section 8

If the same individuals control theoretically competing corporations, an obvious potential exists for collusive anticompetitive conduct such as pricefixing or division of markets. Section 8 of the Clayton Act was designed to minimize the risks posed by such interlocks. Initially, section 8 prohibited any person from serving as a *director* of two or more corporations (other than banks or common carriers) if either had "capital, surplus, and undivided profits aggregating more than $1,000,000" and the corporations were, or had been, competitors, "so that elimination of competition by agreement between them" would violate any of the antitrust laws. The Antitrust Amendments Act of 1990 amended section 8's original language to increase the amount required to trigger the statute from $1 million to $10 million (a figure to be adjusted annually by an amount equal to the percentage increase or decrease in the gross national product).

Section 8 establishes a per se standard of liability in the sense that a violation of the statute may be demonstrated without proof that the interlock harmed competition. Until recently, however, the statute's prohibition against interlocks was quite limited in scope because it barred only interlocking *directorates*. Nothing in the original language of section 8 prohibited a person from serving as an *officer* of two competing corporations, or as an officer of one firm and a director of its competitor. The Antitrust Amendments Act of 1990, however, expanded the scope of the statute by including senior "*officers*" (defined as officers elected or chosen by the board of directors) within its reach.

Although government enforcement of section 8 was historically lax, recent years have witnessed some signs of growing government interest in the statute. The Supreme Court, however, has indicated that section 8 should not be interpreted in an expansive fashion that strains the statutory language. *Bank America Corp. v. United States*[8] stemmed from a Justice Department attempt to police interlocking directorates between banks and insurance companies. Never before had an interlock involving a bank been challenged under section 8 because of the specific statutory language prohibiting interlocks between corporations "other than banks." Concerned about the increasing areas in which banks and a variety of other businesses were competing in rapidly changing financial markets, the Justice Department argued that the statutory exception should apply only when both of the companies at issue were banks. Had the department been successful, the consequences for the banking industry could have been significant, given the long history of interlocking directorates between banks and other business corporations. The Supreme Court, however, rejected the government's broad reading of the statute, holding that the "most natural reading" of the statute was that the interlocking corporations must all be corporations "other than banks." The Antitrust Amendments Act of 1990 retained the statutory language exempting banks.

Signs of renewed government interest in section 8 produced significant concern in an era of conglomerate merger activity. Given the wide diversification that characterizes many large corporations, it would be increasingly easy to demonstrate some degree of competitive overlap among a substantial number of large, diversified corporations. Critics alleged that section 8 has operated to discourage qualified persons from serving as directors when no potential for actual competitive harm exists. In response to such criticism, the Antitrust Amendments Act of 1990 specified that individuals may serve as officers or directors of competing corporations when the "competitive overlap" between them is an insignificant part of either company's total sales.

The Robinson-Patman Act

Background

Section 2 of the Clayton Act originally prohibited *local and territorial price discrimination* by sellers, a practice monopolists frequently used to destroy smaller competitors. A large company operating in a number of geographic markets would sell at or below cost in markets where it faced local competitors, and would then make up its losses by selling at higher prices in areas where it faced no competition. Faced with such tactics, the smaller local competitors might eventually be driven out of business. Section 2 was aimed at such **primary level** (or *first line*) price discrimination.

During the 1930s, Congress was confronted with complaints that large chain stores were using their buying power to induce manufacturers to sell to them at prices lower than those offered to their smaller, independent competitors. Chain stores were also inclined to seek and obtain other payments and services their smaller competitors did not receive. Being able to purchase at lower prices and to obtain discriminatory payments and services arguably gave large firms a competitive advantage over their smaller competitors. Such price discrimination in sales to the competing customers of a particular seller is known as **secondary level** (or *second line*) price discrimination.

In addition, the customers of a manufacturer's favored customer (such as a wholesaler receiving a functional discount) may gain a competitive advantage over *their* competitors (for example, other retailers purchasing directly from the manufacturer at a higher price) if the favored customer passes on all or a portion of its discount to its customers. This form of price discrimination is known as **tertiary level** (or *third line*) price discrimination.

Congress responded to these problems by passing the Robinson-Patman Act in 1936. The Robinson-Patman Act preserved Clayton Act section 2's ban on primary level price discrimination. It also amended section 2 to outlaw secondary and tertiary level direct price discrimination, as well as indirect price discrimination in the form of discriminatory payments and services to a seller's customers. Since its enactment, the Robinson-Patman Act has been the subject of widespread dissatisfaction and criticism. Critics have long charged that the act often protects competitors at the expense of promoting competition. Government enforcement of the act has been haphazard over the years, with prominent officials in the Justice Department and the Federal Trade Commission sometimes voicing disagreement with the act's underlying policies and assumptions. This government stance, when combined with Supreme Court decisions making private enforcement of the act difficult, raises questions about the act's future usefulness as a component of our antitrust laws.

Figure 31-2 summarizes the levels of price discrimination addressed by the Robinson-Patman Act.

FIGURE 31-2
Levels of price discrimination

Type of Discrimination	Type of Harm	Example
First Line	Injury to the seller's competitors	A seller subsidizes its low prices in an area of high competition by raising its prices in areas where it has little competition.
Second Line	Injury to the competitors of the favored buyer	A high-volume chain store induces its suppliers to give it discriminatorily low prices, enabling it to undersell its competitors.
Third Line	Injury to the competitors of the favored buyer's buyers	A wholesaler receiving discriminatorily low prices from its manufacturer passes the savings on to its retailers, enabling them to undersell their competitors.

Jurisdiction

The Robinson-Patman Act applies only to discriminatory acts that occur "in commerce." This test is narrower than the "affecting commerce" test employed under the Sherman Act. At least one of the discriminatory acts complained of must take place in interstate commerce. Thus, the act probably would not apply if a Texas manufacturer discriminated in price in sales to two Texas customers. Some lower federal courts have indicated, however, that even wholly intrastate sales may be deemed sufficiently "in commerce" if the nonfavored buyer bought the goods for resale to out-of-state customers.

Section 2(a)

Section 2(a) of the Robinson-Patman Act prohibits sellers, in certain instances, from *discriminating in price* "between different purchasers of commodities of like grade or quality." Such discrimination is prohibited when its effect may be to (1) "substantially ... lessen competition or tend to create a monopoly in any line of commerce," or (2) "injure, destroy, or prevent competition with any person who either grants [*primary level*] or knowingly receives [*secondary level*] the benefit of such discrimination, or with the customers of either of them [*tertiary level*]."

Price Discrimination

To violate section 2(a), a seller must have made two or more sales to different purchasers at different prices. Merely quoting a discriminatory price or refusing to sell except at a discriminatory price is not a violation of the statute, because no actual purchase is involved. For the same reason, price discrimination in lease or consignment transactions is not covered by section 2(a). Actual sales at different prices to different purchasers will not be treated as discriminatory unless the sales were fairly close in time.

For purposes of deciding whether discriminatory prices have been charged to two or more purchasers, the degree of control a parent corporation exercises over its subsidiaries sometimes assumes major importance. For example, a parent that sells a product directly to one customer at a low price may be found to have engaged in price discrimination if a wholesaler actively controlled by the parent contemporaneously sells the same product at a higher price to a competitor of the parent's customer. On the other hand, contemporaneous sales by a parent to a wholly owned subsidiary and to an independent competitor at different prices are not treated as price discrimination, because no true sale has been made to the subsidiary.

Finally, section 2(a) does not directly address the legality of *functional discounts*. Such discounts are sometimes granted to buyers at various levels in a product's chain of distribution because of differences in the functions those buyers perform in the distribution system. As indicated in the *Texaco* case, which follows shortly, the legality of such discounts depends on their competitive effect. If a seller charges wholesale customers lower prices than it charges retail customers, the Robinson-Patman Act is not violated unless the lower wholesale prices are somehow passed on to retailers in competition with the seller's retail customers.

Texaco, Inc. v. Hasbrouck

Ricky Hasbrouck and 11 other plaintiffs were Texaco retail service station dealers in the Spokane area. They purchased gasoline directly from Texaco and resold it at retail under the Texaco trademark. Throughout the relevant time period (1972-81), Texaco also supplied gasoline to two gasoline distributors, Dompier Oil Company and Gull Oil Company, at a price that was at various times between 2.5 cents and 5.75 cents per gallon lower than the price Hasbrouck paid.

Dompier and Gull sold the gasoline they purchased from Texaco to independent retail service stations. Dompier sold the gasoline to retailers under the Texaco trademark; Gull marketed it under private brand names. Gull's customers either sold their gasoline on consignment (in which case they set their own prices) or on commission (in which case Gull set their resale prices).

Gull retained title until the gas was sold to a retail customer in either case. Some of the retail stations supplied by Dompier were owned and operated by Dompier's salaried employees. Both Dompier and Gull picked up gas at the Texaco bulk plant and delivered it to their retail customers, a service for which Dompier was compensated by Texaco at the common carrier rate.

Hasbrouck and the other dealers filed a price discrimination suit against Texaco under section 2(a) of the Robinson-Patman Act. At trial, Texaco argued that its lower prices to Gull and Dompier were lawful "functional discounts." The jury awarded the plaintiffs $1,349,700 in treble damages. When the Ninth Circuit Court of Appeals affirmed the jury award, Texaco appealed.

Source: 496 U.S. 543 (U.S. Sup. Ct. 1990)

Stevens, Justice

Section 2(a) contains no express reference to functional discounts. It does contain two affirmative defenses that provide protection for two categories of discounts—those that are justified by savings in the seller's cost of manufacture, delivery, of sale, and those that represent a good faith response to the equally low prices of a competitor. In order to establish a violation of the Act, plaintiffs had the burden of proving four facts: (1) that Texaco's sales to Gull and Dompier were made in interstate commerce; (2) that the gasoline sold to them was of the same grade and quality as that sold to plaintiffs; (3) that Texaco discriminated in price as between Gull and Dompier on the one hand and plaintiffs on the other; and (4) that the discrimination had a prohibited effect on competition.

The first two elements of plaintiffs' case are not disputed in this Court. Texaco does argue, however, that although it charged different prices, it did not "discriminate in price" within the meaning of the Act, and that, at least to the extent that Gull and Dompier acted as wholesalers, the price differentials did not injure competition. Texaco's first argument would create a blanket exception for all functional discounts. Indeed, carried to its logical conclusion, it would exempt all price differentials except those given to competing purchasers. The primary basis for Texaco's argument is the following comment by Congressman Utterback, an active sponsor of the Act:

> In its meaning as simple English, a discrimination is more than a mere difference. Underlying the meaning of the word is the idea that some relationship exists between the parties to the discrimination which entitles them to equal treatment, whereby the difference granted to one casts some burden or disadvantage upon the other.... [W]here no such relationship exists, where the goods are sold in different markets and the conditions affecting those markets set different price levels for them, the sale to different customers at ... different prices would not constitute discrimination within the meaning of this bill.

We have previously considered this excerpt from the legislative history, and have refused to draw from it the conclusion Texaco proposes. Although the excerpt does support Texaco's argument, we remain persuaded that the argument is foreclosed by the text Ache Act itself. In a statute that plainly reveals a concern with competitive consequences at different levels of distribution, and carefully defines specific affirmative defenses, it would be anomalous to assume that Congress intended the term "discriminate" to have such a limited meaning. Since we have already decided that a price discrimination within the meaning of section 2(a) "is merely a price difference," we must reject Texaco's first argument.

In *FTC v. Morton Salt Co.* (1948), we held that an injury to competition may be inferred from evidence that some purchasers had to pay their supplier "substantially more for their goods than their competitors had to pay." Texaco, supported by the United States and the Federal Trade Commission as *amici curiae*, argues that this presumption should not apply to differences between prices charged to wholesalers and those charged to retailers. Moreover, they argue that it would be inconsistent with fundamental antitrust policies to construe the Act as requiring a seller to control his customers' resale prices. The seller should not be held liable for the independent pricing decisions of his customers. As the Government correctly notes, this argument endorses the position advocated 35 years ago in the Report of the Attorney General's Nation Committee to Study the Antitrust Laws (1955).

After observing that suppliers ought not to be held liable for the independent pricing decisions of their buyers, and that without functional discounts distributors might go uncompensated for the services they performed, the Committee wrote:

> On the other hand, the law should tolerate no subterfuge. For instance, where a wholesaler-retailer *buys* only part of his goods as a wholesaler, he must not claim a functional discount on all. Only to the extent that a buyer *actually* performs certain functions, assuming all the risk, investment, and costs involved, should he legally qualify for a functional discount.

We generally agree with this description of the legal status of functional discounts. A supplier need not satisfy the rigorous requirements of the cost justification defense in order to prove that a particular functional discount is reasonable and accordingly did not cause any substantial lessening of competition between a wholesaler's customers and the supplier's direct customers. The record in this case, however, adequately supports the finding that Texaco violated the Act.

The hypothetical predicate for the Committee's entire discussion of functional discounts is a price differential "that merely accords due recognition and reimbursement for actual marketing functions." Such a discount is not illegal. In this case, however, both the

District Court and the Court of Appeals concluded that there was no substantial evidence indicating that the discounts to Gull and Dompier constituted a reasonable reimbursement for the value to Texaco of their actual marketing functions. Indeed, Dompier was separately compensated for its hauling function, and neither Gull nor Dompier maintained any significant storage facilities.

Both Gull and Dompier received the full discount on all their purchases even though most of their volume was resold directly to consumers. The extra margin on those sales obviously enabled them to price aggressively in both their retail and their wholesale marketing. To the extent that Dompier and Gull competed with plaintiffs in the retail market, the presumption of adverse effect on competition recognized in the *Morton Salt* case becomes all the more appropriate. The evidence indicates, moreover, that Texaco affirmatively encouraged Dompier to expand its retail business and was fully informed about the persistent and marketwide consequences of its own pricing policies. Indeed, its own executives recognized that the dramatic impact on the market was almost entirely attributable to the magnitude of the distributor discount and the hauling allowance. The special facts of this case thus make it peculiarly difficult for Texaco to claim that it is being held liable for the independent pricing decisions of Gull or Dompier.

The competitive injury component of a Robinson-Patman Act violation is not limited to the injury to competition between the favored and disfavored purchaser; it also encompasses the injury to competition between their customers. This conclusion is compelled by the statutory language, which specifically encompasses not only the adverse effect of price discrimination on persons who either grant or knowingly receive the benefit of such discrimination, but also to the "customers of either of them." Such indirect competitive effects surely may not be presumed automatically in every functional discount setting, and, indeed, one would expect that most functional discounts will be legitimate discounts that do not harm competition. At the least, a functional discount that constitutes a reasonable reimbursement for the purchasers' actual marketing functions will not violate the Act. Yet it is also true that not every functional discount is entitled to a judgment of legitimacy, and that it will sometimes be possible to produce evidence showing that a particular discount caused a price discrimination of the sort that the Act prohibits. When such anticompetitive effects are proved—as we believe they were in this case—they are covered by the Act.

Judgment for Hasbrouck affirmed.

Commodities of Like Grade and Quality

Section 2(a) applies only to price discrimination in the sale of *commodities*. Price discrimination involving intangibles, real estate, or services must be challenged under the Sherman Act (as a restraint of trade or an attempt to monopolize) or under the FTC Act (as an unfair method of competition). The essence of price discrimination is that two or more buyers are charged differing prices for the *same* commodity. Sales of commodities of varying grades or quality at varying prices, therefore, do not violate section 2(a) so long as uniform prices are charged for commodities of equal quality. Some *physical difference* in the grade or quality of two products must be shown to justify a price differential between them. Differences solely in the brand name or label under which a product is sold—such as the seller's standard brand and a "house" brand sold to a large customer for resale under the customer's label—do not justify discriminatory pricing.

Anticompetitive Effect

Only price discrimination having a *probable* anticompetitive effect is prohibited by section 2(a). Traditionally, courts have required a higher degree of proof of likely competitive injury in cases involving primary level price discrimination (which may damage the seller's competitors) than in cases involving secondary or tertiary level discrimination (which threatens competition among the seller's customers or its customers' customers). To prove a primary level violation, a market analysis must show that competitive harm has occurred as a result of the seller's engaging in significant and sustained price discrimination with the intent of punishing or disciplining a competitor. Proof of predatory pricing is often offered as evidence of a seller's anticompetitive intent. The *Brown & Williamson* case, which follows shortly, addresses predatory pricing claims under the Robinson-Patman Act and emphasizes that likely harm to competition—not merely to a competitor—remains the critical focus.

In secondary or tertiary level cases, courts tend to infer the existence of competitive injury from evidence of substantial price discrimination between competing purchasers over time. Some qualifications on this point are in order, however. Price discrimination for a short period of time ordinarily does not support an inference of competitive injury. Likewise, if the evidence indicates that nonfavored buyers could have purchased the same goods from other sellers at prices identical to those the defendant seller charged its favored customers, no competitive injury is inferred. Finally, buyers seeking treble damages for secondary or tertiary level harm must still prove that they suffered actual damages as a result of a violation of the act.

Brooke Group Ltd. v. Brown & Williamson Tobacco Corp.

Brown & Williamson Tobacco Corp. (BOO) and Brooke Group Ltd. (referred to here by its former corporate name, Liggett Corp.) are two of only six firms of significant consequence in the oligopolistic cigarette manufacturing industry. In 1980, BW's share of the national cigarette market was roughly 12 percent. This share placed BW a distant third behind market leaders Philip Morris and R. J. Reynolds. Liggett's share was less than half of BW's. Liggett pioneered the development of the economy segment of the national cigarette market in 1980 by introducing a popular line of "black and white" generic cigarettes (low-priced cigarettes sold in plain white packages with simple black lettering). As Liggett's sales of generic cigarettes became substantial, other cigarette manufacturers started introducing economy-priced cigarettes. In 1984, BW introduced a black and white cigarette whose net price was lower than Liggett's. BW achieved this lower price by offering volume rebates to wholesalers.

Liggett sued BW, claiming that BW's volume rebates amounted to price discrimination having a reasonable probability of injuring competition, in violation of section 2(a) of the Robinson-Patman Act. Specifically, Liggett alleged that BW's rebates were integral to a scheme of predatory pricing, under which BW reduced its net prices for generic cigarettes below average variable costs. Liggett further alleged that this pricing by BW

was designed to pressure Liggett to raise its list prices on generic cigarettes, so that the percentage price difference between generic and branded cigarettes would narrow. As a result, according to Liggett, the growth of the economy segment would be restrained and BW would thereby be able to preserve its supracompetitive profits on branded cigarettes. Liggett further asserted that it could not afford to reduce its wholesale rebates without losing market share to BW. Therefore, Liggett claimed that its only choice, if it wished to avoid prolonged losses on the generic line that had become its principal product, was to raise retail prices.

After a 115-day trial, the jury returned a verdict in Liggett's favor for $49.6 million in damages. The district court trebled this amount. After reviewing the trial record, however, the district court concluded that BW was entitled to prevail as a matter of law. The court therefore set aside the jury's verdict and entered judgment in BW's favor. Liggett appealed. The Fourth Circuit Court of Appeals affirmed, holding (apparently) that there cannot be liability for predatory price discrimination that allegedly takes place in the context of an oligopoly such as the cigarette industry. The Supreme Court granted Liggett's petition for a writ of certiorari.

Source: 113 S. Ct. 2578 (U.S. Sup. Ct. 1993)

Kennedy, Justice

Liggett contends that BW's discriminatory volume rebates to wholesalers threatened substantial competitive injury by furthering a predatory pricing scheme designed to purge competition from the economy segment of the cigarette market. This type of injury, which harms direct competitors of the discriminating seller, is known as primary-line injury. [P]rimary-line competitive injury under the Robinson-Patman Act is of the same general character as the injury inflicted by predatory pricing schemes actionable under section 2 of the Sherman Act. [T]he essence of the claim under either statute is the same.

Accordingly, whether the claim alleges predatory pricing under section 2 of the Sherman Act or primary-line price discrimination under the Robinson-Patman Act, two prerequisites to recovery [exist]. First, a plaintiff seeking to establish competitive injury resulting from a rival's low prices must prove that the prices complained of are below an appropriate measure of its rival's costs. [Second, the plaintiff must demonstrate] that the competitor had a reasonable prospect [if the claim is brought under the Robinson-Patman Act], or ... a dangerous probability [if the claim is brought under section 2 of the Sherman Act], of recouping its investment in below-cost prices. Recoupment is the ultimate object of an unlawful predatory-pricing scheme; it is the means by which a predator profits from predation. Without it, predatory pricing produces lower aggregate prices in the market, and consumer welfare is enhanced. That below-cost pricing may impose painful losses on its target is of no moment to the antitrust laws if competition is not injured.

For recoupment to occur, below-cost pricing must be capable ... of producing the intended effects on the firm's rivals, whether driving them from the market, or, as was alleged to be the goal here, causing them to raise their prices to supracompetitive levels within a disciplined oligopoly. If circumstances indicate that below-cost pricing could likely produce its intended effect on the target, there is still the further question whether it would be likely to injure competition in the relevant market. The plaintiff must demonstrate that there is a likelihood that the predatory scheme alleged would cause a rise in prices above a competitive level that would be sufficient to compensate for the amounts expended on the predation. These prerequisites to recovery are not easy to establish, but ... they are essential components of real market injury.

Liggett ... allege[s] ... that BW sought to preserve supracompetitive profits on branded cigarettes by pressuring Liggett to raise its generic cigarette prices through a process of tacit collusion with the other cigarette companies. Tacit collusion, sometimes called oligopolistic price coordination or conscious parallelism, describes the process, not in itself unlawful, by which firms in a concentrated market might in effect share monopoly power, setting their prices at a profit-maximizing, supracompetitive level by recognizing their shared economic interests and their interdependence with respect to price and output decisions.

In *Matsushita Electric Industrial Co. v. Zenith Radio Corp.* (1986), we remarked upon the general implausibility of predatory pricing. *Matsushita* observed that such schemes are even more improbable when they require coordinated action among several firms. However unlikely predatory pricing by multiple firms may be when they conspire, it is even less likely when, as here, there is no express coordination. Firms that seek to recoup predatory losses through the conscious parallelism of oligopoly must rely on uncertain and ambiguous signals to achieve concerted action. The signals are subject to misinterpretation and are a blunt and imprecise means of ensuring smooth cooperation, especially in the context of changing or unprecedented market circumstances. This anticompetitive minuet is most difficult to compose and to perform, even for a disciplined oligopoly.

[O]n the whole, tacit cooperation among oligopolists must be considered the least likely means of recouping predatory losses. In addition to the difficulty of achieving effective tacit coordination and the high likelihood that any attempt to discipline will produce an outbreak of competition, the predator's present losses in a case like this fall on it alone, while the later supracompetitive profits must be shared with every other oligopolist in proportion to its market share, including the intended victim. In this case, for example, BW, with its 11-12% share of the cigarette market, would have had to generate around $9 in supracompetitive profits for each $1 invested in predation; the remaining $8 would belong to its competitors, who had taken no risk.

[However,] [t]o the extent that the Court of Appeals may have held that the interdependent pricing of an oligopoly may never provide a means for achieving recoupment and so may not form the basis of a primary-line injury claim, we disagree. A predatory pricing scheme designed to preserve or create a stable oligopoly, if successful, can injure consumers in the same way, and to the same extent, as one designed to bring about a monopoly. However unlikely that possibility may be as a general matter, when the realities of the market and the record facts indicate that it has occurred and was likely to have succeeded, theory will not stand in the way of liability. The Robinson-Patman Act ... suggests no exclusion from coverage when primaryline injury occurs in an oligopoly setting. We decline to create a per se rule of nonliability [under the Robinson-Patman Act] for predatory price discrimination when recoupment is alleged to take place through supracompetitive oligopoly pricing.

Although Liggett's theory of liability, as an abstract matter, is within the reach of the statute, we agree with the [lower courts] that Liggett was not entitled to submit its case to the jury. Liggett ... failed to demonstrate competitive injury as a matter of law. The evidence is inadequate to show that in pursuing [an alleged below-cost pricing] scheme, BW had a reasonable prospect of recovering its losses from below-cost pricing through slowing the growth of generics.

The only means by which BW is alleged to have established oligopoly pricing ... is through tacit price coordination with the other cigarette firms. Yet the situation facing the cigarette companies in the 1980s would have made such tacit coordination unmanageable. Tacit coordination is facilitated by a stable market environment, fungible products, and a small number of variables upon which the firms seeking to coordinate their pricing may focus. By 1984, however, the cigarette market was in an obvious state of flux. The introduction of generic cigarettes in 1980 represented the first serious price competition in the cigarette market since the 1930s. This development was bound to unsettle previous expectations and patterns of market conduct and to reduce the cigarette firms' ability to predict each other's behavior. The larger number of product types and pricing variables also decreased the probability of effective parallel pricing.

Even if all the cigarette companies were willing to participate in a scheme to restrain the growth of the generic segment, they would not have been able to coordinate their actions and raise prices above a competitive level unless they understood that BW's entry into the [economy] segment was not a genuine effort to compete with Liggett. If even one other firm misinterpreted BW's entry as an effort to expand share, a chain reaction of competitive responses would almost certainly have resulted, and oligopoly discipline would have broken down, perhaps irretrievably. Liggett argues that [BW's] maintaining existing list prices while offering substantial rebates to wholesalers was a signal to the other cigarette firms that BW did not intend to attract additional smokers to the generic segment by its entry. But a reasonable jury could not conclude that this pricing structure eliminated or rendered insignificant the risk that the other firms might misunderstand BW's entry as a competitive move.

We hold that the evidence cannot support a finding that BW's alleged scheme was likely to result in oligopolistic price coordination and sustained supracompetitive pricing in the generic segment of the national cigarette market. Without this, BW had no reasonable prospect of recouping its predatory losses and could not inflict the injury to competition the antitrust laws prohibit.

Judgment for BW affirmed.

Defenses to Section 2(a) Liability

There are three major statutory defenses to liability under section 2(a): *cost justification*, *changing conditions*, and *meeting competition in good faith*.

Cost Justification

Section 2(a) specifically legalizes price differentials that do no more than make an appropriate allowance for differences in the "cost of manufacture, sale, or delivery resulting from the differing methods or quantities" in which goods are sold or delivered to buyers. This defense recognizes the reality that it may be less costly for a seller to service some buyers than others. Sales to buyers purchasing large quantities may in some cases be more cost-effective than small-quantity sales to their competitors. Sellers are allowed to pass on such cost savings to their customers.

Utilizing this *cost justification* defense is quite difficult and expensive for sellers, however, because quantity discounts must be supported by *actual evidence of cost savings*. Sellers are allowed to average their costs and classify their customers into categories based on their average sales costs. The customers included in any particular classification, however, must be sufficiently similar to justify similar treatment.

Changing Conditions

Section 2(a) specifically exempts price discriminations that reflect "changing conditions in the market for or the marketability of the goods." The *changing conditions* defense has been narrowly confined to temporary situations caused by the physical nature of the goods. Examples include the deterioration of perishable goods and a declining market for seasonal goods. This defense also applies to forced judicial sales of the goods (such as during bankruptcy proceedings involving the seller) and to good faith sales by sellers that have decided to cease selling the goods in question.

Meeting Competition

Section 2(b) of the Robinson-Patman Act states that price discrimination may be lawful if the discriminatory lower price was charged "in good faith to meet an equally low price of a competitor." This *meeting competition* defense is necessary to prevent the act from stifling the very competition it was designed to preserve. For example, suppose Sony Corporation has been selling a particular model of video recorder to its customers for $350 per unit. Sony then learns that Sharp Electronics is offering a comparable recorder to Acme Appliance Stores for $300 per unit. Acme, however, competes with Best Buy Video Stores, a Sony customer that has recently been charged the $350 price. Should Sony be forced to refrain from offering the lower competitive price to Acme for fear that Best Buy will charge Sony with price discrimination if it does so? If Sony cannot offer the lower competitive price to Acme, competition between Sony and Sharp will plainly suffer.

Section 2(b) avoids this undesirable result by allowing a seller to charge a lower price to certain customers if the seller has reasonable grounds for believing that the lower price is necessary to meet an equally low price offered by a competitor. Sellers may meet competition *offensively* (to gain a new customer) or *defensively* (to keep an existing customer). The meeting competition defense is subject to significant qualifications, however. First, the lower price must be necessary to meet a lower price charged by a competitor of the *seller*, not to enable a customer of the seller to compete more effectively with that customer's competitors. Second, the seller may lawfully seek only to *meet*, not *beat*, its competitor's price. A seller cannot, however, be held in violation of the act for beating a competitor's price if it did so unknowingly in a good faith attempt to meet competition. Third, the seller may reduce its price only to meet competitors' prices for products of *similar quality*.

Courts also have held that the discriminatory price must be a response to an individual competitive situation rather than the product of a seller's wholesale adoption of a competitor's discriminatory pricing system. However, a seller's competitive response need not be on a customer-by-customer basis, so long as the lower price is offered only to those customers that the seller reasonably believes are being offered a lower price by the seller's competitors.

Indirect Price Discrimination

When Congress passed the Robinson-Patman Act, it also addressed **indirect price discrimination**, which takes the form of a seller's discriminating among competing buyers by making discriminatory payments to selected buyers or by furnishing certain buyers with services not made available to their competitors. Three sections of the act are designed to prevent such practices.

False Brokerage

Section 2(c) prohibits sellers from granting, and buyers from receiving, any "commission, brokerage, or other compensation, or any allowance or discount in lieu thereof, except for services rendered in connection with the sale or purchase of goods." This provision prevents large buyers, either directly or through subsidiary brokerage agents, from receiving phony commissions or brokerage payments from their suppliers. The courts and the FTC originally interpreted section 2(c) as prohibiting any brokerage payments to a buyer or its agent, regardless of whether the buyer or agent had in fact provided sale-related services that would otherwise have been performed by the seller or an independent broker. This narrow interpretation drew heavy criticism, however, because it operated to create a closed shop for independent brokers by denying large buyers any incentive to create their own brokerage services. This interpretation also made it difficult for small, independent retailers to create cooperative buying organizations and thereby match more closely the buying power of their large competitors. More recent decisions have responded to these criticisms by allowing payments that are for services actually performed by buyers and represent actual cost savings to sellers.

Section 2(c), unlike section 2(a), establishes a per se standard of liability. No demonstration of probable anticompetitive effect is required for a violation. Neither the cost justification nor meeting competition defense is available in 2(c) cases. Individual plaintiffs still must prove that they have suffered some injury as a result of a 2(c) violation, however, before they are entitled to recover damages.

Discriminatory Payments and Services

Sellers and their customers benefit from merchandising activities that customers employ to promote the sellers' products. Section 2(d) prohibits sellers from making *discriminatory payments* to competing customers for such customer-performed services as advertising and promotional activities or such customer-provided facilities as shelf space. Section 2(e) prohibits sellers from discriminating in the *services* they provide to competing customers, such as by providing favored customers with a display case or a demonstration kit.

A seller may lawfully make payments or provide services to customers only if the payments or services are made available to all competing customers on *proportionately equal terms*. This means that the seller must inform all customers of the availability of the payments or services and must distribute them on some rational basis, such as the quantity of goods bought by the customer. The seller must also devise a flexible plan that enables its various classes of customers to participate in the payment or services program in an appropriate way.

As does section 2(c), sections 2(d) and 2(e) create a per se liability standard. No proof of probable harm to competition is required for a violation; no cost justification defense is available. The meeting competition defense provided by section 2(b) is applicable, however, to actions under sections 2(d) and 2(e).

Buyer Inducement of Discrimination

Section 2(f) of the Robinson-Patman Act makes it illegal for a buyer *knowingly to induce or receive* a discriminatory price in violation of section 2(a). The logic of the section is that buyers who are successful in demanding discriminatory prices should face liability along with the sellers charging discriminatory prices. To violate section 2(f), the buyer must know that the price the buyer received was unjustifiably discriminatory. This means that the price probably was neither cost justified nor made in response to changing conditions. Section 2(f) does not apply to buyer inducements of discriminatory payments or services prohibited by sections 2(d) and 2(e). Such buyer actions may, however, be attacked as unfair methods of competition under section 5 of the FTC Act.

In *Great Atlantic and Pacific Tea Co. v. FTC*,[9] the Supreme Court further narrowed the effective reach of section 2(f) by holding that buyers who knowingly received a discriminatory price do not violate the act if their seller has a valid defense to the charge of violating section 2(a). The seller in *Great Atlantic* had a "meeting competition in good faith" defense under section 2(b). This fact was held to insulate the buyer from liability even though the buyer knew that the seller had beaten, rather than merely met, its competitor's price.

Antitrust Exceptions and Exemptions

Introduction

A wide variety of economic activities occur outside the reach of the antitrust laws. This is so either because these activities have been specifically exempted by statute or because courts have carved out nonstatutory exceptions designed to balance our antitrust policy in favor of competition against other social policies. With critics charging that a number of existing exemptions are no longer justifiable, recent years have witnessed a judicial tendency to narrow the scope of many exemptions.

Statutory Exemptions

Labor Unions and Certain Union Activities

Sections 6 and 20 of the Clayton Act and the Norris-LaGuardia Act of 1932 provide that *labor unions* are not combinations or conspiracies in restraint of trade and exempt certain union activities, including boycotts and secondary picketing, from antitrust scrutiny. This statutory exemption does not, however, exempt union combinations with nonlabor groups aimed at restraining trade or creating a monopoly. An example of such nonexempted activity would be a labor union's agreement with Employer A to call a strike at Employer B's plants. In an attempt to accommodate the strong public policy in favor of collective bargaining, courts have also created a limited nonstatutory exemption for legitimate union-employer agreements arising from the collective bargaining context.

Agricultural Cooperatives and Certain Cooperative Actions

Section 6 of the Clayton Act and the Capper-Volstead Act exempt the formation and collective marketing activities of *agricultural cooperatives* from antitrust liability. Courts have narrowly construed this exemption, however. Cooperatives including members not engaged in the production of agricultural commodities have been denied exempt status. One such example would be a cooperative including retailers or wholesalers who do not also produce the commodity in question. The agricultural cooperatives exemption extends only to legitimate collective marketing activities. It does not legitimize coercive or predatory practices that are unnecessary to accomplish lawful cooperative goals. For example, this exemption would not prevent the antitrust laws from being applied to a boycott designed to force nonmembers of the cooperative to adopt a pricing policy established by the cooperative.

Joint Export Activities

The Webb-Pomerene Act exempts the *joint export activities* of American companies, so long as those activities do not "artificially or intentionally enhance or depress prices within the United States." The purpose of the act is to encourage export activity by allowing the formation of combinations to enable domestic firms to compete more effectively with foreign cartels. Some critics assert that this exemption is no longer needed because there are fewer foreign cartels today and American firms often play a dominant role in foreign trade. Others question whether any group of American firms enjoying significant domestic market shares in the sale of a particular product could agree on an international marketing strategy, such as the amounts that they will export, without indirectly affecting domestic supplies and prices.

Business of Insurance

The McCarran-Ferguson Act exempts from federal antitrust scrutiny those aspects of the *business of insurance* that are subject to state regulation. The act provides, however, that state law cannot legitimize any agreement to boycott, coerce, or intimidate others. Because the insurance industry is extensively regulated by the states, many practices in the industry are outside the reach of the federal antitrust laws.

    In recent years, however, courts have tended to decrease the scope of this exemption by narrowly construing the meaning of "business of insurance." For example, in *Union Labor Life Insurance Co. v. Pireno,*[10] the Supreme Court held that the exemption did not insulate from antitrust scrutiny a peer review system in which an insurance company used a committee established by a state chiropractic association to review the reasonableness of particular chiropractors' charges. The Court stated that to qualify for the business of insurance exemption, a challenged practice must have the effect of transferring or spreading policyholders' risk and must be an integral part of the policy relationship between the insured and the insurer. Therefore, only practices related to traditional functions of the insurance business, such as underwriting and risk-spreading, are likely to be exempt.

Calls from some quarters for repeal of the McCarran-Ferguson Act have led to the introduction of bills in Congress to that effect in recent years. These proposals for legislation typically contemplate, however, that insurers could continue to participate in certain joint activities, such as collecting and exchanging information on fraudulent claims, pooling historical loss data, and developing standardized policy forms. The ultimate fate of the McCarran-Ferguson Act and its business of insurance exemption remained unclear as of the time this book went to press.

Other Regulated Industries

Many other *regulated industries* enjoy various degrees of antitrust immunity. The airline, banking, utility, railroad, shipping, and securities industries traditionally have been regulated in the public interest. The regulatory agencies supervising such industries have frequently been given the power to approve industry practices such as rate-setting and mergers that would otherwise violate antitrust laws. In recent years, there has been a distinct tendency to deregulate many regulated industries. If this trend continues, a greater portion of the economic activity in these industries could be subjected to antitrust scrutiny.

State Action Exemption

In *Parker v. Brown*,[11] the Supreme Court held that a California state agency's regulation of the production and price of raisins was a state action exempt from the federal antitrust laws. The **state action exemption** developed in *Parker v. Brown* recognizes states' rights to regulate economic activity in the interest of their citizens. It also, however, may tempt business entities to seek "friendly" state regulation as a way of shielding anticompetitive activity from antitrust supervision. Recognizing this possibility, courts have placed important limitations on the scope of the state action exemption.

First, the exemption extends only to governmental actions by a state or to actions compelled by a state acting in its sovereign capacity. Second, as indicated in the *Ticor Title Insurance* case (which follows shortly), challenged activity cannot qualify for immunity under this exemption unless the activity is "clearly articulated and affirmatively expressed as state policy" and "actively supervised" by the state. In other words, the price of antitrust immunity is real regulation by the state. The Supreme Court placed a further limitation on the state action exemption by holding that it does not automatically confer immunity on the actions of municipalities.[12] Municipal conduct is immune only if it was authorized by the state legislature and its anticompetitive effects were a foreseeable result of the authorization. The Court's decision caused concern that the threat of treble damage liability might inhibit legitimate regulatory action by municipal authorities. As a result, Congress passed the Local Government Antitrust Act of 1984. This statute eliminates damage actions against municipalities and their officers, agents, and employees for antitrust violations and makes injunctive relief the sole remedy in such cases. It does not, however, bar damage suits against private individuals who engage in anticompetitive conduct with local government agencies.

Federal Trade Commission v. Ticor Title Insurance Co.

The Federal Trade Commission filed an administrative complaint against six of the nation's title insurance companies, including Ticor Title Insurance Co. The complaint alleged that the title insurers engaged in horizontal price-fixing in their setting of uniform rates for title searches and title examinations. (According to the FTC, these uniform rates pertained to aspects of the business that did not involve insurance, as opposed to the setting of uniform rates for insurance against risk of loss from defective titles. The latter type of ratesetting, which was not challenged by the FTC in this case, would directly involve insurance and would likely be shielded from antitrust scrutiny by the McCarran-Ferguson Act.)

The challenged uniform ratesetting for title searches and title examinations occurred in various states through rating bureaus organized by the title insurers. These rating bureaus allegedly would set standard rates for search and examination services notwithstanding possible differences in efficiencies and costs as between individual title insurance companies. Though privately organized, these rating bureaus and the rates they set were potentially subject to oversight by the various states in which they operated.

Price-fixing by the title insurers was alleged, in the FTC complaint, to have occurred in four states:

Connecticut, Wisconsin, Arizona, and Montana. The administrative law judge (ALJ) held that price-fixing had occurred in each of those four states, but that the requirements of the state action exemption from liability applied to the title insurer's actions in Arizona and Montana. As for the title insurers' actions in Connecticut and Wisconsin, the ALJ concluded that the requirements of the state action exemption were not met and that the title insurers therefore should face legal responsibility for their antitrust violations. The FTC commissioners, reviewing the ALJ's decision, concluded that the state action exemption did not apply to the title insurers' actions in any of the four states. On appeal, the Third Circuit Court of Appeals held that the state action exemption shielded the title insurers' actions in all four of the states.

The Supreme Court granted certiorari. (On the question whether the Third Circuit correctly stated and applied the law regarding the state action exemption, the FTC and the title insurers (referred to below simply as "Ticor") confined their briefing—and the Supreme Court largely confined its discussion—to the regulatory regimes existing under Wisconsin and Montana law.)

Source: 112 S. Ct. 2169 (U.S. Sup. Ct. 1992)

Kennedy, Justice

[I]n *Parker v. Brown* (1943), we upheld a state-supervised market sharing scheme against a Sherman Act challenge. We announced the doctrine that federal antitrust laws are subject to supersession by state regulatory programs. Our decision was grounded in principles of federalism.

In *California Retail Liquor Dealers Association v. Midcal Aluminum, Inc.* (1980), we announced a two-part [state action immunity test] applicable to instances where private parties participate [with the state in allegedly anticompetitive conduct]: "First, the challenged restraint must be one clearly articulated and affirmatively expressed as state policy; second, the policy must be actively supervised by the State itself." *Midcal* confirms that while a State may not confer antitrust immunity on private parties by fiat, it may displace competition with active state supervision if the displacement is both intended by the State and implemented in its specific details. Actual state involvement, not deference to private price fixing arrangements under the general auspices of state law, is the precondition of immunity from federal law. Immunity is conferred out of respect for ongoing regulation by the State, not out of respect for the economics of price restraint.

The rationale was further elaborated in *Patrick v. Burget*. [In that case, it was noted that the *active supervision* element of the test set forth in *Midcal*] "mandates that the State exercise ultimate control over the challenged anticompetitive conduct" [and establishes that] "mere presence of some state involvement or monitoring does not suffice." [*Patrick* also contained the observation that the] "active supervision prong of the *Midcal* test requires that state officials have and exercise power to review particular anticompetitive acts of private parties and disapprove those that fail to accord with state policy."

Our decisions emphasize that the purpose of the active supervision inquiry ... is to determine whether the State has exercised sufficient independent judgment and control so that the details of the rates or prices have been established as a product of deliberate state intervention, not simply by agreement among private parties. [T]he analysis asks whether the State has played a substantial role in determining the specifics of the economic policy. The question is not how well the state regulation works but whether the anticompetitive scheme is the State's own.

In the case before us, the Court of Appeals relied upon [an erroneous] formulation of the active supervision requirement [in] rul[ing] that the active supervision requirement was met and in [holding] that the [title insurers'] conduct was entitled to state action immunity from antitrust liability. Where prices or rates are set as an initial matter by private parties, subject only to a veto if the State chooses to exercise it, the party claiming immunity must show that state officials have undertaken the necessary steps to determine the specifics of the price-fixing or ratesetting scheme. The mere potential for state supervision is not an adequate substitute for a decision by the State. Under these standards, we must conclude that there was no active supervision in either Wisconsin or Montana.

[I]n Wisconsin and Montana, the rating bureaus filed rates with state agencies and ... the so-called negative option rule prevailed. The rates became effective unless they were rejected within a set time. It is [asserted by Ticor] that as a matter of law in those States inaction signified substantive approval. This proposition cannot be reconciled, however, with the detailed findings, entered by the ALJ and adopted by the Commission[ers], which demonstrate that the potential for state supervision was not realized in fact. The ALJ found, and the Commission[ers] agreed, that at most the rate filings were checked for mathematical accuracy. Some were unchecked altogether. In Montana, a rate filing became effective despite the failure of the rating bureau to provide additional requested information. [There was a similar occurrence in Wisconsin.] These findings are fatal to Ticor's attempts to portray the state regulatory regimes as providing the necessary component of active supervision. The findings demonstrate that whatever the potential for state regulatory review in Wisconsin and Montana, active state supervision did not occur. In the absence of active supervision in fact, there can be no state-action immunity for what were otherwise private price fixing agreements.

This case involves horizontal price fixing under a vague imprimatur in form and agency inaction in fact. No antitrust offense is more pernicious than price fixing. In this context, we decline to formulate a rule that would lead to a finding of active state supervision when in fact there was none.

Judgment of court of appeals reversed in favor of Federal Trade Commission; case remanded for further proceedings and consideration of other issues.

The Noerr-Pennington Doctrine

In the *Noerr* and *Pennington* cases, the Supreme Court held that "the Sherman Act does not prohibit two or more persons from associating together in an attempt to persuade the legislature or the executive to take particular action with respect to a law that would produce a restraint or a monopoly."[13] This exemption recognizes that the right to petition government provided by the Bill of Rights takes precedence over the antitrust policy favoring competition. The exemption does not, however, extend to sham activities that are attempts to interfere with the business activities of competitors rather than legitimate attempts to influence governmental action.[14]

Patent Licensing

There is a basic tension between the antitrust objective of promoting competition and the purpose of the patent law, which seeks to promote innovation by granting a limited monopoly to those who develop new products or processes. In the early case of *United States v. General Electric Company*,[15] the Supreme Court allowed General Electric to control the price at which other manufacturers sold light bulbs they had manufactured under patent licensing agreements with General Electric. The Court recognized that an important part of holding a patent was the right to license others to manufacture the patented item. This right effectively would be negated if licensees were allowed to undercut the prices that patent holders charged for their own sales of patented products.

Patent holders cannot, however, lawfully control the price at which patented items are resold by distributors purchasing them from the patent holder. Nor can patent holders use their patents to impose tying agreements on their customers by conditioning the sale of patented items on the purchase of nonpatented items, unless such agreements are otherwise lawful under the Sherman and Clayton Acts. Finally, firms that seek to monopolize an area by acquiring most or all of the patents related to that area of commerce may face liability for violating Sherman Act section 2 or Clayton Act section 7, because a patent has been held to be an asset within the meaning of section 7.

Foreign Commerce

When foreign governments are involved in commercial activities affecting the domestic or international commerce of the United States, our antitrust policy may be at odds with our foreign policy. Congress and the courts have created a variety of antitrust exemptions aimed at reconciling this potential conflict. The Foreign Sovereign Immunities Act of 1976 (FSIA) provides that the governmental actions of foreign sovereigns and their agents are exempt from antitrust liability. The commercial activities of foreign sovereigns, however, are not included within this **sovereign immunity** exemption. Significant international controversy exists concerning the proper criteria for determining whether a particular governmental act is commercial in nature. Under the FSIA, the courts employ a *nature of the act* test, holding that a commercial activity is one that an individual might customarily carry on for a profit.

The **act of state doctrine** provides that an American court cannot adjudicate a politically sensitive dispute whose resolution would require the court to judge the legality of a foreign government's sovereign act. This doctrine reflects judicial deference to the primary role of the executive and legislative branches in the adoption and execution of our foreign policy. The act of state doctrine recognizes (as does the doctrine of sovereign immunity) the importance of respecting the sovereignty of other nations. Unlike the doctrine of sovereign immunity, however, the act of state doctrine also reflects a fundamental attribute of our system of government—the principle of separation of powers.

Finally, the **sovereign compulsion doctrine** provides private parties a defense if they have been compelled by a foreign sovereign to commit, within that sovereign's territory, acts that would otherwise violate the antitrust laws due to their negative impact on our international commerce. To employ this defense successfully, a defendant must show that the challenged actions were the product of actual compulsion—as opposed to mere encouragement or approval—by a foreign sovereign.

Figure 31-3 summarizes the various antitrust exceptions and exemptions

FIGURE 31-3
Antitrust exceptions and
exemptions

Exception/Exemption	Activities Covered	Source
Statutory Labor	Legitimate union activities	Clayton Act, Norris-LaGuardia Act
Nonstatutory Labor	Collective bargaining agreements	Judicial decision (policy favoring collective bargaining)
Agricultural Cooperatives	Legitimate cooperative activities	Clayton Act, Capper-Volstead Act
Export Trade Associations	Joint export activities	Webb-Pomerene Act
Insurance	Business of insurance	McCarran-Ferguson Act
Regulated Industries	Anticompetitive activities shielded by federal regulation	Regulatory statutes
State Action	State authorized and supervised anticompetitive activities	Judicial decision (federalism)
***Noerr-Pennington* Doctrine**	Attempts to induce anticompetitive governmental action	Judicial decision (First Amendment)
Patent Licensing	Legitimate activities of patent holders	Judicial decision (patent laws)
Sovereign Immunity	Governmental acts of foreign sovereigns	Foreign Sovereign Immunities Act
Act of State Doctrine	Sovereign acts of foreign sovereigns	Judicial decision (separation of powers)
Sovereign Compulsion Doctrine	Private acts compelled by foreign sovereigns	Judicial decision

Ethical and Public Policy Concerns

1. Refer to the facts of the Mozart case in this chapter. Assume that some Mercedes dealers sold their customers nonauthorized parts at the same price that they charged for genuine Mercedes parts, but without telling customers that the parts installed were not genuine Mercedes parts. Is such a practice ethically justifiable? Would your answer change if you were convinced that the nonauthorized parts were equal in quality to genuine Mercedes replacement parts?

2. Refer to the facts of problem case 9 at the end of this chapter. Is paying a disguised bribe to win a contract ethically justifiable under such circumstances? Would your answer change if such bribes were a customary means of doing business in Nigeria rather than a violation of Nigerian law?

Problems and Problem Cases

1. Crossland started his own vending machine business in the early 1960s. In 1973, he bid successfully for the vending business at Fort Bliss, Texas. This expansion exacerbated his company's existing financial problems. In 1974, after months of negotiations, Crossland signed a contract under which he agreed to become a franchisee of Canteen Corporation. The agreement called for Canteen to provide Crossland's business with badly needed capital by buying all of Crossland's vending equipment for $350,000 and leasing it back to him. Crossland continued to have financial problems and ultimately reached the point at which his company owed

Canteen $420,000. Crossland sued Canteen, arguing that Canteen had violated the Sherman and Clayton Acts by tying the lease-back of the equipment to the sale of the Canteen franchise. Was Canteen correct in arguing that both claims should be dismissed?

2. Sterling Electric manufactured electric motors and replacement parts for them. No one else made parts compatible with Sterling motors. After being acquired by A. O. Smith Corporation, Sterling instituted new distribution programs. Its new agreement with distributors who stocked its parts required that these "stocking" distributors buy and aggressively promote minimum quantities of Sterling motors, in return for their being able to buy parts for less than the prices Sterling charged "referral" distributors who merely passed on orders for Sterling parts. On October 1, 1982, Sterling terminated Parts and Electric Motors, Inc. (P&E), a stocking distributor, for insufficient motor purchases. P&E then filed suit against Sterling, arguing that the motor purchase requirement was a tying arrangement prohibited by the Sherman and Clayton Acts. At trial, P&E introduced evidence that the purchase requirement forced dealers to increase their motor purchases by more than $250,000. Was the jury verdict in P&E's favor proper?

3. In 1961, Ford Motor Company acquired Autolite, a manufacturer of spark plugs, in order to enter the profitable aftermarket for spark plugs sold as replacement parts. Ford and the other major automobile manufacturers had previously purchased original equipment spark plugs (those installed in new cars when they leave the factory) from independent producers such as Autolite and Champion, either at or below the producer's cost. The independents were willing to sell original equipment plugs so cheaply because aftermarket mechanics often replace original equipment plugs with the same brand of spark plug. GM had already moved into the spark plug market by developing its own division. Ford decided to do so by means of a vertical merger under which it acquired Autolite. Prior to the Autolite acquisition, Ford bought 10 percent of the total spark plug output. The merger left Champion as the only major independent spark plug producer. Champion's market share thereafter declined because Chrysler was the only major original equipment spark plug purchaser remaining in the market. The government filed a divestiture suit against Ford, arguing that Ford's acquisition of Autolite violated section 7 of the Clayton Act. Should Ford have been ordered to divest itself of Autolite?

4. Siemens, a diversified firm with interests in the medical equipment field, notified the Justice Department in 1979 that it intended to acquire control of Searle Diagnostics (SD), a manufacturer of nuclear medical equipment. Ten years earlier, Siemens had failed in an attempt to start its own nuclear medical equipment division. In 1972, it had considered trying to reenter the field but concluded that it would not be able to recoup the investment reentry required. The top four firms in the nuclear medical equipment market accounted for 77 percent of total sales in 1979. This figure, however, was down from 1975, when they accounted for 92 percent of total sales. Although SD was still first in 1979, it had seen its market share fall from 50 percent to 22 percent during the same five-year period. These facts, together with the fact that SD had lost money in 1978 and 1979, led SD's parent firm to agree to the sale to Siemens. The Justice Department sought a preliminary injunction against the merger, arguing that it would violate section 7 by eliminating both perceived and actual potential competition. The department, however, presented no evidence that any attractive toehold purchase was available to Siemens or that Siemens, as an acknowledged likely entrant, had any actual impact on the conduct of existing firms in the market. Was a preliminary injunction appropriate?

5. In 1983, Warner Communications, Inc., the second-largest distributor of prerecorded music (18.9 percent market share) in the United States, agreed to merge part of its record operations and form a joint venture company with Polygram Records, Inc., the sixth largest (7.1 percent market share) distributor. The Federal Trade Commission applied for a preliminary injunction to block the joint venture. The FTC presented evidence that the top four distributors collectively commanded 67 percent of the domestic market and that if the joint venture were completed, their collective market share would increase to 75 percent. In addition, the FTC presented evidence showing a trend toward concentration in the industry and the existence of high barriers to entry by new competitors. The trial court ruled that the FTC had failed to demonstrate the likelihood of ultimate success necessary to justify a preliminary injunction. Was that ruling correct?

6. First Comics, Inc., wanted to enter the comic book publishing business. First hired World Color Press to print its comics because World had a less expensive method of printing than other comic book printers did. World allegedly promised to charge First the same price it charged its larger customers such as Marvel Comics Group and DC Comics. When First discovered it was being charged 4.3 cents per copy more than Marvel, First demanded reimbursement or a future credit. When World refused, First filed a price discrimination suit against World under the Robinson-Patman Act. Does the Robinson-Patman Act apply to this case?

7. Indian Coffee Company, a coffee roaster in Pittsburgh, Pennsylvania, sold its Breakfast Cheer coffee in the Pittsburgh area, where it had an 18 percent market share, and in Cleveland, Ohio, where it had a significant, but smaller, market share. Late in 1971, Folger Coffee Company, then the leading seller of branded coffee west of the Mississippi, entered the Pittsburgh market for the first time. In its effort to gain market share in Pittsburgh, Folger granted retailers high promotional allowances in the form of coupons. Retail customers could use these coupons to obtain price cuts. Redeeming retailers could use the coupons as credits against invoices from Folger. For a time, Indian tried to retain its market share by matching Folger's price concessions, but because Indian only operated in two areas, it could not subsidize such sales with profits from other areas. Indian, which finally was forced out of business in 1974, later filed a Robinson-Patman suit against Folger. At trial, Indian introduced evidence that Folger's Pittsburgh promotional allowances were far higher than its allowances in other geographic areas, and that Folger's Pittsburgh prices were below green (unrousted) coffee cost, below material and manufacturing costs, below total cost, and below marginal cost or average variable cost. Was the trial court's directed verdict in favor of Folger proper?

8. Peugeot Motors of America, Inc. (PMA), the exclusive domestic importer of Peugeot products, controlled all U.S. Peugeot distributors except EAD, the exclusive distributor for Peugeot cars in the southeastern United States. EAD filed suit against PMA, arguing that PMA had violated sections 2(d) and 2(e) of the Robinson-Patman Act by providing cash incentives, training facilities, and parts repurchase programs (allowing dealers to return for credit a part of their obsolete parts inventory) to PMA's dealers without making such incentives, facilities, and programs available to EAD's dealers. The evidence at trial indicated that Memphis, Tennessee, was the only place in the United States where an EAD dealer was within 50 miles of a PMA dealer, and that less than 1 percent of national Peugeot sales were cross-border sales between PMA and EAD territories. EAD's president testified that he did not know the reason for any of the cross-border sales. He also admitted that some such sales occurred for reasons other than competition between the two sets of dealers. The trial court directed a verdict in favor of PMA. Was the trial court correct in doing so?

9. In 1982, a subsidiary of W. S. Kirkpatrick & Co. won a Nigerian Defense Ministry contract for the construction and equipment of an aeromedical center at a Nigerian Air Force base. Environmental Tectonics Corporation (Environmental), an unsuccessful bidder for the same contract, filed RICO and Robinson-Patman Act claims against Kirkpatrick. Environmental alleged that Kirkpatrick had won the contract by paying a 20 percent "commission" to bribe certain Nigerian officials. The parties agreed that the bribes, if paid, would violate Nigerian law. Was the trial court correct in holding that the act of state doctrine barred Environmental's claim?

10. Pocahontas Coal Company filed suit against a number of other companies engaged in the mining and production of coal in West Virginia. Pocahontas alleged that the defendants were involved in a conspiracy to control the production and pricing of coal. One of Pocahontas's specific claims was that the defendants had violated section 8 of the Clayton Act by "deputizing" various persons to sit on the boards of competing subsidiaries. The defendants moved for summary judgment on the section 8 claim, noting that Pocahontas's complaint contained no factual allegations that any of the defendants were competitors, failed to name any of the alleged "deputies," and was ambiguous because it alleged that certain persons were "officers and/or directors" of competing companies. The trial court offered Pocahontas the opportunity to clarify the complaint by bringing forth additional information on these points. Did the court properly grant the defendants summary judgment when Pocahontas declined to do so?

Endnotes

1. *Times-Picayune Publ. Co. v. United States*, 345 U.S. 594 (U.S. Sup. Ct. 1953).
2. 337 U.S. 293 (U.S. Sup. Ct. 1949).
3. 365 U.S. 320 (1961).
4. See, for instance, *United States v. Phillipsburg National Bank*, 389 U.S. 350 (U.S. Sup. Ct. 1970).
5. 374 U.S. 321 (1963).
6. *United States v. Falstaff Brewing Corp.*, 410 U.S. 526 (U.S. Sup. Ct. 1973).
7. *United States v. Marine Bancorporation, Inc.*, 418 U.S. 602 (U.S. Sup. Ct. 1974).
8. 462 U.S. 122 (U.S. Sup. Ct. 1983).
9. 440 U.S. 69 (U.S. Sup. Ct. 1979).
10. 458 U.S. 1 19 (U.S. Sup. Ct. 1982).
11. 317 U.S. 341 (U.S. Sup. Ct. 1943).
12. *Community Communications Co. v. City of Boulder*, 455 U.S. 40 (U.S. Sup. Ct. 1982).
13. *Eastern R.R. President s Conference v. Noerr Motor Freight, Inc.*, 365 U.S. 127 (U.S. Sup. Ct. 1961); *United Mine Workers v. Pennington*, 381 U.S. 657 (U.S. Sup. Ct. 1965).
14. *California Motor Transport v. Trucking Unlimited*, 404 U.S. 508 (U.S. Sup. Ct. 1982).
15. 272 U.S. 476 (U.S. Sup. Ct. 1926).

Chapter Thirty-Two

BUSINESS IN THE

POLITICAL PROCESS

ADM

The Archer-Daniels-Midland Co., often called simply ADM, is a giant food and agricultural products company which had revenues of $12.6 billion in 1994. For many years ADM has had a reputation for working quietly and effectively behind the scenes in Washington, D.C. The story of ethanol is illustrative.

Ethanol is methyl alcohol, the ingredient added to alcoholic beverages. It is made from corn by adding yeast to ferment sugars and starches. It can be combined with gasoline, usually at about 10 percent of the mixture, to create a "reformulated" fuel which can power ordinary cars and trucks. Ethanol is one of a number of so-called oxygenates, or oxygen-containing substances which can be mixed in gasoline to reduce polluting emissions. Ethanol, coming from corn, saves oil and uses renewable resources. ADM dominates the production of ethanol in the United States with about a 60 percent current market share.

MTBE, or methyl tertiary butyl ether, is an oxygenate derived from natural gas which competes with ethanol. ADM does not make MTBE; it is made by the large oil companies from natural gas. The oxygen in both ethanol and MTBE improves gasoline combustion and reduces tailpipe emissions of smog-producing compounds. Just which one is better is a matter of opinion. Various studies have claimed more environmental benefits for one oxygenate over another.[1] But policy in Washington D.C. is not always, or even often, based on scientific merit.

Over the years Congress has bestowed upon ethanol

production a series of subsidies, incentives, and boosts not given to MTBE. In 1990 lobbyists for ADM managed to get Congress to subsidize ethanol in two ways: first, a 5.4 cent per gallon tax break and, second, a tax credit for companies that blend ethanol and gasoline. The creation by government of these tax incentives made ethanol about 30 percent less expensive than MTBE.

Also in 1990, Congress put a section in the Clean Air Act amendments requiring that nine cities with the worst air pollution use gasoline reformulated with an oxygenate, beginning in 1995, to reduce tailpipe emissions. This promised to create a huge market for both ethanol and MTBE.

But the large oil companies prefer to reformulate with MTBE. They are already geared up to produce it in large quantities because for many years they have been making a related compound which maintains octane levels in gasoline with no lead. Also, water condenses out of ethanol so oil company tanks and pipelines cannot be used for fuels aside from ethanol, necessitating capital investments that are unnecessary with MTBE.

Just before the deadline for reformulating fuel with either ethanol or MTBE in 1995, ADM won a political victory that angered the oil companies. The chairperson of ADM, Dwayne O. Andreas, is known as a generous contributor to politicians and political parties. Over the years he had made large campaign contributions to members of Congress who supported ethanol subsidies. Between 1992 and 1994, Andreas, his wife, ADM executives, and ADM's political action committee had given

---

Business, Government, and Society, Eighth Edition, by George A. Steiner and John F. Steiner. © Irwin/ McGraw-Hill, The McGraw-Hill Companies, 1985, 1988, 1991, 1994, 1997.

continued

event. Only eight days later the Environmental Protection Agency issued a ruling which required gasoline manufacturers to add ethanol in 30 percent of reformulated gasoline. This ruling would have created a huge new market for ethanol. But it seemed to violate a two-year-old negotiated agreement between the EPA, oil companies, and environmentalists that would not have given preference to either ethanol or MTBE. Under fire by the oil companies, the EPA said that use of ethanol provided environmental benefits, but there was great speculation that White House interest had played a role.

The oil companies, furious, called on their political allies in Congress to deny funding for the EPA to enforce its rule. A bill that would have done this came to a vote in late 1994 and when the Senate split 50-50 Vice President Al Gore broke the tie by voting against it. Yet ADM had not won. The oil companies filed a lawsuit claiming that the EPA had no authority under the original Clean Air Act amendments to require ethanol over MTBE and a federal court agreed.[2] This blocked the rule and allowed the oil companies to use MTBE in reformulated gasoline without restriction.

The ADM story illustrates that corporations can achieve tangible benefits to the bottom line with lobbying and campaign contributions. It also illustrates that even companies with tremendous political resources can be checked and countered in Washington politics. In this chapter we will discuss the history and nature of business participation in the political process.

How the Structure of American Government Affects Business

Throughout American history, business has sought and exercised political power in a government that is extraordinarily open to influence. This power, whether used for good or ill, is exercised on constitutional terrain created by the Founding Fathers over 200 years ago. The Constitution of the United States, as elaborated by judicial interpretation since its adoption in 1789, establishes the formal structure of government and broad rules of political activity. Its formal provisions predispose a certain pragmatic, freewheeling political culture which marks day-to-day political life.

Several basic features of the Constitution shape the political system. Each stands as a barrier to the concentrated power that the Founders feared would lead to tyranny. Each has great consequences for corporate political activity.

First, the Constitution sets up a federal system, or a government in which powers are divided between a national government and fifty state governments. This structure has great significance for business, particularly for large corporations with national markets and operations. These corporations are affected by political actions at different levels and in many places. One example of the significance of the federal system is the story of cigarette warning labels. The supremacy clause in the Constitution stipulates that when the federal government passes a law it preempts state laws in that area. In the 1960s, when New York and other states tried to require warning labels on cigarette packages, the tobacco companies supported two labeling laws passed by Congress.[3] If Congress had not acted, each state could have become a political battleground pitting antismoking forces against the cigarette makers over the wording of the warnings.

Second, the Constitution establishes a system of *separation of powers*, whereby the three branches of the federal government—legislative, executive, and judicial—have checks and balances over each other. The states mimic these power-sharing arrangements in their governments. For business, this means that the actions of one branch do not fully define public policy. For example, after Congress passes a law, corporations lobby regulatory agencies in the executive branch to get favorable implementation of its provisions.

Third, the Constitution provides for *judicial review*. This is the power of judges, ultimately those of the Supreme Court, to review actions of government officials and to refuse to uphold those which conflict with their interpretation of the Constitution. A classic example of judicial review occurred in the spring of 1952 when United States military forces in Korea were hard-pressed and a strike by the steelworkers' union threatened to shut down steel production. President Harry Truman ordered his Secretary of Commerce to take possession of and run the steel industry. However, the Supreme Court held that Truman had exceeded his constitutional powers and the steel companies were returned to private hands.[4] In addition to reviewing government actions, the Supreme Court also defines and redefines the great clauses of the Constitution.

The government structure created by the Constitution is open. It has many points of access, and it invites business and other interests to attempt influence. Because no single, central authority exists, significant government action often requires widespread cooperation among levels and branches of government that share power. The system also is particularly vulnerable to blockage and delay. Because significant actions require the combined authority of several elements in the political arena, special interests can block action by getting a favorable hearing at only one juncture. To get action, on the other hand, an interest like business must successfully pressure many actors in the political equation. Thus there has developed a pragmatic political culture in the American system, in which interests are willing to bargain, compromise, and form temporary alliances to achieve their goals rather than stand firm on rigid ideological positions.

The First Amendment is an additional feature of the Constitution critical to business. It protects the right of business to organize and press its agenda on government. In its elegantly archaic language is stated the right "to petition the government for redress of grievances." The First Amendment also protects rights of free speech, freedom of the press, and freedom of assembly—all critical for pressuring government. Without these guarantees, the letter-writing campaigns, speeches, newspaper editorials, and advertisements that business orchestrates might be banned. Imagine how undesirably different our system would be if the public, angered by "windfall" profits, pressured Congress to restrict the lobbying rights of some industry. While the corporate right of free speech is expansive, it is greatly restricted in one area. The Supreme Court has defined monetary campaign contributions as a form of speech[5] and, as will be explained later in this chapter, these contributions are severely restricted because of fears that corporate money will corrupt elections.

A History of Political Dominance by Business

Though not ordained in the Constitution, the preeminence of business interests in the political pressure equation has been an enduring fact in America. Some historians believe that the Revolutionary War of 1775-1783 was fought to free colonial business interests from smothering British mercantile policies.[6] The Founders who later drafted the Constitution were an economic elite. John Jay and Robert Morris, for example, were among the wealthiest men in the colonies. It comes as no surprise that the government arrangements they fabricated were conducive to domination by business interests. The prominent historian Charles Beard argued that the Constitution was an "economic document" drawn up and ratified by propertied interests for their own benefit.[7] His thesis was and remains controversial, in part because it trivializes the importance of philosophical, social, and cultural forces in the politics of constitutional adoption.[8] Nevertheless, the record of business in American politics subsequent to the adoption of the Constitution is one of virtually unbroken predominance.

Business interests were important in the new nation, but did not dominate to the extent that they would later. There were few large companies. The economy was 90 percent agricultural, so farmers and planters were a major element in the political elite. Their interests balanced and checked those of infant industry. Of course, the fledgling government was a tiny presence. Economic regulation was virtually nonexistent.

In this setting two fundamentally different political ideologies clashed, and one was victorious. The outcome of this clash defines to this day the general character of business political activity and the nature of opposition to it. The two ideologies first emerged during the debate over ratification of the Constitution. Later, each came to be championed by an officer in the cabinet of the first President, George Washington.

Secretary of the Treasury Alexander Hamilton led advocates of the ideology of *industrialism*. Industrialism was derived from the basic tenets of capitalism and equated progress with economic growth and capital accumulation. Hamilton advocated interpreting constitutional powers broadly to create a strong, pro-business federal government. Hamilton mistrusted the common citizen, having once said that "the people is a great beast"; he advocated rule by an economic elite.[9] During Washington's administration, from 1789 to 1796, Hamilton implemented a visionary program to stimulate the economy which included plans to finance the Revolutionary War debt, establish a national bank, and raise tariff protection for American manufacturers. His actions laid essential groundwork for the unexampled economic growth that came in the next century.

Hamilton was opposed by agrarian interests. These were led by Thomas Jefferson, Washington's Secretary of State. Jefferson and his followers developed the ideology of agrarianism, which extolled the virtues of a rural nation of free landowners. Jefferson had a deep reverence, akin to mysticism, for the wisdom of ordinary farmers, once writing that they kept alive a "sacred fire" of virtue that God had deposited in their breasts.[10] He trusted in rule by commoners. He also believed that heavy industrial development had undesirable consequences. Farmers left the land to become laborers exploited by factory owners. They moved to cities where slums, poverty, and crime dissipated their lives. Government became a plutocracy. In contrast, Jefferson wanted to preserve the simplicity of rural life which bred values of egalitarianism, humanitarianism, and simple justice. He disagreed with Hamilton's expansive interpretation of the Constitution and argued that the federal government should stay small and have limited powers.

Though the two ideologies were hotly debated in the 1790s, agrarianism rapidly faltered. History conspired against it. Rapid economic development in the new nation soon turned the agrarian ideology into an ideal rather than a practical alternative. Although Jefferson served as President from 1800 to 1808, it was already too late to reverse Hamilton's commitment of government machinery to the ideology of industrialism. As the century progressed the economy grew, and with it the political power of business. The ideology of agrarianism, with its emphasis on rural life, citizen democracy, and human rights, lived on in American society as a subordinate set of values which inspired reformers.

Throughout the nineteenth century, business interests grew in strength. When the Civil War decimated the power base of southern agriculture, a major counterweight to the power of northern industry vanished. In the period following the Civil War, big business dominated state governments and the federal government in a way never seen before or since. It was a time of great imbalance, in which economic interests faced only frail obstacles. It was commonplace for corporations to manipulate the politics of whole states. West Virginia and Kentucky were dominated by coal companies. New York, a number of midwestern states, and California were dominated by railroads. Montana politics were controlled by the Anaconda Copper Mining Company. In Ohio, Texas, and Pennsylvania oil companies were predominant; the great critic of Standard Oil, Henry Demarest Lloyd, wrote that "the Standard has done everything with the Pennsylvania legislature, except refine it."[11] Business was also predominant in Washington, D.C. Through ascendancy in the Republican party, major corporations had decisive influence over the nomination and election of a string of pro-business Republican Presidents from Ulysses S. Grant in 1868 to

William McKinley in 1900.[12] In the Congress, senators were suborned by business money; some even openly represented companies and industries. One observer noted that in 1889,

> a United States senator ... represented something more than a state, more even than a region. He represented principalities and powers in business. One senator, for instance, represented the Union Pacific Railway System, another the New York Central, still another the insurance interests of New York and New Jersey.... Coal and iron owned a coterie from the Middle and Eastern seaport states. Cotton had half a dozen senators. And so it went.[13]

Nineteenth century political cartoonist Joseph Keppler (1838-1894) was a critic of big business who particularly resented the ascendancy of moneyed interests in politics. This cartoon, which appeared in the magazine *Puck* on January 23, 1889, reflected his exasperation with the situation in that period.

The Bosses of the Senate

Under these circumstances corruption was rampant. Grant's first term, for example, was stained by the famous "whisky ring" scandals in which liquor companies cheated in paying taxes and a member of Grant's cabinet solicited bribes in exchange for licenses to sell liquor to Indian tribes. In Grant's second term the Credit Mobilier Company gave away shares of stock to members of Congress to avoid investigation of its fraudulent railroad construction work.

The soaring political fortunes of business in the post-Civil War era invited reaction. A counterbalancing of corporate power began which continues to this day. Late in the century, farmers sought to reassert agrarian values with the Populist party. They floundered, but not before wresting control of a number of state legislatures from corporations. Two other formidable adversaries emerged. One was organized labor. The other was the powerful Anti-Saloon League, which advocated prohibition of alcoholic beverages. Like labor, the Anti-Saloon League became a strong national foe of business. Brewers and distillers were not its only adversaries. Big corporations in many industries worked against prohibition because they opposed the principle and onset of more government regulation.

After 1900, reforms of the progressive movement curtailed overweening corporate power. For example, the Seventeenth Amendment in 1913 instituted the direct election of senators by voters in each state. Corporations fought the amendment. Before, senators had been chosen by state legislatures, a procedure that invited corrupting influence by big corporations. For example, in 1884 representatives of Standard Oil called members of the Ohio legislatures one by one into a back room where $65,000 in bribes were handed out to obtain the election of Henry B. Payne to the Senate. One witness saw "canvas bags and coin bags and cases for greenbacks littered and scattered around the room and on the table and on the floor ... with something green sticking out."[14] Corporations also fought suffrage for women. The battle was led by liquor companies, which feared that women would vote for prohibition. But there was broader fear of women voters. It was widely believed by businessmen that women would vote for radical and socialist measures. The powerful Woman's Christian Temperance Union, which had as many as 10,000 local chapters by 1890, frightened business by standing against liquor, child labor, and income inequality. But after adoption of the Nineteenth Amendment in 1920 the women's vote brought no great change in national politics.

The great political reforms of the progressive era were reactions to corruption in a political system dominated by business. It would be a mistake, however, to conclude that because of reforms and newly emerged opponents the primacy of economic interests had been eclipsed. While business was more often checked after the turn of the century, it remained preeminent. Corruption continued. In 1920 Warren G. Harding, a back-room candidate selected by powerful business interests at a deadlocked Republican party convention, was elected President. His Vice President was Calvin Coolidge, the rabidly antilabor ax-governor of Massachusetts. Harding's administration was so beset by scandals in which officials accepted money for granting favors to corporations that Congress was considering impeaching him when he died of a stroke in 1923. The worst scandal involved Secretary of the Interior Albert B. Fall, who accepted bribes from oil company executives in return for the right to pump oil from government reserves in Teapot Dome, Wyoming. The Teapot Dome affair came to light only after Harding's death, but so besmirched his reputation that it was eight years before his grand tomb in Marion, Ohio, could be dedicated.

By that time the stock market had crashed and catastrophic economic depression racked the country. Conservative business executives argued that the depression would correct itself without government action. After the election of Franklin D. Roosevelt in 1932, corporations fought his measures to regulate banking and industry, strengthen labor unions, and enact social security. Du Pont, General Motors, and other firms supported the anti-Roosevelt Liberty Lobby, which opposed New Deal measures. Against social security, for example, business lobbyists argued that children would no longer support aging parents, that the required payroll tax would discourage workers and they would quit their jobs, and that its protection would remove the "romance of life."

Many executives hated Roosevelt. They said that he was bringing communism to the United States and called him names such as "Stalin Delano Roosevelt."[15] But business had lost its way. Corporate opposition to New Deal measures ran counter to public sentiment. It became ineffective and was sometimes disgraceful. In 1935, for example, utility lobbyists sent Congress 250,000 fake letters and telegrams in a losing effort to stop a bill. Subsequently they ran a whispering campaign saying Roosevelt was insane.

Much New Deal legislation was profoundly egalitarian and humanitarian and reasserted the tradition of agrarian idealism. Because business lacked a positive philosophy for change, its political power was greatly diminished. According to Edwin M. Epstein, "corporate political influence reached its nadir during the New Deal."[16] Roosevelt was hurt by the hate and felt that through his major New Deal programs he had saved capitalism in spite of the capitalists.

The New Deal was a political sea change born out of the Great Depression. One lasting legacy of the era was the philosophy that government should be used to correct the flaws of capitalism and control the economy so that prosperity would no longer depend solely on unbridled market forces.[17] Government would also be used to create a "welfare states to protect citizens from want. Whereas in the past, government had kept its hands off corporations, now it would actively use interest rates, regulation, taxes, subsidies, and other policy instruments to control them. Whereas in the past, most domestic spending had been for infrastructure programs that promoted business, spending would increasingly focus on social programs such as social security. These changes laid the groundwork for an increasingly large, powerful, and activist federal government.

In the 1940s industry's patriotic World War II production record and subsequent postwar prosperity quieted lingering public restiveness about corporate political activity. During the 1950s corporations once again predominated in a very hospitable political environment. In the years between 1952 and 1960, Dwight D. Eisenhower was a pro-business President with a cabinet dominated by political appointees from business. A pro-business conservative coalition of southern Democrats and Republicans in Congress ensured legislative support. Corporations could promote their policy agendas by influencing a small number of leaders. Charls E. Walker, an official in the Eisenhower administration and currently a business lobbyist recalls how only four men shaped economic policy.

> These four officials were President Eisenhower, Treasury Secretary Robert Anderson, Speaker of the House Sam Rayburn, and Senate majority leader Lyndon B. Johnson. These four men would get together every week over a drink at the White House and the President would say, "I think we ought to do this or that." Then Mr. Sam or LBJ might say, "Well, that's a real good idea; send it up and we'll get it through." And they would. They could deliver because at that time they had great influence in Congress, partly because of the seniority system.[18]

But changing political trends soon forced business into more aggressive and sophisticated forms of political intervention. During the 1960s and 1970s, national politics became dominated by a liberal reform agenda. New groups arose to challenge business, reforms in Congress made that institution more openly democratic and responsive to business's foes, business was bridled with massive new regulatory programs, and the government dramatically increased the scope of its activities.[19] During this period the business agenda suffered defeats at the hands of public interest groups and increasingly powerful agency heads in government. These defeats encouraged corporations to become more aggressive and sophisticated in their political activity.

The Rise of Antagonistic Groups

During the late 1960s the climate of pressure politics began to change with the rise of new groups focused on consumer, environmental, taxpayer, civil rights, and other issues. A few of them, such as Ralph Nader's Public Citizen, Inc., the Natural Resources Defense Council, and the Consumer Federation of America grew to have large dues-paying memberships and considerable power to advance a broad agenda advocating restriction and regulation of business. The presence of these groups fundamentally altered the political arena for business. Whereas a decade earlier corporations could dominate Washington politics with quiet, behind-the-scenes influence with key leaders, they now faced an array of hostile groups which, although having less financial resources than business, took advantage of the prevailing climate of public opinion to wrest control of the policy agenda away from business. These groups created the political pressure necessary to enact the many new regulatory programs of this era.

The rise of groups hostile to business is part of a broader trend in which new groups of all kinds, including business and trade associations, have been stimulated by the growth of the federal government. Government growth is reflected by huge jumps in federal spending. In 1960 the federal budget was $92 billion. By 1980 it had reached $591 billion, an increase of over 600 percent. In 1994 it was $1.3 trillion.[20] As government grows, interest groups proliferate around policy areas. One estimate is that there are now around 23,000 organized interest groups, roughly 400 percent more than in the 1950s.[21]

Consumer groups exemplify the trend. Until the late 1960s there were two major groups, both long-established: the National Consumer's League and Consumer's Union.

But between 1967 and 1985 forty-three new groups were formed.[22]   These new groups expanded the policy area of consumerism and their political pressure led to proliferation of federal consumer regulations and the creation of two new federal regulatory agencies (the National Highway Traffic Safety Administration and the Consumer Product Safety Commission).

Most public interest/environmental/reform groups appeal to a liberal constituency and are antagonistic toward business. A survey in the 1970s of lobbyists from eighty-three such groups found that 74 percent placed themselves from liberal to radical on the political spectrum and only 10 percent were conservative.[23] Over twenty years later another study found that this ideological tendency continues. Only 19 percent of environmental group leaders, for example, think that corporations "are serving the public interest."[24]

Citizen lobbies generally are unable to match the financial resources of business, but they do have some advantages. Many focus on dramatic, emotional, or confrontational issues and get wide media coverage. They also get the support of the general public by identifying themselves with the lofty ideal of the public interest in opposition to the so-called special interests of business. Although GM, Ford, and Chrysler and their suppliers employ 1.5 million workers and major oil companies have tens of millions of shareholders, such large companies and industries are regarded as self-seeking interests in contrast to public interest lobbies—no matter how small the membership in the latter.

Diffusion of Power in Government

A second change in the climate of politics, in addition to new groups, has been the diffusion and decentralization of power in Washington, D.C. Three major reasons for this are (1) reforms in Congress, (2) the decline of political parties, and (3) increased complexity of government.

Traditionally, both the House and Senate were run autocratically by a few party leaders and powerful committee chairs. But the stubborn resistance of southern Democrats to civil rights legislation in the 1960s eventually led in 1974 to an uprising of junior members of Congress, who passed a series of procedural reforms that democratized Congress by taking power from a few party leaders and diffusing it widely. After 1974 subcommittees could hold hearings on any subject they wished; they developed large staffs and often became small fiefdoms of independent action. Instead of an institution dominated by a few leaders, Congress was described by one observer as "like a log floating down a river with 535 giant ants aboard, and each one thinks he or she is steering."[25] Business lobbyists had to contact nearly every member of a committee or subcommittee to get support for a measure, rather than just the chair.

At the same time, changes outside Congress further undermined party leaders. One change was the rise of political action committees (PACs) formed by interest groups and corporations to contribute campaign money. Previously, Senate and House members who were loyal to party leaders could count on substantial campaign money from the Republican and Democratic parties. After 1974, however, special-interest PACs began contributing such large amounts that legislators could act independently of party leaders and still raise campaign funds.

Other factors have eroded party authority also. The media, and particularly television, has to some extent replaced the parties as sources of information about candidates and issues. Politicians can bypass their parties simply by speaking directly to the public on emotional issues. Also, the electorate is more highly educated and independent than it was in past eras and many voters identify only weakly with the parties. Increasingly they split their ballots and use decision cues other than party labels.

In the 104th Congress, particularly in the House under the leadership of Republican

Speaker Newt Gingrich, there was an effort to reimpose party discipline to pass the Republican "Contract With America." Political parties have also once again become significant sources of campaign funding for candidates through a 1979 amendment of election law that lets them collect and spend large amounts of so-called soft money. But parties have not returned to the central position they once occupied.

An additional cause of power diffusion is simply that the federal government has grown in size and complexity. In Washington today a maze of competing power centers, including elected officials, congressional committees, cabinet departments, regulatory agencies, political parties, courts, and interest groups affects the business environment. The relationships among these power centers continuously shift as partisan tides, personal ambitions, power struggles, and emerging issues glide across the political landscape.

The sum total of government activity has a much greater impact on the business environment than in historical times. Government action affects taxes, interest rates, import/export rules, antitrust policy, defense spending, regulatory compliance costs, health care costs, relationships with foreign nations, the dollar exchange rate, research and development, technology transfer, and other factors.[26]

Today, corporations are far more politically active than in past eras. Since the political environment changed fundamentally in the late 1960s and early 1970s business has been forced to become more sophisticated in its influence efforts. Behind-the-scenes contacts and big campaign contributions less frequently suffice to triumph over opposing interests. In addition, the sheer growth in size and scope of government means that its actions could be critical to business operations. Many bills passed by Congress, such as tax, trade, and appropriations laws, have a direct impact on earnings. For example, when Congress increased the federal excise tax on beer in 1991 there was a 2 percent decrease in beer sales and 31,000 jobs were lost.[27] The change of a few words or the insertion of a special exception in legislation can be worth millions of dollars. Therefore, business leaders are adopting coordinated strategies for political contributions, establishing early warning systems to track policy issues, using computerized communications to mobilize political support, training managers to watch political trends, and hiring influential Washington insiders to work with company lobbyists.

The Universe of Organized Business Interests

There are literally thousands of groups that represent business. What follows is a summary of this universe.

The most prominent groups are peak associations which represent many different companies. The largest is the U.S. Chamber of Commerce, which was founded in 1912. The Chamber is a federation of 3,000 local and state chapters; 1,200 trade associations; and 215,000 companies. The next largest is the National Association of Manufacturers, founded in 1895, which as the name suggests, represents manufacturers. It has a membership of 13,500 companies. Both the Chamber and the NAM have staffs of lobbyists who carry a conservative business agenda to Congress. But because their memberships are primarily small firms, when issues divide big and small firms, they are sometimes unable to support the positions taken by the largest corporations. Hence, several powerful organizations have arisen to represent the views of the largest corporations.

The Business Council was started in 1933 in response to Franklin D. Roosevelt's desire to have a business advisory body for the Department of Commerce. Its membership is limited to about 100 chief executives of the largest corporations who are picked to represent geographic regions and major industries. The council does not take positions on policy issues or lobby in the traditional sense. Its members meet in forums with high government officials several times each year to exchange ideas. The council's influence is very low key. A second group, the Committee for Economic Development (CED), is directed by approximately 250 trustees, most of whom are chief executives of the biggest corporations. Subcommittees of trustees are set up to focus on a few key policy areas and their members commit themselves to speak out and lobby on behalf of CED positions. A third group, the Business Roundtable founded in 1972, is led by 200 CEOs of the largest corporations. Like the CED, the Business Roundtable focuses on a limited number of issues critical to large corporations and the member-CEOs personally lobby members of Congress and mobilize the lobbying resources of their companies behind Roundtable positions.

Other peak associations represent groups of medium-size or small businesses. The American Business Conference (ABC) was started in 1981 to represent fast-growing, midsize firms. Its membership is strictly limited to 100 CEOs of corporations that have grown at two times GDP plus inflation over the past five years and have revenues between $25 million and $2 billion. The names of member companies are confidential. The ABC does not lobby for particular industries or companies, but for a broad agenda favoring rapid growth.

In addition to these seven peak associations, more than 6,000 *trade associations* represent companies grouped by industry. Virtually every industry has one or more such associations. Illustrative are the American Boiler Manufacturers Association, the Compressed Gas Association, the Corn Refiners Association, the National Turkey Federation, and the Institute of Makers of Explosives. In addition to lobbying for the industries they represent, these associations also act as early warning systems in Washington for companies, hold training conferences, publish data, and provide other services.[28] Trade associations for large industries, such as the American Petroleum Institute, have larger staffs and more financial resources than most consumer or public interest groups.

About 700 corporations now have staffs of government relations experts in Washington, compared with fewer than 200 in the late 1960s. These *Washington offices* are set up mainly by big companies. General Electric, for example, has a staff of twelve lobbyists organized into teams which specialize in lobbying on government activity that affects the company's separate business lines. Some lobbyists specialize in contacting Republicans; others work more with Democrats. The office also provides GE managers with information about how changes in Washington may affect future operations. Although a few smaller firms have Washington offices, they are expensive, and small companies tend to rely on trade associations or hired lobbyists.

Business interests also form *coalitions* to create broader support. There are, today, hundreds of business interest coalitions in Washington. For example, in 1995 when a bill was introduced in Congress to regulate obscenity on the Internet a group of 300 on-line service, telephone, newspaper, and cable companies formed a lobbying coalition called the Online Operators Policy Committee. Such coalitions of instant allies form around policy issues. They are both numerous and ephemeral.

Business gains strength when it is united, but there is frequent disunity. Skirmishes occur, for example, between domestic and foreign firms, truckers and railroads, manufacturers and retailers, banks and insurance companies, and raw material producers and end-product manufacturers. An example of the latter is that the American Sugar Alliance, representing 68,000 sugar growers and refiners, is fighting to preserve federal price supports on sugar in opposition to big corporations such as RJR Nabisco, Coca-Cola, and the Kraft Foods division of Philip Morris, which claim that higher sugar prices raise the cost of manufacturing cookies, candy, and soft drinks.

The Government Relations Process

There are two basic areas of business involvement in politics. The first is government relations, or lobbying, in which business influences policy by contacting government officials. The second is the electoral process, in which business contributes money to political campaigns at all levels of government. Naturally, these areas are related.

Lobbying

A lobby may be defined as the point of access of a corporation, trade association, or other interest group to a part of government. A lobbyist is a person who presents the position of a corporation, interest group, or trade association to a government official. The word "lobbyist" grew into usage in the nineteenth century to describe the practice of standing in the lobbies of legislatures attempting to buttonhole legislators. Today, of course, the influence process is much more sophisticated.

The exact number of lobbyists is elusive. The American League of Lobbyists estimates that approximately 10,000 persons engage in regular, face-to-face contact with senators, representatives, and top executive branch officials.[29] Lobbyists are loosely regulated. The House of Representatives prohibits them from giving gifts of any size to members, including, for example, meals and travel. The Senate prohibits any gift from other than a family member or longtime personal friend over $50 or any series of gifts over $10 which add up to over $100 per year. Campaign contributions are not, of course, categorized as gifts. Beyond anti-bribery laws and these limits on the value of gifts to members of Congress, there are few legal restrictions on lobbying.[30] It is difficult to restrict lobbying, because political advocacy is speech protected by the First Amendment.

Although business lobbyists have been condemned for pleading selfish interests, ignoring the public interest, and corrupting officials, most scholars of American politics believe that they perform two valuable functions. First, lobbyists give legislators useful technical information about bills, and second, they give them politically relevant information about how constituents and interests stand. These functions are useful to busy legislators who cannot themselves fully investigate every provision in the roughly 12,000 bills considered in Congress each year. Every industry has quirks and problems, of which industry lobbyists have special knowledge. Says former Representative Bob S. Bergland:

> Lobbyists perform a useful function. For example, I served on two committees of the House, but there were dozens of bills on the floor from committees [of] which I was not a member. I oftentimes would not know how they would affect my district. I would call lobbyists and ask them. If they level with you it's terribly important.[31]

It is possible for a lobbyist to mislead a lawmaker with biased information. But this is counterproductive. Lawmakers shut out lobbyists who mislead them. A lobbyist who lacks integrity loses access to the very people he or she earns a living from influencing. In addition, effective business lobbyists must defend their proposals on the basis of public benefit since lawmakers and regulators, as a rule, cannot justify acting simply to promote corporate self-interest.

In addition, legislators may recruit lobbyists to further their agendas. In the 104th Congress, for example, the Republican leadership in the House of Representatives met regularly on Thursday mornings with corporate lobbyists to discuss strategy for passing elements of the "Contract With America." As a result of these meetings, the lobbyists in this so-called Thursday Group put together coalitions of corporations, trade associations, and conservative groups; raised funds for expensive lobbying efforts; and then worked to pressure House Members to vote for bills related to the contract. The biggest of these was a coalition of 300 groups put together to lobby for tax cuts. This coalition, in a fund-raising campaign run by Merrill Lynch, raised $500,000 for the effort. It fielded twenty lobbyists to work on undecided representatives for their votes and member groups such as the National Association of Realtors and the National Restaurant Association mobilized their members to write, call, and visit these members.[32]

How Business Lobbies Government

Business uses many lobbying techniques. Personal contact with officials is important and lobbyists cultivate relationships. They telephone, write letters, and visit. They attend committee meetings in the House and Senate and it is common practice for them to catch a representative's eye and give a thumbs-up or thumbs-down signal as various provisions come to a vote. Unless they are former senators or representatives they are not allowed on the floor of either chamber, but they can stand in hallways and confer with legislators. In recent congressional sessions lobbyists in hallways with laptops have drafted debating points and legislative language and sent it in to legislators on the floor.

Direct contact with legislators, however critical, occupies only a minor portion of the typical lobbyist's day. Legislators are too busy to be available often or for long meetings. So most of a Capitol Hill lobbyist's personal contacts are with staff rather than with lawmakers. Lobbyists sponsor and attend parties and fund-raisers. They serve in political campaigns for the obvious advantage it gives them in working with elected officials later. Corporations and trade associations also sponsor charity events, seminars, speaking engagements, and trips for members of Congress and the executive agencies.

Corporations employ in-house lobbyists who earned an average base salary of $95,000 in 1994.[33] They may also hire lobbying firms to press their cases. The most prominent of these firms employ former administration officials, exlegislators, and knowledgeable insiders of both political parties to offer a potent mix of access, influence, and advice. Lobbying firms may serve many clients at once, some with interests that conflict. For instance, the firm Patton, Boggs, & Blow represents U.S. Tobacco, the UST subsidiary which makes smokeless tobacco, along with Blue Cross of California, a hospital trade association, and three life insurance companies. But in the pragmatic culture of Washington such appearances of conflict are often not grounds for withdrawing an account.

There are many styles of contact lobbying. The Motion Picture Association of America capitalizes on the glamour of Hollywood with a private theater in Washington, D.C., in which senators and representatives view films prior to public release. Much effective lobbying is less pretentious. The Fertilizer Institute, a group representing chemical and agricultural corporations, finds strength in plain directness. A staff member in the House described its lobbyists this way:

> They pick out little issues, sink their goddamn teeth into them, and they are relentless. They sit in everybody's office until they talk to them, and bang the shit out of you until they get what they want.... They're up there making their case day after day.... They just wear out their shoe leather.[34]

Lobbyists for corporations and trade associations may also conduct *grassroots lobbying*, or efforts to influence a decision by having customers, employees, or other constituents, including the general public, pressure government officials for action. A classic grassroots campaign occurred in 1983 when Congress required banks to withhold income taxes on the interest earned by customer's savings accounts. The banking industry generated 22 million postcards and letters against the new law and Congress repealed it.

There are many ways to generate grassroots support. Mass mail can be generated by calls from phone banks, mailings with preprinted cards to send to a legislator, or newspaper ads suggesting that people contact their representative. In 1995 the National Association of Manufacturers held a "fly-in" by 200 corporate chief executives to talk to senators and representatives about the need for products liability law reform. Some lobbying firms specialize in creating grassroots pressure for corporate clients. Bonner & Associates, for example, was paid $400,000 by the American Bankers Association to generate 10,000 phone calls from the congressional districts of ten members of a House committee considering lowering credit card interest rates. The proposal failed.[35]

Defense contractors generate grassroots support for major weapons systems by having suppliers in many states and congressional districts. For instance, Lockheed Corp.'s F-22 advanced tactical fighter is being built by 1,150 subcontractors in forty-five states.[36] Textron and Boeing, which make the V-22 Osprey tiltrotor airplane for the Marine Corps., have 2,500 suppliers in forty-six states.[37] The plane crashed on its first flight, was opposed by the Pentagon, and killed seven crashing into the Potomic River during a demonstration flight, but it survives because there are enough votes in Congress to maintain its appropriation.

The Corporate Role in Elections

In the first presidential campaign, George Washington spent no money and campaigned little to get elected. Since then, the length and cost of political campaigns for federal offices—president, vice president, senator, and representative—have soared. In 1992 total campaign expenditures were about $3.2 billion. This is a large sum, but should be kept in perspective: it is only five one-hundredths of our gross domestic product and less than the cost of one nuclear-powered aircraft carrier.[38]

Throughout the nineteenth century companies made direct contributions from their treasuries to candidates, a practice which reached its zenith in William McKinley's campaigns. The election of 1896 matched the pro-business, Republican McKinley against the radical Populist William Jennings Bryan. Bryan, a spellbinder on the stump, scared the eastern financial community by advocating the silver standard, a radical and unwelcome change in the currency system.   Marcus Hanna, campaign manager for McKinley, capitalized on this fear. He systematically assessed 0.25 percent of the assets of each bank from the trembling financiers and raised about $3.5 million.[39] This doubled the amount raised in previous elections and was sufficient to elect McKinley. In 1900 Bryan opposed McKinley again, this time on a platform attacking trusts. So Hanna assessed giant trusts such as Standard Oil and U.S. Steel, based on their assets. A new record sum was raised, and McKinley won by an even larger margin. Hanna believed his system had elevated the ethics of campaign finance above the borderline bribery and petty extortion which had long characterized it, but progressive reformers sought to derail the business juggernaut. In 1907, they passed the Tillman Act to prohibit banks and corporations from making direct contributions to federal candidates, and this remains the law today.

American political culture is still heavily influenced by the egalitarian ideals of Jeffersonian democracy. Huge campaign contributions by business strain popular belief in a rough equality among interests. The Tillman Act was the first of many efforts to protect the electoral system from lopsided contributions by business. But money, and especially corporate money, plays an essential role in funding elections. It is a resource that may be converted to power. Candidates use it to reach and persuade voters. Contributors use it to buy access, influence, and favors. Because money is elemental in electoral politics, new sources and methods of giving arise whenever federal laws limit unsuitable contribution methods.

After 1907 the Tillman Act, a well-intentioned reform, was quickly and continuously circumvented. Companies found numerous indirect ways to funnel money into elections.

These included giving salary bonuses to managers for use as campaign contributions, loaning money to candidates and later forgiving the loans, paying for expensive postage-stamp-size ads in political party booklets, loaning employees to campaigns, and providing free services such as air travel or rental cars. Also, since individual contributions were not limited by the Tillman Act, wealthy donors stepped in. These "fat cats," who included many corporate executives, legally gave unlimited sums.

In response to growing appearances of impropriety, Congress passed the Federal Election Campaign Act (FECA) in 1971 which required full public disclosure of campaign contributions and expenditures. But immediately after its passage, the election of 1972 once again made corporate money in politics a major reform issue. It was in 1972 that the record among known contributions was set when W. Clement Stone, an insurance company executive, gave $2 million to the Nixon campaign. Then, investigations related to the Watergate scandals revealed that twenty-one corporations had violated the Tillman Act by making direct contributions totaling $842,000, also to the Nixon campaign.

In reaction to this illegality and to the appearance of influence buying that was created by large fat-cat contributions, Congress extensively amended the FECA in 1974 (the first of five amending acts over a decade). This revised FECA attempted to curb wealthy donors by placing ceilings on both campaign contributions and expenditures. Congress also established public financing for presidential candidates and created the Federal Election Commission to enforce the law.

The 1974 additional FECA amendments set up a regulatory framework designed to limit large contributions by business interests. However, more than twenty years later it is now evident that federal election law, which occupies 254 double-columned, small-print pages in the *Code of Federal Regulations* and has an eighty-seven-page index, has failed to control as intended large corporate, special-interest, and individual contributions. The reason is that the new FECA regulations were, after 1974, quickly undermined by three unanticipated developments.

First, in 1976 the Supreme Court severely compromised the FECA's design for controlling campaign money. In *Buckley v. Valeo*, the Court held that giving and spending money in political campaigns is a form of expression protected by the guarantee of free speech in the First Amendment.[40] The Court upheld the FECA's *contribution* limits, saying that the government had a legitimate interest in avoiding corruption and the appearance of corruption that was invited by unlimited contributions. But it invalidated *expenditure* limits, and with them the act's ability to control campaign spending.

The Federal Election Campaign Act, as it now stands, attempts to limit contributions from wealthy contributors and special interests by restricting contributions to candidates for federal office (president, vice president, senator, and representative). For example, individuals may contribute $1,000 per election per candidate, $5,000 per year to PACs, $20,000 per year to national political party committees, and $25,000 per year total to all sources. Contributions by political action committees and party committees are also restricted (see Figure 32-1). Direct contributions from corporations remain illegal. Presidential campaigns are heavily funded by the U.S. Treasury using money raised by the check off feature on federal income tax forms which allows taxpayers to earmark $3 of their taxes for a presidential election fund. In the primaries, presidential candidates may accept individual, PAC, and party contributions which comply with the legal limits in Figure 32-1, and these are then matched by U.S. Treasury funds up to a legal ceiling. In the general election, presidential candidates who accept public funding cannot accept other contributions from any source. All major party presidential candidates since 1976 have accepted U.S. Treasury funds. In 1996 the FEC estimates that presidential candidates will have spending limits of $36 million in primaries and $60 million in the general election.[41]

FIGURE 32-1
Federal campaign
contribution and
expenditure limits

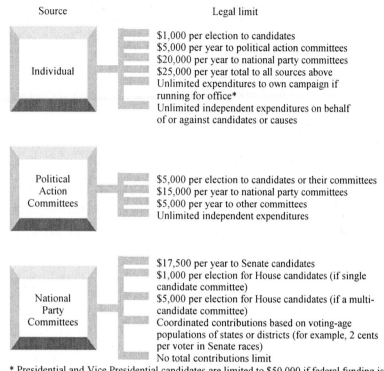

Source

Legal limit

Individual

$1,000 per election to candidates
$5,000 per year to political action committees
$20,000 per year to national party committees
$25,000 per year total to all sources above
Unlimited expenditures to own campaign if
running for office*
Unlimited independent expenditures on behalf
of or against candidates or causes

**Political
Action
Committees**

$5,000 per election to candidates or their committees
$15,000 per year to national party committees
$5,000 per year to other committees
Unlimited independent expenditures

**National
Party
Committees**

$17,500 per year to Senate candidates
$1,000 per election for House candidates (if single
candidate committee)
$5,000 per election for House candidates (if a multi-
candidate committee)
Coordinated contributions based on voting-age
populations of states or districts (for example, 2 cents
per voter in Senate races)
No total contributions limit

* Presidential and Vice Presidential candidates are limited to $50,000 if federal funding is accepted.

Second, the proliferation of interest groups in the 1960s and 1970s created more organized interests to fund campaigns. Because the FECA—even after the *Buckley* decision—limited individual contributions, the era of fat cats seemed over, though as we shall see, only temporarily. So interest groups and corporations raced to set up political action committees (PACs), which could legally contribute to candidates. The number of PACs grew rapidly, and with them the amount of money entering elections.

And third, corporations and lobbyists adapted to the new FECA regime by learning how to exploit, circumvent, and live with its regulations. Their machinations paralleled those that followed the reforms of the Tillman Act in 1907 and showed once again that political money is like water in a stream: dammed up in one place, it flows around and over in another.

What follows is a discussion of some of the ways that corporations now funnel money to politicians and government officials.

Political Action Committees

When Congress limited individual contributions, it left open a loophole permitting organizations to establish political action committees (PACs), or committees composed of organization members who receive money from other members and contribute it to candidates. Corporations previously had not formed PACs, although unions had used them since the 1940s, but since individual contributions by corporate executives had been strictly limited by the FECA they emerged as a device which could get business money to candidates. In 1974, the first year the new FECA amendments went into effect, eighty-nine companies formed PACs. The number rose rapidly. By 1980 there were 1,204 corporate PACS, in 1988 the number peaked at 2,008, and since then has declined slightly to 1,674 in

1995. Leveling off and decline came as corporations' experience with PACs diminished expectations of what they could accomplish. Other interests have also used PACs and in 1995 there were 4,016 PACs altogether, including 334 labor union PACs and 815 trade association and other membership-group PACs.[42]

How PACs Work

To set up a PAC, a corporation must follow legal guidelines. The corporation sets up an account for contributions, a "separate segregated fund" to which it cannot legally donate 1 cent (because of the prohibition since 1907 of direct corporate campaign contributions). The money collected by a PAC is disbursed to candidates based on decisions made by PAC officers, who are corporate employees. Corporations may, and typically do, pay the administrative costs of PACs.

Corporate PACs must get their funds from contributions by employees and others. The law stipulates the solicitation procedure and requires that those eligible to contribute be divided into two groups. Group 1, or stockholders, executives, managers, and their families, may be solicited as often as desired. Solicitations may be done in person or by mail. Contributions are made by check or in some companies through monthly payroll deductions. Many corporations suggest amounts based on a percentage of salary, usually about ¼ to 1 percent of annual salary. Group 2, or hourly paid employees and their families, may be solicited only twice a year by a corporate PAC, and then only by mail to the home.

Foreign nationals may not legally contribute to PACs because they are barred from spending to influence U.S. elections. Some U.S. subsidiaries of foreign corporations have PACs but, in these, all PAC officers and contributors are U. S. citizens. A corporation may set up numerous PACs at divisions around the country, but combined contributions to any recipient may not exceed single-PAC limits of, for example, $5,000 per election per candidate (see Figure 32-2). There are no upper dollar limits to total PAC contributions each year, and there is no limit to so-called independent expenditures on behalf of candidates without their request or cooperation.

Corporate PACs frequently coordinate their contributions with company lobbyists. Lobbyists contend that PAC contributions to a candidate create an expectation of access, or a hearing of the corporation's position, should the candidate be elected or reelected. Most corporate PACs pursue a strategy of giving relatively small contributions to a large number of House and Senate candidates, favoring incumbents (who tend to be reelected), but often giving to their opponents as well. This pattern of giving, designed to ensure access to candidates of either party when elected, is another sign that in Washington politics pragmatism eclipses ideological purity.

Many people believe that, because corporations have so much money, corporate PACs contribute huge amounts and dominate campaign giving, but this is incorrect. In the 1994 midterm elections all House and Senate candidates received a total of $741 million in contributions. Of this, corporate PACs gave only $41 million or 6 percent; individuals gave the largest share at $403 million or 54 percent.[43] Figure 32-2 shows that corporate PACs accounted for only 37 percent of the $189.4 million total contributions of all PACs. But note that PACs in other categories, particularly trade associations, directly represent business interests, thus raising total business contributions.

Circumventing Contributions Limits

Although federal law prohibits corporate contributions and imposes strict contribution limits on individuals, PACs, and national party committees, there are a number of ways to legally breach its boundaries.

FIGURE 32-2
PAC contributions to
federal candidates,
1993-1994 election
cycle

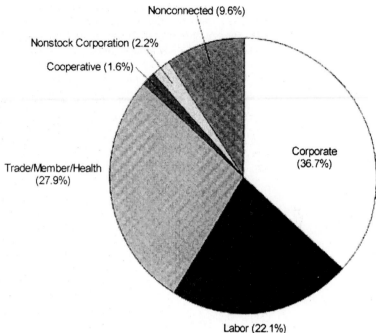

Top Ten Corporate PAC Contributors to Federal Elections, 1993-1994

1.	United Parcel Service Political Action Committee	$2,647,113
2.	American Telephone & Telegraph Company Political Action Committee	$1,294,244
3.	Federal Express Corporation Political Action Committee	$816,600
4.	RJR Political Action Committee RJR Nabisco Inc.	$784,400
5.	Philip Morris Companies Inc. Political Action Committee	$652,666
6.	Union Pacific Fund for Effective Government	$636,803
7.	Nations Bank Corporation PAC	$626,000
8.	Lockheed Employees' Political Action Committee	$592,611
9.	General Electric Company Political Action Committee	$559,043
10.	Morgan Companies Political Action Committee	$531,550

Source: Federal Election Commission press release, March 31, 1995, p. 24.

A time-honored fund-raising technique that is unregulated by the FECA is *brokering*. Brokering takes place when a lobbyist, corporate executive, or group representative acts as an intermediary between candidates and contributors. For example, a Washington lobbying firm might sponsor a $1,000-a-plate dinner for a senator. Buying such a dinner is a campaign contribution under the law. If 400 people attend, the firm has brokered a $400,000 contribution (minus expenses) to the senator. Or a corporate executive, limited to a $1,000 personal contribution, might encourage wealthy friends and relatives to contribute to a House member. Brokered money is a growing source of campaign funds. As long as individual or PAC contribution limits are not exceeded, there is no legal limit to how much money they can raise.

A second technique for circumventing legal contribution limits is *bundling*. It is legal for any individual (even a nonemployee) to contribute to a corporate PAC and to earmark the contribution, or stipulate which candidate is to receive it. The PAC then acts as a conduit for these earmarked funds, which do *not* count against contribution limits. Bundling is used to pass on a collection of checks "bundled" together and given to a politician. A PAC may legally give only $10,000 per election cycle to a congressional candidate ($5,000 in the primary and $5,000 in the general election), but there is no limit to the amount of earmarked contributions for which a PAC may act as a conduit.

A third legal technique for exceeding contribution limits is targeting, which takes place when contributions by multiple PACs are coordinated. Targeting is often practiced by groups of PACs in a specific industry, which focus their contributions on key legislators on committees that oversee industry matters. The Business-Industry Political Action Committee (BIPAC) coordinates giving by over 1,000 corporate and trade association PACs. It issues recommendations on whom to support based on ratings of how legislators vote on business issues. In the midterm elections of 1994, BIPAC was instrumental in generating corporate PAC contributions for a large number of Republican challengers to the House of Representatives.

A fourth channel for business money entering politics is soft money, or money which is contributed to state and local party building with the intention of influencing federal elections. A 1979 amendment to the FECA placed contributions for the purpose of state and local party-building activities outside federal law. Such activities include voter registration drives, printing campaign materials (such as bumper stickers, lawn signs, and slate cards), and administrative expenses (such as rent, utilities, and office supplies).

Soft-money contributions are given to national party committees. Because soft-money contributions are not limited under FECA, both corporations and individuals may give unlimited amounts. For example, between July 1992 and March 1994 Time Warner gave the Democratic National Committee $28,333 in soft-money contributions and a group of its executives contributed another $475,000. The national party committees then parcel out these contributions to states and localities where they are indeed expended to support state and local parties, but the state and local party money that would otherwise have been spent for this support is now freed to be used in ways that help to elect federal candidates.[45]

The Federal Election Commission has set up strict allocation guidelines for expenditure when soft money is sent to state parties. For example, if the state party prints a leaflet listing both state and federal candidates and one-third of its space is devoted to the latter, then soft money may be used to pay two-thirds of its cost and money raised under FECA limits must be used to pay for the other one-third.[46]

Both the Democratic and Republican parties raise millions of dollars in soft money each year. In the first six months of 1995, for example, Democratic committees had raised $10.8 million and Republicans $16.8 million.[47] Many of the largest contributions come from some of the same contributors who gave sums of $100,000 or more prior to the enactment of contribution limits in the 1970s and so the advent of soft money has brought fat cats back into federal elections. The key to understanding soft-money contributions is that although they are ostensibly made for state and local party building their real purpose is to help elect and influence federal candidates.

A fifth method for circumventing contribution limits is through *leadership PACs* set up by senators and representatives to receive contributions. Corporate PACs and executives who have reached legal direct contribution limits with these legislators can give additional money to their PACs. The senators and representatives running leadership PACs then make contributions from them to other candidates' campaigns, thereby increasing their influence over colleagues. There are approximately thirty such leadership PACs. A few legislators also set up foundations to which corporations and executives contribute.

There are more legal methods for channeling money into politics in excess of FECA contribution limits. Individuals and PACs may make *independent expenditures* for or against candidates in addition to direct contributions. Lobbyists frequently pay honoraria to members of Congress for brief speeches. A typical situation is one in which the member of Congress appears at a breakfast attended by executives and lobbyists from a corporation. During breakfast the member speaks briefly, fields questions, and is paid $2,000. House members may keep honoraria up to 27 percent of their salary; senators cannot accept them but may donate them to charity. Corporations are also allowed to contribute directly to help pay for presidential party-nominating conventions.

Using a variety of these methods, a corporation, executive, or corporate PAC can contribute much more than the nominal legal limits set forth in Figure 32-1. A PAC wishing to influence a Senate candidate, for example, can give $5,000 in the primary, $5,000 in the general election, $5,000 to the senator's leadership PAC, $15,000 to committees of the candidate's party, $5,000 to a trade association PAC that might be supporting the candidate, and make unlimited independent expenditures.

Including both lobbying expenses and campaign contributions on both national and state levels and from all sources, the amount of corporate money entering politics adds up to an unknown, but large, total. Washington, D.C., and the states are awash in money spent to buy influence by corporations, trade associations, and their PACs.

The Influence Process

In America there is a historic apprehension that business money will corrupt legislators and officials. The roots of this fear lie in the egalitarian values of the agrarian ideology which entered our political culture during the colonial era and remains strong to this day. Because of these values, even where business's influential efforts are legal, the large sums of money involved raise apprehensions.

Critics argue that corporate money creates unwholesome obligations to special interests. Large contributions from individuals and PACs are blatant efforts to buy votes; they are investments from which donors expect a return. Charles Keating, the owner of Lincoln Savings and Loan and a large campaign donor, once confirmed the critics worst fears when he said, "One question, among many, has had to do with whether my financial support in any way influenced several political figures to take up my cause. I want to say in the most forceful way I can: I certainly hope so."[48] Keating's remark was ingenuous. The reality of influence is more subtle.

Bribery is illegal. If it could be proven that lawmakers or regulators accepted money as a condition for official action, a crime would be documented. This does not mean that contributions associated with lobbying efforts are made without expectation of a return. Large contributions create a debt on the part of legislators and officials who receive them. But because of bribery laws the etiquette of legislator-lobbyist relations requires that collection of the debt be discrete. To avoid suspicion of bribery, financial contributions are not mentioned in connection with requests for action. Former Senator Tom Eagleton (D-Mo.) explains:

> I've never had ... a guy come into this office or over the phone say, "Tom, such-and-such vote's coming up next week. You remember I gave X in your last campaign, and I'm certainly expecting you to vote that way." I've never had anything that direct, blunt, or obscene. However, let's change the phraseology to this: "Tom, this is so-and-so. You know next week an important vote's coming up on such-and-such. I just want to remind you, Tom, I feel very strongly about that issue. Okay, my friend, good to hear from you." Now a senator receives "gentle" calls of that sort.[49]

A book of advice for lobbyists admonishes them to "never discuss a financial contribution in the context of legislation" and suggests that the subjects "be parsed into separate discussions."[50] Needless to say, these are subtle distinctions. When Senator Alan Cranston was rebuked by the Senate in 1991, it was because he had agreed to intervene with federal regulators on behalf of Charles Keating and had done so, sometimes, in the same meeting where Keating's soft-money contributions were delivered. Cranston denied that he had violated Senate norms and accused other senators of doing what he did. He argued that the concept of a decent interval between contribution and service for a constituent was vague and undefinable. Other senators did as he had but were not thrust into the limelight. His lawyer argued that Cranston was like the magician who was reprimanded by his fellows "for showing lay people how the tricks were done."

Because of this artful contributor-recipient etiquette (or magic technique) it is difficult to prove or measure business influence in the political process. Often there exists correlation, but correlation does not prove cause. Did a contribution cause a lawmaker to vote?   Or did the contribution reward earlier support or reward a like-thinking representative? As a lobbyist once said, determining influence is "like finding a black cat in the coal bin at midnight."[51] But the problem of simultaneous cause is a problem mainly for scholars. The long historical perspective on business influence makes clear that, overall, business influence causes many policy changes.

Conclusion

The political environment for corporations today is difficult, complex, and uncertain. Despite this, business retains its historically dominant position among interests.

Business dominance is not new. The power of business in politics today is typical of its power in the past, but in some ways less threatening to the ideals of Jeffersonian democracy.   There is an imbalance of resources between corporate interests and other interests such as poor people, small farmers, environmentalists, and consumer advocates. But an equal or greater imbalance has existed since the end of the colonial era and business is today forced to deal with more, and stronger, opposing interest groups than at any time in the past.[52] Similarly, corporations and executives are today circumventing the spirit of election laws with large contributions. But they have been doing so since early in the century and the disclosure requirements in FECA create more openness than in the past.

The challenge for American society is to balance the First Amendment right of corporations to political expression against the societal interest of maintaining corruption-free elections and government decisions.   So far, our society has been successful in maintaining a rough balance.

Endnotes

1. See, for example, the review in Government Accounting Office, *Energy Policy: Options to Reduce Environmental and Other Costs of Gasoline Consumption*, GAO/RCED-92-260), September 1992, pp. 29-32.
2. *Ethyl Corp. v. Carol M. Browner*, U.S. Court of Appeals, D.C. Circuit, 94-1516 (1995).
3. The Federal Cigarette Labeling and Advertising Act (1965) and the Public Health Cigarette Smoking Act (1969).
4. *Youngstown Sheet & Tube Co. v. Sawyer*, 343 U.S. 579. The basis for the Court's ruling was that Congress had once considered giving presidents the power to seize industries in similar circumstances, but had not done so.
5. In *Buckley v. Valeo*, 424 U.S. 1 (1976).
6. See, for example, Clarence L. Ver Steeg, The American Revolution Considered as an Economic Movement," *Huntington Library Quarterly*, August 1957.
7. Charles Beard, *An Economic Interpretation of the Constitution of the United States*, New York: Macmillan, 1913.
8. See, for example, Robert E. Brown, *Charles Beard and the Constitution*, Princeton: Princeton University Press, 1956; and Forrest McDonald, *We the People: The Economic Origins of the Constitution*, Chicago: University of Chicago Press, 1963.

9. Quoted in Vernon Louis Parrington, *Main Currents in American Thought*, vol. 1, New York: Harcourt, Brace, 1958, p. 300. Originally published in 1927.

10. *Notes on Virginia*, 1782, Query XIX, in Saul K. Padover, ed., *Thomas Jefferson and the Foundations of American Freedom*, New York: Van Nostrand, 1965, p. 111.

11. "The Story of a Great Monopoly," *The Atlantic*, March 1881, p. 322.

12. The exception was the electron of the Democrat and reformer Grover Cleveland in 1884. But even Cleveland had strong support from the business community, Andrew Carnegie and James J. Hill among them. His administration never threatened basic business interests.

13. William Allen White, *Masks in a Pageant*, New York: Macmillan, 1928, p. 79.

14. Quoted in Henry Demarest Lloyd, *Wealth against Commonwealth*, New York: Harper, 1898, pp. 377-78.

15. William Manchester, *The Glory and the Dream*, vol. 1, Boston: Little, Brown, 1973, p. 126.

16. *The Corporation in American Politics*, Englewood Cliffs, N.J.: Prentice-Hall, 1969, p 31.

17. For the story of how this philosophy developed during the New Deal years see Alan Brinkley, *The End of Reform: New Deal Liberalism in Recession and War*, New York: Knopf, 1995.

18. Quoted in Gene E. Bradley, "How to Work in Washington: Building Understanding for Your Business," *Columbia Journal of World Business*, Spring 1994, p. 53.

19. These factors are analyzed by David Vogel in *Fluctuating Fortunes: The Political Power of Business in America*, New York: Basic Books, 1989. Vogel argues that the following changes led to political reverses and put corporations on the defensive: (1) public perception that economic prosperity would continue and business could afford more social investment; (2) a downturn in support for business in opinion polls; (3) the rise of public interest groups; and (4) the growth of a "new class" of educated, middle-class professionals who favored more regulation of business.

20. Bureau of the Census, *Statistical Abstract of the United States: 1994*. Washington, D.C.: U.S. Government Printing Office, September 1994, table 504.

21. Burdett A. Loomis and Allan J. Cigler, "Introduction: The Changing Nature of Interest Group Politics," in Cigler and Loomis, *Interest Group Politics*, 4th ed., Washington, D.C.: Congressional Quarterly Press, 1995, p. 11.

22. Loree Bykerk and Ardith Maney, Consumer Groups and Coalition Politics on Capitol Hill," in Cigler and Loomis, *Interest Group Politics*, p. 266.

23. Jeffrey M. Berry, *Lobbying for the People*, Princeton: Princeton University Press, 1977, p. 94.

24. S. Robert Lichter, "Liberal Greens, Mainstream Camouflage," *Wall Street Journal*, April 21, 1995, p. A5.

25. Gene E. Bradley, "How to Work in Washington," p. 55.

26. Bradley, "How to Work in Washington," p. 51.

27. Richard Klemp, "Lobbying: Can It Be Both Effective and Ethical?" *Vital Speeches*, July 15,1993, p. 592.

28. Andrew A. Procassini, *Competitors in Alliance: Industry Associations, Global Rivalries and Business-Government Relations*, Westport, Conn.: Quorum Books, 1995, p. 125.

29. Authors' telephone interview with Patti Jo Baber, executive director, November 28, 1995. There are approximately 8,000 lobbyists registered in the House of Representatives and 9,200 in the Senate.

30. A 1995 law requires lobbyists to register with Congress if over a six-month period they spend more than one-fifth of their time and more than $5,000 on influence efforts. Corporations must register if they spend over $20,000 in six months. Registration requires disclosure of which policies lobbyists are trying to influence, who employs them, and how much they are spending.

31. In Myron Struck "Deaver Probe Revives Doubts about 'Revolving Door' Ethics," *Insight*, June 9, 1986, p. 17.

32. Peter H. Stone, "Follow the Leaders," *National Journal*, June 24, 1995, pp. 1641-42.

33. Peter H. Stone, Prom the K Street Corridor," *National Journal*, August 19, 1995, p. 2108.

34. Burt Solomon, Measuring Clout," *National Journal*, July 4, 1987, p. 1708.

35. Peter H. Stone, "Green, Green Grass," *National Journal*, March 27, 1993, p. 754.

36. David C. Morrison, "Under Fire," *National Journal*, July 15, 1995, p. 1818.

37. David C. Morrison, "Osprey a True Survivor," *National Journal*, June 24, 1995, p. 1655.

38. GDP figure cited in Robert J. Samuelson, "The Price of Politics," *Newsweek*, August 28, 1995, p. 65.

39. See Herbert Croly, *Marcus Alonzo Hanna: His Life and Work*, New York: Macmillan, 1912, p. 220. A grateful McKinley engineered the appointment of Hanna to the U.S. Senate.

40. 424 U.S. 1.

41. Figures are from "Public Funding," *FEC Record*, May 1995, p. 2. General election figures are for the major parties only. In addition, the major parties will receive an estimated $23.5 million for their nominating conventions and campaign activities.

42. FEC *Record*, "1995 Year-End PAC Count," April 1996, p. 18.

43. FEC press release, April 28 1995, pp. 4-5.

44. Rick Wartzman, "Clinton, Having Assailed Unlimited Donations to Party Groups, Benefits Greatly from Them," *Wall Street Journal*, June 22, 1994, p. A16.

45. These national party distributions are contributions subject to state laws. State laws vary widely, but thirty states permit direct corporate contributions.

46. These allocation guidelines are found in 11 CFR sec. 106.5, 1994.

47. "GOP Receipts More than Double Democratic Party Receipts," FEC *Record*, November 1995, pp. 14-15.

48. In Herbert E. Alexander, *Financing Politics*, 4th ed., Washington, D.C.: Congressional Quarterly Press, 1992, p. 68.

49. Quoted in Hedrick Smith, *The Power Game*, New York: Ballantine Books, 1988, p. 255.

50. Bruce C. Wolpe, *Lobbying Congress: How the System Works*, Washington, D.C.: Congressional Quarterly Press, 1990, p. 45.

51. Alan M. Dershowitz, "It's a Sin to Let the Public Glimpse Reality," *Los Angeles Times*, November 1991.

52. See, for example, the discussion of "neopluralism" in Gary Mucciaroni, *Reversals of Fortune: Public Policy and Private Interests*, Washington, D.C.: Brookings Institution, 1995, pp. 180-83.

Chapter Thirty-Three

REFORMING CORPORATE

GOVERNANCE

GM

For years GM has been described by industry observers as a sluggish, stodgy, bureaucratic sleeping giant. GM's board of directors reflected this picture until April 6, 1992, when it decided to wake up management with a thunderbolt aimed at the top. Such actions are rare in corporate history. However, the storm that led to this unprecedented move had been brewing for some time.

GM's normally docile board became troubled in the fall of 1991 by a slump in automobile sales that led to a $4.5 billion loss. The company's U.S. market share had been stagnant at 35 percent despite the introduction of a number of new cars and trucks and the expenditure of billions of dollars for new plant and equipment.

Robert C. Stempel, GM's chief executive officer, was removed as chairman of the board's executive committee, a powerful advisory and decision-making group composed of chairmen of all the board's committees. He was replaced by an outside director, John G. Smale, retired CEO of Procter & Gamble Co. Mr. Stempel remained as GM's chief executive responsible for day-to-day operation of the company. Lloyd E. Reuss, GM's president and Stempel's choice for his successor, was demoted and replaced by John F. Smith, Jr., former chief of the firm's international division. William E. Hogland was named the new chief financial officer (CFO).

The board made it very clear that it was taking these steps because of the need for a more aggressive management approach to reinvigorate the company and regain profitability. It was apparent that the board intended to keep a close watch on the performance of Stempel and his staff and threatened to take further action if results were unsatisfactory. Smale, a ten-year member of GM's board, began talking with other outside directors in the fall of 1991 about the firm's troubles. Regular meetings of outside

directors were called which excluded inside directors. Their concerns were reinforced by pressures from major investors. Finally the board took the action described above.

Under pressure from board members for not moving more rapidly to correct GM's problems, Robert Stempel resigned on October 26, 1992. At the board meeting on November 2, 1992, John Smith was named CEO and John Smale was given the title of chairman of the board. This was the first time in thirty years that the job of board chairman was divided at GM. Then, on January 1, 1996, the board named John Smith to be chairman and CEO.

As will be discussed in this chapter, boards of directors have been subject to sharp criticism for not doing their jobs. They have responded by taking action to improve their performance, but rarely have they removed a CEO except in unusual circumstances such as the company going into bankruptcy or where criminal acts or egregious ethical failings have occurred. Now, since the board of the largest industrial corporation in this country acted decisively in a case where management performance was unsatisfactory, a precedent has been established and more boards are reviewing more carefully the performance of their CEOs. The action of the GM board, therefore, was a milestone in corporate governance history and a fitting backdrop for this chapter.

Boards of directors have the ultimate responsibility for the performance of our corporations. To perform effectively in their economic and social responsibilities, it is essential that corporations be governed effectively. One of the important trends in corporate life today is that pressures on boards to perform their governance task more effectively are producing results, perhaps not as rapidly as many activists would like, but positive results nonetheless.

This cartoon appeared around the time that the General Motors board acted to change top management.

"A person should know his own limitations I wouldn't even attempt to run General Motors."

We begin this chapter with a definition of governance and contrast it with management. Then the corporate charter as the legal basis for governance authority is described. This is followed with a review of current structures of boards and the broad duties ascribed to directors. We then note the more important specific criticisms of boards and recommendations for reforming them.   Special attention is then given to compensation of CEOs. Finally, we include a note on a comparative survey of boards of directors in other countries.

Corporate Governance Defined

Corporate governance is the overall control of activities in a corporation. It is concerned with the formulation of long-term objectives and plans and the proper management structure (organization, systems, and people) to achieve them. At the same time it entails making sure that the structure functions to maintain the corporation's integrity, reputation, and responsibility to its various constituencies.[1]

In this definition, governance is the concern of the board of directors. However, top management is also clearly involved. But management has other dimensions that are quite distinct from the operations of the typical board of directors. Management is a hands-on operational activity.   It is concerned with supervising day-to-day action and with the prudent use of scarce resources to achieve desirable aims. The typical board of directors does not become involved in such activities. While governance is shared by boards and top management, our focus in this chapter is essentially but not exclusively on boards of directors.

The Corporate Charter

The corporate charter is the legal authority for corporate managers and directors to function in conformance with the above definition. All American corporations except a few quasi-public enterprises chartered by the federal government (for example, the Tennessee Valley Authority) are chartered by the state in which they incorporate.   At the Constitutional Convention of 1787, the Founders of this nation debated a federal chartering power but decided that existing state controls were adequate to regulate corporate activity.

All states have general incorporation laws and compete with one another to attract the tax revenues of large corporations.   Delaware has been the longtime victor in this competition and has chartered almost half the largest industrial corporations in this country. Over the years states have become more permissive in giving corporations authority, and today a corporation can get a charter to engage in just about any business that is legal.

Corporate charters specify the rights and responsibilities of stockholders, directors, and officers. Fundamentally, corporate charters lodge control over the property of the enterprise in stockholders who own shares in the assets of the company and vote those shares in naming a board of directors to run the firm. The directors have a fiduciary responsibility to protect the interests of the shareholders. They are responsible for appointing officers to run the day-to-day affairs of the company. The legal line of power runs from the state, to shareholders, to directors, to managers.

The charters also include detailed provisions about such matters as annual meetings, methods of choosing directors, and authority of directors to issue stock. For instance, charters are specific about calling meetings of shareholders, declaration of dividends, election and removal of officers, proposing amendments of the articles of incorporation, and so on. Such charter provisions are meant to protect the interests of shareholders. A vast body of law that seeks to do the same thing has also been created over time.

The Structure of Boards of Directors

The average corporate board in 1995 had twelve members. Giovani Agnelli, founder of Italy's huge Turin-based Fiat conglomerate, once observed: "Only an odd number of directors can run a company, and three is too many."[2] This is an extreme position, but most small firms and many large ones do have small boards of directors. Banks and other financial institutions tend to have large boards, but the general trend is for smaller boards.

Board membership may include both inside (management) directors and outside (nonmanagement) directors. In recent years the number of outside directors on boards has grown because of pressures to put members on the board who are independent of the CEO. In 1995 the average company had three inside and nine outside directors.

In a detailed report of 831 companies, Korn/Ferry said the number of boards with at least one woman member rose from 11 percent in 1973 to 63 percent in 1995.[3] However, women make up only 7 percent of all directors and there is a tendency for companies to tap the same women. During the same period, boards with ethnic-minority representation grew from 9 percent to 44 percent of all boards surveyed.

In the past, board members were usually suggested by the CEO to the board for approval. Today, nominating committees on most boards have this responsibility but the CEOs still play a prominent part in the process. Once selected, the names of the nominees are presented to the shareholders in the annual call for the stockholder meeting, and management solicits the proxies of the stockholders. A proxy is a permission given by each stockholder to the management to vote the stock as management sees fit. Most stockholders give their proxies to management, which in turn votes the stock at the annual meeting.

In this model, which differs from the classical legal line of appointment noted earlier, managers and directors choose directors. In 1973 only 2.4 percent of boards had nominating committees but in 1995 it was 71 percent! In very small corporations the stockholders typically still choose directors, who in turn choose managers. Often the majority of stockholders in these companies are the managers and the board members.

Boards are divided into committees. Today virtually all companies have audit committees to review for the board the financial affairs of the company and other activities in the company, such as conflicts of interests of officers, that merit board attention. Most (95 percent) have compensation committees that make recommendations to the board concerning pay and bonuses of top executives. Sixty-seven percent have executive committees authorized by the board to decide on its behalf about matters needing attention between board meetings.

Other committees include finance; public affairs, corporate ethics; benefits; corporate strategy; legal affairs; social responsibility; conflict-of-interest; science, technology, and research; and personal or human resources. Very few, if any, companies have all of these committees.

The Duties of Directors

Charters require that corporate affairs be "managed" by a board or "under the direction of a board." The board of directors clearly is the ultimate corporate authority except for matters that must have the approval of shareholders, such as the election of the board itself or an increase in capitalization.

The Business Roundtable, in an important policy statement in 1990, set forth the responsibilities of corporate boards of directors.[4] Overall, said the policy statement, "the principal responsibility is to exercise governance so as to ensure the long-term successful performance of their corporation." Specific responsibilities are as follows:

1. Select, regularly evaluate and, if necessary, replace the chief executive officer. Determine management compensation. Review succession planning.
2. Review and, where appropriate, approve the financial objectives, major strategies, and plans of the corporation.
3. Provide advice and counsel to top management.
4. Select and recommend to shareholders for election an appropriate slate of candidates for the board of directors; evaluate board processes and performance.
5. Review the adequacy of systems to comply with all applicable laws/regulations.

In a similar statement in 1978 the Business Roundtable advocated these specific studies for boards: "It is the board's duty to consider the overall impact of the activities of the corporation on (1) the society of which it is a part, and (2) the interests and views of groups other than those immediately identified with the corporation. This obligation arises out of the responsibility to act primarily in the interests of the share owners—particularly their long-range interests."[5]

Cutting across these functions, it seems to us, are requirements to make sure that there is an appropriate flow of information to the board and that internal policies and procedures of the company are fully capable of responding to board decisions. Peter Drucker has added the following other dimensions to these functions if a board is to be effective: asking critical questions, acting as a conscience, a keeper of human and moral values; serving as a window on the outside world; and helping the corporation to be understood by its constituencies and by the outside community.[6]

These responsibilities are generally accepted by directors and managers.

How individual boards and members perform these duties will vary much. Jay Lorsch, a professor at Harvard Business School, observes, "Traditionally, corporate leaders have considered a powerful, active board to be a nuisance at best and a force that could improperly interfere in the management of the company at worst. They have preferred directors who are content to offer counsel when asked and to support management in times of crisis."[7] That is becoming less true as pressures have led to more active boards. Still, many companies' boards today perform in the traditional way.

Core Criticisms of Current Corporate Governance

Criticisms of boards of directors have increased substantially in recent years because they are not perceived as governing as they should. This is especially true in large corporations that are more exposed to public attention.

Specific criticisms cover a wide range of views. Individual stockholders say they have no influence either on boards or on management and their interests are not really protected. Critics assert that other stakeholders, such as employees, communities, and society as a whole, are not given the attention in decision making they deserve. Indeed, it is said, decisions are often made that are diametrically opposed to the best interests of these stakeholders. It is asserted that boards do not evaluate properly the performance of managers and permit all sorts of unethical practices to go on in their companies. Boards do not get enough information from management to make informed decisions and therefore are mere rubber stamps of management. Board members do not spend enough time on company business and often have a conflict of interest.

Boards of directors are under pressure to do better. For example, they are being driven because of potential legal liabilities from stockholder suits, government regulations and threats of government controls, social pressures, takeover threats, institutional stockholder pressures, and growing competition in global markets. Many stakeholders of the corporation demand greater board accountability. The issue is not director power, but performance.

To illustrate, the board of directors of the giant food processing company Archer-Daniels-Midland Co., was severely criticized in 1995 for not responding properly to current problems of the company such as criminal antitrust investigations for possible price collusion and illegal management compensation. Institutional investors, stockholders, and others joined a chorus of complaints that directors were too well-paid and cozy with management. Indeed, major institutional investors threatened to oppose the reelection of all directors.[8] In January 1996 a board committee made sweeping recommendations to reform the structure and duties of the ADM board.

Proposals for Reforming Corporate Boards of Directors

The literature on corporate boards contains many recommendations for reforming the functioning of boards.[9] Following are some of the major ones.

Federal Chartering

Some observers argue that it is time for federal chartering of large corporations. They say that state incorporation laws are too permissive and that state governments are unable or unwilling to exercise needed controls over corporations. It is preposterous, they argue, to go on letting little New Jersey charter Exxon, one of the largest industrial corporations in the world. The state simply cannot exercise needed surveillance.

Advantages of Federal Chartering

Critics believe that federal chartering of corporations will provide society with an important constraint on managerial power, making corporations more accountable to society than they are now. Ralph Nader, a prominent critic, points out that there is plenty of evidence of corporate abuses that clamor for reform. He has in mind such things as worker health and safety hazards, contamination of community water and air, and interest-group lobbying of Congress for special treatment.[10] Nader is not alone. Bruce R. Scott, a professor at the Harvard Business School, suggests that federal chartering is needed to have companies a "guarantee employment security for all employees with at least ten years service, subject to safeguards in case of gross negligence or misbehavior."[11]

Disadvantages of Federal Chartering

But serious doubts and drawbacks exist. First, federal chartering may confuse the political goals of critics with the economic goals of enterprise and hamper the achievement of both by placing new regulatory costs and restraints on business. Second, federal chartering would require the creation of a new, powerful regulatory authority in government and raise new questions of control. For instance, what would be the performance criteria for the diverse business operations to be regulated in a large corporation? Would massive new regulations and tough implementation result in so much uncertainty and restraint on corporations that they could not function efficiently?

Concluding Comment

Federal incorporation might improve control over corporations in such matters as pollution, discrimination, anticompetitive practices, unethical conduct, and so on. However, there are plenty of other remedies to deal with such matters in the absence of federal chartering. Why launch a new federal program with all of its potential complications when abundant current remedies exist for controlling corporations? Critics argue, of course, that such controls are not sufficient. Their opponents say that they are and that if more are needed, the federal government can be depended upon to impose them.

Separate the Board Chairperson and the CEO

In many European companies the chairperson is not the CEO. In 80 percent of our large corporations the CEO also chairs the board. More and more observers of corporate boards are coming to the conclusion that the two jobs should be separated. But there is much opposition to the idea, especially among CEOs.

Both directors of corporations and outside observers believe that when the CEO also chairs the board he or she has too much power. The power to control the agenda and the information that directors get is overwhelming. The tendency of CEOs to dominate directors was referred to colorfully as the "mushroom concept" by John T. Connor when he was chairman of Allied Chemical. "Put him in a dark place," said Connor of a director, "feed him plenty of horse manure, and when his head rises up through the pile to get attention or ask a question, cut it off quickly and decisively."[12]

After a three-year study in which hundreds of directors participated, Professor Jay W. Lorsch of the Harvard Business School concluded that separating the two jobs would go a long way to help directors perform better. It would help prevent crises because, with an outside director as chairperson, the board would likely get more and better information about company affairs. Also, in the event of a crisis involving the CEO, the board would be more organized to deal with it. But beyond that, splitting the jobs would underscore the notion that managers serve at the discretion of directors, not the other way around. At board meetings directors would feel freer to raise questions and be critical of management.[13] Many top executives support this view.

Critics of this proposal point out that although the two top people usually get along well, there are many unpublicized cases of failure. If the CEO and chairperson positions are split, and if rivalry or dislike develops between the two, then the split works to the detriment of the business and the board functions less well. Critics also note that having an outside director serve as chairperson does not always work well. Incumbent CEOs say that to split the roles would complicate their jobs. They are concerned that their immediate predecessors might be appointed chairperson. That situation would indeed be fraught with danger and should not be permitted by a board where the split has taken place.

Splitting the two jobs is certainly not a panacea for assuring excellence in board functioning. Personalities can clash. The task of determining which officer should do what, and when, raises many fundamental issues of responsibility and accountability. The transition of a board from a single to a dual leadership takes time and patience.

Selecting Directors

The selection process varies among boards. In some, the CEO makes recommendations to a nominating committee, the committee accepts the suggestions, and the board approves. In others, the nominating committee makes selections, which are then discussed with the CEO and the board.

If the board had an outside director as chairperson it would be his or her responsibility to assure that the nominating committee was finding appropriate people for membership. The advice and counsel of the CEO would still be sought, of course. But this process would end the misperception, if there was one, that board members were appointed by the CEO and therefore were in some sense beholden to that person.

Monitoring the Performance of the CEO

The responsibilities of the board of directors set forth by McDonald's Corporation lists first, "Evaluating the performance of the Company and its executive management."[14] This is, or should be, a major function of the board. Today, as a result of corporate performance problems 75 percent of the boards surveyed by Korn/Ferry say they have clear objectives for evaluating the CEOs performance and 67 percent say they have a formal process for evaluating his or her performance. However, only 23 percent give the CEO written as well as oral feedback and that is done largely by the compensation committee or its chairperson.

There is a question about how well-defined the objectives set for CEOs are and how comprehensive and forceful such evaluations are in practice. Too frequently evaluation feedback is a casual conversation about compensation between the CEO and the chairperson of the compensation committee.

The Dayton Hudson Corporation has been a leader in the practice of evaluating the CEO realistically. Today many other companies, such as Alcoa, General Motors, Honeywell, and Zenith Electronics Corp., have detailed evaluation. Criteria essential for an effective evaluation of CEOs would include the following:

- The board should develop a clear job description for the CEO position.
  The board and the CEO should meet and agree upon the CEO's performance objectives.
- The performance evaluation should be conducted annually.
- Specific board meetings should be established for the CEO evaluation.
  The long-term performance of the company should be compared with similar organizations.
- The CEO's goals should be evaluated against his or her personal goals and against the goals set for the company.
- The CEO should appraise his or her performance and present it to the board.
- The CEO should have an opportunity to discuss the evaluation with the entire board.[15]

Board Self-Evaluation

General Motors has a Director of Affairs Committee whose duties, among other things, include evaluating the board's performance in an annual report to the full board. There are, of course, many ways to do this (e.g., questionnaires filled by outside directors, full board discussions, and so on) but the important point is to do it. Gordon Donaldson, a Harvard Business School professor, calls this a "strategic audit," and has set forth a detailed procedure for doing it.[16]

The evaluation should assess how well the board relates to the CEO, how well it understands the basic strategies of the company, how effective the directors believe the board to be in governance, how appropriate the information the board gets from the CEO is, how well the committees are performing, and similar questions. The Korn/Ferry survey revealed that 65 percent of the companies responding had written guidelines on corporate governance, but only 26 percent of all boards formally evaluated their performance on a regular basis.

Understanding and Approving Major Company Strategies

It is difficult to understand how a board can feel comfortable in its performance unless it is certain that it understands, reviews, and approves the major strategies designed for the company. In a number of companies this process is conducted at a two- or three-day offsite meeting of the board to discuss only strategy.

The question arises, of course, At what point does such a legitimate process encroach upon the detailed management of the company? This is a difficult line to draw, but one that must be understood and drawn in such a way that the CEO feels comfortable.

Director Compensation

In recent years sharp criticism has been directed at director compensation. It has been said with some justification that "directors get paid too much for what they do, but not enough for what they should do." What are the facts?

The Korn/Ferry survey showed that the average total 1995 annual compensation reported for outside directors, including committee fees, was $39,707. For companies with sales over $5 billion the average was $49,700. In a few large companies compensation was $100,000 or more. In very small companies directors may not get any compensation.

Giving compensation in the form of stock is growing. Sixty-two percent of all companies compensate directors with some form of company stock. Thirty-one percent of the respondents give directors only stock options. But twenty-eight percent said the practice of stock options was growing. Twenty-four percent give only stock grants. Cash and stock options are not the only forms of compensation. Some companies pay for accident insurance, life insurance, charitable contributions upon death of a director, medical insurance, and pensions.

Most controversy about compensation in recent years centers on pensions for directors. Almost half of all companies, according to Korn/Ferry, grant pensions. Coca-Cola, for example, gives outside directors pensions of $50,000 a year for a period equal to the number of years served and directors are eligible after five years and when they reach 55 years of age. B. F. Goodrich gives its directors $26,000 a year for life after serving ten years and reaching 55 years of age. This practice has been condemned by stockholders in a number of stockholder proposals contained in annual company proxy statements. Many large companies have responded to stockholder complaints and have stopped offering pensions to newly appointed outside directors. Among them are Merck & Co., American Express, Woolworth Corp., Melville Corp., and The McGraw-Hill Companies.[17]

Critics contend that pensions tend to make directors less independent, are far too generous, and lead directors to stay on the board too long. Corporations argue that pensions, as well as other compensation, are needed to attract and retain the type of person the company wants on the board. A prestigious commission established by the National Association of Corporate Directors (NACD) agrees with the critics. In a report submitted in June 1995, which will be influential in this argument, the NACD urges corporations to consider the following:

- Pay directors primarily in stock.
- Set substantial stock ownership requirements for board membership.
- Abolish all benefits programs because they "often reward longevity rather than performance."
- Prohibit outside directors or their firms from consulting arrangements or financial services with the company.
- Disclose completely the pay of directors in the annual proxy statement.[18]

The basic recommendation of critics seems to be that compensation should be adequate and that it should be tied in some way to the long-range, not the short-range, performance of the company. What is adequate will vary among companies and may always remain controversial. How to link pay to performance is challenging but probably can be done better through stock which cannot be redeemed for a specified time in the future.

Institutional Investor Participation in Governance

An old, but still expressed, concern of corporate reformers is to give individual stockholders more influence in governance. Except in smaller corporations that is difficult. Power has shifted to management, as explained years ago by Adolph Berle and Gardener Means in their seminal book *The Modern Corporation and Private Property*.[19] However, in recent years there has been an extraordinary increase in stock holdings of pension funds which can be and have been used to influence governance among the companies whose stock they own. In late December 1995 the total equity holdings of pension funds (private plus state and local government employee retirement funds) amounted to $1.8 trillion dollars, a rise from $444 billion in 1975. This amounted to 38.7 percent of the total value of all stocks in Standard & Poors 500 largest companies which was $4.6 trillion at the end of 1995.[20] (When holdings of other institutional investors such as mutual funds are added, the total stock ownership of an institutional investors amounts to well over 50 percent of outstanding equities.)

Pension fund manager activism in corporate governance began in the mid-1980s, especially with the decision of the California Public Employees Retirement System (CalPERS) to take a more active interest in how companies were managed and the creation of the Council of Institutional Investors (CII). The CII endorsed a "Shareholder's Bill of Rights" that demanded a voice in all "fundamental decisions which could affect corporate performance and growth."[21]

Because of the large holdings of institutional investors they are increasingly rightfully concerned about the governance of the companies in which they have a large share of stock. Their interest, however, is not unchallenged. One CEO undoubtedly spoke for other CEOs and directors when he said: "... we have a group of people with increasing control of the *Fortune* '500' who have no proven skills in management, no experience at selecting directors, no believable judgment in how much should be spent for researcher marketing—in fact, no experience except that which they have accumulated controlling other people's money."[22]

Should pension fund managers seek to influence corporations? If not, why not? If so, in what way? There are many pension fund managers whose interest is essentially short-term improvement in the values of the stocks they hold. If they are not satisfied with the management of the companies whose stock they hold the stock can be sold. This is possible when the shares owned in any one corporation are small. When the assets of a fund reach $83 billion, as with CalPERS, and where they own large shares of a company's stock they are essentially "locked in" as owner-investors. Fundamentally this means, said Dale Hanson former manager of CalPERS, the security owner should take the long view of investment, not the short view. In this light it makes sense to seek to influence companies whose performance is deficient but whose long-term promise is bright. CalPERS and a number of other major pension fund managers do precisely that.

The larger pension funds do not attempt to get involved in the day-to-day management of companies but rather seek to encourage the companies to improve their procedures and, on occasion, their basic strategies. For example, CalPERS had some influence, with other pension fund managers, in the change of top management at General Motors as described at the beginning of the chapter. How much is not publicly known. When the change was made the board prepared a twenty-eight-point governance credo.[23] CalPERS sent it to 200 large companies in which it held substantial stock and asked the boards to compare what they were doing with each of the items in the credo. The items were largely the same as the recommendations discussed in this chapter.

Most companies replied to the questionnaire with reluctance and when they were received CalPERS evaluated them on a scale of A+ to F. The scores were made public. CalPERS said that it was not seeking to get all companies to adopt the GM procedures. Rather it wanted only to get boards to think about how they operated. The exercise was viewed essentially as a "wake-up" call to outside directors. Among the companies receiving A+ were Dayton Hudson, Exxon, Merck, Time Warner.[24] CalPERS has another "wake-up" call in their issuance of an annual listing of nine or ten companies whose performance is judged to be very poor. For companies in this category the pension fund managers seek a meeting with directors and management to try to influence them in making strategic changes to improve long-term performance. Institutional investors have apparently been successful in pushing companies such as Eastman Kodak, Sears, U.S. Steel, and IBM to refocus their core business strategies.[25]

Other Recommendations for Reforming the Board of Directors

The above by no means exhausts the list of suggestions for reforming the board. Space does not permit their evaluation, but it is useful simply to note them.

- There should be a majority of outside directors.
- Members of corporate boards of directors must not serve on so many other boards that they cannot spend the proper amount of time to deal with the issues of each board on which they serve. Some observers recommend allowing service on only one other board.
- The chairperson should assure that at board meetings there will be open dialogue among board members and the CEO.
- The selection process of directors should assure that each is sufficiently knowledgeable to serve effectively.
- The board should have the basic responsibility for selecting its own members.
- The independent members of the board should select a lead director. This person, among other things, could serve at all times as a direct link between the CEO and the outside directors.

- The independent directors should meet alone on a regularly scheduled basis to discuss company issues.
- The independent directors should take responsibility for establishing board procedures.
- Finally, and of cardinal importance, the board should spend as much time as necessary in the selection of the CEO.

Not all the above recommendations are accepted without reservations. But they all are worthy of consideration.

Employee Governance Activities

Employees traditionally have not had much impact on corporate governance. In recent years, however, there have been three avenues through which they have done so, although none have been of major importance except with some individual companies. They are direct representation on boards, employee stock option plans (ESOPS), and the power of pension plan holdings discussed above.

Labor Union Representation on Boards

Unlike European companies, employee representation on corporate boards of directors in the United States is not common and is of relatively recent origin. The major precedent for this was in 1980 when the Chrysler Corporation got into deep financial difficulties and asked the United Automobile Workers (UAW) union to accept a significant wage concession. It did, and one of the trade-offs was an offer by Lee Iacocca, chairman of Chrysler, to nominate Douglas Fraser, the head of UAW, to the board. Labor unions generally have little interest in seeking board representation but this particular commitment worked well.

In more recent years there have been a few comparable instances. In 1993 National Steel Corp., Bethlehem Steel Corp., and Wheeling-Pittsburgh Steel Corp. accepted union representatives on their boards as part of a contract settlement with union strikers. Several airlines have done the same thing. Unions believe that such representation will permit them to have some say in the strategic direction of the company and provide them with better information about the financial operations of the company.

These arrangements work better when the representative focuses attention on the overall interests of the company and not on special-interest representation. If the latter the possibility of serious conflicts on the board is high. This was not the case with Douglas Fraser and Chrysler's board and that is one reason, along with his talents, why his membership was successful both for the union and Chrysler. Corporate managers generally are not in favor of union members on their boards who are interested only in union affairs.

ESOPS (Employee Stock Option Plans)

More and more companies have ESOPS, and their association with boards of directors raises different governance issues than union leader membership. ESOPS originated in the Tax Reduction Act of 1975 and were further encouraged by additional laws passed by both the Congress and individual states. Basically, employers may establish trust funds on workers' behalf in order to receive stock that can be allocated to individual employees. Tax advantages have made these plans popular. They have exploded in number and asset value until today the National Center for Employee Ownership says there are approximately 10 million employees in over 9,500 plans.[26]

Studies of worker attitudes do not show great eagerness to have board representation. They are most interested in job security, satisfactory wages, congenial working conditions, and some participation in decision making at lower levels. They have not pressed for representation on boards, and most companies have not forced the issue.

Activism of Worker Pension Plans

The acquisition of company stock by worker pension plans gives employees leverage to influence corporate governance. For example, union-initiated proxy battles have increased in recent years as their pension fund holdings have mounted. The issues are not necessarily concerned with bargaining but with such matters as management's compensation, management's protections from possible takeovers (called poison pills), stock offerings, breaking up the company into several new corporations, and other major corporate strategies.

The Teamsters, the United Food & Commercial Workers, and the Clothing Workers have been among the more active pension funds attempting to be influential in corporate governance. For example in 1994 the Teamsters initiated proxy battles concerning poison pills among major truck companies.[27] Managers claim unions are using the proxy machinery to make gains they failed to achieve in direct labor negotiations. Unions say this is not so.

Corporate Executive Compensation

Virtually all corporations have compensation committees that set the pay and benefits of top executives. What is perceived as excessively generous pay and benefits for CEOs has today inspired widespread popular outrage. This is not a new phenomenon. In 1939 President Franklin D. Roosevelt railed against the "entrenched greed" of corporation executives, and the criticism has periodically arisen since.

How Much are CEOs Paid?

First of all it must be recognized that there is no consensus about the dollar value of all pay and benefits to a chief executive. The salary paid to a CEO as well as an annual bonus is clear enough and publicly reported. Problems arise in calculating the value of stock options, which are a large part of most CEO compensation, and other benefits such as deferred pay and perquisites. A stock option is a right to buy the company's stock at a fixed price and conditions determined by the board of directors. Usually the price is at or close to the current price and there is a limit on the time granted to the receiver to buy the stock, usually ten years. Thus, if the stock of XYZ corporation today is $10 and rises to $50 dollars within the time limit, say, ten years, the CEO can buy that stock at $10 and reap the gain between this price and the future market price. If the stock does not rise above $10 the option is worthless.

Standard & Poor's Compustat, a division of The McGraw-Hill Companies, examined the proxy statements of 371 companies and found that the average salary and bonus of CEOs rose about 10 percent over 1993 to $1.4 million in 1994.[28] The largest in the S&P survey was to Charles Locke, Morton International, whose total salary and bonus was $12 million. All of the ten largest were over $4 million.

When stock options are calculated the compensation numbers for some CEOs explode. When the exercise of stock options is calculated Charles Locke's compensation in 1994 rose to $25.9 million. The highest nineteen registered incomes were over $10 million. But that is not all. For instance, Lawrence A. Bossidy, eighth on the list of highest paid CEOs in 1994, was given two large stock-option grants on 1.8 million shares of Allied-Signal Inc. stock. If the stock of the company rises 10 percent annually over the 10-year term of the options, he will gain over $100 million on just these options. Kenneth L. Lay, CEO of Enron Corp., was nineteenth on the 1994 highest-pay list, but was awarded stock options which, if the stock rose 10 percent a year over ten years, could be cashed in at $76 million.[29]

Such lofty compensation is not rare today. For example, Walt Disney Co. Chairman Michael D. Eisner cashed options on December 1, 1992, with a value of $197.5 million. He had been granted the options at $3.59 a share many years before and sold at over $40 a share. In 1991 Anthony J. F. O'Reilly, CEO of H. J. Heinz Co. had total compensation of $74.8 million. Coca-Cola Co. gave CEO Roberto Goizueta a 1-million-share restricted stock grant in 1991 estimated to be valued at $59.2 million.[30] Large compensation has not been confined solely to CEOs. Many other executives have received huge incomes.

Criticisms of CEO Compensation

Critics complain that CEO compensation often has little or no correlation with company performance as measured by stockholder returns or profits. Most studies of linkage find some correlation between company size and compensation, but very little correlation between pay and company performance. For example, Graef Crystal, an adjunct professor at the University of California Berkeley, says that in every study he has made "performance counts for very little compared to size." He says there is minimal relationship between pay and performance.[31] Michael C. Jensen at the Harvard Business School and Professor Kevin J. Murphy at the University of Rochester studied CEO compensation (salary and bonus) of 2,505 publicly held corporations from 1974 through 1988 and concluded that "annual changes in executive compensation do not reflect changes in corporate performance."[32] Daniel J. Miller, of Central Connecticut State University has found some, but not much, correlation between compensation and performance.[33]

Critics complain there is something unseemly about high and expanding executive compensation at the same time companies discharge thousands of workers. In the spring of 1995 Ronald W. Allen, Delta Air Lines' chairman announced the elimination of 15,000 jobs representing about 20 percent of the airline's work force. At the same time he told his board he wanted to forego a pay raise and any bonus. This is not typical. More often executive pay is not cut and the stock price on the market rises when employee reductions are announced. This raises a significant question: Should the CEOs compensation be reduced when large layoffs are announced, or should he or she be rewarded for making a difficult decision to make a company more profitable?[34]

Critics charge that in too many compensation committees the members are CEOs of other corporations, cronies of the CEO, and/or consultants who have profited from business with the company. In all cases, it is alleged, the bias is clearly in favor of boosting the compensation of the CEO.

Critics also charge that executives of American corporations get paid far more than their counterparts in foreign countries. A study by Towers Perrin, a consulting firm, revealed that total pay for European CEOs in 1944 averaged $389,428, far below U.S. levels.[35]

In Defense of CEOs

Executives defend huge compensation on several grounds. First, stock options have been a larger part of compensation in recent years. As a result, the bull market in stock prices in the 1980s and 1990s provided opportunities for executives to exercise options given years before at low prices. If these past option grants are exercised and compensation is calculated for the year in which they were exercised, say the CEOs, of course the amount looks large.

Second, many of the large compensation packages were justified by gains of stockholders during their tenure. For example, the stock price of Coca-Cola increased by nearly fourteen times during the years Goizueta has been chief executive of the company. Similarly, Michael Eisner with his associates produced an extraordinarily successful turnaround of Disney. Net income of the company increased from barely break-even in 1984 to over $1.3 billion in 1995.

Boards of directors point out that if they do not pay their CEOs what executives in comparable companies are getting they stand to lose them, and that would be costly. Anyway, they say, the compensation is not out of line with other professionals, such as top lawyers and Wall Street investment bankers.

Finally, comparisons with foreign countries are not always relevant. For one thing, different analysts reach different conclusions about the precise value of annual compensation when the future estimated value of stock options is included. Comparisons with foreign companies is confused by fluctuating exchange rates, different perquisites and their values, dissimilar governance systems, and varying practices with respect to long-range compensation.

What Should Directors Do about Compensation?

There are several reforms that can be introduced to improve the system for setting executive compensation. First, the compensation committee membership must be made independent from the influence of the CEO and other biased interests. Needless to say the committee should be composed solely of outside directors and in large companies have an outside compensation consultant.

The criteria for determining compensation should be designed to provide greater incentives for the CEO to meet company objectives, which, among other things, should be formulated with the long term in view. This can be done in a number of ways. For example, if stock options are given, the time before which they may be exercised can be extended. Cash compensation may be related to achieving specific goals, such as corporate profits.

Other Reforms and Proposals for Reform

In response to widespread criticism of executive pay, and to restrain unnecessary and unwanted congressional legislation, the SEC issued new regulations concerning executive pay in June 1992 that require companies to show in charts and graphs precisely all details of senior executive compensation. The board of director's compensation committee is required to explain the performance factors used in determining pay. As we have said, there is no generally accepted formula for calculating the value of unexercised options. However, the SEC now requires that companies calculate and report to stockholders a range of values.

Criticism of compensation also initiated action by Congress. A new tax law introduced as of January 1, 1994, bars publicly held corporations from deducting as a cost of doing business a top officer's compensation in excess of $1 million a year. Nevertheless, many corporations pay executives more despite the fact that it is not tax deductible as an expense. The Financial Accounting Standards Board (FASB), an organization that sets guidelines for accounting practices has been considering what to do about stock options. The recommendation to them is to account for stock options as an expense, the same as other compensation. The big problem, of course, is how the cost of the options should be calculated.

Stockholders have introduced resolutions in proxy statements to cap executive compensation. For instance, stockholders introduced a resolution at Pacific Telesis Group in 1994 to limit a combined salary and other compensation to no more than 150 percent of the salary provided to the President of the United States. It did not pass.

To Whom are Directors Accountable?

Jay Lorsch in his study found that directors clearly identified shareholder welfare as their number-one priority. Second was the company's long-term future. Lorsch said, "... the majority of directors felt trapped in a dilemma between their traditional legal responsibility to shareholders, whom they consider too interested in short-term payout, and belief about what is best, in the long run, for the health of the company."[36]

The laws are clear that directors are accountable to stockholders. It is their duty to protect stockholder interests and provide an adequate return on their investment. But to which shareholders do directors owe this responsibility? Short-term stock traders? Corporate raiders interested in a "fast buck"? Large institutional investors who focus on short-term appreciation in their portfolios? Investors in friendly leveraged buyouts? Employees in stock option plans? Individual long-term stock investors?

In response to unfriendly takeovers in the 1980s, twenty-five states, not including Delaware, enacted laws that broaden the legal authority of boards to consider in their decision making stakeholders other than shareholders. These other stakeholders may be communities, governments, suppliers, lenders, employees, and others. What these states are saying, and others will likely follow, is that corporations exist to provide more than a return to owners. This legal position, in contrast to the stark doctrine of stockholder supremacy, focuses the accountability of directors on the overriding role of the corporation in society. Directors obviously face difficult problems in balancing claims of different stakeholders and in defining their responsibility to them.

These considerations inject considerable ambiguity into the question, To whom are directors accountable? Lorsch suggests that directors attempt to develop decision criteria for dealing with the dilemmas they face.

Comparative Survey of Boards of Directors

Corporate boards of directors around the world are being pressured by shareholder activists to reform their structures and functioning. The fundamental structures of boards and the duties they purport to perform are similar to the United States, but there are major differences in both structure and performance.

For example, in Germany, the Netherlands, and other European countries the board chairperson and the CEO are separated. Most European countries have laws mandating labor representation on boards. In Germany, there are two boards. There is a board of supervisors whose members represent labor unions, banks, and business. It is responsible for broad policy and reviewing major management decisions. A second board is responsible for the day-to-day operation of the company and is subject to review by the supervisory board.

Criticism of the functioning of boards is similar to that in the United States. For example, shareholders push for higher profits, greater dividends, discharging inefficient managements, more disclosure of information, linking executive pay to performance, more outside directors with more power, and greater accountability of boards to shareholders.

Space does not permit detailed examination of each of these, but a few examples will illustrate the issues. Disclosure of executive pay is nowhere as illuminating as in the United States. The discharge of inefficient top managers by the board does not occur as frequently as in the United States. Outside directors are neither as numerous nor as influential in decision making as in the United States. In Japan boards are almost exclusively insiders who are in top-management positions or are heads of major departments. Boards in many foreign countries are linked more into elitist groups than in the United States. Chinese business networks are largely personal networks organized through family kinships. In France the relationships are held among graduates of elitist schools. South Korean business networks are dominated by elite business families.[37]

One final point of interest concerns pension funds. These funds have not been as active in corporate governance as in the United States, but are beginning to feel pressure from their constituents to do so. The movement is likely to be accelerated by increased purchases of shares of European companies by U.S. pension funds such as CalPERS. Also, there are pressures in Great Britain to require that pension funds vote at annual meetings.[38]

Concluding Observation

The roles of boards of directors of our corporations have changed dramatically in the past few years, a trend destined to continue in the future. Years ago membership on a typical corporate board of a large corporation was viewed as an honorary position with few responsibilities and a chance to get away from the office to socialize with peers. Today more and more boards are asserting their authority over corporate governance.

In this chapter we have discussed reforms that have been suggested for more effective board governance. The successful implementation of these reforms will improve corporate governance. This in turn will improve our economic strength at home and abroad and raise the standard of living of the American people.

Endnotes

1. National Association of Corporate Directors, *Evolution in the Boardroom*, NACD Corporate Directors' Special Report Series, August 1978.
2. Quoted in Paul Betts, Heads Begin to Roll at Fiat," *Paris Financial Times*, June 18, 1990.
3. These and the following numbers about boards of directors came from Korn/Ferry International, *22nd Annual Board of Directors Study, 1995*, New York: Korn/Ferry International, 1995.
4. The Business Roundtable, *Corporate Governance and American Competitiveness*, New York: Business Roundtable, March 1990.
5. The Business Roundtable, *The Role and Composition of the Board of Directors of the Large Publicly Owned Corporation*, New York: Business Roundtable, 1978, pp. 11-12.
6. Peter F. Drucker, "The Bored Board," *Wharton Magazine*, Fall 1976.
7. Jay W. Lorsch "Empowering the Board," *Harvard Business Review*, January-February 1995, p. 107.
8. Joann S. Lublin, "Is ADM's Board Too Big, Cozy and Well-Paid? *Wall Street Journal*, October 17, 1995; and Kurt Eichenwald, "Investor Revolt Takes Stage," *Los Angeles Times*, October 19, 1995.
9. See for example, Paul B. Firstenberg and Burton G. Malkiel, "The Twenty-First Century Boardroom: Who Will Be in Charge?" *Sloan Management Review*, Fall 1994; and Murray Weidenbaum, "The Evolving Corporate Board," St. Louis, Mo.: Washington University Center for the Study of American Business, May 1994.
10. See, for example, Ralph Nader, "Reforming Corporate Governance," *California Management Review*, Summer 1984.
11. Bruce R. Scott, "Can Industry Survive the Welfare State?" *Harvard Business Review*, September-October 1982.
12. John T. Connor, "An Alternative to the Goldberg Prescription,'' remarks before the American Society of Corporate Secretaries, March 14, 1973.
13. Jay W. Lorsch, *Pawns or Potentates*, Boston Mass.: *Harvard Business School Press*, 1989.
14. *McDonald's Corporation Proxy Statement and Notice of 1995 Annual Meeting of Shareholders*, 1995.

15. Report of the NACD Blue Ribbon Commission on *Performance Evaluation of Chief Executive Officers, Boards, and Directors*, Washington, D.C.: National Association of Corporate Directors, 1994.
16. Gordon Donaldson, "A New Tool for Boards: The Strategic Audit," *Harvard Business Review*, July-August 1995.
17. Joann S. Lublin, "Five More Big Companies to Stop Giving Pensions to Outside Members of Boards," *Wall Street Journal*, February 12, 1996.
18. Reported by Joann S. Lublin, "Give the Board Fewer Perks, a Panel Urges," *Wall Street Journal*, June 19, 1995.
19. New York: Macmillan, 1932.
20. *Flow of Funds Accounts, Third Quarter 1995*, Washington, D.C.: Board of Governors of the Federal Reserve System, 1995; and telephone conversation with Standard & Poors, New York.
21. "Council of Institutional Investors," New York: Council of Institutional Investors, undated.
22. Charles Wohlstetter, "Pension Fund Socialism: Can Bureaucrats Run the Blue Chips?" *Harvard Business Review*, January-February 1993, p. 78.
23. *GM Board of Directors Corporate Governance Guidelines*, Detroit: General Motors Corp., adopted January 1994, revised August 1995.
24. Judith H. Dobrzynski, "An Inside Look at CalPERS' Boardroom Report Card," *Business Week*, October 17, 1994.
25. Robert C. Pozen, "Institutional Investors: The Reluctant Activists," *Harvard Business Review*, January-February 1994.
26. In addition there should be added 2 to 3 million employees holding company stock in their 401(K) pension plans. An additional 2 to 3 million participants should be added to these totals because of their stock options. Source: Telephone conversation with Cory Rosen, President, National Center for Employee Ownership, Oakland, Calif., March 25, 1996.
27. Aaron Bernstein, "Labor Flexes Its Muscles—as a Stockholder," *Business Week*, July 18, 1994.
28. John A. Byrne, with Lori Bongiorno, "CEO Pay: Ready for Takeoff," *Business Week*, April 24, 1995.
29. Ibid.
30. Amanda Bennett, "A Little Pain and a Lot to Gain, the Boss's Pay," *Wall Street Journal* Tower Perrin, "1991 CEO Compensation Survey ... ," *Wall Street Journal*, April 22, 1992.
31. Graef Crystal, "Almost Any Way You Figure It, Executive Pay Remains Irrational," *Los Angeles Times*, December 3, 1995.
32. Michael C. Jensen and Kevin J. Murphy, "CEO Incentives—It's Not How Much You Pay, but How," *Harvard Business Review*, May-June 1992, p. 139.
33. Daniel J. Miller, "CEO Salary Increases May Be Rational After All: Referents and Contracts in CEO Pay," *Academy of Management Journal*, October 1995.
34. Molly Baker, "I Feel Your Pain?" *Wall Street Journal*, April 12, 1995.
35. Cited in Paula Dwyer, "Continental Divide over Executive Pay," *Business Week*, July 3, 1995.
36. Jay W. Lorsch, *Pawns or Potentates*, Boston, Mass: Harvard Business School Press, 1989, p. 49.
37. James C. Abegglen, *Sea Change: Pacific Asia as the New World Industrial Center*, New York: Free Press, 1994.
38. For a comprehensive study of this subject see Jonathan Charkham, *Keeping Good Company: A Study of Corporate Governance in Five Countries*, New York: Clarendon Press, 1994.

Case Study: U.S. v. Michael R. Milken

Introduction

Michael R. Milken has been called a "financial genius" with the stature of J. P. Morgan, a generous philanthropist, and a devoted family man. His entrepreneurship in building the junk bond market was instrumental in the development of many successful companies. He therefore holds a place of importance in the history of corporate governance. On the other hand government prosecutors, in one of the most sensational financial trials of the century, filed an indictment in 1990 and said he was a felon who violated many security laws. His defenders say he might have been guilty only of minor technical violations of the securities law. Which characterization was most fitting? We discuss this question in this case.

Background

Michael Milken was born in Encino, California, July 4, 1945, to Ferne and Bernhard Milken. Bernhard Milken was an accountant and from an early age Michael watched his father prepare tax returns. After graduating from Birmingham High School in neighboring Van Nuys in 1964, Michael entered the University of California Berkeley where he majored in business administration. He graduated from Berkeley in 1968 and enrolled for an M.B.A. at the Wharton School of the University of Pennsylvania which, at that time, was renowned for its curriculum in finance and accounting.

Milken was a superior student, brilliant, hardworking, and intensely ambitious. While at Berkeley, he did not engage in the so-called free speech movement sweeping the campus at the time, but chose to work hard on his studies (he graduated Phi Beta Kappa) and then found a job with Touche Ross, an accounting firm. One of his fraternity brothers at Berkeley (he was a Sigma Alpha Mu) said "he was monomaniacal about money. To be a millionaire by age thirty was his goal. I thought I shared the same goal, but Mike was different. He wanted to be *rich.*"[1]

In 1969, while at Wharton, Milken had a summer job at the Philadelphia offices of Drexel Harriman Ripley and later joined the firm's New York office. This company traced its origins to 1871 when it was Drexel, Morgan and Company. The two firms later split and eventually became Drexel, Burnham and Lambert, one of the most powerful investment bankers on Wall Street. Throughout his career in the investment business Milken remained with Drexel.

The Financial Markets in the 1970s and 1980s

When Milken joined Drexel in New York the bond market was in the doldrums. Interest rates on high-grade corporate bonds rated AAA had risen from an average of 4.49 percent in 1965 to 7.04 percent in 1970, remained at that relatively high level through the mid-1970s and began to rise again reaching 14.17 percent in 1981. The doubling of rates resulted in a drop of bond prices of about 50 percent. Prices of low-rated bonds fell even more. In 1974 stock prices fell significantly with the result that investors looked to places other than bonds and stocks to put their money.

Since they did not find other investment opportunities that suited their interests they placed their money in low-paying money market funds. At the same time, pension and insurance company funds were swelling in size. The result was a rising amount of available cash for investment. There were three major sources of potential but not satisfied demand for these funds. (1) Small and medium-size firms found difficulty in raising money. Neither the bond nor stock markets were hospitable for new offerings, and banks were loath to lend them money. (2) Deregulation of the S&Ls, especially the Garn-St. German Depository Institutions Act of 1982 which permitted the S&Ls to invest up to 40 percent of their assets in nonresidential real estate, opened a significant potential demand for securities. (3) The relaxed regulatory atmosphere of the Reagan administration accommodated the thirst of promoters for money to acquire other companies for profit through leveraged buyouts. (The word "leverage" refers to the use of bonds or debt to pay for the common stock of a company to be taken over. The acronym LBO encompasses a variety of financial transactions concerned with acquisitions and mergers.)[2]

The growing supply of and unsatisfied demands for money established a foundation for the sale of bonds, especially low-grade or junk bonds. Highgrade bonds could be sold, but junk bonds were not well-regarded as investments. (Junk bonds are simply securities bearing high-interest rates to reflect a higher risk. They carry low ratings or are unrated by investment-rating services.) Conservative investment bankers avoided underwriting such securities and that opened the door for new financial entrepreneurs. All they had to do was persuade holders of cash to invest in the low-grade bonds, not an easy task in light of the investment atmosphere of the times.

Thus, Milken began his career at the relative bottom of the stock and bond markets and at a time when available money supply was growing but demand could not be met, especially among small, medium-size, and newly formed firms.[3] Milken was a superb salesperson and believed he had logic on his side for persuading people to invest in junk bonds.

Michael R. Milken.

The Case for Investment in Junk Bonds

Milken's interest in junk bonds extended back to his Berkeley days. There he studied research findings of W. Braddock Hickman, published in 1958, which concluded that lower-rated bonds, under certain circumstances, would yield more to an investor than higher-rated securities. If investors bought lower rated bonds at their lows and held them to maturity the net yield would be greater than on higher-rated securities. One reason for this is that at the bottom of the market cycle for bonds the price of lower-grade bonds falls much more than for higher-grade bonds. Since the default rate in the past for lower-grade bonds was not high, an investor who held them through to maturity, or sold at the top of the market, received net returns higher than if he or she had purchased higher-grade bonds.[4] Thomas R. Atkinson of the National Bureau of Economic Research confirmed the Hickman research and added an additional finding, that most defaults of bonds occurred one year before they reached their highs.[5]

Milken's interest at Drexel focused on the junk bond market but he had to persuade buyers to invest in them. As Robert Sobel, a professor at Hofstra University wrote,

> Milken had to convince the potential buyer that the rating was not reflective of their true value, and that the yield justified a purchase. Such bonds couldn't even be efficiently priced, since most had thin markets. Milken had to sweat out every sale in those days, while the gentlemen salesmen of highly rated bonds made their placements with ease. A Milken spiel must have sounded to them like the line of a tout at a bucket shop.[6]

Milken's Activities at Drexel

Milken's focus on junk bond sales paid off and he was a major contributor to Drexel's profits. However, in 1973 Drexel needed a cash infusion which it got by merging with Burnham & Co. to become Drexel Burnham Lambert. Milken's success was appreciated by

Burnham who became president of Drexel and when he was asked by Milken for permission to establish a bond unit to concentrate on junk bonds it was granted. A compensation arrangement was made which eventually yielded extraordinary income to Milken. He could keep $1 for every $3 he made for Drexel and distribute it as he saw fit to pay personnel in his unit. In addition, his unit would receive fees for any new business it attracted. By 1976 Milken made $5 million a year under this arrangement.[7]

In 1978 Milken moved his department to Beverly Hills, California. There, his operation became the center of the junk bond market.

Growth of the Junk Bond Market

In 1970 total junk bonds outstanding were $7 billion, mostly low-grade securities exchanged for formerly high-rated bonds downgraded as a result of financial difficulties of the issuing company. By 1978 the total junk bond market had grown to $9.4 billion, a larger proportion of which was for new issues. Thereafter the total rapidly increased until it reached $15 billion in 1980, $59 billion in 1985, and $210 billion in 1990.[8]

Milken gradually dominated the junk bond market. Robert Sobel wrote:

> ... he [Milken] virtually owned the junk market, and anyone wanting to play there had to go through him. He not only bought and sold the bonds, but he also knew where they were. This meant that he could contact a customer and talk him into a buy, and then call the owner of the bond and invite him to sell. Milken could set prices within a very wide band, since buyer and seller would have no precise idea of how much the bond was worth. Only Milken could know when to deal with those bonds, and only he had pricing power. His customers lacked this information and control.[9]

During the 1970s and early 1980s there was a boom in mergers and acquisitions. Generally, this arrangement was consummated when a company or person bought enough of the stock of a company to gain control of it. When the acquisition was without the approval of the management and stockholders of the targeted corporation, the action was called "hostile." Each case was different in detail but junk bonds were frequently used to help an individual or a company finance the purchase of enough stock to control a company.

The hostile takeover movement was highly distasteful to traditional investment bankers, corporate leaders, employees of the company acquired, and the public. This was partly due to the fact that hostile takeovers often were designed only to enrich the "raider." To prevent a hostile takeover a management might incur substantial debt to pay off the raider by buying his stock at a price much higher than he paid for it. Or, if the hostile takeover succeeded, a corporation might be loaded with excessive debt to pay for the raider's stock; employees might be discharged and careers ruined to cut costs; and sometimes the company sold in pieces with the hope that sales would yield profits for the raider. The issuance of junk bonds became associated in the public mind with such repugnant activities.

In reality, the vast majority of junk underwritings were for corporate restructuring and expansion. Sobel calculated that of 1,100 junk issues between 1980 and 1986 only 3 percent were used in unwelcome takeovers.[10] Milken helped finance well-known corporate raiders such as Victor Posner, Carl Icahn, and T. Boone Pickens. His name became linked with hostile takeovers. Milken also helped finance newly developing firms that became successful giants, such as Turner Broadcasting, MCI Communications, and McCaw Cellular.

The Ethical Climate in the 1970s and 1980s

The late 1970s and 1980s, with but minor bumps, were boom years in financial markets. Vast opportunities existed to make enormous sums of money and large numbers of people became rich virtually overnight. The era was stamped with human greed. Ivan Boesky, a well-known and large-securities trader who was later sent to prison for insider trading and other crimes, said to a graduating class at the University of California Berkeley in 1986, "Greed is all right, by the way. I want you to know that. I think greed is healthy. You can be greedy and feel good about yourself."[11]

There were many investment bankers who held steadfastly to high ethical standards but there were others who did not. Many were guilty of insider trading (using confidential information to acquire stock before the information became available to the public), conflicts of interest, misinforming clients, and fraud. Many were prosecuted and sent to jail.[12]

The U.S. Government Indictment of Milken

In the late 1980s a series of prosecutions for illegalities darkened the financial markets. Among those prosecuted was Ivan Boesky, who in November 1986, pleaded guilty to a series of financial crimes and was given a prison sentence. He freely cooperated with government prosecutors and pointed fingers at Drexel and Michael Milken with whom he had frequent dealings. Drexel was investigated in late 1988 and agreed to accept government charges of wrongdoing and paid a large fine. Part of the agreement was to give Michael Milken a leave of absence. In January 1990 Drexel filed for bankruptcy and in that year Milken was charged with criminal acts.

In the meantime, the junk bond market collapsed. Savings and loan institutions and others dumped junk bonds on the market and prices plummeted. There was no one around like Milken to maintain liquidity in that market.

In March 1990 Benito Romano, U.S. District Attorney in New York, who followed Rudolph Giuliani after he left to run for mayor of New York, brought a 98-count, 110-page, indictment against Michael Milken, his brother Lowell, and Bruce Newberg, a close associate in the Beverly Hills office. The indictment contained charges of unlawful securities trading including price manipulation, fraud in the sale of securities, mail fraud, wire fraud, tax fraud, devious schemes to defraud, and other related crimes "in a pattern of racketeering activity."[13]

The Boesky Arrangement

The first indictment concerned a charge of secret arrangements between Milken and Ivan Boesky, a major security trader, which the government claimed resulted in a series of illegal securities trades. The illegal activities included trading profits from "insider trading,[14] buying and selling bonds to support hostile takeovers without disclosing the purposes of these actions, bogus and fraudulent stock and bond trading, mail fraud, and violating the federal tax and securities laws to defraud investors." Space permits but a very few and brief illustrations of the government's charges of illegality.

Fischbach Corporation

An illustration of the unlawful actions of the Boesky and Milken arrangement, said the government, was the takeover of the Fischbach Corporation. This was a construction business, including electrical and mechanical contracting. Victor Posner, a well-known corporate raider, wanted to acquire Fischbach through the Pacific Engineering Corporation (PEC) which he controlled. In early 1980 PEC filed a Schedule 13D form with the Securities and Exchange Commission disclosing that it had acquired over 10 percent of Fischbach's common stock.[15] Fischbach's management resisted the attempted thrust of PEC and threatened to sue. PEC and Fischbach resolved their differences in a standstill agreement which barred PEC from acquiring more than 24.9 percent of the stock unless a third party not connected with PEC or Posner declared an acquisition of 10 percent or more of Fischbach's stock. If that happened, then the standstill agreement was no longer effective. PEC then proceeded to acquire 24.8 percent of the stock.

In December 1983, Executive Life Insurance Co., a purchaser of large quantities of junk bonds from Milken, filed a 13D with the SEC revealing it had acquired 14.4 percent of Fischbach's stock. This purchase of stock, of course, was enough to end the standstill agreement. However, Fischbach said that insurance companies had to file a 13G, not a 13D, which was correct, and since Executive Life did not do so the standstill agreement still was in force. This was enough to throw the issue into the courts.

The government claimed that Milken then caused Boesky to buy over 10 percent of Fischbach's stock, which he disclosed on 13D to the SEC. The government charged that Milken agreed to cover any losses of Boesky in the transaction. This action, of course, nullified the standstill agreement. The government claimed that Boesky did not reveal on his 13D that the shares were bought on behalf of Drexel Enterprises. This was illegal "stock parking." (Stock parking refers to a person or company buying securities from or on behalf of another person or company without revealing the owner's identity.) Thus, said the government, filing falsely and fraudulently deceived Fischbach and the public. Drexel also bought shares of Fischbach for its own account and later sold them to PEC. In February 1985 Drexel underwrote and sold $56 million of junk bonds to finance the further acquisition of Fischbach by Posner and his group. Posner was able to take control of Fischbach in September 1985.

Fischbach shares dropped in the market and Boesky's losses were substantial. He pressed Milken for reimbursement of losses because Boesky said Milken had said he would cover any losses. Milken later arranged a series of trades in the junk bond market that resulted in profit for Boesky.

Altogether, charged the government, this experience revealed a secret conspiracy among Milken, Drexel, and Boesky's organizations to commit unlawful acts. Among the illegal actions were concealing the purposes of the transactions, unlawfully breaking the standstill agreement, and fraud in the sale of securities.

Golden Nugget

During the first half of 1984 Golden Nugget, a Las Vegas casino, and one of Milken's clients, decided to acquire MCA and quietly began accumulating MCA shares. Golden Nugget bought several million shares at a cost of approximately $99 million but only up to 4.9 percent of MCA's outstanding stock. Then the casino decided it did not wish to go through with the acquisition. It wanted to sell its shares but did not want to dump them on the market for fear of depressing the stock price, which had risen substantially on rumors of the takeover. The casino called on Milken for help; he in turn called on Boesky to buy large amounts of Golden Nugget's stock with the promise, Boesky said, to take care of any losses. "These purchases and sales," said the government, "were done to conceal from the investing public that Golden Nugget was selling its MCA common stock, and thereby to artificially support the price of that stock during the period of those sales." Milken was accused of committing mail fraud as shown in mailings that confirmed the trades of Golden Nugget and Boesky.

Diamond Shamrock Corporation

In this case Diamond Shamrock Corporation and Occidental Petroleum Corporation in January 1985 had agreed in principle to merge the two companies. Drexel was hired to advise Occidental on the merger. At about the same time the government charged that Milken caused Boesky to buy approximately 3.6 million shares of Diamond common stock and sell "short" about 10,000 shares of Occidental common stock.[17] The profits and losses to Boesky were to be split with Drexel. Shortly thereafter Milken caused Boesky to buy 180,700 shares of Diamond and sell short 327,100 shares of Occidental, and to split profits and losses. Neither Diamond nor Occidental knew about these trades. Boesky lost money on the trades and shortly thereafter, said the government, Milken conducted a series of "sham and bogus trades at artificial prices" with Boesky to repay money owed to Boesky on the Occidental and other company losses. Furthermore, Milken had Drexel "... reimburse the Boesky organization secretly for certain of these losses, enabling the Boesky organization falsely and fraudulently to claim the entirety of these losses on its federal income tax returns."[18]

The government alleged that Milken knowingly committed securities fraud by using inside information to profit. He violated his duty to Occidental, engaged in fraudulent security trading, and committed tax and mail fraud, said the government.

Storer Communications, Inc.

Storer, a cable and VHF television station in Miami, Florida, agreed to a leveraged buyout by Kohlberg, Kravis, Roberts & Co. (KKR), an investment firm in New York, in December 1985. KKR sought the help of Milken in the $1.5 billion LBO with bonds and preferred stock. Drexel earned a fee of $49.6 million. (This was the largest LBO up to that time but was surpassed a few years later when KKR bought R. J. Nabisco for $25.1 billion.) Milken caused Boesky to buy 124,300 shares of Storer common stock and secretly agreed to share profits and losses with him. The government charged Milken not only with insider trading but also with failing to disclose the stock acquisition to Storer and KKR. Boesky ultimately made $1.1 million on the trade.

Very briefly here are a few similar charges. Wickes Companies, Inc., was in the home-products business with headquarters in Santa Monica, California. Milken caused Boesky to buy 1.9 million shares of Wickes to lift the stock price to a point that triggered a commitment to redeem preferred stock. This was alleged to be illegal stock manipulation. Princeton/Newport Partners, located in Princeton, New Jersey, and Newport Beach, California, was engaged in investing the assets of the partners in securities and commodities. Milken was accused of causing them to commence a series of trades to manipulate the price of securities underwritten by Drexel. Transactions were also arranged to generate "bogus tax losses which Princeton/Newport fraudulently used to reduce the federal income tax liability of its partners."[19]

David Solomon, the head of a mutual fund, was an important client of Milken's. In December 1985 he needed to offset capital gains with losses for his personal account. The government charged that Milken helped him by selling him bonds that Drexel had in its inventory and later buying them back at a lower price. Milken also agreed to include Solomon in deals at a later date to make up for his losses in the bond transaction. Milken was charged with fraud. The government charged that Milken and his associates (Lowell J. Milken and Bruce L. Newberg) participated in criminal activities that showed a pattern of racketeering activity in violation of RICO and as a result making all their earnings subject to forfeiture.[20] The government calculated that for the years 1984 through 1987 total fees and trading profits amounted to $1.845 billion.[21]

In Defense of Michael Milken

A comprehensive defense of Milken was made by Daniel Fischel, a professor of law and business at the University of Chicago Law School, and formerly on the defense team of Milken, in his book *Payback.*[22]   Fischel wrote that the government did not produce evidence that Milken had "... engaged in any conduct that had ever before been considered criminal. After the most thorough investigation of any individual's business practices in history, the government came up with nothing. In fact, the government never established that Milken's 'crimes' were anything other than routine business practices common to the industry."[23] He concluded: "The unholy alliance of the displaced establishment and the 'decade of greed' rich-haters, aided by ambitious but unscrupulous government lawyers like Rudy Giuliani, combined to destroy him. The whole episode is a national disgrace."[24]

Here is a sampling of the defense as set forth by Fischel and others. As noted above, the government claimed that Boesky bought Fischbach stock on the initiation of Milken who promised Boesky he would cover any losses. Boesky did not reveal that on the 13D he filed with the SEC Milken had an interest in his purchase. This was stock parking. But, said Fischel, this was common practice. Historically, such practice has either been ignored or treated only as a minor technical infraction of the security laws. No one ever suggested this was a serious crime. Furthermore, even if Milken had promised to cover losses, that was no infraction of law. Stockbrokers often help clients cover losses suffered from their recommendations. This is done, among other things, to keep clients happy.

The arrangement of Boesky and Milken was quite innocent, said Fischel. The attempted takeover of Fischbach was well-known and Boesky simply asked Milken his advice about the wisdom of an investment. There was speculation that Boesky bought the stock hoping that Fischbach management would buy his shares well over his cost. This had been done with Executive Life when the company bought back its shares at a premium with the hope that the standstill agreement would, therefore, not be nullified. There was no conspiracy here.

Both Boesky and Milken claimed there was no agreement that Milken would cover Boesky's losses. It is true that Boesky became concerned when the price of Fischbach fell on the market and called Milken about it. Milken's reply was, "Don't worry about it." That certainly was no commitment to cover Boesky's losses. (Boesky ultimately lost approximately $2 million which was later covered by profitable investments recommended by Milken.) This was a common routine accommodation for a client.

There were no explicit agreements for stock parking or reimbursement for loss. "Such ambiguous disputes," said Fischel, "should not be the basis of criminal felony prosecutions."[25] The Golden Nugget case is another illustration of Milken wanting to help a client. There was no proof that Boesky, who bought the casino's shares of MCA, was acting as an agent of Milken.

In the Occidental Petroleum case Milken was accused of insider trading by having Boesky trade in Occidental common stock to make a profit. Boesky suffered losses because the merger with Diamond Shamrock never occurred. If there was insider trading, asks Fischel, why did Milken not inform Boesky that the merger was off so that he could get out?

The charge of tax fraud in the Solomon case, said the defense, made no sense. The loss of Solomon was a real loss and no fraud was committed when he so declared on his income tax. There was no evidence that Milken had agreed to help Solomon make up that loss.

To conclude, Fischel argued that the government was unable to present any evidence that crimes had been committed by Milken. Furthermore, the offenses he was charged with "had rarely, if ever, been subject to criminal prosecution at the time of Michael's acts."[26] No witnesses linked Milken to securities manipulation, he said.

Milken Pleads Guilty

On April 24, 1990, Milken pled guilty to six felonies. Four involved Boesky and two involved Solomon. One concerned the failure to disclose Drexel's interest in Boesky's organization holding securities of Fischbach Corp. A second concerned defrauding investors in the Golden Nugget case. A third related to a criminal conspiracy with Boesky to park securities to conceal the true owners. A fourth involved security fraud in the Golden Nugget case. A fifth involved assisting Solomon to file false tax returns. A final one dealt with mail fraud related to dealings with Solomon.

Fatico Hearings

On September 27, 1990, the court announced that it would conduct *Fatico* hearings. These are hearings, said Judge Kimba Wood, that permit the plaintiff and defendant to present a limited amount of additional information to enable the court, before determining the sentence, "to have as full a picture as possible of Michael Milken's character in sentencing him on the six counts to which he pled guilty."[27]

The government made six charges of which the court accepted only two as being convincing and relevant to the purpose of the *Fatico* hearings. They involved obstruction of justice and concealing transactions to clients as required by law.[28]

Storer

As part of the financing of the LBO of Storer by KKR, Drexel agreed to sell PIK preferred stock. (PIK means that dividends would be paid in preferred stock, not cash.) Warrants were issued as "sweeteners" to induce investors to buy the stock. The warrants permitted holders to purchase Storer common stock at a profit if the merger was successful. Approximately 67 million shares were issued, each worth 7.4 cents a share at the time.

The government claimed that Milken did not use the warrants to sell the preferred stock. Rather he allocated substantial amounts of the warrants to Drexel-affiliated partnerships in which he and his family had sizable interests. Some he offered to employees of Drexel clients to curry their favor. By late 1988 the partnerships had earned approximately $270 million in profits.

The contention of the government was that Milken's interests were concealed from KKR and Storer and they should have been revealed. This point is supported, said the government, by the fact that Drexel's salespeople did not know the warrants were available.

The defense argued that the distribution was within the discretionary power of Drexel as it saw fit in marketing the Storer securities. Furthermore, the CEO of Drexel knew about the warrants and gave his approval to Milken to distribute them as he did because it did not violate Drexel policy. Furthermore, KKR representatives knew that Drexel had no obligation to offer the warrants to any particular investor. Finally, the sale of the preferred stock was crucial to getting the Storer board to approve the merger.

The loss of Solomon was indeed real and no fraud was committed when he so declared on his income tax. There was no evidence that Milken had agreed to help Solomon make up that loss.

The Blue Ledger Book

This document contained entries between Milken and David Solomon, a mutual fund manager and substantial purchaser of Drexel's junk bonds. The books held evidence, said the government, of bogus security trades to generate phony losses for Solomon's personal account. The losses were used in the 1985 tax returns of Solomon and, of course, were illegal.

Terren Peizer, a close associate of Milken, testified that Milken came to him, a few days after subpoenas were served on Milken, and asked him whether he still had the ledger book. Peizer said yes, and Milken then said to give it to Lorraine Spurge, one of Milken's closest confidants. Thereafter, the book disappeared. On another occasion, Peizer testified he was looking for documents in response to the government's subpoena. Milken said to him, in words to the effect, "if you don't have them, you can't provide them."[29] James Dahl, another close associate of Milken's testified that Milken went with him to the men's room, turned the water on, and said to Dahl "there haven't been any subpoenas issued and whatever you need to do, do it."[30] Then he turned off the water and looked to Dahl for response. Dahl said okay and went out. There had been no subpoena for Dahl to produce the documents at that time, but Milken had received subpoenas prior to this interchange.

The defense argued that there was no witness who testified that Dahl had been given specific directions by Milken to withhold documentary evidence. Furthermore, both Peizer's and Dahl's creditability was in doubt because their testimony on other facts proved to be wrong. A number of perfectly legal interpretations of these discussions is possible, argued the defense. For example, Dahl might have misinterpreted Milken's meaning because of the noise of the running water, or Milken merely was telling a trusted employee that a subpoena had been issued.

The government presented other charges, but Judge Wood said they were not relevant to the purpose of the *Fatico* hearing. The defense also presented evidence about the longtime and substantial charitable generosity of Milken.

Comments of Judge Wood on the Fatico Hearing

Judge Wood said she found the testimony of Peizer and Dahl to be creditable and Milken was guilty of obstructing justice. Also, she found that Milken had deliberately concealed from KKR information about his disposition of Storer warrants and thus violated the law. She noted in detail in her resume of the Fatico hearings the reasons for these conclusions and why she excluded the other charges made by the government at that hearing.

Judge Kimba Wood's Sentencing Opinion[31]

Judge Wood handed down her sentencing opinion on November 21, 1990. She noted,

> It is unusual for a judge to be presented with both such a wide range of possible sentences and such a stark contrast between the defendant's version and the government's version of the defendant's conduct.
> Defendant has claimed that his wrongdoing consisted of a few instances of over-zealous service to his clients, mere technical disclosure violations and ... accommodating a client (the Solomon tax help) who needed tax losses.
> The government in contrast claimed defendant was one of the most villainous criminals Wall Street had ever produced and he abused his position as head of the most powerful department in one of the most powerful firms on Wall Street to regularly distort the securities market and enrich himself and Drexel, and, finally, that he obstructed justice.

The judge said, in connection with the defense, although the crimes benefited Milken's clients that was no excuse for violating the law. "There is no escaping the fact that your crimes also benefited you." The argument was not accepted that the violations were merely technical and that the defendant's conduct was not really criminal or only barely criminal.

"These arguments," said Judge Wood, "fail to take into account the fact that you may have committed only subtle crimes not because you were not disposed to any criminal behavior but because you were willing to commit only crimes that were unlikely to be detected.... Your crimes show a pattern of skirting the law, stepping just over the wrong side of the law in an apparent effort to get some of the benefits from violating the law without running a substantial risk of being caught.... You did not order employees to destroy or remove documents, but you communicated the advisability of their doing so in subtle terms that preserved some deniability on your part."

In determining Milken's sentence she said, "I have taken into account that long before your current legal problems you took a significant amount of your own personal time to serve the community by working with disadvantaged children rather, for example, than using all of your personal time to acquire possessions. You also successfully encouraged your colleagues at work to do the same." Furthermore, she added "... competitors found you to be forthright, honorable and honest in your dealings with them over the years." But on the other side, she said, "... you were head of your department and ... you used others in your department to effect unlawful schemes. By your example, you communicated that cutting legal and ethical corners is, at times, acceptable."

Judge Wood made it clear that her sentence was not only to punish for criminal acts but also "to be effective in deterring others from committing them." She then sentenced Milken to ten years in prison, three years of probation, and community service. Milken served less than two years of his prison sentence. He paid a total of $1.1 billion in penalties.

Concluding Comment

It is somewhat troubling to read the documents in this case and see two distinct pictures of a man. Can they be balanced?

Questions

1. Describe the state of the financial markets when Milken first began his career with Drexel.
2. What was the basis of Milken's conviction that junk bonds were good investments?
3. What was going on in the financial markets that helped Milken persuade managers to use junk bonds in their financing and enabled him to market these securities?
4. What were the basic charges of the U.S. District Attorney of New York against Milken?
5. What was the basic response of the defense to these charges?
6. Do you agree or disagree with Judge Woods's sentencing opinion?
7. Do you believe this was a case of (a) violation only of minor technicalities, (b) occasional unethical behavior, or (c) demonstrable criminal acts?

Endnotes

1. Robert Sobel, *Dangerous Dreamers: The Financial Innovators from Charles Merrill to Michael Milken*, New York: Valley, 1993, pp. 6-63.
2. For a fuller definition of LBO, see Carolyn Kay Brancato and Kevin F. Winch, *Leveraged Buyouts and the Pot of Gold: Trends, Public Policy, and Case Studies*, report prepared by the Economics Division of the Congressional Research Service for the Subcommittee on Oversight and Investigations of the Committee on Energy and Commerce, U.S. House of Representatives, Washington, D.C.: U.S. Government Printing Office, December 1987.
3. Ibid., for a detailed discussion of the financial conditions of the 1970s and 1980s.
4. W. Braddock Hickman, *Corporate Bond Quality and Investor Experience*, Princeton, N.J.: Princeton University Press, 1958.
5. Thomas R. Atkinson, with the assistance of Elizabeth T. Simpson, *Trends in Corporate Bond Quality*, New York: National Bureau of Economic Research 1967.
6. Sobel, *Dangerous Dreamers*, p. 72.
7. Ibid., p. 75.
8. Edward A. Altman, "Defaults and Returns on High Meld Bonds: An Update through the First Half of 1991," in the Merrill

Lynch magazine, *Extra Credit*, July/August 1991, p. 19; printed in Sobel, *Dangerous Dreamers*, p. 127.

9.   Sobel, *Dangerous Dreamers*, p. 93.
10. Ibid., p. 128.
11. Quoted in James Steward, *Den of Thieves*, New York: Simon & Schuster, 1992, p. 261.
12. Ibid.
13. *United States of America v. Michael R. Milken, Lowell J. Milken, and Bruce L. Newberg, Indictment*, U.S. District Court, Southern District of New York, S 89 Cr. 41 (KBW) undated. The charges described in this case are from this document unless otherwise specified.
14. Insider trading, a violation of the securities laws, takes place when people who have access to confidential information use that knowledge to trade in securities for their own benefit prior to the release of the information to the public.
15. The Williams Act of 1968 requires, among other things, that anyone acquiring 5 percent or more of a company's common stock must disclose that fact, state the purpose of the acquisition, and whether any additional shares are to be bought.
16. *Milken Indictment*, p. 21
17. Selling short means that stock is sold that is not owned in anticipation of a decline in the stock price. Usually the sold stock is borrowed from a broker for delivery to the purchaser. If the stock later does decline in price, the short seller "covers" the trade by buying the stock and giving it to the broker. If the stock price rises the short seller, of course, loses.
18. *Milken Indictment*, p. 28.
19. Ibid., p. 63.
20. RICO refers to the Racketeer-Influenced and Corrupt Organizations statute passed by Congress in 1970. It was directed at Mafia activities and it is not at all clear that Congress intended it be applied to so-called white-collar crimes. The law is harsh. If one is convicted of crimes under this law he or she can be penalized of all property and profits made in the alleged illegal activities.
21. *Milken Indictment*, p. 88.
22. Daniel Fischel, *Payback: The Conspiracy to Destroy Michael Milken and His Financial Evolution*, New York: Harper-Business, 1995.
23. Ibid. p. 158.
25. Ibid., p. 79.
26. Ibid., p. 169.
27. *U.S. v. Milken*, U.S. District Court, S.D. New York, December 13, 1990, p. 110. FATICO was established by *United States v. Fatico* in 1979.
28. The discussion of these charges is from *United States v. Michael R. Milken, Lowell J. Milken, and Bruce L. Newberg*, U.S. Dis. Ct., S.D. New York, 759 S. F.Supp. 109 (S.D. N.Y. 1990).
29. Ibid., p. 114.
30. Ibid., p. 113.
31. The following quotations are from Judge Kimba M. Wood, *Opinion, United States v. Michael Milken*, U.S. Dist. Ct. S.D. N.Y, November 21, 1990.

Chapter Thirty-Four

FROM NATURE:

ENERGY POLICIES

If it is very easy to substitute other factors for natural resources, then there is in principle no (energy) "problem." The world can, in effect, get along without natural resources, so exhaustion is just an event, not a catastrophe.

Robert Solow, "The Economics of Resources or the Resources of Economics"[1]

Introduction

Natural resources must be available for businesses to make the goods and provide the services that people need. Their availability depends on market forces (the laws of supply, demand, and price), technical capabilities, and government policies. In the long run, smooth transitions from the use of one set of resources to another should take place if markets are to function without unnecessary government interference and if technological change takes place in response to market signals. In the short run, however, there can be unexpected price hikes and resource scarcity. Severe economic problems and adjustment difficulties accompany these conditions. Governments make the situation worse when they try to cushion people from the effects of higher prices; doing so leads to inappropriate long-run decisions that prolong the crisis (e.g., decisions to purchase energy-inefficient capital equipment).

Major energy price shocks shook the world in 1973 and 1979. With the decline of the Cold War, energy policy issues, with their focal point in the Persian Gulf, are an important factor that managers should consider. This chapter focuses on these issues.[2]

The Crisis in the Persian Gulf

The following headline appears in your morning newspaper: "Iraq Takes Control in Kuwait: Bush Embargoes Trade."[3] Your heart sinks as you wonder what this development will mean (see Figure 34-1). Between them Iraq and Kuwait control nearly 20 percent of the world's proven oil reserves (see Figure 34-2).

Business and Society, Second Edition, by Alfred A. Marcus. © Irwin/McGraw-Hill, The McGraw-Hill Companies, 1993, 1996.

FIGURE 34-1
Evolution of the Gulf
Crisis, 1990

July 17   President Saddam Hussein of Iraq accuses Persian Gulf countries that exceed their oil production quotas of "stabbing his country in the back."

July 18   Tarez Aziz, Iraqi foreign minister, denounces Kuwait to Arab League nations claiming that it has "stolen" $2.4 billion worth of Iraqi oil.

July 24   Iraq, maintaining that oil prices should rise to $25 a barrel, deploys thousands of troops on the Kuwaiti border.

July 25   Iraq, refusing to give assurances that it will not attack Kuwait, demands payment of $2.4 billion in compensation from Kuwait.

July 27   While Iraq continues to demand that Kuwait meet its "legitimate rights," the Organization of Petroleum Exporting Countries (OPEC) agrees to increase oil prices to $21 a barrel.

August 2 Iraq, unsatisfied, sends its troops and tanks into Kuwait, launching an attack on that country.

FIGURE 34-2
Proven oil reserves
and production, 1990

	Proven Reserves (billions of barrels)	Production (millions of barrels per day)
Saudi Arabia	255.0	4.9
Iraq	100.0	2.8
Kuwait	94.5	1.6
Iran	91.5	2.9
Soviet Union	58.4	11.6
United States	34.1	7.6
Rest of Middle East	117.9	4.1
All others	259.0	28.1
World total	1,012.0	63.6

Source: Adapted from *BP Statistical Review of World Energy, 1990.*

Declining U.S. Production

In the spring of 1990, U.S. production of crude oil was falling and alternative production methods and technologies, while offering some promise, were not ready to take up the slack. The United States was distracted by changes in the Soviet Union and looming budget battles that were only peripherally related to the energy problem. Output from Alaska's North Slope had peaked at about 2 million barrels a day in 1988 and production of domestic crude oil, 7.6 million barrels a day, was at a 26-year low. In 1989, only 542 exploratory wells had been dug, a decline from 2,334 in 1984. Because of restrictions on offshore drilling and drilling in Alaska wildlife reserves, the drilling that did take place occurred in areas where less oil was likely to be discovered.

The implications were serious. By 1989, the cost of imported oil in the United States had increased by 28 percent. This hindered efforts to close the trade deficit; nearly $50 billion of the trade deficit, or about 45 percent, was spent on foreign oil.

The United States imported 46 percent of the oil it consumed in 1989, substantially more than the 31.5 percent it imported in 1985 and very near the 1977 record of 47.7 percent. The Department of Energy estimated that by the year 2000 domestic production would fall to less than 6 million barrels a day and that the bill for imported oil would increase to more than $100 billion annually in constant dollars if oil prices increased as anticipated to nearly $28 a barrel. The United States would be importing over 75 percent of the oil it consumed. For a nation that imported very little petroleum prior to 1970, this change was remarkable.

Exotic alternatives to imported oil did not show much promise, so the long-term prospects for the United States to get away from heavy dependence on foreign oil were not particularly good. The ultimate example of an exotic alternative was cold fusion, the possibility of extracting vast sums of energy from the forging together of subatomic material.[4] The commercial prospects for cold fusion lay only in the distant future. Still, it might have promise for offering cheap and abundant power that would help eliminate world dependence on petroleum from unstable regions.

Where then was American energy going to come from in the future? Oil companies were trying to revive old domestic petroleum fields by expanding the use of horizontal drilling, which would enable them to capture oil that could not be reached by conventional methods. Though the costs of horizontal drilling were about twice the costs of drilling a conventional well, production rates could be four to five times as great, enabling the companies to rapidly recover the expenses (in the best of cases within a year). The 1989-1990 market for horizontal drilling equipment had increased 18 times from what it had been the year before. Independent oil companies such as Oryx Energy, Union Pacific Resources, and Burlington Resources were taking the lead in using this new method while some of the large integrated companies like ARCO, Amoco, and Texaco used it to a lesser extent. Horizontal drilling had the potential to revive moribund fields in Colorado, North Dakota, and Wyoming. The payoff would be an increase in U.S. proven reserves, considered to be about 27 billion barrels, by several billion barrels.

Nevertheless, an increase in American oil reserves by several billion barrels did not put the United States anywhere near the capability of the Persian Gulf powers to supply the world with oil. There was no doubt that American oil vulnerabilities, which began when the United States first imported substantial amounts of foreign petroleum, were rising.

A Proposal for a Broad-Based Energy Tax

The Bush administration was considering a broad Based energy tax as one means of reducing the budget deficit. This tax would affect nearly every energy source—gasoline, oil, natural gas, nuclear power, and hydroelectric power. It would mean an increase of about 5 to 6 cents on a gallon of gas, an addition to the existing federal gas tax of 9 cents a gallon. It would bring in an additional $20 billion to the Treasury, or about 40 percent of the funds needed to reduce the budget deficit.

At the time, the energy tax did not seem out of line, since the fuel cost of a mile's driving in the United States had plunged from 4 cents per mile in 1979 to 2 cents per mile in 1989. U.S. gasoline prices were about one-third what they were in other nations, chiefly because of lower U.S. gasoline taxes.

The energy tax had an additional benefit: by discouraging energy use, it helped the environment. The biggest cause of pollution is energy use, which contributes to oil spills, acid rain, smog, and greenhouse warming. Some Democrats favored the energy tax because it encouraged conservation and the development of alternative fuels and technologies, but other Democrats bitterly resisted it, claiming that the tax burden would fall most heavily on the poor.

The Organization of Petroleum Exporting Countries (OPEC)

To understand the role of energy in the international economy, it is important to examine actions of the major producers. They belong to the Organization of Petroleum Exporting Nations (OPEC), which came into existence in 1960 following decisions by the multinational oil companies to reduce the price of oil.[5] From 1970 to 1973, the already dominant position of OPEC in terms of world oil production and reserves (three-fourths of the world's oil discoveries between 1945 and 1973 had been in OPEC countries) grew. OPEC was supplying over 80 percent of the free world's exports. The five founding members (Saudi Arabia, Iran, Iraq, Venezuela, and Kuwait) were operating close to maximum sustainable capacity (see Figure 34-3).

FIGURE 34-3
Selected statistics of
OPEC nations, 1990

	Crude Oil Production (thousands of barrels per day)	Share of Oil in GNP (%)	Population (millions)	Per Capita Purchasing Power ($)	Trade Balance (billions)
Saudi Arabia	6,436	54	14.1	6,430	6.6
Iran	3,076	20	57.0	1,400	1.8
Venezuela	2,103	22	19.7	2,150	10.1
United Arab Emirates (UAE)	2,062	40	2.3	11,870	2.1
Iraq	1,948	50	18.8	1,940	4.0
Nigeria	1,779	42	118.8	310	1.7
Libya	1,350	45	4.2	5,860	−0.1
Indonesia	1,249	9	190.1	490	5.7
Kuwait	1,222	31	2.1	9,700	5.2
Algeria	765	25	25.4	2,130	1.3
Qatar	385	30	0.5	13,200	0.9
Ecuador	285	15	10.5	920	0.9
Gabon	280	40	1.1	31,000	

Source: Adapted from Directorate of Intelligence, Central Intelligence Agency, *Handbook of Economic Statistics, 1991* (Washington. D.C.: U.S. Government Printing Office, 1991). p. 32.

Massive Price Increases

The first massive price increase followed the outbreak of the Arab-Israeli War in October 1973. The Organization of Arab Petroleum Exporting Countries (OAPEC), consisting of Saudi Arabia, Abu Dhabi, Libya, Algeria, Kuwait, Bahrain, Qatar, and Dubai, curtailed production by 10 percent and did not permit oil shipments to the United States. However, after 1977 substantial increases in production from Mexico, the North Sea, and Alaska, and increases in non-OPEC production alleviated the pressure on oil prices. As markets became weaker, OPEC's share of world crude production went down.

At the time of the Iranian revolution, real oil prices actually had started to fall. Between 1979 and 1980, however, petroleum prices again doubled. Iranian oil production dropped off because of the revolution. Various countries, led by Japan, tried to take precautions against a possible decline in the flow of oil out of Gulf, and additional pressure on prices came from a buildup in stocks by these countries in 1979 and 1980.

Decline in Demand

World oil demand reached a peak in 1979. Demand fell thereafter because of energy savings and interfuel substitution, non-OPEC supplies, including natural gas liquids from the Soviet Union, and the deep worldwide recession of 1980-1982.[6] In response to these changes, mistrust among the OPEC nations grew. They were unable to meet in November 1980 in Baghdad because of differences about the Iran-Iraq War. OPEC's radical camp—

consisting of Iran, Algeria, and Libya—vehemently opposed the United States and favored short-run OPEC revenue maximization. The Gulf Cooperation Council (GCC), a moderate faction led by Saudi Arabia (see Figure 34-4) sought a less restrictive pricing policy leading to long run revenue maximization. An independent group consisting of the remaining OPEC members frequently altered its position.

FIGURE 34-4
Members of the Gulf
Cooperation Council,
1989

	Oil Reserves (billions of barrels)	Population (millions)	GDP per Capita ($)	Armed Forces
Saudi Arabia	255.0	14.1	6,400	65,700
UAE	97.7	1.6	15,200	43,000
Kuwait	94.5	2.1	11,250	20,300
Qatar	4.5	0.4	14,700	7,000
Oman	4.3	1.5	5,900	25,500
Bahrain	0.1	0.5	7,200	3,350

Source: Oil and Gas Journal, Institute for Strategic Studies.

The first price reduction in the 23-year history of OPEC occurred at the March 1983 London meeting when prices were reduced from $34 to $29 a barrel. Individual OPEC countries resorted to separate deals with consuming nations to maintain their market shares. The cartel began to unravel. It lost control of the oil market during 1985-1986 because its members could not enforce an acceptable market-sharing scheme.[7] Under these circumstances, the Saudis and some of their Gulf neighbors decided that they had to increase their share of the world oil market to maintain revenues. The Saudis were able to sell at low prices without suffering substantial revenue losses because price declines were offset by production increases. In taking the actions it did, Saudi Arabia risked hostile retaliation from the OPEC radicals—Iran, Iraq, and Libya (see Figures 34-5 and 34-6).

FIGURE 34-5
Major oil exporters,
1970-1990

	Hundreds of Thousands of Barrels per Day				
	1970	1975	1980	1985	1990
OPEC					
Saudi Arabia	3.6	6.8	9.3	2.6	6.1
Iran	3.5	4.9	0.9	1.7	2.2
Venezuela	3.4	2.0	1.8	1.2	2.0
UAE	0.8	1.7	1.7	1.0	2.2
Iraq	1.5	2.1	2.5	1.2	1.7
Nigeria	1.1	2.7	2.0	1.3	1.2
Libya	3.3	1.5	1.8	1.0	1.3
Indonesia	0.7	1.1	1.2	0.7	0.9
Kuwait	2.8	2.0	1.6	0.9	1.2
Algeria	1.0	0.9	0.9	0.5	1.0
Non-OPEC					
Soviet Union	1.9	2.6	3.2	3.3	3.2
Mexico	0.0	0.1	0.8	1.6	1.3

Source: Adapted from Directorate of Intelligence, Central Intelligence Agency, *Handbook of Economic Statistics, 1991* (Washington, D.C.: U.S. Government Printing Office, 1991), p. 87.

FIGURE 34-6
Oil revenues of OPEC
nations and the
Soviet Union,
1975-1990

| | **Billions of U.S. Dollars** | | | | |
	1975	1980	1985	1989	1990
Saudi Arabia	27	99	26	24	45
Iran	19	13	15	11	16
Venezuela	8	18	13	9	14
UAE	7	19	12	11	17
Iraq	8	25	11	15	9
Nigeria	7	24	12	9	14
Libya	6	23	10	6	10
Indonesia	4	13	12	6	8
Kuwait	8	19	9	9	6
Algeria	4	15	13	6	9
Qatar	2	6	3	2	3
Ecuador	1	2	2	1	1
Soviet Union	8	28	34	30	27

Source: Directorate of Intelligence, Central Intelligence Agency, *Handbook of Economic Statistics, 1991* (Washington, D.C.: U.S. Government Printing Office, 1991), p. 32.

Why Most Cartels Fail

cartel
Producers' groups, with
control over critical
commodities, that come
together to restrict supply
in order to raise prices.

Like OPEC, numerous other **cartels**, formed to control the price and supply of a commodity, have existed on international markets, but most ultimately failed.[8]

In theory cartels have within them the seeds of their own destruction because in response to higher prices, people search for alternative suppliers, reduce their use, and try to locate substitutes. When the market for a cartel's product diminishes, the problems it faces in continuing collusion grow. If everyone in the cartel sells at a discount, the cartel rapidly disintegrates. When the cheating becomes rampant, cartel members abandon further cooperation.[9]

The Gulf War and Oil

This state of affairs within the oil producers cartel of which Iraq was a part, was not to the liking of Saddam Hussein, who needed cash to rebuild his country's war-torn economy. It serves as the background for his invasion of Kuwait.

Exploiting Oil Vulnerabilities

At the end of the 1980s, Iraq began to lay the groundwork for exploiting oil vulnerabilities. It held direct talks with the Iran aimed at resolving the remaining issues in the decade-long hostility between the two nations. Iraq and Iran then agreed on the decisions that it wanted OPEC to make. Both wanted higher oil prices and lower production levels to earn more foreign currency to help rebuild their economies. To accomplish these purposes, they believed Saudi Arabia's power must be diminished within the region and in OPEC. Iraq and Iran felt that the Saudis, with the world's largest oil reserves, had acted in concert with the United States to keep oil prices low.

The next turn of events was the plummeting of oil prices from $22 a barrel in January 1990 to $16 in July 1990. OPEC producers added nearly 3 million extra barrels of oil a day into inventories in the second quarter of 1990. Prices for low-grade crude briefly slipped below $10 a barrel. The 13-member states of OPEC reported declining revenues at a rate of $100 million a day. Iraq claimed that it lost a billion dollars a year for every one-dollar reduction in the price of a barrel of oil. There were fears among the OPEC nations that prices would go down even more, to as low as $7 a barrel.

Iraq, along with Venezuela and Indonesia, placed the blame for the weak petroleum markets on Kuwait and the United Arab Emirates (UAE), whom they accused of cheating on their production quotas. Iraq had little faith in Saudi Arabia, which was trying to mediate the situation. Saudi Arabia was searching for a new strategy that would get Kuwait and the UAE to cut back their production. Reflecting the uncertainty, the futures price of crude oil crept up—by 11 cents a barrel—to $16.58 on the New York Mercantile Exchange.

Iraq's debt from the war with Iran was an immense $80 billion, and it wanted to see oil prices go up to $25 a barrel so it could pay off the debt and fund its military expansion. Kuwait, on the other hand, had diversified investments in the West and did not want to see the world economy, already tottering on the edge, slip into recession. Kuwait sought continued stability of world oil prices at about $14 a barrel. The dispute between the nations over oil prices opened an old rift between them. Lacking what it regarded as a suitable outlet to the sea, Iraq had been demanding that Kuwait lease to it Bubiyan Island, an empty sandbank, at the top of the Persian Gulf. The territorial dispute was only part of the reason that the two nations were at odds. At a more fundamental level, the Baathist ideology of the ruling clique committed Iraq to a form of pan-Arabism that does not recognize the territorial integrity of neighboring Arab states.

In response to the Iraqi-inspired demands, OPEC agreed to a new oil price ceiling of $21 a barrel, which was based on a production limit of 22.5 million barrels. Iraq, however, was still not satisfied even though an increase in the price to $21 a barrel would have been difficult summer of 1990 because of large petroleum inventories and lagging consumption worldwide. Worldwide consumption had increased by only 1 percent in 1990 and it had actually declined by 2 percent in the United States, the world's largest consumer of energy. Kuwait responded to the situation by affirming its acceptance of the OPEC oil production quota and agreeing to negotiate its border dispute with Iraq, but to no avail. When Iraqi troops moved to the Kuwaiti border, the Gulf sheikhdoms looked to the United States for protection. Neither Kuwait nor its GCC allies could defend themselves in a military confrontation with Iraq. Using the pretext of long-standing disagreements with Kuwait, Saddam Hussein invaded the nearly defenseless neighbor and quickly overwhelmed it.

World Response to the Iraqi Invasion

With Kuwaiti reserves representing about 10 percent of the world total and Iraqi reserves another 10 percent, Iraq controlled more than 20 percent of the world's oil. It threatened the oil resources of the remaining Gulf states, which together constituted nearly 70 percent of the world's oil. The United Nations condemned Iraq and imposed an economic boycott. This condemnation brought together nations that previously had been adversaries, including the United States and the Soviet Union. It united the moderate Arab states of Egypt and Saudi Arabia with hard-line and intransigent Syria, Iraq's traditional foe.

Certainly, Iraq faced difficult economic circumstances at home: an inflation rate estimated at 22 percent in 1988, a decline in the GDP of 4 percent, and huge foreign debts that were the legacy of Iraq's 10-year war with Iran. In attacking Kuwait, however, Saddam Hussein threatened the economic security of all nations. The Persian Gulf region powered the world's automobiles and factories by supplying more than a quarter of the world's daily need for oil. Forty-seven percent of the oil used in Europe came from this area, and

63 percent of the oil used in Japan. If Iraq became the master of the Gulf, it would be virtually free to determine how much of this oil was to be supplied, to whom, and at what price.

World oil prices skyrocketed to $27 a barrel the day after the August 2, 1990, invasion. Each $4 increase in the cost of a barrel of crude raised U.S. gasoline prices by about 10 cents a gallon. The airline, chemical, and steel industries, which were heavy users of petroleum and petroleum by-products, would suffer. For each penny change in the price of a gallon of jet fuel, United Airlines's annual expenses went up by $22.5 million. American automobile manufacturers—in the midst of a movement toward larger, more powerful, and less fuel-efficient cars, and spurred on by relatively low gas prices since 1986—were likely to lose ground to Japanese competitors. While Japanese manufacturers consistently achieved average fuel efficiency standards of more than 30 miles per gallon, U.S. car manufacturers appeared to be stuck at about 27 miles per gallon. According to Environmental Protection Agency (EPA) estimates, 9 of the 10 most fuel-efficient model cars in 1991 were made in Japan; the tenth was not an American car, but the Volkswagen Jetta.

Japan's Preparation

Japan was in many ways better prepared to deal with the Gulf War crisis than the United States. Since 1973, energy policy had been one of its highest domestic political priorities.[10] Now, in 1990, the Japanese government darkened hallways in government buildings and turned down office air conditioners. Japan's Ministry of Trade and Industry (MITI) required drivers not to exceed 50 miles per hour and buildings to be no cooler than 28° Celsius (82.4° F). MITI reaffirmed its commitment to the conservation programs it had initiated following the 1979 oil price hike. Since 1979, it had kept close tabs on the energy consumption of nearly 5,000 factories by requiring from 1 to 10 energy conservation engineers on selected factory floors. The engineers had to spend up to a year studying for an exam that 80 percent would fail. Those who passed sent regular reports about energy use to MITI. The engineers devised plans and took steps to make Japanese factories more energy efficient. By means of energy conservation and industrial restructuring, Japan had reduced its energy use to the point where it was producing 2.24 times the real output for the same energy input as in 1973 (see Figure 34-7). While nearly 80 percent of Japan's energy supplies in 1973 came from oil, this figure had dropped to less than 58 percent by 1990.

FIGURE 34-7
Major consuming
nations, 1960-1990

			Hundreds of Thousands of Barrels per Day			
	United States	**Japan**	**West Germany**	**France**	**United Kingdom**	**Canada**
1960	9.8	0.6	0.7	0.6	1.0	0.8
1970	14.7	4.0	2.6	2.0	2.0	1.5
1980	17.1	5.0	2.6	2.3	1.6	1.8
1985	15.7	4.3	2.3	1.8	1.6	1.4
1990	16.9	5.3	2.4	1.8	1.8	1.7

Source: Directorate of Intelligence, Central Intelligence Agency, *Handbook of Economic Statistics, 1991* (Washington, D.C.: U.S. Government Printing Office), pp. 85, 87.

With the goal of reducing demand and diversifying resources, Japan developed cooperative technical and economic agreements with most of the OPEC and many non-

OPEC producers. It made numerous investments in the development of industry and infrastructure in the Persian Gulf, and the Gulf states in turn purchased large amounts of Japanese securities.[11] To finance the energy price increases that occurred (see Figure 34-8), Japan expanded exports.

FIGURE 34-8
The costs of oil
imports, 1980-1990

Billions of Dollars

	United States	Japan	West Germany	France	United Kingdom
1980	$76.9	$58.9	$35.1	$30.7	$14.0
1985	51.4	40.6	24.1	18.8	10.5
1990	64.5	33.4	19.0	14.8	15.1

Source: Directorate of Intelligence Central Intelligence Agency, *Handbook of Economic Statistics, 1991* (Washington D.C.: U.S Government Printing Office 1991), p. 89.

Production in the basic materials industry, particularly aluminum and petrochemicals, was stagnant because world economic growth was weak and the competitiveness of these segments of Japanese industry, given higher energy prices, declined. Japanese economic growth took place in processing and assembly industries and in the expanding service sector, which were less energy-intensive.

Energy Rationalization Law
The basis for Japan's extensive energy conservation efforts.

The **Energy Rationalization Law** of 1979 was the basis for Japan's energy conservation efforts. It provided for the financing of conservation projects and for a system of tax incentives. It has been estimated that over 5 percent of total Japanese national investment in 1980 went for energy-saving equipment.[12] In the cement, steel, and chemical industries the figure was more than 60 percent of total investment. Japanese society shifted from petroleum to a reliance on other forms of energy including nuclear power and liquefied natural gas (LNG). By 1995, oil provided less than 60 percent of Japan's energy needs. Nuclear power provided 14 percent and LNG 12 percent, both up from 7 percent in 1982.

The main reduction in energy use took place in industry. Many companies invested heavily. Nippon Steel Company installed a $5.6 million coke dry quencher that reduced consumption by 25 percent. Asahi Glass rebuilt production equipment and redesigned production processes to cut energy use by 40 percent in a decade. Japan's northern subway system recycled heat from engines for use in air-conditioning to save energy. Hino Motors added switches to its machine tools so that they would not idle when not in use. It recycled machine oil and reduced shop lighting and air-conditioning. Tokyo Electric Power Company converted to nuclear power, cutting its use of oil by two-thirds. In 1990, Japan's 38 nuclear power plants supplied 9 percent of the country's total energy needs, an increase from almost nothing in 1973.

MITI also encouraged companies to switch from oil to more plentiful coal and natural gas, which could be obtained from politically stable nations. It allowed oil and gas companies and the utilities that supplied electricity to keep their prices artificially high so long as they diverted the excess profit to energy research. In essence, the permission to do so created an energy tax which had many important benefits. The tax stimulated energy research and discouraged energy use. In 1987, the tax revenues provided more than $830 million for energy research that helped Japan develop advanced solar-cell technology, new means for transporting and storing liquid natural gas, and better methods for producing electricity from gasified coal and sea water.

Geographic compactness, population density, and superior public transportation provided Japan with advantages that the United States did not have. Japan benefited from a movement away from energy-intensive heavy industry toward financial services and consumer electronics, which used less energy. Japan, which already was more energy efficient than the United States in 1973, improved its efficiency by one-third. Japanese conservation efforts following the oil shocks of 1973 and 1979 insulated it to a greater extent than other countries from energy price hikes. The share of oil in total Japanese energy demand declined from 77 percent in 1973 to 57 percent in 1987. This decline took place despite the increasing wealth of individual Japanese consumers, who bought more television sets, refrigerators, air conditioners, and other appliances. The Japanese also drove more and bought more cars in the interim. Between 1973 and 1987, Japanese economic output more than doubled, but its reliance on oil imports fell by 20 percent. American reliance on foreign imports increased during this period from 36 percent to 43 percent of total oil consumed.

Oil Price Shocks and Recession

All but one of the eight post-World War II recessions in the United States had been preceded by an oil price increase. At the outset of the Gulf War, consumer confidence was down and factory orders were declining. If the Federal Reserve Board increased the money supply and lowered interest rates, it risked exacerbating inflation. This happened in the 1970s after the first oil price shock when loose monetary policies helped raise inflation to double-digit levels. The Dow-Jones Industrial Average tumbled 183 points in the three days following the Iraqi invasion of Kuwait. Some analysts estimated that oil prices would climb to $50 or $60 a barrel.

The United States, which was dependent on foreign supplies for almost 50 percent of its oil, obtained only about 6.6 percent of it from Iraq and about 1.5 percent from Kuwait. Its largest foreign suppliers were Venezuela, Nigeria, and Canada. The Japanese, 99 percent dependent on foreign oil, imported about 12 percent of it from Iraq and Kuwait.

Oil, nonetheless, was a pervasive part of the American economy. U.S. fuel and oil costs constituted from 4 to 8 percent of all shipping costs. These in turn affected food prices and the prices of nearly all goods bought and sold. Petroleum-based liquid asphalt constituted about half the costs of road resurfacing. Raw materials used in adhesives, coatings, and similar products contained petroleum derivatives. Other products with petroleum derivatives were trash bags and precision plastic parts used in computers. Chemical companies were heavy users of petroleum derivatives. For businesses, the cost increases of the petroleum price hikes varied widely depending on the products they made, where these products fell in the crude-oil production chain, and how much petroleum-based material the products contained.

During the Arab oil embargo between October 1973 and January 1974, the price of oil jumped from $3 to $13 a barrel. This caused the inflation rate in industrial nations to nearly double from 7.9 percent in 1973 to 14 percent in 1974 and the GNP growth rate to fall about 1.75 percent. From the end of 1978 to the end of 1979, oil prices again spiked upward this time from $16 a barrel to $39 a barrel. Inflation rates grew from 7.8 percent at the end of 1978 to 13.6 percent in the first half of 1980. The GNP started to decline in 1979 and did not come back until 1983 when the developed countries, determined to fight inflation, let the unemployment rate slip to 8.5 percent.

Differences from Earlier Price Hikes

As much as the situation in 1990 was similar to earlier price hikes, it also was different. In 1973, when Arab oil producers refused to ship oil to the United States and other Western nations, Saudi Arabia was the instigator of the boycott. This time, with the United Nations, by virtue of a 13-0 Security Council vote, deciding to impose widespread trade restrictions on Iraq, the Saudis were supporting the effort by promising to provide 2 million extra barrels of oil a day to replenish world supplies. The 2 million extra barrels of oil a day represented about half of what the world needed to completely make up for the loss of 20 percent of its supply from Iraq and Kuwait.

Other differences between 1990 and earlier oil shocks existed. U.S. dependence on OPEC oil was now greater (28 percent in 1990 compared with about 13 percent in 1974). However, the industrialized nations had succeeded in diversifying their sources of energy. In 1974, about half of the world's oil came from OPEC countries; in 1990 only about a third came from OPEC. Additional production potential had been developed in the meantime on the North Slope of Alaska, the North Sea, Mexico, and elsewhere. Industrial nations had learned from earlier oil crises how to improve the efficiency with which they used petroleum—in 1990 they used 40 percent less oil to produce one dollar of real GNP.

The United States and other nations had also accumulated large oil reserves that could last as long as 200 days. The United States had a 590-million-barrel reserve, the Japanese a 140-million-barrel reserve, and the Germans a 100-million-barrel reserve, which cushioned these nations against a supply shortage. The reserves could be used to stabilize oil markets. The main problem with the reserves was whether they could be used as anticipated. Two-thirds of the petroleum reserve in the United States consisted of a "sour" variety unsuitable for many U.S. refineries. It had not been tapped in the past and analysts were uncertain who would buy the oil, what they would do with it, and if there would be hoarding and speculation.

Finding Alternative Supplies

Over the long term, conservation in conjunction with technological innovation would drive down oil prices; high prices could not be sustained. The problem was in the short term, when alternative supplies were needed but not necessarily easy to find.

Mexico

Pemex
The publicly owned oil company of Mexico.

In the long term, Mexico was a supplier of great potential. The true extent of its oil resources, ranging anywhere from 45 billion barrels of oil to 260 billion, could not be properly estimated. However, Mexico was ill-prepared to provide the world with extra petroleum. Since the debt crisis of 1982, investment in **Pemex**, its publicly owned oil company, had plummeted. The decline in drilling for oil in Mexico had been extreme. In 1989, only about half the number of exploratory wells were opened as in 1987.

Canada

Once considered a country whose oil reserves had great potential, Canada was having difficulty these reserves. Its proven reserves were estimated at about 4.2 billion barrels, but it was believed to have vast untapped reserves in its Northwest Territories. However, this oil was not easily accessible and it was extremely expensive to develop. Canada also had

tar sands
Mixture of clay, water, bitumen, and oil that is found in abundance in western Canada.

huge deposits of **tar sands** in its western provinces, but these deposits, a mixture of clay, water, and bitumen, had to be refined before they could be used. The refining process was not only expensive and capital-intensive, but also it could be extremely damaging to the environment.

Russia

Russia, which produced 20 percent of the world's oil, could not be called on for additional production because political disruption and outdated technology had ground its oil industry to a halt. Russia's oil industry suffered from declining exports and chronic shortages of basic equipment such as pipes and valves. Although Russia had 60 billion barrels of oil reserves (more than twice the amount of the United States) and the world's largest proven natural gas reserves (about 45 percent of the world's total), it was not likely to add much in the way of new energy production, because it lacked the capability to efficiently produce and market either oil or natural gas.

United States

The U.S. oil industry, too, was in the doldrums in 1990. After a century of high production, no vast pools of undiscovered oil existed in the United States. Worse still, the infrastructure needed for oil exploration and production had been deteriorating. For instance, the capability to build pipelines and manufacture drill bits had declined to about 50 percent of what it had been 10 years earlier. Skilled professional engineers, scientists, and oil-field workers were needed to enhance production from existing wells and to find new oil. Many had retired after the last oil boom of the 1970s and, with low oil prices in the 1980s, they had not been replaced. With its constant booms and busts, the oil industry was no longer as attractive to scientists or blue-collar field workers who did the hard work of getting the oil out of the ground. Non-OPEC producers such as Mexico, Canada, Russia, and the United States could be expected to produce at most an additional 200,000 to 400,000 barrels per day.

Other Nations

Besides Saudi Arabia, which was able to take up about half the slack of the oil lost from Iraq and Kuwait, the world could rely on Venezuela for approximately 600,000 barrels a day and on the UAE for another 800,000 barrels, leaving a shortfall of about 500,000 barrels. As oil prices rose, demand fell and a variety of producers, notably Nigeria, Indonesia, and Libya, made up the difference. As a result, this supply interruption, unlike others in the past, did not involve real shortages of oil.

The Need for an Energy Policy

Clearly, the United States needed an energy policy to reduce its dependence on foreign oil. It had made substantial progress between 1976 to 1986, when it cut its ratio of energy use to GNP by 2.8 percent per year, but by 1987 this progress had come to a halt. Much of the improvement came about because the United States had eased out of energy-intensive heavy industries, by investing money overseas and building plants abroad, and had replaced them with service industries that used less energy. Progress also took place because automobiles obtained 50 percent more miles per gallon than they had in 1973. However, the improvements in automobile efficiency themselves as post-1985 gasoline prices dipped to inflation-adjusted lows. With cheaper driving possible, people were driving more.

Americans on average used more gasoline than people in other countries with comparable standards of living. They consumed about 350 gallons per person in 1989, while Germans consumed only about 150, not just because the Germans had more efficient vehicles, but because Americans drove more miles and had more cars. In the United States as well as the rest of the world, the ratio of cars per person was rising.

At the time of the Gulf War, however, the U.S. government resisted the idea of mounting a major effort to establish a new energy policy. The Bush administration did not want people to be reminded of the sacrifices they had been asked to make during the Carter years. In a famous gesture designed for direct comparison with the Carter administration, President Bush continued to use a gas-guzzling speedboat during his summer holiday in Maine.

The Bush administration's first stab at devising a policy relied solely on voluntary cooperation. It put inflating automobile tires to their proper pressure at the head of a list of conservation measures. An admittedly weak and ineffectual gesture, the administration claimed it would save 100,000 barrels of oil a day if drivers carried it out. Another measure advocated was more car and van pooling; 20 percent more ride-sharing would save another 90,000 barrels of oil a day. The administration also called on people to observe speed limits, thus saving 50,000 barrels a day, and to drive the most energy-efficient car (if there was a choice), saving 40,000 barrels a day.

To increase the oil supply, administration officials asked oil companies to extract additional oil from Alaska's North Slope. They also considered reopening for exploration Alaska's Arctic National Wildlife Refuge, which had been closed in the aftermath of the *Exxon Valdez* oil spill. The Energy Department indicated that it would be willing to mediate a dispute that prevented oil production from the ocean floor along the California coast. A Chevron-led consortium could pump up to 100,000 barrels a day from platforms built near Santa Barbara, but state and local authorities denied permits on environmental grounds.

gasohol
A blend of gasoline and ethanol (corn alcohol.)

The Energy Department also announced that it would switch its own vehicles to **gasohol**—a blend of gasoline and 10 percent ethanol—and would encourage ethanol producers to produce at full capacity. The administration called upon industries to switch from petroleum to more plentiful natural gas whenever possible. Overall, these programs were designed to increase the oil supply by 270,000 barrels a day.

On August 31, 1990, the administration announced that it would support the first national advertising campaign in a decade to promote conservation. It was also considering a tax credit designed to stimulate the recovery of hard-to-get oil from existing fields and a plan to expedite the processing of permits for oil exploration in the BeauLort Sea near Alaska. President Bush went so far as to declare that the United States "must never again enter any crisis—economic or military—with an excessive dependence on foreign oil." But he went no further, and he refused to back up his words with additional actions.

Reluctance to Do More

The U.S. government was reluctant to do more for a variety of reasons. These reasons included the Bush administration's free-market ideology, public opinion polls indicating the unpopularity of other options, and domestic political interests, already agitated about the budget deficit, which were ready to exact a high price for steps the Bush administration might take. On the grounds that the government should not intervene in energy markets, the administration opposed an auto fuel efficiency bill introduced by Senator Richard Bryan, Democrat from Nevada, that would have forced auto manufacturers to improve fleet fuel efficiency standards to 40 miles per gallon by the year 2001.

The bill, first designed as an environmental measure, would have saved 2.8 million barrels of oil per day by the year 2005, more than all the oil the United States had been importing from the Persian Gulf. Energy Secretary James Watkins admitted that two-thirds of the oil burned each day in the United States came from transportation, with the largest share from 171 million private cars and trucks; but he pointed out most automakers opposed fuel economy legislation on the grounds that the public was demanding larger, that is, "safer," cars, which would be impossible to build if the bill took effect.

The administration supported the auto industry's claims with studies asserting that the proposal would result in additional highway accidents and deaths. William Reilly, head of the EPA under Bush, came out against the fuel efficiency standard. On September 25, 1990, supporters of this proposal lost a procedural vote in the Senate, ending hope for passage in 1990.

According to a Gallop poll, 80 percent of Americans favored tougher conservation measures, but 62 percent were opposed to higher gasoline taxes designed to encourage conservation. Despite public opposition, congressional Democrats reintroduced the idea of a tax on energy consumption into the budget talks. The 9 cents per gallon tax they proposed was supposed to enhance revenues, but this purpose would be defeated if people actually curtailed their driving. Republicans ultimately accepted this proposal and it became part of the budget agreement.

Congress, however, refused to consider taking the broader step of gradually increasing American gasoline taxes to levels normally found in other industrialized countries. In France, the United Kingdom, Germany, and Japan, motorists routinely spent $45 to $50 for 12 gallons of gas to fill their tanks. More than 75 percent of this expense was tax. However, the idea of adjusting markets to reflect the true social costs of petroleum use was not one that was accepted by either Congress or the administration.

The American public expressed other opinions that made it difficult for the government to develop a more elaborate energy policy. Fifty-seven percent of Americans, despite the Persian Gulf crisis, continued to oppose the construction of more nuclear power plants, and only 48 percent favored easing restrictions on offshore oil drilling. Tax breaks to stimulate the oil industry were out of the question with enormous budget deficits and the windfall earnings of the oil industry from high petroleum prices. Solar power obtained a boost with a 30 percent increase in research funding sponsored by Congress and endorsed by the administration, but this increase appeared insignificant compared with the funding for solar power in countries such as Japan. The Bush administration considered a tax credit for alternative energy investments, which was supported by environmentalists, but administration economists warned that such measures would not result in sufficient additional revenues to justify the budgetary costs.

Long-Term Energy Alternatives

In the long run, the United States—or any country—has a number of promising options, if the country is willing to take advantage of them. Perpetual heavy reliance on imported oil from unstable regions is neither necessary nor inevitable.

Natural Gas

With 4,000 trillion cubic feet of gas reserves under the ground in the United States, Canada, and other countries, natural gas is far more plentiful than oil (see Figure 34-9). From an environmental perspective, natural gas is cleaner burning and less polluting. However, additional conversion of industries in the United States from oil to natural gas had been limited to the equivalent of about 160,000 barrels of oil a day.

FIGURE 34-9
U.S. primary energy
production by type

	Thousands of Barrels per Day Oil Equivalent		
	1970	**1980**	**1990**
Coal	7,359	9,785	11,989
Crude oil	11,380	10,170	8,825
Natural gas	10,686	9,838	8,814
Hydroelectric/nuclear	1,394	2,774	4,525

Source: Adapted from Directorate of Intelligence, Central Intelligence Agency, *Handbook of Economic Statistics, 1991* (Washington, D.C.: U.S. Government Printing Office, 1991), p. 84.

The extent to which natural gas is an attractive automobile fuel replacement depends on its price and whether it can be adapted for use in internal-combustion engines. As oil prices rise, natural gas prices also go up. Existing cars can run on natural gas only if engine modifications are made and a compressed-gas storage tank is added. If natural gas prices rise too rapidly, however, the conversion of existing autos will not be worth the expense.

Another disadvantage of natural gas over regular fuel is that it is more difficult to store and transport. It is not yet a practical replacement for gasoline. Mobil Corporation developed an advanced process at its New Zealand subsidiary which could convert natural gas directly into gasoline at a cost of just under $35 a barrel. The New Zealand plant produced 15,000 barrels of gasoline a day, providing for one-third of New Zealand's needs.

Energy Conservation

An even better alternative than natural gas from an environmental perspective is conservation. Historically, people used 2 percent less oil for every 10 percent rise in fuel prices. A 30 percent drop in consumption following the last energy price hike took place because people cut the amount of energy they used in response to the higher prices.

The potential for conservation is great. People had increased the amount of energy they used during the 1980s because energy prices had fallen. On average, Americans drove 1,000 more miles per year than they did in 1980. Since 1987, the cars they used have become 7 percent heavier, 10 percent more powerful, and one-half mile per gallon less fuel efficient. Reversing these trends could mean savings of 200,000 barrels of oil a day.

An increase in oil prices would compel U.S. airlines to lower consumption. Next to labor, jet fuel is the second biggest expense for the airlines. Jumbo jets average less than half a mile per gallon. In 1990, the average fuel cost of a flight from New York to Los Angeles was $7,000, and these fuel costs pushed the airlines toward record losses of over $1 billion. To cut energy consumption, they called on pilots to fly at higher altitudes where the air is thinner. They warned the pilots to take the most direct route between locations even if the flight was choppier for passengers. A light touch on the throttle, once the plane was at cruising speed, was also recommended. In addition, pilots were asked not to keep engines idling at airports, even if it meant shutting off air conditioners and annoying passengers.

Immediately after the Iraqi invasion, high fuel prices along with a looming recession depressed energy consumption in industrial countries. The flattening of world oil demand delayed shortages that might have arisen from the Persian Gulf crisis.

Price increases also have stimulated technological innovation such as the energy saving fluorescent light bulb. The bulb costs about $15, screws into standard sockets, and has about the same color and intensity as a regular 60-watt bulb, but it uses only 15 watts of electricity and lasts 10 times longer. With greater sales volume, the price of the new bulb might come down to $10. If 25 percent of the power generated in the United States came from fluorescent light bulbs instead of incandescents, the need for new capital-intensive power plants, which burned conventional fuels or relied on nuclear power, would decline.

Many utilities and, more importantly, many of the public utility commissions that regulated them accepted the idea of rewarding the utilities for marketing such efficiency enhancing mechanisms. Boston Edison offered the fluorescent bulbs to customers for $3 a piece, going door to door and installing them to make sure that they would be used.

Good at innovation, entrepreneurs can design and deliver a package of new energy saving technologies to industrial users. To do so, they have to be in close touch with their customers. It takes about 35 steps, for example, to change industrial motors and their components. The changes could yield savings of roughly half the energy the motors consumed with the payback arriving in about one year. But to design and carry out the changes, the entrepreneurs have to address many areas, including consumer education, the selection and installation of the equipment, financing, and maintenance. They might have to offer a performance guarantee through an insurance company, stating that if the savings were not realized the entrepreneurs would absorb a percentage of the shortfall.

Coal

Conservation and natural gas are the best alternatives to petroleum, but the most abundant alternative is coal. Proven coal reserves in the United States are large enough to last another three centuries at current consumption levels. Unfortunately, coal is dirty. It contributes carbon dioxide to the atmosphere when burned, which may lead to global warming. Safety, too, is a matter of concern, especially in the mining of coal. Few opportunities are left for coal use; 57 percent of the electricity produced in the United States comes from coal-fired generating plants, while oil supplies only 5 percent.

Coal could replace gasoline as a vehicle fuel, but only to a limited extent and at a very high price. South Africa, which could not rely on other nations to supply it with petroleum when sanctions had been imposed for its apartheid policy, had converted coal for this purpose for many years. However, the process of making coal into gasoline is dirty and expensive, and the South African government was forced to heavily subsidize it.

Tar Sands

Canadian tar sands are another alternative. An estimated 300 billion barrels of oil are recoverable from the Athabasca region in northern and western Canada. Syncrude Canada Ltd., a partially owned subsidiary of Exxon, converted tar sands into 180,000 barrels of oil a day. Suncor, Inc., a unit of Sun Company of Philadelphia, produced 60,000 barrels of oil a day from tar sands. Oil prices only have to remain substantially higher than $25 a barrel for these ventures to be commercially viable. Venezuela also is capable of producing a superheavy crude from tar sands found in its Orinoco Belt, but without the addition of water, the product is difficult to transport.

Oil Shale

oil shale
Petroleum deposits trapped in rock commonly found in the western United States.

Another alternative is **oil shale**. The United States has proven reserves of 600 billion barrels of shale oil, about the same as all of OPEC's proven reserves. However, the costs of extracting usable oil from shale are estimated to be as high as $100 for an equivalent barrel of oil. The extensive process used to break up and crush the rock to capture the small residues of trapped oil is extremely expensive and damaging to the environment. An operating shale oil plant is highly capital-intensive and would require immense government subsidies. Even with vast government subsidies, Unocal's Parachute Creek plant lowered costs only to the equivalent of $40 a barrel of imported oil.

Ethanol

During the 1970s, the United States had turned to gasohol, a mixture of gasoline and grain alcohol (ethanol), in the hope that this product would expand the market for corn, reduce pollution, and lessen American dependence on foreign oil. Adding ethanol to gas raises the octane level and causes gasoline to burn more cleanly. In Midwestern farm states (e.g., Minnesota), gasohol sales peaked at nearly 33 percent of the auto fuel market in 1985. Since then, the sale of gasohol declined to less than 10 percent. Rumors circulated that gasohol could destroy carburetor seals, hurt engine valves, and erode the paint from car surfaces. Although these rumors were untrue, the real problem with gasohol remained its price. At about $1.50 a gallon, it simply is not competitive with gasoline.

Propane

Yet another option is propane, a fuel used in more than 300,000 vehicles despite its never having benefited from government subsidies. Very low in pollution, especially ground level pollution that plagues big cities, 85 percent of propane is derived from domestic oil and natural gas production as a by-product. The remaining 15 percent comes from non-OPEC countries such as Canada and Mexico. Mostly used for heating, propane is a much neglected fuel for motor vehicles. It could, with existing supplies, propel up to 3.5 percent of the vehicles on American roads with little difficulty. The problem is obtaining additional supplies.

Solar Power

Solar power also might play a role in reducing U.S. dependence on foreign energy supplies. Solar power comes in many forms. Rapid technological advances have made photovoltaic prices competitive in limited applications (see Case 34-A on ARCO Solar). Another solar option is a trough-like collector that can be used to produce electricity in very sunny climates. In Southern California, solar collectors had been manufactured successfully by Luz International, Ltd. The price of a kilowatt hour of solar-generated power fell from 24 cents in 1980 to 8 cents in 1990. Another decline of 2 cents per kilowatt hour would make solar-generated power competitive with other forms of electric generation. The potential for replacing foreign petroleum with solar power, however, is small, because the utilities in the sun-drenched regions of the Southwest, which would buy solar power, use little petroleum to generate electricity.

Geothermal Power

geothermal power
Energy trapped in coastal areas where the earth's crust has created unique geologic conditions.

Geothermal power, created where the earth's crusts have established perfect geologic conditions of heat, temperature, and pressure, also can play a role in reducing U.S. energy dependence. Unocal Corporation has reserves off the coast of Southern California which were the equivalent of 216 million barrels of oil. The company plans to spend millions of dollars exploring for additional geothermal energy off the Pacific coasts of California, the Philippines, and Indonesia. Geothermal power, however, has major limitations. First, it cannot be transported but must be consumed near its source. Generating electricity with geothermal energy is very expensive; the cost is about 9.5 cents per kilowatt hour from Unocal's Salton Sea facility compared with 4.5 cents to 7.5 cents from more conventional sources.

Nuclear Power

While nuclear power was once a promising option for the United States, no new construction of nuclear plants is planned; and some older U.S. plants are being decommissioned. Growth in sales of new nuclear plants is mostly confined to Asia. Safety and waste storage issues, along with greatly diminished public acceptance, makes nuclear power a less viable option than it was in the past.

Confined to generating electricity, nuclear power has been incapable of direct applications in the transportation sector. Nonetheless, researchers have made progress in advanced nuclear power plant prototypes, and a comeback of this power-generating source is possible if technological progress occurs and air pollution issues (e.g., sulfur dioxide and greenhouse gas emissions) become severe.

A Tax on Energy

A tax on energy use would not only stimulate innovation and energy-saving behavior but also make the alternatives more competitive with oil and thus more attractive. It would reduce the payback period for all types of conservation measures and stimulate alternative production. The market, not the government, would choose which alternative to emphasize based on a host of factors of concern to users, including cost and convenience.

However, no U.S. administration was willing to seriously consider such a tax. If the price of gasoline in the United States had risen as fast as other items on the Consumer Price Index during the 1980s, by 1990 Americans would have been paying $2 a gallon for gasoline, a figure much closer to what people in other countries were paying. The higher price would have encouraged Americans to drive fewer miles in smaller cars and to take other energy-saving measures. Instead, the relatively low price for American gasoline was sending the exact opposite message.

Energy Supply and Demand in the Future

In the long run, a number of scenarios were possible. On the one hand, oil resources would remain heavily concentrated in the Persian Gulf region, and no cheap, clean, and plentiful alternative would come to the forefront. Prospects for continuing expansion of non-OPEC production would remain limited. U.S. production would be below its 1970 peak even with high prices. Without Alaska, U.S. output would have been 25 percent less than it was in 1985. The only substantial non-OPEC discoveries in the post-1973 period, despite heavy exploration, had been in Mexico, but Mexico had only about 10 percent of the world's reserves. U.S., Canadian and North Sea oil would be depleted after three decades of production at current levels, while Persian Gulf producers could sustain current output levels for more than a century. A different scenario saw energy prices, like all resource prices, falling over time. The premise of a fixed stock was mistaken. Natural resources had to be seen as inexhaustible, nonbinding constraints on production. Although humans tended to exploit the cheapest stock of natural resources first, diminishing returns were more than offset by increasing knowledge about how to obtain new stock and how to utilize the existing stock more efficiently. In 1945, it appeared impossible that more oil could be discovered in the United States. The country was more "drilled up" than any other, it was claimed, and remaining reserves were then estimated to be only 20 billion barrels of oil. Nonetheless, the United States, excluding Alaska, produced over 100 billion barrels of oil over the next 40 years. Efforts by any nation or group of nations to withhold production were not likely to work in the long run because of the varied interests of the nations holding petroleum reserves. This also put downward pressures on long-term oil prices.

Breaking the Connection between Energy Consumption and Economic Growth

A key challenge is to break the connection between energy consumption and economic growth,[13] but the feedback effects between energy and the economy are very complicated.[14] Consumption of energy is both necessary for economic growth and a consequence of it. Different nations have different energy-to-GNP ratios. There is a substantially higher energy consumption pattern in the former Communist bloc countries than in Western Europe. Per capita consumption of energy in the United States is greater than in other industrialized nations; the U.S. ratio of energy to output far exceeded that in France, Germany, and Sweden, which have similar per capita income and output. The explanations for the different ratios among countries are complex. They include different pricing policies, the extent to which the countries are import-dependent, their product mix, and the state of their technology. The composition of GNP, exchange rates, climate, and geography play a role as do environmental, demographic, and sociological factors. The people in countries with lower ratios of energy to output than the United States appear to have a greater willingness to change lifestyles and to substitute other economic goods for energy.

Stages in economic development are significant. Underdeveloped countries typically have low energy-to-GNP ratios. As they became more developed, their energy-to-GNP ratios increase, becoming greater than those of developed countries. When economic growth slackens in developed nations, the energy-to-GNP ratio tends to fall.

Historically, growth rates in energy usage in the United States closely paralleled growth rates in the GNP.[15] Earlier in the 20th century, U.S. growth rates for energy consumption and GNP were nearly identical, 3.2 percent and 3.3 percent, respectively. For industrial nations, a 1 percent annual increase in energy usage paralleled a 1 percent annual increase in gross domestic product (GDP) from 1960 to 1973. Between 1973 and 1981, however, when GDP grew at an average annual rate of 2.3 percent, consumption of total primary energy grew by mere .2 percent per year. This decline in energy intensity reflects structural changes in the use of energy, responses to policies and prices, and cyclical effects. Intensity of energy use is lower, which has made a substantial dent in the link between economic growth and energy consumption.

Conclusions

The world economy requires energy from highly unstable regions of the globe. In the long run, the availability of energy is assured, as long as lower-grade resources exist and labor and capital substitutions can take place. The market will work to raise prices so long as imperfections in the market do not exist and governments do not take inappropriate actions that prevent adjustment. In the long run, the U.S. and world economies have changed from more intensive to less intensive energy use. In the long run, energy scarcity is not an important problem. Even in the short term, as long as major wars or some other cataclysmic event do not cause widespread disruption of energy shipments, shortages are not likely to occur.[17] If a country does not have adequate domestic supplies, it can import the resources it needs by offering to pay a sufficiently high price. The real problem in the short term is unexpected price shocks caused by large-scale, unanticipated curtailments in supply, which increase prices. The world experienced two oil price shocks in 1973 and 1979 and very nearly experienced a third at the time of the Gulf War.

This chapter has looked at energy shortages and their causes and effects. The focus was on the crisis surrounding the Gulf War. The role of major producing (OPEC) and consuming nations has been analyzed. OPEC's near collapse in the mid-1980s was discussed, and the factors that permitted it to continue to function have been analyzed. Why most cartels fail in the long run has been addressed, and the long-term prospects for energy supply and demand in the world have been assessed.

Discussion Questions

1. Describe U.S. oil vulnerabilities at the outbreak of the Gulf War.
2. Why did some Democratic politicians oppose a broad-based energy tax? Is this position corrects
3. What countries are members of OPEC? What factions exist in the cartel? What are some different interests of these factions?
4. Why was OPEC forced to accept lower oil prices during the 1980s?
5. Why didn't Iraq want lower oil prices? Why were lower prices not wholeheartedly supported by Saudi Arabia and Kuwait?
6. What caused the Gulf War?
7. Discuss Japanese energy policies. How have they differed from U.S. policies?
8. Why didn't the Gulf War cause rapidly escalating oil prices similar to those of 1973 and 1979?
9. Where are alternative petroleum supplies likely to be found?
10. What kind of energy policy should the U.S. government have?
11. What are the long-term alternatives to petroleum? Assess their practicality.
12. Construct alternative scenarios of future demand and supply for energy. What do you think is likely to happen?

Endnotes

1. R. Solow, "The Economics of Resources or the Resources of Economics," *American Economic Review*, 1974, p. 10; quoted in V. K. Smith, ed., *Scarcity and Growth Reconsidered* (Baltimore: Johns Hopkins University Press, 1979).
2. Much of this chapter is adapted from Alfred Marcus, *Controversial Issues in Energy Policy* (Beverly Hills, Calif.: Sage Press, 1992).
3. G. Brooks and T. Horwitz, "Gulf Crisis Underscores Historical Divisions in the Arab 'Family,'" *The Wall Street Journal*, August 13, 1990 p. A1; G. H. Anderson, M. F. Bryan, and C. J. Pike, "Oil, the Economy, and Monetary Policy," *Economic Commentary*, Federal Reserve Bank of Cleveland, November 1, 1990; "Iraqi Invasion Raises Oil Prices, Threatens U.S., Other Economies," *The Wall Street Journal*, August 3, 1990, p. A1; A. Murray and D. Wessel, "Iraqi Invasion Boosts Chances of Recession in the U.S. This Year," *The Wall Street Journal*, August 6, 1990, p. A1; "Oil's Economic Threat Is Less Than in '70s," *The Wall Street Journal*, August 20, 1990, p. A1; "Rising Oil-Import Bill Will Slow Trade Gains," *The Wall Street Journal*, March 5, 1990, p. A1; C. Solomon and R. Gutfeld, "Petroleum Reserve Has Lots of Oil, but Using It Could Be a Challenge," *The Wall Street Journal*, September 5, 1990, p. A1; C. Solomon, "Sudden Impact: Prices at U.S. Gas Pumps Soar," *The Wall Street Journal*, August 6, 1990, p. B1; A. Sullivan, "Gasoline Exports Rise Despite Concern over Supplies," *The Wall Street Journal*, September 17, 1990, p. B1; A. Sullivan, "It Wouldn't Be Easy, but U.S. Could Ease Reliance on Arab Oil," *The Wall Street Journal*, August 17, 1990, p. A1; A. Sullivan, "OPEC May Face Long Wait to See Higher Oil Prices," *The Wall Street Journal*, July 30, 1990, p. A4; J. Tanner, A. Murray, and B. Rosewicz, "Crude-Oil Prices Fall as Saudis and Others Plan to Boost Output to Offset Shortages," *The Wall Street Journal*, August 9, 1990, p. A3; J. Tanner, "Crude-Oil Prices Register Sharp Drop on Worries of Possible Glut in Supply," *The Wall Street Journal*, April 6, 1990, p. C6; J. Tanner, "Petroleum Use Starting to Fall, Agency Reports," *The Wall Street Journal*, October 5, 1990, p. A3; J. Tanner, "OPEC Adds Capacity, Easing Risk that Cost of Oil Will Soar in '90s," *The Wall Street Journal*, November 22, 1990, p. A1; J. Tanner, "Supplies of Oil Start to Shrink, Firming Prices," *The Wall Street Journal*, September 6, 1990, p. A3; J. Tanner, "Surge in Oil Output Could Lead to a Glut Even if Persian Gulf Standoff Drags On," *The Wall Street Journal*, November 12, 1990, p. A3; J. Taylor, A. Q. Nomani, and S. W. Angrist, "Hedgers Enjoy an Edge as Oil Prices Swing," The Wall Street Journal, August 29, 1990, p. B1; "How Big an Oil Shock?" *The Economist*, August 11, 1990, pp. 12-13; M. Wald, "America Is Still Demanding a Full Tank," *New York*

Times, August 12, 1990, p. E3; M. L. Wald, "Effect of Fall in Soviet Oil Output," *New York Times*, September 6, 1990, p. D1; A. Murray and D. Wessel, "Iraqi Invasion Boosts Chances of Recession in the U.S. This Year," *The Wall Street Journal*, August 6, 1990, p. A1.

4.   "The Fusion Thing," *Economist*, Feb. 8, 1992, pp. 85-86.

5.   M. V. Samii, "The Organization of the Petroleum Exporting Countries and the Oil Market: Different Views," *Journal of Energy and Development* 10 (1985), pp. 159-73.

6.   D. Gately, "The Prospects for Oil Prices Revisited," *Annual Review of Energy* 11 (1986), pp. 513-88; D. Gately, "Lessons from the 1986 Oil Price Collapse," in Economic Activity, 2nd ed., W. C. Brainard and G. L. Perry, eds. (Washington, D.C.: Brookings Institution), pp. 237-87.

7.   W. Lowinger, G. Wihlborg, and A. Willman, "An Empirical Analysis of OPEC and Non-OPEC Behavior," *Journal of Energy and Development* 11, no. 2 (1986), pp. 119-41; Gately, "The Prospects for Oil Prices Revisited"; Gately, "Lessons from the 1986 Oil Price Collapse."

8.   D. J. Teece, "Assessing OPEC's Pricing Policies," *California Management Review* 26 (1983), pp. 69-87; H. Tsai, The Energy Illusion and Economic Stability: Quantum Causality (New York: Praeger, 1989).

9.   Gately, "The Prospects for Oil Prices Revisited," pp. 513-88; Gately, "Lessons from the 1986 Oil Price Collapse," pp. 237-87; Lowinger et al., "An Empirical Analysis of OPEC and Non-OPEC Behavior," pp. 119-41; Tanner, "OPEC Adds Capacity."

10.   E. Ramstetter, "Interaction between Japanese Policy Priorities: Energy and Trade in the 1980s," *Journal of Energy and Development* 11, no. 2 (1986), pp. 285-301.

11.   Ibid.

12.   B. Mossavar-Rahmani, "Japan's Oil Sector Outlook," *Annual Review of Energy* 16 (1988), pp. 185-213.

13.   Central Intelligence Agency, Directorate of Intelligence, *Handbook of Economic Statistics, 1991* (Washington, D.C.: U.S. Government Printing Office, 1991), p. 84.

14.   U. Erol and E. Yu, "On the Causal Relationship between Energy and Income for Industrialized Countries," *Journal of Energy and Development* 13, no. 1 (1988), pp. 113-39; Tsai, *The Energy Illusion and Economic Stability*; Y. Wang and W. Latham, "Energy and State Economic Growth: Some New Evidence," *Journal of Energy and Development* 14 (1989), pp. 197-221.

15.   J. Darmstadter, J. H. Landsberg, H. C. Morton, and M. J. Coda, *Energy, Today and Tomorrow: Living with Uncertainty* (Englewood Cliffs, N.J.: Prentice Hall, 1983); E. Kanovsky, "The Coming Oil Glut," *The Wall Street Journal*, November 30, 1990, p. A14; S. H. Schurr, ed., *Energy in America's Future: The Choices Before Us* (Baltimore: Johns Hopkins University Press, 1979).

16.   Tsai, *The Energy Illusion and Economic Stability*.

17.   R. Pindyck and J. Rotemberg, "Energy Shocks and the Macroeconomy," in Alm and Weiner, eds., Oil Shock, 1984, pp. 97-121; R. S. Pindyck, ed., *Advances in the Economics of Energy and Resources* (Greenwich, Conn.: JAI Press, 1979).

Case 34-A: ARCO Solar Inc.[1]

In early 1988, top management at Atlantic Richfield (ARCO) had an important decision to make concerning the future of the company's solar energy division. (Financial statements are shown in Figures 34-A-1 and 34-A-2.) The wholly owned subsidiary, ARCO Solar Inc., was a world leader in photovoltaic cell production (photovoltaics are semiconductors that produce electricity directly from sunlight), yet in the 11 years since ARCO had purchased the company, it had never turned a profit.[2] ARCO instituted a restructuring plan in 1985 that called for the company to divest itself of operations unrelated to its core oil, gas, chemicals, and coal businesses; yet, the solar technologies being developed by ARCO Solar seemed within a few years of profitability. At the same time, ARCO enjoyed a reputation as a model of good corporate citizenship for continuing to support photovoltaic research and development for so long.

ARCO: A Brief History

Atlantic Richfield was originally incorporated in 1870 as the Atlantic Refining Company and, until the 1960s, was exclusively an oil and gas business. The company was renamed when it merged with the Richfield Oil Corporation in 1966. In 1961, ARCO expanded into the chemicals and plastics business, and by 1977 was well established in the coal business. By 1988, ARCO was one of the largest integrated petroleum enterprises in the industry.

ARCO subsidiaries conducted oil and gas exploration, production, refining, transportation, and marketing. The chemicals, plastics, and coal operations along with the oil and gas businesses constituted the core of ARCO's business.[3]

FIGURE 34-A-1
Atlantic Richfield:
Consolidated balance
sheet (in $ millions)

	December 31 1987	1986
Assets		
Current assets:		
Cash	$ 174	$ 122
Short-term investments	3,761	2,275
Marketable equity securities	758	0
Accounts receivable	709	348
Notes receivable	57	246
Refundable income taxes	0	764
Inventories	801	779
Prepaid expenses and other current assets	204	209
Total current assets	6,464	4,743
Investments and long-term receivables:		
Affiliated companies accounted for on the equity method	898	920
Other investments and long-term receivables	289	338
	1,187	1,258
Fixed assets:		
Property, plant, and equipment, including capitalized leases	26,663	26,175
Less accumulated depreciation, depletion, and amortization	12,258	11,325
	14,405	14,850
Deferred charges and other assets	614	753
Total assets	$22,670	$21,604
Liabilities and Stockholders' Equity		
Current liabilities:		
Notes payable	$ 1,373	$ 872
Amounts payable for securities purchased	626	0
Accounts payable	1,147	957
Taxes payable, including excise taxes	243	225
Long-term debt and other obligations due within one year	422	874
Accrued interest	229	356
Other	427	466
Total current liabilities	4,467	3,750
Long-term debt	6,028	6,661
Capital lease obligations	286	307
Deferred income taxes	3,641	3,562
Other deferred liabilities and credits	2,254	2,065
Minority interest	216	0
Stockholders' equity:		
Preference stocks	2	2
Common stock ($2.50 par value:	544	543
shares issued—1987, 217, 484, 404; 1986, 217, 279, 037		
shares outstanding—1987, 177, 686, 928; 1986, 177, 510, 339)		
Capital in excess of par value of stock	1,034	1,073
Retained earnings	6,683	6,173
Treasury stock, at cost	(2,438)	(2,445)
Foreign currency translation	53	(87)
Total stockholder's equity	5,878	5,259
Total liabilities and stockholders' equity	$22,670	$21,604

FIGURE 34-A-2

Atlantic Richfield:
Consolidated statement
of income and retained
earnings (in $ millions
except per share
amounts)

	1987	1986	1985
Revenues:			
Sales and other operating revenues, including excise taxes	$16,829	$14,993	$22,492
Interest	308	283	176
Other revenues	471	498	412
Total revenues	17,608	15,774	23,080
Expenses:			
Costs and other operating expenses	10,760	9,495	14,770
Selling, general, and administrative expenses	1,107	1,223	1,295
Taxes other than excise and income taxes	702	629	1,114
Excise taxes	547	506	769
Depreciation, depletion, and amortization	1,661	1,646	1,762
Interest	985	972	622
Unusual items	0	0	2,303
Total expenses	15,762	14,471	22,635
Income from continuing operations before gain in issuance of stock by subsidiary	1,846	1,303	445
Gain from issuance of stock by subsidiary	322	0	0
Income before income taxes, minority interest and discontinued operations	2,168	1,303	445
Provision for taxes on income	932	688	112
Minority interest in earnings of subsidiary	0	0	0
Income from continuing operations	1,224	615	333
Discontinued operations—net of income taxes:			
Loss from operations	0	0	(21)
Loss on disposal	0	0	(514)
Net income (loss)	$1,224	$615	$(202)
Earned per share:			
Continuing operations	$6.68	$3.38	$1.55
Net income (loss)	$6.68	$3.38	$(0.97)
Retained earnings:			
Balance, January 1	$6,173	$6,264	$8,782
Net income (loss)	1,224	615	(202)
Cash dividends:			
Preference stocks	(4)	(5)	(8)
Common stock	(710)	(701)	(766)
Cancellation of treasury stock	0	0	(1,542)
Balance, December 31	$6,683	$6,173	$6,264

ARCO expanded into nonpetroleum businesses with limited success. In 1967, ARCO bought the Nuclear Materials & Equipment Company, a producer of uranium- and plutonium-bearing fuels, which it sold in 1971. ARCO also, at one time or another, owned a newspaper, an air-conditioning company, a plant cell research institute, and a building products operation. All were eventually sold.

The 1970s were a turbulent time for the petroleum industry. The energy crises of 1973-1974 and 1979 precipitated a national search for energy alternatives to petroleum. One of the most attractive alternatives was solar energy. The supply was not controlled by foreign countries and it was a clean source of energy. It was also abundant: the sunlight striking the earth in a year contains approximately 1,000 times the energy in the fossil fuels extracted in the same time period.[4] With gasoline and heating-oil prices rising beyond anything previously experienced, there was a great deal of public enthusiasm for solar power.

The enthusiasm seemed justified. Photovoltaic (PV) cells, which produce electricity directly from sunlight, were invented in 1954, and were first used to power U.S. satellites at a cost of over $1,000 per peak watt (a measure of a cell's output at maximum sunlight). By 1974, the price had dropped to $50 per peak watt; by 1977 it was $17 and was continuing to decline as the cells were improved.[5]

ARCO initiated a study of the potential of the solar energy field in 1972. By 1976, with oil apparently on the way out and solar power a promising energy source for the future, the company's studies culminated in a decision to enter the solar field. ARCO did so in 1977 with the purchase of Solar Technology International, Inc., a tiny Chatsworth, California, operation with eight employees. Solar Technology was renamed ARCO Solar Inc.

ARCO Solar Inc.

Solar Technology International was founded in 1975 by an engineer, J. W. (Bill) Yerkes, with $80,000 he pulled together by mortgaging his home and obtaining loans from relatives. The company produced PV panels that powered microwave repeater stations, corrosion-prevention systems in pipelines, navigational aids, irrigation pumps, electrified livestock fences, and trickle chargers for batteries on boats and recreational vehicles. When Yerkes sold the company to ARCO in 1977 for $300,000, he stayed on as ARCO Solar's first presidents

In 1979, the company bought a 90,000-square-foot building in Camarillo, California, and built the world's first fully automated production line for PV cells and panels. By 1980, the company was the first to produce panels generating more than a megawatt of power in a year. Sales had more than doubled from the previous year.

To interest electric utilities in photoelectric power generation, the company constructed demonstration projects where PV's potential for supplying large amounts of energy could be proven. In 1981, the company installed a prototype power generation facility on the Navajo reservation in Arizona and New Mexico that was large enough to power 200 homes. The project was judged a success, and the company moved from a largely research mode into a marketing stage.

An even larger demonstration project was conceived, and by the end of 1982, the company had constructed a PV power facility three times larger than the biggest such plant then in existence. The $15 million, one-megawatt plant near Hesperia, California—large enough to power 400 homes—was constructed on 200 acres of high desert, an area with no strong winds that might blow sand on the panels, thereby blocking sunlight and wearing down the mechanisms.[7]

The power at Hesperia was generated by 108 "trackers," double-axis computer-controlled structures that turn to follow the sun. Each tracker had 265 one-by-four-foot 40-watt PV modules, each of which were made of 35 individual single-crystal silicon cells. The trackers' ability to follow the sun boosted their power output by 40 percent over what a stationary panel could generate.[8] The electricity generated by the plant fed into the Southern California Edison grid and was purchased by the utility.

The plant was constructed in six months, a record for a power plant. Even more impressive, the plant was completed under budget, an uncommon occurrence for a new power-generating facility.

Encouraged by the success of the Hesperia project, the company began construction of a 16-megawatt plant on the Carissa Plain, near Bakersfield, California. The six-megawatt first phase of the project, completed in early 1984, occupied 640 acres. The project utilized several technical improvements in the PV module and tracker construction, which increased each tracker's peak power output by 50 percent, reducing the number of trackers needed. As in Hesperia, a utility bought the power generated by the plant, thus avoiding the cost of generating power from its most expensive fuel, gas or oil. This rate (around 6 cents/kwh) was less than what it cost ARCO Solar to generate the power, but a 37 percent federal and state tax credit for the solar installation brought the cost down enough to justify it as a demonstration of PV's potential.[9]

Meanwhile, ARCO Solar took the industry by surprise by announcing it would begin selling thin-film amorphous silicon products in 1984, much earlier than industry analysts had thought possible. "Genesis," a one-square-foot amorphous silicon cell, was the first use of thin-film technology beyond the tiny cells used in calculators and watches. Developed by a 100-person ARCO Solar research team whose existence had been kept secret, the five-watt module had a 6 percent conversion efficiency and a 20-year design life. It sold to distributors for about $45. Genesis generated enough electricity to maintain batteries in recreational vehicles, cars, and boats, or to power security systems or other low-power remote applications.[10]

Genesis made ARCO Solar the world leader in the race to commercialize thin-film technology. The company's sales doubled again in 1984, and its international network of distributors continued to expand. By 1986, the company was selling 400 Genesis modules per month.[11]

ARCO Solar increasingly turned its attention to thin-film technology. The efficiencies of the thin-film cells steadily improved: by 1985 the company's researchers had a thin-film cell with a record 13.1 percent efficiency, and were predicting 20 percent efficiencies by 1990. Sales volume continued to climb due to the success of the Genesis modules.

In 1986, the company entered into joint ventures with a Japanese company (Showa Shell Sekiyu) and a German firm (Siemens) to manufacture and market ARCO Solar products in the Pacific and Europe. ARCO Solar was now the largest manufacturer of PV products in the world.[12]

But even though sales continued to climb, the company still remained unprofitable. Research and development continued to require a large commitment (35 to 40 percent of sales revenues), and though ARCO Solar's products had improved greatly, the market for PVs, due to the oil glut, was not growing as the company had hoped.

The PV Industry

When ARCO entered the industry in 1977, it was only one of a number of oil industry giants investing in the infant industry. Exxon had become involved in 1969, Shell in 1973, Mobil in 1974, and Amoco in 1979. Chevron, Union Oil of California, Occidental Petroleum, Phillips, Sohio, Gulf, Sun, and Texaco were also funding PV research.

These oil companies, flush with profits from the rising price of oil, were interested in expanding into new businesses that showed promise. In the late 1970s, solar energy seemed to be the energy source of the future.

As an energy source, PVs competed directly with fossil fuels. With oil prices rising and the equivalent price of PV electricity falling, the new technology's future looked promising. Worldwide sales of PV products rose rapidly, from around $11 million in 1978 to an estimated $150 million in 1983. Industry analysts forecasted a billion-dollar PV industry by 1990 and PV electricity at half the equivalent price of oil. The government's 1976 "Project Independence" goal of PV electricity at 50 cents per peak watt seemed achievable in the not-too-distant future.[13]

However, things began to sour for the industry in the early 1980s. By 1982, the price of oil began to fall (see Figure 34A-3). As the nation learned to conserve energy, the demand for electricity fell below projections in many areas, and utilities, not needing new capacity, lost interest in PV demonstration projects. The oil glut that developed in the 1980s made fossil fuels plentiful again, and it made renewables like PVs appear unnecessary. The utilities that needed to expand wanted an established, uninterruptable source of power, and were unwilling to invest in an unproven technology.

FIGURE 34-A-3
World crude oil
prices, 1977-1987

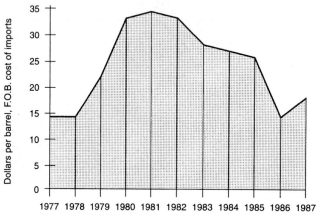

Source: Solar Energy Industries Association.

Another threat to PVs arose in the early 1980s: a severe cutback in the federal government's commitment to solar energy research and development (see Figure 34-A-4). President Ronald Reagan, elected to the White House by a landslide and committed to slashing federal nonmilitary spending, cut heavily into the funding that facilitated much of the progress in PV technologies. Federal funding for solar energy, which rose from $2 million in 1972 to $2 billion in 1978, was cut by more than half in 1982 from its 1981 level. With two exceptions, federal funding continued to drop every year for the rest of the decade.[14] In 1987, the imposition of the Gramm-Rudman-Hollings budget cuts reduced the PV research budget to the lowest level ever. The burden of financing solar energy research, of which the federal government had shouldered 75 percent in 1980, fell increasingly on industry alone.

Besides cuts in research funding, the federal tax credits that encouraged consumers and business to invest in solar technologies expired in 1985. The 40 percent residential tax credit and 15 percent tax credit for industrial, commercial, and agricultural installations, had helped the solar industry's sales to rise rapidly. While the commercial tax credits were extended in 1986 after an intensive lobbying effort by the solar energy industry, the residential credits were not renewed when they expired in 1985.[15]

By the mid-1980s, the decline in crude oil prices was forcing the oil industry to slash capital spending and lay off employees. Several oil companies, particularly those that were forced to sell service stations and refineries, took a hard look at their portfolios, and some decided to get out of the solar energy business. Exxon's Solar Power Company, for example, ceased operations in 1983. Standard Oil wrote off its investment in 1986. By 1988, ARCO and Amoco were the only major U.S. oil companies that still played a significant role in the PV industry.[16]

FIGURE 34-A-4
Federal appropriations for photovoltaic research and development, 1977-1987

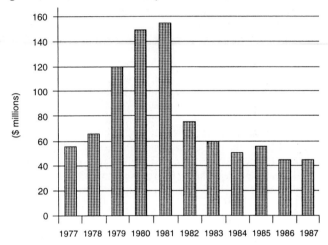

Source: Solar Energy Industries Association.

Competition in the PV Market

In addition, foreign competition grew tougher throughout the decade. While U.S. government R&D funding fell throughout the 19805, this was not true of some foreign governments. By 1985, the Japanese government was spending 19 percent more on PV R&D than the U.S. government. In 1988, for the first time, both the West German and Japanese governments spent more on PV research than the United States.[17] And their investments were paying off; the U.S. companies' share of the world PV market fell from 80 percent in 1981 to 60 percent in 1983 to about 35 percent in 1987. In 1985, only 5 of the top 20 PV firms in the world were located in the United States, though ARCO Solar was number one worldwide. At the same time, the market itself seemed stagnant. After growing rapidly in the late 1970s and early 1980s, world PV sales stalled at the $125 million to $150 million level in the mid-1980s. With all its promise, solar power still accounted for only 0.1 percent of the electricity generated each year.[18]

As they had in other industries, the Japanese showed their expertise in taking an existing technology and commercializing it. In the late 1970s, most attention in the PV industry was directed toward developing cheaper, more efficient single-crystal cells. These cells had the highest conversion efficiencies of any of the PV technologies, but they were also very expensive.

The Japanese, however, used a new type of cell (amorphous silicon), which was much less efficient than the single-crystal cells (3-5 percent efficiency versus 15-20 percent or more efficiency) but much cheaper to produce. They used amorphous silicon cells to power small consumer electronic products like calculators. By 1985, the Japanese were selling

100 million amorphous-silicon-powered calculators and other small electronic products per
year. Their experience in amorphous silicon cell production gave them the early lead in PV
manufacturing technology, along with economies of scale and lower production costs. In
1985, the Japanese manufacturers shipped seven megawatts of amorphous silicon, almost all
of it in consumer products, compared to 0.5 megawatts by U.S. producers.[19]

The most lucrative markets for PVs, though, was utility or grid power generation. In
1987, PVs were economical in grid systems only for what is known in the utility industry as
"peaking power," more costly power sources that are used only during peak load periods.

The other major potential market was in providing power for areas without grid
systems. Three-quarters of the world's population are without grid electricity, yet many
people live in areas where sunlight is abundant and intense. Thousands of small, solar
energy systems were already operating in these areas and the potential market seemed huge.
The Department of Energy estimated that the potential market was 10 to 20 times the
current sales level.[20]

Most of the U.S. producers' attention was directed toward developing a cell that could
generate electricity at a price competitive with fossil fuels. The price of PV electricity was
falling, but whereas electricity from coal cost about 4 to 8 cents per kilowatt-hour (kwh) and
oil or natural gas 5 to 10 cents/kwh, PV electricity cost about 25 to 30 cents/kwh (see
Figure 34-A-5).[21]

FIGURE 34-A-5
Cost of a solar cell
per peak watt of
electricity generated

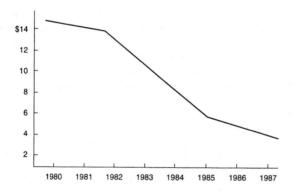

Source: Solar Energy Industries Association.

By the mid-1980s, thin-film technologies, like amorphous silicon, seemed to hold the
most promise. These technologies, which used a fraction of the material required to
produce single-crystal cells and less labor, were continually being refined to yield more
efficient cells. By 1986, thin-film technologies had been developed to the point where they
seemed to be within a few years of reaching 7 to 8 cents/kwh, which would make PVs
competitive with fossil fuels and nuclear power (see Figure 34-A-6).

There was another reason for optimism. By 1988, the search for new energy sources
began to regain the momentum it had in the 1970s, though for a different reason. The threat
posed by global warming had begun to draw attention. Experts warned that consumption of
fossil fuels had to be reduced significantly to address the problem. Also, the Three Mile Island
and Chernobyl nuclear accidents severely damaged the nuclear power industry's credibility
and chances for a large role in the future of electricity generation appeared unlikely. Hydroelectric
power, while clean and safe, had limited expansion potential. Solar energy's potential was once
again apparent.

FIGURE 34-A-6
Efficiencies
of experimental
amorphous silicon
cells

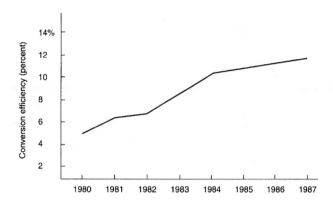

Source: Department of Energy, "National Photovoltaic Program: 1987 Program Review."

ARCO, the Industry Leader

By 1988, ARCO Solar was the undisputed world leader in the PV industry, with 20 percent of the $150 million market (see Figure 34-A-7). The company was leaner than it had been, with 350 employees, half the number in 1983, and sales forecasts were optimistic; the company had a growing backlog of orders. The company's research labs had made advances in a new type of thin-film material, copper indium diselenide (CIS), which promised nondegradability and had even better efficiencies than amorphous silicon. The company was four to five years ahead of the competition in CIS technology, and a line of CIS cells was planned.[22]

FIGURE 34-A-7
U.S. photovoltaic
shipments
(in Megawatts)

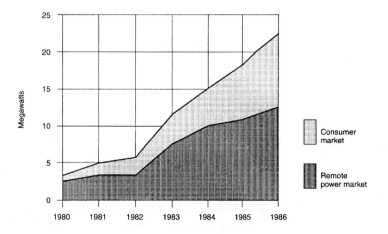

Source: Department of Energy, "National Photovoltaic Program: 1987 Program Review."

Though ARCO Solar was the world's leading producer of PV cells, it had never made a profit. Its $30 million in annual revenue was matched every 15 hours by its parent company. Though ARCO Solar's president was confident the company could stand on its own feet within two or three years, some analysts believed that the $200 million ARCO had invested in its solar subsidiary had hurt the parent company's status on Wall Street.[23]

Other criticisms began to surface in the press. Bill Yerkes, the founder and first president of the company, told the *Los Angeles Times* that "the company was screwed up two years after [ARCO] bought it. We went from making cells for $10 a watt and selling them for $15 to making cells for $32 a watt and selling them for $5."[24] Other former employees cited additional examples of instability: the company's headquarters had shifted five times, and six men had been president in 12 years (three presidents in the first 3 years alone).

What Should ARCO Do?

In 1985, ARCO underwent a restructuring that signaled a shift in corporate strategy. Anticipating continued low oil prices, the company cut costs by $500 million, repurchased 24 percent of its outstanding common stock, and wrote off $1.5 billion in losses on the sale of assets and the expenses incurred by personnel reductions. The chairman of the board retired and the CEO stepped down.

The new CIS thin-film technology showed promise of being the basis of a line of PV cells that would be truly competitive with fossil fuels for utility-scale power generation in the next few years. Given the rising concern over global warming, an economically competitive PV cell for large-scale power generation could be a bonanza.

ARCO also enjoyed its reputation as a socially responsible corporation for continuing to support solar energy when so many oil companies had dropped out. Although critics had claimed in the late 1970s that the oil companies were buying up the solar technology in order to suppress it, "Big Oil," with its deep pockets, was now generally acknowledged as being good for the PV industry. ARCO was a hero of sorts in the renewable-energy community.

Should ARCO sell ARCO Solar? Top management had a difficult decision to make.

Appendix: How Photovoltaic Cells Work

A Photovoltaic cell produces electricity directly from sunlight. When the sunlight strikes the surface of the semiconductor material of which the cell is made, it energizes some of the semiconductor's electrons enough to break them loose. The loose electrons are channeled through a metallic grid on the cell's surface to junctions where they are combined with electrons from other cells to form an electric current.

The electrons from different semiconductor materials are broken loose by different wavelengths of light. Some wavelengths of sunlight reach the earth's surface with more intensity than others. Consequently, much of the effort of photovoltaic research has been to find semiconductor materials that are energized by the most intense light wavelengths and have the potential to provide the most energy.

Single-crystal silicon cells were the first type widely used, powering satellite radios as early as 1958. These cells are energized by some of the most intense sunlight wavelengths, and have achieved conversion efficiencies (percentage of light energy converted to electricity) of more than 20 percent. Other, nonsilicon, single-crystal cells have achieved efficiencies of more than 27 percent.[25]

While efficient, these single-crystal cells are also expensive to produce and the crystals are difficult to grow. Much of the crystal is wasted when sawed into pieces for individual photovoltaic cells. Because they cost so much, their use has been limited mainly to applications where electricity is necessary and there are no other alternatives, such as in the space program.

To reduce production costs, researchers began to search for ways to fabricate silicon into cells that did not require the expensive and wasteful single-crystal techniques. One result of their efforts are *polycrystalline silicon cells*, which sacrifice some efficiency in return for cheaper manufacturing methods. The most efficient polycrystalline cells to date achieve better than 15 percent efficiencies. Together, single-crystal and polycrystalline cells account for two-thirds of those sold.[26]

Perhaps the most promising PV technologies are the "thin-film" techniques, in which cells as large as four square feet—as opposed to crystalline cells which are approximately ¼ inch in diameter—are produced by depositing a film of PV material less than one-hundredth the thickness of a crystalline cell on a suitable base, or substrate. These cells are only about half as efficient as single-crystal cells, but because they can be produced for about one-fourth the cost or less, they offer the greatest potential for large-scale use.

Thin-film silicon cells (called amorphous silicon) accounted for 37 percent of the world market for photovoltaics in 1987. One drawback to amorphous silicon cells, however, is that they typically lose about one-sixth of their power output in the first few months of use. Certain other thin-film materials, such as the promising copper indium diselenide (CIS) and cadmium telluride (CdTe), may not suffer from this light-induced degradation.

The world leader in CIS technology is ARCO Solar. The company has developed a four-square-foot CIS cell with a 9 percent conversion efficiency, demonstrating that large-scale applications of thin-film technology are feasible. A Texas company, Photon Energy, has developed an inexpensive, simple process for applying CdTe to panels as large as ARGO's, achieving a 7 percent efficiency. The company has managed better than 12 percent efficiencies in the laboratory and expects to do even better in the near future.

Besides improving conversion efficiencies by developing new photovoltaic compounds, researchers have been breaking efficiency records by "stacking" cells; these "mechanically stacked multijunction" (MSMJ) cells are actually two cells pasted together. The top cell extracts the energy from one part of the light spectrum, and the lower cell uses the energy from a different part. An MSMJ cell composed of a single-crystal gallium arsenide cell and a single-crystal silicon cell achieved a better than 30 percent efficiency in the late 1980s, and researchers believe that a three-layer cell with a 38 percent efficiency is possible.[27] Efficiency improvements via stacking of more economical thin-film cells are also being investigated.

The continuing improvements in conversion efficiencies are especially remarkable considering that in 1982, theoretical physicists believed that the maximum achievable efficiency of a solar cell was only 22 percent; at that time, the highest efficiency achieved was 16 percent. Theoreticians now estimate that 38-40 percent is the limit, although the physics of thin-film technology is not completely understood.

Other Sun-Powered Energy Sources

Photovoltaics are not the only way of utilizing the sun's energy.[28] They are not even the major producer of electricity from sunlight, a distinction that belongs to solar thermal technologies. Solar thermal systems work by using the heating rays of the sun to warm air, water, or oil for space heating or thermal power generation. Luz International of Los Angeles is the world's largest producer of solar thermal electric plants. The company's seven plants in California's Mojave Desert produce go percent of all solar-generated power in the world. Company officials estimate that solar thermal plants occupying just 1 percent of the Mojave could supply all of Southern California Edison's peak power requirements. Solar thermal facilities, which on sunny days can achieve conversion efficiencies twice that of some PVs, generate power at a cost equal to late-generation nuclear plants, and the cost is dropping.

Biomass technologies focus on developing fast-growing plants that can be burned to extract the solar energy the plants store. A promising biomass technique involves growing certain types of algae in shallow ponds located in the desert. The algae produce an oil that can be extracted and used as fuel.

Ninety percent of the wind-generated electricity in the United States is produced by wind turbines located in three mountain passes in California. These three passes have been credited with having 80 percent of the world's usable wind supply, though experts estimate that under the right conditions, wind power could generate up to 5 percent of the nation's electricity. The California turbines accounted for 1 percent of California's electrical production in 1989. Production of new wind-powered facilities has been sluggish since tax credits for such construction ended in 1985 and because wind power is not competitive with fossil fuels at current prices.

Hydroelectric power, the cheapest power source, is the largest generator of electricity among the renewables. It has limited potential for further expansion, though, since all the most convenient rivers have already been dammed.

Altogether, renewables (solar, biomass, wind, hydro, and geothermal) account for about 9 percent of the electric power generated in the United States.

Discussion Questions

1. In deciding what to do about ARCO Solar, what factors should the company consider?
2. What is the potential of ARCO Solar's products?
3. Even if the products proved to be very promising, should ARCO sell its solar division? Why or why not ?
4. What role should long-term energy price factors play? What role should social responsibility play?

Endnotes

1. This case was written by Mark C. Jankus with the editorial guidance of Alfred Marcus and Gordon Rands, both of the Curtis L. Carlson School of Management, University of Minnesota.
2. Donald Woutat, "Atlantic Richfield Plans to Sell ARCO Solar Unit, Cites Poor Prospects for Growth," *Los Angeles Times*, February 25, 1989, p. IV-1.
3. ARCO Annual Reports, 1977-1989.
4. "Waiting for the Sunrise," *Economist*, May 19, 1990, p. 95.
5. Solar Energy Industries Association, *15 Years in Business with the Sun* (Washington, D.C.: SEIA, 1989).
6. Bruce A. Jacobs, "Bill Yerkes—The Sunshine King," *Industry Week*, July 8, 1985, p.66; James Bates, "Sale of ARCO Unit Casts Shadow on Future of Solar Energy Venture," *Los Angeles Times*, March 7, 1989, p. IV-1.
7. "1-MW Solar Facility Planned in California," *Electrical World*, May 1982, p.25.
8. Don Best, "PV Power Goes On-Line in Hesperia," *Solar Age*, April 1983, p.37.
9. "Solar Plant Is Largest," *Engineering News-Record*, April 7, 1983, p. 16; Alyssa A. Lappen, "Solar Lives!" *Forbes*, August 15,1983, p. 104.
10. Don Best, "ARCO Goes Amorphous," *Solar Age*, November 1983, p.15.
11. Karen Berney, "Why the Outlook Is Dimming for U.S.-Made Solar Cells," *Electronics*, September 23, 1985, p.32; Bill Yerkes, "Big Oil's Future in Photovoltaics," *Solar Age*, June 1986, p. 14.
12. Don Best, "ARCO Solar Enters Joint Venture with Japanese Firm," *Solar Age*, May 1986, p.20.
13. Kenneth R. Sheets, "Solar Power Still the Hottest Thing in Energy," *U.S. News & World Report*, May 2, 1983, p. 45.
14. Solar Energy Industries Association, *15 Years in Business with the Sun*.

15. Berney, "Why the Outlook Is Dimming for U.S.-Made Solar Cells," p. 32.
16. Matthew L. Wald, "U.S. Companies Losing Interest in Solar Energy," *New York Times*, March 7, 1989, p. 1.
17. Ibid.
18. Barbara Rosewicz, "ARCO is Trying to Sell Solar-Panel Unit, Reversing Move into Alternative Energy," *The Wall Street Journal*, February 27, 1989, p. B-3; Best, "ARCO Solar Enters Joint Venture with Japanese Firm," p. 20; Lad Kuzela, "Days are Sunny for Jim Caldwell," *Industry Week*, October 13, 1986, p. 75; "Waiting for the Sunrise," *Economist*, p. 95.
19. Berney, "Why the Outlook is Dimming for U.S.-Made Solar Cells," p. 32.
20. Department of Energy, "National Photovoltaics Program: 1987 Program Review," April 1988.
21. David E. Carlson, "Low-Cost Power from Thin-Film Photovoltaics," in T. B. Johansson, ed., *Electricity: Efficient End-Use and New Generation Technologies, and Their Planning Implications* (Washington, D.C.: American Council for an Energy Efficient Economy, 1989).
22. Mark Crawford, "ARCO Solar Sale Raises Concerns Over Potential Technology Export," *Science*, May 26, 1989, p. 918.
23. Bates, "Sale of ARCO Unit Casts Shadow," p. IV-1.
24. *Los Angeles Times*, March 7, 1989, p. IV-11.
25. Neelkanth G. Dhere, "Present Status of the Development of Thin-Film Solar Cells," *Vacuum* 39, nos. 7-8, p. 743.
26. "Waiting for the Sunrise," *Economist*, p. 95.
27. Dana Gardner, "Solar Cells Reach Efficiency Highs," *Design News*, April 24, 1989, p. 38.
28. Information in this section is adapted from James R. Chiles, "Tomorrow's Energy Today," *Audubon*, January 1990, p. 58.

Chapter Thirty-Five

TO NATURE: ENVIRONMENTAL

PHILOSOPHY

AND ECONOMICS

The Second Law of Thermodynamics states that there is always a waste byproduct of any process. It is the Law of Entropy, of irrevocable dissipation, not only of energy but of matter. The ultimate fate of the universe is chaos. All kinds of energy are gradually transformed into heat, and heat becomes so dissipated that humans cannot use it.

Adapted from Nicholas Georgescu-Roegen, "Energy and Economic Myths"[1]

Introduction

Environmental and pollution problems are transforming the world economy. They not only drive technological innovation but also help shape the legal and economic context of management in the United States and abroad. This chapter introduces environmental issues and discusses the challenges that they pose to managers.

Three environmental challenges are addressed. The first is a philosophical challenge emanating from the ethical viewpoints of environmentalists, which is increasingly understood and appreciated by broad segments of the public but which is at odds with some of the tenets of business philosophy. The second challenge is in the area of public policy, where economic approaches have been developed and applied to pollution problems. They attempt to balance the costs and benefits of environmental protection. Their strengths and weaknesses need to be better understood by managers. The third challenge relates to the adequacy of scientific information for resolving thorny environmental issues. Ultimately, it is the adequacy of this information that determines how capable public officials are of resolving environmental disputes.

Waste Production as a By-Product of Business Activity

Businesses produce waste in the process of extracting raw materials from nature, transforming the raw materials into useful products, and transporting the finished products to markets. These essential business activities yield by-products which have undesirable qualities that have to be absorbed by nature. Thus, the physical environment not only provides goods and materials to the economy but the goods and materials flow back again to the environment as wastes or residuals.[2]

In making business decisions, managers need to keep the costs and risks of waste generation in mind. They also need to be aware that preventing and managing wastes provide opportunities for business gain. Managers are in a position to profit from handling society's wastes creatively.

People have long recognized that nature is of critical importance as a source of material inputs to economic activity, but they have been less aware that the environment also plays an essential role as a receptacle for society's unwanted by-products. A simple materials balance model illustrates the relationship between the economy and the environment (see Figure 35-1). The production sector, which consists of mines and factories, extracts materials from nature and processes them into goods. Transportation and distribution networks move and store the finished products before they reach the point of consumption. The environment provides the material inputs needed to sustain economic activity and carries away the wastes generated by it.

FIGURE 35-1
From nature to nature:
The flow of
materials

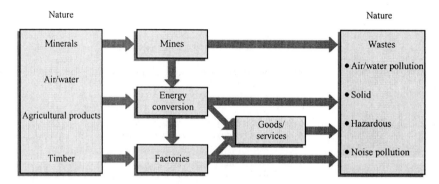

Source: A. Freeman, R. Myrick, A. Haveman, and V. Kneese, *The Economics of Environmental Policy* (New York: John Wiley, 1973).

Energy conversion supports materials processing by providing electricity, heating, and cooling services. It also aids in transportation and distribution. The environment provides essential elements for materials processing, including air and water, fossil fuels, agricultural products and timber, and minerals. The numerous byproducts of these processes must be absorbed or assimilated by the environment. The byproducts include air pollutants such as hydrocarbons, carbon monoxide, sulfur dioxide and particulate matter; solid wastes such as bottom and fly ash from combustion; radioactive wastes; and noise.

The useful energy from energy conversion helps make food, forest products, chemicals, petroleum products, metals, and structural materials such as stone, steel, and cement. The processes by which these materials are made, however, produce wastes, noise, and rubbish. Some waste materials are recovered by recycling, but most are absorbed by the environment. They are dumped in landfills, burned in incinerators, and disposed of as ash. They end up in the air, water, or soil.

Through this process, households have useful products to consume, but households also generate waste, a large portion of which is discarded as garbage. All wastes find their way back to nature.

The law of the conservation of energy dictates that the material inputs and energy that enter the economy cannot be destroyed.[3] But they do change form, finding their way back to nature in a disorganized state as unwanted and perhaps dangerous by-products. The ultimate limits to economic growth—the splendid affluence achieved in developed countries—does not simply come from the availability of raw materials in nature. Nature's limited capacities to absorb wastes set a limit on how much an economy can produce.

Environmental Philosophy and the Environmental Movement

The environmental movement has made people conscious of the environmental degradation caused by production. At the start of the 1990s, the worldwide movement was showing strength and vitality that it had not been shown since the 1970s.[4] One of its primary attractions was that it provided a political alternative to the traditional ideologies of laissez-faire capitalism and socialism. People of different political persuasions could unite behind environmental causes. A New York limes/CBS poll in 1989 found that 79 percent of the American population agreed that "environmental improvements must be made regardless of cost." In 1981, when the same question was asked, only 45 percent accepted this statement (see Figure 35-2).

FIGURE 35-2
Emerging public
consensus on
the environment

- Americans believe the condition of the environment is worsening and consider the environment a top priority.
- Most believe that business, government, and consumers have not done enough to protect the environment.
- Most believe that creating a cleaner environment can actually create jobs and help the economy.
- Despite the recession, nearly three fourths of the public favor protecting the environment even at the risk of slower economic growth.
- Most have taken some personal action to improve the environment and consider themselves environmentalists.
- Trend-setting environmental consumers have changed their personal economic behavior to protect the environment.

Source: Environment Opinion Study; also see *The Environment: Public Attitudes and Individual Behavior*, a study conducted by the Roper Organization, July 1990, New York.

Labeled the Earth Decade, the 1990s were supposed to spawn a "new environmentalism" with features different from the "old." The new environmentalism also gained expression in the request made of companies to subscribe to the Principles of CERES (Coalition for Environmentally Responsible Economics). CERES is a coalition of leading social investors like the Calvert Social Investment Fund, environmental groups like the Sierra Club, public pension bodies including the states of New York and California, labor organizations, and other public interest groups. Started in the wake of the *Exxon Valdez* oil spill in 1989, CERES published its principles, which asked companies to reduce their wastes, use resources prudently, market safe products, and take responsibility for past harm (see Figure 35-3). Among the most prominent companies to subscribe to these principles are General Motors and Sun Oil.

The philosophy out of which the new environmentalism springs is an amalgam of diverse sources and ideas that combines numerous points of view. Some of the key aspects of this philosophy are noted in a sketch of the history of the movement as reflected in the ideas of some of its influential thinkers.[5]

Conservation versus Environmentalism

The conservation movement, which predates the environmental movement, has been anthropocentric (human- as opposed to nature-centered), technologically optimistic, and chiefly concerned with the efficient use of resources. It adheres to the tenets of scientific management; that is, it seeks to avoid waste by promoting the rational and efficient use of nature's riches and maximizing long-term yields, especially of renewable resources. More over, the leaders of the conservation movement as a whole have not generally questioned the system of political authority or the character of the economic system.

FIGURE 35-3
Coalition for
environmentally
responsible economics:
environmental
principles

Protection of the biosphere: Minimize the release of pollutants that may cause environmental damage.

Sustainable use of natural resources: Conserve nonrenewable resources through efficient use and careful planning.

Reduction and disposal of waste: Minimize the creation of waste, especially hazardous waste, and dispose of such materials in a safe, responsible manner.

Wise use of energy: Make every effort to use environmentally safe and sustainable energy sources to meet operating requirements.

Risk reduction: Diminish environmental, health, and safety risks to employees.

Marketing of safe products and services: Sell products that minimize adverse environmental impact and are safe for consumers.

Damage compensation: Accept responsibility for any harm the company causes the environment; conduct bioremediation, and compensate affected parties.

Disclosure of environmental incidents: Public dissemination of accidents relating to operations that harm the environment or pose health or safety risks.

Environmental directors: Appoint at least one board member who is qualified to represent environmental interests; create a position of vice president for environmental affairs.

Assessment and annual audit: Produce and publicize each year a self-evaluation of progress toward implementing the principles and meeting all applicable laws and regulations worldwide. Produce and distribute annual environmental audits to the public.

Source: *Chemical Week*, September 20, 1989; CERES Coalition Handbook.

The environmental movement, in contrast, following the lead of George Perkins Marsh (1801-1882), has shown that the unintended negative effects of human economic activities on the environment are often greater than the positive effects. There are links, for example, between forest cutting and soil erosion and between the draining of marshes and lakes and the decline of animal life. Other early environmentalists such as John Muir (1838-1914) and Aldo Leopold (1886-1948) argued that humans are not above nature but a part of it. Nature is to be revered for the spiritual experience it provides. Humans should preserve nature not simply for its economic use but for its own sake—that is, what humans can learn from it.

The environmental movement has stressed technological limitations. Humans should neither control nor dictate to nature. The political and ideological dimensions of the antitechnological attitude have led to a questioning of the logic of private investment decisions, production, expansion, and economic growth. Environmentalism is often ascetic in its orientation: human beings should live simply, without display, excess, or ostentation.

Science and the Environment

Rachel Carson's best-selling *Silent Spring* helped ignite the modem environmental movement by alerting the public to the dangers of unrestricted pesticide use. She discussed the accumulation of insecticide residues in the fatty tissues of fish and birds that eat fish, the resistance insects develop to the toxins, the dispersion of the toxins far from their source, and the interaction of the toxins in the human body. Carson brought together the findings of toxicology, ecology, and epidemiology in a form accessible to the public. Melding scientific, moral, and political arguments, she made the connection between environmental politics and values and scientific knowledge.

Barry Commoner's *Science and Survival* continued in this vein,[6] but he explicitly expanded the scope of ecology to include everything in the physical, chemical, biological, social, political, economic, and philosophical worlds.[7] All these elements fit together, and they had to be understood as a whole. The symptoms of environmental problems are in the biological world, but their source is in economic and political organizations, and the solutions are political.

This combination of science and environmental politics has not been an easy one.[8] Many in the scientific community have opposed it, and many in the environmental community have been hostile to what science has had to offer. Scientists generally feel that they are obligated to improve the material condition of humanity. Environmentalists, on the other hand, often question whether additional material progress is necessary. Some environmentalists interpret the ecological perspective to mean that nature establishes immutable limits to human progress.

The distinction between engineering and the physical sciences on the one hand, and biology and the life sciences on the other, is important. Engineers and physicists generally have had greater faith in technology than biologists and life scientists, who are more sensitive to nature's limitations. Environmentalists generally criticize the "linear, nonintegrated, hyper-specialized" character of engineering and the physical sciences as being responsible for many environmental problems. They hold that the narrowness of these disciplines means that environmental consequences and costs are not considered when human interference with natural processes takes place.[9]

Economics and the Environment

Environmentalists also tend to criticize businesses for their notions of efficiency emphasis on economic growth. For example, environmentalists argue that managers often do not adequately consider the unintended side effects of growth. Managers need to supplement estimates of the economic costs and benefits of growth with estimates of effects that cannot be measured in economic terms. According to environmentalists, the burden of proof should rest with proponents of the new technologies. The new technologies should not be implemented simply because they advance material progress. In affluent societies, mere economic expansion is insufficient.

steady-state economy
One that maintains a constant level of people and goods with the lowest possible use of matter and energy.

E. J. Mishan, an economist who contributed to the development of cost-benefit analysis, criticized society's obsession with growth.[10] Growth is promoted for many reasons—to restore the balance of payments, to make the nation more competitive, to create jobs, to reduce the deficit, to provide for the old and sick, and to lessen poverty. The public is encouraged to focus on statistics of productivity, balance of payments, and growth, while ignoring the obvious costs. The goal of many environmentalists is a **steady-state economy**, where population and per capita resource consumption stabilize. Herman Daly defines a steady-state economy as one in which "constant stocks of people and artifacts [are] maintained at some desired level ... by the lowest feasible flows of matter and energy[11] (see Figure 35-4).

FIGURE 35-4
Business and environmental viewpoints compared

	Business	Environmentalists
Imperative	Preservation of the organization	Preservation of natural systems
Key stakeholders	Shareholders, employees, customers	Natural systems, future generations
Basis for decisions	Short- to moderate-term return on investment	Long-term preservation of natural systems
View of natural resources	Means to achieve ends Use efficiently based on cost	Ends unto themselves Use only if needed and with proper safeguards in place
Regulating mechanisms	The market	Natural systems, Government
View of economic growth	Desirable, depends on increased resource consumption	Not desirable when it requires resource consumption or pollution above sustainable limits

The environmentalist Paul Hawken foresees "the next economy" as one based on products that last longer because they have been better designed. These products should be lighter, stronger, and easier to repair; they also should consume less energy; and they will be traded again and again.[12]

Human services do not require much energy or material throughput and yet contribute to economic growth. Environmental cleanup and energy conservation also contribute to economic growth while having a positive effect on the environment. Environmentalists maintain that growth can continue, but only if the forms of growth are carefully chosen.

Free time would have to be a larger component of an environmentally acceptable future economy. Free time removes people from potentially harmful production. It also provides them with the time needed to make alternative production processes and techniques work, including organic gardening, recycling, public transportation, and home and appliance maintenance for the purposes of energy conservation.

The problem with reducing the rate of economic growth, as many environmentalists admit, is what it might do to the aspirations for economic mobility by the poor. Rising output satisfies the demands of the poor and middle class for better living conditions without challenging the privileges of the wealthy. Without economic expansion, the struggle for economic advancement might lead to social disorder.

Another requirement of an environmentally acceptable economy, then, is that people accept a "new frugality," a concept that also has been labeled "joyous austerity," "voluntary simplicity," and "conspicuous frugality."[13] (See the special feature, "Amory Lovins: The Soft Energy Path," about how environmentalists deal with trade-offs between energy and environmental requirements.)

The Warnings of Environmentalists

Environmentalists believe that the earth is in great danger. They see a catastrophe coming soon. The earth cannot tolerate the additional contaminants of industrial civilization. Environmentalists project current resource use and environmental degradation into the future to demonstrate that civilization is running out of critical resources[14] (see the special feature, "The Radical Environmentalism of Bill McKibben"). Human intervention, in the form of technological innovation and capital investment complemented by substantial human ingenuity and creativity, is insufficient to prevent this outcome unless drastic steps are taken soon. Numerous civilizations have been destroyed because they abused the environment.

Environmentalists use the laws of physics (the notion of entropy) to show how society systematically dissipates low-entropy, high-concentration forms of energy by converting them to high-entropy, low-concentration waste that cannot be used again except at very high cost. They also rely upon the laws of biology (the notion of carrying capacity) to show that the earth has a limited ability to tolerate the disposal of contaminants. They draw on engineering and management concepts to argue that exceedingly complex and dangerous technologies cannot be managed by humans without disastrous consequences for humanity and the environment.

Their philosophy does not blend in easily with the optimistic tenets of management theory and the materialistic beliefs of businesses. Environmentalists point out that nearly every economic benefit has an environmental cost, and that the sum total of the costs in an affluent society often exceeds the benefits.

Special Feature

Amory Lovins: The Soft Energy Path

For some environmentalists, the energy price shocks of 1973 and 1979 necessitated a reformulation of environmental values. This reformulation was guided by the theories and conclusions of Amory Lovins, a physicist whose books and writings on the "soft energy path" (SEP) were highly influential.[15]

After the 1973 oil embargo, environmentalists were on shaky ground. They opposed offshore oil drilling, the Alaskan pipeline, and additional coal burning, and favored auto emission reductions that had the potential to decrease automotive fuel efficiency. Their views appeared to increase U.S. vulnerability to OPEC. Lovins answered the criticism by proposing policies for an alternative energy future based on renewable resources and energy efficiency. His program promised to reduce pollution and at the same time increase economic growth.

Lovins argued that environmental problems were mainly problems of energy. Human beings had a choice between the so-called hard energy path (HEP) of the past and the soft energy path (SEP) of the future. HEP involved capital-intensive, nonrenewable energy sources that threatened the environment. SEP was based on the efficient use of energy in housing design and other areas. It also was based on obtaining increasing amounts of energy from renewable sources such as sunlight, geothermal energy, wood stoves, wind, water, waves and tides, plants, alcohol, and solar photovoltaics, which promised to be

the ultimate soft technology. Lovins struggled against the presumption that the more energy people used, the better off they were. Another part of his analysis concerned the diseconomies of scale in distributing energy from central sites to dispersed consumers. Thus, the SEP was socially more decentralized in character.

Lovins was a major critic of nuclear power, which he opposed because of potential malfunctions, accidents on a scale not found in any other industry, radioactivity, and problems linked to reprocessing, terrorism, sabotage, and theft. Safety in the nuclear industry required a corps of highly trained, dedicated personnel. Alvin Weinberg, one of the founders of the nuclear power program in the United States, referred to this group as a "technological priesthood."[16] The managers of nuclear production in the United States had to be experts who stood apart from the rest of society and maintained rigorous standards to pre' vent accidents. Extensive psychological testing might be required to recruit these experts; to control them, it might be necessary to monitor their personal, psychological, and financial affairs. Capital punishment might be imposed for crimes committed by nuclear personnel. Lovins therefore believed that nuclear power could only succeed in centrally planned economies where control over individuals was greater and where bureaucratic power could override economic limitations.

continued

Ultimately, it was the economic weaknesses of nuclear power that Lovins stressed. Nuclear power simply was not competitive in the free market. The basic premise of his position was that conservation and renewable resources would win in the marketplace only if the competition was fair.[17] Fair competition meant that the full social and environmental costs of a technology had to be included in the price consumers paid for energy. Lovins advocated what economists had proposed for the electric utilities, that is, marginal cost pricing that would charge users the full cost of new supplies. He also advocated flat or inverted rate structures, which would require large users to pay as much or more per unit of energy as small users.

Lovins's basic approach was in harmony with economic values. Price signals emanating from the marketplace would provide people with the incentives they needed to adapt and conserve. Environmentally benign alternatives to fossil fuel would be introduced in the context of a free market. The role of the government was to remove economic and political barriers and allow creative individuals to find solutions.

The noninterventionist approach of Lovins to economic policy was in contrast to that taken by most environmentalists. It was more in line with a theory of business management in which the market, not government, was sovereign. Lovins, however, provided managers with a major challenge. Implementing SEP meant replacing or substantially modifying virtually the whole capital stock of society—appliances, autos, housing, and highways. OPEC and SEP provided an impetus for environmentalists to accept new technologies and emerging industries, such as telecommunications, computers, and information processing that appeared environmentally benign. It also freed them from a politics of negativism and confrontation with the organized forces of society.

Not all environmentalists were happy with this approach.[18] They had technical disagreements; for instance, they pointed out that there would be competition between using biomass (plant material) for fuel and using it for food under the soft path. Further, even if the entire U.S. corn crop were converted to alcohol, it could provide only about 7.5 percent of the nation's need for motor fuel and only a little more than 1 percent of the total energy needed.[19] Environmentalists also pointed out that coastlines and mountain tops would have to be cluttered with windmills, and that endless acres of land would have to be devoted to biomass-derived fuels. Some environmentalists even argued that Lovins was wrong, and that the use of some nuclear power was benign because it produces large amounts of energy on a relatively small amount of land.

Public Policy and Economic Approaches

Public policy and economic approaches to environmental issues counter claims made by the environmentalists. They argue that limits to growth can be overcome by human ingenuity, that benefits afforded by environmental protection have a cost, and that government programs to clean up the environment are as likely to fail as the market forces that produce pollution.[20]

Overcoming the Limits to Growth

The traditional economic view is that production is a function of labor and capital. In theory, resources are unnecessary since labor and/or capital are infinitely substitutable for resources. Impending resource scarcity results in price increases that lead to technological substitution of capital, labor, or other resources for those that are in scarce supply. Price increases also create pressures for efficiency in use, which leads to reduced consumption.[21]

Thus, resource scarcity is reflected in the price of a given commodity. As resources become scarce, their prices rise accordingly, and price increases induce substitution and technological innovation.

People turn to less scarce resources that fulfill the same basic technological and economic needs provided by the resources no longer available in large quantities. To a large extent, the 1973 price shock induced by the Arab oil embargo and the 1979 price shock following the Iranian Revolution were alleviated by higher prices leading to the discovery of additional supplies and by conservation. By 1985, energy prices in real terms were lower than they were in 1973.

People respond to signals about scarcity and degradation. They respond not only to price signals and not only in economic terms, but also in political, sociological, and psychological terms.[22] Governments express people's collective sentiments and start programs to counter the impending scarcity and degradation. Social movements begin to affect people's expectations and lifestyles. People's attitudes and values change. These feedback loops, which are expressive of human change in the face of information about natural resource scarcity and environmental degradation, are inadequately factored into the simple deterministic models.

Special Feature

The Radical Environmentalism of Bill McKibben

In Bill McKibben's best-selling book *The End of Nature*, the reverence for nature and resentment of intrusions from human technologies is absolute.[23] His concern is that technology and businesses have made everything on earth "manmade and artificial." Nature is being completely "crowded out" by human interference. McKibben expresses a sense of sadness and loss because "nature's independence" has been destroyed.[24] Humility toward nature is what he offers because nature is spiritually superior to human beings. McKibben believes that nature has rights over which human beings have no intrinsic authority. Humans should be prevented from doing whatever they want to nature. They should be stopped from exercising their dominion over nature for the sake of material progress.

What is surprising about McKibben is the extremism of his ideas, his willingness to sympathize with the notion that "individual suffering—animal or human—might be less important than the suffering of species, ecosystems, the planet."[25] For much of history, most humans have not experienced nature as kind and gentle but as harsh and dangerous, and therefore human beings have felt compelled to subordinate nature in order to protect themselves.

McKibben's extremism is partially a consequence of his desperation. As he sees it, there can no longer be "personal solutions." A person cannot escape from industrial society by "moving to the woods" because the woods are no longer inviolate. The solutions McKibben believes are necessary could entail infringements on individual rights that differ from the market-based solutions proposed by some environmentalists.

Extrapolating past consumption patterns into the future without considering the human response is likely to be a futile exercise. As far back as the late 18th century, Thomas Malthus made pessimistic predictions about the limits to growth, but the lesson of modern history is one of technological innovation and substitution in response to price and other societal signals, not one of calamity brought about by resource exhaustion. In general, the prices of natural resources have been declining despite increased production and demand. Prices have fallen because of discoveries of new resources and because of innovations in the extraction and refinement process.[26]

Policy analysts and economists also question the motives and intentions of environmentalists. For example, the interests of the well-to-do are served by arguing that the prospects for additional growth are limited, thus closing channels for those who are less well off. The argument that growth is limited is also in the interests of those who want to manage humankind toward sustainability. According to some economists, a triad of the affluent—"members of the leisure class, intellectuals, and professionals"—may increase social tension and decrease the prospects for peaceful and democratic settlement of national and international conflicts because of their antigrowth pronouncements.[27]

Balancing the Costs and Benefits

Environmentalists might believe that total elimination of risk is possible and even desirable, but economists and policy analysts argue that the benefits of risk elimination have to be balanced against the costs.

Measuring risk is itself very complicated. It involves determining the conditions of exposure, the adverse effects, the levels of exposure, the level of the effects, and the overall contamination. Long latency periods, assessing the implications for human populations of laboratory studies of nonhuman animal species, and the impact of background contamination complicate these efforts. Simple cause-and-effect statements are out of the question.[28]

The most that can be said is that exposure to a particular contaminant is likely to have caused a particular disease. Risk has to be stated in terms of probabilities, not certainties, and it has to be distinguished from safety, which is a societal judgment about how much risk society is willing to bear. When comparing technological systems, different types of risks (e.g., from mining, radiation, industrial accidents, and climate impacts) have to be compared.[29] This type of comparison further complicates the judgments that have to be made.

Reducing risk involves asking the extent to which the proposed methods of reductions are likely to be effective, and how much they will cost. In theory, decision making could be left to the individual. Society could provide people with information (e.g., warning labels) and each person would then decide what to do—whether to purchase a product or service depending upon the environmental and resource consequences. However, relying upon individual judgments in the market may not adequately reflect society's preference for something of value such as air quality. Thus, social and political judgments are needed.

However much science reduces uncertainty in making social and political judgments, gaps in knowledge remain.[30] Scientific limitations open the door for political and bureaucratic biases that may not be rational. In some instances, politicians have framed legislation in ways that seriously hinder, if not entirely prohibit, the consideration of costs (e.g., the Delaney Amendment and the Clean Air Act). In other instances (e.g., the Presidents' Regulatory Review Council), they have explicitly forced cost factors to be considered. Moreover, cost factors can be considered in various ways. Analysts can carry out cost effectiveness analysis in which they attempt to figure out how to achieve a given goal with limited resources, or they can carry out more formal risk-benefit and cost-benefit analyses in which they have to quantify both the benefits and the costs of risk reduction.[31]

Qualitative Judgment in Cost-Benefit Analysis

Economists and policy analysts are the first to admit that formal, quantitative approaches to balancing costs and benefits do not eliminate the need for qualitative judgments. Cost benefit analysis was initially developed for water projects in which the issues were much less complicated than those society now faces.[32] For example, today we must determine the value of a magnificent vista obscured by air pollution or the loss to society if a plant or animal species becomes extinct. We ask what the opportunity costs are of spending vast sums on air pollution—sums that could have been invested in productivity enhancement and global competitiveness.

Equity issues, both interpersonal and intergenerational, cannot be ignored when doing cost-benefit analysis. The costs of air pollution reduction may have to be borne disproportionately by the poor in the form of higher gasoline and automobile prices. The costs of water pollution reduction, on the other hand, may be home to a greater extent by the rich because these costs are financed through public spending. Regions dependent on dirty coal may find it in their interests to unite with environmentalists in seeking pollution-control technology. Pollution-control technology might save coal-mining jobs in West Virginia and the Midwest where the coal is dirty but impede the development of the coal-mining industry in the West where large quantities of clean-burning coal are located.[33]

intergenerational equity
Concern that interests of future generations will be ignored because they are not currently represented in the market.

Intergenerational equity also plays a role. Future generations have no current representatives in the market system or political process. To what extent should current generations hold back on their own consumption for the sake of posterity? Should Bentham's "achieving the greatest good for the greatest number" be modified to read "sufficient per capita product for the greatest number over time?"[34]

These questions are particularly poignant given the fact that most people living on earth today do not have "sufficient per capita product." Achieving moral consensus is extremely difficult in a worldwide community where there are many differences in cultural values. The extent to which political coercion should play a role in achieving global standards on such matters as consumption and procreation must be considered. Neither economics nor policy analysis has simple answers to these ethical issues, which require choosing an appropriate ethical rule.

Market and Government Failures

Most policy analysts and economists accept that markets ordinarily are the superior means for fulfilling human wants. In a market, transactions are made between consenting adults only when both, or several, parties feel they are likely to benefit. Society as a whole gains from the aggregation of individual transactions that take place because of the calculations individuals make about their own welfare. The wealth of a society grows by means of the invisible hand that offers spontaneous coordination with a minimum of coercion and explicit central direction. The intervention of government may be justified only under special circumstances (e.g., if markets are not perfectly competitive, market participants are not fully informed, or property rights are not appropriately assigned).

The lack of appropriately assigned property rights serves as a major justification for government intervention for the sake of natural resource and environmental protection. Since nature lacks a discrete owner, its rights may be violated by market exchanges between consenting parties. As a "common property resource," it is subject to overuse and degradation. Lacking a discrete owner, it is inadequately protected from transactions affecting it unless government is empowered to intervene.

externality
Imposition on society of costs that have not been incorporated into the price system.

free-rider problem
Enjoying the benefits, without paying the cost, of someone else's activities; applied to the damages done to nature, it means that collective action on natures difficult to organize because no single member of a group has a significantly large interest.

Policy analysts and economists view this degradation of nature stemming from the lack of specific property rights as a type of **externality**, that is, the imposition on society of costs that have not been incorporated within the price system. The costs to society are costs to the nonconsenting third parties whose interests in nature have been violated. The parties consenting to the deal inflict damage without compensating the third parties because, without clear property rights, no entity will stand up for the rights of violated nature.

Nature's owners are a collectivity that is hard to organize. They are a large and diverse group that cannot easily pursue remedies in the legal system. In attempting to gain compensation for the damages done to nature, they suffer from the "free-rider" problem, which makes collective action difficult. The **free-rider problem** can be understood as, "Let someone else take care of it." No member of the group has a sufficient interest in the damage to pursue the matter further. Each only has a small amount to gain. Thus, only government intervention can protect the ownership rights of the collectivity in the natural world from harm.

Policy analysts and economists, however, point out that although collective action problems provide a rationale for government involvement, government involvement will not necessarily be effective in addressing the problem. Just as the market can fail so can the government.

Politicians may receive inadequate signals from concerned citizens. Voters may not understand the issues well enough to formulate coherent options to present to politicians. Political decision making also may be dominated by interest groups and biased information, partisanship, ideology, personal deals and arrangements, and financial constraints. In addition, the laws are carried out by civil servants who may not succeed because the goals of the legislation are too diverse or other problems exist that prove unmanageable: insufficient resources, overwhelming political opposition, higher priority for other issues, or sabotage caused by bureaucratic infighting.[35]

Economists and policy analysts speak of the "deadweight costs" of any government program that must be balanced against the proposed benefits. The term internalities describes these inefficiencies in public decision making.[36]

The Burden on Scientific Information

Policymakers face the burden of insufficient or inadequate scientific information. The political process puts an immense burden on science to give definitive answers to such questions as the potential for generating energy from exotic technologies like fusion and solar power and the risks to exposed populations from various chemicals. Science rarely stands up fully to this challenge.

Society needs all kinds of knowledge. It needs to know the true extent of resource limitations, the risks from environmental contaminants, and the expense of cleaning up these contaminants. It also requires knowledge about the strengths and weaknesses of solutions inside and outside the government to environmental problems. Unfortunately, many uncertainties persist.

Real-World Example

The Catalytic Converter Controversy

An example of the burden that scientific information puts on the political process is the catalytic converter controversy. To understand this controversy, it is necessary to go back to President Nixon's statement in 1970 about the Environmental Protection Agency (EPA), in which he stressed the need to merge pollution control programs so as to manage the environment "comprehensively." Nixon argued that energy and environmental issues should be considered together, but his plan for comprehensive environmental management was never realized.

At the time EPA was created in 1990, Senator Edmund Muskie, Democrat from Maine and head of the powerful Senate Subcommittee on Air and Water Pollution, was searching for "handles" that would force the automobile industry to achieve air quality goals by a specific date.

He addressed a problem of regulatory administration that scholars have called "vague delegation of authority."[37] According to this doctrine, the typical regulatory statute has indefinite provisions. In effect, Congress says to the bureaucracy, "Here is the problem—deal with it." The regulatory agency, however, lacks the binding authority needed to coerce industry into complying with statutory requirements. The remedy for problems attributable to vague and ill-formed legislation is to draft statutes that have clear goals and explicit means of implementation.

Clean Air Act

The 1970 Clean Air Act mandated that auto manufacturers achieve a go percent reduction in hydrocarbon and carbon monoxide emissions by 1975, and a go percent

continued

reduction in nitrogen oxide emissions by 1976. Similar legislation passed in 1992 by California required that 2 percent of a car company's sales in that state have "zero emissions" by 1998 and that low percent have "zero emissions" by 2003.

The air quality goals in the 1970 Clean Air Act, however, were "based on incomplete data and large margins of safety."[38] The required go percent reductions were taken from calculations of the highest levels of carbon monoxide emissions ever recorded in Chicago, the highest levels of nitrogen oxide emissions ever recorded in New York, and the highest level of hydrocarbon emissions ever recorded in Los Angeles.

Meanwhile, President Nixon warned the American people about the possibility of energy shortages. In 1973, he said that the United States had only 6 percent of the world's population, but it used one-third of the world's energy. Then, the Syrian and Egyptian armies launched their surprise attack on Israel, and the Arab oil-producing nations imposed an oil embargo. U.S. consumers experienced long waits in line for gasoline, truck drivers blockaded highways to protest fuel shortages and price increases, and the National Guard in some states had to be called out to maintain order.[39]

Extending Deadlines

President Nixon urged Congress in 1974 to modify the Clean Air Act, saying that the interim 1976-1977 auto emission standards should be extended so that manufacturers could concentrate on fuel economy. The automobile emission deadlines already had been extended once before, in 1973. Congress passed a law extending emission deadlines for another year, and the auto manufacturers were given the right to ask for still another one-year extension.[40]

To meet the emissions standards then in effect, auto makers had returned existing engines. The problem was that the returning reduced fuel economy by about 10 percent. EPA officials believed that if auto companies used catalytic converters, there would be no fuel penalty. The National Academy of Sciences backed up the EPA. Its studies showed that go percent reductions were possible in cars equipped with catalytic converters with no fuel penalty.[41]

Acid Emissions

The Ford Motor Company then asked for another extension, because sulfuric acid emissions had been discovered in catalytic converter discharges. John Moran, a health effects researcher located at Research Triangle Park—EPA's scientific complex near Durham, North Carolina—held an unauthorized press conference in the fall of 1973, alerting the public to the danger. He made public a study showing that although catalytic converters reduced hydrocarbons and carbon monoxide, they emitted significant amounts of sulfuric acid with probable adverse effects on public health. Moran's study pointed out that the converter, which was supposed to eliminate the health hazards caused by air pollution, caused a health problem. The acid emissions were minute, but in regions of high traffic density, they could be dangerous.

Moran's statements were attacked by EPA staff. They held their own unauthorized press conference and accused Moran of leaking information about health risks because he wanted EPA headquarters to continue funding his emissions-testing program. They claimed that only at sufficiently high concentrations were adverse health effects associated with sulfuric acid, but these concentrations were too small to make a difference and unlikely to occur anyway.

In 1975, Congress held hearings on amendments to the Clean Air Act. All the participants in the debate—environmentalists, industry, representatives of the administration, and experts—used the language and rhetoric of science to advance their positions and buttressed their arguments with some form of scientific study.[42] Ultimately, catalytic converters were allowed, but not without substantial delay in implementing the Clean Air Act. Predictably, environmentalists were disappointed, but General Motors, surprisingly, was also upset. It had spent hundreds of millions of dollars on catalyst research, built an expensive plant for fabricating catalytic converters, and signed long-term contracts to obtain the precious metals used in the converters—all steps that its U.S. competitors, Ford and Chrysler, had not taken.

How Scientific Knowledge is Generated and Used

residual risk
Decisions made with partial knowledge where some element of risk is not completely understood.

Environmental issues compel consideration of how scientific knowledge is generated and used in public policy debates. Most important choices are made under conditions of **"residual risk"** or limited knowledge: complete knowledge is not available, but the decisions are not the result of mere guesswork either. Even if total knowledge were available, the appropriate actions to take based on this knowledge would not be apparent. Moreover, existing knowledge changes over time, allowing uncertainties to develop that make it more difficult to know what to do.[43]

Choices about policy and implementation are thus made and remade in response to a sorting-out process of what is known and unknown. This process depends on the imperfect capabilities of individuals, groups, and organizations to perceive risk and to act on the basis of their perceptions. Implicit in the process is an evaluation of "societal negligence." Derived from the classic formulation of Judge Learned Hand, Hand's **rule for assessing societal negligence** postulates that in evaluating risk, a "reasonable" person considers (a) the probability of injury, (b) the gravity of the injury should it occur, and (c) the burden of taking adequate precaution. Judge Hand argued that if the expected injury (probability × gravity) exceeds the costs of precaution and the defendant takes no action, then the defendant is negligent.[44]

Hand's rule for assessing societal negligence
In evaluating risk, a reasonable person considers the probability of injury times the gravity should it occur compared with the costs of precaution.

Extended to society at large, the costs of precaution should be balanced against the probability of harm times the costs of harm. Environmentalists are likely to emphasize the probability and costs of harm while downplaying the burdens of precaution. When the expected danger is great, the movement's prevailing philosophy of more government involvement, slower growth, and simpler living can be implemented. In contrast, corporations are likely to focus on the burdens of precaution, since these burdens fall disproportionately on them and have far-reaching implications for their products and how these products are made.

The government should be guided by rational and scientific judgments, but be cause the uncertainties are great, both elected officials and bureaucrats are swayed by the viewpoints of environmentalists and business. Environmentalists and business groups contribute information to the debate, and they sponsor studies and interpret existing studies in accord with their point of view. Neutral experts also contribute information to the debate. In the end, public officials caught in the middle, having to make binding decisions based on uncertain information.

Conclusions

Waste products are made when businesses produce any good or service. These waste products have to be disposed of properly. The capacities of natural systems to absorb this waste are an ultimate limit on the economic expansion a society can achieve.

This chapter has described different approaches to environmental problems. Environmentalists emphasize the limits of nature's capacity to absorb waste. Public policy analysts and economists show how these limits can be overcome by the price system and government; they admit that regulation is needed in some instances but warn that the value of regulation has to be balanced against the costs. Cost-benefit analysis is the way policy analysts/economists prefer to deal with environmental issues, but cost-benefit analysis, as public policy analysts and economists will admit, has qualitative components. It does not get around important normative considerations that play a critical role.

The knowledge that public officials have about environmental issues is also important. This chapter concludes with a discussion of the scientific and other uncertainties encountered in implementing environmental policies.

Discussion Questions

1. Describe the flow of materials from nature to nature. What effect does this flow have on economic growth?
2. Describe the major tenets of the conservation movement. Compare its tenets with those of environmentalism.
3. What contributions did Rachel Carson and Barry Commoner make to the environmental movement?

4. How do environmentalists view economic growth? How are their views on this topic different from the views of economists?
5. What is the soft energy path? How does it differ from the hard energy path?
6. What if the price system was fixed as Lovins advocated? Would energy choices made by society be different? Why or why not?
7. How do you view the environmentalism of Bill McKibben? Does nature deserve absolute respect?
8. According to policy analysts/economists, how are limits to growth to be overcome?
9. What are some of the arguments for and against cost-benefit analysis? What are the appropriate uses for cost-benefit analysis?
10. What do the deadweight costs of any government action have to do with solving environmental problems?
11. What does the regulatory problem "vague delegation of authority" refer to? How does the 1970 Clean Air Act approach this problem?
12. In 1975, when Congress held hearings on the Clean Air Act, what should General Motors have done? What kind of arguments should it have made? What types of analysis should it have used to support its arguments?
13. What does the term residual risk suggest? How important is it in describing environmental issues?
14. What is Judge Learned Hand's rule? To what extent is it helpful in determining if society has been negligent?

Endnotes

1. N. Georgescu-Roegen, *Energy and Economic Myths* (New York: Pergamon, 1976).
2. A. Freeman, R. Myrick, H. Haveman, and A. V. Kneese. *The Economics of Environmental Policy* (New York: John Wiley, 1973); A. V. Kneese, *Economics and the Environment* (New York: Penguin Books, 1977).
3. Georgescu-Roegen, *Energy and Economic Myths*.
4. D. Kirkpatrick, "Environmentalism: The New Crusade," *Fortune*, February 12, 1990, pp. 44-55; R. Irwin, "Clean and Green," *Sierra*, November/December 1985, pp. 50-56; J. Crudele, "Environmental Issues Could Be Hot Item of '90s," *Minneapolis Star and Tribune*, March 18, 1990, p. 2D; R. Buchholz, A. Marcus, and J. Post, *Managing Environmental Issues: A Case Book* (Englewood Cliffs, N.J.: Prentice Hall, 1990).
5. R. Carson, *Silent Spring* (Cambridge, Mass.: Houghton-Mifflin, 1962); R. Paehlke, *Environmentalism and the Future of Progressive Politics* (New Haven: Yale University Press, 1989), pp. 13-41, 76-143; R. Nash, ed., The American Environment (Reading, Mass.: Addison-Wesley, 1968); R. Revelle and H. Landsberg, ed., *America's Changing Environment* (Boston: Beacon Press, 1970); L. Caldwell, *Environment: A Challenge to Modern Society* (Garden City, N.Y.: Anchor Books, 1971); J. M. Petulla, *Environmental Protection in the United States* (San Francisco: San Francisco Study Center, 1987).
6. B. Commoner, *Science and Survival* (New York: Viking Press, 1963).
7. B. Commoner, *The Closing Circle: Nature, Man and Technology* (New York: Bantam Books, 1971).
8. Paehlke, *Environmentalism and the Future of Progressive Politics*, pp. 13-41, 76-143.
9. Ibid.
10. Cited in Paehlke, *Environmentalism and the Future of Progressive Politics*.
11. Ibid., p. 130.
12. R Hawken, J. Ogilvy, and R Schwartz, *Seven Tomorrows: Toward a Voluntary History* (New York: Bantam Books, 1982); Paehlke, *Environmentalism and the Future of Progressive Politics*.
13. Paehlke, *Environmentalism and the Future of Progressive Politics*, p. 136.
14. D. Mann and H. Ingram, "Policy Issues in the Natural Environment," in *Public Policy and the Natural Environment*, ed. H. Ingram and R. K. Goodwin (Greenwich, Conn.: JAI Press, 1985), pp. 15-47.
15. A. B. Lovins, *Soft Energy Paths: Toward a Durable Peace* (New York: Friends of the Earth International, 1977).
16. Paehlke, *Environmentalism and the Future of Progressive Politics*.
17. Ibid.
18. J. R. Emshwiller, "Energy-Efficient Guru Sees Fertile Field for Start-Ups," *The Wall Street Journal*, October 30, 1990, p. B2.
19. Paehlke, *Environmentalism and the Future of Progressive Politics*.
20. A. Nichols and R. Zeckhauser, "The Perils of Prudence," *Regulation*, November/December 1986, pp. 13-25; J. F. Morrall, "A Review of the Record," *Regulation*, November/December 1986, pp. 25-35; Buchholz, Marcus, and Post, *Managing Environmental Issues: A Case Book*.
21. A. Kneese, "The Economics of Natural Resources," in *Population and Resources in Western Intellectual Traditions*, ed. M. Teitelbaum and J. Winter (Washington, D.C.: The Population Council, 1989), pp. 281-309.
22. Mann and Ingram, "Policy Issues in the Natural Environment."
23. B. McKibben, *The End of Nature* (New York: Random House, 1989).
24. D. Kevies, "Paradise Lost," *New York Review of Books*, December 21, 1989, pp. 32-38.
25. Cited in Kevies, "Paradise Lost," p. 35.
26. Kneese, "The Economics of Natural Resources."

27. W. Rostow cited in Mann and Ingram, "Policy Issues in the Natural Environment," pp. 146-48.
28. W. Lowrance, "Choosing Our Pleasures and Out Poisons: Risk Assessment for the 1980s," in *Technology and the Future*, ed. A. Teich (New York: St. Martins Press, 1990), pp. 180-207.
29. Mann and Ingram, "Policy Issues in the Natural Environment."
30. A. A. Marcus, "Risk, Uncertainty, and Scientific Judgment," *Minerva* 2 (1988), pp. 138-52.
31. L. Lave, *The Strategy of Social Regulation* (Washington, D.C.: The Brookings Institution, 1981).
32. Kneese, "The Economics of Natural Resources."
33. Mann and Ingram, "Policy Issues in the Natural Environment."
34. Ibid.
35. A. Marcus, *Controversies in Energy Policy* (Beverly Hills, Calif.: Sage Press, 1992).
36. Mann and Ingram, "Policy Issues in the Natural Environment," p. 41; J. Q. Wilson, *American Government: Institutions and Policies* (Lexington, Mass.: D. C. Heath, 1980).
37. See R. Noll, *Reforming Regulation: An Evaluation of the Ash Council Proposals* (Washington, D.C.: Brookings Institution, 1971); and T. Lowi, *The End of Liberalism* (New York: W. W. Norton, 1969).
38. Ibid., p. 30.
39. Ibid., p. 91.
40. *Energy Supply and Environmental Coordination Act of 1974*, Public Law 93-319 (88 Stat. 248) 1974.
41. *Report on Automotive Fuel Efficiency* (Washington, D.C.: EPA February, 1974); J. Quarles, *Cleaning Up America* (Boston: Houghton Mifflin, 1976), p. 194; and *Committee on Motor Vehicle Emissions, Semi-Annual Report* (Washington, D.C.: National Academy of Sciences, February 12, 1973).
42. Public Law 91-604 (84 Stat. 1676), December 31, 1970. See S. Hays, "Clean Air: From the 1970 Act to the 1977 Amendments," *Duquesne Law Review* 17, no. 1 (1978-79), p. 40.
43. Marcus, "Risk, Uncertainty, and Scientific Judgment."
44. R. Cooter and T. Ulen, *Law and Economics* (Glenview, Ill.: Scott, Foresman, 1988).

Chapter Thirty-Six

WORLDWIDE

ENVIRONMENTAL ISSUES

The ... principle of ecology is holism ... The biosphere is a unity ... Following immediately from this ... principle is the fact of interdependence. Everything within any ecosystem ... can be shown to be related to everything else; ... there are no linear relationships; every effect is also a cause in the web of natural interdependence; ... ecologists ... convey this sense of pervasive community and interrelationship [with] ... "You can never do just one thing."

William Ophuls, Ecology and the Politics of Scarcity[1]

Introduction

Both environmental problems and corporate activities are worldwide in character. To compete on a global level, U.S. managers need to understand how pollution problems manifest themselves outside the country. This chapter discusses the environmental movement in Western Europe, one of the major trading areas for the United States. It examines two key issues, solid wastes and atmospheric pollution, which are among the most pressing issues confronting businesses in the 1990s. Some of the practical steps managers can take to constructively cope with environmental problems are discussed in the final section of this chapter.

The Greening of Western Europe

Environmental problems vary in different countries and regions of the world. Managers must be savvy about the nuances of these problems if they are to be successful.[2] This section focuses on Western Europe. Environmentalism has been a strong force in that part of Europe. In the Soviet bloc, communist governments focused on production. The consequences of their nearsighted actions were disastrous, as those who must clean up the rivers, towns, forests, and even the soil after the fall of communism can testify.

American companies need to understand that there is a large growth market in Europe for environmentally friendly products. The German government has stamped more than 3,000 products with the Blue Angel insignia, indicating environmental approval. In the United Kingdom, John Elkington's *Green Consumer Guide*, a review of ecologically safe products, was on the bestseller list for nine months in 1990-91. Procter and Gamble, an American company, has adapted to the situation in the United Kingdom by marketing diapers that have been pulp-bleached without toxic chlorine gas.

The West European environmental movement started somewhat later than the American movement, but in important respects (e.g., the sale of environmentally safe products and electoral politics) it has gone much further than its American counterpart (see

Figure 36-1 comparing pollution control expenditures). For U.S. firms doing business in Western Europe in the 1990s, environmental concerns are increasingly important.

FIGURE 36-1
Pollution control expenditures in EC and non EC countries 1990 (in 1980 U.S. dollars per capita)

European Community Nations		Non-European Community Nations	
Netherlands	$1,170	Japan	$1,260
West Germany	1,110	Canada	1,260
France	740	United States	800
United Kingdom	650		
Italy	120		

Source: Adapted from Directorate of Intelligence, Central Intelligence Agency, *Handbook of Economic Statistics, 1991* (Washington, D.C.: U.S. Government Printing Office, 1991), p. 28.

The Consequences of Activism

In 1985, the European Community (now the European Union) changed its governing legislation to give it specific authority in the area of environmental protection (see Figure 36-2). The 12 member states had to create or amend their own legislation in accord with community directives to standardize environmental policies and prevent the creation of pollution havens in the poorer countries.

FIGURE 36-2
The European Union (EU)

Purpose: Single market, free movement of goods

Council of Ministers
    Legislative body: 1 member from each state

European Commission
    Advisory body of 17 commissioners, appointed to 4-year terms
    Specific portfolio of policy areas:
    Proposes new legislation to Council of Ministers
    Regulations: Directly enforceable in member state
    Directives: Instructions to member states to adopt laws
    Makes sure member nations enforce regulations and directives

European Parliament
    Popularly elected representatives from all states
    Expanded powers under 1987 amendments to force Council of Ministers to accept legislation aimed at harmonizing European laws

European Court of Justice
    Can institute action against member states for failure to implement all European laws

Treaty of Rome of 1987
    Expressly authorized legislation on environmental matters
    100 environmental laws adopted
    Unanimity not necessary; member state implementation still can differ in timing, content, intensity of enforcement

The European Community (EC) took major environmental initiatives in a number of areas.[3] Strict limits on emissions from new power plants, for example, signified increases in capital investment and production costs for business. Regulations for the release of toxic substances by chemical plants into waterways were also expected.

The EC's activism had some interesting consequences. For example, it put limits on the British government's program of privatization. The United Kingdom's Water Authorities were unable to meet the EC's water quality standard. The government had to comply with the standards before it could sell $11 billion in shares of the Water Authorities to the public.[4]

Another consequence comes from the 1985 EC law affecting automotive emissions. Initially the EC applied U.S. Style standards that called for expensive three-way catalytic converters only on large cars. Small cars could meet the requirement by having lean-burn engines. At the time, the West German government provided tax breaks to customers who bought cars with the converters, and the EC decided to move toward the U.S. standard by 1993, when all cars are required to have catalytic converters. This decision provides competitive advantage to GM, which had been anticipating the change in the standard, and was a blow to companies like Fiat, Renault, Peugeot, and Ford, which had been specializing in the lean-burn engines.[5]

The EC decision on auto emission standards also provided a boost to manufacturers of auto emissions equipment. A subsidiary of Allied Signal, an American company that supplies catalysts, expanded production capacity in northern France to meet anticipated demand. Cars with catalytic converters require special injection systems that feed the engine precisely mixed doses of fuel, and Robert Bosch of Germany, the world's largest producer of fuel injection systems, planned to spend $500 million to expand its plants in Germany, France, and Belgium.[6]

The Environment and Trade

European activism also affected Coca-Cola and Pepsi, the large American beverage companies, which saw Europe as a huge growth market. The average European drinks less than a third the volume of soft drinks of the average American. U.S. companies rely almost exclusively on aluminum cans and plastic bottles that are less expensive, lighter, and more transportable than glass bottles. In the United Kingdom, France, Spain, and Italy, cans and plastic gained acceptance, but Germany, Denmark, Switzerland, and the Netherlands relied mostly on reusable bottles. Denmark went so far as to ban cans and plastic bottles; the West German government was considering a quota system that would limit them to 20 percent of the soft drink and 10 percent of the beer market. In these countries, environmentalists allied themselves with local bottlers to prevent the introduction of alternative packaging.

According to the European Court of Justice, these countries had the right to limit or ban cans and plastic bottles because the measures protected the environment, which was a mandatory requirement under the Treaty of Rome, 1987. The treaty committed the EC to "harmonious and balanced development of economic activities, sustainable and noninflationary growth, respecting the environment." Restrictions on trade between member nations were prohibited with the exception, among other things, of the "protection of life or health of humans, animals, or plants." The treaty stated that the environment could not be used as an "arbitrary discrimination, or a disguised restriction on trade." Nonetheless, the European Court allowed member nations to set high environmental standards, so long as they did so in a consistent fashion.[7]

Ideally, the European Union (KU) would like to move toward common standards in all member nations, but over the years it increasingly recognized the differences among individual countries on environmental matters. For instance, the German government imposed very harsh restrictions on the import of products treated with pentachlorophenols (PCPs), which were used as a disinfectant and preservative in a great number of industries. Since German regulations in effect banned PCP throughout the KU, member states argued that Germany was preventing free trade. The European Court, despite EU rules on harmonization, allowed the German standards to stand. In general, the court's tendency was to permit countries to have their own environmental standards so long as these standards did not openly flout free trade.

The European Environmental Movement

The European environmental movement was different in many ways from the environmental movement in the United States. Europeans opposed to nuclear power had fought pitched battles with the police, and many people were injured and some killed. The German Greens, a political party, were an explosive mixture of pacifists, antinuclear activists, feminists, and proponents of alternative lifestyles. The Greens arose as political parties in nearly all the Western European countries. They won 28 seats in the West German Bundestag (Lower House of the German Parliament) in 1983. Four years later, they won 8.3 percent of the popular vote and elected 44 deputies to this body. The Greens used the quasi legislative European Parliament to forge greater cohesiveness and discipline among different national movements. They increased their representation in the European Parliament from 11 in 1984 to 27 in 1989. As the movement switched to the electoral arena, conflict intensified between its moderate and militant factions.[8]

As in the United States, local issues often dominated the agenda: declining forests in Germany, expansion of France's superfast railways in Belgium, opposition to hunters in Italy, and preservation of historic sites from the ravages of pollution in Greece and Ireland. Overall, European environmentalists proved successful in halting many projects.[9]

The Greens had a strong moralistic tone and borrowed economic ideas from all shades of the political spectrum. Many were apolitical and hostile to the traditional left (i.e., socialists). They were divided chiefly over the question of growth, which remained a core value of worker parties throughout Europe. The Greens favored sustainable development and quality of life which permitted less room for improvement in the plight of the lower classes. Extreme right-wing parties, also seeing a resurgence in Europe, borrowed themes and slogans from the Greens including romanticism about nature and nostalgia for the allegedly simpler times of the past. The conservatives and social democratic parties also used their ideas when they considered it appropriate. No party in Europe could ignore them.[10]

The Effects of the Recession

The slowing of economic growth and continued high levels of unemployment since 1990 dampened some of the enthusiasm for the environment in Europe. Recent developments in Germany, the United Kingdom, and France are sketched.[11]

Germany

The environment, on the top of national opinion polls as the issue of main interest to German voters throughout the 1980s, slipped to third place behind unemployment and crime in 1994. Environmental research lost a third of its national funding. Nonetheless, Germany proceeded with a number of innovations. These included the world's most advanced recycling law, which makes manufacturers responsible not only for the return of the packaging used in consumer goods from automobiles to hair dryers, but also for the material used in production, which should be environmentally benign.

During the hot summer of 1994, two German states temporarily introduced speed limits on the autobahns, an unprecedented move in a nation that had no speed limits since Hitler abolished them in 1934. The government continued to push forward with trail blazing transportation technology for the world's first magnetic levitation trains, which are scheduled to begin operation in 2005.

Germany's main political parties supported the principle of an **ecological-social market**, in which the environment was considered part of the economy. Those who caused pollution had the responsibility of paying for it. The government stood behind the goal of reducing carbon dioxide emissions by 30 percent by the year 2005.

ecological-social market
Market that integrates the natural world and the economy, and requires those responsible for pollution to pay for it.

United Kingdom

The brutal summer of 1994 also affected attitudes toward the environment in the United Kingdom. In southern England, numerous asthma sufferers were admitted to hospital emergency rooms. People from all sides of the political spectrum from Earth First to the Confederation of British Industry agreed that former Prime Minister Margaret Thatcher's vision of a "Great Car Economy" was unworkable. The government introduced new restrictions on driving and on vehicles that caused excessive pollution. Rail subsidies were increased, incentives for alternative fuels introduced, and a voluntary initiative called the Greener Car Forum started. This forum brought together groups from automobile and oil companies, government and environmentalists to consider an "ecostar" label for vehicles.

The government's imposition of a value-added tax (VAT) on domestic fuels generated substantial opposition from groups concerned about the effects of this tax on older people and the poor. Recycling was stalled, but the country was making rapid progress in water treatment. Corporate environmentalism (see the last section of this chapter) also was advancing rapidly. British firms were noted for their voluntary acceptance of environmental quality standards, **eco-auditing**, open corporate reporting on environmental issues, and strong Green support for their products.

eco-auditing
Independent examination and assessment of a company's environmental practices for conformance to company procedures, state laws, and regulations.

France

The Greens commanded only 7 percent of the total popular vote in the 1994 parliamentary elections, but a poll showed that 80 percent of the French considered environmental protection an urgent problem, up from 59 percent six years earlier. In 1994, France passed a comprehensive law aimed at increasing public participation in environmental decisions, minimizing risk, preventing pollution, and managing waste disposal. The law called for the creation of a national commission to publicly debate environmental issues and a substantial increase in the tax on dumping waste.

The business community formed a new association, Enterprises for the Environment, which tried by means of seminars, training sessions, and publications to persuade small businesses to be aware of their environmental duties.

A Comparison with the United States

President Clinton's Council on Sustainable Development
Brings together representatives from various interest groups to develop methods to benefit the environment and the economy.

Most U.S. environmental initiatives attempted to address the adversarial nature of U.S. regulation.[12] **President Clinton's Council on Sustainable Development** (PCSD) brought together representatives from business, government, and environmental groups to make policy recommendations on ways to simultaneously promote environmentalism and economic growth. The PCSD included five cabinet members, representatives of the Environmental Defense Fund, the Natural Resources Defense Council, the National Wildlife Federation, and the Sierra Club as well as companies such as Ciba-Geigy, Dow, Georgia-Pacific, Chevron, and S. C. Johnson. The Eco-efficiency Task Force of the PCSD started demonstration projects on environmentally responsible printing, automobile painting, chemical product stewardship, and ecoindustrial development.

The EPA and Energy Department worked with the Eco-Efficiency Initiative of Business for Social Responsibility, an association representing 800 companies, to implement the Clinton administration's Climate Change Action Plan. The goal was to keep global warming gases at 1990 levels by the year 2000. This business-government partnership relied on voluntary programs to achieve its goal. It helped develop new relations between companies and their suppliers on the one hand, and new electric utility company programs on the other, to stimulate energy efficiency.

Carol Browner, head of the EPA in the Clinton administration, also created a partnership program with business. The Common Sense Initiative was an ambitious effort to change environmental enforcement. Instead of focusing on individual pollutants, the initiative tried to examine the overall impact that pollution reduction requirements had on entire industries such as the pulp and paper industry. The intent was to promote a comprehensive approach toward environmental policy making rather than to respond to particular incidents. The purpose also was to give industry the flexibility to respond in a more cost-effective way.

In general, the U.S. government was trying to move away from a legalistic, adversarial approach to regulation and to create dialogue between environmentalists and business. The Clinton administration, however, supported no new environmental initiatives. Under pressure from industry, it did not give its approval to legislation that would have reduced chlorine discharges into U.S. waterways. Chlorine breaks down into dioxin and other toxic chemicals which, through fish in the waterways, end up as food people eat. The administration's concern was that the compound was basic to 15,000 chemicals sold in the United States and supported 1.3 million jobs.

The election of Albert Gore, a noted environmentalist, to the vice presidency generated hopes among environmentalists, but other issues such as health care, welfare, and international tensions claimed the Clinton administration's attention. However, when the Republican majority in the new Congress of 1995 passed a moratorium on new federal regulation and called for further risk-benefit and economic-impact analysis, Carol Browner and other administration officials came to the defense of existing programs. The ongoing struggle over environmental policies in the United States and the rest of the world continued to generate uncertainties in the business community as each nation pursued a separate course.

Two Important Issues: Solid Wastes and Atmospheric Pollution

Two important environmental issues illustrate the slogan "Think Globally and Act Locally." Solid wastes are primarily a local issue but they have global implications. Atmospheric pollution is a global issue but it has its origins, like many environmental problems, in personal consumption decisions made at the local level.

Solid Wastes: Overview

Americans generated 160 million tons of trash each year, which was roughly equivalent to 3.5 pounds of solid waste per person per day (see Figure 36-3). The volume of this waste was 80 percent greater than it was in 1960, and by the year 2000 it was expected to increase another 20 percent. There was no sign that this volume of waste would decrease.

Currently, it would take 1,000 football fields 30 stories high to store the waste generated annually by Americans.[13]

FIGURE 36-3 Estimates of the annual waste generated in the United States and other countries in the late 1980s		**Municipal Waste (Thousands of Metric Tons)**	**Industrial Waste (Thousands of Metric Tons)**	**Nuclear Waste (Heavy Metal in Metric Tons)**
	United States	208,800	760,000	1,900
	Japan	48,300	312,300	770
	W. Germany	20,230	61,400	360
	United Kingdom	17,700	50,000	900
	France	17,000	50,000	950

Source: Directorate of Intelligence, Central Intelligence Agency, *Handbook of Economic Statistics, 1991*, (Washington, D.C.: U.S. Government Printing Office, 1991), p. 174.

Landfills

The three main methods of disposing of municipal solid waste were landfills, incinerators, and recycling. Eighty percent of the solid waste in the United States goes into landfills, which have a designated life span of only 10 years. More than two-thirds of the nation's landfills have closed since the 1970s.[14]

While modem sanitary techniques and lined landfills greatly reduce the risk of environmental contamination, many existing landfills were built without these precautions and are little more than holes in the ground. Moreover, many were built on or near wetlands; it was believed that the water would wash away and purify the wastes. However, now it is generally recognized that the waste material contains inks, paints, dyes, and a host of chemicals that can leach into the groundwater and cause serious drinking-water contamination.[15]

Advances in sanitary landfilling are meant to mummify the wastes to prevent leaching. However, mummification has its own set of problems. For example, biodegradable plastics are meant to break down and may be harmful because of the complexity of their construction. They simply degrade to smaller pieces without reducing the amount of space in the landfill that they occupy. Plastics constitute less than 10 percent of the total volume of material finding its way into landfills, paper is 37.1 percent, and yard waste another 20 percent (see Figure 36-4).[16]

NIMBY ("not in my backyard") Opposition from local people to placing hazardous wastes or other environmental risks in their communities.

Finding new landfill space is difficult in the United States because of the **NIMBY ("not in my backyard")** syndrome. In the Northeast, finding a site for a new landfill is virtually impossible. Alternatives to operating landfills have to be found.

Incineration

One alternative to landfills is incineration, which can reduce the volume of waste by go percent. Other alternatives are recycling and source reduction, which prevent wastes from permanently entering the waste stream. In Germany and Japan, about 50 percent of the waste is recycled, and almost all of the rest is burned in incinerators. However, the United States has had trouble moving from a system that relies on land-filling to one that relies on incineration and recycling.[17]

FIGURE 36-4
Materials discarded into
the municipal solid
waste stream
(in millions of tons)

Materials	1970 Tons	1970 Percent	1984 Tons	1984 Percent	2000* Tons	2000* Percent
Paper and paperboard	36.5	33.1%	49.4	37.1%	65.1	41.0%
Glass	12.5	11.3	12.9	9.7	12.1	7.6
Metals	13.5	12.2	12.8	9.6	14.3	9.0
Plastics	3.0	2 7.	9.6	7.2	15.5	9.8
Rubber and leather	3.0	2.7	3.3	2.5	3.8	2.4
Textiles	2.2	2.0	2.8	2.1	3.5	2.2
Wood	4.0	3.6	5.1	3.8	6.1	3.8
Other	—	0.1	0.1	0.1	0.1	0.1
Food wastes	12.7	11.5	10.8	8.1	10.8	6.8
Yard wastes	21.0	19.0	23.8	17.9	24.4	15.3
Miscellaneous inorganics	1.8	1.6	2.4	1.8	3.1	2.0
Totals	110.3	100.0	133.0	100.0	158.8	100.0

*Estimated

Source: Adapted from Franklin Associates, EPA, Office of Solid Waste, *Characterization of Municipal Solid Waste in the United States, 1960-2000*, PB-178323, 1986.

To what extent is incineration a viable option in the United States? Originally billed as a panacea for landfill overcrowding, groundwater contamination, and alternative energy generation, it has met with many obstacles. During the 1970s, incineration was synonymous with terms such as "resource recovery" and "waste to energy." Energy prices rose throughout this period, making previously uneconomical power sources appear reasonably priced. Thus, energy-generated revenues associated with incineration played a major role in justifying construction. Incinerator developers and their financial supporters estimated that the energy generated and sold eventually would amount to over half of the revenue needed to cover the costs of incineration. The Public Utilities Regulatory Policies Act of 1978 offered a guaranteed market for the energy produced.

In the 1980s, however, energy prices plummeted, ending hopes that the energy produced would make a major difference in covering the costs of incineration. The Tax Reform Act of 1986 ended incentives such as investment tax credits (which had financed up to 10 percent of construction costs), accelerated depreciation allowances, and favorable financing policies for industrial revenue bonds.[18] Thus, incineration in the late 1980s was faced with decreasing economic justification as well as growing public opposition.

Public opposition was based chiefly on environmental and health considerations. Incinerators emit many pollutants, both toxic and nontoxic, including dioxins, DDT, lead, mercury, arsenic, and benzene. People in the vicinity of incinerators absorb these chemicals through breathing, eating, and drinking the contaminated substances.[19]

Public opposition to incineration also was based on reports of operational problems, mechanical failures and shutdowns, and cost overruns in construction. Hidden costs of construction included water sewer lines and surface roads that had to be constructed to accommodate the increased traffic to and from incinerators. Another concern was the ash left after combustion. If it was categorized as hazardous, disposal costs would increase from 5 to 10 times.[20]

In addition, opponents of incineration claim that municipality guarantees to provide the needed waste for incineration are a deterrent to starting effective recycling and waste' reduction programs. After the huge financial commitment to incineration has been made, they assert local officials will be loath to do anything to threaten the success of incineration. If insufficient waste is available, an incinerator is likely to be a financial failure.

Proponents of recycling also claim that while incineration generates a small amount of energy, recycling saves much more. For instance, recycling aluminum saves about 90 percent of the energy needed to make aluminum from virgin materials. Recycling paper saves about half the energy needed to make new paper.[21]

Recycling

Recycling programs in the United States have met with moderate success. The passage of the Resource Recovery Act in 1970 gave symbolic recognition to the public's interest in recycling, but recycling rates in the United States in the 1970s never exceeded 5 to 7 percent of the waste generated, and by the end of the 1980s amounted only to about 10 percent of the nation's total waste stream.[22]

Some solid waste professionals claim that up to 80 percent of the nation's wastes can be recycled; however, the exact amount is difficult to determine due to lack of precise information about the composition of the waste stream. Recycling rates vagary from material to material; up to 80 percent of the nation's aluminum is recycled but virtually none of the wet garbage (e.g., organic material like table wastes) is recycled.

secondary materials
Recycled goods that consumers and manufacturers would have to buy if recycling is to succeed.

Recycling requires a high degree of coordination among consumers, business, and government. Consumers need to provide waste material and to separate it. They then need to buy products made from recycled, or **secondary materials**. Although consumers express a willingness to buy recycled products, this willingness has not been reflected in increased product sales. In addition, the amount of recycling has been limited by consumer disdain for paper that is not pure white and other materials that are less attractive when made from secondary materials.

For recycling to succeed in a major way, businesses too would have to choose secondary materials over virgin materials. They would also have to develop products for secondary materials and processes for handling them. However, recyclable materials are often highly dispersed, and the cost of collecting them can be labor-intensive and expensive. Moreover, they often are of low grade and contain impurities, factors that raise the costs of preparation for remanufacture.

Most manufacturing facilities are set up to use virgin materials; they cannot use secondary ones. Thus, companies would have to make expensive new capital investments if they were to use recycled materials. These investments would have to compete with other business opportunities for corporate funds.

As long as current markets for secondary materials are limited, recycling programs will have difficulty gaining ground. There is only so much demand for cereal boxes made from recycled newsprint. The capital investment to develop equipment and processes for recycled materials is high. Also, the volatility of the secondary materials market discourages many companies from entering it; the flow of materials is often unpredictable and price can be alternately depressed or greater than that for virgin materials.

tipping fee
The price charged to dispose of waste material in a landfill or incinerator.

Recycling will take off only if manufacturers believe that it is profitable. For example, many companies recycle high-grade computer paper because it fetches high prices and saves the **tipping fees** of landfill disposal. Recycling even low-grade office waste, which contains multiple materials, yields a decent price and avoids tipping fees.

Government can promote community recycling efforts, fund R&D, and buy recycled products. It also can promote recycling by removing the tax advantage that virgin materials have. Mining, timber, and energy companies are given depletion allowances of between 5 to 22 percent of the value of the minerals produced. They also have capital gain advantages that lead to investment in virgin materials production. The social costs of depleting nonrenewable resources, on the other hand, ate not included in the price of the virgin materials.

The federal government's role in recycling is largely symbolic. EPA, for instance, is committed to a 25 percent recycling goal, but spends only 1 to 2 percent of its budget on recycling programs.[23]

Source Reduction

source reduction
Attempt to eliminate waste before it is generated.

The purpose of **source reduction** is to eliminate waste before it is generated; it is unique because it is not an end-of-the-pipe solution. The actual potential for source reduction is unknown. Businesses can modify their production processes to be less wasteful, and many have done so when it appears profitable. 3M for example has a highly successful "Pollution Prevention Pays" program.[24]

Businesses can modify their products to use less material and packaging. Consumers too can change their lifestyles in many small but meaningful ways. They can shop for goods that contain less packaging and use nondisposable alternatives whenever feasible. Since recycling brings with it environmental problems (processing already used materials, transporting them to markets, and reusing them), source reduction is a better solution to the waste problem (see Figure 36-5). But source reduction is very threatening to an acquisitive society that thrives on convenience.

FIGURE 36-5
Waste management hierarchy

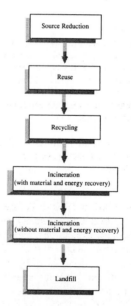

Source: L. Blumberg and R. Gottlieb, *War on Waste* (Washington, D.C.: Island Press, 1989).

Special problems are posed by beverage bottles and diapers. They were once reused, but now are commonly thrown out. Wholesalers and retailers do not want the bother of handling reusable bottles. Many working mothers, hospitals, and day care centers would find it unthinkable to give up plastic diapers and other throwaway baby products.[25]

Manufacturers have created whole systems around throwaway products and packaging, and Americans have become accustomed to their convenience. Certainly, though, if the amount of garbage is reduced at the source, less of it would have to be processed at landfills and incinerators.[26]

Atmospheric Pollution: Overview

The pollutants historically regulated by the government are hydrocarbons, nitrous oxides, carbon monoxide, sulfur dioxide, and particulate matter. Emitted from automobiles and smokestack industries like steel, chemical, and petroleum refining, these pollutants mainly threaten human health. Sensitive individuals are likely to suffer increased incidence of cardio-pulmonary diseases such as asthma under conditions of high exposure. However, the threats to the atmosphere from ozone depletion and carbon dioxide buildup are somewhat different and more serious.

Ozone Depletion

CFCs (chlorofluorocarbons) Chemicals used in aerosol propellants, coolants, solvents, and foaming agents that destroy the earth's ozone cover.

Scientific evidence strongly supports the theory that **chlorofluorocarbons (CFCs)** are destroying stratospheric ozone (see Figure 36-6). Other naturally occurring and manufactured agents such as carbon dioxide produced by decaying vegetation and nitrogen-based fertilizers also contribute to the phenomenon. Still other agents and natural processes counteract ozone depletion, increasing the complexity of the issue. The methods used to validate the theory and to measure the amount of ozone being depleted by CFCs suggest that a multitude of relevant agents are responsible, but primarily implicate CFCs.[27]

FIGURE 36-6
How CFCs contribute to ozone depletion

Application	Percentage
Aerosol propellants and other miscellaneous uses	5%
Solvent cleaning of metal and electronic parts	12%
Sterilization of medical equipment and instruments	4%
Production of plastic foam insulation products	28%
Mobile air conditioners	19%
Refrigeration and space air conditioning	9%
Unallocated production	22%

Source: Adapted from U.S. EPA, 1986; see Daniel Dudek et al., "Business Responses to Environmental Policy: Lessons from CFC Regulation" (Washington, D.C.: Environmental Defense Fund, 1989).

Invented in 1930 to be used as cooling agents for the Frigidaire division of General Motors, CFCs are chemically stable, low in toxicity, and nonflammable. For many years they were believed to be completely safe and hundreds of applications for them were found. Sold under trademarks such as Freon (made by Du Pont), CFCs are used as aerosol propellants, coolants in refrigerators and air conditioners, cleaning solvents for electronic components, and foaming agents in the manufacture of furniture and mattresses, styrofoam, and building insulation. Despite the fact that the United States has banned CFCs for use in aerosol propellants, about one-third of all CFCs in global use are produced and consumed in the United States for these other uses (see Figure 36-7).

Substantial evidence indicates that CFCs are harming the ozone layer of the stratosphere, the upper atmosphere between 15 and 30 miles above the Earth. Stratospheric ozone, which acts as a shield by absorbing radiation from the sun, allows only safe levels of ultraviolet (UV) rays to reach the earth's surface. Even conservative estimates raise serious concerns about increased levels of surface radiation as the earth's protective shield of ozone is reduced.

FIGURE 36-7
Economic scope of
CFC application in
the United States

Use	Value (Billions of Dollars)	Employment (Thousands)
Refrigeration	$ 6.0	52
Air-conditioning	10.9	125
Mobile air-conditioning	2.0	25
Cooling servicing	5.5	472
Plastic foam	2.0	40
Food freezing	0.4	<1
Sterilants	0.1	<1
Totals	$26.9	715

Source: Adapted from Alliance for a Responsible CFC Policy, 1986. See Daniel Dudek et al., "Business Responses to Environmental Policy: Lessons from CFC Regulation" (Washington, D.C.: Environmental Defense Fund, 1989).

Estimates of the actual percentage of ozone depletion range from a low of about 4 percent to a high of over 31 percent. A five- to seven-fold increase in skin cancer is expected for every percentage point decrease in ozone. Other potential harmful effects from the destruction of the ozone layer include increased incidence of cataract formation, reduction in crop yields, elimination of marine life, and the weakening of materials, including plastics.[28]

Significant actions are underway in the United States and around the world to reduce the risks of CFC-related ozone depletion (see Case 36-A, "Dupont and the Clean Air Act of 1990"). They include EPA regulations and international agreements, such as the Montreal and London Protocols, to reduce and monitor CFC production, use, and disposal, and develop safe substitutes for CFCs (See Figure 36-8). Ultimately, CFC use is slated to be phased out in the United States and throughout the world by the year 2000, and substitutes are being developed.[29]

FIGURE 36-8
CFC alternatives and
consequences of
their use

Application	Substitute	Trade-Offs
Refrigeration and air conditioning	Ammonia	Toxic, explosive
	Sulphur dioxide	Combustible, less efficient
Plastic foams	Pentane	Flammable, smog precursor
	Methylene chloride	Suspected carcinogen
Food freezing	Cryogenic systems	Less energy efficient

Source: Adapted from Alliance for a Responsible CFC Policy, 1986. See Daniel Dudek et al. "Business Responses to Environmental Policy: Lessons from CFC Regulation," (Washington, D.C.: Environmental Defense Fund, 1989).

Carbon Dioxide Buildup

Human activities of the past hundred years also are altering the composition of the atmosphere, threatening a global warming trend. Many scientists already are convinced that warming has started and that it will get worse through the next century. Since 1900, scientists estimate a warming trend of between 0.5 and 2 degrees centigrade per year.[30]

Global warming is caused by the **greenhouse effect**, the trapping of infrared energy, or heat, in the stratosphere by carbon dioxide and other greenhouse gases. These gases are transparent to sunlight, thus letting the energy penetrate the earth. Absorbing most of the sunlight, the earth converts the light energy into heat. Unabsorbed light is reflected back into space as heat. As it rises from the earth, it strikes the carbon dioxide and other greenhouse gases. Some heat is reflected back toward the earth, causing the warming effect. (The effect is the same as that of a greenhouse where the panes of glass allow higher energy light waves to enter easily, but do not allow the heat of lower energy waves to escape through the glass.)

Major emphasis is placed on carbon dioxide, which is 50 percent of the problem. Carbon dioxide is measured in the atmosphere at approximately 344 parts per million (ppm). This amount is large considering that only 100 years ago the concentration was only 293 ppm. Thus, an increase of about 15 percent has occurred in the last 100 years.

The major reason for the increase in carbon dioxide is the burning of fossil fuels—oil, coal, and gasoline. Scientists tend to be pessimistic about reducing the use of fossil fuels (see Figure 36-9).

FIGURE 36-9
CO^2 emissions, auto registrations, and energy consumptions: major industrial nations

	United States	Canada	West Germany	United Kingdom	Japan	France
CO^2 emissions (metric tons per capita)	5.34	4.58	3.00	2.67	2.20	1.56
Auto registrations (units per thousand persons)	571	448	462	353	241	395
Energy consumption (barrels of oil equivalent per capita)	57	61	32	27	24	29

Source: Adapted from Directorate of Intelligence, Central Intelligence Agency, *Handbook of Economic Statistics, 1991* (Washington., D.C.: U.S. Government Printing Office, 1991), p. 28.

The other gases contributing to the greenhouse effect are methane, CFCs, nitrous oxides, and ozone (see Figure 36-10). The atmosphere contains 100 percent more methane than it did during glacial periods. This increase is caused by the harvesting of rice paddies, the use of landfills, and the flaring of natural gas wells. CFCs emitted from the earth are found in the atmosphere at one part per billion. Nitrous oxides in minute traces are found in the atmosphere because of the use of fertilizers, natural processes (the emittances of soil microbes), and the burning of fossil fuels. The last major gas that contributes to the greenhouse effect is ozone. Even though the ozone layer provides ultraviolet protection at high levels in the atmosphere, it is dangerous at lower levels, where it is more commonly known as smog.

There are a number of natural processes that counteract the greenhouse effect. For instance, carbon dioxide is absorbed by the oceans and by tropical rain forests and other forms of vegetation, and it is reflected back into space by the clouds. The oceans are considered to be the major sink for carbon dioxide which is readily dissolved into seawater and where aquatic plants absorb it and hold on to it. The quantity of carbon dioxide absorbed by the oceans, however, is unknown. because of the vastness of the oceans, scientists find it difficult to estimate the exact quantities of carbon dioxide plants absorb and oxygen they produce through photosynthesis.

FIGURE 36-10
Contributors to the
greenhouse effect

Gases Contributing to Greenhouse Effect		Human Activities Contributing to Greenhouse Effect	
Gas	**Percent**	**Activity**	**Percent**
Carbon dioxide	50%	Energy use and production	57%
Methane	20	Use of CFCs	17
CFCs	15	Agricultural products	14
Nitrous oxide	10	Deforestation	9
Ozone	5	Other industrial practices	3
	100%		100%

The rate of absorption by terrestrial plants is estimated to be 500 billion tons of carbon dioxide annually worldwide, but this estimate is also uncertain. Because of deforestation, it could be decreasing rapidly.

Unlike the oceans and the rain forests, clouds naturally counteract heat retention not by absorbing carbon dioxide but by reflecting sunlight back into space. If the infrared light from the sun does not reach the earth, heat cannot be created, and if the heat on the earth's surface does not go up, the greenhouse effect cannot occur. However, when infrared light does reach the earth, clouds reflect the heat back toward the earth, thus warming it.

Major uncertainty exists about the role of clouds in counteracting the greenhouse effect. Ultimately, this matter is extremely complicated because it depends on subtle distinctions about cloud thickness and structure.

Impact of the Greenhouse Effect

The greenhouse effect can have many impacts on the world. Some of the major predicted consequences are listed below. These predictions assume that the levels of carbon dioxide and the other greenhouse gases will be emitted at the present rate:[31]

- In Greenland and the North Pole, some of the permafrost and ice will melt, causing the oceans to rise and threatening floods of coastal areas.
- The midwestern United States will be hit hard by drought conditions; the warmer weather will increase evaporation and cause drier soils.
- With the increased evaporation, river levels will lower, causing a shortage in water supplies, lower generation of power, and a disruption in agricultural irrigation.
- The nations of Central and Eastern Europe and Russia will gain approximately 40 days in their growing season, which could make them net exporters of grain to the rest of the world.
- The increased temperatures will cause a wider area of rain forest growth, moving the African rain forests north and bringing rain to Chad, Sudan, and Ethiopia, breaking their prolonged dry spell.
- An increase in snow and frigid rain in Antarctica would create a thicker ice level, which would help counteract some of the greenhouse effect by reflecting more sunlight and counteracting the rise in sea level.

Canada and the United States have the highest emission levels of greenhouse gases per capita among the developed nations. The highest level of greenhouse gas emissions per capita in the world, however, is found in what was formerly East Germany. Brazil and the Ivory Coast have the highest levels of emissions per capita among developing countries. Per unit of GNP, the emissions of greenhouse gases in Brazil and India surpass the levels found in the United States. Contributions by country are shown in Figure 36-11.

FIGURE 36-11
Sources of
greenhouse gasses

Country	Percent of Total
United States	21%
Former Soviet Union	14
European Union	14
China	7
Brazil	4
India	4
Others (total)	36

Limiting Carbon Dioxide Buildup

A first approach to limiting carbon dioxide buildup is to make energy supply and use more efficient. Examples of available technology for conservation are efficient light bulbs in commercial buildings, better insulated buildings, and vehicles that obtain more miles per gallon. A fleet average of 40 miles per gallon, with no increase in miles driven, would cut U.S. auto-related carbon emissions in half.[32]

Another option to reduce the use of fossil fuels is to use different sources of energy. Alternatives such as nuclear power, hydropower, solar technologies, and natural gas produce far less carbon dioxide.

Methanol has been proposed as an alternative motor-vehicle fuel. Methanol made from biomass (primarily wood, organic wastes, or agricultural produce) would not contribute to greenhouse emissions as long as the biomass feedstock was replaced.

Hydrogen fuel cells appear to be a good long-term alternative for motor-vehicle propulsion if the serious technical difficulties can be overcome. A hydrogen-based fuel cell would emit only water vapor and nitrous oxides, the latter at significantly lower levels than fossil fuels. A big problem, however, is tank storage. Smaller tanks must be devised so that the driving range of hydrogen cars is not sacrificed. Another problem with the fuel tank is safety.

A final method to reduce carbon dioxide buildup is to put a stop to the deforestation of the world's rain forests. The burning of the rain forests emits an estimated one billion tons of carbon dioxide a year; at the same time the earth loses one of its major sinks to absorb carbon dioxide. Encouraging the reforestation of areas denuded of natural tree cover is a gesture of important symbolic significance, but it cannot make a significant dent in carbon dioxide buildup.[33]

The Need for an International Treaty

An international treaty on global greenhouse gases, modeled on that of the Montreal and London accords for CFCs, was needed. However, the circumstances that produced these accords were much different than the circumstances surrounding the buildup of greenhouse gases.

First, the Montreal and London accords were reached amid growing international recognition of the scientific basis for the ozone depletion theory. Negotiations gathered momentum after scientists observed a rapidly growing ozone hole over the Antarctic. With respect to global warming, however, great uncertainties remained. Firm evidence was needed to convince people in all nations to take climate change seriously. But the evidence might appear too late. According to the adage, throw a frog into a cauldron of boiling water and it will jump out to save its life, but boil it gradually and it will stay put until it dies.

The second difference between the circumstances surrounding ozone depletion and carbon buildup was that many companies favored a worldwide agreement to limit CFC production. They did so not only because of a sense of corporate social responsibility but because, as manufacturers of expensive CFC substitutes, they stood to gain from new products, methods, and substances.[34] If regulation was inevitable, these manufacturers preferred that it be uniform in coverage and enforceable, so that no company could cheat and offer cheap CFCs as competition to the higher-priced alternatives and so they could plan for a transition to the new era.

Carbon dioxide buildup, however, was unlikely to see a convergence of scientific recognition and industry support. The industry situation was very different. CFCs were produced by a relatively small number of companies and had a relatively narrow range of uses. In comparison, fossil fuel producers and the uses of their products were numerous. Moreover, fossil fuels were very hard to replace.[35]

Implementing the Rio Climate Change Treaty of 1992

Rio Framework on Climate Change
The 1992 treaty establishing long-term goals on stabilizing greenhouse gases at safe levels for humans.

The 1992 Rio Framework on Climate Change, signed by 159 nations, established a *long-term* goal of stabilizing greenhouse gases at levels safe for humans. Eventually, these emissions would have to be cut by 60 to 80 percent. In the short term, nations were expected to list existing emissions and adopt national climate plans. The Europeans and Japanese wanted a freeze at 1990 levels, to which the Bush administration was adamantly opposed, preferring instead a wait-and-see attitude because more study was needed.

Most of the national plans adopted after the Rio treaty were modest: the funding of energy efficiency projects, R&D, and work on renewable energy. No nation in the world had passed a carbon tax, though the European Union considered one that began at a $3 a barrel oil equivalent and would go up to $10 barrel in seven years. No agreement was reached, however, on how to distribute the tax burden among member states, and the proposal was affected by many conflicts.

Since countries with growing economies like Greece, Spain, Portugal, and Ireland forecast inevitable increases in emissions, the expectation was that Germany, Belgium, the Netherlands, and Denmark would have to compensate them. The United Kingdom, which had only recently raised its energy taxes, did not support the tax. The governing institutions of the EU were not unanimous about a carbon tax either: the Environment Commission favored it, but the Economic and Financial Affairs Commission, concerned about jobs and the competitiveness of European industry, and the Customs Union, which already felt overburdened by the need to harmonize tax policies among EU member nations, opposed it.

Economic analysis showed that the tax, if it did not involve increased government revenues, would have little impact because energy constituted only 2 percent of industrial costs. However, in energy and energy-intensive industries, such as iron, steel, clay, and glass, the impact would be very high. Trade groups in those industries made emotionally charged arguments against the tax. Environmentalists and the energy-efficiency and renewable-energy industries did not have the capacity to counter these forces. Ultimately, passage of a carbon tax in the EU was made conditional on the introduction of a carbon tax in competitor nations: the United States, Japan, and the newly industrialized nations of Asia.

In principle, the EU remained committed to using taxes for environmental purposes.[36] In practice, this idea met with many difficulties. A European Commission report in 1995, *Economic Growth and the Environment*, argued for a shift to taxes from regulation. Taxes and environmental charges, the report maintained, were the best means to make an economy sustainable. They conformed to the move from government to the marketplace and sent a clear message to businesses and other economic actors. Less hemmed in by bureaucratic rigidities, businesses would be free to respond to market signals.

Implementing a tax system, however, remained a formidable challenge. Revenues from environmental charges would decline as companies reduced their pollution to avoid payment. The use of taxes might make it more difficult to integrate the economies of Central and Eastern Europe. The EU would have to answer the question of how to use the revenues: Should they be used to subsidize R&D and smooth the transition toward new and cleaner industries?

What Companies Can Do

Pollution and environmental problems posed numerous challenges for business. These challenges occurred at the highest levels in the firm: business strategy and organization. They also affected corporate staff in the public affairs and legal departments and influenced people in traditional functional areas such as operations, marketing, accounting, and financed

Environmental considerations must be part of company wide decision making from the beginning; they are not something to be considered only at the end. Companies may have to think long term even if profits suffer in the short term. Management support at the highest level is essential because changes of the magnitude called for by environmental issues cannot be accomplished without it.

Companies such as Du Pont, 3M, and Pacific Gas & Electric have made well-regarded responses to environmental expectations in the past.[38] Their responses may have relevance for other companies. Based on these responses, a list is provided of actions companies can take.

Strategy and Organization

Companies can take the following actions:

1. *Cut back on environmentally unsafe operations.* Du Pont, the leading producer of CFCs, has announced that it will voluntarily pull out of this $750 million business by the year 2000, if not sooner.
2. *Carry out RID on environmentally safe activities.* Du Pont has announced that it is spending up to $1 billion on the best replacements for CFCs.
3. *Develop and expand environmental cleanup services.* Building on the expertise gained in cleaning up its own plants, Du Pont has formed a safety and environmental resources division to help industrial customers clean up their toxic wastes. The projected future revenues are $1 billion by 2000.
4. *Compensate for environmentally risky endeavors.* Applied Energy Services, a power plant management firm, donated $2 million in 1988 for tree planting in Guatemala to compensate for a coal-fired plant it was building in Connecticut. The trees were meant to offset emissions that might lead to global warming.
5. *Make structural changes.* The CERES Principles call on companies to appoint an environmentalist to the corporate board and to conduct an annual public audit of the company's environmental progress. The environmental auditing movement has taken off, and many companies now routinely, if for no other reason than to prevent liability, conduct audits.[39]

Public Affairs

Companies can take the following actions:

1. *Avoid losses caused by appearing insensitive to environmental issues.* A cost to Exxon of an apparent lack of concern about the Exxon Valdez oil spill was that 41 percent of Americans said that they would consider boycotting the company.

2. *Attempt to gain environmental legitimacy and credibility.* Edgar Woolard, the chairman of Du Pont, has been vocal in his support for environmental protection and regularly delivers speeches on corporate environmentalism. Cosponsors of Earth Day have included Apple Computer, Hewlett-Packard, Shaklee, and the Chemical Manufacturers Association. McDonald's has shown that it is a proponent of recycling.

3. *Collaborate with environmentalists.* Du Pont and PG&E executives meet with environmental groups. PG&E rented a computer model from the Environmental Defense Fund (EDF) that shows the relationship between conservation and electricity costs.

The Legal Area

Companies can take the following actions:

1. *Prevent confrontation with state or federal pollution control agencies.* W. R. Grace faces expensive and time-consuming lawsuits from its toxic dumps, and Browning-Ferris, Waste Management, and Louisiana-Pacific confront violations that have damaged their reputations.

2. *Comply early.* Since compliance costs only increase over time, the first companies to act will have lower costs. This enables them to increase their market share and profit and win competitive advantage.

3. *Take advantage of innovative compliance programs.* Instead of source-by-source reduction, EPA's bubble policy allows a factory to reduce pollution at different sources by different amounts provided that the overall result is equivalent. 3M therefore has installed equipment on some production lines and not on others at its tape manufacturing facility in Pennsylvania, thereby lowering its compliance costs.[40]

Operations

A company can take the following actions:

1. *Promote new manufacturing technologies.* Louisville Gas and Electric has taken the lead in installing smokestack scrubbers, Consolidated Natural Gas in using clean-burning technologies, and Nucor in developing state-of-the-art steel mills. PG&E has agreed to rely on a combination of smaller-scale generating facilities like windmills or cogeneration plants, along with aggressive conservation efforts. It has canceled plans to build large coal and nuclear power plants.

2. *Encourage technological advances that reduce pollution from products and manufacturing processes.* 3M's "Pollution Prevention Pays" program is based on the premise that it is too costly for companies to employ add-on technology and that they should attempt instead to eliminate pollution at the source.[41] Add-on technology is expensive because it takes resources to remove the pollution, the pollution removal then generates new wastes, and more resources are needed to remove the additional waste.

3. *Develop new product formulations.* 3M's rapid-fire agent to extinguish petroleum fires did not meet EPA requirements. Thus, the company had to develop a new formulation, which was 40 times less toxic but equally effective and less expensive to produce.

4. *Modify production equipment and change manufacturing operations to achieve source reduction.* Besides new product formulations, 3M also has modified its equipment and changed operations. Its Kenlevel metal-plating process does not require the use of cyanide, is up to 50 percent more energy efficient, and creates a competitive advantage.

5. *Eliminate manufacturing wastes.* With fewer wastes, add-on equipment becomes less necessary. 3M's philosophy is to invest in reducing the number of materials that trigger regulation. It has, for example, replaced volatile solvents with water-based compounds, eliminating the need for costly air-pollution equipment. Amoco and Polaroid have similar pollution-reduction programs.

6. *Find alternative uses for wastes.* When Du Pont halted ocean dumping of acid iron salts, it discovered that the salts could be sold to water treatment plants at a profit.

7. *Recycle wastes.* Firms with active recycling programs are 3M, Safety-Kleen (solvents and motor oil), Wellman (plastic), Jefferson Smurfit (paper), and Nucor (steel).

Marketing

A company can take various actions in this area:

1. *Cast products in an environmentally friendly light.* A 1989 Michael Peters Group survey found that 77 percent of Americans say that a company's environmental reputation influences what they buy.[42] Companies such as Procter &c Gamble, ARCO, Colgate-Palmolive, Lever Brothers, 3M, and Sun Oil have tried to act on the basis of this finding. Wal-Mart has made efforts to provide customers with recycled or recyclable products. The number of new green products introduced in the United States has increased, and many new product introductions have green features.[43]

2. *Avoid being attacked by environmentalists for unsubstantiated or inappropriate claims.* British Petroleum claimed that a new brand of unleaded gasoline caused no pollution, a claim that it had to withdraw after suffering much embarrassment. The degradable-plastics controversy should provide producers with another warning about the perils of unsubstantiated or inappropriate claims. The Body Shop, a London-based chain of skin and hair care stores that provides literature on ozone depletion and global warming to its customers and has collected signatures on a petition to save the rain forests, is a third example. Companies have to be honest with their customers and have to educate them without charges of fraud.

Accounting

A company can take the following actions:

1. *Demonstrate that antipollution programs pay.* 3M's experience is that pollution-prevention programs must pay so that companies will be motivated to carry them out successfully. Environmental pressures force American companies to spend large sums of money that they could otherwise use for capital formation, new product research and development, and process improvements that raise productivity. Thus, every company should use a minimum of resources to reduce pollution and at the same time encourage innovation.

2. *Show the overall impact of the pollution-reduction program.* Companies have an obligation to account for the costs and benefits of their pollution reduction programs. By 1989, 3M reported that it had reduced wastes by 50 percent and had saved the company over $4 million. Its pollution prevention program added almost 6 cents a share or $13 million to the company's profits. This figure does not include the value of reused material or savings coming from reduced disposal costs.

Finance

The actions that a company can take in this area include the following:

1. *Gain the respect of the socially responsible investment community.*   Socially
   responsible rating services and investment funds try to help people invest with a "clean
   conscience."[44]   Their motto is that they can do well while they are doing good.
   Socially responsible investments can be profitable in the long run because companies
   that can deal creatively with pollution, safety, and employment problems are likely to
   be innovative in other areas as well (see Chapter 4).
2. *Recognize true liability.* Smith Barney, Kidder Peabody, and other investment houses
   have environmental analysts who search for a company's true environmental liability.
   They looked closely at ITT's $30 million charge against earnings a plant in Georgia
   that made creosote-soaked railroad ties and telephone poles. The land on the plant site
   had been damaged and would have to be cleaned up.
3. *Recognize business opportunities.* Smith Barney's indexes of solid waste stocks rose
   59 percent and hazardous waste stocks more than 42 percent in 1989 while the overall
   stock market rose only 27 percent. In the long run, the prospects for solid waste
   companies (e.g., Waste Management, Laidlaw Industries, and Browning Ferris) are
   supposed to be very good because of a scarcity of landfill in some parts of country, and
   because cities like New York have no alternative ways to get rid of their garbage. In
   the short run, these companies were having some difficulties.[45]   Their prospects
   ultimately will improve as the federal defense and energy departments and individual
   companies will have to clean up toxic wastes sites they have created.

Environmental Service and Technology Companies

Business should get better, especially abroad, for environmental service and technology
companies. The worldwide market is estimated to be growing to $300 billion annually.
However, development of this industry has not been easy because regulatory barriers,
cultural differences, and other factors have affected market access.   The Asian Pacific
region offers the greatest opportunities, with a market of $40 to $50 billion annually and a
growth rate of 15 to 20 percent. The region's largest economy, Japan, however, has proved
hard to penetrate, so the best accessible markets are Taiwan, Hong Kong, Singapore,
Australia, and New Zealand.[46]

Latin America also offers good opportunities with a growth rate estimated at 15 to
20 percent per year. Current spending, however, is only $4-5 billion and lax regulatory
enforcement remains a problem.

Eastern and Central Europe have the greatest demand for environmental services and
technology. Annual growth rates in spending of 20 to 30 percent are possible, but base
spending in 1995 is estimated to be only $6-7 billion. Therefore, much of the funding must
come from international organizations.

Annual spending increases in Western Europe are estimated to be between 7 and
10 percent compared with 4 to 6 percent in North America.   The estimated annual
expenditures in 1995 for environmental services and technologies were $60 to 70 billion in
Western Europe and $90 to 110 billion in North America.

In sum, firms have many opportunities, covering all aspects of their business, to meet
the challenge posed by pollution and environmental problems. In time, the environmental
service and technology sector is bound to take off and become an important force in solving
the world's environmental problems.

Conclusions

This chapter has tried to make the following points:

1. Pollution problems are worldwide, and businesses operate in settings throughout the world where environmental conditions, environmental movements, and environmental laws vary. Managers must be aware of the differences because awareness may provide them with opportunities for gain and the potential to avoid liabilities.

2. Two of the most pressing pollution problems affecting the globe are solid-waste disposal and atmospheric pollution. Solid-waste disposal is a local problem. By creating programs to reduce and recycle wastes, companies can do something about it now. Atmospheric pollution is a global problem with long-term consequences. International treaties are needed to deal with problems like the hole in the ozone layer and global warming. Companies require long-term plans for these uncertain contingencies.

3. The actions companies can take to cope with environmental problems extend from strategy making and organization to marketing, finance, accounting, and operations. Efforts to reduce pollution are in accord with various other efforts to enhance quality, lower costs, and introduce new products and technologies. They fit into a strategic approach to problem solving where companies provide value to customers through low-cost (waste minimization) and differentiated (green) products. Companies should prune their product portfolios and stress pollution-reducing alternatives to take advantage of the opportunities and avoid the inevitable risks. The future of the world's environment is in their hands.

Discussion Questions

1. Discuss environmental policies in the European Union. What have been some of the consequences of these policies for business?
2. In what ways is the European environmental movement different from the environmental movement in North America? What are the consequences of these differences for business?
3. To what extent does the United Kingdom provide fertile ground for the expansion of U.S. firms experienced in the technologies and know-how of environmental protection?
4. What other countries in Europe might provide fertile ground for the expansion of experienced U.S. firms.
5. What are the three main methods of disposing of solid wastes? What are the advantages and disadvantages of each?
6. What business interests are represented by the different methods of waste disposal? What public policies would these different business interests tend to favor? What challenges do they face in building their business?
7. Why hasn't recycling been more successful?
8. What are the prospects for source reduction? What special problems and opportunities does it offer brines.
9. What are the public risks posed by ozone depletion? What are the challenges to business? Will business be able to meet these challenges?
10. What risks are posed to the world by carbon dioxide buildup? What must businesses do to confront this issue? What should government officials do?
11. Why has it been so difficult for the EU to introduce a carbon tax?
12. Environmental issues pose numerous challenges to business. Discuss actions that companies can take in different functional areas.
13. Which of the environmental actions that companies can take are most important? Which are the easiest to take? Which are companies least likely to take? Why? Have any examples of company actions been left out of this chapter?
14. As a practicing manager, what kind of environmental policy would you draw up for your company? How would you ensure that the company carries out this policy?
15. Define strategic environmental management. How can companies convert environmental challenges into opportunities for business expansion and profit?

Endnotes

1.   W. Ophuls, *Ecology and the Politics of Scarcity* (San Francisco: W. H. Freeman, 1977), pp. 21-22.
2.   R. Buchholz, A. Marcus, and J. Post, *Managing Environmental Issues: A Case Book* (Englewood Cliffs, N.J.: Prentice Hall, 1992).
3.   Shawn Tully, "What the 'Greens' Mean For Business," *Fortune*, October 23, 1989, pp. 159-64.
4.   Ibid.
5.   Ibid.
6.   Tully, "What the 'Greens' Mean for Business," pp. 159-64; S. McMurray, "Chemical Firms Find that It Pays to Reduce Pollution at Source," *The Wall Street Journal*, June 11, 1991, p. A1.
7.   Martin Wright, "Environmental Law: Free Trade," *Tomorrow*, Oct.-Dec. 1994, p. 98.
8.   Roger Cans, "Les Saga des Verts Europeans," *Le Monde*, June 1, 1989, p. 1; H. de Bresson, "La Tentation du Pouvoir," Le Monde, June 1, 1989, p. 9.
9.   Ibid.
10. Ibid.
11. Theresa Waldrop, Martin Wright, and Martha Johnston, "The Way Ahead for Germany, Britain, and France, *Tomorrow*, Oct.-Dec. 1994, pp. 82-92.
12. Joel Makower, "Friend of the Earth?" *Tomorrow*, Oct.-Dec. 1994, pp. 46-52.
13. "Buried Alive," *Newsweek*, November 27, 1989, pp. 66-76; Louis Blumberg and Robert Gottlieb, "The Growth of the Waste Stream," in *War on Waste*, ed. Louis Blumberg and Robert Gottlieb (Washington, D.C.: Island Press, 1989), pp. 3-26.
14. Directorate of Intelligence, Central Intelligence Agency, *Handbook of Economic Statistics, 1991* (Washington, D.C.: U.S. Government Printing Office, 1991), p. 174.
15. Blumberg and Gottlieb, "The Growth of the Waste Stream."
16. William Rathje, "Rubbish!" *Atlantic Monthly*, Dec. 1989, pp. 99-109; Blumberg and Gottlieb, "The Growth of the Waste Stream."
17. Louis Blumberg and Robert Gottlieb, "The Resurrection of Incineration" and "The Economic Factors," in *War on Waste*, ed. Louis Blumberg and Robert Gottlieb (Washington, D.C.: Island Press, 1989), pp. 26-58 and pp. 123-55.
18. Ibid.
19. Jeffrey Stevens, "Assessing the Health Risks of Incinerating Garbage," *EURA Reporter*, Oct. 1989, pp. 6-10.
20. Ibid.
21. Blumberg and Gottlieb, "The Resurrection of Incineration" and "The Economic Factors."
22. Louis Blumberg and Robert Gottlieb, "Recycling's Unrealized Promise," in War on Waste, ed. Louis Blumberg and Robert Gottlieb (Washington, D.C.: Island Press, 1989), pp. 191-226.
23. Ibid.
24. David Brunner, Will Miller, and Nan Stockholm, "3M Company: Creating Incentives Within the Individual Firm," in Corporations and the Environment: How Should Decisions Be Made, ed. David Brunner et al. (Stanford, Calif.: Stanford Business School, 1981), pp. 97-110.
25. Louis Blumberg and Robert Gottlieb, "The Squeeze on Reuse Strategies," in *War on Waste*, ed. Louis Blumberg and Robert Gottlieb (Washington, D.C.: Island Press, 1989), pp. 226-58; C. Lehrburger, "The Disposable Diaper Myth," *Whole Earth Review*, Fall 1988, pp. 60-66; E. Lyman, "Diaper Hype," Garbage, Jan.-Feb. 1990, pp. 36-40.
26. Kirsten Oldenburg and Joel Hirschhom, "Waste Reduction," *Environment*, March 1987, pp. 16-20, 39-45; Azita Yazdani, "Waste Reduction," Environment, Nov. 1989, pp. 2-4.
27. E Sherwood Rowland, "Chlorofluorocarbons and the Depletion of Stratospheric Ozone," *American Scientist*, Jan.-Feb. 1989, pp. 36-45.
28. S. Fred Singer, "My Adventures in the Ozone Layer," *National Review*, June 30, 1989, pp. 34-38; Joseph Morone and Edward Woodhouse "Threats to the Ozone Layer," in *Averting Catastrophe*, ed. Joseph Morone and Edward Woodhouse, (Berkeley: University of California Press, 1986), pp. 76-96.
29. Forest Reinhardt, "Du Pont Freon Products Division," in *Managing Environmental Issues: A Casebook*, eds. R. Buchholz, A. Marcus, and J. Post, (Englewood Cliffs, N.J.: Prentice Hall, 1992), pp. 261-86; Daniel Dudek et al., "Business Response to Environmental Policy: Lessons from CFC Regulation" (Washington, D.C.: Environmental Defense Fund, 1989); Stuart Gannes, "A Down to Earth Job: Saving the Sky," *Fortune*, March 14, 1988, pp. 137-41.
30. Anthony Ramirez, "A Warming World," *Fortune*, July 4, 1988, pp. 102-7.
31. "A Cool Look at Hot Air," *The Economist*, June 16, 1990, pp. 17-20; Gordon MacDonald, "Scientific Basis for the Greenhouse Effect," *Journal of Policy Analysis and Management* 3 (1988), pp. 425-44; Irving Mintzer, "Living in a Warmer World: Challenges for Policy Analysis and Management," *Journal of Policy Analysis and Management* 3 (1988), pp. 445-59; Lester

Lave, "The Greenhouse Effect: What Government Actions Are Needed?" *Journal of Policy Analysis and Management* 3 (1988), pp. 460-70; Peter Brown "Policy Analysis, Welfare Economics and the Greenhouse Effect," *Journal of Policy Analysis and Management* 3 (1988), pp. 471-75.

32. William Chandler, Howard Geller, and Marc Ledbetter, *Energy Efficiency: A New Agenda*, American Council for an Energy Efficient Economy, 1988, pp. 19-65; Jose Godemberg et al., "An End-Use Oriented Global Energy Strategy," *Annual Review of Energy*, 1985, pp. 613-88; Janet Marinelli, "Cars—The Technology Already Exists to Make Cars that Get 50+ MPG," Garbage, November/December 1989, pp. 28-37; Steven Plotkin, "The Road to Fuel Efficiency in the Passenger Vehicle Fleet," *Environment*, July/August 1989, pp. 19-20, 36-42; Robert Whitford, "Fuel Efficient Autos: Progress and Prognosis," *Annual Review of Energy*, 1984, pp. 375-408.

33. Roger Sedjo, "Forests Might be Able to Moderate or Postpone the Buildup of Atmospheric Carbon," *Environment*, Jan.-Feb. 1989, pp. 15-20; Robert Repetto, *The Forest for the Trees? Government Policies and the Misuse of Forest Resources* (Washington, D.C.: World Resources Institute, 1988), pp. 1-43; Buchholz, *Managing Environmental Issues*.

34. Reinhardt, "Du Pont Freon Products Division."

35. "A Cool Look at Hot Air."

36. Martin Wright, "The EU's Market Instrument Vision," *Tomorrow*, March 1995, p. 78.

37. Frank Friedman, "Implementing Strong Environmental Management Programs," in *Practical Guide to Environmental Management*, ed. Frank Friedman (Washington, D.C.: Environmental Law Institute, 1988), pp. 27-57; William Petak, "Environmental Management: A System Approach," *Environmental Management* 3 (1981), pp. 213-24; Charles Priesing, "A Framework for the Environmental Professional in the Chemical Industry," *The Environmental Professional* 4 (1982), pp. 299-315; Buchholz, *Managing Environmental Issues*.

38. David Kirkpatrick, "Environmentalism: The New Crusade," *Fortune*, February 12, 1990, pp. 45-55.

39. Reinhardt, "Du Pont Freon Products Division,"; Kirkpatrick, "Environmentalism: The New Crusade,"; "Olin Corporation's Regulatory Audit Program," in *Current Practices in Environmental Auditing* (Cambridge, Mass.: Arthur D. Little, 1984), pp. 13-33; Report to U.S. Environmental Protection Agency, "Allied Corporation's Health, Safety, and Environmental Surveillance Program" in *Current Practices in Environmental Auditing* (Cambridge, Mass.: Arthur D. Little, 1984), pp. 33-53; Christopher Duerksen, *Environmental Regulation of Industrial Plant Siting* (Washington, D.C.: The Conservation Foundation, 1983), pp. 17-49, 79-109; Friedman, *Practical Guide to Environmental Management*, pp. 85-97 and pp. 133-43.

40. Brunner, "3M Company: Creating Incentives Within the Individual Firm," pp. 97-110; A. Mazur, "Controlling Technology," in *Technology and the Future*, ed. Allan Teich (New York: St. Martin's Press, 1990), pp. 207-20; Michael Greenberg et al., "Network Television News Coverage of Environmental Risks," *Environment*, March 1989, pp. 16-43; Deborah Stone, "Casual Stories and the Formation of Policy Agendas," *Political Science Quarterly*, Summer 1989, pp. 281-301.

41. Brunner, "3M Company: Creating Incentives Within the Individual Firm."

42. Kirkpatrick, "Environmentalism: The New Crusade."

43. Marketing Intelligence Service.

44. R. Irwin, "Clean and Green," *Sierra*, Nov.-Dec. 1985, pp. 50-56.

45. Bill Birchard, "Waste Disposal Industries Are Suffering, While Pollution Prevention Firms Are Thriving," *Tomorrow*, March 1995, pp. 59-62.

46. Terry Rothetmel and Douglas Shooter, "Where to Go and What to Know," *Tomorrow*, Oct.-Dec. 1994, pp. 52-55.

Case 36-A: Du Pont and the Clean Air Act of 1990[1]

By the time Congress recessed for the 1990 Memorial Day holiday, it was clear that new clean air legislation would soon be passed, legislation that would have a greater impact on Du Pont than any legislation ever had.[2] Both the House of Representatives and Senate had passed amendments to the nation's Clean Air Act. After the holiday, lawmakers would reconvene in a conference committee to reconcile the two versions and to accommodate the Bush administration's concerns.

As one of the 10 largest companies in the United States and, according to government reports, the nation's fifth-largest polluter, E. I. du Pont de Nemours & Company had more at stake than perhaps any other company (Figure 36-A-1 shows a financial statement). Nearly every type of atmospheric pollution identified in the proposed legislation was generated by a Du Pont subsidiary. Du Pont's main substitute for chlorofluorocarbons (CFCs) would be banned under the new legislation a decade sooner than the company had hoped. Provisions designed to address the acid rain problem would threaten parts of

Du Pont's coal operations. Operating costs for the company's chemical division would rise significantly if the law's new requirements concerning toxic air emissions survived the conference committee in their strictest form. And Conoco, Du Pont's gasoline subsidiary, would be affected by provisions mandating cleaner-burning gasoline.

FIGURE 36-A-1
DuPont's financial performance, 1987-1989

Industry Segments (in millions)	Sales			After-Tax Operating Income		
	1989	1988	1987	1989	1988	1987
Industrial products	$ 3,702	$ 3,082	$ 2,636	$ 629	$ 355	$ 319
Fibers	5,966	5,465	5,012	729	676	601
Polymers	5,581	5,423	4,783	455	531	475
Petroleum	12,314	10,995	10,560	538	391	277
Coal	1,818	1,757	1,770	223	226	157
Diversified business	6,153	5,638	5,170	307	275	271
Total company	$35,534	$32,360	$29,931	2,881	2,454	2,100
Interest and other corporate expenses:						
Net of tax				(401)	(264)	(314)
Net income				$2,480	$2,190	$1,786

(dollars in millions except per share amounts)	1989	1988	1987
Sales	$35,534	$32,360	$29,931
Net income	2,480	2,190	1,786
Earnings per share	3.53	3.04	2.46
Dividends per share	1.45	1.23 1/3	1.10
Net return	15.7%	14.6%	12.9%

Source: Adapted from Du Pont's 1989 annual report.

The question now facing Du Pont was how to respond to the legislation.

The Clean Air Act of 1970

The Clean Air Act (CAA) of 1970 was intended to protect people and property from the ill-effects of air pollution.[3] The three titles of the law dealt with pollution from both stationary (industrial plants, buildings, and factories) and mobile sources (cars, trucks, buses, and airplanes). The CAA originally required the nation's air to be clean by 1975. However, this proved impossible, and the law was amended in 1975 and 1977 to allow more time for industry either to comply or to deal with newly discovered pollutants and ambiguities in the law. By 1982, most of the nation's air quality control regions had met the established limits for four of the six major pollutants: lead, nitrogen oxides, particulates, and sulfur oxides. Ozone and carbon monoxide proved more intractable, and some parts of the country had failed to attain the standards set for these pollutants by the end of the decade. However, progress had been made overall. The EPA reported that between 1978 and 1987, the level of carbon monoxide dropped 32 percent, lead by 88 percent, nitrogen dioxide by 12 percent, ozone by 16 percent, particulates by 22 percent, and sulfur dioxide by 35 percent.

Environmentalists, however, were dissatisfied with this progress, citing the threats that airborne pollutants posed to forests, waterways, and wildlife when precipitated out of the atmosphere in the form of so-called acid rain. But their efforts to amend the CAA in the 19805 failed, largely because of the deregulation ideology of the Reagan administration. By

1990, however, the political situation had changed. The Senate finally passed a clean air bill in April 1990 and the House completed voting on its version in late May.

The administration estimated that the bill would cost U.S. industry—already spending $33 billion a year on air pollution control—at least another $21.5 billion annually, more than General Motors, General Electric, Ford Motor, IBM, and Exxon collectively earned in 1989.[4] The amendments designed to combat acid rain could mean double-digit electricity rate increases for the heavily industrialized Middle West. Thousands of the nation's coal miners could expect to lose their jobs. Antipollution equipment could raise the price of a new car by $600. On the other hand, the estimated expected benefits were also significant because air pollution was contributing to the premature deaths of over 50,000 people per year and costing the nation $10 billion to $25 billion annually in health care.[5]

In the ranks of industry there certainly would be winners and losers. For each company that would have to spend some of the $20 billion or more that the CAA was supposed to cost, several other companies would win substantial dividends as the recipients of that spending.[6]

Du Pont and the New Clean Air Act

The new legislation would have profound consequences for Du Pont. The corporate giant, founded in the early 19th century as an explosives manufacturer, had $35.5 billion in sales in 1989, 10 percent higher than in 1988. The company had made a name for itself by harnessing science for commercial purposes. Du Pont's laboratories were the birthplace of nylon, Teflon, Orlon, Dacron, Lycra, and Kevlar. Du Pont helped General Motors develop Freon and became the first producer of the ubiquitous chemical. The company produced a wide range of products, from pesticides to biomedical equipment.

The new CAA had economic implications for most of Du Pont's businesses, but the chlorofluorocarbon, chemical, coal, and gasoline businesses were particularly affected.

Chlorofluorocarbons

Chlorofluorocarbons (CFCs) are a group of chemical compounds prized by industry for their wide range of uses, stability, economy, and nontoxicity. Du Pont's Freon Products division is the largest producer of CFCs in the world, supplying half the U.S. demand and 25 percent of worldwide demand. Though CFC sales are significant (Du Pont's are about $750 million), their future is limited because of the threat they pose to the earth's stratospheric ozone layer, which protects the planet from harmful ultraviolet radiation. In 1974, a wave of concern following the discovery of this threat led to a ban four years later on the use of CFCs as aerosol propellants. Concern waned again until 1985 when the "ozone hole" over Antarctica was discovered. Stratospheric ozone measurements showed that the ozone layer was being depleted faster than had been predicted. Political leaders from around the world agreed to a phaseout of CFCs in the Montreal Protocol in 1987. The Protocol calls for a 50 percent reduction in production by 1998.

In 1988, Du Pont vowed to completely end production of CFCs in the year 2000. The company shifted its attention to developing a marketable substitute, spending $5 million in 1985, more than $30 million in 1988, and planning to spend more than $1 billion on the effort by 2000. Known substitutes like propane, carbon dioxide, or pentane were dangerous, inferior, or more expensive. A promising possible substitute that Du Pont called 132b had to be scrapped when it was discovered the compound caused sterility in male rats.

By early 1990, the company rested its greatest hopes on a class of chemicals called HFCs and HCFCs. These chemicals performed many of the same tasks as CFCs, but because their molecular composition allowed them to break down before they reached the upper atmosphere, they had either zero (HFCs) or only 2 to 10 percent (HCFCs) of the ozone-depleting capacity of CFCs. Though more expensive, these compounds were not prohibited under the Montreal Protocol and appeared to be the most viable alternative. Unfortunately for Du Pont, the new House and Senate bills would freeze production of most HCFCs in 2015 and ban nearly all production in 2030. Both dates were decades earlier than the 2030-2050 timeframe Du Pont had deemed reasonable.

This posed a serious obstacle to Du Pont's plans for the substitute chemical. Customers would be hesitant to adapt to a substitute that would itself be phased out. For example, HCFC-22 could be used in automobile air-conditioning systems, but only if the systems were substantially redesigned to handle the higher operating pressures necessary to use HCFC-22. General Motors executives estimated the necessary retooling would cost their company $600 million.

In March 1990, citing competitive issues, the company sent a letter to its Freon customers urging them to contact their congressmen to protest the legislation for an earlier-than-planned phaseout of HCFCs. Publicly, Du Pont executives were silent about how the company would respond. But even before Congressional debate on the issue began, Du Pont had designed its first new HCFC plant to produce small quantities of the chemical.

Du Pont managers were now faced with hard decisions about where to focus the CFC and CFC substitute division's energies. How hard should it lobby Congress to end the early ban on HCFCs? To what extent should it redirect its research and development efforts to other possible substitutes?

If Du Pont was going to redirect its corporate development strategy, it needed an assessment of the scientific and technical issues that was clear, understandable, and definitive. However, the state of scientific and technical knowledge was in such a state of flux that reaching such an understanding would not be easy.

Chemicals

Two major provisions of the proposed CAA legislation had substantial implications for Du Pont's chemical operations. Du Pont was the largest U.S. chemical company and had 80 or more plants around the country that could be affected.

First, the Senate bill would require chemical plants to stop production unless they could reduce toxic emissions to the point where people living near the plant faced no more than a 1-in-10,000 risk of getting cancer from them. Several Du Pont plants in Texas and Louisiana, which emitted carcinogens like carbon tetrachloride (which is used to produce synthetic rubber), had been cited by the EPA for posing an unacceptable cancer risk to nearby residents. Some of these cited plants already controlled their toxic emissions through state-of-the-art technology; additional safety measures to further reduce emission levels would be very expensive.

Achieving the Senate risk level would be very difficult, but even more difficult would be proving that it was achieved-risk analysis itself is a tricky business. Experts practicing it use different assumptions, which can be contested not only in the legal system but in the court of public opinion, where estimates of risk raise emotions and arouse public controversy.

Unlike the Senate bill, the House bill did not specify an acceptable level of risk, relying instead on the EPA to conduct further risk-assessment studies and make recommendations to Congress. These studies could take years to complete and digest, time that Du Pont could use to plan for the needed changes. Du Pont favored the House bill, but the company feared that too close an identification with the House's position might backfire; environmentalists would use industry backing as a tactic to obtain more stringent regulations from Congress.

The second major provision affecting chemical operations was contained in both versions of the bill; it required that every production line nationwide install the best available emission control technology. The measure was designed to reduce toxic fumes by 90 percent. If companies on their own could not meet the 90 percent reduction, the EPA would set standards for them, defining the best available control technology and requiring the companies to install it.

Toxic fumes are blamed for 2,700 potential cancer cases annually (0.2 percent of all reported cases) as well as other health problems. The cost to industry of the best-technology requirement was pegged at $5 billion per year. However, Du Pont, acting on its own initiative, had already begun spending hundreds of millions of dollars to reduce its emissions voluntarily to 60 percent of their 1987 levels by 1993. This effort was in addition to the company's ongoing reductions in air pollutants, which it had tracked since the early 1970s. If Du Pont were to continue with its own plan, it might be able to meet the 90 percent reduction guideline that would exempt it from EPA-specified emission-control measures. On the other hand, if the company failed to satisfy the reduction requirement, it would have spent millions of dollars on control equipment only to find that the EPA might require different equipment. Whether to continue with its own plan or wait for the EPA regulations to be clarified was a key issue for the chemicals division.

Coal

After a decade of debate, Congress and the administration were ready in 1990 to combat acid rain. Formed when sulfur and nitrogen oxides precipitate out of the atmosphere, acid rain damages forests and lakes, particularly those in the Northeast. A major culprit in the formation of acid rain is the high-sulfur coal used by some coal-burning energy utilities and industrial plants. Du Pont's Consolidated Coal subsidiary is one of the two biggest high-sulfur coal producers in the country, with highsulfur coal accounting for 60 percent of its production.

Congress and the administration were largely in agreement on the provisions that would address the acid rain problem: Utilities would be forced to cut sulfur dioxide emissions by 10 million tons annually by the year 2000, at a cost of about $4.1 billion per year. The president's proposal included an innovative pollution-trading system, which would allow utility companies that cut their emissions by more than the required amount to sell their unused pollution "rights" to utilities that could not meet the standards.

Because many utilities would find it cheaper to buy low-sulfur coal than to invest in costly emission-control technology, Consolidated Coal executives estimated that $40 million to $50 million in annual revenue would be lost, 750 to 800 company coal miners would lose their jobs, and perhaps two of the company's four high-sulfur coal mines would be forced to close starting in 1995. Again, it was unclear what Du Pont should do. Protesting to Congress at this late date was likely to be futile. There had to be some opportunity for creative adjustment to this change in government policy.

Gasoline

The proposed CAA amendments that dealt with gasoline seemed to offer a business opportunity to Du Pont's Conoco subsidiary. The opportunity stemmed from the fact that a gasoline meeting the standards proposed for the mid-1990s had not yet been developed. Both the Senate and House versions of the legislation would require that cleaner burning gasoline be sold in nine of the nation's smoggiest locations: Los Angeles, New York City, Houston, Chicago, Milwaukee, Baltimore, San Diego, Philadelphia, and much of Connecticut.[7] Together, these areas comprise 25 percent of the U.S. gasoline market, but a very small portion of Conoco's market. The Senate version specified what the reformulated gasoline should contain, while the House version allowed refineries more leeway as long as they met the minimum performance standards.

If the oil industry failed to persuade lawmakers to change the reformulation requirement, there would be a large market for any company that came up with an acceptable, working formulation. Conoco researchers started working on the problem shortly after President Bush unveiled his clean air proposal requiring cleaner fuels.

After being caught off-guard when the Senate passed the reformulation amendment, industry trade groups and companies undertook an unprecedented, multimillion-dollar lobbying effort to defeat a similar amendment in the House.[8] Conoco neither contributed to this lobbying effort nor initiated its own effort. A $1 million newspaper ad campaign attacked both the gasohol lobby, which was pushing for the reformulation provision, and Congressman Bill Richardson (Democrat, New Mexico) who sponsored the provision. Several oil companies set up 800 telephone numbers, encouraging their shareholders to call or to send prepaid mailgrams to Congress protesting the amendment. The oil companies also urged their employees and dealers to deluge Congress with mail on the subject. The American Petroleum Institute (API), an industry trade group, circulated API-financed research that discounted the benefits of reformulated gasoline.

The lobbying blitz backfired. According to an environmental lobbyist involved with the legislation, not only did the oil industry lack credibility, but House members were irritated by its heavy-handed tactics. The barrage of mail and attention on the issue confirmed the belief of many lawmakers that Congress needed to define exactly how gasoline should be reformulated rather than leave it to the oil industry to decide.

What Next?

The CAA amendments in their final form would substantially determine how Du Pont would spend its environmental-equipment budget, which was slated to be $500 million by 1991. But other costs would also increase as a result of the legislation (e.g., the company's electric bill). By some calculations, Du Pont—which uses about on percent of all the electricity generated in the United States—could expect to spend up to $40 million more per year in energy costs alone. There were opportunities as well. Du Pont's fledgling environmental services business was projected to expand tenfold during the 1990s, up to $1 billion per year. Though management had to consider how to approach the legislation in the short term, how to prepare for its implementation in the long term was more serious. With new clean air legislation virtually sure to pass (see the appendix for a summary of the major provisions of the Clean Air Act of 1990), Du Pont would have to respond.

Its basic business strategy would be affected in at least six ways:

1. How could Du Pont contain costs so as to continue to bring value to customers and remain competitive? What advantage was to be won from an aggressive pollution prevention program in its core chemical businesses?
2. Could Du Pont innovate fast enough in areas like CFC substitutes and reformulated gasoline to move ahead of the competition and capture new markets?
3. Would Du Pont have to rethink its portfolio of business products, deciding that some were not worth further investment or keeping for the long term because they had substantial pollution problems and posed the risk of significant environmental liabilities?

4. What kind of reorientation in corporate strategic thinking was required? How should Du Pont present itself to the public?
5. What kind of company was Du Pont going to be? How should it explain the reorientation to employees concerned about their jobs and their future?
6. What long-term political strategy would Du Pont have to adopt to achieve its goals?

Appendix: Major Provisions of the Clean Air Act of 1990[9]

Toxic Emissions

Only seven chemicals have been regulated since 1970, but over the next 10 years the majority of polluting plants must use the best technology available to reduce their emissions of 189 toxic chemicals by 90 percent.

For any remaining cancer risks, the EPA is required to set health-based standards that produce ample margins of safety (e.g., a cancer risk of not more than 1 in 10,000) for people living near factories. Coke ovens are eligible for extensions until 2020 if they made extra-stringent reductions in the first round.

The alternative fuels program should significantly reduce toxic emissions from vehicles. Additional cuts from cars or fuel will be required after an EPA study. Benzene and formaldehyde must be controlled.

Acid Rain

In the first phase, the 111 dirtiest power plants in 21 states must cut sulfur-dioxide emissions by a total cut of 5 million tons in 1995. Two-year extensions can be given to plants that commit to buy scrubbing devices that allow continued use of high-sulfur coal.

In the second phase, more than 200 additional power plants must make sulfur-dioxide cuts by the year 2000, for a total nationwide cut of 10 million tons. This deadline can be extended until 2004 for plants that use new clean-coal technology.

An innovative trading system is created in which utilities that make extra-deep pollution reductions get credits, which can be sold or swapped to utilities that want to increase their emissions. Bonus pollution credits are awarded to dirty utilities that install scrubbers and to power plants in high-growth and extremely low-polluting states in addition to the hard-hit Middle West.

A nationwide cap on utility sulfur-dioxide emissions is imposed after the year 2000.

Utilities must cut nitrogen-oxide emissions by 2 million tons a year, or about 25 percent, beginning in 1995.

No help is provided for ratepayers beyond changes in the trading system. Coal miners and others put out of work because of clean-air rules may qualify for extra weeks of unemployment pay under a $250 million, five-year job assistance program.

Smog

Some 96 areas missed the deadline for meeting health standards for ozone, a main ingredient of smog. The new bill requires that all but nine areas comply by November 1999, except for Baltimore, and New York, which must comply by 2007, and Los Angeles, which must comply by November 2020. Areas that are moderately polluted or worse must cut smog 15 percent within six years. After that, areas with serious pollution must make 9 percent improvements every three years until they meet the standards.

Tougher tailpipe standards for automobiles are phased in, starting with the 1994 models, to cut nitrogen oxides by 30 percent and hydrocarbons by 40 percent. Even deeper cuts are required for the year 2003 models if the EPA finds they are cost-effective and needed. These standards have to be maintained for 10 years or 100,000 miles.

Warranties on pollution-control equipment must last eight years or 80,000 miles for catalytic converters and electronic diagnostic equipment, and two years or 24,000 miles for other pollution gear.

Special nozzles are required on gasoline pumps in almost 60 smoggy areas. Also, fume-catching canisters are to be phased in on all new cars, starting in the mid-1990s. Gauges are also required on cars to alert drivers to problems with pollution-control equipment.

Industrial polluters that emit as little as 10 or 25 tons of smog-forming chemicals a year may have to make cuts, depending on the severity of smog in their areas. The present law sets the limit at 100 tons a year. Another 43 categories of. smaller pollution sources, including printing plants, are also regulated.

Alternative Fuels

Beginning in 1995, all gasoline sold in the nine smoggiest cities must be cleaner-burning, reformulated gasoline that cuts emissions of hydrocarbons and toxic pollutants by 15 percent. By the year 2000, the reductions must equal 20 percent.

Starting with 1998 car models, fleets of 10 or more cars in the two dozen smoggiest cities must run 80 percent cleaner than today's autos while trucks must be 50 percent cleaner. Requirements could be delayed three years if clean vehicles are not available.

By the model year 1996, automakers must begin producing at least 150,000 superclean cars and light trucks annually under a California pilot program designed to launch vehicles that can run on nongasoline fuels, such as natural gas and methanol. By the year 2001, even cleaner models must be produced.

Discussion Questions

1. What should Du Pont's strategy be toward the proposed legislation?
2. What types of changes in Du Pont's business strategy will the Clean Air Act of 1990 signify?
3. What opportunities do you see for Du Pont in the Clean Air Act?
4. How will the passage of the bill affect Du Pont compared with its competitors?

Endnotes

1. This case was written by Mark C. Jankus under the editorial guidance of Alfred A. Marcus, Curtis L. Carlson School of Management, University of Minnesota. See R. Buchholz, A. Marcus, J. Post, *Managing Environmental Issues: A Casebook* (Englewood Cliffs, N.J.: Prentice Hall, 1992).
2. Barbara Rosewicz and Richard Koenig, "How Clean Air Bill Will Force Du Pont into Costly Moves," *The Wall Street Journal*, May 25, 1990, p. A1.
3. *The Clean Air Act: A Primer & Glossary*, pamphlet, Clean Air Working Group.
4. Barbara Rosewicz and Rose Gutfeld, "Clean Air Legislation Will Cost Americans $21.5 Billion a Year," *The Wall Street Journal*, March 28, 1990, p. A11.
5. David Wessel, "Air Bill's Cost-Benefit Data Look Very Foggy Close Up," *The Wall Street Journal*, May 25, 1990, p. A7.
6. Rose Gutfeld, "Firms, Environmentalists Gear Up for Crucial Round," *The Wall Street Journal*, May 25, 1990, p. A7.
7. Allanna Sullivan and Rose Gutfeld, "Bill Would Require Oil Companies to Sell Advanced Fuel," *The Wall Street Journal*, May 25, 1990, p. A7.
8. Jil Abramson, "Big Oil May Have Misfired in Heavy Lobbying Drive," *The Wall Street Journal*, May 25, 1990 p. A6.